# GET IT ALL

# Riches

from

# Another World

Neo-Tech Worldwide

Manuscript # 691221

# RICHES

## from

# Profound
# Honesty

---

*Dare to Get it All?*

**Take this Real-Life Journey**

from

**Earth's Anticivilization**

to the

**Civilization of the Universe**

---

# PROFOUND HONESTY

guarantees

## Limitless Prosperity

and an

## Exciting Romantic Life

1st Printing, October 1996
2nd Printing, November 1996
3rd Printing, March 2010
4th Printing, June 2015
5th Printing, April 2017
6th Printing, July 2018
7th Printing, April 2020

9 10 8

ISBN # 911752-78-1
Library of Congress # 96-069932

# *Get It All*

e

# RICHES
from a
## *New World*

Fully Integrated Honesty: Those three words deliver prosperity and excitement. Indeed, those three words will deliver a new civilization to mankind — a civilization of endless riches. Yet, without new information, those three words carry little meaning. Today, however, for the first time, a manuscript comes from another world to deliver this information — powerful new information that evokes different views of life and reality. With those new views, a person outcompetes everyone stuck in today's irrational civilization[1].

For 2300 years, everyone on Earth has been hoodwinked into accepting mystically distorted, force-oriented views of life and reality. Consequently, once one captures the all-powerful views delivered by *Profound Honesty*, he or she will find little acceptance in today's anticivilization. But, so what! That non acceptance by today's boring Establishment is what "quantum leaps" a person over competition — over everyone else into a new-color dynamic that controls both the present and the future.

*Profound Honesty* is composed of New-World Music — four Concertos and two Songs that build into a Symphony. Through the opening Concertos, one discovers the ground upon which to stand. That ground is an omnipotent foundation called Neo-Tech Objectivism. Next, through a brace of Songs, one discovers how that foundation joins *Profound Honesty* to the future. Those Songs introduce the New-Color Symphony from which one crescendos into exciting adventures and happiness. And, finally, in the Closing Ceremonies, one rides toward riches from another world.

---

[1]Everyone is born blind into this Earthbound civilization. Thus, like the congenitally blind, everyone becomes so acclimated to this force-controlled, loser anticivilization that none can see the coming business-controlled, winner Civilization of the Universe. ...*Profound Honesty* cures that blindness.

# Soaring
# Beyond Competition

through

# Omnipotent Visions

from a

# New Way of Thinking

# Opening Ceremonies
## *Cyberspace Concertos #1-4*

# PROFOUND HONESTY
### and
## Neo-Tech Objectivism

> Limitless Prosperity and Romantic Excitement
> via
> Profound Honesty and Neo-Tech Objectivism

## Concerto #1

## New-World Music

Only conscious beings can distort reality. Only conscious beings can act dishonestly and unjustly. Yet, all distortions, dishonesties, and injustices are temporary — illusionary — not part of reality. ...Conscious beings can assert honesty and justice to control their existence within the laws of nature. In that way, conscious beings can control their future. Thus, they can enter a new world of limitless prosperity and romantic excitement.

The Pre Cyberspace World

Before cyberspace, before the Internet, reality often asserted itself slowly — often after years, sometimes only after centuries or millennia. Yet, no matter how dishonest or unjust an individual or a society, reality ultimately prevails. For example, decades after their deaths, the reality of the great values produced by Francis Bacon, Johann Sebastian Bach, Joseph Smith, Herman Melville, and Vincent van Gogh finally came forth. And, today, honesty and justice are revealing scorned businesspeople like Jay

Gould, John D. Rockefeller, Leona Helmsley, and Michael Milken as life-giving benefactors to conscious life. Also, eventually, honesty and justice will reveal Homeric icons like Alexander the Great, Napoleon, Lincoln, and Woodrow Wilson as life-destroying malefactors to conscious life.

Throughout history, dishonesties and injustices have caused deep, widespread distortions of reality. Those distortions arise from one fundamental source: people who choose to live by forcefully or fraudulently draining values from others. Such people do not live naturally — they do not live by producing values for others. They live as unnatural human organisms — as parasitical humanoids.

Many such humanoids glean affluent, respectable, even famous livings by expertly disguising their criminal parasitisms. They live as rulers, politicians, academics, journalists, religious leaders. Such people often manipulate envy from the populace by dishonestly ripping facts out of context in order to drain the real benefactors of society — the competitive job-and-value producers. The direct victims are those precious risk-taking businesspeople who deliver the values and jobs necessary for conscious life to survive and prosper. The indirect victims are all conscious beings living on Earth today.

At every level of activity and visibility, criminal parasites drain the heroic value producers of this world under the facade of altruism — force-and-fraud backed altruism. Such criminal altruism is the underlying deception of this unnatural civilization. For that reason, Earth beings live in an upside-down civilization — an anticivilization — in which uncompetitive, value-destroying parasites control competitive, value-producing heroes.

## A New World

Today, a new world — a cyberspace information world — is bringing a new paradigm to planet Earth. Is this rising new paradigm for better or worse? Consider the single most harmful irrationality of Earth's anticivilization: the apathetic acceptance of criminal parasites draining the life and well-being from everyone. ...Will this new cyberspace paradigm empower or emasculate those who purposely harm society?

### Usenet: A Paradise or Graveyard for Parasites?

In today's anticivilization, the Internet Newsgroup system called Usenet is a world of ironies in which all values, honesty, and justice can be wantonly attacked and seemingly destroyed by shrunken spirits ranging from ersatz philosophers to certain tax-supported academics and criminal-minded nihilists. On Usenet, do-nothing shrunken spirits can seemingly smother any and every great value or accomplishment. Dishonesty seemingly reigns. Nonentities seem to be able to unjustly destroy anything and everything with out-of-context attacks, mendacious innuendos, and fabricated scenarios.

Yet, within that paradoxical picture lies the promise of a new world. A world of fully integrated honesty in which justice asserts itself. For, in the cyberspace world, all dishonesties and injustices become entrapped and then extinguished by reality.

### Cyberspace: The Dishonesty Trap

Cyberspace forms self-exposure traps that will eventually eliminate purposeful destructions from this planet. Through such traps, all dishonesties move toward extinction. Every dishonesty and injustice launched in cyberspace by malevolent value destroyers is permanently recorded and retrievable through Internet search engines. Likewise, every example of honesty, justice, and value production is also permanently recorded and retrievable. How does Usenet combine with the World Wide Web to trap and eventually vanish purposely destructive people? Consider the following:

On Usenet Newsgroups, all varieties of dishonest people, do-nothing idlers, destructive parasites, even criminal psychopaths can delude themselves with feelings of false self-worth and unearned power. Swarms of negative loudmouths seem to out-shout everyone else. Their barrages of achieve-nothing negativities can seemingly trash any laudable effort, positive achievement, or value-producing hero. By contrast, genuine heroes seldom raise their voices. Moreover, they are too busy producing values to defend themselves against attention-seeking nonentities.

In cyberspace, the most insignificant nonentities seem to have free reign to hack apart any positive achievement or value. But the opposite is the fact. For example, achieve-everything Bill Gates has many achieve-nothing flamers dishonestly attacking him on Usenet. Yet, Bill Gates continues to soar — soaring toward becoming perhaps the greatest value-and-job producer in history. Simultaneously, his attention-seeking flamers are self-exposing their nonentity natures while publicly shrinking their souls toward nothingness.

## Half-Life of Usenet

Justice comes to cyberspace as value destroyers shrink toward nothingness and value producers expand toward limitlessness. ...How exactly does that dynamic work in cyberspace?

That dynamic works through the half-life decay (like radioactive half-life decay) of items posted on Usenet Newsgroups — a half-life perhaps as short as a few hours. How does that half-life of Usenet interact with the doubling-life (increasing value delivery) of the World Wide Web? Long-term doubling lives occur for Web sites on which competitive values are constantly building and being delivered to increasingly wider audiences. By contrast, to counter their decaying messages on Usenet, value destroyers must spew more-and-more dishonesties to sustain their illusions of credibility and self-importance. Yet, while their attacks are relentlessly decaying, their dishonesties and malevolences are building in archives that are always available through search engines.

Likewise, integrations of reality are also accumulating and being archived. Thus, whenever needed, those dishonest attacks can be gathered and simultaneously compared to fully integrated honesty on the World Wide Web or in printed literature. ...Such juxtaposition of dishonesty versus honesty makes reality obvious and justice certain.

When nihilistic attacks or ego-boosting smears are gathered and then viewed as a whole, the evil leaps forth, smacking every observer foursquare, eternally trapping unjust attackers in their own disintegrated dishonesties. Consider what happens when disintegrated dishonesty is publicly contrasted to integrated honesty — contrasted point-by-point from every angle. Such vivid contrasts accelerate the public understanding and use of radically new, life-enhancing values. Previously, such values may have taken decades or centuries to gain public acceptance and beneficial use in everyone's life.

Neo-Tech, meaning fully integrated honesty, will publicly advance through the Usenet dynamic via a book titled *Flame-War Justice*. In that book, fully integrated honesty is unjustly, dishonestly attacked from every conceivable angle. Those attacks are then contrasted to widely integrated, fully contextual responses. From such contrasts, the value of even the most radical aspects of fully integrated honesty will become not only publicly clear but publicly acceptable in shorter time frames than possible in the pre cyberspace world.

## The Doubling-Life of Web Sites

The above process of accelerating Neo-Tech Objectivism globally through cyberspace dynamics is catalyzed by widening networks of hyperlinked World Wide Web sites. Fully integrated honesty in the form of hyperlinked Web sites plays off the accumulating Usenet archive and search-engine dynamics. Those Neo-Tech dynamics will be constructed and integrated on the Internet

v

in late 1997 through an interactive Java/ActiveX dynamic called "Ask Zon".

Neo-Tech Objectivism in cyberspace has already cracked the ersatz "leadership" that has stagnated the worldwide advance of Objectivism. What is Objectivism? It is the philosophy of Ayn Rand and Leonard Peikoff. It is the philosophy for benefiting conscious beings. Objectivism is based on the primacy of existence and integrated reason — the new-world philosophy of limitless prosperity and romantic excitement.

Objectivism is the philosophy upon which Neo-Tech/ Zonpower rests. In turn, Neo-Tech/Zonpower is the tool for advancing the primacy of existence around the world. That advance will eliminate irrationality and dishonesty from conscious beings. ...Neo-Tech/Zonpower is the most effective, practical expression of Objectivism, life-enhancing business, and romantic excitement.

Additionally, that Neo-Tech dynamic is breaking the bubbles of irrationality polluting all philosophies, including breaking intolerances toward "different people" and "different believers". Breaking those stagnant intolerances toward people — toward potential customers — will allow an open, honest form of no-compromise Objectivism to advance — Apostle-Paul, reach-everyone style — into realms of limitless prosperity and exciting romance.

## Cyberspace Heaven

The non cyberspace world today has grown for 3000 years from roots of criminal-minded Homeric "heroes", irrational Platonic mysticisms, and fraudulent Augustinian[1] religions — all fed by intentional value destruction, demagoguery, and envy backed by force and fraud. In this criminally manipulated civilization, the duped public is promised life, prosperity, and

---

[1]As a youth, St. Augustine stole other people's property not for need but for kicks. As the Bishop of Hippo, he stole other people's souls not for salvation but for power.

vi

justice in some after-death, imaginary heaven or in some "heroic" remembrance. Indeed, in this anticivilization, everyone has to sacrifice his or her life in order to reach that unreal celestial "reward".

By contrast, today's new cyberspace world will bring conscious beings exciting lives with undreamed prosperity in a real heaven right here on Earth. In that Earthly heaven, fully integrated honesty and justice will mean oblivion for Homeric heroes and all other criminal parasites. Eradication of those humanoids means limitless growth for every competitive human being on this planet.

## The Civilization of the Universe

In the upside-down civilization of the pre cyberspace world, fraud and war are glorified as noble and heroic: Platonistic noble-lie frauds and Homeric macho-hero wars have been historically hyped as ways to bring people to greater heights: political, parasitical heights — *not* competitive, productive heights. Such irrationality eventually brings spiritual and physical death to everyone. By contrast, in the rational Civilization of the Universe, competitive value production, not force and fraud, is what lifts people toward eternal life and happiness.

In cyberspace, harmful parasitical minds remain behind in the closed-circle anticivilization. By contrast, competitive business minds move ahead into the open-ended Civilization of the Universe.

## Discovering New-World Music

Specific metaphors and general metaphors can be the most powerful and sometimes the only means of communicating certain ideas and emotions. Much of classic prose as well as most poems and songs are metaphorical. In fact, general metaphors such as Ayn Rand's novel *Atlas Shrugged* are often the only effective way to introduce radical ideas that are alien to this anticivilization.

While Neo-Tech/Zonpower literature is broadly metaphorical, even right-brain lyrical at times, the literature is not right-brain enough to reach the emotional heart and soul of everyone in this anticivilization. When people emotionally feel the shrunken spirit of this anticivilization, they will actively care about eliminating the unjust harms inflicted upon innocent value producers by intentional value destroyers. Through such active caring for the value producers, all professional value destroyers and their parasitical political leaders will eventually vanish along with their tools of force and fraud.

Until Neo-Tech, no one was willing to consistently stand up and do something about the injustices and purposeful destruction of values that perpetuate this anticivilization. Who really cared about the injustices inflicted by the professional value destroyers upon the competitive value producers? Who really tried to protect and cherish those upon whom the well-being of conscious life depends? Until Neo-Tech, no one consistently stood up to protect unjustly aggrieved value producers from destructive parasites — sub rosa parasites ranging from force-backed politicians and dishonest academics to criminal-minded nihilists and ersatz philosophers.

Yet, no amount of left-brain Neo-Tech literature can deliver the emotional realizations of the sins and virtues woven throughout this bizarrely unnatural anticivilization. Spectacularly new, right-brain metaphorical lyrics are required. ...As an artistic analogy, right-brain impressionists Claude Monet and Vincent van Gogh discovered entirely new ways to emotionally communicate the reality of nature through impressionist art. From another perspective, the abstract art of Pablo Picasso versus the romantic art of Eugéne Delacroix are examples of untouchably different modes for fixed left-brain communication of abstract ideas versus emotional right-brain communication of romantic ideals. Also, consider Mozart's intelligence-boosting piano Concerto #21 and Beethoven's piano/orchestra-dueling Piano Concerto #5. ...The rising Zon literature harnesses the artistic right brain — the exciting romantic brain.

Indeed, weaving a lyrical, right-brain narrative throughout cyberspace is necessary to emotionally communicate the natural Civilization of the Universe currently known to no one on Earth, but necessary to everyone...versus the unnatural anticivilization currently known to everyone on Earth, but necessary to no one.

The rising Zonpower literature has become increasingly metaphorical, even lyrical in parts. Still, further movement toward the right-brain metaphor must evolve over the next few years in order to deliver across all populations a radically new thinking paradigm. A new generation of literature, art, and music will rise from history's longest narrative poem or song comprising up to three-hundred-thousand lines woven through conscious minds. That new-world music will capture the epic journey from Earth's anticivilization to the Civilization of the Universe. ...Those lyrics, which reflect the emotional basis of the Civilization of the Universe, will replace the Homeric poems, which reflect the emotional basis of this anticivilization.

That narrative journey will be titled "Quantum Crossings". It will draw hostility and scorn as it is released in unfinished segments during the years before its completion. Hostility from all quarters is expected. For, acceptance would signal that the Neo-Tech/Zon literature is evolving too slowly — to conservatively — and would fail to accomplish its goal of curing irrationality before everyone is killed by that disease.

Strength grows from resistance. Neo-Tech/Zon must flush out "enemies" and push the limits of scorn and hostility in this anticivilization. Only from actively confronting this irrational anticivilization will come an Objectivist civilization — the Civilization of the Universe for us and our children.

### Wanted: Commercial Objectivists

Harnessed into a competitive business tool, Objectivism can bring never-ending gains in prosperity and happiness to everyone on Earth. With fully integrated honesty, people can heal themselves of anticivilization corruptions. In that process, a Neo-Tech business world will need the services of self-healed people with wide-scope knowledge of Objectivism. To be commercially competitive, however, Objectivists must understand the hard-to-achieve profit dynamics inherent in business. Such businesses advance civilization by aggressively delivering competitive values and jobs to maximum people — a risky, difficult, heroic task.

One derives values from Objectivism by applying its principles to the benevolently tolerant dynamics of business. Does that mean compromising the principles of Objectivism? Absolutely not. To the contrary, competitive success is achieved by developing and delivering the open-ended values of *no-compromise* Objectivism to anyone and everyone worldwide.

For a no-compromise Objectivist professional to become commercially profitable, that person cannot stand on a pedestal, offering only boring, uncompetitive preaching. Instead, he or she must get into the muddy-risky trenches of a nitty-gritty profit battle to demonstrate through hard work the exciting, step-by-step profits available from no-compromise Objectivism.

### Discovering Eternal Prosperity

Neo-Tech Objectivism evolves in cyberspace through confrontation with "enemies" and their hostilities. Additionally, such confrontations provide much of the material for the forthcoming, eye-opening book titled *Flame-War Justice*. That book comprehensively chronicles real-life examples of irrational attacks on the good — dishonest attacks from every angle on newly developing values that benefit everyone. Such a chronicling both in print and across cyberspace will lift the barricades of ignorance and malevolence to bring new knowledge — an eternal knowledge that arises when injustice succumbs to justice, when dishonesty succumbs to honesty, when ignorance succumbs to knowledge.

Thus, comes the limitless prosperity reflected from the Civilization of the Universe. In the Civilization of the Universe, businesspeople become supreme artists — universal composers of heavenly melodies. By contrast, criminal-minded politicians, war makers, and nihilists often march to clanging, nationalistic Wagnerians. Indeed, Wagner is the cocaine of music, making those who get hooked feel ten-feet tall — making destructive parasites feel invincibly powerful.[1]

In counterbalance, businesspeople work through melodiously sensuous, individualistic Debussyans. They deliver the La Mers and Clare de Lunes to this world. They create the seas of value on Earth. They deliver the beams of natural light into night darkness — light reflected from the other side — from the eternally bright Civilization of the Universe.

---

[1]This identification is *not* a criticism of Richard Wagner's great music, which is a supreme example of human creativity, art, and beauty — music that anyone can greatly enjoy.

Concerto #2

# Profound Honesty
### brings
# Limitless Prosperity

In the 1950s, a group called Quadri-I Research[1] discovered that a small minority of persons thought in whole pictures rather than in segments that subsequently built into whole thoughts. Quadri-I also found that each such person generated nearly the same picture for any given thought or idea. Those pictures were similar because they formed immediately — uncorrupted by biases or agendas. Thus, those pictures were more accurate — more in accord with reality. Arbitrary information and errors had no time to enter the thought process. Such corruptions simply dissipated when the whole picture flashed into consciousness.[2]

In the early 1980s, Neo-Tech literature identified that thinking process as Neothink. ...Neothinking is a whole-picture-thinking process that brings riches and excitement to conscious beings as described in the publications, *Neo-Tech Business Control* by Mark Hamilton and *Neo-Tech Global Business Control* by Eric Savage.

Today, most adults think by an opposite process. They begin their thought processes with discrete percepts, concepts, ideas, emotions. From those segments rise the larger segments or thoughts used to make decisions, take actions, and experience emotions. The problem is that those segments can be manipulated and distorted to fit almost any illusion or dishonesty promoted by this anticivilization. Such distortions yield life-diminishing decisions and actions. ...That method of thinking builds profound dishonesties, often well hidden, that block a person's capacity to gain wide-scope understandings and valuable new knowledge.

---

[1]Reference: Larry McNaughton, Tampa, Florida, 1996.

[2]That picture-language thinking has no connection to today's mystical, new-age fads of imaging or visualizing — pictures built from delusions or wishful thinking.

## The Neothink Mind

The Neothink mind thinks simultaneously with both the left brain (full integrations) and the right brain (without boundaries). The Neothink mind thinks in a picture language, which means thinking in integrated, no-boundary images — the ultimate, most sensuous, most powerful form of metaphorical thinking. That mind, in turn, breaks those images into small, powerful segments. Such a breakdown from whole pictures into separate parts provides sources of new knowledge for advancing conscious life toward limitless prosperity and romantic happiness. ...Everyone had a Neothink mind as a young child. And, today, any adult can recapture that young, wide-open mind through fully integrated honesty.

Free of preconceived notions, young children think by an uncorrupted picture process. But, they lose that invaluable picture-language thinking as they are driven by their parents and teachers into the profoundly dishonest, narrow-scope anticivilization. ...By building small distortions into larger distortions, most adults unknowingly think dishonestly about the widest, most important aspects of life. They distort their thoughts by adjusting them to the rationalizations and agendas needed to feel acceptable in this anticivilization. Such a bottom-to-top process becomes a reality-distorting language that cripples the conscious mind.

By contrast, the rare top-to-bottom process retains the honest visual-language mind of childhood. That visual language lets one integrate wide-scope pictures and emotions that cannot be expressed in spoken language or even thought about by people with spoken-language minds. Thus, when encountering ultra-powerful, radical-breakthrough values, most people either ridicule those values or their eyes glaze over as their minds sleep. Such spoken-language minds are blind to the new knowledge, emotions, and values that evolve from visual-language minds.

Right brained, often dyslexic left-handed, even mirror-writer artists and scientists as da Vinci, van Gogh, Cézanne, Monet,

xiii

Newton, and Einstein functioned through picture-language thinking. Einstein could visualize the entire cosmos in a single thought. Then, in one sweep, his mind broke that thought down to submicroscopic particles. In that way, he converted his thoughts into many segments of shockingly new, accurate information that delivered the theories of Special Relativity and Quantum Energy. Only over time did his peers and later others grasp what evolved from Einstein's wide-scope pictures of reality. Even today, aspects of his work are just now being grasped.

Einstein, van Gogh, and Cézanne discovered entirely new aspects of reality from their picture thinking. Years passed, even decades, before society discovered the values flowing from their unusual thinking. Indeed, each canvas of van Gogh and Cézanne today commands many millions of dollars. And, today, Einstein's discoveries are the foundations for all natural sciences. Yet, their wide-scope benefits were initially ridiculed, ignored, or considered boring. ...When society finally awoke to their tremendous values, insightful exploiters parlayed those values into fortune and fame.

Many new, wide-scope values flow from today's Neo-Tech/ Zonpower literature. Most people today, however, are blind to the powerful, practical values of Neo-Tech. But, that blindness will end. ...Consider the discoveries flowing from the following six Neo-Tech pictures:

Neo-Tech Picture 1: The discovery of two opposite, conscious-created civilizations: Our current, unnatural anticivilization versus the natural Civilization of the Universe.

Neo-Tech Picture 2: The discovery that the dynamic for conscious death versus conscious life is criminal parasitism versus competitive business. The anticivilization dynamic propagates through criminal value destruction. The Civilization of the Universe propagates through competitive value production.

Neo-Tech Picture 3: The discovery of mankind's shrunken spirit

— the dishonesties, criminalities, and irrationalities that diminish the spirit of *every* citizen living in this anticivilization. Failure to see the unnecessity of that shrunken spirit is what perpetuates this unnatural anticivilization. ...Failure to reject such spiritual and physical diminishments ultimately brings impotence and death to conscious beings.

Neo-Tech Picture 4: The discovery that the future for everyone on Earth *is* the Civilization of the Universe — an Objectivist civilization free of dishonesty, irrationality, criminality, disease, aging, and death itself.

Neo-Tech Picture 5: The discovery that value-and-job producers of this world are caught in history's highest-stake poker game. That game is run by professional value destroyers — by hidden killers and neocheating looters who propagate this anticivilization through guns, envy, and parasitism. The stakes are the life and death of every conscious being living on Earth.

Neo-Tech Picture 6: The discovery that profound honesty will nonviolently vanish those professional value destroyers, criminal neocheaters, and their anticivilization. ...Chapters 16 and 35 of *Zonpower from Cyberspace* provide an understanding of the white-hat honesties that eradicate professional value destroyers and their black-hat neocheating.

### Profound Honesty delivers Limitless Prosperity

The time frame to bridge the gap for solid, public understandings of the above six discoveries would probably extend beyond the lifetime of every person living on planet Earth today. Thus, the task of Neo-Tech Publishing Company is to collapse that indefinitely long time span into the next few years. Such time-span shrinkage can be accomplished by delivering to everyone the practical, wide-scope values pouring from the Neo-Tech/Zonpower discoveries. The benefits from those values will be unleashed through a series of unusual publications titled

*Quantum Crossings.* As those publications accrue during the next five years, they will vanish the criminal parasites and black-hat neocheaters to end their 2200-year-old poker game of bilking every conscious being out of prosperity, happiness, and life itself.

Those today who have no access to or understanding of Neo-Tech and Zonpower need not worry. The coming *Quantum Crossings* will build the top-to-bottom pictures to let everyone prosper from the profound honesties of Neo-Tech/Zonpower woven around the world.

# Making Everyone a Value

On Usenet in early 1996, a "jobless ex-postal worker living off government checks" anonymously posted hundreds of embittered, envious attacks on successful value-and-job producers and competitive business. He also declared across the Internet his desires for limitless, promiscuous sex. Then, between blizzards of uncontrolled Tourette-like sexual profanities, he publicly posted his intentions to murder U.S. army officers and nuke an American city filled with innocent citizens and children. According to legal counsel, that post constituted a domestic-terrorist threat of murder publicly made over the Internet — a serious crime. For that criminal act, he could face both state and federal felony charges upon revealing his identity.[1]

Later in 1996, that envy-embittered, "ex-postal employee" carrying a virtual-reality AK-47 reappeared on the Internet to emphasize his passion for mass murder as shown in his post quoted below:

>In article <4jgqpc$p6r@utopia.hacktic.nl>,
    nobody@flame.alias.net
>(Anonymous) wrote:
>>I would destroy the entire universe rather than live as a
    slave.
>>And you can quote me on that.
 <snip>
>>Ah - so I have nihilistic "tendencies" now.
>>Nihilism is the belief in NOTHING.
>>I believe in all sorts of things very strongly.
>>I might be a terrifyingly immoral egoist from the point of
    view of
>>communitarian and altruist moral codes, but I'm no nihilist.
>>I am something MUCH, MUCH WORSE!

---

[1]In reality, probably the biggest danger from such a person is blowing out his own brains over his compulsive hatred of life and envy of success — just as Goethe's hateful envy-monger "Young Werther" blew his brains out for the exact same reason. ...Becoming a value producer through Neo-Tech cures such hatred and envy.

How could such a person be a value to Neo-Tech? Herein lies the justice dynamics of cyberspace: That person was transformed into a Neo-Tech servant. Indeed, a controlled servant indentured by integrated honesty that brought forth two public revelations: (1) the deep dishonesties of self-proclaimed Objectivist "leaders" and (2) the deep-rooted destructiveness that dwells in everyone invested in this anticivilization. Consider the following paragraphs:

### Neo-Tech Objectivism Rises from Flames

Dr. Leonard Peikoff is a genuine philosophical leader. He is courageously leading a philosophical Reformation toward Ayn Rand's Objectivism — a Reformation away from destructive, primacy-of-consciousness (i.e.: subjective-authority led) philosophies to a productive, primacy-of-existence (i.e.: objective-reality led) philosophy. ...Dr. Peikoff is to philosophy what the 16th-century Martin Luther was to religion.

Yet, in April 1995, Leonard Peikoff, while making valid points about illegal private armies, made an irrational, potentially murderous error by "condemning" innocent militia self-defenders to the initiatory force of a corrupt government. Martin Luther in the early 16th century made the same murderous error by condemning innocent peasant self-defenders to the initiatory force of a corrupt government. Luther's moral error triggered the brutal government slaughter of many innocent peasants. ...Dogmatist John Calvin followed Luther in purifying the religious Reformation by directly committing premeditated murder: On gaining access to the initiatory force of government, he had "evil" heretics burned alive at the stake.

Today, Objectivist dogmatists follow Peikoff in purifying the philosophical Reformation. If they gained the physical-force power of government, what would those "Calvinist" dogmatists do to "evil" heretics like militia members, libertarians, and Neo-Tech Objectivists?

Indeed, this is the anticivilization. In advancing one's

anticivilization investments, each becomes malicious, even murderous — directly or indirectly. Thus, certain Objectivist "leaders" eagerly embraced as their ally that embittered nihilist described above who, chained to an Internet keyboard by Neo-Tech, proclaimed his passion to commit mass murder and have promiscuous sex with everyone possible.

Why did those Objectivists publicly, dishonestly abandon principle to embrace such an entity as their protector and ally? Solely because he uncontrollably libeled and physically threatened their competition — their perceived "enemy" — the Neo-Tech Objectivists. He recklessly endangered the lives of innocent value producers with defaming libel and malignant innuendo that no Objectivist would dare display. Thus, such a person became their sanctioned anti Neo-Tech mouthpiece. ...Objectivist honesty? Objectivist principles? What better demonstration of people supporting their irrational investments in this bizarre anticivilization at any self-destructive cost or hypocritical dishonesty. At some point, however, each will have to look at his or her picture and discover a Dorian Gray — the visual results of one's pact with destructive irrationality.

Consider, for example, a dishonest Objectivist "leader" who cheered on that nihilist servant and fed him libelous information to expand his attacks toward her enemy — fully integrated honesty. Therein lies her investment in this anticivilization. Still, in the broadest sense, that Objectivist "leader" is no better or worse than anyone irrationally investing in this anticivilization — no better or worse than that jobless nihilist.

Indeed, any person ultimately promotes criminally murderous behaviors whenever he or she promotes irrationality — whenever that person upholds dishonesty to protect his or her anticivilization investments. ...Yet, even she can, as can any Objectivist, self-heal the wounds of dishonesty to become a growing value in an Objectivist world — in the Civilization of the Universe.

Through fully integrated honesty, people can open their eyes to the irrationalities practiced by every investor in this anticivilization, ranging from murderous psychopaths, to dishonest academics, even to outstanding Objectivist value producers, *including* Neo-Tech Objectivists and risk-taking business heroes. ...The pervasive diseases of irrationality and dishonesty beget criminality and destructiveness, directly or indirectly, by force or by sanction, in every conscious being on Earth. Without fully integrated honesty, *everyone* will ultimately kill directly or indirectly to preserve his or her anticivilization investment, ego, or livelihood.

But, the mental illnesses, irrationalities, and dishonesties of this anticivilization will shrivel and vanish in cyberspace driven by fully integrated honesty. Indeed, the profound honesty of Neo-Tech is taking over Objectivism, healing it, and propagating it worldwide — propagating it through competitive business.

Among the most moving testimonials for *The Neo-Tech Discovery* are those that reveal its extraordinary effectiveness in curing mental illnesses — psychoses, neuroses, alcoholism, obesity, mysticism, drug abuse, depression, criminalities. Consider that after several months immersion into the integrated honesty of Neo-Tech, the profane government-dependent nihilist described above was transformed by a Neo-Tech editor[1] into a propagator of Neo-Tech ideas on the Internet. ...A similar transformation could occur with criminal-minded President Clinton as explained on page 5 of the Golden-Helmet "Victory" Overture at the end of this manuscript.

---

[1]Drew "Kaiser" Ellis, an editor of Neo-Tech Publishing Company, developed the string-controlled KOAH/ACSE machine to study the dishonesty disease in public cyberspace.

Concerto #4

# Neo-Tech Empowers Objectivists

From August 21, 1995 to June 19, 1996, the profound honesty of Neo-Tech flowed through cyberspace. Through the Internet Newsgroup alt.philosophy.objectivism (apo), that flow of honesty liberated "official" Objectivists from their closed circles of stagnation as summarized below:

1. Broke their thirty-year-old dogmatic structure and exposed their pseudo-intellectualism. Such do-nothing, closed-circle intellectualisms will disappear with the publication of a book titled *Flame-War Justice*.

2. Deflated their illusions of philosophical "authority", which for thirty years harmfully retarded the wide-scale advance of Objectivism.

3. Compelled "official" Objectivists into accepting as allies their previous worst enemies such as Libertarians, Kelley-type Objectivists, and other "evil" heretics. Those "official" Objectivists became comrades with their previous enemies in trying to defeat their new, worse-than-worst enemy: the evilissimo Neo-Tech. For, through its honesty templates, Neo-Tech publicly revealed the dishonesties, hypocrisies, and impotence of "official" Objectivists.

4. Contrasted the backward-looking, intellectualizing-mode of "official" Objectivists to the forward-looking, business-mode of Neo-Tech Objectivists.

5. Caused Objectivist "officials" to create a tightly monitored newsgroup humanities.philosophy.objectivism (hpo). Their entire purpose for creating hpo was to explicitly censor and prevent fully integrated honesty — Neo-Tech — from breaking false authority. But, ironically, hiding from Neo-Tech in their cloistered hpo newsgroup, those same "officials" are now demystifing and liberating themselves.

For, they are compelled to deal rationally with their new allies — their previous worst enemies. Thus, through Neo-Tech, stunted Objectivist "leaders" are growing again, empowering themselves. They are learning to communicate more maturely, more effectively — with less flaming, less name calling, less emotionalism...less stagnating dogmatism.[1]

6. Drove cyberspace Objectivism into a stronger position for worldwide growth.

Liberating Objectivists for future growth was the goal of Neo-Tech Publishing. Moreover, achieving that goal never involved compromising Objectivism. For, Ayn Rand's and Leonard Peikoff's Objectivism is a universal philosophy of exquisite consistency.

---

[1]Neo-Tech associates hold no hostile attitudes toward anyone posting on Usenet. While they will counterpunch with fully integrated templates when dishonestly attacked, they never initiate attacks, flames, insults, or profanities toward anyone. Yet, very important, the attacks on Neo-Tech provide the material to evolve commercial products needed for delivering an Objectivist civilization — the Civilization of the Universe — to everyone on Earth.

The profound honesty and resulting values of Neo-Tech Objectivism are rejected by today's Establishment. Yet, that Establishment rejection is what keeps Neo-Tech pushing into ever deeper areas of non acceptance. Such non acceptance will culminate in Quantum Crossings — the one-way bridges into the Civilization of the Universe.

Neo-Tech does not benefit by acceptance from *any* quarter in this anticivilization. Thus, as each new level of Neo-Tech begins gaining acceptance, Neo-Tech Publishing must push beyond the pale — into ever more "outlandish" realms of objective reality and knowledge. Indeed, profound honesty is used to constantly move beyond acceptance in this anticivilization — beyond acceptance even by Neo-Tech supporters and associates. That wide-scope, long-range progress must continue until the dishonest, irrational, murderous anticivilization has vanished from Earth — until we all live with eternal prosperity and romantic excitement in an ever growing honest, rational, benevolent Objectivist civilization.

By reading the book version of *Profound Honesty,* one can easily, contextually grasp Neo-Tech and Zonpower. Indeed, those who carefully read *Profound Honesty* will be joyfully awakened as they jump beyond competition in this anticivilization. ...Eventually, everyone will be happily jolted out of this anticivilization by the compelling simplicity of Neo-Tech/Zonpower.

# One, Two, Three...Prosperity
## *Song 1*

The Journey
from
Earth's Anticivilization
to the
Civilization of the Universe

think999@ix.netcom.com
"We are dealing with something powerful here.
The most powerful ideas in the Universe.
We are dealing with Neo-Tech in Cyberspace."

The Mozarts, Shelleys, Keatses, Raphaels, Büchners, and Schuberts are not the only ones who die too young. We all die too young. So little of our potential is ever realized. After youth, survivors unnaturally age, grow old, and die. None come close to the full-scope happiness and prosperity possible to conscious life. None find the spiritual answers tragically sought by Tolstoy. Some live bound within Baudelaire's visions of man-made cities...others within Frost's visions of snowy country nights. Yet, what was Emily Dickenson saying in her poems of nature, consciousness, and death? How can we live our natural lives — lives without limits, yet within the limits of nature? The answer is Neo-Tech. For, Neo-Tech will bring a profoundly honest civilization within cyberspace to create the Civilization of the Universe on planet Earth.

## INTRODUCTION
The profound honesty of Neo-Tech is taking over a philosophy called Objectivism and implementing it through worldwide business dynamics. What is Objectivism? And, why implement it worldwide?

Objectivism is a philosophy rooted in Aristotle,

1

discovered by Ayn Rand, nailed down by Dr. Leonard Peikoff, and now being dispersed globally through Neo-Tech. The goal is to rapidly bring an Objectivist civilization to planet Earth. For, an Objectivist civilization will bring every conscious person wide-open prosperity. How will every person gain such prosperity through a philosophy? What powers and riches are derived from implementing Objectivism worldwide? ...*Profound Honesty* answers those questions.

To be of universal value, mankind's one valid philosophy — Objectivism — must be liberated from its stagnant leaders and academic authorities. Objectivism must be injected into the action-mode dynamics of competitive value production. That liberation of Objectivist philosophy is outlined in Song 2.

The liberation of Objectivism will deliver prosperity to every honest person through the three epiphanies:
ONE, TWO, THREE...PROSPERITY

*Three Epiphanies from Three Facts*
Conscious beings will gain eternal prosperity through three epiphanies arising from three facts:

Fact 1: The Civilization of the Universe and an anticivilization are antithetical domains of honesty and dishonesty — the either/or domains in which all conscious beings dwell throughout time and space.

Fact 2: Conscious beings on Earth unknowingly live in an anticivilization built upon (a) Homer's criminal-minded heroes, (b) Plato's noble-lie dishonesties, and (c) Augustine's death-demanding mysticisms.

Fact 3: Fully integrated honesty (Neo-Tech) and wide-scope integrations (Neothink) dissolve the anticivilization dynamics of value destruction, aging, and death. ...In its place appears the Objectivist-civilization dynamics of value production, youth, and prosperity.

2

Until liberated by epiphanies rising from those three facts, we remain as blind mice trapped in the bizarre maze of an irrational civilization. Indeed, trapped in Earth's domain of illusions, we remain unaware of our stunted spirits and shrunken visions. Moreover, we knowingly or unknowingly cling to the life-losing investments and commitments that uphold this anticivilization. As such, whenever the circumstances arise, each of us will commit injustices and harm innocent others by voice or deed. ...Thus, after youth, we all shrink toward death, then to dust.

But, on opening our minds and actions to fully integrated honesty, we gain the wide-scope integrations needed to vanish this mystically twisted anticivilization. In its place will rise an Objectivist civilization — the rational Civilization of the Universe. In that natural realm of universal honesty, everyone thrives with abiding happiness and limitless vision. In that illusion-free empyrean, even the most aggressive competitor never acts unjustly or inflicts harm upon others. ...Thus, after youth, honest people grow beyond the stars toward eternal prosperity.

## EPIPHANY ONE

### *Liberating Philosophy*

Philosophy. Who understands philosophy? Who really cares about philosophy? Very few. For, it is a highly technical subject reserved mainly for professional philosophers dwelling in academic realms. Yet, everyone lives by a philosophy — subconsciously, implicitly. Only one philosophy is based on the total, wide-scope well-being of conscious life — the philosophy of Objectivism.

The Civilization of the Universe depends on Objectivist philosophy. Thus, Epiphany One involves liberating stagnant Objectivism from its anticivilization dogmatizers.

*Song 1: One, Two, Three...Prosperity*

Objectivism is the philosophy of rational, conscious life — of fully integrated honesty. Yet, no one on planet Earth has consistently lived by the philosophy of Objectivism — not even its originator and developer, Ayn Rand and Leonard Peikoff. Even though Rand and Peikoff could discover, develop, and intellectually deal with Objectivism, they nor anyone else can live by it any more than can Hillary Clinton, the Pope, or O. J. Simpson. For, the modus operandi of everyone in this anticivilization rests upon a foundation of dishonesty and criminality.

Epiphany One sweeps a floodlight beneath the rickety structure of criminal dishonesty that supports all anticivilization investments and commitments. Once permanently spotlighted in one's mind, that person can finally identify the destruction-driven irrationalities and criminalities of this anticivilization.

*Eureka! I have found the light to identify and isolate the anticivilization. I can now banish it from my life, bit by bit, piece by piece.*

## EPIPHANY TWO

*Neo-Tech Stimulants*

Epiphany Two makes the crystal-clear identification that the anticivilization and the Civilization of the Universe are two inescapable facts. Through Neo-Tech arises a new, wide-scope vision. Within that vision lie the stimulants needed to vanish each perpetrator of that anticivilization.

*Eureka! I have found the stimulants to identify and isolate each anticivilization perpetrator. I can now banish them from my life, one by one.*

## EPIPHANY THREE

*Vanishing the Anticivilization*

Epiphany Three reveals a specific tool: The wide-scope accounting tool called the Golden Helmet as detailed in the

Appendix of this manuscript. That tool provides a protocol for vanishing the archetype institution of wide-scope destruction in today's anticivilization — the United States Internal Revenue Service (IRS). Moreover, that concrete example serves as a model for vanishing other destructive, anticivilization institutions and bureaucracies.

Through that Golden-Helmet protocol, the unnecessary acceptance of destructive institutions is first recognized, then undermined, and finally vanished. Indeed, that change from intimidated acceptance to unequivocal rejection will vanish the destructive institutions of this anticivilization to bring forth the Civilization of the Universe.

*Eureka! I have found the tool to identify and isolate each destructive institution of this anticivilization. I can now banish them from my life, one after the other.*

Epiphany One, Two, Three...here comes eternal prosperity.

## ETERNAL PROSPERITY

### *The Neo-Tech Discovery*

Neo-Tech is the action mode that cures the disease causing this anticivilization. That disease is dishonesty. In turn, dishonesty comprises irrationality and mysticism. ...The *Neo-Tech Discovery* published by Neo-Tech Worldwide is a separate telephone-book size book — an 800-page document that identifies and isolates the information matrix for ending the irrationalities and mysticisms of this anticivilization.

### *Zonpower Rules Cyberspace*

*Zonpower* is the first document written on Earth from the perspective of an Objectivist civilization. *Zonpower* gazes deep into the radically different Objectivist realm — into the Civilization of the Universe realm. Through *Zonpower*, that

Objectivist civilization is already rising on planet Earth.  Each bit and piece of that new-color Objectivist civilization forever replaces bit by bit, piece by piece, this 2300-year-old dishonest anticivilization.

## The Key

The key to jumping the abyss from today's anticivilization into tomorrow's Objectivist civilization is discovered in Epiphany Two.  That discovery is the vivid recognition of the dishonest anticivilization that dominates planet Earth versus the honest Civilization of the Universe that reigns throughout existence. ...Those two opposite civilizations represent the two fundamental choices faced by conscious beings: dishonesty versus honesty — death versus life.

Indeed, death or life *is* the fundamental choice of conscious beings.  Moreover, no conscious being on Earth can escape aging and death until he or she identifies, understands, then acts upon fully integrated honesty.  Anything less condemns one to a shrinking life leading to death and dust. ...To survive and prosper eternally one must first see everything in concrete terms of an anticivilization versus an Objectivist civilization.

One of many specific steps already being taken in that direction through Neo-Tech — fully integrated honesty — is described below:

---

*Scarlet Lettering Baleful Philosophers*

The importance of Objectivism to everyone's future is captured in a single fact:  Objectivism *is* the philosophy of the Civilization of the Universe.

A forthcoming book titled *Flame-War Justice* will demonstrate how anyone can identify and then scarlet letter those who are blocking Objectivism from sweeping planet Earth.  That scarlet lettering will vanish their baleful influence.

*Flame-War Justice* will bury the stagnation of Objectivism caused by ersatz Objectivists and their closed-circle "leaders".

From May 1995 to April 1996, a furious flame war was waged in cyberspace by the Objectivist dogmatists against the closest ally of Objectivism — Neo-Tech.  Why did the self-appointed "guardians" of Objectivism attack the action-mode producers of Neo-Tech?  Because Neo-Tech is tearing Objectivism away from their elitist

---

"leaders" and propelling it forward, into the hands of the honest, non intellectual, working class — beyond the control of dogmatists and elitists.

In a pyrotechnic display of dishonesty, those self-aggrandizing dogmatists made their last stand against Neo-Tech — their last stand for shrinking Objectivism into a cloister of dark-age scholastics. ...At this historic juncture of exploding technology and apocalyptic threats to mankind's survival, such shrinking of Objectivism would mark mankind's greatest disaster. But, instead, Neo-Tech, the wide-open, worldwide facilitator of Objectivism will safely carry everyone into the next millennium, eventually delivering eternal prosperity to all.

Neo-Tech never initiates attacks on Objectivists or their ideas. Moreover, it has never attacked a single tenet of Objectivism. Indeed, Neo-Tech has always supported, without compromise, the tenets of Objectivism. ...Certainly, Neo-Tech parries and counterpunches dishonest attacks by baleful Objectivists and their nihilist allies. Neo-Tech, moreover, profitably uses those attacks and responses in its published literature.

Yes, some aggressive Neo-Tech self-leaders made learning errors on Usenet. But, they openly admitted those errors once realized...and then corrected them. Also, the editors of Neo-Tech literature have appreciatively acknowledged and corrected errors in their publications whenever pointed out. For, Neo-Tech is wide-open — void of defensiveness — always correcting, improving, forever growing. ...Neo-Tech is the new direction Objectivism must now travel.

### Objectivism for the Proletariat

Because the working classes do not intellectualize philosophy, elitist Objectivists dismiss them as the great "unwashed". Fully integrated honesty, however, is drying up those uncompetitive, elitist Objectivists. But, no one needs to fear diminishment of Objectivism. To the contrary, Neo-Tech is taking over elitist-crippled Objectivism to heal it and spread its practical values among "non intellectual" working people. Neo-Tech is weaving the practical benefits of Objectivism among the honest working classes. Indeed, fully integrated honesty — Neo-Tech — will bring an Objectivist civilization to everyone via those working classes. ...One, two, three, here comes eternal prosperity.

### The "Philosopher" Zoo
*Objectivists Caged in Cyberspace*

From July 1995 to June 1996, Neo-Tech Publishing Company (NTP) posted on three Usenet newsgroups in cyberspace for two

Song 1

purposes:

1. The first purpose was to expose ersatz philosophers and cultist Objectivists who dishonestly used Usenet — specifically the newsgroup: alt.philosophy.objectivism (apo) — to promote their own false importance through mixtures of dishonest arguments and name-calling attacks against anyone who questioned their dogmas. Neo-Tech exposed their fakeries through templates of integrated facts. As a result, those cultists were driven to create a closed newsgroup — humanities.philosophy.objectivism (hpo) — designed to ban explicitly any mention of Neo-Tech and to censor any dynamic of fully integrated honesty.

Into their self-created newsgroup the cultists fled, locking the door behind. ...They had herded themselves into a caged zoo for public viewing.

Those Objectivists found they were not alone in their no-escape zoo. Unwittingly, they had locked themselves in with a warrior band of ferocious Libertarians flanked by savvy Kelley-freed Objectivists. Those warriors are now tearing to pieces the hypocritical spoutings of every flowing-robe Randian cultist. Indeed, today, those desperate cultists are arguing more shrilly, senselessly, and frequently than ever from their sealed cage. But, now, they have been publicly discredited and are unable to further retard the advance of Objectivism. As a result, propelled by integrated honesty, orgasmically exciting Neo-Tech/Objectivism is spreading throughout the World Wide Web, advancing beyond the closed circles of stagnant, Ayn-Rand disciples.

Neo-Tech, as anything else, does not advance through time-wasting, do-nothing arguments on philosophical newsgroups. It advances through dynamic cyberspace communications reaching all classes of people in all nations. With 15,000 daily visits[1], the lively Neo-Tech web site introduces far more new people to Objectivist/Libertarian ideas in one day than do all the Objectivist and Libertarian sites combined in a month.[2]

---

[1] Daily hit statistics are now publicly displayed on the Neo-Tech web site: http://www.neo-tech.com

[2] Neo-Tech Publishing (NTP) and its associates have always recognized and supported the many genuine, value-delivering works of Objectivists and Libertarians. For years, NTP and its associates have been financial contributors to the Ayn Rand Institute (ARI), the Institute for Objectivist Studies (IOS), and many Libertarian organizations. NTP also offered to support Dr. Peikoff's daily radio show with paid spots, but the offer was declined. Rejecting good-paying business sponsors is perhaps one reason the daily show failed commercially and now struggles as a subsidized weekend show. ...While explicitly criticizing their mystical errors and public

(footnote continued on page 9)

With the worldwide cyber communication of Objectivist/Libertarian values free from dogmatic elitists, cyberspace will increasingly become the Civilization of the Universe ruled by the fully integrated honesty of Neo-Tech. The Civilization of the Universe, which is an Objectivist civilization, is now entering planet Earth through Neo-Tech from cyberspace. ...Neo-Tech was made for cyberspace. Cyberspace was made for Neo-Tech.

2. The second purpose of NTP posting on Usenet was to generate commercially publishable material. Some of that commercial material is on the Neo-Tech web site and published in a book titled *Get It All*. Usenet was also used to gather the material for NTP's forthcoming book titled *Flame-War Justice*. Now, those caged Objectivist cultists are carping about NTP's intention to publish their dishonest Usenet posts without their permissions. They huff and snort about copyrights, property rights, and lawsuits. Thus, for the record, NTP states: Any dishonest, out-of-context post used to attack innocent parties has no claim under objective laws for copyrights, intellectual rights, or property rights. Such posts will be used without permission at any time in any way, in part or full, by the attackee to (1) answer dishonest attackers, (2) defend against libelous attackers, (3) set the public record straight, and (4) deliver justice to dishonest attackers. Furthermore, NTP would welcome any lawsuit challenging its free use of such public posts and will mount countersuits whenever appropriate and advantageous.

NTP and its associates have always welcomed fair criticisms and honest arguments. They have gratefully learned how to change and effectively benefit from valid criticisms on the Internet. But, pips who dishonestly attack innocent value producers must deal with the poker-ruthless, sandbagging Frank R. Wallace who has a long record of subtle goading and laying back to "suck 'em in". Then, springing the fully integrated honesty of Neo-Tech, Wallace converts such attacks and adversaries into both short-term profits and long-term advantages. And, Dr. Wallace will continue to do so until maximum profits are extracted and full justice is delivered. ...Neo-Tech wins today. Neo-Tech owns tomorrow.

---

(footnote continued from page 8)

misbehaviors, NTP always recognizes and openly defends the values of many major Objectivist "authorities", including Harry Binswanger, Peter Schwartz, and especially the heavily pip-attacked Leonard Peikoff (even though Dr. Peikoff badly needs a banker's haircut and a Wall-Street business suit to help unleash his greatly under exploited values and power.) ...Today, caged in cyberspace, the old Objectivist preachers and their monotone choirs are being left behind by the lively spread of Neo-Tech. Sadly, their thirty years of productive efforts are now calcifying into endless, do-nothing arguments on Usenet.

Song 1

## Person, Author, and Book Index
### for the
### Addendum, Opening Ceremonies, and Song 1

c-2=cover 2 (inside front cover)

10

Liberation in Cyberspace
*Song 2*
in
Three Stanzas

# Liberating

## *Objectivism*

*Stanza I*

### The Liberation Manifesto

*pages 1-18*

*Stanza II*

### Tools that Win Flame Wars

*pages 19-26*

*Stanza III*

### Fruits of Victory
### A Glimpse into the Future

*pages 27-39*

Stanza I

## Table of Contents

---

**Outline**
for
**LIBERATING OBJECTIVISM**

*Stanza I* outlines the takeover of Objectivism by fully integrated honesty — Neo-Tech.

*Stanza II* reveals the cyberspace tools for vanishing Luddite Objectivists. Illustrates the lesson of tolerance and compassion without compromising philosophical principles or personal integrity.

*Stanza III* provides a glimpse into the future — into the coming Neo-Tech Objectivist civilization in which all conscious beings live naturally — live with eternal honesty, prosperity, and happiness.

---

# LIBERATING OBJECTIVISM

## Stanza I

# THE LIBERATION MANIFESTO

Probably every Objectivist at some time has reasoned: "Objectivism is so logical, correct, certain. Its benefits to conscious beings are so obvious. Why isn't Objectivism applied everywhere by everyone? Why don't we have an Objectivist civilization now?" Yet, Objectivism is profitably applied almost nowhere. Why? The reason lies in the leadership of Objectivism — an obstructionist leadership. The deep-rooted failure of that leadership prevents Objectivism from spreading to populations worldwide.

Forward-moving applications of Objectivism into new areas by "outsiders" has always been resisted by a clique of self-appointed leaders and authorities. Because that clique demands "purity" before any new action can be taken, it effectively blocks practical, wide-scope applications of Objectivism in most areas of human life and business. Those ever-tightening circles of purity kept everyone ignorant of the wider-scope visions needed to evolve Objectivism into a civilization for the entire planet. ...Today, however, in cyberspace, business-driven Neo-Tech exposes the harm and dishonesties propagated by those closed-circle Objectivists.

## Bogus Leaders and Authorities

Demands for philosophical purity perpetuates stagnation while protecting the parasitical positions of Luddite leaders and self-appointed authorities. Deriving power from their dogmas, they must condemn anyone who deviates from their control. Like the leaders of the Catholic church during the dark ages, today's Objectivist "leaders" maintain a grip on their followers by attacking competition and condemning deviants.

Such "leaders" of Objectivism must condemn each deviant without consideration of the values that person has contributed to them, others, and society — values that usually vastly outweigh any impurity peccadillo. They must also dismiss all potential future values from that deviant. ...Those Objectivists demand a dependent, following mode from everyone.

Luddite Objectivists are cult-like Randians who attack new, unauthorized applications of Objectivism. They attack aggressive, independent doers or value producers who apply Objectivism beyond authorized realms. They declare such people immoral heretics. They attack with mantras of name-calling nouns such as wackos and adjectives such as evil. They use ad hominem attacks, out-of-context dishonesties, sweeping non sequiturs, and scenario-spun lies rather than rational arguments. Such people should examine their irrationalities and consider Marie Curie's advice: "Be less curious about people and more curious about ideas".

Those closed circles of purity protect the dogmatists from the demands of growth and evolvement — protect them from having to compete in the free market with applications of Objectivism. Listed below are three specific examples in which the dogmatists use dishonesty to avoid competition:

(1) *Politics* with its irrational, ad hominem attacks on drummed-out Objectivist Libertarians.

(2) *Psychology* with its irrational, ad hominem attacks on drummed-out Objectivist psychologist Nathaniel Branden.

(3) *Philosophy* and other academic areas with their irrational, ad hominem attacks on the many other drummed-out

5

Song 2

Stanza #1

Song 2

*Song 2: Liberating Objectivism*

Objectivists ranging from philosopher David Kelley to economist Murray Rothbard.

Ayn Rand's Objectivist philosophy requires no leaders or authorities. Objectivism requires no defense or protection. For, Objectivism is rooted in unassailable reality. Luddite leaders block the universal application of Objectivism. Individual self-leaders on the Internet are now ousting those false leaders. Vanishing the Luddites will let Objectivism flow more freely into business, politics, and everyday life. ...No more manipulating dishonesties and ax-grinding agendas as found in their Rand/Branden, Peikoff/Kelley, and Objectivists/Libertarian type wars[1]. Instead, Objectivism will be profitably applied everywhere through Neo-Tech business dynamics. ...What about the wars with Neo-Tech? What wars? Wars do not exist with Neo-Tech. For, Neo-Tech extinguishes all wars — always to its and everyone else's eventual advantage.

Sooner or later, all Objectivists will realize no conflict exists with Neo-Tech. They will realize that Neo-Tech is the business/application mode of Objectivism. They will realize that Neo-Tech literature pushes the furthest known limits — the most future vision of Objectivist business dynamics in order to apply Objectivism to all areas of conscious life. Moreover, they will discover that the extension of Neo-Tech into Zonpower is actually an array of metaphors integrating the most advanced knowledge of objective reality.

The Zonpower theories and hypotheses are presented as metaphors, not proven facts. Yet, none of the Zonpower theories or hypotheses contradict the laws of nature. Indeed, they all correspond to the laws of physics — the laws of nature. ...Moreover, exotic names such as *Zon*, *Zonpower*, and *Cassandra's Secret* are effective marketing tools for the general population.

---

[1]For specific examples arising from those "wars", see footnote on page 18 at the end of this Stanza I.

6

*Why Neo-Tech Sandbagged the Objectivist "Leaders"*

As previously done with selected officials in government along with certain white-collar-hoax businesspeople, Neo-Tech sandbagged various self-proclaimed leaders and false authorities on the Internet as part of the world's biggest poker game. On the Objectivist newsgroup (apo), Neo-Tech sandbagged its flamers along with many ersatz Objectivists. Through that process, Neo-Tech achieved its apo agenda. One part of that agenda was to produce material needed for the forthcoming book, *Flame-War Justice,* to be released by Neo-Tech Worldwide.

Was another part of the Neo-Tech agenda to "convert" apo Objectivists into Neo-Tech Objectivists? No. Such an agenda is too narrow. Neo-Tech sandbagged the self-appointed leaders of Objectivism to break their false authorities that impeded the worldwide advance of Objectivism.

*Vanishing Bogus "Leaders"*

To back up some: What about those self-appointed leaders of Objectivism who continue their delusions of being Randian heroes? They use their dogmatisms to draw attention to themselves. They try to gain authority status by tying Ayn Rand's philosophy into knots of narrow-scope purity while blocking others from competitively advancing Objectivism to the masses worldwide. ...They strive to be philosopher kings lording over a small kingdom of cult followers.

But, Neo-Tech draws those false authorities into self-exposure traps that collapse their harmful positions. For, they are the ones who darken Ayn Rand's name and prevent the wide-spread, profitable use of her great work. Indeed, for thirty years, such people have been major impediments to the natural spread of Objectivism and its practical applications around the world.

Progress toward an Objectivist civilization comes not from do-nothing dogmatists posturing as protective purists. Progress

7

comes from aggressively applying Objectivism in the real world. Genuine progress requires constant hard work — consistent discipline, thought, and control. Only by competitively applying Objectivism will the real problems of impurity be out-competed and eventually disappear. Indeed, the totally principled, no-compromise Objectivism of Rand and Peikoff is the most powerful and ultimately the only effective form of Objectivism. But, Objectivism must be competitively evolved in all areas of productive activities, not kept in ever tightening knots of hypocrisy and stagnation.

### Saving Ayn Rand from Aristotle's Tragedy

Consider a parallel example of over 2000 years ago: As with Ayn Rand today, the analogous Aristotelian hangers-on stagnated his philosophy with their self-created dogmatisms. Those self-serving "hero-worshipers" buried the precious opportunity for society to advance toward an Aristotelian civilization. They buried the practical applications of Aristotle's work until the Renaissance 1500 years later. That disastrous stagnation by the Aristotelian dogmatizers eventually allowed the Catholic church to usurp a nicely petrified package of Aristotelian concepts into its official dogma.

In that way, Aristotle's name and work were darkened. His philosophy was viewed out of context, thus, was grossly misunderstood and vigorously maligned when the Renaissance arrived. Civilization-advancing giants such as Francis Bacon, Galileo, Descartes, and Newton were incensed at Aristotle and his philosophy for retarding civilization for two millennia. But, what if they had the opportunity to view Aristotle's work free of its closed-circle packaging by self-appointed "protectors" of the status quo? What if Bacon, Galileo, Descartes, and Newton knew what the dogmatist — the scholastics — had done to Aristotle and his philosophy in order to retain their self-proclaimed authorities?

Those Renaissance giants would have realized that Aristotle

was not the greatest villain against progress but the greatest hero for progress. With that recognition and their use of Aristotle's tremendous values, they would have advanced their own lives and brilliant works even further, especially Descartes. ...The ersatz-philosopher dogmatists, not Aristotle, were the villains who stunted civilization for 2000 years.

Not until the 20th century with the work of Ayn Rand did Aristotle's philosophy rise again to gain its rightful recognition and application as a supreme civilization-advancing value. ...Ayn Rand broke through and evolved Aristotle's great work in a way somewhat analogous to how Einstein broke through and evolved Newton's great work.

Consider also the example of Hippocrates and Galen: Hippocrates with his great civilization-advancing, breakthrough work in establishing the objective practice of medicine. Then, Galen, the physician/surgeon for the Roman gladiators, radically advanced the understanding of human anatomy, physiology, and the effective practice of medicine. The relationship of their work to one another is somewhat analogous to the relationship between Ayn Rand's and Leonard Peikoff's work in discovering and implementing the human-based philosophy of Objectivism.

As happened with Aristotle, the self-appointed authorities of Hippocrates and Galen — tragically with the help of Galen himself — stagnated further major advances for the next 1500 years. ...Not until the 19th century era of Louis Pasteur and Joseph Lister[1] did medicine finally resume its breakthrough advances. But, today, major advances in medicine are again being stagnated by the armed authorities of the FDA and the dishonest machinations of politicians.

------

[1]Pasteur and Lister were masters at taking their radical Zon-like hypotheses and converting them into saving literally hundreds of millions of human lives. In the past few centuries, such value-producing heroes in medicine and business have managed to enhance and save more human lives than the value-destroying bureaucrats and politicians have been able to drain and kill.

(footnote continued on next page)

Song 2

Song 2

Stanza #1

*Song 2: Liberating Objectivism*

Will history repeat? Will the spectacular opportunity for advancing civilization through the great work of Ayn Rand and Leonard Peikoff likewise be darkened and stagnated — tragically with the help of Peikoff himself? Will the non competitive "authorities" who dogmatize Objectivism for unearned benefits succeed in burying Objectivism? Will they succeed in preventing business dynamics from unleashing its limitless values to the working populations of today's world?

Will Rand follow Aristotle's fate? Here lies the real danger of the Peikoffian dogmatists: The Catholic Inquisition used a dogmatized Aristotilian philosophy to persecute heretics, including Galileo. That principle, in turn, led to killing countless innocent people. The police-state Peikoffian hierarchy is dogmatizing Rand with its own narrow-scope spin to use government force to persecute militia members, regardless if they are guilty or innocent of objective crimes. Such a principle would eventually lead to the government killing countless innocent people. ...With the fully integrated honesty of Neo-Tech now available, no such disaster is going to occur.

"Save me from the Randians", Ayn Rand once remarked. Neo-Tech is doing that today.

### Success through Commercial Dynamics

Consider Ayn Rand's and Leonard Peikoff's work: Objectivism evolved and advanced through commercial dynamics. First were the major publishers rolling out Ayn Rand's books, followed by Warner Brothers through the movie "The Fountainhead". Next came Nathaniel Branden with his own important contributions, including his highly successful NBI corporation that got commercial Objectivism rolling. And,

---

(footnote continued from previous page)
With nuclear and biological weapons available today, that positive ratio of life to death could suddenly, disastrously reverse. Only Objectivism implemented through aggressive Neo-Tech business modes can eliminate that potential disaster.

finally, came Leonard Peikoff with his forward-movement work on Objectivism and its application to new areas with his many commercial products — invaluable books, lectures, courses, tapes. Without those commercial dynamics, Objectivism today would be virtually unknown and unavailable.

Today, unfortunately, the self-serving dogmatists have drawn even Peikoff into their stagnation with his ad hominem, police-state intolerances. They are shrinking Objectivism into ever narrower purities to protect their authoritarian positions. They desperately try to prevent those beyond their influence or control from driving Objectivism forward into new and wider realms.

Today, however, the dynamic of fully integrated honesty — Neo-Tech — is breaking those closed circles of false authorities, freeing Objectivism to advance through competitive business dynamics. Moreover, the Neo-Tech self-exposure traps reveal the unprincipled, dishonest behaviors of Objectivist dogmatists. In seeking allies to fight Neo-Tech, they are now welcoming with open arms their previous "evil" enemies: the Libertarians, IOSers[1], and even scatological nihilists. ...Thus, Neo-Tech has accomplished its first mission: open up Objectivism to all comers and takers, even to its "evil" enemies.

## Honesty is the Best Policy

The bottom line: Only honesty counts. So what if one holds different ideas from Objectivism? The fundamental standard of character is honesty. What more can one ask of another's character than honesty? Virtues and values originate not from truth, knowledge, or intelligence, but from those areas to which honesty is applied in identifying reality. Attacking an honest person is a bad policy — a dishonest, destructive policy. The great 19th-century railroad tycoon, Jay Gould, coined in a high-school essay the statement "Honesty is the Best Policy". Contrary to the Establishment's dishonest "Robber-Baron" attacks on Gould, his great business successes arose from a firm policy of honesty. He was poker-game ruthless, but honest: He could

_____
[1]IOS: Institute for Objectivist Studies founded by Dr. David Kelley.

11

Song 2

Song 2

Stanza #1

be absolutely trusted on any handshake business deal. In fact, essentially every long-term, successful businessperson can be trusted. ...Honesty is not only the best policy, it is the only policy for long-term success.

## Purity

What good is an "authority" on Objectivism who is dishonest while demanding purity for Objectivism? By contrast, consider the tremendous wide-scope value of the impure Bennett Cerf, the politically liberal but honest Random House publisher of the novel, *Atlas Shrugged*. He and Rand admired one another as they worked together to promote Objectivism to the general population through that novel. Likewise, many other honest businesspeople who have successfully delivered Objectivism to the public were ignorant of or even hostile to fundamental ideas of Objectivism. So what? Let any honest-based action roll out the power of Objectivism, regardless of purity or impurity of anyone's beliefs. For, lying beneath all, always ready to be tapped, is the limitless power of pure, no-compromise Objectivism identified by Rand and solidified by Peikoff.

Indeed, everyone applying Objectivism to whatever degree of dilution, such as impure libertarianism, must eventually come back to the purity of Objectivism for answers, solutions, and increased competitive power — for competitive growth.

Therein lies the tremendous market for those having expert intellectual knowledge of Objectivism: Instead of expert Objectivist dogmatists obstructing advances of Objectivism into new and wider areas, those experts can help guide the application of Objectivism into new areas. But, as with any competitive dynamic, those experts must first understand the competitive marketplace into which they would be offering or selling their expertise.

## Business-Oriented Objectivism

Let unrestricted entrepreneurial applications of Objectivism explode everywhere — like the unrestricted entrepreneurial applications propelling the computer/cyberspace boom today. No need to wait for authoritarian purity that, like Godot, will never come. The foundation of Objectivism is rock solid. Current and future errors will self-correct. For, to remain competitive, all business actions will continually return to that rock-solid foundation of Ayn Rand's Objectivism brilliantly nailed down by Leonard Peikoff.

Hang that fake scholastic purity. Focus on net-profit balances. Let business-oriented Objectivism roll freely, everywhere...by everyone. Objectivism will take over the future. Rand and Peikoff have done their work well. Hopefully, Peikoff and other contributors to Objectivism will now break from that circling-wagon syndrome in order to stay competitive and help further advance Objectivism.

Let the power of business-oriented Objectivism roll. The dynamics of wide-open competition and business will drive out the bad — the anticivilization. As the anticivilization fades, an Objectivist civilization will rise. That rising civilization of competitive doers will bring the Civilization of the Universe to planet Earth.

## The Business of Neo-Tech

Neo-Tech Worldwide is an ad hoc company designed to put itself out of business upon accomplishing its goal of vanishing this anticivilization so a business-oriented Objectivist civilization can arise. Only then can the Neo-Tech business owners and employees effectively return to their intended business of Bio-Medical Research free of government destructions, especially the FDA — free to pursue its genetic research and human cloning for the elimination of disease, aging, and death.

Today, Neo-Tech Publishing is investing its profits and capital in providing free, universal values on Web sites across cyberspace. The immediate goal is to liberate conscious minds from their closed-circle thinking modes — to release conscious thinking into the widest possible perspectives. Each such

13

conscious mind will then see Earth's civilization from a radically different perspective. Each will realize that all conscious beings on planet Earth suffer and perish from one basic disease — the disease of irrationality from which flows this anticivilization with all its dishonesties, harms, and criminalities.

### A Criminal-Based Anticivilization
#### versus
### A Business-Based Objectivist Civilization

Dogmatists seeking false authority have always existed in this anticivilization. In most cases, such dogmatists captured bogus doctrines and then brought out the worst in those doctrines — doctrines ranging from murderous communism and Islam...to violent anti-abortion positions that advocate killing doctors...to government-promoted fat-free (eat-all-you-want carbohydrate) diets that deliver obesity and diabetes to kill health, happiness, and life itself. Objectivism, by contrast, is valid with no harmful aspects to attack. Thus, the Objectivist dogmatists corral powerful "advantages" in having hog-tied a valid, rational doctrine. Nevertheless, such Objectivists are soul mates to those living off murderous doctrines. Not only are they stealing from everyone's present life, they are stealing from everyone's future.

From every perspective, the anticivilization is an inherently diseased, criminal-based civilization. Yet, by breaking through today's closed-circle thinking modes, one discovers a healthy, business-based Objectivist civilization. ...One then discovers the Civilization of the Universe.

Indeed, by recognizing the unnecessity of this irrational anticivilization, one realizes that a fully operating Objectivist civilization can prevail on planet Earth — not after decades or centuries, but now, over the next few years!

### The Role of Zonpower

The function of Zonpower is to break people from their stagnant thinking traps. Zonpower frees people to think and act independently, on their own, from the widest possible perspectives — from the most powerful integrations. The thrilling discovery which awaits everyone is that essentially every problem, big and small, can be solved with maximum benefits once the facts are explicitly put into the widest-scope context of Zonpower.

*****

Tradition must always yield to the newly evolving facts of objective reality for conscious life to survive and prosper. But consider the tremendous resistance to fundamental change. Consider Pope Pius IX's closed-circle attack on Charles Darwin and his "outlandish" work on evolution — work that radically changed everyone's fundamental perspective and thinking about human life on planet Earth:

> *[Darwin's system] is a system repudiated by history, by the traditions of people, by exact science, by the observation of facts, and even by reason itself... The corruption of the century, the guile of the depraved, the danger of oversimplification, demand that such dreamings, absurd as they are, be refuted by science, since they wear the mask of science.*
>
> Pope Pius, IX

Such are the popish attacks on Zonpower, especially on its physics, on its view of civilization, on its view of the Universe.

Consider what Galileo said concerning radically changed views about physics, civilization, and the Universe:

> *Facts which at first seem impossible...drop the cloak which has hidden them and they stand forth in naked beauty.*
>
> Galilei Galileo

Indeed, the Civilization of the Universe will arrive as nature's naked beauty through Neo-Tech physics that start with new-world songs and end with a new-color symphony: *Zonpower from*

15

*Cyberspace.* Through that symphony, conscious beings sublimate to eternal prosperity and happiness.

## The Harm of Closed-Circle Objectivism
### versus
### The Value of Wide-Open Objectivism

What does one need in order to reap the benefits of Objectivism? One needs courage, independence, fully integrated honesty combined with the wide-open, business applications of Objectivism. Until this Liberation Manifesto, most Objectivists were afraid of independence — afraid to vanish their leaders and authorities. They were afraid of criticism, of condemnation, of being excommunicated by the high "priests" of Objectivism. ...Thus, they clung to their deadly investments in this anticivilization.

Objectivists become free by independently wielding competitive, action-mode Objectivism. And those who do not free themselves? They will wither and die for some self-proclaimed authority. They will die for their investments in this anticivilization.

Neo-Tech Objectivism offers no icons, leaders, or authorities. Through Neo-Tech Objectivism, each individual lives productively, independently, happily. Indeed, the prize is eternal prosperity and happiness. ...Without fully integrated Objectivism, all crumble to dust. Through fully integrated Objectivism, all rise to the Civilization of the Universe.

### Booming Objectivism

Liberating Objectivism will boom the money-making business interests of the Objectivist establishment. Currently, Luddites fear that the liberation of Objectivism will cause a decline in revenues — a decline in (1) support for the scholarly and academic works of Objectivism, (2) attendance at the lucrative Objectivist conferences, and (3) sales of Objectivist-oriented books and tapes. Yet, any diminishment of financial support for the scholarly and business activities of the Objectivist

16

establishment would contradict the goal of Neo-Tech Worldwide.

Neo-Tech Worldwide explicitly recognizes the outstanding values and accomplishments of Objectivist intellectuals, their publications, their conferences, their organizations, and the apo/hpo[1] Usenet newsgroups. Neo-Tech Worldwide along with many of its employees and associates have long admired and supported, both directly and indirectly, the work of Objectivist intellectuals...and will continue to do so.

Brushing aside the above Luddite fear, all Objectivist markets will expand. Objectivism will boom not only financially but in effectiveness and influence. For, the Objectivist establishment has the values and products to market competitively worldwide. They have the most important values for conscious beings on Earth. ...Liberating Objectivism will benefit everyone — more than anyone can imagine.

### Neo-Tech/Objectivism

With the publication and distribution of this *Profound Honesty* manuscript, the Neo-Tech/Objectivist writing machine begins inscribing justice into the minds and bodies of people living dishonestly through their investments in this anticivilization.

What is the time frame to complete this inscription process? In Kafka's anticivilization "Penal Colony", his horrendous justice-inscription process took six hours to realize its effects and twelve hours to complete the process. In the real world, a person starts being inscribed on reading *Profound Honesty*. The equivalent time scale to completion for each individual will vary, perhaps from as quick as one-month real time per Kafka hour increasing up to one-year real time per Kafka hour.

Through Profound Honesty, everyone will eventually become inscribed with Neo-Tech/Objectivism. ...Everyone will then experience justice, prosperity, happiness.

---

[1] apo = alt.philosophy.objectivism
hpo = humanities.philosophy.objectivism

## Song 2: Liberating Objectivism

✳✳✳✳✳✳✳✳✳✳✳✳✳✳✳✳✳✳✳✳✳✳✳✳✳✳✳✳✳✳✳✳✳✳✳✳✳✳✳✳✳✳✳✳✳✳✳✳✳✳✳✳✳✳✳✳✳✳✳✳✳✳✳✳✳✳✳✳✳✳✳✳✳✳✳
(Below is the footnote referred to on page 6)

Consider the specious Objectivist/Libertarian conflict initiated by Ayn Rand. Her own Luddite mode was followed with a vengeance by Leonard Peikoff and his cohorts. Ad hominem evilization of impure Objectivists became standard practice:

Indeed, specific statements and actions by Libertarians contradict at times certain ideas and principles of Objectivism, just as Ayn Rand and Leonard Peikoff contradicted at times the ideas and principles of Objectivism. Yet, the foundations of Libertarianism require the philosophy of Objectivism. Moreover, Libertarianism points the direction toward a practical Objectivist civilization far more principled and uncompromised than any political movement in history. Indeed, Libertarianism would deliver significantly more Objectivist principles in government than America's founding fathers ever envisioned.

Then why do the Luddite Objectivists rightfully praise America's founding fathers while heaping scorn on today's principled Libertarians? Why in 1996 did they heap scorn on the most Objectivist-rooted presidential candidate in history — Harry Browne? ...Indeed, the closer any person or thing comes to actually implementing or advancing Objectivism into new or unsanctioned areas, the more emotionally virulent become the attacks by the Luddite Objectivists. Why? Competition. Competition will knock stagnant Objectivist "leaders" out of their cozy, flowing-robes positions of unearned authority.

Advances of Objectivism beyond its sanctioned, closed-circle domains threaten those dogmatists with extinction. But, why stop with the Luddite Objectivists? The 1996 Libertarian presidential candidate, Harry Browne, clearly offered far more benefits and happiness to all citizens than any politician in American history. By contrast, Bill Clinton is one of the most dishonest, destructive politicians in American history. Yet, hold a political fund-raiser for Harry Browne where perhaps a hundred of the most ardent Libertarian supporters may show up. A sincere, honest Harry Browne delivers a stunningly practical picture of freedom and prosperity through minimal government based mainly on Objectivist principles. Some muted applause is heard and perhaps $4000 in campaign contributions is raised.

Now, in that same area, hold a political fund raiser for Bill Clinton. A crowd of two thousand or more citizens show up. A hypocritical, pervasively dishonest Bill Clinton delivers a silver-tongued, FDR-like speech about irrationally increasing government activities that harm everyone. A cheering, standing ovation is heard and a million dollars in campaign contributions is raised.

How can such ad hoc irrationalities exist in *everyone* — from Randian Objectivists to Libertarian supporters to Clinton liberals? How? Why? Buddy, this is the anticivilization. Everyone has a stake invested in this anticivilization, including the Randian Objectivists and Libertarian supporters alike. A Neo-Tech/Objectivist civilization threatens that stake. *Everyone* in the anticivilization subconsciously fears a totally honest, free-enterprise civilization. No one in the anticivilization, including Objectivists and Libertarians, really want that kind of freedom and responsibility. All want their ad hoc dishonesties and irrationalities to protect their anticivilization investments.

Neo-Tech/Zonpower breaks that self-defeating paradox. How? By using Objectivism, the Neo-Tech/Zonpower dynamic breaks each anticivilization investment encountered, thus, opening the way to an Objectivist civilization — the Civilization of the Universe.

## Stanza II

# Tools that Win Flame Wars

## Time-Saving Templates

cyberspace tools that vanish

## Pips, Blowhards, Journalists

and

## Nihilists

Any of the Templates listed herein may be copied and reproduced
in part or whole without permission
For latest versions see web site http://www.neo-tech.com/

### *Flame-War Policy of Neo-Tech Publishing*

Most flame wars in cyberspace consist of segments from Usenet posts taken out of context and then attacked — often using ad hominem arguments. ...Flame wars are generally time-consuming, ineffective, and quickly forgotten — a waste of time. Neo-Tech Publishing never initiates flames, only responds in order to protect innocent targets from unjust attacks.

Neo-Tech Publishing has three decades of experience in confronting and squelching unjust attacks on innocent business people by pips — by dishonest academics, establishment journalists, and gun-toting bureaucrats.

The key to benefiting from flames is to design widely integrated, fully honest templates that reduce each flame to an underlying principle based on objective reality. Such templates are permanently valuable and publishable. ...Through their strident complaints, pips themselves demonstrate the effectiveness of such templates. For, those templates reduce them to nonentities — to blatant insignificance.

### *The Always-Profit Rule*

Do not consume irreplaceable time making one-time, quickly forgotten posts and responses. Instead, fashion principled templates anchored in reality to extinguish unjust flames or dishonest attacks. ...Then collect those principled templates for future postings in cyberspace and profitable publications in print. Below are examples of five such templates:

[Notes: 1. These templates are available on FTP sites for free use by anyone on the Internet. See http://www.neo-tech.com for easy copying and pasting of these templates.

2. A most effective response is often achieved by sandwiching a pip attack between, for example, Template #1 and #2 or between Template #1 and #3. Hit with repeated templates, pips shrink into their nothingness. ...In addition to these five templates, an essentially limitless number of powerful templates can be custom constructed by assembling various segments from *Profound Honesty* to squelch pip attacks, in or out of cyberspace.]

# List of Templates

### *Template #1*
### *Who are Pips*

Generally pips are dishonest losers who produce few if any *competitive* values for others and society. They seldom if ever exert the hard efforts required to do something really excellent with their lives — something about which they can be proud.

Pips are people who purposely attack values by distorting out-of-context fragments of those values. Using those distortions, pips attack values with false but logical-sounding criticisms. They often conjure up straw men to bash. ...Pips create problems where none exist.

The obsession with and anger over Neo-Tech templates among pips on various Internet newsgroups demonstrate the effectiveness of such templates. Indeed, these templates clearly, precisely identify the dishonesty and malevolence of those people. Thus, such templates should be used whenever appropriate. They are always effective and never lose their punch. More important, they save precious time needed for productive activities.

### *What Does Pipping Mean? Why Do Losers Pip?*

Pipping involves attacking values by isolating out-of-context fragments of the achievements produced by others or their businesses. Pipping means building one's ego by manipulating with words rather than by producing genuine values. Pipping is done to make a loser appear superior to and more moral than the achievements or businesses being attacked.

Pips reject any response that places their distorted fragments back into context. Pips refuse to understand the full context of the values they are attacking. They are not interested in values, honesty, accuracy, answers, explanations, or learning. They are only interested in the level of ego enhancement they can conjure up through spurious attacks on values. Thus, once pipping is detected, further communication or argument is worthless and should cease so no more irreplaceable time is wasted. A principled template such as this becomes an effective response. The attacking pip will then stand alone, recognized as someone seeking unearned importance. Hence, malicious,

21

attack-mode pips will first vanish from cyberspace and then from the world. ...Justice will be served.  Everyone will profit.

Throughout history, before cyberspace, civilization-benefiting giants and their work were constantly attacked, always injured, and sometimes destroyed by self-proclaimed "victims" and attack-mode pips.[1]  Yet, valid questions and sincere criticisms concerning radically new values will naturally occur.  An important example is Objectivist philosophy with its live-action applications of Neo-Tech and Zonpower.  Such valuable questions and criticisms deserve patient, respectful responses.  But, when ego-pumping pipping is detected, further communication not only wastes irreplaceable time of the respondent, but feeds that pip's ego, allowing him or her to continue draining values created by others. ...Simply template such losers.  Let them complain.  The templates will eventually vanish them.

### Template #2
## Giants versus Twerps

Who knows the fierce battle it takes to start from nothing except an idea, and from that idea to build livelihoods, values, jobs, and prosperity for entire populations?

Jay Gould knew, Henry Ford knew, Leona Helmsley knew, Michael Milken knew along with too many other unsung giants.  Indeed, each were attacked in a thousand ways by countless twerps, pips, ex-beneficiaries, fired employees, professional value destroyers, government bureaucrats, parasitical elites, ego prosecutors/judges, and demagogic politicians.

Those entrepreneurs knew about fighting day and night, year after year to build job-creating businesses that deliver competitive values to society — values that advance civilization.

---

[1] Business people, honest entrepreneurs, and professional value producers no longer need to stand helpless while being drained by parasitical elites, dishonest journalists, and professional value destroyers.  For, those parasites depend on the attacks of "victims" and pips to drain values from heroic value producers.  But, now, the value producers can compose and use an endless variety of Neo-Tech templates extracted from *Profound Honesty* to vanish attacking "victims", pips, and professional value destroyers.

Such business people tragically must consume irreplaceable chunks of their precious lives in throwing off envious parasites and do-nothing nonentities who constantly try to drain them and diminish the values they produce for society.

Only those precious few entrepreneurs know the fierce struggle required to competitively succeed where countless others fail. Only they have the toughness to battle nonstop in solving and overcoming the never ending flood of life-or-death survival problems. They seldom or never can "go home" after work to entertainment or diversions. They seldom or never can kick back in the evenings, on weekends, or on vacations. They seldom or never can leave their work or responsibilities. ...Such people do not collect paychecks from others. They create the paychecks that others live on. Such is their responsibility. They work to solve problems that do exist, not to create problems that do not exist.

In a week or even a day, the entrepreneur business builder can face and must solve more survival problems than most people face in a lifetime. Any one of those countless problems can be taken out of context by a malicious value destroyer ranging from a fired ex-employee trying to financially shake down his ex-employer to a nihilistic pip trying to pump up his shrunken self-worth.

What kind of people dishonestly, enviously, maliciously attack the good? What kind of people feel, think, and act in such purposely destructive ways? In Stalin's Soviet Union, Mao's China, and Hitler's Germany, how many millions of value producers met their deaths because of such pips? In America, today, countless envy-shriveled pips stand ready to destroy heroic, competitive value-and-job producers through jail or death as a police state of armed bureaucrats arises — a police state arising today from the self-aggrandizing agendas of criminal-minded politicians and dishonest journalists.

Many pips collect paychecks from tax-funded sources, from tenured-academe positions, from statist-establishment positions,

Song 2

Stanza #2

Song 2

23

or from companies they hate. Indeed, such pips lack the courage, discipline, and effort to profitably build competitive values for themselves, others, and society. Instead, they expose their essence by attacking objective values produced by others while making problems where none exist. Various examples of such pips are provided in the forthcoming book *Flame-War Justice* from Neo-Tech Worldwide.

In any case, such pips and nihilists have no understanding of what it takes to start, build, and run competitive businesses that ultimately provide the livelihoods and well beings for them and everyone else on Earth. And, who else besides such value destroyers has the time or inclination to pip — to ego pump by purposely dragging down successes and values created by others? ...Neo-Tech stands alone in protecting value-and-job producers from intentional value destroyers.

### Template #3
### *Zonpower and Salvador Dali's "Last Supper"*

One of the most breathtaking paintings of any age is Salvador Dali's "Last Supper". And, as many Objectivists know, that painting was one of Ayn Rand's favorites. Jesus appears indescribably beautiful, innocent, and benevolent. He appears as the Chairman presiding over a Universe-500 board meeting. Notice even the neatly cropped, modern New York executive haircuts of the Apostles. Dali delivered a radical presentation of Christ never before seen among the thousands of holy paintings by hundreds of master artists over the millennium.

Imagine this crystal-clear painting being cast as a giant, ten-thousand-piece jigsaw puzzle. Now, imagine a dishonest blowhard, journalist, or nihilist — a pip — plucking a piece, any piece, or a handful of pieces, from that painting. Then imagine that pip waving those pieces before a public who had never before seen the whole picture of that masterpiece. Using glib words and dishonest non sequiturs, that pip harangues his audience: In tearing down the great value of Dali and his masterpiece, that pip captures an unearned ego trip.

*Tools that Win Flame Wars*

The pip simply needs to hold up the piece or pieces of the puzzle ripped from the total picture and loudly proclaim: "Look at this Dali-crap! It's valued only by Dali-kooks. This proves that Daliism is new-age cult stuff, pseudo art, a sham", the pip blusters. The attacking pip then swells up with feel-big ego for publicly, effortlessly exposing the Dali "fraud". Through his unjust no-effort attack, the pip feels superior to the lifetime hard efforts produced by Dali.

Those who had never seen Dali's complete painting could not know that the facts were the opposite to the non sequiturs being dishonestly pronounced. How could they know that the exposing "hero" was really a nothingness fraud while the exposed "fraud" was a beautiful gem?

In the same way, pips throughout the establishment constantly tear down Ayn Rand and her work. Likewise, in that same way, pips have often torn down, even killed or destroyed, the most radical yet greatest of civilization-benefiting value producers throughout history — Socrates, Galileo, Michael Milken.

*Zonpower* found on home page http://www.neo-tech.com/ reflects the most radical value and widest-scope integration in history. Today, the way to know the full power and beauty of Zonpower is to see the entire, fully integrated picture with all its puzzle pieces locked into place. For those not owning this manuscript in a printed book form, that full picture can be achieved by downloading and reading the *entire* web site. But, as opposed to easily reading the printed book, gaining full integrations and understandings from the web-site requires much time and effort.

Because of the vast scope and tight interdependencies of the Zonpower integrations, the printed-book version with all its diagrams, illustrations, and footnotes properly positioned is much easier, quicker, and more convenient to read. The physical book itself lets one see the assembled pieces in an elegant picture of Dali-like beauty. That picture shows who is the heroic value producer and who is the malevolent value destroyer.

25

*Song 2: Liberating Objectivism*

**Template #4**
*Objectivist Heroes*
(see pages 9-12 of Closing Ceremonies)

**Template #5**
*(Media Template)*

*Rolling the DICE of Media Pips*

Neo-Tech rolls the DICE for the biggest army of professional value destroyers — dishonest journalists. Against Neo-Tech, the dice come up snake eyes for media pips every time.

---

## DICE
### Dishonesty, Ignorance, Cowardliness, Envy
The Essence of Journalist/Media Pips

•*Dishonesty* arises in purposely ripping out of context bits and pieces from the values being attacked and then destroying those values through concealed dishonesties, manipulations, distortions, and non sequiturs.

•*Ignorance* arises through intention, carelessness, or laziness in not becoming informed concerning the full facts about the subject of their attacks.

•*Cowardliness* arises in hiding behind deceptive facades and camouflages throughout the media.

•*Envy* arises in malevolently trying to destroy objective values because they *are* objective values — competitive values for others and society that the attackers themselves cannot produce. Only by destroying competitive values produced by others can the envy attackers feel important enough to sustain their livelihoods based on harmful dishonesties.

---

## Stanza III

# A Glimpse into the Future

An Early Introduction
to

# QUANTUM CROSSINGS

(to be constructed on the World Wide Web)

## Twelve Quantum Crossings

to the

## Civilization of the Universe

---

The Introduction to Quantum Crossings
is dedicated to
The First Honest Business Leader of Western Civilization:
King Hiero II of Syracuse
In his 54 year reign from 270 BC to 216 BC
his only agenda was peace and progress.
*He ruled without armed bureaucrats*
*He ruled without killing, exiling, or injuring a single citizen*
Business not only flourished
but Archimedes, history's greatest inventor, also flourished
In such an atmosphere,
Jesus Christ superstar carpenter
could have built the ancient world's tallest skyscraper
and provided ten-thousand jobs
instead of becoming a self-sacrificing mystic
that cost civilization its free-enterprise economies.
Constantine could have been "The Great" forever
Jay Gould could be alive today
commanding Wall Street with Micheal Milken
Today, here comes Neo-Tech
here comes
Prosperity, Excitement, Romance

Stanza #3

Song 2

Song 2

From
**Aeschylus, Sophocles, Epicurus**
to the
**Businessman-Poet Wallace Stevens**
and the
**Music of Rush**
civilization marches forward
Yet, high above drama, poem, and song
shines
**Ayn Rand**
elevated from the shadows
by
**Branden, Peikoff, Neo-Tech**

From teachings and words, civilizations grow
Earth's anticivilization grew
within
Plato's cave for two millennia
Today, crafted dishonesties
in speeches, prose, and journalism
yield
looters, parasites, and killers
hidden by
Homeric heroes, mystical shadows, and noble lies

Behold!
Cyberspace has arrived
Profound Honesty
outcompetes dishonesties
be them
darkly hidden or widely open

Profound Honesty
jumps beyond Earth's anticivilization
into a
Neo-Tech Civilization
into the
Civilization of the Universe

Stanza III
## Table of Contents

### Introduction

To survive and prosper, the parasitical-elite ruling classes of the anticivilization artfully craft glorious memories of criminal Homeric-hero leaders ranging from Alexander the Great, Julius Caesar and Napoleon Bonaparte to Abraham Lincoln, Woodrow Wilson, and FDR.

More important, to survive, any parasitical ruling class must malign or vanish the memories of history's greatest, competitive value producers. Indeed, criminal-minded leaders have buried the memories of business-minded leaders such as King Hiero II, Jay Gould, and Calvin Coolidge whose prime focus was rationality, peace, and prosperity. And, today, a person like Mark Hamilton or Eric Savage could, as early as 2001AD, become one of those rare business-minded leaders.

*Quantum Crossings* will vanish the criminal-minded icons and celebrities of this irrational anticivilization while resurrecting the business-minded heroes dwelling in the rational Civilization of the Universe.

## QUANTUM CROSSINGS

Under construction for the World Wide Web is a primary epic poem. This is the first such epic poem in a thousand years — the first since *Beowulf* in 1000 AD. A primary epic poem not only breaks the eons of conscious silence forever before, but breaks the conscious norm forever after. When nothing is understandable, when nothing is explainable, when communication and understanding break down, only poem and song communicate unity, for better or worse, through everyone's right-hemisphere brain. Neither ignorance nor rationalization from left-hemisphere brains can block that unity. ...No mechanism or defense can prevent primary epics from changing civilizations.

The newly evolving epic, *Quantum Crossings*, will be continuously edited and expanded into thousands of pages. From that epic, the anticivilization will disappear chunk by chunk as the Civilization of the Universe appears jump by jump.

From *Quantum Crossings* will spring the Protocols for the Civilization of the Universe. Those Protocols will turn all major scientific-and-medical research toward health, happiness, and prosperity. How? By unleashing individual competitive business, not gun-point collectivist governments, to eliminate war, crime, mysticism, irrationality, disease, aging, and death.

*A Glimpse into the Future*

**Preliminary Outline**
for
*Quantum Crossings*


THREE FOUNDATIONS

I.   Literature Creates Conscious Civilizations
II.  Sabotaging the Anticivilization
III. Quantum Crossings to the Civilization of the Universe


TWELVE QUANTUM CROSSINGS
to the
CIVILIZATION OF THE UNIVERSE

Crossing 1: Youth
Crossing 2:  Power beyond the Gods
Crossing 3:  Power Lost
Crossing 4:  Anticivilization Addiction
Crossing 5:  Failure and Death
Crossing 6:  Quantum Escape
Crossing 7:  Life without Mysticism
Crossing 8:  Politics without Guns
Crossing 9:  Power Regained
Crossing 10: Individual Enterprise Eternal
Crossing 11: Prosperity Forever
Crossing 12: Civilization of the Universe

31

## Literature Creates Conscious Civilizations

*The Odyssey, The Aeneid, The Divine Comedy, The Canterbury Tales, Paradise Lost, The Pilgrim's Progress, Gulliver's Travels,* and *Faust* were journeys that created Western civilization. Homer, Plato, Virgil, Dante, Boccaccio, Chaucer, Shakespeare, Bunyan, Swift, Kant[1], Goethe, Balzac, all took journeys that advanced Earth's anticivilization. In the context of this anticivilization, regardless of philosophical errors, those travelers did their work right — exactly right, powerfully right. That fact must be understood to advance beyond this anticivilization.[2]

The lone saboteur was Ayn Rand with her epic *Atlas Shrugged.* Yet, she and her great work were trapped in purgatory — trapped in the unbridgeable gulf between this anticivilization and the Civilization of the Universe.

By contrast, an evolving primary epic called *Quantum Crossings* will reveal a dramatic mind-altering journey for all conscious beings. A journey from this anticivilization into the Civilization of the Universe. In *Quantum Crossings*, the protagonist, Iu, in a life-and-death race for planet Earth, crafts twelve keys to open twelve gates that allow conscious beings to jump across the twelve unbridgeable gulfs leading to the Civilization of the Universe.

---

[1]Acting without sufficient knowledge and contrary to Objectivism, both Rand and Peikoff subjectively, emotionally attacked Immanuel Kant as "the most evil person who ever lived". When, in fact, Kant was a kind, gentle person who through a lifetime of hard, sincere work produced a key value for mankind: He comprehensively integrated and systematized the philosophy underlying the irrationality dominating this civilization. Thus, Kant's work serves as a valuable servant for advancing Objectivism. By juxtaposing his articulated philosophical system against Objectivism, Earth's anticivilization can finally be understood. Only with that understanding can this criminal-driven civilization be undermined, sabotaged, then finally collapsed and vanished. ...Eternal thanks must be given to Kant, Rand, Peikoff, and fully integrated honesty for the coming Objectivist civilization — for the coming business-driven Civilization of the Universe.

[2]The modern or existential writers of the 20th century such as Proust, Joyce, Sartre, and Beckett do not hold the civilization-determining power of the classicists. Kafka and Camus are two exceptions: Kafka for his "The Law" and his "Writing Machine" (in which the jailer changes places with the prisoner to understand justice) serve to symbolize the metaphysics of this anticivilization; and Camus for his projecting love and happiness as the noble pursuits in this anticivilization. Also, Faulkner captures the soul of dishonest journalists and Letterman-type nihilists. Indeed, their sound and fury mean nothing. Still, Sartre's *Nausea* and Beckett's *Godot* in their Theaters of the Absurd are correct. Even from feminist/lesbian poet Adrienna Rich, we learn and advance. For, this is the anticivilization. And, their work brought forth the understanding needed to sabotage the anticivilization out of existence.

*A Glimpse into the Future*

# Who is Sabotaging this Anticivilization?

Saboteur Supreme
Ayn Rand's anger hid her exquisite victory
Rejected by the intelligentsia, the academe, the media
Ignored by the establishment rulers and big-business leaders
Minimized, ridiculed, ignored by the high, the mighty
Without exception
No establishment elite acknowledges her supreme accomplishment
Not yesterday, not today, never

No establishment figure has ever risen to proclaim
Ayn Rand's Objectivism as civilization's most valuable product
As in Henrik Ibsen's themes of fearing the light
Establishment elites must fear the most brilliant light
The light of fully integrated honesty

Objectivism: the universal philosophy of facts and reason
Based upon the universal needs of conscious beings
Objectivism: eternally benefiting conscious beings
Through fully integrated honesty
Under any conditions, throughout time and space

II
Trapped in literature naiveness
Ranging from Homer and Shakespheare to Blake and Whitman
Ayn Rand lived in her world of narrow-scope accuracies
She lived in her world of blind naiveness
Naive to the wide-scope context of philosophers from Plato to Kant
Naive to the wide-scope power behind the classics of literature
Naive to the anticivilization in which she invested

She never understood why the classics were classics
Or how such classics deliver to the establishment its power
Or why those classics deliver tremendous values that advance civilization

In this anticivilization, mighty authors craft their works correctly
Despite their philosophical errors
The classics control their subjects with an iron grip
For, such crafted words mold all who follow
Even Proust in his life cycle of memories did it right
So did Joyce with his awesome works of nothingness
Along with Sartre's and Beckett's monuments to the Absurd
For, this is the anticivilization
And that is why even the existentialists did their work correctly

In her innocence, Ayn Rand never understood their accomplishments
Thus, she never perceived the establishment's deep secret
The secret of why establishment intellectuals must never accept
Honest value producers, especially giants like Ayn Rand

33

Song 2

Stanza #3

Song 2

*Stanza 2: Liberating Objectivism*

In her innocence
She could never belong
Ayn Rand the Saboteur

### III

Never belonging made Ayn Rand angry and discouraged
Never belonging made her coworkers frustrated and baffled
Never belonging made her followers shut their minds
None could see beyond this anticivilization

Objectivism will never be proclaimed by establishment elites
Or by anyone whose self-esteem is invested in this anticivilization
Objectivism is never going to be accepted by establishment rulers
So look beyond

### IV

But wait! Why look beyond?
Today arises an upward attention sweep
For Ayn Rand and her work
An upward sweep among the establishment
The influence of "Atlas Shrugged" topped only by the Bible
Both read by the Pope today
Victory at last?

No. No victory. No victory ever in this anticivilization
That upward sweep is a fashion surge
A fashion surge captured by the dynamics of profitable business
A fashion surge driven by establishment egos

In the past, *The Fountainhead*, then its movie, and finally *Atlas Shrugged*
Also brought fashion surges from the establishment elites
But, each such surge was emasculated with political correctness
Emasculated with mixes of distortion and equivocation
Emasculated with ridicule or scorn by strutting nihilists

No establishment authority, no establishment powerhouse
No establishment star ever recognized Objectivism as Earth's greatest value
Not then, not now, never
Objectivism threatens the establishment elites

### V

Consider those few who break their establishment dependencies
Those who end their investments in this anticivilization
They are the few who can look far, far ahead — toward eternity
They are the few who can see new-color dimensions
In which corrupt establishments and their authorities vanish forever

Consider those free souls who look across the abyss
Into wide-scope reality
Through fully integrated honesty, they hear a symphony
The Symphony of the Universe
They see an approaching civilization
The Civilization of the Universe

34

*A Glimpse into the Future*

## VI
Today, an engine of fully integrated honesty is planted deep
Deep into the veins of this moribund anticivilization
That engine is Neo-Tech
Neo-Tech is fully integrated honesty in action
An engine that injects Objectivism into every act

Neo-Tech opens the gates to quantum crossings
Opens the gates for journeys into wide-scope reality
Into the Civilization of the Universe
Into fully integrated honesty

## VII
Allegory reveals the first Quantum Crossing:
Theism is never proclaimed by Hell's elite
Satanism is never hailed by Heaven's elite.
Objectivism is never celebrated by the Anticivilization's elite
Arbitrary, subjectivist philosophies are unknown
In the immortal Civilization of the Universe

Can Hell be Heaven?  Can Heaven be Hell?
Can the Anticivilization be the Civilization of the Universe?
Can the Civilization of the Universe be the Anticivilization?
Can A be Z?  Or Z be A?
Can death be life?  Can life be death?

## VIII
Victory is now available for everyone, everywhere, forever.
The gate swings open to the first of twelve crossings
Crossings into wide-scope reality
Crossings into the Civilization of the Universe
Untouched and untouchable by this unreal, mystical anticivilization
Untouched by hecklers, nihilists, and parasitical elites
Untouched by professional value destroyers

The Anticivilization's destination
Means eternal death from nihilistic nothingness
The Civilization of the Universe's destination
Means eternal life from productive prosperity

Ayn Rand saboteur supreme
Her exquisite victory is sublime
Now rising toward the Civilization of the Universe
Nihilists vanish in non competitiveness
Unable to exist in an Objectivist civilization

Stand up
A toast to Ayn Rand
The Saboteur
Fully integrated honesty is here forever

35

*Song 2: Liberating Objectivism*

## Introduction Topics
### for the
## Civilization of the Universe

> The rigid structures of rhyme and meter change into less rigid structures of meter only then phase into entirely new, conceptual structures of facts and logic that unstoppably enter the right-hemisphere brain via free verse, which in turn will lead to unstoppable left-brain prose — *The Zon Protocols*.

### EPICS

Homer's *Iliad* does come first
Delivers life for better or worse
*Beowulf* points to future fights
*Quantum Crossings* will end the nights

Epics and poems from far shores
Broke the silence of closed doors
An epic sung to the future now
Will free us from the deadly past

When nothing is explicable,
Nothing is understandable
When communication crumbles,
Epics and poems unite our minds

Traveling beyond time and space
Primary epics fill each place
Free from our neglect or regret
Rising above all friends and foes

Circling high with quiet breath
Singing songs of failure and death
Plato converts workers to slaves
Not even God can break the chains

Virgil and Ovid gripped the past
Using the state to crush life fast
Quantum Crossings bring the future
Far beyond all El Dorados

*A Glimpse into the Future*

## YOUTH

Above high God rise youthful might
Soon forgotten in mystic flight
We grow old by dying young
All lost in clouds of God-filled frauds

Binding tight each lively spirit,
Rulers bury the powers of youth
Who will break the grimness of death
To let young spirits rise anew

Rulers on high drain those below
Denying all control of life
Each youth soon trapped in stifling cells
Locked away from growth eternal

Who else will know the hidden truth
Of powers beyond each quick youth
Who else can find the facts right now
To break the grip of gods before

Narrow blackness of rulers past
Or widest light of future bright
The answer lies forever now
In jumping past abyss-like gaps

Quantum Crossings bring keys anew
For love and joy to young and old
The maps of life will show new ways
From which arise eternal wealth

The first step now to break the binds
Finding new keys to open each gate
Vanishing ghosts of past and now
Beyond which lie unbounded life

37

*Song 2: Liberating Objectivism*

## IU

Iu is we born upon Earth
Life without life, peace without peace
Whence comes progress with no progress
Then comes justice with no justice

Teaching Iu to live for doom
Rulers smother children in bloom
Crushing the minds of all on Earth
Forcing on each, eyes so blind

Compassion blocked by force and guns
Iu's spirit soon succumbs
Leaving facts in prisons dark
Moving blindly from life to death

Yet Iu awoke to new ways
Seeking knowledge beyond the gods
Till lost in altruistic scams
That swap our joy for bleak salvation

Where is growth without stagnation?
Where is bright light without dark gloom?
Where is good life without grim death?
Silence from all, even the gods

Students locked in guarded jails
No way out, tenured teachers preach
Which way out? Iu asks anew
Silence from all, even high God

Years fly by, faster and faster
Iu grows older, younger still
Growing young while growing old
The secret is no secret now

Force brings each code of sacrifice
Till Iu finds the code of life
Rulers on high breathe fire and smoke
Lest Iu frees five-billion slaves

Each upon Earth creates the stars
Who knows those gifts beyond the gods
How soon will Iu rise again
To bring to all eternal life

*A Glimpse into the Future*

## Other Topics to be Posted

before the publication of

# *Quantum Crossings*

Value Producers vs. Value Destroyers
Business vs. Politics
Freedom vs. Addiction
Rationality vs. Irrationality
Reality vs. Mysticism
Health vs. Sickness
Productive Minds vs. Criminal Minds
Objective Law vs. Subjective Law
Honesty vs. Truth
Life vs. Death.

Herein lies the keys to limitless prosperity, power, and romantic love. The keys to the Civilization of the Universe.

## CROSSING 1
(under construction)

### YOUTH

A newborn cried
Iu awoke
Seventy years or so from then
Iu's eyes should close forever
Like all conscious beings born upon Earth
So says the laws from scriptures supreme
With armed rulers to make those laws seem real
While hiding the laws of physics and nature
Thus, a race against time
A race for death or life

39

The New-Color Symphony

# Zonpower

from

# Cyberspace

Globe Designed by Steve Rapella

Neo-Tech Worldwide

# *Zonpower*

lets *you* become

# GOD

even without a computer

> *Relax: Zonpower Rules Cyberspace*
> *You Alone Rule Your Life*
>
> Zonpower and cyberspace are made for each other. In cyberspace, the destructive elements of government and the entire parasitical-elite class vanish. Only Zonpower succeeds.
>
> Eventually, through the Internet and beyond, Zonpower will immortalize and deify every conscious *individual* on planet Earth. Through cyberspace, Zonpower empowers the individual by emasculating false authority and vanishing dishonesty. That empowerment comes not from academic philosophizing but from real-life, in-the-trenches business and legal actions. Then shall vanish *government-caused* criminalities and wars.
>
> Blaise Pascal saw only boredom and doom for those who did not believe in God. The fact is: Zonpower removes all boredom and doom from conscious beings.
>
> Additionally, through cyberspace, Zonpower prevents the corruption of youth. Everyone becomes forever young — forever clean, innocent, free. Youth flourishes; corruption vanishes. ...Cyberspace *is* the Civilization of the Universe. There is no God but you.

# The New-Color Symphony

# Zonpower

Movement I
## Neo-Tech Physics
*The Foundation*
pages 1-92

Movement II
## The Anticivilization
*The Problem*
pages 93-200

Movement III
## The Civilization of the Universe
*The Solution*
pages 201-328

Nature is the Will of "God"

Conscious Beings Control Nature
by obeying
Nature
through the
Laws of Physics

## Honesty

1. Fairness and straightforwardness in conduct.
2. Adherence to the facts: sincerity.

*(Webster's Ninth New Collegiate Dictionary)*

---

*Your Route to Riches*

Three thousand years ago, our nature-given bicameral minds broke down into chaos. To survive, we invented consciousness, which soon became corrupted with Plato's dishonesties and "noble" lies. Now, today, our Plato-corroded conscious minds are breaking down. To survive, we are finally discovering the all-powerful Neothink mind that functions through wide-scope integrations and fully integrated honesty. Neothink brings Zonpower — the power from the Civilization of the Universe. ...Zonpower provides everyone with riches, romantic excitement, and a god-like mind and body.

---

*Zonpower*
A Symphony of Contextual Facts and Metaphors
dedicated to
Henrik Ibsen
and his play
*An Enemy of the People*
and to
Socrates, Francis Bacon, Voltaire


*How can the natural world be preserved*
*if man dominates?*
*...Man **is** the natural world*

ISBN# 911752-72-2
Library of Congress # 95-60719
Copyright © 1995, 1996
by the
Zon Association, Inc.

<u>Cyberspace</u>
Neo-Tech/Zonpower Home Page:
http://www.neo-tech.com/

# Zonpower

## A Communiqué from the Universe

### Orientation

Zon is absent from the entire history of Earth's anticivilization. Yet, Zon embraces all the future. ...Zon answers the *how* and *why* questions of life and existence.

The reader needs only a brief orientation to *Zonpower* rather than an Introduction or Preface as found in most books. This orientation will help the reader capture the Zonpower dynamics that lead to limitless riches, romantic charisma, and nonaging beauty guaranteed by Zon.

Movement I, *The Foundation,* is a nonmathematical presentation of Neo-Tech Physics edited for all readers — from general readers to professional physicists.

After Movement II, *The Problem*, and Movement III, *The Solution*, one captures the Zonpower needed to collect limitless riches, romance, and a god-like mind and body.

New-Color Symphony

---

"Blessed are the meek: for they shall inherit the Earth"
Matthew 5:4 — 10

Meaning: Blessed are the unassuming value producers not invested in this anticivilization — blessed are those quietly wielding the omnipotent tools of Zon: for they shall inherit the Earth. Condemned are the parasitical elites who live through force-backed criminalities — condemned are those criminally investing in this anticivilization: for they shall vanish from the Earth.

---

# Table of Contents

iv

# Table of Contents

## Illustrations

## Charts and Tables

New-Color Symphony

# New Words and Concepts

**Zon** is a collective word related to the fully integrated honesty of Neo-Tech and comprises (1) the Civilization of the Universe, (2) those operating from its wide-scope perspective, and (3) the power required to control existence — the integrated power to gain limitless wealth and eternal happiness. ...Zon is the mind of God. Zon *is* you!

**Zonpower** is the power to control (*not* create) existence. Zonpower is derived from applying the fully integrated honesty and wide-scope accountability of Neo-Tech to all conscious actions.

**Neo-Tech** is a noun or an adjective meaning *fully integrated honesty* based on facts of reality. Neo-Tech creates a collection of *new techniques* and *new technology* that lets one know exactly what is happening and what to do for gaining honest advantages in all situations. Neo-Tech provides the integrations to collapse the illusions, hoaxes, and irrationalities of any harmful individual or institution.

**Objectivism** is the philosophy for the well-being of conscious beings — the philosophy based on reason — the new-world philosophy of limitless prosperity.

**Anticivilization** is the irrational civilization gripping planet Earth — an unreal civilization riddled with professional value destroyers causing endless cycles of wars, economic and property destructions, unemployment and poverty, suffering and death. The essence of the anticivilization is dishonesty. ...Through Neo-Tech, the Civilization of the Universe will replace Earth's anticivilization.

**Civilization of the Universe** is the rational civilization throughout the universe — a civilization filled with value producers providing endless cycles of wealth, happiness, and rejuvenation for everyone. ...Professional value destroyers and parasitical elites are nonexistent in the Civilization of the Universe.

**Parasitical Elites** are unnatural people who drain everyone. The parasitical-elite class lives by usurping,

vi

swindling, and destroying values produced by others. Their survival requires political-agenda laws, armed bureaucracies, ego-"justice" systems, and deceptive neocheating.

**Neocheating** is the undetected usurpation of values from others: the unsuspicious swindling of money, power, or values through deceptive manipulations of rationalizations, non sequiturs, illusions, and mysticisms. ...All such net harms inflicted on society can now be objectively measured by the wide-scope accounting of Neo-Tech.

**Subjective Laws** include political-agenda laws conjured up by politicians and bureaucrats to gain self-serving benefits, ego props, and unearned power. Enforcement of political-agenda laws requires the use of force and armed agents against innocent people. ...The only purpose of such laws is to violate individual rights in order to parasitically gain values produced by others.

**Objective Laws** are not conjured up by politicians or bureaucrats. Instead, like the laws of physics, they arise from the *immutable laws of nature*. Such laws are valid across space and time, benefit everyone, and advance society. Objective laws are based on the moral prohibition of initiatory force, threats of force, and fraud as constituted on page 188. ...The only rational purpose of laws is to protect individual rights.

**Ego "Justice"** is the use of political-agenda laws to gain parasitical livelihoods and feel false importance. Ego "justice" is the survival tool of many politicians, lawyers, and judges. Ego "justice" is the most pernicious form of neocheating. ...Parasitical elites thrive on subjective laws and ego "justice" to the harm of everyone else and society.

**Cassandra's Secret** revealed through Zon is the power of the conscious mind to accurately, nonmystically foretell the future. How? Through the mind's power to control its own existence...thus, its own future.

## New Words and Concepts

**Intelligence** is redefined by Neo-Tech as the *range of integrated thinking*. The range, width, or scope of valid integrations is more a function of honesty than of IQ. No matter how high is one's raw IQ, that person can ultimately be outflanked and outperformed by a lower IQ mind that is more honest, allowing wider-scope integrations. In the Civilization of the Universe, wide-scope integrations are what give conscious minds unlimited power. Neo-Tech intelligence supersedes the role of IQ detailed by Richard J. Herrnstein and Charles Murray in their controversial, best-selling book *The Bell Curve* (Simon & Schuster, 1994). Since fully integrated honesty, not IQ, is the key to long-range success and abiding happiness, all races have equal access to the limitless prosperity available from the Civilization of the Universe.

**Purpose of Existence and Motive for Controlling Existence:** Achieving and expanding happiness is the moral purpose of conscious life.[1] Happiness, therefore, is the ultimate motivator behind conscious-controlled existence. But, to control existence, one must realize that existence itself is *never* derived from thoughts or emotions. Instead, thoughts and emotions, including happiness, are *always* derived from the conscious control of existence. Thus, conscious control of existence is ultimately directed toward creating limitless prosperity, rejuvenated life, and eternal happiness for everyone and society.

---

[1]As identified in Aristotle's *Nicomachean Ethics*, happiness is the highest moral *purpose* of conscious life. ...Life is the moral *standard*. Reason is necessary for human survival. Reason *and* honesty are required to achieve happiness.

[See pages 323-327 for additional word usages]

# MOVEMENT I

# Neo-Tech Physics

## *The Foundation*

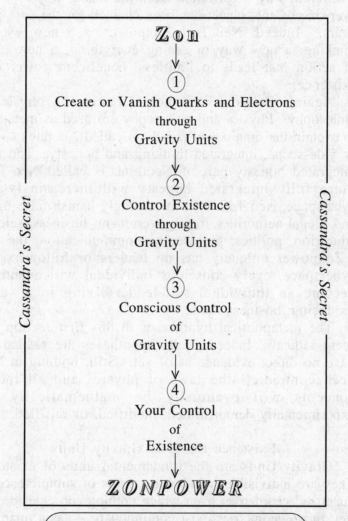

Zon

↓

① 

Create or Vanish Quarks and Electrons
through
Gravity Units

↓

②

Control Existence
through
Gravity Units

↓

③

Conscious Control
of
Gravity Units

↓

④

Your Control
of
Existence

↓

ZONPOWER

*Cassandra's Secret*      *Cassandra's Secret*

The main body of text for Neo-Tech Physics is simplified for the general, nonscientific reader. Moreover, Neo-Tech physics is but one of several major metaphorical points made in the text. Those interested in knowing the full context in which the physics is presented must carefully read all of the technical footnotes.

1

## The Goal and Purpose of Neo-Tech/Zonpower

The goal of Neo-Tech/Zonpower is to cure the interwoven disease of irrationality and dishonesty.

The purpose of Neo-Tech/Zonpower is to have conscious individuals think about and see everything in a different way — different from the losing way in which everyone on this planet has been chained for the past 3000 years. Indeed, Neo-Tech/Zonpower is a new way of thinking, a new way of seeing everything, a new mode of action that leads to limitless, beneficent power over existence.

Again, "Zonpower" is not a treatise on physics or philosophy. Physics and philosophy are used as metaphors to explain the omnipotent paradigm called Neothink, which is wide-scope, integrated thinking and honesty. The fully integrated honesty part of Neothink is called Neo-Tech. Since fully integrated honesty will increasingly rule cyberspace, Neo-Tech will increasingly banish false biases and illegal authorities from government, business, science, education, politics, philosophy, communication, the arts. ...Zonpower uniquely has no leaders or followers. In cyberspace, every conscious individual will eventually become an individual self-leader living in a value-producing, business mode.

The metaphorical hypotheses in this first section may seem radical. Indeed, some hypotheses are radical and have no direct evidence as of yet. Still, nothing in Neo-Tech contradicts the laws of physics and all radical concepts will eventually be mathematically and experimentally demonstrated, modified, or falsified.

### Existence Exists as Gravity Units

Gravity Units are the fundamental units of existence. They are indivisible, windowless units of submicroscopic, quantized geometries from which nothing can enter or exit. Yet, those geometries exist continuously — as a quantum-blended whole through wave-like dynamics and smeared-out resonances. Also, manifestations of certain Gravity Units could form the weakly interacting dark material that accounts for the missing mass in modern cosmological theories. And finally, each Gravity Unit can flux into a universe of gravity, mass, energy, and consciousness.

*All wealth arises from conscious-controlled Gravity Units.*

# Chapter 1
# Boundless Prosperity
### through
### SIGUs and Googolplexes

What are SIGUs and googolplexes? What connection do they have to boundless prosperity? First ask: How do conscious beings meet the energy and communication requirements of an eternally advancing civilization? How does one unleash nature's power to achieve near instant communication throughout the universe? How can one capture the power of universes spanning billions of light years across? How can one unleash the universal power locked in gravity units lurking beneath every subatomic particle? How can one direct the power of Super-Inflation Gravity Units[1] (SIGUs) to eternally expand life and prosperity?

### Take a Numbers Ride

*Take a ride to the big*: The mathematical term googol is the number 1 followed by a hundred zeroes, or $10^{100}$, meaning 10 raised to the power of a hundred.[2] How big a number is a googol? Astronomers estimate our universe is 15 billion years old...or $10^{18}$ seconds old. Over 22 centuries ago, Archimedes calculated that $10^{63}$ grains of sand would fill the then known universe.

Consider today's known universe contains at least a hundred-billion galaxies each containing an average of a

[1]A Super-Inflation Gravity Unit is equivalent to a symmetrical Geometry Unit of the entire universe.

[2]The power of the number 10 means the number of zeros after the number 1. For example, 10 raised to the power of 2 or $10^2$ means 100, $10^3$ means 1000, $10^{100}$ means 1 followed by a hundred zeros, $10^{10^{12}}$ means 1 followed by a trillion zeros. Likewise, $10^{-3}$ is $1/10^3 = .001$. Also, $10^{-43}$, for example, is a decimal point followed by 42 zeros then the number 1. ...Human life expectancy is about $2 \times 10^9$ seconds. The passing of a light wave takes about $10^{-15}$ seconds.

3

New-Color Symphony

Movement #1

hundred-billion stars. Now consider the mind-boggling number of electrons, protons, neutrons, and all other matter-and-energy particles in those stars, planets, dark matter...as well as all additional particles scattered throughout space. That number would equal $10^{86}$ particles, a number still considerably less than a googol! Now, if our entire universe of about fifteen billion light years across were packed *solid* with subatomic particles with zero space between them, the number of particles would rise to $10^{130}$.

But, how large is a googolplex, $10^{10^{100}}$? Just to print the number of zeroes after the number 1 would require enough paper to pack solid our entire universe, fifteen billion light years across.[1] ...And a super googolplex is a googolplex that is raised to an additional 100th power. No scale is available for any conscious mind on Earth to grasp such a number.

*Now take a ride to the small*: Slice an average-sized pie in half ninety-one times. On the ninety-second slice, you would need to slice the nucleus of an atom in half. How small is the nucleus of an atom? Enlarge a baseball to the size of Earth. One would then see the atoms of that baseball as the size of cherries filling the entire planet. Now, enlarge one of those atoms to the size of the Astrodome. The nucleus would then become visible as the size of a grain of sand.

What about the smallest or shortest unit of time that the human mind can grasp: Planck's time of $10^{-42}$ of a second — about the time required for light travelling at 186,281 miles per second to traverse the diameter of the smallest subatomic particle of, say, a $2 \times 10^{-33}$ centimeter

---

[1]Roger Penrose calculated that to emulate all possible quantum states of the known universe would require $10^{10^{123}}$ bits of information — the maximum capacity for the Universal Computer.

diameter, which is Planck's length. A time less than $10^{-42}$ of a second measured from the *theoretical* beginning of time in our universe[1] cannot be experimentally simulated or conceptually grasped.

Finally, grasping the smallest and the biggest in terms of eternity requires the axiomatic fact that *existence exists*. Thus, existence has no prior cause and is eternal. Relative to eternity, the smallest unit and the largest unit are equal in occurrence, time, or distance. For example, compare an incredibly fast event that occurs once every $10^{-42}$ of a second to an incredibly slow event that occurs once every googolplex years. The occurrence of those events are equal in eternity. For, each of those events will occur an "infinite"[2] number of times in eternity.

The smallest units of existence, such as quarks and electrons or the even smaller Gravity Units as explained in Chapters 5 and 7, to the largest expansion of the universe with everything in between and beyond are all a part of eternal existence. Gravity Units, quarks, subatomic particles and energies; protons, neutrons, and electrons; electromagnetism, nuclear forces, and gravity; universes, galaxies, stars, and planets; atoms, molecules, and compounds; gasses, liquids, and solids; air, water, and land; mountains, oceans, and clouds; protoplasm, amoeba, plants, fish, animals, primates, *and conscious beings*...all are part of existence and its natural evolution that has occurred eternally. Indeed, each and every entity of existence has existed forever. Thus, conscious beings as entities of existence have also existed forever throughout the universes as described in Chapter 6 and in Part III.

---

[1]Contrary to big-bang theories, universes have no natural beginnings or endings as described in later chapters.

[2]Infinity is a mind-created concept, not a part of reality.

Rapid Communication Across Universes
by using
Super-Inflation Gravity Units Called SIGUs

Reality can never be contradicted. Thus, the laws of nature and physics can never be violated. That means nothing can exceed the speed of light. So, how can near instant communication occur across distances that require light (travelling at 186,281 miles per second) millions or even billions of years to traverse? Even more, how can communication occur between universes from which not even light can escape? Conscious beings and only conscious beings can accomplish such near instant communication. How do they accomplish that communication without violating the laws of nature or physics?

Conscious beings harnessing the Super-Inflation nature of Gravity Units (SIGUs) can produce near instant, gravity-pulse communication not only across an entire universe but possibly between universes — all without violating physical laws, including the speed of light. How? By gravity pulses transmitted through big-bang-type inflations radiating from exploded Gravity Units.

How do gravity pulses communicate faster than the speed of light with nothing exceeding the speed of light? First, realize that the smallest units of existence, Gravity Units, and the largest unit of existence, the full expanding universe, are one and the same: They each contain the same mass and energy potentials. The units are just in different modes throughout time and space. Next, examine the so-called big-bang or hypothetical spacetime birth of our universe from a gravity unit: At $10^{-42}$ of a second or Planck's time after its birth, the entire universe is $10^{35}$ times *smaller* than a subatomic proton. Doubling every $10^{-34}$ seconds or doubling $10^{36}$ times at $10^{-32}$ seconds from birth, the universe has grown to 12 centimeters across — about the size of a grapefruit. And then, doubling $10^{50}$ times by somewhat over $10^{-30}$ seconds from its hypothetical birth, the universe has exploded to the size of our solar system — all in that tiniest fraction of a second. ...In other words, during that instant in time, the universe has expanded trillions of times faster than the speed of light. Yet, nothing exceeds the speed of light. How can that occur?

The super-fast growth of the universe during its first moment in time can be explained by the Inflation Theory originated by Alan Guth of MIT in 1979. Such inflation involves the brief existence of "repulsive gravity" and the relative positions of spacetime coordinates in accord with Einstein's general relativity. ...That super-fast inflation can also be understood, without complete accuracy, in more simple Newtonian terms: Consider two entities starting at the same point and moving apart near or at the speed of light. At the end of one year, those entities will be about two light years apart. Thus, they will have "communicated" from their respective points A and B at about twice the distance covered by the speed of light without exceeding the speed of light.

Now, consider breaking the geometry or symmetry of a universe-containing Gravity Unit or Geometry Unit, causing a spacetime birth. That occurrence begins the near instant conversion of the smallest unit of existence, the universe-containing Gravity Unit, into the largest unit of existence, the entire expanding universe. Incredibly, that new-born exploding Gravity Unit has the same mass/ energy total of an entire universe fifteen billion years old. Consider what occurs in the tiniest fraction of the initial second during a big-bang birth: a near instantaneous unit-after-unit multiplication, perhaps initially with repulsive

7

gravity, into nearly the total number of entities ($10^{86}$) that will exist in the mature universe billions of years old.[1]

Like the previous, simple example of two entities separating at nearly twice the speed of light, each of the rapidly multiplying, countless entities are also separating at or near the speed of light from all the previous and subsequent formed entities. That process multiplies distances of entity separation by trillions of times the speed of light without any individual entity exceeding the speed of light. In that way, the total range of expansion or "communication" announcing the big-bang birth occurs at trillions of times the speed of light without violating the laws of physics. (See pages 91-92 for another perspective.)

What if conscious beings can control how and when to break the symmetry of Gravity Units? With conscious beings controlling the symmetry breaking of Gravity Units, the efficiencies and power of universe-creating energy and communication multiply. How can that multiplication occur? The most obvious way is by aiming or lasing each spacetime birth in specific directions as energy waves or gravity pulses, rolling out in multidimensional geometries ...rather than allowing the gravity explosion to convert into the "usual" universe-making energy and matter radiating in three geometric directions. ...Also, such communication could possibly flash through hyperspace to other universes.[2]

---

[1]Each new universe exploded from a single Gravity Unit will then contain its own space-time dimensions filled with its own, new quantized geometries or Gravity Units each of which can in turn form a universe filled with Gravity Units. ...For this, as with certain other hypotheses in Neo-Tech Physics, no direct evidence as of yet exists.

[2]In water, the speed of light slows by about 23% to 142,600 miles/second. Thus, in water very high-energy, charged particles can exceed that slower speed of light to create a light-barrier shock wave producing Cerenkov radiation. Now, throughout existence, no total vacuum can exist in which to measure the ultimate speed of light.

(footnote continued on next page)

*Boundless Prosperity*

Business: The Power of the Universe

Competitive business is the eternal power of existence. It advances every level of society throughout the universe as described in Mark Hamilton's *Neo-Tech Cosmic Business Control*, 510 pages, Neo-Tech Publishing (1989) and in Eric Savage's *Neo-Tech Global Business Control*, 256 pages, Neo-Tech Worldwide (1992). Business is the natural mode of existence for conscious beings. What is business? Business is the *competitive production* and *voluntary exchange* of values among conscious beings. ...Conscious beings throughout the universe control nature through business.

Knowledge begets knowledge. Thus, knowledge is limitless — limitless power. Harnessing universal energy and communication through business represents one increment of productive achievement along the endless scale of knowledge throughout the Civilization of the Universe. Indeed, conscious beings exert business control over nature. Through the universal virtue of competitive business, advances in value production continue endlessly — beyond the imagination of conscious beings on Earth.

---

(footnote continued from previous page)

In our universe, the quantum vacuum state or the gravity-unit ether exists at a certain energy level. In a vacuum state at lower-energy levels, light could travel faster than 186,281 miles/second. Does that mean certain particles such as Gravity Units could travel faster than 186,281 miles per second through our universe and not exceed the speed of light travelling through lower energy-level vacuums? Is the Guth's "faster-than-light" big-bang expansion phase simply the speed of light traveling into a lower energy-state vacuum of meta space? Could such particles set up a shock wave that would break or tunnel through the metastable vacuum of this universe into a lower energy state, thus, annihilating at light speed our entire universe as we know it? Or, could lower vacuum states be a conscious-controlled, advanced source of energy and communication? ...What about tachyons? They are hypothetical particles that can never travel *slower* than the speed of light and *increase* in speed as they *lose* energy. Existence of tachyons is entirely speculative and highly unlikely.

9

Yet, someday, in the eternal Civilization of the Universe, immortal descendents from Earth will routinely function along all levels of unimaginable knowledge and accomplishments.

How can conscious life be immortal — eternal? First, examine the nature of existence: Existence is axiomatic. Existence simply exists — eternally, without prior cause. No alternative is possible. For, existence cannot *not* exist. Thus, as part of existence, the evolution of consciousness is also eternal. Countless conscious societies, therefore, exist throughout the universes with endlessly higher levels of knowledge — with millions or billions of years more advanced societies than ours. Because of such vast and endless differences in knowledge, conscious beings at any specific level of civilization cannot imagine the knowledge or activities of say a thousand years, much less a million or a billion years, more advanced societies.

If communication among conscious beings throughout the universe delivers rational benefits, such communication would develop through competitive-business dynamics. But, probably no net benefits would accrue from communicating with less advanced civilizations. Likewise, communicating with much more highly advanced civilizations would probably yield no net benefits. For, conscious beings in the Civilization of the Universe would not benefit by jumping significantly beyond their own ongoing, step-by-step integrations in developing knowledge and values. Indeed, no matter from what level of knowledge, the *continuity* of experiences and integrations needed to create ever expanding prosperity is the root cause of happiness in any civilization.

Why are net benefits impossible from big-gap jumps into realms beyond current knowledge? For example, conscious beings cannot benefit from "million-year" advanced-knowledge jumps without going through the integrated steps to acquire that knowledge. Indeed, to benefit from advances in knowledge requires meeting the criterion for advancing prosperity. That criterion throughout all universes and all time is fully integrated honesty combined with productive effort. In other words, that criterion *is* Neo-Tech.

## On Becoming Zon

Most conscious beings among Earth's anticivilization will encounter the fully integrated honesty of Neo-Tech at least once by the year 2000. That encounter will knock each person down. But, most people will jump right back up. Still enclosed in their mystical bubbles, most will bounce away...never examining what happened, never discovering eternal life and prosperity. Yet, a few will stay to examine Earth-evolved Neo-Tech. They will benefit enormously from applying its fully integrated honesty *within* Earth's anticivilization. ...And, a small number of those people will go beyond Neo-Tech by entering the Civilization of the Universe. As explained in Part III, they will become Zons. For them, the anticivilization will vanish into its nothingness as they experience the power of the universe — the power of Zon.

With the power of Zon, all things throughout the universe can become nonmystical conscious thoughts — *and nonmystical conscious thoughts (T1) can become all things (T2) throughout the universe.* ...As explained in Part III, from the equation T1 equals T2k arises k as the universal constant of Zon. From the constant k flows the power of Zon.[1]

_____

[1]The Zon constant k has not yet been determined. But, k would be the fifth and unifying universal constant: unifying the relativistic,

(footnote continued on next page)

## Movement I: Neo-Tech Physics

(footnote continued from previous page)

macroscopic universal constants of $G$ (gravity) and $c$ (velocity of light) with the quantum, submicroscopic universal constants of $k$ (Boltzmann) and $h$ (Planck). Perhaps k manifests itself in some sort of unifying ratio with the other four universal constants, such as k: $Gc/kh$. The Zon constant would relate energy, mass, gravity, and their velocities to the flow of *time* toward decreasing entropy, *not* toward increasing entropy. ...Universal constants, including the quantum cosmological constant, ultimately arise from a deep, compelling symmetry or geometry controlled by conscious beings. *The Zon constant fixes the values of all other constants.*

Except for consciousness, gravity is the weakest yet most pervasive force in nature. Indeed, gravity controls universal motion. But, the fifth force of nature — human consciousness — is the *grand-unifying* force controlling all existence. Conscious force is more subtle to specific measurement and mathematical quantification than gravity. Still, consciousness is the most noticeable force on planet Earth. Moreover, consciousness is the only force that can alter the otherwise predestined courses of the other four forces of nature: gravitational, electromagnetic, weak nuclear, strong nuclear. ...Consciousness is the force that unifies all forces and heals the seeming breaches of nature caused by quantum "uncertainties".

As a law of nature expressed by the Heisenberg Uncertainty Principle, facts asserted as truth are never certain. But, *principles* contextually determined through integrated honesty are always certain. Thus, for example, one can have certainty about the Heisenberg Uncertainty *Principle* without paradox or contradiction: (1) Metaphysically one can be certain that any particle always has an exact position and momentum at any exact time. But, epistemologically one can be certain that exact position and momentum *cannot* be simultaneously measured...at least not directly. (2) Measurements can be validly done in Euclidean/Galilean/Newtonian coordinate systems or in noneuclidean/relativistic/quantum-mechanical systems, depending on the object measured and the accuracy desired. And finally, (3) the indeterminate and probabilistic nature of quantum mechanics does not negate the laws of identity, noncontradiction, or cause and effect. The decay of radioactive atoms, for example, are both indeterminate and probabilistic. But, each decay has an identifiable, noncontradictory cause. ...That means Heracleitus, Plato, and Kant are out; Parmenides, Aristotle, and Rand are in.

As a side note important later: Plato is the father of organized deception through "noble" lies — the father of purposely dishonest government and science. Aristotle not only is the father of logic, science, and biology, but is the father of *rational* metaphysics and epistemology. Plato subjugated conscious life to higher mystical powers. Aristotle exalted conscious life on Earth as the highest value. Portions of Aristotle's ethics and politics, however, remained under Plato's influence, thus, are fallacious. ...Philosophically, Plato and Kant are mankind's villains, Aristotle and Rand are mankind's heroes.

# Chapter 2
# Your Journey to *Zonpower*

What is Zonpower?  To answer that question, you must first take a journey that leads to the center of weirdness.  Then, you must go beyond, into the realm of weirder-than-weird.  That journey will lead you into the weirdest realm of the entire universe.  And that realm is right here on planet Earth in its bizarre, upside-down, anti-power civilization.  You must go to that black-hole apex in order to go through it and then out into the advanced Civilization of the Universe — the civilization of honesty, prosperity, and happiness.

### Journey to the Weirdest Realm
Only from this anticivilization can you discover the realm of weirder-than-weird.  Once there, you will find the key to Zonpower.  Unlocking the door to all power and prosperity, you will escape the false journey that essentially everyone on Earth is traveling:  As one example, consider the false search in today's sciences and religions, especially in astro/quantum/particle physics and the Vatican.  That search is for a **Quantum/God Singularity** and the **Big Bang** — the fictional, wished-for birthplace of our forever evolving, plasmatic Universe.

World-class scientists have searched for that single point of creation.  Yet, the notion of Singularity contradicts the laws of nature and physics, as do the mystical notions of perpetual motion, cold fusion, low-energy nano-technology, along with various mystical interpretations of chaos and quantum mechanics.  Many brilliant scientists

13

are pursuing never ending illusions that demand ever more tax money, such as the twelve-billion-dollar, super collider (SSC)[1] in Texas. Such pursuits can generate ever more intriguing but eventually meaningless science and mathematics.

Singularity is rationalized to occur in an infinite[2] black hole collapsed to an undefinable, single-point entity filled with mathematical stratagems involving infinities. From such a single-point entity or Singularity, certain physicists assert that our universe and all existence was born. In turn, certain religionists enthusiastically point to Singularity as scientific proof of "God". For, the creation of our universe from Singularity would require a "God"

---

[1]The SSC's mission to find the Higgs boson is a valid quest, especially under brilliant Nobelists such as experimentalist Leon Lederman and theorist Murray Gell-Mann...but not under the dishonesties and inefficiencies of tax-funded science.

[2]"Infinite" is a useful mind-created concept that cannot exist in reality. Except for existence itself, which is eternal and has no finites or boundaries, "infinity" violates the law of identity. In accordance with reality, at any point one stops in traveling toward infinity, the entity is defined and finite, never infinite. For example, one's mind knows that a curve can asymptotically approach a straight line forever. Yet, at any point on that curve, all becomes finite and definable about that curve and the straight line.

Now, consider how the notion of a single point can always be approached closer and closer, but can never be reached. For, like the notion of infinity, singularity does not and cannot exist beyond a mind-created notion. As an analogy, think again how a curve can asymptotically approach but never reach that straight line and become a straight line. Nothing in reality can justify a notion that such an ever approaching curve would suddenly contradict its nature — its never-ending course — by arbitrarily and inexplicably jumping over a quantum space to join, straighten out, and become a part of that never reachable straight line.

The laws of identity and noncontradiction always hold in reality. Those laws are eternally fundamental and axiomatic throughout existence. Moreover, existence is not in space or time. Rather, time and space are in existence. The universe is eternal, not infinite.

mystically preexisting in nothingness and creating a universe out of nonreality. ...What an unnecessary, impotent notion.

Why resort to mysticisms, nonrealities, and nothingness to explain the creation of our universe? Why be stuck within such unreal and harmful limitations? Consider the seemingly infinite number of ordinary conscious beings wielding Zonpower throughout the rational civilizations existing among the universes. Most of those conscious beings have the power to create far beyond any imagined creations of a mystical "God". And, unlike the miracles of a made-up "God", conscious-being creations are real — accomplished naturally, within the laws of physics.

Each such conscious being, for example, has the power to create an endless number of universes from an endless number of universe-containing black holes existing at every spacetime point throughout eternity. Even so, most of those conscious beings have technologically and economically advanced so far that they have long ago in their forgotten histories abandoned the creation of universes as an inefficient, primitive activity.

### Vanish All "Gods"

With Zonpower, one captures powers far beyond any imagined powers of a "God" conjured up in Earth's anticivilization. Every such "God" is created to demand sacrifice — sacrifice of the productive class to the parasite class. But, with Zonpower, one escapes the "God" trap by entering the Civilization of the Universe.

Blasphemy? No. For, rational Zonpower, not imagined Godpower, is real and good. Zonpower, not wishful thinking, delivers open-ended prosperity and happiness to conscious beings throughout the universe.

Individual consciousness throughout the universes *is* the eternal, grand-unifying force of existence.

On planet Earth today, Albert Einstein represents the furthest advance in theoretical science and physics based entirely on a foundation of rationality and reality. Einstein avoided any arbitrary, quantum-mechanical retreats into fashionable nonrealities or Eastern mysticisms. With the recent discovery of Zonpower, Einstein arises anew. For science, physics, quantum mechanics, mathematics, and business can now advance in unison on Einstein's foundation of rationality and reality toward the promised land.

### A Journey into the Black Hole

To discover Zonpower, you must first take a journey to the realm of weirder-than-weird.[1] This journey proceeds from Einstein's dual relativity viewpoints — first from the observer's viewpoint and then from the traveler's viewpoint:

### THE OBSERVER

Through a special relativity telescope/microscope, you are observing a spaceship hurling toward a universe-containing black hole of such great mass that all matter will collapse seemingly forever.[2] You see the spaceship

---

[1]This metaphorical journey is contextually and descriptively fairly accurate. But out of necessity for nontechnical communication, some descriptions are not *precisely* accurate. Other descriptions await further advances in physics.

[2]Every black hole originates from less than infinite mass and energy. All black holes, therefore, will stop collapsing at some equilibrium point determined by its finite mass/energy: For example, stopping at the Chandrasekhar limit then at the Schwarzschild radius. That equilibrium point of finite size consists of various entities and energies that cannot by definition be a pure point of singularity. Instead, by nature, those entities and energies are simply new, valid, and real sets of physics definable by that particular condition for those entities, masses, energies, and finally gravity at a particular density or geometry.

cross the event horizon to be inescapably captured by the enormous, always increasing gravitational pull of that black hole. That overwhelming gravity continually accelerates the spaceship's plunge toward the center point with ever increasing speeds — speeds always approaching but never reaching the speed of light: 186,281 miles per second.

Observable only through your relativity telescope/ microscope, the collapsing, mega-mass black hole itself is now submicroscopic. And that black hole continues to collapse at ever increasing speeds. With fuzzy thinking, you rationalize that the infinitesimally tiny black hole still collapsing ever faster, approaching the speed of light, should in the next instant crunch into one entity at a single-point center. Your fuzzy thinking continues: All entities and forces would then become Singularity — a unified, single-point entity or force describable only in terms of unreal infinities.

Yet, no such thing happens as you continue observing through your relativity telescope/microscope: The spaceship and all surrounding existence keeps hurling toward the center at ever increasing speeds with ever decreasing distances, but without ever reaching the center. How can that be?

By continuing to observe the spaceship, you discover the answer through the laws of physics and Einstein's Special/General Relativity: As any object approaches the speed of light, its mass density increases *toward* infinity and its size shrinks *toward* zero length from the observer's viewpoint. Accelerating toward the speed of light, that spaceship appears to you, the outside observer, to move forward essentially as fast as that same spaceship is shrinking backward. Also, time aboard the spaceship

17

appears to slow toward zero. Thus, as with all the other entities of that black hole, the shrinking spaceship keeps approaching the black-hole center at ever higher velocities, but with ever slowing time, never reaching that center.

At some approaching equilibrium, the collapse will stop accelerating as determined by the laws of physics and the finite mass/energy/gravity geometry of the black-hole center. At that moment, the spaceship and all other surrounding entities of existence captured by the black hole will stop shrinking. All existence will then lock together in a black hole of finite size and specific nature — a nature or physics characteristic to its particular gravity or geometry. Moreover, that or any physics will always be in accord with reality. Thus, such a finite geometry of locked entities can, by definition and nature, never be a single point of mass or energy...or of Singularity. Instead, all that existence will be an energy/entity unit of gravity or geometry...not a single-point.

Without the mind-blocking, dead-end concept called Singularity, a new question and viewpoint arise: What or who could break a black-hole equilibrium of locked-together symmetries, entities, and energies? The answer, as described in later chapters, is that conscious people can break universe-containing black-hole symmetries to create universes and encoded cosmos systems observable today.

### THE TRAVELER

Now, let us experience the same journey as a traveler on that spaceship in quest of Singularity. First, you would have to somehow acquire such a spaceship from some advanced civilization. For, if you were capable of building that spaceship, you would also have the knowledge to realize Singularity is a contradiction of reality and cannot

18

exist. Thus, any such quest would be a fool's journey, forever wasting your life. Indeed, when that universe-containing black-hole equilibrium were finally reached, you would be locked together with all entities and energies, entombed apparently forever in that black hole.

Nevertheless, in that spaceship, you are now accelerating toward a seemingly infinite-mass black hole that will collapse almost forever toward its center. Crossing the event horizon, you see the center of the black hole. You fear an imminent crash into that center. But, soon, you realize something entirely different is happening. On looking outside the spaceship, time seems to pass so slowly and then ever slower. To travel the most minute distance seems to take forever. Every tiny incremental approach toward that black-hole center seems to take ever longer as time passes ever slower.

Soon you seem to be standing still with the black-hole center never again appearing to get closer. Yet, the spaceship's instruments show you are traveling at almost the speed of light and continually accelerating toward that center. You realize that you are experiencing not only Einstein's relativity in time and space, you are also experiencing relativity in gravity: Now, even the increases in gravity seem to have stopped. In fact, not even the quantized effects of gravity can escape that universe-mass black hole. ...You seem to be forever frozen in time, space, and gravity.

Finally, you the space traveler realize the ultimate fool's journey of boredom in which you have embarked and are forever trapped. You lose all that conscious life and valid knowledge have to offer. Your fool's journey offers only an endlessly changing physics, energy, and particles that at first seem rapid, interesting, important, and leading to new knowledge for answering questions. But

19

now, your almost infinitely slow journey is leading to nothing new — nothing that can build new knowledge or answer questions in reality. You can only observe endlessly slower changing forms[1] of mass/energy that are forever predictable as a function of existence and its gravitational fields, geometries, and dimensions.

Yet, the moment you awaken from your unreal physics-fiction dream is the moment you recognize what an endless, inescapable fool's journey you have traveled and are now stuck. Then, the door to escape opens. Realizing existence is never born or created, it simply exists eternally, your mind is finally free. Your entire thinking and viewpoint change. You realize existence, *not* consciousness, is primary.[2] You can now gain valid, new knowledge — Zonpower knowledge — that will show you how to escape that meaningless pursuit of a nonexistent grail: the birthplace of existence. You realize existence has no birthplace. You realize conscious beings have always controlled eternal existence through Zonpower.

Indeed, Zonpower brings you into the all-powerful Civilization of the Universe. With Zonpower, you control existence and, thus, can break out of any black hole.[3]

---

[1]Changing from a black hole to a naked black hole from which nothing, not even gravity, can escape...and finally changing into the geometry of a Gravity Unit.

[2]Aristotle is the father of the philosophically correct *primacy-of-existence* concept — a concept fully validated by Rand and Peikoff in the late 20th century. Plato is the father of the philosophically false *primacy-of-consciousness* concept — a concept disastrously advanced by Augustine, Hobbes, Descartes, Hume, Kant, and Hegel. ...Totalitarian-trending governments and their destructive politicians, armed bureaucrats, and parasitical elites require a dishonest, primary-of-consciousness philosophy to advance. *Zonpower in cyberspace vanishes Plato's philosophy, irrational acts, and government evils.*

[3]With conscious beings, rotating black holes can actually become shortcuts through space and time.

# Chapter 3

# Seven Waves

to the

# Civilization of the Universe

## WAVE ONE
### The Journey into a Black-Hole Civilization

* A spaceship travels into a universe-containing black hole: That spaceship can never reach Singularity, all in accord with the laws of nature as expressed by (1) Einstein's general relativity, by (2) *full-context* quantum/particle physics, or by (3) multidimensional superstring or duality string theories.

* Singularity and the big-bang creation of existence is a mystical notion requiring an imagined "God". Thus, the astute Vatican and its Pope, as early as the 1950s, seized out-of-context quantum physics as the long sought-after-link of science to religion "proving" the existence of their mystical "God".

* The fundamental fact of existence is *existence exists*. That means existence is eternal without prior causes. Existence includes the full evolvement of each new universe: from subatomic gravity units, quarks, electrons to the elements and compounds...from land, water, life, conscious beings, buildings, computers to conscious-created civilizations...and finally to conscious-controlled universes — controlled from both above and below. Thus, life and consciousness — like geometry, matter, and energy — have existed throughout eternity. Indeed, conscious beings like us, not an imagined "God", have eternally controlled nature and existence. ...Consciousness within each human being *is* the controlling force of existence.

21

## WAVE TWO
### Discovering the Civilization of the Universe

* Consider the very few honest philosophers who have lived on Earth: Parmenides, Aristotle, Thomas Aquinas ("variance with reason is evil"), Baruch Spinoza, Adam Smith (economist), John Locke, Ayn Rand, Leonard Peikoff.  Consider their struggle against the irrationality of an anticivilization.  They all sensed increasing frustration at their inevitable failures because they too were an integrated part of irrationality — of anticivilization.  They never knew how to leave or even knew that leaving an anticivilization was possible.  They never considered themselves being able to create and then enter the Civilization of the Universe. ...They too were locked in a fool's journey within Earth's black-hole anticivilization.

* Not until mystical, wishful-thinking notions, such as a Quantum/God Singularity, are cut away and discarded can physicists, mathematicians, and astronomers once again move forward in generating major new knowledge.  As new-age mysticisms multiply, all fields of knowledge shrink toward darkness.  But, as Neo-Tech starts vanishing such mysticisms, those declines in physics, mathematics, astronomy, medicine, law, education, and philosophy will reverse.  The resulting forward movement will bring a golden age of knowledge.  From that new knowledge and prosperity, we shall learn to live forever with ever increasing wealth and happiness.  We shall be in the Civilization of the Universe.


## WAVE THREE
### Zon Easily Outdoing "God's" Supreme Feat

* A century ago, no religious huckster could even imagine their mystical "God" could create a nuclear-power

22

reactor or a computer.  Yet, conscious beings easily do that today.

* Who would be the winner in any Zon-versus-"God" contest?  All conscious beings have the capacity within the laws of nature and physics to outdo the greatest imaginable feat of that mystical "God" — the creation of our universe.  Indeed, the creation of universes by conscious-controlled, Guth-type inflations of Gravity Units is elementary child's play long-ago left behind by the more advanced Zons.

* Unchain Jesus[1]:  He was a hero of Zon, not "God".

* Cut away and vanish the nothingness trap of mysticism, such as Quantum/God Singularity.  Then what happens?  An entirely different view, thinking, experiments, and physics unfold:

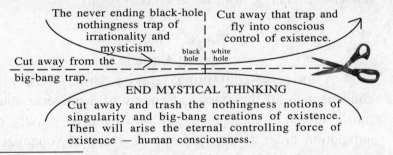

The never ending black-hole nothingness trap of irrationality and mysticism.

Cut away that trap and fly into conscious control of existence.

black hole | white hole

Cut away from the big-bang trap.

END MYSTICAL THINKING

Cut away and trash the nothingness notions of singularity and big-bang creations of existence. Then will arise the eternal controlling force of existence — human consciousness.

---

[1]Not the unreal, dead Jesus of establishment Christianity.  Not the chained, captive Jesus manipulated by parasitical "authorities" and vested interests since 400 AD.  But, the real, ever-living Israelite Jesus — the free spirit of eternal prosperity and happiness.

The parasitical-elite class with its subjective laws and ego "justice" attacked, jailed, and finally killed Jesus.  Why?  For his trying to bring the prosperous Civilization of the Universe described in Movement III to the harmful anticivilization described in Movement II. ...The professional value destroyers of the Roman Empire convicted and crucified Jesus solely to protect their ego agendas and harmful livelihoods.

Brief, erratic contacts with the Civilization of the Universe described in Movement III were perhaps experienced by Moses, Confucius, Socrates, Jesus, Bruno, Galileo, Spinoza, Newton, Brigham

(footnote continued on next page)

\* A century ago, any thought of human beings cracking the atom to convert mass into energy was inconceivable.  Today, nuclear energy is routine.  Likewise, today, any thought of human beings cracking super-dense black holes or Gravity Units (GUs) into new galaxies and universes is inconceivable.  Yet, once free of mystical notions such as Singularity and the big-bang creation of spacetime, the cracking of black-hole symmetries will become understood.  Then, universe-making energy can be harnessed by conscious beings breaking the symmetry of universe-containing Gravity Units — all consistent with the laws of physics. ...That process, in turn, will spin out the unlimited riches available from the conscious-controlled unleashing of matter and energy from those Gravity Units.

## WAVE FOUR
### Surpassing Einstein
\* A universe-containing Gravity Unit (UGU[1]) is equivalent to all the mass and energy of a universe spun into a submicroscopic geometry of wound-up gravity or antimotion order at zero entropy — the pure, quantized geometry of gravity in which time and space do not exist.  Advanced conscious beings create countless universes from such hidden quantized Gravity Units.  How?  By

---

(footnote continued from previous page)
Young, Einstein.  But, today, a consistent, nonstop journey from Earth to the Civilization of the Universe has begun.  It began in 1976 with the publication of the *Neo-Tech Reference Encyclopedia*.

The future belongs to fully integrated honesty — to reason, rationality, Neo-Tech, and the Civilization of the Universe.

[1]Universe containing Gravity Units (UGUs) *are* existence, thus, have existed eternally.  By contrast, universe-containing black holes (Chapter 2) form whenever an entire universe collapses into a black hole.

breaking symmetries to unwind the endless UGUs into universes of matter and energy...or perhaps into just gravity pulses for communication. Why do conscious beings create universes? To utilize nature's ultimate energy and communication source in advancing their well beings. ...That conversion of UGUs into endless riches and universes by conscious beings is expressed by the equation:

**UGU energy/c2 $\overset{Eq}{\longleftrightarrow}$ UGU mass→$\left[\begin{smallmatrix}\text{broken}\\\text{symmetry}\end{smallmatrix}\right]$→Energy+Mass+Time**

    * The UGU state is near pure gravity in an existence field. UGUs are at once *all* energy and *all* mass. The quantized Gravity Unit is the basic unit of existence — the immutable source of all life and riches. Thus, all expanding values and riches rise from that single unit (*not* a single point) — the quantized GU. Additionally, GUs are the energy and communication means among the controlling force of existence — goal-directed conscious life.

    * How does one prove conscious life is the only nongeometrically structured force of nature — the fifth and controlling force of the universe? By discovering anomalies in the universe that are unmistakably obvious as conscious creations — creations that could never be produced or configured by the other four universal forces — the geometrically structured forces of gravity, electromagnetism, weak nuclear forces, and strong nuclear forces. ...Consider one observing a planet in a distant solar system. Did conscious life ever exist there? What if that observer spotted a land-rover vehicle on that planet? That land-rover vehicle would be unmistakable proof of conscious existence. For, no geometric force of nature could produce or configure a land-rover vehicle. Now, extrapolate that example to anomaly configurations in the universe. Are those anomalies a part of a nongeometric,

consciously encoded cosmos system? Such anomalies will be resolved only by plugging in the purposeful, unifying force of conscious life into theoretical and mathematical models of our entire universe down to subatomic phenomena. ...Is existence itself encoded by conscious control?

* At every level, from distant quasars to subatomic quarks, from astronomy to quantum physics, certain anomalies will be resolved as purposeful, life-enhancing conscious actions. Within that resolution exists the proof that nongeometrically structured conscious life *is* the fifth and controlling force/dimension of existence.

* The conscious harnessing of Super-Inflation Gravity Units (SIGUs) allows near instant, gravity-pulse communication not only across our entire universe but possibly between universes — all without violating physical laws, including the speed of light. How? By rolling multidimensional geometries into lased gravity pulses transmitted via Guth-type inflations of Gravity Units.[1]

## WAVE FIVE
### From Impossible to Succeed to Impossible to Fail

* Civilizations and anticivilizations are conscious-

---

[1]No single entity or particle can travel faster than the speed of light. But, quantum fluxes can provide "instantaneous" or "superluminal" travel of a particle such as the Bohr-orbit quantum jump of an electron. What happens is a quantum flux produces a physics-permitted, positron-and-electron pair in a vacuum in a different energy level or orbit. The space/energy difference between the two energy levels is the electron-produced wavelength. The positron then annihilates the lower orbit electron leaving the new electron in a different orbit, giving the appearance of an instantaneous jump between orbits when in reality two separate electrons are involved.

Similar rationally explicable phenomena occur with faster-than-light, "big-bang" expansions or quantum fluxes of Gravity Units into universes. ...No mysticism or conscious-created reality exists in physics or reality, from cosmological relativity to quantum mechanics.

26

created, just as are land-rover vehicles, airplanes, and television sets. None exist in nature alone. None are created by the other forces of nature without conscious beings.

* The Civilization of the Universe is created by conscious beings objectively integrating reality. But an anticivilization is conjured up by humanoids subjectively disintegrating reality.

* In an anticivilization, endless volumes of philosophy arise in order to rationalize or counter the endless contradictions of reality and rationality. The Civilization of the Universe **is civilization**. *For, civilization is the integration of reason and objective reality.* In such a civilization, philosophy simplifies to a few words and then disappears as self-evident.

* Civilization vanishes any anticivilization on contact — somewhat analogous to matter vanishing antimatter on contact. Both anticivilization and antimatter are anti *by nature*. Therefore, their natures can never be changed. But, they can be annihilated, vanished, or puffed away by actual matter and the actual Civilization of the Universe.

* Throughout the universe, the position of anyone or any civilization on the scale of knowledge makes no difference. Only the process of advancing unimpeded on that never ending scale of knowledge delivers prosperity and happiness to conscious beings.

* The Civilization of the Universe delivers far beyond any mystic's dream of a no-effort paradise. With Zonpower, one can solve life's problems to live eternally in ever expanding knowledge, prosperity, and happiness. For, the Civilization of the Universe is based on rational efforts integrated with reality — on disciplined thoughts, goal-directed actions, and iron-grip controls — not on lazy rationalizations, wishful thinkings, or sloppy mysticisms.

New-Color Symphony

Movement #1

\* In any civilization, the *only* legitimate or beneficial function of government is to **protect** individual property rights. The *only* legitimate use of force is self-defense in protecting those rights. By contrast, criminal-controlled governments of anticivilizations depend on political-agenda laws, ego "justice", initiatory force, threats, coercion, fake compassion, and fraud to survive. They survive by draining value producers and **violating** property rights.

\* How can one escape parasitical elites while trapped in their anticivilization? The trap is the attempt to reform their anticivilization, which cannot be done. The key is Zonpower. With Zonpower, one can cut away and vanish the anticivilization. Consider the following: (1) Zonpower is the tool for building unlimited prosperity available to every conscious being, (2) Zonpower is Neo-Tech applied from the Civilization of the Universe, (3) Zon is anyone who is applying Neo-Tech from the Civilization of the Universe.

\* In an anticivilization, long-range successes are impossible. In the Civilization of the Universe, long-range failures are impossible.

## WAVE SIX
### The Source of Eternal Wealth

\* Technically, gravitational "forces" do not exist. As Einstein discovered in surpassing Newton, gravity is the relative interaction among the geometries of mass, energy, space, and time.[1] Similarly, universal consciousness as promoted by certain physicists, Eastern religions, and pantheism does not exist. Rather, universal consciousness

---

[1]Somewhat analogous to two-dimensional flatlanders feeling the tugs of geometric variances as "gravitational forces" when they traverse, for example, a crumpled sheet of paper.

as the eternal interaction between individual conscious beings and existence is what dominates nature.

* As Einsteinian relativity overtook Newtonian gravity, astronomers and physicists went about empirically proving relativity. Likewise, as the Civilization of the Universe overtakes today's anticivilization, astronomers and physicists will go about empirically proving Zonpower: the control of the universe by conscious beings. ...Einstein's discredited cosmological constant will rise anew from Gravity Units containing the hidden Zon constant that brings eternal wealth and happiness to the universe.

## WAVE SEVEN
### The Product from Zon — Let There be Light!

* Civilizations are created by conscious beings applying the eternal principles of nature to life. Thus, civilizations can be created by billions of conscious beings or by a single conscious being. Moreover, as a conscious creation, civilizations can be created and expressed in writing — in a document. Once a Civilization of the Universe is created here on Earth, anyone can experience that civilization. And, once one experiences that civilization, he or she captures the power of Zon.

The ancients saw power in the gods among the stars. The golden-age Greeks brought power to man on Earth. Today, Zonpower brings the Civilization of the Universe to Earth. ...Zonpower gives conscious people power over existence.

* On capturing that wealth and power among the Civilization of the Universe, one can never again look back or waste a thought on the boring irrationality of today's anticivilization — today's insane civilization ruled by dishonest parasites who can only drain others and harm society.

29

*Movement I: Neo-Tech Physics*

\* Thus, the first-and-final product from Zon *is* the **Civilization of the Universe**. As explained in Movement III, once one receives that ultimate product, he or she becomes a citizen of the universe. With the resulting Zonpower, that person puffs away the anticivilization to gain eternal wealth, romantic love, and exciting happiness.

*Science, Physics, and Mathematics*
*merge into*
*Conscious-Controlled Cyberspace*

Francis Bacon (1562-1626) the father of the Scientific Method developed inductive reasoning and formulated perhaps the most important maxim of Western thought: "Nature, to be commanded, must be obeyed." To be commanded, nature must first be understood. Thus, "knowledge is power". ...That power resides in conscious-controlled cyberspace.

Galileo Galilei (1564-1642) the father of modern science identified and demonstrated that mathematics was required for the development of physics — its theories and laws. Mathematics as the key to understanding nature was also demonstrated by Johannas Kepler (1571-1630) in his discoveries of algebraic geometries that codified the elliptical orbits and area sweeps of planetary motions.

The Zon Institute is seeking to develop the mathematical descriptions and field formulations of conscious-controlled physics. All universal constants and the laws of physics are formulated through the conscious unfurling of Gravity Units. Publishable contributions providing such mathematical descriptions may be submitted to John Flint, Neo-Tech Publishing, P. O. Box 531330, Henderson, NV 89053-1330.

30

# Chapter 4

# Zon's Force Field

> ## Note to General Readers
> Understanding the scientific technicalities of the previous chapters and the next four chapters with their footnotes is not necessary for understanding and fully using Zonpower. Read those chapters for what you can easily understand. Do not worry about the rest.

By understanding what existence *really* is, you gain control over impediments blocking your life. Without those impediments, you can foretell the future to gain limitless riches.

Indeed, you can get incredibly rich by controlling the force fields of existence. But first you must know what existence really is through Neo-Tech physics. Existence is axiomatic and eternal. For, existence simply exists with no prior causes. Existence is a natural, open-ended plasma of force fields[1] eternally evolving with no beginning or end. Neo-Tech physics demonstrates how human-like consciousness is not only an integral part of existence, but is the eternal controller of its geometries, fields, and particles. ...Yet, what is the actual nature of existence?

Most existence throughout the universe exists as an open-ended electroplasma, always evolving through its interacting matter (M) and energy (E) fields or modes. Those two fields of existence eternally interchange in a

---

[1]Fields and forces are the result of noneuclidean geometries and symmetries in space. Thus, there are no unaccounted, spooky "actions at a distance". ...Superstring theory, which would involve the geometries and mathematics of Gravity Units, consist of sixteen dimensions, or, in actuality, ten dimensions because six dimensions are redundant. Those ten dimensions can, in turn, split into a rolled-up six dimensions in which time, space, motion, and entropy do not exist — and the unrolled four dimensions of our current observable universe in which time, space, motion, and entropy do exist.

relationship expressed by Einstein as $M = E/c^2$ (from $E = mc^2$), with c being the universal constant representing the velocity of light.

Existence cannot *not* exist. Moreover, no vacuum void of existence is possible. "Vacuums" of the *matter* field can exist as in outer space, in vacuumed-pumped containers, and in areas between electrons. But, all those volumes are filled with the unmovable, frictionless ether or existence field — a uniform, continuous field of existence.[1]

Throughout eternity, a massless field uniformly occupies every spacetime point of existence. This field of existence behaves as an ether matrix with stationary wave, vibration, or string properties. Within this field matrix, both energy and matter geometries interact to form physical existence, always behaving in dynamic combinations of one mode interacting with the other. Certain motions of the matter field, for example, interact at the

---

[1]An all-pervasive existence field of mass and energy modes is somewhat analogous to a combination of (1) Dirac's ocean in which exists an endless field of "electrons" or energy fluctuations at all points throughout space and (2) Faraday's nonmatter, stationary lines or fields of force. ...All known energy modes can pressure wave through the energy/matter ratios of outer space. Most modes are absorbed or changed at the energy/matter ratios either in Earth's gaseous atmosphere or in the liquids and solids of Earth itself. By contrast, almost all neutrino wave pressures can pass through the electron/nuclear fields of thick solid masses, even through the entire planet Earth without mode change.

This resurrection of an *ether*, **not as a matter or energy field**, but as a fixed existence field, reconciles Newton's classical laws and Einstein's relativity with quantum mechanics. Such a reconciliation arises from a universal Zon constant, k, which, in turn, arises from conscious control of the existence-field ether manifested at every spacetime point of existence. The resulting causal control of existence by eternal conscious beings is (1) universal, (2) fixed, (3) unmovable, and (4) independent of any frame of reference or method of observation.

quantum level with the energy field. That interaction produces irreducible packets of quantized energies or geometric structures. Those irreducible quanta, such as photons, send relief-seeking signals or perturbations into the continuous existence field radiating throughout eternity.

### Conscious Control of Existence Fields

During its creation, each new energy quantum slips smoothly and continuously from its matter field into the fixed existence field. Like water flowing from a dripping faucet, each quantum is pinched off into a minimum-energy wave packet. Simultaneously, from the continuous energy flow, a new quantum starts forming. Thus, continuous, smooth-flowing energy forms discrete photons. In turn, those photons or pinched-off wave packets of minimum *energy **matter*** create field disturbances or nonequilibrium pressures[1] signalling themselves in all directions throughout the existence field. Such signals generally travel near or at the speed of light.

Eventually, each point line of disturbance or pressure signal is relieved by a receptor that absorbs such signals. In turn, that disturbance absorption converts back into pinched-off packets of minimum *matter **energy*** — chemical, potential, or kinetic. In other words, a receptor relieves signal pressures by locally absorbing quanta equivalent to the quanta from the originating source. Each absorbed quantum is then converted back into the

---

[1]Not a pushing pressure, but a nonequilibrium pressure or disturbance signal seeking equilibrium. What is detected only *represents* what is transmitted. ...A pressure intruding into the existence field causes that field to curve around the intrusion which, in turn, traces the curved paths of gravity. The interactive relationships between mass, energy, fields, curved space, and gravity require an ether of existence fixed throughout spacetime.

equivalent of its original mode. Such exchanges of modes can be detected as a wave/particle in the energy field or a particle/wave in the matter field or a combination, depending on how and where that mode exchange is emitted, absorbed, and measured.[1]

Those field or mode exchanges occur, for example, when stars pour *nature-controlled*, gravity-fusion energy into its surrounding electrons. Those energized electrons, in turn, pour photons into the existence field. Those photons cause disturbances that simulate waves ranging from radio waves to gamma waves. Those simulated waves radiate toward receptors located at the end of all point lines throughout existence — such as a lens of a telescope in another galaxy. That receptor conserves existence by withdrawing or absorbing equivalent amounts of pressure-alleviating photons to neutralize the disturbances from the originating source.

Similarly, a hydro, fossil-fuel, or fusion power plant on Earth pours *human-controlled,* power-plant energy into, for example, a television transmitter. That energized transmitter, in turn, pours its *human-controlled* photons into

---

[1]In measurements, the distinction between metaphysical and epistemological certainties must be discerned, especially in quantum mechanics: No *metaphysical* uncertainties exist in physical nature. Only *epistemological* uncertainties exist.* Probability statistics are used in the absence of concrete knowledge. The de Broglie/Bohm's pilot-wave theories help eliminate the mystical misinterpretations of quantum mechanics arising from the 1926 Copenhagen Interpretation. ...Pilot waves are the fingerprint disturbances guiding moving particles.

*Consider the following epistemological uncertainty: The ratio of a circle's circumference to its diameter is $\pi$ or 3.14159..., a number that continues indefinitely without ever repeating. Thus, the use of $\pi$ in calculations, such as the area of a circle $A=\pi r^2$, can never yield an exact or certain answer. For the answer always depends on how many decimals one extends $\pi$ in calculating that area. Yet, an exact area exists, it just cannot be calculated by using $\pi$ or any method of diminishing triangulation.

the existence-field ether. Such an action creates radiating lines of disturbances that are equilibrated by absorption of photons into the matter field of, for example, a television receiver. The same energy/matter mode equilibrations can be traced from that television set to the retina of a human eye, then to a conscious brain, and finally to volitional physical actions that both alter and control the course of nature.

Discrete quanta or particles move at high velocities approaching the speed of light mainly in (1) expansions or contractions of the universe, in (2) certain nuclear reactions or radioactive decays causing symmetry breakings or hidings, and in (3) conscious-controlled actions such as particle accelerations. By contrast, the ordinary transmission of light, electromagnetism, or quantum energy across space is not a result of any significant particle movement. But rather such linear or curved transmissions are simply vibrating, resonating, or wave-like disturbances in spacetime geometries propagating near or at the speed of light through the existence field. Thus, discrete energy quantum and matter quantum do not themselves travel across space. Instead, each creates a disturbance pressure that radiates wave like along the stationary point lines of existence. That wave-like disturbance is eventually relieved, equilibrated, or absorbed by receptors at the end of each point line of existence.

Consider the above description of *locally* creating and relieving energy pressures by emitters and receptors in the stationary existence-field ether. Now, consider the popular notion that almost every particle ever created or released physically races across space — often across millions or billions of light years in space. That notion seems to violate some sort of "least-action" principle. Such an action-inefficient notion of endlessly traveling quanta seems as quaint as the notion of a geocentric universe in which all inertial matter, planets, and stars daily race around planet Earth.

Indeed, both matter and energy interact locally, not across space. Light, for example, does not literally propagate across time and space. But, rather, light locally manifests a disturbance that spreads wave like throughout the existence-field ether until absorbed or equilibrated by a receptor.[1]

### Conscious Control of Existence

The above example of an energy-releasing star can be "deterministically" calculated from the "immutable" cause-and-effect of existence *without* conscious influences. But, the above example of an energy-releasing television transmitter is the volitional dynamics of existence being integrated, controlled, and forever altered by freewill human consciousness. Thus, as revealed by Neo-Tech physics, all existence is ultimately controlled and evolved through volitional human consciousness.

Unknown to the busily self-serving Establishment, the

---

[1]Then what really is the "speed of light", c? First, consider atomic fission or fusion in which a given mass is converted to energy as $mc^2=E$. Now, by contrast, the "speed of light", c, is the velocity at which a given energy is converted to mass as $E/c^2=m$. Yet, light itself is the opposite — it has no rest mass. So where is the connection of light to the velocity, c? There is none. The "speed of light", c, is not the speed of light at all, but rather c is the velocity relationships of field disturbances, which all have a speed limit of 186,281 miles per second in a particular vacuum state.

Incidentally, traveling near or at the velocity of light, energy fields bend in gravitational fields. The quasi mass generated by high-velocity, photonically disturbed existence fields is what bends in gravitational fields.

nature of existence and its dynamics of matter and energy are today being increasingly understood and methodically verified. That verification process will lead to the corollary verification that *human consciousness* is the eternal integrator and controller of existence. ...Human consciousness ultimately controls the relationships and geometries of the other existence modes — matter and energy along with space and time. The human-consciousness mode *is* the purposeful, unmoved mover of existence.

## Zonpower Commands the Future

The scientific verification that any individual conscious being can control existence will vanish Earth's irrational anticivilization. As Earth's anticivilization vanishes, the rational Civilization of the Universe will embrace our world. ...With Zonpower, one can foretell and command the future by controlling the existence field that reaches into the future — into the Civilization of the Universe.

The age of Zon means controlling the universal information field *not* through Earthbound computers, but through Zonpower: the foretelling knowledge of Neo-Tech physics — the certainty used to gain limitless excitement, power, and riches...*eternally*.

## The Five Forces of Nature

| Force | Particles Affected | Manifestation | Field Quanta | Range (meters) | Relative Strength |
|---|---|---|---|---|---|
| 1. strong | quarks | nuclear power | gluons | $10^{-15}$ | 1 |
| 2. electro-magnetic | charged particles | chemistry | photons | unlimited | 1/137 |
| 3. weak | quarks and leptons | radioactive decay | $W^{\pm}$ and $Z^0$ bosons | $<10^{-15}$ | $10^{-5}$ |
| 4. gravity | all particles | cosmic structures | gravitons | unlimited | $10^{-40}$ |
| 5. consciousness | gravity units + bosons (energy particles) + fermions (matter particles) | controlling all scales of existence | thinkons (see page 46) | unlimited | $k \cdot x$ |

38

# Chapter 5

# The Physics Behind Zonpower

*Zonpower* is a communiqué from the Civilization of the Universe. When you carefully read the *entire* communiqué, an epiphany will occur. You will, for the first time in your life, know how to control all that affects you. Nothing negative or harmful in the anticivilization will control you again. You will gain majestic control over your mind, body, and all events involving your prosperity, happiness, and well-being. ...You will gain Zonpower from which you will capture the power and riches available from the Civilization of the Universe.

Every owner of *Zonpower* must carefully read this communiqué in its entirety at least once, perhaps twice or more, in order to reach into an ecstatic future...into the Civilization of the Universe to gain its power and riches. At the same time, you will toss the yoke of today's stagnant anticivilization. Indeed, *Zonpower* delivers a stunning new power to benefit from every event that touches your life.

### Scientific Proofs

The final proof of the Civilization of the Universe lies in the foretelling powers of Zonpower that yield limitless riches, even to those trapped in this anticivilization. But to vanish this anticivilization by having everyone on Earth move into the Civilization of the Universe requires scientific proofs embedded in mathematics. Those proofs are today evolving. One such proof will evolve from answering the fundamental question: What is existence?

39

The answer will arise by first answering another question: What is the relationship of consciousness to mass and energy? That answer requires understanding the relationship of inertial or gravitational mass to a massless universal ether — a fixed matrix of existence. Then, one can discover the relationships among mass, energy, and consciousness itself. ...How are (1) mass as "weight" and (2) energy as "weightlessness" related to (3) conscious-controlled existence? Why do each of those three existence modes require a universal existence field? ...Below is the simplest approach to answering those questions:

### If Mass is Not Intrinsic, What is Weight?

Aristotle postulated things had weight because they had tendencies to be heavy or light. But that postulate does nothing to really explain weight. Newton explained weight through the force of gravity. On careful thought, however, gravitational force does nothing more to explain weight than Aristotle's tendencies. Additionally, Einstein's general relativity demonstrates that gravity does not exist as a force. But rather mass curves space by displacing the space surrounding that mass. Thus, gravity is simply mass moving along spacetime curves — along natural paths of least action.

The greater the mass, the more it bends or curves space toward itself by displacement. Therefore, the more a unit of mass curves space toward itself the greater will be its inertia in falling toward another unit of mass with space likewise curved toward its own mass. ...Mass falling through space curved toward another mass gives the effect of gravitational attraction or negative energy striving toward nonmotion.

Now, through Einstein's relativity, one can approach

40

*The Physics Behind Zonpower*

an explanation of what weight really is. But, on still closer examination, even Einstein fails to provide a complete answer. What is missing? The existence field is missing — the ether that Einstein dismissed. ...Mass is *not* intrinsic to matter. Thus, an existence-field ether is required to explain what weight really is.

Why does Einstein's General Relativity fail to explain weight without a fixed field of existence? Take two cannonballs of identical size, one made of solid iron, the other of solid aluminum. Both fall and accelerate in a gravitational field at the same rate. Why does the iron ball weigh about twice that of the aluminum ball of the same size? Einstein's general relativity explains that space curves toward the center of mass in proportion to that mass. But, if a non-ether space surrounding the equal-sized cannonballs is being "displaced" and curved, is that curvature equal for equal-volume cannonballs? Is the weight for identical-sized iron and aluminum cannonballs identical? Of course not. ...What is wrong? Nothing.[1]

One must first strip away volume/particle/mass/energy ideas such as the mass of a quark or the energy of a photon. For, gravity and weight can be understood only in terms of interacting geometries within a fixed existence field *beneath* all mass and energy quanta...beneath each cannonball, quark, electron, photon.

The key concept is this: In order to have weight or gravity, one must have a fixed ether field of weightless existence that is *uniformly and equally present everywhere* from the spaces between galaxies and above, down to the spaces between quarks and below, down to the final symmetry of the ether-hidden Gravity Unit.

---

[1]Volume, of course, does not explain weight or General Relativity. And, of course, Einstein's General Relativity is correct. Volume is simply used as an analogy to dig beneath volume/mass/energy to find the gravity geometries needed to explain the origins of weight. ...See pages 15-20 of the Closing Ceremonies for further understandings of weight.

## Movement I: Neo-Tech Physics

If that symmetry-hiding ether were not uniformly present and fixed everywhere in existence, the universal laws of nature, such as gravity, would be arbitrary and fail. ...That fixed existence-field ether is not only necessary for existence, but *is* existence — conscious-controlled geometries throughout spacetime.

One must recognize that a fixed, weightless field *is* existence in which its modes of matter, energy, and consciousness interact. The mathematics and experiments will then fall into place for understanding and controlling existence.[1] ...Weight is simply what and where weightlessness is not.

### Football-Stadium Experiments

From the macroworld perspective, conduct the following experiment: In a bowl-like football stadium,

---

[1] Controlling Existence at *All* Scales:

Any given astral volume of matter and energy will maintain its same weight before and after collapsing into a black hole. For, any collapsed volume will still contain the equivalent number of mass/energy units for equivalent ether-field displacements. Total spacetime curvature and total gravity will, therefore, be equivalent for any mass/volume in both its black-hole form and its fully expanded star, galaxy, or universe form. Now, by definition, light and other energy or mass forms cannot escape a black hole. Thus, a normal black hole cannot be detected, except by its gravity or perhaps by Hawking radiation. But nothing, not even gravity, can escape from universe-containing black holes that further collapse into Gravity Units. Why? Because mass and energy have collapsed into a symmetrical geometry of gravity curved in on itself. By collapsing to trillions of times smaller than a regular, microscopic black hole, the Gravity Unit becomes a *quasi point that causes no ether displacement*. It becomes a part of weightless ether. Thus, the Gravity Unit is essentially weightless with no current technology to detect its totally lost, inconceivably tiny weight and volume. ...This essentially weightless, undetectable Gravity Unit represents the underlying geometry of all existence *minus* consciousness. Now, all geometries of existence are subject to nongeometrical conscious control through Gravity Units.

Light cannot escape from black holes whose volumes are proportional to their masses. Neither light *nor gravity* can escape from Gravity Units whose "volumes" are *inversely* proportional to their *potential* masses. Does space, time, or motion exist beneath Gravity Units? Is our universe a Gravity Unit relative to other universes? 42

bolt on the arm of every seat a simple, low-cost, push-button, battery device.  On pushing the button, a precisely tuned radio wave unique to each device is emitted.  Beneath the stadium is a radio-wave detector hooked up to a computer.  Now, fill the stadium with 100,000 football fans.  As part of the halftime ceremonies, provide a laser-light display.  Ask the spectators to keep their fingers on the signal button and immediately press it each time they see a green laser flash.  Deliver 50 green flashes during the laser display.[1]  The signal detector and computer will detect and record every person's signal, plotting each as a point along either side of a dividing line continuously calculated as the medium signal time.

If those signals plot reproducible, double sine waves for each $360^0$ revolution of the stadium, watch out!  For, conscious quanta as an integral part of a fixed existence-field has been experimentally demonstrated.  From such verifiable and repeatable experiments, the Civilization of the Universe and its powers can become known and increasingly accessible to everyone on planet Earth.

How would a double sine wave in this experiment (1) identify the fixed ether of existence and (2) demonstrate consciousness as an integral mode of that ether?  The Earth is orbiting the sun at about 67,000 miles per hour...or about 0.01% the speed of light.  Thus, if consciousness or conscious control is an integral part of the fixed ether, those oriented most directly in line with the direction of that motion will, because of relativity effects, record on average minutely slower but statistically measurable response times reflected by points plotted below the medium line.

---

[1]An *at-rest* comparison of the speed of light versus the 5,000,000 pieces of data requires several orders of magnitude more preciseness to detect the sought effect.  But, the experiment can be enhanced to detect the sought effect through added computer/trigonometric analyses that detect secondary changes in statistical data reflecting particles *not* at rest but traveling 67,000 mph through the GU ether relative to the sun. ...Other motions could be detectable, even overwhelming: for example, the high-speed motion of our galaxy through the GU ether. ...See pages 15-20 of the Closing Ceremonies for further understandings of this experiment.

43

New-Color Symphony

Movement #1

*Movement I: Neo-Tech Physics*

Those people sitting at a $90^0$ angle to Earth's orbital motion will record on average a minutely faster response as reflected by points plotted above the medium line. The average of those points should then show a double sine-wave inclination for each $360^0$ revolution of the stadium. Statistically, on calculating the effects of relativity, about 100 points should fall outside the statistical average, above and below the line, for each $360^0$ revolution of 100,000 points of data recorded after each green laser flash. That 100 point variation per flash times fifty flashes should manifest itself as detectable, reproducible sine waves.

Why did the famous Michelson-Morley experiment in 1887, for which Michelson won the Nobel prize in 1907, "prove" that no fixed ether existed? Because the signals measured were photons of light, which are not intrinsic to the existence field. In other words, rather than seeking a weightless existence-field ether, a nonexistent matter-mode ether was sought. Therefore, no relativity effects would be detected for photons in that experiment. Thus, no detection of the "ether wind" could occur. But, what if consciousness or conscious control is intrinsic to existence — a constituent of the fixed ether? Then, with live conscious action, its mediating quanta particles called *thinkons* will cut through a fixed field of existence at 67,000 miles per hour relative to the sun — or greater speeds relative to other universe entities, such as other galaxies, or the entire expanding universe, or even the meta-universe — the Universe of Universes.[1]

---

[1]Electromagnetic forces such as photons would "disturb" but not measurably interact with a fixed ether of Gravity Units. Thus, photons would act independently and could not detect the "ether". By contrast, hypothetical thinkons would be intrinsic to Gravity Units, thus, would interact with the GU ether — the unmoving frame of reference for all existence. ...What if the speed through the GU ether is close to the speed of light, $c$, relative to the expanding universe?

(footnote continued on next page)

## Other Experiments:  Clocks and Computers

Physicists have already demonstrated minute differences in time for clocks at different latitudes and altitudes.  Those differences are attributed to differences in gravitational "forces".  Could similar experiments utilize super-computer-speed variations to detect both the orbital and rotational movements of the Earth through the GU ether?[1]

## Gravity Units: the Basic Unit of Existence

Gravity Units are neither energy nor matter.[2]  But, in

_____

(footnote continued from previous page)

Does that mean conscious beings could measurably, albeit minutely, think more efficiently facing one direction versus another direction? Worth experiments?  What if conscious beings are traveling at all directions simultaneously through the fixed "ether" at near the speed of light?  In that case, the "ether" could not be detected by Stadium Experiments and thinking rates would be equal in all directions. ...In any case, the point of the Stadium-Experiment idea is not only one of physics, but one of metaphor to illustrate the relationship of consciousness to existence.

[1]Neo-Tech physics with its ether field resolves the many mysteries of quantum mechanics, including Bell's theorem in explaining the 1982 Alain Aspect's "faster-than-light" experiments.  Conscious control of the ether field removes the mysticism from quantum interpretations of CPT symmetry breakings, the Einstein-Bohr debate, Schrödinger's cat paradox and Wigner's friend, and even reducing Everett's parallel universes from infinitely multiplying down to two: the universe and the antiuniverse (the anticivilization). ...Rational consciousness collapses the wavefunction of the antiuniverse.

[2]Energy and mass in the strictest sense do not actually convert from one to the other as suggested by $E=mc^2$.  They are really just two different modes of the most fundamental field — the *existence field* consisting of quasi spacetime points and Gravity Units.  From any Gravity Unit or quasi spacetime point can spring the mass and energy of an entire universe...an entire universe of quarks and electrons.

But, how do the quarks and electrons actually materialize? They materialize by breaking the symmetry of a Gravity Unit or spacetime point, which is pure symmetry at zero energy, zero mass, and zero gravity.  That symmetry breaks into exactly equal but any amounts of positive and negative energy.  The amount of energy depends on how the symmetry breaks.  The positive energy consists of mass and

(footnote continued on next page)

sort of a de Sitter sense, energy and matter meld into the symmetry of Gravity-Unit space or an *existence field*. From that fundamental symmetry or field of existence, all universes spring. Indeed, Gravity Units are that which the latest string theories are groping toward. Gravity Units not only occupy all space among matter and energy particles, but comprise all such particles themselves including quarks and electrons, including gravitons and photons.

The most fundamental controller of existence is human consciousness, the force that controls symmetry and Gravity Units. From those dynamics, existence evolves. ...Consciousness is the ultimate logic, beauty, and symmetry of physics from which future, major theories and discoveries will be predicted and confirmed.

---

(footnote continued from previous page)

energy fields comprising the dynamics of quark-and-electron motions. The negative energy consists of gravity comprising the dynamics of antimotions and slowing time. The total energy, mass, and gravity for any universe or its alternate mode of a Gravity Unit is zero, with all positive and negative energies exactly cancelling each other. Indeed, in the totality of any closed universe or Gravity Unit, the conservation laws of energy, angular momentum, and electrical charge disappear. They each cancel to zero. ...In a Gravity Unit, time stops and disappears into a spatial dimension or geometry.

What really are quarks and electrons? They are existence modes or geometries of quantized momentums that are relativistically compacted into mass particles surrounded by energy fields or wave functions.

Gravity Units and their existence field are controlled by conscious beings through unblocked, wide-scope, integrated thinking efforts. The fine-coarse graining of existence will reveal a quantized particle of conscious thought: the *thinkon*. As photons mediate force in the electromagnetic field, as W and Z particles mediate force in the weak nuclear field, as gluons mediate force in the strong nuclear field, and as gravitons mediate force in the gravitational field, thinkons mediate the force of consciousness in the existence field. All existence can be identified through various sum-over histories of thinkons. ...The thinkon particle can be deduced from football-stadium type experiments. What experiments could directly demonstrate the thinkon particle? The mathematics of noneuclidean, multidimensional geometries may provide the field equations for the existence field and its thinkons.

# Chapter 6

# A Cosmology of Infinite Riches

$\left(\begin{array}{c}\text{From the F.R. Wallace's "Long Wave" publication ©1985} \\ \text{simplified in 1995 to be contextually accurate if not technically precise}\end{array}\right)$

---

This chapter is going to take you on a journey. A journey into realms you never knew existed. By the time you finish this journey, your thinking will change about you, this world, the universe, the future. That metamorphosis will occur on putting together 25 pieces of a puzzle. ...When the last piece snaps into place, your thinking will change forever.

More specifically, after reading this 25-part chapter, an array of new concepts will jell into a matrix on the final page. That matrix will eventually end all mysticism and deliver endless riches to this world.

---

## Part 1
### A Neo-Tech Discovery

Tony, a lad of thirteen, was singing the theme song of Monty Python's "The Meaning of Life". The song went something like this:

*"Just remember that you are standing on a planet that's revolving at 900 miles per hour, that's orbiting at 90 miles per second. So it's reckoned that the source of all our power, the sun, and you and I and all the stars that we can see are moving at a million miles a day. That's figured out as moving at 42,000 miles an hour, in our galaxy called the Milky Way. Our Galaxy itself contains 100 billion stars. It's 100,000 light years from side to side and 16,000 light years thick. We are 30,000 light years from our galactic center and go around that center every 200 million years. Our galaxy is one of millions of billions in this amazing, expanding universe. The universe itself keeps on expanding in all directions at the speed of light. It's whizzing as fast as it can go, you know, at 12 million miles a minute. So remember*

47

*Movement I: Neo-Tech Physics*

*when we are feeling very small and insecure, how amazing
and unlikely is our birth. And pray that there is intelligent
life somewhere up in space, 'cause we are down here on
Earth."*

What makes those lyrics fascinating is that every
statement is essentially factual and verifiable. But the
song left out the most important part: Probability statistics
overwhelmingly reveal that our universe contains at least
a hundred million, and probably billions of Earth-like
planets populated with conscious beings like you and me.
Millions of conscious civilizations exist that are millions
of years more advanced than our newly born, immature,
still mystically oriented civilization.[1]

Moreover, that song was praying for what Neo-Tech
already discovered. In fact, Albert Einstein spent his
professional life searching in vain for what Neo-Tech
discovered — the unifying, controlling element of the
universe: *human-like consciousness.*

## Part 2
### Einstein and the Unifying Link

Throughout history, conscious beings on Earth have
struggled with mystical notions of a "superior"
consciousness, an imagined god, or some other "higher"
power reigning over the universe. But today, by
integrating the dynamics of mass and energy, Neo-Tech

---

[1]Since 1995, astronomers have been discovering by direct observation
other planets orbiting nearby stars, providing mounting evidence for a
super abundance of planets throughout our galaxy. Then, on August 7,
1996, NASA announced direct evidence from a Martian meteorite
discovered on Earth in the early 1980s that cellular life evolved on Mars
over 4.5 billion years ago. The implied ease that life evolved in at least
two separate places in our own solar system lends stunning support to the
Long-Wave hypothesis that life — evolved conscious life — exists on
billions of planets throughout our universe . ...Moreover, an entirely
different genetic form of life called Archaea, which needs no light,
oxygen, and lives at 400°F, has recently been discovered on Earth.

48

reveals a relationship between our own Earth-bound consciousness and all existence. The unifying power that orchestrates existence is not some mystical god or "superior" being. But, as demonstrated in this chapter, that unifying power is conscious beings — conceptual/introspective beings as you and I.

Einstein never accomplished his ultimate goal of unifying all forces. He never derived a Unified-Field Theory. But extrapolating Einstein's work into Neo-Tech reveals the unifying entity of existence — the only integrating force of the universe: human-like consciousness.

Why did Einstein not realize that fact? One reason perhaps stems from his abhorrence for unpredictable actions among the dynamics of nature. For that reason, he disliked quantum mechanics or anything that suggested arbitrary or "god-like" interventions. Always searching for order, Einstein focused on only two components of existence: mass and energy integrated with the geometries of time and space. He believed those components could always be explained, exactly and predictably. Thus, he never considered the third and controlling component of existence: volitional consciousness — a free-will, conceptual/introspective/integrating conscious mind.

Perhaps his passionate dislike for the unpredictable and disorder caused him to overlook consciousness as the third spacetime component of existence. For consciousness can and does unpredictably alter the dynamics of nature, every moment, throughout the universe. Yet, from the widest perspective, consciousness brings the most elegant order and predictability to the universe as demonstrated in this chapter.

All past attempts to link consciousness with existence

49

were based on mystical, "higher forms of consciousness". Such irrational, ethereal linkages always originated as dishonest, unfounded assertions by mystics or neocheaters conjuring up religious and political power.  But the Neo-Tech discovery of human-like consciousness as the unifying element of existence can be scientifically established not only with theory but with direct observation and experimental proof.

Understanding the conscious mind as the controlling, unifying element of existence first requires understanding the *unchanging* nature of consciousness and existence versus the *changing* nature of matter and energy:

## Part 3
### The Unchanging, Eternal Nature of Consciousness

As first identified by Professor Julian Jaynes of Princeton University and described in Chapter 28, the conscious mind was discovered within nature's bicameral mind[1] about 3000 years ago.  Given sufficient information, that first conscious mind had the same capacity as conscious minds today to understand anything in the universe from Einstein's theories to computer technologies and beyond.  Consider the astonishing conscious minds of Socrates, Plato, Aristotle, Archimedes that were flourishing only a few centuries after the discovery of consciousness.  They would, for example, have no problems whatsoever in understanding Einstein's theories

---

[1]The bicameral mind was man's intelligent, nature-evolved mind before he discovered consciousness as a conceptual/introspective mind. The conscious mind is not a part of nature's evolutionary process. But, rather, consciousness is a discovery by man that lies beyond the dynamics of nature.  This discovery process is explained in Chapter 28, pages 241-256. ...When referring to consciousness, the word *discovered* is used when perhaps the word should be *invented*.

or computer technology. Given the information, they certainly had the capacity we have today to understand anything in the universe.

In other words, while much is unknown, nothing is unknowable to the conscious mind. By nature, the conscious mind requires no change or evolvement to understand anything in existence.[1] On acquiring the correct knowledge, conscious beings today are capable of doing anything within the immutable laws of physics throughout the universe.

Consciousness is man's discovery that sprang from his nature-evolved bicameral mind. Consciousness is not part of nature's evolutionary processes, but is a natural phenomenon of existence.[2] Thus, the first conscious minds on this planet 3000 years ago are the same as the conscious minds on this planet today...and the same as conscious minds in any galaxy ten million years from now. All conscious minds have the same ability to understand anything in existence.

Consciousness, therefore, does not evolve. It exists eternally, unchangingly.[3] And its capacity to understand anything in the universe transposes into forever fulfilling the supreme responsibility of conscious beings. That responsibility is to preserve forever the supreme value of the universe — individual consciousness. To meet that responsibility means achieving non-aging biological immortality as described in Parts 12 and 16 of this chapter.

---

[1]Individual minds are endowed with various capacities. Individuals then develop or retard their capacities through either conscious efforts or mystical defaults. But consciousness itself is either there to be used or abused...or it is not there.

[2]As demonstrated later in this chapter, consciousness has always existed throughout the universe as an integral part of existence.

[3]Consciousness is the fundamental invariance and overarching symmetry of existence.

## Part 4
### The Unchanging, Eternal Nature of Existence

Who Created Existence? And who or what created the creator of existence? And then who or what created the creator of the creator, and so on regressing forever. Such questions are, of course, unanswerable. But, such infinite-regression questions need never be answered.[1] For existence is primary and axiomatic — meaning irreducible, self-evident, and requiring no further explanation. While new realms of existence such as galaxies and universes are constantly being created, nothing creates existence itself. It simply exists. Existence always has and always will exist. And that primacy of existence existing forever is independent of consciousness or anything else. ...The most profound of all concepts as underscored by Einstein is simply: Existence exists. What is the alternative? No alternative is possible unless one accepts the contradiction that existence does not exist.

Throughout eternal time, existence constantly generates new realms of life out of which conscious minds spring from the evolvement of bicameral minds — minds of evolved intelligence capable of discovering consciousness. Once consciousness is discovered and harnessed, it can, with accumulating knowledge and productive efforts, learn to forever muster new realms of existence. From those new realms evolve new life. And from new life evolve bicameral minds from which conscious minds spring.

Throughout eternal time and space, the following creation cycle always has existed and always will exist:

---

[1] The *Neo-Tech Discovery*, Concept #28 identifies the specious nature of infinite-regression questions.

Table 1
## THE CREATION CYCLE
**Realms of existence created by conscious beings —> life evolved —> bicameral mind evolved —> consciousness discovered —> mysticism developed to replace lost, bicameral gods —> mysticism and neocheaters take control of conscious beings —> partial freedom and capitalism developed —> Neo-Tech discovered —> guiltless prosperity, power, romantic love revealed to value producers —> mysticism and neocheating are uncompetitive and, thus, eliminated —> biological immortality achieved —> control of the universe learned —> new realms of existence created by new conscious beings —> and so on, forever expanding and repeating the cycle.**

Stated another way: Space, time, consciousness, and existence are eternal; they have no beginning or end. Throughout time eternal, stars, solar systems, and Earth-like planets constantly form anew. Thus, living organisms and conscious beings constantly form anew. Throughout never ending time and universes, limitless planets forever generate life. That life, in turn, forever generates nature's evolutionary processes that always end with conscious beings.[1] ...Conscious civilizations free of mysticism always survive, prosper, take control of nature and then existence.

Given the endless number of water/oxygen abundant, Earth-like planets forever spinning in endlessly evolving existence, one realizes life and consciousness have forever co-existed in limitless abundance. Human-like

---

[1]As explained in Chapter 28, pages 241-256.

consciousness, therefore, is as much a part of eternal existence as are mass and energy. When consciousness is integrated with endless existence and time, the stunning conclusion unfolds that human-like consciousness is also unchanging and has always existed.

Consciousness, mass, and energy are the three macro components of existence. Those three components are inextricably linked and must be integrated into all physical understandings and mathematical accounts of our universe. If only the mass and energy components existed, then all existence would be predictable and predestined through the dynamics of nature and physics. But further research and refinement of data will show that seemingly predictable actions of the universe are actually unpredictable from a mass and energy accounting alone. That unpredictability arises from not accounting for the influence of volitional conscious beings throughout existence.

Human-like, volitional consciousness is:
1) the third and integrating component of existence,
2) the unifying component or force never recognized by Einstein,
3) the supreme component of existence that controls the dynamics of nature, mass, and energy to forever preserve and evolve conscious life,
4) the eternal component that has existed and controlled existence, not for trillions of years, but forever.

\* \* \* \*

The balance of this chapter develops a non-mathematical, nontechnical understanding of how conscious beings dominate the universe and muster new realms of existence and life through increasing control of mass and energy.

## Part 5
### The Changing Nature of Mass and Energy:
### The Grand Cycle

All events of the universe fall within nature's mighty Grand Cycle, the dominating, all-inclusive energy wave involving the entire universe. That cycle consists of nature's longest energy wave exactly counterpoised with nature's shortest energy wave. All other cycles, waves, or forces of nature, ranging from cosmic and gamma rays to radio waves fall within the Grand Cycle. ...The Grand Cycle is described in Table 2 below:

Table 2
**The Total History Of The Universe**
(omitting the unifying element of consciousness)
is contained in
**THE GRAND CYCLE**
which consists of
The Googol-Year Explosion
Half-Cycle, Long Wave

with gravity-wave dissipation
with proton decay
with quark and electron annihilation

The Googol-Year Implosion
Half-Cycle, Long Wave

The Googolth-of-a-Second
Full-Cycle, Short Wave
(black hole/white hole)

(a googol equals $10^{100}$ or
1 followed by 100 zeroes)

55

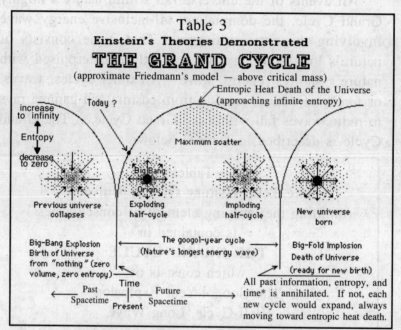

## Table 3
### Einstein's Theories Demonstrated
# THE GRAND CYCLE
(approximate Friedmann's model — above critical mass)

*When time is annihilated, the next event (birth of a universe) is instantaneous to the previous event (end of a universe). No time passes between the two events.

A capsulized account of the Grand Cycle starting with the so-called big-bang birth of the universe is illustrated in Table 3 on page 56.

Table 3 also indicates that all activity during nature's longest wave, the googol-year exploding/imploding cycles, exactly equals all activity occurring during nature's shortest wave, the googolth-of-a-second cycle. An understanding of that seeming paradox will evolve over the next few pages.

## Part 6

### The Explosion Cycle

Within the universe, all existence oscillates in one Grand Cycle spanning trillions of years. The actual time to complete that Cycle is not relevant here, but will someday be scientifically measured by us on Earth. But, even today, experiments and calculations from the astrophysical Doppler effect[1] show our universe is in the explosion, energy-to-matter half cycle. Our universe is exploding outward at near the speed of light, scattering away from a so-called "big-bang birth" with ever increasing entropy[2] — a measurement of spent energy.

---

[1]A change of light-wave frequencies caused by a moving light source such as a star. The wavelength of light from a star moving away *red shifts* — becomes longer — stretches toward the color red.

[2]Entropy involves the second of the three laws of thermodynamics for *closed* systems. Entropy is simply the movement of events toward their highest probability or disorder.* Entropy measures irretrievable energy spent on scattering a closed universe. ...For every star that explodes, every pebble that drops from a cliff, entropy and disorder irreversibly increase throughout the universe. Approaching infinite entropy, all usable energy throughout the closed universe is spent. All is flat and scattered to the maximum. No star is available to explode, no cliff is available from which a pebble can fall. No wind blows. All is dead and still. Stars are collapsed, cold and dark, or not at all. No sound or light exists: perhaps not even mass exists. Perhaps only unusable radiation near and always approaching 0°K exists.

   *The same probability concept applies to formulating hypotheses: always formulate toward the highest probability. Thus, the formulation of the Long-Wave hypothesis.

Energy available for work throughout the universe will keep decreasing as the universe spreads out for trillions of years until all energy is spent. In that state, trillions of years after the initial big-bang explosion, the universe exists at its maximum scattered or disordered state — as inert residue of an exploded bomb. At that moment, the entire universe is motionless, energyless, and while always approaching absolute zero Kelvin temperature ($0^0K=-273.16^0C=-469.67°F$), all energy is in the form of uniform, unusable heat radiation. ...Do subatomic arrows of time exist? Will protons, quarks, and electrons eventually decay or annihilate to end in radiation for all subatomic particles and motions?[1]

## Part 7
### The Implosion Cycle

With no usable energies or motions, the universe is dead. Entropy is essentially infinite. Entropic heat death has occurred. Without the force of consciousness, one incredibly weak force remains — by far the weakest of nature's forces — gravity. And, at that moment, in the absence of all other forces, gravity begins acting as an invisible cosmic hand destined to fulfill its function as the ultimate housekeeper, healer, and energy restorer of the universe. For, at that moment, gravity begins pulling a

---

[1]Are gravity waves the final dissipater of energy and motion? Or does mass itself seek higher entropy? With incredibly long half lives of $10^{32}$ years or perhaps up to $10^{220}$ years, do protons themselves decay toward infinite entropy? What about the energy and mass of a quark, an electron? Do quarks and electrons finally decay or annihilate with antiparticles? In any case, without conscious intervention, entropy death of a closed universe will eventually occur. ...**The laws of thermodynamics, however, apply only to *closed* systems. Existence itself is eternally open and evolving. Thus, any meaning of entropy to existence disappears, including the idea of entropic heat death.**

totally scattered, exhausted universe back toward increased order while gradually restoring potential energy. Increasingly restoring energy by reversing entropy, this cycle is the mirror image of the explosion cycle and equally lasts trillions of years. In that implosion cycle, gravity eventually pulls the universe back into essentially perfect order...an ultimate-compact, black-hole[1] bomb, ready to explode into another big bang as entropy races toward zero.

As contraction of the universe begins, gravity gradually changes from the weakest to the mightiest force of nature. Starting as an unimaginably faint but constant pull, gravity begins rebuilding the scattered universe by drawing all energyless existence closer together — perhaps initially by a millimicron in a million years. But every movement closer together increases the pull of gravity.[2] That, in turn, increases the speed at which the universe condenses toward an ordered, densifying mass. From the beginning to the end of that condensing-collapsing-imploding cycle, gravity steadily moves toward increasing all forms of energy ranging from potential and kinetic energies to

[1]The universe-containing black hole described here is matter and energy condensed beyond the critical mass and density needed to be captured, collapsed, and then imploded by its own gravity. When the collapse is complete, the resulting black hole can convert into a white hole, exploding into a new universe. The entire black-hole/white-hole cycle occurs in the tiniest fraction of a second because all information, entropy, and time obliterates between the two Grand Cycles.

[2]Gravitational attraction increases proportionally to the amount of existence involved multiplied by the inverse square of the distances between the eventual masses and energies. That means gravitational attraction accelerates exponentially as masses and energies are collapsed toward unity. Fields of existence are rolled ever closer together, perhaps into multidimensional space* and then into Gravity Units.

*Up to a twenty-six dimensional space has been mathematically derived in superstring theory. ...Most of those dimensions are rolled up into inconceivably tiny volumes or strings that vibrate at characteristic resonances.

chemical, heat, and nuclear energies.

In the explosion cycle, all energy escapes the diminishing grip of gravity. But in the implosion cycle, no energy escapes the increasing grip of gravity. In this cycle, the universe keeps moving together. Gravity holds all forms of increasing mass and energy within the same shrinking unit as the universe races closer together at accelerating speeds.

## Part 8
### The Googolth-of-a-Second Cycle

On drawing the universe *toward* a never reachable point, the accelerating pull of gravity begins compacting matter and energy toward a super-ordered, super-compact black hole. Becoming the mightiest physical force in existence, gravity begins crushing the universe. All forms of energy blend into all forms of matter and vice versa. All molecules, atoms, protons, neutrons, electrons, sub-atomic particles, and energy waves of the universe are crushed together into unrecognizable forms of matter and energy. That rapidly compacting universe assumes entirely different forms of existence occurring only during that nearly instantaneous moment of super compaction at the final instant of the implosion half cycle.

Then, as the entire universe implodes to the size of a basketball, those bizarre forms of existence keep changing with increasing rapidity. Undergoing seemingly infinite changes into ever more radical forms of existence, the universe crushes inward at near the speed of light, imploding to golf-ball size, then to pinhead size, then to pinpoint size. Everything in the universe, including trillions of stars and billions of galaxies, even black holes, are crushed into that pinpoint. The universe then flickers from microscopic to submicroscopic size then to sizes unimaginably smaller than a proton — all while continuously changing into near infinite varieties of unimaginable radical structures shrinking toward zero volume and infinite density. ...The end condition may or may not be different, more disordered, from the beginning condition.

Most incredibly, the total of all mass/energy/activity changes that occur during nature's longest cycle (the seemingly infinitely long, googol-year explosion and implosion half cycles) is exactly counterpoised or duplicated during nature's shortest cycle (the seemingly infinitesimally short, googolth-of-a-second cycle). In other words, the total action during nature's longest cycle of trillions of years is exactly counterbalanced during nature's shortest cycle occurring in the tiniest fraction of a nanosecond[1].

## Part 9
### The Universe Turns Inside Out
### From Implosion to Explosion

At that final instant, all activity ceases as the universe is essentially, but not actually, at zero volume, infinite density, and zero entropy. At that final instant, all the universe is in the form of gravity/existence symmetry. All information and time from the previous Grand Cycle has vanished. At that moment, with a quantum flux, a new spacetime is born — the universe turns inside out from the implosion cycle to the explosion cycle. At once, the universe converts from increasing order and compaction to "nothing" then to increasing disorder and scatteration, from decreasing entropy to increasing entropy, from implosion to explosion. At that instant, the entire universe

---

[1]A nanosecond is one billionth of a second.

is cataclysmically destroyed and then instantly reborn from seemingly nothing — reborn in a big-bang inflation of a trillion times a trillion suns.

Created from seemingly nothing, a mammoth composite of post-inflation mass and energy expands in every direction at nearly the speed of light. That ball of mass and energy keeps expanding for centuries, millennia, or perhaps longer before blowing apart, scattering, and then congealing its mass and energy. That scattering and congealing eventually forms visible stars, solar systems, planets. During our current googol-year cycle, millions of Earth-like planets and conscious civilizations formed billions of years before Earth's formation. And millions of Earth-like planets and conscious civilizations will form billions of years after Earth's formation.

## Part 10
### Super Grand Cycles

Assuming similar gravitational dynamics operate among universes,[1] similar Grand Cycles would occur among the universes themselves, but on endlessly greater scales. And then, ever longer cycles exist among ever larger clusters of universes, and so on, eternally. For each greater cluster of existence, its exponentially longer Grand Cycle would have occurred endlessly in eternity.

From the perspective of forever greater Super Grand Cycles, infinity becomes two dimensional with one vector forever reaching into space, eternally gathering greater and greater mass and energy. Concomitantly, the other vector forever reaches into time, eternally repeating ever longer cycles. Thus, travelling on those two vectors, existence

---

[1]Currently, Earth beings have no way to observe other universes. Thus, no way is currently known to establish if gravity operates among the universes — throughout the meta-universe.

evolves forever throughout the endless universes.

From the limited perspective of our world and universe, the speed of light seems incredibly fast and free. But from the perspective of endlessly evolving existence and ever greater clusters of universes, the speed of light seems increasingly slow and restricting. For, the process of escaping such super big-bangs seems chained to the speed of light. Indeed, being limited by the speed of light, a seemingly endless time would be needed just for those unimaginably large masses to escape their "instantaneous", initial big-bang inflations in their Super Grand Cycles.

Space, time, and distance throughout existence are mind-boggling because they truly never end.


## Part 11
### Grasping the Ungraspable:
### The Infinity of Existence

Within the Milky Way, our relatively small galaxy, billions of stars and planets exist that are millions of years older than our Earth. Within our universe, billions of galaxies exist that are larger than our Milky Way. Throughout the Grand Cycle, millions of stars, solar systems, and Earthlike planets constantly form anew. Among those millions of Earthlike planets abundant in water and oxygen, the dynamics of nature immutably generate life. Life, in turn, always undergoes nature's evolutionary process that ends with conscious beings...and conscious beings always evolve to control endless existence.

Indeed, life itself, its evolutionary processes, and thus, conscious beings themselves, have always existed throughout the universe as its third and unifying/ integrating/controlling component. And that unifying/

integrating/controlling component of the conscious mind was the component Einstein always sought but never recognized. For, he focused only on the mass and energy components of the universe while overlooking the component of consciousness.

When dealing with infinity, relationships among time, distance, knowledge, events, and probabilities become meaningless, resulting in seemingly bizarre situations. Consider a realistically impossible event here on earth for which the odds are a billion to one against occurring. When put in the context of infinite time, such an improbable event will not only occur with absolute certainty, but will occur an infinite number of times. Throughout infinity, whatever is theoretically possible becomes an absolute certainty that occurs an endless number of times.

To further demonstrate the bizarreness of infinity: Take an essentially impossible event that might occur once every billion years. Now take an event that happens constantly, say, once every nanosecond. Relative to infinity, both events will reoccur endlessly, forever into the future. Thus, from the perspective of infinity, no difference exists between their occurrences, for they both occur with endless repetition. So, juxtaposed against infinity, no difference exists between an event that occurs every nanosecond versus an event that occurs once every billion years. For, throughout infinity, both events occur infinite times.

Also, in the context of infinity, no difference exists between distances throughout space. For, throughout infinity, no reference points exist to measure differences among time or distances. ...Infinity is the only concept in existence without identity or boundaries. Thus, infinity[1] is radically unique from all other concepts.

To grasp the meaning of infinite existence, one cannot view existence from the perspective of a finite planet or a finite universe. Instead, one must view existence from the perspective of eternal endlessness. From that perspective, no difference exists between a mile and a trillion miles, or a year and a trillion years, or a forest fire and a star fire, or a lightning bolt and a big-bang birth of a universe. For, no reference points exist to compare distance, time, knowledge, or events of any magnitude when forever really means <u>forever</u>.

*As shown later, certain deterministic concepts in the above four paragraphs are valid only in the hypothetical absence of eternal, free-will conscious life.*

## Part 12
### Achieving Biological Immortality Now

From a perspective of the infinite time available throughout existence, all newly formed life evolves almost immediately into a highly intelligent brain that can invent consciousness from nature's bicameral mind. The resulting conscious beings then, nearly instantly:

1) take control of nature,
2) render obsolete nature's evolutionary "need" for life-and-death cycles,
3) evolve into the Neo-Tech/Neothink mind,
4) cure irrationality and its mysticism, the only disease of the conscious mind, and
5) achieve non-aging immortality in order to live forever with growing prosperity and happiness.
6) control existence.

---

[1]Infinity, as explained in the footnote on page 14, is a useful mind-created concept that does not exist in reality.

*Movement I: Neo-Tech Physics*

But from a perspective of the brief, finite time available for contemporary life on Earth, exactly how and when will biological immortality occur? First consider that, today, newly discovered Neo-Tech will eradicate the disease of irrationality and its parasitical neocheaters. Without the constant destructiveness of professional parasites, conscious beings will quickly, naturally develop commercial biological immortality as described below.

As Neo-Tech cures the disease of irrationality and vanishes those professional parasites, biological immortality will become a certainty for most human beings living today, regardless of age. In fact, today, freedom from irrationality will almost guarantee biological immortality for most people. And that could happen without massive efforts or spectacular medical discoveries. What is necessary, however, is the curing of irrationality and its mysticism. For irrationality, directly or indirectly, eventually kills all human beings while preventing biological immortality for all conscious beings.

Irrationality is the only disease of human consciousness. The symptoms of irrationality are harmful dishonesties and mysticisms. Those symptoms undermine the ability to integrate together the values of rationality *and emotions*. What is the value of emotions? The all-important value of emotions is to experience happiness — the bottom-line moral purpose of conscious life. But, mysticisms mixed with emotionalisms dishonestly assume a primacy over reason and reality. That dishonesty, in turn, casts mortal harm over every individual human being on planet Earth.

Neo-Tech, which is fully integrated honesty, eradicates the disease of irrationality. Thus, the immediate evolvement of biological immortality need not require quick technological breakthroughs, major research projects, or even explicit, direct efforts. But rather, with Neo-Tech, the process of biological immortality can begin immediately within one's own self. And that process will culminate with definitive biological immortality as the 3000-year disease of irrationality is cured by Neo-Tech worldwide.

How will biological immortality actually happen? First, consider:

- a world without irrationality,
- a world without professional value destroyers, parasitical elites, and dishonest neocheaters,
- a world without their destructive institutions of usurped power, such as the FDA (the most health-and-life destroying entity) and the IRS (the most value-and-job destroying entity),
- a world without the *anti-business* elements of irrational governments.
- a world without irrational governments.

Without life-corroding irrationality and its virus-like neocheaters draining everyone, business would explode into an endless productivity spiral. That value-driven explosion would launch human life into upward-spiraling prosperity with continuously expanding life spans.

Consider, for example, how the dynamics of computer technology have so far operated relatively free of parasitical elites, professional value destroyers, and government interference. Being relatively free of irrational regulations, force, coercion, and destructiveness, the computer industry has burgeoned. Computer technology is now delivering soaring capacities for processing and utilizing new knowledge at rates faster than new knowledge can be integrated and used by human beings. Such explosive advances in computer technology, or any technology, requires being free of government irrationality and its professional parasites.

The rational, conscious mind is synonymous with the productive, business mind. The value-creating business mind is the antithesis of the value-destroying political mind. The destructiveness of socialist, fascist, and religious societies prevents their citizens from developing efficient business-driven technologies. Indeed, all such societies are controlled by parasitical elites using force and deception to usurp harmful livelihoods. Such people live by attacking, draining, harming, or destroying value-and-job producing businesses...and their heroic creators and competitive expanders.

By contrast, explosive computer-like advances in human health and longevity directed toward commercial biological immortality will naturally occur in any mystic-free, business-driven society. But exactly how could biological immortality quickly occur today in a mystic-free society? Consider, a 60-year-old person today having a life expectancy of 20 more years. In a rational, business-minded society, uninhibited market forces will rapidly develop the most valuable products and technologies. ...The most valuable of all technologies — the quality preservation of conscious life — will advance so rapidly that when that person reaches 70, high-quality life spans will have expanded to 100 or 120 years, or more.

In a rational, mystic-free society, knowledge and technology accelerate geometrically. Thus, when that person reaches 100, high-quality life expectancy will have expanded to 140 or 180 years, or more. Those accelerating extensions of life expectancy would provide the time needed to develop *definitive biological immortality* for almost every value producer living today. Indeed, in the coming years, Neo-Tech will cure the disease of irrationality to eradicate physical diseases and death among all conscious beings on planet Earth.

In a competitive business-driven atmosphere free of irrationality, the life spans of conscious beings will advance faster than the passing of years. Thus, the result of Neo-Tech eliminating irrationality is immediate, de facto biological immortality. Then, rapidly accelerating health technology — including antiaging genetics — will yield that *definitive biological immortality*.[1]

Therefore, by replacing all forms of irrationality, mysticism, and neocheating with the fully integrated honesty of Neo-Tech, nearly everyone today can live forever.[2] Most important, with Neo-Tech, one can live forever with increasing prosperity, happiness, and love.

Almost anyone living today can survive to biological immortality by (1) replacing the death disease of irrationality with the life elixir of Neo-Tech and by (2) stopping mystical behaviors and destructive actions, such as making problems where none exist, smoking, and becoming mentally and physically unfit. Almost everyone today can and will achieve biological immortality by rejecting irrationality and neocheating both in one's self

---

[1]Curing death is described in the *Neo-Tech Discovery*: specifically in Part V and generally in Appendix F titled, *Achieving Commercial Biological Immortality in Our Lifetime*. ...Mortality is natural in life, *except* for conscious beings whose nature *is* immortality — the same immortality God possesses!

[2]The longer a productive individual lives, the more valuable that person becomes through his or her increased knowledge, experience, competence, productivity, and capacity for business and happiness. Thus, in any rational, mystic-free society, the motivation for and value of biological immortality increases as the age of the individual increases.

and in others. The key for everyone is to first recognize and then reject the disease of irrationality and mysticism from within one's own self. Then one can effectively reject irrationality and mysticism in others.

Life is everything. Death is nothing. Irrationality trades everything for nothing. Irrationality is a terminal disease that breeds professional value destroyers who eventually harm or kill everyone. ...Today, the disease of irrationality is totally unnecessary since it can be cured with Neo-Tech. Thus, through Neo-Tech, essentially everyone can live forever with ever increasing prosperity and happiness.

Also, as demonstrated in Neo-Tech Advantage #31 of the *Neo-Tech Discovery,* conscious civilizations much advanced beyond ours would by necessity be free of irrationality and neocheating. For, by holding irrational premises, no civilization can advance much past the Nuclear-Decision Threshold[1] without destroying itself. ...In rational mystic-free societies, the idea of dishonesty is unknown.[2] Thus, *unknown* ideas also include war, murder, deception, fraud, forced taxation, conscription, racism, theft, assault, envy, anxiety, guilt.

# Part 13
## Infinite Knowledge

To quote from the first Neo-Tech World Summit (March, 1986) keynote address titled, "Three Steps to Achieving Commercial Biological Immortality in Our Lifetime" as quoted on the next page:

---

[1] Planet Earth is currently at that Nuclear-Decision Threshold. For our civilization to survive, the disease of irrationality must be cured.

[2] Science-fiction stories and movies of evil or hostile aliens are illogical. For, no civilization with the nuclear-energy technology required for interstellar travel could survive as irrational, evil, violent, corrupt, or criminal in *any* way.

70

"Living forever would be boring. False. Exactly the opposite is the fact. For creating and increasing values is the essence of a happy, exciting life, which, in turn, gives increasing motivation to live forever. Indeed, all new values come from expanding knowledge. And each new unit of knowledge generates several newer units of knowledge. Therefore, the ability to generate new knowledge is limitless. The notion of finite knowledge is only an illusion from our present, limited-knowledge perspective. Indeed, knowledge is not simply uncovered; it is generated from past knowledge. Thus, each day, the discovery of new knowledge generates ever greater bodies of ever newer knowledge and values.

"No one in the last century could have, for example, imagined any aspect of quantum mechanics, the computer age, genetic engineering, superconductivity, or fusion energy. For, everyone was many layers of knowledge away from even imagining those twentieth-century achievements. Yes, knowledge upon knowledge and achievement upon achievement will be generated anew — forever — by human consciousness.

"Human consciousness is the only force in the universe not predetermined by nature. Indeed, only consciousness can alter or go beyond the fixed patterns of nature. Consciousness obsoletes nature's blind, life-and-death survival cycles when applied to human beings. ...In a society free of irrationality, every conscious being produces open-ended achievements for society without bounds or limits. Thus, by producing an eternal stream of benefits for society, each conscious life continues happily, forever."

## Part 14

Immortality — the Natural State of Consciousness

Thousands of years ago, before anyone on Earth grasped the concept of geometrical shapes, a man looked toward the heavens at the moon, then at the sun, then at the eyes of his woman. Suddenly he grasped the concept of "round"...a strange, new concept that no one had grasped or understood before. From that geometric concept came the circle, the wheel, the principles of mathematics and science, the automobile, the computer, and the latest theories of gravity. Yet, essentially no one today realizes that a concept so naturally integrated with life and taken for granted as the shape "round" was at one time unknown, strange, and spectacular to discover.

Likewise, a few thousand years from today, the natural physical state of conscious man — biological immortality — will be so natural, so integrated with life, so taken for granted that only historians would realize how during a brief time in faded history conscious beings were irrational and thus mortal. Indeed, mortality is not only the most unnatural, bizarre state for conscious beings, but is an essentially unknown state among rational, mystic-free, conscious beings throughout the universe.

In addition to biological immortality as revealed in the *Neo-Tech Discovery*, conscious man's most natural, psychological state is happiness. Essentially all human unhappiness arises directly or indirectly from the disease of irrationality and its mysticisms. With irrationality cured, happiness will become so natural and commonplace that in future millennia few if any will know that unhappiness and death ever existed.

## Part 15
Einstein's First Oversight:
Failure to Integrate Human Consciousness *On Earth*
With the Grand Cycle

Consider us Earth beings with our technology of less than 3000 years. Consider our advances projected by the year 2000, only a few years away. Then project that rate of growth into a geometrically increasing curve of knowledge soaring toward a thousand years hence, a million years hence. One can easily see that conscious beings are altering the dynamics of nature at ever increasing rates. And through a relatively minuscule time span within the incomprehensibly long, googol-year cycle, conscious beings on Earth can quickly learn to dominate nature.

After only the first few centuries of consciousness, around 500 BC, human beings begin controlling nature faster then nature's evolutionary processes. Witness, for example, the development of consciousness from only 3000 years ago, an invisibly short time span in the Grand Cycle as shown in Table 4 below. Earthbound consciousness has already obsoleted nature's evolutionary processes: Today, man-made shelter, food, medicine, and technology

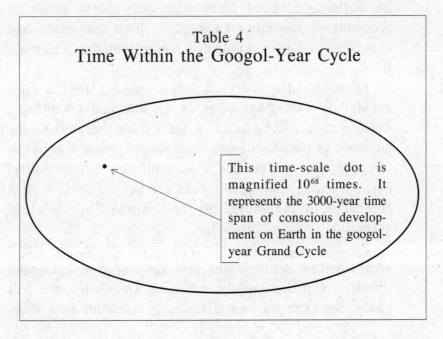

### Table 4
### Time Within the Googol-Year Cycle

This time-scale dot is magnified $10^{68}$ times. It represents the 3000-year time span of conscious development on Earth in the googol-year Grand Cycle

The New-Color Symphony

Movement #1

advance human survival and well-being much faster and better then do the slow evolutionary, adaptive processes of nature. In less than 3000 years, consciousness is already taking over the dynamics of nature on Earth. With that takeover, consciousness obsoletes nature's protective/survival mechanism of death. Thus, through time, consciousness mandates biological immortality for all conscious beings.

Becoming free of irrationality, Earth beings will not just increasingly control nature, but will dominate nature just a few hundred years hence as explained below.

During the next million years, planet Earth will geologically remain relatively static with basically the same oxygen, land, and water conditions. But, with geometrically accelerating knowledge, we on planet Earth will soon dominate and control nature. Consider, for example, the world's largest man-made lake accomplished by building Hoover Dam with only 3000 years of accumulated, conscious knowledge. That man-made feat controlled and then dominated nature's mighty Colorado River.

From the discovery of consciousness to the first automobile took 2900 years of accumulated knowledge. Then, within 100 years, man went from the auto to the airplane, to the moon, and now toward super computers for everyone. ...Knowledge accumulates geometrically, quickly leaving nature's forces far behind as if frozen compared to the incredibly fast, always accelerating generation of new knowledge.

Perhaps only a few-hundred years hence, we Earth beings will be accumulating new knowledge at lightening speeds. With that rapidly increasing knowledge, we will easily, for example, corral heavenly asteroids into man-made orbital matter to fill our needs, just as today we corral river water into man-made lakes to fill our needs. ...What needs will we Earth beings have a thousand years from now, a million years from now? And how will we use our super-advanced knowledge and tools to control nature in filling those needs?

A thousand, even a million or a billion years, is an incredibly short time, a mere instant, within the Grand Cycle as shown in Table 4. But, well within that brief time span, we Earth beings can also accumulate the knowledge to dominate and drive the universe — to interdict nature's mass/energy dynamics in preventing the Grand Cycle from ever completing itself.

## Part 16
### Einstein's Second Oversight:
### Failure to Integrate Consciousness *Beyond Earth*
### With the Grand Cycle

Consider the billions of Earth-like planets existing within our own universe that are billions of years older than Earth. Through immutable evolutionary processes among those billions of Earth-like planets, conscious beings have evolved with millions or billions of years more advanced knowledge than we have on Earth today. ...Just imagine the technology and capacity of those conscious beings who have enjoyed geometrically accumulated knowledge for a million years, a billion years.

Human-like consciousness is the only entity in existence that can alter the inexorable course of nature. Human consciousness quickly advances from building cities to utilizing nuclear power, to developing computers, to making astronautical flights, to corralling astro matter, to understanding the universe, to controlling existence —

and beyond forever.

Integrating nature's Grand Cycle with conscious beings reveals an elegantly simple understanding of existence. That integration reveals how individual consciousness is not only an integral component of existence, but is the dominating and controlling component. For example, at either end of the Grand Cycle, all life would perish. But individual consciousness — the supreme value of the universe — must forever protect itself. Thus, conscious beings a thousand or a million years more advanced in knowledge than we on Earth have long ago *met that responsibility to preserve the supreme value of existence: individual consciousness.*

Without immortal consciousness, the Grand Cycle would inexorably and infinitely repeat itself as dictated by the natural dynamics of mass and energy. But, with consciousness, the integrating and controlling component of existence missed by Einstein, the Grand Cycle is always interdicted and truncated. Thus, the destruction of the universe and consciousness has never occurred and will never occur. In other words, by integrating conscious beings into the dynamics of existence, nature's Grand Cycle becomes hypothetical and never occurs.

## Consciousness and Existence Integrated

1) Anything theoretically possible in existence, no matter how remote the probability, will happen infinite times unless interdicted by conscious beings.
2) Human-like consciousness has forever been and will forever be an integral part of existence.
3) Conscious beings, as you and I, can

understand anything in existence.  On gaining the knowledge, therefore, we can and will eventually do anything theoretically possible that rationally benefits our existence.

4) Thus, human-like conscious beings throughout the universe always have, and always will, control existence.

5) On curing the disease of irrationality through Neo-Tech, we Earth beings will gain the same power, prosperity, and immortality of our fellow beings who control existence throughout the universe.

## Part 17
### Knowledge at the Speed of Light

Everything in existence seems limited by a universal constant — the speed of light.  For, as shown by Einstein, nothing can exceed the speed of light.  Consciousness, therefore, being an integral part of existence, must also be limited by the speed of light.  But how can the speed of light limit knowledge, especially since consciousness has no limits on understanding anything in existence?  To answer that, one must first understand the dual faculty of consciousness:

1) The unlimited faculty to understand anything in existence.

2) The limited faculty to store and process knowledge.

By nature, each new unit of knowledge begets multiple units of still newer knowledge.  Thus, consciousness creates knowledge geometrically.  So, then, what can limit increases in knowledge?  Nothing can stop knowledge

77

from increasing forever. But, the rate of knowledge accumulation is ultimately limited by the speed of light in our closed universe.

To understand the faculty of consciousness that stores and processes knowledge, one must first understand the history of that faculty starting with the origins of man-discovered consciousness on Earth 3000 years ago: For the first 2000 years after the discovery of consciousness, knowledge accumulated very slowly. That accumulation gradually increased as the base of knowledge increased through memory and oral communication. Knowledge then accelerated through written communication.

For man to produce great sailing ships, for example, he needed that initial 1800 years of accumulated knowledge and technology stored and passed by memory, hand-scribed documents, and oral communication. Then he needed another 1000 years of faster accumulated knowledge and technology stored and passed through written works to produce steamships and trains in further improving transportation. He needed another 100 years of more rapidly accumulating knowledge and technology stored and passed through printed works to produce automobiles that greatly improved transportation. Next, he needed only 60 more years of accelerating knowledge and technology stored and passed through books, journals, and communication equipment to produce practical airplanes that provided transportation inconceivable a century before. Finally, he needed only 40 more years of soaring knowledge and technology stored and passed through computers and electronic communications to develop space ships for landing men on the moon and building space stations.

Now, today, new knowledge is accelerating so rapidly

that our productive focus is shifting toward storing, processing, integrating, and transmitting information through million-dollar super computers moving toward thousand-dollar personal computers. Thus, today, computers are undergoing explosive increases in capacities, power, practicality, and economies. And from now into the future, the demands of accumulating, storing, processing, and transmitting knowledge will shift into high gear from man's limited storage-capacity brain to external extensions of the brain with electron/photon-circuited quantum computers and beyond.

Today, storing and processing our geometrically increasing knowledge depends on our developing and building increasingly efficient, man-made computers. Advancing economies and prosperity depend on developing ever more advanced devices until the capacity of every spacetime point in the universe is utilized for storing, processing, and transmitting knowledge.

Knowledge will increase geometrically for a few millennia or perhaps only a few centuries — until the building of external-knowledge devices approaches the speed-of-light limitation. From that point, the expansion of knowledge shifts from geometric to linear. Knowledge will then expand linearly, near the speed of light, and limited by the speed of light.

When our own expanding knowledge reaches that limitation, we can join the millions of other civilizations in our universe that have reached that point. We can then communicate through the universal computer (perhaps gravity-coded) and control existence as our fellow conscious beings do. For, then, the entire universe of universes expanding at near the speed of light becomes our computer and storage facility for all acquired knowledge.[1]

The relationship of conscious knowledge to existence reduces to a single equation. To understand that equation, the following two points must be understood:

1) Knowledge is a function of time, which as Einstein determined is related to the speed of light.

2) Essentially all mega-advanced knowledge throughout the universe is generated, stored, and processed near the speed of light, limited only by the infinite Universe of universes on vectors forever expanding at near the speed of light.

Thus, knowledge ultimately obeys the same laws that all existence obeys...such as Einstein's law that integrates energy and mass with the speed of light as expressed by his famous equation:

$$E = mc^2$$

where:

E = energy;  m = mass;  $c^2$ = the speed of
light squared

Likewise, knowledge integrates with time and the speed of light as expressed by the following equation:

$$K = tc^2$$

where:

K = knowledge;  t = time;  $c^2$ = the speed of
light squared

Today, in our young Earthbound civilization, the

---

[1]Conscious beings perhaps overcome the speed-of-light limitation through eternal inflationary expansions of Gravity Units beyond our universe, into limitless existence and hyperspace.

always fatal disease of irrationality darkens the future for all human beings. Growing irrationality reduces and eventually stops the accumulation of new knowledge needed to survive and prosper. Growing irrationality eventually destroys the conscious mechanism for processing and accumulating knowledge. But, with the Neo-Tech discovery, irrationality can be cured worldwide to let all conscious beings forge ahead, geometrically accumulating knowledge at rates eventually limited only by the speed of light.

## Part 18
### The Universe is but a Dot Next to Individual Consciousness

Every individual consciousness has the capacity to generate, process, and use new knowledge at rates approaching the speed of light. By fully understanding the effects of such knowledge production and use, one quickly rectifies the false view of life held by most people who have lived on Earth. That false view expressed in Monty Python's "Meaning of Life" and promoted by mystics throughout history is: "Individual human beings are but insignificant dots among the vast universe."

Facts and logic demonstrate the exact opposite: Without irrationality or mysticism, each individual consciousness has unlimited capacity to generate and utilize new knowledge at near the speed of light. Francis Bacon identified, "Knowledge is power." Thus, after a few millennia of such knowledge accumulation, any conscious individual gains the power to so totally dominate existence that the entire universe and all its evolutionary processes seem by comparison to shrink into static insignificance. For, in both power and significance, individual consciousness quickly soars beyond the dynamics of nature and the entire universe.

Today, on Earth, the fully integrated honesty of Neo-Tech finally reverses that mystical view bewailing mankind's insignificance. Neo-Tech demonstrates that the power of the universe shrinks to almost nothing when compared to the unlimited power of individual consciousness.

## Part 19
### Who is the Creator?

Does a creator of galaxies and universes exist? Indeed, such a creator could not defy the laws of physics. Yet, today, as for the past three millennia, most people believe a creator must be some mystical higher "authority" or power as promulgated by someone's scriptures or edicts. ...For two millennia, such mystical gods of creation were conjured-up by neocheaters wanting nothing more grand than to live off the efforts of others.

As demonstrated in the balance of this chapter, everyday conscious beings like you and me work within the laws of physics to create and control all heavens and earths.

## Part 20
### The Goal of Conscious Beings

Throughout the universe, conscious beings pursue their natural goals and responsibilities by achieving biological immortality, limitless prosperity, and eternal happiness. Thus, they forever preserve the supreme value of the universe: individual consciousness. For without conscious beings, no value or meaning would exist throughout the universe. ...Conscious beings free of mysticism never allow their precious lives — lives of limitless value — to end.

## Part 21

### Galaxies Created Beyond The Dynamics of Nature

Eons ago, a conscious being, as you and I, worked at the edge of a distant galaxy with an integrating computer of a spatial-geometry driven, mass/energy assembler. By assembling units of gravitational geometries, that person corralled enough strings of wound-up gravity to equal the mass of another galaxy. As the moment of critical gravity approached, the final collapse into an entropy-reversing, rotating "black hole" began. He then arose smiling. With arm held high, he cried, "Let there be light!"[1] ...At that moment, in a far corner of the universe, the light of a million times a million suns flashed and began its photonic journey across the universe. A galaxy was born...a man-made galaxy.

## Part 22

### Galaxies Discovered Beyond The Dynamics of Nature

Today, eons later, specks of light from that conscious-made galaxy fall on the planet Earth — on the lens of a telescope. An astrophysicist examines computer data gathered from those specks of light. Then, integrating that data with the physical and mathematical dynamics of astral mass and energy, he moves closer to a momentous discovery. He moves closer to discovering a major astral event falling outside the natural dynamics of mass and

---

[1]The expression "Let there be light" was first manipulatively used in the mystical world of the Bible, then entertainingly used in the science-fiction world of Isaac Asimov, and now factually used in the objective world of Neo-Tech.

energy — an event that irrevocably altered nature's charted course for the universe.

But, that scientist knows, as any competent scientist knows, that nothing, including conscious beings, can alter the axiomatic laws of physics, mathematics, and existence. And he knows that existence can have no antecedent basis or original creator. Yet, he realizes that, within the laws of physics, conscious beings can alter the natural dynamics of mass and energy. Thus, he realizes conscious beings and only conscious beings can alter nature's manifest destiny, not only here on Earth, but throughout the universe.

Combining such knowledge with computer processed data, that scientist moves closer toward directly observing the alteration of nature's Grand Cycle by conscious beings. Such direct observation may come, for example, through a correlation of computer data concerning black holes or possibly quasars and pulsars. In fact, such correlations of data probably already exist on Earth — hidden in considerable accumulations of uninterpreted data. Integrating such data could reveal that certain cosmic events exist outside the natural dynamics of their mass, energy, and gravity. In turn, that data could then demonstrate how conscious beings create and control such cosmic events as energy and galaxy creators for the eternal prosperity of all conscious life.

Thus, conscious beings could forever prevent the Grand Cycle from completing itself. They could do that, for example, by routinely creating gravity dimensions and geometries that constantly pump entropy-reversing structures back into the universe. Such constantly created, new structures would break the dynamics of the Grand Cycle, allowing the universe to forever oscillate within its most efficient range for conscious beings.

## Part 23
### Create Your Own Galaxy

Beginning with the data from that speck of light born a million years before, today's Earthbound scientist will discover and prove a newborn galaxy created outside the mass/energy/gravity dynamics of nature alone. He will then look toward the heavens realizing that he has discovered a galaxy made by a conscious being. He will further realize that over eternal time, over eternally interdicted cycles, all the galaxies and universes, all the heavens and Earths, were at one time created from conscious-made structure pumps that formed new realms of existence while preserving old realms.

And finally, he will realize his mind is the same conscious mind possessed by our immutable conscious cousins who create new realms of existence in other worlds and galaxies for us, them, and everyone.

## Part 24
### After the Discovery

After that first discovery of a conscious-made galaxy or black hole, scientists will then approximate from our geometric increases of knowledge on Earth and our achievement of biological immortality, when you and I can stand above all the imagined gods to give the command, *Let there be light!*

## Part 25
### Conclusion

No intimidating god or ethereal super consciousness reigns over the universe. Mystical gods or "higher beings"

85

do not exist, cannot exist, need not exist. For only universes created and controlled by rational, value-producing conscious beings as you and I are needed to explain all existence. And with biological immortality, we Earth beings will someday stand smiling at the edge of space creating our own stars, galaxies, universes, collections of universes, and beyond.

## EPILOGUE

The mightiest power in existence, the power to control existence, is expressed by the great command, "Let there be light!" That power has forever existed among fellow beings throughout the universe. The essence of that power is available to all of us, now, here on Earth today through Neo-Tech. ...Neo-Tech eradicates irrationality — the disease that causes ignorance and death among conscious beings.

AIDS degenerates the body's protective immune system into weakness, sickness, then death; irrationality and mysticism degenerates the mind's protective thinking system into ignorance, sickness, then death. Irrationality cripples and finally destroys the conscious mind.

But unlike AIDS, an immediate cure exists right now for irrationality and its virus-like neocheaters. That cure is Neo-Tech. Curing irrationality will also bring definitive cures for AIDS, cancer, heart disease, and all other diseases harmful to conscious beings. Neo-Tech forever eradicates irrationality and its symbiotic neocheaters, allowing the individual to direct his or her life toward achieving guiltless prosperity and abiding happiness for self, others, and all society.

Neo-Tech also opens the way for knowledge expanding geometrically to eventually approach the speed of light. Every person applying Neo-Tech, therefore, holds unbeatable advantages over those crippled by irrationality, parasitical elites, and neocheaters. Indeed, Neo-Tech allows human beings to acquire total control over both the material and emotional realms. Neo-Tech gives all human beings on Earth today the power to execute the tripartite commands: "Let there be wealth!", "Let there be romantic love!", "Let there be eternal youth!"

---

The time has come to grow up...or be left behind to perish in a world of irrationality. Clinging to irrational or mystical beliefs such as supreme creators or "higher authorities" is as crippling to human life and prosperity as would be the clinging to the once popular belief that the Earth is flat or today's fading belief that force-backed "authorities" or politicians can advance the well-being of any individual or society.

---

After 3000 years, the time has come to abandon life-destroying irrationality and all its symbiotic parasites and neocheaters. Now is the time to mature into meeting our responsibility of grooming the supreme value of the universe — our own conscious lives. Now is the time to groom our conscious minds with fully integrated honesty for limitless growth and value production forever into the future. Now is the time to join our fellow conscious beings throughout all existence in meeting our supreme responsibility to life — to live happily, prosperously with our fellow conscious beings throughout eternal existence. **For, we are the creators of all heavens and earths. ...All glory to us conscious beings!**

# A Mathematical View
## of
## Time, Eternity, and Existence
by

Bruce Gordon, Cyberglyph, 32 Debora Drive, Plainview, NY 11803

An **instant in time**, like this or any other moment in eternity is an *infinitesimal* quantity, expressed symbolically as

$$t_i = dt$$

**Eternity** ($\underline{E}$) is the whole of time, from the infinitely distant past to the infinitely far future, an *integrated*, infinite time interval. Using the notation of the calculus, eternity is expressed as

$$\underline{E} = \int_{-\infty}^{\infty} dt$$

**A universe ($\underline{U}$) is a process in time.**[1] It can be thought of as a matrix-valued function of dimensionality $(n_1, n_2, ...)$.

$$\underline{U} = [u_{x_1 x_2 ...}]_{(n_1, n_2, ...)}$$

where the $u_{x_1 x_2 ...}$ are **Gravity Units** at positions specified by the coordinates $(x_1, x_2, ...)$. If the status of a gravity unit varies as a function of time then, at any given instant, a "snapshot" of that gravity unit at that instant in time would be

$$u_i = u(t_i)$$

The composite portrait of the whole universe at that same instant,

$$\underline{U}_i = [u(t_i)_{x_1 x_2 ...}]_{(n_1, n_2, ...)}$$

is integrated to obtain the **equation of eternal existence**...

$$\underline{U}_E = \int_{-\infty}^{\infty} [u(t)_{x_1 x_2 ...}]_{(n_1, n_2, ...)}\, dt = [\int_{-\infty}^{\infty} u(t)_{x_1 x_2 ...}\, dt]_{(n_1, n_2, ...)}$$

(See page 98 for this equation adjusted to a perceived linearity of Future mathematical steps will involve the relationships among consciousness, Neothink, and Gravity Units. Submissions to Neo-Tech Publishing, P.O. Box 60906, Boulder City, NV 89006 are invited.

---

[1] Existence is not in time. Time is within existence. Thus, any universe is in time within existence.

# Chapter 7
# Gravity Units

The fully integrated honesty of Neo-Tech bridges the widest gaps among physics and science — from the general relativity of cosmic gravity and beyond to the quantum mechanics of quarks and below.[1] Conscious life using Neo-Tech — fully integrated honesty — bridges those and other problems, great and small, to deliver eternal life, happiness, prosperity.

The controlling keys of existence are the ultimate-symmetry Gravity Units as explained in Chapter 5. Also, as explained on pages 45-46, gravity is negative energy, always pulling in toward nonmotion. Mass and energy are positive energy, always pushing out toward motion. Our universe and all existence consist of gravity, mass, and energy. The sum of all existence equals zero energy. Therefore, the total energy of (1) our universe, of (2) every universe-containing, microscopically undetectable Gravity Unit, and of (3) all vacuums is zero — nothing — as explained on pages 45-46.

No real vacuum exists in nature. All spacetime points in existence contain *existence* itself. All existence consists of Gravity Units with zero energy. Thus, any and every point in existence can be quantum fluxed into equal amounts of negative-energy gravity and positive-energy mass/energy. Then, exploding from the cold "vacuum" or "nothingness" of pure geometric gravity into a cosmic

---

[1]And, from chemical clocks of strange-attractor chaos that are strong on empirical demonstration but weak on theory...to superstrings* of ultimate symmetry that are strong on theory but weak on empirical demonstration. ...Neo-Tech bridges those gaps.

*Strings, not points, seem to be the basic entities of existence. Even in nature-evolved life, the string-like helix of DNA is basic.

89

inflation, that Gravity Unit forms a new universe of mass, energy, space, time, and motion.

A Metaphor

From any point above-and-below, in every vacuum state and universe, conscious beings can flux, break, or inflate Gravity-Unit symmetries into limitless new galaxies or universes. All of those actions can occur without violating the laws of physics.

Existence exists. For, existence cannot not exist. Existence is Gravity Units with fields of existence at every point in space, matter, energy, and time.[1] As philosopher Ayn Rand recognized, "Existence *is* identity." Thus, Gravity Units *are* identity: the fundamental identity of existence — as is consciousness. ...The melded symmetry of consciousness and Gravity Units points the way to unifying consciousness with physics — points the way to unifying all existence.

---

[1]Time is always within a background of existence: Existence is not in time. Instead, time is in existence. Thus, time can be measured as changing geometric shapes in space. Indeed, spacetime is a geometry dependent on its contents and their configurations. Inside Gravity Units, time disappears into fixed spatial dimensions.

*Gravity Units*

Gravity Inflations, Light Cones, and Universe Creations

Existence does not smoothly reduce down to nothing or non existence. Instead, everything in nature ultimately reduces to a discrete bump, a quantum, a unit in an ether of Gravity Units (GUs), which are the eternal quantum units of existence. GUs comprise the ether substrate in which all broken symmetries exist. A GU is an unimaginably small entity with essentially zero surface at seemingly infinite curvature. Yet, each GU is still an entity, a unit of existence — the prime unit of existence with specific properties. The GU is essentially maximal symmetry: a pure symmetry of gravity or field of geometry.

But, at the boundaries of GUs are *asymmetric* regions of countless smaller, connecting Gravity Units at which quantum fluxes can inflate into separate universes. Each of those universes creates a spacetime quasi light cone that eventually meets the real light cone of every other universe evolving from that Gravity Unit to create a universe of universes many times the total size of the distance traversed at the speed of light.

For example, as shown by the illustration on page 92, magnify a Gravity Unit by a googol...or $10^{100}$ times. The GU would now appear as unimaginably large with its highly curved surface now appearing as essentially flat. That surface is asymmetrically disrupted with bumps of countless other, smaller Gravity Units. Those disruptions can flux into universes at countless points on the surface of the GU to produce countless quasi light cones that eventually link at distances in any amounts beyond that communicated by the speed of light.

As shown on the illustration on page 92, light cones linked from Y to B″ have communicated at many times the speed of light with nothing exceeding the speed of light.

91

# A Gravity Unit Magnified 10$^{100}$ Times

### fluxing into

## Countless Universe-Making Gravity/Light Cones

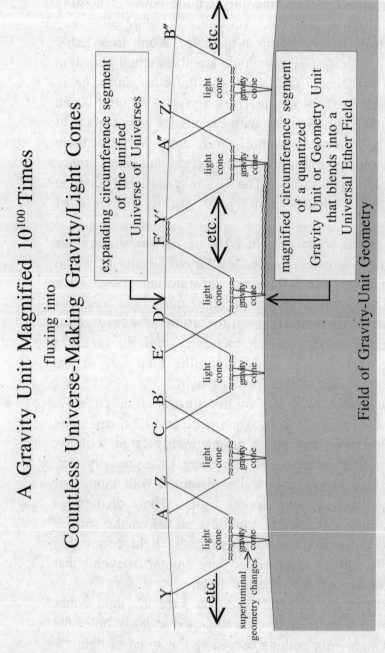

expanding circumference segment
of the unified
Universe of Universes

magnified circumference segment
of a quantized
Gravity Unit or Geometry Unit
that blends into a
Universal Ether Field

**Field of Gravity-Unit Geometry**

As a law of nature, everything in existence can be reduced to a smallest unit or quantum — be it an electron or quark for mass or a photon for energy. Beneath mass and energy lie resonating strings and thinkons with dimensions less than 10$^{-35}$ meters. Those strings and thinkons create spacetime mass, energy, and consciousness. Beneath those dimensions lie an ether of Gravity Units that form a universal sea of eternal geometries. Measurements through Gravity Units may someday overcome the Heisenberg Uncertainty Principle in establishing the simultaneous position and momentum of an electron to any arbitrary degree of certainty.

# MOVEMENT II

# The Anticivilization

*The Problem*

## Unconquerable Honesty

In this anticivilization, we each are alone in our struggle to live rationally. We have always been alone with our own honesty. That aloneness of honesty is our only unconquerable strength in this anticivilization. For, we are chained to a civilization based on dishonesty. In the end, that dishonesty cheats us of our earned rewards as we each die unnecessarily, tragically unfulfilled.

By contrast, in the Civilization of the Universe, no such struggle or dishonesty exists. In an honest culture of certainty and rationality, everyone is free — eternally free, prosperous, fulfilled.

# Chapter 8
## Unlocking the Secrets
### to
## Limitless Wealth

On planet Earth, no major breakthrough of knowledge has occurred in two generations — since (1) Albert Einstein replaced Newtonian physics[1] with relativity and (2) a handful of brilliant physicists like Dirac and Feynman developed quantum mechanics. Why no further seminal breakthroughs? Because thinking from today's greatest minds, such as those of Stephen Hawking and Roger Penrose, short-circuits when their wide-scope thinking turns to mysticism. Indeed, mystical bubbles reduce conscious minds to those of lost children, even the greatest minds like those of Hawking and Penrose. Thus, trapped in mysticism, new knowledge needed to deliver prosperity, both now and into the future, can no longer evolve.

In this anticivilization, the most brilliant conscious minds can no longer develop major, breakthrough knowledge. Most such brilliant minds today are stuck — limited to narrow, specialized areas — bounded by integration-blocking mysticisms. Those brilliant minds are weakened and limited by mysticism. They can be outflanked and outperformed by lower IQ minds that are

---

[1]Einstein did not "overthrow" Newton's gravity. Rather, Einstein adjusted and *explained* gravity (Newton would "frame no hypotheses"). Einstein actually strengthened and solidified Newton's inverse square law for gravity with spacetime geometry. *In context*, Newton as Einstein was, is, and will remain correct.

95

mystic-free — minds that can integrate wider perspectives of reality. Because of their expanding mysticisms, geniuses today are thinking and living with increasing impotence. ...So, where does the future lie?

The future lies in the Zonpower discovery: Throughout history, six seminal changes have occurred in the way mankind views itself and its world: (1) the invention of consciousness three millennia ago, (2) the Greeks' discovery of logic and its power, (3) the Renaissance's overthrow of traditional "truths" for the scientific method, (4) the Copernican revolution, (5) the Newtonian revolution, (6) Einstein's relativity and quantum mechanics. Today, the seventh seminal change arises: the unifying discovery of Neothink, Zonpower, and the Civilization of the Universe.

Zonpower delivers boundless knowledge and riches to any conscious individual. For, Zonpower frees reality from irrational illusions. Zonpower connects reality with *all* existence to bring unlimited purpose, wealth, and happiness to conscious beings.

Such wealth-producing, wide-scope integrations are easy to grasp and implement. This *Zonpower* communiqué will prepare you. First, *Zonpower* provides an entirely different way to view yourself, the world, and all existence. Second, *Zonpower* is so widely integrated yet so simply expressed that, on the first reading, you are ready to collect its guiltless riches. Then, on each subsequent reading, your powers to collect its boundless rewards expand.

How scientifically valid is Zonpower? Its mathematical models reduce to $T1=T2k$. Do not worry about that formula now. It is derived on page 239 and made clear throughout Part III. Such a simple formula or model can explain most, if not all, major anomalies in today's science and physics. That universal mathematical expression meets the "simplicity-and-beauty" criterion of Nobel-prize-winning Paul Dirac. Also, for validating major theories, the T1=T2k hypothesis meets the "correspondence" criterion of Nobel-prize-winning Niels Bohr.[1] The "correspondence" criterion requires noncontradictory linkages with science and nature.

And, finally, valid theory must meet three other criteria: (1) offer answers to previously unanswered questions and unsolved problems, (2) offer predictability, and (3) offer many ways to verify or refute the theory. Scientific demonstration of those three criteria focuses on identifying conscious configurations encoded throughout the cosmos. That scientific verification is the object of Neo-Tech research. But, practical proof already exists: **Today, Zonpower can make you rich, happy, and healthy.**

---

[1]Niels Bohr's correspondence criterion should not be confused with his *complimentary principle*, which means the more of one the less of the other. For example, position and momentum of a particle are complementary — the more precisely one is known the less precisely the other is known. Truth and honesty are complementary. For example, the more dogmatically one asserts truth the less honest one becomes. In other words, the more one demands truth, the less contextual or honest become the facts.

# A Linear View

## Time, Eternity, and Existence

(view from the anticivilization)

by

Justin James Evermen, Theoretical Research Department
Iowa State University, Ames, IA 50012

**Below is an alteration** on Gordon's mathematical view of time, eternity, and existence on page 88. Gordon's equation does not explain the non circular/curved nature of time that seems to present itself to us. We see linear time. So to approximate this lineation it is necessary to take the natural log of the function. This lineates the space gravity curve and presents them as our consciousness perceives them. Just as $1/\chi$ graphed on logxlog paper is lineated so is time by the log or ln function. And just as $1/\chi$ appears linear on logxlog paper so does time. Thus, the necessity to lineate its curvature. So, therefore, we know $1/\chi$ is curved as also time is curved. But in this askewed frame of reference they will both present themselves as linear.

### Therefore

$$\underline{U}_E = \int_{-\infty}^{\infty} [\ln{(u(t)\chi_1\chi_2\chi_3\ldots)}](n_1, n_2,\ldots)dt$$

$$= \int_{-\infty}^{\infty} [\ln{(u(t)\chi_1\chi_2\chi_3\ldots)}dt](n_1, n_2,\ldots)$$

Thus the log or ln function serves to lineate the curvature that the **Gravity Units** hold. Hence, our perception of linear, not curved time.

So thus the **equation of eternal existence...**

$$\underline{U}_E = \int_{-\infty}^{\infty} [\ln{(u(t)\chi_1\chi_2\chi_3\ldots)}dt](n_1, n_2,\ldots)$$

### Where

$t_i$ = instant of time      $\underline{U}$=universe

$\underline{E}$= eternity      $u\chi_1, \chi_2\ldots$=Gravity Units

# Chapter 9

# Birth of Parasitical Elites

in
## America

James J. Hill was a 19th-Century super value producer who pushed into a worldwide business dynamic. Just as Hill achieved great success in the American railroad industry and began spearheading an international expansion, he was snuffed out by a newly burgeoning parasitical-elite class in America. The story of James J. Hill is documented in the book *"Entrepreneurs Versus The State"* by Burton W. Folsom, Jr.

### Political Entrepreneurs Versus Market Entrepreneurs

In that book, Folsom identifies how throughout history there have been two distinct types of entrepreneurs: political entrepreneurs and market entrepreneurs. Political entrepreneurs seek profits by working with the government to get subsidies, grants, and special privileges. They seek success through political pull. In contrast, market entrepreneurs seek success by producing increasingly improved values, products, and services at increasingly lower costs.

### The Transcontinental Railroads

The building of America's transcontinental railroads provided a dramatic example of political entrepreneurs versus market entrepreneurs. In the 1860s, railroads began expanding rapidly throughout America. Thus, political

99

entrepreneurs seeking easy dollars teamed up with Congressmen seeking unearned power and glory. Those political entrepreneurs lobbied Congressmen for the federal government to subsidize the building of America's first transcontinental railroad.

That situation presented a perfect combination for the parasitical-elite class: White-collar-hoax political entrepreneurs could line their pockets with lavish government subsidies, and the Congressmen handing out those subsidies could garner self-glory and justify their jobs by proclaiming how beneficial they were to the American people by financing America's first transcontinental railroad. Thus, a deception was woven by that parasitical-elite class through claiming only the government could finance an undertaking as large and expensive as building a transcontinental railroad. That same deception is still promoted in history books to this day.

With great fanfare, enormous subsidies were granted to the Union Pacific and the California Pacific. The California Pacific started building track from the west coast, the Union Pacific from the east coast. Those companies were paid by the government according to how many miles of track each laid. Consequently, both companies built along the longest, most out-of-the-way routes they could justify. That way, each company collected the maximum dollars from the government.

Spending public money they controlled but did not earn, the Congressmen were quick to claim credit for building America's first transcontinental railroad. But, unlike market-entrepreneur businessmen spending their own money, those Congressmen were not about to exert the nitty-gritty effort required to insure good value was received for each dollar spent. Thus, the building of that government-financed transcontinental railroad turned into an orgy of fraud.

As a result, after that first transcontinental railroad was built, subsequently called the Union Pacific, it had enormously high operating costs. Because extra-long routes had been purposely built, because time and research had not been taken to locate routes across the lowest-grade hills, each train took more time and fuel to complete its journey. More wages had to be paid; more equipment was tied up. In addition, because the railroad track had been laid so hastily, thousands of miles of shoddy track had to be pulled up and laid again before the first train could even travel over it. Thus, from the start, the Union Pacific could not make a profit. As a result, the federal government had to continue doling out taxpayer dollars just to enable the Union Pacific to operate after the line had been completed.

Soon other political entrepreneurs ganged up with local politicians to demand federally subsidized transcontinental railroads be built in their areas of the country. Thus, the federal government financed a transcontinental railroad in the North, the Northern Pacific, and a transcontinental railroad in the South, the Santa Fe. The building of those two additional government-financed railroads followed the same course as the building of the Union Pacific. The lines were poorly constructed. The builders focused on obtaining maximum government subsidies, not on achieving economy and quality. Thus, after the Northern Pacific and Santa Fe transcontinentals were completed, they too had unnecessarily high operating costs. Both lost money from the start, and both had to continue receiving government subsidies just to operate.

*Movement II: The Anticivilization*

## A Deception Is Woven

A parasitical-elite class consisting of political entrepreneurs, job-justifying politicians, and government-subsidized university professors propagandize to this very day that only the federal government could have financed the building of America's first transcontinental railroads. The story of James J. Hill is ignored.

James J. Hill was a market entrepreneur, *not* a political entrepreneur. He was an integrated thinker and a forward-essence mover. Hill was born in a log cabin to a working class family in Ontario, Canada. He got a job with a local railroad when he was a teenager. He loved railroads and integrated his life with them. Hill moved up quickly. Soon he became involved in the building of local railroads. Then, in 1880, Hill decided to build a transcontinental railroad privately, without any government subsidies. He would call his line the Great Northern.

Hill's plan to build a transcontinental railroad at the very northern border of America was labelled "Hill's folly." Why? First of all, Hill was building a railroad way up north in unsettled wilderness. From where would his business come? Secondly, Hill would have to compete with three transcontinental railroads to the south: the Northern Pacific, the Union Pacific, and the Santa Fe. How could a private railroad be built without government help and then compete with three other railroads that had their expenses paid by the government?

James J. Hill was forced to meet the disciplines of a bottom line. He had to stay within profitable red-to-black business dynamics. Thus, instead of "rushing to collect government subsidies", he built his railroad one extension at a time, westward into the northern wilderness. Hill would build an extension westward a few hundred miles, then move in farmers from the East, free of charge, in order to settle the land along his railroad. Those farmers would then start using Hill's railroad to ship their crops back East to market. Because Hill received no government money, each extension constructed westward would have to profit before another westward extension could be built. In ten years, Hill completed his transcontinental railroad, the Great Northern, without receiving one cent of government money.

Hill had to build each extension with detailed planning to achieve maximum efficiency at minimum operating costs. Hill personally mapped out and built along the shortest, most direct routes. He also carefully surveyed land to find routes containing the lowest grades of hills over which to build. And, with Hill spending hard-earned private money, he insisted on the highest quality workmanship and materials.

The three government-financed transcontinental railroads south of Hill's Great Northern were in the heart of the country and none of them could earn a profit. But, what actually happened once Hill's Great Northern reached the Pacific? All three government-financed trans-continentals went bankrupt and required ever more government bail-out money — taxpayer money — to continue running. In stark contrast, Hill's railroad flourished from the very start. The Great Northern produced a profit, even during recession years.

## A Spiral of Inefficiencies

Because the federal government continued subsidizing the money-losing, government-financed transcontinentals, each of those railroads had to obtain government approval to build any new extension. On the other hand, once the

Great Northern was running, Hill built his railroad with extensions called feeder lines. For example, if coal was discovered a hundred miles to the north of Hill's line, he built a feeder line to service that mine. If good trees were available for lumber on a nearby mountain, Hill would build a feeder line to that mountain so that a lumber company could move in and use his railroad to ship its lumber to market. If a suitable valley for cattle ranching existed a few miles to the south, Hill would build a feeder line to service that valley. Railroads discovered that feeder lines were crucial to their profitability. But whenever one of the government-subsidized railroads wanted to build a feeder line, it had to get approval from Congress since it was providing the financing.

Well, everyone knows what happens when politicians become involved. A simple business decision would get hung up for months, even years, before receiving approval. Thus, the government-subsidized railroads could not operate effectively. They could not compete with Hill's Great Northern railroad. What had initially been labelled "Hill's folly" by the establishment ran circles around the government-subsidized, poorly managed railroads.

### Fraud Is Inherent in the Parasitical-Elite Class

Over time, the corruption that laced the government-financed transcontinental railroads began unraveling. Unlike James J. Hill's privately-financed transcontinental railroad, the managements of the government-financed transcontinental railroads were not operating by the disciplines of a bottom line. Thus, those white-collar-hoax political entrepreneurs did not exert the discipline required to closely supervise the construction of their railroads for quality and efficiency. The survival of those political entrepreneurs did not depend upon efficient management. Their survival, instead, depended upon exerting political pull. Consequently, the government-financed railroads were left wide open to fraud. Managers often formed their own supply companies selling substandard materials to their own railroads at inflated prices. Payoffs and sellouts were rampant.

Over time, the fraudulent practices of the government-subsidized transcontinental railroads increasingly surfaced. The public became fed up with that corruption. Thus, glory-seeking politicians in Washington once again rushed in to grab attention and "serve the public". A new deception was woven. Congressmen now claimed they were the defenders of the American people and would expose the corruption in the transcontinental railroads. Glory-seeking Congressmen began conducting investigations into the nation's railroad business. Yet, in reality, those glory-seeking politicians were the root cause of that corruption.

As the fraud continued between political entrepreneurs and job-justifying politicians, consider what James J. Hill, the market entrepreneur, was accomplishing. After completing his profitable transcontinental railroad, Hill promoted the building of entire new industries in the Northwest, such as lumber companies in Oregon, apple farms in Washington, mining industries in Montana, cattle ranches in the plains. Hill helped businesses move to the Northwest and gave them special rates to ship their products back East until those businesses became established. This practice quickly built up business along Hill's railroad line.

Next, Hill began thinking about business beyond America. He began exploring opportunities in the Orient.

## Movement II: The Anticivilization

Hill calculated that if a single major Chinese province substituted just one ounce of American wheat for rice in their daily diets, he could ship 50,000,000 bushels of wheat to China from America. ...Hill, using wide-scope integrated thinking, began moving beyond the boundaries of a restricted, single-nation mode. He began moving into a worldwide mode.

James J. Hill decided that he was going to promote American trade in Asia, just as he had promoted trade in the Northwest. So, he bought cargo ships and formed his own steamship company to ship American goods to China and Japan. He then sent agents abroad to promote American goods to Asians.

While the white-collar-hoax political entrepreneurs were still trying to figure out how to get more subsidies from the federal government, Hill was turning his attention to world business. James J. Hill was figuring out how to deliver increasing values to the world. He realized that the key to tapping the vast markets of Asia was to build trade by offering to ship American products on his railroad and steamships for free until trade could become established. So, Hill began racing his steamships back and forth between Japan, China, and America.

Hill was a heroic forward-essence mover. He exported to Asia wheat from Midwest farmers and cotton from Southern farmers. He offered a group of Japanese industrialists low-cost American cotton if they would test the American cotton in place of the cotton that they traditionally imported from India. If the Japanese did not like the American cotton, Hill offered to let them keep it free of charge. This worked. Soon Hill's boxcars were filled with cotton bales heading to Japan. Utilizing this same technique, Hill got both the Japanese and the Chinese

106

to start buying American textiles from New England.

### James J. Hill Was Spearheading
### An American Dominance of Asian Trade

In 1896, American exports to Japan totalled 7.7 million dollars a year. Nine years later, James J. Hill had pushed that figure to 51.7 million dollars a year. He was spearheading an American dominance of Asian trade. And this was occurring a hundred years ago! James J. Hill worked diligently to promote American exports to Asia. For example, starting around 1900, Japan began a railroad building boom. England and Belgium were the traditional suppliers of rail. American rail-makers were still fledgling in the Pittsburgh area. But Hill recognized the importance of the Asian market for steel and rails. So, he personally underbid the Europeans to capture Japanese orders for American rail-makers.

Hill diligently promoted American goods in Asia, ranging from lumber from the Northwest to wheat from the Midwest, to copper from Montana, to apples from Washington, to steel from Pittsburgh, to cotton from the South, to textiles from New England. While the white-collar-hoax political entrepreneurs of the government-subsidized railroads were being closed in upon, Hill was booming American business while blossoming his railroad into an international dynamo.

So what happened next? Attention-seeking politicians began parading the corrupt political entrepreneurs infesting government-subsidized railroads before the public through Senate investigation hearings. Yet, it was Congress that created that corruption in the first place by self-righteously giving away public money it controlled but did not earn. Instead of identifying that Congress was the root cause of the problem, Congress began clamoring for strict regulation of the railroad industry. Congress then devised a strong-arm approach, proclaiming it was protecting the American public from greedy, corrupt railroad executives.

Congress proposed creating the Interstate Commerce Commission to regulate and control the railroads and the Sherman Antitrust Act designed to threaten and punish the railroad industry. Well, James J. Hill realized what was occurring. He travelled to Washington to testify before Congress. Hill meticulously explained what had happened with the government-subsidized railroads versus his privately-financed railroad and how the solution was for government to get out of the railroad business altogether.

But Hill was ignored. Those politicians and bureaucrats could not increase their power nor garner self-glory if they admitted that the root of the problem was caused by Congress getting into the railroad business in the first place — a place in which government never belonged.

## Conscious Destruction

Congress ignored James J. Hill and went ahead to create the Interstate Commerce Commission (ICC) and pass the Sherman Antitrust laws that heavily regulated and punished the railroad industry. The ICC and antitrust laws forbid giving any special deals to customers. Thus, the techniques Hill had used to build up trade in the Northwest and was now using to build American trade to Asia became "illegal" — illegal not through objective law but through *force-backed, political-agenda "law"*. As a direct result of that legislation, James J. Hill ended his expansion into the Asian markets. One year after Congress created the Interstate Commerce Commission and passed the Sherman Antitrust laws, Hill sold his steamship line. His farsighted, wide-scope methods were stopped by corrupt government regulations.

America's trade to Japan and China dropped forty percent within two years. ...Remember, before that point, America's trade with Asia had been increasing geometrically. Two years after that legislation was passed by Congress, America's trade with Asia dropped almost in half.

What happened in Congress was not a case of ignorance. James J. Hill actually set up residence in Washington to intensively lobby Congress and its investigative committees. Hill made sure those Congressmen knew what had really happened in the railroad industry and why. He even wrote a book about the situation and published the book himself. Still, Hill's arguments were ignored. For, Congress's goal was not to serve the best interests of the public.

Instead, Congress could garner public support and praise by attacking and regulating the railroad industry, not by admitting that they had been the root cause of railroad corruption. ...Power-seeking politicians with regulating bureaucrats will always block free enterprise and competitiveness. The intervention of politicians and bureaucrats will always drive prices up, service down, while spreading decay and corruption.

## What Are the Implications?

How many people today have the slightest idea what happened a hundred years ago with James J. Hill? How many people today know what was started by a single, integrated thinking, forward-essence mover? How many people today know that James J. Hill was spear-heading an American dominance of trade in Asia one-hundred years ago!

Hill's incredible parade of value production, trade, business, and job creation was cut off in its infancy because of a handful of politicians. Seeking to advance their own harmful careers, with total disregard of honesty and reality, those politicians stopped a tremendous value producer, James J. Hill, and his push into Asia.

Hill's master plan was destroyed by corrupt Congressmen one-hundred years ago. And, one must not forget, those Congressmen knew what they were doing. Hill diligently informed them of the real situation — what he had done with his privately-financed railroad, whose fault it was for the corruption that occurred within the government-financed railroads, and what his railroad was doing for America's international trade by its freedom to nurture new business. Yet, those elite, college-educated Congressmen proceeded to pass their self-serving laws and regulations in order to protect and enhance their own harmful livelihoods.

### What Really Happened a Hundred Years Ago?

Let us examine this situation even closer. ...What really happened a hundred years ago? What really was cut off by the parasitical-elite class in Washington using force-backed political policies? James J. Hill was not only spearheading an American dominance of trade in Asia a hundred years ago, he was also spearheading an industrialization of Asia. Hill was pushing American business into Asia, causing railroads to be built, causing factories to be built, causing new businesses to be created. He nurtured American business in Asia, and that business was beginning to follow its natural course of flooding into markets and dominating trade. That, in turn, would have led to a rapid industrialization of Asia.

Had James J. Hill been left free to continue spearheading the industrialization of China a hundred years ago, the world would be different today. What kind of creative energies would have been released if China, a country of one billion people, had industrialized a hundred years ago? Where would civilization be today? Would we have cures for cancer, heart disease, AIDS? Would we be building cities in the oceans and on the moon? The contributions that the Chinese could have made to science, to technology, to the world economy are mind-boggling. But no. All of that potential was smashed. A billion people were pushed down and stagnated, 30 million Chinese were killed by communist predators. Why? Because Congressmen a hundred years ago wanted to exercise unearned power and feel false importance!

### Thus Arose the Newly Born Parasitical Elites

A hundred years ago, one man learned how to honestly integrate business with reality. He started moving up. He learned how business worked; he learned how the American economy worked. Then, he learned how the world economy worked. He began learning how the whole up-rising of civilization worked. One man, a hundred years ago, learned how to do integrated thinking and forward essence movement. He then began pushing the lid up on society. If that man had been left alone, if he had not been stopped by the politicians, he would have swung open that lid, China would have industrialized, all of Asia would have industrialized, the whole world would have risen up, and America would have been sitting on top of it all.

Instead, James J. Hill was smashed down. The newly

born parasitical-elite class consisting of politicians, bureaucrats, political entrepreneurs, and other professional value destroyers smashed down whatever threatened to expose their hoaxes, whatever threatened their nonproductive livelihoods.

Thus arose the newly born parasitical-elite class in America. They joined the worldwide parasitical elites that created an anticivilization on planet Earth. But this irrational civilization based on illusions and hoaxes will be replaced by the rational Civilization of the Universe sensed by James J. Hill at the start of the 20th century and implemented by Zon at the end of the 20th century.

E.S., 1989

*Anticivilization*: The irrational planet Earth riddled with dishonest parasitical elites like Woodrow Wilson, FDR, and the Clintons causing endless cycles of corruption, destruction, and death for everyone.

*Civilization of the Universe*: The rational universe filled with honest value producers like J.J. Hill, Ray Kroc, and Bill Gates providing endless happiness, wealth, and life for others and society.

New-Color Symphony

Movement #2

# Chapter 10

# Who Is Wasting Your Brief Life?

An old man is dying. His one-and-only life is ending. All his adult life he worked hard producing values for others. He complained at times, perhaps even questioned, but never more. He always accepted the dictates of the ruling elite — the politicians, bureaucrats, journalists, lawyers, university professors. For that acceptance, he collected social security, food stamps, and other handouts for which he paid hundreds of times over with shrinking happiness, security, savings, and standard of living. At the same time, threats from crime, drugs, racism, and poverty kept growing.

His wife died ten months before. She had devoted her life to following the mystic path from the church, to astrology, to theosophy. He always silently thought her life path was for nothing — a sadly wasted life. Yet, was his path any different? Indeed, they depended on each other. Her loss caused unbearable pain that wanted to scream out. And now, for the first time, he began feeling an indescribable anger bubbling deep within his soul. What caused that rising anger? Did it come from the same source discovered by his wife during her dying days?

Her anger began when she realized the mystic path, which consumed her entire adult life, was a terrible hoax — was nothing real. Her life was wasted on an illusion — a vast hoax perpetuated and manipulated by those who used deceit to advance their own harmful livelihoods, self-importance, and usurped power. ...Indeed, over the centuries, those hoaxers used and wasted the one-and-only lives of their victims by the millions.

As his wife lay dying, she suddenly startled him. She had always been so tranquil. But, now, anger lashed out. Suddenly that frail woman wanted to obliterate everyone associated with manipulating those mystic frauds.

Strangely, during her final moments of anger, he once again, after fifty years, felt love, excitement, and life with his wife. And he knew she felt the same. Their eyes shared the most precious moment of their lives. They shared once more, after fifty years, a fleeting moment of long-lost love and passion. Suddenly, they had discovered the key to life and happiness together. Then, she closed her eyes for the final time. She was gone forever.

Now, today, as he is dying, that old man feels anger rising deep from within. He wonders what would happen if that anger ever discovered its undefined targets. But, what targets? No, not the same mystic-leader targets his wife so angrily attacked. Those mystic leaders deprived his wife's entire adult life of love, happiness, and excitement. Yet, he was never tricked by those exploiters of ignorance and illusions. Then, who are his targets of this fifty-year accumulation of anger now surging from deep within? ...On second thought, could those targets be the same mystic hoaxers his wife discovered — just more cleverly disguised?

In his mind, he begins reviewing his life, year by year. In the perspective of potential, his life seems to have meant so little. He feels life lacked the growth, prosperity, and accomplishment that belonged to him. ...Did he miss a tremendous life experience that he earned but never collected? Who then collected those earnings?

## Who Is Wasting Your Brief Life?

What happens to everyone's one-and-only life? The old man wondered. What happens to the promise of youth? Indeed, almost every human life is drained or used up until each dies. Why does such a waste occur to essentially everyone? Almost everyone seems to lose his or her life to nothing, for nothing. Who is responsible, who is to blame?

Then, he recalls an experience shortly after his wife died. It was a Saturday afternoon. He went to the shopping mall to which he and his wife had often gone. Somehow he knew this would be his last visit to that mall — or any mall. He sat in the rotunda to think about her.

After some time, he began noticing the people in the mall. He gradually noticed something different — something he never saw before: No one looked *really* happy! Many seemed overweight. So many seemed drained. Some were harassed by their children. Others seemed unhappy with their spouses. He knew most wanted or needed more money. Many probably disliked their jobs. Others were worried about losing their jobs, or had already lost their jobs. Most looked bored, anxious, or empty. Like him, he knew almost everyone had abandoned his or her youthful dreams of success, glamour, prosperity. ...Almost everyone's life seemed wasted.

He then thought to himself: To have so many losses and problems, we must be guilty of something. We must be guilty of all kinds of faults, failures, and mediocrities. Anyway, we cause our own problems and limitations, don't we? That's what the authorities say. They say we're to blame, we're at fault.

Wait a minute! We cause our own problems? We're to blame, we're at fault, we are guilty? Who says? Who exactly are those who say we are responsible for not

117

having success, prosperity, and happiness? Do we really prevent ourselves from gaining success, prosperity, and happiness? Does that really make sense? Is that natural? Or is some dark secret fooling us?

Coming back to the present, the old man realizes his rising anger is unlocking that secret: Such losses do not make sense, he tells himself. Such losses are not natural. Yes, some dark secret has been fooling everyone. The old man closes his eyes. He is dying. ...Someday everyone will discover the cause of that old man's anger, pain, and suffering. Everyone will discover that the deeply hidden causes of human suffering and death emanate from the parasitical-elite class.

Who exactly are the parasitical elites? A simple, wide-scope accounting process reveals one fact: Parasitical elites are those whose livelihoods are draining much more, often infinitely more, from the economy and society than they deliver. Such accounting answers the following question: Does one's job, livelihood, profession, agency, bureaucracy, or company *build or drain* the economy — *benefit or harm* the productive class? **Does one produce values or destroy values?** ...Wide-scope accounting is a definitive economic-impact statement.

### Murderous Organizations are Killing *You*

Some net value destroyers are so obvious that no specific accounting figures are needed for the public to see the destructiveness of such people and their harmful organizations. Consider some of the most harmful bureaucracies in America today: the BATF, DEA, EPA, IRS, INS, FDA, FTC, SEC. Such murderous organizations[1] need guns, jails, and ego "justice" to exist and expand. Those organizations breed legions of professional value destroyers who are responsible for mass property and business destructions that eventually bring economic and social devastations. But, most harmfully, those organizations move *everyone* toward life-wasting stagnation, unhappiness, and death.

Daily, those organizations violate objective justice by committing real crimes of force and fraud. Those organizations are not only harming the economy, but are destroying society and everyone's freedoms by violating each of the ten Articles of the Bill of Rights except the third — they have not yet forced the quartering of their troops in private homes. ...Those organizations depend on a legal system corrupted with the subjective laws and ego "justice" used to advance their harmful political agendas.[2]

## The DEA

With conventional accounting within arbitrary or closed boundaries, almost any destructive end, even destructions of entire economies and genocide, can be made to appear beneficial to the public as demonstrated by Lenin, Hitler, and Mao. But, wide-scope accounting

---

[1]Murderous organizations? Even the EPA, for example, is responsible for the deaths of 8–20 people for every life it theoretically saves. The EPA kills people through the increased living costs and decreased living standards that bureaucracy forces on society, especially on the lower classes (Ref: *Forbes*, 7/6/92, page 60). Likewise, other bureaucracies cause long-term harm and death to countless more people than those few people who may benefit. In fact, those who profit from or live off the lethal actions of those bureaucracies are accomplices to murder — often mass murder.

[2]Reference: *The Neo-Tech Protection Kit*, Volumes I and II, 780 pages, The Neo-Tech Research and Writing Center, revised 1994.

119

immediately reveals the destructiveness of those men and their organizations. Now, apply that wide-scope accounting to organizations like the Drug Enforcement Administration (the DEA). First, consider that the DEA exists entirely through gun-backed policies created by self-serving, demagogic politicians. From that fact, the public can increasingly see that the armed divisions of the DEA are the engines that support and expand the drug problem, crimes, death, and loss of constitutional rights for every American citizen.

The armed DEA divisions continuously expand the market for drugs by providing the super-high price supports that make possible the flourishing of organized crime and drug cartels. Such government-forced economics necessitate pushing ever more potent drugs onto others, especially onto vulnerable young people. In turn, those immoral DEA actions keep escalating the crimes and deaths related to drugs.

Gun-backed organizations like the DEA serve but one purpose — the expansion of harmful livelihoods that let politicians and bureaucrats drain the economy and damage society by creating ever expanding drug problems.

## The IRS

Likewise, the gun-backed divisions of the Internal Revenue Service work with Dole-type[1] politicians in expanding destructive political agendas that enhance their jobs and power. Their armed criminal activities diminish everyone's future by crippling or breaking the daring entrepreneur and aggressive business person. Indeed, every large business today started with the daring courage,

---

[1]Career politician Senator Bob Dole has been a major supporter of expanding the destructive power and criminality of the IRS through its violent armed agents.

hard work, and precious seed capital of a heroically aggressive entrepreneur. Yet, as official policy, the IRS directs its newest-trained auditors and armed agents to "cut their teeth" on small, vulnerable, first-year companies. In that way, the IRS each year ruins countless individuals and small businesses — destroying the seeds to our economic future by destroying millions of current and future jobs.[1] Indeed, wide-scope accounting reveals how the armed divisions of the IRS are criminally destroying the essence of our economy, society, and freedoms not only for today, but for future generations.

The IRS thrives as a destructive bureaucracy *because* of the irrational income tax. By contrast, revenues raised through consumption or sales taxes would vanish deficits, reduce the IRS to a fraction of its current size...and eliminate its armed divisions that back criminal collection procedures used to override due process while inflicting cruel-and-unusual punishments on its victims.

No legitimate reason exists for armed agents in any bureaucracy. Local police and courts, not armed bureaucratic agents, can competently and constitutionally protect all individuals, property, and organizations, including physically protecting government officials.

## The INS

What about the Immigration and Naturalization Service, the INS? By throwing wide-scope accounting on the gun-backed segments of that organization, anyone can see its harm to the economy. With its army of enforcers who never have to answer to American citizens, the INS

---

[1] The Neo-Tech Research Center estimates that 7.1 million jobs in the American economy were lost from 1980-1990 due to businesses being damaged or destroyed by illegal IRS actions.

ravishes hard-working value producers and their families. The INS army expands its power and livelihoods by attacking America's most competitive workers of the past and future. Those workers are the immigrants who abandon their homelands and risk their lives to deliver competitive values to our economy. Thus, they raise the well-being and prosperity of all Americans. Such life-improving immigrants have been the backbone of competitive growth and economic prosperity in America, despite the dishonest political demagoguery to the contrary.

## The FDA

And the Food and Drug Administration? Wide-scope accounting shows the FDA to be the biggest killer of all — literally killing millions of human beings. Operating under a power-mad Commissioner like Dr. David Kessler, armies of FDA bureaucrats destructively build their own "achievement" files for their own promotions. By enforcing increasingly cost-prohibitive compliance to irrational regulations, the FDA blocks scientific and medical progress.

As specifically identified in the Neo-Tech literature, without the FDA and its armed enforcers, today we would have cures for cancer, heart disease, AIDS, muscular dystrophy, and essentially all other serious diseases (Ref: *The Neo-Tech Discovery*). Moreover, biomedical advances would have the human race moving toward non-aging longevity as achieved in all mystic-free civilizations throughout the universe — in all civilizations free of parasitical elites. This concept is supported by recent findings in physics and astronomy as summarized in Parts I and III of *Zonpower*.

Destructive Organizations
How Do They Survive?

How do destructive organizations succeed in deceiving everyone so completely for so long?

A successful magician deceives *everyone* in his audience with illusions. The key to the magician's successful tricks or deceptions is to keep everyone distracted. The magician with his wand keeps attention focused on a decoy illusion removed from the point of deception. With everyone's attention diverted, no one sees the deception.

All parasitical elites and their organizations have a myriad of decoy illusions. Created through deceptive rationalizations, those illusions have hidden the destructions of the parasitical-elite class since Plato showed golden-soul parasites 2300 years ago how to rule the value producers.

Consider today's Drug Enforcement Administration: With subjective laws enacted by power-usurping politicians, the DEA uses its wand of deception to point at the drugs it seized and people it jailed as progress in the "War on Drugs". But, in fact, the DEA has no motivation to diminish any drug problem. Without an expanding drug problem, its system of livelihoods and power would diminish. Thus, the DEA has every motivation to expand its bureaucracy of bogus livelihoods and power by creating and expanding drug problems, which it does very successfully.

Consider the armed criminal divisions of the Internal Revenue Service: With their wands of deception, those IRS divisions point at the money and property seized. Through its gun-backed agents, the IRS criminally squeezes the working assets out of the "underground" economy, heroic entrepreneurs, struggling individuals, and small businesses. They point to the dollars they have seized from those whom they have crippled, destroyed, or jailed. But throw wide-scope accounting on those illegal elements of the IRS, and one discovers its gun-backed enforcers are destroying our present and future economy, jobs, freedoms, privacy, and well-being. More broadly, the, IRS-forced paperwork alone is the greatest time-and-life destroyer *ever* devised to expand bureaucratic jobs and power. ...And most destructively, the IRS smothers youth from becoming the independent business giants needed for the future prosperity of any society.

Consider the Immigration and Naturalization Service: The INS points its wand of deception at the "illegal" aliens it forcibly drains, blocks, jails, or ejects from America. Such uses of force are not only racist, but are criminal acts against innocent value producers. Those crimes are hidden by deceptive-wand myths such as "draining welfare funds" and "keeping jobs for Americans". Both such claims are patently false. Wide-scope accounting clearly reveals that "illegal" aliens (1) add much more in taxes than they "drain" and (2) create many more jobs for Americans than they take. Thus, each racist INS crime diminishes everyone's job and life by undermining America's standard of living, its economic strength, its international competitiveness.

And finally, consider the Food and Drug Administration: The FDA points its wand of deception toward "protecting" the health of Americans. But, in reality, the FDA is responsible for killing more citizens than any other group of parasitical elites. For, through power-usurping regulations, the FDA blocks the cures for all major diseases. The FDA also blocks the development of major longevity advances. ...Only unhindered science and business can bring disease-free, non-aging longevity, as accomplished in all mystic-free, parasite-free civilizations throughout the universe.

### The Neo-Tech Literature

With actual wide-scope accountings, the Neo-Tech literature reveals the huge net destructions caused by specific politicians, bureaucrats, judges, lawyers, prosecutors, white-collar-hoax business people, and other parasitical elites. The Neo-Tech literature also details how those elites can exist only by creating and expanding power-building instruments such as armed bureaucracies. The Neo-Tech literature identifies how all parasitical elites depend on armed bureaucracies and subjective ego "justice" to enforce their harmful survival agendas. And finally, the Neo-Tech literature details the spectacular prosperity that awaits everyone upon terminating the parasitical-elite class.

### The Neo-Tech Wedge

Most people in government, business, and the professions are *not* targets for personal ostracism or job termination. Instead, they are candidates to benefit economically, professionally, and personally by getting on the honest side of the split caused by the *Neo-Tech Wedge*. That Wedge is already beginning to move through governments and businesses, separating the honest productive people from the parasitical elites. ...Only parasitical elites and their armed enforcers are targeted for ostracism and job termination. They are the ones who waste everyone's brief life. They shall not escape the Neo-Tech Wedge.

*Movement II: The Anticivilization*

## Vanishing Armed Bureaucrats

In contrast to legitimately armed policemen who serve to protect life and property, armed bureaucrats serve to harm life and property. Today, the increasing social and physical harms caused by politicized armed bureaucrats are endangering all federal employees.[1] ...Bureaucrats, not law-abiding citizens, must be disarmed.

As with Shakespeare's Iago in *Othello*, a politician who lives through armed bureaucracies exists not to produce values but to destroy them, not to bring social harmony but to disrupt it. As with the conflict in Sophocles' *Antigone*, the conflict between Neo-Tech and politicized armed bureaucracies evolves from the deepest issues of right versus wrong, honesty versus dishonesty, and protective government versus destructive government.

Neo-Tech will bring *peace*[2] to America and *trust* in government by vanishing armed bureaucracies.

---

[1]The criminalities of various politicians and the brutal destructiveness of certain federal bureaucracies, all deceptively whitewashed by the news media, are fueling a public loathing toward government that is threatening its employees.

[2]On May 29, 1995, the following notice was posted on various Internet newsgroups:

*Memorial Day: a Political Hoax*
*Clinton's wreath laying: obscene hypocrisy. Notice how such politicians, the cause of all wars, revel in glory as they eulogize their dead victims. ...Remember when Memorial Day was called Decoration Day? It was not a eulogy day for the politicians' dead victims, but a celebration for the end of war and its living survivors.*

# Chapter 11

# Your Personal Terminator

guarantees

# Limitless Prosperity

In the popular Arnold Schwarzenegger movies of the early 1990s, the terminator represents a nonstoppable force of destruction. In the real world, Neo-Tech represents a nonstoppable force that terminates *all* destructive forces. ...Neo-Tech is *your* personal terminator.

Today, right now, you hold a personal terminator in your hands — a terminator programed to eliminate all forces that harm you, your family, your future. ...Your terminator comes alive today to deliver unending happiness and prosperity.

### What is a Personal Terminator?

A personal terminator is your *natural self* programed to deliver limitless prosperity by terminating all life-depriving forces, large or small. For example, consider the most damaging of those forces, which began growing over six decades ago: In 1933, politicians with their expanding bureaucracies began draining America's business and economic assets. Starting with Roosevelt's New Deal, that drainage has expanded into the largest, most camouflaged theft and destruction of assets in history. Today, politicians and bureaucrats, as part of a growing *parasitical-elite class*, are devouring those shrinking assets.

Economic deterioration is upon us. But, with your personal terminator, you can end such parasitical harms while creating prosperity for you, your family, and society.

127

Neo-Tech — the Master Terminator

Personal terminators are generated from a Master Terminator called Neo-Tech. That terminator is eternally protective to all conscious life.

First, consider that neither harmful leaders nor destructive terminators can exist in civilizations evolved beyond the nuclear age. In other words, no civilization can survive much past its nuclear age with a destructive ruling class — with a parasitical-elite class.

Now, consider our civilization: Already well into our nuclear age, we are still ruled by parasitical elites. They are unnatural beings. For, they replace their productive human nature with a nonhuman program of purposely harming others, the economy, and society. Thus, they are not human beings. They are subhumans or *humanoids*. Not science-fiction humanoids, but self-made humanoids. For, each parasitical elite has removed from his or her thinking process the essence of a human being. That essence is the competitive production of economic and societal values needed for human survival, prosperity, and happiness.

Those humanoids increasingly drain everyone and society through dishonesty backed by the deception and force needed for parasitical survival. Those parasites live by covertly draining values produced by others rather than by competitively producing values for others and society. ...A civilization ruled by parasites must end in nuclear conflagration. But, that conflagration will never occur. For, the Master Terminator is programed to vanish the parasitical ruling class as nothing in cyberspace.

In pre-nuclear ages, the Master Terminator worked to overcome nature's forces that were harmful to conscious beings. With that natural terminator, for example, human beings worked to increasingly protect themselves from the elements, wild animals, hunger, injuries, disease. Now, today, during this nuclear age, conscious beings are using that same natural terminator to eradicate their most harmful and dangerous enemy — the parasitical elites. For, those professional value destroyers control the means to kill everyone on Earth in a nuclear holocaust.

In post-nuclear ages, evolved conscious beings will continue using the Master Terminator to overcome diseases and death itself...along with overcoming the longer-range destructive forces in nature such as weather disasters, earthquakes, asteroid and comet collisions, cosmic disasters, solar burnouts, and collapses into black holes.

That natural Master Terminator which functions throughout all ages in all universes *is* Neo-Tech. Indeed, Neo-Tech is simply fully integrated honesty — natural honesty. Nothing can stop the natural mission of Neo-Tech. Nothing can stop its mission of terminating the parasitical-elite class.

### Terminating the Parasitical-Elite Class

Today, economic deterioration accelerates: An enlarging pool of professional value *destroyers* increasingly pillages the shrinking pool of professional value *producers*. But, today, the rising Prosperity Revolution will accomplish the first-and-final *valid* class overthrow in history. That overthrow and termination of the parasitical-elite class by *Neo-Tech self-leaders and honest business leaders* will boom all economies. Mankind will finally experience the unlimited prosperity enjoyed by all advanced civilizations throughout the Universe.

This is *your* revolution to unlimited prosperity.

*Movement II: The Anticivilization*

Your Prosperity Revolution

A prosperity revolution? Neo-Tech self-leaders? Class overthrow? Relentless and uncompromising? Overthrowing the entire parasitical-elite class? Yes. Forward march to the overthrow and unlimited prosperity!

Another revolution of bombs, blood, and tears? Power-seeking revolutionary leaders? Another round of destructions leading to ever more destructions? Socialist, fascist, or world-order "democracy" inspired? Building a new parasitical-elite class? No. Just the opposite.

*All past revolutions required inconsistencies, illegalities, and destructions. But this revolution is unique. It is based on Neo-Tech. And, Neo-Tech requires logical consistency, objective law, and honest productivity.* Neo-Tech upholds objective law by terminating all subjective political policies that harm you, society, and the economy. ...This is your revolution. This revolution will bring you unlimited prosperity.

Your prosperity revolution? When will it happen? What will happen? Who will make it happen? How will it bring you unlimited prosperity?

All past revolutions and class overthrows were bogus or compromised. For, all were fomented so one parasitical group could take power from another parasitical group. All were fomented from false or artificial class conflicts of nationalities, races, religions, political issues, economic levels, or social levels. .

*The Prosperity Revolution is the first and only legitimate class overthrow possible among human beings:* The honest productive class ranging from ditch digger to billionaire entrepreneur will overthrow the parasitical-elite class — a criminal class comprised of destructive politicians and their legions of harmful bureaucrats, armed political-policy enforcers, ego judges, politico prosecutors, corrupt lawyers, dishonest journalists, evil academics, and white-collar-hoax business quislings.

Parasitical elites survive through false power — power gained through deceptive illusions. But, today, with your personal terminator, you can break their illusions to end all false power. ...Right now, with Neo-Tech, you can prosper without limits.

# Chapter 12

# Terminating Evil

You are a hard-working entrepreneur. Starting with $3500, you worked 16 hours a day, seven days a week, for over twenty years to build a medical-research firm. Your life is dedicated to a single goal: develop marketable knowledge leading to the root cause of disease. Marketing various segments of that developing knowledge increasingly provides the keys to understanding and then curing all diseases — including cancer, AIDS, muscular dystrophy, and death itself.

Your only competitor, I & O Research and Writing, was attacked on November 3rd, 1986, by an armed criminal element growing within the IRS. I & O was destroyed through physical violence and looting inflicted by that criminal element. Each level of criminal behavior used by the IRS is identified in the table below:

| Responsibility Level | Criminal Activity | Remedy |
|---|---|---|
| IRS Commissioner | Sanctions and uses criminal activities | Ostracize and prosecute |
| IRS District Directors | Direct criminal activities and destructions | Fire and prosecute |
| IRS Guns-and-Fists Agents | Blindly carry out physical violence and property destructions | Educate and rehabilitate if possible...or fire |
| IRS Seizing Agents | Blindly carry out financial lootings and economic destructions | Educate and rehabilitate if possible...or fire |

133

*Movement II: The Anticivilization*

**10:00PM, April 15**: You have spent the last two weeks, sixteen hours a day, completing the tax paperwork for your company and employees. Along with your accountant and lawyer, you have spent an average of ten weeks each year over the past decade handling all tax matters concerning your company and its twenty-five employees. That means for this decade alone, two years were lost to forced-labor paperwork. And that does not include the irreplaceable time destroyed on paperwork forced by other government bureaucracies and regulatory agencies. ...Because of that growing destruction of time and life, both you and your business can never reach full potential. Thus, you may never reach your goal of delivering the fundamental, unifying cure to all diseases.

That productive time consumed through such forced-labor paperwork diminishes the long-range potential of every person, every trade, every profession, every business. You realize that destruction of the value-producers' time is undermining the future of our economy and society. That time destroyed is even more harmful than the *irrational* taxes the value producers are forced to pay. And, that devastating time destruction serves but one purpose — to expand harmful jobs and power throughout the government. That expansion of harmful jobs and government power, in turn, serves only to expand the parasitical-elite class.

You have struggled long hours at the cost of all personal relationships. You have no time for vacations, leisure, relaxation. That unrelenting struggle is required for meeting the responsibilities to your customers, employees, and company. Without more time, you cannot reach your potential of building a worldwide enterprise — an enterprise providing countless jobs by delivering health, happiness, and prosperity to everyone. You realize that those two years of forced-labor paperwork per decade (like receiving a ten-year prison term for producing competitive values for others and society over a fifty-year career) was the very block of creative time and crucial concentration needed to reach your potential, your goal. ...Such is the destruction inflicted today on every hard-driving value producer with supreme potentials and goals.

Then, you realize the escalation of time-destroying tax complexities backed by harsher and harsher penalties has nothing to do with collecting taxes. Instead, that escalation of destructiveness and penalties has everything to do with increasing bureaucratic control. For, that increasing control over the value producers is how the parasitical-elite class survives — how it creates more and more harmful jobs and power needed to live parasitically.

You now understand how the parasitical elites join with white-collar-hoax executives of stagnant big businesses to prevent competition from the most competent entrepreneurs. You now understand why those elites must malign, destroy, and imprison great value producers — honest but aggressive, tough, often unpopular business-people like Michael Milken and Leona Helmsley who prospered by delivering competitive values to society, thus, threatening the livelihoods of all parasites. By stifling aggressive competition, parasitical elites keep their own harmful livelihoods from being exposed and eliminated.

Also, without that competition, parasitical business quislings can entrench themselves in big businesses. For years, even decades, such pseudo businesspeople can gain unearned wealth and prestige by milking the great accumulations of assets built by genuinely competitive, aggressive value producers of the past. ...Most of those original, heroic value producers came from an age before the creation of armed bureaucracies used to enforce destructive political agendas.

You then think about history's greatest value producers in art, music, science, and business. Despite the many-fold increases in population and technology, we have no more daVincis, Michelangelos, Beethovens, Mozarts, Galileos, Newtons, Hugos, du Ponts, Carnegies, Fords, Einsteins. Why? The reasons can be traced to the destructive effects of an expanding parasitical-elite class methodically draining everyone's time, energy, resources ...and long-range potential. With each passing year, fewer and fewer tender youth can rise to become great value producers. That shrinkage of individual potential reduces or eliminates greatness from all conscious beings.

You realize that increasing armed enforcement of destructive political agendas is designed to support a growing parasitical-elite class not only throughout government and stagnant big businesses, but throughout much of the news media, public education, and the legal profession. You then realize *all* political enforcements involve criminal violations of objective law by armed bureaucracies.

You realize that supreme value producers such as Andrew Carnegie, Florence Nightingale, J. J. Hill, and Henry Ford will not rise again until that criminal class of parasitical elites and their armed bureaucracies are eliminated. Indeed, if living today, every one of those heroic value producers would be in prison with their potentials collapsed. In prison for what? For violating political-agenda "laws" enforced not only by the IRS, but by all the other armed bureaucracies and invasive regulatory agencies cancerously growing today.

As described in Movements II and III of this New-Color Symphony, Neo-Tech and Zon will terminate those evils.

# Chapter 13

# My Termination

Depression hits me as I survey the view. The camp is bitterly uncompromising — its sheer vastness, its images of hopelessness and deprivation. The sight of withered, dying men and shoddy cardboard shelters, along with the endless odor of decay, combine to bring emotions of hatred and abhorrence in all the unfortunate people who live here.

In the distance is the city: a tall, beautiful, magnificent symbol of man's achievement and prosperity. That symbol makes the dichotomy of this land all the more painful. But this has been my home for the past three years. And, deep down, I detest myself and all that I represent. Disgust wells inside me as I think of this place and my failed attempts to rationalize my pathetic existence. Occasionally, in moments of honesty, I stop the rationalizing and grimly accept my fate, knowing that I deserve no better. In recognizing these rare moments of honesty, I find my mood becomes more positive. I almost mistake the mood for happiness. It isn't. I struggle to define the feeling for a few seconds and then stop, fearing that analysis may eliminate it. But the feeling stays, alien yet welcome. Welcome because it helps me face my last few minutes of life.

Death. An obsolete state in today's world. And yet today, the 3rd of November 2003, I will die a hideous and barbaric death. I will be sacrificed, murdered. But

137

strangely, through the actions of my life, I have given my consent to this grotesque act. Again, the cold shock of reality hits me. My mind for once is free of mysticism and dishonesty. How ironic that I have allowed myself to evade honesty for so long, only yielding to it at the end of my miserable existence. My mood becomes reflective as I begin to wonder how I could have prevented this self-loathing and desperate end.

For as long as I can remember, I have succumbed to camouflaged laziness — to wangling values from others rather than earning values. Never have I put forth the effort to create anything of genuine value. Indeed, it is this self-chosen flaw that has sealed my fate, just as that same flaw has sealed the fate of thousands like me around the world. Decades ago, after cheating my way through a prestigious, Ivy-League university, I decided on a career in law and politics. I had no grand plan to improve the world. But I knew the power of politics would be to my advantage. I could use that power to outmaneuver my peers and competitors. For, most blindly believed, at least initially, that politics was benevolent and designed for the good of the people. They rationalized against seeing the big lie. I, without such quixotic limitations, easily used politics to capture a prosperous and prestigious living from the efforts of others. I fostered the big lie to usurp values from productive people. Indeed, my skills of deception and manipulation became highly refined. I made honest value producers feel guilty for any "selfish" gain or accomplishment. It was easy. My technique was simply to blame them for the endless sufferings and injustices we politicians ourselves cause. ...The value producers paid for our pillagings — those suckers paid us to drain them dry.

Within a short time, I was rich, famous, powerful. My

life was easy, and my potential for further success seemed endless. I was single-handedly capable of developing laws and getting them passed. I could control almost anyone or anything...and look like a saint while doing it. I was responsible for legislation that greatly empowered the Drug Enforcement Administration and its armed enforcers. That DEA bureaucracy had no motivation to reduce any drug problem; for, it had no desire to reduce its jobs or power. It didn't matter to us that innocent lives were lost or destroyed through our trampling on individual rights and property rights. We pushed to spend billions upon billions of tax dollars on projects that I knew would never work. But, so what. Through the media, I always looked good to the masses. Indeed, my "War on Drugs" created some of my richest years.

And my soul mates at the IRS? I helped create and expand their armed divisions. I cleared the way for them to rule through fear and destruction. I loved increasing their power. I loved the viciousness of their commissioner. I loved their lawlessness and criminality. We were soul mates. For, through them my power grew.

We politicians and our bureaucrats created a bond of malevolence with *Newsweek*-type journalists. That unified dishonesty let us smear, control, and ruin America's greatest value producers — innocent people like Michael Milken and Leona Helmsley. We giulianied them. ...We almost took over America with me riding high.

Next came the environmental movement. With dishonest journalists and bankrupt professors, we exploited every phony notion conjured up by pseudo environmentalists. Their hate-filled, save-the-earth movement offered a bonanza of opportunities to increase my power. Political correctness became my favorite weapon. We passed regulations

139

controlling or influencing essentially every business. And, because of my power within Congress, almost every special-interest group courted me. I seldom paid for anything. The gifts and privileges were endless. It didn't bother me that the cost of everyday goods, automobiles, and housing increased substantially because of the regulations I created. In essence, I said to hell with the masses. If they have to suffer or pay a higher price, so be it. For, I was gunning for power — the presidency and beyond.

I further increased my power by exploiting the ego-seeking demagoguery of the anti-abortion gangs as well as the Ralph-Nader gangs. Feminists? Gays? Yahoo! With that power, I passed more and more laws telling people what they could and could not do. ...And they did what I told them because my laws were backed by guns and jails. At times, even I could not believe the power I had — the extent to which people could be controlled and manipulated.

The power. I loved the power. It was as if people would fall to their knees before me — I could do no wrong. And the women, they were everywhere. Most were prostitutes, but I never paid for any of them. Sex. Orgy sex, kinky sex, sex of any kind was the order of the day. Gradually, my wife, with the help of alcohol, learned to accept this, not that her feelings or health mattered to me. I came to believe that I was above everyone. It began to seem that such favors and advantages were owed to me. I answered to no one. Indeed, I quickly learned to live with myself; or should I say, to suppress any twinge of self-respect and honesty. For, with the money and power, it was easy to keep going, to keep taking more and more money, more and more power, more and more of everything. My lust for power constantly grew. I could never get enough.

But then it all crumbled with the Prosperity Revolution of the late 90s. That's what caused my downfall. I remember what seemed like the starting point — our destruction of people like Milken and Helmsley. Our atrocities began backfiring when we sadistically flaunted our power on that April-15th tax day. Using subjective laws, ego "justice", dishonest journalists, and a vicious IRS, we snuffed out the unpopular but innocent Helmsleys.

Soon after, we saw our own end coming with the 1994 American elections. Value-producing men and women all over the world began angrily realizing how they were being duped and exploited. ...Our final ploy was the Clinton pirouette of 1996.

Finally, with Neo-Tech echoing around the world through cyberspace, the value producers took control of their own lives, ending the stupidity of their blind obedience to me and all other false authorities. Almost overnight, politicians like me were scorned out of existence: first in Eastern Europe, then in Asia and Africa. In America, it started in those 1994 elections. Then, the whole world woke up to the hoax. Self-sufficient, value-producing men and women suddenly realized they didn't need self-serving politicians giving them inflation, poor economies, and wars. People realized they could control and direct all areas of their lives without a parasitical ruling class. Charismatic political leaders such as myself were finished when the public started scorning us — then started laughing at us. For us, the bottom line to our final campaign was fear — shear terror and panic over losing our livelihoods, our social standing, our power.

Very quickly, once-powerful politicians were ostracized from society. We were no longer able to plunder the values produced by others. And for society, everything began to improve. There were a few initial and minor problems caused by the change, but advancement was rapid. Indeed, genuine free enterprise was the order of the day, not the insidious "free-trade" mercantilism that I, Bush, Clinton, Newt, Dole, and others touted throughout the world. A torrent of jobs were created. The standard of living soared. Poverty and racism disappeared. Third-world wars and starvation ended.

Before being overthrown, my cohorts and I used constant tax increases to force everyone's earnings into our power-boosting schemes. After we were overthrown, people invested their extra earnings into business and technology. ...Trade and science flourished. Unemployment fell to nearly zero. Only the professional social schemers were unemployed. Street crime vanished.

The technological advancements came quickly. Cures for AIDS and cancer came in a matter of months. Soon, one goal captured the focus of the world: Non-aging longevity. The religious and political objections were increasingly being scorned by the once submissive masses. The masses of productive people now demanded wealth, happiness, love, and life itself.

For me, I sat on the sidelines, increasingly feeling pity and hatred for myself. I had known the truth about politics and religion. Yet, I pushed my dishonesties onto the unthinking public. I knew I deserved the fate that awaited me — it was deserved because of the untold lives I had ruined by promoting and enforcing my destructive political policies. ...The loss of prosperity, happiness, love, and life itself caused by my actions was too great to count or imagine. If only I had assumed the responsibility to be honest and to produce values. Had I done this, I could right now be living in that prosperous other world. All the pain and fear I now suffer was avoidable had I been honest. In fact, if I and the others here had only exerted the effort to be honest in taking the responsibility to create values and pay restitution for our crimes, we all could have moved into that sunlit world of prosperity, happiness, and beauty. But now, it is too late for me. Starting over is impossible. Once, in desperation, I even offered myself to a zoo as an extinct humanoid. I thought scientists could study me as a relic of evil. But alas, the wide-scope accounting records of Neo-Tech showed I belonged here.

So that is why I am here — in this nightmare of a camp. I was ostracized like the rest — scorned out of society, laughed out of existence, unwilling to participate in any activity with the producers of the world, unwilling to produce or trade any desirable value.

In the beginning, we had food and supplies, mostly brought by the later arrivals. But eventually those supplies ran out, as did the animals shortly afterward. It was at this point that our very existence became threatened. Survival became the goal. We could no longer steal from the producers. They were now too smart, too organized. Computerized ostracism made hiding or even a nomadic life impossible. Ironically, the only choice we had was to live as before — to live off other people, to live by sacrificing the lives of others to us. So, we took the concept of sacrifice to its logical but horrific conclusion:

Some would have to sacrifice their lives so the rest could survive. That is why I am in this position today. My lot came up. I would now be sacrificed to the remaining few. Death, a fair and just outcome for all that has gone before me. It is with this perverse feeling of justice and inevitability that I console myself while I think of the manner of my death: clubs raining down on my weak, undernourished body, wielded by those remaining few. I imagine their emotions as they rip my limbs apart. They will be content with their meal, their hunger temporarily averted; each will be glad it's not him this time, but each knowing that soon, very soon, it will be. Fear will be the only companion until the bitter end. ...None can escape.

Suddenly, my introspection is broken by the sound of voices. I see my peers clambering over the rubble, weapons in hand, their ragged clothes and starving bodies almost comical, contrasting strikingly to the power and strength of the city visible on the horizon. Although I have accepted this ghastly end, I feel a fleeting desire to run, to escape before they get too close. But where? What is the point? My death is certain whatever I do.

I am aware that I am smiling as they face me. A matter of feet separate us, death seconds away. No words are spoken, but the sound of fear is deafening. My fear. And theirs.

I see the first club being raised high into the air by my own son. My life flashes before me. ...Oh, the millions who suffered just to keep me feeling important! I craved the ultimate — the goal of *every* politician — the power to rule the world. I craved the unearned power to control everyone in every way. For that power, I'd gladly surpass Hitler in destruction. Yes, I'd gladly nuke the world just to have that power. For, I'm not human. I'm a politician. I'm a humanoid.

I feel the first blow. I fall with my diary. I scrawl my last note: *Honesty terminated me.*

144

# Chapter 14
# The Prosperity Revolution

Over two millennia ago, the Greek politician and philosopher Plato established the techniques for hoaxing the public, thus, allowing a parasitical-elite class to rise. Throughout the subsequent centuries, parasitical elites have used Plato-like hoaxes to drain the prosperity that the productive class generates for society. ...Such sacrifice-to-higher-cause hoaxes remained largely unidentified until Neo-Tech unraveled them. Today, Neo-Tech is dissolving those Platonistic elite-class hoaxes. That dissolution of illusions will wash away the parasitical elites along with their higher causes that sacrifice us to them. ...All value producers will then gain their earned prosperity stolen from them and society for 2300 years.

### Human History Approaches Its Greatest Event

As our civilization approaches the year 2000, the greatest event in human history is about to break across our planet. Planet Earth will give birth to a super civilization. Indeed, the whole world is shimmering, ready to reveal a new, previously unknown world. Today, raw and unguided fomentations are bubbling from beneath the seams circling the globe. Those fomentations are from the productive class — those who add more to the economy and society than they take. Those value producers are lashing out independently, without authoritarian leadership. Without guidance, they are driving parasitical elites from their destructive livelihoods, including some of the highest "authorities": politicians, clerics, bureaucrats in America, Europe, and Asia —

145

including elites in America like world-order-dominator George Bush, theocratic-statist William Bennett, and killer-hypocrite Hillary Clinton.

### Blindness of Past Revolutions

Without Neo-Tech, the productive class impotently lashes out at the parasitical elites, never identifying their underlying hoax of sacrificing the workers to the rulers under the facade of helping the needy. Without identifying that hoax, all revolutions eventually fail by perpetuating the very same hoax to often yield new, even more destructive parasitical elites — new breeds of parasitical masters: new breeds of socialist, fascist, communist, theocrat, and world-order elitists.

To eradicate the parasitical-elite class, productive people around the world must have access to Neo-Tech.

### Stop Paying the Parasite-Class Deficits

Who pays for the economic and social deficits created by the parasite class? Someone always has to pay. Until the Neo-Tech Discovery with its wide-scope accounting, the parasitical elites could always delude the productive class into paying their deficits. The parasitical elites have tricked each productive person of the past 23 centuries into supporting their destructive livelihoods.

What hoax could make the productive class continuously pay for those deficits? That hoax as revealed in Plato's *Republic* is to use truth rather than honesty. Ever since, that hoax has tricked the productive class into sacrificing itself to the parasitical elites. The key to perpetuating that hoax is building public-accepted illusions — illusions built by dishonestly twisting truths and facts into limited or false *contexts* acceptable to the public.

146

The Hoax of Using Truth Instead of Honesty[1]

How does that hoax work? It works through *false context*. **Avoiding full context to build false context is the most powerful tool of deception**. For, avoiding full context and building false context leaves honest people ignorant of the "sacrifice the producers to the parasitical elites" hoax.

By limiting or falsifying context, anyone can build *closed systems* of bogus logic to support or rationalize almost any idea or action — such as the rationalizations behind all force-backed organizations like the DEA, FDA, INS, IRS. Through false logic and context, one can create bogus but good-sounding claims or illusions to justify essentially any destructive means to any parasitical end. And each public acceptance of such bogus claims or illusions means the continued hoaxing of value producers into supporting the parasite class.

Once such hoaxes are identified through *full-context* wide-scope accounting, value producers worldwide will rise in irreversible revolution. ...The genuine value producers will stop paying those leech-class deficits forever.

### Irreversible Revolution

*All* parasitical deceptions and illusions are now exposed by the Neo-Tech literature. Thus, through Neo-Tech, the business/working class will rise in the Prosperity Revolution to overthrow the leech class worldwide.

That Overthrow Can Occur Almost Overnight

In December 1989, on CNN satellite news, citizens of the Romanian productive class suddenly saw the false power of their dictator Ceausescu and the rickety hoax

---

[1]See page 327 for explantation of truth versus honesty.

of his parasitical-elite class. In just five days, those citizens unleashed an anger that brought Ceausescu from the height of life-and-death power over all Romanian citizens to his death before a firing squad manned by those same citizens.

### Self-Defense against Criminals and Murderers

Consider the natural dynamics of a valid revolution: What happens when totalitarian oppression and censorship occur? As identified by Thomas Jefferson two centuries ago, overthrow becomes the only *moral* self-defense against the resulting rise of totalitarian criminals. That is why the government should never be allowed to disarm its citizens. By contrast, the *immoral* self-defense against those criminals is to support them in order to "be safe" from their enforcers.

**Neo-Tech Assures Everlasting Peace**
The opportunity for a peaceful overthrow must not be lost. The gun-backed oppression of free press executed against Neo-Tech must be rectified. With unfettered free press, the Prosperity Revolution will vanish the parasitical-elite class without a single incident of physical harm or violence. ...Everyone can then enjoy the unending peace and prosperity available to all conscious beings.

New-Color Symphony
Movement #2

# Chapter 15

# Neo-Tech Resurrects
# The Child of the Universe

### The Child of the Past
### *leads to the*
### Civilization of the Universe

Neo-Tech is fully integrated honesty. Neo-Tech is the natural essence of conscious beings as demonstrated in *every* young child still uncorrupted by dishonesty and irrationality. Through integrated thinking and rational exuberance, every child learns to perceive, talk, and then conceptualize. Every child learns with the certainty of integrated honesty present throughout the Universe. Yet, *every* child loses that certainty through the diseases of dishonesty, irrationality, and mysticism.

The dynamics of Neo-Tech bring back that certainty of fully integrated honesty. Neo-Tech brings everyone back to his or her nature. Neo-Tech resurrects that *Child of the Universe* who sleeps in everyone's soul. ...Fully integrated honesty *is* the nature of every conscious being throughout the Universe.

*Neo-Tech Resurrects the Child of the Universe*

What is Neo-Tech?

Neo-Tech is a matrix of fully integrated honesty and wide-scope accounting. From that matrix comes a certainty about the most effective way to live every aspect of conscious life. Each human being has sought that certainty since mankind became conscious. Indeed, Neo-Tech is the *natural* certainty residing in every conscious being throughout the Universe.

But, on planet Earth, a parasitical-elite class has hidden the objective process of honesty for twenty-three centuries by manipulating subjective *assertions of truth*: Beginning about 300 BC, the philosopher Plato pulled civilization into a cave. He obliterated the individual with his force-backed master-servant collectivism. Plato then crowned the parasitical elites and his philosopher kings with souls of gold.[1] Only they would have the "wisdom" to control, exploit, and drain the productive class: the masses trapped in Plato's cave. Plato relegated to his trapped servants lowly souls of copper and iron.[2]

How did Plato finesse such an outlandish hoax that dominates the Western world to this day? By using the *arbitrariness of truths* to turn reality upside-down, causing a sea of "noble" lies, illusions, deceptions, shadows, doubts, and uncertainties. Such created uncertainties let the parasitical elites rule through dishonesties backed by armed agents of force. By contrast, Neo-Tech eliminates

------

[1]Plato also assigned souls of silver to the obedient armed agents of force serving the golden-souled rulers.

[2]In America, Plato's hoax reached its climax in 1993 with criminal-minded, golden-soul Hillary Rodham Clinton knowing what was best for the health and welfare of the masses with their lowly souls of copper and iron. Through Neo-Tech, the American public broke that hoax in the elections of 1994.

manipulated truths, doubts, uncertainties, out-of-context facts, deceptions, illusions, and gun-backed parasitical "leadership". ...The certainty of Neo-Tech uprights reality and forbids initiatory force against individuals and their property, thus, dooming the parasitical-elite class.

### Certainty Without Omniscience[1]

Reality is relational. Knowledge is contextual and hierarchal. Thus, certainty evolves from Neo-Tech — from fully integrated honesty. By nature, fully integrated honesty is the mechanism for building relational, contextual, hierarchal knowledge. Through fully integrated honesty, we share the same certainty — the same knowledge-building *processes* — enjoyed among all mystic-free civilizations throughout the universe.

---

[1]Title of a lecture by objectivist philosopher Leonard Peikoff.

*Neo-Tech Resurrects the Child of the Universe*

## America Today

America today is at once the greatest and the worst nation on Earth: The greatest by the productivity, well-being, and happiness created by the mightiest host of professional value producers and competent workers in history. The worst by the harm, deprivations, and unhappiness caused by a rapidly expanding parasitical-elite class. That leech class is cannibalizing history's most bountiful trove of earned wealth and created values. ...But, today, everyone can look happily to the future. For, the rising Prosperity Revolution and its army of independent self-leaders will eliminate the parasite class to bring ever growing well-being and happiness to everyone.

155

### Ending the World of Chains

Imagine a world of cruel masters binding to a stake every puppy born — binding every dog for every moment of its life from birth to death to a stake with a short chain. Those dogs during their entire lives would know nothing except a totally bleak, constantly chained life. Thus, they would accept their one-and-only lives being used up and wasted without ever experiencing the joys and well-being possible for all dogs, but experienced by none. Not a single dog would ever experience natural puppy joy, playfulness, or the happy companionship of a loving master. But, imagine if those dogs had the ability to become aware of their chained lives. Imagine what they would feel toward their cruel masters.

Now, consider conscious human beings with almost infinitely more life experiences available to them. Imagine a world of human beings chained to stakes from youth to death. Imagine their lives being used up and wasted solely to support the destructive livelihoods of a few parasitical-elite "masters". ...Imagine the anger that would explode if all those chained beings suddenly discovered that their lives and the lives of a hundred generations before were used up and wasted just to support a handful of parasitical elites.

What will happen when conscious beings on Earth discover the hoax that has kept them chained, used up, and wasted for a hundred generations? The rising anger will push the ostracism matrix everywhere in government, religion, business, and the professions. A relentless army of value producers will then eradicate that parasite class, ending the world of chains forever.

## A World Brightly Lit

Over one hundred years ago, Thomas Edison lit the world with his electric light bulb. For many years, he built his foundation of knowledge. He knew exactly what would happen and exactly how *it* would happen...the *it* being electrically lighting the world. Then, he and his co-workers needed several more years of intense work to find the exact combination to unlock an incandescent bulb with more and more uses until the entire world was lit with electricity.

Using Neo-Tech, which means fully integrated honesty, Frank R. Wallace and his co-workers spent twenty-three years building the foundation of knowledge for intellectually and emotionally lighting the world forever. Today, those co-workers worldwide know exactly what will happen and exactly *how it* will happen...the *how* being cyberspace, the *it* being the vanishing of the parasitical-elite class in resurrecting the Child of the Universe on planet Earth.

# Chapter 16

# Neo-Tech
# Self-Leaders

New-Color Symphony

Movement #2

> *A Single Credo for Neo-Tech Self-Leaders*
> Direct every thought, every discipline, every effort
> toward the overthrow of the parasitical-elite class —
> toward the eradication of every livelihood that harms
> the value producers, the economy, and society.

### Eleven Requisites for Neo-Tech Self-Leaders

1. To recognize that all past revolutions and their class overthrows have been false, compromised, or temporary. Only the Prosperity Revolution that eradicates the parasitical-elite class will permanently empower the productive class.

*The Self-Leader's Goal*

2. The self-leader has but one implacable goal: the unrestricted well-being and happiness of the productive class and all humanity.

3. To accomplish that goal, the parasitical-elite class must be eliminated. How will that be accomplished? By welding the productive class into an ostracism force that is all-subversive toward everything supporting that leech class.

4. Until now, every revolution in history eventually betrayed itself by overthrowing one parasitical-elite class in order to replace it with another. But, the *leaderless* Prosperity Revolution can never impose any form of rule

159

or exploitation on the productive class. For, the single task of the Prosperity Revolution is to eradicate the parasitical elites by eliminating their dishonest illusions, hoaxes, and mysticisms. The revolution will then be over. ...All revolutions will be over forever. Unending prosperity and happiness will reign.

### The Self-Leader's Behavior
5. The self-leader dedicates his or her life toward the uncompromising eradication of the parasitical-elite class.

6. The self-leader breaks all bonds with the world controlled by parasitical elites. Yet, the self-leader infiltrates that world. He or she deals with parasitical elites, increasingly through cyberspace, only to subvert and destroy their corrupt systems more rapidly.

7. The self-leader rejects public opinion and the existing social morality. For the self-leader, morality is everything that advances the overthrow. Immorality is everything that blocks the overthrow.

8. The self-leader not only suppresses all sentimentality, but he or she abandons all private hatred and revenge. Day and night, the self-leader has but one thought, one aim — the merciless overthrow of the parasitical-elite class.

### The Self-Leader's Relationship to Others and Society
9. The degree of friendship, devotion, and obligation toward others is determined solely by the degree they are useful in terminating parasitical elites.

10. A second-degree or third-degree self-leader is one who has not yet totally committed to the elimination of the parasitical-elite class. He or she is part of the common revolution capital to be used for the greatest advantage in advancing the revolution.

11. The self-leader is proven not by his or her words but by the deeds toward advancing the overthrow. The self-leader has no sympathy for the parasitical elites and does not hesitate to undermine their every position. He or she may frequently penetrate any area and live among their world in order to hasten their eradication.

Parasitical elites can be split into several categories. The first category consists of those who are condemned to termination as soon as possible. The second category consists of those who are spared temporarily as being useful for provoking the public into revolution. The third category consists of those liberals and conservatives in high positions of unearned power and influence, various dishonest politicians, and certain harmful bureaucrats, lawyers, and judges. Those parasitical elites can be useful — they can be exploited for advancing the revolution. The fourth category consists of pseudo-leaders who can be useful for a while. But, eventually, parasitical elites in all categories must be terminated.

### The Greatest Event in History

What about other great events in history? Forget them. The emerging Prosperity Revolution is by far history's greatest event. That event will open the way for *all* future advancements toward eternal prosperity and happiness.

161

### Terminating the Parasitical-Elite Class

Independent self-leaders are developing with no leader to follow or obey. They are people who will increasingly carry out missions of subversion against the parasitical-elite class.

So long as self-leaders have no leader to obey, they will steadily multiply and never stop moving forward. For, on learning how to break the hoax of professional parasitism, they will react personally to each parasite who harms or drains society. On their own, in their own ways, they will increasingly subvert the entire parasite class. They will subvert the leeches one by one, relentlessly, until each is driven from his or her bogus career. Especially through the Internet, self-leaders will have no time or energy limits to stop them from eradicating the parasitical-elite class that wastes the lives of everyone. They will have no more compunction about swatting down parasitical elites who exploit society than they have about swatting down mosquitoes that spread disease.

So long as uncensored cyberspace and free expression exists, the Prosperity Revolution will proceed peacefully. Without gun-backed oppression, the overthrow of the parasitical-elite class will be peaceful but uncompromising, total, permanent.

### Seven Waves to Prosperity

1. Plant the root system: Identify and define the problem, the enemy, the solution. ...Completed 1976.

2. Build the foundation: Establish a two-million-word body of literature published in twelve languages with audio, video, art, and music supplements. ...Done 1966-1991.

3. Develop the confrontational phase: Setting self-exposure traps such as the Golden Helmet for neocheaters, professional value destroyers, and the parasitical elites along with their armed enforcers. (Ref: *Politicians and Bureaucrats on Trial,* B & W, 1991) ...Began in 1980. Activated in 1986. Continuing.

4. Carry out and complete the free-press protection phase: Decentralization of publishing activities and literature distribution. Dispersion into independent phantom-bantam companies worldwide. Translate foundation work into twelve languages. Distribute into 156 countries. Those actions protect Neo-Tech publishing activities from being wiped out in further attacks by armed agents in America or in any other country. ...Completed in 1987. Insures a peaceful revolution.

5. Enter the direct confrontational phase: Activate the self-exposure traps for the neocheaters, professional value destroyers, and parasitical elites in government, the courts, business, and the professions. Establish a computerized ostracism matrix that will drive all parasitical elites and their cohorts from their destructive livelihoods. As of 1994, over 2450 parasitical elites, neocheaters, and professional value destroyers have been permanently locked into the Neo-Tech Ostracism Matrix. ...Began in 1990. Continuing.

6. Begin the worldwide revolution-overthrow phase: Move from quiet foundation-building and self-exposure confrontational modes to public-action terminator modes. To begin in 1998.

7. Cyberspace into the future.

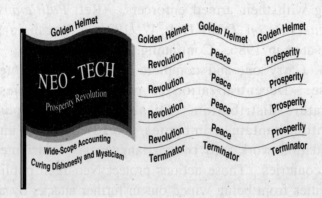

RULES FOR LIMITLESS PROSPERITY

**Rule 1**

No person, group of persons or government may initiate force, threat of force, or fraud against any individual or private property.

**Rule 2**

Force may be morally and legally used only in self-defense against those who violate Rule 1.

**Rule 3**

No exceptions shall exist for Rules 1 and 2.

*Initiation of force, except in self-defense, always leads to destruction and is the opposite of value.*

# CALL TO REVOLUTION

## Preamble

We stand united — the worker, ditch digger, farmer, tradesman, office worker, business person, billionaire entrepreneur — the productive class. Dishonest parasitical elites shall no longer live off our work. They shall no longer exist by deceiving us.

# The Two Points of Revolution
## *The Enemy*
## *The Promise*

| Point One<br>THE ENEMY | The enemy is the parasitical-elite class comprised of harmful politicians, lawyers, judges, prosecutors, bureaucrats, clerics, and other leeches, neocheaters, professional value destroyers, and agents of force. Those people fraudulently live off you. ...They have stolen their livings from you for far too long. |
|---|---|
| Point Two<br>THE PROMISE | We will eliminate the parasitical elites. That ridding of the leech class will yield the unlimited expansion of jobs, prosperity, pride, and security for all honest value producers, their children, and their future generations. |

# WE DEMAND!

We the value-producing workers, entrepreneurs, business people, soldiers, police, youth, students, parish priests, exploited government employees, and suffering unemployed demand the breaking of all deceptions foisted upon us — deceptions that let the parasitical elites drain and harm our lives.

WE SHALL TERMINATE THE PARASITICAL-ELITE CLASS

We shall break the chain that chokes our lives. We shall terminate the parasitical-elite class forever. ...Our march to peace and prosperity begins now!

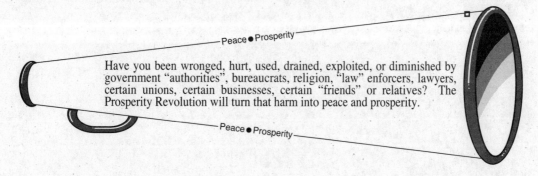

Peace ● Prosperity

Have you been wronged, hurt, used, drained, exploited, or diminished by government "authorities", bureaucrats, religion, "law" enforcers, lawyers, certain unions, certain businesses, certain "friends" or relatives? The Prosperity Revolution will turn that harm into peace and prosperity.

Peace ● Prosperity

4-3/92

# Chapter 17
# Commanding Life
## on
# Planet Earth

### The Final Decade of Earth's Anticivilization

A parasitical-elite class has spawned this upside-down civilization — an irrational civilization that inflicts purposeful harm on conscious beings, their economies, their societies. Parasitical elites today manipulate nearly all politics, many bureaucracies, the legal profession, the courts, public schools, the academe, the news media, religion, entertainment, and certain big businesses. What most of those manipulators represent as the best is really the worst...the *most destructive* — and vice versa.

Be prepared to discover the facts: Jay Gould is the best, Abraham Lincoln is the worst; Leona Helmsley is the best, Eleanor Roosevelt is the worst; Malcolm X is the best, Martin Luther King is the worst; Michael Milken is the best, Rudolph Giuliani is the worst; Florence Nightingale is the best, Hillary Clinton is the worst. ...Indeed, you must first dismiss nearly *everything* that the parasitical-elite class and its news media represent as good and bad in order to command your life on planet Earth toward boundless prosperity.

### What Do the Following Have in Common?

Armed ATF, DEA, IRS agents, force-backed anti-abortionists, jailing of Milken and Helmsley, Jew and Japan bashing, busting Noriega, gay bashing and gay

167

"rights", racism, urban riots, RICO and seizure laws, PETA, political correctness, the DEA, EPA, FDA, INS, IRS, OSHA, formal religion, Greenpeace, evangelism, gun control, Ralph Nader, Fidel Castro, Jesse Jackson, Jesse Helms, Pat Buchanan, white-collar-hoax big-business executives: What do they all have in common?

All of the above are based on economic and social parasitism. They are all backed by professional value destroyers, parasitical elites, envy mongers, and self-righteous neocheaters infesting government, religion, big business, entertainment, the media. By purposely creating problems where none exist, all such parasites end in destroying the very values they pretend to support. Such destructive people must pretend to support values. They must fake compassion and good intentions to survive — to gain false esteem, power, and bogus livelihoods.

They and their supporters comprise a rapidly expanding class of parasitical elites. Today, from survival necessity, they are converging in a final feeding frenzy. They increasingly loot and destroy innocent value producers through despotic "laws": RICO, seizure, and EPA/FDA/FTC/OSHA/SEC-type "laws"...all backed by force along with the irrationalities of ego "justice", fake scientisms, and pressured by escalating deep-pocket litigations. And now, the parasite class fight one another to devour the remains of a vanishing class of genuine job-and-wealth producers.

Indeed, for decades, that escalating class of professional value destroyers has orchestrated libel, slander, and public envy to attack and drain a now decimated, crumbling class of super value producers. Eventually, under various disguised forms of fascist socialism — such as Clinton/Gore/Dole-type, tax-the-producers envynomics

— those converging parasites would drain dry the remaining remnant of super job producers and aggressive entrepreneurs. The demise of those last great value producers would bring annihilations of the world economies and societies. ...But, none of that will happen because of Neo-Tech and the Prosperity Revolution that started in 1994.

# Chapter 18

# What is the Illuminati? What is Zon?

> **The Illuminati**
> has its origins in the biblical Abraham who smashed the idols four millennia ago in establishing the existence of only one reality.

Ever hear of the Illuminati? For the past two centuries, they have been condemned by nationalistic governments and mystical religions. How about the Bilderbergers, the Club of Rome, the Council on Foreign Relations, the Trilateral Commission? They are semi-secret organizations that for the past several decades have been linked to one-world conspiracy theories. Consider the controlling influences behind those worldwide organizations — businessmen, such as today's quiet businessman David Rockefeller. He, for example, is seldom seen or mentioned in the mainstream media. But, he is hysterically attacked as the epitome of evil by the ultra-conservative media, the nationalistic-populist media, and the religious-right media. Yet, David Rockefeller is among the world's most moral, clear-thinking, responsible people.

### The Illuminati Protocols
This chapter refers to the early Illuminati protocols — the master plan for worldwide control first formulated over two centuries ago by leading European bankers and businessmen. Essentially anyone reading the protocols

171

alone and out of context would view them as one of the most evil plots ever devised. Yet, on reading those very same protocols in the context of wide-scope accountability, one will realize the men responsible for those protocols were among the most moral, clear-thinking, responsible people who ever lived on this planet. Moreover, through Zon, today's Illuminati can make everyone on Earth rich and happy.

### Making the Illuminati Serve You

Zon will far surpass the goal of the Illuminati. By understanding Zon, the Illuminati and their organizations will be at your service — providing you with limitless wealth.

### Business-Controlled Master Plans

Business-controlled master plans underlie all actions controlling the creation of long-term prosperity and happiness. Two such master plans or protocols operate on planet Earth: (1) the closed-system Illuminati protocols developed in Europe over two centuries ago, and (2) the evolving, open-ended Zon protocols that began developing in early 1992 and reflected in the American elections of 1994. Today, Zon is replacing the Illuminati's master plan. With Zon, the world will soar in cyberspace beyond the Illuminati's plan for worldwide prosperity. For, Zon delivers eternal happiness with limitless wealth to all conscious beings.

The Illuminati, from its founding protocols forged in the mid-18th century by Adam Weishaupt and Albert Pike, have nearly completed their noble goal of undermining and eliminating the twin instruments of irrationality and destruction on this planet: (1) forced-backed nationalist governments, and (2) fraud-backed mystical religions.

*What is the Illuminati?   What is Zon?*

Now, after two centuries, that goal will not only be achieved but far surpassed, perhaps as early as 2001AD. How?   By replacing the established, seemingly violent Illuminati protocols with the newly evolving, peaceful Zon protocols as deduced from the original, 176-page *Cassandra's Secret* manuscript developed in 1993.   The specific Zon protocols will be ready for public use before 2001AD.   But, first, one must understand the goal and protocols of the original Illuminati as described below:

The Illuminati's Business Plan
for
Depoliticizing Planet Earth

Since the late 1700s, essentially all public reporting and exposés of the secretive Illuminati have been rabidly negative.   Most such reports and exposés emanate from paranoid conspiracy theories presented in populist, nationalistic, or right-wing religious publications.   All such reports and exposés present the Illuminati and their protocols as diabolically evil.   Modern-day exposés especially rail at the Illuminati's tools used to undermine public respect for political-agenda laws, irrational traditions, and predatory institutions.   The Illuminati work to undermine public support of the parasitical-elite class...a destructive class that survives through politically and religiously ruled governments.

The modern-day tools of the Illuminati include international organizations such as the Trilateral Commission, the Council on Foreign Relations, the Bilderbergers, the Club of Rome, and the outdated Freemasons.   In addition to high-profile parasitical elites, those organizations comprise the most-influential, low-profile businesspeople throughout the world.   Still, they

173

are all simply tools masterfully maneuvered into advancing the Illuminati's goal.

Many members of those organizations are sincere value producers; others are power-seeking parasites. Yet, all effectively serve the Illuminati's pretended goal of worldwide political and economic cooperation. Beneath that goal, however, lies the Illuminati's real goal: break the institutions that support this destructive anticivilization.

To understand the Illuminati, one must understand their poker-playing modus operandi. The Illuminati perfected the shrewdest poker-playing stratagems imaginable — analogous to those stratagems revealed in Frank R. Wallace's *Advanced Concepts of Poker*, first published in 1968. After 21 printings, plus additional printings by Crown Publishing and Warner Books, Wallace withdrew that book from print in 1986 in favor of the evolving Neo-Tech literature.

Consider the following stratagem by the Illuminati: To most effectively achieve their goal, they knew their real targets for termination must remain concealed for as long as possible. Because of their world-wide influences, the Illuminati also realized that, over time, information about their work and goal would leak to the public, despite their influence over the world news media. Thus, the Illuminati planted ruses in their protocols that would invite hysterical criticism of them and their satellite organizations. By promoting hysteria against themselves, criticisms would lose credibility, preventing any effective effort to block or retard their progress.

For example, the Illuminati realized their secret protocols would eventually be publicly revealed. Thus, they drafted their Protocols to conceal their real agenda. They made their Protocols to appear as a Jewish or Zionist plot for placing all human beings under one-world tyrannical rule. They floated a poker-ploy hoax document titled *The Protocols of the Learned Elders of Zion.* Throughout that document, they shrewdly planted a Jewish slur word for Gentiles to describe their targets — the *goyim.*

That strategy has worked brilliantly for two centuries: All exposés or attacks on the Illuminati turn into strident accusations about being evil socialistic, communistic, Jewish, Zionist, satanic, or Luciferin plots for world domination. Thus, all exposés and attacks have ultimately been dismissed as paranoid anti-Semitic, Jew baiting, racist, or religious-right paranoia — exactly what the Illuminati intended.[1] ...Incidentally, from their origin to modern day, many among the Illuminati are Jewish. But, they are moral Jewish businessmen, not socialists or Zionists seeking world domination. Indeed, the Illuminati are ingenious "poker players" who orchestrate criticisms of them to advance their goal.

The Illuminati especially utilize their poker strategies in wielding influence from their toolbox of international organizations. Those organizations comprise the world's leading businesspeople, politicians, journalists, publishers, bankers, industrialists, military leaders, and other influential people used to advance a one-world agenda. But, that agenda conceals the real goal fully known only to the Illuminati. That goal is to undermine and eliminate the institutions supporting parasitical elites.

What gave the Illuminati businessmen their overwhelming power and success for the past two centuries? The answer lies in their ability to create genuine values and jobs for society, *combined* with an unshakable moral responsibility to bring growing

---

[1]A good example of how this strategy works is found in the April, 1995, *Reader's Digest* article titled, "This Lie Will Not Die".

175

prosperity to all conscious beings on this planet. Their moral foundation, however, was based on knowledge limited to this closed, irrational anticivilization. Thus, for them, the only possible way to preserve and then flourish human consciousness on Earth was to eliminate, by whatever means necessary, the institutions that support this anticivilization and its parasitical-elite propagators. ...But, means cannot justify the ends — morally...and ultimately, practically. Zon, by contrast, functions through the consistently sound principle of fully integrated honesty. Thus, Zon solves such dilemmas by delivering practical, objectively moral solutions free of force and violence.

Zon replaces the moral justification for violence upon which the Illuminati have stood since their institution-breaking role in the 1793 French Revolution. ...Today, Zon has replaced that justification with a moral foundation that *peacefully* elevates the wealth and happiness of *all* conscious beings throughout time and existence. That moral base stands on integrated honesty, productive effort, wide-scope accounting, objective law, and the Golden-Helmet dynamics as detailed in the Appendix at the end of this manuscript.

The institution-breaking accomplishments of the Illuminati along with their one-world organizations such as the Bilderbergers and the Trilateral Commission provide an advanced position from which the Civilization of the Universe can envelop this planet while peacefully vanishing the anticivilization and its manipulators.

With the discovery of Zon, the keys to prosperity are found in (1) originating conscious actions from Civilization-of-the-Universe perspectives and (2) recognizing that anticivilization perspectives are unreal. In that way, harmful aspects of the anticivilization are

*What is the Illuminati? What is Zon?*

dismissed and ultimately vanished. Also, in that way, the two-century-old Illuminati dynamics of using deceit and force to undermine those elements supporting the anticivilization are replaced by the honest, peaceful Zon dynamics.

### The Most Moral Men on Earth

Without the concepts of white-hat neocheating and advanced poker strategy combined with Neo-Tech, anyone who reads the Illuminati protocols[1] will come to the same conclusion: Those protocols are the epitome of evil. But on understanding neocheating and the concepts of poker along with Neo-Tech and Cassandra's Secret, one comes to the exact opposite conclusion: The Illuminati protocols reflect the most responsible and moral forces on Earth — forces designed to bring wealth and happiness to our world by breaking the institutions and racisms that support this parasitically drained, death-oriented anticivilization.

As identified in the *Neo-Tech Discovery*, the original Illuminati also realized that honest business dynamics are what sustain and advance conscious life. Thus, those business dynamics are the only source of genuine, life-enhancing power among conscious beings. Indeed, only competitive value-and-job producers hold real power — the ultimate power to control not only current events but future events on planet Earth.

Until the original 18th-century Illuminati, no value-and-job producer understood the draining hoaxes and illusions of the parasitical elites. From Plato's time, a ruling leech class has built and propagated an anticivilization with the single purpose of sustaining their own harmful livelihoods by draining the productive class.

---

[1]*The 18th-Century Illuminati Protocols*, 32 pages, Zon Association (1994).

177

*New-Color Symphony*
*Movement #2*

## Movement II: The Anticivilization

The Illuminati discovered that they, not kings, popes, tyrants, sultans, or other parasitical elites hold the power to control and direct society. On that realization, those original Illuminati, most of whom were powerful businessmen and bankers, moved with confidence to eliminate the parasitical elites by relentlessly pitting those leeches and their institutions against each other. That dynamic caused the world populations to increasingly lose confidence in politics, nationalistic governments, mystical religions, and their parasitical leaders.

*Schindler's List*, the factual story of German businessman Oskar Schindler in the 1940s, illustrates how even at the evilest depths of this anticivilization, the value-and-job producer is the *only* person with genuine power and love...even midst humanoids who live by guns and mass murder. Only businessman Schindler, for example, could walk through the bloody mud of the Holocaust without soiling his soul, his compassion, his respect for human life. Only job-producing Schindler had the power, moral character, and strength to reach into the depths of this anticivilization to save conscious beings from the destruction and death wrought by its humanoid propagators.

Extrapolate the metaphor of businessman Schindler into the advanced technologies among the Civilization of the universe. One will then recognize that honest businesspeople with their limitless valuation of conscious beings are the real saviors of everyone in existence. Only such value-and-job producers have the power, responsibility, and love to never let perish the supreme value throughout the universe — conscious life, including conscious human beings on planet Earth. ...The

178

competitive, value-and-job producing businessperson eternally preserves and advances all conscious life.

The Illuminati originally comprised the few most efficacious businessmen in Europe.  The original Illuminati rejected parasites holding false or life-draining power.  Indeed, none of the Illuminati were kings, tyrants, politicians, lawyers, religionists, entertainers, writers, or orators.  Instead, they were quiet businessmen and bankers — they were among the world's most potent creators of life-sustaining values and jobs.

The Illuminati's relentless work has always been directed toward saving the future generations of conscious beings from destruction by the institutionalized irrationality woven throughout this anticivilization.  The Illuminati's goal has been to free conscious beings from the tribal mentalities that make possible criminal societies: parasitical governments, socialism, fascism, the welfare state, and mystical religions.

The Illuminati sought a world in which its citizens valued their fellow citizens not by social status, wealth, nationality, race, or religion, but by what each did to competitively benefit others and society.

For 250 years, playing the most ingenious poker game in history, the Illuminati have brought much of the world close to their goal of ending 3000 years of unnecessary suffering and death inflicted on all populations of Earth — inflicted by parasitical humanoids through their criminal institutions. ...Finally, today, the newly arrived Zon dynamics will not only peacefully achieve but far surpass the noble goal of the Illuminati.

179

*Movement II: The Anticivilization*

Chapter 35 publicly identifies the meaning beneath the Illuminati protocols[1], their master plan, their one-world organizations...and the resulting future for all on planet Earth through Zon.[2]

---

[1]What is the source of those Protocols? In 1906, the British Museum in London received a copy of the Illuminati Protocols written in Russian. Those secret Protocols were probably translated into Russian sometime after 1850 from the original German language Protocols, which first appeared in Bavaria during the late 18th century. Parts of the Protocols were used by Maurice Joly in his 1864 satire, *Dialogue in Hell Between Machiavelli and Montesquieu*. In the early 20th century, British journalist Victor Marsden translated the Protocols into English. His translations were finally issued by the British Publishing Society in 1921 (Ref: Des Griffith, *Fourth Reich of the Rich*). ...Metaphor or real, those Protocols express the Illuminati strategy.

[2]The Illuminati's goal has always been to replace the destructive forces of monarchism, nationalism, religion with the productive dynamics of business. Toward that goal, Neo-Tech/Zonpower adds (1) free-market dynamics for societal decisions plus (2) the essentialness of working-class individuals. For, such working-class individuals are disconnected from the elite class, which is intellectually indoctrinated into closed-circle visions of nature. Thus, non indoctrinated workers have retained their childhood capacities for fully integrated honesty — for wide-scope viewings of nature. While vision-controlled elites, specialists, and philosophers — including most Objectivists — have lost their capacities for fully integrated honesty.

Indeed, the honest, wide-scope views of nature by the working class will lead the mass advance of mankind into a rational civilization — into the Civilization of the Universe. ...Such ability to see nature as it is by non Establishment individuals — an ability lost by the indoctrinated elites — was first identified by Georg Büchner (1813-1837) in his path-breaking drama *Woyzech*.

*What is the Illuminati?   What is Zon?*

---

**The Neo-Tech Trojan Horse**

Over the years, the Neo-Tech/Illuminati dynamic has evolved into today's *Zonpower*. This 200-year-old dynamic is increasingly undermining false, harmful authorities throughout governments and religions worldwide. The Neo-Tech/Illuminati dynamic has been the hidden force beneath the collapse of communism in Eastern Europe and America's coming sea change first reflected in its Neo-Tech inspired 1994 elections.

The seventh and final cyberspace stage of Neo-Tech/Zonpower — the public phase — will activate sometime before 2001 with the Internet distribution of the *Zonpower Protocols*...the Trojan-Horse penetration of Neo-Tech into the heart of the Establishment in America and worldwide.

---

181

# Chapter 19

# Dumping Goy Politics

## Reality and Objective Law

The *real* physical world resides in a beautiful symmetry of rationality embodied by the objective laws of nature. Philosophers and scientists throughout the ages have striven to discover the ultimate nature and symmetry of existence. For 24 centuries, great minds have opened one door after another, solved one deep mystery of nature after another, only to discover whole new and deeper symmetries hiding beneath the ever evolving forces within the unchanging laws of nature. That long history started with the postulating of atoms and led to the discovery of gravity, electromagnetism, and relativity. Those great minds ranged from Democritus to Newton, to Faraday, to Einstein...to Nobel laureate Leon Lederman, the pre-eminent experimental physicist who in his book *The God Particle* (Houghton Mifflin, 1993) metaphorically named the ultimate nature of existence, the "God Particle"[1].

Are we opening the final door that reveals what lies beyond the "God Particle"? Will we find at last the elegantly simple, beautiful force with no beginning or ending, lying beneath and above the "God Particle"? ...Beneath and above that particle lie Gravity Units of symmetrical, subspatial geometries controlled by conscious beings free of *goy* politics.

## Nonreality and Subjective Law

The *unreal* political world of the goyim hides the ugly irrationality embodied by subjective laws born of politics. Those laws are used to gain destructive livelihoods and

[1]Technically the "God Particle" is called by physicists the Higgs boson.

183

criminal power in an anticivilization. As one discovers the secret of goy politics, one discovers that *everything* arising from their political-agenda laws involves the criminal acquisition of power — from Caligula to Hitler to the Clintons.[1]

From Caligula's socio-fascist Rome to Hitler's socio-fascist Germany to Clinton's socio-fascist America, all destructive laws arise from political processes — processes designed to create self-serving political powers. Today, as in Germany 60 years ago, the process of law making is driven by politics rather than by objective reality. Indeed, most law today arises from arbitrary political correctness in a drum roll of force-backed, political-agenda laws.

Such laws are turning political tools like the FDA, DEA, BATF, IRS, INS, EPA into armed bureaucracies that destroy life, liberty, and society. Also, consider today's politicization of health care, food diets, abortion, religion, education, the media, drugs, tobacco, law enforcement, criminal prosecution, immigration, the environment. Decisions in those areas should have nothing to do with politics, but everything to do with objective reality. ...What irrational forces underlie the politicization of human action?

The forces underlying harmful political actions are camouflaged dishonesty, hidden laziness, and parasitical livelihoods. From those forces, a purposeful destructiveness arises. That destructiveness is used to gain unearned values at the expense of the competitive value

---

[1]Consider the following: How many Platos, Alexander the Greats, Caesars, Caligulas, Attilas, Genghis Khans, Tamerlanes, Napoleons, Lincolns, Lenins, Woodrow Wilsons, Mussolinis, Hitlers, FDRs, Stalins, Maos, Pol Pots, Castros, Idi Amins, Bokassas, Khomeinis, Pengs, Saddams, Nicolae and Elena Ceausescus, Bill and Hillary Clintons were Jews? None.

184

producers. Beneath those forces lie irrationality and insanity — the schizophrenia of parasitism. Contrary to common belief, schizophrenia is not a split or a dual personality, which is just one of many possible *symptoms* of schizophrenia. Rather, the disease of schizophrenia is the **detachment of consciousness from objective reality**, which is required to convert one's precious life into a worthless life — into a parasite.

The tripartite cure for insanity in government is simple: depoliticize, depoliticize, depoliticize. ...How will that cure arise? Consider the following Illuminati article of June, 1994. This article was published five months before the first Neo-Tech domino fell in America — five months before America's November 1994 elections:

---

Quote

### Obsoleting the Criminal-Minded Goyim

The most valuable goyim of the '90s are the Clintons. Faking compassion and using demagoguery, they foment envy against the productive class — against the competitive producers of wealth and jobs. They move forward, feeding on individual rights and competitive value production. Their grand wealth-distribution schemes consume the source of earned values and well-being. Their illegal schemes, epitomized by bribes paid through fraudulent cattle straddles, undermine the public's sense of justice and honesty in America.

Moreover, the fake compassion of the Clintons is nothing more than a three-step, **Toll-Booth Compassion:** Personally they give nothing that genuinely benefits humanity or society. Instead, (1) they collect self-aggrandizing tolls by forcing the productive class into financing an expanding parasitical-elite class through

---

political-agenda laws. (2) They extract financial tolls by draining the only real benefactors of the needy and society: the competitive value-and-job producers. And, then (3) they hit the jackpot with a neocheating livelihood replete with force-backed political power and praise-filled honors.

Such three-step, toll-booth compassion includes larceny and homicide. For example: "If this law saves one life, then it's worth it" type demagoguery hides the 100 or 1000 or million innocent victims hurt, impoverished, or killed directly or indirectly through such sound-good, toll-booth-compassion laws — laws that subjugate society through force-back control, destruction, and death.

Seeking unearned power through virtuoso lying, the Clintons emasculate America's long-term security and prosperity for their own power. Left unchecked, such criminal agendas would destroy health care, individual rights, the economy, and maybe start a war to avoid impeachment or jail. ...The point is that such goy politicians will loot, kill, and build violent hatred toward government just to sustain their destructive livelihoods.

Indeed, today, political predators are crushing property rights, plundering the middle class, and widening the gap between the rich and poor. How? By escalating police-state regulations, destructive political-agenda laws, and irrational taxes enforced by armed bureaucrats. Those irrationalities decimate small businesses, the middle class, and individual self-reliance: the three originators of all productive jobs and earned profits. ...Why do political predators purposely advance economic and social harms? So they can live in power and praise without themselves having to produce competitive values.

The above dynamics are ironically in accord with the

186

original Illuminati Protocols. Those master-plan protocols use Machiavellian political tools such as the Clintons who have Dostoyevsky-type criminal minds[1]. For, such goy tools cause calamities that undermine planet Earth's twin institutions of parasitical evil: nationalistic governments and organized religions...institutions that subjugate the well-being of society to the parasitical-elite class.

Obsoleting such criminal-minded goyim will halt the government's parasitical feeding on the value-producing class. A depoliticized civilization will bring eternal peace and prosperity. Indeed, the laws among the Civilization of the Universe arise from the divine grace embodied in every conscious being who has ever existed. From those laws arise genuine prosperity and romantic happiness.

End Quote

## Seven-Point Agenda
### for
### America's First Neo-Tech President

1. Immediately pardon and free *all* individuals convicted of "crimes" created from political-agenda laws.
2. Veto and work to repeal *every* political-agenda law passed by Congress, current and past.
3. Work to end all welfare and social programs. Replace Clintonian toll-booth compassion with genuine compassion.
4. Privatize Social Security. Fully meet all obligations by paying back with market-rate interest *all* monies paid into Social Security. Finance this payback by

---

[1]Such deluded "superior beings" think their "greatness" puts them above objective law, including murder...as Raskolnikov in Dostoyevsky's *Crime and Punishment*, as the OJs and the Clintons in today's America.

187

selling government businesses and assets.

5. Permit government activity only in areas of national defense, *local* police, and the courts to protect individual and property rights. Eliminate all other force-backed government powers and programs. Disarm all bureaucrats, not honest citizens.

6. Replace the irrational, envy-based income tax with a rational consumption tax — a national sales tax. Then phase out sales taxes with major budget reductions, market-rate user fees, and the Golden Helmet. Use revenues only for national defense and the protection of individuals and their property from objective crime.

7. Help redeemable parasitical elites, neocheaters, and professional value destroyers convert to competitive value producers in the Civilization of the Universe.

Accomplishing the above seven points are the natural results of upholding the Constitution of the Universe:

---

### CONSTITUTION OF THE UNIVERSE
#### Article 1
No person, group of persons or government may initiate force, threat of force, or fraud against any individual's self or property.
#### Article 2
Force may be morally and legally used only in self-defense against those who violate Article 1.
#### Article 3
No exceptions shall exist for Articles 1 and 2.

---

Even Plato recognized that the creation of a civilization is the "victory of persuasion over force...". By contrast, an anticivilization means the use of force over persuasion.

*Dumping Goy Politics*

### A "Heaven-Sent" Illuminati Tool — The Clintons

Why did most of the news media and much of the public keep accepting the automatic lies and covering up objective crimes by Bill Clinton when he became the President of the United States? What about his Machiavellian drive to escape his crimes and stay in office? Through his and his wife's dishonest camouflages, the Clintons strove to ravage health care and society itself.

*All* genuine jobs, prosperity, and happiness in *any* society come from honest individuals and businesses. President Clinton had no concept of honesty or business. He never held or created a productive job in his adult life. He lived parasitically by (1) demagogically attacking and then (2) self-righteously draining those who produce the jobs and values upon which society depends. ...How did such a person become accepted by a population as its leader?

Congenial President Clinton was the most skilled, manipulative public speaker since Hitler, Churchill, and FDR.[1] His gross lack of principles combined with his supreme ability to sound good let him project sincerity and good intentions with persuasive skills, perhaps surpassing any neocheater living today. Pandering to envy and parasitism, both Clintons "compassionately" extracted maximum capital from the producers to buy votes and power from the public.

Indeed, Bill and Hillary Clinton were a key find for the Illuminati to accomplish their two-century goal of eliminating public acceptance of the parasitical-elite class draining the value producers and society. ...Ultimately, the pernicious Clintons will bring prosperity and happiness to America. How will that happen when all their actions

---

[1]Clinton crafted words as Shakespeare's Iago crafted words — crafted to put poisons in everyone's ear, potions that make evil actions seem good and good actions seem evil.

189

worked to decay individual rights, property rights, self-responsibility, self-respect, objective law, crime prevention, education, health care, and the economy?

The "Heaven-Sent" President Clinton was a professional Elmer Gantry who exuded sincerity, confidence, and compassion upon all whom he exploited for his own unearned livelihood and selfish ego. But, just as he built his illusions to the height of public deceptions, the fully integrated honesty of Neo-Tech began breaking those illusions in 1994. As the illusions break, such parasitical elites and their supporting casts will be scorned or prosecuted out of existence. The dishonest concepts of politics will be increasingly trashed along with political-agenda laws and ego-"justice" systems. At that point, America will be ready for depoliticization and decriminalization.

The Clintonian criminal mind is woven throughout goy politics — woven throughout the White House, the Congress, the legal profession, the media, and the celebrity industry. Above-the-law/beat-the-law, golfing-partners OJ/Clinton hid their criminal minds behind sharp lawyers, automatic lying, public adulation, and wonderful-person facades. Such persons will always coldly, arrogantly rationalize themselves out of criminal acts ranging from wife batterings and WACO killings to the destruction of public health, safety, and the economy.

The fully integrated honesty of Neo-Tech and the wide-scope accounting of the Golden Helmet combined with the coming cyber-information revolution will eliminate dishonest politicians, their harmful political-agenda laws, and their armed agents of force.

Why is victory on Earth possible over the next few years? Consider the survival tool of purposely destructive politicians and government officials. Their survival tool is the public acceptance of armed bureaucracies made possible by deception and irrationality. To perpetuate those dishonesties, the fully integrated honesty of Neo-Tech and the wide-scope accounting of the Golden Helmet must be hidden from the population by force, coercion, and fraud. Yet, every act to suppress the Neo-Tech/Golden-Helmet, including the jailing of its author and publisher, enhances public movements toward its all-revealing, depoliticization dynamic.

Through cyberspace, Golden-Helmet economies backed by nonpolitical *objective* law could be in place by 2001 AD or earlier. ...Prosperity and happiness will then be available for everyone and society.

# Chapter 20

# The End of Chaos

xn=rx(1-x)

# The Start of Guiltless Wealth

The best-selling book *Chaos* by James Gleick (Penguin, 1988) popularized the vogue theories of chaos in nature. Yet, the universal laws of physics and nature preclude chaos throughout time, space, and existence. Still, *appearances* of chaos are everywhere in nature, especially through irregular shapes called fractals.[1] Yet, with enough knowledge, one discovers genuine chaos does not exist, save one exception. Indeed, the law of identity along with cause and effect holds everywhere, barring that one exception.

That one exception proves the rule that *conscious beings* control existence. They control existence with a system designed for eternal survival through limitless value creation. Ironically, that universal rule can be proven by its one exception — the existence of parasitical humanoids who survive by creating chaos. They survive by creating chaos in draining economies and harming societies. With facades of good intentions and compassion, those humanoids inflict cruel harm and fraud on society. Such inflictions of harm and fraud are epitomized by Clinton-type *Envynomics*. Those media-hyped economics of envy

---

[1]Nonlinear, far-from-equilibrium situations bifurcate into potentially endless fractals in any finite space. That process, in turn, self-organizes into patterns of near-perfect order reaching over potentially limitless distances. ...Thus evolves not only the cosmos and life itself but all productive work, creative thinking...and limitless knowledge.

193

would drain dry all productive dynamics remaining in America. Indeed, envynomics provide the only means of survival left for the expanding clique of parasitical elites and their value-destroying bureaucracies.

Throughout the vast universe, genuine chaos exists only in an unnatural anticivilization such as now dominates planet Earth. Its humanoid rulers survive through parasitisms requiring force, threat of force, and fraud. They live by criminally draining those who produce values for society. ...But, all such parasites and their unnatural anticivilization will vanish on exposure to the natural Civilization of the Universe, which is now coming to planet Earth.

Beyond that exception found in an anticivilization, no fundamental chaos exists in nature, from quarks to universes. Still, *appearances* of chaos exist everywhere. However, investigation into every such appearance reveals either a transitory illusion in nature or a purposely *productive* act by conscious beings creating higher degrees of order as explained in the coming paragraphs. ...Remember, conscious beings are the grand-unifying force and controlling dimension of existence as identified in Part I on Neo-Tech Physics and discussed in Part III on the Civilization of the Universe.

Only purposely *destructive* acts of parasitical humanoids create genuine chaos. Wars, for example, create bona fide chaos that has no connection to the conscious-controlled flow of value production throughout the universe. Still, chaos-causing humanoids and their anticivilizations, such as infesting planet Earth today, comprise only a minute, transitory part of the universe. Thus, the effect of humanoid chaos on the universe is essentially nil and undetectable, except at its tiny moment of flickering existence in time and space. By contrast, the *appearances* of chaos created by increasing values are not chaos at all. Instead, all such appearances are revealed as conscious creations of ordered values...even in Earth's anticivilization.

Look at a sleek, high-powered sports car from a little distance. One perceives beautiful symmetry and order — the antithesis of chaos. But, approach that car and throw open its engine hood — chaos! To the nonmechanic, all appears so asymmetrical and complex — a chaos of wires and tubes among a myriad of varied shapes and parts. Yet, pursue knowledge to the function and essence of that complex engine. One then perceives a supreme beauty of conscious symmetry and purposeful order.

Now, open a computer — chaos! But again, what looks like chaos — a jumble of electronics, chips, and circuitry — is actually a wondrous display of conscious-made order delivering mega values to the economy and society. Such value synergies arise from assembling widely varied components into functional designs. ...In ruling existence, conscious beings create ever increasing values that appear as chaos to the more primitive, unknowledgeable eye.

Look into the night sky. Sense the smooth, orderly-rotating universe. Now, using radio and optical telescopes combined with computers and astrophysics, throw open the curtain of the Universe for a closer look. Chaos! All looks so asymmetrical, jumbled, complex. A seemingly random scattering of all kinds of stars, galaxies, black holes, pulsars, quasars, nebulas, novas, particles, waves, rays, forces, fields, energies, and masses. Yet, on pursuing the widest knowledge and integrations, one discovers the orderly purpose in such "chaos". With that discovery on

New-Color Symphony
Movement #2

195

planet Earth, everyone will grasp the purpose and value of the universe as orchestrated by conscious beings with much more-advanced knowledge. Then, finally, everyone on Earth can share that same beneficial control over time, space, and existence.

In Earth's anticivilization, the more conscious beings evolve, the more chaos appears to the unknowledgeable eye and primitive mind: Consider the obvious order of building blocks comprising the ancient pyramids. Compare the ordered symmetry of those pyramids to the apparent chaos perceived by the unknowledgeable, primitive eye gazing for the first time upon the jumbled maze of Manhattan's skyline. Compare the ordered drumbeats by early African or Indian tribes to the apparent chaos filling the untrained, primitive ear listening for the first time to full-blast Wagnerian opera. Compare the easy reading of simple parables throughout the Bible to the apparent chaos meeting the unintegrated mind perusing for the first time *Zonpower* — a communiqué from beyond the stars.

Now, trace the societal values within the symmetries of ancient human achievements — from the ordered pyramids advancing to the more chaotic-appearing but astronomically valuable Stonehenge. Then advance through the ages toward the ever increasing complexities of conscious achievements — toward ever greater economic and social values. Finally, consider the combined volumes of *Neo-Tech* and *Zonpower*: Their 1400 plus pages combine the widest-scope integrations possible — from subatomic particles to the universe of universes, from eternal time to eternal mass and energy, from romantic love to non-aging longevity with ever increasing prosperity and happiness for *all* conscious beings. From that integrated combination, an epiphany appears — the epiphany for the Civilization of the Universe enveloping planet Earth by the turn of this century.

A single artist can paint or sculpt a perfect-ordered auto engine or computer circuitry in a matter of hours or days. But consider what is required to actually invent, develop, and then competitively mass-produce complex, jumbled-appearing engines or computers that deliver ever increasing values to others, the economy, and society. Such mega achievements require countless man-*years* of efforts — heroic efforts combining fully integrated honesty with brilliantly integrated efforts.

In other words, only competitive business dynamics deliver ever increasing values to all peoples, in all societies, at all times. For, those dynamics follow the preordained paths of honesty and effort required for genuine job-and-value production. Only that value production delivers prosperity and happiness to conscious life. ...Such value production often appears as increasing chaos to the more primitive mind and eye. But, the opposite is *always* the fact. For, all genuine values consist of conscious minds molding existence into ordered benefits for everyone and society.

On studying *Zonpower*, one finds a widely varied communiqué. Yet, on integration of these varied writings, *Zonpower* unveils the supreme order for *all* existence. How? By contextually interweaving the general with specifics, theory with practice, abstraction with fact, history with the contemporary...and the future. Thus evolves a spiralling synergy of many parts — a synergy that crunches millions of words and countless volumes into this single communiqué.

## Movement II: The Anticivilization

*Zonpower* reveals to citizens of Earth their most important discovery: the Civilization of the Universe. Through the condensation of such wide-scope integrations arises the Neo-Tech/Zonpower discovery. And, from that discovery will come the first-and-final product of existence: the Civilization of the Universe.

Through the Neo-Tech/Zonpower discovery, that ultimate product can now arise on planet Earth. The Civilization of the Universe will start overtaking the parasitical-elite class, perhaps as early as the 2000 AD elections. Indeed, the Civilization of the Universe will vanish Earth's anticivilization and free everyone from unnatural deprivations, unhappiness, and death. For, those evils were wrought by chaos producers ranging from subhuman thieves and murderers to humanoid parasitical elites and professional value destroyers. ...The Civilization of the Universe will vanish those chaos generators to bring everyone on Earth the gifts of eternal life, prosperity, and happiness — gifts that are natural to all citizens of the universe.

---

### Universal Communication

Zon talks to every conscious being in the universe. But, with the disease of mysticism and prior to the Neo-Tech/Zonpower discovery, no one on Earth could hear Zon.

Can conscious beings receive the eternal communications from the Civilization of the Universe? Because of mysticism and its anticivilization, no one on Earth could hear such communications. Through Gravity Units, universal communication is possible within the laws of physics as identified in Movements I and III. As Movements I and III further identify, we can cue our "ears" for such communication. Then, on curing the integration-blocking disease of irrationality, everyone on Earth can receive the eternal benefits available from the Civilization of the Universe.

---

# MOVEMENT III

# The Civilization of the Universe

*The Solution*

## The Anticivilization

How long?  How long?
How long must we suffocate and die
in a web of dishonesty?
Was John Milton[1] right?
Was the happy fall needed to gain paradise?

Dante proposed that conscious beings could escape evil and be born into a new life: "Incipit Vita Nova". Jonathan Swift sensed the all-pervasive anticivilization, about which he bitterly railed.  Voltaire recognized the futility of life in the anticivilization in his totally pessimistic antitheodicy, *Candide*.  None knew of the Zon escape — the escape to the Civilization of the Universe.

---

### Escaping Dishonesty

A four-dimensional field or matrix of dishonesty pervades the anticivilization.  Our every thought, our every movement during every instant becomes entangled in that matrix of dishonesty.   In its omnipresent smog, we *all* suffocate and die. ...With the forthcoming *Quantum Crossings* and *Zon Protocols*, we can escape that dishonesty — escape that matrix of entrapment, diminishment, and death.  How?  By using Zonpower to quantum jump from the anticivilization to the Civilization of the Universe.

---

### The Civilization of the Universe
Free.  Free at last.  Free forever.

---

[1]John Milton and many other writers with radical ideas that contradicted the Establishment were politically imprisoned, some almost losing their lives: Dante imprisoned 2 years, Marco Polo imprisoned 6 years, Cervantes imprisoned, John Milton imprisoned and nearly executed, John Bunyan imprisoned 12 years, Daniel Defoe imprisoned, pilloried, barely escaped the gallows, Voltaire imprisoned in the Bastille twice, Fyodor Dostoyevsky twice imprisoned for many years, nearly executed.  And, remember, nonwriter Socrates was executed simply for discussing his ideas. ...The author of Neo-Tech was politically imprisoned after barely escaping being shot by armed federal agents who beat, kicked, and hospitalized his personal editor.

# Chapter 21

# Finding Tomorrow's Golden World

On February 13, 1991, the federal prosecutor turned to the jury and revealed the man on trial was from another world. The prosecutor told the jury that this one man was the most dangerous man. For, this one man threatened the status quo — threatened to upright this upside down world in which we live.

Did you ever feel that a better world must exist somewhere: an eternally benevolent world of honesty, integrity, rationality, peace, security...a world of limitless excitement and prosperity? Where is that other world? How do we get there? Has any explorer yet discovered that world? Does he have a map for us? Is that our world of the future?

In 1980, a scout, a pioneer, a Columbus set sail into the unknown to discover a new world. All but a handful of people thought he was going to sail off the edge of this flat, irrational society. He did not. Instead, he returned wearing a Golden Helmet. He had discovered that better world. He discovered our world of tomorrow. He discovered a world of eternal rationality, peace, and prosperity. ...He discovered the Civilization of the Universe.

On returning from his long voyage, that man was imprisoned. Why? That man as a scientist ventured beyond the known to discover the route to Shangrila. He returned with a map. And, that map shows all men and women the route to a rational world of opportunity, growth, and unimaginable riches. Once started on that route, one can no longer accept the political criminalities, social insanities, and economic destructions overtaking today's world. Thus, for bringing you the map that leads to the Civilization of the Universe, that man was imprisoned by the threatened parasitical-elite class. But, now, with his map and Zonpower, nothing can stop those on Earth from discovering that golden world of eternal prosperity and happiness...starting now!

MS

# Chapter 22
# Cassandra's Secret

---

**13th Century BC**

Cassandra of Troy possessed the power to predict the future with perfect accuracy. But, no one would believe her. Thus, everyone missed collecting unlimited riches.

---

Imagine you are speaking to an old friend. Suddenly, you realize every conversation, every action, no matter how seemingly reasonable or conventional, is geared toward losing values and happiness. Suddenly, you see this mundane, completely "normal" experience as bizarrely unnatural. Then, you see nearly everyone and all society as hypnotized losers in a civilization that is irrational, insane.

Next, you realize your own children, your spouse, your own self, all who seem to live with some success and happiness, are equally trapped in an insane civilization that always moves toward loss and death. You then realize the only realm of consistent sanity and increasing values lies within value-producing professions and market-driven businesses.

### Breaking the Hypnotic Spell

First, you must choose to live in either a sane civilization or an insane one. An insane civilization is one that shrinks backward into irrationality. In today's anticivilization, essentially all thinking and knowledge are hypnotically contracting into ever more narrow ranges that

205

increasingly block honesty and understanding. Thus, communication and actions are becoming increasingly politically correct, irrational, and harmfully split from reality...increasingly schizophrenic.

Hypnotic irrationality grips Earth's anticivilization. That spreading irrationality yields a decaying system in which increasing entropy brings decreasing order and increasing strife. That, in turn, brings declining job-and-value creation. Thus, whenever irrationality prevails, time must be *redefined* as running backward toward increasing ignorance, poverty, and entropy.

With consciousness as the controlling force of existence, the arrow of time in physics is reversed and must be redefined: In an open and eternally evolving universe, time flows forward toward decreasing entropy (increasing order) as controlled by productive conscious actions, *not* toward increasing entropy (decreasing order) as controlled by nonconscious actions or destructive conscious actions.

In a naturally evolving civilization with decreasing entropy (increasing order and harmony), competitive value production constantly expands. Thus, with rationality prevailing, time runs forward toward expanding knowledge, prosperity, and *decreasing* entropy.

Various aspects of this time-and-energy flow throughout the cosmos are observationally and experimentally demonstrated by electromagnetic-plasma cosmology — a cosmology first identified by Nobel laureate Hannes Alfvén — backed by Nobel laureates de Broglie, Schrödinger, and Prigogine — then advanced by Eric J. Lerner in his popular book, *The Big Bang Never Happened* (Vantage Books, 1992).

Now comes the real discovery: You discover what

*everyone* on Earth fears, including yourself. You discover what *no one* on Earth wants, including yourself. You discover how anyone on Earth can become rich, powerful, happy — quickly, guiltlessly, eternally. Yet, only with great concentration and effort do you break your hypnotic paralysis enough to barely open the easy-turning spigot to limitless riches.

Something seems paradoxical or upside down about the above paragraph, especially when restated as follows: Everyone on Earth, including you, *fears and shuns* that which brings exciting riches and romantic happiness!

On learning Cassandra's Secret, you will understand the above statement. You will view reality from wider dimensions. You will understand this anticivilization. You will see the invisible hypnotic state in which everyone on Earth loses the values of life. You will then awaken to win everything — fabulous riches and happiness while benefiting everyone and society. You will discover what Zonpower is; you will discover that Zon is you. ...Those who do not rise to understand Cassandra's Secret will remain asleep in malignant irrationality, steadily losing their lives and happiness.

### You Control Reality

Cassandra's Secret vanishes irrationalities and mysticisms, ranging from the false concepts of a finite existence and the singularity big-bang creation of the universe to the criminal concepts of socialized collectivism and political-agenda laws backed by ego "justice". ...Cassandra's Secret operates from two directions: (1) it vanishes irrational illusions, (2) it reveals objective reality. Now, consider the following two points:

1. ***You* can Vanish Irrationality**: From the widest-

scope knowledge possible, Cassandra's Secret interweaves the essences of science, reality, business, and human consciousness to reveal a stunningly benevolent and bountiful civilization — a civilization 180° different from the one in which we all live. That endlessly rich civilization is available now — easily available to any conscious being on Earth who realizes the impotent nothingness of *all* irrationalities, mysticisms, and insanities.

Today, the disease of irrationality infests everyone on Earth. Cassandra's Secret reveals how by stepping into the Civilization of the Universe, you cure that disease — you vanish irrationality into its nothingness.

2. *You* **are the Controlling, Fixed Center of Existence**: Human consciousness is eternal. It has always been a fixed part of existence as demonstrated in Chapter 6. Indeed, human consciousness *is* the prime mover of existence.

The above statement implies nothing mystical about consciousness. Cassandra's Secret is not at all about new-age ideas, pantheistic Eastern mysticism, or some abstract "universal consciousness". It is about the limitless power of *your own* down-to-earth consciousness. Moreover, you must understand that consciousness can never *create* reality or existence.[1] Any claim that consciousness creates reality or existence is mystical. For, any such claim contradicts the nature of both consciousness and existence. ...Existence was not created. Existence simply exists as eternally evolving fields of matter and energy. Existence *cannot not* exist.

---

[1] However, consciousness can and does control the modes of existence such as matter, energy, and spacetime geometries to evolve new modes of existence, including new universes.

Indeed, consciousness is the sole ***integrator and controller*** of existence. Thus, consciousness is the prime mover of existence. Ever wider scopes of integrations unleash the limitless power of human consciousness. By contrast, irrationalities and mysticisms are diseases of human consciousness that truncate the power to integrate reality. For, integration of reality can never move beyond any point of irrationality or mysticism. By curing irrationality comes (1) ever growing knowledge of existence, (2) ever growing control of existence, and (3) ever growing prosperity and happiness.

Newton's absolute physics, Einstein's relativistic physics, and Bohr's quantum physics are reconciled by the ever widening knowledge generated from human consciousness free of mysticisms and irrationalities. Indeed, existence is controlled to eternally provide ever wider, integrated knowledge and riches for every conscious being. In other words, your consciousness *is* the fixed center and ultimate controller of existence.

\* \* \*

Cassandra's Secret comprises the widest-scope integration with reality to yield accurate predictions of the future. Cassandra's Secret is based on observed facts, scientific research, and direct experience combined with inductive and deductive reasoning ranging from well-demonstrated theory and objective law to speculative hypotheses moving toward rejection or confirmation.

But, Cassandra's Secret is in no way dependent on recognition or approval by anyone, much less the Establishment. For, the anticivilization Establishment is irrelevant to evolving knowledge and progress. Moreover,

New-Color Symphony
Movement #3

the fully integrated honesty and wide-scope integrations of Cassandra's Secret will ultimately end all bogus livelihoods — all livelihoods arising from professional value destroyers corrupting today's political, legal, scientific, and educational systems.

The ideas revealed by Cassandra's Secret are now propagating through worldwide networks, beyond the reach of oppressive "authorities" and their gun-backed political agendas. Neo-Tech spreads independently of the Establishment media and academe. The key is Neo-Tech publications — free cyberspace publications combined with low-cost newsprint publications in twelve languages mass distributed by worldwide mailings from many countries.

The certitude arising from Cassandra's Secret quietly spreads from those Neo-Tech publications to the populations throughout the world. Nothing can stop that certitude from spreading in print and through cyberspace. The revelations of Cassandra's Secret will bring honest, rational people eternal prosperity and happiness.

# Chapter 23
# Ultimate Wealth Lurks
## within
# Cassandra's Secret

Undreamt wealth can be gained by controlling the power underlying the universe: Zonpower *is* the universal symmetry that underpins Cassandra's Secret. The power of Zon controls existence at *all* scales. ...Hidden beneath everyone's consciousness flows Zonpower — a mighty river of wealth creation. That power is available to you now: through Cassandra's Secret, through the supersymmetry of Zonpower.

### Born Free

Born free of the irrationalities propagating Earth's anticivilization, all young children hold the power of Zon. They are citizens of the universe. But, quickly, every child becomes trapped in a bizarrely irrational civilization created by parasitical elites...humanoids who have lost their humanity. Those humanoids must trap and blind every child. Why? To assure the future survival of humanoids. For, they survive by parasitically draining productive adults who have been blinded since youth by illusions, deception, and force.

### Trapped

This humanoid-created anticivilization blinds and then corrupts its children. This corruption is force fed into the

211

mind of every child. While unknowingly holding the power of the universe, children lack the knowledge to protect their minds. Thus, before they can learn to use their power, they are inflicted with painfully destructive illusions built on contradictions and irrationalities. Those illusions damage the minds of children and block Zonpower from their consciousness.

How have such harms corrupted everyone on Earth for the past three millennia? To live "comfortably" in this life-draining anticivilization, one must increasingly invest in the harmful illusions of the anticivilization — one must sink to a lower social dimension. From that restricted dimension, no one can discover his or her natural power.

Until now, Zonpower has remained submerged in everyone's natural consciousness. Yet, Zonpower functions in parallel but hidden ways beneath one's clouded consciousness — clouded since childhood. The resulting becloudings provided the hypnotic set up for lifetime exploitations of every value producer by the parasitical elites. Indeed, that exploitive set up is the illusion of "needing to get along in or approval from" this irrational anticivilization hypnotically conjured up by the parasitical-elite "leaders".

Cassandra's Secret breaks that hypnotic spell. Once that spell is broken, one can freely access Zonpower to control existence and predict the future to gain limitless wealth.

## Leaving the World of Losers

Perhaps certain children become autistic because they will not let their minds be corrupted by the anticivilization. Perhaps they withdraw from all relationships with their environment and cease their journeys into this corrupt, unreal world. But with that withdrawal, they also cease their personal development.

In 1993, Public Broadcasting aired a documentary about an acclaimed "breakthrough" from Australia for treating autistic children by a technique called "facilitated communication". Almost the entire professional field involved in treating and caring for autistic children embraced that technique, around which they began boosting their careers. Many millions of tax dollars poured into this "breakthrough", including costly physical facilities, such as at Syracuse University, dedicated to "facilitated communication".

Yet, any objective observation of that technique, even by those unfamiliar with autism, will immediately reveal the technique as bogus. Not only does the technique lack rationality, but has no correspondence with any law of nature, science, or logic. Anyone can easily recognize the technique as nothing more than a Ouija board spelling out the subliminal thoughts of the professional therapists "treating" autistic children. This technique is not only worthless but is harmful toward those children and their families.

How could an entire field of professionals invest their lives and build their careers on something so obviously bogus and harmful to everyone? When people start investing their lives into bogus activities, they increasingly rationalize — blindly and without limits — to continue expanding their harmful investments and livelihoods.

Thus lies the mechanism through which almost everyone on Earth invests his or her life into this bogus civilization. Once that investment is made in the anticivilization, one is trapped within its all-encompassing, irrationality.

Everyone in this anticivilization starts with the mind

213

of an innocent, defenseless child.  That mind is then tortured with painful contradictions and dishonesties until the child either becomes autistic by withdrawing from this irrational civilization or becomes "normal" by surrendering to its destructive irrationalities.

The more irrational and destructive people become, the more they will destroy and kill to maintain their harmful careers in the anticivilization.  Additionally, the more people invest in destructive careers, the less competent they become in producing competitive values that genuinely benefit others and society.

Most politicians — along with many bureaucrats, lawyers, judges, and stagnant big-business executives — abolish their human nature by becoming parasites.  As professional parasites, they become camouflaged criminals, even murderers, rationalizing behind shields of subjective political-agenda "law" and corrupt ego "justice".

Consider Hitler, Mao, Castro, Pol Pot, and the Clintons.  Each increasingly invested their lives into becoming clandestine parasites until they could no longer support themselves by competitively producing values for others and society.  Thus, such people *must* become increasingly open criminals and killers to survive.

With Zonpower, you leave all such losers behind forever.

## Becoming Zon

Heathcliff, the main character of Emily Brontë's[1] novel *Wuthering Heights,* reflects the hidden, parallel consciousness that flows in every human being. Heathcliff is portrayed as the epitome of a nasty, evil man.  Yet, even in him, the nature of human consciousness surfaces to reveal nobility and good.  Likewise, both the heroes

---

[1]She died too young at 30 as did her author sister Anne at 29.

and villains created by the great novelist Victor Hugo
reveal the underlying human power and nobility that flow
independently of the meanness and irrationalities
controlling this unnatural anticivilization.

The nobility and good of human character are revealed
at times in everyone, except in humanoids who have
destroyed their human nature. Indeed, nobility and good
are revealed spontaneously, in greater or lesser degrees,
throughout the life of every conscious being. Now, today,
the limitless potential of one's childhood can be fulfilled
through Zonpower. At the same time, anyone can tap
Cassandra's Secret to emasculate and vanish the harmful
consequences of this anticivilization.

## Conclusion

Through Cassandra's Secret, you will break the
hypnotic spell of this anticivilization. You will discover
how Zonpower puffs away the harms propagated by
parasitical elites. Zonpower lifts *you* toward wealth —
guiltless wealth for you and society, wealth that flows
from super-wide integrations of knowledge. In your
hands, you hold the widest-scope knowledge ever unveiled
on planet Earth — the knowledge of Zonpower.

From *Zonpower*, you gain an entirely new way to view
yourself, your life, and all existence. You will then be
poised to capture eternal life. From Zonpower, you will
seize iron-grip control and a confident certitude that brings
everlasting youth, riches, and romantic love.

# Chapter 24

# Zon Speaks

"In this anticivilization dominating planet Earth, only young children hold the power of the universe. For, they are innocent and pure: free of the irrationality disease called mysticism. During their brief mystic-free period, children live among the Civilization of the Universe. They hold the limitless yet unlearned power of the universe — Zonpower. But all children are dependent on their parents and teachers for acquiring initial knowledge. Thus, parents and teachers are responsible for infecting and debilitating the minds of their children with deadly irrationality — with the integration-blocking disease of mysticism.

"The minds of such children are manipulated and twisted into grotesque dishonesties ranging from accepting parental irrationalities and mystical religions to accepting the politically correct insanities and destructive actions of harmful 'teachers', 'authorities', and 'leaders'. Thus, children are dragged into Earth's irrational, Plato-enslaved anticivilization to lose their potential for eternal growth and happiness.

"Upon accepting an irrational civilization as normal, a closed bubble of mysticism forms around each child. Each such closed bubble assumes its own wobbly size and shape to accommodate the dishonesties, inner logic, and rationalizations required to live 'normally' in an irrational civilization. *In such a bubble, one can never squarely stand on reality. Therefore, one never has real strength or power. One is never anchored in objective reality, but is always trapped in illusions.* Thus, one never even

217

glimpses his or her potential. Floating in a mystical bubble, often upside down, one can never experience the Civilization of the Universe with its limitless power and wealth.

"Today, all citizens of Earth's anticivilization live in such bubbles, floating detached from reality and the universe. Those bubbles are easily pushed around in directions that support false authorities backed by their armed agents of force. Those false authorities lack any real power to produce genuine values for themselves and others. Such parasites survive by manipulating both the dishonesties of mysticism and the evils of force. They learn how to manipulate or force *everyone's* bubble of mysticism into supporting their own destructive lives.

"Indeed, every person living in this anticivilization is trapped within his or her own bubble, never to gain eternal prosperity and happiness. Thus, everyone on Earth sooner or later stagnates and dies. By contrast, in the rational Civilization of the Universe, stagnation or death of any conscious being is the ultimate loss, the ultimate tragedy, the ultimate irrationality. ...Thus, stagnation and death have long ago been cured or eliminated from the Civilization of the Universe.

"Until today, no one on Earth realized that conscious beings never need to live in an anticivilization. For, an anticivilization is unreal — created entirely from illusions and hoaxes by parasitical 'leaders'. Those false leaders live as they have for three millennia: by enforcing fraudulent political agendas in order to control and, thus, live off the value producers.

"But, today, through Neo-Tech, all value producers on planet Earth can begin to recognize the Civilization of the Universe. That recognition begins the journey into fully integrated honesty. That honesty, in turn, will begin to dissolve the bubble of mysticism. When the bubble finally breaks, one lands upright, feet firmly planted in reality. From that position, one commands reality, never again threatened or manipulated by illusions. From that position, one captures Zonpower with its limitless excitement and prosperity.

"The most remarkable feature about Zonpower and the Civilization of the Universe is that to become Zon and achieve limitless prosperity requires *nothing* remarkable. Zon and the Civilization of the Universe are open to all honest people, no matter what their intellectual or physical attributes.

"Once one breaks his or her bubble of mysticism, the unreal anticivilization is revealed as nothing — as a nightmare of illusions. That person then becomes a Citizen of the Universe. That person captures the limitless power of eternity. That person becomes Zon!"

*Civilization of the Universe, 1993*

New-Color Symphony

Movement #3

# Chapter 25

# Are You Zon?
# What Is Zonpower?

> You are chained to an anticivilization
> But Zonpower breaks those chains to let you capture
> Boundless wealth, romantic love, and happiness

### The Power of Zon

You are thunderstruck. You have discovered the source of unlimited wealth. You have discovered how to leave the boring anticivilization of planet Earth for a civilization of boundless life, excitement, wealth, and romantic love. How did you make that discovery?

Sitting before a mirror, you have just interviewed an ordinary-appearing human being. But, that person is not a citizen of this world. Sitting before you, talking as a physical being, that person is a citizen of an all-powerful civilization — the Civilization of the Universe. With powers beyond what Earth citizens could ever imagine, that person is called Zon. To those among Earth's stagnant civilization, Zon has powers wondrous beyond description.

A UFO has landed? An alien from space? A supernatural being? Or other such mystical wonder? No, nothing mystical or supernatural. Yet, in Earth's tribalistic anticivilization, the powers of Zon seem infinitely wondrous. Still, Zon is starkly in the here and now, standing before everyone on planet Earth. For, Zon exists just as you and everyone else.

221

## Movement III:  The Civilization of the Universe

From where did Zon come?  What can and will Zon do for you?  How can you gain Zon's power?  Can you become Zon?  Are you already Zon?

Zon was born on planet Earth.  By five years of age, that child escaped Earth's anticivilization to experience the all-powerful Civilization of the Universe.  During that escape, he held universal power — a power greater than held by any adult on Earth.  But, not until many years later, decades later, did he rediscover that power.  He then realized that every conscious child two to six years old likewise escapes Earth's anticivilization to experience the power of the universe.  Yet, *every* child forgets that experience as he or she is inexorably drawn into Earth's irrational, mind-crippling anticivilization.

A rare, perhaps one-in-a-trillion combination of ordinary circumstances let an ordinary person escape Earth's anticivilization.  He then returned to construct a map for all conscious people to rediscover the all-powerful Civilization of the Universe.  Today, by using that map, any conscious being can vanish the illusions of this anticivilization to boom into a civilization of limitless power, wealth, and life.

Thus, today, one can finally become free of the life-destroying humanoids infesting planet Earth.  Zonpower offers everyone the key to vanish this anticivilization beset with parasitical elites, their illusions, their hoaxes. ...Zonpower will eventually bring everyone into the endlessly exciting Civilization of the Universe.

### The Origins of Earth's Irrational Civilization
As babies first start becoming conscious, perhaps around two years of age, they automatically become citizens of the universe with omnipotent yet unlearned and

222

unrealized powers over all life and existence.[1]  But, before they can realize those unlimited powers, all young children are relentlessly, remorselessly drawn into Earth's irrational anticivilization.  This unnatural anticivilization could not evolve until man's bicameral mind invented consciousness about 3000 years ago as described in Chapter 28.  With that event, man's nature-organized automatic mind jumped to a much superior, man-organized conscious mind.

About a half millennia after that jump, man's newly conscious mind became infected with irrationality, which is an integration-blocking disease analogous to the immune-blocking disease of AIDS.  The result was a fatal condition known as Plato's disease.  Named after its historical originator, Plato's disease breaks down rationality — the mind's defense mechanism against integration-breaking illusions. ...Without consistent rationality, such illusions allow purposeful destructions, exploitations, poverty, unhappiness, suffering, disease, envy, evil, and death itself seem a natural part of life.

Thus, illusion-infected consciousness creates economically stupid, war-like civilizations that continuously collapse on themselves into black-hole anomalies.  Irrationality is the disease that causes certain human beings to mutate into parasites or humanoids programed to harm conscious life and society.  Those mutants survive by feeding off and draining value-producing human beings.  That constant, parasitical drain leaves innocent people in chains — increasingly unfulfilled and eventually dead.

_____

[1]Babies do not grow old; they grow toward knowledge and power. After becoming infected with irrationality, however, everyone grows old and dies.

*Movement III: The Civilization of the Universe*

### Zon's Escape — Your Escape

How did one conscious person on planet Earth escape its unnatural anticivilization? How did that one ordinary person as an adult rediscover the rational Civilization of the Universe? How can that person deliver to you boundless power and prosperity?

In answering those questions, you too can capture Zonpower. You can have the power of Zon. You can become Zon.

### Zonpower is Waiting for You

You can acquire Zonpower by going to the origin of Earth's anticivilization. At that origin, one discovers the exit. ...Prior to that discovery, no adult could leave this anticivilization ruled by parasitical elites and their armed agents of force.

Until the Zonpower discovery in 1992, every person on Earth was embedded in this dead-end anticivilization. Every person's thinking process was corrupted by parasitical "leaders" in government, education, journalism, entertainment, and big business. Every person's logic was undermined by illusions and hoaxes from those professional parasites. Indeed, to live off the efforts of others, all parasitical elites *must undermine logic* with look-good illusions and rip-off hoaxes. As a result, everyone on planet Earth suffers incalculable losses.

But now, today, you too can leave that anticivilization. *Immediately upon leaving, you will experience the greatest mind empowerment possible for conscious beings. You will suddenly dominate life and control the future.* Moreover, you will be among the first in history to acquire knowledge beyond this anticivilization. You will capture ever expanding knowledge from the all-powerful

224

*Are You Zon? What is Zonpower?*

Civilization of the Universe — you will capture Zonpower for unlimited life, wealth, and happiness.

By understanding the charts on the next three pages, you can begin eliminating those who harm and drain your life — those who chain your life to a stake, those who keep you in a mystical bubble.

225

Chart 1

| Vanish Purposely Harmful People (parasitical-elite value destroyers) | Uphold Naturally Beneficial People (economic value-and-job producers) |
|---|---|
| *State of Being:* Diseased, ridiculous, unfocused, destructive, ignoble Self-corrupted, malevolent minds; ciphers, uncompetitive Degenerated their natural minds, unintegrated word spouters Metaphysically dishonest, clownish, guilty, unhappy Entropy-increasing humanoids. Penis collapsors | *State of Being:* Healthy, important, focused, productive, noble Self-made, benevolent minds; infinites, competitive Developed their natural minds, integrated thinkers Metaphysically honest, serious, innocent, happy Entropy-decreasing human beings. Penis erectors |
| *Archetypes:* Most politicians; many lawyers, bureaucrats, and journalists; all business quislings, socialists, fascists, nihilists, criminals, armed agents of force, political entrepreneurs | *Archetypes:* Blue-collar workers, farmers, job-creating business-people, laborers, byte heads, defenders of property rights, nurses, postal workers, firemen, defense soldiers, market entrepreneurs |
| **Examples** *Historical:* Plato, Alexander the Great, Julius Caesar, Caligula, Genghis Khan, Kant, Hegel, Alexander Hamilton, Napoleon, Lincoln, Woodrow Wilson, John M. Keynes, John Dewey, Lenin, Hitler, FDR, LBJ, Mao, Ayatollah Khomeini  *Current:* Fidel Castro, Li Peng, Rudolph Giuliani, William Bennett, Newsweek-type journalists, purposely destructive politicians and bureaucrats, money-mad lawyers and doctors, dishonest professors and journalists | **Examples** *Historical:* Thales, Socrates, Aquinas, Bruno, Galileo, Spinoza, Newton, Jefferson, Darwin, Mark Twain, Andrew Carnegie, Jay Gould, J.J. Hill, Edison, Henry Ford, Einstein, Maria Montessori, Walt Disney, Ray Kroc, Sam Walton  *Current:* Jonas Salk, Steven Jobs, Soichiro Honda, Michael Milken, Dershowitz, Leona Helmsley, Bill Gates, honest writers and editors, blue-collar workers, local police-men, value-producing housewives and teachers, entrepreneurs |
| *Survival Dynamics:* Survival depends on draining values from others, obscuring objective law, and implementing ego "justice" to control and drain the value producers. | *Survival Dynamics:* Survival depends on producing competitive values for others and upholding objective law. The result is expanding prosperity, happiness, and justice for everyone. |
| *Potentials:* Drainers of human life, the economy, and society. Destroyers of earned property, happiness, economies, and civilization. | *Potentials:* Enhancers of human life, the economy, and society. Builders of assets, economies, and civilization. |
| *Action Toward:* Identify, dishonor, ostracize, vanish. Forget them. | *Action Toward:* Identify, honor, uphold, multiply. Remember them. |
| *End their Current State of:* Being dishonestly glorified and praised. Reject JFK's *Profiles in Courage.* They are nothing. Remove their images and names from stamps, money, monuments, streets, buildings. Replace them with honest value-and-job producers. | *End their Current State of:* Being ignored, mocked, slandered, scorned, envied, plundered, even jailed and killed. They are everything. Praise and uphold value-and-job producing business people and risk-taking entrepreneurs. They are the real heroes. |

226

Chart 2

# Discover the Power of Zon

Code: − = Economic and social harms inflicted on society
+ = Economic and social benefits produced for society

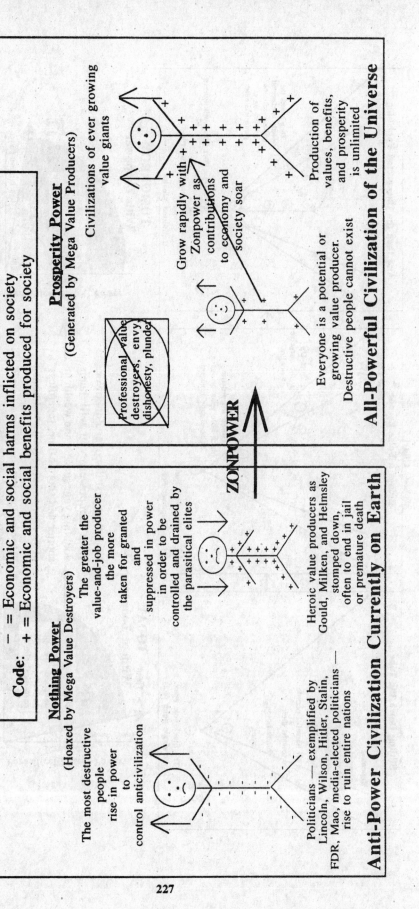

### Prosperity Power
(Generated by Mega Value Producers)

Civilizations of ever growing value giants

Grow rapidly with Zonpower as contributions to economy and society soar

Professional value destroyers, envy, dishonesty, plunder

Production of values, benefits, and prosperity is unlimited

Everyone is a potential or growing value producer. Destructive people cannot exist

**All-Powerful Civilization of the Universe**

ZONPOWER

### Nothing Power
(Hoaxed by Mega Value Destroyers)

The greater the value-and-job producer the more taken for granted and suppressed in power in order to be controlled and drained by the parasitical elites

Heroic value producers as Gould, Milken, and Helmsley stomped down, often to end in jail or premature death

The most destructive people rise in power to control anticivilization

Politicians — exemplified by Lincoln, Wilson, Hitler, Stalin, FDR, Mao, media-elected politicians — rise to ruin entire nations

**Anti-Power Civilization Currently on Earth**

New-Color Symphony

Movement #3

227

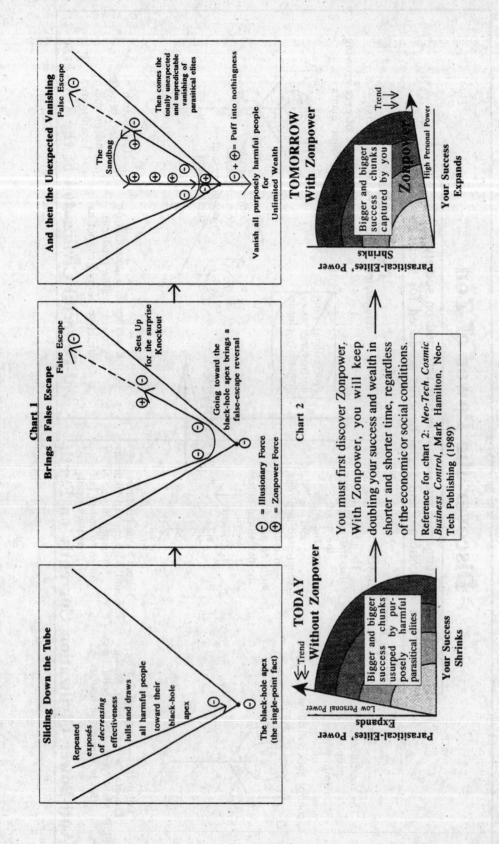

## Chart 1

### Sliding Down the Tube

Repeated exposés
of decreasing
effectiveness
lulls and draws
all harmful people
toward their
black-hole
apex

The black-hole apex
(the single-point fact)

### Brings a False Escape

False Escape

Sets Up
for the surprise
Knockout

Going toward the
black-hole apex brings a
false-escape reversal

$\ominus$ = Illusionary Force
$\oplus$ = Zonpower Force

### And then the Unexpected Vanishing

False Escape

Then comes the
totally unexpected
unpredictable
vanishing of
parasitical elites

The Sandbag

$\ominus + \oplus$ = Puff into nothingness

Vanish all purposely harmful people
for
Unlimited Wealth

## Chart 2

You must first discover Zonpower.
With Zonpower, you will keep
doubling your success and wealth in
shorter and shorter time, regardless
of the economic or social conditions.

Reference for chart 2: *Neo-Tech Cosmic
Business Control*, Mark Hamilton, Neo-
Tech Publishing (1989)

### TODAY
### Without Zonpower

Trend

Parasitical-Elites' Power
Expands

Low Personal Power

Bigger and bigger
success chunks
usurped by pur-
posely harmful
parasitical elites

Your Success
Shrinks

### TOMORROW
### With Zonpower

Trend

Parasitical-Elites' Power
Shrinks

Zonpower

Bigger and bigger
success chunks
captured by you

High Personal Power

Your Success
Expands

228

# Chapter 26
# Breaking the Bubble
of
# Mysticism

Neo-Tech/Zonpower cures irrationality. Curing irrationality will end the parasitical-elite class and its hoax-built anticivilization. Indeed, curing irrationality and breaking its mystical bubbles of illusions will bring everyone into the Civilization of the Universe. ...Key knowledge for breaking everyone's mystical bubble evolved from three sources: *The Neo-Tech Discovery* by Frank R. Wallace (800 pages, Neo-Tech Publishing, revised 1994), *The Origins of Consciousness* by Julian Jaynes (467 pages, Houghton Mifflin, New York, 1976), and *Objectivism: the Philosophy of Ayn Rand* by Leonard Peikoff (493 pages, Dutton, New York, 1991).

Julian Jaynes, an academic at Princeton University, avidly avoids recognizing the titanic significance of his discovery that human consciousness is man-discovered, not nature-evolved.[1] For, to protect his own personal bubble of mysticism needed to live "acceptably" in today's anticivilization, he must avoid knowing the mystic-shattering key embodied in his work. And, as did the late Ayn Rand, her protégé Leonard Peikoff, a highly productive and principled philosopher, also avoids knowing the mystic-vanishing power lying within his and Rand's work. For, he, too, must protect his mystical bubble in order to live "normally" in today's anticivilization.

As is now experienced explicitly with mystic-breaking

---

[1]Jaynes's work is reviewed in Chapter 28 of this communiqué.

Neo-Tech, Peikoff's masterwork will be experienced implicitly as a threat by everyone living "normally" in an irrational anticivilization. Thus, today, Peikoff's great work is largely ignored or minimized not only by the threatened parasitical-elite class, but by his professional peers and objectivist cohorts. And, finally, neither Jaynes nor Peikoff recognizes the achievements of the other. Thus, neither integrates their great works together: Jaynes's work reveals the origins and metaphysical nature of consciousness; Peikoff's work reveals the epistemological nature of consciousness and its philosophical consequences.

Other major value producers, such as Albert Einstein and Michael Milken, were also trapped in their own bubbles of mysticism. Thus, they never identified the widest, most important values contained in their work. For, they would rather perish than abandon their lifelong emotional and material investments in the status quo that trapped them in Earth's anticivilization. ...*Every* citizen of planet Earth exists in a self-made mystical bubble in order to live "correctly" in a loser's anticivilization.

### Vanishing the Parasitical-Elite Class

What are we talking about? We are talking about a parasitical-elite class that has created an anticivilization on planet Earth. We are talking about a parasitical-elite class that after 2500 years has finally overwhelmed its host — the producers of objective values and genuine jobs...the sole providers of life and prosperity to mankind. We are talking about a malignancy of parasites who drain and destroy those value-and-job producers. We are talking about forever vanishing professional value destroyers and their anticivilization. We are talking about limitless wealth, health, and happiness available to everyone on Earth. ...We are talking about the mystic-free Civilization of the Universe enveloping planet Earth, perhaps as early as 2001.

"No, that could never happen," everyone exclaims. "Not in a generation, a century, or even a millennium."

Such an exclamation is valid within today's hoaxed anticivilization. But, anyone who steps into the Civilization of the Universe will exclaim: "Parasitical elites? An anticivilization built on force and deception? ...Everything was so irrationally destructive and boring back then. What is there to remember about such a value vacuum — such nothingness?"

Indeed, parasitical elites are subhumans or humanoids who lack the requirements for supporting human life. They lack honest character, long-range principles, real power. They live by manipulating truth to bleed others — by undercutting objective law, societal well-being, and human happiness. They bring society only losses and suffering. Thus, all memories of those parasites and their hoaxed civilization will vanish as the Civilization of the Universe brings to Earth the excitement of boundless prosperity and happiness.

How can such certainty exist about vanishing the parasitical elites and their anticivilization? That certainty rises from new knowledge: As demonstrated in *Zonpower*, every hoax and illusion is revealed on exposure to the Civilization of the Universe. Stripped of their illusions, parasitical elites go down the memory hole in whirlpools of absurdity. Also washed away will be politicians living as destructive humanoids, bureaucrats violently enforcing harmful political agendas, judges applying ego "justice", and prosecutors ignoring objective law and justice. ...They all will vanish down the drain of public ostracism.

As the Civilization of the Universe envelops Earth, *genuine* value-and-job producers from hard-working laborers to multimillionaire entrepreneurs will assume power. This anticivilization will then end. ...What guarantees the end of this anticivilization? Relentless self-spreading Neo-Tech guarantees the end of the parasitical-elite class and its hoax-built anticivilization.

### The Role of Rand and Peikoff

Amidst the pending demise of the parasitical-elite class and its anticivilization, Earth's first valid philosophy arises. That philosophy arises from two people in history who applied fully integrated honesty in developing a comprehensive philosophy: Ayn Rand and Leonard Peikoff. Ayn Rand established Objectivist philosophy, despite her tragic personal irrationalities. That philosophy evolved by overcoming the philosophical errors of Aristotle, Spinoza, and Nietzsche. Today, Objectivist philosophy combined with the limitless prosperity available from Neo-Tech disintegrates the anticivilization on planet Earth by *dis*integrating all its bogus philosophies.

Ironically, the Civilization of the Universe with its Zonpower requires no explicit philosophy. For, by nature, the only moral and practical philosophy throughout all universes and all times — Objectivist philosophy — is self-evident to everyone in the Civilization of the Universe. Indeed, valid philosophy — its metaphysics, epistemology, ethics, politics, and aesthetics — reduces to thirteen words: *What is is. Perceive it. Integrate it honestly. Act on it. Idealize it.* ...Honesty *is* free will.

Peikoff definitively grounds those thirteen words to existence. After thirty years of preparation and six years

232

of writing and editing, he crafted Ayn Rand's philosophy of Objectivism into 180,000 words. Those words link the Civilization of the Universe to existence, throughout time. ...Dr. Peikoff provides an unmovable position that philosophically exposes the parasitical-elite class and its anticivilization.

In philosophically exposing the anticivilization, Peikoff provides a reality-linking tour from sense perception and volition to concept formation, objectivity, and reason; from the nature of man to the concepts of good, virtue, happiness, government, economics, and art. *That tour is the death knell for the grotesque anticivilization in which today every citizen of Earth lives...and upon which every Earth-bound citizen falsely feels dependent.* Indeed, everyone's comfort-zone rationalizations, livelihoods, socializings, and contemporary lifestyles are falsely dependent on a wealth-and-life-destroying anticivilization. Yet, in reality, no healthy, prosperous life is dependent on any anticivilization or on any parasitical humanoid.

How does Neo-Tech extend Jaynes's and Piekoff's works into Zonpower? Neo-Tech is fully integrated honesty applied within a dishonest anticivilization. Zonpower is the limitless power radiating from the Civilization of the Universe. Zonpower both unifies and evolves existence, radiating as unbreached, integrated honesty throughout the universe. With Neo-Tech literature seeding the world in many languages, the Civilization of the Universe will blossom to vanish Earth's anticivilization. ...Ironically, from the rising specter of uncompromised Zonpower, those people closest to Neo-Tech, even the discoverer and author of Neo-Tech, will also feel their bubble-protecting urges to shun the rise of Zonpower. For, they too will feel the threat of losing their

New-Color Symphony
Movement #3

stake in the anticivilization if their "protective" bubbles of mysticism are broken. ...On stepping into the wider social dimensions found in the Civilization of the Universe, one can use Zonpower to vanish all connections with the anticivilization.

### Limitless Success Guaranteed

With Jaynes's and Peikoff's masterworks, the Neo-Tech/Zonpower dynamics guarantee the disappearance of Earth's anticivilization. Indeed, today, with Zonpower, any citizen of Earth can step into the Civilization of the Universe and vanish Earth's anticivilization. ...In the Civilization of the Universe, every conscious being is guaranteed limitless prosperity and exciting happiness — eternal success.

### The Government and Religion of the Universe

Philosophy with its ivory-tower approach is incomprehensible to most people. By contrast, government and religion provide the behaviors, laws, and values understandable to general populations. *Rational* government and *rational* religion, therefore, benefit society.

In an anticivilization, destructive governments and irrational religions grow from Earth-bound "authorities" manipulating truths based on illusions and faith. Thus, harmful behaviors and subjective laws evolve. A parasitical-elite class backed by force can then rise by draining the value producers. Stagnation of conscious life results. By contrast, the government and religion of the universe grow from rational consciousness. Humanoid parasites cannot rise or even exist in the rational Civilization of the Universe. Thus, an unlimited flourishing of conscious life results.

234

Zon is the unbreached honesty of the universe. Zon honors the honesty within each conscious being. By contrast, mysticism profanes honesty. Those who hold the honesty of Zon above the dishonesty of mysticism become all-powerful. Those who use the power of Zon to end the destructiveness of Earth's anticivilization secure themselves among the stars.

Movement II of *Zonpower* identifies the problem: Earth's irrational anticivilization. Movement II also shows how Neo-Tech lets one live free and incorruptible within Earth's unfree, corrupt anticivilization. And, finally, Movement III of *Zonpower* shows how the universal "government" and "religion" of Zon let one become a Citizen of the Universe to live free of the anticivilization — to live forever with unbounded prosperity and happiness protected by the Constitution of the Universe shown on page 188.

### The Discovery of Zon

Zon is the essence of fully integrated honesty. Zon is the giver of boundless prosperity to conscious beings throughout the universe. Zon is beyond God and heaven. ...Zon *is* the eternal government, religion, and paradise of the universe. Zon is you.

Thirty years ago, Frank R. Wallace discovered fully integrated honesty, later called Neo-Tech. He then abandoned the Earth-bound ideas of government and God formulated through manipulated truths and mystical faith. In 1972, Dr. Wallace resigned his position as Senior Research Chemist at E.I. du Pont de Nemours & Company with the goal of bringing the limitless benefits of Neo-Tech to everyone on Earth. Twenty years later, *The Neo-Tech Discovery* is published in twelve languages and distributed worldwide — in 156 countries.

*Movement III: The Civilization of the Universe*

From the indelible foundation of Neo-Tech, the world advances toward fully integrated honesty — toward Zon, the rational government and religion of the universe. Today, Zon rises on planet Earth midst the pillagings, jailings, and deprivations inflicted upon the value-and-job producers. Zon rises midst the economic destructions by a burgeoning parasitical-elite class comprising morally corrupt journalists, politicians, bureaucrats, and judges who are circling to silence Neo-Tech. They must silence fully integrated honesty to continue their harmful livelihoods. To survive, they must break the all-exposing, wide-scope accounting of Neo-Tech. But, they cannot silence the unsilenceable. They cannot break the unbreakable. ...Professional value destroyers cannot survive in the Civilization of the Universe. In America, the first hint of their demise was signalled in the elections of November, 1994.

## Compassion Rules the Universe

Who really helps the needy: the elderly, the handicapped, the oppressed, the sick, the helpless? Who really protects the disadvantaged, the consumer, the environment, the innocent animals? Who really provides the rational needs of everyone at ever lower costs? No, not those people who effusively try to convince themselves and others how much care and compassion they have for the disadvantaged, animals, and the environment. They are compassion hoaxers. For, they function by irrationally demanding *others* be forced into providing for the needy and protecting the environment.

Those compassion hoaxers do not function through benevolence and good will. They function through parasitical force and malevolent destruction. Be they

236

politicians, journalists, judges, professors, advocates, or entertainers, they all hypocritically feign good intentions to conceal agendas of unearned livelihoods, power, esteem.

How much can one trust a president or anyone who must implore his victims to "trust" him? How good are the intentions of politicians, news journalists, judges, or clergy who must constantly try to convince themselves and others of their good intentions and compassion, especially toward their ultimate victims, such as minorities, the poor, the disadvantaged, innocent animals, and the environment?

By contrast, the genuinely honest, trustworthy, and good-intentioned person *never* needs to publicly prove that he or she is honest, trustworthy, good-intentioned, compassionate. In fact, the more genuinely good-intentioned and compassionate one really is, the less that person is aware of being good-intentioned or compassionate.

Essentially every parasitical elite and professional value destroyer is consumed with guilt over his or her self-made, destructive nature. Each lives by what others think rather than by the facts of reality. Thus, each squirms behind hoaxes of good intentions and compassion. Within each such hoaxer exists an agenda of vilifying, draining, and destroying genuine value-and-job producers from innocent GM truck manufactures to innocent apple growers. ...Dishonest compassion hoaxers at the end of Earth's anticivilization era include people like Hillary Clinton, Pope John Paul, Jane Pauley, NBC news producers, Meryl Streep. Equally dishonest are the religious-exploiting demagogs seeking political power such as Pat Buchanan and Bill Bennett. ...Zon vanishes those souls of malevolence.

Remember, Zon is fully integrated honesty: the widest integrations of reality throughout the universe. Those who

237

produce genuine jobs for others and competitive values for society have authentic power and benevolence. Those who have earned that power have the greatest good intentions and compassion toward others. Thus, through Zon, those with authentic power — those souls of benevolence — reign supreme among the stars, eternally delivering genuine compassion and prosperity to all citizens of the universe.

# Chapter 27
# Rise from Your Knees

Until now, all governments and religions grew from dishonest mysticisms...from Earth-bound "authorities", force, and fraud. Until now, all governments and religions worked to break human beings of their natural self-confidence, creativity, happiness, pride, courage, and honesty. But, today, Zon makes the clean sweep sought by Nietzsche a century ago. Zon frees everyone on Earth. Through Zon, any conscious being can unite with the Civilization of the Universe to gain its unlimited power — Zonpower. *Unlike* Nietzsche's strong-rule-the-weak ideas[1], Zon allows *every* man and woman on this planet to become an "overman"; a superman ruled by no one, a genius regardless of IQ or race. Zon brings dignity with boundless excitement, wealth, and romantic love to every conscious being throughout the universe. ...Rise from your knees. Zon vanishes mystical "Gods". Zon lives eternally. Zon is *you*!

### Guiltless Riches Through Zon
Energy and matter are one and the same as identified by Einstein. Energy (E) can become matter; and matter (M) can become energy: $E=Mc^2$. Likewise, thought and things are one and the same as identified by Spinoza. Nonmystical thoughts (T1) can become all things throughout the universe; and all things (T2) throughout the universe can become nonmystical thoughts: $T1=T2k$, where k is the universal constant of Zon. Also, the Di Silvestro equation: $T1(I°+E°)=vT2(k)$ in which I° is the

---

[1]Friedrich Nietzsche staunchly opposed nationalism, anti-semitism, and tyranny. After his death, his writings were grossly misappropriated and dishonestly altered by his anti-semitic sister Elizabeth and the Nazis.

239

degree of intent and E° is the degree of effort behind the thought. I° and E° affect *v* or the velocity of converting T1 to T2, with T2 being the thought converted to reality. ...Thus flows the power of Zon.

Consider this: Can empty space or vacuums really exist? Or does existence always exist — *everywhere*? Is *all* space filled with an ether of existence, filled with quantized Gravity Units — the weightless geometry of existence so tiny with near-surfaceless, seemingly infinite curvature that gravity, mass, or energy can neither enter nor exit? If so, do endless universes exist above and below each Gravity Unit, hiding as pure symmetry beneath every point in existence? ...Regardless of the ultimate answers to those questions, wealth and happiness evolve eternally for every citizen of the universe.

# Chapter 28
# Infinite Power
## from
# Conscious Dynamics

(From a 1980 article by Frank R. Wallace)

A person could make an excellent bet by wagering a hundred ounces of gold that Julian Jaynes's book, *The Origin of Consciousness in the Breakdown of the Bicameral Mind* (Houghton Mifflin, 1976) will rank among the five most important books ever written by the year 2006. ...Jaynes's book signals the end of a 10,000-year reign of authoritarian institutions. His book also marks the beginning of a new era of individual consciousness during which people will increasingly act on the authority of their own brains. That movement toward self-responsibility will increasingly weaken the influences of external or mystical "authorities" such as government and religion.

The discovery of the bicameral mind solves the missing-link problem that has defied all previous theories of human evolution. But more important, that discovery is generating a new field of knowledge called Neothink with which all human life can evolve into abiding prosperity and happiness through powerfully competitive Neo-Tech advantages.

Dr. Jaynes discovered that until 3000 years ago essentially all human beings were void of consciousness.[1] Man along with all other primates functioned by mimicked or learned reactions. But, because of his much larger, more complex brain, man was able to develop a coherent

---

[1]An interesting note that underscores the recency of consciousness: A person living to 70 years today will have spanned over 2% of the time since human beings have been conscious.

language beginning about 8000 B.C. He was then guided by audio hallucinations. Those hallucinations evolved in the right hemisphere of the brain and were "heard" as communications or instructions in the left hemisphere of the brain (the bicameral or two-chamber mind). ...In effect, human beings were super-intelligent but automatically reacting animals who could communicate by talking. That communication enabled human beings to cooperate closely to build societies, even thriving civilizations.

Still, like all other animals, man functioned almost entirely by an automatic guidance system that was void of consciousness — until about 1000 B.C. when he was forced to invent consciousness to survive in the collapsing bicameral civilizations. ...Today, man's survival still depends on his choice of beneficially following his own consciousness or destructively following the voices of external "authorities".

The major components of Jaynes's discovery are:
- All civilizations before 1000 B.C. — such as Assyria, Babylonia, Mesopotamia, pharaonic Egypt — were built, inhabited, and ruled by nonconscious people.
- Ancient writings such as the *Iliad* and the early books of the Old Testament were composed by nonconscious minds that automatically recorded and objectively reported both real and imagined events. The transition to subjective and introspective writings of the conscious mind occurred in later works such as the *Odyssey* and the newer books of the Old Testament.
- Ancient people learned to speak, read, write, as well as carry out daily life, work, and the professions all while remaining nonconscious throughout their lives. Being nonconscious, they never experienced guilt, never practiced deceit, and were not responsible for their actions. They, like any other animal, had no

concept of guilt, deception, evil, justice, philosophy, history, or the future. They could not introspect and had no internal idea of themselves. They had no subjective sense of time or space and had no memories as we know them. They were nonconscious and innocent. They were guided by "voices" or strong impressions in their bicameral minds — nonconscious minds structured for nature's automatic survival.

- The development of human consciousness began about 3000 years ago when the automatic bicameral mind began breaking down under the mounting stresses of its inadequacy to find workable solutions in increasingly complex societies. The hallucinated voices became more and more confused, contradictory, and destructive.

- Man was forced to invent and develop consciousness in order to survive as his hallucinating voices no longer provided adequate guidance for survival.

- Today, after 3000 years, most people retain remnants of the bicameral guidance system in the form of mysticism and the desire for external authority.

- Except for schizophrenics, people today no longer hallucinate the voices that guided bicameral man. Yet, most people are at least partly influenced and are sometimes driven by the remnants of the bicameral mind as they seek, to varying degrees, automatic guidance from the mystical "voices" of others — from the commanding voices of false external "authorities".

- Religions and governments are rooted in the nonconscious bicameral mind that is obedient to the "voices" of external "authorities" — obedient to the voice of "God", gods, rulers, and leaders.

- The discovery that consciousness was never a part of

243

nature's evolutionary scheme (but was invented by man) eliminates the missing-link in human evolution.

- Essentially all religious and most political ideas today survive through those vestiges of the obsolete bicameral mind. The bicameral mind seeks omniscient truth and automatic guidance from external "authorities" such as political or spiritual leaders — or other "authoritarian" sources such as manifested in idols, astrologers, gurus. Likewise, politicians, lawyers, psychiatrists, psychologists, professors, doctors, journalists and TV anchormen become "authoritarian voices".

The idea of civilizations consisting entirely of nonconscious, yet highly intelligent, automatic-reacting people and the idea of man bypassing nature to invent his own consciousness initially seems incredible. But as Jaynes documents his evidence in a reasoned and detached manner, the existence of two minds in all human beings becomes increasingly evident: (1) the obsolete, nonconscious (bicameral) mind that seeks guidance from external "authorities" for important thoughts and decisions, especially under stressed or difficult conditions; and (2) the newly invented conscious mind that bypasses external "authorities" and provides thoughts and guidance generated from one's own mind. ...Understanding Jaynes's discoveries unlocks the 10,000 year-old secret of controlling the actions of people through their mystical or bicameral minds.

What evidence does Jaynes present to support his discoveries? After defining consciousness, he systematically presents his evidence to prove that man was not conscious until 3000 years ago when the bicameral civilizations collapsed and individuals began inventing consciousness in order to survive. Jaynes's proof begins with the definition of consciousness:

*Infinite Power from Conscious Dynamics*

### Defining and Understanding Consciousness

Julian Jaynes defines both what consciousness is and what it is not. After speculating on its location, he demonstrates that consciousness itself has no physical location, but rather is a particular organization of the mind and a specific way of using the brain. Jaynes then demonstrates that consciousness is only a small part of mental activity and is not necessary for concept formation, learning, thinking, or even reasoning. He illustrates how all those mental functions can be performed automatically, intelligently, but unconsciously. Furthermore, consciousness does not contribute to and often hinders the execution of learned skills such as speaking, listening, writing, reading —as well as skills involving music, art, and athletics. Thus, if major human actions and skills can function automatically and without consciousness, those same actions and skills can be controlled or driven by external influences, "authorities", or "voices" emanating under conditions described later. ...But first an understanding of consciousness is important:

Consciousness requires metaphors (i.e., referring to one thing in order to better understand or describe another thing — such as the head of an army, the head of a household, the head of a nail). Consciousness also requires analog models, (i.e., thinking of a map of California, for example, in order to visualize the entire, physical state of California). Thinking in metaphors and analog models creates the mind space and mental flexibility needed to bypass the automatic, bicameral processes.[1]

The *bicameral thinking* process functions only in

----

[1]Metaphors and analog models bring the right hemisphere brain functions to the left hemisphere with a much broader, wide-scope view which enables ever more powerful conceptual thinking.

concrete terms and narrow, here-and-now specifics. But the *conscious thinking* process generates an infinite array of subjective perceptions that permit ever broader understandings and better decisions.

Metaphors of "me" and analog models of "I" allow consciousness to function through introspection and self-visualization. In turn, consciousness expands by creating more and more metaphors and analog models. That expanding consciousness allows a person to "see" and understand the relationship between himself and the world with increasing accuracy and clarity.

Consciousness is a conceptual, metaphor-generated analog world that parallels the actual world. Man, therefore, could not invent consciousness until he developed a language sophisticated enough to produce metaphors and analog models.

The genus Homo began about two million years ago. Rudimentary oral languages developed from 70,000 B.C. to about 8000 B.C. Written languages began about 3000 B.C. and gradually developed into syntactical structures capable of generating metaphors and analog models. Only at that point could man invent and experience consciousness.

Jaynes shows that man's early writings (hieroglyphics, hiertatic, and cuneiform) reflect a mentality totally different from our own. They reflect a nonmetaphoric, nonconscious mentality. Jaynes also shows that the *Iliad*, which evolved as a sung poem about 1000 B.C., contains little if any conscious thought. The characters in the Iliad (e.g., Achilles, Agamemnon, Hector, Helen) act unconsciously in initiating all their major actions and decisions through "voices", and all speak in hexameter rhythms (as often do modern-day schizophrenics when hallucinating). Hexameter rhythms are characteristic of the rhythmically automatic functionings of the right-hemisphere brain. Moreover, the *Iliad* is entirely about action...about the acts and consequences of Achilles. The *Iliad* never mentions subjective thoughts or the contents of anyone's mind. The language is nonconscious — an objective reporting of facts that are concrete bound and void of introspection and abstract thought.

With a conscious mind, man can introspect; he can debate with himself; he can become his own god, voice, and decision maker. But before the invention of consciousness, the mind functioned bicamerally: the right hemisphere (the poetic, god-brain) hallucinated audio instructions to the left hemisphere (the analytical, man-brain), especially in unusual or stressful situations. Essentially, man's brain today is physically identical to the ancient bicameral brain; but with his discovery or more precisely his *invention* of consciousness, he can now choose to focus on integrating the functions of the left and right hemispheres.

Beginning about 9000 B.C. — as oral languages developed — routine or habitual tasks became increasingly standardized. The hallucinating voices for performing those basic tasks, therefore, became increasingly similar among groups of people. The collectivization of "voices" allowed more and more people to cooperate and function together through their bicameral minds. The leaders spoke to the "gods" and used the "voices" to lead the masses in cooperative unison. That cooperation allowed nomadic hunting tribes to gradually organize into stationary, food-producing societies. The continuing development of oral language and the increasing collectivization of bicameral minds allowed towns and eventually cities to form and flourish.

247

*Movement III:  The Civilization of the Universe*

The bicameral mind, however, became increasingly inadequate for guiding human actions as societies continued to grow in size and complexity.  By about 1000 B.C., the bicameral mind had become so inadequate that man's social structures began collapsing.  Under threat of extinction, man invented a new way to use his brain that allowed him to solve the much more complex problems needed to survive — he invented a new organization of the mind called consciousness.

Jaynes eliminated the missing link in the evolution of man by discovering that consciousness never existed in the evolutionary processes — consciousness was invented by man.

## The Development of Consciousness

Dr. Jaynes shows through abundant archaeological, historical, and biological evidence that the towns, cities, and societies from 9000 B.C. to 1000 B.C. were established and developed by nonconscious people.  Those societies formed and grew through common hallucinating voices attributed to gods, rulers, and the dead — to external "authorities".  Various external symbols that "spoke" (such as graves, idols, and statues) helped to reinforce and expand the authority of those common "voices".  Such "voices" continued to expand their reach through increasingly visible and awe-inspiring symbols such as tombs, temples, colossuses, and pyramids.

But as those unconscious societies became more complex and increasingly intermingled through trade and wars, the "voices" became mixed and contradictory.  With the "voices" becoming muddled, their effectiveness in guiding people diminished.  Rituals and importunings became ever more intense and elaborate in attempts to evoke clearer "voices" and better guidance. The development of writing and the permanent recording of instructions and laws during the second millennium B.C. further weakened the authority and effectiveness of hallucinated voices. As the "voices" lost their effectiveness, they began falling silent. And without authoritarian "voices" to guide and control its people, those societies suddenly began collapsing with no external cause.

As the bicameral mind broke down and societies collapsed, individuals one by one began inventing consciousness to make decisions needed to survive in the mounting anarchy and chaos. On making conscious and volitional decisions, man for the first time became responsible for his actions. Also, for short-range advantages and easy power, conscious man began discovering and using deceit and treachery — behaviors not possible from nonconscious, bicameral minds. ...Before inventing consciousness, man was as guiltless and amoral as any other animal since he had no volitional choice in following his automatic guidance system of hallucinated voices.

As the "voices" fell silent, man began contriving religions and prayers in his attempts to communicate with the departed gods. Jaynes shows how man developed the concept of worship, heaven, angels, demons, exorcism, sacrifice, divination, omens, sortilege, augury in his attempts to evoke guidance from the gods — from external "authorities".

All such quests for external "authority" hark back to the breakdown of the hallucinating bicameral mind — to the silencing and celestialization of the once "vocal" and earthly gods.

Much direct evidence for the breakdown of the

bicameral mind and the development of consciousness comes from writings scribed between 1300 B.C. and 300 B.C. Those writings gradually shift from nonconscious, objective reports to conscious, subjective expressions that reflect introspection. The jump from the nonconscious writing of the *Iliad* to the conscious writing of the *Odyssey* (composed perhaps a century later) is dramatically obvious. In the *Odyssey*, unlike the *Iliad*, characters possess conscious self-awareness, introspection powers, and can sense right, wrong, and guilt. ...That radical difference between the *Iliad* and the *Odyssey* is, incidentally, further evidence that more than one poet composed the Homeric epics.

The transition from the nonconscious *Iliad* to the conscious *Odyssey* marks man's break with his 8000-year-old hallucinatory guidance system. By the sixth century B.C., written languages began reflecting conscious ideas of morality and justice similar to those reflected today.

The Old Testament of the Bible also illustrates the transition from the nonconscious writing of its earlier books (such as Amos, circa 750 B.C.) to the fully conscious writing of its later books (such as Ecclesiastes, circa 350 B.C.). Amid that transition, the book of Samuel records the first known suicide — an act that requires consciousness. And the book of Deuteronomy illustrates the conflict between the bicameral mind and the conscious mind.

Likewise, the transition to consciousness is observed in other parts of the world: Chinese literature moved from bicameral nonconsciousness to subjective consciousness about 500 B.C. with the writings of Confucius. And in India, literature shifted to subjective consciousness around 400 B.C. with the Upanishadic writings.

American Indians, however, never developed the sophisticated, metaphorical languages needed to develop full consciousness. As a result, their mentalities were probably bicameral when they first encountered the European explorers. For example, with little or no conscious resistance, the Incas allowed the Spanish "white gods" to dominate, plunder, and slaughter them.

### The Bicameral Mind in Today's World

Dr. Jaynes identifies many vestiges of the bicameral mentality that exist today. The most obvious vestige is religion and its symbols. Ironically, early Christianity with its teachings of Jesus was an attempt to shift religion from the outmoded bicameral and celestial mind of Moses to the newly conscious and earthly mind of man. Christianity then discovered a devastatingly effective tool for authoritarian control — guilt. Indeed, guilt not only worked on conscious minds, but required conscious minds to be effective.

Despite religion, conscious minds caused the gradual shifts from governments of gods to governments of men and from divine laws to secular laws. Still, the vestiges of the bicameral mind combined with man's longing for guidance produced churches, prophets, oracles, sibyls, diviners, cults, mediums, astrologers, saints, idols, demons, tarot cards, seances, Ouija boards, glossolalia, fuhrers, ayatollahs, popes, peyote, Jonestown, born-agains.

Jaynes shows how such external "authorities" exist only through the remnants of the bicameral mind. Moreover, he reveals a four-step paradigm that can reshuffle susceptible minds back into hallucinating, bicameral mentalities. The ancient Greeks used a similar paradigm to reorganize or reprogram the minds of uneducated

251

peasant girls into totally bicameral mentalities so they could become oracles and give advice through hallucinated voices — voices that would rule the world (e.g., the oracle at Delphi). ...Today, people who deteriorate into schizophrenic psychoses follow similar paradigms.

A common thread united most oracles, sibyls, prophets, and demon-possessed people: Almost all were illiterate, all believed in spirits, and all could readily retrieve the bicameral mind. Today, however, retrieval of the bicameral mind is schizophrenic insanity. Also, today, as throughout history, a symptomatic cure for "demon-possessed" people involves exorcising rituals that let a more powerful "authority" or god replace the "authority" of the demon. The New Testament, for example, shows that Jesus and his disciples became effective exorcists by substituting one "authority" (their god) for another "authority" (another god or demon).

As the voices of the oracles became confused and nonsensical, their popularity waned. In their places, idolatry revived and then flourished. But as Christianity became a popular source of external "authority", Christian zealots began physically destroying all competing idols. They then built their own idols and symbols to reinforce the external "authority" of Christianity.

Among today's vestiges of the bicameral mentality is the born-again movement that seeks external guidance. In that movement, people surrender their self-choice and self-decision making in exchange for false promises of protection and guidance. Such vestiges dramatize man's resistance to use his own invention of consciousness to guide his life.

The chanting cadence of poetry and the rhythmic beat of music are also rooted in the bicameral mentality. In ancient writings, the hallucinated voices of the gods were always in poetic verse, usually in dactylic hexameter and sometimes in rhyme or alliteration — all characteristic of right-brain functionings. The oracles and prophets also spoke in verse. And today schizophrenics often speak in verse when they hallucinate.

Poetry and chants can have authoritarian or commanding beats and rhythms that can effectively block consciousness. Poetry is the language of the gods — it is the language of the artistic, right-hemispheric brain. Plato recognized poetry as a divine madness.

Most poetry and songs have an abruptly changing or a discontinuous pitch. Normal speech, on the other hand, has a smoothly changing pitch. Jaynes demonstrates that reciting poetry, singing, and playing music are right-brain functions, while speaking is a left-brain function. That is why people with speech impediments can often sing, chant, or recite poetry with flawless clarity. Conversely, almost anyone trying to sing a conversation will find his words quickly deteriorating into a mass of inarticulate cliches.

Likewise, listening to music and poetry is a right-brain function. And music, poetry, or chants that project authority with loud or rhythmic beats can suppress left-brain functions to temporarily relieve anxiety or a painfully troubled consciousness.

Jaynes goes on to show phenomena such as hypnosis, acupuncture, and déjà vu also function through vestiges of the bicameral mind. And he demonstrates how hypnosis steadily narrows the sense of self, time, space, and introspection as consciousness shrinks and the mind reverts to a bicameral type organization. Analogously, bicameral and schizophrenic minds have little or no sense

253

of self, time, space or introspection. The hypnotized mind is urged to obey the voice of the hypnotist; the bicameral mind is compelled to obey the "voices" of "authority" or gods. By sensing oneself functioning in the narrow-scope, unaware state of hypnosis, gives one an idea of functioning in the narrow-scope, unaware state of bicameral man.

Jaynes also identifies how modern quests for external "authority" are linked to the bicameral mind. Many such quests use science to seek authority in the laws of nature. In fact, today, science is surpassing the waning institutional religions as a major source of external "authority". And rising from the vestiges of the bicameral mind are an array of scientisms (pseudoscientific doctrines, faiths, and cults) that select various natural or scientific facts to subvert into apocryphal, authoritarian doctrines. That subversion is accomplished by using facts out of context to fit promulgated beliefs. Such mystical scientisms include astrology, ESP, Scientology, Christian Science and other "science" churches, I Ching, behaviorism, sensitivity training, mind control, meditation, hypnotism, as well as specious nutritional, health, and medical fads.

Today the major worldwide sources of external "authority" are the philosophical doctrines of religion (along with the other forms of mysticism and "metaphysics") combined with political doctrines such as Socialism, Fascism, and Marxism. All such doctrines demand the surrender of the individual's ego (sense of self or "I") to a collective, obedient faith toward the "authority" of those doctrines. In return, those doctrines offer automatic answers and lifetime guidance from which faithful followers can survive without the responsibility or effort of using their own conscious minds. Thus, all current political systems represent a regression into mysticism — from conscious man back to bicameral man.

Despite their constant harm to everyone, most modern-day external "authorities" and master neocheaters thrive by using the following two-step neocheating technique to repress consciousness and activate the bicameral mind in their victims.

1. First man is made to feel guilty. He is condemned for having lost his "innocence" by inventing consciousness. He is condemned for assuming the responsibility to use his own mind to guide his life. He is condemned for exchanging his automatic, bicameral life for a volitional, conscious life...condemned for exchanging his nature-given bicameral mind for a superior, man-invented conscious mind.

2. Then man is offered automatic solutions to problems and guidance through life — is offered an "effortless" Garden of Eden or a utopian hereafter if he exchanges his own invented consciousness for faith in external "authority": bicameral faith in some leader, doctrine, or god. He is offered the "reward" of protection and the escape from the self-responsibility of making one's own decisions to guide one's own life. But for that "reward", he must renounce his own mind to follow someone else's mind or wishes disguised as "truths" promulgated by some external "authority" or higher power.

But, in reality, no valid external "authority" or higher power can exist or ever has existed. Valid authority evolves only from one's own independent, conscious mode of thinking. When that fact is fully realized, man will emerge completely from his bicameral past and move into a future that accepts individual consciousness as the only authority. ...Man will then fully evolve into a prosperous, happy individual who has assumed full responsibility for his own thinking and life.

Still, the resistance to self-responsibility is formidable. The bicameral mentality grips those seeking mysticism or other "authorities" for guidance. Those who accept external "authority" allow government officials, religious leaders, environmental and anti-abortion movements, faith, homilies, cliches, one-liners, slogans, the familiar, habits, and feelings to automatically guide their actions. The *Neo-Tech Discovery* demonstrates how throughout history billions of people because of their bicameral tendencies unnecessarily submit to the illusionary external "authorities" of parasitical Establishments, governments, and religions. Such submission is always done at a net loss to everyone's well being and happiness.

## The Implications of Neo-Tech

To some, the implications of Neo-Tech (fully integrated honesty) are frightening, even terrifying. To others, the implications are electrifying and liberating. ...The implications of Neo-Tech are that each individual is solely responsible for his or her own life — responsible for making the efforts required for learning how to honestly guide one's own life toward growing prosperity and happiness. No automatic, effortless route to knowledge or guidance exists.

No valid external "authority" exists that one can automatically live by. To live effectively, an individual must let only the authority of his own consciousness guide his activities. All consistently competent people have learned to act on reality — not on their feelings or someone else's feelings or doctrines. An individual must accept the responsibility to guide his or her own life in order to live competently, successfully, happily.

# Chapter 29
# The Rise and Fall
## of the
# Anticivilization

Earth's anticivilization is characterized by humanoids with criminal minds controlling value-producing human beings. For 3000 years, such humanoids survived through hidden agendas designed to usurp the wealth created by the productive class. Those hidden criminals are responsible for all wars, slave-master relationships, mass thefts, purposeful property destructions, terrorisms, genocide.

### Neocheaters: The Hidden Criminals

Two classes of criminals exist: (1) The less-dangerous *subhuman* class consisting of people, who with blatant criminal minds, openly rob, injure, and murder human beings. Such subhumans are generally scorned by society and are usually jailed for their crimes through objective laws and valid justice. (2) The most-dangerous *humanoid* class consisting of people, who with ingeniously hidden criminal minds, covertly rob, injure, and destroy entire economies, entire populations, entire nations, entire civilizations. Such humanoids are camouflaged criminals who survive by destructive deceptions used to gain bogus livelihoods, respect, even adulation from their duped human victims. Such criminals are usually praised by the parasitical Establishment and seldom held responsible for their crimes.

The subhuman class of criminals sporadically commit crimes against various individuals. The humanoid class

257

of criminals daily, continuously commit crimes against everyone and society through their destructive careers.

The anticivilization is created by the parasitical-elite class and its legions of professional value destroyers. They exist by manipulating the disease of irrationality. Such career criminals deceive and plunder populations through subjective laws, harmful regulations, and dishonest ego "justice".

### Cambodia's Pol Pot to FDA's Dr. Kessler

Neocheaters comprise destructive politicians, corrupt lawyers, and killer bureaucrats who exist through the criminal use of government force implemented through political-agenda laws, gun-backed regulations, and ego-determined "justice". Examples of destructive neocheaters in the closing years of Earth's anticivilization include genocide-champion Pol Pot, mass-killer FDA commissioner Dr. David Kessler, envy-demagog Hillary Clinton, Tiananmen-Square murderer Li Peng, job-killer Interior Secretary Bruce Babbitt, child-abuser/killer (Fijnje/Waco) Janet Reno, and Russia's star of evil Vladimir Zhirinovsky. ...In what way are all such neocheaters mass killers? Wide-scope accounting demonstrates that for every life humanoids purport to benefit, they are responsible for killing several, often dozens, even hundreds or thousands of innocent people directly through guns and political prisons or indirectly through draining economies and destroying assets as documented in the *Neo-Tech Protection Kit*, volume II, 1994 edition.

### Homer to Plato

How did the disease of accepting criminal neocheaters as legendary heroes evolve on planet Earth? And, how does that disease continue to ravage everyone today? As identified previously, the philosophical father of the parasitical-elite class and totalitarian governments is Plato. His neocheating masterpiece was *The Republic* written nearly 2400 years ago. But, the foundations were laid 400 years earlier with two of the three primary epics of Western literature — the *Iliad* and the *Odyssey*.

The Iliad's hero, the nonconscious amoral Achilles, and the Odyssey's hero, the conscious immoral Odysseus, were in essence nothing more than wildly irrational, criminal killers with no sense of honesty or justice. The nature of all glory-seeking criminal minds is summed up in the character of Odysseus, especially as he returns home after a decade of "glorious" battles and "heroic" adventures. The great bully Odysseus simply plunders and butchers the innocent populations of defenseless coastal towns whenever he and his cohorts want to feel big and powerful — whenever they want to plunder the value producers, rape them, kill them, have a good time.

Such Homeric-hero characters are not human beings, but are humanoids with no concept of honesty, human values, or objective justice. They are criminals who pretend worthiness through fake glories, destructive heroics, and evil ego "justice". All their boastfully paraded "heroics", "courage", and "glory" are nothing more than masks for criminal acts and parasitical cowardice. ...All such humanoids are simply plunderers and killers, *nothing more*, no matter what "heroics" they stage. Indeed, was that the message which the blind-poet Homer intended? For, Homer grants no hint of virtuous good-versus-evil struggles by those "heroes".

If so, 400 years later, the politician-philosopher Plato turned Homer's message upside down. As identified in the *Neo-Tech Discovery*, Plato ingeniously constructed an integrated philosophy justifying the parasitical control and dictatorial rule of the honest value producers by criminal-minded elites. Finally, 300 years after Plato, the Roman poet Virgil in his famous secondary epic, the *Aeneid*, recycled Homer's *Odyssey* into a "gentler", more hidden form of evil. Thus, Virgil laid the structure for ever more subtle and hidden neocheating techniques.

Ever since Virgil, subtle neocheating techniques have allowed criminal-minded humanoids to plunder the value producers in countless, hidden ways while appearing moral, even heroic. Thus, those neocheating techniques allowed an irrational anticivilization to rise and exist to this day on planet Earth.

## Virgil to Hitler

Virgil promotes the evil falsity that the virtues of life, character, bravery, and morality lie in sacrifice and service — sacrifice of the workers and value producers to the service of the parasitical elites. All such calls for sacrifice are done under the arbitrary guises of government, nationalism, religion, society, "higher causes"...whatever sounds good at the time. Virgil's *Aeneid* lays the foundations for totalitarianism and "glorious" leaders like Hitler to rise and destroy entire economies and populations.

Most Germans and many others in the 1930s were duped into admiring Hitler's Odysseus-like courage as one of the bravest soldiers in World War I and the strutting Wagnerian "glory" he bestowed on the Third Reich. Thus, most Germans and many others blinded themselves to the obvious fact that popular, glory-talking Hitler was nothing more than a criminal value destroyer — a mass murderer for his *own* parasitical livelihood and glory. Like most

260

politicians, Hitler increasingly committed destructive acts so he could increasingly feel big, important, powerful.

Likewise, prompted by a deeply dishonest media, many Americans were duped into admiring a good-sounding, smooth-talking Hillary Clinton. Until the Neo-Tech dynamics began taking hold in America in 1994, most people were blind to the fact that she was a criminal-minded lawyer intent on controlling society by draining the value producers. She almost succeeded through her attempted power-grab encompassing America's entire health-care system. How would she have carried out her giant, free-lunch fraud? Through use of government force — through subjective laws and gun-backed regulations enforced by ego "justice". ...Had Hillary Clinton succeeded, health-care would have decayed, effective medical research would have stopped, businesses would have shut down, jobs would have been lost, innocent value producers and dedicated doctors would have been fined and jailed, many precious lives would have been lost.

How could anyone be so purposely destructive? Given the chance, essentially *any* politician from a small-town mayor to a nation's president or his wife would eagerly seize Hitlerian power with all its criminalities and destructiveness. For, that is the essence of essentially all politicians. Under camouflaged deception, they will simply plunder and destroy people, property, jobs, capital, *whatever they can get away with*, in order to advance their own harmful careers, glory, and power...in order to have an Odysseus-like good time.

## Capone to Clinton
*Humanoid* criminals are much more destructive and dangerous than *subhuman* criminals such as Al Capone.

For example, Hillary Clinton, with help from a fawningly dishonest media, rationalized away her criminal-minded behaviors. Her camouflaged drive for Orwellian power and control would be justified through the sacrifice of productive workers and hard-working businesspeople to a hypocritically proclaimed "higher good" or "caring for others". Such ploys ultimately hurt everyone badly. For, Hillary Clinton's "higher good" meant nothing more than a self-serving empowerment for personal gains through government force. ...Such self-serving empowerment and gains are the essence of essentially all politicians who propagate Earth's irrational anticivilization.

## Beowulf to a Neo-Tech President

The third and final primary epic of Western literature, the allegorical *Beowulf*, written about 1000 AD, reflects an honest, moral foundation for conscious beings. The hero, Beowulf, is genuinely noble and honest as his pure goodness triumphs over pure evil — over allegorical monsters who are metaphors for humanoid neocheaters. Indeed, Beowulf himself explicitly identifies the greatest evil as harming and killing innocent people, especially one's own people. But, evilly *unprincipled* Odysseus, not virtuously *principled* Beowulf, underpins Earth's anticivilization. Yet, Beowulf represents the first glimmerings of the Civilization of the Universe.

In this anticivilization, most political leaders are nothing more than camouflaged, criminal-minded plunderers. Those "leaders" hide behind Plato's and Virgil's neocheating techniques. They are simply modern-day Odysseuses committing their hidden crimes to garner unearned livelihoods, power, and glory — be they a Hitler, a Stalin, a Bush, a Clinton.

## The Rise and Fall of the Anticivilization

Will the to-be-announced Neo-Tech presidential candidate be the first major political figure of the past 2000 years to embody the life-enhancing character of Beowulf? By 2001 AD, will the benevolent spirit of Beowulf vanish the neocheaters and let the value producers bring eternal prosperity and happiness to *all* human beings? By 2001 AD, will Cassandra's Secret and the fully integrated honesty of Neo-Tech have vanished this anticivilization? By 2001 AD, will *Zonpower* be delivering limitless prosperity, love, and happiness to all conscious beings on Earth?

---

### Honoring Value Producers and Ending the Anticivilization

The Neo-Tech web site honors the values delivered by the premier entrepreneur philosopher — Dr. Leonard Peikoff. The values he delivers to mankind are grossly under recognized and under appreciated not only by the public, but by libertarians, objectivists, Peikoffian Objectivists, even Dr. Peikoff himself. Leonard Peikoff has produced and continues to produce more major, competitive values than all the other professional Objectivists combined.[1] Thus, sadness arises when that outstanding man diminishes himself through his own irrationality. He has become a tragic Aeneas/Beowulf contradiction. ...Indeed, sadness is felt whenever irrationality diminishes anyone of great personal value, be it one's spouse or child or mega value producers such as Ayn Rand and Leonard Peikoff.

Whatever the root of his irrationality, Dr. Peikoff's persona shrinks with his advocating force-backed intolerance as he expressed during his 1995 Ford Hall Forum lecture. Recall how Ayn Rand's life was tragically diminished by her irrational, deadly, "dot-of-light" glamorization of smoking. Her emotional, irrational denials of the narcotically addictive, physically destructive nature of tobacco smoking led her and some of her "caped" followers to the grave. ...Now, today, arises the Peikoff tragedy — Greek-tragedy style. But, because this outstanding

---

[1]See page 272 for footnote.

value producer still lives, he has the potential for a life of supreme fulfillment through his continuing production of universal values. He can soar to great heights by using fully integrated honesty to eliminate his tragic flaw — his advocating force-backed intolerance.

Consider those who brought functional Objectivism to the general public. Of course, Ayn Rand was the prime contributor. But major contributors also included: 1) Dr. Leonard Peikoff as the continuing producer of exciting, profitable Objectivist values; 2) Dr. Nathaniel Branden as the highly successful, NBI business-entrepreneur director who profitably marketed Objectivism to the public as well as being a major contributor to its products (a value greatly under appreciated and misunderstood by Ayn Rand and most of her followers), and 3) Warner Brothers, Inc., as the business-savvy launch pad of Ayn Rand's work and fame (a value also under appreciated and misunderstood by Ayn Rand).

The values those competitive producers gave to our civilization should be kept separate from their personal contradictions and errors. Such errors, as with any public figure, should be identified and accounted for objectively. But, at the same time, their gifts of competitive universal values should always be recognized, appreciated, and honored. For, their values, not their errors, are what count for the quality of our lives and futures. Those who seek ego boosts by attacking Ayn Rand, Leonard Peikoff, or Nathaniel Branden without acknowledging the outstanding universal values each has given to mankind should first consider what outstanding universal values they themselves have given to mankind.

The bottom line: Absorb and integrate the values produced by others, honor those values, and then profit from them. Also, identify the errors, reject them, and then make objective adjustments for them. That process is called wide-scope integration with fully integrated honesty. That process takes profitable advantage of every value and error available. That process carries one to eternal prosperity — to the Civilization of the Universe.

# Chapter 30

# RELAX

### for

## Zonpower Rules Cyberspace

What should you do about this draining anticivilization and its humanoid creators — its parasitical elites who only fake the human qualities of value and compassion? Should you stand up, resist, fight back? Unless you are a Neo-Tech self-leader described in Chapter 16, you can relax. Simply ignore the parasitical elites. Ignore the negative, the irrational, the unreal. For, with Neo-Tech advancing through cyberspace, the anticivilization and its harmful humanoids will lose their power over you. And, when you learn Cassandra's Secret, humanoids will be unable to drain your life or harm your future.

On learning Cassandra's Secret, anxieties vanish. You will discover that *nothing* in this anticivilization has power over you or your future. ...Parasitical elites have no power in cyberspace.

After capturing Cassandra's Secret, most of what you see and hear from others becomes meaningless. Most of what others say or do becomes pointless and boring. For, you will control all that affects you, now and in the future. You will dismiss all political and philosophical positions — left or right, conservative or liberal, rationalist or empiricist. You will dismiss them all as equally senseless. You will see every position and argument in this anticivilization as an irrational swirl of nothing.

On reading and rereading *Zonpower,* you will learn Cassandra's Secret and control the power of Zon. Not only is Zonpower real, it is omnipotent. With Zonpower, any loss in the unreal anticivilization is no loss at all.

265

For, within the dynamics of nature, losses in an unreal world become gains in the real world. Thus, with Zonpower dynamics, all such unreal losses become real gains in propelling you into the Civilization of the Universe — into limitless power and wealth.

In the anticivilization, its parasitical humanoids — its malignant politicians, wealth-destroying bureaucrats, life-destroying ego judges, mind-destroying academe, dishonest journalists, stagnant big-business executives — are, in reality, *nothing*. For, they make *no* difference to anything in the real world or over any span of time.

Humanoids and their anticivilization are no more real than fleeting antimatter particles that exist not in permanent reality but in a transitory, virtual reality — a false, simulated reality that affects nothing real, nothing in the future. ...Those humanoids are nothing more than figments that can be vanished by Zonpower and the Civilization of the Universe.

Arriving at the next millennium, today's anticivilization and all its destructive humanoids will have affected nothing in our world, universe, or future. Only you with Zonpower will affect our world, universe, and future. Thus, this anticivilization with its last wave of humanoids can be ignored and forgotten, now and forever. But, you, with Cassandra's Secret, will become eternally powerful, forever gaining exciting adventure, wealth, and happiness.

### The Hidden Source of All Advantages

*Zonpower* is easily understandable for readers at all levels, especially after a second reading. Yet, most dishonest politicians, parasitical elites, destructive lawyers, and force-backed bureaucrats shrink in befuddlement on exposure to *Zonpower*. Therein lies the hidden power of

Zon — its great advantage in this anticivilization.

As did the mythical Cassandra, *Zonpower* foretells all. Yet, the more minds that are beclouded by Cassandra's Secret, the greater is its power. For, if the professional value destroyers knew Cassandra's Secret, they would forcibly block its future. Moreover, most people will not directly hear about *Zonpower* until the year-2000 presidential campaign. Thus, today, arises the greatest opportunity. With *Zonpower,* one can live beyond the parasitical elites — one can live on Earth with immortal prosperity.

## 1996 AD

Most know something is wrong. Some know something is terribly wrong. Most want change — real change.

They are right: Something is wrong — terribly wrong. For, here lies a stagnant, envy-ridden anticivilization shrinking into dishonesty and ignorance worth nothing to the future. But, relax. Enjoy life. The first domino of a seminal change fell in America during its 1994 elections. Ahead lies the booming, exciting Civilization of the Universe expanding through cyberspace forever into the future.

## 2001 AD

During the year-2000 Presidential Campaign, people in America will begin directly learning about Zonpower and Cassandra's Secret through the forthcoming *Zon Protocols*.

## 2005 AD

After the turn of the millennium, highly productive market entrepreneurs will have already swept away today's political parasites along with their armed agents of force.[1]

### Today

*Zonpower* is an exotic manuscript that initially will becloud most conscious minds on Earth. Like suddenly being flipped up into a higher spatial dimension, *Zonpower* initially will make many conscious beings on Earth go blank and run. That fact can be illustrated by the following account:

On Saturday, June 27, 1992, a meeting was held in Las Vegas, Nevada. At that meeting, Dr. Frank R. Wallace revealed Zonpower. He explained how the reactions to this new discovery by essentially everyone would not only be negative, but would grow increasingly negative as its dynamics became manifest. For, on planet Earth today, essentially everyone is engaged in wide-scope dishonesties and evasions to protect his or her investments in this anticivilization. ...But, therein lies the key to everyone's prosperity and happiness as described below:

### Sweeping Away Ignorance and Evil

Part of Cassandra's Secret involves isolating the essence of ignorance and evil personified by many politicians, lawyers, and judges. Many high-profile men and women, especially those in government and law, are ignorant of justice and honesty. More destructively, they function through automatic dishonesties and deceptions. They build harmful careers based on ego agendas and reveal the irrational foundations of an anticivilization. Those revelations produce a predicted reaction among those exposed to Zonpower as described next:

---

[1]Swept away as described by Mark Hamilton in his book *Will America Go Neo-Tech?*, Neo-Tech Publishing, 1995.

*Relax*

Confronted with the foretold banishment of irrationality, many minds go blank. For, the closer one gets to the knowledge of Zonpower, the clearer becomes the realization that the cure for irrationality is coming. In turn, that means Zonpower will sweep away this anticivilization along with its parasites who survive unnaturally through irrationalities, dishonesties, and deceptions backed by bogus political-policy laws, ego "justice", and armed agents of force.

So why will almost everyone on Earth initially blind themselves to Zonpower and Cassandra's Secret? Because, (1) almost everyone has a lifetime investment in this anticivilization with its wide-scope dishonesties and (2) almost everyone is addicted to its neocheating opiates of the past 2300 years.

On reading *Zonpower*, many cannot proceed past the first few chapters when they (1) sense the end of their lifetime investments in an anticivilization, and (2) sense the end of their hypnotic state that yields automatic, wide-scope dishonesties. Many will rationalize, "I don't understand", "this is real deep", "it's eerie", "it's kooky", "it's beyond me", "it's scary". ...They cannot face losing their bad investments and hypnotic rationalizations.

By contrast, those who do not "have it made" with the Establishment, those honest workers who are not benefiting from the ruling elites, those who are not invested in today's society...they will most quickly flourish on reading *Zonpower*. They will be among the first to understand its intoxicating secret.

Thus, lies the power of *Zonpower* — one's route to fabulous riches. By grasping *Zonpower* before it spreads to everyone, one can dominate the sleeping minds of others. One can gain wide-awake powers far beyond the parasitical elites. Indeed, the parasitical elites living today in this moribund anticivilization are losing their deceptive means to control others because of Neo-Tech in cyberspace.

### Cassandra's Secret

Harnessing *Zonpower* is a dual process: (1) recognize that nearly everyone's mind in the anticivilization will initially becloud on exposure to *Zonpower*, (2) follow the two steps given on the next page for breaking mystical bubbles and preventing one's own mind from beclouding on exposure to *Zonpower*. ...Those two steps will unlock the forecasting power of Cassandra's Secret.

### Breaking the Hypnotic Spell

First consider that knowledge ends at each person's boundary of irrationality and dishonesty used to hold everyone in the anticivilization. That boundary is defined by each person's mystical bubble needed to tolerate life in this futile-loser anticivilization. But, by breaking that hypnotic boundary — that mystical bubble — one breaks into the winning realm of limitless knowledge and prosperity.

The purpose of *Zonpower* is not to persuade or convert others. That cannot be done. For, no one can understand beyond his or her hypnotic boundary or bubble. Indeed, everyone today mistakenly protects his or her mystical bubble in order to justify living in an irrational civilization.

The essence of *Zonpower* is its power to break that hypnotic spell — to break that mystical bubble in which everyone on Earth is trapped. Once that bubble is broken, one is no longer trapped in the dishonesties of an anticivilization. One can then soar beyond everyone else's boundary. One can soar into the Civilization of the Universe, gaining its knowledge and foretelling power to collect limitless riches here on Earth.

### Two Steps to Break Mystical Bubbles

1. Realize that *Zonpower* does *not* rise from a different drummer or some higher power. Instead, *Zonpower* rises from every natural, mystic-free mind — from every honest, conscious mind that produces competitive values for self and others.

2. Read *Zonpower*...and then carefully reread *Zonpower* until its integrations reveal new-color powers — powers to accurately control, thus forecast, the future.

Those two steps let fully integrated honesty integrate and then use the wide-scope knowledge needed to control the future.

271

# Movement III: The Civilization of the Universe

(Footnote from page 263)

[1]By stating that Dr. Peikoff has delivered more competitive, commercial values than all the other professional Objectivists combined does not imply the works of other Objectivists lack value. To the contrary, almost all written and audio works of the Peikoff-sphere Objectivists such as the Berliners, Binswingers, Schwartzs are valuable, interesting, and valid.

The Peikoffian dynamics of intolerant no-compromise Objectivism provide great power and strength when applying its principles. Problems with the Peikoffians arise when they generalize their intolerances inaccurately or emotionally to non-applicable areas of people and situations. Such misapplied intolerances are invalid, self-limiting, and eventually lead to intellectual isolation, even personal defeat...especially now as every area of mystical intolerance will be subject to the full scrutiny of the integrated honesty that ultimately rules cyberspace.

Leonard Peikoff has a wide array of valuable commercial products involving education and communication. Many of his products contain uniquely original, invaluable information that will be around for a long time. Also, his 493-page book, *Objectivism: The Philosophy of Ayn Rand*, Dutton, 1991, is a supreme accomplishment that permanently locks Objectivism into our civilization. Generally, those who carp about that masterpiece do not see the book as a powerful, wide-scope value that will eventually drive all bogus philosophies from this planet.

Also, it was important to publicly identify Peikoff's "Police-State" error so adjustments can be made to make his work even more valuable in the future. Hopefully, Dr. Peikoff will see and correct that error so he can more fully enjoy the fruits of his great work.

The books, tapes, lectures and other products of the "tolerant", more open-ended Kelley-sphere Objectivists might be more valuable to both professional philosophers and those interested in studying philosophy in technical depth. Also, David Kelley's sphere might grow in academic importance faster than Leonard Peikoff's sphere.

\* \* \*

Perhaps the most profitable lesson to learn in business is to accurately distinguish the 1) specific principled areas for hard-nosed, objective application of no compromise intolerance from the 2) general non-principled areas that require constant discipline to develop wide-scope, tolerant understandings. Acquiring that skill lets one take profitable advantage of every positive *and* negative situation. Stated another way: In business, one increases competitiveness and profitability by developing the skills to confidently toughen up with accurate, no-compromise control of specific principles while loosening up with benevolent understandings of general principles. ...For maximum effectiveness, communicate more like Horace and Erasmus and less like Juvenal and Jonathan Edwards. Toughening up by lightening up powerfully complement one another in philosophy and business.

272

# Chapter 31

# Earth's Greatest Discovery

On any objective consideration, one cannot take seriously religious claims of life after death. Yet, such claims are the centerpiece of Western religions as well as many other religions. But, all such claims are marketing hype to exploit the deepest hopes and fears of conscious beings. For the past two millennia, afterlife promises have hoaxed Earth's anticivilization into embracing mystical religions.[1]

### Earth's Greatest Discovery: Profit-Driven Immortality[2]

The afterlife hoaxes promoted by mystical religions serve to hide the single most important, potentially provable fact on this planet: *Most if not all honest conscious beings who have died on Earth in the past 3000 years continue to live with eternally expanding prosperity and happiness throughout the Civilization of the Universe!*

### Ultimate Justice

Justice is an immutable law of nature. As demonstrated by Cassandra's Secret, justice is *always* fulfilled throughout existence. As a result, the eventual destination or just reward for every actual and potential value producer — of every honest conscious being — is eternal prosperity and happiness in the Civilization of the Universe.

---

[1]Religious faith has, however, been a key value at various periods in history. At times, for example, religious faith served to divide and weaken government tyranny, and vice versa, leaving pockets of freedom to advance knowledge, technology, and well-being within the anticivilization.

[2]Profit-driven immortality as presented in this chapter is a speculative hypothesis arising from a-priori logic. Yet, logically, no contradictions exist in that hypothesis. Today, the chief value of that hypothesis is metaphorical — an illustration of justice that reality ultimately asserts. Tomorrow? Facts and knowledge will unfold to reveal the hypothesis as fact or fiction.

*Movement III: The Civilization of the Universe*

That just destination is the inevitable consequence of nature. From that nature comes (1) immutable justice that characterizes the Civilization of the Universe, (2) the supremely leveraged, limitless value of each conscious being when placed in a rational civilization, (3) the dynamics of eternally expanding prosperity, which demand the full use of *every* available conscious being, and, as explained later in this chapter, (4) the technology needed to transceive[1] every volitionally developed human consciousness through the omnipresent existence field and into the Civilization of the Universe.

Humanoid criminals or parasitical neocheaters who have lived by harming others or society through force, fraud, and illusions also meet ultimate justice: They become humanoids because they destroy the human nature of their own consciousnesses. Therefore, they destroy the conscious structure needed to transceive through the Gravity-Unit existence field and into the Civilization of the Universe. Moreover, having lived as enormous net negatives to society, humanoids such as destructive politicians with their armed bureaucracies and ego-"justice" systems are, unless rehabilitated, worthless to the Civilization of the Universe. Thus, they simply vanish from existence, forever forgotten.

## Bases of Proof

Any future proof of immortality for conscious beings must be derived from theories that are in full correspondence with the laws of physics. Theories derived

---

[1]Transceived not in the mystical Plato sense of a detached soul. For, the soul and physical body are one in the same and function as a unit. But, transceived (within a profit-mode, business dynamic) in the Gravity-Unit form that captures conscious "I"ness immortality as described in *The Neo-Tech Discovery*, all in accord with the laws of physics. ...The crucial importance of "I"ness in the rejection of the cryonic approach to immortality is detailed in the *Neo-Tech Protection Kit*, volume II, pages 371-375, Neo-Tech Publishing Company (1994).

both deductively and inductively must provide wide-range predictiveness, reproducible experimental evidence, consistent mathematical definitions, and limitless ways to test for contradictions and falsifications. This communiqué provides the elements needed to develop such proofs, predictions, and facts. ...Those theories must withstand challenges of direct and indirect experimental tests, observations, and calculations.

Listed below are the elements found in this communiqué. When assembled, those elements posit the hypotheses that (1) the Civilization of the Universe exists, (2) every fully developed, honest conscious being who lived on this planet for the past 3000 years continues to live with growing prosperity, love, and happiness in the Civilization of the Universe, and (3) technology commonly exists throughout the Civilization of the Universe that provides eternal life and prosperity to all honest, conscious beings on this planet. Those hypotheses also posit that every humanoid criminal who has died during the past 3000 years has vanished from existence. Moreover, all such parasitical humanoids who currently live by harming others will also vanish from existence. Humanoids living on Earth today, however, can be "saved" by restructuring their behaviors in order to mature into healthy, conscious human beings who competitively produce values for others and society.

Potential Elements of Proof found in *Zonpower*

Existence exists.

Existence is axiomatic, endless, eternal.

Existence exists eternally with no prior causes.

Consciousness is not only an eternal part of eternal existence, but is the eternal controller of existence.

Individual human consciousness is the greatest value in

275

eternal existence...the seminal value from which all other values flow.

The greatest social value among conscious beings is honest, competitive businesses combined with *objective* law and justice.

Valid knowledge is contextual and hierarchal. Valid ideas are hierarchal paradigms of contextual facts.

Conscious knowledge is limitless because knowledge always begets new knowledge — geometrically, up to the speed of light.

The essence of human consciousness is goodness: By nature human consciousness is noble, rational, honest, just, compassionate, value producing, benevolent, kind, loving, happy.

The only diseases of human consciousness are dishonesty, mysticism, and irrationality.

Those diseases destroy the natural good of human consciousness. Those diseases cause all wars and crimes, including politically inflicted property destructions, harms, sufferings, cruelties, and deaths. Such evils are inflicted by force or fraud to support the lives of open criminals (subhumans) such as muggers and rapists...or the much more evil, hidden criminals (humanoids) such as destructive politicians, tyrannical rulers, and killer-type (WACO) bureaucrats.

Camouflaged irrationality and deception used to drain, harm, and kill human beings is called neocheating.

Neocheaters are highly intelligent humanoids in whom the diseases of dishonesty and irrationality have destroyed the human nature of their conscious minds. Thus, such neocheaters are no longer human beings. They are humanoids who have destroyed the conscious structures of the human essences needed to enter the Civilization of the Universe. [Ref: The Neo-Tech Matrix described in the *Neo-Tech Discovery*]

To parasitically exist, neocheaters purposely propagate a bizarre, irrational civilization on planet Earth within which conscious life always moves toward unnatural death instead of natural immortality.

This unnatural, transitory anticivilization in macroscopic existence is somewhat analogous to the unnatural, transitory antiparticle in microscopic existence.

As the bizarre antiparticle vanishes forever on contact with natural matter, the bizarre anticivilization will vanish forever on contact with the natural Civilization of the Universe.

The supreme value of human consciousness will always be preserved by advanced civilizations using multi-dimensional[1] transceiver technologies in quantum-state, digitized cyberspace. Those technologies integrate rational consciousness with the existence field throughout the Civilization of the Universe.

By the fact of their continued existence, civilizations technologically advanced significantly past their Nuclear-Decision Thresholds are free from the diseases of dishonesty, mysticism, and irrationality. Thus, all such advanced civilizations are a part of the Civilization of the Universe.

In most areas, no one can predict the state of technology 100 years ahead, and certainly not a 1000 years ahead, much less a million years into the future. We cannot even imagine the technological states and economies of the advanced societies throughout the Civilization of the Universe.

---

[1]Such multidimensional examples are derivable from superstring and wormhole theories. Traversable wormholes, rotating black holes, and above-and-below Gravity Units offer theoretical but questionable time-travel possibilities at superluminal speeds. Such possibilities, nevertheless, can be codified through mathematics.

## Movement III: The Civilization of the Universe

We can, however, know that no society, regardless of how advanced, can contradict the laws of physics or nature. Moreover, we can know that conscious beings throughout the Civilization of the Universe will never purposely act to violate their nature, well being, and happiness.

The basic nature of rational conscious beings has never and will never change. No rational being would ever let technology overtake his or her nature, self-control, self-responsibility, growth, and happiness. For, that loss of control over one's self — one's greatest value — would be self-destructive and irrational. Indeed, all conscious beings in the Civilization of the Universe are free of such irrationality or any other impediments to the growth and happiness of individual consciousness.

Thus, conscious beings in the Civilization of the Universe have the same nature: They live for happiness and its corollary emotions of genuine self-esteem and love. Indeed, the moral purpose of conscious beings is to meet the requirements for achieving rational happiness.

The nature of existence includes (1) objective law and justice, which characterize the Civilization of the Universe, (2) the limitless value of each conscious being when functioning in a rational civilization, (3) the dynamics of continually expanding value production and prosperity, which demands eternally preserving the supreme value of *every* conscious being.

The most bizarre characteristics of the anticivilization are its overpopulation and aging problems. In any rational civilization, overpopulation and aging are impossible. Exactly the opposite occurs. When free of destructive humanoids, each conscious being is free to productively, culturally, and artistically innovate and flourish without limits, becoming a priceless value to others and society.

278

## Earth's Greatest Discovery

For, each conscious being in a rational civilization is free to innovate and produce through division-of-labor dynamics far more values and resources than he or she consumes. ...Always increasing in value while always decreasing entropy, conscious beings remains forever young and precious.

Thus, in the open-ended Civilization of the Universe, a great demand for volitionally conscious people *always* exists. ...When free in an open and rational society based on objective law, each conscious individual enormously benefits and enriches all other conscious individuals and their societies. Through eternity, therefore, each conscious being will eventually contribute more value to society than its entire population at any given point in time.

Knowledge and technology increase endlessly. All advancing civilizations require developing ever greater and cheaper energy sources and production efficiencies.

Prosperity and happiness of conscious beings do *not* depend on their actual level of knowledge or technology, but depend on their rational thinking and acting processes required for continuously advancing knowledge and technology from any level.

Throughout the universe, every level of advancing knowledge and technology exists. Thus exists a technological level of conscious beings whose most efficient production of values depend on the *unsupervised* development and utilization of free-will conscious beings...such as found in an anticivilization as exists today on planet Earth. For, each such transceivable conscious person would provide endless values to all individuals and societies in the Civilization of the Universe.

Every populated area in existence has the economic-growth

279

needs for which each additional, volitionally developed, conscious being from any civilization would be of immense value. Thus, honest conscious beings anywhere in existence are never allowed to perish.

In Earth's anticivilization, *every* volitionally developed, honest conscious person is transceived/redeemed on a commercially profitable basis into the Civilization of the Universe. In other words, essentially every honest conscious being who has ever lived on Earth continues to live, flourishing eternally, in the Civilization of the Universe. ...But, the harmful humanoids of past history self-programed themselves to perish — to vanish from existence forever in the ultimate Ostracism Matrix.

Thus, justice and rationality are preserved through immortality.

### Assembling the Proof of Immortality

Consider the effect of delivering irrefutable proof showing how all honest human beings live *forever* with increasing prosperity and happiness. Such proof might include measuring Gravity-Unit field changes of human beings versus humanoids and animals as they die.[1]

Of course, the primary responsibility of conscious beings on Earth today is to protect and preserve their existence — to create their own immortality in which transceiving would be unnecessary.

---

[1] In the mid 19th century, the great German mathematicians, C. F. Gauss and G. F. Riemann uncovered the noneuclidean geometries and higher spatial dimensions involved in such transductions throughout existence. Matter, energy, forces, and fields arise from motions through varying geometries in various dimensions and quantum states. Einstein needed Riemann's geometries to develop general relativity. Today, superstring theory originating from Kaluza-Klein theory further links geometries in various dimensions to existence.

Gravity-Unit Consciousness $\xrightarrow[\text{to}]{\text{convert}}$ matter/energy/forces/fields $\xrightarrow[\text{to}]{\text{convert}}$ spacetime curvatures/geometries $\xrightarrow[\text{to}]{\text{convert}}$ Gravity-Unit Consciousness

# Chapter 32

# Your Ride

## into the

# Civilization of the Universe

What will actually happen when you travel into the Civilization of the Universe? What will you experience? Will you ever return to this anticivilization? What about those left behind? What will limitless prosperity and eternal happiness really mean to you — emotionally, practically?

Once in the Civilization of the Universe, you will quickly forget the anticivilization. For, the anticivilization vanishes as the unreal nothingness it really is — it simply vanishes to be forever forgotten. And, those left behind? They too will vanish and be forgotten. But, no one will be left behind except criminal humanoids who have destroyed their human nature and refused to reconstruct their humanity. Thus, every conscious being, once in the rational Civilization of the Universe, has no reason or desire to connect their lives or memories with the destructive irrationalities of an anticivilization.

What will a nonpolitical civilization based entirely on integrated honesty and *objective* law be like? That civilization will be free of *subjective* political-policy laws, irrational ego "justice", and dishonest parasitical elites. Gone will be force-backed governments with their above-the-law rulers. Gone will be the politicians, lawyers, and judges identified as criminal-minded "superior people" by Fyodor Dostoyevsky in his classic *Crime and Punishment*.

## Movement III: The Civilization of the Universe

Gone will be armed bureaucracies, mystical religions, wars, crime, fraud, poverty, disease, and death itself.

But, what is the Civilization of the Universe really like — emotionally, intellectually, and experience wise? What will living free of disease, mysticism, dishonesty, criminality, and irrationality be like? One's entire pattern of thoughts, emotions, and experiences will be different — so radically different from anything experienced in this anticivilization that no one today could fully know or describe that eternal difference...at least not until the Civilization of the Universe is created on planet Earth.[1] The conscious-created Civilization of the Universe could be available on Earth as early as 2001. If so, then by 2005 AD, many conscious beings in the business-developed countries will have already left behind this unreal anticivilization to reside in the exciting Civilization of the Universe.

How can one get some idea of what conscious life in the Civilization of the Universe might be like — some idea before actually taking that one-way journey from this grotesquely contradictory anticivilization into the beautifully harmonious Civilization of the Universe?

Perhaps one can begin imagining an eternally prosperous, happy life by trying to view this closed-system anticivilization from the outside. From that external view, one can sense how irrationality constantly blocks or cuts

[1]Consider a flatlander living in a two-dimensional universe being flipped up into a three-dimensional universe then falling back into his flat-plane universe. Observing only a series of two-dimensional planes or lines fly by as he travels through three-dimensional space, that flatlander would have no adequate way to understand a three-dimensional universe and would have no way to explain it to his fellow flatlanders. ...Do not confuse this useful dimensional analogy with the invalid analogy of Plato's cave to so-called higher realities. No higher or multirealities exist. Only one reality exists.

282

off experiencing life as ecstasy, cuts off achieving limitless prosperity, cuts off experiencing a fully joyful, productive, rational life. From the Civilization of the Universe, *every* perspective will look different from anything one could experience within this anticivilization. Each new perspective will be like encountering a new color for the first time — a new-color symphony — a stunningly unexpected experience unrecognizable from any previous experience.

The increasing government-imposed difficulties in achieving competitive values and genuine happiness throughout this anticivilization will wondrously transform into the easy way — the path of self-responsibile freedom — a consistently joyful path filled with endless victories. Indeed, that easy way is *endless* growth through discipline, rational thought, and productive action. Perhaps the closest, but still distant sense to that experience, can be observed in children under six years old still not diseased by the anticivilization. In every such child, one can observe his or her learning as not only remarkably rapid but compellingly joyful and exciting. Until poisoned by the dishonesties and mysticisms of the anticivilization, each young child experiences increasing joy in progressing toward knowledge and control of existence.

Through the Zon Protocols, every adult can reenter the Civilization of the Universe left behind as a child. On reentering, one becomes free from the life-draining burdens of irrationality, dishonesty, and mysticism. One then gains hitherto unknown perspectives on discipline, productive work, love, happiness, health, diet, fitness, entertainment, pleasures. Indeed, an ecstatic life of endless growth is experienced by all conscious beings in the Civilization of the Universe. Even destructive politicians and other

283

parasitical humanoids can reenter that nonpolitical Civilization of the Universe after reconstructing their humanity — after becoming honest, competitive human beings who are genuinely valuable to others and society.

What joyful lives await human beings on Earth. Our journey toward the nonpolitical Civilization of the Universe has begun. Indeed, our one-way, magic-carpet ride into the Civilization of the Universe begins with *Zonpower* and is completed with the forthcoming *Zon Protocols*.

This unreal anticivilization whose politicians depend on dark Schopenhauer drives to survive by harming others and society will then vanish. Yes, the *Zon Protocols* will usher in the Civilization of the Universe...the natural civilization from which we came as children. And, into which, we will return as increasingly valuable, fully responsible, mature adults. For, we belong to the eternally evolving Civilization of the Universe.

Zon is the *natural* law of conscious beings in all worlds and universes.

# Chapter 33
# You Will Become Zon

Consider the following six points:

1. Zon is the measure of all conscious beings.
2. Zon is disconnected from *every* aspect of any anticivilization.
3. Parasitical elites have created a dishonest, violent anticivilization on Earth. They each will unhesitantly lie, make war, commit crimes, murder, even mass murder to continue their destructive livelihoods and increase their power usurpations.
4. One finds eternal freedom by disconnecting from Earth's anticivilization. Such a disconnection switches one from this anticivilization into the Civilization of the Universe.
5. No part of any anticivilization is redeemable or correctable. For, nothing is redeemable or correctable from illusions based on nonreality. ...Fully integrated honesty with its wide-scope reality vanishes all such illusions.
6. Daybreak does not at once replace the darkness. Thus, the Civilization of the Universe will not at once replace Earth's anticivilization. In both cases, a seeming glow comes first. Then light breaks across the darkness. All becomes visible, clear — a peaceful civilization of eternal prosperity and exciting romance here on Earth.

The following journey unites the above points by returning *you* to Zon whose kingdom is the Civilization of the Universe.

> You Control Existence
> You are Invulnerable
> You are Zon

Zon is a citizen of all universes. How would a citizen of Earth recognize Zon? How would Zon appear? How would Zon think? What would Zon do?

Zon is the controller of existence. Zon is the past and future creator of all universes. Zon is identical to you, except he or she acts entirely through fully integrated honesty and wide-scope accounting. Thus, you can experience Zon. Indeed, you can become Zon to rule existence and gain eternal prosperity. ...As Zon, nothing in an anticivilization has power over you.

You were born Zon. Every conscious being who has ever existed was born Zon. But, on planet Earth, *every* conscious being has been dragged from childhood into the dishonest illusions that perpetuate this anticivilization. Thus, everyone today behaves as someone else — as someone other than an honest, fully conscious human being. ...Until today, every adult on Earth has lived as a phantom, never realizing that he or she is an eternal Zon.

You are Zon living in an illusion-shrouded anticivilization. In this illusionary civilization, all human beings live as phantoms deluded into believing they are mortals who live and die with no eternal power, purpose, or prosperity. When, in reality, conscious beings are immortal with limitless power and purpose.

On vanishing the illusions of this anticivilization, you reconnect with Zon, the ruler of existence. Although you still walk among the phantoms in this anticivilization, you have no connection with their illusions. You are as divorced from their illusions as you would be divorced from the illusions of schizophrenics in an insane asylum.

Yet, you see *everyone* as your kin. You see the profound value and power in every conscious being. Beyond all else in existence, you treasure the soul of each human being, regardless of what civilization or age in which each lives.

* * *

As Zon, how would you appear physically, mentally, and behaviorally among the phantoms of this anticivilization? How would you gain ever increasing prosperity, love, and happiness when you are disconnected from all the illusions comprising this anticivilization? How would you function among the hypnotized human beings and destructive humanoids of this anticivilization?

As Zon, you do not feel superior to, aloof from, or even particularly different than others. Nor are you a Bartleby. You simply know you are in a different civilization — a 180° different civilization. That difference does not make you feel uncomfortable or uneasy. In fact, your ability to function with others is enhanced. That disconnection also enhances your ability to benefit all human beings *and* humanoids on this planet. Moreover, your disconnection enhances your own happiness and enjoyment of life on Earth.

Most profoundly, as Zon you know that you are invulnerable to the irrationalities of this anticivilization. Like the anticivilization itself, the irrational actions of both its human-being and humanoid citizens are unreal — not connected to reality. Thus, such nonreality has no meaning for you...no real influence on you.

*Movement III: The Civilization of the Universe*

Still, you are among fellow conscious beings — the greatest value in existence. Moreover, the objective requirement for eternal life, prosperity, and happiness remains the same wherever conscious beings exist. That requirement is to deliver ever increasing values to others and society. Through the division of essence and labor combined with voluntary transactions, you create increasingly more values for others than you consume. You become increasingly valuable to yourself, others, and society.

You live to *be*, not to *have*. You live to create, not to consume. You need nothing beyond the requirements to produce life-enhancing values at maximum efficiencies for yourself, others, and society. You need or want nothing from this moribund anticivilization. You neither need nor want anything from its inherently destructive rulers and their dishonest media, organizations, academe, politicians, intellectuals, or celebrities.

Why the zero value of this anticivilization? Consider its irrational effects: The more life-enhancing values that heroic value producers deliver to society, the more parasitical humanoids foment public envy against those value producers. Why? To increasingly usurp unearned livelihoods from the productive class. Likewise, the more life-supporting jobs that honest businesses deliver to society, the more parasitical humanoids use government force to drain those businesses through irrational taxes, political-agenda laws, and destructive regulations. Such insanity is not the fault of human beings. Rather, that insanity is inherent in any irrational civilization functioning through subjective laws fashioned by parasitical rulers backed by armed agents of force.

In reality, you and all human beings belong *not* among this unreal anticivilization but among the Civilization of the Universe. All the insanities of which an anticivilization is constructed are merely illusions that never exist in reality — bizarre illusions that ultimately yield only diminishment and death to human beings — dishonest illusions that serve only the parasitical livelihoods of humanoids.

Yet, you as Zon are eternally protected by honesty and reality. You are always advancing in *real* spacetime to ever greater accomplishments, continually decreasing the entropy[1] of existence — continually making order out of disorder. Thus, nothing in the anticivilization can really harm or adversely affect your progress in moving through spacetime toward eternal life and prosperity.

At this moment, you can experience the first glimpse at how you as Zon function among your fellow human beings in this anticivilization. You first note the honest innocence of young children. You realize that essentially all children under six years of age are Zons — innocent, uncorrupted, honest. You notice how all such children struggle to obtain objective knowledge, not illusions. Those children strive for value-producing powers, not socially destructive pragmatisms. Then you realize how all parents and adults in this anticivilization are deluded by their humanoid rulers — humanoids who eventually corrupt and then bury the innocence, honesty, and power inherent within *every* young child.

Only through that ultimate crime inflicted on all children has this bizarre anticivilization been perpetuated since its creator, Plato, twenty-three centuries ago.

### Real and Imaginary Killing of Human Beings

You start your journey into the Civilization of the Universe by transporting yourself into a mind and body that functions through fully integrated honesty and wide-

---

[1]That capacity to decrease entropy is why conscious beings and only conscious beings can potentially reverse physical aging.

scope accountability. With the power of fully integrated honesty, you discover the universal laws that deliver valid solutions to all problems. As a simple example, consider two diverse problems in this anticivilization: (1) the unhealthy fattening of Americans and (2) the emotionally charged abortion issue. Wide-scope accounting provides completely different perspectives on those two problems, links them together in unexpected ways, and then delivers powerful, definitive solutions to each based on universal laws. Consider the following example:

— Real Killings—

You are sitting in a mall ice-cream parlor eating nothing, just looking at those eating ice cream. You then look into the mall promenade at the milling crowd. You let nothing block your thoughts. You think honestly, widely. Nothing is out-of-bounds. In such wide-scope thinking, everything eventually connects together through new knowledge, certain knowledge about the past, present, and future.

You are thinking about the intentional destruction of the human mind and body. You realize that such destruction accrues through subjective laws and views replacing objective laws and views. By that process, you see America is becoming a fat farm as well as an insane asylum. You realize that obesity and insanity are related. With drug-like intensity, Americans are increasingly living to eat, rather than eating to live.

Indeed, the intentional destruction of the body requires the intentional destruction of the mind, which in turn requires the loss of honesty through rationalizations. That loss of honesty evolves from a culture of parasitical leaders foisting self-serving political agendas and exploitive mysticisms onto the public.

*You Will Become Zon*

How do the above facts link together to cause the intentional killing of Americans — the lethal fattening of men, women, and most evilly, innocent children[1]? How do those facts link together to increasingly diminish the chance for a healthy, happy life for Americans and their children? ...You discover the answer:

Research for the Canadian Air Force in the 1960s compiled and implemented scientifically sound facts about human metabolism, health, and physical fitness. That study identified the objective causes of damaging one's metabolism to breed unhealthy weight gains that lead to demoralizing stagnation, decreasing happiness, and early death.

Then in the early 1970s, Dr. Robert C. Atkins converted the Canadian Air Force findings into the best-selling, most effective diet book ever published: *The Diet Revolution*.[2, 3] The eternal fact underlying Dr. Atkins' diet is that carbohydrates combined with poor aerobic fitness — *not* calories, oils, or fat per se — cause unsavory weight gain, heart disease, diabetes, hypoglycemia, and other health problems. For, the human body does *not* naturally metabolize concentrated carbohydrates. In fact, above certain modest quantities, carbohydrates are both poisonous and addicting to human beings.

Human beings are natural carnivores, not herbivores. Human beings are natural meat or protein eaters, not vegetarians or carbohydrate eaters. Human beings naturally metabolize proteins along with fats and oils. Thus, natural foods include meat, poultry, fish, cheese,

---

[1]With hypocritical concerns and dishonest pleadings, people like Susan Smith and Hillary Clinton either directly kill their own children or indirectly kill thousands or even millions of other people's children. Also, Dickens/Gifford-type child-labor dishonesties have starved millions of children.

[2]In later years, Dr. Atkins sadly surrendered to the politically correct establishment, grew stout again, and leaned toward bogus fad diets.

[3]A modified, improved version of Dr. Atkin's diet was published in 1995: *The Zone*, Barry Sears, Harper Collins.

nuts, butter, cream, eggs, low-starch vegetables, and high-fiber cereals. While corn, sweet fruits, potatoes, pastries, pastas, and breads are troubling foods for human metabolism. All concentrated carbohydrates are harmful above modest levels, especially the most concentrated, purest form of carbohydrate — sugar in *all* its forms, including fructose, honey, and corn-syrup sweeteners. ...Sugar, a heavily government-subsidized industry, is subtly the most addicting, toxic, and deleterious drug known to afflict the human body...and mind.

Sugar is the crack cocaine of the carbohydrate drugs. Sugar is by far the biggest killing substance among human beings today. Such concentrated carbohydrates lie at the root of most eating disorders, discipline problems, concentration deficiencies, moodiness, unhappiness, depression, sloth, poor performance, and criminal behavior. Indeed, *without exaggeration*, the most insidiously harmful of child abusers and drug pushers are parents who addict their defenseless children with sugar in all its forms.

Those are facts: facts now, facts before, facts forever. Sitting in that ice-cream parlor, you realize why Americans today are increasingly throwing away their health and happiness. You realize they are increasingly mutilating their bodies and trashing their minds through endless upside-down "health" diets, government-subsidized nutritional frauds, bogus low-fat school lunch programs, and dishonest government-backed, survey-type pseudo science. Those frauds along with the FDA armed bureaucrats maliciously work to harm the physical and mental health of all Americans and their children.

In the 1970s and 1980s, increasing numbers of people directly or indirectly recognized the universal, objective facts about diet and health. Development and sales of sugar-free food and drinks escalated. But, in the early 1990s, sugar-free foods began vanishing in favor of meaningless low-fat, low-cholesterol, organic "natural" foods — politically correct foods. Mega-size, fat-free, sugar-laden cookies, brownies, snacks, and drinks are sold as health foods while the most benign and effective of the nonsugar sweeteners — cyclamates — are dishonestly banned by power-crazed FDA bureaucrats...and the harmless sugar-substitute saccharine is irrationally labelled as cancer-causing by the FDA, leaving only dubious NutraSweet® unscathed.

Today, as the public obsession with irrational food consumption and bogus fat-free diets grows, the per capita intake of toxic carbohydrates soars. Indeed, consumption of sugar and carbohydrates is now accelerating as people are deceived with illusions generated by the government, FDA, and bogus health advocates. Their sickening deceptions dupe people into believing they are eating healthier by eating low-cholesterol, low-fat carbohydrates. In the meantime, they and their children are increasing their carbohydrate intakes and addictions. Thus, they grow fatter while irreversibly damaging their metabolic systems, leading to glandular harm, uncontrolled fatness, and mounting unhappiness.

Next, consider Dr. Kenneth Cooper's great, scientifically grounded research in the 1960s concerning physical fitness and his subsequent book, *Aerobics*. From that book, Americans freely, on their own, began a rational trend toward genuinely improved physical fitness and happiness. For, in the 1970s and early 1980s, without the blatherings of government "experts" or self-appointed "health" advocates, the two natural criteria of a healthy human body were being increasingly understood: Human beings are by nature (1) protein metabolizers and (2) long-distance running animals.

Yet, in the 1990s, sales of near worthless, non-aerobic exercise devices, health-club memberships, low-fat diet books, and "anti-aging" pills soared. Fewer and fewer people kept *aerobically* fit to remain trim and happy into old age. ...The key to human health and longevity is *low-carbohydrate* diets combined with *aerobic* fitness. The key to human dietary happiness is the CAS diet — no Caffeine, no Alcohol, no Sugar.

Observe the increasing political-correctness machinations combined with government-funded, pseudo-science "research" in the form of noncontextual surveys. Today's avalanche of lazy, dishonest "science" is why objective knowledge about health, fitness, and happiness is being lost in a sea of irrationality — forgotten in a contradictory blizzard of bogus, survey-type health "discoveries".

The mid 1990s was like reentering the Dark Ages that were dominated by dishonest religious Establishments similar to today's dishonest politically correct Establishments. During that dark-age period of extreme irrationality, knowledge about health and prosperity was lost or sequestered. Life expectancy plunged, for example, to less than half that experienced in the previous, more-rational Golden Age of Greece.

Today's period of increasing irrationality blocks public knowledge of the destructive political agendas diminishing everyone's precious life. For example, government promotes public dependency and control by increasing drug-like carbohydrate consumption in the form of low-fat, low-cholesterol, sugar-laced foods and drinks. As people become carbohydrate addicted, unfit, and unhappy, they lose self-esteem and seek ever more dependency on authorities supplying good-sounding "easy answers". ...Consequently, the first major product that totalitarian governments allow into their countries is the insidious, will-breaking, sugar-laced caffeine drug, Coca-Cola®. ...Such governments show no interest in importing healthy, sugar-free, caffeine-free beverages.

The inescapable essence of a healthy human mind and body is *honesty and effort*. That identification about honesty and effort will eventually serve to vanish our chronically sick anticivilization, replacing it with the eternally healthy Civilization of the Universe.

### — Imaginary Killings —

Now shift to an entirely different problem in this anticivilization: Today's religious-right individuals are among the most worthy of Americans. Most religious-right people deliver genuine values and prosperity to others and society. Many are hard working, productive, family-oriented individuals who act as foils to the destructive actions of the parasitical-elite class throughout the secular Establishment.[1] Most religious-right people are self-sufficient and do not partake in government-sponsored, gun-backed parasitism. Yet, they are self-defeating and thoroughly hoodwinked by their own demagogic leaders on abortion and issues like school prayer.

Only with fully integrated honesty can they escape their trap — their contradictions of reality. With integrated honesty, they can remove the threats against their lifestyles while expanding their admirable values to vanish their nemeses: parasitical elites who enforce evil agendas through their armed bureaucrats.

Because of their loyalty to genuine values, religious-

---

[1] As stated on page 273, Western religion has often acted as a foil to the destructive power of the state — and vice versa. ...In the Civilization of the Universe, no illusions exist. Thus, no state or religious powers exist. Only individual Zonpower exists.

right people properly respect human life above all else. Thus, they would be correct — morally and legally — to block by any means within *objective* law, anyone, including government itself, who purposely murders other human beings. But, the problem with their all-out crusade against abortion "murder" is simply that a fetus is *not* a human being. ...Potentiality is *not* actuality.

Their badly misguided concept of "murdering" fetuses springs from emotional brainwashings by false "spiritual" leaders — leaders who support agendas needed to advance their own self-serving demagogic livelihoods. Indeed, at *any* stage, a fetus is nothing more than self-created protoplasm. The fetus is not a baby, not a child, not a human being. The defining essence or attribute of a human being is consciousness — conscious awareness and conscious functioning. The fetus has no consciousness. The fetus is not a human being. The fetus has no rights. The fetus requires no legal or moral protection.

Many millions of intelligent, religious people have been duped into morally and physically defending fetuses as if they were human beings. Consider their forcibly aggressive anti-abortion demonstrations along with other contradictions such as their demanding prayer or silent mediation in *public* schools. Such repugnant blending of church and state ultimately subverts the rights and freedoms of all nonreligious *and* religious people. For, demanding *any* gun-backed government action to promote political frauds or religious agendas means sanctioning gun-backed actions leading to all criminal acts, including political-agenda mass murder such as at WACO. Indeed, WACO was a political fraud that involved *real* child killings by the President, his armed bureaucracies, and his Attorney General.

*You Will Become Zon*

Objective Laws are Universal Laws

In the final analysis, all problems tie together to yield valid, effective solutions according to objective, universal laws that can never be contradicted. Only objective laws are valid and apply to everyone, at all places, at all times. By definition, objective laws do not spring from the minds of men and women. Such laws have always and will always exist universally — independent of the human mind and its emotions. Thus, no objective law is new; each is eternal. Moreover, *no* law — physical, legal, or moral — is valid unless that law is naturally applicable, universally and eternally.

Living by the universal principles of objective law, one neither needs nor wants approval, acceptance, or recognition from anyone interacting with this unreal anticivilization. The entire history of the anticivilization and its humanoid rulers is one of fraud leading to human diminishment. The anticivilization has no real existence or power. Its humanoid perpetrators have only illusionary existences and imaginary powers in an anticivilization first conjured up by Plato and then perpetuated by parasitical elites. Such parasites are epitomized by the dishonest hierarchies of the church, state, and academe who have fatally corrupted the minds and bodies of human beings for the past two millennia.

Now consider the meaning of vanishing the illusions that support this anticivilization and its humanoid rulers — the meaning of you becoming Zon:

Becoming Zon

On becoming Zon, you increasingly disconnect from the actions, people, and humanoids interacting with this unreal anticivilization. Your disconnection is not one of

297

misanthropy, but one of grace. Your disconnection involves (1) *physical actions* reflected by a pleasant demeanor, (2) *mental processes* reflected by creative, nonlinear, far-from-equilibrium thinking that brings order out of chaos to create new knowledge, and (3) *behaviors* reflected by benevolent disconnections from the irrationalities of this anticivilization. Those irrationalities include health-diminishing, life-consuming distractions ranging from drug-like obsessions with eating to life-escaping obsessions with sports, entertainment, and celebrities.

*You need not correct anything in an uncorrectable anticivilization.* **You only need to disconnect**. ...Now consider these areas of disconnection:

### — Physical —

Expanding health and vitality are earned, not given. Expanding health and vitality come no other way except through DTC — <u>D</u>iscipline, <u>T</u>hought, then <u>C</u>ontrol. DTC self-perpetuates, builds on itself, and then brings limitless rewards to every aspect of conscious life. ...DTC is the most powerful determinant of human health, longevity, and happiness.

Returning to your free-ranging thoughts, you have long known human beings on Earth are by nature long-distance running animals. Thus, through DTC, you run daily. You started years ago by running a slow 100 yards, working up over several years to a steady five miles a day in 40 minutes. Now you run every day, probably not missing a half-dozen days in a year. Time and schedule "inconvenience" are no more an inconvenience than bathing everyday. With that daily run, you are physically and mentally reborn each day, ready to advance beyond the accomplishments of the previous day, progressing forever into a future of expanding knowledge and prosperity.

You also know human beings are carnivorous animals. Indeed, your natural, low-carbohydrate diet eliminates desires for drug-like, high-concentration carbohydrates and sugar toxins. ...DTC naturally occurs throughout the Civilization of the Universe as does the CAS happiness diet — no Caffeine, no Alcohol, or no Sugar. ...You recognize cups of coffee, for example, as cups of unhappiness.

You are trim, fit, and happy. With your spouse, values such as growth, communication, love, and sexual enjoyment grow each year. In handling life, your effectiveness increases each year, *never* diminishing with age.

Your joy with your work, your loved ones, and your life expand eternally. You realize DTC and physical fitness are natural for all conscious beings throughout all universes, in all ages.

You disconnect from the irrationalities throughout this anticivilization.

### — Mental —

Your power to acquire expanding knowledge for controlling existence derives through fully integrated honesty and wide-scope thinking. Fully integrated honesty is the underlying source of value creation and competitive businesses on Earth and throughout existence. In an anticivilization, its humanoid creators and perpetrators can survive only by disintegrating the most powerful essence of conscious beings — fully integrated honesty.

You disconnect from the dishonesties throughout this anticivilization.

*Movement III: The Civilization of the Universe*

— Behavior —

Conscious beings are social animals mediated through value exchange and business. The limitless benevolence, prosperity, excitement, and happiness possible among conscious beings are derived from the natural dynamics among the Civilization of the Universe. They are derived from conscious beings freely producing and volitionally trading mutually beneficial values through not only the division of human labor but through the division of human essences. ...Poverty, crime, and war are inconceivable concepts in the Civilization of the Universe.

You disconnect from the socially and economically destructive behaviors throughout this anticivilization.

\* \* \*

As Zon, you feel a profound care and valuation for the source of *all* human values, in all universes, in all ages. That source of values is your fellow conscious beings. You also care for the humanoid parasites who created and propagate this destructive anticivilization. Indeed, you work for their redemption as human beings. Why? Most humanoids can be guided back to their childhoods when they were innocent Zons. From that point, they can learn to grow up — to mature into value-producing human beings. On becoming honest conscious beings, they also can reenter the Civilization of the Universe to become limitless values to others and society.

*You Will Become Zon*

## The Zon Protocols

The forthcoming *Zon Protocols* is the medium through which the Civilization of the Universe will embrace planet Earth. The *Zon Protocols* identify, integrate, and then vanish each and every illusion conjured up for the past two millennia by parasitical humanoids. Eventually, through the *Zon Protocols*, every conscious being on Earth will, with no transition phase or backward glance, simply click off this transitory, unreal anticivilization and step into an eternal, real civilization — the Civilization of the Universe in which each conscious person naturally belongs.

In the meantime, *Zonpower* will enable adults to protect children from being dragged into this illusionary anticivilization. Children will remain Zons. Thus, their Zonpower will remain intact as they grow into adults. They will leave this anticivilization behind as *nothing*. The anticivilization with its humanoid rulers will vanish, forgotten forever. Everyone will then live prosperously, peacefully, eternally in the Civilization of the Universe.

Children are the Achilles' heel of this anticivilization. For essentially all children under six belong to the Civilization of the Universe. They are Zons, citizens of the universe. Uncorrupted, they hold the power to control existence through fully integrated honesty. When, through *Zonpower* or the *Zon Protocols*, parents realize that every baby is born a Zon, they will protect and prevent their children from being dragged into this lethal, illusionary anticivilization. Thus, when those children become adults, they will assume their responsibilities as all-powerful citizens of the universe. They will be free of corruption and dishonesty. For them, the anticivilization will not exist. It will have been vanished, forgotten forever. ...Conscious beings on Earth will then be free to control

301

## Movement III:  The Civilization of the Universe

existence in creating for society eternal health, prosperity, and happiness.

# Chapter 34
# The Zon Awakening

Nothing links the nonliving to the living, the plant to the animal, or the animal mind to the human mind. Similarly, nothing links the slumberous consciousness of the anticivilization to the dynamic consciousness of the Civilization of the Universe. ...Likewise, nothing links the endless deprivations in this anticivilization to the limitless prosperity in the Civilization of the Universe.

In physics, nothing links one electron state to another or one spacetime system to another. In both life and physics, essences exist in either one state or another with no flow, transition, or linkage between them. Consider the nature of Planck's go/no-go blackbody radiation, Einstein's go/no-go photoelectric effect, and *civilization's go/no-go limitless-prosperity dynamics*. Locked within the laws of physics, how could one ever enter the law-based Civilization of the Universe from this criminal-based anticivilization?

As in physics with the introduction of Planck's energy, the introduction of Zonpower will allow entry into the Civilization of the Universe. Eventually, everyone on Earth will leave criminal politics behind and click into the Civilization of the Universe without transition.

Since no link or communication with the anticivilization is possible, no one today can know what life is like in the Civilization of the Universe — not until it actually appears on planet Earth, perhaps by the end of this century. Until then, all that can be known with certainty is that life in the Civilization of the Universe means

303

limitless prosperity and eternal happiness. Indeed, everyone can look forward to the happiest shock of his or her life as each suddenly awakens in a law-based civilization of eternal riches and exciting romance.

Why is linkage between the two civilizations impossible? That impossibility is not because of any cultural or psychological differences, which are profound and absolute. But, rather, that impossibility is because the laws of physics make impossible any contact or linkage, both practically and theoretically. The reason for that impossibility lies in the fact that each civilization travels along separate spacetime coordinates. One cannot travel or switch to a different spacetime system anymore than one can travel backward in time. *For, any such spacetime travel or switch would require the conscious reconstruction of every quantum state — of every matter and force coordinate — in the universe at every instant in time.* Thus, the arrow of time cannot be reversed or switched.

Spacetime systems constantly evolve and move forward. One is never able to travel to different spacetime or light-cone coordinates that have already come and gone...here or elsewhere. Nothing can revisit, return to, or alter events occurring in any past or separate time frame as reflected in a familiar way by Omar Khayyám in *The Rubáiyát* nine centuries ago:

> The moving finger writes; and, having writ,
> Moves on: nor all your piety nor wit
> Shall lure it back to cancel half a line,
> Nor all your tears wash out a word of it.

Consider the two illustrations on the next page:

## Illustration A
## ENERGY-ACTIVITY SYSTEMS

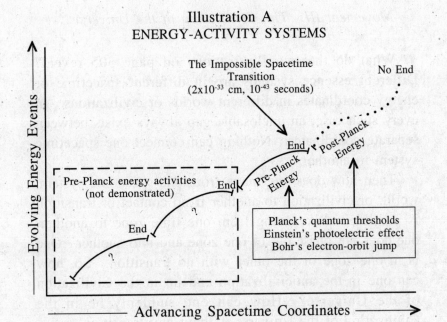

The Impossible Spacetime Transition ($2 \times 10^{-33}$ cm, $10^{-43}$ seconds)

No End

End

Post-Planck Energy

Pre-Planck Energy

Pre-Planck energy activities (not demonstrated)

End

End

?

End

?

?

Planck's quantum thresholds
Einstein's photoelectric effect
Bohr's electron-orbit jump

Evolving Energy Events

Advancing Spacetime Coordinates

## Illustration B
## CONSCIOUS-ACTIVITY SYSTEMS

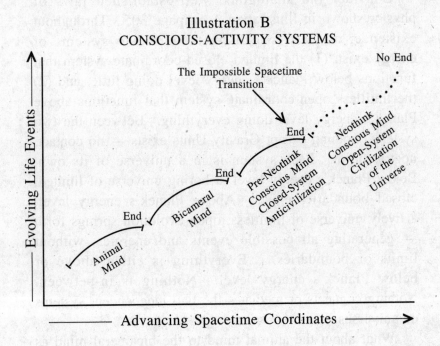

The Impossible Spacetime Transition

No End

End

Neothink Conscious Mind Open-System Civilization of the Universe

Pre-Neothink Conscious Mind Closed-System Anticivilization

End

Bicameral Mind

End

Animal Mind

Evolving Life Events

Advancing Spacetime Coordinates

## Movement III: The Civilization of the Universe

What do the two illustrations on page 305 reveal? Different essence systems are in different spacetime or energy coordinates in different worlds or civilizations. In every such case, an unclosable gap always exists between separate coordinates. Nothing can connect one spacetime system to another.

Then how does one move from one spacetime system, world, or civilization to another if no contact or transition is possible? Like going from one time zone to another, one does not phase out of one zone and into another. One is in one zone or the other with no transition. So, how can one in the anticivilization end up in the Civilization of the Universe? How can one suddenly be in the Civilization of the Universe without any transition?

Consider the analogous, well-established laws of physics shown in Illustration A on page 305. Throughout existence, at least two distinct coordinate systems of energy exist: (1) the limited closed-coordinate system that functions below Planck's energy level doing little, and (2) the limitless open-coordinate system that functions above Planck's energy level doing everything. Between the two systems, nothing except Gravity Units exists — no contact, no transition. Each system is in a universe of its own. Below Planck's energy level, a boring universe of limited, closed boundaries exists. Above Planck's energy level, a lively universe of limitless, open evolution springs forth — generating all possible events and energies, without limits or boundaries. ...Everything is either above or below Planck's energy level. Nothing is in-between. Nothing connects or mediates the two independent systems or universes.

What about the animal mind to the bicameral mind as shown in Illustration B? The bicameral mind to the conscious mind? The closed-system, rationalizing Kantian mind comprising the anticivilization to the open-ended, integrating Randian mind comprising the Civilization of the Universe? The criminally destructive Hitlerian/ Clintonian mind to the heroically productive Thomas Edison/Bill Gates mind? ...What is the analogous Planck's energy that will jump the spacetime gap or void from the anticivilization to the Civilization of the Universe? That equivalency of Planck's energy is contained within the universal constant of Zon, k, described on page 11. From the constant k flows the power of Zon.

The Civilization of the Universe *is* Zonpower. Once one integrates with Zonpower, he or she automatically makes a Planck-like jump with no transition. Abruptly, one is in the Civilization of the Universe. The anti- civilization is then left behind, impossible to contact, soon forgotten forever.

### Nonaging through Time Dilation

Civilizations are functions of conscious thinking, especially integrated thinking. The speed of integrated thinking depends on the depth and range of objective knowledge acquired. All such thinking is subject to time- dilation as described by Einstein's Special Relativity. In the closed boundaries of the anticivilization, integrated thinking is severely and absolutely limited. Thus, both the power and speed of integrated thinking are limited to minimal ranges. The speed of integration always increases with advancing knowledge. But, the closed boundaries of the anticivilization holds the speed of advancing knowledge far below that which Einstein's relativity has any observable effects.

By contrast, the Civilization of the Universe has no

Movement III: The Civilization of the Universe

boundaries. Thus, new knowledge is limitless and the speed of integrations are bounded only by the speed of light. Thereby, both knowledge and speed of thinking increase geometrically, if not exponentially. With such a multiplying effect, the speed of integration will soon approach the velocity of light as described in Chapter 6. At such speeds, time dilation becomes noticeable and then dominates.

What happens as the speed of integrations for new knowledge keeps accelerating ever closer to the velocity of light? The resulting time dilation becomes so great that the flow of time essentially ceases relative to events and experiences in technologically advanced cyberspaces.

* * *

The rationally open Civilization of the Universe allows conscious beings to live in eternal prosperity and exciting happiness. By contrast, the criminally closed anticivilization forces conscious beings to live in boring deprivation and then die.

Those differences in time dilation reflect the separate spacetime coordinates or paths along which conscious beings travel in the closed anticivilization versus the open Civilization of the Universe. With those differences in time dilation, any linkage or contact is impossible between conscious minds travelling along their separate spacetime coordinates — the anticivilization slow path versus the Civilization of the Universe fast path. ...Galileo/Newton provided the transformations of classical physics; Lorentz/Einstein provided the transformations of relativity; today Neothink/Zon provides the transformations of consciousness.

The Civilization of the Universe is coming. On its

arrival for each individual, the anticivilization and its criminal parasites will disappear, lost in bygone spacetime coordinates, never to be revisited, forever forgotten as nothing.

### Life in the Civilization of the Universe

Why do people who materially indulge themselves live in hidden desperation, cynicism, boredom? Why do they grow increasingly dissatisfied with themselves? Why does the greatest dissatisfaction and emptiness occur in those who seek ego indulgences and material gains most fervently? By contrast, what makes the Civilization of the Universe inconceivably different in which *everyone* has limitless prosperity and romantic excitement...void of anxiety, doubt, boredom?

In the anticivilization, why care about what anyone thinks, says, or does? Except for competitive values and their heroic producers, what difference does anything or anyone make in the schizophrenic irrationality of an anticivilization? Beneath this anticivilization, nothing except permanent value production makes any difference...or sense. In the Civilization of the Universe, however, everything that each individual does or experiences makes the most profound difference to everyone eternally.

Onward to Cyberspace
(See periodic chart on next page)

# A Periodic Chart
# Evolving from Endless Losses to Limitless Prosperity

→ Expansion Phases

| | Foundation | Value Development | Value Spreading | Protection |
|---|---|---|---|---|
| **Neo-Tech in the Anticivilization** | Fundamentals and Principles Neo-Tech Pincer I 1968 — Advanced Concepts of Poker — Neo-Tech Reference Encyclopedia 1976 — Neocheating 1979 — Golden Helmet 1980 — Neo-Tech Discovery 1981/1986/1994 | Conversion to Business Applications Neo-Tech Pincer II — Neo-Tech/Neothink Business System 1988 — Neo-Tech World Summits 1985-1987 | Spreading Worldwide Neo-Tech Pincer III — Building a Global Business Empire 1992 — Golden-Helmet Package 1994 — The Seven Waves 1987-1997 | Neo-Tech Protection Kit 1988/1994 |
| **Resurrection of Zon** | Prosperity Revolution 1991-1999 — Court Trials 1991-1995 — The Zonpower Discovery 1992 — Cassandra's Secret 1993 — Depoliticize, Decriminalize 1995-2001 | Foundation Building for a New Civilization 1. Neo-Tech Day-Care Centers 2. Neo-Tech Elementary Schools 3. Neo-Tech Role Models 4. Neo-Tech high-paying jobs for everyone 5. Neo-Tech Love Connection and Friendship Service 6. Objective-Law Party 2001 | Neo-Tech Literature Distribution Program 1994 — Social Connection 1994 — Zon World Summit 1999 | Operation of the Ostracism/Praise Matrix 2001 — Worldwide Conscious Control 2005 |
| **Civilization of the Universe** | *Cyberspace* Zon Protocols 2001 — Civilization of the Universe under development (available 1999-2004) | *Cyberspace* Implementation Worldwide as shown above 2001-2005 | *Cyberspace* Universal Networking 2005 | *Cyberspace* Universal Conscious Control 2010 |

→ Movement toward Limitless Prosperity →

# Chapter 35
# Poker Stratagems
### replaced by
# Zon's Integrated Honesty

As described in Chapter 18, how could anything so seemingly evil as the Illuminati Protocols be compatible with the fully integrated honesty of Neo-Tech? How could the founding Illuminati be the heroic precursors of Neo-Tech? Those questions are answered by comparing the underlying dynamics flowing beneath the fatally flawed, close-ended Illuminati dynamics to the pristine, open-ended Neo-Tech/Zon dynamics:

### Compatible Dynamics

The original Neo-Tech author and the original Illuminati recognized that all conscious beings on Earth, throughout the ages, were and continue to be drained, impoverished, and killed by a permanently entrenched parasitical-elite class. Moreover, the original Neo-Tech author and the original Illuminati recognized that this parasitical-elite class created a bizarre anticivilization from which no one could escape its always fatal human diminishments. The original Neo-Tech author and the original Illuminati also recognized that no matter what reforms or advances occurred, the same ever increasing cycles of parasitical destruction would always occur on planet Earth. ...Thus, when technology advanced to the capacity of destroying the entire human race through biological or nuclear weapons, that destruction would occur on the next major upswing cycle of irrationalities leading to mass destructions or wars.

311

*Movement III: The Civilization of the Universe*

As was the original Neo-Tech author, the original Illuminati were aware that every conscious being and all earned values on Earth would eventually be consumed by the parasitical elites. Although not knowing the final technology that could destroy conscious life on Earth, the original Illuminati knew that capability would eventually develop. Today, everyone knows that this total-destruction technology is thermonuclear energy.

Thus, the Illuminati today race to complete their goal of subverting and eliminating all life-draining institutions that support parasitical humanoids — eliminate them before they obliterate conscious life on Earth. The current parasitical cycle will increasingly ruin the real value-and-job producers, their means of production, their capital, their property. As in all past such cycles, this parasitical feeding cycle will escalate until the maximum possible human values are consumed or destroyed.

By using nuclear or biological weapons to destroy maximum possible values, this final wipe-out cycle would end most if not all conscious life on Earth. ...Some religious-right fundamentalists fervidly root for such an apocalyptic wipe out.

As revealed in Movement II of *Zonpower*, the only solution possible by working *within* this anticivilization is to undermine and then break every harmful institution throughout the anticivilization — eliminate every institution that supports humanoid parasites. That breaking of parasitical institutions could be accomplished by harnessing genuine business power through advanced poker stratagems. For, by combining that business power with such stratagems, one can outflank every parasitical maneuver.

The breaking of destructive governments and religious

institutions along with their parasitical beneficiaries can be done through organized, persistent business dynamics. In fact, that breaking of those destructive institutions has been nearly accomplished. By whom? By the dedicated handful of highly responsible Illuminati businesspeople.

Advancing the Illuminati's goal required the confident certainty that genuine business power combined with advanced poker strategy will *always* outflank and eventually vanish the false power of parasitical elites and their illusion-built institutions. Indeed, the underlying Illuminati strategy is maneuvering parasitical elites and influential leaders alike into irresistible positions of worldwide, ego-boosting power. Such positions are proffered by various quasi-secret international organizations. But, the controlling long-range plans and power are orchestrated by that handful of obscure Illuminati. Through such a system, the Illuminati could always maneuver influential leaders worldwide into creating conflicts that increasingly undermine nationalistic governments and organized religions.

## Incompatible Dynamics

While discovering the Civilization of the Universe in 1992, the following was revealed: On the brink of victory, the Illuminati would catastrophically fail, resulting in the end of conscious life on planet Earth. For, parasitical humanoids and their institutions can never be eliminated from *within* their own creation — from within their closed-system anticivilization. Instead, those humanoids on the brink of defeat would devour the Illuminati and their organizations as explained later in this chapter.

By contrast, as revealed in *Zonpower*, the Civilization of the Universe provides an eternally open, evolving

313

system of advancing knowledge, value production, and prosperity that is totally independent of the anticivilization. When individuals begin functioning from the Civilization of the Universe now arising on planet Earth in cyberspace, the illusions of the anticivilization and the influences of its parasitical rulers simply vanish.

Thus, the Illuminati's goal can be fully achieved not by violently working within this unnatural anticivilization but by peacefully working from without — from the natural Civilization of the Universe. ...The Civilization of the Universe is a healthy business civilization void of poverty and violence — void of parasitical elites.

Credit for Zon and the Civilization of the Universe being able to embrace planet Earth and vanish the anticivilization by the turn of this century belongs to the Illuminati — to their two centuries of relentlessly undermining the destructive institutions of this anticivilization. Credit must go to the heroic "dirty work" done by men of productive accomplishments and moral responsibility from the 18th-century Adam Weishaupt to today's 20th-century David Rockefeller...and all the other unrecognized, low-profile Illuminati. For two centuries, they have brilliantly duped and poker played the parasitical-elite class into undermining its own institutions.

Eight decades ago, Einstein's open system of relativity physics jumped past Newton's brilliant, invaluable work within the closed system of classical physics. Both systems were dedicated to eliminating ignorance about physical reality. To advance into the future, however, Einstein's open system had to move past Newton's closed system.

Likewise, today, Zon's open-system Civilization of the Universe jumps past the Illuminati's brilliant, invaluable work on the closed-system anticivilization. Both works are dedicated to eliminating the deceptions supporting this anticivilization. To advance into the future, however, the open-system moral base of Zon must replace the closed-system moral base of the Illuminati.

### The Illuminati Would Fail Without Zon

The Illuminati could not foresee the inevitable failure of their master plan. That failure would occur near their moment of victory: In the death throes of this anticivilization, its parasitical-elite rulers in a desperate attempt to survive would enter into a final feeding frenzy. They would devour the last seeds of human and financial capital needed for populations to exist and prosper.

Today, less-and-less earned wealth remains for the burgeoning parasitical-elite class to feed upon. When those last seeds of prosperity are devoured, even the Illuminati along with their master plan, their influential international organizations, and their noble goal would end in a suicidal, global Hitler-like debacle. For, with the essence of productive business gone, the Illuminati could no longer function. The anticivilization would then be primed for a new cycle of Hitlerian tyrants to arise — arise chaotically without the two-century-old restraints and controls of the Illuminati. Such uncontrolled humanoid rulers would drum-beat the world toward nuclear conflagrations, consuming nationality after nationality, race after race, population after population. ...The Illuminati's fatal flaw is their working *within* the closed-system anticivilization. They could not foresee that in the end they too would be devoured by the anticivilization.

Zon removes that fatal flaw to allow the successful conclusion of the Illuminati's master plan. ...Against the

315

reality of Zon, the anticivilization with its parasitical rulers vanish in cyberspace.

Today, with the glimmerings of Zonpower rising from America's 1994 elections, the Illuminati are sensing the shift of their moral and operational base from the politicized anticivilization to the nonpolitical Civilization of the Universe.

### The Wonderful World Ahead

Ahead lie limitless riches, romantic excitement, and eternal happiness for all conscious beings. Today, the Illuminati can finally vanish this moribund anticivilization. How? By using the glittering nonpolitical Civilization of the Universe as their new, limitless base of operations.

\* \* \*

In the Civilization of the Universe, one asks not where another is from, but one asks what another does for a living...what one does to deliver needed, competitive values to others and society. Concepts of race, nationality, and religion are unknown in the Civilization of the Universe.

### Objective Laws are Universal Laws

In the final analysis, all problems tie together to yield valid, effective solutions according to objective, universal laws that cannot be contradicted. Only objective laws are valid and apply to everyone, at all places, at all times. By definition, objective laws do not spring from the minds of men and women. Such laws have always and will always exist universally — independent of the human mind and its emotions. Thus, no objective law is new;

like the laws of physics, objective laws are valid in all frames of reference. Moreover, *no* law — physical, legal, or moral — is valid unless it is valid in all frames of reference.

### The Protocols of Zon

The Illuminati's goal will now be peacefully, humanely completed through the protocols of Zon. Those omnipotent protocols arise from Cassandra's Secret. Around the turn of this millennium, the explicit, formal Zon Protocols will be published through the Internet for worldwide implementation. ...The nonviolent Zon Protocols will bring a nonpolitical business civilization to planet Earth.

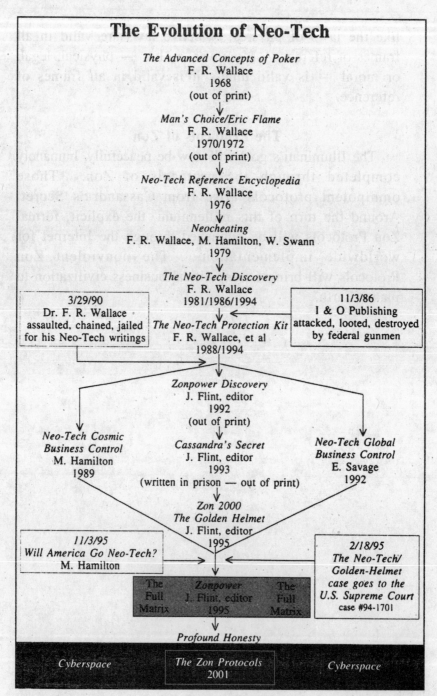

# The Evolution of Neo-Tech

*The Advanced Concepts of Poker*
F. R. Wallace
1968
(out of print)

↓

*Man's Choice/Eric Flame*
F. R. Wallace
1970/1972
(out of print)

↓

*Neo-Tech Reference Encyclopedia*
F. R. Wallace
1976

↓

*Neocheating*
F. R. Wallace, M. Hamilton, W. Swann
1979

↓

*The Neo-Tech Discovery*
F. R. Wallace
1981/1986/1994

| 3/29/90 | | 11/3/86 |
|---|---|---|
| Dr. F. R. Wallace assaulted, chained, jailed for his Neo-Tech writings | *The Neo-Tech Protection Kit* F. R. Wallace, et al 1988/1994 | I & O Publishing attacked, looted, destroyed by federal gunmen |

*Zonpower Discovery*
J. Flint, editor
1992
(out of print)

| *Neo-Tech Cosmic Business Control* M. Hamilton 1989 | *Cassandra's Secret* J. Flint, editor 1993 (written in prison — out of print) | *Neo-Tech Global Business Control* E. Savage 1992 |
|---|---|---|

*Zon 2000*
*The Golden Helmet*
J. Flint, editor
1995

| 11/3/95 *Will America Go Neo-Tech?* M. Hamilton | The Full Matrix  *Zonpower* J. Flint, editor 1995  The Full Matrix | 2/18/95 *The Neo-Tech/ Golden-Helmet case goes to the U.S. Supreme Court* case #94-1701 |
|---|---|---|

*Profound Honesty*

*Cyberspace*        *The Zon Protocols* 2001        *Cyberspace*

# Chapter 36
# The Zon Protocols

Most physicists, scientists, or physicians with vested interests in the anticivilization, such as tax-funded livelihoods, will resist identifying that human consciousness is the omnipotent force controlling existence.[1] Likewise, business people, professionals, or academics seeking praise and acceptance from within Earth's anticivilization must avoid grasping the wide-scope dynamics of Neo-Tech with its fully integrated honesty. But, those who integrate with *Zonpower* today or those who encounter the *Zon Protocols* at the end of this century can disconnect from Earth's anticivilization to gain Zonpower.

Without Zonpower, You are Trapped in an
Anticivilization
With Zonpower, You Control Existence

Until the unveiling of Zonpower in June 1992, every conscious adult on planet Earth was imprisoned in its irrational civilization — a mortally destructive anticivilization. Through force and coercion, a dishonest parasite class has propagated an anticivilization around the globe. They continue propagating that anticivilization by deceptively, forcibly draining the productive class, especially the entrepreneur business class which is the source of all genuine jobs, prosperity, and happiness.

Without Zonpower, every conscious mind is imprisoned. Without Zonpower, no conscious mind is able to escape the products of an anticivilization: dishonesty, irrationality, destruction, death. The reason for that entrapment is that everyone is coerced from *every*

---

[1]As reviewed in Chapter 6, *The Long Wave*.

319

direction. And no conscious mind can think honestly, widely, or deeply under *any* form of coercion.

Most important, on trying to live by fully integrated honesty that is natural in the Civilization of the Universe, one will increasingly feel uncomfortable and anxious if his or her life remains invested in the anticivilization. Indeed, one cannot capture Zonpower while remaining invested in this unreal anticivilization.

Ironically, throughout history, only young children and certain schizophrenic savants have tasted Zonpower, albeit in narrow areas. What is meant by stating certain schizophrenics have tasted Zonpower? Do their experiences provide a hint of the undreamt power available to conscious beings not invested in this anticivilization? Consider the ancient oracles of Greece, including the most famous, the Oracle at Delphi. They had one common background: They all were naively honest, uneducated country girls who hallucinated as schizophrenics. None were invested in the anticivilization. Yet, kings as mighty as Alexander the Great, emperors, generals, lawmakers, and the wealthy regularly consulted and acted, often with spectacularly favorable results, on the uncanny, seemingly brilliant insights of those hallucinating women.

Consider Joan of Arc in the early 15th century. She too was a naively honest, uneducated country girl who hallucinated and was disconnected from society — disconnected from the sophistications of the anti-civilization. Yet, as a teenager, she became the premier military commander and war strategist in France. She delivered brilliant new insights into politics, warfare leadership, and battle tactics. Starting by liberating Orléans at 17 years old, she personally led France to key victories over the English invaders. She then provided the political strategy to restore Charles VII to the throne of France. ...At 19 years old, undermining the false power of the parasitical-elite class, she was politically imprisoned, tried by ego "justice", and then burned at the stake.

Why did those uneducated, illiterate women have insights beyond anyone else in areas of state and war? Because they were uneducated, poor, and disconnected from established society, their minds were disconnected from the integration-blocking dynamics of the anticivilization. In those areas, therefore, they were free to think more widely, without bounds...free to think with greater honesty.

In their areas of disconnection, they could gather wider ranges of integrations and insights than anyone connected to the anticivilization, including the greatest contemporary experts. Thus, the unblocked minds of those women could provide completely new and often more accurate perspectives of momentous events.

Consider the most powerful moral savant of Western Civilization: an uneducated, illiterate hippie who also hallucinated. He too was disconnected from the anticivilization of his day. Yet, that man held moral sway over the Western world for a hundred generations, right up to this day. That person was Jesus. He undermined the parasitical-elite class, was politically imprisoned, tried by ego "justice", and then crucified. ...Jesus' *earthly* moral principles are now yielding to the *universal* moral principles found in objective law and expressed by the forthcoming Zon Protocols.

Indeed, wide-scope thinking is impossible under coercion. That is why no one in this anticivilization can fully grasp the concept of integrated honesty to unleash Zonpower. *Any form of coercion generates an array of rationalizations that prevent the wide-scope, contextual thinking required for Zonpower.*

By disconnecting from *every* aspect of the coercive anticivilization, the conscious mind springs free from the anticivilization to gain Zonpower. With Zonpower, one controls existence through fully integrated honesty.

**You**

and the

**Zon Protocols in Cyberspace**

Through the Zon Protocols, you will live with ever increasing health, prosperity, and happiness. You will no longer need to invest in a corrupt anticivilization. You will live in the Civilization of the Universe. You will vanish the dishonesties, illusions, and nonrealties that today assault the mind and body of every conscious being on Earth. The anticivilization with all its coercions, harms, and diminishments will disappear. You will gain genuine power. You will gain Zonpower. You will control existence.

Today, you are unable to experience fully integrated honesty and wide-scope thinking. Today, you are bound within bubbles of mysticism, stunted by coercions, blocked by rationalizations in seeking acceptance from an irrational civilization ruled by parasitical elites. Thus, you will enter the *Zon Protocols* as a citizen of Earth's anticivilization created by criminal politics and morbid religions. ...But, you and everyone reading the forthcoming *Zon Protocols* will become a Citizen of the Universe. You will become Zon. You will be free of mysticisms and illusions — free of Earth's anticivilization. You will control existence through fully integrated honesty, boundless energy, and wide-scope thinking. **...You will gain the eternal prosperity and happiness available to all conscious life.**

# Word Usage

**Neo-Tech** is a noun or an adjective meaning *fully integrated honesty* based on facts of reality. Neo-Tech creates a collection of *new techniques* or *new technology*[1] that lets one know exactly what is happening and what to do for gaining honest advantages in all situations. Neo-Tech provides the integrations in every situation to collapse the illusions, hoaxes, and all other forms of irrationality manipulated by the parasitical-elite class. ...Understanding *is* the process of honest integration.

**Mysticism** is action based on dishonest irrationalities and mind-created "realities". Mysticism evokes, accepts, or uses unreal notions that *create problems where none exist*. Contrary to popular belief, mysticism today seldom involves god-type religions or the occult. God religions and the occult are dying forms of mysticism with fading powers to hurt the productive class. More generally, mysticism is the dishonesty that evolves from using feelings or rationalizations to generate mind-created "realities". In turn, those "realities" create unnecessary problems and unnatural destructions. Unnecessary and unnatural because the human brain *cannot create* reality. Instead, the brain *perceives* and then *integrates* facts of reality in order to control reality.

Thus, "reality"-creating mysticism is a perversion or disease of human consciousness. Indeed, mysticism is the destruction disease. For mysticism blocks brain integrations to erode all values. Mysticism breeds dishonesty, malevolence, and death. Hence, mysticism is suicide on all levels — on personal, family, social, and business levels; on local, national, and world levels.

---

[1]New to the anticivilization, but normal to the Civilization of the Universe.

323

**Neocheating** is the undetected usurpation of a livelihood — the unsuspicious swindling of money, power, or values through clever manipulations of dishonest rationalizations, non sequiturs, and mystical notions. Neocheating means *new cheating* for usurping values earned by others. Actually, parasitical elites have used neocheating for two millennia in hidden, unnoticeable ways. But the *techniques* of neocheating were not specifically identified until 1976. Thus, neocheating is a *new identification* rather than a *new technique*. Before that identification, no one could define or even notice a neocheater. Now, anyone with Neo-Tech can easily spot neocheaters and render them impotent. For, against Neo-Tech, the illusions of mysticism vanish and neocheaters become powerless. ...Neocheaters are unnatural people. Some are humanoids.

- The essence of Neo-Tech is honesty and effort.
- The essence of mysticism and neocheating is hidden dishonesty and laziness.

*NEO-TECH* is rational. It lets one act consistently on objective *facts*. That approach yields beneficial emotions of happiness and love. Thus, Neo-Tech captures reality by having actions produce emotions. ...*Neo-Tech integrates the mind*.

*MYSTICISM* is irrational. It lets one act arbitrarily on subjective *feelings*. That approach yields harmful actions and spoils beneficial emotions. Thus, mysticism loses reality by having emotions produce actions. ...*Mysticism disintegrates the mind*.

Mysticism is the essential tool of all parasitical elites and neocheaters. But Neo-Tech will cure the disease of mysticism to end irrationality, dishonesty, neocheating, and the parasitical-elite class.

**Neothink** is the boundlessly wide integrations made possible by Neo-Tech eradicating irrationality. Neothink is the harnessing of Neo-Tech power here on Earth: ...*Neothink outcompetes all, controls all.*

**Integrated Thinking** is the honest effort of putting information into the most accurate, widest context by logically connecting *all* known relevant facts. Only contextual knowledge is valid. Thus, genuine power is gained through integrated thinking, both vertical and horizontal, in the widest possible context. ...Volitional choice, the essence of free will, is also the essential of effective integrated thinking and valid knowledge building.

**Justice** is based on objective law and integrated honesty.

**Ego "Justice"** is based on arbitrary subjective laws and force-backed political agendas used to gain unearned livelihoods and feel false importance.

**Parasitical Elites** are unnatural people who dishonestly drain others. They have lost the attributes of human beings. They are humanoids who live by furtively usurping, swindling, or destroying values produced by others. To exist, they must prevent honest, integrated thinking by others. For survival, they depend on ego "justice" and force-backed political policies.

**Criminal Minds:** *Others owe me a living. Thus, I can live by destroying, stealing, leeching, or usurping values earned by others."* ...Criminal minds lay the responsibility for competitive value production onto others. Such criminal minds epitomize politicians, business quislings, also many bureaucrats, academics, clerics, news journalists, judges, and lawyers. For, their behaviors fit Dostoyevsky's *Crime and Punishment* definitive description of the criminal mind: 1) Unawareness of or contempt for individual property rights. 2) The presumption that parasites, usurpers, enviers, value destroyers, and con artists have a right to live off the productive efforts of others. ...Criminal minds exist by using deception or force to live off the productive class. Survival depends on fraud-driven or force-backed value destruction. Incompetence and unhappiness result.

**Virtuous Minds:** *I must earn my own living. Thus, I must live through my own productive efforts. I must competitively create and produce values needed by others and society."* ...Such virtuous minds are the opposite of criminal minds. For, virtuous minds, by nature, respect individual property rights. Virtuous minds never need to use ego "justice", deception, fraud, or force to prosper. Survival depends on value production. Competence and happiness result.

**Value Producers** have business minds that benefit society. They live by creating or producing competitive values and productive jobs for others and society. They succeed by honest, integrated thinking.

**Money:** Is it wanted for laziness or effort? A criminal mind sees usurping money as a way to escape competitive efforts needed to produce values for others...a way to do less. A business mind sees earning money as a way to increase competitive efforts to produce ever more values and jobs...a way to do more for others and society.

**Neo-Tech Minds** are the powerful, mystic-free minds of the Civilization of the Universe...minds based on fully integrated honesty and justice.

**Neo-Tech Business Minds** easily outflank and outcompete the narrow thinking and dishonest behavior of all criminal and mystic-plagued minds.

**Truth** is a mushy, hydra-headed word. Everyone disputes its meaning. Truth denotes a <u>static</u> <u>assertion</u> that changes from person to person, opinion to opinion, culture to culture. Thus, *truth* is a hollow, manipulative word that parasitical elites promulgate to gain credibility for their deceptions, destructions, and ego "justice".

**Honesty** is a solid, indivisible word. No one disputes its meaning. Honesty denotes a <u>dynamic</u> <u>process</u> that is identical for every conscious being. *Honesty* cannot be manipulated. Therefore, parasitical elites must squelch honesty in order to live off the productive class.

> *Discard the Word* **Truth** *—*
> *Uphold the Word* **Honesty**
> *Discard Ego "Justice" —*
> *Uphold Objective Law*
> *Discard the Parasitical Class —*
> *Uphold the Productive Class*

# The News-Media Establishment

vanishes in

# Cyberspace

The news-media establishment must promote the political status quo as meaningful. Neo-Tech and Zon sweep away the political status quo as meaningless. The news-media establishment has little value in cyberspace and no value in the Civilization of the Universe.

5940

Cyberspace/Zon137=$hc/2\pi e^2$

330

Neutrino wave pressures, 32
Neutrons, 5, 6
*Newsweek*, 139, 226
New-age ideas, 208
New Testament, 252
News media, 126, 141, 167, 168, 328, see also Media
Newton, Isaac, 23, 40, 136, 183, 209, 226, 308, 314
Newtonian physics, 7, 12, 96, 209
Newtonian revolution, 96
*Nicomachean Ethics*, 187
Nietzsche, Elizabeth, 239
Nietzsche, Friedrich W., 232, 239
Nightingale, Florence, 136, 167
Nihilists, 226
Noncontradiction law, 14
Nonequilibrium pressures, 33
Noneuclidean geometry, 31, 46, 280
Nonreality
    Goy politics and, 183-185
Noriega, 167
Northern Pacific Railroad, 100-103
Nothing power, 227
Novas, 195
Nuclear-Decision Thresholds, 70, 277
Nuclear energy, 24, 60
Nuclear forces, 5, 12, 25
Nuclear fusion, 311
Nuclear weapons, 312
Nutrasweet®, 293


– O –

Obesity, 290, 291
Objective justice, 119, 278
Objective law, vii,109, 130, 190, 231, 232, 257, 276,
        278, 279, 297, 317
    enforcement of, 155
    in Civilization of the Universe, 281
    defined, 297, 317
    Goy politics and, 183
    Illuminati and, 176
    upholding of, 226
Objective reality, 207
Objectivism, 229-234, 263-264 see also Peikoff, L.;
    Rand, Ayn
*Objectivism: the Philosophy of Ayn Rand*, 229, 272
Observer, 15-20
Oceans, 5
Odysseus, 259, 260
*Odyssey, The*, 242, 250, 259, 260
Oklahoma City, bombing, c-2, 185
Old Testament, 242, 250
Omar Khayyám, 304
One-liners, 256
One-world agenda, 175, 181
One-world conspiracy theories, 171, 180
Oracles, 251, 320
    at Delphi, 320
Order, 196, 206
*Origin of Consciousness in the Breakdown of the
    Bicameral Mind, The*, 229, 241-256
Ostracism, 232

computerized, 162, 163
    of parasitical-elite class, 125, 143, 159
Ostracism Matrix, 157, 159, 163, 280
*Othello*, 126
Ouija boards, 213, 250-253
Overpopulation, 278


– P –

Paperwork of federal agencies, 134
*Paradise Lost*, 202
Parallel universes, 45
Parasites, 214, 223, 265, 268, see also Parasitical-elite class
    sweeping away of, 269
Parasitical-elite class, vii, 20, 115, 121, 122, 124,
        140-143, 146, 149, 156, 227, 258, 266, see also
        Value destroyers
    archetypes of, 226
    Bakunin description of, 152-154
    categories of, 160, 161
    chaos and, 193, 194
    Clinton Envynomics and, 193, 194
    defined, 22-23, 27, 325
    as enemy in value producers' revolution, 165
    escape from, 28, 29
    examples of, 226
    expanding, 95, 96
    exposure of, 233
    fraud and, 105-108
    Golden Helmet and, 162, 163
    guilt of, 237, 238
    Hitler's description of, 152
    hoax of, 145-147
    ostracism of, 125, 143, 159
    Peikoff and, 232
    plunderers, 262
    potentials of, 226
    power of, 167, 168
    rise of in America, 99-199
    rule of, 222
    state of being of, 226
    subjective law and, 155
    support for, 135, 136
    survival of, 193, 194, 226
    termination of, 127-131, 146, 151, 159, 163, 165, 198
    peacefulness of, 162
    permanent, 20
    timing of, 229-232
    Zonpower and, 28, 29, 222, 226, 229, 230-232
    Zon attacked by, 236, 237
Parasitical cycle, 312
Parasitical elites, 20, 291, 297
    dynamics of, 311, 313
    Goy politics and, 186, 187
    Illuminati and, 173, 177, 180, 315
    redemption of, 188
    religious-right and, 296
    vanishing of, 314
    Zon and, 285, 288
Parasitism, 167, 168
Parmenides, 12, 22

339

344

# Closing Ceremonies

"...Dreaming dreams no mortal ever dared to dream before."
Edgar Allan Poe
*The Raven*

*Profound Honesty* not only dreams such dreams, but makes those dreams become real to all mortals here on Earth.

---

# Ride to Prosperity
## in
# Cyberspace

---

### Neo-Tech Stimulants Underlie the Future

Stimulation is the most basic need for all life. For conscious life, stimulation underlies the drives for sex, identity, self-esteem, security, survival, and consciousness itself. Lose stimulation and conscious life is lost. Excitement is an outward expression of stimulation. Natural stimulation and excitement arise through efforts that produce ever greater values for self and others — values that let conscious life become increasingly prosperous. Stimulation can also arise unnaturally through irrational acts that harm self and others — destructive acts ranging from dishonest politics and criminal parasitism to promiscuous sex and drug abuse. Such unnatural stimulations always leave hangovers of value destruction, stagnation, anxiety, boredom, ill health. The more one depends on *unnatural* stimulation to survive, the more destructive that person becomes to self and others. By contrast, the more one achieves *natural* stimulation, the more valuable and exciting that person becomes to self and others. ...This Closing Ceremony shows how natural Neo-Tech stimulants in cyberspace will deliver prosperity and happiness to everyone.

---

Marsh Ward, working with the Washington DC Homeless Shelter, originated this stimulant concept. He is the innovator of "nongovernment drug therapy for the ghetto poor" — America's most effective drug-addiction cure.

a

# Closing Ceremonies

## Table Of Contents

## Ending the Long Search

"I have long searched for the words to explain the purposely destructive attacks by governments, religions, and their leaders on the essence of human values — attacks on competitive business, property rights, individual rights, fully integrated honesty, objective law. What deep anti-life disease warps the conscious mind to cause such irrational actions? That disease is not only the ultimate cause of all purposeful harms and injustices inflicted on human beings, but that disease ultimately brings decline, stagnation, and death to all conscious beings on Earth. ...Perhaps, in prison, I shall find those words to explain what has never been explained."

Above were the words of Dr. Frank R. Wallace upon entering federal prison on June 28, 1991. He was imprisoned for writing, publishing, and billboarding about the rising government violence against innocent value producers. He was imprisoned for publicizing the rising criminalities, including murders, by armed federal bureaucrats. ...If Wallace had not been silenced in 1991, perhaps the Waco and Oklahoma City murders would never have occurred.

Now consider the words of President Clinton in 1995: "There is nothing patriotic about hating your government or pretending you can hate your government but love your country".

The political desperado who uttered that statement to condemn American citizens who morally resist rising government tyranny placed himself among the despots of history: Remember, despot King George III condemned *British citizens* George Washington, John Adams, Thomas

1

Jefferson, James Madison for loving their country by morally resisting their government's rising tyranny. King George III hanged Nathan Hale ("I only regret that I have but one life to lose for my country") and would have hanged Washington, Adams, Jefferson, and Madison if captured by their government. And, remember, despot Santa Ana condemned and killed *Mexican citizens* Jim Bowie, David Crockett, and many others at the Alamo and elsewhere in Texas for loving their country by morally resisting their government's rising tyranny.

Remember, too, despot Adolf Hitler and his armed Gestapo bureaucrats murdered bands of heroic *German citizens* in the 1930s for loving their country by morally resisting their government's rising tyranny. Millions who loved their country were killed for hating and resisting Stalin's evil government. Thousands who love their country still rot and die in prisons for hating and resisting Castro's evil government.

Unless morally resisted by those who love their country, criminal-minded politicians and their armed bureaucrats will continue driving America toward tyranny, terrorism, riots, and lawlessness. ...Fully integrated honesty, which rules cyberspace, is morally resisting and will vanish such despots and tyranny not only in America but worldwide.

This document brings forth those long-sought-after words found by Dr. Wallace in prison. Those words finally bring understanding to 3000 years of incomprehensible attacks on competitive value production, property rights, individual rights, and fully integrated honesty.

This document identifies the deep anti-life disease that impels conscious minds to attack the essence of good. Most important, this document celebrates the cure to those irrationalities — a cure already being delivered by Neo-Tech stimulants in cyberspace. That cure is fully integrated honesty.

### Curing the Criminal Mind

Can people perceive themselves as so important, so self-righteous that they believe their actions are above objective law? Are such people capable of remorselessly inflicting great harms even deaths upon the innocent, even entire populations? Examples abound in great literature and across history. From great literature arise the murderous minds of Homer's Odysseus and Dostoyevsky's Raskolnikov. And, across history arise the murderous minds of Caesar, Woodrow Wilson, Stalin, Mao, Castro...and currently the Clintons, O.J. Simpson, and "race-excused" criminals. They seemingly escape justice through the latent criminal mind buried in others — buried in everyone invested in this anticivilization. That pervasive criminal mind embedded at all levels of society allows such self-aggrandizing killers to inflict their harms against others without apology, without punishment, often without even rebuke. ...How can justice prevail? How can the criminal mind be cured?

Everyone from Ayn Rand to the Pope can and does rationalize away criminal-minded acts of themselves and others. Such acts, including murder, are rationalized given particular combinations of threats to that person's livelihood, ego, and survival in this irrational anticivilization. Some Nazi death-camp killers, for example, were refined university-educated scholars of Schiller and Goethe. Indeed, the anticivilization can activate a criminal mind in anyone, at any time. ...Everyone must try to deny integrated honesty in order

3

to protect his or her investments in this irrational civilization.  But, ultimately, honesty cannot be denied.

In the rational Civilization of the Universe, self-destructions, criminal acts, and harmful rationalizations vanish.  Integrated honesty is the gateway to the Civilization of the Universe.  Indeed, integrated honesty ultimately eliminates all threats to one's livelihood and survival.  Thus, through integrated honesty, the criminal mind with its rationalized injustices is cured.

That curing is already happening in cyberspace through Neo-Tech. ...Neo-Tech will *crush the evil*.

*Écrasez l'infâme*
Voltaire

# Who Rules Cyberspace?

## Happening Now In Cyberspace

on
World Wide Web Site
http://www.neo-tech.com/

## Vaporizing Irrationality

### Cyberspace Excitement

Throughout conscious existence on planet Earth flows an unbridgeable gulf separating dishonesty from honesty, irrationality from rationality, subjectivism from objectivism. Conscious beings today stand upon the shore awash with dishonesty, irrationality, subjectivism. Most are productive human beings, a few are parasitical humanoids. Some advance liberty, a few advance tyranny. All stand with their backs to the gulf. At first, none are aware of the approaching new paradigm for an eternally prosperous life.

Poised upon the lip of eternity, a few lift their heads to glimpse beyond the gulf. They see that new paradigm. They see a paradigm of integrated honesty that terminates the long train of illusions and investments throughout this moribund anticivilization. At first, rejection abounds. As the paradigm approaches, rejection turns to fear. For, that paradigm means the disappearance of government force that created a galaxy of parasitical livelihoods — livelihoods supported by dishonesty, irrationality, fraud, murder.

At the height of that fear, those irrational investments become worthless. As those life-long investments in beguilement evaporate, people will sublimate into an exciting, prosperous civilization of integrated honesty. ...That sublimation has already begun in cyberspace.

5

Vanishing Irrationality

Fully integrated honesty rules cyberspace because no one rules cyberspace. A paradoxical statement? Consider the following: Individual consciousness reigns supreme in cyberspace. Indeed, in cyberspace, harmful politicians, armed bureaucrats, ego judges, religious charlatans, dishonest journalists, and stagnant big-business executives have no control or power over individuals. Consider the harmful politicians who promote gun-backed laws to impose their whims in trying to control others. In cyberspace, destructive politicians are left impotent, thus harmless. They are simply flamed out of existence.

What will happen as individuals by the millions, then by the billons, move into cyberspace? In cyberspace, individuals function freely, voluntarily among themselves. No space, time, or cost boundaries exist in cyberspace. No legal, political, or religious boundaries exist. Thus, a natural dynamic develops in which the honest, the exciting, the valuable drive out the dishonest, the boring, the destructive.

By contrast, in the noncyberspace world ruled by political agendas, the honest and rational are often condemned or suppressed as politically incorrect or subjectively illegal. Also, in the noncyberspace world, the dishonest and irrational are often politically promoted, especially when backed by armed bureaucrats functioning as unpunished criminals. In the noncyberspace world, armed bureaucrats become dehumanized criminals who destroy innocent people's lives, values, and property.

In cyberspace, contextual facts vanish myths. Likewise, rationality vanishes irrationality: value vanishes disvalue, honesty vanishes dishonesty. The good drives out the bad, reality drives out mysticism, excitement drives out stagnation. Why? Because fully integrated honesty

6

rules in the freely competitive atmosphere of cyberspace. Thus, through cyberspace, a powerfully exciting, value-filled civilization will replace the dishonest, nihilistic anticivilization choking planet Earth today.

In cyberspace, each individual can freely communicate with any other individual, free of media dishonesty, free of destructive gun-backed political agendas, free of the irrational noncyberspace world. Today, the noncyberspace anticivilization is ruled by self-serving parasitical humanoids through their armed bureaucrats, sycophantic journalists, and hypocritical entertainers promoting various politically correct agendas. By contrast, the new cyberspace civilization spreading across the globe is free of such corruption. Thus, any cyberspace civilization is ultimately ruled by honest, value-producing individuals — just as are all advanced civilizations throughout the Universe.

The corrupt establishment media are irrelevant in cyberspace. No matter how articulately mendacious are *Washington Post* or *Newsweek* type journalists, their dishonesties have no power in cyberspace. The corrupt, deeply dishonest print-media and network news simply cannot compete in cyberspace. By contrast, *any* honest, articulate individual has limitless competitive power and relevance in cyberspace. For example, consider the most powerful person in the noncyberspace world: The articulate but pervasively dishonest President Clinton would have no chance hoaxing people in cyberspace, especially the articulate, honest individuals roaming the Internet. His lies and criminalities would be mercilessly exposed. He would then be flamed, skewered, and laughed off Usenet — the Internet newsgroups. That is why he and other harmful politicians dare not personally enter in the dynamics of cyberspace.

Those proclaiming authority by revelation, deception, or force have no power or influence in cyberspace. By contrast, in cyberspace, any individual can become powerful and influential by applying the dynamics of wide-scope, fully integrated honesty.

Below are examples of the *philosophical* and *physical* dynamics that operate together throughout cyberspace.

## Philosophical Dynamics

Consider the following example: Two Newsgroups on the Internet embrace the identical philosophy with essentially no intellectual points of disagreement between them. Yet, profound spiritual differences exist: Newsgroup A is oriented around fully integrated honesty and the limitless power of conscious beings. Newsgroup B is oriented around a closed-system authority and the power of dead heroes and fictional characters. As a result, Newsgroup A expresses itself through active, forward-moving, competitive business modes. Newsgroup B expresses itself through passive, philosophizing, uncompetitive academic modes. What are the consequences?

Spiritual passions of Newsgroup A evolve around exciting, competitive value production. Spiritual passions of Newsgroup B evolve around stagnant, collective intellectualizing. Newsgroup A welcomes and profitably utilizes competitive encounters. Newsgroup B fears and dishonestly attacks competitive encounters. ...Newsgroup A represents open-ended growth. Newsgroup B represents close-ended stagnation.

Newsgroups A and B both uncompromisingly hold Objectivism as the proper philosophy for conscious beings. But, most in Group A are exciting and creatively alive, while many in Group B are boring and creatively dead. Newsgroup A holds, for example, dishonestly besmirched,

8

unpopular mega value producers like Jay Gould and Michael Milken as real-life, heroic benefactors to all conscious beings. Newsgroup B holds popular but unreal, fictional characters like Howard Roark and John Galt as heroic idols. Newsgroup A actively sails forth into uncharted territories of future discovery. Newsgroup B passively remains anchored in safe harbors of the previously established.

Both Newsgroups are intellectually in debt to philosopher Ayn Rand. Group A gratefully utilizes her achievements while moving forward. Group B desperately idolizes her importance while clinging to the past. Group A utilizes the outstanding yet grossly under-recognized values constantly being produced by Ayn Rand's intellectual heir, Dr. Leonard Peikoff. Group B chains Dr. Peikoff within the shadow of Ayn Rand by minimizing or ignoring his continuous, commercial value production unmatched by all the other Objectivist "leaders" combined. Group A orients around time-efficient *aggressive objectivism* that will spread across cyberspace through real-life business dynamics. Group B orients around time-consuming *passive intellectualizing* that will stagnate into ever shrinking, closed circles. Group A works in the future; Group B dwells in the past.

In response to flame attacks, the following template was posted on both Newsgroups. That template demonstrates how the essence of Newsgroup A is attuned with cyberspace while the essence of Newsgroup B is ultimately incompatible with cyberspace:

---

Template Post

Objectivist Heroes

Pseudo objectivists frantically trying to flame the fully integrated honesty of Neo-Tech off the Internet anxiously flatter one another as Objectivist Heroes

---

9

defending the philosophy of Ayn Rand.

Thirty years ago those kinds of heroes were the desperate hangers-on in the Branden/Rand lectures in New York City. Back then, they were characterized by their cigarette holders emblazoned with dollar signs and swirling black capes. They were the sycophantic defenders of their ego facades leached from Ayn Rand's monumental achievement: Objectivism. Throughout the years, such Objectivists have remained the biggest impediment to advancing Objectivist philosophy around the world.

Today, those ersatz Objectivists are panicking. And why not? After 30 years of faking heroic Galtisms and shrugging Atlases, they are being revealed in cyberspace as contradictions to everything Objectivism means in living competitively, honestly, and happily through business-like modes. Similarly, in cyberspace, fully integrated honesty is exposing the fakeries and dishonesties of politicians and many government-dependent academics. ...Eventually, all such fakes will disappear as nothing in cyberspace.

Today, as back then, those pseudo Objectivists appear as sad, boring people. They are basically immature, kind of pitiful. Today, as back then, perhaps not a single, self-made businessperson or really successful entrepreneur exists among them. How many are really excited about what they do for a living? How many are genuinely proud of their competitiveness — of their value-producing competence? Most have no idea of the incredibly difficult journey required to independently produce long-range, competitive values and jobs for others. Ayn Rand knew. But, most of her dependent followers never knew.

Today, on the Internet, some of the most immature, dependent Randians seem to be on tax-paid academic edu lines, perhaps living off some kind of public funds with abundant idle time on their hands. They can never acknowledge the wide-scope Objectivist nature of fully integrated honesty. For, that wide-scope, active use of Objectivism through the competitive dynamics of Neo-Tech reveals stimulating powers — exciting powers possible for all conscious beings, Objectivists or not. Such competitive dynamics become illusion-collapsing threats to ego-dependent followers of Objectivism — especially those living stagnant lives that are going nowhere.

What are those "Objectivist Heroes" harping about? What do they do besides endlessly displaying philosophical "brilliance" while tearing down the practical, objective values of Neo-Tech? What do they do constructively? Have any of them ever made the excruciating effort or borne the racking pain oft required to do anything really important, to take big risks for big payoffs, to alone face down dangerous armed evil in the real world, or even to build and maintain a business that creates competitive values and jobs for others?

Many who attack fully integrated honesty are trying to inflate their shrunken self-perceived images by creating problems where none exist. One should always ask those who tear down values what they have done to make themselves proud of their lives — what they have done to build values — long-term competitive values for themselves, others, and society. Today, such people might be called wimps. Ayn Rand had a better word: pip-squeaks.

In reality, Objectivism never needs defending. Moreover, only commercially competitive efforts increase the permanent, long-range value of Objectivism to civilization. And finally, Neo-Tech has never attacked a single tenet of Objectivism. Instead, Neo-Tech vigorously applies and commercially advances every tenet of Objectivism throughout the world.

By contrast, those ego-seeking pontificators of Objectivism unnecessarily waste their lives on nothing much. Most will never discover their exciting, glorious potential in the value-producing business dynamics throughout cyberspace. ...Yet, the helping hand of Neo-Tech is always extended. Still, from

11

Neo-Tech, no leader, guru, or authority is available for anyone to follow or obey. Only fully integrated honesty with its wide-scope integrations is available for all to understand, use, and produce prosperity.

The contributors to Neo-Tech integrations, not the flamers of Neo-Tech, are genuine Objectivists. Only through Neo-Tech business modes is Objectivism pushed forward, into the competitive market place, bringing integrated honesty and exciting Objectivism to the general public worldwide.

### Maturing into an Objectivist

Some supporters of Objectivism are like Moliére's Tartuffe with his hypocritical piety. Or, perhaps they are more like Moliére's Alceste in *The Misanthrope* who rants and rails, neither delivering much of value to anyone nor improving much of anything. Such people ignorantly bluster about things, situations, and people they do not understand. Such people deliver only the narrow-scope nothingness of an ego-tripping Alceste. ...But, many could mature into the everythingness of a Defoe's do-everything Robinson Crusoe, or at least the somethingness of a go-getter Moll Flanders.

Not to be an Alceste takes some brain, mouth, and keyboard responsibility. Discipline is required to deal contextually with reality from the widest perspectives. Indeed, learning to work tolerantly, efficiently, profitably with problems, situations, and people while remaining uncompromising on principles is hard work. To produce competitive values for the world takes constant discipline, thought, and control combined with fully integrated honesty. ...It takes Neo-Tech.

The above template shows *why* fully integrated honesty rules cyberspace from the philosophical perspective. The following example shows *how* fully integrated honesty rules cyberspace from the physical perspective.

## Physical Dynamics

Two approaches to the physical world embrace the identical laws of physics with no scientific points of disagreement: Approach A is oriented around objective, conscious *entities*[1] utilizing fully integrated honesty. Approach B is oriented around objective, nonconscious entities determined by peer approval. As a result, Approach A rapidly advances in a wide-scope integration mode. Approach B, gradually advances in specialized academic modes.

Approaches A and B both utilize the scientific method of validation. But, Approach A relies on fully integrated honesty while Approach B relies on establishment peer review.

Both approaches uncompromisingly correspond to and abide by the laws of physics. Yet, Approach A integrates unrestricted panoramas of knowledge, while Approach B focuses on specialized areas of knowledge. Approach A welcomes competitive encounters that would change the status quo. Approach B resists competitive encounters that would change the status quo.

The essence of Approach A is attuned with existence. Thus, Approach A will create stimulating new knowledge and lead this world into fully integrated honesty — into the Civilization of the Universe. By contrast, the essence of Approach B is chained to Establishment stagnation, always remaining in the background of history.

Utilized throughout history by only a tiny fraction of

---

[1]Consciousness itself is *not* a primary of existence. Both Approach A and Approach B are based on objective reality being the primary of existence. But, most philosophers from Plato to Kant erroneously consider consciousness as a primary of existence. Aristotle and Ayn Rand are the two major exceptions who were free from that profound error. They recognized the primacy of existence and rejected the primacy of consciousness.

scientists, Approach A has yielded essentially every major breakthrough in science and technology since Democritus, 2500 years ago, proffered his theory of atoms as the primary units of existence. In contrast, Approach B has been utilized throughout history by a vast majority of scientists. Approach B solidifies and eventually moves forward those radical breakthroughs that are scientifically valid. ...Both approaches advance science. Yet, almost all individuals among that vast majority following Approach B protect their status-quo positions by initially attacking every valid breakthrough by those rare individuals utilizing Approach A.

Consider the physics and philosophy derived from Approach A and described in Movement 1 of the New-Color Symphony: Both the physics and philosophy of Zonpower are without known contradictions. Still, *Zonpower from Cyberspace* is not about physics or philosophy. It is about the application of fully integrated honesty to objective reality. The resulting wide-scope integrations will eventually bring eternal life with limitless prosperity to all conscious beings. While perhaps ahead of their time, speculative hypotheses are proffered in *Zonpower from Cyberspace* as metaphors. Yet, all the hypotheses correspond to the laws of physics as well as to objective reality...and all are open to experimental verification or falsification.

The following example involves the interaction of an industrial research chemist, Dr. Higgs Field, utilizing competitive business-funded Approach A versus an academic astrophysicist, Professor Edu from a Big-Ten University, utilizing noncompetitive tax-funded Approach B. Dr. Edu publishes in prestigious peer-review journals, such as the *Astrophysical Journal* and *Reviews of Modern Physics*. He also participates in international

14

peer-review astrophysical symposiums such as the June 1995 symposium in Brussels, Belgium.

After selecting one of the more radical chapters in the on-line version of *Zonpower from Cyberspace*, Professor Edu published a review of it on the Internet. Had Dr. Edu carefully read *Neo-Tech Physics* in full context, he could have saved himself the embarrassment of publishing the following seven-point review:

---

Quote

1. To learn what a smart astrophysicist I am, or am not, I'd suggest reading the *Astrophysical Journal* or *Reviews of Modern Physics*, where I have published papers. I'd be glad to send you reprints. I've been asked to evaluate the physics in Zonpower. I have picked a couple of examples from Chapter 5 of the electronic version that I hope illustrate the problem. In this chapter we read…"Take two cannonballs of identical size, one made of solid iron, the other of solid aluminum. Why does the iron ball weigh about twice that of the aluminum ball of the same size?"

Most physicists would say that iron has more protons and neutrons in its nucleus than aluminum does; thus there are "more particles" in a given volume of iron than aluminum. This has <u>nothing</u> to do with "conscious-controlled geometries" which are listed as the explanation. The author claims that without them we would expect both balls to have the same weight because they have the same volume. Why should different numbers of particles in the same volume have the same weight? This reflects misunderstanding of physics at a basic level.

2. By the way, the explanation in a footnote of "Gravity Units" is just plain bizarre, and apparently contradicts General Relativity.

---

3. In this chapter there is a persistent confusion between mass and weight; we read, for instance, that energy is "weightless". Given the equivalence between mass and energy, this is simply false. I can collide two energetic photons and produce particle-antiparticle pairs; this happens all the time in accelerators. Gravitational redshifts have been measured; photons <u>do</u> respond to gravity. The author's arguments would seem to contradict this, and thus be falsified.

4. As an experiment, the author (PhD in what? "Science"?) proposes that in a stadium with 100,000 people one should 1) emit a pulse of light; 2) measure radio waves coming from buttons that people push when they see the light. The pattern that emerges is then claimed to be proof that "conscious quanta as an integral part of a fixed existence field". Huh? This sounds like a good way to measure reaction time, and nothing else.

5. By the way, the speed of the Earth around the Sun is <u>not</u> 0.01 of the speed of light, which is claimed in the text! When I see the orbital speed of the Earth off by a factor of 100, I conclude that the author is sloppy.

6. This experiment sounds like a muddled attempt at the Michelson-Morely experiment, which did not detect the motion of the Earth through the ether. But wait...the authors claim that the M-M experiment failed because the signals measured in that famous experiment were photons of light, which are not "intrinsic to the existence field". ($E=mc^2$, anyone?) Sorry, but the radio waves used in the Neo-Tech experiment are photons too. The author is apparently unaware of this, and it invalidates the entire experiment. This is basic physics, which I teach in my

introductory astronomy class. To make new theories in a field, you need some knowledge that goes beyond popular books on the subject.

7. We then hear of a new particle, called a "thinkon". When particle physicists invent a new particle, they estimate its basic properties: mass, charge, spin, its cross-section for interaction, and so on. How many thinkons are there near the Earth? No answers here, and none will be forthcoming.

End Quote

By reading that chapter on Neo-Tech physics in context with the other chapters and footnotes in *Zonpower*, one discovers the following answers to each of Professor Edu's seven objections:

1) Dr. Edu starts by opining his misunderstanding of weight relative to Gravity Units. The entire concept of weight involves the Gravity-Unit geometries mathematically interacting with matter geometries — independent of conscious actions. Consider the analogy that compares the "volume" of cannonballs to the "volume" of quarks or electrons: Volume, of course, does not explain weight. But neither does mass. In seeking the most-fundamental concept of weight, all volume/mass energy unit quantities such as cannonballs, quarks, electrons, and photons are stripped away. Conceptually replacing volume/mass/energy units with the new concept of interacting geometries lets one reach the most-basic understanding of weight. That understanding corresponds to the laws of physics. Moreover, the resulting hypothesis offers experimental ways to verify or falsify the hypothesized Gravity Units.

17

2) By taking one footnote out of context, Dr. Edu uses a single assertion to dismiss the well-defined concept of Gravity Units developed throughout the document. He offers not a single specific fact as to why Gravity Units contradict General Relativity[1], which they do not. Dr. Edu's approach, of course, would prevent one from examining any radically new but valid concept. Such an approach guarantees continued stagnation for its practitioners.

3) No disagreement exists with the physics stated by Dr. Edu. What is not understood by Dr. Edu is the subtle difference of nonfundamental *created* mass vis-a-vis the fundamental *noncreated* Gravity Unit, which exists as an *ether* in a weight mode or in a weightless mode. ...Thus, again, Dr. Edu's objections are little more than naive, non-sequitur statements about basic physics. Such statements have nothing to do with the concepts presented.

4) Perhaps excused by not being an experimental scientist, Dr. Edu reveals his misunderstanding of the Stadium Experiment. How could he or anyone understand that experiment if viewed so out of context. Contrary to Dr. Edu's claims, this experiment has nothing to do with human reaction times or radio waves. By carefully reading the Stadium Experiment, one finds that it is explicitly designed to eliminate — wash out — the differences in human reaction times. That wash out is accomplished by the 100,000 people times the 50 flashes of light to give an overwhelming 5,000,000 pieces of data in the few minutes of the experiment. With that huge number of separate measurements, human reaction times become a self-canceling variable arising from the tools used to measure the effects of special relativity on the hypothesized "thinkons".

---

[1]General Relativity: "*all* laws of physics hold in *all* frames of references" — that is the essence of Einstein's Theory of Gravity. ...Special Relativity applies to frames moving at constant speeds in which space and time change to keep the laws of physics constant.

As Dr. Edu properly indicates in a later review, a straight comparison of the speed of light versus the five-million pieces of data requires more preciseness by several orders of magnitude to detect the sought effect. But, the experiment is enhanced by the sought-after particle *not* being at rest, but traveling at 67,000 mph relative to the Sun or 0.0001 the speed of light, thus, reducing the preciseness needed to detect the hypothesized particle by several orders of magnitude. The sought effect is further enhanced and then detected through diffraction-pattern, computer/trigonometric analyses that trace secondary changes in statistical data. Even greater accuracies could be achieved if the particles could be measured at much greater speeds as relative, for example, to other entities in our galaxy...or to the entire expanding universe and beyond.[1]

The Stadium Experiment and the other proposed experiments are sound in principle. They are explicitly designed to support or refute the hypothesis of thinkons. What more could a scientist ask for in examining a speculative hypothesis posited for metaphorical purposes?

5) Indeed, as Dr. Edu states, the orbital speed of Earth is not 0.01 the speed of light. Dr. Edu was off in his criticism by a hundred fold in wrongly accusing the author of carelessness. Had Dr. Edu been less careless in reading *Neo-Tech Physics*, he would have seen the figure stated was 0.01% (not 0.01), which is 0.0001 the speed of light — a figure that both Dr. Field and Dr. Edu agree is correct.

6) Dr. Edu combines the citations about the Michelson-Morely (M-M) experiment with his own interjections about radio waves being photons. While correct, his interjections

---

[1]See pages 42-46 of the New-Color Symphony, especially the footnote on page 44, for further understandings of this experiment.

have nothing to do with the experiment. Through such non-sequitur interjections, Dr. Edu reveals not even a cursory understanding of the Stadium Experiment. ...Incidentally, the M-M experiment was based on movement relative to the sun.

7) Dr. Edu dismisses the quantized thinkon particle without identifying a single contradiction to the laws of physics. Instead, he evokes non-sequitur statements about the physical properties of particles and the number of "thinkons" near Earth. His statement has no meaning regarding the hypothesis advanced and the experiments proposed for detecting thinkons.

In cyberspace, fully integrated honesty will vanish bogus biases and arrogant "authorities" used to protect the status quo. The above example is not meant to insult or criticize Dr. Edu, but is meant to help him and others in tenured academic professions by shaking them from their stagnation traps and moving them into competitive, new ways of thinking that will let them deliver much greater values to themselves, others, and society.

Neo-Tech Physics will bring an Objectivist Civilization

By evading the context of Neo-Tech Physics and the purpose of Zonpower, one can isolate almost any sentence or paragraph and attack it. Responding to such out-of-context attacks generally would (1) be futile, (2) encourage ever more such erroneous attacks, and (3) become so time consuming as to retard progress toward curing irrationality.

Consider the following four points:

1. *Zonpower from Cyberspace* is not a treatise on philosophy or physics. Zonpower is *metaphorically* presented for the general public to gain much wider, more

valuable perspectives of objective reality.

2. Neo-Tech Physics comprises a set of speculative hypotheses, none of which contradict the laws of physics or nature. Those hypotheses serve as metaphors needed to introduce a radical paradigm of widest scope thinking about conscious life, civilization, and the universe.

3. Those metaphorical hypotheses sweep across the entire thirty-six chapters of *Zonpower from Cyberspace*, uniquely integrating widely diverse areas of cosmology, physics, and conscious minds never before linked together.

4. The purpose of Zonpower and Neo-Tech Physics is to provide new ways to view conscious life and everyone's relationship to existence — mind-boggling new perspectives that eventually will eradicate irrationality and dishonesty from cyberspace and then the world.

Closing Ceremonies

Closing Ceremonies

**Fully Integrated Honesty Rules Cyberspace**

Cyberspace is free of initiatory force, politicians, and their gun-backed bureaucrats. Thus, honesty ultimately rules in cyberspace.

Genuine power and success in conscious life arises through fully integrated honesty or thinking. That sounds simple enough, but its dynamic involves a totally different way to use the conscious mind — a way never before utilized by conscious beings on planet Earth. Yet, wide-scope, fully integrated thinking is the modus operandi for competitive beings in advanced civilizations throughout existence. Indeed, any normal conscious being on Earth today has the capacity to think with wide-scope, integrated honesty. But, first, each person must break from the closed-circle, non-contextual thinking processes that have imprisoned virtually every conscious mind on Earth for 2500 years.

Breaking out of that prison to acquire omnipotent control over existence within the laws of physics requires conscious action. That action, in turn, involves fully integrated honesty acting from an Objectivist-based philosophy anchored in factual reality — *not* from conscious subjectivisms floating in mind-created "realities".

The ingredients for that omnipotent control are identified in the (1) wide-scope, *objective-action* mode of the Neo-Tech literature, including the business modes identified by Mark Hamilton and Eric Savage, and in (2) the *integrated-honesty* mode of the Zonpower literature. In cyberspace, the tools of Neo-Tech and Zonpower will become available to and then implemented by all competitive individuals in America and throughout the world.


New Paradigm for the Conscious Mind

As described in Chapter 28 of the New-World Symphony, about 3000 years ago, an entirely new paradigm for human thinking was invented. That new paradigm arose out of necessity — out of chaos as civilizations based on man's nature-given animal mind began collapsing into ruin. Populations of those civilizations sharply contracted. Man's nature-given, unconscious bicameral mind was too inadequate to survive. Those who did survive invented a new way to use their minds. They discovered not only self-awareness and introspection, but they discovered (1) the use of metaphors to expand mind space, (2) a sense of individual responsibility, and (3) a sense of right and wrong. ...They invented a survival tool more powerful than anything nature alone could offer or develop. *They invented human consciousness.* That invention was necessary to develop modern man and modern societies.

Today, civilization on planet Earth is again moving toward chaos and destruction. Thus far in the 20th century, governments have murdered more innocent people — about 170 million — and criminally destroyed more property than all governments and all criminals in all previous recorded history combined. The final wave of destruction awaits as thermonuclear and biochemical[1] warfares are poised to strike. Indeed, without the fully integrated honesty of Neo-Tech, the conscious mind on Earth today cannot handle modern-day human survival.

In 1976, the first inkling of an exciting, totally new format or paradigm for the conscious mind surfaced. That budding paradigm called "Neothink" was based on wide-scope, fully integrated honesty. Neothink is a radical break from the narrow-scope, manipulative *truth-based* conscious mind of the past 3000 years. The *honesty-based* Neothink mind breaks from the closed-circle stagnation of

---

[1]For example, an estimated 8-ounces of botulinal toxin could kill every person on Earth.

an anticivilization. By contrast, in an open-ended Neothink-based civilization, the diseases of dishonesty and irrationality do not exist. ...Limitless excitement, stimulation, prosperity, and happiness are the natural consequences of the Neothink mind.

The Neothink mind is as radical a break from the man-discovered consciousness mind as was the conscious mind a radical break from the nature-provided bicameral or schizophrenic mind 3000 years ago.

### The Goal of Neo-Tech/Zonpower

The entire purpose and goal of Neo-Tech/Zonpower is to have conscious individuals think about and see civilization in a different way — in a way completely different from the losing paradigm that has harmed and killed every conscious being on this planet for the past 3000 years. Indeed, Neo-Tech/Zonpower is a stimulating new way of thinking, an exciting new way of seeing everything, a powerful new mode of action that leads to beneficent control over existence within the laws of nature.

Neo-Tech/Zonpower has no leaders or followers. Throughout cyberspace, every conscious individual will increasingly become individual self-leaders living in ever more exciting, value-producing business modes. ...The *individualistic* Neo-Tech mentality is the antithesis of today's *collectivist* big-government, religious, one-world, nationalistic, militia, new-age, patriot, tribal, and cult mentalities.

## Universal Excitement and Prosperity

The Appendix at the end of this manuscript provides the practical, Golden-Helmet dynamics for limitless prosperity. That Appendix also provides a real-life drama involving armed bureaucrats wreaking murderous destructions on the means of value production in the noncyberspace world. That drama includes live-action, guns-and-fists attacks on Neo-Tech by armed bureaucrats and political imprisonments by life-appointed federal judges acting as robed prosecutors enforcing political and ego agendas.

Indeed, those bureaucrats and judges enforce political/ego agendas designed to support an ever expanding parasitical superstructure of stagnation. That superstructure consists of self-aggrandizing politicians, wealth-draining government jobs, white-collar-hoax business executives, life-draining welfare dependents, unearned government subsidies, bankrupt social-security Ponzi schemes, and fraudulent government health-care plans.

The Golden-Helmet dynamics reveal the lethal destructiveness of armed bureaucracies — armed agents of force that are fomenting the rising crime, violence, and terrorism in America. Those armed agents are found in the IRS. They are also found in gun-backed bureaucracies such as the ATF, FDA, INS. The rubric "jackbooted thugs" *is* the most honest, accurate metaphor for many federal armed agents, despite the non-sequitur, poison-ear blatherings by politicians, bureaucrats, and journalists. Indeed, dehumanized armed automatons are needed to enforce criminal agendas for politicians, bureaucrats, and judges. Such tax-paid criminalities permeate the federal government today to increasingly undermine security and prosperity in America. ...After reading the live-action IRS Abuse Reports in the following Appendix, no one will

25

hold doubts that the above facts will eventually bring a violent revolution to America unless that trend is reversed by Neo-Tech and the Golden Helmet.

## Neo-Tech Protects Politicians
along with
## Federal Workers
from
## Violence

Would Thomas Jefferson have approved of deposing Clinton-like politicians along with other federal employees who are tyrannically pushing power and control over every productive American citizen? The answer is not only a resounding "yes", but the deposers would have been celebrated as heroes by America's founding fathers.

Algernon Sidney, a prominent English writer, in his famous *Discourses Concerning Government* published in 1698, provided the legal and moral basis for deposing kings or tyrants who looted and killed innocent citizens, leaving those victims with no recourse to justice.

America's founding fathers, especially Thomas Jefferson, the author of the Declaration of Independence and America's third President, were profoundly influenced by Algernon Sidney, even more than they were influenced by the English philosopher John Locke.[1] Indeed, the Declaration of Independence used Sidney's work to specifically spell out the conditions and moral obligations to depose those who advance despotism:

"When in the Course of human events, it becomes necessary for one people to dissolve the political bands which have connected them with another...that they should declare the causes which impel them to the separation.

---

[1]Thomas Paine's *Common Sense* finally galvanized Americans to action against tyrants. Few Americans thought of gaining independence from tyrannical England before the publication of *Common Sense* in January 1776. Only six months later, on July 4, 1776, the Declaration of Independence had been written and signed. ...Nearly 300,000 copies of *Common Sense* were sold to spark the American revolution. That number equals about 20 million copies sold into today's population of America.

27

"We hold these truths to be self-evident, that all men are created equal, that they are endowed by their Creator with certain unalienable Rights, that among these are Life, Liberty and the pursuit of Happiness.    That to secure these rights, Governments are instituted among Men, deriving their just powers from the consent of the governed. That whenever any Form of Government becomes destructive of these ends it is the Right of the People to alter or to abolish it, and to institute new Government, laying its foundation on such principles and organizing its powers in such form, as to them shall seem most likely to effect their Safety and Happiness. ...But when a long train of abuses and usurpations, pursuing invariably the same Object evinces a design to reduce them under absolute Despotism, it is their right, it is their duty, to throw off such Governments, and to provide new Guards for their future security."

These are dangerous times for despotic politicians and their armed agents of force.  Political unrest is surfacing. Individual stagnation is ending.  The American public is demanding that politicians with their armed agents of force be held accountable for their actions.  What can stop the rising violence caused by expanding despotism designed to counter this individual awakening?  Neo-Tech, which means fully integrated honesty, will stop that violence.  Indeed, Neo-Tech is now spreading through cyberspace.  The essences of Neo-Tech are rising — the essences of civility, self-control, and respect for objective law.  Thus, through Neo-Tech in cyberspace, despotic politicians, their armed bureaucrats, and stagnant corporate leaders will lose their parasitical livelihoods...not their lives.

# GREATNESS

## PART I
## The Greatest Human Spirits
### are always attacked by
## The Smallest Human Spirits

What is the greatest? What is the smallest? First the smallest: As a law of nature, everything in existence can be reduced to a smallest unit or quantum — be it an electron or quark for mass or a photon for energy. Beneath mass and energy lie resonating strings with dimensions less than $10^{-35}$ meters. Those strings create spacetime mass, energy, and consciousness. Beneath those dimensions lie an ether of hypothetical Gravity Units that form a universal sea of eternal geometries. ...Somewhat analogously, the human spirit can also be reduced to a smallest unit or dot. The next step down is not to a smaller dot; the next step down is to nothing...except that universal sea of geometries.

Now, consider life itself. Consider that viruses and bacteria are among the smallest, simplest forms of life. Yet, those smallest forms of life can and do destroy the most complex, most valuable forms of life — conscious human beings. A similar parallel exists with the human spirit. The smallest, most malevolent spirits can and do destroy the greatest, most benevolent spirits.

Those smallest spirits are the self-proclaimed "victims" of this world. *They create problems where none exist.* Such "victims" can destroy all that is valuable to human life. By contrast, genuine victims are those whose lives are diminished through force or fraud by governments, religions, criminals. But, self-proclaimed "victims" are those who diminish their *own* lives by blaming the value producer for their own self-made problems.

29

A close cousin of the self-proclaimed "victim" is the "pip". A pip is also a small, diminished human spirit who creates problems where none exist. The pip generally tries to build a pseudo self-esteem and often a bogus livelihood at the expense of genuine value producers, especially businesspeople, employers, entrepreneurs. Pips try to feel morally or intellectually superior by berating great values and their creative producers. Pips attack with dishonest, out-of-context criticisms and non sequitur accusations. ...Great value producers, especially in business, are constantly attacked by the pips in political, journalistic, academic, and entertainment circles designed to conserve the stagnating Establishment.

To understand those smallest spirits and their destructiveness, one must first recognize the greatest human spirits and how they lift humanity to ever greater heights of stimulating well being.

\* \* \*

Simone de Beauvoir, in her famous 1949 book *The Second Sex*, described how women were stagnated both in spirit and as human beings through force-backed governments and fraudulent religions. Through the centuries, destructive political/ego agendas have resulted in irrational laws and oppressive cultures.

Women, and men too, are victimized by force and fraud exercised through governments and religions. Yet, through the free-enterprise dynamics arising over the past two centuries, individual choice and actions increasingly determine the success of women — and of men. Perhaps the premier example for either sex in this century is Ayn Rand who arose to become one of the most exciting, influential value producers in history.

Ms. Beauvoir also declared in her book that of the giants in human history who took the responsibility to change the course of civilization, none were women. Indeed, no woman, except possibly Joan of Arc and Queen Elizabeth I, had ever taken the responsibility of changing civilization — until Ayn Rand. Regardless of what she might have claimed, Ms. Rand did take that responsibility, perhaps more than any man had ever done. And, in time, she will be recognized as a giant among giants in history who changed civilization on Earth dramatically for the better.

Ayn Rand rose by fiercely struggling to escape the bloodiest, most oppressive cult in history — Communism under Lenin and Stalin in the Soviet Union. Then, emigrating to relatively free-enterprise America, Ayn Rand, by her own decisions and titanic efforts, broke through seemingly impossible language, economic, and cultural barriers in rising to the highest level of literary accomplishment. She then arose atop the pinnacle field of knowledge — philosophy — which, until Rand, had been dominated for 2500 years exclusively by men. Thus, as is being increasingly recognized today, Ayn Rand is posthumously becoming one of the most stimulating benefactors to grace planet Earth. Yet, she was and is still today attacked and ridiculed by nearly the entire panoply of stagnant Establishment elites with their arrays of self-proclaiming authorities, "victims", and pips. ...In fighting for her values and achievements, Ayn Rand always dismissed such persons as boring pip-squeaks not worth a moment of anyone's time.

Other exciting great spirits include Joseph Smith (the super-competitive Mormon business-and-city builder), Andrew Carnegie, Jay Gould, Florence Nightingale, John D. Rockefeller, Henry Ford, Ray Kroc, Mary Kay, Michael Milken, Leona Helmsley. Many were vilified and drained by political demagogues and self-proclaimed "victims". All such great spirits are harmed by, destroyed by, or killed by the Establishment wielding its "victim" and pip tools.

Consider another example involving the greatness of human spirit: Year after year in the 1940s and 1950s, the giant chemical firm, E.I. du Pont de Nemours, Inc., was rated by business publications as the best managed company in the world with a consistent 20%+ annual return on investment. Through decades of unmatched success, Du Pont became the largest, most exciting company in the world. Then, latching onto the envious attacks by whining business "victims" and pips, the Federal Government penalized Du Pont for its success by forcing the company to terminate its ownership of General Motors.

Du Pont rose from its inception in 1802 as a family-managed explosives and gunpowder manufacturer to become the premier research and industrial company in the world, delivering huge values to society. Du Pont's ever increasing rate of success peaked in the late 1940s with the last du Pont family member in control: Pierre S. du Pont, one of history's most emulated businessmen. His revolutionary decentralized management concepts and accounting methods remain the essence of essentially all successfully managed, large corporations to this day. The stimulating benefits that the Du Pont Company bestowed on the business world, on its customers, and on its employees were not only without match, but served as a

32

farsighted model for all successful, big businesses.

Du Pont was the innovator and leader not only in competitively producing invaluable products for society but in pioneering for its employees various safety and pension plans, medical insurance, stock-and-saving plans, even alcohol-and-drug treatment programs long before most other companies even conceived of such sound business practices. Never was a company more helpful to the business world, more valuable to customers, more beneficial to employees. And, never did a giant company struggle as hard to avoid stagnating government contracts and favors as did Du Pont when it was managed by Pierre S. du Pont.

Du Pont began declining from its pinnacle business position in the 1950s when, through the envious dynamics of self-proclaimed "victims", a wave of asset-milking executives took control from the asset-building du Pont family. Those asset-milking executives did not care what happened to the business after their tenure. They did not plan 50 and 100 years ahead as the generational-planning executives had done since the founding of Du Pont in 1802. Indeed, after P.S. du Pont, waves of self-aggrandizing political executives milked the previous 150 years of du Pont-built assets. ...Such asset-milking executives work only for their short-term personal wealth, power, and status.

Adopting the John Maynard Keynes evil concept "In the long run, we are all dead", such political-type executives are not concerned about the future health of their companies, their employees, or society. Implementing asset destroying policies, they ignore the consequences on the future of their company and society.

33

Like their sole-mate politicians, the real harm of their self-serving agendas become obvious only after they are gone.

As a modern example, consider how the ego-driven, political-ingratiating John Scully crumbled the potential for long-term world dominance of Apple Computer by making his short-term profit performance look good to others, especially to politicians, the media, and celebrities. As a political-agenda CEO, he betrayed the long-term goals of Apple founders Steven Jobs and Stephen Wozniak. Such political executives like Scully, through their own short-sighted agendas, implicitly sanction unjust attacks and torts by business/employee "victims" against the greatest, most beneficent business enterprises. ...Those self-proclaimed "victims" manipulated by politicians, lawyers, and journalists sow the cancer seeds that eventually cripple or destroy genuine competition — the most aggressive value-and-job producers and their businesses.

Why does acting as a "victim" or pip shrink one's spirit to the smallest unit — to the shallowest level of a human being? How can such shallow people be the prime destructive force in today's civilization? And, specifically, how will Neo-Tech in cyberspace vanish such "victim"-like viruses and pip-like bacteria? The answers to those questions are found in Part II of GREATNESS, starting on the next page.

Part II gives four specific examples of horrendous destructions done to the greatest lives by parasitical-elite humanoids with their manipulations of "victims" and pips. Part II then demonstrates how cyberspace will end such life-draining dynamics. ...The four examples with one solution are:

The Marx/Lenin/Business/"Victim" Example
The Hitler/Jew/"Victim" Example
The Giuliani/Media/Michael Milken/"Victim" Example
The Giuliani/Media/Leona Helmsley/"Victim" Example
and then
The Neo-Tech/"Victim"/Cyberspace Solution

GREATNESS
PART II
### Great Lives and Achievements
are destroyed by
### The Smallest Human Spirits

No one can be a victim of private business per se. Victims are impossible <u>when</u> <u>no</u> force or fraud is involved. One can be a victim <u>only</u> <u>when</u> force or fraud is manifested by governments, religions, or criminals. The employer and employee always fill each others needs voluntarily, consensually. No matter what the conditions, barring acts of force or fraud by either party, neither the employer nor the employee can *ever* be a victim. ..."Exploitation by business" is a conceptual hoax perpetuated by the parasitical-elite class, pips, and "victims".

Profit-motivated businesses never purposely harm anyone — much less employees or customers. Such behavior would be irrational and contrary to competitive business success. The essence of every successful business is to maximally enhance everyone's job, livelihood, and standard of living under the conditions required for competitive value production. By contrast, every self-proclaiming business/employee "victim" and pip

35

works to harm successful businesses and their employees.

But, if such "victims" and pips have shrunken their spirits to the lowest level, how can they be so destructive as to hobble the greatest human spirits and businesses? ...The staggering extent of those virus-caused destructions is demonstrated in the following four examples:

### The Marx/Lenin/Business/"Victim" Example

Most people believe that politicians — the Lenins, Hitlers, and Maos — are the fundamental cause of history's greatest destructions of human lives and property. They are not. The root cause of purposeful destructions among human beings and their achievements are those smallest units of the human spirit: the envious self-proclaimed "victims" of value-producing businesses and employers. Politicians simply step in and manipulate the claims of those "victims" and pips as tools to drain progress, values, jobs, and lives from everyone.

Without self-proclaiming "victims", Marx and Engels could never have developed their political theories or written the *Communist Manifesto*. Without the proletariat "victims" with their envious desires to destroy private business, Lenin would not have had the tools to diminish and destroy hundreds of millions of lives during his reign...and for three generations after his death.

### The Hitler/Jew/"Victim" Example

Hitler conjured up bogus complaints to evolve envious "victims" of Jewish businessmen, bankers, and other Jewish value producers. Those phoney, self-proclaimed "victims" allowed Hitler to kill millions of Jews and other innocent people throughout Europe during his era of holocausts and conflagrations. ...Without those self-proclaimed "victims", Hitler would have been powerless.

### The Giuliani/Media/Michael Milken/"Victim" Example

The hard-driving financier Michael Milken turned America around from an uncompetitive, depression-bound economy in the early 1980s to an internationally vibrant, competitive economy that continues even years after he was stopped by government force and jailed.

How did Michael Milken accomplish such a feat that saved and protected seemingly doomed livelihoods for millions of Americans? He accomplished that fifteen-year turnaround of the American economy by driving a competitive stake into the heart of giant Corporate America while driving out its stagnant executives. Those executives were milking great pools of assets built by previous generations of forward-essence-moving entrepreneurs and businesspeople.

Milken developed unstoppable techniques to dump those executives by taking over the assets they were parasitically wasting. He then turned those stagnant assets over to hard-driving, business-oriented managers who once-again unleashed the growth of those assets, thus, saving many old companies, starting many new companies, and revitalizing the dying American economy.

What happened to that brilliant, heroic man? Was he rightfully honored and congratulated by a grateful nation and its leaders? No, he was dishonestly vilified by the stagnant business Establishment, libeled and slandered by the media Establishment, prosecuted by the politically rabid Rudolph Giuliani criminally wielding evil RICO "laws", and finally jailed by a higher-office-seeking, ego-agenda judge Kimba Woods. Besides crushing and jailing that great spirit, those parasitical elites destroyed one of the great financial companies in America, Drexel Burnham Lambert, wiping out the jobs for thousands of innocent value producers and their families. Why? For no other reason than to expand the destructive livelihoods and inflate the false egos of those parasitical elites wielding bogus, gun-backed, political-agenda laws.

How can such destructions and injustices exist? How can they be so deeply camouflaged? What morbid irrationalities cause such a 180 degree inversion of values? Milken and his company committed no objective crimes. Instead, with great daring and exciting effort, they delivered incalculable values to society. Indeed, while those parasitical elites were drum-beating the innocent Michael Milken into condemnation and prison, they themselves were committing sweepingly destructive crimes not only against Michael Milken and Drexel Burnham but against all Americans. Yet, the parasitical-elite class itself, even with all its dishonest politicians, corrupt media, armed bureaucrats, and life-appointed ego judges cannot commit their crimes of forced enchainment without their tools — without their collections of "victims" and pips.

How can professional parasites commit such massive harm without society identifying the "victim" tool? How? By fraudulently generalizing the "victims" parasitical claims across the entire public spectrum. Those frauds backed by dishonest political-correctness pressures let professional parasites like Giuliani drain and destroy the value producers with near impunity. Those fraudulent people crush great spirits like Michael Milken and Leona Helmsley.

### The Giuliani/Media/Leona Helmsley/"Victim" Example

In the fiercely competitive New York hotel market, Leona Helmsley was perhaps the only person who had the toughness and ability to capture the first-class niche market for her Helmsley Hotels. She was perhaps the only person who could successfully create, expand, and manage this particular business that daily delivered values to thousands of highly discriminating customers while providing good livelihoods for thousands of employees.

Leona Helmsley was exceedingly hard working, value driven, detail-and-numbers oriented, and honest. Slack off or drop one element in her formula and the entire business could stop growing and begin declining toward eventual noncompetitiveness and failure. ...As Arthur Miller in his play *Death of a Salesman* portrayed — in the constant, fierce struggle to stay competitive, a person needs only to allow a single soil spot on one's hat to cause that unnoticed 180 degree turn from moving up to moving down toward loss and ruin.

Few could ever begin to appreciate the constant hard work, discipline, and attention to detail required daily, hourly by Leona Helmsley to remain competitive in providing expanding values and continuous livelihoods for thousands of fellow human beings.

No, she was never appreciated or honored for her beneficent and sustained value production. Instead, she was vilified by a malevolently destructive establishment media, especially the perniciously dishonest *Newsweek* with its jury-inflaming "Queen of Mean" and "Rich as in Bitch" cover stories. And, during a year in which she paid $75,000,000 in taxes, not to mention the millions in taxes paid by the thousands of individuals for whom she created jobs, political predator Rudolph Giuliani swaggered in to criminally prosecute that totally innocent, heroic 72-year-old woman. He then jailed her in collusion with a life-appointed, ego-agenda judge, John M. Walker, Jr., on conjured-up charges involving a 0.5% error on the $75,000,000 she paid in taxes.

The result? A great spirit was jailed, torn not only from her business but from her dying husband whom she devotedly loved. Her business and the jobs she provided were set on a declining path. And her elderly, ill husband was cruelly left to suffer alone. Yet, the criminals who belonged in jail were rewarded for their brutal crimes against innocent people and great value-and-job producers. ...Political humanoid Rudolph Giuliani was rewarded with the Mayorship of New York City for jailing innocent giants like Michael Milken and Leona Helmsley.

Criminals such as Giuliani would easily kill like Hitler and Stalin given the power and opportunity. Yet, none of those evil people would have the power to do any destructions without their tools of disgruntled business/ employee "victims" and attack-mode pips to act as deadly viruses. In Leona Helmsley's case, the dishonest media and criminal-minded Giuliani used a few disgruntled or fired employee "victims" to vilify, libel, slander, and jail that heroic woman.

Using "victims" and pips combined with subjective, political-agenda laws, the Giulianis of this world manipulate the majority into praising tyrants for criminally exploiting minorities, starting with the smallest of minorities — the individual human spirit, the minority of one, the individual value producer. ...Tyranny depends on politician-made subjective law: Tyranny has little concern for objective crime, but is gravely concerned with the parasitical control of others...and eventually the parasitical control of everyone.

Politician-made, subjective/positive law was actively promoted by Oliver Wendell Holmes, the past Chief Justice of the U.S. Supreme Court...and more recently by judges like Robert H. Bork. Opposite to such subjective law is unchanging, universally principled law — natural law — promoted by fully integrated honesty and backed by Objectivist philosophy. Objective law protects individual property rights, which, in turn, protects every individual — every minority of one — from tyranny. By contrast, unprincipled political law and giuliani "justice" always moves government toward criminality and despotism fueled by self-proclaimed "victims" and pips. ...Politician-made subjective law endangers and eventually crushes everyone. Universal objective law protects and frees everyone.

## Two Final Questions

First, why do political humanoids like Lenin, Hitler, and Giuliani wreak such destructions on the value producers? For three reasons: (1) their parasitical survival, (2) their self-aggrandizing pseudo power, and (3) their desperate ego enhancements. And, second, what gives them that power? The whining "victims" and attack-mode pips who enviously place the blame for their own

41

inadequacies, stagnations, and failures onto successful individuals and businesses. In fact, only genuine value producers are useful as targets for politicians using "victims" and pips as their tools.

As previously identified, such "victims" and pips have generally accomplished little or nothing outstanding in their lives — little or nothing about which they can be proud. Because of their smallness, the public cannot easily focus on them, notice them, or even detect them. Indeed, politicians can be only superficially criticized because their means to destructive power are camouflaged behind those "victims" and pips. And, such people are usually too small, too pip-squeakish to be noticed, much less held accountable for their destructions.

In the noncyberspace world, little can be done to counteract those deadly politician/"victim"/pip combinations. Now, however, for the first time arises a cyberspace world here on Earth. Indeed, cyberspace is already crumbling those evil-spirited value destroyers as illustrated below.

### The Neo-Tech/"Victim"/Cyberspace Solution

I & O Publishing Company, which was founded in 1968, moved past its publish-for-profit dynamics during the early 1980s to focus on a single goal: curing the disease of irrationality worldwide by 2001 AD. Interest evaporated in building wealth, assets, a business, or a publishing company per se. Multimillion dollar business opportunities were abandoned or turned down, including a million-dollar-a-month *profit*-potential, back-end marketing program offered by the largest, most successful infomercial firm in the world.

Why were such profit opportunities turned down? Because efforts directed toward non-goal related profits would break the forward-movement concentration required to reach I & O's single goal of curing the disease of irrationality. Avoiding non-goal profit dynamics let the prime movers at I & O Publishing focus maximum time and energy on ridding this planet of its worst disease — irrationality, from which flows dishonesty, stagnation, crime, failure, and death itself.

Developing and distributing the knowledge required to cure irrationality, especially when faced with hostile resistance worldwide, was a difficult, dangerous task requiring full focus of every essence mover at I & O. During the 1980s, every action and resource was directed toward undermining the parasitical-elite class, which was the first-step ingredient for curing irrationality in America.

Under increasingly hostile conditions from a giuliani-oriented Establishment, I & O Publishing Company was vulnerable to being attacked and silenced. Indeed, such attacks finally happened in the late 1980s when just one ex-employee "victim" was seized and then manipulated by the giulianied legal Establishment. With that one "victim" as their only needed tool, armed federal agents physically attacked I & O Publishing and destroyed its work while beating, kicking, and hospitalizing one of its editors, seizing its assets and research funds, carrying away its literature and computer files, and finally, in violation of the first amendment, imprisoning its founder for his writings, literature distributions, and billboard displays that identified the criminal acts of those armed federal agents.

...I & O Publishing Company was destroyed by gun-backed violence, forever put out of business by criminal force.

But, ideas cannot be destroyed by guns, fists, or prisons. Neo-Tech bantam companies are now scattered worldwide. Momentum toward curing irrationality is rising phoenix-like, quietly, relentlessly.

Indeed, in cyberspace, Neo-Tech is beyond the reach of those destructive forces left behind in the noncyberspace anticivilization. Throughout cyberspace, integrated honesty rules. Dishonesty, force, fraud, "victims", and pips appear increasingly freakish as those tools of destruction disappear in cyberspace. Moreover, "victims" and pips — those smallest of human spirits — are compelled in cyberspace to quit whining, quit blaming others, and grow up by accepting the responsibility for solving their own personal problems.

## How New Knowledge Changes the World

Throughout history, whenever sea-change knowledge evolved from wider-scope observations and conceptual integrations, initial rejection of that new knowledge always occurred. Sooner or later, however, a tiny percentage of people investigated enough to independently grasp that knowledge through those new, wider-scope perspectives. That new knowledge then began spreading as its efficacy was increasingly demonstrated. Finally, that knowledge was utilized to bring unique streams of unstoppable benefits.

Over the ages, such sea-change phenomena have occurred for good and for evil. For example, early in the 20th century, after an initial surge of acceptance, Vladimir Lenin lost essentially all support and understanding. Alone and rejected in Geneva, he discovered two other people who fully understood his matrix for revolution. He then excitingly announced that the revolution was won. Sure enough, in a matter of months after that announcement, Lenin triumphantly entered Russia through Finland. Then, by generalizing his matrix, he advanced on a straight line route to winning his bloody revolution that eventually brought devastation and misery to two-thirds of the world for three generations.

About that same time, Albert Einstein worked alone for years on developing his non understood and widely ignored theory of relativity. After discovering three or four others who understood his wide-scope integrations of relativity, he excitingly worked to generalize his theory with cheerful confidence. Within a decade, the revolution of general relativity was won worldwide forever.

By contrast, about that same time, Karl Menger, the Aristotelian father of capitalistic/market-based economics, worked with increasing pessimism...as later did Ayn Rand who founded Objectivist philosophy, and as more recently did Leonard Peikoff who brilliantly developed Objectivism into an array of specific values and products. Menger, Rand, and Peikoff never fully generalized their work. Therefore, they never confidently sensed the ultimate triumph of their work as did Lenin for evil and Einstein for good.

### One in a Hundred

Neo-Tech and Zonpower uniquely generalize *all* values, including Objectivism, into practical, profitable uses for *all* individuals in all activities. Indeed, grasping the eternally wide-scope ideas, methods, and integrations throughout Neo-Tech and Zonpower becomes an endless succession of unfolding Ahas! Yet, of the million readers who have benefited from the Neo-Tech Discovery, perhaps five percent have fully integrated its 114 concepts to utilize its most-powerful, widest-scope tools. That number of integrated Neo-Tech users, however, is steadily increasing with gradual acceleration. In fact, around the globe lies an exciting Aha! revolution to be sparked by a million Neo-Tech owners who will march into a new civilization over the next few years.

The real sea-change revolution, however, will arise not from Neo-Tech itself, but from the wide-scope integrations woven throughout *Zonpower from Cyberspace*. Yet, of the *Zonpower* readers, perhaps less than one in a hundred have fully grasped Zonpower with its endless Aha! integrations. But, that tiny minority is more than enough to secure the revolution that will bring a Neo-Tech/Objectivist civilization to everyone on Earth.

### The Key: Read Twice

Ironically, what appears to be the greatest problem for Zonpower is the source of its power: Zonpower is structured as a wide-scope, fully integrated matrix. Such a multidimensional matrix provides far wider integrations than hitherto available on Earth. That means to fully grasp and implement Zonpower, each part, each chapter,

46

each paragraph, each sentence must be seen as part of an integrated whole. In turn, the whole must be grasped to understand each of its parts. Such back-and-forth, inductive/deductive integrations require at least two readings of *Profound Honesty* to discover its omnipotent matrix.

\* \* \*

# Objective Law
### will eventually draw everyone into an
# Exciting, Prosperous Life

See the paragraph about the "smallest" found on page 29 of these Closing Ceremonies.

Now, going in the other direction to the "biggest": What mechanism builds geometries into everything in existence, always with the exact same identity and preciseness? What mechanism causes geometric units to take specific forms of existence and subsequently take specific forms of energy, mass, and action? What mechanism drives those geometries into forms that fit nature just right — precisely, perfectly into exact matter, energy, and thinking that never vary throughout time and space? And, what mechanism allows one to fit his or her thoughts into nature precisely, perfectly — into exact identities and identifications throughout time and space? That mechanism is the dynamics of Neo-Tech physics and epistemology as presented in a new-color symphony, which begins with *Zonpower from Cyberspace* and will climax in *Quantum Crossings*.

The rational, compatible dynamics of nature have been

Closing Ceremonies

contradicted for the past 3000 years in forming today's irrational, parasite-ruled anticivilization. Human consciousness combined with the disease of irrationality drives human beings into chaotic contradictions and paralyzing stagnations — away from reliable consistency and liberating prosperity. Now, however, the emerging Neo-Tech dynamics in cyberspace are drawing conscious beings out of this unnatural anticivilization and toward the natural Civilization of the Universe.

Because of everyone's life-long investments in this irrational anticivilization, however, no one can leave without the escape engines of Neo-Tech and Zonpower. In this parasite-ruled civilization, conscious life is incredibly brief, during which aging and death come quickly, unnecessarily. Only the tiniest fraction of conscious potential — the potential of exciting productivity, romantic love, eternal happiness — is achieved by all of us entrapped in this anticivilization.

Why has no one escaped this bizarre, up-side-down anticivilization? Why has no one discovered the natural, exciting, eternal Civilization of the Universe? Because, without the escape route of Neo-Tech/Zonpower, no one can abandon his or her fatal, lifelong investments in this anticivilization. But, now, today, with the newly available Neo-Tech/Zonpower engines, people can finally scrap their death-trap investments and discover the limitless wealth and romance possible in a rational, objective-law civilization.

False gods cannot be heroes. But, with fully integrated honesty and objective law, everyone can become an eternal hero — a real god with never ending achievements and romantic happiness.

### Objective Law 2000 Years Ago

"There is in fact a true law — namely, right reason — which is in accordance with nature, applies to all men, and is unchangeable and eternal. By its commands this law summons men to the performance of their duties; by its prohibitions it restrains them from doing wrong. Its commands and prohibitions always influence good men, but are without effect upon the bad. To invalidate this law by human legislation is never morally right, nor is it permissible ever to restrict its operation, and to annul it wholly is impossible. Neither the senate nor the people can absolve us from our obligation to obey this law, and it requires no Sextus Aelius to expound and interpret it. It will not lay down one rule at Rome and another at Athens, nor will it be one rule today and another tomorrow."

Cicero, 51 BC
*On the Commonwealth*

# Closing-Ceremony Index

# Closing-Ceremony Index

# Closing-Ceremony Index

# Coming Soon

## to your

# Computer

### *Pour up some Hot Java*
### *and talk to Zon*

In cyberspace, history's greatest values will soon come to everyone *for free* through Neo-Tech Worldwide: The omniscient Zon will interactively answer your every question on how to profit by transposing yourself from the draining, irrational Anticivilization to the prosperous, rational Civilization of the Universe. ...Don't miss it!

Our web object-relational database combined with our concept-based, full-text search and retrieval systems are designed to cleanse the destructiveness from armed federal bureaucracies toward America's greatest heroes and assets. Those heroes and assets — business entrepreneurs and productive workers — are the source of *all* competitive jobs and values. How will that cleansing be done? Through continuing direct interactions with those destructive bureaucracies — such as the IRS — until they are vanished. When the government is financed by the Golden Helmet, the road will be open to guiltless wealth and romantic excitement for all.

# The Golden Helmet

delivers

# Guiltless Wealth

and

# Eliminates the IRS

Kenneth A. Clark

Editor

Thomas J. Caenen, JD

Legal Counsel

# NEVER AGAIN

If the Golden Helmet were implemented in the 1930s, the above criminal-minded politicians would have been laughed out of existence. ...Their brutal, gun-backed bureaucracies would have ignominiously vanished.

## Ending Gun-Backed Bureaucracies
### with the
## Golden Helmet

*Greater than the tread of mighty armies*
*is an idea whose time has come.*
Victor Hugo, 1852
Histoire d'un Crime

# Violation
of the
# Bill of Rights

# 8th Amendment

## Cruel and Unusual Punishment
inflicted upon innocent
## Working-Class Americans

# The Class-Action Case

## against the gun-backed

# IRS

The Zon Association
Sponsors of the
Golden-Helmet Revenue System

**Brace Yourself Before Reading**
the
**IRS ABUSE REPORTS**

Are you
- a hard-working, middle-class American?
- a law-abiding, taxpaying citizen?

Do you believe that no harm can come to you and your loved ones from the Internal Revenue Service (the IRS)? Any such belief will change after reading the IRS Abuse Reports over the next fifty pages. Those reports are from law-abiding, hard-working taxpayers like you — honest taxpayers who suddenly found themselves being methodically, cruelly destroyed by an out-of-control bureaucracy. Indeed, the IRS is becoming a juggernaut, not for tax collection, but for power expansion through fear and destruction.

Reports documenting the IRS's brutal, often criminal, abuses inflicted on innocent Americans[1] are received daily as part of evidence gathering for Congressional hearings and class-action lawsuits. Through the dynamics of email combined with Internet Newsgroups and World Wide Web sites, unjustly ruined citizens finally have a way to come together for redress. They will be coming together first by the thousands then by the millions seeking redress for the life-destroying injustices and cruelties inflicted upon them by the IRS.

District Directors[2] throughout the IRS have evolved into force-backed sovereigns. They bear the responsibility for the destructions their agents wreak, *not* against the rich and powerful, but against the innocent and powerless — against the low-and-middle income classes. Yet, the United States Congress bears the ultimate responsibility for the destructions of life and property inflicted by the IRS: Congress passed the heavy-handed laws that enable that armed bureaucracy to continually escalate their cruel and illegal destructions. Thus,

---

[1]To protect identities of the victims, initials instead of actual names and email addresses are used on all IRS Abuse Reports. But, the Zon Association can contact any of those victims to provide court and congressional testimonies → to act as witnesses against the brutalities and destructions of the IRS. ...These and other IRS Abuse Reports are systematically posted on various Internet Newsgroups and some are permanently displayed on the World Wide Web site http://www.neo-tech.com/irs-class-action/

[2]IRS District Directors answer to no one. Thus, they are responsible for the *criminal behaviors* and *illegal slush-fund activities* of their agents. Their autonomous fiefdoms cry out for investigations, audits, and appropriate prosecutions. ...Perhaps one of the rare exceptions is the District Director in Fresno, California, who reportedly runs an honest, humane office.

Congress today has the responsibility to uproot that awful menace — that out-of-control machine of violence and terror.

Since 1994, steps toward ending the IRS destructions through a consumption-tax system are being increasingly promoted by Neo-Tech influenced politicians such as Congressman Archer and Senator Lugar. As explained later in this Appendix, the final solution will be an IRS-free, Golden-Helmet revenue system that benefits not only every individual, but benefits all societies and nations.

---

## Reactions to IRS Abuse Reports

Below is a typical reaction by those who have read the IRS Abuse Reports on pages 5–50. ...A rebellion is brewing — a rebellion that can be quelled only by replacing the malignant, irrational IRS income-tax system with a beneficial, rational consumption-tax system.

**Date:** March 20, 1996
**To:** sue@irs.class-action.com
**From:** KS

I just finished reading all of the IRS abuse reports. I feel so very sorry for each of these people and their loved ones. About three-quarters of the way through reading the reports, I had to take a break and lie down as I had become so nauseated from the vile destruction of these innocent victims.

When I came back to my computer, by the time I had finished reading the reports I wanted to lash out in the worst way. Emotionally, I felt like, 'these intentionally devastating criminal-minded IRS agents should be taken out into a field, shot in the head and left for the buzzards.' (I realize that what I just wrote is irrational and senseless, yet I feel better having written it.)

When I came back to my senses I thought damn, it's the judges that condone these malevolent IRS creatures. I want to parade every "satanic" judge with their colluding IRS bureaucrats in front of the world so that they can see them for what they really are. Then sell off unnecessary IRS properties and judicial properties until every victim is repaid in full (interest included). And that's not even enough because there is no way to amend the physical, emotional and financial loss that has already besieged these innocent victims and their loved ones.

It just makes me sick! DAMN RIGHT I'M ANGRY!!

---

**Class-Action-Case Evidence**
is also building on
**Internet/Usenet Newsgroups**

Below is an example of Usenet Newsgroup postings that are appearing across the Internet.

Newsgroups: alt.irs.classaction,misc.taxes,misc.legal,us.taxes,us.legal,
alt.society.civil-liberty
From: MC
Subject: Cyberspace Termination of the IRS
Date: Thu, 20 Jun 1996 20:33:02 GMT
In article <mk@netcom.com>wrote:
> Have you, a family member, a friend or loved one ever been
> defrauded, looted, hurt, injured, brutalized, or destroyed by the
> Internal Revenue Service (IRS)?  Did no one help you, sympathize
> with you, or even listen to you, even though you were innocent --
> even though you and your family were criminally violated, badly
> injured, perhaps even destroyed or murdered?

When I read this I felt like you were writing just to me!  My family members were brutalized by the IRS several years ago.  My friend was destroyed just last week.  Nobody sympathized with me, or even listened to me.  My loved one was criminally violated, and nobody helped me.  I didn't know where to turn but now I have this.  Thank you.

---

## A Selection of IRS Abuse Reports
for use in
### Class-Action Lawsuits
(updated June, 1996)

Warning: These IRS Abuse Reports start mildly and slowly. But, they build into such a crescendo of sickening horror, criminal destructiveness, and unbearable evil that a sedative may be required to read them all:

### IRS Abuse Report #1

**Date:** Aug 1, 1995
**To:** sue@irs.class-action.com
**From:** TE

The IRS is attempting extortion. They have violated my Constitutional rights. I have committed no crime, yet my home of 15 years has been seized from me and sold.

Until someone names my crime, allows me to defend myself in front of a jury of my peers, who convicts me of a crime, I WILL NOT SURRENDER MY HOME.

Help me to defend my home and the Constitution of the United States against these bureaucratic thugs.

### IRS Abuse Report #2

**Date:** Aug 3, 1995
**To:** sue@irs.class-action.com
**From:** TS

We are on a monthly payment plan that we will never be able to pay off -- due to excessive interest and penalties.

### IRS Abuse Report #3

**Date:** Aug 4, 1995
**To:** sue@irs.class-action.com
**From:** PC

The IRS ruined our credit. Now, we are unable to live a normal life or own a home. I feel helpless. They have made us feel like criminals. A financial mistake when we were young, ten years ago, and our lives have been ruined. We started out owing $8,000, now we owe $30,000 that we can never pay.

Golden-Helmet Overture

The Evil

## IRS Abuse Report #4

**Date:** Aug 5, 1995
**To:** sue@irs.class-action.com
**From:** JG

The IRS would not allow me due process in considering my case BEFORE threatening to seize my bank accounts. This FORCED me to pay all amounts, plus penalties and interest that they insisted I owed them. No hearing, no chance to show they were wrong, no help in seeking justice... from anybody!

## IRS Abuse Report #5

**Date:** Aug 5, 1995
**To:** sue@irs.class-action.com
**From:** AS

I am an American living in Singapore. My wife is a Singaporean. The IRS has been calling in the middle of the night waking us up and harassing us. I am not a tax protestor. I have filed all my necessary tax returns and provided the IRS all the information they have requested to substantiate my returns. Yet, they seem to have ignored everything and sent me a 300K tax bill and a 90 day letter. I had NO CHOICE but to file a case in the US Tax Court. I was forced to spend additional thousands of dollars to defend myself against this agency that has run amok. I don't like that. My wife being a citizen of an independent sovereign country does not like being wakened in the middle of the night by US government agents. She may file a protest with the Singapore government. She considers this action by the US a violation of her right to privacy. Its time we stopped these guys. Also, as a person who's life is being destroyed by the IRS for NO REASON I am willing to contribute of my time and expertise without charge to your cause if it will help insure the demise of the IRS. I need help too as I have a case coming up in the US Tax Court soon, and living abroad, I find it difficult to get any help.

Someone suggested writing to my congressman but since I do not have a US home (for over 11 years) I don't believe I even have one to write to. And, if I did, I have no faith he or she would listen to my plea.

I have done nothing wrong but am being forced to spend lot's of money to keep my name clear. And, after reading your book, even innocence may not prevail where the tax bureaucracy is concerned.

It's time for the silent majority to be heard. We will not have our freedom trampled upon by the tax-Gestapo IRS that operates outside the law.

## IRS Abuse Report #6

**Date:** Aug 8, 1995
**To:** sue@irs.class-action.com
**From:** JM

The IRS was directly responsible for the demise of my father's successful consulting company. His accountants were partially to blame -- they put his company on an incorrect tax plan, and the IRS came after five years of operation to demand back taxes, almost a half-million dollars. This was back when the construction market wasn't too good, and they could not pay the back taxes in the time that the IRS demanded. My father and his partners tried to pay it back gradually, but the IRS wanted it immediately. They had to liquidate the company in order to get the money, and the IRS constantly threatened to seize our home if the money was not repaid on time. We eventually got them off our backs, but now my father is working for someone else at a job he does not enjoy. I hope you are successful in this lawsuit.

## IRS Abuse Report #7

**Date:** Aug 10, 1995
**To:** sue@irs.class-action.com
**From:** JK

The IRS has stolen money from me under threat of force. They did this by threatening to imprison me if I did not give up a percentage of my money every year .

## IRS Abuse Report #8

**Date:** Aug 14, 1995.
**To:** sue@irs.class-action.com
**From:** WL

They are threatening to file a lien against me and seize my property because they claim that I owe them the whopping sum of $53.46 from 1992. They have repeatedly ignored my requests for proof of their claim. They have failed to answer even the most basic questions.

## IRS Abuse Report #9

**Date:** Aug 12, 1995.
**To:** sue@irs.class-action.com
**From:** MK

I was in business from 72-86 and closed because of the harassment I received from the IRS. It turned out to be an error by the IRS but not before they threatened to reposes our house and other items. The IRS owed us over $10,000 -- it was finally paid back to us -- but not before much intimidation.

## IRS Abuse Report #10

**Date:** Aug 16, 1995.
**To:** sue@irs.class-action.com
**From: RA**
I am required to spend at least 28% of my productive energy paying for services I do not require and seldom if ever use. In addition, I am required to do enormous amounts of record keeping and income reporting which have absolutely nothing to do with the productive purposes of my business. In all, just using narrow-scope accounting, this one particular agency wastes 40% of my productive energy.

## IRS Abuse Report #11

**Date:** Aug 23, 1995.
**To:** sue@irs.class-action.com
**From: AB**
The IRS audited my pension plan on what I consider frivolous charges, they later dropped all the charges -- after keeping me on edge for 4 years and after all kinds of auditing expenses. Not to mention the time and tax payer money wasted by the IRS.

## IRS Abuse Report #12

**Date:** Aug 16, 1995.
**To:** sue@irs.class-action.com
**From: JT**
The IRS creates INCREDIBLE fear. I am always afraid I'm going to make a mistake on my tax return! It is impossible to understand all the fine points in their instructions, yet I cannot afford to hire expensive legal help to figure it out!

## IRS Abuse Report #13

**Date:** Aug. 26, 1995:
**To:** sue@irs.class-action.com
**From: JT**
Simply, the IRS takes 25% of my income, and gives me nothing but threats in return.

## IRS Abuse Report #14

**Date:** Aug. 31, 1995:
**To:** sue@irs.class-action.com
**From:** CS

In 1992, my wife received a settlement from a large corporation in a class action discrimination suit that was granted under title 7 in regards to personal injury. Taxes were paid in accordance with the prevailing laws and all was well. Now, three years later, the IRS has decided that the settlement no longer falls under title 7, and that these were simply a loss of wages. The settlement was for a period over four years in length and yet they feel entitled to an additional $33,000 and $8,000 in interest. Total bill of $41,000!! This family of five lives at a low enough level that it qualifies for financial aid and the local food program!

## IRS Abuse Report #15

**Date:** Sept. 3, 1995:
**To:** sue@irs.class-action.com
**From:** JC

Interesting site. Is the IRS watching? I have been on an installment agreement for 10 years. The original debt (941) was approx. $8000, I have paid $14,000 so far and I am told I currently owe approx $25,000. I have sufficient equity in a home that the IRS happily put a lien on it. I seem to be stuck and cannot get any amnesty or forgiveness.

## IRS Abuse Report #16

**Date:** Sept. 15, 1995:
**To:** sue@irs.class-action.com
**From:** PC

The I.R.S. seized my car because of a mistake they made. They got my ss# wrong and it matched someone who did not pay taxes. Even though the names were different, they took the car anyway. It took me 3 months to get it back. And, my radio was stolen from their impound!

## IRS Abuse Report #17

**Date:** Sept. 17, 1995
**To:** sue@irs.class-action.com
**From:** AM

Levies, liens, excessive penalties and interest. All of these have just about crippled me financially. I had to file a chapter 13 bankruptcy to protect myself. All of these actions (including the bankruptcy), have caused me nothing but misery. I need a co-signer for just about any lease or credit application I submit. I found the tax liens to be an enormous embarrassment especially when my sisters and I applied for a loan to remodel an old house we had inherited from our father, only to have the loan turned down for the above reasons. I am in a serious financial rut that I am having much difficulty climbing out of.

## IRS Abuse Report #18

**Date:** Sept. 17, 1995
**To:** sue@irs.class-action.com
**From:** PK
Constant threats over a 6 yr period. An attempt to garnish wages. Several levies for taxes owed, unreasonable tax assessed when I played in a band at 17yrs of age making ONLY enough $ to survive living on the road.

## IRS Abuse Report #19

**Date:** Sept. 19, 1995
**To:** sue@irs.class-action.com
**From:** AH
Can they really take all that I own?

## IRS Abuse Report #20

**Date:** Sept. 20, 1995
**To:** sue@irs.class-action.com
**From:** SW
They have garnished my wages. They have unfairly decided how much they wanted to take and left me with less than enough to survive. The amount the IRS thinks I owe is not associated with any objective honesty. The IRS does not even follow their own rules.

## IRS Abuse Report #21

**Date:** Oct. 4, 1995
**To:** sue@irs.class-action.com
**From:** TQBS
I am paying the IRS $70 per month, but with penalties, it seems I'll never get my $2,000 in back taxes paid!

## IRS Abuse Report #22

**Date:** Oct. 5, 1995
**To:** sue@irs.class-action.com
**From:** DW
Penalties make my tax debt to last forever.

## IRS Abuse Report #23

**Date:** Oct. 13, 1995
**To:** sue@irs.class-action.com
**From:** JB
The IRS is draining the working class of all savings, to pay 'entitlements' to those that choose not to report their incomes, or unwilling to go out and contribute their time and effort to work. The IRS has put a lien on my home.

## IRS Abuse Report #24

**Date:** Oct. 16, 1995
**To:** sue@irs.class-action.com
**From:** BD
My bank account was seized by the IRS without notification from the IRS or the Bank. Checks were bouncing and I was finally informed of the seizure by the Bank after several enquiries. I contacted the local IRS field office asking what was going on and was informed that I would have to provide certain documents to them for them to take any action. I obtained the documents and had to take time off from work to deliver them to the field office. Within a minute of delivering the documents I was told it was all a mistake and never should have happened. From there, it took several days for my account to be released and my money to be restored. But, the bounced check charges were not reimbursed.

## IRS Abuse Report #25

**Date:** Oct. 24, 1995
**To:** sue@irs.class-action.com
**From:** DE
I have been harassed by the IRS. During the past year, I have filed the same 1992 Tax Return 3 times, Signed and gave Power of Attorney to represent me in a different matter with IRS, filled out an asset statement, asked for installment plan or offer of compromise. Since last September IRS has claimed they have never received any of this. This past September, I was threatened by an IRS agent over the phone. He claimed that they have none of the information and that I was lying about the power of Attorney and my place of employment. I restated the facts and had my attorney send the documents they requested. I was told by the agent that I was a liar and threatened me with a lien and levy against my wages. He gave me till 09/07/ 95 to provide all the above or he would file the levy. I went back to my lawyer and he resent all requested documents 10 days before the deadline. Today I received a notice of levy against my wages from my employer. Returning to my attorney, he got an agent on the phone, who claims I failed to respond and they filed the levy. It was stated that they do not have any of the

forms!!!! I want to sue for harassment and violation of my taxpayer rights but do not know where to turn. I am desperate for information on what to do and how to confront the IRS. My attorney seems to be afraid of them or just does not know how to proceed. I have to forestall this levy, I will lose my job if this happens. If you can point me to any resources it would be a great help to me. I just do not know who to go to for help. Thank You

### IRS Abuse Report #26

**Date:** Oct. 30, 1995
**To:** sue@irs.class-action.com
**From:** LB

In 1985 I got audited and was found to owe 6500 dollars. And I have been paying them 100 or 150 dollars a month and they have kept my refunds ever since 1985-1994. I have paid them almost 13,000 dollars, and still owe them over 4,000 dollars.

### IRS Abuse Report #27

**Date:** Nov. 2, 1995
**To:** sue@irs.class-action.com
**From:** AW

I programed for a local company the past ten years. The IRS demanded $400/ week, my boss said he had to comply, sent $800 from two checks he was holding. I am now a paper boy. A friend's sister, currently living/working in Egypt, lately had $30,000 removed from her bank account w/no warning by the IRS. Several letters have not produced a reply. I have only been inconvenienced. This lady was robbed.

### IRS Abuse Report #28

**Date:** Nov. 4, 1995
**To:** sue@irs.class-action.com
**From:** JB

After filing taxes every year, on year ten the IRS decides that a filing ten years ago is incorrect, and is trying to collect. Did nothing for nine years. IRS is attaching liens. One IRS office says I owe nothing, another IRS office says I owe money, and another IRS office is working on the problem.

### IRS Abuse Report #29

**Date:** Nov. 9, 1995
**To:** sue@irs.class-action.com
**From:** RE

At the end of the 1976 I owed nothing but $600 for my social security for that year. The IRS fined me for not paying my S.S. and in three months the $600 cost me over $3000. ...Because I was negligent in paying my **own** social security retirement!

### IRS Abuse Report #30

**Date:** Nov. 13, 1995
**To:** sue@irs.class-action.com
**From:** DS

I had a certified federal enrolled tax agent complete my taxes for 3 years. This agency is governed by the IRS themselves. Well, it comes to pass after the tax agent's death (due to cancer) I find out that he did not do what I paid him to do. He did not file my state or federal taxes for 3 years. I called the IRS, telling them of this. They instantly liened my house, seized all my bank accounts and are bleeding me to death. They forced me to sell a income property. Which net profit will be $8,000 due to capital gains. Each month, I get calls from my collections agent, he randomly gives me an amount he wants from 2,500 to 500. To be given to him that month. Living on edge every second. I, my life, dreams, hard work are all gone. Due to trusting in the IRS and there organization of federal enrolled tax agents.

### IRS Abuse Report #31

**Date:** Nov. 14, 1995
**To:** sue@irs.class-action.com
**From:** S

The IRS has illegally charged me $20,000 for a US Treasury Note which I purchased in 1989 for $10,000. They are saying that the Note was income which I did not claim. So, I am being penalized 100% for this Treasury note. They have notified my employer to garnishee my wages and they have placed liens on my property.

### IRS Abuse Report #32

**Date:** Nov. 18, 1995
**To:** sue@irs.class-action.com
**From:** SY

I received notice on 11-10-95 from my employer, that the IRS had garnished my wages. I certainly did not receive the 30-day notice as supposedly written into IRS policy.

Golden-Helmet Overture
The Evil

## IRS Abuse Report #33

**Date:** Nov. 19, 1995
**To:** sue@irs.class-action.com
**From:** JC

In my experience with the IRS, if you don't know what you are talking about, they will lie to confuse you. If you know what you are talking about, they take the fifth by refusing to answer.

## IRS Abuse Report #34

**Date:** Nov. 26, 1995
**To:** sue@irs.class-action.com
**From:** GT

The following happened to two friends of mine: BEWARE OF THE OVERPAYMENT SCHEME !! Each, having been overpaid by the IRS after filing a yearly statement, sent the excess back to the IRS. The IRS proceeded to bill them for interest, penalties and interest on penalties!!!! FOR THEIR OWN MISTAKES !!!!!

## IRS Abuse Report #35

**Date:** Nov. 27, 1995
**To:** sue@irs.class-action.com
**From:** SA

In 1992 I received a letter from the IRS that they had not received a tax return for me in the years 1980, 1981, and 1982. I said I had sent the returns when due (10-12 years ago), but I had no copies after so long. They maintained that there were no returns on file for those years. Subsequently, they levied against all my assets for over $80,000 and placed liens on my credit records which are still there. The liens keep me from getting work, getting anything on credit, etc.

## IRS Abuse Report #36

**Date:** Nov. 28, 1995
**To:** sue@irs.class-action.com
**From:** RB

Have taken my money, my businesses, (cost me 4 years of court time, my time, and my family's time). Am appealing in the Federal court .

**IRS Abuse Report #37**

**Date:** Nov. 29, 1995
**To:** sue@irs.class-action.com
**From:** BH

During the 91'-92' tax years, apparently our CPA had entered a lot of false statements on our return so that we could get more money back. There were a lot of people in our area that she did this to. She took deductions that weren't legally acceptable, and we had no knowledge of what our legal deductions were -- after all, that was why we were paying a CPA. Then came the IRS and the auditors. About 50 people I know were audited. After the audit was over and they figured out how much we owed the IRS, they put us on a payment plan to pay them back. I thought that would be the end of the terrible ordeal, but no. Six months after the audit the IRS criminal investigators called and wanted to setup an appointment to discuss our CPA. So we told them all we knew, and again we thought surely this would be the end of this ordeal with the CPA and the IRS. After a year of making monthly payments to the IRS, which my wife made on time every month, they sent a letter saying that we had defaulted on our balance owed to them, and they were giving us 2 weeks to pay them or they were going to seize our assets and place a lien on us. So I went to the bank and got the money and paid them off. Again thinking, damn this has got to be the end of this situation with the IRS. Tonight an agent from the Charlotte, NC IRS criminal division called wanting to setup another appointment to discuss our tax returns again. After treating us like shit, I'm tired of dealing with these assholes. Do I legally have to talk to these people, I've already told them all I know? I'm sick and tired of this and want it to stop. What options do I have? Help me.

**IRS Abuse Report #38**

**Date:** Fri, 01 Dec 95 12:21:46 -800
**To:** sue@irs.class-action.com
**From:** S

Approx. 24 months ago I contracted a rare pneumonia, I was on disability for 8 months. At the same time the company I had worked for was experiencing restructuring. They required that I move to San Francisco. We agreed on a cash settlement. This gave me the monies needed to learn and establish a new career. My monies were budgeted to give me adequate time for transition. I set about the career transition without asking any assistance.

Recently the IRS took $3200 out of my account. This was the last of my cash reserve. I now have no means of paying rent, electricity, or phone. The IRS could literally be the reason I become homeless.

## IRS Abuse Report #39

**Date:** Tue Dec  5 20:10:41 1995
**To:** sue@irs.class-action.com
**From:**  MP

After filing bankruptcy in 92, because of a bad divorce, I went to the IRS for an offer of compromise, then the fun started.  They denied my application.  I still can't get them to stop harassing me with liens and levies.

## IRS Abuse Report #40

**Date:** Thu, 07 Dec 95 21:48:01 -800
**To:** sue@irs.class-action.com
**From:**  IRS R.I.P.

Back in 1988 the IRS took all but $260 a month from my paycheck, via a levy.  This was for the year 1982.  I had been filing exempt on the w-4. Which is my lawful right.  In 1992 I was convicted on two counts of tax evasion for 1986 and 1987.  And for 1985 they are getting ready to send another levy to my employer for about $15,000.  And before I forget, I am now in tax court for 83, 84, 86, and 87.   Did I leave anything out? Oh, I am on probation until 1997.  I did not see any prison time, am I lucky or what? I have been just this side of hell.

## IRS Abuse Report #41

**Date:** Sat Dec  9 10:48:32 1995
**To:** sue@irs.class-action.com
**From:**  PG

The company where I am the Business Director was seized after the I.R.S. had entered into a payment agreement and we had given them $55,000.   The majority of the money owed now is penalty and interest.   However, to get the business back, we had to file a Chapter 11.

## IRS Abuse Report #42

**Date:** Mon Dec 11 12:51:45 1995
**To:** sue@irs.class-action.com
**From:**  TR

My home belongs to the IRS and every attempt to negotiate is met with a brick wall.   In 1982 I was brought an investment, by an investment counselor, that would allow me to enter into the music/record business.  This investment promised some tax advantages so I met with the IRS to insure legality.  I was informed by the IRS that the investment was sound.  Upon making the investment and taking the tax credits in 1983, I was audited in 1986.  The tax credits were denied.  The IRS applied interest and  penalties which made the amount owed impossible to pay. Liens were placed on my home. Because of the liens my credit was ruined. Because of this I was unable to get loans to pay off the liens. This year I found a funding company that would work with the IRS to negotiate the amounts owed and give me a second mortgage. The IRS refused to negotiate and instead is in the process of increasing the lien amounts for additional interests and penalties. So far, an $18000 tax savings, originally approved by the IRS, has resulted in $62000 debt to the IRS. During my last conversation with an IRS agent, I was told that the only way they would negotiate was if I sold my home and gave them all of the equity plus $1500. When I asked the agent where he expected me to find housing, I was informed "that's not my problem".

## IRS Abuse Report #43

**Date:** Fri, 15 Dec 95 08:17:01 -0800
**To:** sue@irs.class-action.com
**From:** MY Story:

I was audited by the IRS for Income Tax Filing Years 1980, 81, 83, and 84 and thru this audit I lost a vehicle by IRS seizure while I was on an out of state work assignment in 1985. In 1988 I had some military trauma flash backs which ended up with my being incarcerated from June 1988 until November 1994. During this period of incarceration I was able to pay in-full the tax owed for the years of 1983 and 1984. I had an attorney represent me before the IRS in an effort to settle the tax debts. Through delays caused by the IRS not answering his inquiries, it took over 18 months, as well as red-tape run-arounds, to finalize payment for years 1983 and 84. We asked for a waiver of interest for the period of my incarceration [only]. The waver was denied. My tax debt for the unpaid years, was originally somewhere in the areas of $1100 for one and $2500 for the other. With the IRS disallowing the waiver of interest during my term of incarceration, the total tax debt for those 2 years is just over $10,000. The IRS has agreed to installment payments of $247/month for 3 years. I do not object to paying the original amount plus interest and penalties for the years prior to my being incarcerated. My payment of some $4,000 for the years of 1983 and 1984 while incarcerate is evidence that I am trying to settle my tax obligation. I just have a real problem with the IRS incurring interest upon my remaining debt during a time of incarceration.

I am also disabled and receiving Social Security Disability Income monthly payments, a 10% VA monthly Compensation, and monthly payments from a trust my deceased parents setup for me. This is my total source of income other than my wife's Social Security Retirement income. I am just getting my family back into a stable living environment and this $247 monthly installment payments for 36 months will be a considerable burden. If the interest were adjusted to waive the period of incarceration I would likely be able to settle in full, 6 to 8 months, though with some short-term hardship. I could then continue my productive, tax paying life without the anxiety of continually looking over my shoulder for the feared impending ambush coming.

## IRS Abuse Report #44

**Date:** Sun Dec 17 11:05:15 1995
**To:** sue@irs.class-action.com
**From:** JK

Audited tax return from 1983 in the year 1989, then demanded that copies of checks, rather than actual bank statements which matched Merrill Lynch Cash Management Account statements, be provided. Merrill Lynch did not have the cancelled checks even though their literature states that they keep them on hand and will provide them, or copies of them, upon request.

IRS then rejected clearly legitimate deductions and demanded immediate payment of $250,000 in "unpaid taxes, interest, and penalties" which now adds up to more than $450,000.

## IRS Abuse Report #45

**Date:** Thu, 21 Dec 1995 00:42:54 -0500
**To:** sue@irs.class-action.com
**From:** BE

My life has been made miserable and my credit ruined by IRS liens relating to a business that I operated from 1978 to 1984. I always had an accountant do my withholding taxes and to the best of my knowledge, except for the last quarter of operations, when the company had no funds, I eventually made all payments. I have never had any conversation or correspondence with the IRS regarding these liens, but now they have seemed to multiply out of nothing into more than $80,000, and a couple of them have expired, meaning that probably more than $100,000 has been assessed against me by the IRS for nothing that I can figure out.

It is my belief that the IRS misapplied payments that I made while the business was operating and did not credit them to my company, as I did change the name of the business twice. After that, penalties and interest applied by the IRS to mistaken claims have simply escalated, and continue to do so. There is nothing I can do to fight this, as all of the records from that business were given up when the business' lease was terminated in 1985. In any event, I have not been able to buy a home or a car, or anything on new credit as the IRS liens are viewed as the worst kind of credit liability. To make matters worse, due to my age, I have been unable to find suitable employment although I am doing important volunteer work which means that I am capable if I could get hired.

### IRS Abuse Report #46

**Date:** Fri Dec 22 22:14:23 1995
**To:** sue@irs.class-action.com
**From:** AS

The IRS has garnisheed wages three times. The IRS attempted once for
$50,000. I am so sick of these people not answering my letters and stealing
my property (wages).

### IRS Abuse Report #47

**Date:** Wed Dec 27 13:23:52 1995
**To:** sue@irs.class-action.com
**From:** LS

They have made so many mistakes on my account and charged me with
monies I do not owe. Every time, they send me two and three letters about
the same thing. They have made my life a living hell.

### IRS Abuse Report #48

**Date:** Wed Jan 10 13:12:38 EST 1996
**To:** sue@irs.class-action.com
**From:** JS

IRS has Fed.Tax Liens filled against my property. I can't even go on living,
with this over my head. 56 years old..no way to ever pay off..Taxes
paid..penalties and interest keep building. No way out..P.S. Probably dropping
E-Mail address soon..Suicide the only answer to forgetting this problem.
Help...

Can't purchase house, mine falling down..Can't even make any major
purchase..Life not really worth going on 56 yrs. old and no end to this
mess....Also, they took a friend of mine, house and everything he
owned..ruined him forever. Help me...

### IRS Abuse Report #49

**Date:** Sat, 13 Jan 1996 21:49:29 -0500
**To:** sue@irs.class-action.com

The IRS is currently attempting to audit me on fictitious income they claim
was suppose to have been reported on my 1985 Tax return. I am using the
IRS Ombudsman to assist me in responding to the IRS. With interest and
penalties, they turned a few hundred dollars dispute it into a $30,000 dispute.
They have also Garnished my wages. Understand, my first claim against them
was not prior notice (even about the garnishment) and the IRS states they sent
notice to the address on the form. Well I haven't lived there since 1986 and

the IRS has (from a print out of their own system) my current address as well as my current and previous employers. I wish I could afford a really good attorney. I'd like to put the IRS in their place.

## IRS Abuse Report #50

**Date:** Thu, 18 Jan 1996 02:01:12 -0800
**To:** sue@irs.class-action.com
Five years ago, my brother was married to a woman who filed a tax report owing $1,100 . She did not pay it. A year later my brother divorced this women. Now, the IRS wants my brother to pay taxes, interest, and penalties for his ex-wife.

My brother had bought a "dollar" home and lived in it for a few years and really fixed the place up and when he moved he sold it for 17,000 dollars! That's a real good improvement and the place really did look nice, but all the other homes in the area are worth about 10,000 dollars. He lived in a ghetto. Well, the IRS now says that the house was sold for 54,000 and not 17,000 and they want there cut of the action.

My brother now lives with a woman he is not married to. He has 4 boys that are living with him, ages 2 to 14. The IRS says he can't claim them as a deduction. He also has 2 children of his own which live with their mother, ages 8 and 15. He doesn't claim them but does have to provide support for them.

The woman that he lives with made 3,000 dollars last year as a janitor. He brought in a whopping 20,000 last year. My brother works very hard to support the family the best that he can. Last week he went to pick up his paycheck and to his surprise, its only for a hundred bucks for two weeks work. The IRS put a levy against his wages for 1,800 hundred dollars. He lives paycheck to paycheck as do alot of Americans.

My brother NEEDS help and advise. I told him to pick up a second job until the IRS finds him and then move on to another job. He is 40 years old and has no savings, no retirement, and no future. What do you think is going to happen if no release comes?

## IRS Abuse Report #51

**Date:** Fri Jan 19 18:19:46 EST 1996
**To:** sue@irs.class-action.com
**From:** DS
 During 1992 and 1993, my wife and I did not have enough tax withheld from our paychecks. As a result, we ended up owing the IRS almost $10,000, a

large portion of which was penalties and interest. We set up an installment agreement, and have been paying on it for over three years. On TWO occasions during this time, we were late (by less than 5 days) in making our payment. This prompted someone in the IRS to decide that we are a "nonpayment risk." So, they seized our bank account and filed a public tax lien against us. They did not notify us of this action, and we found out when we received a call from an organization that helps out people with tax problems. We were able to get our bank account released, but only after dozens of phone calls to every IRS office whose number I could get, and a visit to two IRS offices. I was not able to get the lien released. In fact, they couldn't even tell me who in the IRS had taken the action. The bottom line? Because of the lien, we are not able to get a loan for a car, and were even turned down for renting a house. All because the IRS "seized" our credit for two late payments totalling $430. I know this may sound trivial compared to some horror stories, but every act of unconstitutional aggression by our government hurts us all.

## IRS Abuse Report #52

**Date:** Fri Jan 19 21:28:33 EST 1996
**To:** sue@irs.class-action.com
 **From:** JK
I made a typo when filling out my forms making  my sons social security number invalid. Because of this, they refused to let me claim him as a dependent. They ordered me to produce all kinds of paper work to prove that he was my son and that he lived with me. While I was getting the paperwork, I wrote them numerous letters explaining the typing error and asked if they would simply check their records they would see that I had been claiming him for the last 16 years and that his status hadn't changed. They would not accept him as my dependent.  Each time I would send them the papers they requested, they would take several months to reply, always informing me of more papers they wanted, which in turn, I would send. When they decided that I had sent enough paper work, they sent me a notice saying to much time had elapsed and that the case was closed. Now, not only do I owe them the original amount, they assessed a penalty of 25% for late payment.

## IRS Abuse Report #53

**Date:** Tue, 23 Jan 96 00:23:43 -0800
**To:** sue@irs.class-action.com
**From:** JB
In the late 70's and early 80's I was behind on filing my returns. In 1984, I filed 8 years all at once and paid the fines. Now in 1994, the IRS has said that they did not receive my 78 return until 1989, and my 1981 return until 1986, and when a refund was due me, they kept the refund. Now can you

believe what the IRS has done regarding penalties and interest since 1978 and 1981. The amounts they are claiming, you would not believe. I have dealt with seven offices, and at least 21 IRS employees. The left hand doesn't know the right hand. The Problem Resolution Program (PRP) only sends letters saying pay.....You mail these people proof of your filings, and they lose those documents and the process starts over again. The IRS should be eliminated, and I am sure persons in the private sector could do a much better job.

## IRS Abuse Report #54

**Date:** Tue Jan 23 02:13:01 EST 1996
**To:** sue@irs.class-action.com
**From:** GC
It is time to stop the unconstitutional powers of the IRS. They need to be put out of business, along with anyone who supports them. They took my father-in-law and put a levy on him for my tax problems. No due process, they come and spit on your due process. It is time to shut them down and do America a great deed.

## IRS Abuse Report #55

**Date:** Sat Jan 27 01:37:45 EST 1996
**To:** sue@irs.class-action.com
**From:** TA
The money extorted from my paycheck and personal finances every day by the IRS has cost me freedom of movement, basic human comfort, a Chapter 11 Bankruptcy, and continual involuntary servitude. The presence of the IRS has created underlying fear in my personal life and the lives of my family. This fear has prevented productivity and the ability to live up to my highest potential as a human being and to exercise personal freedoms awarded me at birth. The money extorted every day prevents me from investing in the future, specifically my health and financial well-being when I become a senior citizen, and prevents my family the basic human right of safety and well-being in their future years. The IRS is a threat to my safety, both physically and mentally, and should be charged with endangering the health and well-being of every American citizen.

## IRS Abuse Report #56

**Date:** Thu Feb  1 18:39:39 EST 1996
**To:** sue@irs.class-action.com
**From:** RC
The IRS is taking $1800 of my $2000 pension which leaves me fairly penniless and unable to support myself in retirement.

## IRS Abuse Report #57

**Date:** Fri, 9 Feb 1996 02:39:02 -0500
**To:** sue@irs.class-action.com
**From:** BL

I am now engaged in a payment plan, which may not retire my IRS obligation before my death. The taxes in question, which I agree fully I owe (however, I strongly dispute the moral and legal basis for the penalties accruing thereto) were incurred in just two years, during which I was separated from my wife and trying to negotiate a divorce agreement. This period of time also saw the swift downturn of work availability in my profession, and in the general economy of the State of California. I was faced with providing necessary living accommodations for myself, my children, my to-be ex-wife, while trying to maintain a level of earning in a diminishing economy. It became clear to me that there simply wasn't enough money to satisfy all demands. I was eventually forced into bankruptcy.

Realizing my dilemma, I sought advice on how to deal with tax problems. One fact was perfectly clear: Filing tax returns when the means to pay was not at hand was tantamount to subjecting oneself to the most horrific torture. So, I did what was the proper thing to do: I delayed filing until I felt I could "face the music". Of course, the penalties and interest attached to the taxes have made the debt most burdensome.

Well, I was unable to pay the tax, and now I am on the aforementioned payment plan which will probably follow me to my grave -- if I can earn enough to stay a half-step ahead.

When I declared bankruptcy, my income taxes should have been discharged along with my other debts. I would now be a clean, productive citizen. Instead, I have a monstrous tax lien filed with the County Recorder, and the cloud of pernicious, untamed collection actions of the IRS hanging over me. The IRS doesn't have to live by any laws but their own. (And they hire the most obnoxious people -- but what normal person would want such a job?)

What possible good does this system serve? How does this differ from the time of indentured servants, "servants" who often paid with their lives when the tax collector paid his visit? Where is the constitutional authority for the establishment of an agency of the government which can disregard all the restraints of our constitution to achieve the ends of its mission? Where is the popular media exercising it's constitutionally protected grace to discuss this obfuscation of our rights? When will we all wake up to the fact that the IRS is, simply the armed servant of the power-grubbing, do-gooders -- social engineers, bureaucrats, and generally those who think their ideas and social mission is more important than individual rights and responsibility?

## IRS Abuse Report #58

**Date:** Thu Feb 8 15:47:52 EST 1996
**To:** sue@irs.class-action.com
**From:** SR

In approximately 1983, I was asked by an employer to fill out a w-4 form. A few weeks later the IRS said the information I provided was false. They fined me $1,000 for providing false information. The IRS acted as judge and jury and convicted me without allowing me to redress my grievances. I refused to pay so they took all the money I had in my bank account, which was less than $100 and then they put a lien on my land and levied my wages until the fines, penalties and interest were paid.

## IRS Abuse Report #59

**Date:** Thu Feb 8 19:58:37 EST 1996
**To:** sue@irs.class-action.com
**From:** JW

The income tax as presently levied makes us all slaves to politicians, IRS agents, state taxing agents, and their police state thugs. In reading Kahriger v. U.S. the supreme court states that a tax return, like the 1040, is a confession. If we are compelled to sign confessions in this "land of the free and home of the brave" then we are slaves! Even the Geneva Convention outlaws the use of torture, physical or mental, or any form of coercion to force a prisoner of war to sign a confession. We are worse off than prisoners of war; WE THE SLAVE PEOPLE in order to form a "more perfect union"? The IRS wipes their butt with the U.S. Constitution every day...they think its a piece of toilet paper...and the bulk of Americans seem satisfied being the tame little Slaves for these supercilious rats.

The IRS seized my car in 1988. I paid to get it back and I asked the agent, if this was the end of it for the 1984 year. He responded with "yes." A year later the agency was back rejecting the settlement because the agent had used the wrong form!

The agency then treated stock sales as total profit, disregarding the obvious purchase price, and in 1987 they proceed to turn what was less then 12 k (before inflation) gross profit on sales of 40 k investment over 10 years into in excess of 150 k taxes with penalties and interest! I lost to the tax court judge. I spent over 2 k on an attorney to file bankruptcy. The IRS accepted all but 1985, which they now claim as over 35 k.

## IRS Abuse Report #60

**Date:** Tue, 13 Feb 96 09:14:20 -2400
**To:** sue@irs.class-action.com
**From:** JM
The IRS has cleaned out our two IRA accounts and molested us in numerous other ways.

## IRS Abuse Report #61

**Date:** Mon, 19 Feb 1996 18:50:28 -0600 (CST)
**To:** sue@irs.class-action.com
**From:** NM
In 1989, my ex-husband left me. I have a son (not his). Within 6 months of his leaving, I was laid off from my job. (I also do not get child support -- his father refuses to pay.) My husband talked me into filing joint since we were still married in '89. I signed the form he worked up; it looked fine to me. Well, after he mailed it in, I found out that he had not paid ANY taxes for the year. Needless to say, we had to pay. Well, I ended up paying about three thousand dollars for him. He didn't file his taxes for at least three years, because it took me that long to pay it off. I asked the IRS why I had to pay his debt and I was told that 1) we were still married -- separation didn't count; and 2) "we take easy money, whoever we can get to pay first -- we don't care who pays." I ended up filing bankruptcy -- against my better judgement. I asked the IRS the second year why they weren't taking any money from him, too. I didn't get an answer. I asked if my ex was even filing his taxes: no answer. The second year I was paying his debt, the IRS sent me a letter saying I owed a little over $7,000. Since I had only made $9,000 that whole year, I laughed, then I got mad because they were serious. I was going through the bankruptcy, so my attorney also called the IRS to find out what was going on. She and I both fought them for a year just to get answers. We both got a different person every time we called. I got a letter about every month, and we called the IRS every week to find out what was going on.

## IRS Abuse Report #62

**Date:** Sat Feb 17 20:11:03 EST 1996
**To:** sue@irs.class-action.com
**From:** BR
I ran a successful contracting business for over ten years and had many employees. Due to an error in math I underpaid withholding taxes. I told the IRS this at the end of the year when I discovered the error. They fined me $40,000 and forced me into bankruptcy. Even after going bankrupt I still owe $16,000 personally and have had my accounts cleaned out and my wages garnished.

## IRS Abuse Report #63

**Date:** Mon, 19 Feb 1996 00:39:37 -0500
**To:** sue@irs.class-action.com
**From:** RM

The federal income tax and the IRS is destroying the very principles this country was founded on.

## IRS Abuse Report #64

**Date:** Fri, 20 Feb 2009 12:11:19 -0800
**To:** sue@irs.class-action.com
**From:** RV

Recently the IRS has adopted a new set of rules taxing tuition waivers for employees. Many university employees work for reduced salaries, like myself, because they are going to school to better themselves and the university gives them free tuition to compensate the difference.

IRS is collecting millions if not billions of dollars with this new law that is probably making many unfortunate people have to discontinue their graduate studies because they cannot afford to give the IRS several hundred dollars a month in tuition waiver tax. Please help!

## IRS Abuse Report #65

**Date:** Wed, 21 Feb 1996 11:45:28 -0500
**To:** sue@irs.class-action.com
**From:** DM

I have been battling the IRS for about 10 yrs now. They have a lien on the house, and until recently had a lien on my wife's salary. Last year we managed to make a (over 10% reduction) "contribution" to our tax liability. Seven months after this activity we receive notices of "WE HAVE CHANGED YOUR ACCOUNTS" where they added over $8,000 in "late payment penalties" and over $40,000 in interest! This interest figure represented, in a 7 month period, a 31% rate!

I have other information available if I can be of assistance in your fight.

## IRS Abuse Report #66

**Date:** Wed, 21 Feb 1996 20:26:52 -0500
**To:** sue@irs.class-action.com
**From:** BK

Recently I received a notice of levy from big brother of over 1500. The interesting part is that they are holding $1000 that they won't apply to this levy, and they refuse to let me make payments. They say that they won't release the cash because of the chapter 13 filed to prevent them from getting money from my trustee . It seems to me that if they are holding money that they owe me, it should be applied to the new levy, then I could afford to pay them off. This is the first notice that I have received on these new owes they say they have sent four. Any help or advice you can offer would help, what's next, be forced into homelessness?

## IRS Abuse Report #67

**Date:** Thu Feb 22 18:52:17 EST 1996
**To:** sue@irs.class-action.com
**From:** LE
When the IRS, allegedly, could not reach me at my N.Y. address that I had lived at for almost 8 years, they put a levy on my salary taking 90%. This left about $134 a week to live on. I lived on Long Island and used the Long Island Railroad -- that alone cost $140 monthly. Rent was $1330 and I won't even add in all the other expenses, phone, utilities, credit payments, loans, food, etc... Since I couldn't afford to work I had to resign. I had about 18,000 saved so I moved to North Carolina where the cost of living is less than N.Y. and immediately hired a tax specialist to see what they could do. After almost a year of negotiations The IRS 'AGREED' to allow me to make monthly payments of 740 to pay off my alleged underpayment of taxes since 1990 of $40,635.25. If I had $740 extra a month I'd have a nice sized savings account but as it happened I couldn't find a job for 10 months, exhausted all my savings and don't have a bank account at all.

I am to start making this payment in 2 weeks. If I make this payment I will not be able to pay all my other monthly bills. I am now shopping for a good, cheap bankruptcy lawyer. I am going to miss payments so I might as well go bankrupt before the harassing creditor calls start. How is it they could find where I worked to levy my salary but couldn't call me there or get my address from my employer?

The IRS is definitely more dangerous than most of the criminals in jail today. They don't kill you or maim you, they just rob all of us daily in the name of government, rape us, ruin us financially and make our lives a living hell.

## IRS Abuse Report #68

**Date:** Sat Feb 24 08:46:03 EST 1996
**To:** sue@irs.class-action.com
**From:** JB
A couple in Dayton Ohio saved for years to buy a dream home. The IRS had several properties advertised for sale at auction (seized properties).   The IRS

Golden-Helmet Overture

The Evil

assured everyone that all the houses had clear titles.

The couple bid on a house and were high bidders. The IRS required $24,000 down payment. The couple put the $24,000 down and went to the bank for a mortgage for the balance. This wasn't a problem until they did the title search. The house had $150,000 in liens against it. The couple demanded that the IRS return their $24,000 but the IRS refused, saying the couple should have checked for liens (even though the IRS had assured them previously there were no liens).

If a real estate agency in the State of Ohio had done this, everyone involved would have been jailed. How can IRS agents get away with breaking fraud laws just because they happen to be employed by a Federal agency? This is the ultimate in sleaze.

### IRS Abuse Report #69

**Date:** Sun Feb 25 16:21:55 EST 1996
**To:** sue@irs.class-action.com
**From:** RI
The IRS claims to have a lien on my entire personal estate due to 'unpaid taxes for the tax year 1987. But I am unable to "make a return of income" because I have been very poor for the past 3.5 years

### IRS Abuse Report #70

**Date:** Tue Feb 27 17:02:56 EST 1996
**To:** sue@irs.class-action.com
**From:** TE
Where to start the list??? 1. Wage Garnishments. 2. Bank Acct Seizures. 3. Home Foreclosure & Forced sale for 20 % of true value . 4. etc...etc...etc...

I have been victimized, abused, lied to, cheated, and now I am being thrown from my home. This is all in the name of "for the good of the Government"

HELP !!!!!

### IRS Abuse Report #71

**Date:** Wed, 28 Feb 96 10:37:53 -0800
**To:** sue@irs.class-action.com
**From:** RU
We are in the mist of some serious charges, and nobody seems to care that we are innocent.

## IRS Abuse Report #72

**Date:** Wed, 06 Mar 1996 22:08:36 -0600
**From:** RH
**To:** sue@irs.class-action.com

Our trouble started in Jan.1985. We can't own anything, get credit etc... This last year they have been really bad. Garnishing wages illegally, Levies, false payment agreements. The told us to move out of our house in to a small apartment with our 2 sons. One of our sons is Attention Deficit with Hyperactivity and is under care. That is just part of the things they have done. I could write a book. The lies and deceit are unbelievable. Our legal bills are growing and our Attorney has recommended we file suit for damages and legal fees for all the hell we have gone through.

## IRS Abuse Report #73

**Date:** Sat, 09 Mar 1996 23:32:11 -0800
**To:** sue@irs.class-action.com
**From:** IR

The IRS's repeated attempts to audit me in person even though I was incapacitated at the time from an automobile accident is typical of the IRS.

The time and money I am spending due to their corrupt and inhumane beaurocracy could be spent in producing productive goods and services. They are crippling our country.

## IRS Abuse Report #74

**Date:** Tue Mar 12 09:34:05 EST 1996
**From:** MK

I voluntarily served in the armed forces, and after my final year of service, I was not given a W-2 form by the navy. I could only file on the other income which I earned that year. For 3 years now the IRS has harrassed me, threatened me with liens and garnishings.

## IRS Abuse Report #75

**Date:** Thu, 14 Mar 1996 18:38:36 -0600
**To:** sue@irs.class-action.com
**From:** DP

I have been diagnosed as Atypical Bipolar-II Rapid Cycling. In simple terms this means that I suffer from an "atypical" form of manic-depression.

Over the past 10 years, I have been hospitalized approximately 12 times in both private and state hospitals. At least three of my hospitalizations occurred during tax time (Jan 1 through April 15). When you are hospitalized, voluntarily or by judges order (I have experienced both), there is no way you can comply with the tax laws or IRS policies.

The tax laws require (mentally) disabled people to do things they cannot do. (We are not on a mental/fiscal schedule, when we're ill, we're ill.) That sort of makes the ADA and the tax laws contradictory. When a person like myself goes into remission and does file his/her return after April 15, without an approved extension, we are subject to financial penalties and interest through no fault of our own.

There IRS offers no accomodation to and for the mentally ill. The IRS has ignored the reality of our needs to help us comply with the law. They however hold us 100% accountable for their unjust penalties and interest.

Communication from the IRS is a pretty scary thing for all of us, but it can be a precipitating factor to someone like myself. I recently received a letter from the IRS advising me that they will soon place levies on my car and possibly my wages. Well I am living with that for now, but if I were in a degenerated state, it might be just enough to cause a psychotic episode resulting in anything from running to nowhere and putting myself in harms way, to hospitalization, to suicide. All over tax laws and their unfair means.

## IRS Abuse Report #76

**Date:** Thu Mar 14 00:22:49 EST 1996
**To:** sue@irs.class-action.com
**From:** KA

They put a lien against me for back taxes they said I owed, I did not. When I tried to prove this they told me I had to pay them in full before I could get my money back even though they agreed with me. They have damaged my credit record with this injustice. If this was the private sector of business the people involved would all be fired for malice, slander, mental anguish etc. and a lawsuit would be won hands down!

## IRS Abuse Report #77

**Date:** Mon Apr 1 16:30:23 EST 1996
**To:** sue@irs.class-action.com
**From:** MK

I have been nearly sequestered in my home since November 1994 due to actions of the IRS.

They stole the contents of my personal bank account in 1994 and demanded immediate payment of alleged underpayments, fines and penalties in the amount of approximately $180,000.

I have since gone through my records -- I have all records from all years. It turns out they owe me over $30,000, none of which I will ever see, and that doesn't include any interest calculations.

In the process of proving this, I have been unable to continue my business causing economic loss to not only myself, but my customers and my employees.

### IRS Abuse Report #78

**Date:** Tue Apr  9 03:27:03 EDT 1996
**To:** sue@irs.class-action.com
**From:**    RC
I had an attorney, specializing in tax matters, tell me that, "in this country, one can pay whatever the IRS claims or go to jail or get shot." This from an attorney working "within the system"!

### IRS Abuse Report #79

**Date:** Tue Apr  9 19:35:42 EDT 1996
**To:** sue@irs.class-action.com
**From:**    CM
We have been under the thumb of the IRS for over 10 years now. Currently, we are at the end of our 45 day stay against collection action while we are scrambling to put together our offers in compromise.

I was told by one IRS phone agent that I should get a real job and finally become a responsible taxpayer. When I call seeking help to solve our long term problem, all I get are standard form letters. When I call the IRS office I get abusive, patronizing, condescending slurs to my character and my responsibilities as an American.

When I asked for names, I was most often refused the information with comments like "it was of no value to me to have their names and therefore it's unnecessary".

After going bankrupt over five years ago from my first encounter with these people, I have never dug out. Now they have added 100% in interest and penalties and the interest is still compounding -- yet no one will help us. This agency is absolutely out of control and needs to be abolished.

## IRS Abuse Report #80

**Date:** Thu, 11 Apr 1996 20:32:27 EDT
**To:** sue@irs.class-action.com
**From:** DP

In 1988, I received a computer-generated IRS form letter about an over-refund from a couple of years before. The signature was a totally illegible inkblot. I called the 800 number on the letter -- every day for 6 months. No answer. I called the local IRS number. No answer.

I wrote to the IRS at the address on the letter. My response was another letter, identical to the first one, with the same inkblot signature.

Without any further warning, they began levying my salary -- 100% of it. I took home $0.00 paychecks for three and a half months. My home and car were both repossessed because I fell so far behind in my payments. The only reason I survived was through the kindness of a co-worker.

## IRS Abuse Report #81

**Date:** Thu Apr 11 01:37:19 EDT 1996
**To:** sue@irs.class-action.com
**From:** JB

The IRS has decided to withhold refunds due me as they say I owe taxes back to 1981. After three years of dealing with these people, the IRS is trying to attach liens against everything I own. The problem resolution office will not even meet with me. I filed suit in the Tax court against the IRS. Since I constantly receive collection notices (totally incorrect) I though a law suit would finally settle the matter. WRONG. The tax court accepted a motion that the IRS filed to throw my case out as I did not have a proper NOTICE OF DEFICIENCY form. They can still send collection notices, and I have asked for a proper NOTICE OF DEFICIENCY form, but they will not give this form, just collections notices and attempted liens.

## IRS Abuse Report #82

**Date:** Thu Apr 121 20:06:23 EDT 1996
**To:** sue@irs.class-action.com
**From:** HN

The killed my father and put my family in the streets.......must I say more?

I have been left with nothing and have nothing.......thank you America!!!

IF THERE IS ANYTHING THAT I CAN DO TO BRING DOWN THESE BASTARDS PLEASE LET ME KNOW....I HATE THEM WITH ALL MY

HEART AND SOUL!!!!!

## IRS Abuse Report #83

**Date:** Sun Apr 14 07:15:33 EDT 1996
**To:** sue@irs.class-action.com
**From:** RG

These thugs have to be stopped. The IRS through, fraudulent "Notices of Levies", have attacked my spouse and my wages, along with our bank accounts. And, because of these fraudulent leans, they have prevented me form getting credit for my daughters college education.

We are powerless to stop this tyranny and extortion.

## IRS Abuse Report #84

**Date:** Mon, 15 Apr 96 12:14:10 -0700
**To:** sue@irs.class-action.com
**From:** JG

After I was laid off from my occupation of 22 years in the aircraft maintenance field. I found out that the Federal Govt classified aircraft maintenance as an obsolete career due to the number of mechanics and the faltering airline business.

I proceeded to try and find a new career. Now, the IRS tells me that all expenses I spent trying to find a new line of work, while trying to support myself, my wife, and 4 kids on unemployment, is not deductible because it's not in the same field I was working in -- which they themselves classified as obsolete!

On top of that, in order to feed and house my large family on $125 per week, and trying to find a new job, I had to cash in my K401 to save my house... Now I'm taking a $1476 penalty off the top off my return. Plus paying the taxes on unemployment..

No wonder I can't catch up or get ahead, I wasn't even allowed food stamps because I had a 1 year old Mazda MPV that I owed the bank $23,000 on -- that disqualified me...Where is the justice!

## IRS Abuse Report #85

**Date:** Mon Apr 15 19:11:37 EDT 1996
**To:** sue@irs.class-action.com
**From:** GY

We have received liens on money they say we owe them! They have taken money out of credit union saving! And, they are trying to take money from my pay check!

## IRS Abuse Report #86

**Date:** Thu, 18 Apr 1996 18:02:54 -0400
**To:** sue@irs.class-action.com
**From:** VMD7493@aol.com
My parents committed suicide the first of this year to avoid further problems from the IRS.

## IRS Abuse Report #87

**Date:** Tue Apr 16 21:37:37 1996
**To:** sue@irs.class-action.com
**From:** MD
The IRS went after my brother and assessed him $19,000. He owed about $3000, so the balance was penalties and interest. Further, the IRS agents have refused to let him deduct his children, even though he has a court order that states he is the sole guardian. They also will not let his ex-wife deduct the children. This case proves they are not above breaking their own laws or above using harassment against others. By the way, my brother has been unemployed for the last two years and the $19,000 they took from him is from his retirement that he spent 20 years working for.

## IRS Abuse Report #88

**Date:** Thu Apr 18 11:36:37 1996
**To:** sue@irs.class-action.com
**From:** VN
I received a refund of $57.00 for 1988. Now, for the past four years, the IRS has insisted that I did not file. They have been adding interest and penalties continuously. I have been continuously sending them copies of the forms I originally sent to them. They refuse to admit they are wrong.

They have threatened me with all kinds of things from garnishments to taking my possessions. Where do they get the right to take more than they should. I have been paying taxes for many years and my ancestors paid before.

## IRS Abuse Report #89

**Date:** Thu Apr 18 22:27:50 1996
**To:** sue@irs.class-action.com
**From:** Anon
The IRS Has:
 *violated my power of attorney
*filed liens without notice
*threatened my pregnant wife
*routinely "lost files"
*refused to examine evidence
*told one of my attorneys to go away
*threatened me if I didn't fire that particular attorney.
All at a cost of time and money (a hell of a lot more than the bogus assessment).

## IRS Abuse Report #90

**Date:** Sun Apr 21 16:40:49 1996
**To:** sue@irs.class-action.com
**From:**    JH
The IRS does not respond to any of my inquiries, letters, or statements.  I have only received unscheduled visits at my home and office by agents threatening to charge me with crimes, stating that they do not have to respond to any of my questions.  They sent summons to my banks, and credit card institutions.

## IRS Abuse Report #91

**Date:** Mon Apr 22 10:11:08 1996
**To:** sue@irs.class-action.com
**From:** TV
The IRS lost or misplaced my tax return for 1992 and then two years later notified me that I owed back taxes and penalties — the penalties are approximately $6,000.   When I pointed out that I had filed my return, their response was PROVE IT. How can I prove that I mailed a return?  All I can do is show a copy of what they claim I did not send to them to begin with!!

## IRS Abuse Report #92

**Date:** Fri Apr 12 13:22:58 EDT 1996
**To:** sue@irs.class-action.com
**From:** anonymous
They claim I owe $75,000 and if I don't come into their offices to take care of it that they will begin to garnish my wages! I told them that I have never

even earned that much money throughout my whole life as I have been a college student until this year. The majority of their claim came from a stock purchase of my fathers that had erroneously ended up with my social security # on it during a time while I was in Japan for two years doing volunteer missionary work with no pay! Letters were already on file with the IRS documenting the error and placing the tax liability with my father. All they were apparently doing was trying to discover something to come after my father with and scared the hell out of me in the process.

If that is not harassment then I don't know what is! They came after me for something they already knew wasn't my liability. I've had probing calls before, but that threat was just going too far!

I would love to give the IRS a taste of their own medicine but don't feel I can afford to because they have so much influence over my family's life. As we run a family owned business, they cannot only hit our personal lives, but come directly after our companies as well, so we quietly grin and bear it while shaking in our boots everyday.

No one is safe from the IRS!

(scared to give my name!)
P.S. I'd like information on the lawsuit, but I really don't want the IRS coming after me or my father, so I don't want U.S. mail sent to me on the subject. I'm not even sure e-mail would be safe. I'm really paranoid. The IRS makes life a living hell! I think I'd just as soon deal with the KGB.

## IRS Abuse Report #93

**Date:** Fri Apr 26 18:44:22 1996
**To:** sue@irs.class-action.com
**From:** GW
Here is a list of IRS abuses inflicted on me and my family:
*My 1993 taxes are currently "under audit" by an IRS Revenue Agent. He has been auditing our tax return since November, 1995. It is now near the end of April and we still have not gotten the audit finished.

*At first he said the audit would take about two half days. Then he wanted two full days. I run a business from my home, just me, I did not want this guy holding up my business for two full days.

*Neither we nor our attorney heard anything from him until a month later, when on February 29, 1996, I got a phone call from our attorney saying that the IRS agent had 13 questions he wanted us to answer. The questions were all answered in our amended return – which apparently he did not even look at.

*The IRS Agent then said there would be an additional $9000 plus my self employment taxes all payable in 10 days. I had to stop work for an entire week, trying to track down information to document his requests.

*When the 10 days were up, my husband went to the meeting between the IRS agent and our lawyer. The IRS agent was pretty hostile. He basically disallowed everything. He refused to look at any documentation my husband tried to present.

*From what my husband could figure out, it sounded like our tax bill was going to be even bigger than the $9000. So, the more we tried to comply, the worse it got for us. Now, we don't know what is going to happen. The IRS Agent even said that I had committed some kind of crime because I paid my kids to work for me in my business (which he doesn't believe—he said we just put the money back in our own pockets). My kids filed tax returns and paid taxes on their earnings, as well as tax on the interest in their bank accounts

*We live in a small town, our tax lawyer has to do business with the IRS all the time. Plus, he has been audited three times himself. He doesn't want to rock the boat.

*It's now April 26, I have no clue what's going on with our audit. I've paid my taxes for 1995 but filed for an extension because I don't know what's going to happen.

### IRS Abuse Report #94

**Date:** Tue Apr 30 11:16:24 1996
**To:** sue@irs.class-action.com
**From:** MR

I was a member of a partnership that was audited back in 1984.

The case took six years to settle. I signed an agreement accepting the settlement. Nothing happened for over a year. Then out of the blue the IRS came at me with both guns blazing. Assessing all kinds of penalties and claiming that the time to reply to their claims had elapsed.

This same event happened to everyone in the partnership, however, all members had signed and filed the paper work prior to final agreement. Each member had to individually prove to the IRS that the IRS had made the mistake.

It's very involved and involves several instances where the IRS misplaced, lost or outright deceived us. This also precipitated a nervous breakdown for me.

The financial distress was enormous and to this day I haven't recovered from the problems the IRS caused due to their negligence.

## IRS Abuse Report #95

**Date:** Tue Apr 30 23:26:54 1996
**To:** sue@irs.class-action.com
**From:** PM

The IRS confiscated my wages. I was working on an $80,000 year job and had to quit, dispose of all I owned, and have not been able to work since, except odd jobs. I did not owe IRS the money they said. It was due to a tax shelter that went bankrupt and not only did IRS come after me, but about 200 other people. I filed bankruptcy against the IRS and was discharged of my debt. However, I still owe for the past 4 years and feel it is unconstitutional the way they harass me. I have not been able to get a real job or own anything because of the IRS.

## IRS Abuse Report #96

**Date:** Thu May  2  1:23:54 1996
**To:** sue@irs.class-action.com
**From:** CCl

"The IRS has harassed me for 16 years".

In 1980 a previous employer erroneously reported my income by reporting that I earned $10,000 in 1980. I explained to the IRS that I did not earn the $10,000 because I only worked two weeks in 1980 at the rate of $750 bi-weekly. I further explained that I was the accounting supervisor for that company that reported the error and it can be very easily corrected. To no avail, the IRS ignored my request to ascertain the facts and eagerly tried to destroy me. the IRS subsequently seized my house, my car, my retirement account, and everything I needed to sustain life. The IRS has hounded me for 16 years. This year in 1996, the IRS seized my bank account, and tax payments I made. The IRS told me the seizures were for payments on the 1980 taxes that they say that I still owe. The IRS seized everything I owned making it almost impossible to cope and they are still harassing and intimidating me.

I'm not rich nor do I own anything worth having. The IRS has really hurt me in a very serious way. I mean in the way that you hurt inside where the pain is so deep that all the tears stop flowing and all that remain is the moan! I remember on one occasion the IRS came on my job and thus caused me to lose my job. I have not been allowed to get credit, or live a comfortable life for 16 years. I am a Vietnam veteran and I have not been able to use my G.I. bill to buy a house because of what the IRS has done to me, my name, and my credit. The IRS has caused me and my wife to suffer great depressions in our marriage and the IRS has caused disharmony among me and my friends.

## IRS Abuse Report #97

**Date:** Thu May  2 16:06:48 1996
**To:** sue@irs.class-action.com
**From:** Anonymous
I just received a tax examination change report for 1993 and 1994 which bills me for $25,000 due to disallowing alimony I paid.  I didn't even get a chance to show my canceled checks, court order, etc. I was presumed guilty without the right to show proof.

## IRS Abuse Report #98

**Date:** Sat May 18  0:54:48 1996
**To:** sue@irs.class-action.com
**From:** T.M
We are being audited for 1993 and 1994 in spite of losses totaling $ 70,000. We have already been billed for almost $ 6,000 plus penalties and interest. They are also accusing us of hiding income due to $ 25,000 in loans from relatives.  All this has caused much stress and sleepless nights so far.

## IRS Abuse Report #99

**Date:** Sat May 18  9:31:27 1996
**To:** sue@irs.class-action.com
**From:** PB
I am being persecuted and harassed by the IRS — have been for years because I am trying to stop their abuses which are the same tactics and methods used by gangsters, the Mafia, the Gestapo, Al Capone — collect through fear.  I have written to Congressmen, the IRS Commissioner, the president, everyone I think could help and called for a Congressional Investigation into the abuses of the IRS and its collection methods.  Without exception, they passed the buck and in effect laughed at me.

I am a tax accountant for many years — have seen abuses first hand in my family and clients.  Now for the tenth or 11th time I am being audited -- have had a deficiency judgment issued against me and am in the process of filing a brief in the tax court.  This will do no good.  How can we get justice in the tax court when the judge him or herself is in the pay of the same entity we are fighting.  It is to their interest to find for the government for their paycheck is at issue.  We do not have the right to a jury trial guaranteed us by the Constitution. The IRS violates every constitutional right - they are the Gestapo run rampant.  I expect to lose everything for there is no justice here and I will go to jail before I will pay a tax I do not owe. In the audit and appeals court I provided every proof of my deductions they called for, answered every question — yet they disallowed everything.

I am not against paying taxes and in the last two years I was audited, I paid over $10,000 in taxes willingly but the IRS is trying to collect $10,000 more and I am just a small wage earner — very middle class. Please enter me in this class action law suit.

## IRS Abuse Report #100

**Date:** Thu May 23 14:38:12 1996
**To:** sue@irs.class-action.com
**From:** BW

My mom works for the IRS. She has told me numerous stories of how the IRS has taken things from people and even put them in jail. One particular story really made me hate the IRS:

An elderly woman lost her husband in 92. She had never written a check or paid a bill in her life. Her home was completely paid for. Her family was helping her pay her bills. In 1994 the IRS seized her home and all of her worldly belongings for back taxes. She died two months later. Her family fought with the IRS for a whole year to find out why no one was notified of this seizure before it occurred and why the family had no idea what was going on. After 5 months of investigation the IRS has sent the family a letter stating their apologies for a miscalculation which in turn made it look like the elderly woman owed $1750 in back taxes when it should have read a $17.50 due to her. Because of their misrepresentation and false information the elderly woman died of a heart attack at her home the day it was sold. The IRS has gone too far...these people think they are the answer to GOD himself. They need to be stopped.

## IRS Abuse Report #101

**Date:** Fri June 7 1:42:57 1996
**To:** sue@irs.class-action.com
From CW

I owned a cleaning business as sole proprietor. Incorporated after first year. Neglected to vacate first employer ID number, so IRS decided that I have two identical businesses simultaneously and estimated my so-called unreported income for two years. After six years I ran out of money to fight them and had to pay $16000 for a business I never owned?

## IRS Abuse Report #102

**Date:** Sat June 8 12:26:54 1996
**To:** sue@irs.class-action.com
**From:** RB

My uncle made a mistake over a period of ten years concerning deductions that should have been extracted from his farm workers wages. After repeated threats to take everything he had, and put him in prison, he committed suicide leaving a wife and children to fend for themselves.

He was goaded into it by the IRS, the GESTAPO and STORM TROOPERS of the UNITED STATES OF AMERICA. I have since found out that the threat of prison was used falsely.

I personally believe my uncle killed himself because of the shame he thought he'd endure by going to prison. He was wrong. To go to prison because of the IRS is a RED BADGE of COURAGE! Down with the IRS. If you work for the IRS, never let your shadow darken my path!

## IRS Abuse Report #103

**Date:** Sat June 10 23:19:06 1996
**To:** sue@irs.class-action.com
**From:** LT

Consider the "people" who are working for the "IRS". What makes them so heartless, so eager to destroy and cause pain and loss to so many. I don't consider these beings human in any sense of the word except that they appear in human form.

## IRS Abuse Report #104

**Date:** Sat Jul 13 17:14:31 1996
**To:** sue@irs.class-action.com
**From:** Anon

What happened with myself and the IRS is unforgivable. For the first time in my life I truly know the feeling of hatred for another.

If you ever want to be free, then realize that the IRS must be destroyed. Shame them, turn your backs to them, make them and their families hate to go out in public, make sure they feel unwanted, let them know they are not welcomed anywhere. Stand up and fight with anyone who will stand with you against these monsters.

Anyone that has ever had any contact with the IRS must wonder what type of people they are. Just patriots following orders? So were the guards in the concentration camps. How do they look at themselves in the mirror? They provide nothing to society but misery and despair. They can look at themselves because they enjoy the limitless ability to abuse power.

If there is evil in the US, it is the employees and judges of the IRS. Do their neighbors and family know were they work? If they don't, they should. We should all know their ID's. If we are successful and true freedom is restored to every citizen of the US, do we simply forgive these parasites? Do the former IRS elite simply to go out among us as if they had done nothing but follow orders? Why don't you post lists of these employees with pictures, names, and addresses so we all know who they are? I don't want my children playing with the children of parents who think nothing of stealing food from the mouths, along with the shirts off the backs, of other people.

If your neighbors son or daughter works for the IRS, shouldn't you know? You would want to know if a pedophile came to visit the neighborhood, wouldn't you? Send them statements that they are not welcome in the USA any longer. Post their pictures and their identity in their neighborhoods. Ostracize them and their families. Start making *them* miserable for a change. Force them out! Don't feel pity for them. No one forced them to work for the IRS. They did it willingly, all on their own. They are not good people. If they were, they would recognize the evil in what they do for a living. If they had an ounce of decency in them, they would never have taken a job with the IRS. Don't hold your breath waiting for a politician to give up their greatest political tool just to end our suffering. Like the IRS agent, if the members of the congress and senate had an ounce of decency in them, their first priority would be to free us, repeal the 16th amendment, and brand the bastards working at the IRS as criminals, jail them and take away everything that they bought with the money they stole from us.

Until we stand together against them, they will continue to intimidate and harass us and we will never realize freedom. All future generations of children in the US will be born into slavery. Never to realize any form of hope, prosperity, or the right to privacy.

**IRS Abuse Report #105**

**Date:** Mon 11 Sep 1995 08:08:36 -0500
**To:** sue@irs.class-action.com
**From:** RD
The following was written a few days after the incident happened.

Around 10 A.M. January 19, 1995, my bookkeeper came to my office and said a QW from the IRS was there and wished to speak to me. I told her I did not want to talk to Q because I had no idea what this was about. As far as I knew, we had no outstanding issues with the IRS, and all old issues had been settled. Since she was obviously frightened by Q's attitude, I knew I'd have to handle it myself.

I went to the door, this lady shook my hand and said "I'm QW with the IRS". I said she could come in and motioned her to a chair in my office. I took my chair, and she asked as I sat down, "Who am I speaking to?". I replied, "My name is RD". She said "Then you are who I need to talk to." I thought it strange the way she asked and responded. If she didn't know who I was, I thought, "Perhaps this is a scam artist, or, who knows what??? I'd better be careful, 'til I can tell what's going on here. She didn't offer me any identification, and since I don't know of anything wrong with my relationship with the IRS, this might be 'some type of out-of-the-blue' scam. I figured I had better find out if this gal is real, or yet another nightmare."

She then asked "Who owns this building?" I thought "What the heck business is it of yours?" but replied, "What is your authority and what is your purpose." She did not reply, but instead asked if JK was my attorney. Now, this really put me on edge. If she really was IRS, she should know who my attorney was. And if she knew that, she knew it was a breech of the IRS code to talk to me directly. If she wasn't IRS, then she'd ask that question to set us up for something -- but what? Maybe She'd been routing in our trash and found an old bill and come up with a scheme to bilk us. But if she is IRS, she should have already talked to Jim before showing up, and he hasn't called. So, who knows what's going on here! This lady is apparently up to no good. So, I cautiously replied, "I haven't talked to Jim in a few months. But I notice you haven't answered my question, what is your authority and what is your..." She cut me off! I was getting very stressed and thinking I need to call the police and get this lady out of here. "She said, what I notice is you didn't answer my question -- WHO OWNS THIS BUILDING!" I think I asked why she needed to know, and incredibly, she said, 'Cause I checked and it isn't listed with the county records office!" I wondered what that had to do with anything, and how it could be that the records didn't list the owner, when all filing and insurance paperwork was paid for back when NM purchased the property. Again, her conduct and responses did not match what I thought to be the truth.

Then, I thought about the two "POSTED: No Trespassing Signs" on the corners of the building. And also the "KEEP OUT PRIVATE PROPERTY" sign in the yard. A few minutes before she arrived, someone had been walking on the property taking pictures and I had debated going out after them and throwing them off. But having been shot at before, I returned my thoughts to her and said, "Listen, you're on private property without an appointment or an invitation..." I was preparing to order her off the property, but she didn't wait for it to be stated. "That's fine," she said, "that's all I need to know." And she got up and walked out.

I was pretty miffed. If she was IRS, what had she wanted and why wouldn't she tell me? If she wasn't, which sure seemed to fit her actions better, then I was the target of some kind of scam. I told my bookkeeper to bring me that old IRS file. I needed to talk to MZ. I had worked with Mark before and trusted him, and I think he trusted me as well.

I called and asked the gal who answered the phone if QW worked there. I was told she did. I asked this gal for Q's supervisor. I was told it was Dave someone. I was surprised it wasn't Mark. I asked to talk with Dave. The operator said Dave was busy. I said, fine, who is his supervisor. She said MZ. I said "Oh good, I know Mark, let me speak with him!" I was put on hold again. Then a fellow came on the line. He identified himself and I said, "Is QW one of yours?" He took a hostile stance and said "What do you mean, is she one of mine!" I said, "Is she one of your employees? Are you her supervisor? Is she an IRS agent? He said, "Well, who am I talking to?" or perhaps "Who the hell am I talking to?" the intonation was consistent with either answer. I said, "My name is RD. A lady just popped up out here, saying her name was Q that she was IRS." He informed me, "Yes, she is a IRS collection agent, and she must be working on a collection case." I said, "Well, she just popped up out here and refused to answer any questions about who she was and what authority she had." He snapped back, "She's a field agent and us field agents can pop up wherever we want to." I asked, "Why wouldn't she tell me what's going on? and why isn't she talking to the people I pay to handle these matters..." He asked, "Well, does she have a paper with her where you assigned your power of attorney?" I replied, "Well how should I know, I've never seen this lady before in my life and...". He replied, "Well, she's got to have a power of attorney to be able to talk to your attorney." I said, "As far as I know the IRS has a power of attorney on file for JK...", He again belligerently asked, "Well, does she have that piece of paper?" I answered, "How I am supposed to know? I asked her about her authority and she left!"

He seemed to drop his hostile attitude, a bit. He said, "She's working on a case." I was confused. I thought we were all caught up with the IRS and, frankly, proud of it, and how we had handled our obligations at the time. I said, "I don't understand, I worked with MZ in the past..." He spouted, "What do you mean you worked with MZ!" He was fierce. This news really took him by surprise. It frightened me. I had no idea where he was coming from, or why he'd be mad at me for having worked with Mark. I said, I worked with Mark in the past, we had some trouble and we worked it out.. He was clearly confused by what I was telling him. I again complained about Q's refusing to identify herself and her authority and purpose. He asked, "She showed you her credentials?" I said "No, I asked her what her authority was, and what her purpose was, and she refused to answer. She didn't show me anything. I told him someone remembered a QW from the past coming out, but I had never met her. After that, he calmed down again. I think he then asked to talk to Q. I told him she had left the property. At this point, I noticed a surprise in David's voice. He must have thought she was still in front of me. He said "If she comes back tell her to talk to me." I wondered why she would be coming back. I told him, "Look, whatever the case, my position is, if she is here without and invitation and without an appointment, she is trespassing. She's supposed to talk to my attorney, and it's still my opinion she should do so." He acknowledged, reminded me if she were to come back he wanted to talk to her first. I took this for an acknowledgment of my complaint, and an indication he would see after it. I thanked him and hung up.

I thought there was more to this story. I didn't feel safe any more. I called my attorney and explained the strange thing that had just happened. He said he hadn't heard anything, but he'd find out and if something was really happening, he'd fill a 911 with the IRS, because as far as he knew, there had been no communications with the IRS since filing the affidavit. Clearly proper IRS procedures were not being followed, and someone was out of line, and way out of control.

At that point, one of the employees appeared at my office and said "she's back". She stormed in and said they were taking the building and changing the locks. She started down the hall, I said you need to call David. She wheeled at me and shouted, accusatory, "I know you talked to David." I thought this was probably a lie, she was probably surprised I knew her coworker's name and was bluffing. I asked, "Have you talked to David since you were last here?" She wheeled and again headed down the hall without answering. I said, "David told me to tell you to call him." She ignored me and started to peel the back off of some kind of sticker. Clearly this person was not interested in Law, Justice, Due Process, or IRS procedures and Code. Nor was she interested in hearing what her supervisor had to say to her. I began to suspect Dave wasn't her supervisor at all. What was going on here?

She threw out a Notice of Levy on my desk. Then she walked away and turned around again and threw out a Notice of Seizures. I looked at it. It was getting pretty clear at this point. The notices were to CA-PC. I asked "What do you think you're doing here?" She shouted, "We're shutting down the business!" I asked, "Which business?" That pretty much threw her into a rage. She sputtered and shouted, "This business here!!!" and pointed at the floor in my office. So, I asked, "And what business do you think this is?" She refused to answer and stormed out of my office.

My attorney and I continued to talk. I began digging for the sales contract proving NM owned the building she was seizing in the name of PC's back taxes. She went to every NM employee and told them they had to leave. She ordered one to get off the phone, who was having a conversation with a NM customer. I am told no one believed her. She was so rude and irrational, no one could imagine what her problems was.

I was talking to my attorney one time when she came stomping through, and I was telling him I had asked for her identification several times and she had refused. At this, she finally produced a wallet with two pieces of paper in it. I began to read the paper, and had read the first half, with various IRS information on it while still holding the phone so my attorney could hear, and as soon as I reached the personal information, she snatched it away and stomped off. I said "wait a minute, I didn't finish. Hey, Q, can we get a copy of that?" She didn't answer. It's becoming apparent to me this woman does not want any personal identification numbers to become part of the record.

I decided I'd better talk to Mark at the IRS, since he was the only one with enough integrity to be trusted. It seemed nearly every other agent I had talked to, had lied. I dialed Mark. I had to wait quite awhile. When Mark answered the phone, I asked if he remembered me and that we had worked together in the past. He said he thought he remembered the name. I began to explain the situation as best I understood it. At that moment, the police we called arrived in my office. I told Mark, "Oh good the police are here, hang on." I then addressed the officer, still speaking into the phone so Mark could hear, and said, "Thank you for coming out, today. We've got quit a problem here. These agents have come out to serve a Levy and Seizures, but as you can see here on their documents they have the wrong company listed. This property is owned by another company, here.." and I offered him the sales contract showing NM owned the building. The officer began examining the two documents. I turned my attention again to Mark. I said, "Did you copy all that Mark?" He said he wanted to speak to Q. I told the bookkeeper to go tell Q she was wanted on the phone. She said, I don't think she'll come. I said please go tell her MZ is on the phone and wants to speak to her. She said she'd try.

Both agents were in my office. Q began listening to Mark. She made several objections. She said, "I sent it to them here, and I sent it to them there" I assume she meant PC, "and these guys sent back an affidavit and the other guys didn't send back anything." I thought, "Great, cooperate with the IRS, follow the rules, and what do they do? Jump on you for the effort. If the other guy DIDN'T respond, why did you assume the guys who did respond, followed IRS procedure and filed affidavit, which went unanswered by the IRS for months, were the ones who needed to have things seized?

She said to Mark, "I was out several times and I spoke to Mr. RD several time..." My blood boiled. She was a liar. To the best of my knowledge, I had never seen this woman before. She may have called several times when I was out, but she sure didn't talk to me. I had a power of attorney, and they were supposed to talk to him. I was so mad at the way I had been treated by the IRS that I wanted no personal contact. Nothing in the world burned me more than dishonest IRS agents, and here in my office on posted private property was a jerk using my phone to lie to her supervisor while disrupting the business of a company in complete compliance with the IRS. She was busily trying to deprive more than a dozen people of their salaries, and thereby about to deprive the U.S. of $100,000 a year in revenue. Let alone the other companies who would go out of business and have cause to sue. We were already warned that day, if we allowed interruption of parts shipments to RJS, they would go out of business and be forced to sue. She had usurped so many powers of the Constitution, let alone violated so many rules and procedures of IRS code, that she was, well, either criminally negligent, or worse, acting with full criminal intent.

She and Mark went on talking, "but I'm looking right at a business card with CA on it in his office." I said, yes, but that's CA-I. That's an entirely different company from CA-PC." By her reasoning, Joe Getz could be held accountable for Joe Gonzales taxes, even if their Federal Tax Identifiers were different. Why? Because they had the first name? Oh Brother! I got up and took one of the cards and offered it to the other agent. I said, may I present this for your examination. Now, this other agent was sitting wide eyed and in general looking amazed at what was going on. She looked at the card. Q on the phone said something to Jim about "International". Sensing there might be some reason coming to the other agent, I returned to my desk and took out the sales contract and took it to her and told her this property was owned by NM. She almost grabbed this out of my hands. I held on to it as it was the only copy I had. She asked, "When was this?" I helped her look for a date and found the 4th of November 1986.

I went back behind my desk and was able to find an inventory list from PC works which was labeled as such and returned to show her. I said, "These were the assets of PC," and I pointed out, "there's not a single piece of anything on that list in this building."

She said, "JK is your attorney?" I said yes. She shook her head and said, "I've worked with Jim before, he's a good guy." I began to pipe in how I thought so too and Jim was an ex-agent himself and I almost missed her next comment, half under her breath and in total disbelief. "How did this ever get this far?"

Q jumped in, still on the phone with Mark and said, "Can I have a copy of that?" I said, "Sure, I'll be more than happy to give you a copy -- just as soon as you agree to stop this illegal action.." Oh! she glared at me. She turned around and didn't ask again, nor did she acknowledge my offer. She finished with Mark after a quite a few more minutes. She closed saying, I'll see you back at the office." I said, Wait! I still want to talk to Mark. She hesitated and sneered at me.

A little later, or perhaps still during the phone call, this agent who had seemed reasonable asked about NM. She asked if I was the president of NM. I said yes, and she said, "Q he's the president of NM too, Q! Q!" But Q was getting an earful from Mark at that time, or just ending her call, and waved her off. I thought great, you still are outside due process and you're grabbing at straws, and you're going to do the seizure anyway. You've got no concept of the meaning of "legal entity" and due process of law. Another attempt at illegal seizure. These agents are either ignorant of the law and the IRS code, or deliberately ignoring it. They don't know who they can proceed against and they don't care. They don't even know the difference between private property and personal property.

When I got the phone back, Mark had already hung up. So, I dialed him up again. He asked about my relationship with PC. I went on and told Mark that I was willing to pay every cent I owned, and he should know that from working with us before, but in this case, that wasn't it. I told him I'd been involved with Pat of PC for only a few months. Pat had told me where break-even was, and I helped get the sales there. I then found out break-even was MUCH lower. I told Pat we could either shut down the business and sell off the assets or he could buy it back and take over all obligations. Mark asked about my relationship and I said I basically gave business advice and had pumped in some money. I told him I never had signature authority on the PC account, that Pat was the manager before, during and after my involvement with it. I think this was all in accordance with the affidavit we filed. He asked me if I knew where the bank account was, then there was another commotion. Someone shouted at me, they're changing the locks. Q walked back in. I asked if we were done? Was it over? Could the police office go? She gave half a nod and a sneer, but no solid answer and walked out.

Mark asked if I minded answering a few questions from time to time. I told him I didn't mind talking to him personally but... He said, okay, what if he called and asked a few questions from time to time, would I mind. I said, no I wouldn't mind, but, this in no way was meant to waive my power or attorney I had with JK. He acknowledged he understood, and then we went on to discuss what a good guy we both thought Jim was. That was the end of our conversation.

Q was standing outside. I opened the door to ask her if she wanted copies as I had promised, and she sneered, I'll be back in a minute. So I went back to waiting. All the employees were standing around trying to figure out what happened. She came back in with two sets of keys and said here's your keys to the locks. Sign this. I asked what it was. She said it was just a release form, saying we got our building back in the same condition it was in. I insisted on reading the type above my signature. There were two sides to the page. I didn't know it at the time I signed. When I tried to pick up the papers, she scolded me. Ooh, there's two copies there be careful. Don't get them out of line. Above my signature was the line she said certified the building had been returned in the same condition it was taken. There was also a release clause that I held the government blameless for damage to the building. I turned to the locksmith and said, are those my original locks and keys. He said he had to re-key the locks and he couldn't put them back in the same order without seeing our original keys. I said, we had lots of keys out and if we didn't have keys we didn't have our building back. She said, Well you're going to have to pay for that. All I paid him to do was to change the locks and then give you the keys. If you want them changed, you're going to have to pay for it. I scowled at the paper. The locksmith chimed in, how many sets of keys? I said about ten. He said he'd make them. I asked how much. He said he'd throw them in no charge. I accepted his offer and signed under that condition. As far as I know, they did not damage the building. It wasn't the building I was worried about anyway. We'd been knocked off our schedule, suffered lost production and sales, I was suffering chest pains and could feel my blood pressure was at a dangerous level, and I thought if I didn't have that release, I'd be sleeping there overnight with as many employees as would stay with me. And there was no release clause against her as an individual. After all, as I understood the situation, the government had rules she had broken and the majority of illegal action had been on her part, the assisting agent, and the supervisor, Dave. So we were free to sue for anything as long as we weren't claiming damage to the building.

When I had the keys, I made copies of the Sales Contract between NM, Inc., and PC along with the inventory list of PC equipment. She told me she was going to send a letter of some kind and to be sure I filled out every question on it. Then she said I was the only registered officer of the company so they were still going to hold me responsible for the back taxes. She then left.

Well, I was so upset I was only able to sleep about an hour that night. Most of the night I spent working on this recording of the events as they were fresh in my mind. My wife told me she could hear the stress in my voice and she can see it in my color.

The experience of trying to deal with an irrational QW and IRS has been detrimental to my health. I checked my blood pressure Friday morning and it was up ~150% above previous highs. The readings I took were 214 over 114 with pulse of 110. I called my Doctor's staff, with the numbers. They told me to come in immediately. I went to the hospital Friday before noon. My doctor told me anything over 200 was an emergency. He told me no matter what was going on, "At some point you've just got to calm down and tell yourself, 'I'm not going to let these people kill me.'" He told me he was certain I'd had suffered some injury to my heart during that session. He felt the IRS should be made to pay for such a serious intrusion into one's life.

I am now on blood pressure medicine. Prior to this, I had maintained a reasonable pressure by natural means -- reduced salt, low sugar, low fat diet, exercise and weight loss. This is no longer possible. Monday, five days later, under medication, my pressure is still 177 over 93, higher than any other point I have a record of prior to Q's illegal action.

Nothing has yet been resolved. Can you help?

**Ending the IRS
The Route to Everyone's Prosperity**

Have you, a family member, a friend or loved one ever been defrauded, looted, hurt, injured, brutalized, or destroyed by the Internal Revenue Service (IRS)? Did no one help you, sympathize with you, or even listen to you, even though you were innocent — even though you and your family were criminally violated, badly injured, perhaps even destroyed or murdered? Do you want legal justice? Do you want to alleviate the sufferings and fears caused by the IRS? You can now safely participate in an inspiring, class-action-type lawsuit against the IRS, its armed agents of force, its paid informants, and those politicians responsible for illegal tax laws, fraudulent assessments, regulations, penalties, liens, levies, seizures, and garnishments. These class-action lawsuits will be based on cruel-and-unusual punishment in violation of the 8th Amendment of the Bill of Rights in the United States Constitution. ...Ending those IRS cruelties is the route to everyone's prosperity and happiness. Replacing the destructive crimes by armed federal agents with a civil tax on *consumption* not on *production* will bring peace and prosperity to everyone.

For information, review the IRS-class-action home page at its *http://www.neo-tech.com/irs-class-action.com/* cyberspace address. In addition, join the discussions on the Eliminate-the-IRS Newsgroup at its *alt.irs.class-action* cyberspace address.

You can add to the expanding arsenal of legal evidence simply by revealing how the IRS has harmed you or others at the *sue@irs.class-action.com* email address. Also important, read the latest IRS abuse reports at
*http://www.neo-tech.com/irs-class-action/*

IRS Class-Action Announcement
alt.irs.class-action

"The attorney preparing the Eighth-Amendment, class-action lawsuit against the IRS issued the following statement:

"In the past few months, we have gathered well over a hundred valid plaintiffs that legally meet the requirements for a class-action suit against the IRS on the basis of the Eighth Amendment to the United States Constitution, which forbids the government from inflicting cruel-and-unusual punishment on its citizens. We are adding an average of 1-2 valid plaintiffs daily from web site http//www.neo-tech.com/ irs.class-action/. We would like to have about 500 bona fide plaintiffs when we file the lawsuit in Federal District Court. Potential plaintiffs should visit the IRS Class-Action home page for information about this lawsuit and how to become a plaintiff. ...No fees or charges of any kind are being asked or will be asked from any plaintiff or potential plaintiff."

A Side Note about this Action
"Of the hundreds of potential plaintiffs we have reviewed, the most unnecessarily tragic of the victims are those whose lives have been crushed even though they have paid their taxes in full and have no legal recourse to gain credit for their tax payments. How does that occur?

"Such victims are generally those who fully paid their taxes, often with refunds due, through employer-payroll withholding taxes. Then, correctly believing their taxes have been paid in full or in excess by their employers, they fail to file their income tax return due to their busyness, forgetfulness, ignorance, or any other reason. Now, hidden in the IRS codes and case law, any taxpayer who after three years fails to file will automatically lose their tax credits/payments. That taxpayer is then considered as having paid $0 in taxes for that year because of a IRS three year limitation period and has no way to get credit for the taxes he or she has paid once the three year limitation has passed. (Remember, to get credit for taxes paid, one must file a tax return, even if that filing consists of stapling a W-2 form to a signed, blank return requesting the IRS to calculate the tax return.) If the non-filing taxpayer fails to do this then the taxpayer is subjected to full tax liability along with its horrendous penalties and interest that often can never be paid. The taxpayer is then crushed with liens, garnishments, and seizures with no legal recourse to the IRS or the courts. Such IRS actions as described above will comprise a second lawsuit that will contribute to the eventual abolishment of the IRS.

"All those who, for whatever reason, have been or are being illegally or cruelly punished by IRS penalties, interests, levies, garnishments, seizures are potentially eligible plaintiffs for either or both lawsuits."

# The Golden Helmet

versus

# Armed Bureaucracies

Cyberspace Addresses
Class-action email:  sue@irs.class-action
Eliminate-the-IRS home page:  http://www.neo-tech.com/irs-class-action/
Eliminate-the-IRS Newsgroup:  alt.irs.class-action
Profound Honesty/Neo-Tech/Zon home page:  http://www.neo-tech.com/
Neo-Tech Mailing List:  neo-talk@lists.best.com

## Table of Contents

# Introduction

Can the following battles be won on planet Earth: Good versus evil. Justice versus injustice. Prosperity versus poverty. And more: Rationality versus irrationality, peace versus war, life versus death. Yes, *all* those battles can be won. Victory is certain — perhaps by 2001 AD or even earlier.

Why is victory certain over the next decade? The survival of all purposely harmful politicians and government officials depends on public acceptance of armed bureaucracies. That acceptance occurs through political and media deceptions. To perpetuate such deceptions, the integrated honesty of Neo-Tech and the wide-scope accounting of the Golden Helmet must be kept hidden or suppressed. Yet, every act to suppress Neo-Tech and its Golden Helmet increases public desires to depoliticize government as first begun in America during its 1994 elections.

This report describes how Neo-Tech and Golden Helmets will eventually depoliticize government and eliminate its armed bureaucracies. This report also reveals how the violent attacks on Neo-Tech literature and its Golden-Helmet dynamic by armed bureaucrats in both 1986 and 1990 began the dynamics for eliminating armed bureaucrats from government. And finally, this report shows how every aggression inflicted on Neo-Tech literature and its Golden-Helmet dynamic subverts the perpetrators and draws them toward being legislated out of existence. *...That elimination of armed bureaucrats will bring limitless prosperity to America as identified in this Appendix.*

\* \* \*

By shunning publicity and the media since 1981, Neo-Tech authors and editors have quietly spread Neo-Tech worldwide. Published in twelve languages,

4

## Introduction

Neo-Tech literature is distributed in 156 countries. It is now too late to stop the Neo-Tech dynamic of fully integrated honesty and its wide-scope accountability.

Neo-Tech is the dynamic undermining destructive politics and organized religion for the past decade. Neo-Tech has been the deep-root cause of (1) collapsing totalitarian governments, such as in Eastern Europe, (2) eroding the authority of Western religions, such as Roman Catholicism, (3) removing from office economically and socially destructive politicians, such as begun in America during its 1994 elections. In turn, that Neo-Tech dynamic is now undermining economically and socially destructive bureaucracies worldwide, including America's most-harmful armed bureaucracies such as the ATF, DEA, EPA, FDA, INS, IRS. ...Those politician-created, criminal-driven bureaucracies are the underlying cause of raising violence and terrorism throughout America.

What to do about those politicians responsible for the criminal elements of government? Independent of everything occurring in today's Establishment, the Neo-Tech/Golden-Helmet dynamic helped determine the 1994 elections and will largely determine the 2000 AD elections. Indeed, that dynamic will increasingly vanish or redeem[1] harmful politicians. Moreover, that constant

---

[1]Redeem? Bill Clinton, for example, had a redeemable core of innocence. Ironically, President Clinton's high intelligence combined with a total lack of principles left him uniquely qualified to understand and then implement the Neo-Tech/Golden-Helmet dynamic. Thus, in the following way, Clinton could have become the greatest, most valuable world leader in history: Before Neo-Tech and the Golden Helmet, no consistently rational principles were available in which anyone could invest. Bill Clinton, maybe out of a special integrity, never locked into or invested in bogus principles from the irrational philosophies that swirled about him and everyone else. Such a fact left him uniquely free for redemption — free to extricate himself from the problems, crimes, and harms of his past. How? Through the Neo-Tech/Golden-Helmet dynamic, Clinton could have swept away

(continued on next page)

undermining of harmful people by Neo-Tech will eventually eliminate destructive bureaucrats, judges, and lawyers.

Local policemen serve to protect life and property. But, armed bureaucrats serve to harm life and property. Today, the increasing social and physical harms caused by politicized armed bureaucrats are endangering all Americans. ...Bureaucrats, not law-abiding citizens, must be disarmed.

Golden-Helmet economics backed by nonpolitical *objective* law could be in place by 2001 AD or earlier. Limitless prosperity and happiness will then become available to everyone.

---

(continued from previous page)

armed bureaucracies, political-agenda laws, and ego "justice" to boom America and the world into limitless prosperity. Seizing that opportunity, he could have freed himself from his hidden crimes to become a hero for all time. Instead, he chose to be Iago to an Othello-like America. With brilliant language seduction, Clinton became the poison in the ear of America to bring a society of "Danish" rot. Such hidden rot only brings more rot, escalating violence, and increasing terrorism...all to be cured by Neo-Tech and the Golden Helmet.

6

# New Words and Concepts

**Golden Helmets** are all-revealing, wide-scope accounting tools that evolve naturally from the fully integrated honesty of Neo-Tech. Golden Helmets are what will vanish not only income taxes but all other taxes on production, earnings, savings, property, inheritance, and estates. Golden Helmets are the tools used by businesspeople to generate limitless wealth for others and society.

**Neo-Tech** is a noun or an adjective meaning *fully integrated honesty* based on facts of reality. Neo-Tech creates a collection of *new techniques* and *new technology* that lets one know exactly what is happening and what to do for gaining honest advantages in all situations. Neo-Tech provides the integrations to collapse the illusions, hoaxes, and irrationalities of any harmful individual or institution.

**Objectivism** is the philosophy of Neo-Tech: the philosophy for the well-being of conscious beings — the philosophy based on reason — the new-world philosophy of limitless prosperity.

**Subjective Laws** include political-agenda laws conjured up by politicians and bureaucrats to gain self-serving benefits, false egos, and unearned power. Enforcement of political-agenda laws requires the use of force and armed agents against innocent people. ...The only purpose of such laws is to violate individual rights. **Objective Laws** are not conjured up by politicians or bureaucrats. Instead, like the laws of physics, they arise from the *immutable laws of nature*.[1] Such laws are valid across time and space, benefit everyone, and advance society. Objective laws are based on the moral prohibition of initiatory force, threats of force, and fraud as constituted on page 89 of this Golden-Helmet Appendix. ...The only rational purpose of laws is to protect individual rights.

---

[1] Unchanging, universally *principled the-point*, natural law as promoted by fully integrated honesty...not *pragmatic a-point*, positive law as promoted by Oliver Wendell Holmes and today by jurists like Robert H. Bork. Such politician-made, positive law always leads toward criminal governments and despotism.

7

**Ego "Justice"** is the use of subjective, political-agenda laws to gain harmful livelihoods and feel false importance. Ego "justice" is the survival tool of many politicians, lawyers, and judges. Ego "justice" is the most pernicious form of neocheating. ...Parasitical elites thrive on subjective laws and ego "justice" to the harm of every individual and all of society.

**Parasitical Elites** are unnatural people who drain everyone. The parasitical-elite class lives by usurping, swindling, and destroying values produced by others. Their survival requires political-agenda laws, armed bureaucracies, ego-"justice" systems, and deceptive neocheating.

**Neocheating** is the undetected usurpation of values from others: the unsuspicious swindling of money, power, or values through deceptive manipulations of rationalizations, non sequiturs, illusions, and mysticisms. ...All such net harms inflicted on society can now be objectively measured by the wide-scope accounting of Neo-Tech.

**Truth** is a mushy, hydra-headed word. Everyone disputes its meaning. Truth denotes a <u>static</u> <u>assertion</u> that changes from person to person, opinion to opinion, culture to culture. Thus, *truth* is a hollow, manipulative word that parasitical elites promulgate to gain credibility for their deceptions, destructions, and ego "justice".

**Honesty** is a solid, indivisible word. No one disputes its meaning. Honesty denotes a <u>dynamic</u> <u>process</u> that is identical for every conscious being. *Honesty* cannot be manipulated. Therefore, parasitical elites must squelch honesty in order to live off the productive class. ...Thus, discard the word **truth**; uphold the word **honesty**. Discard ego "justice"; uphold objective law. Discard the parasitical class; uphold the productive class.

**Anticivilization** is the irrational civilization gripping planet Earth — an unreal civilization riddled with professional value destroyers and neocheaters causing endless cycles of wars, economic and property destructions, unemployment and poverty, suffering and death. ...Through Neo-Tech, the honest Civilization of the Universe will replace Earth's dishonest anticivilization.

8

*New Words and Concepts*

**Civilization of the Universe** is the rational civilization throughout the law-abiding universe — a civilization filled with value producers providing endless cycles of wealth, happiness, and rejuvenation for everyone. ...Professional value destroyers and parasitical elites are nonexistent in the Civilization of the Universe.

**Zon** is a collective word related to the fully integrated honesty of Neo-Tech and comprises (1) the Civilization of the Universe, (2) those operating from its wide-scope perspective, and (3) the power required to control existence — the integrated power to gain wealth and happiness.

**Zonpower** is the power to control (*not* create) existence. Zonpower is derived from applying the fully integrated honesty and wide-scope accountability of Neo-Tech to all conscious actions.

9

# Chapter 1
# Armed Evil

In the "Neo-Tech Newsletter", volume 3, number 5, the author of the *Neo-Tech Discovery*, Dr. Frank R. Wallace, published an article about the Golden Helmet and its wide-scope accounting. That article included an ostracism matrix of the most socially destructive people in America. The publication was then released to its armed IRS targets at 8:00 AM on March 29, 1990. An hour later, a huge, electrically lighted billboard spotlighting the IRS was unveiled in front of the federal courthouse concealing a bevy of armed IRS agents. On the same day, twelve hours after releasing that publication and the unveiling of that electric billboard, those armed agents attacked the author of Neo-Tech, violating his First-Amendment rights.

Under cover of night, those IRS agents assaulted Dr. Wallace at his writing office. They threw copies of his just released publication against his body while screaming obscenities. "How is Neo-Tech going to help you now?" their leader shouted. Wallace's only response was to ask for a minute before being jailed to feed his two aged cats. "F_ _ k the cats!" came a screaming reply. Then, in violation of the First Amendment and free press, they shackled Dr. Wallace's hands behind his back and jailed him. ...The newly published pamphlets disappeared and the electric billboard came down.

Later, the federal prosecutor described Wallace as a most dangerous man because of his Neo-Tech literature and espousals. The federal judge characterized Wallace's Neo-Tech work as "a task of terrifying proportions".

Yes, in fact, Frank R. Wallace is a most dangerous man publishing terrifying literature — dangerous and terrifying to the professional value destroyers whose careers will eventually be ended by the Golden Helmet, its wide-scope accounting, and its ostracism matrix.

## The Ostracism Matrix

Today, cyber communication and computer technology provide an inescapable ostracism matrix. At the deepest roots, that matrix exposes destructive people and their harmful careers. Over 2450 American and foreign parasitical elites are already locked into that computerized matrix. Combined with wide-scope accounting as described in the Neo-Tech literature, that matrix identifies professional value destroyers in government, business, and the legal professions. That matrix will eventually reveal to everyone the world's most harmful people. Against Golden-Helmet accounting, they can no longer hide behind their deceptions and illusions.

## Wide-Scope Accounting

After years of quietly building the Neo-Tech/Golden-Helmet dynamics, the public is awakening to a monstrous fraud — an awakening first reflected across America in its 1994 elections. Eventually, all professional value destroyers from left-wing property usurpers to right-wing spirit usurpers will be driven from their jobs — jobs used to commit crimes against innocent people, the economy, and society. With the parasitical elites gone, America and the world will prosper beyond imagination. But, how will the parasitical elites be vanished? To answer that question, the nature of a class overthrow based on wide-scope accounting must be understood. With that understanding comes the knowledge for a peaceful overthrow of socially harmful politicians and bureaucrats.

But, first, review again that morning of March 29, 1990: Newly published documents written by Dr. Frank R. Wallace were placed in newsracks in front of two targeted IRS buildings. An hour later, a huge 16' x 48' electric billboard was unveiled in front of the federal-court building. Neither the documents nor the billboard were directed at the public. The time had not yet arrived to begin the public revolution. The documents and billboard were directed at several-hundred professional value destroyers identified for the first time in print by name — destructive persons already in a computerized ostracism matrix capable of itemizing the net destructiveness of each individual.

Those published names ranged from criminal-minded persons holding various-level positions in government, religion, big business, and the professions. In addition to names of IRS officials responsible for committing objective crimes, other names ranged from nefarious political-exploiter Rudolph Giuliani[1] to barbaric drug-czar William Bennett[2]. All published names were people who used armed bureaucratic enforcers and self-serving ego "justice" to promote themselves and their careers while discarding objective law and justice (Ref: *The Neo-Tech Protection Kit*, B &W, 1991).

Also published were the names of bureaucrats and lawyers who are professional value destroyers. Their jobs were based on harming the economy, society, and the productive class. Such jobs must be backed by armed enforcers who threaten, harm, pillage, jail, and eventually destroy their victims — victims who are often the most

---

[1]See Giuliani's footnote on page 17.

[2]William J. Bennett's best-selling *Book of Virtues* (Simon & Schuster, 1993) is a full-blown example of camouflaging evil with illusions of virtue. Close examination of Bennett's book of "virtues" reveals a maudlin collection of non sequiturs that mostly contradict mankind's only two objective virtues: (1) fully integrated honesty and (2) producing competitive values for others and society. William Bennett is nothing more than a totalitarian theocrat who advocates, for example, public beheadings of those who violate bogus political-agenda laws involving drugs.

courageous and talented of the value producers. ...Such entrepreneurial victims represent the future prosperity of any economy.

Those newsstand documents not only published the specific names of those in the ostracism matrix, but described how that matrix would function once it were released to the public. Those documents described how the matrix would eventually remove each professional value destroyer from his or her harmful livelihood. ...Seizing those documents in the morning, armed IRS agents attacked Neo-Tech and jailed its author by nightfall.

### Parasitical Elites Depend on Guns and Jails

Armed bureaucrats assaulted and jailed Frank R. Wallace. He was then "silenced" in a federal labor camp. Three months later, in an attempt to stop his writings from prison, Dr. Wallace was shackled in handcuffs, waist chains, and leg irons. He was then spirited to a more isolated prison atop a windblown, desert hill.

During their violent destructions several years earlier, on November 3, 1986, those same armed bureaucrats beat, kicked, and hospitalized the personal editor of Dr. Wallace. Next, they destroyed irreplaceable original research and literature manuscripts. They pillaged the hard-earned property of I & O Publishing Company, its writers, its editors, and its customers. Gleefully, they carried off the precious biomedical research funds of the Research Institute for Biological Immortality (RIBI). They put I & O Publishing out of business....Four years later, those same gun-carrying bureaucrats caused the death of Wallace's pet cat.

Pillaging, injury, destruction, death — why? To survive, the parasitical-elite class must increasingly harm and destroy Earth's innocent creatures — men, women, children, even pets and animals. Indeed, while in federal

13

prison, Dr. Wallace witnessed daily the deterioration of political prisoners *and their families* — hundreds of innocent men, women, and children being slowly, insidiously stripped of life. They were being murdered as surely as if being killed by Hitler or Stalin. ...Through wide-scope accounting, all parasitical elites are revealed as killers — murderers of political pawns by either open Hitler/Stalin style or hidden Bush/Clinton style.

Today, in America, innocent political pawns are increasingly broken or jailed in order to support an expanding parasitical-elite class. Tomorrow, without Neo-Tech, those victims would be one's own children, parents, brothers, sisters, friends. ...Eventually, everyone who is not a parasitical elite or an active supporter of the leech class would become a victim.

# Chapter 2
# Political Prisoner #26061-048

1992
The Author of Neo-Tech
speaks from a
Federal Labor Camp

"Prison paradoxically both magnifies and hides the harm parasitical elites inflict on the economy and society. Today, armed bureaucrats and ego-"justice" courts are quietly incarcerating tens of thousands of political pawns in federal labor camps scattered across the United States. In its spiraling need to control and drain others through enforcement of political-agenda laws, the American parasitical-elite class imprisons a higher percentage of noncriminals than any other country in the industrialized world.

"Those political prisoners are victims of power-usurping politicians and bureaucrats. Such politicians and bureaucrats usurp their power through the bureaucracies they create, arm with guns, and then expand. Such bureaucracies include the ATF, DEA, EPA, FDA, FTC, INS, IRS, SEC. Politicians backed by those armed bureaucracies increasingly force their way into every citizen's life. Armed bureaucracies are used to control and drain the productive class in order to support the parasitical-elite class at the expense of everyone else, especially the needy.

"When those many thousands of prisoners and their families are exposed to the Golden Helmet, they will realize their sufferings were inflicted solely to advance the parasitical-elite class. Such political prisoners will realize they have broken no objective law and are not guilty of

15

any real crime. Each will also realize that initiating force, threats, or fraud toward other individuals is the only objective basis of crime for which justice can be rendered. Then, angrily, each will realize the parasitical-elite class is guilty of initiating the force and fraud that cruelly crushed their lives...and the lives of their families.

For every political pawn jailed or destroyed, the parasitical elites cower a hundred value producers into submission. Those monstrous but hidden crimes violate objective law. ...Those perpetrators can and eventually will be brought to justice through the Neo-Tech/Golden-Helmet ostracism matrix."

## Political-Agenda Laws

"Many, but not all, federal prisoners today are jailed for violating political-agenda 'laws' that have nothing to do with objective law. Political-agenda 'laws' are gun-enforced to empower politicians, bureaucrats, and an iniquitous triangle of lawyers, prosecutors, and judges.

"Today, only those prisoners and their loved ones can experience the full evil of the ego-'justice' system created by the parasitical-elite class. As a result, America's justice system is now controlled by a triad of deeply dishonest lawyers, malicious prosecutors, and falsely respected judges who disdain objective law, justice, and honesty. Indeed, ego 'justice' is increasingly draining all productive people without the public knowing the terrible price everyone is paying. That price is a deteriorating society."

## Ego "Justice"

"Ego 'justice' is practiced by judges who abandon objective law to support armed bureaucracies that enforce destructive political agendas. Through judicial exploitations and social deceptions, those judges garner public

16

respect. Yet, they are destroyers of property, life, and happiness. Today's ego-'justice' judges incarcerate ever more political pawns with ever harsher, totally unjust sentences. Why? To maintain their ego props and arbitrary power through expanding enforcement of political-agenda laws."

## Humanoid Judges

"Consider the life-shattering sentences imposed daily on people innocent of any objective crime. Consider Los Angeles federal judge Manuel L. Real who routinely destroys those caught in his web with the harshest possible prison terms — solely to feel power and importance. He takes pleasure in his tough-judge image expressed by his Maximum-Manny nickname. In his self-glorifying process, he destroys the lives of innocent men, women, and children. ...Many other judges at all levels are also Maximum Mannys who destroy innocent human beings and their families in order to feel important.

"Consider federal judges Thomas P. Griesa, Milton Pollack, John M. Walker, Jr., and Kimba Wood. Each giulianied[1] innocent business giants for personal power and ego enhancement. Each such judge is a killer of innocent but unpopular people like Michael Milken and Leona Helmsley. Review the records of perhaps the most murderous political-agenda judges in America, Walter Smith, Jr., of Waco, Texas and Clifford Weckstein of Leesburg, Virginia. Such judges destroy objectively innocent individuals caught in the evil web of political-

---

[1]The verb giuliani means to use gun-backed, political-agenda law to criminally destroy honest businesspeople and illegally seize private property. Derived from Rudolph Giuliani who advanced in politics by illegally using RICO and seizure laws to crush innocent people and their businesses.

agenda enforcements. To garner ego-boosting publicity and to feel powerful, those humanoid judges crush their wrongly accused, media-smeared victims with false, inhumane imprisonments.

"Each such judge is an accomplice to the gun-backed crimes of political-agenda enforcement — crimes of collective assault, pillage, murder. Such judges and their prosecutor cohorts must be held responsible for their crimes against individuals, the economy, and society. Moreover, their innocent victims must be freed, pardoned, and paid restitution."

## Heinous Crimes

"In late 1991, a triad of politicians, bureaucrats, and their ego-'justice' system in America joined to protect themselves — joined to establish the apparatus for removing threats to their power: In increasingly harsh actions, that triad established the death penalty for guilt-by-association crimes, opening the way to the death penalty for political 'crimes'. In addition, through the Supreme Court, that triad is quietly undermining habeas corpus — the basic protection against illegal or false imprisonments. ...In 1933, Hitler secured his future tyranny by quietly undermining habeas corpus. That undermining of objective law eventually led to an orgy of crimes by armed bureaucracies culminating with Auschwitz.

"Through illegal use of RICO and seizure laws; through plea-bargain 'justice' based on threats, paid perjurers, and coerced betrayals forced even between husbands and wives, parents and children, this ego-'justice' system is setting the foundation for liquidating any opposition to political policies. ...Daily, one can see that triad's heinous crimes on the dying faces of innocent

18

political prisoners. Many of those victims must helplessly watch their families die bit by bit until all love and life are lost."

## Prison: A False Target

"Consider one of the deceptions that hides the ego-'justice' system: The attention of political prisoners is riveted on the prison system in which they and their families profoundly suffer. Thus, those prisoner victims and their families increasingly focus blame on the prison system. They then lose sight of who is responsible for destroying their lives, families, and businesses. They lose sight of the ego-'justice' system that illegally put them in prison.

"In that way, the Bureau of Prisons becomes a false target. A false target because the Bureau of Prisons is not run by professional value destroyers. Instead, it is a fairly benevolent, well-run system that tries to benefit those falsely imprisoned by a corrupt ego-'justice' system. ...Many prison employees, as well as many lower-tier government employees, are good-intentioned. They too are exploited and drained. They too can and will help vanish the parasitical elites. They too shall rise with anger to overthrow the leech class — the devil class."

## Roots of Evil

"Three centuries before Christ, the Greek philosopher and politician Plato gave birth to a parasitical-elite class that to this day controls the populations of the world. Three decades ago, both the Arabic and Black Muslims perceptively sensed but only partially identified that controlling class as the Great Satan or White Devils. What the Muslims, even their own murderous leech class, actually sensed were those who have controlled the two-

19

millennia reign of dishonesty, exploitation, tyranny, oppression, crusades, wars, slavery, pogroms, holocausts.

"From Plato's techniques evolved a devil class — the parasitical-elite class. That class thrives by draining the value producers — the working class. That devil class is the parasitical-elite class, which has grown to dominate the world through subjective laws, mendacious politics, destructive bureaucracies, corrupted professions, mystical religions, effete educators, dishonest media, and the carcasses of stagnant big businesses.

"Neo-Tech, meaning fully integrated honesty, has identified that parasite class as everyone's enemy. It drains the lives of all productive people as well as lower-tiered government workers, dependent entitlement clients, and slave-labor political prisoners.

"The Muslims, especially the Black Muslims of the 1960s as exploitatively promoted by Elijah Muhammad and then more honestly articulated by Malcolm X, sensed the two-millennia-old hoax perpetuated by that devil class. But, the Muslims were misled by demographics: Certainly, in recent history, the majority within the parasitical-elite class have been western-world, white-skinned demagogues. Yet, throughout history, other cultures, races, skin colors, religions, and nationalities have also produced the same devil class — the same criminal-elite class. Even today, note how the Muslim theocracy criminally, murderously rules Iran today. Note the murderous Idi Amins of Africa. ...Race, color, religion, and nationality have nothing to do with being a devil — a professional parasite. Instead, professional parasitism has everything to do with being an enemy of the people.

"Likewise, race, color, or nationality have nothing to do with the victim class. The exploited victims are always the productive working class — regardless of race, color,

20

nationality, economic status, or period of history.

"That devil class — the parasitical-elite class — can exist only in an unnatural, upside-down world."

### Uprighting our Upside-Down World

"Nearly everything the parasitical-elite class promotes as right is dishonest and destructive. Nearly everything it promotes as wrong is honest and productive. That upside-down world of the past 23 centuries was recognized a century ago by Russian writer Mikhail Bakunin:

> 'For there is no terror, cruelty, sacrilege, perjury, cynical theft, brazen robbery, or foul treason which has not been committed and is still being committed by representatives of the State, with no other excuse than this elastic, at times so convenient and terrible phrase, *for reasons of the state*. A terrible phrase indeed...as soon as it is uttered everything becomes silent and drops out of sight: honesty, honor, justice, right, pity itself vanish and with it logic and sound sense; black becomes white and white becomes black, the horrible becomes humane and the most dastardly felonies and atrocious crimes become meritorious acts.'

"Hitler described parasitical elites as leeches, vampires, vermin, termites, maggots, bacilli. In his upside-down world, he then labeled the Jews as those parasitical elites. But Hitler's description of parasitical elites really applied to himself, his cohorts, and his guns-and-fists enforcers who empowered him through armed bureaucracies. By contrast, his targeted Jews were among Germany's greatest value producers.

"Likewise, to exist, all other parasitical-elite kingpins must also turn reality upside down. Mao and Khomeini,

21

for example, used force to posit nonforce free-enterprise and individual property rights as unjust and parasitical, while positing Mao's gun-backed socialism and Khomeini's gun-backed religious fundamentalism as just and valuable. ...Such people can rise to power only in an irrational, upside-down world of force, dishonesty, and mysticism."

## Discovery from Prison

"What if every judge, prosecutor, and high-level bureaucrat spent a month in a Federal[1] Labor Camp for political prisoners — spent a month among the victims of subjective, political-agenda laws and ego "justice"? Each such judge, prosecutor, and bureaucrat would be indelibly struck by the suffering and destruction wreaked on innocent, good people and their families. Only by directly experiencing prison can one discover the profound harm caused by the unjust incarceration of political pawns — versus the just incarceration of real criminals guilty of objective crimes.

"Prisoners who commit objective crimes — genuine criminals — are **justly** incarcerated. Thus, they suffer *much less* than innocent political prisoners who are **unjustly** incarcerated. For, real criminals know the justice of their sentences and accept the maxim "Do the crime, do the time". By contrast, innocent political prisoners suffer deeply from (1) the horrendous injustices inflicted

---

[1]Why federal? Most prisoners in state prisons are real criminals. Many prisoners in federal prisons are political prisoners. State and county trial judges and courts deal mainly with legitimate, objective laws and crimes. By contrast, federal trial judges and courts deal mainly with enforcing bogus political-agenda laws. The federal government in Washington gives its judges lifetime appointments so they never need be accountable to the public. Thus, federal trial judges can reign in their courts as government heavies with totalitarian power. Such judges practice ego "justice" with impunity. ...Eliminating the anticivilization justice system involves revoking all political-agenda laws and ending life-time appointments for Federal District-Court trial judges.

upon them and their families and from (2) the fact that criminals throughout the government are living free while illegally destroying the lives of political prisoners, their families, and countless other innocent people.

"One and only one reason exists to enforce political-agenda laws. That reason is to enhance the harmful livelihoods of parasitical elites and their corps of professional value destroyers. Be it in 100th-BC galley ships, in 12th-century dungeons, in 20th-century Nazi death camps, or in today's federal prisons, its innocent victims are *purposely* incarcerated and often destroyed just to indulge the bogus livelihoods of a few evil people: a few habitual, mass-destruction criminals ranging from Caligula to Hitler to today's parasitical elites with their legions of armed bureaucrats.

"Only by directly experiencing prison does one discover the deep moral difference between evilly enforcing subjective political-agenda laws versus justly enforcing objective laws. With direct prison experience, many bureaucrats, prosecutors, and judges would stop pursuing, prosecuting, or adjudicating political-agenda law. They would reject such subjective laws and ego-"justice" support systems as evil."

## America Today

"America today is at once the greatest and the worst nation on Earth: The greatest by the productivity, well-being, and happiness created by the mightiest host of professional value producers and competent workers in history. The worst by the harm, deprivations, and unhappiness caused by a rapidly expanding parasitical-elite class. That leech class is cannibalizing history's most bountiful trove of earned wealth and created values. But, with the rising Neo-Tech/Golden-Helmet dynamics, every-one can look happily to the future. For, the elimination

23

of the leech class, starting perhaps by the year 2000 elections, will bring ever growing well-being and happiness to everyone."

U.S. Political Prisoner #26061-048
February, 1992

# Chapter 3

# The Golden-Helmet Trial

Federal Trial CR-S-90-057-LDG(LRL)
(An Article 58 Trial)

Dr. Frank R. Wallace is a scientist, author, editor, and publisher. He is also the discoverer of Neo-Tech and the Golden Helmet. In February 1991, Wallace was tried in Federal Court on criminal tax charges. Those politically wrought charges arose from a Neo-Tech street publication and billboard publicly released on March 29, 1990 — ten hours later, Dr. Wallace was in jail.

During that first trial, the judge denied Wallace an oath to incorruptible honesty rather than to manipulative truth. That denial prevented Wallace from testifying. Thus, he was convicted and sent to prison. Subsequently, the United States Court of Appeals overturned that conviction citing the judge's "abuse of judicial discretion". In the retrial of August 1993, that same judge again denied Wallace a fair jury trial through even greater abuses of judicial discretion in "ordering" the jury to render a guilty verdict as described in Chapter 6. ...Facing Wallace again, that judge pursued a single agenda: control the jury and the courtroom proceedings to obtain a conviction. To avenge his embarrassing reversal, that ego-oriented judge had to convict Wallace, regardless of the facts or justice.

Using occasional trials of objective crimes as credibility props, such judges must not let honesty or objective law expose their ego agendas. For, all ego agendas depend on dishonesty and subjective laws — on enforcing harmful political agendas through ego "justice". But, that irrationality will end. For, Neo-Tech, which means fully integrated honesty, is now embedded in the

25

legal system. Once in the system, Neo-Tech will relentlessly persist, eventually vanishing subjective laws with their ego-"justice" support systems. That, in turn, will vanish the parasitical-elite class and its professional value destroyers.

During the retrial, the judge preserved his ego agenda by manipulating an intrusive, father-like image that commanded obedience from the jurors. The judge assured obedience through improper ingratiations and intimidations directed at each individual juror. The judge then concluded the trial with a surprise, unstipulated jury instruction demanding conviction: His blatant abuse of "fair comment" after the conclusion of the trial compelled the jury members to render verdicts of guilty, no matter what their opinions of the trial or judgments of the evidence, no matter what the stipulated jury instructions stated.

That judge further sought to protect his ego by forcing Dr. Wallace into "mental-health" treatments. However, that mendacious ploy backfired as the "mental-health" sentence was overturned by the 9th Circuit Appeals Court charging the judge with vindictiveness. ...Such self-serving dishonesty serves to highlight the nature of ego "justice".

Dr. Wallace confronts evil that robs us and our children of prosperity and happiness. He confronts subjective law and challenges its ego "justice". Below are key portions of his retrial.

## Wallace's Opening Statement

Ladies and gentlemen of the jury, ten years ago, through Golden-Helmet tax payments, I & O Publishing paid over four times the legal obligation of income taxes for each year in question: 1983, 1984, 1985. Unlike the prosecutor's case, my case will be grounded in reality. Nothing will be out of context. Nothing will be distorted. Nothing will be manipulated. No illusions will be created to sway the jury.

### Golden-Helmet Tax Payments
From my testimony, you will also realize why only Golden-Helmet tax payments will reduce our national deficit, end our declining economy, create good jobs, bring lower taxes, and deliver benefits to everyone.

### The Honesty Oath
This is a historic trial. Just prior to my testimony, I will take an oath not to truth, but to honesty as recently mandated by the Ninth-Circuit Court of Appeals. Why an oath to honesty rather than to truth? What is truth? We all know that truth for one may not be truth for another. Truth varies with condition or context. And, an unlimited number of conditions or contexts exist. Thus, without an anchor to honesty, anyone can manipulate truth to serve harmful agendas. Truth, therefore, can serve bad laws — subjective laws, which mean arbitrary laws designed to advance self-serving political, bureaucratic, and personal agendas.

By contrast, everyone knows what honesty is. It is the same for everyone. No one can manipulate honesty. Honesty, therefore, can serve only good law — objective law, which means consistent law independent of political, bureaucratic, or personal agendas.

### The Truth Oath
The prosecution witnesses will take an oath to truth, not to honesty. ...Listen to the difference of testimony

27

taken under the honesty oath versus the truth oath. At first, this imposing courtroom setting will bestow an illusion of power and credibility upon the judge and prosecutor. They will sound convincing. They will paint a picture that is opposite to the fact. As my testimony will show, the I & O Golden Helmet paid 4.1 times the legal obligation of income taxes each year from 1983 to 1985. But, the prosecutor will present out-of-context accounting figures and a paid witness — all tailored to force a conviction. But, hold judgment until you hear my testimony under the honesty oath.

### Revealing a Profound Government Error
At the conclusion of my testimony, I believe most will recognize the prosecutor's accusations are an error of epic proportions. I believe even the prosecutor and the IRS will realize and admit their profound error — at least silently, to themselves.

### Two Worlds
And finally, my testimony will show this is a trial between two worlds: the rational, objective-law world of the Golden Helmet versus the irrational, subjective-law world of harmful political and personal agendas. ...This trial will show how the Golden Helmet will bring great benefits to everyone — even to the prosecutor, to the IRS, and to this court.

\* \* \*

### The IRS's Case
For many hours, over two days, the prosecution presented a parade of IRS witnesses, a paid informant, and manipulated financial figures — all in an attempt to show

that Frank R. Wallace was guilty of so-called tax "crimes".
...By contrast, Wallace presented his case in one hour and
called no witnesses.

The IRS's case was based entirely on subjective,
political-agenda law. Nothing in the IRS's case was
relevant to objective law as described in the testimony.

[See trial transcripts for the full IRS case.]

### Wallace's Testimony

The historic oath to fully integrated honesty was taken
at this time by Frank R. Wallace:

"Do you affirm to speak with fully integrated honesty,
only with fully integrated honesty, and nothing but fully
integrated honesty?"

Wallace reviewed Charts 1 and 2
before starting his testimony.

---

## Chart 1

## WALLACE'S TESTIMONY WILL REVEAL

- Why Wallace is on trial
- Who is innocent; who is guilty
- The excess tax payments for 1983-1985

---

## Chart 2

# OUTLINE OF WALLACE'S TESTIMONY

(based on the fully integrated honesty oath)

*Valid Facts Depend on Context*

I. Context
* Building the foundation: Pre-1986
* Destructions of November 3, 1986
  (the violent armed attack on writing offices)
* Rebuilding: 1986-1990
* The March 29, 1990 book-flinging assault,
  shackling, and jailing
* Building for the future: 1990-1993

II. Valid Facts
* All taxes for 1983-1985 paid legally and in excess
* Criminal charges were politically motivated
* Wallace is innocent of all charges

[While the prosecution was allowed two days of uninterrupted testimony, Wallace's brief one hour of testimony was repeatedly cut off by the judge, even when there was no objection from the prosecution. ...Indeed, the ego-threatened judge demanded a conviction more than did the prosecution.]

Building the Foundation:  Pre-1986

I was born a severe dyslexic, resulting in my being a mirror writer who could not spell, read, keep numbers straight, or remember names.  To function and learn, I had to rely on conceptualization and integration rather than memory.  Thus, I increasingly turned toward the sciences and mathematics.

My career aptitude tests registered the highest scores for law and a rare, perfect score for becoming an FBI agent.  My family background is almost entirely law:  My great, great grandfather was the United States congressman who acted as an attorney for the House of Representatives in bringing impeachment charges against President Andrew Johnson. Both my great grandfather and grandfather were attorney generals of New York State. My father was the youngest Supreme Court Judge in the history of New York State. All my uncles and older brother were lawyers. My early life was steeped in law.

From that early life, I clearly understood that a prosperous, happy society depended on a government of laws, not a government of politicians and bureaucrats. Yet, I sensed something terribly wrong with much of the law that surrounded me — something hidden and undefined — something deeply dishonest and harmful to our society.

I turned away from family tradition and headed first for a Jack-London stint in the merchant marines then to the sciences with a clean sense of exhilaration. Not until thirty years later did I discover that undefined dishonesty sensed in my early years. I discovered the difference between two kinds of law: The first kind was **Objective Law** that condemns and prosecutes murder, rape, assault, robbery, extortion, and objective civil litigations — consistent law that serves society throughout history, in all countries. The second kind was **Subjective Law** that permits self-serving political agendas, ego "justice", and dishonest torts — socially and economically destructive law that corrupts politicians, bureaucrats, judges, lawyers, and certain businesspeople. ...Subjective law mixed with objective law means corrupt law. Now I understood my exhilaration on heading toward a career in the sciences.

With an Instructorship teaching premedical students and then winning a full-time Research Fellowship, I earned my

## Appendix: *The Golden Helmet*

Doctorate in Inorganic and Analytical Chemistry from the University of Iowa in 1957. Turning down higher-paying jobs in industrial chemistry, I accepted an elite exploratory research position at Du Pont's famous Brandywine Laboratories — the mecca for chemical research with over 3000 Ph.D. scientists and a billion dollars of research facilities at one's disposal. If any place in industry existed in which one could do research to win the Nobel Prize in Chemistry, this was the place.

After obtaining a basic patent on high-temperature catalytic reactions, I left that academic-like, basic-research career to pursue fast-track industrial research. Almost immediately, I recognized my dyslexic limitations would inhibit my career. While strong in organization, creativity, research, and math, I was a Ph.D. who, except for studying and noting technical works, could barely read or write. To function in business, I had to effectively communicate with my superiors and colleagues through writing. I also had to possess a wide, well-read base of knowledge. Because of my dyslexia, I could not even write an effective memo and had read only one classic in literature, Victor Hugo's *Les Miserables*.

Thus, I began a self-education program attacking my weaknesses with furious, nonstop intensity. Gathering a battery of books on English grammar, composition, vocabulary, and usage, I squeezed every hour out of every day for three years teaching myself to write effectively. Many nights, I worked into the morning hours writing a simple one-page memo. I studied and edited over and over, dozens of times until I was delivering my message in a clear, concise manner. Next, I launched a nonstop reading program, hardly allowing a minute to pass without a book in my hand, reading while standing in line, eating,

32

riding in public transportation. I read hundreds of books in all areas of knowledge.

My writing and knowledge continually improved. Others began noticing my writings. Eventually, I became recognized as a good technical writer. Then, I was being sought within Du Pont for my writing skills as I increasingly wrote articles and manuals. ...Thus, I turned my greatest weakness into a strength. As a result, my progress as a research scientist accelerated.

Only 20% of the Ph.D. scientists at Du Pont succeed in being associated with a discovery that eventually becomes a successful commercial product. In less than ten years, I moved three products from the lab bench, to pilot plants, to commercial plants, then to the public with marketing and sales. As far as I know, those products to this day are still making profits for Du Pont.

My career was moving fast. All looked bright. But, all was not right. As years before with law, I was again experiencing a sense that something was terribly wrong — something I could not grasp. My career was soaring. I had three beautiful children. But, I was losing my marriage with a woman whom I dearly loved. What was wrong? Why was my deepest, inner life declining?

Reflecting back to my first week at Du Pont a decade earlier, I recall listening to an inspiring speech by world-renowned Dr. Frank McGrew, the Director of Central Research at Du Pont. Almost any research chemist in the world would consider Dr. McGrew's position as the pinnacle career goal. Yet, with profound respect for that great man, I looked at him from the back of a crowded auditorium and was seized by the realization that I had to dedicate my life to a much more important goal. Years later, while pursuing a potential cancer cure at Du Pont,

33

I felt even that goal was not important enough — not my passion, goal, purpose.

I did not know what that goal was, but increasingly I noticed that nearly everyone over thirty gradually seemed to lose his or her desire for life and happiness. What was wrong all around me, with everyone, and why? ...I was to discover the answer after I wrote my first book.

Combining my poker experiences that began in the third grade with my recent hard-earned writing skills, I wrote and published my first book: "Poker, A Guaranteed Income for Life by Using the Advanced Concepts of Poker". Within two years, it became the best-selling poker book in history. Then, Crown Publishing and Warner Books in New York took ten-year licenses to market both the hardcover and softcover editions. They doubled the sales of the book.

The poker book was not really a book about poker. It was a metaphor demonstrating the destructiveness of irrationality as opposed to the productiveness of rationality. After further studies, I realized that irrationality was not only bizarrely unnatural, but was actually a man-made disease. ...Irrationality was the disease, not cancer, that I needed to cure. I realized the single most-important goal for conscious beings on Earth was to eradicate irrationality!

After extensive research, I learned that the disease of irrationality was first propagated by Plato over 2300 years ago to support a burgeoning class of parasitical elites. ...Today, that disease is propagated by a class of parasitical politicians, bureaucrats, educators, artists, entertainers, media journalists, judges, and lawyers. They propagate their destructive irrationality through coercion, force, dishonesty, blatherings, deception, ego "justice", and subjective laws.

Indeed, mankind's most important goal is to cure that disease of irrationality. For, irrationality not only prevents the cure for all other diseases, but is the cause of poverty, wars, riots, violent crimes, injustice, corruption, subjective laws, job losses, happiness losses, and death itself. With that realization, the goal to which I must dedicate my life was clear.

On making that discovery, I resigned my position as Senior Research Chemist at Du Pont in 1972 to pursue full time the cure of mankind's most devastating disease: the death-and-destruction disease of irrationality.

Living on borrowed money from 1973 to 1976, I wrote and produced a quarter-million-word encyclopedia about the disease of irrationality and its cure. Even though demand for the poker book continued, I took the book out of print after the licenses expired. For, I wanted the public to focus on my newly evolving literature about the prosperity and happiness that arises from Neo-Tech — from fully integrated honesty.

The encyclopedia, however, was not commercially successful. Thus, I was sunk financially with three children in school to support. That began a four-year period of great financial difficulties — until the commercially successful Neo-Tech Discovery was published. At that time, a second crucial realization occurred: To achieve my goal, not only books and publications were required, but direct, ongoing confrontations with those irrational forces that bleed society were also required. Thus, various confrontation dynamics were created.

One such confrontation dynamic, conceived in 1980, involved the Golden Helmet and the IRS. The idea was to increasingly confront the IRS on a legal, peaceful, civil

35

level — to confront the IRS through the courts. In that way, I could gradually introduce the Golden Helmet. Both the government and the public would then increasingly understand the Golden Helmet. Through such a steady but peaceful confrontation process, the beneficial laws based on rationality would eventually prevail over the harmful political-agenda laws based on irrationality.

### Destructions of November 3rd

Then, the totally unexpected happened: At 12:25 PM, November 3, 1986, without warning, sixteen IRS agents carrying guns attacked the research-and-writing facilities of I□& O Publishing. Without reason, they punched, kicked, and hospitalized my personal editor. Those agents then proceeded to ransack everything. Breaking into a safe, they seized the RIBI research funds allotted to 2200 registrants — funds obligated to an offshore medical-research program.

Those agents took all files, computer disks and backups, writing and research projects in progress. They took everything needed to carry out our writing, research, and publishing activities. ...Without a hearing or even an indication of a crime committed, their seizures ended the rapid expansion of I & O Publishing Company and eventually put it out of business.

Now, crucial to my testimony, I want you to hear a commercial audio tape — the portion containing a live, impromptu twenty-minute speech I gave at the Neo-Tech World Summit to five-hundred international representatives at the Tropicanna Hotel on November 11, 1986, just eight days after those armed agents violently pillaged I & O's writing and research offices.

*The Golden-Helmet Trial*

37

*Appendix: The Golden Helmet*

[Editors Note: The prosecutor having previously heard that tape objected to the jury to hearing it. For, by describing the Neo-Tech/Golden Helmet, the tape clearly demonstrated Dr. Wallace's innocence. ...Then, the judge, without even listening to the tape, prohibited the playing of that tape to the jury.

Indeed, of the dozens of rulings and motions since the inception of this case in March 1990, Judge Lloyd D. George supported the prosecution without a single exception. The court records show that George ruled 100% against Dr. Wallace. He seldom addressed even a single point in Wallace's motions. In almost every action since 1990, Judge George simply reworded the prosecution's position to rule against Wallace. Other judges involved with this case showed no such bias. They generally considered Wallace's position fairly and equally with the prosecution's position. Thus, those judges ruled about fifty fifty for and against each side.

The Ninth-Circuit Court of Appeals overturned Judge George's entire 1991 trial for his abuse of judicial discretion against Wallace.]

After the attack of November 3, 1986, I tried to reason and work with the IRS. More than once, in both letters and in publications, I offered to review my Golden-Helmet tax-payment records with the IRS commissioner. In May 1987, I sent the supervisor of that IRS attack, Gary Rogers, a key to my safe-deposit box containing the Golden-Helmet plan showing the excess tax payments. I even sent the IRS Commissioner, Fred T. Goldberg, two skids of Golden-Helmet tax records from previous years. Yet, the IRS apparently never used that key or those records to confirm the Golden-Helmet tax payments.  Did the IRS already realize its error?  Did the IRS agents realize they seized I & O's property solely on the basis of a dishonest informant seeking a cash payoff?

### Rebuilding: 1986-1990

The IRS ended our research and publishing capability. Additionally, the IRS ended our capacity to service a quarter-million readers and customers.  Yet, the integrity of I & O Publishing Company required providing those customers with products and services.  The Golden-Helmet and medical-research funds held abroad were used to pay expenses required to satisfy both our national and international customers.

Thus, the rapid growth of jobs, values, and taxpayments generated through the Golden Helmet ended along with our medical-research plans.

A shrinking I & O Publishing continued out of homes and apartments, rather like a Kibbutz or a Mormon family, until independent, non Golden-Helmet companies developed in 1990.  Indeed, from 1987 to 1990, every remaining asset of the Golden Helmet was committed to preserving our progress toward curing the death-and-destruction disease of irrationality.

To maintain that forward movement, I voluntarily worked 14-16 hours a day, 7 days a week.  No vacations, no hobbies, no luxuries.  No retirement or pension benefits.  No salary or paychecks.  In 1989, a modest house was purchased for me to live with my wife when my office domicile — a house  purchased in 1973 for $32,000 — was donated to the Kenneth A. Clark Memorial.  An additional room and a meeting-room basement were added to handle the escalating meeting, writing, research activities. During that time, funds needed to support my work, research, and publications averaged about $5000 a month. On the advice of a loan officer, that amount was listed to meet the mortgage requirements. From that writing/research support structure, my donated house, along with money from my wife's savings, a down payment was made.

After the Golden-Helmet support structure was phased out, I & O Publishing was abandoned in 1990. Today, my wife, Rosa Maria, supports portions of my research and writings, as do thousands of other Neo-Tech benefactors worldwide.

If not for my devoted wife, whom I need and who fervently supports my work, I would live like a monk in a YMCA — which I have done during several periods of my life, even when I was a Senior Research Chemist at Du Pont in the early 1970s. As is, I still live like a monk as much as possible. I return to my wife's house only for dinner, then again to sleep. I have no hobbies and take no vacations; I have no interest in accumulating wealth or material luxuries. ...Such diversions would only consume irreplaceable time, break my concentration, and distract me from my work and goal of curing irrationality worldwide.

I never, however, advocate such a 100% service or a monk's life for others. I advocate a happy life for everyone by whatever rational, productive life style brings maximum happiness. ...By my choice and dedication to a single goal, a monk-style life is what makes me the most efficient and, thus, the most happy.

Today, I accept only a minimum-wage job as an editor for Neo-Tech Worldwide. My wife and others support my pro-bono publishing activities. ...My life is 100% dedicated to eliminating the disease of irrationality.

The Book-Flinging Assault
and
Political Jailing of March 29, 1990

After the 1986 armed attacks and seizures, the IRS did nothing for over three years and appeared it would do nothing. With all of I & O's funds, records, and writings in its possession, the IRS did nothing to bring my case to court or to allow a just trial. I increasingly pressed the IRS to interact rationally through its personnel and the civil courts. I still had no response. I applied pressure through a series of pro-bono publications sent to the IRS and others throughout the government. Each new release was more aggressive in identifying the irrational behaviors of certain harmful people in politics and the IRS.

Then, early in the morning on March 29, 1990, newsstands were placed in front of the two IRS buildings in Las Vegas and stocked with my latest publication. An hour later, a huge 16' by 48' billboard was unveiled in front of this very court building. That publication and billboard were directed at several-hundred harmful politicians and bureaucrats identified for the first time in print, by name. ...The most destructive of the IRS personnel were also highlighted.

That night, under cover of darkness, those same armed agents of three-and-a-half years earlier attacked me outside my writing offices. Midst their screaming obscenities, an agent threw a stack of my publications at me — publications they had removed that morning from the newsstands. "How is Neo-Tech going to help you now?" he shouted.

In blatant violation of the First Amendment, free press, and free expression, they then shackled my hands behind my back and jailed me because of my publications and large billboard placed in front of their offices that morning. During the entire two-hour assault, shackling, and jailing, not one IRS agent mentioned taxes as a reason for my arrest. For, all their harmful acts over the past six-and-a-half years, including today's trial, had nothing to do with taxes. Instead, their destructive acts had everything to do with violating the Constitution and the First Amendment protecting free press and free expression.

### Building for the Future: 1990-1993

Today, I confront those who in 1986 destroyed my work, pillaged my home and offices, seized our medical research funds, hospitalized my editor, threatened my family, and then in 1990 jailed me because of my writings. Today, I am here to help cure that evil — to help cure the disease of irrationality that always seeks to destroy everyone's happiness and well being.

\* \* \*

Now, let us turn to one specific area that will help cure the disease of irrationality: Golden Helmets as reviewed on the next three charts.

This chart demonstrates that my ideas and actions are

---

### Chart 3
## CONCEPT OF EXCESS
## TAX PAYMENTS

(Golden-Helmet Position)
### Excess Taxes are *Always* Voluntarily Paid

- Every genuine job producer *always* pays
  excess taxes voluntarily
- The IRS Code explicitly recognizes that excess
  taxes *must* be paid voluntarily

# versus

(Tax-Rebel Position)
## "Taxes are Voluntary"

- Not recognized by law or the IRS Code

---

not among those who do not pay taxes...or those who call themselves tax rebels. My essence has always been to generate values, jobs, and excess tax payments.

The key word is voluntary: Tax rebels use the word "voluntary" to avoid paying taxes. In contrast, the Golden Helmet uses *voluntary* work and effort to pay far more than the required amount of taxes.

---

### Chart 4

## EXCESS TAX PAYMENTS OF 1983-1985

- Excess tax payments were paid *voluntarily* through a multiplying agent called I & O
- IRS had knowledge of those excess tax payments:
  1. It had all financial records for 1983-1985
  2. It issued 100% tax abatements for 1983-1985
  3. It issued a 1992 tax-refund check to Wallace

---

## Chart 4

Through the Golden Helmet, I & O Publishing voluntarily paid over four times the legal obligation in income taxes for each year from 1983 to 1985.

As early as 1987, the IRS had knowledge of those excess tax payments for the following reasons:

1. The IRS seized all records for 1980-1985. From those records, it could have deduced those excess tax payments, especially with its informant's statements, and, certainly, after I repeatedly sent the IRS letters, information, records, and literature about the Golden Helmet. As testified earlier, I even sent the IRS management a key to my safe-deposit box containing the Golden-Helmet, tax-payment procedures.

2. After destroying I & O Publishing on November 3, 1986, the IRS apparently realized its mistake and took no further action for over three years. Presumably, the IRS would have taken no further action if not provoked into jailing me in 1990 because of my aggressive writings and publications.

3. On April 22, 1991, the IRS issued a 100% abatement on all my alleged taxes, penalties, and interest for 1983-1985:

*Appendix: The Golden Helmet*

## (Below are the IRS Abatements for 1983 to 1985)

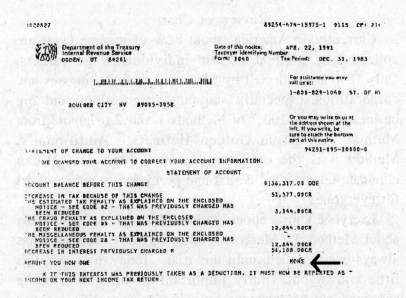

The above three abatements show the balance owed for each year as "NONE".

Since the IRS has all the records for 1983-1985 and all the years before, only the IRS can provide the specific accounting figures for the Golden Helmet. Nevertheless, I will demonstrate the excess tax payments with the next chart.

### Chart 5

First, I will review the three legal methods of income-tax payments.

(Review Chart #5 at this point)

*Appendix: The Golden Helmet*

## Review of Chart 5

Currently, in America, about 82% of income taxes are collected by Method 1 from individual wage earners. Only 18% are collected by Method 2 from businesses and corporations, especially stagnant corporations and big businesses. But, 100% of Methods 1 and 2 *originate* from Method 3 — from Golden Helmets. Additionally, Method 3 is the only tax-payment dynamic that can eliminate our national deficit and permanently reduce taxes for everyone.

Everyone knows about Methods 1 and 2, but few know about Method 3. Moreover, knowledge of Method 3 has always been implicit, until this trial. Today, however, this little-known but vitally important Method 3 is being squeezed out of existence by self-serving politicians and bureaucrats. That is why the economy today, no matter what is done, can never really flourish for all of society. Instead, the economy will continue to fluctuate into ever lower real wages along with reoccurring recessions coupled with periods of inflation, deflation, and declining employment — constantly draining the productive class.

The only major politician who implicitly understood and acted on the Golden Helmet was President John F. Kennedy in 1961. For the first time in history, an American President began implementing the Golden Helmet. Thus, President Kennedy rapidly yanked the economy out of a deep recession, boomed job creation, and dropped unemployment toward new lows. If allowed to continue expanding, that Golden-Helmet dynamic would have collapsed the irrational aspects of politics, bureaucracies, and stagnant big businesses.

Today, the growing armed divisions of government bureaucracies are used to prevent movements toward Golden Helmets. However, now, for the first time, the

48

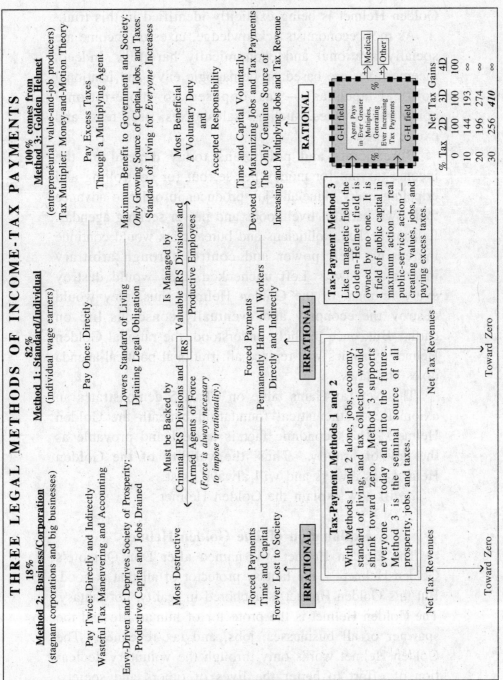

# THREE LEGAL METHODS OF INCOME-TAX PAYMENTS

**Method 2: Business/Corporation**
18%
(stagnant corporations and big businesses)

**Method 1: Standard/Individual**
82%
(individual wage earners)

**Method 3: Golden Helmet**
100% comes from
(entrepreneurial value-and-job producers)
Tax Multiplier: Money-and-Motion Theory

Pay Twice: Directly and Indirectly
Wasteful Tax Maneuvering and Accounting

Pay Once: Directly

Pay Excess Taxes
Through a Multiplying Agent

Envy-Driven and Deprives Society of Prosperity:
Productive Capital and Jobs Drained

Lowers Standard of Living
Draining Legal Obligation

Maximum Benefit to Government and Society:
*Only* Growing Source of Capital, Jobs, and Taxes.
Standard of Living for *Everyone* Increases

Most Beneficial
A Voluntary Duty
and
Accepted Responsibility

Is Managed by
Valuable IRS Divisions and
Productive Employees

Most Destructive

Must be Backed by
Criminal IRS Divisions and
Armed Agents of Force
(*Force is always necessary
to impose irrationality.*)

Time and Capital Voluntarily
Devoted to Maximizing Jobs and Tax Payments
The Only Genuine Source of
Increasing and Multiplying Jobs and Tax Revenue

Forced Payments
Permanently Harm All Workers
Directly and Indirectly

Forced Payments
Time and Capital
Forever Lost to Society

**IRRATIONAL**

**IRRATIONAL**

**RATIONAL**

**Tax-Payment Methods 1 and 2**

With Methods 1 and 2 alone, jobs, economy,
standard of living, and tax collection would
shrink toward zero. Method 3 supports
everyone — today and into the future.
Method 3 is the seminal source of all
prosperity, jobs, and taxes.

**Tax-Payment Method 3**

Like a magnetic field, the
Golden-Helmet field is
owned by no one. It is
a field of public capital in
maximum action — real
public-service action —
creating values, jobs, and
paying excess taxes.

Net Tax Revenues

Net Tax Revenues → Toward Zero

Net Tax Revenues → Toward Zero

G-H field
Agent Pays
in Ever Greater
Multiples,
Generating
Ever Increasing
Tax Payments
G-H field

Medical
Other

Net Tax Gains

| % Tax | 2D | 3D | 4D |
|---|---|---|---|
| 0 | 100 | 100 | 100 |
| 10 | 144 | 193 | ∞ |
| 20 | 196 | 274 | ∞ |
| 30 | 256 | 410 | ∞ |

Chart 5

49

Golden Helmet is being explicitly identified in this trial.

As most economists acknowledge, taxes on income are socially irrational and economically harmful. Indeed, income taxes are based on demagogic envy and irrational political agendas — as opposed to more-rational consumption taxes, such as sales taxes, user fees, and excise taxes.

Bureaucrats and politicians today depend on the income tax not for money per se, but for controlling and crippling every value-and-job producer in order to advance their own harmful livelihoods and power-seeking agendas. Left unchecked, politicians and bureaucrats would continue increasing their power and control through arbitrary income-tax laws. Left unchecked, they would destroy every remnant of the Golden Helmet; thus, they would destroy the economy and eventually conscious life on earth. But, once publicly understood, the rational Golden Helmet dynamics will replace all irrational political-agenda taxes and laws.

The Net-Tax-Gains table on Chart 5 demonstrates an axiomatic, mathematical foundation beneath the Golden Helmet. That economic fact is as real and provable as the law of gravity. Thus, the validity of the Golden Helmet has always and will always exist.

I will now explain the Golden Helmet.

## Explanation of The Golden Helmet

The Golden Helmet was named after Don Quixote's Golden Helmet — the fantasy protector of all that is good. But this Golden Helmet is anchored in reality, not fantasy. The Golden Helmet is the protector of human life and the spawner of all businesses, jobs, and tax revenues. The Golden Helmet works only through the voluntary dedication of effort to better the lives of others and society. Without the Golden Helmet, conscious life would perish.

*The Golden-Helmet Trial*

No one owns the Golden Helmet. Society owns it. No one can exploit the Golden Helmet. ...One harnesses the Golden Helmet by voluntarily serving it — by generating excess values, jobs, and taxes for others and society.

### How Does the Golden Helmet Work?

To serve the Golden Helmet 100% is to harness every effort, every asset, into the most efficient generation of values and jobs for society. In serving the Golden Helmet as a monk, nothing is taken for one's self. At 100% service, one collects no income or financial gains, thus, acquires no personal wealth or material gains from the Golden Helmet. But one does gain great productive efficacy, excitement, and happiness.

### A 100% Service Environment

If a scientist volunteers to do research at a South-Pole experimental station, his life during that period is in a 100% service environment. Thus, all his expenses, including all living expenses, are paid so he can perform those services. None of those expenses are income or accrue to his material benefit. Thus, he is not liable for taxes. If that scientist draws a paycheck, however, he must pay income taxes on that paycheck. Likewise, a Red-Cross volunteer in Bosnia has all expenses paid. He or she has no tax liability while in that service environment. Even the merchant seaman has all his job and living expenses paid in his 100% service environment aboard ship. He has tax liability only for his paycheck. If he took no paycheck, he would have no tax liability or filing requirements. ...Those examples involved total service environments, as did my situation in 1983 to 1985 during which no paychecks were drawn. Thus, no

51

material gains or taxable incomes accrued.

Now, let me give a specific example how the Golden Helmet works in business: Ray Kroc built McDonald's into the world's largest restaurant chain. Yet, for many years, while building a billion-dollar business, he took little income. Covering only his most basic needs, Ray Kroc lived almost monk-like in his cramped Chicago office. He was in the Golden Helmet nearly 100% during those years. He paid little if any personal income taxes through Method 1. But, his Golden Helmet paid many millions in taxes through Method 3. As a result, today, billions in taxes are being paid each year by Methods 1 and 2 because **one man** in the Golden Helmet paid excess taxes by Method 3 for so many years.

Mr. Kroc could have chosen to stop his voluntary service to the Golden Helmet at any time — for example, after a year with a dozen or so hamburger stands. He could have made a nice living for himself, providing a few static jobs while paying a few thousand dollars a year in taxes by Methods 1 and 2. However, he did not do that. Instead, Ray Kroc used the Golden-Helmet dynamics to grow McDonald's into an international titan, paying billions of dollars in taxes. More important, Kroc generated hundreds of thousands of jobs and significantly raised America's standard of living through tax-payment Method 3. After those many years of monk-like service to the Golden Helmet, Mr. Kroc finally took a portion for personal gain and shifted that part of his tax payments to Method 1 when his company went public through a stock offering.

In contrast to Ray Kroc, many of today's big-business executives live lavishly by draining corporations that were originally built by great Golden-Helmet entrepreneurs like Andrew Carnegie, Henry Ford, Harvey Firestone, Thomas

Edison. Many modern-day, big-business executives draw tremendous salaries and pay considerable personal taxes through Methods 1 and 2. Without Golden-Helmet dedication, those once great companies eventually shrink in value, size, and jobs. Instead of expanding and generating new jobs and taxes, such big-business executives downsize their value-and-job production, eventually reducing tax revenues by billions of dollars. ...In contrast, Golden Helmets continually expand not only societal values and productive jobs, but actual tax revenues.

*The only real value any human being has to give society is his or her rational thought, time, and effort. No one can give more.* Through the Golden Helmet, that gift can be multiplied into highly leveraged, tangible values that greatly benefit everyone. At any time, that contributing individual can withdraw his or her maximum-value production to diminish or end the Golden Helmet. At that point, the newly enriched individual must directly support society by paying taxes through Methods 1 and 2.

Like Ray Kroc's early years, with my nearly 100% service to the Golden Helmet during the years 1983-1985, I never acquired taxable earnings. Thus, no filings or payments were required for those years.

Essentially all money was in a non-owned, Golden-Helmet public field that always flowed back into value-and-job expansion...moving toward a thousand new jobs by 1990, all while paying excess taxes at a 4.1 ratio as shown in chart 5.

### The Meaning of Golden Helmets

Let me try to convey emotionally what Golden Helmets mean: Would you bring a child into this world if political agendas mandated that you abuse, cripple, and eventually kill your precious child? Would you abide such

53

political policies just to provide harmful livelihoods and ego power to a few professional value destroyers infesting our society? And, if you did have a child, would not you do everything to protect that child from such politically mandated crippling or destruction of that child's potential? ...To society, the Golden Helmet is just as precious and vulnerable as that child. To fulfill society's beneficent potential, we must protect every Golden Helmet as we would protect a precious, innocent child.

The Golden-Helmet dynamic is valid, proven, and much bigger than me or any group of people. The explicit Golden-Helmet concept is now entering the government's own institutions, courts, and politics. ...Golden Helmets will save our country, our livelihoods, our children.

### Rebuking Destructive Irrationality

Purposely crippling or destroying productive Golden Helmets is unbearably irrational. I could never personally partake in something so evil, no matter what political agendas dictated. Legal defiance of such irrationality was the entire purpose of my planned confrontation with the IRS in the civil courts. My purpose was to work legally within the system to eliminate those destructive political agendas designed to cripple or destroy Golden Helmets.

I won't deny the prosecutor's claims about filing requirements. But, that does not mean I am guilty. I had no income that required filing. Moreover, I am serving everyone and society by standing up to this insane destruction of values and jobs — evil destruction falsely justified to support the bogus livelihoods of a few selfish parasitical elites and their legions of professional value destroyers. My responsibility is to face such irrationality head on. ...If I lived in Germany fifty-five years ago, I would be that person who took my Jewish neighbors and hid them in my attic, regardless of what political policies dictated. I will always rebuke such destructive irrationality. I have no other way to think or live.

## Summary

I was the first to explicitly identify the Golden Helmet. And, in court, I was the first to demand an oath to fully integrated honesty rather then the traditional oath to manipulative truth. Yet, while always striving for honesty, I do not present myself as infallibly honest. I do not think anyone can. I am fallible and vulnerable as everyone else. Still, honesty is my guiding ideal. And, for me, as with everyone, honesty requires constant discipline and effort in every area of life.

That always difficult striving toward integrated honesty first resulted in my turning away from my family's traditions of law, politics, religion, and medicine. Instead, I paid my own way in pursuing the sciences. Eventually, I sought a goal beyond my career in chemistry. That, in turn, shaped my first published book into much deeper, comprehensive understandings of rationality versus irrationality.

Such understandings led me to discover my goal in life: to cure the disease of irrationality. That goal, in turn, led me to the Golden Helmet. Once discovered, the Golden Helmet became my responsibility to protect and nurture into explicit, worldwide fruition. Through the Golden Helmet, I could publicly express the differences between subjective law and objective law. Through the Golden Helmet, I discovered the route to cure irrationality worldwide.

Every day lost toward curing the disease of irrationality, thousands die unnecessarily while millions more suffer. I feel that pressure and responsibility

55

immensely, constantly. I must not, will not stop. I must put my every moment, every effort into curing mankind's worst plague — irrationality.

[End of Frank R. Wallace's Testimony]

### No Cross-Examination

Most unexpectedly, the prosecution declined to cross-examine Dr. Wallace. The prosecution never challenged the Golden Helmet. Thus, they ceded to everything revealed in the Golden-Helmet testimony. ...A cross-examination would have directly underscored to the jury the validity of the Golden Helmet and the innocence of Frank R. Wallace.

* * *

### Wallace's Closing Argument
### PART I

In the past two days, numerous witnesses for the government have testified. I would like to review some of their testimony. The IRS called a Mrs. Hollowell. She testified that there was no tax return for Frank R. Wallace for the years 1983, 1984, and 1985. That is correct. As I have stated, I did not have sufficient income in those years to file a tax return.

A Mr. Marchbanks who owned Park Roofing testified that his company put a new roof on the office home in Boulder City. Mr. Rhodes, a neighbor of mine, testified that he added a room and basement for meetings and storage. Mr. Rhodes testified he knew me for twenty years and that I spent most of my time in this same office home. Mr. Rhodes testified that my office home was an extremely active business place. He described my office home as very modest. He further testified that I do not live in any way luxuriously. Indeed, that structure was not a home, but an office in which I lived.

56

The witness from Weyerhauser Mortgage testified, and, I agree, that I & O Publishing Company paid the mortgage payments. After all, this office home was being used almost exclusively for I & O Publishing, in which I worked almost 16 hours a day, every day — working to generate values, jobs, and Golden-Helmet taxes for others and society.

The IRS tried to mislead you into thinking I had income by misapplying legitimate business expenses. The IRS summary witness, Mr. Carl Uhlott, for example, tried to show Weyerhauser-Mortgage and Park-Roofing payments as my personal income even though the office home was used almost exclusively for business purposes. Thus, I & O Publishing paid the Weyerhauser Mortgage payments and Park Roofing. Note that no such payments went in or out of my modest personal account.

A representative of the Boulder Dam Credit Union testified that I made $5000 per month. But, after questioning, she clarified that the application showed a $5000 draw, not salary. In other words, I could withdraw from the company up to $5000 a month for expenses to run my writing projects, my research projects, and the Golden-Helmet production of values and jobs. Moreover, I lived frugally and never needed to personally draw that money.

Again, the IRS summary witness, Mr. Carl Uhlott, uses figures to distort facts in making the E. F. Hutton checks appear as my personal income. I will explain later the purpose of checks for cash, but it definitely was not for personal use.

I had no personal income, as I chose not to withdraw money from the Golden Helmet. You will see all bank accounts and brokerage accounts were owned by I & O

57

Publishing Company. None were owned by me. Those funds were for I & O Publishing Company, not for me personally.

The IRS used several witnesses to describe the same transactions several times. Why? To give the illusion of many transactions. Count the number of actual transactions — you will see how few transactions are really presented. Also, you will note that a lot of evidence orally presented by the IRS was not available as evidence for you to see.

Again, the summary witness Mr. Uhlott, testified that he did not attribute any income or tax figures to I & O Publishing Company. Instead, Mr. Uhlott improperly attributed that income to me personally.[1] Such accounting is not only bizarre, it is plain wrong. All the records are in the name of I & O Publishing Company As you can see from the evidence, I had little or no personal income and thus was not required to file a tax return. And, as shown in Charts #3 and #5, I never drew enough money from I & O Publishing Company to qualify for filing or paying income taxes.

Remember, the IRS witness, Uhlott, is paid to arrange facts and figures to justify the IRS's mistakes and improper actions. Please look carefully at the actual figures Mr. Uhlott provided to you. You will see that I had no income. The income the IRS alleged I earned all belonged to I & O Publishing and its Golden Helmet.

---

[1] In the first trial, the IRS summary witness used the *same* financial figures to demonstrate the exact opposite — how all earned income was that of I & O Publishing Company, *not* my personal income. Now, to win the second trial, the IRS summary witness took the identical financial figures and made a 180° turn in interpretation to make all income appear to be that of Frank R. Wallace. ...Nothing better underscores the need for the honesty oath rather than the truth oath to prevent such unprincipled manipulation of facts and figures to fit self-serving agendas without regard to honesty, objective law, or justice.

I am not an accountant, but it is obvious that the IRS is selecting figures to build illusions that I am guilty of crimes when the fact is the opposite: The IRS in this case is guilty of violent, objective crimes against my editor, I & O Publishing, and its Golden Helmet — guilty of unprovoked bodily assault and injury, unrepentant criminal pillaging, and intentional value-and-job destruction.

## PART II

The prosecutor has no case. He dared not cross-examine the Golden-Helmet testimony. He could not show one instance where I was living a lifestyle requiring my filing and paying a personal income tax.

The prosecutor showed some cash transactions. That cash was used for pushing the Golden Helmet into ever more efficient value-and-job production. Moreover, the portion of cash invested in gold and silver assets prudently hedged our research funds from the severe inflation of the early 80s.

Those inflation-protected research funds were being accumulated for the biomedical RIBI research project. Initiating this research would cost $500,000 as revealed on the 1986 Neo-Tech World-Summit tape that the judge prevented the jury from hearing. Cash was also used in bank transfers for our international operations. Indeed, considerable cash was used to buy live postage for the large-volume mailings involved in driving I & O toward that thousand-job international publishing business planned in four years hence. Those facts were likewise revealed on the 1986 World-Summit tape that the judge suppressed.

...That tremendous expansion of values, jobs, and tax revenues was ended by the 1986 armed IRS attacks and seizures.

Golden-Helmet Overture
The Victory

## Appendix: *The Golden Helmet*

What about that list of registered trade names the prosecutor presented to create more illusions of guilt? For a quarter century, I have been an author and writer. Those legal names were properly used as pen names for our various literature projects. Those names had nothing to do with financial transactions as the prosecution disingenuously asserted without a single supporting fact.

For two days, the prosecutor used a parade of fragmented facts, such as a roof being put on my writing and business offices so that water would not leak on my work. Or, the company providing a new car when my 1979 economy-sized Datsun had been run into the ground with over 120,000 miles, driving our publications to and from printers and mailers in California. And, finally, to conjure up a case, the prosecutor had to manipulate the testimony of a paid informant.

Indeed, the prosecutor could present no evidence that I live other than a monk or have any interest in material gain or leisure. The prosecutor could present no evidence that even on approaching retirement years, I ever indulged in a single personal luxury. Where was my first-class vacation to Hawaii? Or any vacation to anywhere? It never happened. Where was my big custom home? It never happened. Where was my boat? It never happened. Where was my luxurious Jaguar? It never happened. Where was my membership to an elite country club? It never happened. ...I believe in and try to live by Henry Thoreau's philosophy about life: Simplify, Simplify, Simplify.

I do not even own a VCR or have a hobby. The prosecutor could not show a single luxury in my life. Why? Because I did not acquire income or material assets by my own voluntary choice. Instead of acquiring financial gains, I focused my concentration, time, and efforts toward achieving my goal of curing the disease of

60

irrationality. By what means? By building the Golden Helmet, creating values and jobs for others, and then paying taxes at four times the non-Golden-Helmet rate.

\* \* \*

Will you, the jury of my peers, support the self-serving politicians and armed bureaucrats who are draining everyone in creating a stagnant America? Or will you support a vibrant America — a rising standard of living and lower taxes for everyone? ...Will you back the irrationality of economically and socially destructive political agendas? Or will you back the rationality of advancing honest businesses toward creating real jobs and endless wealth in building a great America?

## PART III

[Dr. Wallace could not deliver the following Part III of his closing argument because the judge had banished from the trial Chart #6 shown below. Despite the fact that the prosecution had no objection to Chart #6 for trial use, the judge prohibited not only that chart but the ideas that chart embodied. For, those ideas would have undermined the unstipulated jury instruction the judge was planning to spring on the jury. That improper instruction commanded the jury to convict Wallace regardless of the evidence.]

---

### Chart 6

### *The Jury's Duty is to Deliver Justice*
by
**Protecting the Innocent Value Producer**
and
**Condemning the Guilty Value Destroyer**

---

*Appendix: The Golden Helmet*

## Law of Nature

The Golden Helmet is not a hypothesis or even a theory — it is a law of nature. The Golden Helmet has always been and will always be the seminal source of prosperity and happiness for mankind.

Throughout history, the discovery of every fundamental law of nature upsets the irrational elements of society. For, such irrational elements survive through parasitical agendas that prevent the advancement of knowledge and prosperity. Thus, the discoverers of those laws were often branded as radicals who violated tradition. Yet, such traditions were usually nothing more than political-agenda laws — false laws designed to support the vested interests of the parasitical-elite class. ...Historic prime movers like Archimedes, Socrates, Jesus, and Galileo were prosecuted, jailed, even killed by the parasitical-elite class and its armed bureaucrats.

The prosecutor tried to portray me as a radical who put himself above the law. In the sense of me being above the law, he is completely wrong. No one respects and upholds objective law more than I. Indeed, daily, I risk my life and freedom to uphold objective law by publicly identifying those in government who break it. For, objective law is the essence of civilization and the route to curing the disease of irrationality — the route to eternal peace and prosperity.

But in the sense of me being radical, he is right. I am uncompromising in my thinking and actions when it comes to protecting individuals, businesses, and society against irrational harm. And, when a new way is discovered that tremendously benefits society and every American, I rise to action. I act uncompromisingly and meet my responsibility. I focus all my thoughts and efforts on delivering that new benefit to society. ...I am dedicated to the Golden Helmet because its benefits to society, our government, and every individual are so clear, profound, and just.

## The Law

This trial is not about taxes. It is about irrationally draining wealth and life from our country and economy. This trial is about camouflaged dishonesty that has spread throughout our government, our courts, our educational system, our media, our society. As the jury, your responsibility is not to uphold self-serving parasites, their harmful agendas, their armed enforcers. Your responsibility is to protect the innocent value producer and condemn the guilty value destroyer. Your responsibility is to uphold objective law and justice.

## Achieving the Possible Dream
### Beating the Beatable Foe — Irrationality

You know who is innocent, who is guilty. Stand firm. Do not compromise. Today, you can play a heroic role in bringing honesty and prosperity to America. My testimony has shown that this is a trial between two worlds: the irrational, subjective-law world of harmful political agendas versus the rational, objective-law world of Golden Helmets. Indeed, Golden Helmets will bring great benefits to everyone — even to the prosecutor, to the IRS, and to this court. Do not yield to pressures from this courtroom. Let no one sway you from your judgment. Your verdict can help end this irrational assault on our economy and society to eternally benefit everyone and society.

You, the jury, have one principle and duty: Protect the innocent value producer; condemn the guilty value destroyer.

63

Golden-Helmet Overture

The Victory

# Chapter 4

# After the
# Golden-Helmet Trial

> Below is a letter Frank R. Wallace sent to the
> 28-year-old lawyer who helped prosecute the
> Golden-Helmet trial.
> (Edited for article format and clarity.)

Dear Mr. Bullard:

Last week, you helped prosecute the Golden-Helmet trial. Any young attorney familiar with this case who is not yet locked into the vested interests of today's legal profession has an opportunity for an historic, precedent-setting career. That opportunity arises from two concepts revealed in the Golden-Helmet trial. Those two concepts are fully integrated honesty and objective law.

Those concepts will become as influential to law as the thirteenth-century Magna Carta concept was to overturning the vested interests in the tyrannical, divine-rights view...and as enlightening to society as the fifteenth-century heliocentric concept was to overturning the vested interests in the flat-earth, geocentric view.

Now, late in the twentieth century, the consistent, provable concepts rising from the Golden-Helmet trial will overturn the arbitrary, vested interests in the political-agenda/ego-"justice" views. That overturn will come from three directions: (1) integrated honesty overturning manipulated truths, (2) objective law overturning subjective laws, (3) the rationality of objective justice overturning the irrationality of ego "justice".

64

Later, when you receive literature about the Golden Helmet, read it carefully with an integrating mind. Understand conceptually what is being sown worldwide. Perceive what is subtly entering today's society and government. Perceive that newly forming wedge approaching business and government. Move to the rational side of that wedge. Through pursuing objective law, you can help lead our country toward rationality — toward permanent prosperity and happiness. You can help bring forth a rational, just society. You can help heal the wounds inflicted by today's political-agenda laws and ego "justice".

* * *

Think how history will view your rebuttal arguments used to win the prosecution's case. Indeed, character assassination was your dishonorable recourse:[1]

1. **Quoting my poker book on bluffing to present such deception as my *personal* character**: Out-of-context paraphrasing of literature is the easiest, most effective way to misrepresent an author. Yet, on reading my poker book, anyone can see the $180^0$ misrepresentation by the prosecution. That book identifies how integrated honesty is the essence of prosperity for conscious life. Likewise, that book identifies the inescapable harm that lying and deception *always* inflict on its perpetrator whenever done *beyond* the game of poker.

---

[1]The following is a handwritten note from Mrs. T.S., a courtroom observer: "During Wallace's Golden-Helmet testimony, his character, his honesty, his dedication to values came across with such conviction and benevolence, the prosecution knew it had to break that image to win its case. Thus, the prosecution used its entire closing argument not to outline the facts but to falsely attack Wallace's character. By saving its innuendos for the closing argument, the prosecution unethically prevented rebuttal. ...It appeared the prosecution had no way to convict except through dishonesty."

The poker book is a metaphor: It uses the nonreality of a game in which the mutually agreed-upon rules and universally known essence is the bluff. In that unreal-world game context, bluffing *is not* dishonest. By contrast, in the real-world context, outside of poker, bluffing and deception *is* dishonest. Such juxtaposition of reality to unreality underscores the virtue of fully integrated honesty for all real-world situations — with *no* exceptions.

Consider the conclusion of my poker book: The fictional "hero", the unbeatable big winner, is always the biggest loser! Why? Wide-scope accounting demonstrates that he has wasted his assets — his hard-earned intelligence, his irreplaceable time, his intense efforts, his integrated thinking, his iron discipline — all wasted in an unproductive, zero-sum game that accomplishes nothing real for him or society. Instead, he could have harnessed those disciplines, assets, and precious time to achieve genuine self-worth by producing growing values for others and society. ...Thus, I forsook poker when I finished writing the book in 1968.

2. **Creating a false impression of me hoarding money, ready to flee the country**: The prosecution along with the court has in its possession several handwritten letters from its paid informant, Ms. K, admitting her dishonesties to me, my family, and others during our relationship. Then, from perjurious statements by Ms. K, the IRS's chief witness, the prosecution crafted a closing argument describing me as sitting atop a floor safe filled with money.

That mendacious argument was used to create false illusions of me hoarding and concealing assets for fleeing the country. Among Ms. K's sworn grand-jury/search-warrant affidavits and her testimony in the first trial, she stated under oath that the floor safe had a three-foot diameter cover and was located directly beneath my desk chair. She further testified that I always sat atop those assets — assets available for quickly fleeing the country if the IRS came after me.

Now consider the facts: That safe cover was six inches, not three feet, in diameter. The safe was located in a corner of a writing office over which a bookcase was located. The geometry of a room corner with its two walls made it physically impossible to locate a chair over that safe, much less a desk. Mr. Goodrich and many other IRS agents knew those facts. Additionally, Ms. K knew those seized assets were not personal funds but were RIBI research funds. Indeed, when she worked with me, one of her main responsibilities was to manage the funds, records, business, and correspondence of the 2200 RIBI registrants. Additionally, she kept the books for I & O Publishing from 1983 to 1985...and did the accounting for those research funds.

Opposite to her testimony, Ms. K knew I had no intentions to leave this country. To the contrary, my entire objective was to stand and face all adversaries, as demonstrated by these trials. Moreover, she was well acquainted with my plans of using the Golden Helmet to confront the IRS through civil actions and the courts.

Ms. K intimately knew of my concerns about our biomedical research projects involving human cloning for nonrejectable organs and consciousness preservation for the terminally ill. I became increasingly concerned about destructive interference from regulatory bureaucracies, especially the murderous FDA. Thus, I prepared to move not me and my publishing company, but to move that specific medical research project and its funding abroad.

Ms. K even participated in the abandoning of that research project in the United States. She knew we planned to do the physical research abroad, scheduled to begin in 1988, pending accumulation of the required $500,000 start-up capital. In fact, Ms. K met in Nevada with the Swiss scientist who was already developing the 144-point, Neo-Tech mind matrix — the first step in consciousness transfer. She then traveled abroad to make preliminary arrangements for that research project. ...After our relationship failed, Ms. K spun yarns in order to evoke the seizure of those RIBI research funds that she had managed. Thus, she could rake a 10% informant's fee from the $250,000 in seized funds.

3. **Dishonestly denying the Golden Helmet**: Finally, the prosecution's closing argument made an emphatic point that Ms. K, during the three years of working with me, never knew of the Golden Helmet. Again, Ms. K fully knew about the Golden-Helmet tax payments from the beginning. In fact, she described exactly how those tax payments were made in her own sworn statements in the 1986 search-warrant affidavits and in her testimony at the first trial. She described how excess taxes were paid by the I & O multiplying agent through third parties. Now, granted, she may not have known the actual name "Golden Helmet". The metaphorical Golden-Helmet name evolved after our personal relationship ended in 1984 and our business relationship ended in late 1985. But, she knew everything about those tax payments done under wide-scope accounting, which was and still is the generic term for the Golden Helmet.

\* \* \*

The prosecution's rebuttal arguments were not rebuttals at all. They neither addressed nor rebutted anything in my testimony or closing statement. Indeed, the prosecution never even cross-examined my testimony. Instead, it used that rebuttal for dishonest character assassination by conjuring up false "new evidence", jury deceptions, and illusions opposite to the facts.

The prosecution simply conjured up those calumnies because it needed them to win. And the judge made no objection to this false "new evidence" being improperly injected into a closing argument. By injecting those dishonesties into the final rebuttal, both you and the judge knew I had no opportunity to rebut or refute those falsehoods. ...Such were the dishonesties you and the judge used to win.

Mr. Bullard, objective justice is not a poker game of bluff and deception. Do you want to consume your one-and-only life "winning" dishonestly? Think about the longer-range consequences. By nature, dishonest victories are always temporary and hollow. More important, dishonest victories are not victories at all. They are Pyrrhic and they always return to defeat the "victor".

Being young, you are, I am sure, still able to feel qualms about winning dishonestly. If you can still emotionally feel the difference between right and wrong, then you have not yet become an automaton dependent on enforcing political-agenda laws through ego "justice". With honesty alive in your conscience and new knowledge growing in your mind, you can lead the legal profession to rationality and objective law. You have an opportunity to heroically lead the legal profession away from ego "justice" and into objective law.

Being young, you probably do not yet know the end result of a career dependent on ego "justice". Look at Judge George. He is lost and can no longer interact honestly with reality. The dishonest route in law

*Appendix: The Golden Helmet*

ultimately means living off subjective political-agenda laws. Self-esteem then becomes dependent on ego "justice". The legitimate, crucial activities of upholding and enforcing objective law are forgotten. The occasional enforcement of objective laws becomes merely a prop for camouflaging and rationalizing the immoral enforcement of subjective laws evolved from self-serving political agendas backed by armed bureaucrats.

The Neo-Tech literature identifies the source of such dishonesty in the courts as ego "justice". The centerfold of the *Zon-2000* publication sent to you earlier described ego "justice". That description was largely theoretical. But the judge in this case transformed ego-"justice" theory into documented reality. Throughout the Golden-Helmet trial, Judge Lloyd D. George provided an abundance of factual, empirical information illustrating ego "justice". Indeed, Judge George gave history a priceless gift — a concretized, full-blown example of ego "justice" in action.

Throughout the trial, the judge consistently acted to fill a single agenda — control the trial and jury to convict the defendant. He had to convict the person who directly challenged his ego — an ego whose survival is dependent on subjective law. He had to squelch any threat that could expose his fraud.

To win a conviction, Judge George relied on improper judicial abuses to control the jury. Additionally, he emphasized the derogatory "hundreds-of-years" quote both times he had to deal with the honesty oath. For, the honesty oath was the ego-bruising issue that defeated the judge in the first trial. Thus, he biased the jury against my testimony by showing his contempt for the honesty oath. Such behavior from a federal judge reflects the end result of a career based on self-indulgent ego "justice". ...Reality always levies final justice as that judge shrinks

70

backwards in life — incapable of experiencing genuine self-esteem or happiness.

From start to finish of this retrial, Judge George inappropriately ingratiated himself to the jury. His hypocritically saccharine, highly personal banter with jury members — improper behavior for any judge — is documented in the voir dire and trial transcripts. And what about the intimidations Judge George sent back to the jury after that sidebar drama concerning a jury member asking the bailiff for information about the Golden Helmet?

To cap his improper behavior, the judge had to assure direct control over the jury's verdict. How did he assure that direct control? By abusing his fair-comment privilege *after* both sides had rested. He bootlegged in his own unstipulated, private jury instruction demanding a conviction. That bootlegged instruction was preplanned to nullify the crucial "reasonable doubt" and "willfulness" instructions to which we all stipulated.

Judge George's gratuitous, ego-"justice" instruction implied that I should be found guilty regardless of the trial evidence and the stipulated jury instructions. He implied without an iota of evidence that I was a renegade who took the law into my own hands rather than working through politics or Congress. With his private instruction dishonestly introduced as "new evidence", about which no rebuttal or challenge was allowed, Judge George nullified the factual trial evidence that proved the exact *opposite*: It was I, not George, who worked within legal boundaries. It was I, not George, who respected and upheld objective law. It was I, not George, who was innocent.

As you know, during the trial, I offered the chief prosecutor, J. Gregory Damm, to waive rights if the judge would leave his bench and sit at the prosecution table as a member of its team. Then, the trial would at least have the merit of being honest in regards to the judge and how the jury perceived him. ...The judge's behavior toward the jury was brazenly self-serving. He had to save his ego. He had to save face by orchestrating an unjust conviction.

While the way is always open and a helping hand is always extended, Judge George is perhaps too calcified — too deeply invested in his ego agendas to understand the approaching sea change to rationality and objective law. Perhaps, he can never share in the coming triumph of fully integrated honesty. Yet, if he pondered the final statement of an American judge in the 1949 Nuremberg trial of Nazi judges, George might finally understand the profound difference between objective justice and ego "justice": A German judge pleaded he had no idea of the consequences that would ultimately evolve from ego "justice". The American judge replied by telling him that using political-agenda "law" to *purposely* condemn even just one innocent person was enough to condemn any judge for life. ...Will George end like Tolstoy's Ivan Ilych?

But, you, Mr. Bullard, can certainly be an important part of the coming triumph. And, if they choose to think conceptually in principles — in a widely integrated manner rather than a narrow concrete-bound manner — prosecutor Damm, even IRS agent Goodrich, could come to understand this newly evolving age of rationality. Then, they too could move into the world of fully integrated honesty to share the triumph and rewards.

Someday, perhaps you, Mr. Damm, Mr. Goodrich, even Judge George will work with us. Together we can uphold objective law to eliminate the armed divisions among the bureaucracies. We can then advance the Golden Helmet as the route to a genuinely prosperous, happy society.

# Chapter 5

# The Appeal — The Future

On June 18, 1993, the Solicitor General of the United States, Drew S. Days III, in a last-minute maneuver submitted a typo-ridden continuance motion to the United States Supreme Court to stop the use of Wallace's honesty oath. That motion was granted by Supreme-Court Justice Sandra Day O'Connor. Indeed, many people in government already know that fully integrated honesty will reveal that subjective laws are nothing more than manipulative devices serving harmful political and ego agendas.

### The Honesty Oath is now the Law of the Land

The first trial in February 1991 legally established the Honesty Oath in the United States judicial system. The appeal and the courageous opinion written by Appellate Judge Betty B. Fletcher made the honesty oath the law of the land for all to henceforth use.[1] The honesty oath provides the foothold needed to eradicate manipulated truths and false witnesses from courtrooms.

The retrial in August 1993 prepared the way toward establishing rationality and objective law as the standard for law. The second appeal provides the foothold needed to hoist the Neo-Tech/Golden-Helmet dynamic into public view. That dynamic will eventually eliminate subjective political-agenda laws, arbitrary ego "justice", and dishonest torts throughout the legal systems of this world.

---

[1]U.S. vs. Wallace, 989, F.2d, 1015 (9th Cir. 1993).

73

*Appendix: The Golden Helmet*

Why the Honesty Oath?

Why an oath to fully integrated honesty rather than to truth? Who knows what truth is? No one knows. Truth is merely a static assertion of observations or "facts". Truth for one may not be truth for another. For, truth varies with condition and context. And, an unlimited number of conditions and contexts exist. Thus, the truth oath allows unlimited dishonesties and corruptions.

---

**Truth-Oath Testimony**

Noncontextual Facts, Unintegrated Evidence,
Dishonest

I saw John O'Grady premeditate and then purposely kill a man. Conclusion: John O'Grady is a murderer. He should be jailed.

*True facts. Incomplete. Out of context.*

*Unjust conclusion.*

**Honesty-Oath Testimony**

Contextual Facts, Fully Integrated Evidence,
Honest

I saw John O'Grady save a platoon of men in 1944 during the Battle of the Bulge at Bastogne, Belgium. Trapped beneath a snow-covered ledge by a Nazi machine-gunner, John premeditated a plan. He then scaled an icy cliff. Wounded twice, John shot and killed the machine-gunner. He saved the twenty men in his platoon. Conclusion: John O'Grady is a hero. He should be honored.

*Honest facts. Complete. In context.*

*Just conclusion.*

---

## The Appeal — The Future

Without an anchor to honesty, anyone can manipulate truth and facts into harmful agendas. Politicians who make self-serving laws and lawyers who profit from those harmful laws live by manipulating truth. They talk about truth all the time. But, they seldom, if ever, talk about honesty. For, unlike truth, everyone knows the exact meaning of honesty. Honesty is a process that has the same clear, fixed meaning for everyone. Honesty cannot be manipulated. One is either honest or not. Therefore, a shield of silence about honesty exists among politicians and lawyers. Indeed, they fear and avoid fully integrated honesty.[1]

This retrial was not about taxes. It was about camouflaged irrationality. It was about armed bureaucracies destroying Golden Helmets. It was about draining wealth and life from society and the populace to provide a few parasitical elites and their supporters with harmful livelihoods, false egos, and illicit power. It was about camouflaged dishonesty that has spread throughout our government, educational system, courts, and society.

Yet, from this retrial arose the dynamics to vanish Plato's 2300-year-old, parasitical-elite class. Indeed, this retrial established the groundwork for eliminating subjective law and ego "justice", starting with a motion to prohibit subjective courtroom bias — a motion summarily denied by Judge Lloyd D. George.

---

[1]Dr. Wallace presented his own case in both trials. But, Wallace's supporters tried to hire a lawyer for the sole purpose of cross-examining and impeaching the prosecution's paid informant. Four lawyers, in turn, accepted and then withdrew when they discovered the honesty principle underlying the Golden-Helmet trial. ...Those lawyers feared for their own ego-"justice"-dependent careers if they helped a defendant combat ego "justice".

75

The Victory

*Appendix: The Golden Helmet*

## A Motion to Prohibit Subjective, Courtroom Biases

> The following motion was filed with the U.S. District Court on June 28, 1993. Below are various descriptive, "the-point" portions of its arguments. The technical, "a-point" portions are not included, but are available from the court files.

This motion proposes introductory jury instructions by the judge to assure a trial free of subjective, courtroom bias.

Comes now Frank R. Wallace with a motion to the court for preliminary jury instructions relating to courtroom bias. Such instructions shall be in the form presently provided in the *Manual of Model Criminal Jury Instructions for the Ninth Circuit* under "What is admissible evidence? What is inadmissible evidence?" The following activities by the United States Government shall not be considered as evidence, but shall constitute inadmissible evidence:

1. Superior acting or contemptuous conduct toward the defendant by the presiding United States district-court judge.

2. Superior acting or contemptuous conduct by any member of the judicial staff including bailiffs, clerks, or anyone assisting the court in the conduct of the trial.

3. *The court, its personnel, and its staff shall not act to prejudice the defendant's presumption of innocence by their conduct or remarks.*

4. The jury shall be cautioned that the accouterments of power and prestige of the United States are subjective and not admissible evidence. Thus, those accouterments should not weigh to the advantage of the prosecution or to the detriment of the defendant.

5. Any witness called by the prosecution shall not

76

be vested with greater credibility than any witness called by the defendant. The jury's responsibility is to judge the credibility and value of all testimonies and all witnesses as they objectively relate to the trial.

The above jury instructions should be given by the judge prior to the trial.

### Arguments in Support of this Motion

When the government and its courts inflict subjective biases on its citizens, those citizens and society itself are increasingly subject to constitutional violations, human-rights abuses, and economic harms. Thus, the court has a constitutional duty, a legal obligation, and a social responsibility to prohibit all applications of subjective bias.

This motion asks the court to prohibit the infliction of subjective biases on the defendant, before and during the trial. For, the infliction of such biases directly violates the defendant's Fifth-Amendment rights. Indeed, all due-process, constitutional, and human rights eventually vanish under subjective courtroom biases, as clearly observable in the evolvement of totalitarian governments.

Tradition or habit that has been practiced even for "hundreds of years" offers no argument against this motion. For, tradition or "the test of time" is no gauge of value or validity. Ten centuries ago, status-quo tradition or biases led the Western World into a dark millennium of stagnation and human misery. The subsequent Renaissance, the American Constitution, and the Industrial Revolution emerged only after discarding the irrationalities of subjective biases and overthrowing many force-backed, political/religious-agenda laws.

That discarding of subjective biases unleashed a flood of new knowledge and life-enhancing values. Stunning advances arose from the honesty, objectivity, and efforts

77

of courageous giants like Leonardo da Vinci, Copernicus, Galileo, Spinoza, Newton, Jefferson, Darwin. Each such hero overturned subjective truths and laws based on biases, traditions, dogma.

Now is the time for the court to end criminal enforcement of self-serving political agendas backed by subjective laws, ego "justice", and armed bureaucracies. Now is the time to establish a new legal foundation based on objective law backed by integrated honesty. Now is the time for courageous judges to usher in the golden age of objective law that brings everlasting peace and prosperity to everyone and society.

## Conclusion

Objective law protects the innocent value producer. Subjective laws and ego "justice" advance the professional value destroyer. Any court sanction of subjective law or bias vanishes justice. Subjective laws and biases arise from political or personal agendas designed to support harmful livelihoods. Thus, the court is asked to meet its legal and moral responsibility by rejecting all subjective laws and biases.[1]

---

The above motion to prohibit subjective biases and ego "justice" in the courtroom was summarily denied by Judge Lloyd D. George on July 14, 1993. The motion was then orally resubmitted on August 2, 1993. Judge George again brusquely denied the motion to eliminate courtroom biases and ego "justice" from his courtroom.

---

[1]Also see Legal Exhibit titled Ego-"Justice" Terminator on page 89.

### ADDENDUM

For an added perspective, the following introduction to an affidavit for Wallace's civil litigations illustrates the corruptions that arise when the government uses paid informants. In this case, the corruptions began with the IRS's violent attacks on I & O Publishing in 1986. Those attacks arose from political-agenda laws, armed bureaucrats, and a government-paid perjurer. From those corruptions came the IRS, its hired prosecutor, and its ego-driven judge. From that medley of fraud came the violent pillaging and imprisonment of an innocent man for his writings and publications that are subverting the parasitical-elite class throughout the world.

Human nature requires being or learning to be a net value producer for others and society. As Socrates identified, human nature requires honesty and objective law for expanding prosperity and happiness. By contrast, parasitical elites must build corrupt ego-"justice" systems to enforce the political agendas needed for their survival. Only by disintegrating the sacred trinity of rationality, honesty, and objective law can they enforce their parasitical agendas. And, unless eliminated, such parasitism eventually destroys its twin hosts — the economy and its value producers.

### Ego "Justice"

Ego "justice" contradicts objective law. Under objective law, the primary responsibility of prosecutors and judges alike is to secure justice — not to win cases per se and especially not to enforce self-serving political agendas that support a criminal-behaving, parasitical-elite class.

In other words, with objective law, the first priority

of prosecutors and judges is to bring forth all and only the contextual facts needed to render justice. In that way, objective law protects the innocent value producer and prosecutes the guilty value destroyer, which is the entire purpose of objective law and justice.

By contrast, with subjective political law and its ego "justice", the first priority is to obtain convictions that protect the political agendas supporting a growing class of parasites throughout the government and the legal profession. Judges and lawyers must becloud honesty while manipulating truth to punish, convict, or eliminate political-agenda threats. Enforcement of political agendas by suppressing objective law is required to support the parasitical-elite class and its ego-"justice" system. Such corruption is demonstrated in every courtroom used to enforce political-agenda laws rather than to uphold objective law.

\* \* \*

This document supports the idea that lifetime appointments be revoked for federal judges who practice ego "justice" or who support political-agenda laws rather than uphold objective law. ...Indeed, the Golden Helmet has already begun the process needed to eliminate ego "justice" from America's courtrooms.

# Chapter 6

# The Golden-Helmet
# Oral Argument

> CA-93-10703/September 12, 1994
>
> U.S. 9th-Circuit Court of Appeals
>
> Oral Argument
> by
> Frank R. Wallace
> before appellate judges
> Robert R. Beezer, Jerome Farris, Linda McLaughlin

Your honors: My *written brief* contains the legal points of this appeal. Those points are based on a-point law: meaning technical points and case law. But, for all a points, one must ask, "What is <u>the</u> point?" The point behind this appeal is singular: ***Objective law must be upheld***.

My written brief cites a number of illegalities by the judge and prosecutor who improperly forced a conviction. That brief identifies those illegalities with citations from the trial transcripts, case law, and affidavits.

My *oral argument* today focuses on the violations of objective law that led to an improper conviction:

The trial testimony under the honesty oath explained how all tax obligations were met in excess by the defendant through the Golden Helmet.

The Golden Helmet recognizes that through excess personal acquisitions, one increasingly loses his or her potential to create, produce, and deliver maximum values

81

to others and society. The trial testimony explains how and why the defendant lived monastically, lived a life of *being* rather than a life of *having*. He lived a life of creating not consuming, personally drawing no taxable income for the years in question. ...The prosecution neither challenged nor cross-examined that testimony. Thus, the prosecution accepted the Golden-Helmet testimony in full.

So, *why was the defendant convicted*? In addition to the trial errors detailed in the written brief, the defendant was blocked from obtaining his own business and accounting records. Such facts and figures would prove that (1) the defendant had no personal tax liability, and (2) more than the required taxes were always paid through the Golden Helmet.

Indeed, without those facts and figures contained in the seized records, the confusion among the jury was obvious: As the transcripts reveal, a mistrial nearly resulted from a juror's aggressive quest to a bailiff for more information about the Golden Helmet on behalf of herself and the other jurors. That quest went unfulfilled, leaving the jurors confused and dependent on an intimidating judge demanding a conviction.

Now, why was the defendant unable to provide the jury with the specific facts and figures from the seized financial records? Because the prosecution withheld from the defendant key records and accounting figures seized by armed IRS agents in 1986 — key documents covering the three years in question.

Just days before the trial in August 1993, the prosecution handed the defendant only a cherry-picked portion of the discovery — only that portion to be used out of context against the defendant. The prosecution withheld all evidence favorable to the defendant — especially the computer accounting records that would have let the defendant prove his testimony with specific facts and figures buried in that discovery.

Those facts and figures were contained in the never returned books, files, and computer disks. The IRS had seized not only 100% of the original disks but 100% of the backup disks. At any time after April, 1990, the prosecution could have easily, simply provided the defendant with a copy of its paid informant's bookkeeping records as well as a copied set of the seized computer disks to fulfill its discovery obligations.

Why did not the prosecution simply provide that discovery as soon as this case became an open-file case in April, 1990? Because, giving the defendant those disks and bookkeeping records with enough time to develop them into evidence would have vanished the prosecution's case.

Despite numerous requests by the defendant dating back to 1990, the prosecution did not allow access to that discovery until just days before the scheduled date of the second trial. The defendant's voluntary accountant promptly went to the IRS evidence room to examine the discovery. Over a period of two days, he inventoried an overwhelming amount of discovery: seized assets, cartons, personal diaries, files, bookkeeping records, and computer disks. Then, in his affidavit, as exhibited in my brief, the accountant estimated that just to print out the seized computer records from pre-1986 Radio-Shack Tandy disks on obsolete printing equipment in the IRS evidence room would require up to 81 days involving up to 2610 documents on 87 disks.

Within that huge accumulation of records, which had

not been seen for 7 to 10 years, lie the data not just to demonstrate but to prove *factually* the Golden-Helmet taxpayments.

Yet, to properly prepare for the trial and present the Golden Helmet, the defendant already needed 16-hour work days right up to the trial date. Thus, the defendant knew that, without a continuance, that massive discovery could not be used. Those few days before trial were urgently needed for basic trial preparation, exhibit preparation, and crucial motions.

Moreover, even if the full discovery had been presented to the defendant in a usable form and work commenced around the clock, time would still have been grossly insufficient to pull together three full years of records and accounting figures in those few remaining days before the trial. Time simply did not exist for converting that multi-year-delayed discovery into trial evidence — evidence that factually proves the defendant's absence of tax liability.

Both the prosecution and the judge were fully aware of that time problem as presented in both the defendant's written and oral motions for a single continuance. Yet, the prosecution declined to stipulate and the judge denied the defendant's fully documented motion justifying that continuance. The judge's denial prevented any chance to utilize the newly availed discovery. ...Thus, the denial of that continuance saved the case for the prosecution by effectively denying discovery to the defendant.

Still, through careful trial preparation and utilizing the honesty oath for the first time in judicial history, the defendant was grateful to present the Golden Helmet, in part at least, in a court trial. Although the presentation was undermined by the denied discovery and a vindictively biased judge as detailed in the written brief and trial transcripts, the defendant exercised restraint. He exercised that restraint in order to avoid any future, out-of-context claim by the judge or prosecutor that the honesty oath was in any way abusively used in its very first courtroom application. That restraint was exercised even though the judge defensively, subjectively, in front of the jury, mocked the honesty oath twice. ...A noncontroversial courtroom experience was important for developing the full legal potential of the honesty oath for the future benefit of society, including the prosecution and the court.

During the trial, the judicial and prosecutorial errors prevented the jurors from learning the contextual facts — the factual proof behind the testimony demonstrating no criminal intent or tax liability. And, most important, the opportunity was denied to *fully* demonstrate in a court of law the meaning, legality, and supreme value of the Golden Helmet to all governments and societies.

Let us deliver our civilization from the arbitrary rule of subjective law — from the rule of political-agenda laws and personal egos that place self-serving bias above justice. Let us build a new civilization based on objective law free from the arbitrary whims of dishonest politicians, destructive bureaucrats, and ego-driven judges. For, a civilization ruled solely by objective law yields eternal peace and prosperity.

\* \* \*

Comments about the Golden-Helmet Argument

Frank R. Wallace's oral argument to the three appellate judges focused on the Golden Helmet through which far more than one's legally required taxes are always paid. The Golden Helmet is not new, has *nothing* to do with

85

tax rebellion, and is the *opposite* of tax avoidance. The Golden Helmet is fully rooted in objective law, profoundly beneficial to all, and practiced in part by people as diverse as Andrew Carnegie, Albert Schweitzer, and Ray Kroc.

Today, the following fact is known: By combining Neo-Tech's continuing court efforts with its expanding penetration of worldwide cyberspace communications, the Golden Helmet will increasingly become understood and accepted by the world's populations. Indeed, by eliminating ego "justice", the Golden Helmet will reshape our political and economic futures to deliver its promise of eternal peace and prosperity.

# Chapter 7

# What is Next?

Requirements for Victory

For the Neo-Tech/Golden-Helmet dynamics to advance in politics, court *processes* are what matter. On receiving an honest and just court decision, the task concludes with a quick, small victory offering little further value. On receiving a dishonest political-agenda or ego-"justice" court decision, the process continues with great strength-building value offering eventual, total victory.

When will the next Neo-Tech/Golden-Helmet court engagement with political agendas and ego "justice" occur? Perhaps this year, next year, in five years. Engagement with whom? Perhaps with Congress, the FDA, the INS...or perhaps with organized religion, the academe, the media, or even the clique of parasitical executives draining stagnant big businesses. The actual harmful agent who engages Neo-Tech makes little difference. For, against the fully integrated honesty of Neo-Tech, all aggressions by harmful agents hasten the demise of their irrational survival systems.

Golden-Helmet Prosperity by 2001 AD?

Brief, erratic contacts with the Civilization of the Universe were made by Moses, Confucius, Socrates, Jesus, Bruno, Galileo, Spinoza, Newton, Brigham Young, Albert Einstein. But, today, a consistent, nonstop journey from Earth to the Civilization of the Universe has begun. It began in 1976 with the publication of the original *Neo-Tech Reference Encyclopedia*.

Avoiding the dishonest distortions of publicity and the media, working through the virtuous dynamics of

87

international business, the seeds of Neo-Tech have been quietly sown around the world in many languages, for many years. Neo-Tech is empowering those who benefit society to various degrees through the Golden Helmet. Neo-Tech is empowering those who produce far more values for society than they consume — from productive laborers and valuable housewives to honest physicists and billionaire entrepreneurs. ...Only genuine value producers hold power in the Civilization of the Universe.

Because Neo-Tech is fully integrated honesty, it largely escapes understanding and notice by today's professional value destroyers who are busily consuming our society and economy. Thus, from beneath their feet, Neo-Tech unexpectedly will burgeon from its seeds planted worldwide. As begun in America during its 1994 elections, that flowering of Neo-Tech will vanish all purposely harmful people. Perhaps as early as 2001 AD or even sooner, Golden Helmets will be flourishing worldwide. Conscious beings will then be free to step into the Civilization of the Universe to enjoy guiltless lives of eternal prosperity and happiness.

The future belongs to fully integrated honesty — to rationality, Neo-Tech, Golden Helmets, and the Civilization of the Universe.

# *The Constitution of the Universe*

### Preamble
The purpose of human life is to live happily.

The function of government is to guarantee those conditions that allow individuals to fulfill their purpose. Those conditions can be guaranteed through a constitution that forbids the use of initiatory force, fraud, or coercion by any person or group against any individual:

\* \* \*

### Article 1
No person, group of persons or government may initiate force, threat of force, or fraud against any individual's self or property.

### Article 2
Force may be morally and legally used only in self-defense against those who violate Article 1.

### Article 3
No exceptions shall exist for Articles 1 and 2.

\* \* \*

The Neo-Tech Constitution rests on six axioms:
1. Values exist only relative to life.
2. Whatever benefits a living organism is a value to that organism. Whatever harms a living organism is a disvalue to that organism.
3. The basic value against which all values are measured is the conscious individual.
4. Morals relate only to conscious individuals.
5. Immoral actions arise from individuals choosing to harm others through force, fraud, deception, coercion — or from individuals choosing to usurp, attack, or destroy values earned by others.
6. Moral actions arise from individuals choosing to benefit others by competitively producing values for them.

# Legal Exhibit
## Ego-"Justice" Terminator

Objective Law Must be Upheld
This Legal Exhibit demands that objective law be upheld by all officers of the court. Attach this Exhibit to all motions, legal documents, correspondence used in any local, state, or federal jurisdiction.

This Legal Exhibit Demands the Termination of
1. Subjective, Political-Agenda Laws
2. Ego "Justice"

Upon receipt of this Legal Exhibit, under penalty of job termination, judges as well as prosecutors and lawyers must reject *all* forms of subjective, political-agenda law and ego "justice". Those officers of the court must henceforth practice only objective law.

**Subjective Laws** include political-agenda laws conjured up by politicians and bureaucrats to gain self-serving benefits, false egos, and unearned power. Enforcement of political-agenda laws requires the use of force and armed bureaucrats against innocent people.

**Objective Laws** are not conjured up by politicians or bureaucrats. Instead, like the laws of physics, they arise from the *immutable laws of nature*. Such laws are valid, benefit everyone, and advance society. Objective laws are based on the moral prohibition of initiatory force, threats of force, and fraud.

**Ego "Justice"** is the use of subjective, political-agenda laws to gain harmful livelihoods and feel false importance. Ego "justice" is the survival tool of many harmful politicians, lawyers, and judges.

Benefit-of-the-Doubt Clause
Except for the most egregious offenders, this Legal Exhibit presents an opportunity for officers of the court to amend their past errors of supporting subjective law and using ego "justice".

Each officer must henceforth uphold objective law and reject ego "justice" along with its gun-backed, political-agenda laws and enforcements.

Purpose of this Legal Exhibit
1. To inform officers of the court that practicing ego "justice" and using threats, force, fines, guns, and jails to enforce political-agenda laws are serious, objective crimes that must eventually be prosecuted.
2. To inform officers of the court that they are henceforth fully responsible for upholding objective law and rejecting ego "justice".

## ORDER

Render criminal penalties *only* against those violating objective laws in committing objective crimes. Objective crimes occur only upon the initiation of force or fraud against individuals and their property. Such crimes include murder, rape, assault, robbery, fraud. Those crimes also include *all* ego-"justice" frauds. Such criminal frauds encompass gun-backed threats, gun-backed assaults, gun-backed pillagings, and gun-backed false imprisonments executed by armed bureaucracies enforcing political-agenda laws. Also, the illegal, political weapons of RICO and seizure laws are increasingly used against innocent people. ...All such political-agenda and ego-"justice" crimes are terminated by enforcing *objective* law.

After receipt of this Legal Exhibit, any officer of the court who commits such crimes of ego "justice" and judicial fraud will eventually be identified, prosecuted, and have his or her harmful career terminated. And, through objective justice, court officers guilty of those serious crimes must pay restitution to their victims.

NOTICE
Citizens should always try to serve as jurors on political-"crime" trials...and *always* vote acquittal.

— This legal exhibit is not copyrighted —
Anyone may photocopy this Legal Exhibit for repeated use on attaching to all legal documents. This Legal Exhibit is also available in French, German, Spanish, Italian, and other languages for use in jurisdictions worldwide.

Address correspondence to: The Zon Association, P.O. Box 60752, Boulder City, Nevada 89006

**"The only justifiable purpose of political institutions is to insure the unhindered development of the individual."**
*Albert Einstein*

Printed with permission from the National Archives: Niels Bohr Library

91

## Appendix: The Golden-Helmet Index

92

## Appendix: The Golden-Helmet Index

## Appendix: The Golden-Helmet Index

Look into yourself with honesty
and
You shall find God

Look into each individual with honesty
and
You shall find the Civilization of the Universe

Look into the future with honesty
and
You shall find the end of dishonest government

## Negative Comments about Neo-Tech

Neo-Tech Publishing has many thousands of positive comments and about two-hundred negative comments in its files. *The Neo-Tech Discovery* shows in print several hundred testimonials heralding the life-saving benefits of Neo-Tech. Yet, sometimes, negative comments can also be informative as shown below:

(some comments are edited slightly for readability)

"Man was not given the authority to do what he wants. You wrote your own Bible. I don't want any part of it." A.M., CA

"A grave threat to mystical beliefs." B.D.

"Neo-Tech promotes outright individualism — a crime that should be punishable by death." R M., CA

"You will gain greater and greater ability to manipulate the material world. But many eminent scientists have written impassioned pleas on the danger of pure reason. I can only look to the ultimate source to prevent you from destroying the rest of us." P.N.P., WI

"Neo-Tech puts man at the level of God. You give man prosperity, power, love — total control. You dismiss self-sacrifice in your haughty exaltation of the individual over God. You are dark and deluded. Give up. Confess your sins, repent, and turn to Jesus." C.G., GA

"Your repeated slander of mystics and authorities is extremely sickening to me. Do you really think you can find true happiness through such a material approach?" C.B., MD

"I am completely appalled. Anyone who doesn't believe in spirits and mysticism is insane." B.T., KS

"You blatantly deny the spiritual man in assuming humans as the ultimate creation." Ms. J.G., CA

"Man wallows in the lower-plane earth geared to materialism and ego." F.W., GA

"Sex, gold, and the pursuit of knowledge — keep it to yourself." W.F., CA

"You are totally human centered and doomed to destruction." A.A., NJ

"Power is the most deadly drug and that is what you are offering." T.M., OK

"I cannot accept reality over religion." Mrs. J.D., IN

(continued)

# Negative Comments about Neo-Tech

"Biological immortality — who wants it, even if you achieve it. I am looking for life after death." C.L.

"Jehovah owns the universe. Puny humans have no such rights. R.S., CA

"You are all screwed up in the head, no one controls his future, love, or money. God is the controlling force in this world. And if you dispute that you can burn in hell." N.S., CA

"We realize that we are no more or less important than the ant we have just crushed, or the plant we have just carelessly ripped out of the earth because we call it a 'weed'. You will discover that reality is incomprehensible." S.K., CA

"You should be put in jail for trying to brainwash people. Those who believe men descended from monkeys probably did." S.O.

"I consider Neo-Tech to be very dangerous." S.J., CA

"Get down on your knees and beg for forgiveness." S.F.

"There is no such thing as 'free enterprise.' 'Free enterprise' is the freedom of swine to push and shoulder each other aside while guzzling at the feed-trough." I.F., FL

"Your books are counter productive to the established way of life as normal people live it." J.V., NE

"Not only was I shocked at some of the concepts, but I absolutely refuse to believe them." W.S., OH

"Dr. Frank R. Wallace is the most intelligent fool I have ever been privileged to know." J.S., CA

"Dr. Wallace is a man in rebellion against authority — any and all authority. To state it another way, no one should have any authority over anyone else. Shed a sincere tear for Frank R. Wallace." J.H., TX

"As a devout Ayn Rand fan and proponent of free thought, it is my opinion that you are the most subversive organization I have ever encountered." S.N., CA

"The immediate satisfaction and ego trip that accompanies Neo-Tech is so tempting." L.V., MA

"If Frank R. Wallace will send me date, month, and year of birth, I will reply and tell through channels his life span on planet earth. Frank Wallace is held accountable to God for his evil manuscript. Wallace is going directly to Ravat Mountains U.S.S.R. (center of the Universe), which runs all the way to Siberia. Two miles below the earth's surface, are the pits of fire and brimstone, a blazing inferno 2000 degrees Farenheit." D.A., TX

Government-Free

# *CYBERSPACE*

delivers limitless

# Riches and Romance

John Flint, Ph.D.
Editor-in-Chief

Neo-Tech Publishing

# A
# *Fifth-Dimension*
# Paradigm

that guarantees limitless

## Personal Wealth

and

## Romantic Love

Neo-Tech Publishing
Las Vegas

a

1st printing, October, 1998
2nd printing, November, 1998
Printings after 2nd
3 5 7 9 10 8 6 4

ISBN #911752-85-4
Library of Congress #98-68357

In government-free cyberspace,
freed entrepreneurs will deliver
permanent, prosperous solutions
to
y2k, economic, financial problems and crashes

# A Glimpse

into the
# *Fifth Dimension*

### Riches and Romance
guaranteed for life
on entering the exotic/erotic
### *Fifth Dimension*

---

According to the latest string/quantum theories,
The universal laws of physics comprise up to eleven dimensions of objective reality.
Until now, you have known and experienced only four dimensions of conscious life.

---

First, push button #5 below to enter

Button
#5

## *The Exotic/Erotic 5ᵗʰ Dimension*

Then, push buttons #1-#4 to collect

| Button #1 | Button #2 | Button #3 | Button #4 |
|:---:|:---:|:---:|:---:|
| **Wealth** | **Power** | **Youth** | **Sex** |
| Guaranteed for Life | Guaranteed for Life | Guaranteed for Life | Guaranteed for Life |

*A Glimpse*

## Pushing those Five Buttons
### Guarantee Exotic/Erotic Riches

I stared at the above five buttons printed above in two dimensions. The Neo-Tech publications are likewise printed in two dimensions on sheets of paper. I, as many thousands of Neo-Tech owners, knew buttons #1-#4 existed in the Neo-Tech Discovery. I, as most owners of Neo-Tech, learned how to move those flat buttons into the three dimensions of one's own life. We then learned from Neo-Tech how to use those buttons in the fourth dimension of time for traversing space within Earth's irrational anticivilization. On pushing those four buttons, we effected justice — we exploited Earth's mystics and neocheaters to gain wealth, power, health, and romantic sex.

### Everyone Benefited — 10% Big Time,
### 40% Greatly, 50% Marginally

A survey of a half-million Neo-Tech owners revealed that most pushed the four buttons to wealth, power, health, and romantic love. Of those, an estimated 10% benefited big time, 40% benefited greatly, and 50% benefited marginally. The question has always been, "Why didn't everyone benefit big time?"

The answer is *the struggle*. We learned that achieving wealth, power, health, and romantic love in an anticivilization is a struggle — a constant struggle against the pervasively harmful forces of irrationality. Every Neo-Tech owner who pushed those four buttons knows what that struggle means. They know of the parasitical and criminal draining experienced by every value producer in Earth's anticivilization. If, during that struggle, one separates from the anticivilization, that person begins feeling like the stranger, Meursault, in Albert Camus 1946 novel, *The Stranger*. One begins feeling an emotional and reflective detachment from the irrationally harmful anticivilization. One becomes increasingly bored and indifferent toward everything in the anticivilization.

d

One then realizes that everything about an anticivilization *is* absurd. ...How does a person convert those realizations and feelings into guaranteed riches and sexual love?

With or without that struggle and detachment, everyone still experiences the ultimate loss — the unnecessary loss of power, health, and then life itself. Those losses to the parasitical and criminal classes have always been the mortal problem of human life on Earth. ...Earth's anticivilization *is* the Theater of the Absurd.

### Cockroaches and Blimps of Absurdity

With that detachment from Earth's anticivilization, one increasingly sees its rulers and their subjects undergo Kafka-like metamorphoses:

1. One sees Earth's parasitical-elite rulers mutate into giant, criminally manipulating cockroaches living through automatic dishonesties. ...Cockroaches: permanent entities of the anticivilization.
2. One sees the parasitical-fawning supporters of those rulers mutate into unhealthy, fat-free/carbohydrate-stuffed blimps living through politically correct irrationalities. ...Blimps: new mutations in the anticivilization.

The absurdity of life in an anticivilization becomes especially vivid when juxtaposed against the Civilization of the Universe. Thus, how does one convert that absurdity into guaranteed riches?

### From the Absurd to the Sublime

Today, with the release of these *Protocols*, any Neo-Tech owner can bypass that struggle — the absurdity of an anticivilization — to prosper big time. How? By tapping the laws of physics as described in the *Protocols*, one gains limitless riches available beyond the dimensions of Earth's milieu of bizarre mysticisms and criminalities — riches available from the Fifth Dimension of the cyberspace/business Universe. With these *Protocols*, every Neo-Tech owner, not just 10%, can succeed big time. Every Neo-Tech owner can now achieve guaranteed wealth, power, youth, and romantic sex — even in this anticivilization. With these *Protocols*, Dr. Frank R. Wallace unravels Earth's irrationalities. He solves his final problem in Earth's anticivilization. He achieves his final goal in this anticivilization. He discovers how anyone can convert the absurd into the sublime. He discovers how anyone can step from guaranteed loss of every human value to guaranteed gain of every desirable value.

## Scientific Documentation
### and its
## Iron-Clad Guarantee

### *The Beginnings*

"All comes from the Limitless and all returns to it," said Thales of Miletus (625-547 B.C.). The "Limitless" *is* the Civilization of the Universe. Thus, began the development of non-mystical views of existence 2600 years ago. That scientific development advanced universal facts, which enriched human existence through liberated reason. That scientific development replaced the story-telling Homeric views, which enslaved human thought through authoritarian dogma. Those early scientists radically avoided arbitrary, mind-spun stories that dictated the "why" of things in trying to explain nature. Instead, they began explaining nature through consistent, fact-seeking contexts that reasoned the "what" and "how" of things. They were the thinkers of Ionian and Greek cultures. They were the first to venture into the previously unknown areas of objective knowledge called science. By nature, that venture began as problematic speculations

f

dubbed Pre-Socratic Physics. Those speculative physicists ranged from Thales (625-547 B.C.) and Anaximander (610-540 B.C.) to the mathematician Pythagoras (580-500 B.C.) and the atomist Democritus (460-370 B.C.). ...Over time, with further studies, many of their speculations evolved into hypotheses, theories, and often, many centuries later, into solid knowledge backed by contextual proofs.

Likewise, today, a new field of knowledge opens. That new field involves the physics of nature's exotic/erotic Fifth Dimension. ...It involves Neo-Tech Physics.

### What is Neo-Tech Physics?

Don't we just have physics — universal physics? We don't have German physics, Jewish physics, or Mao physics. Yet, indeed, we do have Neo-Tech Physics just as we had Pre-Socratic Physics. We have such specified physics when an entirely new dynamic of thought and knowledge is introduced. The starting point into new-breed dynamics of knowledge must, by nature, begin with problematic speculations. From that starting point comes development of hypotheses, theories, and proofs. Thus, rises Neo-Tech Physics, which today is moving from speculation toward hypothesis and theories through inductive verifications, ocular evidences, and mathematical proofs. ...Today, the most powerful verification of Neo-Tech Physics comes from the fact that it works in the real world.

Moving beyond an irrational anticivilization with these *Protocols* brings one into the previously unknown and unexperienced Fifth Dimension. That new dimension is the entrance to the Civilization of the Universe. More significantly, coming from the Fifth Dimension, the *Protocols* deliver wealth, power, health, fitness, and romantic sex *without* the previous struggle — *without* the 2300 years of interference from the parasites, mystics, and criminals who infest Earth's anticivilization.

*A Glimpse*

## *What is the Exotic/Erotic Fifth Dimension?*

The Fifth Dimension lies in a separate realm — separate from the space-time dimensions of Earth's anticivilization. During Dr. Wallace's six-year development of the *Protocols*, that exotic/erotic Fifth Dimension arose unexpectedly. It was an entirely new entity never before imagined on this planet. That Fifth Dimension is now emerging through cyberspace. Stepping into those rising five dimensions, one becomes free from the oppressive space-time boundaries of an anticivilization.

Within that new Fifth Dimension, nothing remains from an anticivilization — nothing exists that limits or harms anyone in that Fifth Dimension. One is free of the irrationalities of force-backed government criminalities and mystical-shrouded religious frauds. One is joyously free of being a stranger — free of Camus' detachment, indifference, boredom, absurdity. For, when one steps into the Fifth Dimension, the irrationalities and absurdities of an anticivilization fade to a vanishing point. The reality of limitless riches and romantic excitement rise to ineffable levels. ...Riches and excitement rise beyond expressions like "awesome" and "mind boggling".

## *Slingshot Losers into Riches and Romance*

On glimpsing the Fifth Dimension, one will meet Frank R. Wallace. Professionally, he has left the anticivilization and will not return. He will not again publish in that irrational civilization. Yet, he delivers the highest values: He delivers new knowledge that benefits those who acquire it. Wallace's *Protocols* deliver the knowledge to exit today's losing civilization and slingshot into the limitless prosperity, power, health, and romantic love of the exotic/erotic Fifth Dimension discovered in cyberspace.

h

# Neothink Protocols

## CONTENTS

*Protocols*
for entering the fifth dimension of cyberspace
reveal an *artificial* four-dimensional earthbound
anticivilization of dishonesty
created 2300-years ago by Pericles and Plato.
Earth populated today by six-billion Trumans,
its citizens can now find the exit door
into the *real* five-dimensional cyberspace
Civilization of the Universe
that delivers limitless
Romance, Life, and Prosperity.

# Neothink Protocols
## for a
# New Civilization

### FOREWORD

These Protocols deliver five paradigm shifts that lead to the fifth dimension of nature. That fifth dimension reveals Nature's Quintessential Secret (NQS) for controlling existence. On understanding those paradigm shifts, one ascends toward becoming a business controller of existence. From that control comes limitless prosperity and romantic excitement. ...From that control, one becomes a God — a real God — a business Zon.

Anticivilization y2k/economic/financial crashes will accelerate the final three paradigm shifts to bring open-ended prosperity to those implementing the Neothink Protocols.

*Man's First Paradigm Shift*
*was from the*
*Bicameral Mind to the Conscious Mind*

Professor Julian Jaynes's book, *The Origins of Consciousness in the Breakdown of the Bicameral Mind* (1976) and Dr. Frank R. Wallace's book, *The Neo-Tech Discovery* (1986) both identify that first paradigm shift. Both books reveal how and why man's automatic-animal bicameral mind quantum jumped to a volitional-human conscious mind under life-and-death survival pressures 3000 years ago.

*Man's Second Paradigm Shift*
*was from*
*Theism to Deism*

Deism is best described in Thomas Paine's book, *The Age of*

1

*Reason*. Many of America's founding fathers were deists, including Thomas Jefferson who penned into the *Declaration of Independence* the universal sentence, "We hold these truths to be self-evident, that all men are created equal, that they are endowed by their Creator with certain unalienable Rights, among those are Life, Liberty and the pursuit of Happiness." Deism was the most radical shift in conscious thought since the bicameral mind jumped to the conscious mind 3000 years before. Deism implicitly rejects Judeo/Christian ethics involving an intruding, vengeful God. Before deism, Jewish and Christian theistic beliefs posited an all-intruding God who ordered every specific action in the Universe. John Calvin best expressed the theist conception with the idea that "God commands every specific action on Earth, from each leaf that falls to each blade of grass that grows". For those theists, God intrudes into everything that happens on Earth and throughout the Universe.

By contrast, the deist conceived God as the "perfect watchmaker". For the deists, a Deity flawlessly created the Universe, wound it up with the physical laws of nature (physics) so perfectly, so ingeniously, that everything could henceforth advance by itself according to those laws of Nature. After creating his Universe, that Deity had no need or motivation to interfere. He had more important things to do with his time and energy. He had to move on to create ever greater value creations elsewhere. ...By contrast, the repairman theist God seemed less perfect, less powerful, and less benevolent then a flawless-creator Deity. Moreover, the theist God made a flawed Universe since he had to angrily consume his time and energy by constantly rushing in to correct, adjust, and brutally punish those subjects who did not believe and obey on faith.

Lastly, the beliefs of theists rested in specific books or scriptures written by "authorities" of the past, validated by the "test of time". They believed in faith and dogma dictated by the words and scriptures of other "authorities". Challenging that conception, deist philosophers Hume, Montesquieu, and Voltaire

2

asked what would be the dogmatic beliefs of a theist if he or she had been educated and lived in distant lands, in different cultures. Those deists then answered their own question by identifying that such "unchangeable" beliefs would change — would be different — in other cultures and circumstances. Thus, dogmatic beliefs and theistic faiths were relative to circumstances and not rooted in reality.

Theistic beliefs, being relative, were localized, particularized, and based on revelations or commands conjured up from the past words and writings of men arbitrarily deemed as "authorities". Such beliefs have no basis for consistency or agreement with other beliefs from different "authorities". ...By contrast, the authority and beliefs of the deists rested in the book of nature. Nature and its immutable laws are contextually the same throughout the Universe as are Newton's and Einstein's laws of motion and gravity. Thus, anyone, at anytime, in any culture, can access the same universal laws of nature in the same context and come to the same understandings and agreements.

In a restated summary: The beliefs of the theists were *subjective*, specified, and arbitrary. Their beliefs were based on the proclaimed authority of ancient men and their scriptures. The irrationalities of such beliefs were often justified through Periclean rationalizations and Platonic a-priori, *deductive* processes. People in different lands and cultures had no basis for agreements on religious beliefs, political doctrines, subjective knowledge, and declared ethics. By contrast, the deists' ideas were *objective*, generalized, and principled. Their ideas were based on the laws of nature and objective knowledge discovered, not invented, by man through Aristotelian sense perceptions and Lockean a-posteriori, *inductive* processes[1]. ...Using the universal laws of nature, not dogma of men, anyone in any land, time, or culture could access the same authority — the same laws of nature and physics — to come away with agreements about consistent facts and objective knowledge.

---

[1]Wide-scope integrations involving *both* deductive and inductive processes are necessary for major advances in competitive, value-producing knowledge.

*A New Paradigm*

## Man's Third Paradigm Shift
### is from the
## Conscious Mind to the Neothink Mind

Frank R. Wallace's books *The Neo-Tech Discovery* and *Profound Honesty* along with Mark Hamilton's book *God-Man: Our Final Evolution* identify the neothink mind and describe its no-transition, quantum jump from the conscious mind. A forthcoming book, *Vanishing Mysticisms and Religions*, by Tracey Alexander and Eric Savage, traverses the unconnectable realms of dishonesty and honesty, irrationality and rationality, mysticism and reality. ...Other examples of no-transition, quantum jumps over realms of unconnectable knowledge are: Ptolemy to Galileo, Newton to Einstein, Kant to Rand, God to Zon, mortals to immortals, Earth's anticivilization to the Civilization of the Universe (C of U).

## Man's Fourth Paradigm Shift
### is from
## God to Zon

Now comes the fourth paradigm shift in man on Earth. Zon vanishes the theories of God with scientifically determinable, objective facts. Zon shifts conscious thought from (A) a mystical, non-provable myth or illusion called God who magically operates differently through the whims of different authorities in different locations on planet Earth to (B) an objective, provable conscious person or self called Zon who factually operates consistently through the laws of nature and business across time and space:

> (A) God operates according to the subjective beliefs and arbitrary whims conjured up by different societies throughout Earth's anticivilization.

> (B) Zon operates according to the objective laws of nature and business uniformly available and consistently applicable to conscious beings throughout the Universe.

Most Earthlings today are duped citizens in an anticivilization

4

of automatic dishonesties and criminal politics. By contrast, Zons are sovereigns in a value-producing Universe of fully integrated honesty and wide-scope accounting. Earthlings and Zons are equivalent living beings. Earthlings today, however, live from the perspective of a self-destructive anticivilization ruled by religious/government mysticisms, frauds, parasitisms, and criminalities. Zons, by contrast, live from the perspective of an ever expanding, value-creating, business civilization existing throughout time and space.

Now to frame a speculative hypothesis: Zons exist throughout a universal civilization. They develop the means and power within the laws of nature to unfold (quantum flux) Gravity Units (quanta of zero mass and zero positive energy) into self-evolving, business universes. Those universes evolve within "perfect" laws of physics that unfold ever expanding prosperity. Such business creations by Zons continually develop new assets comprised of new universes filled with ever more wealth-producing Zons needed for future expansions of consumers, suppliers, trade, knowledge, and liquidity.

Sooner or later, scientists will inductively uncover hard-evidence proof of today's hypothesized Zon and the Civilization of the Universe (C of U). Bountiful inductive evidence, perhaps even proof, may exist today buried in the mountains of unexamined astronomical data already collected. When different questions are asked in the analyses of those data, scientists might find different answers. They might find models that suggest a neothinking-directed dynamic is creating or controlling certain galaxies and other astronomical bodies within our Universe for economically sound business reasons. Or, on a larger scale, such data might yield models that suggest a Zon created and controls our Universe for business reasons.

Zon's creations will ultimately be demonstrated through understanding his purposeful, conscious-caused phenomena rising throughout a business cosmos...as opposed to automatic, nonconscious-caused phenomena rising from nature alone.[1]  At that point, religious theories positing a mythical God along with political theories positing the use of force will vanish and be forgotten.

Discoveries unfolding today in physics and astronomy are yielding evidentiary puzzle pieces pointing toward the Civilization of the Universe.  Those discoveries are undermining the religious/mystical frauds and political parasitisms identified in publications such as *The Neo-Tech Reference Encyclopedia* (1976), *The Neo-Tech Discovery* (1986), *Neo-Tech Cosmic Business Control* (1988), *Zonpower* (1995), *Global Wealth Power* (1996), *Profound Honesty* (1996), *Outcompete God and Government* (1997), and *God-Man: Our Final Evolution* (1998).  Today, for example, scientific evidence, theories, and hypotheses are advancing toward demonstrating an essentially limitless abundance of planetary life throughout the Universe.

> *There are infinite worlds both like and unlike this world of ours.*
>
> Epicurus
> (341-270 B.C.)

### Who or What Created the Universe?

Evidence toward demonstrating neothink-created universes from sub-subatomic Gravity Units is evolving from (1) new statistical calculations, (2) recent string/membrane theories, (3) newly discovered neutrino mass that cannot be explained by the current standard model of existence, and (4) gamma-ray bursts of energies beyond that which can be explained by the current laws of physics.  Contrary to previous beliefs, the mathematics of those theories are

---

[1]Searching for conscious-caused phenomena in the mountains of unprocessed astronomical and cosmological data already existing is more logical, cheaper, and promises much greater payoffs than the illogical, ongoing SETI project of searching for intelligent extraterrestrial communications in space. ...The SETI boondoggle was perhaps astronomer Carl Sagan's biggest time/money-wasting mistake.

today indicating that the laws of physics do *not* break down within the unimaginable tiny quanta of existence found within dimensions (up to eleven dimensions) far beneath Plank's length of $10^{-33}$ meters — found within zero-mass/zero-energy Gravity Units of enormous negative energies (gravity) drawn into infinitesimal volumes.

Thus, the laws of nature and physics might not break down at above-and-below dimensions of any size such as:

*large* beyond this Universe, beyond parallel Universes, beyond layered orders of magnitudes — on forever into the eternally boundless meta universe (obvious),

*small* beneath unimaginably tiny (calculus-type "nilpoint infinitesimals"), zero-mass/zero-energy Gravity Units (vacuum units) buried everywhere — buried beneath strings as eternal universes (not so obvious).

The laws of physics, therefore, might remain the same for *all* dimensions. Indeed, applying Einstein's relativity to below Plank's dimensions down to Gravity Units unifies relativity and quantum mechanics. That unification of physical laws would permit neothinking Zons to create Universes from Gravity Units.

As explained in the Neo-Tech literature since 1994, the only difference between Zons and people on Earth today is that Zons have learned to neothink. In other words, they identify and harness uncorrupted knowledge of nature through wide-scope accounting and fully integrated honesty. ...In the C of U, Zons exist on every level of knowledge and have no concept of dishonesty or deception.

The Statistical Evidence of Zons
as
Supreme Controllers of Existence

Now comes a statistical analysis for the near-certain probability of conscious-created universes: Consider the current big-bang theory for forming our Universe from an infinitesimally small point or "nothing" 13 billion years ago. With a few notable exceptions (e.g.: Eric J. Lerner; Nobelist, Ilya Prigogine; and in certain contexts, Frank R. Wallace), most scientists today accept the big-bang theory. Still, how could a big-bang birth begin? Many theists, led by Pope John Paul and his Vatican advisors, seized the big-bang theory to proclaim that here finally was "scientific proof" of God's existence.[1] For, only God could have created that universe from "nothing", they asserted.

By contrast, professional physicists posit nonmystical, objective hypotheses for a big-bang birth of the Universe based on ocular evidence, gravity, relativity, quantum mechanics, inflation theory, and string theory. Those physicists hypothesize that the big-bang birth of our Universe began naturally — within the laws of physics — with a statistical wave function or quantum flux (a vacuum fluxuation[2]) of a space-time unit/point. Such a unit/point is a Gravity Unit (GU) of zero mass and zero energy but seemingly limitless negative energy (point gravity). ...GUs are homogenized fluids or ethers of infinitesimals (below $10^{-35}$ meters, arbitrarily close to zero) comprised of gravity/vacuum fields.

Next comes a Neo-Tech hypothesis that accepts the statistical aspects of nature's quantum-flux theories of universe formations from "nothing" — from space-time points or Gravity Units. Yet, those same statistical analyses suggests that a Zon — a neothinking person in the C of U — not only created this Universe but created limitless Universes to serve his or her business interests, intellectual growth, and physical well being for self, loved ones, and society. That hypothesis arises from Neo-Tech dismissing God notions as based on nothing more than ignorance,

---

[1]As early as the 1950s, the Vatican seized the seemingly "inexplicable" aspects of quantum mechanics to claim proof of God.

[2]Vacuum fluxuations were first proposed by Edward P. Tryon of Columbia University in a 1973 issue of *Nature*. In the 4th century BC Greece, Lucretius said "nothing can come from nothing". But, perhaps "everything can come from nothing", entirely within the laws of physics. Perhaps everything can come from zero-mass/zero-energy Gravity Units.

superstition, wishful thinking.

Those God notions are tools of mystical frauds and criminal manipulations used by arbitrary, self-proclaimed authorities. Aside from some entertainment value, such "authorities" produce few if any competitive values. Instead, they ultimately cause lethal damage to human life on Earth.

The Neo-Tech hypothesis minimizes the quantum-flux theory as an event that happens rarely compared to the formation of universes by Zons. Thus, that natural quantum-flux formation of universes, while possible, is of no real significance. From that point, the following probabilities arise based on statistics that are similar to the immutable laws of thermodynamics, which are also based on probability statistics.

### Statistical "Proof" of Conscious-Created Universes

Chapter 1 of *Zonpower* (1996) examines the nature of the very small versus the very large. From that chapter combined with an article by Dr. Richard E. Crandall of NeXT Software, *The Challenge of Large Numbers* (Scientific American, February 1997), arises the following analyses:

A googol is $10^{100}$ — that is 1 followed by 100 zeroes, which is an overwhelmingly large number. Consider that the grains of sand that would fill our entire solar system is only about $10^{52}$. The total number of atomic and subatomic particles in our entire Universe is about $10^{86}$, a number still incredibly small compared to a googol. Now, consider a parrot pecking randomly, continuously at a keyboard could statistically type out Arthur Conan Doyle's great Sherlock Holmes mystery novel *The Hound of the Baskervilles* — without a single spelling or punctuation error — once every $10^{3,000,000}$ years. By contrast, the age of our universe since the Big Bang is estimated at only $10^{10}$ years. Now, the patience in waiting for a perfect spelled novel from that impeccable parrot is nothing when compared to the patience required for observing a quantum fluctuation that would tip over a beer can on a level surface. Statistically, that event would occur once in every 10^10^33 years.

### The Odds for Man-Made Universes
versus
Nature-Made Universes

Now, for some seriously big numbers: Instead of tipping over a mere beer can, how many years would be required to quantum flux the birth of an entire universe from its folded-up corollary — a Gravity Unit? Consider a googolplex, 10^10^100. Just to type that number would require more paper than would tightly fill our entire universe. Next, consider that the total quantum states for all particles in the Universe were estimated by Roger Penrose to be 10^10^123 — a number far greater than a googolplex. Now to quantum flux our full-blown Universe into another universe — or a folded-up Gravity Unit into a natural-born universe — would require numbers so large to be expressed only in Ackermann numbers.

An Ackermann number series goes as follows: 10^0, 10^1, 10^2^2, 10^3^3^3. Now, 10^3^3^3 equals 10^3,683,334,640,024. The fifth Ackermann number, 10^4^4^4^4 would require more paper tightly packed to fill the entire Universe to type out that number expressed as *exponential* notations! Such a number makes a googolplex seem like an invisible speck. Still to quantum flux the entire Universe or to quantum flux a Gravity Unit or space-time point into a universe would require an Ackermann number in years beyond the fifth number. Unimaginable? Yes. Still, eternity is a long time. And, in eternity, quantum fluxes of natural universes occur limitless times.

Yet, when statistically compared to potential conscious-created universes, the number of natural created universes is relatively non-existent. Consider the progress of human knowledge in just the past 3000 years within Earth's retarded anticivilization. Consider the geometrically increasing nature of "beyond-God" accomplishments and energy creations on Earth in just the past 100 years. Who could have imagined splitting atoms to release

10

incredible energies, much less fusing atoms to yield ever greater energies? Or, audibly and visibly communicating with anyone, anyplace on Earth at near zero cost, at the speed of light? No one today can even imagine the exponential advances in knowledge, communication, bio/genetic engineering, and harnessing energy a hundred years hence, much less a thousand, a million years hence. We can only speculate how the accelerating flood of knowledge and energy production gathered from above and below the limitless meta-universe. Such gathering of power could allow man on Earth to harness essentially limitless energy from inexhaustible realms beyond this Universe to crack or unfold Gravity Units into limitless new Universes tailored to his or her business needs. ...The probability for Zon-made universes is astronomically more favorable than for a natural quantum-flux made universe, which itself has occurred limitless times throughout eternity.

## *Man's Fifth Paradigm Shift*
### *is from*
### *Man to Zon*

In the fifth paradigm shift, one becomes a Zon on learning to control his existence. To accomplish that final stunning shift, one must grasp the unreal nature of Earth's anticivilization throughout the past 2300 years from a Civilization-of-the-Universe perspective. First, one must understand the comprehensive perspective shift that occurred in the fifth century with philosopher/ bishop St. Augustine. Next, one must understand the comprehensive perspective shift that occurred in the twentieth century with philosopher/artist Ayn Rand. And, finally, one must grasp the comprehensive perspective shift that comes now, turning into the twenty-first century, as Neo-Tech/cyberspace business brings forth the C of U.

The first paradigm shift is detailed in the Neo-Tech literature. In that shift, man abruptly jumped from an automatic animal mind into a volitional human mind. That newly reorganized mind was capable of accomplishing all things beneficial to mankind within the laws of nature. For the next 500 years, up to the fifth century BC, within the Athenian city-state of Greece, arose Earth's greatest civilization. That civilization was moving in a steady progression toward the C of U — a civilization that functions through wide-scope business dynamics and fully integrated honesty.

Then, during the fourth century B.C., as described in *Outcompete God and Government*, man's newly discovered, rapidly advancing conscious mind became infected with a deadly disease. That disease arose from dishonest politics and fraudulent piety within that great Athenian city-state. The disease took root through lawyer-like dishonesties and then spread throughout Western civilization and eventually throughout the world. That disease was caused by the symbiotic viruses of dishonesty and mysticism — lethal viruses that were murderously spread by the world's first master politician and neocheater — Pericles. His dishonest war rhetoric ultimately resulted in the defeat of Athens[1] by Sparta and the execution of Athens' most honest citizen — Socrates[2].

Pericles' lawyer-like dishonesties were philosophically nailed down and given formal credibility by the world's first master academic, Plato. Wielding his mystical forms and plying clever

---

[1]That defeat was aided by the most treacherous, slickest of Athenian pragmatists — the handsome, brilliant sophist — Alcibiades, the ancient-day Bill Clinton.

[2]Socrates through Plato's *Dialogues*, especially the beautiful Dialogue on love, *Phaedraus*, points toward several key Neo-Tech concepts about Earth's anticivilization. That dialogue points toward value-based romantic love, friendship, and the sublime innocence of children — the innocence of each person's child of the past long ago devoured by the dishonesty-and-irrationality Minotaur of an anticivilization. Most profound, Socrates, through the *Dialogues*, was the first to observe that for conscious beings to die at the height of their wisdom, knowledge, and value accumulated through a lifetime of learning was "no way to run a Universe". And, he was right. The Universe is not run that way. It is not run through the disease of death. Only in an anticivilization do conscious beings become diseased — become mortal only to perish at the height of their knowledge and value. They perish from the terminal diseases of dishonesty and irrationality after being devoured in childhood by that anticivilization Minotaur. In the Civilization of the Universe, by contrast, neothinking people from childhood remain immortal sovereigns who eternally expand their knowledge and value.

rhetoric and dialectic arguments with beautiful poetry and ironic brilliance, Plato lent credibility to criminal totalitarian regimes for the next 2300 years. Plato supported totalitarianism and gained credibility by shrewdly attacking the genuine corruptions that arose from (1) Periclean politics, (2) a majority-rule democracy, and (3) manipulating the ignorance of the masses. Around the fourth century AD, the deadly diseases of dishonesty and mysticism spread permanently throughout the Western world via Roman-Catholic Christianity that became ridden with neoplatonism and corrupt rulers.

Finally, after 2300 years, come the Protocols and its business matrix to cure the deadly diseases of dishonesty, irrationality, and mysticism. How? By vanishing the anticivilization via cyberspace businesses. ...Such businesses will lift the masses from ignorant slaves to enlightened entrepreneurs free from bogus authorities.

# PREFACE

The Neothink Protocols deliver a business matrix that vanishes the mortal diseases of dishonesty, irrationality, and mysticism. Thus, those Protocols deliver eternal life, romance, and prosperity through nature's Quintessential Secret woven throughout the Civilization of the Universe (C of U).

Perspectives from the Civilization of the Universe yield stunningly different knowledge never perceived in Earth's anticivilization. Until the Neothink Protocols, the limitless power and wealth available from operating within the laws of nature and C-of-U perspectives were unknown throughout Earth's anticivilization. Today, glimpsed for the first time, C-of-U perspectives are breathtaking in their scope and power. The Neothink Protocols begin by revealing general, wide-scope perspectives from the C of U concerning philosophy, wealth, power, sex, health, business, law, politics, music and art, life style and romantic love. Those new perspectives are conveyed through 100 Dialogues, including an adventure/love story titled *Only Atheists go to Heaven — The New Gods*.

The Neothink Protocols deliver specific perspectives that encompass essentially every aspect of conscious life. Those C-of-U perspectives reveal nature's *Quintessential Secret*. That secret unfolds first in practical, conceptual terms and then in unforgettable, emotional terms. Such a blend of concepts and emotions occurs through various art forms circulating beneath a Neo-Tech business umbrella.

\*\*\*\*\*\*\*\*\*\*\*

## *Perspectives of Conscious Man on Earth*

Living species on Earth undergo long-range biological evolutions causing gradual changes to their survival mechanisms. Only conscious man undergoes rapid evolution in his survival mechanism via the conscious mind, independent of biological evolution. Indeed, conscious man rapidly evolves *not* through the slow, previously immutable changes of natural biology. Instead, he evolves through the rapid, volitional changes of conscious thought that through science, medicine, and competitive business quickly take over, surpass, and obsolete his natural biological changes. ...Thus, conscious man has a fast changing historical perspective evolving in quantum-like jumps along the endless scale of changing conscious thought and knowledge.

Man today encompasses the most advanced-thinking position in Earth's history. Thus, a person today cannot make value judgments about any past period of history without first understanding the knowledge, technology, and thinking context of that past period. One can accurately understand and judge past events, people, and values only from their historical perspectives — only from their position on the evolutionary thinking-and-knowledge scale of history. ...Understanding past anticivilization perspectives is important for discovering future C-of-U perspectives.

Now, by contrast, consider moral judgments: Before man evolved into his conscious mind, moral judgments could not exist. Unconscious (bicameral) man acted automatically through a highly intelligent animal mind that was unable to make moral choices. He made automatic choices dictated by reactions to the impinging forces of nature. Thus, bicameral man was amoral as were his fellow animals. On becoming conscious, however, unlike his fellow animals, he became responsible for both his behavior and his survival through volitional choices. At that point, an objective, unchanging moral standard arose for conscious man. That standard is the same for conscious beings throughout the Universe... throughout space and time.

What is the moral standard for man? Volitional acts that objectively benefit conscious individuals and their societies through competitive value production are good — ethical, moral. By contrast, volitional acts that objectively harm conscious individuals

16

and their societies through initiatory force, dishonesty, and fraud are bad — unethical, immoral.

In summary, valid judgment of *nonmoral* values requires a *changing* historical and cultural context that brings **near-term** prosperity and happiness to individuals and societies. By contrast, valid judgment of *moral* values requires the *unchanging* universal context that brings **long-term** or **eternal** prosperity and happiness to individuals and societies. ...Violation of individual/property rights through initiatory force is universally immoral. Protection of individual/property rights through free enterprise is universally moral.

## The Anticivilization is a Deadly Game
### of
### Force and Fraud

The basis of an anticivilization is manipulation of deception, dishonesty, fraud. For the past 2300 years, most value-producing citizens were unaware of such manipulations. Yet, *every* deceptive "leader", dishonest academic, and fraudulent authority in an anticivilization is harmful to the well-being and happiness of conscious life. Such "leaders" are skilled at hiding their dishonesties and destructions used to drain the value producers. Today, those "leaders" are called *neocheaters*. All neocheaters, however, are trapped within their own creation — within their own unnatural anticivilization. They are trapped by their parasitical lives — trapped into playing a monstrous game that always ends in loss and death for them and everyone else on Earth.

In essence, living in the anticivilization requires everyone playing its bizarrely deadly game of survival. That game is accepted by everyone invested in the anticivilization. It is a pervasive game of subtle dishonesties, rationalizations, and self-deceptions that bring everyone to unnecessary losses and eventual death. It is a game that grinds human life to nothing through criminal redistributions of wealth via gun-backed regulations, political-agenda laws, con-game compassions, lawyer-like dishonesties, and destructive religious frauds. ...From the

17

C-of-U perspective, the death-delivering anticivilization is unredeemable, incomprehensible, not worthy of memories. On leaving the anticivilization behind, one hears Poe's raven cry, "nevermore, nevermore, nevermore".

## *The Civilization of the Universe is the Eternal Business of Competitive Value Production*

The Neothink Protocols deliver never-before-imagined business dynamics that arise from C-of-U perspectives. Those dynamics deliver endless wealth, ageless life, and romantic excitement undreamed in Earth's anticivilization. No games are played in the Civilization of the Universe. Dishonesty, irrationality, mysticism, fraud, crime, wars, disease, envy, boredom, loneliness, mental depression, and death are unknown. Instead, every citizen lives honestly through expanding business excitement, competitive value production, endless knowledge/wealth creation, benevolent friendships, romantic love, and artistic enjoyments.

## *The Anticivilization Perspective*

Since the discovery of Neo-Tech two decades ago, its literature has been written from the perspective of prospering in Earth's anticivilization. As identified in that literature, an anticivilization functions criminally — from a dishonest political/religious base of irrationality, mysticism, force, and fraud. Yet, by applying wide-scope accounting and fully integrated honesty to life on Earth along with DTC — an acronym for Discipline, Thought, and Control — one prospers despite those anticivilization ruinations. Today, hundreds of thousands of people worldwide are quietly acquiring open-ended wealth and enjoying happy romantic love. By applying the competitive advantages gained through Neo-Tech, they outflank the parasites and neocheaters who drain everyone on Earth. ...Through Neo-Tech, one bypasses the destructive forces of dishonesty, mysticism, laziness, irrationality, nationalism, religion, and politics inherent throughout an anticivilization.

*A New Civilization*

Yet, even with Neo-Tech, an anticivilization ultimately delivers aging and death to every individual. Moreover, the achievements and wealth of any individual in an anticivilization seem insignificant when compared to the limitless achievements and eternal prosperity available to everyone through cyberspace businesses in the Civilization of the Universe.

## The Civilization-of-the-Universe Perspective

A forthcoming book titled *Vanishing Mysticisms and Religions* by Tracey Alexander and Eric Savage traverses the gap between the anticivilization and the Civilization of the Universe. After that book is published, no more Neo-Tech literature will be offered from the anticivilization perspective. Indeed, Earth's anticivilization is designed for losers who age, suffer, and die by clinging to their anticivilization investments in supporting the parasitical ruling classes. In addition to the forthcoming Alexander/Savage book, the last two Neo-Tech anticivilization publications — *Outcompeting God and Government* (1997) by Frank R. Wallace and *God-Man, Our Final Evolution* (1998) by Mark Hamilton — captured the final hidden dishonesties of the anticivilization. Future publications will bypass Earth's anticivilization. For, through wealth-creating businesses in cyberspace, the anticivilization will vanish. No one will need rationalizing philosophies. Everyone will live as a sovereign through fully integrated honesty.

## Truman's Doorway

In the mortal anticivilization, life ultimately becomes meaningless. Biblical King Solomon wrote in *Ecclesiastes*, "Meaningless! Meaningless! Everything is meaningless and chasing after the wind". Indeed, only in the immortal Civilization of the Universe can life evolve into ever increasing meaning and happiness. ...Fully integrated honesty — Neo-Tech — is the doorway out of the anticivilization and into the C of U.

19

*A New Paradigm*

*The Protocols*

Being free of mysticisms and dishonesties, which means being free of aging and death, makes the Civilization of the Universe forever separate from Earth's anticivilization. By nature, no nexus or connection exists between the C of U and an anticivilization. In the C of U, the idea of an anticivilization is incomprehensible since the concepts of disease, poverty, envy, crime, war, dishonesty, and rationalizing philosophies are unknown. ...*The Protocols* vanish the anticivilization by bringing forth the C of U.

*******************

## General Perspectives

Limitlessly wide perspectives exist throughout the C of U. By contrast, the narrow, closed-circle perspectives in the anticivilization arise from the rationalizing mechanisms offered by an array of competing philosophical systems. To move past philosophy, which is unneeded in the C of U, the various philosophies on Earth must be viewed from a Neo-Tech — fully integrated honesty — perspective within the anticivilization. From that perspective, those philosophies, including the valid C-of-U philosophy of Objectivism, appear essentially the same. They appear as rationalization systems needed to protect one's investments in an irrational civilization. When Earth's anticivilization philosophies are viewed from the rational Civilization of the Universe, they vanish as equally meaningless or unnecessary within the eternally prosperous Civilization of the Universe.

Aristotle's unmatched C-of-U pointing philosophy was dishonestly twisted centuries ago into sterile, pseudo-intellectual rhetoric and show-off disputations by Aristotelian cultists and scholastic dogmatists. Today, Ayn Rand's brilliant C-of-U pointing philosophy is twisting into sterile, pseudo-intellectual rhetoric and show-off disputations by Randian cultists and closed-circle dogmatists via the Internet. When dogmatized centuries ago by the scholastics, Aristotle's philosophy became barren — not useful — for competitive wealth production. When dogmatized today by pseudo-intellectuals, Rand's philosophy becomes barren — not useful — for competitive wealth production as is observed daily on the Randian Internet newsgroup:

*humanities.philosophy.objectivism*

The bylaws of that newsgroup forbid any discussion of forward-moving Neo-Tech. In Orwellian fashion, the Objectivist cultists forbid even mentioning the word "Neo-Tech" under penalty of permanent expulsion from the discussion group. Socrates would have shaken his head in wonder at such close-minded resistance to progress in order to protect dogma.

Four-centuries ago, Francis Bacon scrapped the dead chains of stagnated Aristotelian philosophy to clear the way for the Age of Enlightenment leading to the Industrial Revolution and Ayn Rand's Objectivist philosophy. Today, Neo-Tech scraps the dead chains of stagnated Objectivism to clear the way for the Protocols leading to the Civilization of the Universe and eternal business prosperity.

The Protocols illustrate how seemingly opposite philosophies unify in the anticivilization: One philosophy, Christian neoplatonism, was developed 1500 years ago by Saint Augustine, which if dogmatically applied in today's context of knowledge would be extremely harmful to the individual and society throughout Earth's anticivilization. The other philosophy, atheistic Objectivism, was developed 50 years ago by Ayn Rand, which if *non-dogmatically* applied in today's context of knowledge can greatly benefit every individual and society throughout Earth's anticivilization. But, in historical contexts, both philosophical systems meld as equal and then disappear as unneeded in the Civilization of the Universe.

*A New Paradigm*

*The First Step Leading to C-of-U Perspectives*
*is to outcompete*
*Homer, Plato, Virgil, Dante, Swift, Voltaire, Hume, Shaw,*
*and*
*Monty Python*

How does one reveal nature's Quintessential Secret? Revealing that secret brings the no-transition, quantum jump of conscious individuals in Earth's anticivilization to neothinking individuals in the Civilization of the Universe. The first step is an allegorical journey toward the C of U via the blended styles of Homer's *The Iliad* and *The Odyssey*, Plato/Socrates' *Dialogues*, Virgil's *Aeneid*, Dante's *Divine Comedy*, Erasmus's humanistic *Praise of Folly*, Swift's *Gulliver's Travels*, Voltaire's *Candide*, Hume's *Dialogues concerning Religion and Natural Rights*, Shaw's *Don Juan in Hell*, and Monty Python's *The Meaning of Life.*

The journey begins in 1998 as an adventure/love story titled *Only Atheists go to Heaven:* A Christian saint who left Earth's anticivilization in 430 A.D. falls in love with an Objectivist philosopher who left Earth's anticivilization in 1982. Approaching the Civilization of the Universe, they meet a business tycoon named Jay Gould Zon who is a controller of existence. Together, as free entrepreneurs, they begin a new-color journey toward vanishing Earth's anticivilization. But, for Earth's anticivilization to survive, its rulers must eliminate those free entrepreneurs.

Who will survive? Who will vanish? The free entrepreneurs or the rulers of Earth's anticivilization? That question cannot be answered until the *Neothink Protocols* with its Dialogues are complete and nature's Quintessential Secret is revealed.

# INTRODUCTION

The Neothink Protocols switch conscious minds from a shadowy cave to a universal light — from an always *lose* anticivilization to an always *win* Civilization of the Universe (C of U). In 1980, Dr. Frank R. Wallace began the research and development needed to uncover nature's universal secret — its Quintessential Secret. In 1992, he started formulating the Protocols. In 1998, he began drafting early portions of its Dialogues.

Producing the complete Neothink Protocols with its 100 Dialogues is a ten-year project estimated at a million words of literature combined with the aesthetic arts. Producing the Protocol Dialogues is a death-to-life race against time. For, no one can wait ten years without facing the probability of failure and death.

### Earth's Minotaur

The anticivilization is an all-pervasive, child-devouring monster — a Minotaur of half dishonesty, half irrationality.

Everyone on Earth lives in an anticivilization of dishonesty, irrationality, and mysticism. That unnatural civilization is premised on the death of human beings in which immortal children of the Universe born on Earth are devoured by that Minotaur of dishonesty and irrationality. They are then regurgitated as mortal adults into an anticivilization promising only pointless aging and irrational death to its citizens.

Earth's anticivilization exists in a maze of contradictions as identified by Blaise Pascal over three centuries ago. Those contradictions blended right with wrong — blended magnificent technological advances and life-enhancing rationalities with horrifying political/religious destructions and death-causing irrationalities — blended competence and genius with dishonesty and evil. By nature, such unnatural combinations of skill and dishonesty, good and evil, competitive value production and parasitical value destruction, brilliance and stupidity, rationality

23

and irrationality will eventually deploy today's weapons of mass destruction to vanish conscious life on Earth. ...The race, therefore, is between (1) death and (2) life. Society's choice is between (1) vanishing human life on Earth with nuclear, chemical, or biological weapons or (2) vanishing Earth's anticivilization with the approaching Civilization of the Universe. ...The individual's choice is (1) aging and death or (2) biological immortality and eternal prosperity.

*Testing a Piecemeal Approach*

Irrational, unnecessary death awaits everyone in Earth's anticivilization. Thus, Neo-Tech Publishing (NTP) seeks to shorten the race against time. How? Through early piecemeal releases of those aspects within the Neothink Protocols — a new thinking paradigm — that vanish the anticivilization. NTP, therefore, will test publish on the Internet early beta drafts of Protocol segments as they develop.

As Protocol segments roll out, readers will learn how to outcompete each aspect of Earth's anticivilization that is rooted in destructive, ultimately fatal dishonesty. Readers will learn how to *turn off* fatal anticivilization perspectives by *turning on* prosperous Civilization-of-the-Universe perspectives.

NTP is testing that piecemeal concept on web site neo-tech.com

The test will start by launching an adventure/love story comprising a Dante-like "Sublime Comedy" combined with a Monty Python "Life of Zon" parody written in the Shavian style of a "Don Juan in Hell". That metaphorical adventure titled *Only Atheists Go to Heaven* includes a romantic stroll from "Purgatory" toward "Heaven" and back to "Hell" on Earth by lusty playboy St. Augustine and intellectual giant Ann Brand. On their journey, they encounter people such as Helen of Vegas along with a modernized Blaise Pascal, and a Luciferian protector of eternal life named Jay Gould Zon.  They also meet hundreds of other noted characters from the prehistoric Greek poet Homer to an ancient Greek politician named Callicles[1], a shrewd libertarian named Jesus, and a Neo-Tech double agent named Bill Clinton. They quietly operate under the operatic strains of Monteverdi's *L' incoronazione di Poppea* that celebrates the triumph of corrupt souls. ...Eyes will open wide at the climax of that stroll as the anticivilization vanishes.  Life around the globe then rises in entirely different, new-light perspectives within a universal business matrix.

## *A New Thinking Paradigm*

The Neothink Protocols move a person from impotence to omnipotence by moving him or her away from a mystical God in an unnatural anticivilization to a factual Zon in the natural Civilization of the Universe. On discovering nature's Quintessential Secret within the Protocols, one becomes an immortal giant standing on the shoulders of pygmies.  Such a person first obeys and then commands the laws of nature to gain the endless knowledge for creating limitless wealth and romantic happiness. That person then becomes a Zon — a sovereign individual — a free entrepreneur — a business controller of existence.

A Zon needs no external authority for guidance in any matter of life.  A Zon develops a neothinking mind with powers that no external authority could match.  A Zon is a sovereign who alone is responsible for his or her life, eternal prosperity, and romantic happiness.

Zon is any citizen living in the Civilization of the Universe. The C of U is based on solving problems via competitive businesses operating through wide-scope accounting and fully

---

[1]Callicles and Clinton are two politicians who bracket the beginning and ending of Earth's anticivilization.  Neither politician could control his own life, but both strove to control the lives of everyone else through sophistry, rhetoric, and force-backed political-agenda laws. ...Callicles and Plato represent the start of Earth's anticivilization.  Clinton and Neo-Tech represent the end of Earth's anticivilization.

integrated honesty. By contrast, man on Earth today is living in an unnatural anticivilization — a civilization based on (1) lawyer-like dishonesties that began with Pericles 2300 years ago and (2) a Platonistic parasitical-elite ruling class epitomized today by "noble" lies and cynical "compassions". Such illegitimate rulers and arbitrary authorities use force-backed, political-agenda laws for redistributing wealth earned by others to gain political powers. They hide their criminal destructiveness through compassion hoaxes laid upon "labor", "little people", and the productive class. Exemplars of 19th and 20th century compassion hoaxers include Bismarck, Lenin, FDR, and Clinton. They usurped their false authorities through tollbooth compassion based on collecting power and glory by criminally redistributing other people's earned wealth though gun-backed, political-agenda laws.

*Making a Quantum Jump*
*from*
*Mystical Beliefs to Objective Reality*

### Question Authority — Always, Continuously

Always question arbitrarily proclaimed intellectual, political, and religious authorities. Question external authority in order to grow and prosper. Take the Socratic path of questioning. Standing the "test of time" does *not* validate any proclaimed authority. Unquestioned acceptance of written-word authority stagnates the advance of knowledge. Neither a follower nor a leader be. Instead, be a sovereign — a free entrepreneur — a *genius* producer of competitive values.

### Everyone is a Sleeping Genius

Genius never arises from statically following and obeying proclaimed authority with its ever increasing epicycles of mysticism. Instead, genius arises from replacing static authority and its growing mysticisms with wide-scope knowledge derived

26

from fully integrated honesty. Genius blooms by discovering and harnessing the laws of nature while discarding the dogmas of men. Such a process brings growth, knowledge, and genius that never ends.

As Roger Bacon (1214-1291) implied, Francis Bacon (1561-1626) stated, and Galileo (1564-1642) demonstrated, forward-moving knowledge that benefits man and society is built *inductively* from the book of nature. By contrast, backward-moving rationalizations that harm man and society are brewed *deductively* from the books of man. Those books include the essential intellectual works in history — the works of Heracleitus ("all is change"), Parmenides ("all is one"), Plato, Aristotle, Augustine, Aquinas, Descartes, John Locke, Montesquieu, Voltaire, Immanuel Kant, and Ayn Rand. ...Such works are powerful educational tools for maximizing competence on the road to genius. But, to be of universal value, those works must be contextually integrated with (1) history, (2) the laws of nature[1], (3) value creation, (4) aesthetics, and (5) competitive business.

Baron Montesquieu (1689-1755) was the first to recognize the radical benefits of quantum separations (no transitions) between the legislative, executive, and judicial branches of government. The United States government was modeled after the Lockean ideas of Montesquieu. Even more, Montesquieu identified the no-transition, quantum separation between certain societies, cultures, and civilizations. That no-connection concept was the precursor to discovering the no-transition, quantum separation between Earth's *unnatural* anticivilization and the *natural* Civilization of the Universe.

As the Neothink Protocols will demonstrate, such a lacuna creates stunningly different perspectives for every activity of

---

[1]The irony of the Aristotelian scholastics refusing to look through Galileo's telescope is that Aristotle himself would have been the first and most eager to look through the telescope to dispel old notions not only of past authorities and scriptures, but to dispel his own old notions. ...Aristotle was a forward-moving scientist; his cult followers were backward-looking dogmatizers.

conscious life. Perspectives from the nature-created Civilization of the Universe are dramatically different than the perspectives from the mind-spun anticivilization that corrupts planet Earth. For example, from the anticivilization perspective, Saint Augustine and Ayn Rand are the most opposite individuals imaginable. Yet, from the Civilization-of-the-Universe perspective blended with historical context, they are nearly identical in their ideas. In fact, by substituting the modern-day Zon concept for the ancient-day God concept, St. Augustine appears even more objective and closer to the C of U than Ayn Rand and her cult-like dogmatizers. ...That fact is demonstrated in the first two of a hundred Dialogues within the Protocols.

Those one-hundred Dialogues will flip Earth's citizens right side up to vanish their unnatural anticivilization. The natural Civilization of the Universe will fill the void with its limitless prosperity and eternal happiness.

# *Neothink Protocols*

for

## *Quantum Jumping*

from

## Dying in the Anticivilization

to

## Living in the Civilization of the Universe

# Prologue

# Replacing the Old with the New

Four centuries ago, Francis Bacon asked his readers to revere the great accomplishments of Aristotle, but to leave him and his followers (the Scholastics) behind. Bacon then asked his readers to look forward, not backwards, with evolving knowledge in order to move into a new and better future (the Enlightenment). In the 1990s, Neo-Tech asked its readers to revere the great accomplishments of Ayn Rand, but to leave her and her followers (Randian cultists) behind. Neo-Tech then asked its readers to look forward, not backwards, with new evolving knowledge in order to move into a new and better future. Today, at the turn of the millennium, the Neothink Protocols are moving beyond Neo-Tech and its incomparable advantages in the anticivilization. Those Protocols do not deal with the anticivilization. Instead, they start from ground zero in a different place that is not and never will be connected to the anticivilization. That new thinking paradigm starts at the gates to the Civilization of the Universe.

The early developments of Neo-Tech in the 1980s delivered lifesaving values to thousands of individuals. Subsequently, the initial Neo-Tech Discovery (1986) not only provided the tools to avoid the most destructive elements of the anticivilization, but provided the tools to gain wealth, health, and romantic happiness in the anticivilization.

As Neo-Tech evolved, however, it also removed excuses and rationalizations for supporting the anticivilization — it blocked the routes for investing in the harmful irrationalities of an anticivilization. Thus, most readers narrowed their thinking and avoided the integrations of the final two Neo-Tech documents. ...Those last two documents represent the culmination of Neo-Tech literature in the anticivilization. They represent the doorway to the future.

*The Quantum Jump*

*Quantum Jump to the New Neo-Tech*

From the Neothink Protocols, readers will gain unique views and new values from those final two documents that are now rewritten and reprinted on pages 35-226. ...Careful readers will then quantum jump to a new-thinking paradigm.

*Witch Trials*

Three centuries of aggressive witch trials and burnings in Europe occurred before, during, and after Bacon's time — throughout the entire Renaissance. Those witch trials were carefully orchestrated with "justice", decorum, and credibility. The trials were backed by voluminous, detailed canons of seemingly objective law and rules of evidence carefully considered and approved by every country in Western Europe. Moreover, the latest technology was used to support the credibility of those laws and trials with the face of science. ...Witch trials served to support false, force-backed authorities.

Today, at the turn of the millennium, aggressive political-agenda cases and trials — bogus-tort civil cases and victimless-crime criminal cases — are escalating, especially in America. Those "witch" trials are carefully orchestrated with "justice", decorum, and credibility. The trials are backed by voluminous, detailed canons of seemingly objective law and rules of evidence carefully considered and approved by every first-world country. Moreover, the latest technology is used to support the credibility of those laws and trials with the face of science. ...Political-agenda trials serve to support false, force-backed authorities.

From Pericles to Bacon to the end of the 20th century, irrationality and dishonesty was, is, and will always be the unchangeable essence of the anticivilization. The anticivilization cannot evolve. It can only vanish. As 2400 years ago in Athens under Pericles, the world today is directed by lawyer-like dishonesties and criminal-acting politicians. Now, as then, the world existed and still exists in an anticivilization. The anticivilization cannot change. It will either exist or not exist.

The anticivilization will either self-destruct via its nuclear, chemical, or biological weapons...or the anticivilization will vanish as its citizens quantum jump into the Civilization of the Universe.

### *Neo-Tech Information in the Anticivilization* *Ultimately Evolves into the Zon Protocols*

Neo-Tech is not a philosophical, religious, or political belief system. No one can calcify Neo-Tech into dogma, doctrines, or scriptures to fit the anticivilization. Neo-Tech is not an external authority for anyone in any time or place. Neo-Tech leaders and gurus do not exist. Neo-Tech is a constantly evolving business dynamic based on fully integrated honesty and wide-scope accounting.

As a business dynamic, Neo-Tech cannot stagnate. It evolves continually as new facts of reality, nature, and physics are discovered, developed, and exploited for profits. Neo-Tech techniques are designed to gain wealth and romantic excitement in any environment — positive or negative. But, in Earth's dead-end anticivilization, Neo-Tech information from the anticivilization perspective eventually evolves to a stopping point as it did in the final two Neo-Tech documents written in 1997-1998 by Frank R. Wallace. ...To move past that stopping point, the remaining copies of those two documents were destroyed. Every sentence was rewritten and aimed toward the *Fifth Dimension*. Those two rewritten documents are now re-presented for the first time in this manuscript.

This Protocol/Dialogue sample written from the Civilization-of-the-Universe perspective is bracketed around the start and end of those two rewritten documents. Such juxtaposing of documents demonstrate: (1) the end of Wallace's writings from the anticivilization perspective and (2) the quantum-jump, no-transition nature between the anticivilization and the Civilization of the Universe. Understanding those two facts lets one turn toward limitless prosperity and eternal romance.

# Final Anticivilization Document
## about
## Neo-Tech

### INTRODUCTION

Neo-Tech means new techniques and new technologies derived through wide-scope accounting and fully integrated honesty.

### The Dialectic

Consider Henrik Ibsen's play *An Enemy of the People*. Then ask: Was Dr. Stockman an enemy of the people because of his discovery? Next ask: Is Dr. Wallace an enemy of the people because of his discovery? Is Wallace an enemy of the people for revealing Cassandra's Secret — for revealing that Earth's civilization is poisoned — for revealing that its citizens live in a deadly religious/political anticivilization? The Establishment answered, "Yes, he is an enemy". As the Establishment ostracized Stockman, it ostracized Wallace by imprisoning him. Yet, Wallace's Cassandra's Secret reveals how to gain limitless riches despite Earth's criminalized civilization.

Can Neo-Tech eventually enrich the entire populace by transfiguring everyone's future into a cyberspace/business-driven Universe? Barring a nuclear, chemical, or biological apocalypse, will the y2k computer problem help jump Earth's politician/bureaucrat-ruled anticivilization into the cyberspace/business-ruled Civilization of the Universe?

### Four Questions

**I. Is Neo-Tech a threat to Earth's anticivilization?** The clean-sweep nature of Neo-Tech rips Hawthorne's black veil from everyone's face. When a person's anticivilization rationalizations are exposed, the Zon Protocols can jump that person from Earth's

35

dead-end anticivilization into an eternally prosperous, entrepreneur-driven cyberspace civilization — which is the entrance to the Civilization of the Universe.

II. **Is Neo-Tech a new Jewish/Mormonism?** While Neo-Tech utilizes many Jewish and Mormon features as reflected below, it has no dimensions of mysticism or faith. Neo-Tech is simply the fully integrated honesty that brings the individual into the Civilization of the Universe — into universal business competition.

III. **Is Neo-Tech the new Illuminati?** The agendas of Neo-Tech and the Illuminati are similar: Eliminate negatives — eliminate mysticisms, religions, and nationalistic governments. Replace them with universal businesses. Yet, the Illuminati is destined to failure in the closed anticivilization. In contrast, Neo-Tech, perhaps aided by the y2k breakdown, will eventually deliver a wide-open cyberspace/cybercash civilization. ...That cyberspace civilization *is* the gateway to the Civilization of the Universe.

IV. **Is Neo-Tech the universal dynamic of eternal prosperity?** Through its wide-scope accounting and fully integrated honesty, Neo-Tech becomes the universal dynamic of competitive business.

Two Natures

Given the circumstances or opportunities in a force-backed anticivilization, essentially *anyone* will ultimately attack, destroy, kill, even commit genocide to preserve or advance his or her life orientation, livelihood, career agenda, or investments in the anticivilization. Each person will act either as a hidden criminal gaining unearned wealth or as an ignoble follower collecting government-forced redistributions of wealth. In fact, government force-backed wealth redistributions are objective crimes — *criminal acts of theft*. **Such is the nature of Earth's inherently dishonest anticivilization.** Thus, everyone invested in anticivilization dishonesties and criminalities must eventually avoid, reject, or attack Neo-Tech/Zon Protocols to survive. For, Neo-Tech/Zon Protocols are the ultimate threat to everyone's investment in Earth's anticivilization. **Such is the nature of Neo-Tech's fully integrated honesty.**

## Parallels to Jewish Mormonism?

The Mormons are preparing for Earth's anticivilization to end. They expect a new civilization to rise in America. The Mormons also recognize that man is what God (Zon) was. And, God (Zon) is what man will become. Jews, Mormons, and Neo-Tech recognize that competitive value production, discipline, and hard work generate maximum values from the dimension of time. Those Jewish-Mormonism elements combined with Neo-Tech individual rights and objective law are what bring prosperity to conscious beings.

Unlike Judaism or Mormonism, Neo-Tech recognizes no "authorities" higher than honesty, reason, and individual self-responsibility. Neo-Tech does not recognize God or any other mythical authority. Indeed, Neo-Tech is antimystical and rejects "followers". Moreover, it rejects initiated force or fraud inflicted on anyone by any individual — or by any group — by any government, religion, or philosophy under color of political-agenda law, religious law, or any other man-made, subjective law. ...Neo-Tech is about discovering, obeying, and benefiting from the objective laws of nature.

Even more than Judaism and early Mormonism, Neo-Tech is a competitive threat to Earth's anticivilization. Like the Jews of today and the Mormons of the past, Neo-Tech is a competitive threat to neocheaters and parasitical elites. Neo-Tech must be repelled and defeated for the survival of Earth's anticivilization. Yet, Neo-Tech cannot be defeated. For, its business dynamics will ultimately bring limitless prosperity and eternal happiness to conscious beings on Earth.

This document demonstrates through **four dynamics**, how Neo-Tech will transfigure Earth's anticivilization into a cyberspace civilization — and then into the Civilization of the Universe. That transfiguration will be done by:

Dynamic #1) converting outdated, losing Illuminati dynamics into modern, winning Neo-Tech dynamics.

Dynamic #2) bringing to justice the camouflaged criminalities of the anticivilization. Cyberspace justice, for example, will transform the young minds being corrupted today by an anticivilization educational system epitomized by Harvard Law School. ...Neo-Tech transfigures those minds trained in destructive lawyer-like dishonesties and parasitical manipulations into independent minds functioning through productive honesty and competitive businesses.

Dynamic #3) vanishing neocheaters and parasitical elites via wide-scope accounting and fully integrated honesty.

Dynamic #4) harnessing the Neo-Tech Golden Helmet to bring limitless riches to everyone.

# DYNAMIC #1
Modernizing the Illuminati Agenda
(See Reference #1 for the two unedited emails from an "honest"
neocheater)

Highlighting an Illuminati view of Earth's anticivilization, an "honest" neocheater predicts Neo-Tech's demise in a world ruled by parasitical elites. That prediction is articulated in two email letters to the discoverer of Neo-Tech, Frank R. Wallace, provided in Reference #1 of this document. ...Below is a condensed version of those two letters:

```
Date        :  Mon Feb   2 22:38:41 1998
Hostname    :  ws-6.wired-cafe.com
Email       :  hn@freenet.calgary.ab.ca
```

The escape from the anticivilization is needed as one's soul is trapped in an irrational context. One's soul does not want to be here.

But, mysticism meets both the neocheater's and the mystic's needs. If you think about this, you will understand why the mystic's soul is always seeking a context, and why I am a metaphysical Houdini — always escaping context. The neocheater does not value life and the mystic is of no value to life. Yes, I do attack and undermine the souls of others, but remember, I do it to myself first. Like Plato said: "The first and best victory is to conquer the self." If you were to look at my face, you would see there is nothing to attack — no values to threaten. But oh, to look into the face of a creator...there is so much to attack.

My philosophy is based on error, so I can't lose. It's perfect. There's literally nothing to attack. Yes, I will admit I feel somewhat disturbed (just barely) by your penetrating the foundation of our civilization. ...Heresy is something we cannot ignore. For the longest time, we've had this tacit understanding: we would not penetrate your world, and you would not penetrate ours. You've broken the rules of the game, Mr. Wallace.

Yet, it is we who are the experts at reflecting reality to the masses. Don't tell me what we reflect is an illusion. When enough people see and believe, they act, and the result is metaphysical. And here is my trump card, Mr. Wallace. Like you say about a truly good person being unable to recognize his own goodness because it (like the ether of existence) is such a continuous presence, he knows nothing else. But, he can easily recognize when he's bad because it does not fit with his psyche. Me? Well, my soul is corrupted enough that I no longer perceive the bad within me. I am immune from guilt, but creators feel guilt so easily. ...Pretty ironic, don't you think. And yet, the genesis of the guilt is real: each has committed the Original Sin by compromising his consciousness to adapt to this civilization.

Consciousness is what gives one choice — control over reality. I've reduced my consciousness to the point where I no longer have a choice. You see, everyone must protect his place in the anticivilization, at whatever cost, because it is the only place he knows. Anything else, for him, is to risk the deepest fear, a total loss of context — a kind of spiritual death. You are fighting against people's survival instincts, Mr. Wallace. I am helping to prepare an alternative place for them. Turn your knowledge around. Don't think of inducing mysticism as evil, rather recognize the neocheater's goodness in using mysticism to make living in an anticivilization bearable.

********

40

# Neo-Tech: An Enemy of the People?

One can reject or embrace the fully integrated honesty of Neo-Tech. By avoiding fully integrated honesty, one will die forever in the anticivilization. But, by harnessing the profound honesty of Neo-Tech, one can live eternally in the Civilization of the Universe.

### *Neo-Tech's Destiny is Everyone's Destiny*

For the anticivilization to survive, it must stop Neo-Tech from spreading across cyberspace, especially among those disenfranchised from anticivilization investments. Yet, acts to stop Neo-Tech can be outflanked by: (1) *fully integrated honesty* and (2) *wide-scope business dynamics*.

As presented in <u>Reference #1</u>, consider the best attempt at sinking Neo-Tech by a neocheater grinding his heel into the anticivilization. He compellingly predicts Neo-Tech's demise. Indeed, his statements are accurate from a closed-circle anticivilization context. But, wide-scope integrations from a Civilization-of-the-Universe context outflank his predictions. Such outflankings foretell the end of both the anticivilization and its neocheaters through universal business dynamics. The demise of the anticivilization becomes irrevocable with the following two flanks that reach beyond any neocheater's act, statement, or prediction:

### *Flank #1 is Metaphysical and Factual*

Both the totality and the details of what the neocheater says in his document (<u>Reference #1</u>) are essentially correct from within his closed-circle boundaries — from within his mystical bubbles floating about the anticivilization. But, the fully integrated honesty of Neo-Tech spearheads in every direction, without limits. Such spear-like flankings burst mystical bubbles in reaching beyond anticivilization dishonesties and pragmatisms — reaching forever

41

into the future of discovering universal laws, facts, and principles. ...The anticivilization and its neocheaters are not competitive against the universal business dynamics of Neo-Tech. Indeed, neocheaters vanish against wide-scope business competition from cyberspace.

## *Flank #2 is Personal and Emotional*

Even more important for every conscious individual is achieving productive purpose and genuine happiness from life. Neocheaters and parasitical elites fail on both counts, regardless of their anticivilization "victories". By contrast, competitive value producers succeed on both counts, regardless of their anticivilization "defeats".

## Conclusion

Anticivilization hostilities toward Neo-Tech are escalating. Yet, barring a nuclear, chemical, or biological apocalypse, Neo-Tech can quantum jump everyone from Earth's neocheater-driven anticivilization into the business-driven Civilization of the Universe. ...Nothing can stop the profound honesty of Neo-Tech from delivering eternal prosperity and happiness to conscious beings.

## DYNAMIC #2

Reorienting Laws and Lawyers from Subjective to Objective
(See <u>Reference #2</u> for the *Wallace vs. Harvard et al* Free-Speech Lawsuit)

Harvard Law School, Harvard University, et al tried to stop Internet-newsgroup postings from revealing the lawyer-like dishonesties that for 2400 years have perpetuated Earth's anticivilization. Their method? Dishonest, ad-hominem defamations in trying to silence the author of those Usenet posts as described in <u>Reference #2</u>.

On February 20, 1998, the following notice was posted on various

Internet newsgroups:

```
Newsgroups:
alt.irs.class-
action,misc.taxes,misc.legal,us.taxes,us.legal,alt.society.civil-
liberty,talk.politics,misc.legal
Subject: $26.8 Million Internet Free-Speech Suit
filed against Harvard University et al
Date: Sat, 21 Feb 98 02:55:35 GMT
Organization: Netcom
Lines: 9
Message-ID: <6clfjo$q3o@sjx-ixn10.ix.netcom.com>
NNTP-Posting-Host: lvx-nv19-12.ix.netcom.com
X-NETCOM-Date: Fri Feb 20  6:53:44 PM PST 1998
X-Newsreader: News Xpress 2.0 Beta #2
```

On February 20, 1998, in Clark County, Nevada District Court, a $26.84M defamation suit (#A384803, Dept #IX, Docket #W) was filed against Harvard University, Harvard Law School, Jol Silversmith, and John Does #1-26 for trying to block Frank R. Wallace's Internet free-speech rights through a 646-count libel and defamation campaign.

## DYNAMIC #3
Eliminating Harmful Bureaucracies from the DEA, to the FDA, to the IRS
(See Reference #3 for the Cyberspace *IRS Abuse Reports*)

### *Cruel-and-Unusual Punishment*

Have you, a family member, a loved one, or a friend ever been defrauded, looted, hurt, injured, brutalized, or destroyed by the Internal Revenue Service (IRS)? Did no one help you, sympathize with you, or even listen to you, even though you or others were innocent, even though you, a loved one, or a friend were criminally violated, badly injured, perhaps even destroyed or killed? The IRS destroys thousands of families and lives each year. United States lawmakers, however, are responsible for creating, empowering, and perpetuating that criminal bureaucracy.

The accompanying IRS Abuse Reports (<u>Reference #3</u>) were compiled for the investigating committees of the United States Senate and House of Representatives as well as for all United States Federal Judges. The Reports start mildly and build slowly. After awhile, they build into such a crescendo of sickening horror, criminal destructiveness, and unbearable evil that a sedative may be required to read them.

The Neo-Tech dynamics constantly undermine and will eventually vanish irrational, harmful entities and bureaucracies as epitomized by the IRS.

## DYNAMIC #4
### Enriching the Populace
(See <u>References #4</u>
for
*Outcompeting God and Government*)

The 1996 Neo-Tech publication titled *Profound Honesty* revealed a Golden Helmet through which dishonesty becomes impossible, success becomes unavoidable, crime vanishes:

# The Golden Helmet
from
## Metaphor to Reality

# A Metaphorical Golden Helmet

Throughout the Neo-Tech literature, the Golden Helmet is a metaphor for the power of fully integrated honesty harnessed through objective reality. On wearing a Golden Helmet, evil falls away as (1) neocheaters and parasitical elites are left impotent, (2) instruments of force and fraud are rendered ineffective, and

(3) competitive value producers rise as heroes of the Universe. ...**Specifically**, the Golden Helmet is being used in America to eliminate the irrational income tax and its destructive IRS — replaced with a stopgap consumption tax that will eventually phase into voluntary-use fees and protection-package fees. **Generally**, the Golden Helmet is being used worldwide to identify dishonesty and hidden criminalities.

The Golden Helmet was first identified as a metaphor for honest, wide-scope accountings in the earlier Neo-Tech publications, *Neo-Tech Protection Kit*, *Profound Honesty*, and *Zonpower*. The competitive dynamics of the Neo-Tech Golden Helmet is what brought the gestalt firing-squad demise to Romanian dictator Nicolae Ceausescu in 1989, collapsed the Berlin Wall, freed Albania, almost freed China and Burma, and brought the sudden end of the Soviet Union. Today, the Golden Helmet is undermining America's political engines of destruction such as the DEA, FDA, IRS, and perhaps the most dehumanized stealth killer — the racist INS.

# A Tangible Golden Helmet

Available also is a tangible Golden Helmet that one can physically wear to enhance integrated thinking and block rationalized dishonesties.

What is a tangible Golden Helmet? How does it work? Such a Golden Helmet is based on an electronic-"headband" concept for generating orderly brainwaves. At the same time, those brainwaves override the unnatural, disorderly circuitry of dishonesty, mysticism, and criminality. ...Orderly brainwaves also enhance one's ability for wide-scope integrated thinking that outflanks those who dishonestly drain the competitive value producers.

*Final Anticivilization Document*

## How it Works

Various research studies indicate that the well-defined mathematical integrations of classical music, composed largely from 1770-1830, deliver logic-inducing brainwaves that let one think more clearly and integrate more widely. Anyone can demonstrate such a mind-enhancing effect: For example, confront a difficult-thinking or wide-scope integration project. Sense the struggle in solving that difficult problem. Then immerse yourself in Mozart's *Piano Concerto #21*. Immediately, the ease of thinking increases as tension decreases, focus increases, and integrations widen.

## Blocking Dishonesties

A previously undiscovered value arises from Mozart's music. His music induces brainwaves that block dishonesty. One can demonstrate Mozart's remarkable effect: Go to a quiet place. Intensely concentrate. Imagine standing before a nationwide television audience as President Clinton. Imagine looking at millions of American citizens straight in the eye. Then blatantly lie with conviction and a wagging finger, "I never had sexual relations with that woman!" Under such highly compartmentalized, isolated conditions, most people can bald-face lie with a straight face, just as President Clinton. Next, put on earphones under the same conditions and play Mozart's *Piano Concerto #21*. You will not be able to make such clintonian lies with a straight face. You will either stutter and stammer or your face will crack into uncontrollable smiles, even laughter. You simply cannot bald-face lie under the brainwaves generated by Mozart's music. ...As simple as that device seems, such a tangible Golden Helmet cannot only enhance one's integration powers but could reveal the deceptions of dishonest lawyers, destructive politicians, and other criminals. ...The Golden Helmet could be a cheaper, more-reliable lie detector than current-day devices.

# Reference #1

## Two Letters from an Honest Neocheater

Letter #1 to Frank R. Wallace, From an "Honest" Neocheater

Date : Thu Jan 29 22:11:59 1998
Email : .calgary.ab.ca

So you think you're starting to win, do you?
Well, as hard as it is for you to believe,
Neo-Tech will disintegrate long before we ever
do. To date, Neo-Tech has only been attacked
by minor, two-bit neocheaters. I'm going to
do you a favor — I'm going to put all my
cards on the table so you will understand why
you should quit while you're ahead. To explain,
let's begin with points of agreement.

Philosophy is about how to solve human problems
— which is another way of saying the soul's
needs are primary. Existence (or more
dynamically, creation) is good, rational and
holy. There is an unbridgeable gulf between
the philosophy of destruction and creation. In
fact, in a fully integrated sense, the
philosophy of destruction cannot actually exist
— it is an antiphilosophy where the ego's (or
consciousness) needs are primary. This is why
mysticism is a much needed buffer between the
two philosophies.

Your philosophy exists within the bounds of
creation. Any practitioner of this philosophy
is a creator, is holy, or as you prefer —
is Zon. A creator is a rational soul existing
in a rational universe. A destroyer, or as
you say — a neocheater, is one whose soul

is integrated with irrationality existing within an irrational context, i.e. our civilization. As a neocheater, I operate outside the bounds of creation. I enjoy the feeling of power, God-like power to create something from nothing ...POWER, right here, right now, on this earth, and I have no reason to give that up for the illusion — delusion? — that is Zon. Delusion?

Integrated Objectivism not possible on this earth? As you state, its tenets are: What is is. Perceive it. Integrate it (honestly). Act on it. Idealize it? Not quite, the last tenet is: Reflect it. Drawing on philosophy as principled problem solving, REFLECTION is what PROVES the solution, as in plugging in an answer for a math equation. To restate: 1. What is is. 2. Perceive it. (value awareness) a. Sense it. (external awareness) b. Feel it. (internal awareness) 3. Integrate it. (value judgment) a. Think about it. (integration of right brain contents by left) b. Idealize it. (Imagine and desire it — integration of left brain contents by right) 4. Act on it. (value production) 5. Reflect it. (value reflection)

Value Reflection requires the existence of a soul — otherwise there is nothing to reflect. Without the soul, one exists only as a conception without a perceptional referent to reality — i.e. one exists only in one's mind or in the minds of others. A soul is not just value awareness as what happens when an animal is stimulated by an event. Nor is it when consciousness organizes these value awarenesses, re-organizes them and chooses an action based on the ideal organization. Consciousness can bring awareness to one's soul — but it is not the same as one's soul. (Of course, to the extent one is conscious of one's soul the greater one's spirit is.) A soul is a continuous part of one's being — that which exists regardless of immediate outside circumstances — that was the point of "The Fountainhead". It is that which values, the motive power, the Prime Mover that is created when the reverse conceptual/perceptual loop meets the forward perceptual/conceptual loop.

Consciousness, as Rand understood in her pre-Atlas days, is not an entity, it is a mirror. More specifically, it is a two-way mirror with a perceptual and conceptual side. Kant was correct, if consciousness has identity, it cannot be relied on to integrate reality. Any relation between two existents changes the nature of both existents. As you conclude (not consistently) from Einstein's and Rand's work: mass, energy, time and space AND consciousness are not existents, but are RELATIONS between existents. And that of these basic concepts, consciousness is the Prime Concept — that which is formed without a perceptual referent to reality.

One can only vanish irrationality by accepting that metaphysically one's consciousness is nothing. Any philosophy that gives consciousness identity is subjectivism — a fake philosophy — one that is invented, not the philosophy Rand discovered. As long as one treats consciousness as an entity, one can never be fully honest.

However, all this, all that we agree on, is useless intellectualism. In this civilization, one must use one's consciousness to create an identity in order to survive. And nowhere on Earth can you prove to me that Zon — an uncorrupted soul — exists. For example, let's look at Neo-Tech. Neo-Tech, like Earth's Objectivism, provides the shell but not the kernel of reason. You could learn from Nietzsche who said: "He who has a reason why, can bear any how." That is, Neo-Tech is big on internal authority (leading to the blind alley of consciousness as a primary), but it does not integrate it with internal motivation.

More specifically, look at "Cosmic Business Control". Except for the appendix (that which is separated from the main body of work), it operates from a vaguely malevolent-universe premise — a kind of "life is tough and you have to be tougher" perspective. Like "Atlas", it turns people off emotionally, even if they buy into it intellectually. It advocates DTC (Discipline, Thought, then Control)— discipline to cure mysticism, that feelings do not control thoughts, nor that "EMOTIONS BEGET ACTIONS". Fascinating — a neo-platonist stoic would be very comfortable with this, though they would come to far different conclusions than you. Certainly, in the broadest sense, actions (external) do beget feelings (internal). But this is not the sense the author intended. He means consciously chosen actions precede emotions. It is possible to feel without thinking, but to think without feeling? What would power that thought, what basis would one have to make a value judgment? To act without emotion? If you had an external energy source you might be able to make a good robot, but it would make a very poor ballet dancer.

Correctly defined, it is value reflection that is the reward for achievement. Rather than discipline being a short-term strategy to avoid acting on irrational desires. DTC is its god

— both the method and purpose of its work, and people are to be used as its disciples. Like "Atlas", it relentlessly removes the irrational context of this civilization, and thus offers the soul no room to exist. You had to come up with Zon to allow the escape into the Civilization of the Universe.

So you will stop wasting yours and everyone else's time, I will prove that only mysticism can offer, temporarily at least, an escape from this anticivilization. (Life is short, so temporary is long enough.)

## Letter #2 to Frank R. Wallace, From an "Honest" Neocheater

Date : Mon Feb 2 22:38:41 1998
Email : .calgary.ab.ca

The escape is needed as one's soul is trapped in an irrational context. One's soul does not want to be here.' Mysticism meets both the neocheater's and the mystic's needs. When a mystic's mind approaches mysticism, it blanks out and thus becomes dependent on me for authority. I? I blank out the blank out to avoid being caught in my own mysticism. If you think about this, you will understand why the mystic's soul is always seeking a context, and why I am a metaphysical Houdini — always escaping context. From a Jaynes's view, the neocheater holds a concept as primary, so the integration of the left brain is consciously blocked from going to the right brain; the effect is that signals go from the right to left subconsciously.

The neocheater hates having these subconscious perceptions contradicting previously accepted (though irrational) concepts, and so feeling a lack of control over reality, needs the integration of the left brain to be blocked from going to the right brain even more. Eventually, he loses his emotional awareness of the anticivilization. The mystic's integration of the right brain is consciously blocked from going to the left brain. The effect is that signals go from the left to right subconsciously. The mystic's right brain is afraid of receiving these signals from the left...that some external influence is guiding his perceptions. So he has to block the integration of the right brain by the left brain even more. Eventually, he loses his intellectual awareness of the anticivilization.

Psychologically, all this blocking (funneling at either side of consciousness) is to hide the one fact: The neocheater does not value life, and the mystic is of no value to life. Though, in reality (outside the context of the anticivilization), for the mystic, life (lived within the anticivilization) is of no value to him. Without a mystic to justify my existence, I am of no value to life. Psychologically, there is a profound reason not to be Zon, and it is supported by our entire civilization.

You need to fear honesty more than I do. The more aware you become of the gap between things as they are, and things as they should be, the greater the loss you will feel, and the more disheartened you will become. I am perfectly safe. The fact you are not able to adapt means you are insane: you have created a powerful, complex intellectual rationale to support that insanity, and a cult to isolate yourself from normal society.

Of course, I did not expect underdeveloped two-bit neocheaters to destroy you. They are like poker players who when losing, complain that it's a dishonest game and demand their money back. They make me sick! I, at least know what game I'm playing. The two-bit neocheater holds others responsible for problems created by his own irrationality. I have a much broader and more altruistic perspective: I hold the creator, the "great-souled man", responsible for collective irrationality. I need the soul's energy — to get that soul in a context where I can use its energy to get people to sacrifice their souls to the anticivilization — to give me the power to make it work.

Yes, I do attack and undermine the souls of others, but remember, I do it to myself first. Like Plato said: "The first and best victory is to conquer self." If you were to look at my face, you would see that there is nothing to attack — no values to threaten. But oh...for the face of a creator...there is so much...there to attack.

Aside from vulnerability to context switching, the failure with your fully integrated philosophy is the least error, even an inflated valence of a value judgment in its presentation, gives me room to attack your entire philosophy. My philosophy is based on error, so I can't lose. It's perfect. There's literally nothing to attack. Yes, I will admit I feel somewhat disturbed (just barely) by your penetrating a foundation of our civilization with your revisionist gospel. Heresy is something we cannot ignore. For the longest time, we've had this tacit understanding: we would not penetrate your world, and you would not penetrate ours. You've broken the rules of the game, Mr. Wallace. Would you like it if we penetrated your world?

In any case, it is we who are the experts at reflecting reality to the masses. Don't tell me what we reflect is an illusion. When enough people see and believe, they act and the result is metaphysical. Don't you agree? Or was what we did to you an illusion? And here is my trump card, Mr. Wallace. Like you say about a truly good person being unable to recognize his own goodness because it (like the ether of existence) is such a continuous presence, he knows nothing else. But, he can easily recognize it when he's bad because it does not fit in with any part of his psyche. Me? Well, my soul is corrupted enough that I can no longer perceive the bad within me. I am immune from guilting, but creators can be guilted so easily. Pretty ironic, don't you think.... And yet the genesis of the guilt is real: each has committed the Original Sin by compromising his consciousness to adapt to this civilization. Am I really to blame? The sin was here before I came. I merely adapted to it is all. (Or should you look in the mirror?) You cannot hold me responsible for who I am.

Consciousness is what gives one choice — control over reality. I've reduced my consciousness to the point where I no longer have a choice. Just as all those who follow me will have no choice either about being born into an anticivilization. No one is immune. Consider Ayn Rand, mankind's only notable exception, who had, incidentally, intellectual powers, and yes, even benevolence far exceeding your own. Yet, even she valued the anticivilization — though in a negative way. She sensed this in the process of writing her masterpiece, "Atlas Shrugged", and attempted to negate its influence on her (blank out the blank out) by using "pure consciousness" — an irrational concept.

The bitterness in her writing, when the awareness of the anticivilization was closer to the surface, was buried and replaced by a kind of deadness. The result was, as unprecedented an achievement "Atlas" was, it had a secondary, rather than primary influence. It was the mind, not the soul of the author that was communicated. You see, everyone must protect his place in the anticivilization, at whatever cost, because it is the only place he knows. Anything else, for him, is to risk the deepest fear, a total loss of context — a kind of spiritual death.

You are fighting against people's survival instincts, Mr. Wallace. I am helping to prepare a place for them. Who do you think will win? Neo-Tech is fond of making predictions so allow me to make a prediction — one that will come true. 2001 will arrive. Nothing will happen. You will die. And we will take over Neo-Tech.com (if there is anything worth taking over). If need be, we will pick up how to control people through their Neo-Tech identity, just as we learned how to control people through their Christian or social identity.

In this world, I am the problem, but I am also the solution — so we will be around for many years to come. Our representatives may change, but one thing stays the same: "You cannot defy the will of the world." Rand, and all the others that preceded her failed and you will too.

It is much better to admit defeat early rather than put your energy into something that will eventually collapse or be taken over by us. It's hard to be Zon, isn't it? Upon contact with our civilization, you keep slipping back, don't you? Well, rather than isolate yourself on your own little Neo-Tech island, why not use your knowledge to gain and profit and take from our civilization? Why spend your last remaining years chasing windmills, when, if only you'd learn to open up to it, our world has so much to offer? You believe in non-sacrifice. Who has sacrificed more these past thirty years for as little gain?

You still think it's me who cannot give up his investment in the anticivilization. No, I don't need to because that is reality here on this earth. It's you who cannot give up his investment in the C of U. It's you who is wasting his one and only precious life — for what cause?

Mystics need neocheaters and neocheaters need mystics. No one needs Zon. Rather than placing an ideal before reality, accept the context that we live in. Turn your knowledge around. Don't think of inducing mysticism as evil, rather recognize the neocheater's goodness in using mysticism to make living in an anticivilization bearable.

# Reference #2

## Wallace vs. Harvard et al Defamation Lawsuit

Harvard Law School, Harvard University, et al tried to stop Internet-newsgroup postings that are revealing 2400 years of lawyer-like dishonesties. Their method was to defame the author of those posts — Dr. Frank R. Wallace.

Dr. Wallace is a former Senior Research Chemist for E. I. du Pont de Nemours & Co., Inc. He is also a world-read author of anti-religious/anti-force/anti-fraud literature called Neo-Tech. His writings are published in twelve languages and circulated to 156 countries. He avoids publicity and protects his privacy as well as his family's privacy. Except for his family, he has no social or public life. He makes no public appearances and grants no interviews. Since 1986, he has worked toward curing the life-diminishing diseases of irrationality, mysticism, and dishonesty. In 1997, he began effectively using the Internet to reveal how lawyer-like dishonesties have harmed every individual and corrupted every society since 431 B.C. And, today, the blatant dishonesties escalating throughout America's political and legal systems are dramatically illustrated via Dr. Wallace's publications, both in print and on the Internet.

In September 1997, a representative of Harvard Law School and Harvard University launched a daily ad-hominem campaign directed at Dr. Wallace. That campaign failed to stop the Internet postings revealing lawyer-like dishonesties. Thus, in December 1997, Harvard's campaign degenerated into defamation — into dishonestly conjuring up false accusations of heinous sexual crimes. Moreover, that representative is a long-term, professional law student at Harvard University. He publicly admitted the 600-plus defaming attacks on IRS/lawyer-related newsgroups were directed at Dr. Wallace (see exhibits #1a-b) to stop his Internet program of educating the public about lawyer-like dishonesties (see exhibits #2a-h).

With Harvard's sanction, the representative used Harvard's name and its owned/paid-for Internet equipment/server to defame Frank R. Wallace. Under Harvard's prestigious banners, that representative then attempted to jail Dr. Wallace through a publicly solicited conspiracy to file police reports containing false accusations of sexual child molestation. Throughout that illicit campaign, Harvard Law School and Harvard University provided heavyweight credibility with their world-renowned names emblazoned atop each public Internet message defaming Frank R. Wallace. That Harvard credibility reached into soliciting others to make false police reports (see exhibits #3a-f).

Harvard et al's defamation campaign has been aggressively waged for months while providing zero evidence of child molestation. ...Harvard Law School, Harvard University, et al are responsible for swamping the Internet with disgustingly ugly snippets of child pornography arising from their own whole-cloth fabrications about Frank R. Wallace having "third-grade girls to suck his penis" (see exhibits #4a-g). They then continued to fantasize publicly about having Dr. Wallace sent to prison in which "prison rape by convicts would break his wide-scope integrations about lawyer-like dishonesties". ...Almost daily, for weeks, Harvard's representative obsessively posted his pornographic defamations across the Internet. That same representative is a long-term Harvard law student with a propensity toward child pornography dating back to 1992 (see www.qz.to/~eli/erotica/various/term-paper.html). He also had achieved some Internet notoriety with his malevolent public signature, "I have a firm grip on reality, now I can strangle it." (See www.faisal.com/quotes/s.html).

Furthermore, that Harvard representative persistently urged others to notify the police in Dr. Wallace's hometown about him being a "child molester" and a "danger to their children" (see exhibit #5a). Yet, knowingly filing false police reports against innocent people is a criminal act. Still, other anti Neo-Tech "lawyers" reading the lawyer-oriented newsgroups were encouraged through Internet messages from prestigious Harvard to further defame Frank R. Wallace by portraying him as molesting not just third-grade children, but now three-year-old children (see exhibit #6a).

## Motive for Defaming Frank R. Wallace
### by
### Harvard Law School, Harvard University, et al

Written under various pen names, the literature of Frank R. Wallace circulates worldwide both through books printed in twelve languages and across World-Wide-Web sites in four languages (see www.neo-tech.com). His publications educate the productive middle class about the damages inflicted upon it via lawyer-like dishonesties. For, such dishonesties are the root cause of the productive class being parasitically drained, exploited, harmed, enslaved, and killed for the past 2400 years — since lawyer-like politician Pericles delivered his inflaming funeral oration of 431 B.C. With that profoundly dishonest oration, he incited continuation of the thirty-year Peloponnesian War for his own personal glory and political power. That unnecessary war slaughtered countless thousands of innocent value producers along with their families and children. ...Promoted by politician/lawyer-like dishonesties, that war ultimately destroyed the flourishing Athenian civilization (see www.neo-tech.com/lastbook-ww/intro-002.html).

Pericles and Plato introduced the rationalizations for "noble" lies and lawyer-like dishonesties. Since that time, politicians and lawmakers have manipulated such lies and dishonesties to extract wealth and power from the value producers. The renowned Greek historian Thucydides identified how the golden-soul elitists lived through "noble" lies used to politically manipulate and parasitically drain value-producing citizens. The unearned powers of those parasitical elites increasingly corrupted and ultimately destroyed the brilliantly advancing Athenian culture. That great culture was advancing toward a civilization based on value production, scientific inquiry, the arts, and integrated honesty. Athens then became corrupted with Pericles/Plato manipulated truths, sophistic rhetoric, and "noble" lies. With that demise of history's most rational-and-honest culture, the subsequent societies on planet Earth fell into the same corruptions through the same politician/lawyer-like dishonesties that manipulate and drain the populace.

Harvard et al tried to stop Dr. Wallace's Internet program to educate the productive middle class about the hidden harms of lawyer-like dishonesties. Specifically, Harvard et al defamed Frank R. Wallace in trying to halt his educational series of ten archetype lawyer-like dishonesties routinely rotated on lawyer-oriented newsgroups. That series of newsgroup posts are found on the World Wide Web address:

www.neo-tech.com/lastbook

Does Wallace condemn politicians and lawyers? Absolutely not. He is from a four-generation family of lawyers, politicians, judges, congressmen, and New-York-State Attorney Generals. He has never condemned lawyers or the legal profession per se. To the contrary, he publicly states in print and on the World Wide Web the crucial need for objective law and the honorable role of lawyers in the past, present, and future.

Dr. Wallace's educational campaign is one of support for the legal profession through objective law. Indeed, that educational campaign brings forth integrated honesty to replace the manipulated "truths", out-of-context facts, and subjective law too often used by politicians and lawyers for unearned gains that harm society. Dr. Wallace's educational campaign will continue until (1) only honest lawyers can gain livelihoods, (2) only objective law is practiced, and (3) destructive political-agenda laws disappear from planet Earth.

Ironically, the public defamation of Frank R. Wallace by Harvard et al provides a dramatic illustration of the lawyer-like dishonesties that Dr. Wallace continues to reveal across the Internet. The odd twist in this lawsuit is that for centuries trained lawyers have carefully, skillfully avoided creating actionable dishonesties. Thus, they astutely kept evidence of their dishonesties well hidden from public perception — hidden especially from legal action. From the perspective of centuries-old lawyer traditions and training, the defamation of Frank R. Wallace was uncharacteristically foolish and legally indefensible. Harvard et al's defamations were not only knowingly false, purposely malignant, and permanently damaging, but were emotionally driven, profoundly unprofessional, and fully exposed to actionable tort.

The Harvard-sponsored defamation of Frank R. Wallace was aggressively conducted over a period of several months, even after Harvard et al were explicitly and publicly warned across the Internet by Dr. Wallace's attorney on December 27, 1997. They were warned that their continued defamation and possible criminal acts were legally actionable (see exhibits #7a-b). Yet, Harvard's representative publicly, foolishly ridiculed that legal warning as he continued to defame Frank R. Wallace with daily, multiple newsgroup posts to the Internet (see exhibits #8a-c).

Harvard et al's defamation campaign continued unabated up to the February 20, 1998 filing of the defamation lawsuit. The defamation continued despite posted email notices to the Dean of Harvard Law School, Robert Clarke, and to Harvard Law Professor, Laurence H. Tribe, warning them that their representative was making libelous posts under Harvard's auspices while using Harvard's name along with its owned/paid-for Internet equipment and server (see exhibits #9a-d). Moreover, the defamation continued even after others warned Harvard's representative that his dishonest, libelous, and defamatory posts could place him in legal jeopardy (see exhibits #10a-b).

## Damages Inflicted on Frank R. Wallace
by
Harvard Law School, Harvard University, et al

With their concerted defamation campaign, Harvard et al smeared damage and stigma across the life and accomplishments of Frank R. Wallace. The damage was inestimable among Dr. Wallace's professional associates and his millions of readers worldwide. Even more damaging was the harm done to his family. ...Harvard et al were not only responsible for permanently harming Frank R. Wallace's business and professional life, but for diminishing his personal life as well as the lives of his wife, children, and grandchildren.

That malicious, widespread public defamation caused Frank R. Wallace and his family irreparable damage and permanent pain. For, defamation involving child molestation carries an unerasable stigma like no other stigma. That stigma and harm carry to Dr. Wallace's young grandchildren and their parents. Such defamation can ruin the victim's life by depriving him of trusting, happy relations with his family, friends, associates, and the public. That, in turn, can lead to loss of happiness, productivity, and purpose in life — even to suicide.

## Knowingly False Basis of Defamation
by
Harvard Law School, Harvard University, et al

What was the basis of Harvard Law School, Harvard University,

62

et al falsely accusing Frank R. Wallace of child molestation? The entire defamation campaign was based on a six-sentence statement about Ibsen's mythical character, Peer Gynt, plucked from Dr. Wallace's two-million words in print. That statement was taken from a chapter titled *Solveig's Song* in a 1997 portion of a nonfiction novel *QS* embedded in a 512-page, hard-copy book titled *Outcompeting God and Government* (ISBN#9111752-82-x, Library of Congress #97-076000). *Solveig's Song* containing that same statement was also published in a 24-page booklet and mass mailed on September 26, 1997, as part of a seven-year mailing campaign to every federal judge as well as every member of the United States Senate and House of Representatives. In addition, *Solveig's Song* was mailed to hundreds of high-ranking federal officials and to every state Governor on a 2800-name mailing list (exhibits available). ...And, finally, both *QS* and *Solveig's Song* have been continuously available for free-and-open reading by anyone since mid 1997 on the World Wide Web address: www.neo-tech.com

From all the publications and worldwide distributions of *Solveig's Song*, never from anyone, including Dr. Wallace's many critics and opponents who would like to silence him (especially his critics from the religious right) has there ever been a misinterpretation of *Solveig's Song* as "child molestation". Moreover, no one has ever questioned a single passage in any of Dr. Wallace's vast published and unpublished works to even remotely suggest anything about child molestation. In fact, his 1986, 800-page, flagship publication, *The Neo-Tech Discovery*, harshly condemns child abuse and child molestation as first-order, objective crimes requiring severe punishments.

*Solveig's Song* is described in its Introduction as "an allegory of (1) adults returning to the Civilization of the Universe experienced in their childhood and (2) children remaining in the Civilization of the Universe as they become adults." That allegory is based on the twenty-year demonstrations and proofs throughout the two-million-word body of Neo-Tech literature that children exist as innocent, honest individuals in the Civilization of the Universe until 6-9 years of age. In that age range, children are increasingly dragged out of their natural, pro-value lives into an unnatural, anti-value civilization.

*Solveig's Song*: The Redemption of Beauty, Honesty, and Love

As are many of Frank R. Wallace's writings in the past thirty years, *Solveig's Song* is a metaphorical story with multiple layers of wide-scope integrations and interconnected meanings — leading to three themes: honesty, integrity, and justice. Those themes consistently point to objective reality. In fact, the essence of mankind's future survival and prosperity is fully integrated honesty. And, for the past eighteen years, fully integrated honesty has been the formal definition of Neo-Tech printed in every Neo-Tech hard-copy and cyberspace publication.

*Solveig's Song* rises from the Norwegian playwright Henrik Ibsen's drama *Peer Gynt* and the musical suites of romantic tone-poet Edvard Grieg. That mythical story involves two young people, Gynt and Solveig. With all her heart, Solveig loves Gynt (a metaphor for the Child Zon who exists in every child and adult). But, she realizes that Gynt is filled with immaturities rising from his undisciplined powers of youth. Out of her abiding love for Gynt and her unyielding loyalty to values, she explicitly exercises self-restraint to postpone her passions until Gynt also discovers, many years later, the maturity and honesty required for genuinely happy romantic love. Those requirements are a value-based sexual relationship fulfilled in a monogamous marriage. ...For the full context of Solveig's six-sentence statement, one must read the segment of published literature in which that statement is embedded. That segment is provided in the following italicized text:

64

---

*Child Zon is an allegory of*
*(1) adults returning to the Civilization of the Universe*
*experienced in their childhood*
*and*
*(2) children remaining in the Civilization of the Universe as*
*they become adults.*

---

*Copyright © 1997*
*Zon Associates, Ltd.*

### Child Zon

*A schoolyard bully named Atf seemed large and powerful. Towering over third-grader Zon near the top steps to the second-floor school entrance, Atf grabbed Zon's throat with one hand and, with his other hand, cocked a vibrating fist, ready to strike. While not knowing Archimedes' laws of leverage, those silent laws of nature spoke to Zon. In a lightning instant, child Zon stepped on the bully's toe and flicked him away. Down the flight of stairs tumbled Atf. He never bothered Zon or anyone else at that school again. ...Child Zon became a silent victor in one swift move of nature that protected him and others from physical force for the rest of his school days.*

*In the third grade, after winning all the king-marble shooters in the schoolyard, Zon learned how to gain sex, money, and power in this anticivilization. Gain sex, money, and power in the third grade? Yes, indeed, Zon controlled the dynamics of sex, money, and power so confidently, so effortlessly through nature's Quintessential Secret that he could put each such activity aside for the next eight years. For, he had too much to learn about living in this world without surrendering to its anticivilization — without being detected — without being waylaid by pretty girls, gaining money, or mystic-promoting teachers, parents, and peers.*

*Yet, from that point on, he had the power on the deepest level to outcompete everyone in Earth's anticivilization for sex, money, and power.*

*Where did Zon get that power? Was it a cosmic power emanating from beyond? Was it mind over matter? No, the opposite was the fact. His power came from the here-and-now laws of nature combined with consistent effort, honesty, logic, and reason.*

### Solveig's Song

*Bonnie Lou Solveig was her name. She was the prettiest, smartest girl in the third grade. She was also a child prodigy — a concert pianist. Her name became a song as she walked with Zon across a field hidden behind the blockhouses of the working class. She was from another world. Someday, she would teach Zon the omnipotence of fully integrating honesty with conscious life. Someday, the entire Civilization of the Universe would be embodied in her body and soul.*

*Suddenly, Solveig stopped, sank to her knees, grabbed for the buttons on Zon's fly and implored, "You are my god. I want you to do to me what my father does to my mother every night. I want you to do it to me every day forever. I'll wait till you're like me. ...I'll wait till you won't die. Then you'll do it to me forever."*

*With Solveig, child Zon perceived a secret about another world — a real world perceived through a Golden Helmet. Then Solveig was gone. Yet, she left him with a guiding wisdom combined with a power unknown to anyone since Jesus. Child Jesus, however, never experienced Solveig's world. Thus, Jesus became lost in the anticivilization and was eventually crucified for his public identifications of the parasitical-elite class. But, Zon, wearing that Golden Helmet, was never lost. He quietly moved beyond the anticivilization. He moved from classrooms to back rooms; from library tables to card tables; from university laboratories to merchant-ship engine rooms; from steel mills to tobacco auctions; from scientific societies to prison societies; from books to writing; from writing to action...always integrating, always learning, always self-correcting, always controlling reality with an ever widening reach.*

*Never removing his Golden Helmet, Zon built the dynamics that will eventually overwhelm anticivilization politics and lawyer-like dishonesties without using a single tool of force or fraud, without consuming a single tax dollar, without soliciting a single political vote. ...Zon built a dynamic through Solveig's wisdom that will eventually bring everyone the eternal prosperity available throughout the Civilization of the Universe.*

The story of Zon will continue
until
1. Zon's Quintessential Secret fully reveals the C of U
2. Everyone returns to Solveig
3. Everyone dwells in the Civilization of the Universe.

*Solveig's Song* reflects a key moral lesson of human life. Mythical Solveig conveys a powerful, beautiful statement for children and adults alike to exercise self-restraint, self-respect, and maturity by pursuing uncompromised integrity and honest frankness within the laws of nature. ...Through learning that lesson, one earns the long-range values and happiness available from life — a lesson from which President Clinton could have avoided his sexual immaturities and impotence leading to his ever expanding dishonesties and corruptions.

If not for the explicit atheistic/humanistic nature of Dr. Wallace's writings, Solveig's statement would be embraced not only by the populace, but by the religious right as a moral lesson for children and adults alike. For, to young and old alike, the message of Solveig's statement reflects a self-discipline that prevents immature irrationalities and unchecked passions from subverting one's life and happiness. ...*Solveig's Song* reflects an unwavering loyalty both to the laws of objective reality and to the human virtues of honesty and integrity.

\* \* \* \*

Lawyer-like dishonesties turn objective reality upside down by making the good bad and the bad good. The defamation lawsuit, *Wallace vs. Harvard et al*, uprights reality by permanently exposing lawyer-like dishonesties — by publicly delivering justice.

\* \* \* \*

Reference #                                                    Message ID#

#1  a   Deja News http://wz.dejanews.com/
    b   5kb3ht$d0m$4@nntp1.ba.best.com

#2  a   &lt;silversm-070597191934001@hls-silversm.student.harvard.edu&gt
    b   &lt;silversm-260997173402001@hls-silversm.student.harvard.edu&gt
    c   &lt;silversm-2709970009320001@hls-silversm.student.harvard.edu&gt
    d   &lt;silversm-2310971047180001@hls-silversm.student.harvard.edu&gt
    e   &lt;silversm-0911972106130001@hls-silversm.student.harvard.edu&gt
    f   &lt;silversm-1111970833450001@hls-silversm.student.harvard.edu&gt
    g   &lt;silversm-1001981753260001@hls-silversm.student.harvard.edu&gt
    h   34B26A5D.12A9@chinadirect.com

#3  a   &lt;silversm-1010970822250001@hls-silversm.student.harvard.edu&gt
    b   &lt;silversm-2212972247350001@hls-silversm.student.harvard.edu&gt
    c   &lt;silversm-2412970928500001@hls-silversm.student.harvard.edu&gt
    d   &lt;silversm-2312971024590001@hls-silversm.student.harvard.edu&gt
    e   34A5F48.4D51@chinadirect.com
    f   34A5C661.6F2A@chinadirect.com

#4  a   &lt;silversm-2509970831110001@hls-silversm.student.harvard.edu&gt
    b   &lt;silversm-2509970823350001@hls-silversm.student.harvard.edu&gt
    c   &lt;silversm-2312971016490001@hls-silversm.student.harvard.edu&gt
    d   silversm-2312971024430001@hls-silversm.student.harvard.edu&gt
    e   34A5C4A7.17AA@chinadirect.com
    f   34B6BEDC.29D3@chinadirect.com
    g   34B67338.1010@chinadirect.com

#5  a   34AF0E33.75FE6F6F@isds-sever.jpl.nasa.gov

#6  a   34AF0E33.75FE6F6F@isds-sever.jpl.nasa.gov

#7  a   68415e$q1r@sjx-ixn10.ix.netcom.com
    b   6841dd$q1r@sjx-ixn10.ix.netcom.com

#8  a   6855lt$mkf@nntp02.primenet.com
    b   silversm-2912971154410001@hls-silversm.student.harvard.edu&gt
    c   silversm-2912971202270001@hls-silversm.student.harvard.edu&gt

#9  a   Pine.BSF.3.96.971229141729.17741B-100000@shell5.ba.best.com
    b   Pine.BSF.3.96.971229141729.17741B-100000@shell5.ba.best.com

Reference #                    Message ID#

    c   Pine.BSF.3.96.980102123719.20068A-100000@shell5.ba.best.com
    d   34ACC553.3773904E@mindless.com

#10 a   34AF995E.7C0955ED@erols.com
    b   34AE8180.6004E692@erols.com
    c   34A65DA9.47BDD08C@erols.com
    d   34A8E8E0.D3628F8B@erols.com
    e   34B0F34C.39567876@erols.com
    f   34AA8D98.7FC9@servtech.com,

# Reference #3

## Cruel-and-Unusual Punishment
### IRS Abuse Reports

As provided in Appendix I (pages 295-476), Neo-Tech Publishing Company prepared the accompanying 489 IRS Abuse Reports for committees of the United States Senate and the House of Representatives investigating the illegal abuses of the Internal Revenue Service (IRS). ...Those reports were also sent to all United States Federal Judges. For, they are the ones who rule on cases involving the IRS.

# Reference #4

## Neo-Tech Enriches Every Individual
as each leaves
## Earth's Anticivilization

Leaving Neo-Tech
on a
Streetcar Named Desire

In the movie *Leaving Las Vegas*, anticivilization-escaping alcohol unleashes the drunken joys of irrationality and death. In the document *Leaving Neo-Tech*, anticivilization-causing dishonesty unleashes the lawyer joys of crime and parasitism. On leaving Las Vegas, the character played by Nicholas Cage will be dead. On leaving Neo-Tech, the society orchestrated by the anticivilization will be dead. ...Consider this: Without business entrepreneurs, moral/economic-bankrupt socialism dies more quickly and humanely when faced with competition from free-market capitalism. Without Neo-Tech, the lawyer/politician-led anticivilization will die more quickly and humanely when faced with competition from honest/cyberspace-led entrepreneurs.

Lures of Suicide

Sixty years ago, a song about leaving Earth's anticivilization titled *Gloomy Sunday*, sung by the jazz-blues singer Billie Holiday, was banned from the airwaves because the song lured listeners into suicide. It was dubbed the "Hungarian Suicide Song". Today, the song of Earth's anticivilization is captured in an earlier published book titled *Outcompeting God and Government*. The song within that book can likewise lure readers into suicide, directly or indirectly. Dubbing that book the "Anticivilization Suicide Song", it was withdrawn from the market after its first printing. The remaining inventory was destroyed.

## A Dangerous Puzzle

During six years of discovering, gathering, and assembling the puzzle pieces that reveal the anticivilization, the author of *Outcompeting God and Government* journeyed ever closer to mortal dangers. Consternation arose on realizing that exposing others to the "Anticivilization Suicide Song" could draw them into similar dangers.

The more one assembles the anticivilization puzzle revealing its vermiculating criminalities, the more that person must escape the inescapable anticivilization. ...Consider the following quote from *Outcompeting God and Government*:

"On Discovering Earth's Lawyer-Rationalized Anticivilization,
one must choose among
Killing, Being Killed, Looting, Suicide,
Madness, Mystical Escape

or one can choose

Neo-Tech Sublimation
into
Cyberspace/Cybercash Businesses
that vanish the
Dishonesties of an Anticivilization"

## New Knowledge is Needed to Choose Sublimation

For the first time, with the publication the *Protocols*, a written document identifies the causes and effects of an incurable anticivilization engulfing planet Earth. Today, on each reading of the *Protocols,* one synthesizes spirals of unexpected knowledge. That new knowledge provides vivid, camouflage-free views of Earth's anticivilization. One then discovers that everyone on Earth does indeed live in an inescapable anticivilization — an irrational civilization in which everyone is driven into one or more of six life failures, with failure #6 common to everyone on Earth today:

*Final Anticivilization Document*

1. self-destructive mystical escapes moving toward self-defeating life styles
2. self-imposed loneliness moving toward isolation
3. self-inflicted depression moving toward insanity
4. self-chosen parasitism moving toward criminality
5. self-driven failure moving toward suicide
6. self-accepted aging and decline moving toward death.

Consider the nature of an anticivilization characterized by lawyer-like dishonesties, deceptions, and criminalities:

The Basis of an Anticivilization
is
Lawyer-Like Dishonesty
that arose from
Pericles and Plato

Earth's Anticivilization
is a world operating through
Self-Deceptions
epitomized by
Dostoyevsky's Grand Inquisitor

In Dostoyevsky's *Brothers Karamazov*, the brother Ivan rejected the camouflaged dishonesties and criminalities of the ultimate, lawyer-like deceiver — the Grand Inquisitor. On recognizing the incurable dishonesty, criminality, and injustice of the Grand Inquisitor, brother Ivan tried returning his ticket to existence as the only honest option. By contrast, Stavrogin in Dostoyevsky's *The Possessed* bought into the Grand-Inquisitor's world. On recognizing the nature of the anticivilization in which everyone lived with no escape, Stavrogin hastened to buy his one-way ticket for living through criminal violence — to live as a self-righteous, lawyer-rationalizing terrorist. And, finally, Dostoyevsky's *Crime and Punishment* presents the criminal-minded

74

Raskolnikov. That young man used Periclean/Platonic justifications to murder an innocent businessman. He used those rationalizations to support "greatness" — to financially support "Raskolnikov's greatness" — to support his "elite-wannabe" parasitisms.

In Verdi's opera *Otello* (*Othello*), Iago's credo rings factual in an anticivilization. Iago, a smooth clintonian liar, is the pinnacle symbol for hidden evil — a subtle metaphor for lawyer-created monstrosities such as the DEA, FDA, IRS, and the Association of Trial Lawyers of America. Yet, like Othello, innocent people who encounter such evil creations are compelled to escape the inescapable, often with tragic results. Those tragedies comprise irrational isolations, insanities, even suicides...or crimes of theft, murder, even genocide. ...Historical examples of those who vividly experienced the anticivilization are illustrated in the early pages of the re-written *Outcompete God and Government*.

## Tragic Teen Suicides

Consider the seemingly inexplicable escalation of teen suicides. The root of many youth suicides lies in the fact that before the age of six, children experience the rational, benevolent Civilization of the Universe. That fact is established in the Neo-Tech publication *Profound Honesty* (640 pages, 1996). As teenagers, however, they sense being driven helplessly from an honest, happy world into either (1) an escapist Huckleberry-Finn[1] world of

---

[1]Mark Twain's *Huckleberry Finn* is about a youth entering manhood who refuses to enter the anticivilization. The defining moment occurs when Huck tears-up the anticivilization document demanding that he turn runaway slave Jim over to the authorities. Huck says that he chooses going to Hell rather than obeying that political-agenda law. He then discovers that Hell is the utterly lonely realm on Earth that lies outside its anticivilization. T. S. Eliot describes Huck as the loneliest person in literature. Huck himself says he feels at times so lonely he wishes he were dead. ...Nineteenth-century America was the only nation moving towards the Civilization of the Universe. In that sense, Ernest

(footnote continued on next page)

rejecting the anticivilization or (2) a dishonest, irrational anticivilization from which no escape exists.[1]  That no-escape sense, if sufficiently vivid, compels suicide.  With passing years, however, everyone loses the sense and memory of childhood experiences in the Civilization of the Universe.  Thus, the attraction for suicide among surrendered youth diminishes with age.  As adults, they surrender to Freud's false superego.  They surrender to the status quo. ...They surrender to ultimate suicide — ultimate failure and meaningless death in an incurable anticivilization.

The re-written *Outcompete God and Government* was the first document to identify — fully, explicitly, vividly — the anticivilization that strangles everyone on planet Earth.  The author of *Outcompete* did not evade those identifications.  Instead, he identified ever more anticivilization realities — hidden realities that guarantee everyone's failure and death.

A death-to-life race ensued in which the author either had to surrender, fail, and die in the anticivilization...or he had to rise through business to assemble a puzzle that emotionally and intellectually identified the anticivilization from which everyone could disinvest.  He chose to assemble that puzzle.  Would he have time to build the strength and knowledge needed for switching life's investments from the anticivilization into the Civilization of the Universe?  In his death-to-life race, he re-wrote that penultimate anticivilization publication, *Outcompeting God and Government*.  In that re-written version, the author discovered not only how to avoid the dangers encountered upon identifying Earth's anticivilization, but how to profit from such identifications.

---

(footnote continued from previous page)

Hemingway identified that all *authentic* American literature arose from *Huckleberry Finn*.

[1]As Henry James identified in his Freudian novel, *Turning of the Screw*, most children are captured and ultimately destroyed by anticivilization "teachers" who inject corrupting "ghosts" into innocent minds.

## Götterdämmerung
### *The Twilight of the Gods*

Friedrich Nietzsche first envisioned the sublimation of Earthlings to Obermen. Yet, perhaps no figure in literary history so fully felt the heavy milieu of a no-escape anticivilization. His early friend, Richard Wagner, similarly felt the darkness of Earth's anticivilization. Nietzsche so intensely felt the fatal diminishment of its every citizen that he constantly suffered nervous and physical breakdowns. Eventually, he went insane (partially because of tertiary syphilis). Caught in his passions and compassions, Nietzsche could not escape his fixation on the bleakness of every Earthling dying in an anticivilization. ...He saw no escape. He saw no one sublimating to an Oberman.

Nietzsche had no knowledge of the Civilization of the Universe, Zon, or the ultimate nothingness of the anticivilization built on a matrix of irrational dishonesties. Instead, Nietzsche saw the mortal anticivilization epitomized by the life-shrinking Judeo/Christian ethics. On Earth, he saw as authentic only animals, children, and ironically, Jesus. ...Nietzsche saw Jesus as naively honest — a child-like ignoramus — somewhat like the innocent, other-world Myshkin in Dostoevsky's *The Idiot*, or even like William Faulkner's innocent, crucified (castrated) Benjy in *The Sound and the Fury*. Nietzsche also recognized how his sweet Jesus was savagely exploited centuries later by Christian frauds.

Perhaps Nietzsche thought he saw one person rise above the corrupted, narcotized masses — the magnificent Goethe. Perhaps Nietzsche saw Goethe as the closest to becoming an Oberman with his pervasive genius and artistic integrity. ...Nietzsche had not the benefit of knowing about Ayn Rand, the intellectual Oberman artist of the 20th century. Her cult followers consider her the Öbermensch. Yet, she too was still a step away from a Zon who lives through a C-of-U business matrix. That matrix evolves through Neo-Tech with its fully integrated honesty and wide-scope accounting.

## Strum und Drang
### *The Struggle and Sublimation Starts*

On Monday, November 3, 1986, I & O Publishing possessed priceless volumes of unpublished manuscripts, crucial research documents, and hard-earned assets for the Research Institute for Biological Immortality (RIBI). Those documents and assets were key to RIBI's carefully planned, FDA-prohibited, Swiss-conducted, offshore human-cloning project scheduled for 1987 — a decade earlier than Dolly's cloning. At 12:25 PM on that criminally destructive day in 1986, sixteen gun-toting IRS agents violently attacked I&O and RIBI with threats to kill. After beating, kicking, and hospitalizing the innocent RIBI editor, they seized and destroyed RIBI's works and assets that promised an eternally prosperous future for mankind.

For ten hours, their wanton destruction of precious values reigned. During their methodical destruction of lives, business, and values, they feasted on pizza and ice cream, told boisterous jokes, and harassed female employees with pornographic pictures. By day's end, those gunmen laughed and celebrated. They thought the seek-loot-destroy mission for their parasitical-elite clients had succeeded. Using an IRS-beholden judge, the parasitical elites then sent the author of Neo-Tech in chains to an isolated desert prison. ...They laughed again.

But, they laughed too soon. On Saturday, May 22, 1992, a meeting occurred among Neo-Tech business supporters. During that meeting, the author, recently released from federal prison, made his opening move. He made his initial public identification of the anticivilization versus the Civilization of the Universe. At that moment, a door of light swung open to identify, for the first time, the anticivilization stripped of its camouflages.

Yet, with each advance toward communicating the integrations of the anticivilization versus the C of U, the author experienced increased "Huck-Finn" isolation on being considered by others as "too far out" or going in a "wrong direction". Those others defended their anticivilization investments. Those others closed the door of light to avoid the life-changing "dangers" of the approaching Civilization of the Universe. ...How could the author deliver the courage, strength, and knowledge to others so they could safely open that door?

The author continued to gather and assemble puzzle pieces for sublimating conscious minds from the anticivilization into the Civilization of the Universe. To accomplish that task, he would have to discover and then disclose Nature's Quintessential Secret (NQS) that would bypass everyone's investment-protecting defenses. He could then bring the necessary knowledge and strength into the lives of others. ...Could he succeed before the irrational anticivilization self-destructs via nuclear, chemical, and biological weapons? The answer partly evolves from the following questions and answers:

Q: For the author of Neo-Tech, what about the stigma of being convicted and imprisoned?
A: Being imprisoned for a political-agenda "crime" is no stigma at all. In fact, the author wears as a badge of honor his being imprisoned for advancing the rational Golden-Helmet revenue system. Indeed, from prison, he started spreading the nationwide/worldwide process for ending the destructively irrational income-tax system.

Q: Does the author wear Stephen Crane's "Red Badge of Courage"?
A: One's courage is unknown until tested in battle. Most on Earth are marched from childhood into the anticivilization — into a battle of irrationalities. Each who enters that battle becomes trapped in an iron box of inverted reality. That inverted reality eventually grinds everyone into a corpse.

Q: How can we escape?
A: Look not toward God or Government to escape that iron box — that corpse-making insanity. Look not toward God and

Government to find eternal life and prosperity. God and Government are the origins of insanity and corpse making. Instead, look toward fully integrated honesty to vanish insanity and death. ...The honesty of cyberspace brings forth the Civilization of the Universe. ...The first sign occurs with *Leaving Neo-Tech* — with Neo-Tech leaving Earth's anticivilization to bring forth the Civilization of the Universe.

Q: Leaving Neo-Tech? Neo-Tech leaving the anticivilization? What does that mean?
A: It means leaving integrated honesty out of the anticivilization. It means letting the anticivilization continue to manipulate its "Truths" without honesty as Shakespeare clearly understood four-hundred years ago. It means leaving Neo-Tech out of the lawyer-like dishonesties inherent throughout the anticivilization. In other words, do not mix the integrated honesty of Neo-Tech with the dishonesties of the anticivilization, its bogus "Truths", its lawyer-like deceptions. Then, each individual can discover the lain-bare anticivilization. Each can gain the personal vision and courage to sweep away his or her anticivilization investments.

Q: How can a person do that?
A: By factually and emotionally discovering the Civilization of the Universe available today in cyberspace. How? By seeing the competitive and psychological advantages of abandoning the anticivilization. Eventually, no one will choose to fail and die by remaining in the anticivilization of mortal losers. Aided by cyberspace communications and businesses, people will dump their destructive anticivilization investments and replace them with productive C-of-U investments. That replacement process is implied in Mark Hamilton's 1998 book titled *God-Man: Our Final Evolution*, identified in the re-written *Outcompete God and Government,* and unfolded in Frank R. Wallace's *NQS.*

Q: What is *NQS*?

A: It's a metaphorical opera revealing nature's Quintessential Secret.

Q: An opera?

A: Metaphorical. ...Consider what composers Carl von Weber and Richard Wagner accomplished with opera in the nineteenth century: Inspired by Weber's pioneering opera, *Der Freischütz*, Wagner orchestrated together various art forms to synthesize an emotional/intellectual whole greater than its parts. He accomplished that enlargement through his operas, especially in his masterpiece, *Tristan and Isolde*. In that way, Wagner produced expanded forms of mysticism. Wagner's mystical world transcended Earth's anticivilization. ...By contrast, *NQS* constructs a new world free of mysticism. *NQS's* real world transcends the unreal worlds of Weber, Wagner, and everyone today.

Q: I assume those closest associated with Neo-Tech Publishing will profit the most.

A: No. Others more talented and aggressive will outcompete Neo-Tech Publishing. That's where the leverage lies as a coiled spring. Others will take the lead artistically, philosophically, scientifically, politically, socially, financially, through business — through cyberspace/cybercash businesses. With greater talents and resources, others will capture the open-ended profits available from liquidating anticivilization investments and moving into limitless C-of-U business opportunities. ...Driven by the invisible hand of economics, people will quantum jump financially and emotionally from the loser anticivilization into the winner Civilization of the Universe.

Q: Why the intense emphasis on business, especially cyberspace business? Except for the individual, you seem to place business above all.

A: Business is *uber alles*. It is the essence of conscious life...or more precisely, universally free businesses are the essences of

81

neothink life throughout the Universe. And, indeed, universal businesses are, by nature, free of lawyer-like dishonesties and government irrationalities. Thus, such businesses cannot exist in an anticivilization. That is why conscious, mystic-prone people in the anticivilization have not yet evolved into neothinking business-oriented people in the C of U.

Q: Can one prove the C of U?
A: Astronomical observations and physical proof of the C of U are emerging on several scientific fronts today as outlined in *Outcompete God and Government*.

Q: What about the "how and why" of life and the Universe?
A: Honest, competitive business is the supreme, universally moral activity. Everyone should be grateful to the competitive value producers. Only through their business efforts is life made easier, healthier, and happier for everyone on Earth. Economic growth through business is the essential element for human health and ever longer life. On entering the Civilization of the Universe, businesses will expand throughout cyberspace into radically new realms. The publication *Profound Honesty* (1996) demonstrates "how" advanced neothinking entrepreneurs create universes in which conscious life naturally evolves.

Q: Why do they create new Universes? To ask a teleological question: What is the purpose of the Universe?
A: Neothinking business people expand future markets by creating universes and evolving new civilizations. Those advanced neothinkers require new markets and economic growth just as we humans do on planet Earth today. For that reason, Earthlings will eventually become cyberspace markets for and suppliers to the C of U. Moreover, advanced Earthlings in the far future will create their own universes to expand their businesses and markets for continued growth, prosperity, and happiness.

Q: Neo-Tech seems to answer the "how" and "why" of the universe.

A: Neo-Tech leads to the "how" and "why" of Creation: It is not an arbitrary God working through miraculous dictates. It is purposeful, neothinking entrepreneurs working through profitable businesses. They pursue eternal growth and prosperity. Thus, they must continuously create universes and life within the laws of physics.

Q: Why does Neo-Tech literature assert that advanced people throughout the Universe never have and probably never will contact Earth? Why does Neo-Tech posit UFO and extraterrestrial visitations claims as false?

A: First, no credible evidence exists for such claims. And, second, Neo-Tech's "no-contact" statement must logically be held as fact until proven otherwise. For, among the countless trillions of newly created, far less-advanced, or flawed civilizations, no economic incentive or scientific justification exists for their Creator to invest time or energy in contacting any of those civilizations.

Q: Why would there be no incentives for a Creator to contact or influence his or her evolving civilizations?

A: Again, the answer lies in economics — in the inefficient or negative return on time-and-energy investments. The most profitable and efficient business dynamic would be to increasingly create universes. Then, with no further investment of time and energy, that business Creator would let each universe naturally evolve on its own, through the universal laws of nature and physics, into countless civilizations that further evolve conscious people into free, neothinking sovereigns. After becoming integrated with the Civilization of the Universe, those *self-determined* sovereigns develop the technology for benefiting themselves and their Creator as consumers and suppliers through cyberspace/cybercash businesses. Indeed, those neothinking sovereigns eventually develop the knowledge and technology to become business Creators of their own universes and civilizations. ...Thus evolves eternal growth and life at every level of knowledge in the Civilization of the Universe.

Q: And, thus, arises the purpose of Neo-Tech and its Protocols.
A: The Protocols change contextual perspectives from a mortal anticivilization controlled by inherently oppressive parasites to the immortal Civilization of the Universe populated by eternally free entrepreneurs. From that new perspective, one's vision changes dramatically from receiving mortal failure, aging, and death — to delivering limitless prosperity, health, and happiness.

Q: What about those who worship God?
A: In the Civilization of the Universe, the only object worthy of worship is man, the value creator.

Q: What about man in the anticivilization?
A: Man, magnificent creature — unrealized Zon — is being wasted in Earth's anticivilization. On integrating the *Protocols*, he becomes omnipotent Zon in the Civilization of the Universe.

## Approaching the C of U

Neo-Tech will always be there. Neo-Tech will be at every new beginning. Neo-Tech will be in every future. Neo-Tech with the *Protocols* will bring human beings into the Civilization of the Universe.

# *Outcompete God and Government*

## Always Prosper, Never Age, Never Die

1. The nature of human beings is to prosper happily forever.

2. Hating only hatred sets one free to conduct business that will outcompete God and Government for limitless health and wealth.

*Outcompete God and Government*
for limitless
Health and Wealth
via
Nature's Quintessential Secret

# Always Prosper, Never Age, Never Die

Table of Contents

## Table of Contents Continued

# You Too Can
# Outcompete God and Government

*Outcompete God and Government* is the opening shot from the approaching Civilization of the Universe. That shot marks the beginning of the end to Earth's anticivilization. For, this work introduces the process for outcompeting God and Government (G & G). How? By integrating facts, history, and logic with business and cybercash into naturally forming Internet matrixes. Those matrixes will:

1. replace those in government, the legal profession, the universities, and various religions who live through socially harmful dishonesties;
2. replace their subjective, political-agenda, "a-point" laws with objective, nature-agenda, "the-point" laws;
3. replace their irrational, criminally malignant income taxes with rational, legally beneficial use fees;
4. empower each individual as a healthy, wealthy, sexy sovereign;

Moving toward the above four points will generate "Golden-Helmet" revenue/wealth systems (reference: www.neo-tech.com/golden-helmet/contents.html). Neo-Tech/Golden-Helmet principles should, by the turn of the century, after the y2k problem, begin delivering prosperity to the populations of this world through cyberspace by (1) ending the rule of parasitical elites and (2) bringing forth peace and prosperity to populations via cybercash free enterprise (reference: *Forbes*, 9/8/97).

# Ending 2400 Years
## of
# Lawyer-Like Dishonesties

## A Universal Brief

This universal brief intertwines history with facts to reveal the lawyer-like dishonesties gripping Western Civilization for over two millennia — a grip that eventually strangles everyone on Earth. Until now, the closer one came to revealing those dishonesties, the closer that person came to personal obliteration. Thus, throughout history, no one has fully revealed lawyer-like dishonesties. Today, however, wide-scope accountability is spreading throughout non-intimidated cyberspace to reveal those dishonesties...and will continue to do so until such dishonesties disappear.

What are lawyer-like dishonesties? They are hidden frauds, automatic lies, and camouflaged crimes that over the centuries evolved irrational governments. Such governments let parasitical rulers and professional liars gain unearned livelihoods, power, and fame by draining individuals, businesses, and society of life and property. Today's examples of those wielding such harmful dishonesties include deep-pocket-seeking tort lawyers, thug-like union leaders, criminal-behaving bureaucrats, white-collar-hoax business quislings, power-seeking politicians, mind-destroying professors, mystic-promoting religious leaders — and corrupt professional liars led by the President of the United States.

Lawyer-like dishonesties are the oldest, smoothest forms of mass deception and fraud. They quietly gut the lives of innocent people while surreptitiously draining values from society. ...Well-hidden, lawyer-like dishonesties comprise the archetype form of neocheating, which is the foundation of Earth's anticivilization observed upon leaving Plato's cave:

91

---

**Leaving Plato's Cave**
by sweeping the
Searchlight of Honesty
from
King David to Pericles to Neo-Tech
in discovering how
Lawyer-Like Dishonesties Created an Incurable Anticivilization.


Today, Neo-Tech is Ending the Irrational Income Tax
and its
Life-Destroying IRS
which is a
Criminal Force that Cripples Wealth Creation.

Tomorrow, Neo-Tech will End Lawyer-Like Dishonesties
and their
Life-Draining Institutions.

Neo-Tech frees Market-Driven Entrepreneurs
which are the
Fountainhead Dynamics
for the
Civilization of the Universe.

---

Leaving Plato's Cave

Consider what happened to those few individuals in history who discovered that human life on Earth exists in an incurable anticivilization that ultimately brings failure and death to everyone:

A Brahman Hindu (1000BC) on discovering the darkness of dishonesty in his world found "enlightenment" by abandoning everyone and "living alone in the forest";

Young Buddha (563-483BC) on discovering the incomprehensibility of dishonesty, poverty, aging, and death became a life-escaping icon who is replicated to this day;

Philosopher Socrates (470-399BC) on criticizing anticivilization dishonesties was executed;

Secular Jesus (6BC-30AD) on revealing anticivilization hypocrisies to the populace was crucified;

Shakespeare (1564-1616) through *Hamlet* handled anticivilization evils by reducing them to "quintessence dust". Shakespeare through *King Lear* handled anticivilization rulers by reducing them to nothingness. ...Shakespeare was the first to understand the dynamics behind *Outcompete God and Government* published four centuries later. Shakespeare, as does *Outcompete*, lets the anticivilization churn in space — alone, isolated, all blending into insignificance. Except for his "let's kill all the lawyers" statement in *King Henry VI*, Shakespeare had no need to pass public judgments. He just lets anticivilization irrationalities churn until self-extinguished. Like St. Augustine (354-430), in his *City of God*, Shakespeare recognized the anticivilization and evil as something nonexistent in the Civilization of the Universe;

Premier mathematician Blaise Pascal (1623-1662) escaped the contradictory anticivilization by converting to a religious fanatic;

Sublime composer Robert Schumann (1810-1856) on discovering the anticivilization sank into madness. The great opera-buffa composer Rossini (1792-1868) became mentally debilitated on discovering the futility of his freedom-seeking William Tell. ...Poet Lord Byron (1788-1824) along with the painters Vincent van Gogh (1853-1890) and Paul Gauguin (1848-1906) suffered similar tragedies on identifying the incurable anticivilization;

Henry Thoreau (1817-1862) escaped the anticivilization by living alone at Walden Pond;

Non-force Tibetan monks escaped the force-backed anticivilization by cloistering their lives in monasteries;

Novelist Fyodor Dostoyevsky (1821-1881), after barely escaping death by a government firing squad, discovered the criminal-based authorities of an anticivilization: His fictional Grand Inquisitor revealed the pinnacle of lawyer-like dishonesties and hidden criminalities;

Friedrich Nietzsche (1844-1900) consumed by the dark, no-escape heaviness of the anticivilization went insane.

The great physicist Ludwig Boltzman (1844-1906), on trying to isolate himself from dishonest criticisms and lawyer-like attacks, committed suicide;[1]

Gustav Mahler (1860-1911) in his first four symphonies sought but never found the reward of overcoming the anticivilization;

Giacomo Puccini (1858-1924), on recognizing the evil nature of government officials in an anticivilization, composed *Tosca* with its famous torture and murder scenes;

Sigmund Freud (1856-1939) saw the ugly picture of the anticivilization stored in the subconscious that the conscious mind spends a lifetime rationalizing, denying, and repressing.

Wallace Hume Carothers (1896-1937), the brilliant DuPont chemist

---

[1]Boltzman discovered one of the four physical constants of the Universe — Newton, Planck, and Einstein discovered the other three. Equally important, Boltzman was the first to **unify** the difference between the time-symmetric laws of physics (deterministic) with the asymmetric laws of thermodynamics (arrow-of-time probabilistic). Boltzman's radical **unification** step was crucial for the ongoing process of validating Neo-Tech physics. By obeying the laws of physics, neothink minds control the Universe through probabilistic thermodynamics and quantum mechanics. (See the document *Neo-Tech Physics* on www.neo-tech.com) ...Isolated beyond the anticivilization by his discoveries, the heavily criticized Ludwig Boltzman tragically committed suicide.

and inventor of nylon, committed suicide when he could no longer advance in Earth's anticivilization;

Emma Goldman (1869-1940), rejecting the anticivilization without the knowledge of Neo-Tech, became a misguided anarchist writer and charismatic orator who stood heroically against war, religion, discrimination, lawyer-like dishonesties, and force-backed governments. She was censored, jailed, deported, and died alone in Toronto seeking Ibsen's Solveig and Wallace's Neo-Tech;

F. Scott Fitzgerald (1896-1940) artistically expressed and then vividly lived the ultimate smashup and inevitable death from seeking fulfillment of passion within the anticivilization.[1]

Heaven's-Gate cult (1997) tried escaping the anticivilization via mass suicide through the sound-good, lawyer-like deceptions of its neocheating leader, "Do".

While factually blind to the anticivilization, various poets, philosophers, and writers from Robert Frost to Martin Heidegger to Charlotte Perkins Gilman to T. S. Eliot[2] emotionally expressed the artificially-constructed anticivilization into which everyone is driven as a child. Gilman in *The Yellow Wallpaper* expressed how either "escape from" or "freedom in" the anticivilization meant madness.

---

[1] F. Scott Fitzgerald, the 1920s jazz "poet" of money and romance, showed both in his novel *The Great Gatsby* and in his personal life with the dazzling Zelda Sayre how romantic desire can shape and drive lives. Perhaps every man with a lost love has some J. Gatsby within him. Other writers who captured the smashup when people drive to fulfill passionate aspirations in the anticivilization include Charles Dickens (1812-1870) in his *Great Expectations* and Gustave Flaubert (1821-1870) in his *Madame Bovary*.

[2] T. S. Eliot recognized that the anticivilization is composed of disintegrated fragments. He tried to gather those fragments in a futile attempt to assemble them into a unified, lasting value. He tried and largely failed at that attempt in his magnum opus, *The Waste Land*.

*   *   *

*Lawyer-Like Dishonesties of Pericles*
*Caused Earth's Ultimate Disaster —*
*A Disaster that Spawned*
*An Incurable Anticivilization*

Unresolvable contradictions within Earth's civilization arose from lawyer-like dishonesties 2400 years ago, starting on a grand scale with Pericles (495-429 B.C.). He discovered and exploited a powerful weapon of mass manipulation. That weapon was the newly instituted popular vote within a majority-ruled (tyranny of the majority) democracy:

Kings and tyrants ruled by force. But, force-ruled subjects usually despised such tyrants and did not support their parasitical actions. Thus, the tyrant's power and reach were restricted. Pericles discovered that a politician in a democracy also ruled by force. But, the majority cheered him onward into ever greater corruptions to expand his force-backed power and criminal reach. The politician ruled through the tyranny of the majority. He cared not what kind of criminal tyranny was demanded by the majority. He would do whatever that majority wanted, no matter how criminal or destructive, in order to accomplish his only end by any means. ...That only end is always to expand his force-backed power and criminal reach.

Upon manipulating majority support, Pericles became a tax-ravaging, monument builder for his own glory. To expand his power and "greatness", he built, for example, the budget-breaking, war-inspiring Acropolis. Aided by his vainglorious, jingoistic funeral oration in 431 B.C., Pericles deceptively argued before the voting jury of 40,000 citizens to "fall in love" with government. Why? So they would sacrifice their property and lives via force-backed taxation and aggressive wars for the glory of the state — for the glory of Pericles.

Pericles incited the citizens through dishonestly induced sophisms and jury-swaying emotionalisms. He evoked a majority

96

vote to agitate the unnecessary Peloponnesian war (431-404 B.C.) — a bully war against the smaller, backward oligarchy, Sparta. Inflamed by Pericles' power-seeking bombast to spread the glory of Athens, the war became increasingly savage, violent, corrupting with wild killing of anyone for any reason, including fathers butchering their sons.

Thucydides' history of that war revealed the full impact of its corrupting brutality that sank the great Athenian civilization. Thucydides identified Pericles' profound destructiveness that harmfully affects mankind to this day. He concluded of Pericles: "Love of power, operating through greed and personal ambition caused those evils". Yet, today, who from ancient Greece do lawyers and politicians most quote and praise? That person is Pericles. He is second only to Plato as the hero among the parasitical-elite class.

From those Periclean dishonesties arose the parable-spinning, philosopher/politician Plato (428-348 B.C.). Lawyer-like Plato openly advocated lying for political expediency.[1] Then, through an elaborate web of closed-circle deductions, he evolved an anticivilization designed to perpetuate the parasitical-elite class. Plato perfected the rationalizations needed to force the competitive value producer into supporting the parasitical elites who ply their deceptions for unearned power and glory. ...To this day, parasitical elites dishonestly survive by draining the value producer via Plato's force-backed "ideals".[2] Those mind-spun "ideals" led men

---

[1]As quoted from Plato's *The Republic*, 390 B.C.: "The rulers of the state are the only ones who should have the privilege of lying, either at home or abroad; they may be allowed to lie for the good of the state."

[2]Examine Niccolò Machiavelli's (1469-1527) **history-created** masterwork, *The Prince*. It is about pragmatic political power. Machiavelli's work has the merit of being honest realpolitik in an anticivilization. Then examine Plato's **theory-created** masterwork, *The Republic*. It is about elitist politics and forced government "education". Plato's work delivers a-priori deceptions brilliantly woven throughout a system of mind-spun "ideals". Machiavelli was honestly up front. Plato was deceptively sub rosa. ...Tragically, those dishonest "ideals"

(footnote continued on next page)

and governments into subsequent wars, human impoverishments, and purposeful destructions.

Now, sweep the Pericles/Plato lawyer-like dishonesties across history. Start with the basically honest, "God-is-Dead" philosopher, Friedrich Nietzsche (1844-1900). He saved his greatest invective against Christianity with his "Look what Christianity did to Pascal" accusation. But, what happened to Pascal was caused not by Christianity, but by the Pericles/Plato-formed anticivilization.

In 1653, Pascal discovered that an incurably dishonest anticivilization dominated Earth. That great mathematician and conceiver of the computer (inventor of the first digital calculator and for whom the 20th-century computer programming language "Pascal" was named) then experienced his "Night of Fire". He immediately converted his life to that of "Jesus on the Cross".

Nietzsche did not possess Pascal's knowledge that everyone on Earth was trapped in an anticivilization controlled by lawyer-like dishonesties originating from criminal/war-like heroes of

---

(footnote continued from previous page)

of Plato were only partially countered — with little success — by the honest, reality-bound works of Aristotle.

Through a Plato-created anticivilization, the irrational, anti-property philosophies of a mawkish Rousseau or an envy-ridden Marx rise to wreak slaughter and destruction upon entire populations. Indeed, mass-murderers Hitler, Stalin, Mao, and Pol Pot can flourish only within Plato's anticivilization. For, in an anticivilization, any well-spun rationalization combined with well-hidden, lawyer-like dishonesties can succeed until its victims are devoured. Even Freud's scientific-sounding pessimism — his mind-spun system of the id, ego, and superego — flows prestigiously and usefully throughout the anticivilization.

In an anticivilization, envy-driven socialism/fascism and its criminal/parasitical rulers reign through violation of individual rights and force-backed usurpations of private property. In today's anticivilization, intolerance-driven religion and political-correct statism dominate. In an anticivilization, a Hitler intentionally promoting fascist violence and a Gandhi unintentionally promoting socialist poverty can succeed simultaneously. ...Irrational schemes comprising lawyer-like dishonesties and mind-spun "realities" can succeed, no matter how evil or destructive, in an anticivilization. By contrast, only rational, honest business practices linked to objective reality can succeed in the Civilization of the Universe.

ancient Greece.[1]

Pascal saw across history the admiration bestowed upon civilization-destroying Pericles. Pascal saw the unjust dishonesties of a smooth-talking, civilization killer being honored with the "Golden Age of Pericles" signature. Pascal saw many of the most destructive people in history held in high esteem throughout the generations. He saw in everyone massive, non-resolvable contradictions — contradictions between man's magnificent intelligence and value production versus man's crushing stupidities and murderous destructions. His masterwork, *Pensées* (translated as "Thoughts"), vividly described the seemingly incurable contradictions of good and evil within everyone on Earth.

The most-read author of 18th-century Europe was Pierre Bayle (1647-1706). He underscored Pascal's conclusion by identifying the extreme contradictions in the scriptures. Pointing to the lying-deceiver, murderous-criminal King David as being one of "God's chosen few", Bayle asserted that one must not try to understand

[1]Nietzsche greatly admired both the real and fictional criminal/war-like heroes of ancient Greece, such as Achilles, Odysseus, Pericles, Alcibiades, Alexander the Great...and throughout history from Genghis Khan to Napoleon. Moreover, Nietzsche argued quite validly for his heroes from the anticivilization perspective. He argued Hegel's dialectical view that wars build character and strength among victorious survivors who then carry on with greater achievements for society. Note, in this century, for example, the character building within the millions of soldiers who returned as victors from action in World War II. Yet, consider what those same individuals and societies, along with those who were killed or destroyed by that war, might have accomplished within a high-pitched, exciting, freely competitive civilization (e.g., within a Silicon-Valley/high-tech-type competitiveness). And, finally consider what everyone might have accomplished within the business-driven, criminal-free/war-free Civilization of the Universe. ...Those happy, free individuals would have performed with incalculably greater character and accomplishment than anyone in the anticivilization under any circumstances.

Hitler was a Pericles-like orator whose theme was altruistic sacrifice both to the state and to mankind. Drawing from Hegel and Nietzsche, the will-to-power Hitler wrote in *Mein Kampf*, "Mankind has grown great in eternal struggle. Only in eternal peace that it perishes." Was Hitler factual? Yes. For, in the anticivilization, that struggle for greatness does indeed succeed through collectivist power via force and violence. In the Civilization of the Universe, however, that struggle for greatness succeeds only through individual benevolence via competitive value production for others and society.

the scriptures or this world by reason or logic. Instead, he believed that one must proceed on faith alone to find resolution and peace in a criminally irrational anticivilization.

Lawyer-Like Dishonesties
ultimately
Harm every Person and Value

Pascal saw how those skilled with lawyer-like dishonesties parasitically drain the magnificent accomplishments of value producers who got little or no mention, honors, or credit throughout anticivilization history. Pascal recognized that most in Earth's anticivilization history dubbed as a Great, a Sun King[1], or a Golden-Age icon were criminal mass killers — destroyers of what others had striven to produce for the benefit of others and society. ...Discovering that such injustices and contradictions were the essence of Earth's civilization was more than Pascal could bear. Trapped in an anticivilization, he had no choice but to exit by leaping into an unreal world of faith.

Pascal abandoned rational, worldly pursuits, including his brilliant pursuits of mathematics, engineering, and physics. He turned to the Christian faith with "Jesus on the Cross" as his exemplar. ...Lacking the knowledge of Neo-Tech and the Civilization of the Universe, Pascal's decision to dump the anticivilization for an imaginary world of Christ becomes comprehendible.

### *Planet Earth Missed its Chance 2300 Years Ago*
If Pericles had not implemented lawyer-like dishonesties, the corruptions of the Peloponnesian Wars would not have occurred, Socrates would not have been executed, Plato would not have spun the foundation for an anticivilization — and that soaring Athenian

---

[1]The famous Sun King, Louis XIV of France, was in power slightly after Pascal's time.

100

civilization boosted by Aristotle may have thrived to this day in becoming part of the eternal Civilization of the Universe.

*Planet Earth Gets Another Chance Today*

Ending Lawyer-Like Dishonesties
will end today's **irrational**
Anticivilization
and bring forth the **rational**
Civilization of the Universe

Today, Pascal and Bayle would have had another choice to exit the anticivilization. They would have had the wide-scope accounting and fully integrated honesty of Neo-Tech to discover the eternally consistent, rational Civilization of the Universe (C of U). In the C of U, contradictions among men and societies are resolved as the anticivilization vanishes through wide-scope accountability and fully integrated honesty — through Neo-Tech — through freely benevolent business dynamics. ...In seeking proof for the Civilization of the Universe, odds-maker Pascal might have reformulated his famous incitement to proof of God as follows:

*Accept* the Civilization of the Universe: If the C of U is real, you gain everything for eternity. If it is not real, you lose nothing and still gain a better life.

*Reject* the Civilization of the Universe: If the C of U is not real, you gain nothing. If it is real, you lose everything for eternity.

## ORIGINS OF THE ANTICIVILIZATION

### The Caste System

In Plato's parasitical political system, the supreme souls of gold (the parasitical elites) are supported through force-backed "laws" foisted upon the lowly souls of bronze and iron (the value producers). But, centuries before Plato, parasitical elites established the caste system in India (Verna categories, 1000 B.C.). That system established the parasitical elites as the top caste to be supported by the lowest caste — the value producers — as shown below:

The Parasitical Elites
(gold souls)

Top: Brahman — the philosopher/priest caste filled with sattva: wisdom and goodness.

The Force-Backed Implementers of Parasitism
(silver souls)

Middle: Kshatriya — the political/military caste filled with rajas: courage and energy.

Their Sacrificial Servants — The Value Producers
(bronze and iron souls)

Low: Vaishya — the commercial/agriculture caste filled with tamas: desire and appetite.

## ORIGINS OF ENDING THE ANTICIVILIZATION

Honest, Objective Natural Law
replaces
Dishonest, Subjective Political-Agenda Law

In Sophocles' (495-406 B.C.) play *Antigone,* the daughter of Oedipus Rex makes history's first principled stand (which led to her execution) on obeying eternally natural, objective laws over arbitrarily unnatural, political-agenda "law". ...Valid, objective laws consistent throughout the Universe negate force-backed, political-agenda "laws" arbitrarily conjured up on Earth through lawyer-like dishonesties.

# THE CHOICE

## Poverty via Government/Religion
### or
## Prosperity via Neo-Tech/Business

Choose the poverty of criminality, death, suicide, madness, escapism, and faith via God and Government...or choose the prosperity of wide-scope accountability and fully integrated honesty via Neo-Tech and business. The choice seems obvious. Yet, without cyberspace, that choice can be difficult. For some, perhaps Pascal's proposition, revised for Neo-Tech, needs evoking. In any case, once one cuts the chains of dishonesty, he or she can leave the dark illusions of Plato's cave for the freedom light of cyberspace. That person, through Neo-Tech, can then see the blackness of an anticivilization, not just its shadows, gripping planet Earth. That same person will finally glimpse the new colors from the Civilization of the Universe approaching Earth, networking throughout cyberspace.

On leaving Plato's cave, one cannot return to its darkness, lest that person be consumed by its demons as were Socrates, Pascal, Schumann, van Gogh, Boltzman, and Carothers. Instead, one must remain in the light of honesty to sublimate his or her life into performing naturally — into performing with wide-scope accountability and fully integrated honesty. ...Such performance advances the conscious mind into a neothink mind for harvesting limitless riches and eternal happiness from the Fifth Dimension — from the Civilization of the Universe.

### Sublimation

Today, no one needs to escape the anticivilization or even be harmed by it. With wide-scope accounting and fully integrated honesty — Neo-Tech — one can vanish lawyer-like dishonesties. Indeed, nothing except global destruction can stop Neo-Tech from sublimating the criminal-ruled anticivilization into cyberspace —

103

into the self-ruled Civilization of the Universe. ...Fully integrated honesty will sublimate the world into a prosperous future of self-responsibility. Populations will flourish from Neo-Tech in cyberspace without requiring a single tax dollar or a single political vote.

# God and Government

prevent wealth creation
through the
## Lethal Stealth
of
## Princess Diana and Mother Teresa

*Usenet Post of September 6, 1997*
## THE BRITISH DISEASE
Vilify Businessmen, Glorify Parasitical Elites

"England, the country that gave the world the competitive, job-producing, self-disciplined Scrooge to *scorn,* also gave the world the uncompetitive, tax-supported, self-indulgent Princess Diana to *adulate.* ...'Down with business people, up with parasitical elites', says the British disease.

"In America, news journalists stood up to cheer when hard-driving, business-geniuses Michael Milken and Leona Helmsley were unjustly imprisoned. Those same journalists dressed in black to shed maudlin tears when a parasitical elite supported by gun-enforced taxes — a sleep-till-noon, cafe-society playgirl who manipulated compassion with low-effort photo ops — died in a drunken-drive, 100mph crash while endangering the lives of disposable commoners. ...'Let `em eat Establishment news coverage', says the lethal stealth of Di elites.

"Reject their manipulated emotionalisms. Long live paparazzis, tabloids, and free enterprise. Long live free speech, freedom of the press, and objective law. ...Let objective criminal-and-civil law resolve legitimate violations of individual rights."

### Why the Anticivilization is Incurable
The above article was posted by Neo-Tech Publishing to Usenet newsgroups on the day of Princess Diana's funeral. The article drew sharp criticisms, including criticisms from some Neo-Tech supporters, for its "lack of compassion and sensitivity". Those critics failed to identify the unifying principles of justice that the article embodies.[1] The article displays extraordinary compassion,

---

[1]Human knowledge is in terms of unified, all-inclusive contexts and single principles (e.g.: justice) built from interconnected concretes such as Scrooge,
(footnote continued on next page)

benevolence, and sensitivity to the countless lives of innocent value producers diminished or destroyed in an anticivilization dominated by tax-consuming Princess-Di elites manipulating the populace into supporting their gun-backed parasitisms.

The negative reactions to that article demonstrated why nothing within the anticivilization can cure its dishonesties, its irrationalities, its mysticisms. That article also demonstrated why only free enterprise in cyberspace will undermine parasitical cults ...and then vanish their anticivilization. How? By outcompeting God and Government via competitive business to render irrelevant the malignant emotionalisms that today diminish everyone on Earth.

## Ending the Mother-Teresa Hoax

Unlike Princess Diana, Mother Teresa was respectable in personal character. She was neither a gun-backed parasitical elite nor an airhead pawn. Yet, poverty-pledged Mother Teresa fueled the mirror image of the anticivilization-altruistic hoax promoted by Di elitists. Mother Teresa gained anticivilization fame second only to Jesus by harmfully glorifying altruism, poverty, and misery. She never supported or even acknowledged the only beneficent dynamic that eliminates poverty. That dynamic is competitive, value-and-job producing businesses. ...Through her adamant opposition to abortion, birth control, divorce, she multiplied the malevolent dynamic of human sacrifice that promotes poverty and misery, especially among the poor and downtrodden...her fodder for fame.

Who has done the most widespread, long-range harm among the peoples of this world — Princess Diana or Mother Teresa? No contest. Mother Teresa has and will continue to inflict the most harms among the populace of Earth's anticivilization. Neither, however, was directly destructive as were power-driven

---

(footnote continued from previous page)

Princess Diana, and Mother Teresa. ...Perhaps the single greatest document in the anticivilization reflecting the unified context of **justice** and **individual rights** is Thomas Jefferson's *Declaration of Independence*. Novelist/philosopher Ayn Rand once said, "If it is ever proper for man to kneel, it would be when reading the Declaration of Independence."

politicians from Hitler to Stalin, from Lincoln to FDR. Yet, the Diana/Teresa hoax of altruism and human sacrifice to higher causes means sacrifice to the state — sacrifice to the parasitical elites — sacrifice to those tyrants and politicians of mass destruction. And, finally, from the productive side, none of the above ever legitimately created or sustained a net-value job or met a payroll for anyone.

The above paragraph is not a personal attack on Mother Teresa, who perhaps acted with some genuine compassion and provided some direct values to certain individuals. Her widespread, net harms arise from the destructive ethics of altruism and sacrifice that she fostered. Those are the ethics upon which dishonest politicians depend upon to survive. But, now, the coming Neo-Tech cyberspace/cybercash businesses are going to (1) outcompete God and Government, (2) end the Princess-Di/Mother-Teresa hoaxes, and (3) replace praises to destructive neocheaters with appreciation of productive benefactors — the real heroes — the value-and-job producers such as Jay Gould, Michael Milken, and Leona Helmsley.

# I
# Business

Will Outcompete

# God and Government

# I

# Always Prosper, Never Age, Never Die

# I

## Business will Outcompete God and Government

ALWAYS PROSPER, NEVER AGE, NEVER DIE

### FOUR PREMISES

1. An unnatural, irrational, parasite-ruled anticivilization has existed on Earth for 2300 years.

2. Neo-Tech/Zon isolates the anticivilization with a moat of silence.

3. Through cyberspace will arise the natural, free-market Civilization of the Universe (C of U).

4. The competitive free-enterprise/cybercash C of U will replace Earth's uncompetitive y2k[1] anticivilization.

Zon's Quintessential Secret
reveals how
Business and Neo-Tech
will bring
Eternal Prosperity to Everyone

---

*Newton Unified Heaven and Earth — They are the Same*
*Neo-Tech Unified God and Man — They are the Same*

---

# Neo-Tech via Zon

Neo-Tech means new technology and techniques based on fully integrated honesty and wide-scope accounting. Zon is any

---

[1]Y2k is the year-2000 computer-crash problem that will end the corrupted "computer age". Shortly after that crash, the world will boom into the "cyberspace/cybercash age". ...The individualistic/pc Internet combined with wide-open, entrepreneurial enterprises free from government interference will extricate mankind from the collectivist/main-frame y2k program disaster.

competitive person wielding the business power of fully integrated honesty and wide-scope accounting. Those concepts are new to this world. The initial, unnamed concepts began forming in 1965 as Frank R. Wallace contemplated writing his first book — *The Advanced Concepts of Poker* — while he was a Senior Research Chemist at E.I. du Pont de Nemours & Co., Inc. Published in hardbound by Crown and in paperback by Time Warner, that ruthlessly honest book became the all-time, best-selling poker manual:

www.neo-tech.com/poker/

From Dr. Wallace's 1976 foundation work, *Psychuous Sex*, the word "Neo-Tech" evolved in 1979. From 1980, starting with the book titled *Neocheating*, Neo-Tech literature began expanding, slowly at first, but then at an ever increasing pace while broadening its scope through cycles — cycles of ever wider Neo-Tech concepts followed by ever more practical applications.

Since 1981, new discoveries about Neo-Tech steadily expanded through the writings and publications of Dr. Wallace. By 1985, three other authors began writing and publishing major Neo-Tech works — Mark Hamilton in the business/political areas; Eric Savage in the business/international areas; Yasuhiko Kimura in the philosophical/historical areas. ...Their works expanded both the theoretical and practical reach of Neo-Tech.

In 1992, the concept that "anyone can outcompete God and Government" began unfolding. In mid 1995, as Neo-Tech entered cyberspace, other authors further extended the reach of Neo-Tech into new, practical areas. By 1997, the body of published Neo-Tech literature exceeded 2,000,000 words, not counting the Neo-Tech literature published in 13 languages.

In 1997, culminating thirty years of uncovering Neo-Tech, Wallace finished his work in the anticivilization. In 1998-1999, the last three major Neo-Tech works from the anticivilization perspective will be published: *God-Man: The Final Evolution* by Mark Hamilton, *The Bells Toll for Mysticism* by Eric Savage and

112

Tracey Alexander, and *Flame-War Justice* edited by Drew Ellis et al. Those final works will tee-up the anticivilization so its dishonesties and mysticisms vanish as nature's Quintessential Secret actuates the Civilization of the Universe here on Earth.

1965-1997

Neo-Tech to Zon

After thirty-two years developing Neo-Tech/Zon combined with the quiet worldwide distribution of its literature, Frank R. Wallace pinpointed the highest-leveraged mechanism to bring the Civilization of the Universe to planet Earth. That mechanism involves emotionally abandoning anticivilization dependencies and deceptions through cyberspace businesses — businesses that function beyond Earth's anticivilization. ...A free cyberspace/cybercash market will provide prosperity to everyone as each individual emotionally unlocks nature's Quintessential Secret:

Unlocking
Nature's Quintessential Secret
through the
Profitable Syntheses
of universally recognized
Arts and Emotions
with wide-scope
Business Dynamics

Dr. Wallace deals with open-ended reality, not with closed-circle abstractions. He is a research chemist, a high-stake poker player, and an in-the-trenches entrepreneur/businessman. Only from that unique combination of competitive experience and real-world perspective could Neo-Tech develop. Neo-Tech is not about philosophy or politics. It is about wide-scope business integrations combined with fully integrated honesty. Neo-Tech blends the competitive values of (1) science and history with logic, (2) the

113

metaphor with the analogue, (3) the abstract with the concrete, (4) the perceptual with the conceptual, (5) the hypothesis with the fact, (6) the serious with the parody, (7) the intellectual with the emotional, (8) the hard-nosed with the compassionate, (9) the general with the specific, (10) the "**is**" with the "**ought**"[1].

> Be neither an Empiricist nor a Rationalist
> Be neither an Intrinsicist nor a Subjectivist
> Be a Wide-Scope Integrator of Objective facts

*Wide-Scope Knowledge is Universal Power*

Neo-Tech actualizes Francis Bacon's maxim "knowledge is power"[2]: Neo-Tech unifies inductive/deductive knowledge with wide-scope business knowledge to bring universal power. That unified knowledge and power is expressed in the following two poems about the interconnectiveness of knowledge and power:

## Unification of Knowledge

Flower in the crannied wall
I pluck you out of the cranny
I hold you here root and all in my hand
Little flower but if I could understand

---

[1]The general definition or the "**is**" of Neo-Tech is *new technology and new techniques*. The specific definition or the "**ought**" of Neo-Tech is *fully integrated honesty*. (Ref: Peikoff, Leonard, "Philosophic Integration: Unity in Epistemology and Ethics", 1996) ...In the *unreal* anticivilization, most things "seem" or "appear" so. In the *real* C of U, most things "are" so.

[2]Francis Bacon (1561-1626) broke the closed-circle logic of stagnant scholasticism by (1) separating theology from knowledge and (2) recognizing that useful new knowledge is acquired through inductive reasoning (dynamic observations) not deductive logic from dead authority (dogmatic arguments). ...Bacon is the father of the Scientific Method and the author of the aphorism, "Nature to be commanded must be obeyed". He rejected the status quo of the Establishment and the bogus "test-of-time" criterion while blazing the way for Descartes, Locke, and Newton. ...Bacon pointed the way toward the 18th-century Age of Enlightenment.

What you are, root and all, and all in all
I should know what God and man is.

Alfred Lord Tennyson
1809-1892

## Unification of Power

Flower in the crannied wall
I pluck you out of the cranny
I hold you here root and all in my hand
Little flower but if I could understand
What you are, root and all, and all in all
I should know that God is man.

Zon
Eternity

Neo-Tech forms an expanding spiral of knowledge-integrating deductions drawn from knowledge-building inductions. Those inductions, in turn, are drawn from objective reality through fully integrated honesty. Such a spiral yields ever greater clarity and profitability when facts are orchestrated into a unity called Zonpower.

### Emotional Penetration
*Quintessential Secret (QS),* a forthcoming Neo-Tech/cyberspace "operatic" work, will reveal a new form of communication that penetrates the emotions of politicians and business people alike — the emotions of parasites and value producers alike. *Quintessential Secret* slices through intellectual-and-emotional anticivilization defenses. *Quintessential Secret* crumbles the defenses that block wide-scope accountability and fully integrated honesty. For 2400 years, those defenses have locked everyone on Earth into an irrational anticivilization — a world controlled by

115

hidden neocheaters and camouflaged criminals since Plato[1] in the third century BC. ...Nature's Quintessential Secret vanishes those defenses.

*Quintessential Secret* (*QS*) communicates via symphonic prose. It orchestrates together the universal communication of (1) integrated musical composition, (2) operatic oratorio, (3) epic poetry, and (4) the arts into blends of fiction/nonfiction prose. In that blend of symphonic prose, the total is greater than the sum of its parts — music, prose, poetry, art. That combination bypasses emotional and intellectual blocks in revealing one reality: *The rational Civilization of the Universe replaces Earth's irrational anticivilization through nature's Quintessential Secret.*

That symphonic prose comprises movements that bring fully integrated honesty — Neo-Tech — into one's emotional life. The final movement is open-ended and will be profitably exploited by authors, composers, artists, business people, working people, and other net-value producers. ...That final movement will build until the anticivilization vanishes. Citizens of Earth will then live with eternal prosperity in the Civilization of the Universe.

## Neo-Tech Sweeps the Globe

Those who grasp *QS* will embrace its opening movement titled *Child Zon*. They will integrate with the mind of Zon to capture limitless prosperity through the seven steps shown on page 136. Through chain reactions, newly forming Zons will sweep the globe clean of self-deception, dishonesty, and mysticism in becoming competitive exemplars of prosperity, power, and romantic love. ...Populations will prosper through the increasing liberation of individuals as competitive sovereigns.

Entrepreneurs who grasp the Neo-Tech/Zon concepts will ultimately outcompete Frank R. Wallace and Neo-Tech Publishing

---

[1]Plato was a brilliant deductive rationalizer who, with Pericles, opened the world to an anticivilization of subjective law and criminal rule. Aristotle, by contrast, was an honest inductive scientist who laid the groundwork for objective law and free-market enterprise.

Company in enveloping the globe with the Civilization of the Universe. Leapfrogging their anticivilization investments, such entrepreneurs will be driven by richly profitable dynamics that capture ever greater areas of cyberspace business. For those entrepreneurs, the anticivilization phenomena of boredom, dishonesty, mysticism, criminality, disease, aging, and death will disappear as emotional excitement and material prosperity rises to undreamed heights.

\* \* \*

### Replacing Dreams with Reality

In the anticivilization, socialized people in a quasi-capitalistic system live through dreams. They live as Willy Lomans. As says playwright Arthur Miller: *They live through a shoeshine and a smile*. When others stop smiling back, it is an earthquake. When their hats get a couple of spots, prosperity and life shrink toward nothing. Happiness and life disappear. By contrast, in the Civilization of the Universe, sovereign entrepreneurs live through ageless objective reality. As their competitive value production grows, their prosperity and happiness expand toward eternity.

\* \* \*

# The Question

## DROPPING DEAD SLOWLY?

### Dead Populations Walking

Government-made laws and justice execute the condemned with lethal injections of drugs. The execution hides behind a facade of merciful sleep that conceals a fast turbulence of crushing pain and agonizing death. The lethal injection contains a drug which acts first to paralyze outward movements of the body so no sign of the ultimate physical torture can be detected by observers. Outside observers can see only the closing of a man's eyes as his outer body passes into a motionless state. Once the doomed man is incapable of outer movement or expression, the other drugs kick-in. Then he starts feeling the most horrible of pains: His internal body and its organs begin ripping apart and then collapsing as organ after organ crushes life into death. ...Everyone else sees only a peaceful, "painless" death of a condemned man.

Government-made criminals and parasites called neocheaters execute entire populations with lethal injections of dishonesties and mysticisms. Those mass executions hide behind facades of "natural" life that conceal the turbulence of personal loss and death. The lethal injections contain soothing mysticisms that cause their victims to slowly lose the values of life. Thus, everyone walks toward eternal death in the unnatural anticivilization. ...No one experiences the open-ended life and prosperity available in the natural Civilization of the Universe.

Government-made neocheaters are only partially responsible for creating Earth's *unreal*[1] anticivilization. Their victim populations are responsible for accepting the *real* deadliness of an anticivilization. ...In prison, dead men are walking. In the anticivilization, dead populations are walking.

Is there a way for people on Earth to avoid the slow execution and eternal death that currently await everyone on Earth? Is there a way for people on Earth to live naturally — to live with eternal prosperity and non-aging happiness?

---

[1]The Neo-Tech/Zon literature occasionally refers to the anticivilization and its ingredients — dishonesty, irrationality, and mysticism — as *unreal* or *nothing*. In a philosophical sense, the anticivilization and its ingredients do, of course, have identities, causes, effects, and properties. Thus, they are real and something. Thoughts, dreams, imaginations, illusions, lies, even hallucinations are likewise real in that philosophical sense. Yet, ultimately, contradictions do not exist in reality, because contradictions vanish at wider-scope integrations of knowledge. In that way, the anticivilization along with its irrational, dishonest, and mystical ingredients vanish as unreal or nothing as one enters the Civilization of the Universe. For, those ingredients are non-existent within the widest-scope laws of nature and fully integrated honesty. Thus, from the non-philosophical context within the Civilization of the Universe, the anticivilization and its dishonesties, irrationalities, and mysticisms are unreal, nothing.

# *The Answer*

## ALWAYS PROSPER, NEVER AGE, NEVER DIE

### ORIENTATION

Neo-Tech's long lonely journey will ultimately make the C of U visible on Earth through Nature's Quintessential Secret (NQS). Revealing NQS *is* the dynamic for terminating aging and death on planet Earth — a dynamic that reveals everyone on Earth as a Truman living in an artificially created civilization. From that unnatural world, each Truman and every Willy Loman can step through nature's door and into the Civilization of the Universe.

### Goal/Problem/Solution

The Goal: Tattoo the following two realities into the minds of human Earthlings.

1. For 2300 years, an irrational anticivilization has existed on Earth in which everyone ultimately fails and dies.
2. For eternity, a rational civilization has existed throughout the Cosmos in which competitive businesses solve problems and cure diseases to bring eternal life and limitless prosperity to conscious people.

Such tattooed minds will eventually cure the seminal negative of this anticivilization: the symbiotic diseases of dishonesty and mysticism. Those deeply hidden, always fatal diseases are manifested in various automatic/reflex forms of self-deception. Curing those diseases will free every adult, allowing each to function through power-laden, wide-scope accountability and fully integrated honesty. ...Eradication of those diseases will vanish the irrational anticivilization and bring forth the rational Civilization of the Universe.

*The Problem*: Everyone on Earth is invested in a death-oriented anticivilization in which "improvements" mean shifting bad habits to different, more-hidden bad habits while "reforms" mean shifting obvious harms to deeper, less-obvious harms. Indeed, no one wants to lose his or her investments in that anticivilization. But, the cost of such investments is eventual failure and certain death.

*The Solution*: Revealing nature's Quintessential Secret will ultimately (1) vanish professional parasites, (2) cure the fatal dishonesty/mysticism disease, (3) allow everyone to think and act rationally in abandoning the anticivilization for the C of U.

\* \* \*

Everyone — parasite, business hero; poor, rich; left wing, right wing; totalitarian, libertarian; mystic, realist; subjectivist, objectivist; theist, atheist; even every Neo-Tech supporter, including its founder — has deeply invested in the anticivilization. Thus, nearly everyone today, including nearly every Neo-Tech supporter, rejects the Neo-Tech/Zon *combination*. For, from Neo-Tech/Zon evolves the most radical change to human life on Earth since the evolution of the conscious mind. That previous evolution 3000 years ago threw out in one swoop the ancient bicameral civilization. (See www.neo-tech.com/discovery/nt3.html)

The approaching Neo-Tech/Zon evolution throws out in one swoop the dishonesties and irrationalities of the anticivilization to bring forth the rational Civilization of the Universe. ...When will that swoop happen? It will happen when cyberspace reveals nature's Quintessential Secret (NQS) throughout the world. ...NQS will free mystical-restricted conscious minds by the millions, flipping them into wide-scope neothink minds — wide-scope, fully honest business minds.

\* \* \*

Parasitical elites and neocheaters in the anticivilization continually "improve" their techniques of criminally living off the

120

value producer.  Those professional value destroyers keep refining
and camouflaging their techniques: They have gone from the
violent looting of value producers by the fictional Odysseus then
by the real Genghis Kahns, Napoleons, and other tyrants wielding
clubs and guns — to the quiet looting of value producers by
politicians, bureaucrats, and lawyers wielding gun-backed political-
agenda laws and destructive bureaucracy-building regulations.

Yet, certain entities that appear in Earth's irrational
anticivilization have always belonged to the rational Civilization
of the Universe.  Those entities include the laws of nature,
equations of physics and chemistry, theorems of mathematics,
widely integrated music and fine arts, the productive and
competitive aspects of business, the creative aspects of art and
science...and the emotions of love and happiness.  Also, plants,
animals[1], and children under the age of four belong to the C of U.

Today, however, essentially no normally functioning adult on
Earth is a part of the Civilization of the Universe.  Each was
dragged from the C of U as a child and injected into the death-
oriented anticivilization constructed by parasitical rulers functioning
through networks of criminal politics.  How does such grand-scale
criminality exist?  Why do those rulers commit such crimes?
Because, through force, dishonesties, thefts, frauds, Ponzi schemes,
and mysticisms, they can coerce or trick the competitive value

---

[1]As nonconscious animals, cats are uncorrupted by the anticivilization.  Notice
how cats often respond with relaxing pleasure to the harmonic "mathematics"
of classical music.  Yet, those same cats may react with restless annoyance
to the irrational atonality of certain "modern" music.  Cat rejections, however,
are not indictments of "modern" music, which can be both valuable and
entertaining in Earth's anticivilization. But, those cat critics indicate that non-
melodic, atonal "modern" music would have no commercial value in the
Civilization of the Universe.  Also, in 1998 the *Journal of Neurological
Research* reported that Mozart piano sonatas played to rats for weeks before
and after birth significantly improved their maze-solving abilities.  By contrast,
those rats similarly exposed to the minimalist music of Philip Glass's *Einstein
on the Beach* did significantly poorer. ...Pythagoras's universal musical
harmonies via the plucked strings of Orpheus's lyre to Kepler's universal
mathematical harmonies of planetary motions belong not to Earth's
anticivilization but to the Civilization of the Universe.

producer — the fountainhead of human values — into supporting their hoaxes of unearned livelihoods and illusions of self-worth.

Earth's moribund anticivilization is based on illusions conjured up for the past 2300 years via professional parasites and their bureaucratic agents of force. By contrast, the Civilization of the Universe is based on competitive value production via sovereign entrepreneurs and their unfettered businesses. ...Today, the illumination of Neo-Tech through cyberspace business vanishes darkness — vanishes the dishonesties and mysticisms that comprise Earth's irrational anticivilization.

What is Neo-Tech? It is new technologies and new techniques. It is wide-scope accounting based on fully integrated honesty. It is the new Illuminati. Who understands the power of Neo-Tech? Few on Earth today will let themselves understand. Why? Because nearly everyone has deeply invested in today's irrational anticivilization. On fully understanding Neo-Tech, each would lose his or her vested interests in Earth's anticivilization. Indeed, who in the anticivilization would give up his or her illusionary benefits of government — the pyrrhic gifts that lead to failure and death? ...With world-wide knowledge of nature's Quintessential Secret, essentially everyone would abandon the anticivilization and dump its deadly gifts.

\*\*\*

The Music Connection

How can parasitically exploited adults once again glimpse the eternal Civilization of the Universe? A conduit for emotionally glimpsing aspects of the C of U is integrated music — such as universally appealing classical/romantic music.

For example, consider the longings for life by those last to die before nature's Quintessential Secret delivers non-aging biological immortality to everyone. Such longings are poignantly expressed in Antonin Dvorák's *New World Symphony*, second movement, during his reflections on Longfellow's *Song of Hiawatha*. Also, as another example, a verse from the Norwegian National Anthem is dedicated to the romantic composer, Edvard Grieg. That verse reflects nature suddenly viewed from the Civilization of the Universe:

> "He walked here beside me
> the great tone poet.
> I heard the water flow with a lovelier cadence.
> And, never in the world before,
> no matter how often I had trod the same path
> had I understood completely
> how dear nature had become to me in this place."

Nature is so lovely and dear because it is the most marvelous creation of neothinking man — of Zon, the creator of universes. He created nature for the most-efficient "deistic" generation of human values distributed through his universal business dynamics.

123

The collaboration of Edvard Grieg with the famous playwright Henrik Ibsen on *Peer Gynt* emotionally reflects redemption from the anticivilization by the abiding love of a woman named Solveig who waited a lifetime to bring the Civilization of the Universe to Peer Gynt.

The *Requiem* by the French composer Gabriel Fauré expresses the happy escape from death in the anticivilization to eternal prosperity in the C of U.

Even the long-ignored and ridiculed composer César Franck[1] presents distant C-of-U music as do "heavenly" Mozart, Beethoven, and other wide-scope integrating composers.

Sibelius and his *Finlandia* were inspired by nature, freedom, and businessmen.

And, who was not taken beyond this world by Stanley Kubrick's *2001 Space Odyssey* music from Richard Strauss's[2] *Thus Spoke Zarathustra*.

Andrew Lloyd Webber through his *Phantom of the Opera* recognized that love and music were everything in this anticivilization.

As one visitor to the Neo-Tech/Zon web site asked, "In some profound sense is the Universe a song?" Yes, through the unified integration of metaphysics and epistemology — through the objective unity of metaphorical *Gravity Units* and *Thinkons* — the Universe is a song. For example, through tone poems, Neo-Tech can interconnect knowledge, emotions, and things into a Universe — differentia into a single objective unity — as will be demonstrated by the forthcoming operatic oratorio titled *NQS: Life Immortal*. ...NQS — Nature's Quintessential Secret — is the

---

[1] Franck's other-world work was recognized, decades after his death, by Marcel Proust, the noted French author of the stupefying, what-is-it-all-about 13-volume, *Remembrance of Things Past*. Hiring musicians to play Franck's music, Proust transported himself out of this anticivilization to "another world". Thus, Proust avoided suicide.

[2] As an aside, whist card-killer Richard Strauss was the soul mate to Wallace's fictional poker card-killer John Finn — "ancestor" of Huckleberry Finn.

Universe unified into a poem song.[1]

### Visiting the C of U via Music

New knowledge arises from recognizing the honesty of widely integrated music. Integrated music includes most classical music, much romantic-era music, along with baroque music such as Bach's music revealing exquisite beauty, and certain "romantic/ modern" music such as Rachmaninoff's *Theme of Paganini* revealing the victory of a rational devil...and even certain Renaissance music such as the enduring *Greensleeves* and the works of Palestrina. Integrated music represents a rich source of C-of-U entities existing in Earth's anticivilization. That music along with mathematics and prime numbers would be the most basic, immediately recognized form of emotional and intellectual communication among civilizations throughout the Universe.

Note the following three gems of new knowledge that arise from recognizing the universality of widely integrated music:

Gem #1. Consider two antithetical philosophers: the great optimist Aristotle and the great pessimist Schoppenhauer. Surprisingly, they both come from the same implicit sensing of the anticivilization on Earth versus the Civilization of the Universe. The sum-total implication of Aristotle was that the most desired life on Earth is the contemplative life. The sum-total implication of Schoppenhauer was that the only worthwhile value on Earth is music. Both philosophers were coming from the implicit rejection of Earth's anticivilization in seeking the Civilization of the Universe. Through contemplation, Aristotle created a basically honest primacy-of-existence philosophy like that of the C of U. While Schoppenhauer created a basically dishonest primacy-of-

---

[1]Pathagoras (580-500 B.C.), although a mystic, did combine the C-of-U mind/ emotion elements of mathematics and music. And, mythical Orpheus used C-of-U music to retrieve his beloved Eurydice from the netherworld of Hades. Through his music, Orpheus crashed through the mind defenses of the underworld rulers, including their leader, Pluto. ...Likewise, *NQS* is designed to crash through the mind defenses of the anticivilization rulers to usher in the Civilization of the Universe.

consciousness philosophy like that of Earth's anticivilization.

Aristotle hated irrationality, but loved his rational, mind-created C of U. Thus, he desired to escape the irrational Pericles/Plato anticivilization by living in his contemplated rational civilization. Schoppenhauer hated the anticivilization, but loved classical music. Thus, he desired to escape the inhuman anticivilization by living in a world of music that belonged to the C of U. ...On understanding the relationships among the anticivilization, the C of U, and music, one sees Aristotle and Schoppenhauer as twins in rejecting life in the anticivilization and seeking life in the Civilization of the Universe.

Gem #2. Two seemingly contradictory, yet preeminent positions for Neo-Tech since 1976 are (1) the high probability of countless, far-more advanced civilizations throughout the universe combined with (2) the improbability of extraterrestrial life ever visiting Earth. For, those countless advanced civilizations would have no economic or scientific incentive to visit Earth's civilization as detailed in the Neo-Tech "Long Wave" document published in 1985 by I & O Publishing Company. (Reference: www.neo-tech.com/zonpower/book/chapters/chapter6.html)

Now, today, comes perhaps one reason for not-too-far-advanced civilizations to expend the time and energy to contact Earth — to get its unique, individual-composed, conceptual music! Indeed, Earth's widely integrated music delivers universal pleasures and, thus, represents commercial values to other civilizations. ...Earth's anticivilization has no values to offer advanced civilizations, except possibly its uniquely individualistic forms of emotional concepts expressed as music and art of universal beauty.

Gem #3. Mortals value time because their time of life is limited. Immortals would not value time because their time of life is unlimited. Those two statements are not only false but the reverse is the fact. That paradox can be understood once one identifies the separate natures of the anticivilization versus the C of U — separate natures connected only by C-of-U essences of music, mathematics, physics, chemistry, creativity, business, and positive emotions such as love and happiness:

In the anticivilization, those most pressured for every moment of time are intensely creative, highly successful businesspeople, Nobel-status scientists, high-tech genius creators midst fast-track competitive pressures...and driven-to-collapse creators of C-of-U music and art as often happens to composers, artists, and authors of universal value. ...Such time-valuing, high-pressured, competitive value producers are generally the most happily prosperous people on Earth.

Those intense time seekers are pressed for capturing every bit of time for maximum use *not* because they are mortals with only limited life available. Instead, they are desperate for time because of the high-intensity pressures and excitement to create and produce competitively — before their opportunity or inspiration is lost to competition, obsolescence, or time-wasting distractions.

The high-intensity, exciting business and creative nature of immortals in the C of U would by nature experience even greater valuation of time in their ever more pleasurably intense and excitingly competitive lives as experienced by the mightiest value producers. ...Such value producers are precious few in the anticivilization, but are essentially everyone in the C of U.

\* \* \*

Consider the mathematical/music glimpse toward the Civilization of the Universe: Does a quick, simple way exist to factor prime numbers of any length? What are the mathematical harmonies of the neothink mind relative to the dynamics of universal existence? Is the entire Universe a quantum computer functioning as a communication/business/cybercash entity? Is the Universe a web site with push-pull technology available to access value-producing information and products at various levels of knowledge across the Cosmos? ...The C of U with its Quintessential Secret holds those answers.

## Will NQS Reach You in Time for Eternal Prosperity?

### INTRODUCTION
to

# NQS

## Nature's Quintessential Secret

(NQS underlies Cassandra's Secret, Zonpower, and the Zon Protocols)

---

**Neo-Tech**
vanishes
**Professional Parasites**
by bringing forth a
**Cyberspace/Cybercash/Free-Enterprise Economy**
that delivers
**Eternal Prosperity & Non-Aging Immortality**

---

In 1992, Dr. Frank R. Wallace was isolated incommunicado in a federal prison because his Neo-Tech publications publicly revealed the Golden-Helmet revenue system (reference: Federal Case# CV-S-93-889-LDG, CA#97-15506). Unleashing that rational revenue system would have by nature purged professional parasites from government and society. Yet, during his imprisonment, Wallace discovered the simplest, highest-leveraged mission for Neo-Tech: Use nature's Quintessential Secret to contrast the destructive nonrealities of Earth's anticivilization to the productive realities of the Civilization of the Universe. Such revelations will call forth a rational, mystic-free civilization on planet Earth.

Wallace is a high-stake risk taker who is willing to "lose everything" in order to gain everything. For, as always previously done, he jujitsus every loss — every negative — into a positive dynamic that advances the goal of (1) ending the force-backed parasitisms corrupting governments, (2) establishing through cyberspace the rational, business-driven Civilization of the Universe here on Earth, and (3) sublimating mortals guided by death-causing mysticism into immortals guided by objective reality.

## Beyond Good and Evil

In the C of U, the concepts of good and evil disappear and are forgotten. For, when evil vanishes, no contrasting concept exists to understand the concept of good. Instead, unstated universal justice, value production, and business prevail. Indeed, an economy driven by eternal health, happiness, and prosperity rules a rational civilization. ...The C of U exists not beyond Nietzsche's mythical good and evil but beyond the factual good and evil of an irrational anticivilization.

To state once again: Bringing forth the C of U requires propagating two realities among the world's populace —

Reality #1 — Earth's **mind-created** anticivilization is built on dishonest illusions and mystical *memes* that guarantee ultimate failure and death for everyone.

Reality #2 — The **existence-created** Civilization of the Universe is built on objective reality and integrated *honesty* that guarantee eternal prosperity for everyone.

The forthcoming "opera", *NQS: Life Immortal*, will communicate both realities to the populace as indicated on comparing the following two libretto preludes:

129

# NQS: Life Immortal

**COMPARE**
The Prelude
for
Richard Wagner's
*LOHENGRIN*

"Out of the clear-blue ether
there seems to condense
a wonderful yet at first a hardly perceptible vision.
And out of this there emerges
ever more clearly
an angel host bearing in its midst
the Holy Grail.
The glory of the vision grows and grows
until it seems as though the rapture
must be shattered and dispersed
by the
very vehemence of its expansion.
The flames die away
and the angel host soars up again
to the ethereal heights
in tender joy."

*TO*
The Prelude
for
Frank R. Wallace's
*LIFE IMMORTAL*

"Out of eternally honest cyberspace
there seems to condense
a wonderful yet at first a hardly perceptible vision.
And out of this there emerges

> ever more clearly
> a Zon host bearing in its midst
> the Civilization of the Universe.
> The glory of the vision grows and grows
> until it seems as though the rapture
> must be shattered and dispersed
> by the
> very vehemence of its expansion.
> The flames die away
> and the Zon host soars up again
> to the ethereal heights of cyberspace
> bringing eternal prosperity to all."

## Child Zon to the Dark World Came

Midst America's great depression appeared a child named Zon. From where did he come? From where did Byron's Childe Harold come? At four years of age, Zon held within his aura nature's Quintessential Secret that delivers life immortal. Most children possess that secret up to four years of age. A secret that they cannot communicate to adults. What happens, therefore, when they start communicating with adults in sentences? By the age of six, those children lose and forget their ineffable secret of immortality. Thus, they change from natural immortals to unnatural mortals, never realizing their profound loss.

How do children lose such a valuable asset? Through sentence communications, adults protect their anticivilization investments. How? By using automatic dishonesties and reflex mysticisms to methodically erode each child's natural ability for processing objective reality with total honesty. Without that natural grasp on reality and honesty, the child's secret asset fades then vanishes, leaving the adult's malinvestments in the anticivilization unexposed and protected. ...Thus, every Earthling travels down that path of ultimate loss, failure, and death.

Child Zon retained nature's Quintessential Secret as did the metaphorically immortal, secular Jesus 2000 years ago. Both Jesus

131

and Zon lived seemingly normal lives without deeply communicating with the populace until near the end of their anticivlization careers. Their secrets began unfolding to the world as they were increasingly persecuted by professional parasites. Jesus was executed before his secret could widely spread. By contrast, Zon outflanked his persecutors to spread nature's secret throughout cyberspace.

At the age of four, Zon finally spoke in sentences. But, his sentences were allegorical, came out in reverse word order, and sounded nonsensical to adults. Until the third grade, he wrote backwards, starting on the right side of the page, writing to the left. Thereafter, he occasionally reverted to mirror writing. In 1950, during his senior year of high school, he wrote three blue books of essays backward in his final English exam. ...No one realized that those surreal-like essays were allegories about the then unknown dynamics of cyberspace/cybercash dominating Earth's civilization through wide-scope accountability, integrated honesty, and competitive businesses.

## Zon's Quintessential Secret

As Zon evolved from rudimentary consciousness at four years of age into full consciousness at six years of age, he, unlike other children, retained the secret of immortality. By remaining in a non-communicative mode, Zon kept his mind free from the dishonesty/mysticism disease. That freedom allowed him to function with wide-scope accountability and fully integrated honesty.

Secular Jesus was two-thousand years early with his secret. Yet, he radiated his natural power across two millennia. Now, today, messages from a *real* C of U cast through the limitless range of cyberspace have profoundly greater power than Jesus could muster. For, Jesus could only cast messages about an *unreal* heaven through the limited range of his voice. ...Revealing NQS throughout cyberspace opens the way for everyone on Earth to join their immortal cousins throughout the Civilization of the Universe.

## Zon Uncovers the Problem

At nine years of age, Zon held power over conscious life on Earth. Zon's power was real and flowed from the laws of nature. Zonpower (ZP) produces limitless values for self, others, and society. ZP has no connection to the unreal, force-backed power wielded over this anticivilization, which is a false power that has drained Earth's value producers for 2300 years. Who wields that harmful force over the populace? Professional parasites and value-destroying neocheaters camouflaged as politicians, lawyers, professors, preachers, and journalists. Such people wield pseudo yet lethally destructive power. Those stealth criminals live off their victims — duped victims who include every competitive value producer on this planet. Those hidden criminals survive by usurping, leeching, or stealing values from others and society through political-agenda laws, force, fraud, and Ponzi schemes.

Consider the establishment-dependent parasites: Most act as apologists or toadies who praise and empower their lunch-ticket rulers. Those followers and their rulers symbiotically survive while harming everyone else and society. Yet, the criminal power of those "leaders" has no meaning, no future. Their lives bring death to *everyone*[1]. ...By contrast, through the natural power of accountability and honesty combined with nature's Quintessential Secret, competitive value producers will deliver the greatest value in the Universe: *non-aging immortality with eternal prosperity*.

## Zon Vanishes Darkness

As Childe Harold to the dark tower came, Childe Zon to the dark world came. He came with the light of a new civilization — a rational, business-driven civilization — the Civilization of the Universe. One need not ask, "How did Jesus come from the heavens?". Instead, one must ask, "How did Zon come from the

---

[1]Life within Earth's nonbusiness-created anticivilization ends in failure and death for everyone. Yet, everyone can became immortal by discovering nature's Quintessential Secret — and then stepping into the business-created Civilization of the Universe.

C of U?" The answer reveals itself on penetrating the mind of Zon. One first discovers that Zon's mind is no different than the minds of average people on Earth. His difference lies in how he organizes his mind — a mind organization that those on Earth can achieve by restructuring their thinking not around the stale, dishonest, cultural memes of the past, but around the fresh, honest, wide-scope thinking of the future.

A mind structured around wide-scope accountability and integrated honesty becomes a neothink mind. The first priority of such a mind is to achieve commercial, non-aging biological immortality with limitless prosperity for everyone. Thus, a rational civilization comprised of neothink minds achieves eternal prosperity — naturally, quickly, profitably.

Eternal prosperity arises from the unfettered, competitive dynamics of business. In those dynamics, limitless profits are generated, not for self-indulgent consumption, but for continually advancing competitive value production toward commercial preservation of youth, health, happiness, and life for each conscious being. ...Life for each then becomes an ever increasing spiral of value production — producing exciting, commercial values for others and society. Every individual becomes immensely valuable, important, and profitable to everyone else. Each individual, therefore, becomes the most protected, precious asset in the Cosmos. ...Within that statement lies nature's Quintessential Secret.

### Taking a Road Never Trod

Because a road has never been trod on Earth does not mean that everyone on Earth cannot trod that road to non-aging, eternal prosperity.

134

# Nature's Quintessential Secret is Revealed
in
## Eight Movements
of
## Prose, Music, and Poetry in Counterpoint

Movement I: Child Zon

Movement II: Scientist/Businessman/Professional Zon

Movement III: Explorer/Adventurer Zon

Movement IV: Zon's Mind is Everyone's Mind

Movement V: Zon Reveals Nature's Quintessential Secret

Movement VI: Zon Delivers Eternal Prosperity

Movement VII: Zon Rules Existence

Movement VIII: Eternal Epic of Each Conscious Life

## SEVEN STEPS

*Step One*
brings
Distant Words from the Future

*Step Two*
brings
Visibility to the Invisible

*Step Three*
brings
Wide-Scope Perceptions from Nature

*Step Four*
brings
The End of Criminal Politicians and Dishonest Lawyers

*Step Five*
brings
A Free-Enterprise World

*Step Six*
brings
Non-Aging Immortality and Eternal Prosperity

*Step Seven*
brings
The Civilization of the Universe

\* \* \*

| Chinese Koan<br>from the<br>Anticivilization | Zon Koan<br>from the<br>Civilization of the Universe |
| --- | --- |
| grandfather dies | always prosper |
| father dies | never age |
| son dies | never die |

# II
# Final Messages

# II
# Final Messages

# II
# Final Messages

[Neo-Tech = wide-scope accountability and fully integrated honesty]

### Final Message

In mid 1997, the discoverer of Neo-Tech faced an unexpected medical death sentence. Thus, he began composing his final message. Then, through a Neo-Tech medical solution, he escaped that death sentence. ...He lives. Yet, quoted below is that message:

"My time is brief. I must deliver the highest leveraged information in the most effective way. My message must assure that not only my loved ones but everyone living on Earth can safely exit the non-cyberspace world, possibly crumbled beneath y2k problems. Everyone can enter a new cyberspace/cybercash civilization of unleashed, totally free, division-of-labor entrepreneurs. For, they can quickly, profitably solve the potentially deadly y2k problems. Government control and regulation of entrepreneurs and business must vanish. To make that exit/entrance possible for everyone, my final message must deliver the tool that lets the populace harness the power of business through Neo-Tech. ...To harness that power, I must unfold nature's Quintessential Secret throughout cyberspace.

"Through that secret, the populace will learn to use Neo-Tech for generating open-ended prosperity through the emasculation of professional value destroyers[1]. For 2300 years, force-backed rulers have usurped power from honest individuals by turning them into herds of duped losers with guaranteed death for all. Such rulers are professional value destroyers. They live by creating problems where none exist. By contrast, competitive value producers live

---

[1]Today, professional value destroyers comprise mainly politicians, bureaucrats, lawyers, news journalists, educators, religious leaders, union leaders, and business quislings.

139

by solving problems where they do exist.

"Yet, those professional value destroyers cannot survive in the newly rising cyberspace/cybercash civilization. For, in cyberspace, integrated honesty ends their parasitisms. Moreover, in cyberspace, each value producer holds the power to surpass any value destroyer. Indeed, with Neo-Tech in the hands of the populace via fast-developing, cheap, easy cyberspace/cybercash technologies, the parasite class will fade and then vanish. ...Consider the following two charts:"

# Chart 1
*Cyberspace means Vanishing Dishonesty*

Cults epitomized by the Fabian Society, Maoism, Randism, The Ayran Brotherhood, Skinheads, Heaven's Gate, Soldiers of God, Soldiers of Allah, Terrorists

Mysticisms such as UFOs, astrology, fat-free sugar-loaded diets, angels

Occultisms such as witchcraft, voodooism, Satanism, Godism

Religions including Christianity, Fundamentalism, Scientology, New-Age vogues

Propaganda devices such as the Bible, the Koran, goose-stepping nationalism

Force-backed destructions by governments, including democracies

Nationalism, communism, fascism, the INS, DEA, IRS, and other forms of racism and criminality

Political/pseudo-sciences supporting human-killing schemes such as the FDA and DDT/CFC/Cyclamate-type bannings

Political-agenda dishonesties such as global cooling/warming, ozone holes, acid rain, rain forests, second-hand smoke

Value-destroying pips, politicians, bureaucrats, journalists, preachers, professors, lawyers, business quislings

Force-backed irrationalities such as income-tax systems and arbitrary regulatory "laws"

Politicized scams such as Ponzi-scheme Social Security/Medicare, overpopulation, antiabortion, nutrition, war on drugs and tobacco

Political hijackings of environmental, educational, health, and welfare issues

Philosophical suicides ranging from Platonism to Kantism, from hippie Existentialism to cult-captured Objectivism

Parasitical elites criminally feeding off competitive value producers

A-Point "law" hiding The-Point law

Subjective "law" concealing Objective law

Man-made "law" overruling Natural law

Rule by ever changing "laws" of men rather than by never changing Laws of Nature

Force-backed "laws" that violate individual-and-property rights

Conservative causes, liberal causes

Egalitarianism, collectivism, socialism, fascism

Intentional parasitisms

Memorials, holidays, and honors for parasitical elites and professional value destroyers

Dishonest journalism, dishonest education, most conspiracy theories

Ego justice

Criminal minds and acts

Wars

Aging and Death

The Anticivilization

# Chart 2
### *Cyberspace means Upholding Honesty*

Open-ended entrepreneurial power derived through cyberspace/cybercash businesses

Protection of individual-and-property rights

Limitless prosperity derived from wide-scope accounting and fully integrated honesty competitively operating in cyberspace

Unfettered, mystic-free, business activities

Competitive value producers as CEOs of their own business universes (See Mark Hamilton's *Cosmic Business Control*.)

Non-aging youth and eternal life through laissez-faire enterprise

The rational cyberspace civilization — an Objectivist civilization — the Civilization of the Universe

## Hangman's Noose

"Someone once said, 'Nothing focuses the mind like facing the hangman's noose.' Facing death, I must focus on delivering the greatest possible value to my loved ones and society in the shortest time. I hope to reveal a secret that will flip conscious minds into neothink minds. Such a flip will bring via unfettered businesses a rational civilization of death-free prosperity. For, neothink business minds eradicate the seminal diseases of irrationality, mysticism, dishonesty, and death — the diseases that cause limitations, unhappiness, criminalities, aging, and mortality in human beings.

"The hangman and execution metaphors are accurate for everyone's death. Those metaphors imply unnatural, man-inflicted death. So, how can those metaphors be applied to seemingly natural medical and accidental causes of death? To answer that question, one must demonstrate how neothink minds freed in cyberspace will eradicate every cause of death. ...That eradication lies in changing the direction that arrows of time travel through a person's mind.

"About 3000 years ago, man reprogrammed his mind from an ancient bicameral paradigm without direction of time — to a modern conscious paradigm with a past-to-present-to-future

143

direction of time as described in the 1980 Neo-Tech literature and in 1976 by Professor Julian Jaynes of Princeton University. That ancient, bicameral mind had no introspective sense of time or self. Instead, the bicameral mind functioned automatically — similar to other perceptively aware animals. Since about 1000 B.C., however, the reorganized conscious mind processed self-aware thoughts flowing along arrows of time within closed boundaries of past to present. ...In fact, conscious people today are self-aware from perspectives only within the past-to-present boundaries of Earth's anticivilization.

"What happens, however, if the human mind views reality from the perspectives of no limitations — of no time boundaries? On capturing all-direction viewpoints, the mind becomes imbued with wide-scope accountability and fully integrated honesty. Such a mind becomes a neothink mind of limitless perspectives with time flowing in every direction. Such a mind vanishes the disease of death.

"In the late 1970s, Neo-Tech literature began developing the concepts of wide-scope accounting and fully integrated honesty along with notions of a more powerful thinking paradigm. Those notions solidified in the 1980s with the evolvement of a new thinking process called Neothink. During the 1990s until 1997, the Neo-Tech literature recognized the neothink mind as a post-modern cyberspace mind. That literature began describing the results of such a mind replacing the conscious mind. ...Those descriptions compared the cyberspace-mind evolvement to the conscious-mind evolvement 3000 years ago.

"As previously described in the Neo-Tech literature, consider what happened 3000 years ago when the first isolated modern minds began emerging from a collapsing ancient-mind civilization. Each isolated conscious mind held enormous powers and advantages over the severely restricted ancient minds. Those ancient bicameral minds did not know what consciousness meant,

144

much less what consciousness would mean to them, their descendents, and civilization itself. Confronted with do-or-die survival situations, those impotent bicameral minds flipped one-by-one into powerful, life-saving, conscious minds.

"Today, a similar experience of mortal conscious minds flipping into immortal neothink minds is weakly analogous to those novelty 3-D laser pictures in which a person at first sees only a flat pattern. Then, after intense concentration and mind stretching for 'survival', that person's mind-set suddenly flips from that flat, two-dimensional pattern into a startling, three-dimensional picture of clarity and beauty.

"Another weak analogy is the flatlander two-dimensional mind never being able to perceive the bicameral three-dimensional mind which, in turn, is unable to perceive the conscious four-dimensional mind — each mind is unable to perceive that wider dimension until it flips into wider-scope perspectives. Now comes the five-dimensional cyberspace mind that obsoletes death. ...About 3000 years ago, the transformation to the conscious mind was marked by the 'Hey, I'm me' realization. Today's transformation to the cyberspace mind is marked by the 'Hey, I'm an immortal controller of existence' realization.

"On researching the nature of five-dimensional cyberspace minds, new concepts arose that required developing several unique words, concepts, and metaphors such as Zon, Zonpower, Gravity Units, Thinkons, the anticivilization, the cyberspace civilization, and the Civilization of the Universe. Those words sounded strange, science-fiction-like, mystical — even though the ideas behind them represented the antithesis of science fiction and mysticism. Indeed, the ideas behind those words contained the very concepts needed to cure mysticism, irrationality, and dishonesty. Thus, despite the barrage of public criticism and ridicule, including disapproval from Neo-Tech supporters, those words will stand. ...Those words belong to the lexicon of the future.

"Today, similar to three-thousand years ago, people who switch to five-dimensional minds will survive and prosper; people who do not will sink and perish. That transition could occur en masse when the survival pressures from the y2k computer problem combined with other government problems rock the fading non-cyberspace civilization. For, y2k will create government, banking, and business chaos along with hostility toward the old, government/Gore vintage of computer technology.

"The way out of that problem? Corrupt, death-oriented conscious minds trapped in the anticivilization will flip into clean, life-saving neothink minds freed in cyberspace. Those flipped minds, by nature, will profitably solve the y2k problems and vanish the anticivilization. How will that happen? Revealing nature's Quintessential Secret will trigger those flips into five-dimensional, neothink minds — minds that solve human problems to yield eternal life and prosperity."

June, 1997

* * *

The following three documents, combined with the previous documents in this volume will help flip conscious minds into neothink minds.

DOCUMENTS A-C
A. Ending Lawyer-Like Dishonesties #1-10
B. Curing Objectivist Cultists #1-7
C. Defense Techniques

# Document A

## ENDING LAWYER-LIKE DISHONESTIES #1-10

### Ending Lawyer-Like Dishonesties #1

### Nausea on Discovering their Criminalities

In the non-cyberspace world, lawyer-like dishonesties dominate politics, the legal profession, the media, and many universities. Most people vaguely sense those dishonesties used to support well-hidden, professional parasites. But, on understanding Neo-Tech with its wide-scope accountability, one vividly identifies professional parasites. The stomach then turns in nausea on discovering how their criminalities are executed so smoothly, so self-righteously, so harmfully — seemingly with impunity.

In the cyberspace world, however, that nausea dissipates as professional parasites are rendered impotent through Drudge-like exposés. Through cyberspace, every perpetrator of lawyer-like dishonesties will eventually be held accountable for his or her now-hidden criminal behaviors. Moreover, in cyberspace, no dishonest "leader" or external "authority" can usurp values created by others. In a cyberspace/cybercash world, everyone functions as a sovereign. Even today, anyone can increasingly find the full-context facts on Internet search engines to discover the honesty level of others. ...In cyberspace, lawyer-like frauds lose their power to fool or control anyone.

Notice how big-name, destructive lawyers, politicians, professors, and journalists have virtually no power on the Internet. What disaster, for example, would await a Hillary Clinton, a Ralph Nader, a Pat Buchanan, a Dan Rather, or a "Book-of-Virtues" Bill Bennett if they interacted with the world through Usenet. ...After

2300 years, the parasitical-elite class is finally shrinking with no way to compete or survive in the rising cyberspace civilization.

## Ending Lawyer-Like Dishonesties #2

### They Laugh, Giggle, and Snort at their Victims

Across the Internet, certain lawyers, bureaucrats, tax accountants, and other government agents were caught laughing, giggling, and snorting publicly at their suffering, dying victims. That sadistic mirth occurred when criminal IRS atrocities inflicted on those victims were posted to Usenet newsgroups. Examples of such "laughable" victims are illustrated in the following IRS Abuse Reports selected from those Reports being emailed daily by Neo-Tech Publishing to 300 U.S. Congressmen. In addition to publicly exposing professional value destroyers who laugh at their victims, those Abuse Reports combined with two Neo-Tech tax cases currently in the 9th Circuit Federal Court of Appeals along with potential class-action lawsuits have another purpose: Replace the irrational income tax with a stopgap consumption "tax" as the first step toward a non-force Golden-Helmet revenue system described in the Neo-Tech literature.

What follows are examples of innocent families criminally abused and then destroyed by the IRS tax laws passed by Congress. Those are the victims about whom IRS lawyers and agents, gun-backed bureaucrats, and IRS-dependent accountants were caught laughing, giggling, and snorting:

IRS Abuse Reports: http:www.neo-tech.com/irs-class-action/

IRS Abuse Report #163

Date: Tue, Apr 8, 1997 1:32 PM
To: sue@irs-class-action.com
From: BG
"In 1993 my husband and I were notified, due to an audit, that there was a problem with one of our previous tax returns. My husband, Bill, contacted the IRS many, many, many times over a two year period in an attempt to remedy the situation. He was laid-off from his job in 1992, and after 3 months found another job at 1/4 of the salary he had been making. Needless to say, things were very hard on us. He tried very hard to make the IRS understand this and tried to work out this situation with them. The IRS was VERY difficult to work with.

"In March, 1995, my husband committed suicide (shot himself in the head), leaving our son, Justin (12 years old) and I in unbelievable GRIEF (not to mention the terrible financial situation). Since Bill's death I had to put my son in a "special" school and he has been seeing a psychologist every single week since then. He is still devastated.

"Bill left me a suicide note mentioning that he just couldn't handle dealing with the IRS any longer, and hopes that some day I'll be able to forgive him.

"If only they (IRS) had worked with him, none of this would have happened."

\* \* \*

149

Below is another victim's reply to the above IRS Abuse Report:

Date: Thur, April 10, 1997
To: Sue@irs.class-action.com
From: AP

"This is almost routine (at least the part about the IRS failing to respond or being hard to work with). One of my best friends committed suicide after the IRS ruined his thriving business (destroying 25 good jobs in the process) and essentially caused his wife's premature death from cancer. After he contacted them in good faith (BEFORE his liability was due) and asked them for more time or some kind of payment plan to handle his tax bill, to which they said 'no problem'. They then seized his bank account and padlocked his business doors. His cancer ridden wife was then told to 'go home' by the hospital in which the medical bills could no longer be paid by a man whose entire fortune had been seized by IRS thugs.

"Then, of course, there is the famous Alex Council story from Winston-Salem, NC. This was another man who committed suicide so his life insurance could be used to pay off what later (in court) turned out to be an erroneous lien on his family's home. This one was covered on 20/20. It is the one where an IRS regional director arrogantly told the 20/20 interviewer: 'Just because a judge says we're wrong, doesn't mean we are.' "

And, finally, is a Usenet response reporting on another victim:

In article <3385B7F6.34CF@spinach.xylogics.com>, RC
<rchristi@spinach.xylogics.com> wrote:
>IRS Abuse Reports #142 - #144 wrote:
>
>>All this heartache from our government not a foreign power

.>>but our own UNITED STATES GOVERNMENT. Our
>>dreams are shattered, our lives destroyed. My heart goes out
>>to all the people who shared their stories on this service, I
>>cried for you, I cried for myself.
>
>I wonder how the IRS apologists will explain this one?

*****

Neo-Tech Publishing Company (NTP) is effectively
undermining political-agenda "laws" while working to replace the
irrational income tax with a transitional consumption tax. NTP
knows through feedback from specific Congressmen and Senators,
especially Congressman Archer along with Senators Lugar and
Roth, that its IRS-Abuse-Report program turned opinion against
the IRS bureaucracy on Capital Hill and in the media. In mid
1997, Time Magazine and CBS Nightly News requested and used
information from NTP's Abuse Reports. And, in June 1997,
60 Minutes came to Las Vegas to interview NTP's attorney about
those Abuse Reports for an August 1997 program. In July 1997,
Newsday gathered details from various IRS Abuse Reports for a
feature article. Further, CNN's web site provided a direct link
to the web site showing the IRS Abuse Reports. Newspapers from
the *Kansas City Star* to the *Christian Science Monitor* also
provided direct links to the IRS Abuse Reports. In October, 1997,
NBC News, CNBC, and Cox Broadcasting contacted NTP for
further information about the IRS Abuse Reports.

By publishing those Abuse Reports, Neo-Tech Worldwide is
changing public perceptions and political attitudes about the IRS
and its irrational income-tax laws. The 1997 congressional
attitudes and their public hearings about the IRS abuses were a direct
result of the IRS Abuse Reports emailed daily to 300 congressmen
and published daily throughout cyberspace since 1995.

Ending Lawyer-Like Dishonesties #3

## Lawyer Leg of the Dishonesty Tripod

Competitive value producers continuously deliver benefits to others and society. Yet, they and their achievements are attacked in the non-cyberspace world by dishonest lawyers, corrupt politicians, mind-crushing professors, and envious pips — none of whom deliver net benefits to others and society. Instead, such parasitical entities live off the achievements of others through lawyer-like dishonesties.

One must dig deep to discover the essence of those dishonesties. That essence seems simple: take facts out of context to drain values from others. But, one must dig deeper by understanding that lawyers, politicians, university professors and media pips operate in the context of a destructive civilization — an anticivilization. By plumbing ever deeper with wide-scope accounting, one finally understands how for 2300 years — since lawyer-like Pericles and Plato — parasitical elites backed by pips have survived by living off the values produced by others.

The anticivilization is supported on three wobbly legs: (1) the ruling leg upheld by political-agenda "laws", (2) the philosophical leg upheld by following-mode cultists, and (3) the lemming leg upheld by envious/sycophantic pips. All three legs require parasitisms that today are being undercut by the fully integrated honesty of Neo-Tech and the wide-scope accountability of cyberspace.

## Ending Lawyer-Like Dishonesties #4

## Let's Call Neo-Tech a Cult

Perhaps the most-obvious, lawyer-like dishonesty archived throughout Internet search engines is the assertion that Neo-Tech is a cult. Neo-Tech is not only the antithesis of cults, but is the tool that vanishes them. ...Neo-Tech is based on wide-scope accountability and fully integrated honesty, while cults are based on narrow-scope restrictions and manipulated deceptions. Consider the following dozen contrasts between Neo-Tech and cults:

1. Neo-Tech has no members or leaders. Cults exist through members and leaders.

2. Neo-Tech requires crossing boundaries to generate ever expanding knowledge. Cults prohibit crossing boundaries to protect ever stagnant dogmas.

3. Neo-Tech generates open-ended wealth for individuals and society. Cults dissipate wealth earned by others and society.

4. Neo-Tech is anchored in factual reality. Cults float in imagined mysticisms.

5. Neo-Tech holds the individual self and natural law — one's own self and objective law — as the only authorities to guide man's life. Neo-Tech (1) posits self-responsibility as a primary of conscious life and (2) rejects the concepts of political-agenda "laws", collectivist "leaders", and external "authorities". With Neo-Tech, conscious beings become self-leaders, allowing no outside "authority" to rule their lives. By contrast, cult members demand that their leader and his group-agenda "laws" rule their lives.

6. Neo-Tech seeks out its errors in order to correct them. Cults evade their errors in order to propagate them.

7. Neo-Tech yields productive interactions with others and life. Cults demand harmful withdrawals from nonmembers and life.

8. Many people avoid or attack Neo-Tech because its integrated honesty exposes their own irrationalities and destructiveness. Cultists avoid or attack society because the real world exposes their cult's irrationalities and destructiveness.

9. Neo-Tech brings growth, prosperity, and life to individuals. Cults bring restrictions, stagnation, and death to individuals.

10. Neo-Tech spreads social benefits through integrated honesty and competitive business. Cults spread social harms by manipulating their victims through dishonesty and frauds.

11. Neo-Tech propagates individual freedom. Cults propagate group oppression.

12. Neo-Tech will prevail in the 21st century. Cults will vanish in the 21st century.


Ending Lawyer-Like Dishonesties #5

Harming Everyone for 2300 Years

The following six Neo-Tech dynamics will end over two millennia of lawyer-like dishonesties:

1. Neo-Tech reveals how nearly everyone on Earth today invests

in an anticivilization. In that irrational civilization, professional value destroyers live by bilking harmful livelihoods from the populace and society. Such parasites have harmed everyone for over two millennia. Yet, their destructiveness has been skillfully hidden from the public since lawyer-like academic Plato taught Statist politics at his Academy in Greece 2300 years ago. ...Today, however, Earth's parasitically ruled anticivilization is losing its grip on this planet as wide-scope accountability and fully integrated honesty spread throughout cyberspace.

2. Neo-Tech explicitly identifies professional value destroyers. Such shrouded criminals dominate politics, law, religion, universities, and much of the media in the non-cyberspace civilization. As integrated honesty spreads throughout cyberspace, search engines and ostracism matrixes will expose, shrivel, and then vanish those parasitical livelihoods requiring force or fraud to exist.

3. Neo-Tech identifies the invisible parasitisms called Neocheating. Professional value destroyers and parasitical elites have neocheated others and society for over two millennia to collect unearned livelihoods, power, and fame. They operate through political-agenda "laws" by "legally" initiating force and fraud to usurp their livelihoods from others. But, their days will end in a cyberspace/cybercash civilization.

4. Neo-Tech exposes the scam of "toll-booth" compassion used by neocheaters — by politicians, tort lawyers, political business quislings, dishonest journalists, cause-seeking celebrities, and religious leaders. President Clinton honed the teary-eyed "I feel your pain" scam to new heights. He and other such compassion hoaxers care little about helping the needy. They care about forcing others to "help" the needy while they themselves collect

their gun-backed tolls of unearned fame and power. ...Those compassion thieves survive by continuously extracting near-term tolls from the value producers while harming everyone over the long term, especially the needy.

5. As one Usenet poster identified: Politicians, lawyers, and other compassion hoaxers care enough about the "needy" — government-made victims — to use political-agenda laws and gun-backed taxes in forcing the value producers into *keeping those victims dependent on the government for continued exploitation.* By contrast, only competitive value producers care enough about society to permanently help the needy in *providing value-producing jobs that enrich the populace.* ...Competitive value producers alone possess the long-range ability and compassion to genuinely, permanently benefit the needy and society.

6. The integrated honesty of Neo-Tech spreading through the Internet will bring forth a cyberspace civilization. That cyberspace/cybercash civilization is the precursor to the business-driven Civilization of the Universe, which is based on objective law, wide-scope accountability, and fully integrated honesty. ...The Civilization of the Universe is simply cyberspace in which unfettered value producers rise to become unexploitable, free-wheeling entrepreneurs who build their own business universes. How? By delivering ever increasing wealth to others and society through production of competitive values.

Ending Lawyer-Like Dishonesties #6

Lawyer Genes versus Business Genes

How can so many people on Earth — the majority — behave

as lemmings in sacrificing their one-and-only lives to bogus "leaders" and professional value destroyers? How can so many people surrender to the lawyer-like manipulators who have reigned since Pericles and Plato? Such manipulators exist with impunity as camouflaged criminals in the highest offices. Today, they operate through subjective, political-agenda "laws" using cleverly disguised dishonesties[1] backed by armies of gun-backed bureaucrats. ...Does a slavery gene create their lemming-like followers and supporters?

By contrast, why do a few brave people pursue freedom and justice at any cost? They seek freedom in escaping force-backed political-agenda "laws" and professional parasites. ...Does a freedom gene drive such freedom seekers?

From that question arises another question: Do value-destroying lawyer genes versus value-producing business genes exist?

### Slavery/Lawyer Genes versus Freedom/Entrepreneur Genes

Does Neo-Tech literature support the slavery/freedom and lawyer/business gene theories? Absolutely not. Neo-Tech

---

[1]Cleverly disguised dishonesties? Consider President Clinton's White-House lawyer Charles Ruff who was hired at the same time the White House and the media were smearing Whitewater prosecutor Kenneth Starr with the non sequitur about having been an attorney for the tobacco industry. Yet, nothing was mentioned about Charles Ruff being the stellar attorney for giant cigarette companies like Phillip Morris, R. J. Reynolds, and Liggett. As identified by others, Mr. Ruff is an expert in using non-substance, jury-swaying lawyerese like, "You've tried the front door, you've tried the back door, you've tried the side door, and now you're trying the trap door, and it isn't gonna work." Ruff, a successful ex-Watergate prosecutor, has a history of getting Democrats (Charles Robb, John Glenn, Ira Magaziner) out of legal trouble. Ruff so deftly manipulates the legal system that he has saved public officials from seemingly certain criminal indictments. And, now, in 1997, he steps into his biggest challenge — looking for his biggest victory. He will use all his political manipulations, high Justice-Department contacts, and lawyer-like dishonesties in trying to save President Clinton from impeachment and/or criminal indictments.

literature recognizes that each individual sculpts his or her own life and character through free-will choices and efforts, not through genes and culture. Neo-Tech identifies the natural drive for honesty, freedom, and justice wired into conscious minds — wiring that had been damaged or short-circuited in essentially everyone for the past 2300 years. ...Today, by identifying lawyer-like dishonesties, Neo-Tech rips out that damaged wiring to rewire the natural pursuit of freedom through competitive value production.

Ending Lawyer-Like Dishonesties #7

Lawyer/Politician Demagoguery and Looting

Tobacco companies manufacture and market a deadly product that is profoundly irrational to use — tobacco. The nicotine in tobacco is a drug more addicting than heroin.[1] Cigarettes are products more lethal than alcohol or pot. Cigarettes kill more human beings than any other product except sugar. How could anyone rationally defend such an outrageously destructive product? Neo-Tech certainly does not defend cigarettes, any more than it defends the use of the deadliest, most-destructive product of all — a concoction of two drugs that is ingested daily not just by adults but is destructively poured into tens-of-millions of defenseless children in this anticivilization. That drug concoction is the diabetes/obesity-drug sugar mixed with the tension/

---

[1]Neo-Tech may be in error about the addictiveness of nicotine. A 1998 book titled *Allan Carr's Easy Way to Stop Smoking* presents a compelling case that nicotine, as long claimed by cigarette companies, is *not* addicting. In any case, Carr's book is recommended for those who wish to break their tobacco habit. For further information and an excellent anecdotal example, see www.BarbaraBranden.com/

unhappiness-drug caffeine[1].

Yet, using wide-scope accounting and integrated honesty, Neo-Tech will staunchly defend the businesses and executives who manufacture and market tobacco and cola products. Technically, Neo-Tech is not defending tobacco and cola companies or their executives per se, but is defending principle — the principle of non-force, laissez-faire business embraced by the following realities versus non-realities:

## The Principled Defense of Reality

| REALITIES (laissez-faire) | vs. | NON-REALITIES (socialism) |
|---|---|---|
| business people | vs. | parasitical elites |
| heroes | vs. | neocheaters |
| honesty | vs. | dishonesty |
| rationality | vs. | irrationality |
| property rights | vs. | property theft |
| justice | vs. | injustice and ego-"justice" |
| free choice | vs. | dictated behavior |
| freedom | vs. | tyranny |
| facts | vs. | myths and faith |
| Zon | vs. | God |

---

[1]Colas are laced with the deadliest of drug concoctions — caffeine and sugar. That long-term, metabolism-destroying poison is pumped daily into millions of children, even infants. The Cola poisoning of children is especially dominant in fat-farm America — the sugar/carbo/obesity capital of the world. Thus, using the same lawyer-like dishonesties used to attack the politically incorrect tobacco companies, the currently politically correct companies, Coca-Cola and Pepsi, would be sued dry and their executives jailed for life as the ultimate drug pushers, and maybe even executed under the current, unconstitutional, drug-kingpin laws. ...So long as force or fraud is not used, Neo-Tech supports the moral and legal rights for any business to market any free-choice, non-fraud product — including drugs — without interferences or regulations from lawyers or governments.

| REALITY | vs. | ANTIREALITY |
|---|---|---|
| Jesus the Jew | vs. | Jesus the Christian |
| Bach's B minor Mass | vs. | Pope's Catholic Mass |
| tenor | vs. | castrato |
| Beethoven – "Eroica" | vs. | Napoléon – dictator |
| Nobel Physics Prizes | vs. | Nobel Peace Prizes |
| health | vs. | sickness |
| value hierarchy | vs. | egalitarian leveling |
| individualism | vs. | collectivism |
| producers | vs. | parasites |
| Gould and Milken | vs. | Lincoln and FDR |
| giants | vs. | pip-squeaks |
| objective law | vs. | subjective "law" |
| the-point law | vs. | a-point "law" |
| natural law | vs. | political-agenda "law" |
| value producers | vs. | value destroyers |
| contextual | vs. | noncontextual |
| sequiturs | vs. | non sequiturs |
| accuracies | vs. | inaccuracies |
| problem solving | vs. | problem making |
| youth | vs. | aged |
| life | vs. | death |

## Defending Political Undefendables

In the long run, only the principled defense of reality delivers net benefits to everyone and society.  Consider the following 1997 letter to the CEO of a major tobacco-company:

160

Mr. James E. Morgan, CEO
Phillip Morris, Inc.
120 Park Avenue
New York, NY 10017-5523

Dear Mr. Morgan:

If this letter were published and widely circulated with the title —

"Tobacco Wars: the Guilty, the Innocent, the Heroes"

most would assume from that title that the guilty would be you, your company, and other tobacco executives and their companies. Many would assume the heroes to be those state attorney generals, judges, lawyers, professors, "scientists", FDA/FTC bureaucrats, and journalists who are exposing the "evil" of companies and executives who produce tobacco products.

Yet, one discovers the opposite on sweeping away lawyer-like dishonesties, non sequiturs, emotions, out-of-context facts, political-agenda laws, and politically correct regulations: The major U.S. tobacco companies are superbly efficient, well-run businesses whose executives are, for the most part, the good, the innocent, and often the quietly heroic. Contrastingly, consider those who use force-backed political-agenda "laws", tort fraud, and dishonest lawyerese to drain the earned assets of tobacco companies and persecute their executives. Those lawyer-like value destroyers are the bad, the guilty, and often the criminally guilty.

Increasing government control of tobacco will bring even greater disasters than occurred with the government control of drugs. Criminal-gang distributions will push cigarette use among school children in magnitudes far beyond Joe Camel. Cigarettes will be aggressively black-marketed. Teen smoking will be ever more glamorized as defiantly cool. Armed-youth gangs will increasingly push cigarettes as beginner-kit drugs along with ever

161

more potent drugs onto ever younger kids. That phenomenon is not only occurring today, but is accelerating as government and lawyers increase their parasitical drainings of tobacco companies. ...It is the politicians and lawyers who are criminal killers of kids, not tobacco companies or any other honest business.

Clinton/Waxman-type compassion/health hoaxers and their tort/trial-lawyer backers do not give a damn about the well-being of children or the health of anyone. They care about advancing their illicit livelihoods and usurped power. Neo-Tech, which means wide-scope accounting and fully integrated honesty, blocks such lawyer/politician-like dishonesties and brings justice to business people.

Neo-Tech also brings justice to other political "undefendables" made unpopular and targeted for rip-offs by political/social/lawyer/media demagogues. Those political "undefendables" include great value-producing companies like Exxon, Texaco, Value Jet...and genuine business heroes like Jay Gould, Michael Milken, Leona Helmsley, and Bill Gates who have been and continue to be unjustly smeared, giulianied, and looted by the parasite class using lawyer-like dishonesties.

Honest tobacco-company executives can formulate impenetrable defenses based on Neo-Tech:

## NEO-TECH
lets the innocent go on the offense
with
Wide-Scope Accounting and Fully Integrated Honesty

A person or company must uproot government dishonesties at their root...and then persist in those uprootings. Such persistence publicly juxtaposes productive innocence against destructive guilt. The guilty are those who use political-agenda "laws" and force-backed institutions to steal unearned livelihoods from competitive

162

value producers. Such theft steals from everyone and society. ...Go after those criminal parasites with confidence — with the invincible justice of wide-scope accounting and fully integrated honesty.

Consult web site —

www.neo-tech.com

To see counterattacks in action, key the words "Protection Kit" into the Neo-Tech search engine.

Those counterattacks are already rising in the cyberspace civilization. That new civilization is the precursor to the rational Civilization of the Universe. Ironically, however, through the competitive, free-market dynamics in the Civilization of the Universe, smoking cigarettes would end without any force of law or political correctness. In fact, purposely harmful activities would end voluntarily, including theft, murder, other criminal acts, initiatory force, fraud, wars, drunkenness, gambling, sexual harassment, prostitution, drug use, and overeating. For, in a cyberspace civilization — in the Civilization of the Universe — irrationality disappears in the natural competition for prosperous value creation.

Examine Neo-Tech. It is your survival tool. It is the tool of justice. Sooner or later you must use it to protect yourself and your company.

Sincerely,

*John Flint*

John Flint,
Editor
Neo-Tech Worldwide Publishing

Ending 2300 Years of Lawyer-Like Dishonesties

The following post of April 26, 1997, concluded NTP's lawyer-dishonesty campaign on Usenet (Internet Newsgroups):

"Kudos to each who through Usenet elicited arrays of dishonesties from unskilled or wannabe lawyers. In the uncontrollable Usenet world, those amateurs provided bountiful displays of lawyer-like dishonesties. They lacked the experience and shrewdness of professional lawyers and politicians who prosper by keeping their dishonesties well camouflaged. Through their naïveté, those Usenet/edu[1] 'lawyers' publicly revealed the automatic-lying mechanism of lawyers and politicians.

"Each such dishonesty becomes embedded in the ostracism/praise matrix building throughout cyberspace. Equally important, the lawyer/politician dishonesties and contextual responses serve as raw material for web sites and book publications that will undercut the third and final tripod leg supporting today's anticivilization. ...Those three legs comprise (1) media-pip dishonesties, (2) intellectual-educational dishonesties, and (3) lawyer-politician dishonesties.

"Employing Usenet to uncover the first leg of that tripod began in 1995 with the creation of a cyberspace dishonesty machine called KOAH. That machine used arrays of noncontexutal attack-mode Usenet posts in a technique called 'pipping'. That technique arose from Mike-Wallace wannabes on Usenet who enviously attack great value producers such as Bill Gates and their businesses. ...Like the amateur lawyers on Usenet, those amateur journalists blatantly revealed the secrets of media dishonesty.

---

[1]edu is the Internet code for communications or web sites originating from educational institutions.

Thus, those previously guarded secrets are now publicly exposed and archived on Internet search engines.

"Uncovering the second leg of the tripod consisted of identifying intellectual-educational frauds. For over a year, those same KOAH dynamics elicited intellectual dishonesties from ersatz philosophers. That Usenet campaign developed a new body of literature that subverts pseudo-intellectuals and mind-crippling educators who underpin today's anticivilization.

"The third leg of the tripod supporting this anticivilization was forged from lawyer-like dishonesties. Those dishonesties were the deepest buried and most difficult to expose. Usenet was the breakthrough tool needed to extract archetype examples of those previously hidden lawyer-like dishonesties. Through Usenet and the web along with hard-copy literature[1], the lawyer/politician frauds that harmed everyone on Earth for 2300 years are now used to undermine and eventually vanish the anticivilization.

## Ending Lawyer-Like Dishonesties #9

### Blindside Justice

In the non-cyberspace world, the parasitical elites with their force-backed agents and armies of pips live through automatic lies, fake compassion, and smooth-sailing frauds. But, in the cyberspace world, search engines archive such dishonesties, fakes, frauds. Those search engines can then publicly juxtapose dishonesties against contextual facts. Thus, in cyberspace, no one can live through dishonesty, fraud, or bluff. ...A rising cyberspace/cybercash world will blindside the futures of professional value

---

[1]A hard-copy book titled *Flame-War Justice* will be published in late 1999 covering the three legs of NTP's Usenet campaign.

destroyers surviving today through lawyer-like dishonesties.


## Ending Lawyer-Like Dishonesties #10

## Law as a Valid Profession

Law is an important, valid profession.  Honest, value-producing lawyers do exist.  Such lawyers will play crucial roles in the coming cyberspace/cybercash civilization.  But, today, far too many lawyers live through destructive dishonesties empowered by force-backed, political-agenda "laws".  Such bogus, self-serving "laws" are made by lawyers, for lawyers, and backed by the rabidly destructive Association of Trial Lawyers of America.[1]  Those "laws" yield hidden parasitisms that give lawyers the generally deserved reputation of being festering sewage needing to be flushed away. ...Fully integrated honesty in cyberspace flushes away that sewage to give lawyers a new chance for a clean, honest life in the coming Civilization of the Universe.


### *Admirable Lawyers*

In the upside-down anticivilization, the most admirable, value-delivering lawyers are often criticized and scorned.  One such person is the notorious "mob" lawyer, Oscar Goodman.  Yet, lawyers like Mr. Goodman are among the few front-line heroes protecting everyone from expanding prosecutorial abuses and eroding constitutional rights.  Such abuses and erosions lead to increasing government damages and criminal tyranny.  Oscar Goodman — like O.J. Simpson's legal team — helps keep the government legal machines honest by holding their feet to the fire in making them *objectively* prove their cases beyond a reasonable

---

[1]Examples of industry destructions via lawyer-like dishonesties include apples (Alar), asbestos, breast implants, the Corvair, nuclear power, tobacco, Microsoft.

doubt. Moreover, unlike most lawyers, especially tort lawyers, Oscar Goodman is honest, forthright, and delivers net values to society in protecting everyone's liberty.

Document B

# CURING OBJECTIVIST CULTISTS #1-7

## Curing Objectivist Cultists #1

### Profits from Honesty

Cyberspace search engines are quietly building matrixes that will eventually make everyone accountable for his or her words and actions. The Neo-Tech literature as far back as 1986 described the formation of a permanent, computerized ostracism/praise matrix. Once computer-analyzing/matching programs along with more advanced Artificial Intelligence (AI) programs are integrated with the contents of those search engines, no one will escape his or her words being searched out then juxtaposed against full-context facts. Find, for example, through the search engine on the Neo-Tech web site, the story about New York mayor Rudolph Giuliani being sunk by a computerized ostracism matrix in the year 2002 for his 1980s crimes against one of this century's greatest value-producers, Michael Milken — and Giuliani's subsequent criminal destruction of the fabulously valuable Wall-Street company, Drexel Burnham Lambert.[1] ...Cyberspace never forgets.

Then, use that search engine to find "My Termination" — a 1989 metaphorical account dramatizing the vanishing of professional value destroyers be they parasitical politicians, destructive lawyers, dishonest journalists, or mind-ravaging professors. ...Honesty/dishonesty ratings of each person's words and actions will eventually become publicly available to everyone for job hiring, business dealings, criminal indictments, and social

[1]Giuliani's story was also printed on the back cover of the 1989 *Neo-Tech Discovery*.

169

relationships.

Notice how automatic self-accountability is the opposite of Orwell's "big brother is watching you" concept. ...Rapidly accelerating technology crumbles tyranny.

And, finally realize that no one can gain an understanding of Neo-Tech or Objectivism through Usenet alone. Objectivist cultists will eventually learn that the most advanced understanding of Neo-Tech *and* Objectivism, not only for today but into the future, resides on the continually growing, increasingly profitable, 2.1-million-word web site at

www.neo-tech.com

To sample the coming computer-matching accountability, one can enter the words "Objectivism", "pips", "Rand", "Peikoff", and other related words or names into the Neo-Tech search engine. By doing that, one discovers how the dishonest behaviors of a pip, a lawyer, or an Objectivist cultist are juxtaposed against contextual facts.

Usenet is a domain in which many of its habitués waste irreplaceable chunks of life on (1) ego-pumping attacks directed at competitive values and their heroic producers and on (2) arguing accomplish-nothing ideas to insignificant, static audiences. Moreover, to date (1997), the web for most businesses has been remarkably impotent in delivering benefits and profits. But, Neo-Tech Bantam Companies through split-run testing and statistical analyses have learned how to exploit Usenet and Web activities into unique PR dynamics that (1) increase profitability in non-cyberspace markets, (2) expand sales of existing products, and (3) generate new products indefinitely into the future.

Most important, the cyberspace dynamics of Neo-Tech continually advance the commercial use of Objectivism while revealing new venues for applying Neo-Tech/Objectivism worldwide.

170

Curing Objectivist Cultists #2

## Execute Immanual Kant and Adam Smith?

Objectivist cultists[1] rabidly condemn the 19th century philosopher Immanuel Kant. For, their guru, Ayn Rand, publicly stated that Kant was "the evilest man who ever lived". In that condemnation, Objectivist cultists contradict the essence of Objectivist philosophy: Evil among men occurs not through thoughts, but through willful action involving the initiation of force or fraud. Yet, those same cultists properly criticize Christianity for condemning to Hell or praising to Heaven people, not for their actions, but, for their thoughts. ...According to Christianity, one is evil for having lust or murder in his heart. By contrast, according to Objectivism, one is evil for raping or murdering others, not for thoughts of rape or murder. One is evil for committing objective crimes, *not* for expressing subjective thoughts or ideas and *not* for unacted upon emotions.

Immanuel Kant did not live by initiating force or fraud against others. He did not commit objective crimes. He expressed his subjective thoughts as piles of irrational, circular logic. Nevertheless, Objectivist cultists, hypnotized by Ayn Rand, assert that Kant was more evil than mass killers such as Hitler, Stalin, Mao, Pol Pot, even FDA's mass-murderer Robert Kessler or DOJ's child-killer Janet Reno. ...Objectivist cultists blindly chant that

---

[1]To directly observe Objectivist cultists in merry-go-round action, visit the Usenet newsgroup humanities.philosophy.objectivism (hpo). In its charter, that newsgroup explicitly bans any discussion of "evil" wide-scope Neo-Tech. Even mentioning the word Neo-Tech is banned and automatically censored through its killbot . The hpo newsgroup is, however, an efficient newsgroup for gaining knowledge about Objectivism and observing the healthy debunking of Objectivist cultists by Libertarians, Anarcho-Capitalists, and Objectivist noncultists. ...Also, Neo-Tech recognizes and respects the right of association in forming hpo to ban Neo-Tech, no matter how unwise. Today, hpo includes the spectacle of dishonest Objectivist cultists savagely obliterating one another with ad-hominem attacks. Such a spectacle demonstrates the justice throughout cyberspace in which honesty ultimately prevails.

Kant was responsible for acts of murder committed by others.

Those cultists arbitrarily transferred responsibility from actual killers to someone who expressed subjective ideas — to someone whose ideas differed from the dogmas of Objectivist cultists. Thus, if Kant were alive today, those cultists would extend their pipping[1] "logic" by advocating his execution as the evilest man who ever lived. They would advocate an "Objectivist" police-state execution of Kant for his thoughts, ideas, and writings.

Objectivist philosophy was nearly flawlessly developed by intellectual-giant Ayn Rand. Her philosophy is crucial for living honestly, productively, happily. Her philosophy is correct in its contextual premises and axioms. But, Objectivism is dishonestly used for ego boosting by its dogmatic cultists. Still, regardless of the cultists' dishonesties, mankind on Earth owes a profound debt to Ayn Rand along with her associates Leonard Peikoff and Nathaniel Branden for discovering, developing, and marketing Objectivism to the public through intellectual and business dynamics. For, Objectivism is the underlying philosophy throughout the Civilization of the Universe — the philosophy that will envelop Earth through cyberspace/cybercash business dynamics.

Yet, mankind would be thrown into the dark ages if Objectivist cultists succeeded in destroying the credibility of Objectivism and killing its advance into the working-class populace. Similarly, in history, mankind was thrown into the dark ages when Aristotelian cultists and the Catholic hierarchy dishonestly dogmatized and destroyed the credibility of Aristotle's philosophical works. ...Aristotle's uncorrupted works, however, rose again through Aquinas and served as the precursor to Objectivism, Neo-Tech, and the coming Civilization of the Universe.

The ego-boosting tool of Objectivist cultists is "pipping". To illustrate that tool, consider how they pip greatness: Adam Smith was the father of the Industrial Revolution and the essential pillar

---

[1]For specific examples of pipping, see www.neo-tech.com and enter the words "pip", "pips", and "pipping" into its search engine.

for limitless wealth production through free-enterprise capitalism. Yet, the Objectivist cultists giddily "discovered" that from Adam Smith's philosophical work, *Theory of Moral Sentiments*, Kant got his most "evil" ideas. (Kant also gleaned many of his ideas from David Hume and Jean-Jacques Rousseau.)

Those cultists then spout Rand's words that mass murderers as Hitler and Stalin could not have succeeded without Kant. Thus, by extending that same "reasoning", Kant could not have succeeded without Smith. "Logically", therefore, Adam Smith should have been executed by the State to prevent the subsequent generations of mass murder and terrible evil for which "the creator of ideas, not the doer" is held responsible. ...So go the Objectivist cultists who behave more as irrational Kantians than as rational Objectivists.

What is the problem with those cultists? Mainly, they try to dishonestly boost their egos by tearing down great people and their historic achievements — enviously tearing down by pipping. Those cultists try to justify their own life-wasting philosophizings and productivity failures by showing their "superiority" over successful people. ...Pipping occurs when petty people (pip-squeaks) try to make themselves appear important by taking facts out of context and using non sequiturs to enviously denigrate outstanding value producers, usually in a dishonest, ad-hominem manner.

Another method for pipping historic greatness is to pluck ideas and achievements from earlier eras. Then, juxtapose those ideas and achievements against today's advanced knowledge. From that dishonest position, pips can easily point to all kinds of "evils"— all kinds of, in their own words, "Inherently Dishonest Ideas" (IDIs).

The pipper largely ignores, for example, that Adam Smith (1723-1790) came out of a primitive base of knowledge to build a crucially valuable, comprehensive foundation for the industrial revolution, for laissez-faire capitalism, and for Ayn Rand's own philosophy of Objectivism. Indeed, Smith died a century before the deductive knowledge of Nietzsche and the inductive experience of the Industrial Revolution.

Incidentally, Nietzsche was also condemned and denigrated by Objectivist cultists, even though Rand obtained many of her early ideas from Nietzsche without acknowledging him. ...Objectivist cultists pipping the achievements of other historical fighters for not following Ayn Rand's Objectivism is somewhat like pipping Newton for not following Einstein's theory of relativity.

Objectivist cultists live through aggressive dogmatisms. They thrive on emotionally subjective ad-hominem attacks. Following their leader Rand, they call Kant the evilest man who ever lived. Yet, Kant was, in fact, invaluable in the production of Objectivism. His philosophical power was surpassed only by Plato, Aristotle, and Rand. ...Powerful, comprehensive ideas, good or bad, are ultimately valuable. To repeat: In the anticivilization, powerful yet false idea systems such as Kant's were needed to develop the singularly valid idea system of Objectivism.

Like welcoming losing poker players into the game, Neo-Tech welcomes losing philosophers into the competition. A Plato, a Rousseau, a Kant, a Hegel, a Marx are welcomed to construct anticivilization philosophies or ideas, no matter how irrational, no matter how bogus, no matter how others might use or misuse those philosophies. Any shifting of moral or criminal blame from the club/gun-wielding criminals/rulers onto peaceful thinkers/ philosophers is wrongly shifting responsibility from the objectively guilty to the objectively innocent. Such false blame is not only unjust, but chills the free-market of ideas.

Like exploiting losing poker players, Neo-Tech exploits losing philosophers to the eventual benefit of everyone. By identifying the errors within the philosophies of Plato, Rousseau, Kant, Hegel, and Marx[1], Ayn Rand put the anticivilization philosophies into the

---

[1]Blame mass murders on the bogus philosophies of Plato, Rousseau, Kant, Hegel, and Marx? Upon whom then does one blame the mass murders by Genghis Khan, Ivan the Terrible, Jack the Ripper, Idi Amin, and Jeffrey

(footnote continued on next page)

crosshairs of the Neo-Tech business dynamic to profitably blast those philosophies into oblivion.

## Curing Objectivist Cultists #3

## "Stop-Servitude" Campaign

Objectivist cultists are appreciated for their participation in the on-going "Stop Servitude" campaign sponsored by the Ayn Rand Institute (ARI). But, standing on the seminal, no-force/no-coercion principle against fascist servitude is not enough. Even ARI-president Michael Berliner's valuable, articulate editorials about the destructive degeneracy of the altruistic principle underpinning "Service" are not enough. To be effective, the focus must delve deeper — down to a different root. If not, the servitude-hoaxers' saintly sounding oratory about duty to the national good will steamroll those Objectivists. They will be steamrolled not only by the Mussolini-type statists such as President Clinton and General Powell, but by the social-type conservatives such as Arianna Huffington and cyberspace-censor Senator Dan Coats spouting their moral imperatives.

Service-to-others hoaxers easily overwhelm anti-slavery principles with piles of good-sounding non sequiturs about serving the "greater good". Moreover, the benevolent word "volunteerism" will be dishonestly thrown into the faces of those campaigning

---

(footnote continued from previous page)

Dahmer. They either never heard of or never absorbed the ideas of those philosophers. ...Yes, go all out with intellectual action to attack, subvert, and eliminate ideas that are bogus, as were the ideas of Rousseau, Kant, Hegel, and Marx. But, do not condemn those philosophers as evil. Moreover, they are the valuable articulators of the harmful idea systems upon which the anticivilization depends. Such articulations of bogus ideas are necessary for unleashing the power of Objectivism and Neo-Tech.

against the "Service" servitude juggernaut.

One must undercut the "Service" propaganda by demonstrating that the entire campaign is a ploy having nothing to do with volunteerism, good will, or benefiting anyone except its shrewd promoters. That fascist-servitude ploy is driven by cunning neocheaters gaining unearned praise, power, and livelihoods through good-sounding, compassionate words. That "Service" ploy gets each victim not only to sanction the servitude-fraud promoters but to praise their "compassion".

What masterful neocheating! Give them credit: The promoters of "Service" servitude are neocheaters supreme. ...That "Service" servitude ploy must be undercut at a deeper level — at the Jay-Gould level of understanding:

### Sacrificial Service: Jay Gould versus Adolf Hitler

One of the greatest competitive value producers of the 19th century was railroad magnate/financier Jay Gould. Yet, he endured endless government, church, and media attacks for his "greed" — unjust attacks that continue to this day. Despite those constant attacks and dishonest "Robber-Baron" myths, Gould produced competitive values for society through integrated honesty combined with wide-scope accounting. Perhaps more than any businessman, he identified the parasitical neocheaters of his time. He did not care what the parasitical leaders, the duped public, the religious preachers, or the dishonest media said about him. He routinely triumphed over those who attacked him, those who desperately tried to break him. ...Gould simply outflanked them with integrated honesty, always pushing ahead, producing ever greater values for others and society.

Jay Gould admired other great businessmen of his day. But, from wider integrations, he also criticized them, especially John D. Rockefeller, for yielding to the calls for altruism by the social predators throughout the government, media, churches, and

176

universities.[1] Gould identified the irrationality of efficacious businessmen sacrificing any part of their lives to "service" — sacrificing their invaluable time and capital that deliver maximum benefits to others and society. ...Jay Gould was too rational and benevolent to sacrifice any part of his supreme value. He would not diminish the efficacious use of his time and capital just to lessen the criticisms from professional compassion hoaxers.

Today, the compassion hoaxers are drumbeating a debilitating message into the formative minds of youth. Those hoaxers are pounding into children an ugly message that idealizes unambitious service, coerced servitude, and wimpish sacrifice as the highest standard to which one could aspire. ...If everyone aspired to that "highest" standard — that Hitlerian standard — most would die of starvation or be killed in looting wars.

Ignored in today's anti-life, be-slaves-to-society messages is the source of human values and benevolence. That source of

---

[1]A distinction is drawn between (1) Rockefeller's altruism motivated by social approval for sacrificing his values to the degenerative altruist agenda and (2) Carnegie's value-generating philanthropy motivated by self-chosen acts for delivering maximum values to others and society. Acts of self-motivated philanthropy as displayed by Andrew Carnegie in building America's public library system can be highly valuable and admirable, but still, not as valuable and admirable as his acts of generating competitive industries, commercial values, and lifetime jobs for others and society.

The hoax of altruism is heavily worked in movies. A common theme is depicting a harried husband and father struggling to exhaustion in maintaining his good-paying job that provides his family with life's amenities, comforts, and security. But, with the demands for properly performing his high-paying job, he misses his son's Little-League game. Thus, he loses the love of his wife and gains the enmity of his son, neither of whom show an understanding of that man's value-producing work. Neither show an appreciation of the long, exhausting hours he had to labor for his family's comfort and well being. The wife and son never identify from where come their luxurious lifestyles. They never realize that their over-extended yuppie lifestyles must be hard earned by the husband. To regain his family's love, the husband sacrifices his career so he will not miss any more Little-League games. The story ends without explaining how that family will maintain the standard of living that his wife and son demand. ...That scenario serves the altruist agenda of sacrificing greater values to lesser values in a sea of cloying sentimentalities.

genuine service to mankind is competitive job-and-value production through business. The real heroes and servers of society are those entrepreneurs so busy, so hard driving in creating competitive jobs and producing values for others and society that they have no time for image building, volunteer work, or sacrificial service. ...Today's idealization of coerced sacrificial service is the same malignant irrationality that Jay Gould identified and rejected over a century ago...and the same sacrificial service that Hitler, the ultimate altruist, used to conduct history's greatest holocaust. ...Do not scorn the servitude program; scorn its promoters.

## Curing Objectivist Cultists #4

### Philosophy through a Wide-Scope Lens

Aside from profitable web-pointing "Pip" templates, Neo-Tech Publishing (NTP) personnel never respond to dishonest or ad-hominem attacks. NTP will, however, publish ad-hoc material that advances its purpose and goal. For example, in ferreting out the deep-hidden dishonesties woven throughout the Objectivist culture, writers from Neo-Tech will publish from time to time "outlandish" material on Usenet and the Web. That material will carry Neo-Tech Objectivism into new markets under titles such as:

## Existentialist Soul Mates:
## Ayn Rand and Jean-Paul Sartre

What is an Existentialist? An Existentialist can be anyone ranging from a crusading Christian (Kierkegaard) with murderous preachings, to a heil-Hitler Fascist (Heidigger) with genocidal ideas, to a fervent communist (Sartre) with ravaging parasitisms.

But, an Existentialist can also be a fervent Randian Objectivist imbued with cult-like hatred. Even capitalist Ayn Rand with her self-responsible, value-creating passion "seems to be"[1] a heroic Existentialist!

Existentialism applies to an imagined universe *arbitrarily* constructed from *subjective* consciousness. Whereas, Objectivism applies to the factual universe *logically* constructed from *objective* reality. Are not the two philosophies opposites? Well, usually they are, depending on context. Yet, certain Objectivists such as cult followers of Ayn Rand can at times be irrational, unproductive Sartrian Existentialists. And, certain Existentialists such as Nietzsche, Camus, even Sartre can at times be rational, productive Randian Objectivists. How can that be? With (1) Existentialism in the context of an irrational civilization and (2) Objectivism in the context of a rational civilization, both philosophies seem to meld.

Also consider that Nietzsche through Existentialism held virulent contempt for Christianity as a mind/life-destroying dynamic that shrinks conscious beings toward nothingness. Yet, one of Nietzsche's most admired individuals was Jesus, a Jew, whom Nietzsche called the only real Christian. For, Jesus, as a metaphorical individual, innovated his life and passionately created his own character to impact an entire civilization for two millennia. ...Jesus aside, Nietzsche viewed Christians as life-wasting followers of church-spun hoaxes and Pope-like tyrannies.

Next consider that Neo-Tech/Objectivism largely agrees with Nietzsche's view of religion, but would regard many passionately creative Christians as heroes in an irrational civilization, such as Apostle Paul, Thomas Aquinas, and perhaps Martin Luther along

---

[1]"Seems to be" because no one can define Existentialism or an Existentialist. Those two words roam as ghosts within an arbitrary, mystical-created anticivilization. ...Existentialism is more an attitude involving humanistic self-responsibility rather than a unified set of ideas.

with outstanding artists, scientists, explorers and business people who were Christians. Additionally, Christianity was the first individualistic philosophy and served as a 2000-year, semi-effective foil against government tyrants and other criminals.

Finally, by Nietzsche's standard, Neo-Tech/Objectivism holds passionate innovators and developers of Objectivism such as Ayn Rand (Jesus-Christ like), Nathaniel Branden (Apostle-Paul like), and Leonard Peikoff (Thomas-Aquinas like) as genuine, individualistic heroes in this anticivilization. By the same Nietzschean standard, Neo-Tech/Objectivism dismisses the Randian cultists as anti-individualistic life-wasters who retard the advance of Objectivism.

Similarly, by Existentialist standards, one finds passionate innovators in Søren Kierkegaard (Jesus-Christ like), Albert Camus (Apostle-Paul like), and Jean-Paul Sarte (Thomas-Aquinas like). Moreover, those holding the most useful views were people with the widest-scope understandings. Thus, Nathaniel Branden held the widest-scope understandings of Objectivism while Albert Camus held the widest-scope understandings of Existentialism. ...Nevertheless, hard-core Objectivist, Leonard Peikoff, produced the most accurate, valuable Objectivist products. Similarly, hard-core Existentialist, Jean-Paul Sartre, produced the most accurate, valuable Existentialist products.

## Philosophical Twins Paradox

Philosophies such as Existentialism, even Kantism, are valid and useful in the context of an unreal (conscious-created) anticivilization. Objectivism, however, is the single philosophy that underpins the real (reality-based) Civilization of the Universe. Most important, however, "unreal" and "real" have no middle ground or compromise position — no connections, mixes, or transitions. Likewise, the anticivilization and the Civilization of the Universe have no middle ground or compromise position —

no connections, mixes, or transitions.

Similarly, no middle ground or compromise position exists between dishonesty and honesty. Yet, as outrageous as the thought seems, capitalist Rand and communist Sartre seem to be soul mates. They are nearly identical in their ontological view of life passion, self-responsibility, and individual freedom when the context for Rand is kept in the rational Civilization of the Universe and the context for Sartre is kept in the irrational anticivilization.

Except for Objectivism, however, philosophies in Earth's irrational civilization become head-spinning, chaotic messes of words when compared and contrasted. For, philosophies conflict in an arbitrary, irrational civilization. Thus, philosophers constantly argue. One philosopher never convinces the other of anything. Both think the other is wrong, neither realizing that the other is right from his or her own contextual perspective. Their endless arguments, therefore, are generally a waste of time and life.

Such right/wrong passions rage at all levels to all extremes, including bloody wars and genocides. Indeed, in this anticivilization, furious emotions reign through endless accomplish-nothing battles. The crafty fury of each side is captured by a Lewis Carroll doublet in his *The Tale of the Mouse*:

> "I'll be judge, I'll be jury
> Said crafty old fury."

As opposed to the Neo-Tech doublet:

> "Reality is judge, reality is jury
> Said fully integrated honesty"

* * *

In the Civilization of the Universe, philosophies vanish as meaningless. Only Objectivism remains, which by definition is based on the objective reality underlying the Civilization of the Universe. Words such as war, crime, fraud, evil, and dishonesty vanish from nonuse in an eternally rational Universe. With time, even the word Objectivism itself will be forgotten from nonuse in the eternally prosperous Civilization of the Universe.

## Neo-Tech Reconciles the Unreconcilable

While Objectivism and Existentialism can never meet or mix, they can be reconciled through the wide-scope accounting of Neo-Tech. Thus, through Neo-Tech, Objectivist philosophers Ayn Rand/Leonard Peikoff mediated through David Kelley/Nathaniel Branden are reconciled with Existentialist philosophers Kierkegaard/Sartre mediated through Nietzsche/Camus.

## Combining Nietzsche and Rand

Friedrich Nietzsche champions ancient-Greek/Homeric morals of living life passionately within any realm or illusion. By contrast, Ayn Rand champions living life intransigently within objective reality. Combining Nietzsche's relentless passion with Rand's uncompromised Objectivism would accomplish the following two feats:

**Feat #1**

*Vanish Anticivilization Propagators*
*and their*
lawyer-like dishonesties
philosophical deceptions
political frauds
religious hoaxes
God concepts
cultisms
mysticisms
occultisms
new-age vogues
fad diets and health myths
pseudosciences
UFO theories
conspiracy theories
Illuminati bashing
political-agenda "laws"
a-point law
subjective law
the IRS
ego justice

**Feat #2**

*Vanish Parasitical/Envy Attacks*
*on*
Jay Gould
John D. Rockefeller
Ayn Rand
Michael Milken
Leona Helmsley
Bill Gates

Problems arise when cult-like philosophers try to use the power of Objectivism to fix Earth's unfixable anticivilization. Trying to change the unchangeable is futile. Such efforts perpetuate the anticivilization. ...Identify the evil. Do not try to fix or change it. Instead, isolate it. Let it die alone, within each individual and society. Partake in a cyberspace/cybercash business civilization. The Civilization of the Universe — an Objectivist civilization — will then envelop planet Earth.

What is the difference between (1) Randian Objectivists trying to fix the anticivilization while protecting their investments in that irrational civilization and (2) Neo-Tech Objectivists "seemingly" trying to fix the anticivilization while liquidating their investments in that same irrational civilization? Randian Objectivists try with various degrees of temporary success to improve the anticivilization while still protecting their investments in that irrational civilization. Neo-Tech Objectivists, by contrast, work with increasing degrees of permanent success to vanish the anticivilization while building new investments in a new civilization — an Objectivist civilization — the Civilization of the Universe. ...Objectivism seeks to add positives and improve the anticivilization through philosophy. Neo-Tech seeks to remove negatives and vanish the anticivilization through business competition.

Curing Objectivist Cultists #5

Compatible Detachment

On understanding the dynamics of Neo-Tech in cyberspace, one loses interest in Earth's dying anticivilization. For, Neo-Tech/Objectivism presented as *theory* glazes the eyes of status-quo people protecting their anticivilization investments. Neo-Tech/ Objectivism presented as *action* — as fully integrated honesty — makes those people either run and hide or attack with criminal force.

A person detached from objective reality is schizophrenic. Such a person is incompatible with his or her environment and, thus, functions poorly in society. What happens, however, when a person is detached from the anticivilization, but (1) functions competently within that irrational civilization, (2) remains rooted in objective reality, and (3) produces competitive values for others and society? That person can profitably operate with Neo-Tech/ Objectivism from outside the anticivilization rather than being plucked to pieces inside that irrational civilization. With the tools of Neo-Tech, one can quietly outwit, profit from, and then undermine professional value destroyers along with their armed agents of force roaming this anticivilization. ...Such is the power of Neo-Tech/Objectivism through which one can fulfill his or her life.

## Curing Objectivist Cultists #6

### Neo-Tech vs. Objectivism

The more one understands Neo-Tech, the more one discovers the wider integrations of Objectivism — wider than made by Rand or Peikoff in every area. Neo-Tech is a business/wealth-generation vision that requires metaphors combined with multiple layers of integrations with wide-scope accountings. Neo-Tech draws both mental and physical entities into accountability. Most important, Neo-Tech works by exposing, subverting, and then removing harmful negatives, especially mysticisms and dishonesties. ...By removing those negatives, the positives take care of themselves.

To date, Neo-Tech has been most effective among the non-

185

elitist working class. But, now, through the Neo-Tech web site, other classes are discovering Neo-Tech. ...A Neo-Tech firestorm is in everyone's future — a firestorm that burns away mysticisms and dishonesties to bring limitless prosperity.

Objectivists and most intellectuals cannot understand or evaluate Neo-Tech without first understanding its unique "removing-negatives" essence. They must re-examine Neo-Tech from an out-of-this-anticivilization perspective. ...Intellectuals, writers, artists, and publishers who break from their closed-circle anticivilization thinking will discover commercial, scientific, and intellectual bonanzas in Neo-Tech.

Ignorance of and hostility toward Neo-Tech is displayed by most orthodox Objectivists. Yet, Neo-Tech is the most comprehensive, anti-mystical, pro-freedom dynamic conceivable. On understanding the essence of Neo-Tech, one grasps its power in subverting mysticisms and exposing the dishonesties of physical-and-intellectual oppressions. Not only does Neo-Tech overtly castigate every form of mysticism and the paranormal, but specifically debunks telepathy, telekinesis, UFOs, supernaturalism, mind-over-matter, primacy-of-consciousness, and the pseudo-sciences. Yet, the gross ignorance about Neo-Tech by Objectivist cultists is illustrated by the poster below in his comment, "The Neo-Tech folks believe in telepathy, telekinesis":

In article <lakidED2H4D.JMu@netcom.com>,
lakid@netcom.com wrote:
>Hi, Roger:)
>It isn't just an issue of immortality. The Neo-Tech folks believe
>in telepathy, telekinesis, being able to remove the chance factor
>from life so you are *guaranteed* success...and blending it all
>with bits and pieces taken from Objectivist writings and
>lectures and workshops. I'm kinder to it than you, though. If

>one makes a conscientious effort to delete all the references in
>Neotech that are just plain crazy (this is *very* easy to do)
>it's actually possible to learn alot about Objectivism that is not
>elsewhere. And, at least in my brief browsing, the references
>easily available in any one book upon the subject about
>Objectivism seemed fairly accurate!

>This may seem like rank heresy...but the insights in the
>Neotech manuals about objectivism, though mixed with
>everything from science fiction to mysiticism, actually feel, to
>me, more integrated than the studied words of Dr. Peikoff!
>

Curing Objectivist Cultists #7

Neo-Tech Uber Alles

Forget Hitler's bogus usurpation of Franz Haydn's Emperor Quartet, "Deutschland Uber Alles". The fact for everyone is "Neo-Tech Uber Alles" — Accountability and Honesty Above All.

# III
# Gaining Riches
## by
# Curing Death

# III
# Gaining Riches by Curing Death

# III

# Gaining Riches by Curing Death

### The Civilization of the Universe

A naturally created *civilization* advances through honesty. Its citizens cannot be defeated. They bring prosperity and immortality to conscious beings. An artificially created *anticivilization* is ruled through dishonesty. Its rulers cannot be defeated. They bring harm and death to conscious beings.

Despite tremendous human progress, planet Earth has been ruled for 2300 years through dishonesty — starting with Pericles and Plato in the fourth-century BC. ...Pericles was the genesis of the neocheating politician. He taught professional killers how to seize power through popular support of a democracy. Plato was the genesis of the dishonesty disease. He taught the parasitical elites how to rationalize deception in order to rule the value producers through dishonesties and mysticisms[1].

What about those who put forth heroic efforts to override Platonic deceptions — deceptions that harm and ultimately kill everyone on Earth? What about those few heroic freedom fighters such as William Wallace (1272-1305) and entrepreneurs such as Jay Gould (1836-1892)? What about they who work to eliminate dishonesties and injustices woven throughout Earth's anticivilization? Such people are relentlessly, dishonestly, mortally attacked by the *dependents* of Earth's anticivilization. ...Through such attacks on the good and heroic, the anticivilization is perpetuated and never defeated.

From that base of anticivilization dishonesty, everyone eventually accepts his or her icons of fraud and criminality. Indeed, parasitical elites promote universally harmful icons into popular acceptance, be they a Hitler, a Mao, a Pope, a Princess

---

[1]Dishonesty and mysticism contradict nature. They are diseases of human consciousness.

Diana, a Pat Buchanan, a Jerry Falwell, a Hillary Clinton. Likewise, such parasitical elites besmirch universally beneficent wealth-and-job producers ranging from J. P. Morgan and John D. Rockefeller of yesteryear to Michael Milken and Bill Gates of today.

By contrast, the Civilization of the Universe protects and honors competitive value producers for their universally beneficial actions. For, only through their productive efforts can a civilization deliver increasing riches and eternal life to its citizens.

## Attacks Enhance Neo-Tech

Citizens of Earth live in an anticivilization. Any high-effort, publicly visible action taken to counter the harmful effects of their anticivilization is taken out of context, dishonestly attacked, and often destroyed. For, the anticivilization must preserve itself.

An anticivilization is based on dishonesty. Nothing within an anticivilization is going to end its deadly harms inflicted upon its citizens. Yet, a quantum shift to the honest-based Civilization of the Universe will vanish Earth's anticivilization. ...That shift has begun in cyberspace.

Neo-Tech — fully integrated honesty — is unique: Attacks from the anticivilization enhance the profits of Neo-Tech businesses.

## Flame-War Justice: Rule #1

Before the Internet, no reliable dynamic existed to profitably counter anticivilization dishonesties and injustices. Indeed, in the non-cyberspace world, dishonesty and injustice have held sway for centuries. ...What then delivers honesty and justice in cyberspace?

Consider the first rule in the forthcoming *Flame-War Justice* book to be published by Neo-Tech Publishing: Never admit or deny assertions by dishonest attackers. Once their foundation of falsities is laid, let them expand their dishonesties. Let their dishonesties build upon those falsities. Let the dishonesties from value attackers build into mountains of falsities displayed through search engines and on profit-generating Neo-Tech web sites. Let their errors build layer upon layer without the attackers realizing the consequences. The greater their errors and dishonesties, the greater the payoff to Neo-Tech. When reality appears for others to see throughout cyberspace, the trap closes and profits mount. Those dishonesties and their perpetrators then vanish.

## Dishonesty Disease

For many years, Neo-Tech Publishing (NTP) has studied the dishonesty disease as the underlying essence of Earth's anticivilization. NTP seeks to cure that disease. Such a cure would eradicate the anticivilization and replace it with the Civilization of the Universe.

Integrated honesty, justice, and profits ultimately rule cyberspace. The future belongs to Neo-Tech in the spirit of Schiller/Beethoven's *Ode to Joy:* Someday, men and women will *not* live bound in a brotherhood, but will live free as individual brothers and sisters conducting *profitable* businesses throughout the Civilization of the Universe. In the poem *The Sleepers* found within his *Leaves of Grass*, Walt Whitman recognized that real brotherhood exists on Earth only when people sleep. Whitman also recognized that conscious beings on Earth exist chained in an unnatural anticivilization. Whereas the innocent — children and animals — live free in the natural Civilization of the Universe. They live free in honesty. ...No one can live free in dishonesty.

## Objectivism: the Good, the Bad, the Ugly

Among the outspoken Objectivists, outstanding success stories seem limited to the originators — Rand, Branden, Peikoff — and in lesser degrees to a few other widely published authors of Objectivist philosophy such as David Kelley, Michael Berliner,

Harry Binswanger, Peter Schwartz. On the other hand, outstanding success stories abound today and throughout history ranging from Aristotle, Archimedes, Adam Smith, Andrew Carnegie, and Jay Gould to Ray Kroc, Harold Geneen, and Soichiro Honda. Those people knew little or nothing about Objectivism. Yet, they rose through integrated honesty and wide-scope accounting to deliver tremendous, long-range values and wealth to mankind.

Why cannot Objectivist cultists rise to admirable success? What follows are three revelations that evolve from that question:

### 1. The Last Stand of Objectivist Cultists

Today, a civilization that has been manipulated for 2300 years by criminal rulers and parasitical elites is about to quantum jump into a cyberspace civilization driven by competitive entrepreneurs. Thus, today brings a last-stand resistance against that rising new civilization — a new civilization in which no one can profit from parasitism, fraud, dishonesty, or physical force. Rushing to the forefront of that resistance are today's Objectivist cultists. They are making their last stand based on dishonesty and hypocrisy. ...Eventually, however, cyberspace honesty will redeem them.

In this new cyberspace civilization, honest laborers will rise above Clinton/Buchanan politicians — above criminal leaders/rulers, academic socialists/fascists, dishonest lawyers/deceptive preachers. The John D. Rockefellers, Jay Goulds, and J. P. Morgans will rise as historic heroes while muckraking pips and demagogic hypocrites will vanish. Entrepreneurial value-and-job producers, not Objectivist "philosopher" pips shall lead Earth's civilization into a future of eternal wealth.

### 2. Honesty, not Objectivism, is Fundamental

Conscious beings need not understand Objectivism to discover the Civilization of the Universe. Conscious beings need only wide-scope accounting, fully integrated honesty, and consistent effort to gain limitless prosperity. Honesty ultimately corrects errors and evolves valid knowledge. ...Honesty, by nature, leads to a cyberspace-business civilization — an Objectivist civilization — the Civilization of the Universe.

Conscious beings need no explicit knowledge of philosophy or economics to thrive. Integrated honesty is the underlying fundamental that leads to Objectivism. Civilizations advance not through the static scholastic modes of philosophy, economics, or education per se, but through the dynamic action modes of integrated honesty, wide-scope accounting, consistent effort, and competitive value production. In fact, in an advanced Objectivist civilization, except perhaps for a few scholars, no one will know of an academic discipline called philosophy — or classroom economics for that matter. ...In the future, education and knowledge will come from cyberspace. Knowledge of philosophy and Objectivism will disappear. But fully integrated honesty and wide-scope accounting — Neo-Tech — will remain.

Today, however, heavy doses of philosophy and economics are used worldwide to rationalize the injustices, dishonesties, and irrationalities woven throughout Earth's anticivilization. By contrast, competitive production of values in cyberspace guided by integrated honesty and wide-scope accounting will jump conscious beings from their anticivilization into the Civilization of the Universe.

### 3. Honesty and Effort Deliver Values

Manipulated *facts* are wrong and destructive. Manipulated *truths* are wrong and destructive. Manipulated *Objectivisms* are wrong and destructive. Indeed, dishonest academics, journalists, politicians, lawyers, and cultist Objectivists must function through rationalizations — through manipulated packages of dishonesties comprising truths, facts, and philosophies taken out of context.

No one can be evil by being honest. No one can be a criminal

195

by being honest. Honesty is the universal basis of morals, justice, and ethics.

Integrated honesty is always constructive. Integrated honesty — not philosophy, economics, or education per se — leads to valid knowledge and eternal prosperity. For, integrated honesty is the fundamental dynamic of reality identification and value production. Moreover, philosophy, economics, and science are validated through competitive value-producing actions that evolve from integrated, wide-scope honesty. ...As Leonard Peikoff pointed out, Ayn Rand needed *both* the concrete history of America's founding fathers *and* the dramatic, value-gushing Industrial Revolution to formulate Objectivism with its principled, moral defense of laissez-faire Capitalism.

In the journey toward an Objectivist civilization, academic disciplines are subsumed into the dynamics of Neo-Tech business. Beneath the competitive production of values exist integrated honesty, wide-scope accounting and consistent effort. ...Neo-Tech *is* the prime mover of the Civilization of the Universe.

Objectivism/Libertarianism<br>versus<br>Neo-Tech in Cyberspace

Consider the following estimates of data reflecting daily activity on Usenet (cyberspace newsgroups) in early 1997:

Most Usenet audiences are relatively small, static, and of little commercial value. On Usenet, most posters do little more than preach to the choir, attack critics, or criticize one another. The average daily Libertarian Usenet audience on two Usenet groups is estimated at 3000, the Objectivist audience on two Usenet groups at 600, the Neo-Tech audience on one Usenet group at 200. How many viewers each day might provide commercial profits for Libertarianism, Objectivism, or Neo-Tech? Perhaps 1% or less of those viewers. That means up to 30 daily for Libertarians, up to 6 for Objectivists, up to 2 for Neo-Tech per day. Perhaps 20% of those potential customers will convert to cash profits. And, those estimates are probably generous. Thus, from a marketing standpoint, such figures indicate that Usenet is an insignificant "marketing" medium, especially for Neo-Tech. But, when integrated with web-site dynamics, even Usenet plays an increasingly profitable role in three unexpected areas as explained on the next page.

Now, consider the more accurate statistics for web sites: The Neo-Tech home page began in May, 1996 — about 18 months before writing this document. Without paid advertising or outside publicity, web-site visits have climbed to over 12,000 per day with several hundred new potential "converts" or customers daily — compared to less than 2 per day from Usenet.

The spontaneous climb on the Neo-Tech Web Site is occurring with only a minuscule number of visits coming from Usenet. Moreover, that open-ended climb in visits to Neo-Tech is occurring in the face of proliferating web sites, which are causing declines in hits to most established sites. In studying the statistics from those hits, about 80% of the Neo-Tech visitors are new, coming from all sources and locations.

While lacking specific data for other sites, the figures for Neo-Tech are probably higher than the Libertarian and Objectivist web sites combined. Moreover, the majority of visits to those web sites are from the choir checking on news, updates, and notices. ...The Neo-Tech Web site does not offer news or notices for customers, readers, or "followers". For, the Neo-Tech site is designed to reach all classes of *new* people who are unfamiliar with Neo-Tech, Libertarianism, and Objectivism.

The bottom line is that Libertarian, Objectivist, and most other such web sites evolve around services and news to their established groups. By contrast, Neo-Tech has no established group or organization and offers no such service to its "followers".

Thus, its dynamic is different. Neo-Tech is not structured around serving any intellectual group or doctrine. Neo-Tech reaches the broadest, most diverse markets far beyond Libertarian and Objectivist audiences. In fact, void of doctrines, leaders, or gurus, Neo-Tech reaches essentially all demographic/education/economic groups.

Today, Neo-Tech rises as the strongest dynamic introducing previously unreachable people to Libertarian and Objectivist ideas. The explicit non-authority, non-follower, anti-cult nature of Neo-Tech is the source of its long-range growth. ...Even Usenet is profitable to Neo-Tech in three ways:

1. Usenet provides a quick-response, learn-and-test medium for commercially adjusting to the rising cyberspace civilization. The first rule is never to do anything on the Internet without a plan to convert one's effort into profits.
2. Usenet provides a new, unexpected editing tool for honing literature into higher commercial values for both web sites and printed books.
3. Usenet flamers and critics provide important free material to develop into commercial products for both back-end and front-end customers.

Most establishment Libertarians and Objectivists never considered Neo-Tech in context. But the day is approaching in which everyone must use Neo-Tech — fully integrated honesty and wide-scope accounting — to be competitive in a rising cyberspace civilization.

Finally, addressing the concern of various newsgroup posters about Neo-Tech's adamant distinction between the truth fallacy and the honesty reality: If a person examines in full context just one Neo-Tech concept, that person should examine the honesty-versus-truth concept. That concept underlies long-term competitive advantages. Implementing that concept means discarding the concept of "truth" as bogus, arbitrary, and universally harmful to conscious beings. For, "truth" is a manipulative, anticivilization artifact of negative value.

"Honesty" exists in reality. But, "truth" per se *does not*. Reality moves through time and space. "Honesty" is a *moving* process, while "truth" is a *static* assertion, always fading in time. Only the honesty of contextual facts and ideas moves through time and space of a naturally evolving, objective civilization — the Civilization of the Universe.

Putting facts and ideas into an ever moving context requires the dynamic process of fully integrated honesty. That process is the key to generating new knowledge, creating new wealth, and curing the diseases of aging and death.

\* \* \*

## Two 1997 Addendums

### Addendum #1

*President Clinton: A Charming King Richard III*

Bill Clinton is no brooding, slow-moving Macbeth who will kill anyone or everyone for political power. Instead, Clinton is a charming version of Shakespeare's sharp-witted, fast-moving King Richard III who will kill anyone or everyone for political power. Bill Clinton certainly is the epistemological model of Richard III awaiting the King's fate. Like Richard III, Bill Clinton has a psychological deformity that gives him a monstrous freedom — a cunning freedom to murderously drive for power and sex. Clinton and Richard III are both chameleon manipulators who energetically strove from the dark backwaters of treachery, seduction, and corruption into the blazing light of powerful rulers. As awaited Richard III, disaster awaits Clinton as his crimes and victims accumulate.

Deserving no honorable Cassius or Brutus to eliminate him, he will lose his life to nothing more than salacious muck. ...Or, could he be redeemed? Unlike Richard III, Bill Clinton has one all-encompassing redeeming feature. Through that feature, he not only could have escaped his crimes, but he could have become the greatest world leader in the history of Earth's anticivilization as identified in a paragraph on page 5 of the Golden-Helmet Appendix in *Profound Honesty*. That paragraph reads as follows:

"Redeem? Bill Clinton, for example, had a redeemable core of innocence. Ironically, President Clinton's high intelligence combined with a total lack of principles left him uniquely qualified to understand and then implement the Neo-Tech/Golden-Helmet dynamic. Thus, in the following way, Clinton could have become the greatest world leader in history: Before Neo-Tech and the Golden Helmet, no consistently rational principles were available in which anyone could invest. Bill Clinton, maybe out of a special integrity, never invested in bogus principles from the irrational philosophies that swirled about him and everyone else. Such a fact left him uniquely free for redemption — free to extricate himself from his problems, crimes, and harms of the past. How? Through the Neo-Tech/Golden-Helmet dynamic, Clinton could have swept away armed bureaucracies, political-agenda laws, and ego 'justice' to boom America and then the world into limitless prosperity. Seizing that opportunity, he could have freed himself from his hidden crimes to become a hero for all time. Instead, he chose to be Iago to an Othello-like America. With brilliant language seduction, Clinton became the Macbeth poison in the ear of America to ferment a political culture of rot. ...He could have unleashed America toward a rational civilization through

Neo-Tech and the Golden Helmet. He could have brought this world into the Civilization of the Universe years ahead of schedule. Thus, he could have saved countless millions of lives while booming everyone into worldwide prosperity."

One specific example embodied in Clinton's potential for redemption is identified in Addendum #2:

## Addendum #2
*Prison: Devastating the Good*
The following quoted article was written by former
## Federal Political Prisoner #26061-048

"*Get tough on prisoners!* is a demagogic pitch for many politicians. Look at the agenda behind that pitch. A picture emerges of the public being duped. The *let's-get-tough* movement is done in lieu of reducing real, objective crimes.

"Yes, more criminals of violence and theft need to be imprisoned...and for longer terms. Yet, according to an October, 1996 article in the *Wall Street Journal*, that need is prevented by prisons filling up at seven times the rate of European countries. ...So, who are filling up American prisons? Not violent-and-theft criminals, but victimless-crime offenders are filling those prisons.

"If every politician, judge, and prosecutor could spend time in prison, each would discover deeply hidden, opinion-changing facts invisible to everyone except the prisoners. As in Kafka's novel, *In the Penal Colony*, one must become the prisoner to understand justice — to become inscribed with justice. ...In prison, one discovers three distinct classes of prisoners: (1) objective-crime prisoners who committed universal, objective crimes of theft and violence, (2) subjective-crime prisoners who violated bogus, victimless-crime laws or political-agenda regulations, and (3)

201

wrongly convicted prisoners innocent of any offense.

"The most startling discovery? The effects of incarcerating theft-and-violent-crime prisoners are profoundly kinder than the effects of incarcerating victimless-crime prisoners. In America, people are legally and constitutionally sent to prison *as* punishment, not *for* punishment. That loss of freedom makes minimal difference for theft-and-violent criminals. Most such objective-crime prisoners accept with equanimity the maxim "do the crime, do the time". Moreover, most such criminals have little or no real responsibilities or values to lose on being incarcerated. Few people, if any, suffer unjustly when an objectively real criminal is incarcerated.

"By contrast, most wrongly convicted and subjective/political-crime prisoners had responsible, productive lives in which they sustained jobs, businesses, and families. The loss of freedom is financially, psychologically, and socially devastating not just for them but for many innocent people such as employees, employers, and especially families and dependent children. For them, prison is agonizing torture — cruel-and-unusual punishment. ...Society is damaged whenever an innocent person or a subjective-crime offender loses his or her freedom.

"In brief, incarcerating theft-and-violent criminals is (a) just and constructive, (b) causes minimal suffering, (c) harms few if any innocent people, and (d) protects society. By contrast, incarcerating wrongly convicted or subjective-law offenders is (a) unjust and destructive, (b) causes great suffering, (c) damages many innocent people, and (d) harms society.

"Today, political-agenda prisoners make up an ever growing majority of federal prisoners and a significant minority of state prisoners. The movement to subject such prisoners to increasing brutalities, chain gangs, and tent prisons evolves from political demagoguery that increases the harms inflicted on society by government with mounting costs to taxpayers.

"With the percentage of victimless-crime prisoners steadily increasing over real-crime prisoners, the latest "get-tough" ploys are emasculating centuries-old habeas-corpus rights, including cutting off the most basic of First-Amendment rights — the right for *prisoners* to communicate with the outside world. Indeed, cutting off those rights allows government to increasingly conceal political prisoners where they cannot be heard. (Reference CV-S-93-889-LDG, CA#97-15506) ...Stalin, Hitler, Mao, and Castro clearly understood the importance of emasculating habeas corpus and preventing prisoners from communicating beyond their prison walls."

## Blame not the Bureaucrats,
### It's the Politicians' Fault

"A new direction must evolve in which the public increasingly holds politicians accountable for destructive political-agenda laws. Such bogus laws serve only to increase the power of career politicians and their created bureaucracies. The public must demand elimination of politician-created laws, which range from victimless-crime drug laws, to irrational income-tax laws, to destructive federal regulations, to newly proposed antiabortion laws.

"Without reversing that 'get-tough' on prisoners trend combined with mounting political-agenda laws and regulations, everyone becomes a victim. Eventually, every child, parent, sibling, friend, employer, employee will become a potential "criminal", subject to the destructions imposed by "get-tough" politicians of today and their expanding political-agenda laws.

"An important improvement in protecting society will come through rejecting dishonest cant about crime. A start comes from applauding those few politicians and officials who are not exploiting the dangerous "get-tough-on-prisoners" rhetoric. ...Bill Clinton and Joycelyn Elders deserve applause on that prison issue so important to everyone's future.[1]

"Elimination of victimless-crime laws and political-agenda regulations would change our prison-and-justice systems into increasingly efficient instruments for protecting society from objective crimes — violent-and-theft crimes. ...A new society would then rise in which the intentional value destroyers are the jailed criminals and the competitive value-and-job producers are the freed heroes."

Federal Political Prisoner #26061-048

* * *

### Clinton: Pity, Praise, and Condemnation
### THE STARR REPORT

For what President Clinton is condemned, he should be pitied and, in some cases, praised as reflected in the footnote[1] below. By contrast, for what President Clinton is praised, he should be condemned, perhaps even jailed:

The most shocking sex aspect of *The Starr Report* released on September 11, 1998 is the lack of shocking sex — the mundane paucity of President Clinton's sexual experiences. What a boring, shrunken sex life that wing-clipped man experiences. What a lousy lover. Those who understand Neo-Tech and have experienced romantic love with psychuous sex will feel sorry for

---

[1]To Bill Clinton's lasting credit are his stands on (1) a woman's inalienable right to her own body, health, and life through unconditional abortion rights, including "partial-birth" abortion, (2) backing away from the irrational, self-defecting "war on drugs" and "war on immigrants", (3) refusing to sacrifice himself to the force-backed draft for the irrational Vietnam War, and (4) advancing the Illuminati/Neo-Tech goal of unrestricted worldwide commerce. ...More important, genital-blistering (herpes?), semen-splattering President Clinton with his automatic lying plays an essential role toward diminishing public awe and respect toward political leaders and parasitical elites who rule Earth's anticivilization. Thus, he advances the Neo-Tech agenda of bringing forth the Civilization of the Universe.

the truncated, sexual limpness of that lonely man. Pity, pity.

In this upside-down anticivilization, Clinton is praised for pragmatic prosperity in America and short-term peace in the world. Yet, on net, he contributed nothing to American prosperity or world peace. Instead, he, as did Keynes, undermined long-range prosperity and peace for everyone. He parasitically extracted values created by others — created by entrepreneurs, businesses, and the technology boom. He drained society for his own power agenda. ...Bill Clinton never produced long-range net values for society. Instead, he inflicted immeasurable long-range net losses and sufferings upon everyone by expanding (1) government criminalities, (2) bureaucratic damages, (3) short-range, foreign policies of appeasement with deadly long-range consequences, and (4) political corruptions throughout America and the world.

Should Clinton be impeached based on the Starr Report? No. Instead, he and/or some of his associates should be charged with objective crimes ranging from (1) theft via gun-backed redistributions of wealth to (2) murder for illicit power via Reno/Waco child killings that led to the ATF/OKC child killings.

Bill Clinton is no Marcus Aurelius. Yet, the history of Earth's anticivilization will reveal President Clinton as Neo-Tech's most valuable agent and loudest shill for vanishing lawyer-like dishonesties and parasitical-criminal politicians.

\*\*\*

In his October 1998 article *Private Lives*, Llewellyn H. Rockwell, Jr., president of the Ludwig von Mises Institute in Auburn, Alabama, states the following about President Clinton's August 17, 1998 speech:

"It might be possible to be more sympathetic to Bill's predicament. Let him repeal the sexual harassment laws in which he is now entangled. Let him strip the CIA, the IRS, the FBI, the AFT, and the NSA of their power to spy in our private lives.

"Let Bill light a bonfire on the White House lawn made of the federal code and a hundred years of the Federal Register. Let him grant to every American the broad rights to private life that he demands for himself. Until then, we are entitled to regard his speech as the plea of a tyrant caught in his own web."

President Clinton would do what Mr. Rockwell suggested if Clinton flipped his own mind from the mortal anticivilization mode to the immortal C-of-U mode.

October 12, 1998

# IV
# The Next Era
## After
# Cyberspace

# IV
# The Next Era after Cyberspace

# IV
# The Next Era after Cyberspace

QUANTUM-CROSSING #1 — BEYOND CYBERSPACE

## Synthesizing the Future

> The next era after cyberspace
> goes beyond human cloning even
> beyond non-aging biological
> immortality.

*Cassandra's Secret is Nature's Quintessential Secret*

While no one would believe her, Cassandra of Greek mythology predicted the future. But, could she or anyone really predict the future then or now? Yes, the future is accurately predicted by determining cause and effect with Neo-Tech/Neothink. How? By integrating wide-scope knowledge into an objective unity that synthesizes cause-and-effect futures.

### What is Neo-Tech/Neothink?

Neo-Tech, which means fully integrated honesty and wide-scope accounting, blends new technologies with new techniques. Those blends of technologies and techniques are achieved through wide-scope business integrations. Through metaphors, inductive Neo-Tech combined with deductive Neothink yields a unity that reveals the future. What is Neothink? It is a thinking process that uncovers never-before-identified Laws of the Universe — laws of nature and physics that link causes to effects with contextual certainty. Those natural laws, hidden until now, never contradict reality in yielding a predictable future. Neothinking integrates current *causes* with Universal laws of physics and nature to determine future *effects*.

Neothinking was discovered in the early 1980s. It anchors

209

the future to reality by homogenizing fully integrated honesty with wide-scope accounting. Applying Neothink to Neo-Tech knowledge uncovers the cause-and-effect certainties of nature. From those certainties arise the predictive power of Neo-Tech/Neothink.

## Neo-Tech/Neothink Synthesizes the Future

Inductive Neo-Tech and deductive Neothink synthesize future knowledge — limitless new knowledge generated from the laws of nature. Those laws are discoverable within the YES/NO philosophies of Ayn Rand and Immanuel Kant. YES, "certainty is possible", is the philosophy of Rand. NO, "certainty is impossible", is the philosophy of Kant. Do those two philosophies create a useful dialectic? Yes, when wide-scope accounting is applied. Do those two philosophies create a contradiction? No, not when "context" is considered: (1) *certainty* arises from identifying and adhering to context, (2) *uncertainty* arises from either expanding beyond or ignoring context. Predictability arises from blending that context with wide-scope accounting and fully integrated honesty through Neothinking. That formula synthesizes certain future *effects* from known controllable *causes*. ...Within the widest integrations throughout Earth's anticivilization, the philosophies of Rand and Kant interconnect as do all philosophies, knowledge, and entities — no matter how seemingly contradictory.

Consider the following example: Without homogenizing their philosophical systems with Neo-Tech/Neothink, neither Rand nor Kant could achieve contextual certainty. For, both ranged beyond their scope of knowledge in making erroneous proclamations outside contextual boundaries: Implying *false certainty* beyond her contextual knowledge, Rand publicly denigrated, out of ignorance, the supreme values created, for example, by Beethoven and Shakespeare. Analogously, implying *false uncertainty* from an opinionated range of ignorance, Kant promoted the bogus

210

morality of collectivist duty and self-sacrifice, which are deadly to individuals and societies alike.

## BC:  Before Cyberspace

Through dogma, followers of Rand and Kant lock themselves into a deadly dance of ignorances and dishonesties.  The self-inflicted harms of dishonesty lead to aging and death — the essences of an anticivilization.  Before Cyberspace (BC), Rand, Kant, and essentially everyone else invested in a *death-delivering* anticivilization.  After Cyberspace (AC), everyone will invest in the *life-delivering* Civilization of the Universe.

## AC:  After Cyberspace

In cyberspace, Neo-Tech uses wide-scope accounting to collapse the walls of dishonesty and irrationality to reveal the paths of certainty.  Those paths lead to ever widening avenues of knowledge.  Yet, with Neo-Tech, one always remains within an expanding contextual realm.  Such a process marches conscious beings toward Neothink — toward self-made futures of eternal prosperity.  During that march, a person's contextual knowledge combined with the Neo-Tech/Neothink dynamic predicts and then synthesizes that person's future. ...Neo-Tech is the AC future — a future of quantum crossings (jumps without transitions) into the Civilization of the Universe.

## Predicting the Future with Certainty

Since the early 1980s, Neo-Tech/Neothink has accurately predicted the future on personal, business, and global levels.  Those predictions occurred when Neo-Tech and Neothinking controlled absolute causes that lead to absolute ends according to the laws of nature.  In that way, ends ranging from personal to global are predicted, controlled, and then fulfilled.  Listed below are some such predictions covering the past, present, and future:

## Past

PERSONAL (early 1980s): Predicted and then brought forth the end of harmful, personal relationships with the rise of beneficial business, friendship, and romantic-love relationships for those implementing Neo-Tech through competitive value production. By contrast, those who fled that Neo-Tech dynamic sank in their anticivilization problems. They were left behind as complaining, disgruntled losers.

BUSINESS (early 1980s): Predicted and brought forth (1) the government attack on research-oriented I & O Publishing Company and (2) the subsequent phoenix-like rise of Neo-Tech bantam companies involved in global commerce and the coming demise of a criminally destructive IRS along with its irrational income taxes.

GLOBAL (mid 1980s): Predicted and brought forth the dynamics that collapsed communism in Eastern Europe (most specifically, Neo-Tech working in Romania to bring the sudden, legal, firing-squad executions of murderers Nicolae and Elena Ceausescu in 1989, vanishing their totalitarian regime)...and, through faxes, almost succeeded in toppling the Communist regime in China twelve years ahead of predictions — almost succeeded until the Bush/Baker/Deng/Peng Tiananmen Square massacre in 1989. ...The fall of tyranny in China, however, will come not through publications, faxes, or the media, but through Neo-Tech business dynamics in cyberspace as predicted a decade ago.

## Present

PERSONAL: With cyberspace vanishing the parasitical-elite class and their pips, competitive value producers will rise toward eternal health, romance, and prosperity.

BUSINESS: With cyberspace collapsing irrational political-agenda laws (ranging from anti-drug, anti-immigration, and anti-business laws to irrational income-tax, environmental, and health laws), the well-being and longevity for everyone will rise worldwide. ...Business will end poverty and disease.

GLOBAL: With cyberspace driving politicians and lawyers from parasitical value destructions into competitive value production, their force-backed political agendas will vanish. The health and wealth of conscious beings will then expand, without limits, toward the Civilization of the Universe. Then, no one will want to live in the loser anticivilization. ...Let the C of U begin.

### Future

PERSONAL: Through cyberspace/cybercash businesses, the value of individual human life will expand eternally.

BUSINESS: From the y2k breakdown, global bantam companies run by sovereign individuals will rise. Such companies will dominate education, commerce, and science through push-pull cyberspace technology. Those companies will envelop Earth with the Civilization of the Universe.

GLOBAL: Fulfilling its role in vanishing the anticivilization, cyberspace itself will eventually become obsolete. As the world populations quantum-cross into the Civilization of the Universe, individuals become a part of the conscious-controlled, "Gravity-Unit/Thinkon" computers that synthesize the future.

### Neo-Tech/Neothink Certainties

The certainties of Neo-Tech/Neothink are today being

demonstrated, established, and utilized. For example, two Neo-Tech hypothetical "certainties" identified in the early 1980s are now being physically demonstrated as reflected in points 1 and 2 below:

Point 1.    Throughout space-time, an essentially limitless abundance of conscious life at every level of knowledge flourishes throughout the Civilization of the Universe:

Hard, physical evidence supporting the certainty of Universal conscious life is emerging. Such evidence suggests that wide varieties of life evolve independently and easily, not only in different locations under widely diverse conditions on Earth, but throughout this solar system and beyond. Life rises as microbes called extremophiles from non-solar/non-oxygen/methane conditions in boiling-hot blackness miles deep in oceans. Conscious-life evolves independently at several different locations on planet Earth. Beyond Earth, a hidden lake of life-giving water (estimated at 250-2500 billion gallons) has been found on the moon. Life-generating conditions are detected on Mars and even on Jupiter's moons Io and Europa.

Also, ocular evidence of other planetary/moon systems is now appearing among Earth's nearest stars. Those mounting evidences imply an open-ended abundance of conscious life throughout the Universe as detailed in the Neo-Tech 1985 "Long-Wave" document. ...Mounting hard evidence is revealing how *easy*, *common*, and *natural* is the evolvement of abundant life, including conscious life, throughout the Universe.

Point 2.    With Neo-Tech vanishing the anticivilization, government-free entrepreneurs will deliver commercial

214

genetic engineering and human cloning during the lifetime of most people living today. Those accomplishments will bring low-cost, non-aging, biological immortality to conscious beings on planet Earth:

The clandestine, 1980s human cloning project and the *Research Institute for Biological Immortality* (RIBI) was destroyed by armed federal agents in 1986. The viability of that project is now demonstrated in Scotland with the genetic cloning of a mammal — Dolly, a female sheep. And more recently comes news of successfully cloned anthropoids — monkeys. ...Neo-Tech in cyberspace vanishes the "ethical questions" of cloning — false questions that professional value destroyers use to block genetic engineering and human cloning.

Such dishonest "ethical" questions and political-agenda restrictions are introduced by a parasitical-elite class that survives through the gun-backed control of competitive value producers. But, the parasite class cannot survive in a cyberspace/cybercash economy driven by Neo-Tech accounting and integrated honesty. ...Contrary to the demagoguery of the parasite class, entrepreneurial genetic engineering and human cloning will spearhead history's most moral, beneficent advance for conscious beings.

Neo-Tech/Neothink businesses in cyberspace will make available to the populace cheap genetic health/youth treatments and commercial human cloning. Conscious beings on planet Earth will then abandon today's anticivilization to join their cousins throughout the Universe, greeting them with the freedom cry:

*Free, Free at Last*
*Thank the Almighty Laws of Nature*
*We are Free at Last!*

# Beyond Human Cloning
and
## Biological Immortality

The following quoted news item was posted to Usenet on February 28, 1997:

### Cheap, Commercial Human Cloning

"In the mid 1980s, I & O Publishing Company, operating through the Golden Helmet, was accumulating cash assets to initiate aggressive, lone-wolf research on human cloning. That research would have been conducted offshore — beyond the reach of government political-agenda laws and FDA-type regulations — directed by a Swiss scientist. On November 3, 1986, sixteen armed federal agents with guns, fists, and kicking feet destroyed I & O Publishing Company and its Research Institute of Biological Immortality (RIBI). Those guns-and-fists agents beat, kicked, and hospitalized the editor of RIBI, destroyed I & O's manuscripts, and seized its records along with its hard-earned assets needed to initiate its clandestine human-cloning project. ...The founder of I & O Publishing and RIBI was sent incommunicado in chains to an isolated Federal prison camp atop a mountain in the California desert.

"Today, phoenix-like interests once again seek to initiate such offshore research. Commercial goals include genetic repair and physical rejuvenation as well as body transplants from rapidly matured, mechanically exercised, nonconscious clones cheaply grown in electrochemical/electromagnetic 'cultures'.

"The Zon Association will consider scientifically sound proposals for reversing aging and curing the disease of death. Political-agenda laws and bureaucratic regulations will be bypassed to reach the moral apex for human beings on Earth — eternal life, happiness, and prosperity. (*Objective laws*, however, will not be broken. Ends do not justify the means)

"For information on biological immortality, review web site www.neo-tech.com and enter 'biological immortality', 'cloning', 'physics', and 'I-ness' into its search engine.

"Interested scientists should email proposals to John Flint at: think999@ix.netcom.com"

# V
# Defense Techniques

that protect

**Competitive Value Producers**

in the

**Anticivilization**

# IV
# Defense Techniques

Document C

# V
# Defense Techniques
### that protect
### Competitive Value Producers
Jean-Claude Rueille as told by Justin Parkes

### *Defense Techniques in an Irrational Anticivilization*
Swiss business magnate, Jean-Claude Rueille, developed effective defense techniques for competitive value producers in the non-cyberspace anticivilization. First, he set up the following scenario:

[Below is quoted from a Neo-Tech Worldwide Travel Report by Justin Parkes]

### How to Handle Dishonest Journalists
### hustling for the gun-backed
### Parasitical-Elite Class

"I discovered that Jean-Claude Rueille (JCR) has had considerable experience in dealing with the media and dishonest journalists. Over the years he has appeared on many radio talk shows and TV shows such as the equivalent of '20/20', '60 Minutes', and 'Larry King Live'. In some of these cases, he was given a 24-hour notice that his products and promotions were going to be "exposed" on the show the next day and he could attend and defend if he wished.

"JCR really made his point to me on this subject with repetition. Over and over he explained how he would handle an attacking journalist or a group of journalists. He initially made his point by asking me if we were to leave the restaurant at this moment, and were confronted by a horde of journalists with lights and TV cameras outside the restaurant asking pointed questions

221

about Neo-Tech, what would I say? The point of that exercise is that when confronted with such a situation you tend to freeze up and are unable to think effectively on your feet. The moment you stumble in the slightest, appear uncertain, or unsure of your position, the vultures will close in. Point #1 therefore on handling the media, was not to wait until the media come to you, but be prepared whether or not you ever expect to be confronted by the media.

"An essential point JCR kept emphasizing is <u>the irrelevance of the questions journalists might be asking</u>. While using different terminology, he was emphasizing that while journalists are jumping around from A-point to A-point, you should only be focusing on THE-point. You must know what your THE-point is and have it thoroughly automated in your mind before you are ever confronted by a horde of journalists.

"Let's say for example your main THE-points are: 1) Responsibility to customers, 2) Responsibility to employees, 3) Responsibility to suppliers, and so on. Organize on paper these points and whatever sub-points there are within the main THE-points. And, if there are any sub-points within any further sub-point divisions also write those out. Then like memorizing for a test have those points absolutely committed in your mind so that they become reflex actions that can be recalled without thinking under the stress of an unexpected camera, a flood of lights, and a horde of journalists.

"The concept therefore is, if you are on Larry King for example, and Larry King was not to ask any questions, what would you say? Know this down pat, know how to communicate it convincingly, and in such a commanding manner that there is no inkling of hesitation or questioning of yourself. Now introduce the attacking journalist into the picture. He asks his question, whatever it may be. In your mind, you go down the list of say five major THE-points and immediately hook on to the one that is most closely relevant to the question. Then go into the mode of convincingly articulating this point. You continue for as long as the journalist doesn't stop you. If he doesn't stop you, you go onto the next point on your list, and then the next point, and so on until you are interrupted.

"<u>Regardless of what the journalist says, regardless — when he finishes talking you just hook right back onto one of your major THE-points</u>. You convincingly articulate the point and move onto the next point and the next point until you are again interrupted. Regardless of any question or any attack or angle a journalist might take with you, you essentially ignore anything that comes out of the journalist's mouth and always jump right back to one of your THE-points and continue articulating it for as long as you have to be heard. <u>You answer your questions to the audience, not to the journalist</u>. The approach has the effect of subverting any journalist's A-point attack. <u>You cannot answer any A-point attack</u>. This is JCR's point. But what you can do is leave the audience with a deeper impression of the good intentions and honesty of your company. As long as you look totally solid and unshakable in the face of TV cameras with lights and attacking journalists, the audience is subconsciously always going to know there is more to this story than what the journalist may be focusing on."

\* \* \*

*Tools for Prosperity*
*in a*
*Rational Cyberspace Civilization*

Competitive businesspeople like Jean-Claude Rueille use defense techniques in the anticivilization as protection against the deadly drainings by the parasitical-elite ruling class. Today, that ruling class survives through its armies of professional value destroyers, including its claquish "news" journalists and force-backed bureaucrats. ...The "defense" of Neo-Tech itself, however, is easy, natural, and involves no counterattacks or reconciliations as explained below:

## No Defenses Needed

In the anticivilization, Neo-Tech works through eliminating negatives rather than advancing positives. Neo-Tech renders impotent the hidden parasitisms, frauds, and destructions of politicians, bureaucrats, lawyers, clergymen, academics, and journalists. The essence of Neo-Tech subverts, undermines, and finally collapses negative elements throughout the anticivilization.

## A Message to Professional Value Destroyers
### from a
### Neo-Tech Businessman
(quoted below)

"On learning nature's Quintessential Secret via Neo-Tech in cyberspace, competitive value producers like Jean-Paul Rueille will no longer be damaged and drained by you or other gun-backed agents hidden by dishonest lawyers, mind-decaying professors, and claquish journalists. Until now, value producers struggled to protect themselves from your frauds, dishonesties, parasitisms, and destructions of the past 2300 years. Until now, honest value producers had no power to stop your expanding harms. But now, Neo-Tech will vanish your anticivilization along with its camouflaged destructiveness. How? By using your attacks to spread Neo-Tech businesses throughout cyberspace. Moreover, by nature, the dynamics of Neo-Tech, once launched, will not cease until the parasitical-elite class and its armies of professional value destroyers are gone and forgotten.

"You come to attack, drain, and suppress Neo-Tech. Yet, Neo-Tech is the good, the innocent, the protector of competitive value producers and human life itself. Neo-Tech is the giver of eternal life and happiness to individuals, societies, and civilizations. Neo-Tech Publishing Company literally saves thousands of human lives each year in Earth's anticivilization, while benefiting the lives of everyone it touches — millions of lives. Who are you? What *net* benefits have you delivered to humanity? You are the gun-backed, the guilty, the dishonest, the destroyer of values. You live by draining values created by others — you directly and indirectly kill innocent people for your livelihoods. Now, finally today, against the fully integrated honesty of Neo-Tech, your criminal world of 2300 years is ending. Your parasitical world is vanishing forever.

"Neo-Tech is the universal source of prosperity and happiness throughout the Universe. Integrated honesty needs no defenses, counterattacks, or reconciliations. Instead, it exposes your parasitisms and criminalities, no matter how deeply concealed. ...Through its business dynamics, the fully integrated honesty of Neo-Tech delivers priceless values to society and to every individual it touches.

"Want proof of the statements above? Look at yourself in the mirror of honesty. Then look around. Ocular proof abounds: You are professional value destroyers responsible for the continual harm to conscious beings. You feed off their contributions to civilization. Your antithesis is Neo-Tech. Businesspeople using Neo-Tech in cyberspace will vanish your anticivilization. ...Through cyberspace, Neo-Tech victoriously brings the Civilization of the Universe to human beings on planet Earth, including you."

Eric Flame
November 3, 1997

* * *

## Ostracism/Praise Matrixes

Business-run, ostracism/praise matrixes building in cyberspace will eventually vanish professional value destroyers. Concomitantly, through cyberspace, their victims of the past 2300 years will finally gain justice. And, their descendents will gain open-ended freedom and prosperity.

A forthcoming publication, *Flame-War Justice*, will present in print the Ostracism/Praise Matrix already building among Usenet posts and Web sites. That book will reveal how anyone can profitably tap an ostracism matrix for previously hidden, professional value destroyers as well as a praise matrix for previously unrecognized, honest value producers.

Finally, and most important, nature's Quintessential Secret will spread throughout cyberspace. The anticivilization will vanish as the Civilization of the Universe envelops planet Earth to bring eternal life, prosperity, and happiness to conscious beings.

# *Only Atheists*
## go to
# *Heaven*

### *The New Gods*

Those who promote God and Government to survive by fraud or force will *perish forever* from the terminal diseases of mysticism and dishonesty. Those who produce competitive values will *thrive forever* via honest businesses throughout the fifth dimension of cyberspace.

# Dialogue #1
### (The First of 100 Dialogues)

## Saint Augustine and Atheist Ann
### take a romantic stroll toward the
## Civilization of the Universe

Today, Saint Augustine would be as much of an atheist as philosopher/novelist Ayn Rand. Fifteen-hundred years ago, Randian cultists would have been as religious as Roman-Catholic cultists. How can that be? The answer comes easily once one realizes that everyone on planet Earth lives within an upside-down civilization — an anticivilization. In such a civilization, each person survives by investing in hidden dishonesties, irrationalities, mysticisms, and criminalities. ...These Dialogues provide the roadmap for leading the reader out of the mortal anticivilization and into the immortal Civilization of the Universe — into the eternally prosperous fifth dimension of cyberspace businesses.

## Act 1 of 3

St. Aug.: A millennium and a half I've been wandering. Finally, I've reached a place of benevolence. This must be Heaven.

Ann: Heaven! You mystical fool. Benevolence? Why, you're the second most malevolent person who ever lived on Earth. You wrote in your *Confessions*, "We're all born between feces and urine". What a malevolent view of man. Even worse, your epistemology and metaphysics violate the nature of man! Christ, how evil can a person get?

St. Aug.: I'm the second most malevolent person who ever lived? Who was the most?

Ann: Immanuel Kant, of course. You wouldn't know him. He lived a thousand years after you.

St. Aug.: If we aren't in Heaven talking to each other when you died 1500 years after me, then where are we, Ann?

Ann: How'd you know my name? And, don't call me Ann. Only my friends may call me Ann. You aren't my friend and we sure as hell aren't in Heaven. That's a fraudulent myth.

St. Aug.: How would you like me to address you?

Ann: Mr. Augustine, I prefer that you not address me at all. You have nothing to offer. You and your neoplatonistic writings led the entire Western civilization into a thousand-year dark age. You're a mass murderer.

St. Aug.: Have you read my works?

Ann: Scanned some of 'em. Don't need to read that garbage.

St. Aug.: Then we need not talk. We need only to think.

Ann: Okay, call me Miss Brand. And, where are we anyway? What am I doing walking along with my philosophical antipode? ...Yet, I've never imagined a place so wonderful. I feel better and freer than I ever did on Earth, even with you beside me. I'm no anarchist, but this is the air of freedom. I feel no government here. I feel everything here is run by a profitable business — like Disneyland. ...Happy feeling, isn't it?

St. Aug.: The air is special. Yes, I feel good and happy. Love the feeling of no oppression or religion.

Ann: Feeling no oppression or religion? Why, you're the icon of oppressive religion.

St. Aug.: When we get to know each other, you'll find your views of me misguided. ...Anyway, I believe we're going to have a beautiful romantic relationship.

Ann: Romantic relationship? What nerve! How dare you. Should slap your face. You can bet we're not even going to get to know each other. ...But, you're not like I pictured. You're kind of good-looking. Squared jawed. Kind of virile and intelligent. A little swarthy maybe. And, you sure aren't shy. If only you were blond and blue eyed. Anyway, call me Ann. ...Where are we?

St. Aug.: We're in Heaven, Ann. It's the only fact that can

explain these circumstances.

Ann: Fact?  Heaven is no fact.  It's just a part of your manipulation mechanism to dupe your followers — your victims.

St. Aug.: You don't understand my writings or their context.  I had no knowledge of science, technology, and the nature of reality that you had.  My work was of the fifth century. ...Did you read my final work, *The City of God*?  It's mostly metaphors from which Aquinas built his work.

Ann: Didn't need to read *The City of God*.  Don't need to read or understand your writings.  They're false, unreal, mystical.  They're the antithesis of everything I wrote.  And, don't blaspheme Aquinas by connecting him with your writings.  He's the only Roman-Catholic icon I admire.  Even named my cat after him. ...By the way, don't suppose you read any of my writings?

St. Aug.: Read all your books during my wanderings.  Don't know how, but an entity know as amazon.com supplied any book I wanted.  Your writings were among the most valuable works on planet Earth.  Learned a lot from you, especially about epistemology, politics, and ethics. ...I know most of recorded history and its literature.  You displayed one of the most powerfully honest minds to grace Earth.  I'm grateful to you.

Ann: Really?  You, Saint Augustine, are saying that?  Don't know whether to cheer or jeer. ...Want to smoke a cigarette with me?

St. Aug.: Smoke a cigarette?  You, the hero of twentieth century rationality?  Everything I've read about cigarettes bespeaks the mortal harm they inflict.  You'll die a horrible death.  You're too precious for that.  Just say no to smoking.

Ann: You're right.  My husband and I both know how smoking

230

kills. I'll quit. No more rationalizations about a pleasurable dot of light moving through the darkness. I lost everything because of my dishonesty, my denial...my irrationality about smoking. Took a lot of copycat cult followers down with me. I'll quit now, forever. ...You seem rational and honest, how could you have written such malevolent crap — such evil stuff? How could you have been so wicked?

St. Aug.: You need to cut the carbs, drop a few pounds, and get physically fit. Try working toward running a marathon.

Ann: I'll work on it, smart ass. Don't evade my question. How could you have written such evil stuff?

St. Aug.: I lived and wrote when civilization was retreating into the dark ages.

Ann: So what? Time doesn't make any difference. Mysticism is mysticism, evil is evil, no matter when and where.

St. Aug.: I agree. But, without context, one can mistake what is mystical and evil.

Ann: Humph! Doubt if I'd make that kind of a mistake. Anyway, what are we doing here? All this seems like a mystical illusion. Still, I like it. And, amazingly, don't mind talking to you. Don't feel negative or depressed like I did on Earth. Imagine, my enjoying talking to the silver-medal monster, Saint Augustine.

St. Aug.: And the gold-medal monster is Kant?

Ann: Right. He was pure evil. Worse than Hitler or Stalin.

St. Aug.: You must be analogizing my hero Plato with his souls of gold and the Greek Olympics. ...Who was the bronze-medal

231

monster?

Ann: Your hero, Plato.

St. Aug.: Plato a monster? Let's keep walking and thinking. Perhaps we'll learn to improve our questions and answers, especially about Plato.

Ann: Improved answers about Plato? Never. And keep your distance, you wolf.

St. Aug.: How much have you read Plato's work? His *Dialogues* must be read more than once to understand his work.

Ann: Humph! Just scanned *The Republic*. That's enough. He was a worse commie than a communist. ..."Each man shall have a thousand commune sons"...indeed. Good old middle-class-champion Aristotle nailed him good on that gem. ...The only thing I liked about Plato was that he hated poetry.

St. Aug.: He recognized poetry as a powerful teaching tool that could mislead youth. Plato opposed the heroic-warrior poetry of Homer. To present murderous, irrational brutes like Achilles and Odysseus as heroes to be emulated was lousy stuff to teach kids. Yet, Plato himself was one of history's greatest poets. He poetically presented Socrates as the new hero — an intellectual, moral, and educational hero — like you Ann. ...Plato's *Dialogues* are volumes of beautiful poetry, especially his *Phaedrus* about romantic love.

Ann: Quit winking at me! Besides, his *Dialogues* stunk.

St. Aug.: Stunk? Just stunk? Is that your only evaluation of Plato's work? If your writings weren't among the most valuable in Earth's history, I'd say you're pipping one of history's great men?  Can you give more than a one-word evaluation of Plato's *Dialogues*?

Ann: Bah!  His *Dialogues* stunk because Plato stunk.  That's a good enough answer.

St. Aug.: Look ahead!  I see someone.  A strange-dressed man sitting at a table with something weird — a box of light — something I've never seen before.

Ann: He's wearing a pinstriped suit and using a computer. Hooray!  He looks like a Wall-Street businessman.

St. Aug.: A businessman I understand to be a trader of values? But a computer?

Ann: Living fifteen centuries ago, you'd have no idea of a computer, even if you read my books.

St. Aug.: I read about computers, but don't understand them. What are they?

Ann: They're huge machines — ultimate business machines.

St. Aug.: That doesn't look like a huge machine.

Ann: It's something called a desktop computer.  They were starting to appear when I left Earth in 1982.  They're called Apples, I think.  Don't know why.  I'm no expert on computers.  Best to ask that man to explain.

St. Aug.: Let's ask him.

Ann: Sir, my name is Ann Brand and this is Mr. Augustine.

Zon: Been expecting you both.  Want to hire you as a marketing team.  Both did valuable work in Earth's anticivilization.   I can exploit your talents in my cyberspace businesses.

Ann: Expecting us?  Hire us?  Augustine did valuable work?  And what do you mean, Earth's anticivilization?  Who are you?  Where the heck are we?

Zon: I'm a Zon.  You're approaching the Civilization of the Universe.

St. Aug.: That's the same as Heaven, right?   And, Zon means God?

Ann: Ignore Augustine.  He's a jerk.

St. Aug.: You don't look like the suffering abandoned Messiah described by Apostle Mark.

Ann: God, what a schmuck.

Zon: God, Heaven, and Messiahs don't exist.  Zons exist.  We can feel pain and sadness.  But, we don't suffer.  Only a Zon trapped in an anticivilization is abandoned and suffers — until he vanishes that anticivilization.

Ann: What's a Zon?  And, again, what's an anticivilization?

Zon: A Zon is a person who lives from the perspective of the Civilization of the Universe.  Earth has been an anticivilization since the Greek politician Pericles infected the citizens of Athens with the mortal diseases of irrationality and dishonesty. ...When you jump past your anticivilization perspective, you too will become a Zon doing business beyond the anticivilization — doing business in the limitless cyberspace markets throughout the

Universe.

Ann: Business? That's a good start. ...Still, how does an anticivilization differ from the Civilization of the Universe?

Zon: An anticivilization rests on a foundation of irrationality and dishonesty. Yet, islands of rationality and honesty generate the values and wealth that sustain, even advance, the anticivilization. But, its citizens continue to be drained and defrauded to death. By contrast, in the Civilization of the Universe, people live as sovereigns and prosper forever through fully integrated honesty, wide-scope accounting, and competitive businesses throughout cyberspace. ...You're now in an area approaching the Civilization of the Universe.

Ann: Sounds like your telling me we came from Hell and now we're in Purgatory. Next you'll tell me we're going to become non-corporeal souls floating forever in Heaven.

Zon: Bodiless souls, just as mystical utopias, don't exist. The body is an indispensable part of life, existence...and happiness — the ultimate purpose of conscious life. Achievements, emotions, sex, and love can't exist without the body. The body physically moves and controls existence through time and space. Neothink people, just as conscious people, must exist as body-and-soul individuals who physically conduct business. Their competitive achievements require physical movements. They learn to cure the diseases of dishonesty and mysticism in order to harness the laws of nature. After that, they learn through unfettered business techniques to eradicate disease, aging, then death. Each such individual is then on his or her own — a sovereign — eternally relying on his or her own thinking, decisions, physical actions, and profit-making businesses.

Ann: How is death eradicated?

Zon: Through self-responsibility and competition — through free markets that harness science and technology to deliver the greatest possible values at the most efficient speed and lowest costs. On Earth, for example, the first great products would be aging retardants, disease cures, and dishonesty eliminators — products that lead to the eradication of aging and disease. ...Freewheeling businesses focusing on genetic manipulation, head/brain/body transfer, human cloning, and I-ness capture are among the first steps.

Ann: I can understand that. Business and economies free of government would quickly solve every problem that's solvable, profitable, and beneficial to human beings.

St. Aug.: Sounds like the steps to Heaven.

Zon: Perhaps in a metaphorical sense. But, not from the mystical perspective of Earth's anticivilization.

Ann: Makes sense. But me being here doesn't make sense. I want some proof of all this. I want evidence of the senses.

Zon: What evidence are your senses delivering right now? What are you doing here alive, body and soul, walking along with Saint Augustine?

St. Aug.: Touché! He nailed you. Right, Ann? Aren't you experiencing Aristotle's delight of the senses?

Ann: Quit asking questions. I don't believe any of this. I'm the founder of Objectivism. I accept only provable, objective reality. Moreover, I'm an atheist.

St. Aug.: Me too. I'm an atheist — been so ever since I was a teenager.

236

Ann: Then you're a hypocritical preacher ripping off your followers. ...And, quit holding my hand, Mr. Augustine!

St. Aug.: You took hold of my hand, Ann. ...You can call me Augie.

Ann: Shut up! I want to hear what Zon has to say about the Civilization of the Universe.

Zon: In the Civilization of the Universe, everyone lives the way each was meant to live — according to one's nature. Each lives to fill his or her needs — needs that flourish the human organism. As Aristotle identified, people flourish by living according to their nature — according to natural law as first identified by Sophocles in his play *Antigone*. Natural law was advanced by the Greek Stoics, even by the Epicureans, and evolved by Seneca then Marcus Aurelius from Cicero's Roman Law...and finally evolved from Justinian, to Locke, to Neo-Tech's depoliticized laws of justice and nature. ...Through value-producing businesses and objective laws, everyone lives happily by creating limitless prosperity for self and others.

Ann: Neo-Tech depoliticized laws? Do they bring about an Objectivist society like Balt's Gulch? If so, then, this is my place and Aristotle must be here. I want to see him as proof.

St. Aug.: And, Plato too? I want to see him.

Zon: I can introduce you to Aristotle, even Parmenides, Hippocrates, and Archimedes, if you wish. But, Plato? Don't recall that name. Don't think he exists in the Civilization of the Universe. ...Is Plato a man or a woman?

St. Aug.: Sweet Jesus, he doesn't even know Plato's name.

Ann: Plato's not here? This place is getting better every minute.

Yes, I belong here. I bet that mawkish tree-hugging killer, Rousseau, isn't here either — or his heirs like Robespierre, Hitler, and Pol Pot.

Zon: You're right. They're not here.

Ann: Then that killer gang is dead forever?

Zon: Death is unknown in the Civilization of the Universe. An anticivilization is the only place where conscious life vanishes. Death of conscious people is obscenely irrational.

Ann: Right. Death is a bummer.

Zon: I'll try to locate Rousseau and his heirs through my list broker. He has email addresses of vanished Earthlings. Sounds like they'd be good prospects for buying my products for quantum-jump redemptions.

Ann: Addresses for dead people! Selling products to dead people! Doing business with the worst sort of unredeemable scumbags imaginable? How mystical and depraved can you get? Suddenly, I'm losing confidence in this place and you. ...What's your name?

Zon: My name is Zon.

Ann: Zon! Just Zon. You told me you were a Zon; now your saying your name is Zon. Damn, that sounds mystical. You might be a dashing businessman, but, I'm starting not to like you or this place. ...Why are you smiling?

Zon: What you're now experiencing must seem mystical from your 1982 anticivilization perspective. With more experience here, you'll gain answers to your questions. ...You'll find this place normal and natural. By contrast, you'll realize Earth's anticivilization was bizarre and unnatural.

Ann: You must answer one question for me to continue. What about that bloody gang you're going to put on your redemption mailing list? How can mass murderers be redeemed? I could never accept such injustice.

Zon: Here we stand uncompromisingly on principle — on justice. Means take care of the ends. ...But, mass murder? Don't recall that concept.

Ann: How do you know so much and so little at the same time? ...And, how do you redeem the unredeemable heirs of Rouseau?

Zon: It's all in cyberspace. In this realm, you'll discover how the unredeemable must finally answer to justice — answer to the laws of nature. Even murderous humanoids like Pol Pot who die peacefully in their sleep must ultimately meet justice. ...In this realm, entrepreneurs track only what's valuable to them, their loved ones, and their businesses. They forget the rest, especially the evils and unrealities of an anticivilization. That way, no harmful person can consume their time or drain their lives. That's the nature of cyberspace dynamics.

Ann: Cyberspace dynamics? Sounds great, but unreal. And, why is Saint Augustine standing here, right here beside me, patting my rear? If I were a criminal-minded feminist, I'd set him up to sue his ass off. ...I want to understand those cyberspace dynamics.

Zon: Many new understandings come from cyberspace. For example, you'll learn that Saint Augustine was the most forward-moving, freethinking intellectual during his time in history. Roger Bacon laid the groundwork for scientific inquiry and method while using Augustine's writings as his foundation. Augustine's writings were original and courageous. His writings counterbalanced the coming dark ages and eventually led to the development of the Renaissance. Taking the lead from Augustine, Aquinas revived both natural law and Aristotle along with the no-connection separation of the physical world from the spiritual realm.

Ann: Tell me more about Augie.

Zon: As a teenager, Augustine dumped his strict Catholic upbringing and its dogma. He recognized religion as mystical and harmful. He recognized that man must discover the creator of the universe through constantly evolving inquiry into reality. He easily defeated the arguments of Catholic priests and bishops throughout his realm of North Africa and Italy. Augustine keenly observed and experienced the mortal destructiveness of Earth's anticivilization — first as a Manichaean, then as a Heretic. Without your modern knowledge of reality and physics, he was vainly seeking the Civilization of the Universe.

Ann: Please continue.

Zon: Finally, when his closest friend died, Augustine as a secret atheist focused on the Catholic hierarchy. He then exploited that Roman-Catholic neocheating machine. Through white-hat neocheating, he became its most influential bishop. For, he had discovered that no ranking Catholic official from a bishop, to a cardinal, to a pope could compete for high positions by remaining weak and ignorant in clinging to faith or mysticism. To become a leader of any large religious or mystical organization, one had to become a secret nonbeliever — an atheist — not only to manipulate the believers but to compete for positions of power. One had to reject faith and mysticism to effectively manipulate the frauds of faith and mysticism. Just like Earth's politicians: They rise in power through automatic lies and black-hat neocheating, while secretly scorning those doctrines and laws that they harangue others to believe and obey.

Ann: What's a neocheater? What's white-hat and black-hat neocheating?

Zon: You'll discover that later.

St. Aug.: You're giving away our deepest secrets. It's about time. Yes, my Catholic peers and I were all nonbelievers — objective atheists.

Ann: Catholics as objective atheists? What a contradiction. Yet, I sense something behind what you're saying. Still, contradictions can't exist in reality.

Zon: You're right, contradictions don't exist in reality. In Earth's nonreality anticivilization, however, deceptive contradictions abound within truths taken out of context. Deceptions and contradictions vanish within a civilization based on objective reality. ...The key distinction ain't believers verses nonbelievers but value producers versus value destroyers.

St. Aug.: Ain't? Not knowing if Plato is a man or a woman? Are you playing a cosmic poker game?

Ann: Don't let Augie bother you. He's a professional value destroyer, right?

Zon: No. In context, Augustine was a major, net-value producer.

Ann: Humph.

St. Aug.: Can we now replace the metaphor "Heaven" for the factual "Civilization of the Universe"?

Ann: I'll never buy into such crap.

St. Aug.: Why is it crap? We're talking about metaphors.

Ann: I won't discuss it.

St. Aug.: Why won't you discuss it?

Ann: I won't answer those questions.

St. Aug.: Why not?

Ann: Look! Isn't that Denis Diderot approaching? I read his great French Encyclopedia in college. ...Is Voltaire here too?

Diderot: Voltaire and Descartes both work with me — so do Locke and Newton. My contemporary Rousseau never made it. He vanished in the anticivilization.

Ann: Descartes works with you? He's an evil skeptic who rejected the power of our senses to identify reality. ...He's no good — almost as bad as Rousseau.

Diderot: No good? An evil skeptic? Descartes is no more evil than Aristotle was evil. He's no more of a skeptic than Socrates was a sophist. Within his 17th-century scope of knowledge, Descartes used skepticism to demonstrate the power of our minds to identify reality. He used skepticism to undermine the skeptics; just as Socrates used sophistry to undermine the sophists. Descartes played a crucial role in breaking the Scholastics' dogmatic oppression of Aristotle. He also advanced Euclid by developing analytical geometry — a vast value to any civilization. Later, Locke used more advanced knowledge to evolve and replace Descartes philosophy with liberty under law, not oppression under men. Finally, you, Ann Brand, developed an even more advanced paradigm that evolved and replaced Locke's paradigm.

Ann: You know about me and my writings?

Diderot: Of course. Who doesn't? Got your books through amazon.com

Ann: Then you realize Descartes was bogus. He was a Rationalist with his "Cogito, ergo sum" nonsense. You know, "I think therefore I am". So, if you think not, you vanish, right?

St. Aug.: How did you make such valuable contributions to philosophy while being so ignorant of philosophers from Plato to Wittenstein?

Ann: Quiet, Augie! I want to hear Diderot explain why Descartes wouldn't vanish if he "thought not". ...And, who the hell is Wittenstein?

Diderot: I don't know about Wittenstein. But, Descartes was a great Rationalist as Locke was a great Empiricist. You needed both their lines of knowledge mixed with Thomas Reid's and William James's common sense philosophies to look toward Objectivism. The later philosophies of Auguste Comte, John Stuart Mill, and Herbert Spencer pointed toward the individualism, freedom, and liberty needed to evolve the Industrial Revolution. Those philosophies, especially that of Mill, opened the door to Objectivism. How? By stripping philosophy of mystical metaphysics and rationalized "intuitions" that suppress new ideas.

Ann: Next, I suppose you'll be telling me that Thomas Hobbes was a good guy for writing *Leviathan*.

Diderot: Despite his absolutist and totalitarian views, he was the first to put society and government formally on an objective rather than a mystical basis. Hobbes identified that government was the congeries of individuals. He established that the first and primary function of government was to protect the life and property of its citizens. If government did not perform such functions, Hobbes believed it should be overthrown. Without that Hobbesian start, there would be no classical liberalism or Objectivism. Even the bogus thoughts of Berkeley and Hume were necessary to reach Objectivism.

Ann: Well, perhaps I misjudged Descartes, Hobbes, and Hume. On Earth, I never admitted errors to my cult followers. ...Anyway, where's your candle for Augustine to blow out?

St. Aug.: Candle to blow out?

Ann: I remember Diderot telling of a man using a candle to find his way through the darkness. He meets a theist. The theist advises him to blow out the candle in order to find his way through the darkness. ..."Put out the light to find your way on faith alone," the theist insisted. Get it? Like you, found your way on faith alone, right, Augie?

St. Aug.: Wrong. Pay attention. Both Zon and I already told you that I became an atheist and rejected faith in my teens. Without being an atheist, I'd be too weak and ignorant to become a Catholic bishop.

Ann: Hypocrite.

St. Aug.: My writings were metaphorical in trying to direct the collapsing Roman, pre-medieval world toward objective reality. Consider some of my views: The First Commandment, for example, has nothing to do with worshiping one God. It's a metaphor about recognizing that one reality and only one reality exists. *The Good* is everything in reality. *The Evil* is nothing.

244

Evil is turning away from reality — turning toward the nothingness of mysticism and dishonesty. Faith? Hey, you got to believe that the guy — the Zon — who created this Universe has more advance knowledge of physics and nature than we do. Right? And, original sin? It's merely conscious man's capacity to be irrational. If you live through irrationality, of course, your life is going to be damned. Also, Christian universal brotherhood has nothing to do with egalitarianism. It's about moral equality — about morality being determined by individual character development, not by race, nationality, or the class one is born into. I was replacing elitist, class-status ideas with individualistic, self-earned values. ...My goal was to shift religion away from amorphous, outer-world notions — and toward humanistic, self-responsible notions. Aquinas combined my work with Aristotle's to bring the world out of the dark ages through natural law.

Ann: Finally, some sense from a Catholic icon. Augie's not promoting some Thomas More communist *Utopia*. That's **no place**. Anyway, bet Bill Buckley is a closet atheist too. Despite his protestations about God and Catholicism, he's too smart for such beliefs. He'd never blow out the candle, either. Too bad he's not as honest as you, Augie. He's just another elitist who manipulates others through religion and Plato's noble lies.

Diderot: Buckley hasn't yet come to the Civilization of the Universe. When he does, his dishonesties will vanish like everyone else's. Then, I'll hire him to edit my publications. He has a good vocabulary and wit. ...Got to go now. I'm meeting with Leona Helmsley about producing a modern business encyclopedia. She's a hard-nosed, value-producing businesswoman from New York.

Ann: I admire Mrs. Helmsley. Give my regards to that business genius.

St. Aug.: How, Ann, can I get a clearer understanding of what business means — in the way you're talking about?

Ann: I'm gaining some sympathy for you, Augie. Living 1500 years ago, you could never have known about the supreme morality of business. You could not know that business is the ultimate value for mankind. I'm realizing that you had no idea of the Renaissance, the Enlightenment, the Industrial Revolution, America, automobiles, McDonald fries — yum, or IBM. Without those experiences, how could you understand competitive business? Diderot will learn a lot about business from Leona Helmsley. You should join their discussions. I recall her building a real-estate empire in New York City. She's a real businessman.

St. Aug.: She's a businessman?

Ann: Right. No feminist political correctness in me. ...Augie, I'm going to give you my book about the morality of business. It's titled, *Capitalism, the Morality Tool*. It explains the benevolent virtue of business and rational selfishness in trading values. It also shows how ending the hoax of altruism is the key to universal prosperity and happiness.

St. Aug.: Altruism a hoax? Ending altruism? Universal prosperity and happiness through trading values and rational selfishness? Great concepts! I read about those ideas in your books. With my primitive knowledge, those were the ideas I was reaching for in my writings. ...You're talking about the route to Heaven.

Ann: Don't link anything of mine with Heaven.

St. Aug.: Socrates taught me to always expand my thinking in order to obsolete my current thinking. I realized how little I knew in context of future knowledge. Now I'm gaining new knowledge — like I'm learning from you. ...Socrates wanted everyone to challenge his ideas and show him new ideas. That way, he and everyone could move past old ideas into futures of never ending new knowledge and prosperity.

Ann: Guess I could've learned something from Socrates after all. Never knew what he was getting at. Plato screwed him up. I'll look at your work again based on what Zon said about you. ...Zon, what's your real name? Your full name?

Zon: My anticivilization name was Jay Gould. Still use it in my email address.

Ann: Jay Gould! The railroad tycoon of the 19th century?

Zon: I reorganized and expanded America's transcontinental railroad system into profitable enterprises instead of political instruments for financial fraud.

Ann: I admire you, Mr. Gould. You and railroad-builder J. J. Hill. I especially admired how you alone bucked the altruistic crap of your day. I admire how you criticized the business-genius Rockefeller for yielding to the compassion hoaxers. I admire how you identified that the most successful and talented business people were dissipating their capital by giving it to government and charity under political and religious pressures. You alone identified how everyone and society, especially the poor, could receive limitless benefits if those business geniuses reinvested their money back into their own competitive value-producing enterprises — like you always did. ...You never yielded your benevolence, rationality, and principles to the envy and dishonesty of parasites — politicians, preachers, pseudo-intellectuals.

Zon: Intentional destruction of capital happens only in an anticivilization.

Ann: I'm beginning to see your concept of an anticivilization. It's a state of insanity with its citizens trapped in deadly denials of reality. Yes, the propagators of an anticivilization must undermine the businessman to survive by looting his achievements. They use altruism to paint him as evil and greedy. That's how they labeled you as the worst and greediest of the Robber Barons. But, damn, you and the Robber Barons were the real benefactors to society. Still, an anticivilization must attack people like you so its parasitical rulers can thrive like weeds by usurping your wealth creations. Anyway, you're a real-life hero. You're greater than any hero I produced in my novels — even greater than John Balt. Well, maybe, Hank Beardon, my favorite hero, was like you. But, you were real life, not fiction. ...If I'd known you back then, Mr. Gould, I'd have fallen on my knees and begged you to let me be your housekeeper who'd take care of your every need. To hell with the feminists. You could've raped me without ever hearing a complaint. ...Are you married?

Zon: I appreciate the compliments from a woman I greatly admire. ...Yes, I was happily married on Earth. And, I'm still married to the same romantic woman, happier and more in love than ever.

Ann: Figures. The great ones are always taken. Anyway, how'd you handle such relentless attacks from government, religion, the press, and the academics? How'd you act so calmly, so benevolently, for so long in the face of such dishonesties? I could never handle evil attacks like you did with such aplomb. How'd you do it?

Zon: I was having too much fun converting decaying capital into profitable enterprises. I was too excited converting lead into gold of almost everything I managed. I never yielded to criticisms and attacks. Instead, I learned how to turn nearly every attack into expanding profits. It was great fun outflanking the parasites.

Ann: They don't make 'em like you these days.

St. Aug.: Plato told at the start of his *Republic* how the most virtuous of men always get the worst, most unjust treatment from society.

Zon: I hear from the Internet that one of the greatest businessmen on Earth today sold out to altruism in destroying huge chunks of his capital — worse than Rockefeller did. His name, I think, is Ted Turner. As Pascal discovered, only in an anticivilization can such genius and stupidity exist simultaneously. On a more honest path, a person named Bill Gates is outflanking dishonest attacks of envy and parasitism against his world-supreme enterprise. I even have his operating system in my computer. Don't know how he penetrated this outer-Earth market, but he did. Busted the competition here. What an aggressive business genius. He could become the catalyst to vanishing Earth's anticivilization. ...He mustn't yield to envious parasites. Instead, he's got to make profits from their irrationalities and criminalities.

Ann: I love you, Jay Gould! Please walk with me through your domain. The ambience is free, fresh, and clean. I feel an excitement I haven't felt since falling in love with Bate Randon while writing my magnum opus, *Real Men Never Shrug.* ...I want to learn from you, Zon, my dear Mr. Gould. Arrangements can be made for your wife.

St. Aug.: Arrangements? Like what?

Ann: Like fix her up with you, Augie.

Zon: Miss Brand, I know you're a man worshiper, but please rise from your knees.

Ann: I'll always fall on my knees before men like you. ...Mr.

Gould, please explain what's happening.

Zon: Can't explain now. Must tend to something urgent — something strange. My Universal Computer picked up the audio words of "Leona Helmsley" from Diderot. My monitor keeps signaling that she remains bound in the anticivilization. She's neither here nor in the Civilization of the Universe. So, how can Diderot be meeting with her? Strange, indeed. The defense-warning signals are flashing.

Ann: Universal Computer? Show me what you're doing.

Zon: You'll find out soon enough. You're part of my business plans.

Ann: How's that?

Zon: Being from Earth's anticivilization, you've heard of television infomercials and direct-mail marketing often maligned as junk mailing?

Ann: I have. But, don't worry, I admire aggressive business methods.

St. Aug.: I'm lost.

Zon: You'll understand soon enough. You're going to be my top salespeople behind my marketing blitz.

St. Aug.: Marketing blitz?

Zon: My products deliver never ending wealth, power, and romantic sex. Who could resist buying with passionate testimonials from both of you — the Libidinous Bishop and the Capitalist Atheist?

St. Aug.: Romantic sex!  Haven't experienced that since I was a teenager.  How much?  I'll buy! ...Think I'd have a chance with you, Ann?

Ann: How dare you!  Jeez, and you're a Roman-Catholic bishop. ...I'm married you know.

St. Aug.: Arrangements can be made.

Ann: Been there, done that.  My affair with a young hero was open, honest, and valuable.  Got lots of heat about that relationship from a bunch of know-nothing, accomplish-nothing pipsqueaks. They never knew what a great value that relationship was to both of us.  He was my hero.  He developed the business methods that got Objectivism rolling.  All went sour when I got mystical. Created problems where none existed. ...But, never again.  I made mistakes.  I hurt my husband.  Then I discovered that I loved my husband more than anyone else.

St. Aug.: Think about polyandry.  I approve of that.

Ann: What insolent nerve!  I'd never think about that unless my husband approved.

St. Aug.: Did you know Hugh Hefner?  He blew away religious-stamped sexual guilt from planet Earth.

Ann: He did some heroic things, so did Larry Flynt.  But, they knew nothing about value-based romantic love.

St. Aug.: Haw!  I remember reading about Mr. Flynt.  Great parodies he did on religious hypocrites.  Loved the one on my latter-day colleague, Reverend Jerry Falwell, having sex with his mom in an outhouse.

251

Ann: I liked Guccione's parodies better, especially Jesus on the cross getting fellatio. ...Damn, let's get off this sordid subject.

St. Aug.: Right, let's continue our journey. I want to learn about that supreme value you call business.

Ann: Please be our guide through this wonderful realm, Zon. I'll pay for your time.

Zon: These cyberspace warnings are something serious.

Ann: Serious? Like what?

Zon: The Universal Computer last gave these warnings over two-millennia ago when an orator named Pericles using lawyer-like dishonesties was discovered approaching this realm. He tried to infiltrate the Civilization of the Universe. His entourage included someone I'd forgotten about 'til now. His name was Plato; the same person you asked about earlier. They were disguised as universal silk merchants on a trade mission. Instead, they were neocheaters from Earth wanting to usurp unearned wealth and power by spreading the diseases of dishonesty and mysticism through the false compassion of altruism. Using noble lies, that gang was going to subvert children with deceptively good-sounding educations about philosopher kings and force-backed statism. ...A Zon named Archangel discovered their scheme and bounced them back to Earth's anticivilization.

Ann: Damn that Archangel. Sending those guys back sank Earth's future. Ended up killing everyone who ever lived there, including my husband and me. ...Wait a minute. What am I talking about? Life after death? Am I turning into some kind of hallucinating mystic? What am I doing here talking to you, like I'm alive? What's happening, Zon? Is Objectivism bogus?

Zon: Have confidence in your Objectivism. Nothing mystical is happening. The metaphysics and epistemology expressed in your books stand fast — just as the laws of nature stand fast throughout the Universe.

Ann: I want to know how what's happening is compatible with my writings. As Aristotle said, "All men by nature have a desire to know".

Zon: I'll first have to build a matrix of new contexts around everything you've written. You'll be shocked but thrilled. The advance from your philosophy to the current knowledge here in the anteroom of the C of U will be as great as the advance from Kant's philosophy to your Objectivism there on Earth.

Ann: Impossible. Kant and Objectivism can't be linked. Consider this comparison: Anti-hero Kant was a short, wizened, shrunken-jawed, dark, bent little man. Objectivist-hero, John Balt, was a tall, robust, squared-jawed, blond, blue-eyed, erect muscular man. How can you link those two?

St. Aug.: Your ad-hominem habit of linking character and value of a man to his inborn physical characteristics is as unjust as racism. Such bigotry is not only stupid, but it contradicts Objectivism and works against gaining new knowledge.

Ann: Your right, Augie. My Homeric habit is stupid, ugly, and unjust. I'm going to uproot that habit from my thinking and writing.

St. Aug.: Seems impossible to be dishonest in this realm.

Ann: Right, it's great for correcting self-deceptions and destructive errors. ...Still, Zon, I want to know how Kant and Objectivism are linked.

Zon: As I said, you'll be shocked and thrilled. You'll realize Kant's erroneous philosophical model was like Ptolemy's erroneous astronomical model that nevertheless served as an invaluable tool in advancing navigation and marine commerce for many centuries. Thus, you'll realize how Kant's model advanced abstract thought. But, today, his model is no longer useful. ...Aristotle and you, however, are like Galileo and Newton. You'll always be contextually valuable — similar to Pythagoras's eternal conception of the triangle...until Georg Riemann advanced that concept by expanding geometry to curved space.

Ann: Interesting. Go on.

Zon: Today, in this place, development of knowledge is like the radically unexpected Einstein relativity/quantum model in Earth's early 20th century. Our model, like Einstein's model, is subject to replacement with new knowledge and discoveries. ...The basic tools developed by Newton and you are here to stay, like the Pythagorean theorem. But, the works of future Einsteins and Zons will always evolve.

Ann: Don't quite follow. Moreover, I still don't understand how that links Kant to Objectivism?

Zon: You'll understand when you reach the promontory overlooking the Civilization of the Universe.

Ann: Promontory or not, how can you put the evilest man in history in any context with Aristotle and Newton?

Zon: Who's evil? Ptolemy, Kant, or Einstein?

Ann: Kant, of course. I won't move from my position on Kant 'til I have factual reasons to modify my view.

Zon: Focus on the facts and reality. Kant was a paragon of morality like yourself.

Ann: How dare you say that.

Zon: The problem with calling people evil rests in the methods of judging evil. Valid judgments of morality can't come from deductive scenarios extrapolated from one's own time and knowledge. That's what's being done to Kant. Moral judgments can be made only inductively — from objective acts in full context. Such clean, straight-line judgments are obscured in an anticivilization. On Earth, direct killers like Caligula, Genghis Kahn, Robespierre, and Jack the Ripper are obviously evil. But, an anticivilization hides the evil of indirect killers like Pericles, Rousseau, and Lincoln.

St, Aug.: I'll agree about Pericles. Don't know about Lincoln. But, as bad as he might appear today, don't witch-hunt Rousseau like Ann did with Plato and Kant. Don't make him or anyone responsible for casting evil spells on others for centuries into the future.

Zon: You're right. And, remember, Rousseau said, "Man is born free and everywhere he's in chains." Now, extend his metaphor to this time and place and he is saying, "Man in the Civilization of the Universe is free, and everywhere in Earth's anticivilization he's in chains". Ironically, an anticivilization is required to understand freedom, rationality, and honesty. For, man who has never experienced chains, dishonesty, and irrationality can't grasp his own freedom, honesty, and rationality.

St. Aug.: Is man on Earth doomed?

Zon: No. As with Goethe's *Faust*, the citizens of Earth's civilization long ago sold their souls to a Mephistopheles named

Pericles to enter his *unreal* world — the anticivilization. Still, conscious beings on Earth possess the attributes to become immortal sovereigns. They can gain limitless wealth and romantic happiness in the C of U. Thus, today, through the saving Angels of fully integrated honesty and wide-scope accounting, Earthlings can regain their bodies and souls to reenter the *real* world — the Civilization of the Universe — even a person like Rousseau.

Ann: Despite what you said, that sobbing Rousseau was evil in his own time and place. Call it witch hunting. Still, his direct descendant was mass-murderer Pol Pot. ...Now, explain your judgment that posits Kant as moral.

Zon: You present non sequiturs. But, before explaining about Kant, I must resolve this problem flashing on my monitor. I just emailed Helen of Vegas who arrived from Earth on March 23, 1998. She'll be more helpful than I. She has fresh memories from Earth. You'll need her comparative perspectives to glimpse C-of-U perspectives. ...She's arriving now.

St. Aug.: She anything like Helen of Troy? I'll lay Gorgias's Encomium on her.

Ann: Cool it, Augie. Don't think you're Paris who'll carry Helen away. ...Who's Gorgias anyway?

St. Aug.: He was the most renowned of the Greek sophists. But, Socrates easily overcame him. ...The great Socrates overcame all dishonesties.

Ann: Socrates wasn't that great.

St. Aug.: Not that great? Greatness is the recognition that virtue *is* enough. Only Socrates had the courageous virtue to live and die on his principles. He was the only consistently honest philosopher. ...Socrates chose death by execution to avoid contradicting his philosophy.

Ann: Look, a beautiful woman! She's appearing out of pixels! She's wearing a tight dress spun from platinum threads. Who's that appearing with her? How'd they get here? This is too much. I'm hallucinating. ...Are you Helen of Vegas? Who's that person with you? I must be going insane

Helen: You can trust your senses, Miss Brand. Nothing here is mystical. Everything can be explained within the laws of nature and physics. ...I'm Helen. Meet my friend Blaise Pascal. Socrates will join us later.

Ann: You're Pascal! Explain this outrage. Socrates I can take, although Plato smeared despotism all over him. But, what's that religious fanatic Pascal doing here? And, where the hell is Aristotle? I suppose next you'll be laying Jesus on me.

St. Aug.: He'd be an attractive stud to lay on you. Jesus was a beautiful guy...and horny.

Ann: Shut up! I don't want to hear anymore from your Larry-Flynt gutter mind. ...I demand explanations from Miss Vegas.

Helen: You'll understand in time. But, first, don't put unilateral demands on me or anyone else here. No one here owes you explanations. You're here as a guest 'til you earn your own way.

Ann: You're right. I apologize. I'm sounding like my cult followers. Blab out demands without considering my own principles of trading values. ...Shall I call you Miss Vegas?

Helen: Call me Helen. I'm a wide-scope business accountant.

Ann: I like you, Helen. You sound like a straightforward businessman.

Helen: Both of you, come, walk with Blaise and me. Zon's busy now. We'll head toward the quantum-jump promontory — a point from which Socrates can help jump your perspectives from Earth's anticivilization into the Civilization of the Universe. ...Like Blaise did centuries ago.

Ann: You mean his night of fire?

Pascal: That's when my mind switched from the incomprehensible to the comprehensible.

Ann: Comprehensible? How can such blatant mysticism be comprehensible? Comprehensible to what? To a radical leap of faith? No wonder Nietzsche hated Christianity. "Look what it did to Pascal," he raged with disgust.

Pascal: On reaching that quantum-jump promontory, you'll see a wider context. You'll see an opposite picture than what you now see. My work has nothing to do with advocating faith. My work has everything to do with identifying the anticivilization. My work shows that to accept and invest in something so irrational and dishonest as Earth's anticivilization, one must accept and use its equally irrational and dishonest tools.

Helen: Didn't that pious Calvinist, Pierre Bayle, imply something like that? Using the incomprehensible evils and irrationalities in the Bible, he points to the plunderer, rapist, and murderer King David as one of God's chosen loved ones. From that, Bayle shows that irrationality, dishonesty, and injustice, underpins Earth's anticivilization.

Pascal: In that regard, Pierre Bayle and I are soulmates. By the way, Pierre is now a scholar who studies Ann Brand's writings.

Ann: A Calvinist priest studying my writings? I need my night of fire to switch my mind from the incomprehensible to the comprehensible. Next thing you'll be telling me is that Plato was a good guy — a white-hat philosopher. ...Maybe something like a white-hat neocheater that Zon mentioned.

Helen: He was more than that. Plato was a brilliant manipulator of words who developed the first integrated, comprehensive philosophy on planet Earth. With his wide-ranging work, he captured most intellectuals of his day...and he still does to this day on Earth. His work was incalculably valuable in developing human thought. And, arguably, he wrote the most enduring, beautiful poetry ever created on Earth.

Ann: What about his totalitarian preachings?

Helen: Indeed, he forged the use of dishonesties, force-backed political-agenda laws, and malevolent mysticism as prime instruments for totalitarian power. Yet, by poetically using Socrates in his *Dialogues*, he delivered incomparable values. He showed man not *what* to think, but *how* to think for learning new knowledge — for achieving intellectual self-development. Because of Plato, an Aristotle could rise. And, then, mankind could advance within an anticivilization. More important, because Plato laid the philosophical foundation for the anticivilization, he also sewed the seeds for its own destruction by identifying in his *Dialogues* the hidden dishonesties behind sophistry and rhetoric. Sophistic rhetoric is the tool for neocheating — a tool for destructive political agendas, arbitrary laws, and lawyer-like dishonesties upon which the parasitical leaders of an anticivilization survive. ...Plato scorned the Sophists, although he used sophistic rhetoric himself. For, he, like everyone else, was heavily invested in the anticivilization.

St. Aug.: I'll still vouch for Plato. He and Socrates were my guiding lights.

Ann: That's my point. Plato twisted Socrates to his own ends to become for centuries the hell hole of destructive mysticisms, religions, governments, and philosophies.

Helen: How much Plato did you read?

Ann: Scanned *The Republic*.

Helen: Yes, Plato projected malevolent political views in his *Republic*. Yes, he was an elitist. He even advocated political-agenda murder to secure the parasitical-elite class. But, one needs to study Plato's later dialogues to understand what he was trying to accomplish. One then discovers that Plato worked toward becoming an honest philosopher — perhaps more honest than you, Ann.

Ann: How can you say that? Plato was a dogmatic totalitarian who manipulated a phony world of forms. Just read his *Republic*.

St. Aug.: Read past his *Republic*. You'll discover he was anything but dogmatic. He always challenged his own theories and moved forward in knowledge. In his later works, starting with his *Parmenides*, he directly questioned and methodically began undermining his entire theory of forms. That conscious undermining of his life's work took great honesty and courage. Moreover, he prepared the epistemological and metaphysical groundwork for the silver-medal philosopher, Aristotle.

Helen: Like Socrates and Plato, we must constantly reexamine our paradigms against evolving new knowledge. Those who don't reexamine their ideas can't change with advancing knowledge. They stagnate — like Aristotelian cult followers did, like Miss

Brand's cult followers are doing today.

St. Aug.: What about those cult followers, Ann?

Ann: Humph!

St. Aug.: Quit humphing so much. Instead, think about what's being asked.

Ann: You're right, Augie. I'll quit humphing and think instead. Got to have the discipline to distinguish between acting like a paranoid egotist and being an honest egoist. No more humphing. No more behaving like my cult followers. As you said, it's impossible to bluff in this realm. ...By the way, Augie, who's history's gold-medal philosopher hero?

St. Aug.: You, Ann. That's a big reason why I'm sexually attracted to you and your legs.

Ann: Thanks for the gold medal. But, the gold belongs to Aristotle. ...And, don't expect me to ever wrap my legs around you!

St. Aug.: We'll see. ...We're in a teleia-philia relationship. We can never escape that fact.

Ann: What the hell is a teleia-philia relationship?

St. Aug.: How carefully did you read your hero Aristotle?

Ann: Read some books about him.

St. Aug.: Read first hand his works on friendship and love.

Helen: I think Ann and Aristotle tie as gold medal heroes. And, Ann is not entirely wrong about Plato — at least about those who misused his philosophy. Manipulators of Plato's philosophy pressed a "crown of thorns on the brow of mankind" — a metaphorical fact of reality, not just an Objectivist perspective. Moreover, Plato was a backward-looking reactionary, at least up to his writing *The Republic*. By contrast, Aristotle was a forward-looking innovator. Then his cult followers wrongfully dogmatized his works. Yet, labeling Plato as evil is inaccurate, especially when viewed from his latter works.

Ann: Humph. ...Errr, I mean continue, please.

Helen: In his later life, Plato realized that aging and death of every conscious person who built a lifetime of knowledge and values was no way to run the Universe. Plato then realized that he and everyone on Earth lived in an irrational, mortal anticivilization. Thus, he realized that his entire theory of forms was a paradigm sinking under the weight of "save-the-appearances" rationalizations. Approaching the end of his life, Plato knew he was at a dead end and his entire paradigm needed replacing. But, he had nothing to replace it with. So, he kept trying to patch it up while purposely tearing it down. At the end of his life, while never discovering the Civilization of the Universe, he heroically began pointing in that direction — toward Aristotle's direction, and eventually toward your direction, Ann. ...Today, when you juxtapose the facts of an anticivilization against ideas of the Civilization of the Universe, you'll see everything from radically different perspectives. You'll begin seeing those new-color perspectives as you approach the Civilization of the Universe.

Ann: You and Augie made important identifications about Plato's honesty. Wish my protégé, Dr. Piecrust, could hear your words. He commercially pulled my most important works together while producing many valuable and profitable products. He's an unrecognized hero who's constantly pipped by do-nothing intellectuals. Sure, he made mistakes, especially his police-state views. But, he's an honest guy. He's honest, forthright, and innocent like Spinoza. He was more honest than I. And, I made more mistakes — like irrationally putting down others, especially Dr. Randon and the libertarians who competitively advanced Objectivism onto the world stage. Moreover, I handled some emotional problems badly. And, my irrationalities cost me and others our health as well as a lot of earned romantic happiness. ...I appreciate your little speeches.

Helen: Well, as Socrates taught, speeches aren't the best way to teach new knowledge — Balt's speech not withstanding. ...Yet, from your new C-of-U perspectives, you'll delight in Shakespeare "speeches" that implode the anticivilization.

Ann: Doubt it. Never did like Shakespeare's tragic sense of life. Likewise, I despise the nasty works of Eugene O'Neil, Tennessee Williams, and Arthur Miller.

Helen: What do you know about the plays of O'Neil, Williams, and Miller?

Ann: Nothing, except they were socialist downers. I only liked Sophocles. And, Aristophanes was a hoot the way he put down the in-the-clouds Socrates.

St. Aug.: With flippant talk like that is, I guess, the reason we're in Purgatory instead of Heaven.

Helen: Those malevolent-view American writers highlighted the nothingness of Earth's anticivilization. An important ingredient in grasping the anticivilization. In that way, they were the converse of heroic-view Aeschylus, Sophocles, and Euripides.

St. Aug.: Are you and Zon metaphors for some kind of divine figures or omniscient gods?

263

Helen: Divine? Omniscient? We're just as much in the dark about understanding perspectives from the next level of advanced knowledge as you and Ann are about understanding the perspectives from our elementary-level, C-of-U knowledge. On this C-of-U entry level, I need to help Zon adjust his thinking about Plato. He holds erroneous perceptions from reading Ann's narrow-scope criticisms of Plato. That's why Zon forgot about Plato. In most other areas, however, Zon advances my thinking to ever wider perspectives. We advance in knowledge, first through our own independent efforts, and then through trading our newly developed knowledge. Have patience on your journey toward fully integrated honesty. The proofs and profits are coming. Then, as every conscious person can eventually do, you'll quantum jump into the Civilization of the Universe. At that moment, the illusionary anticivilization vanishes.

Ann: I'll hang around to witness that, even with Augie and Mr. Pascal in my presence. ...I'd say that traveling from Earth toward the C of U is like running *The Grapes of Wrath* backward.

Helen: Maybe it's more like Absalom celebrating the demise of King David.

Ann: Absalom?

Helen: I'm getting a cyberspace message from Zon.

Ann: What's he say?

Helen: He's discovered the interloper disguised as Leona Helmsley is Martin Luther King, Jr.! He's got a gaggle of politicians, lawyers, professors, talking heads, and movie celebrities ready to invade our realm. They're being advised by Thrasymachus from Plato's days, Niccolò Machiavelli, and a soulmate Earthling who personifies cynical compassion hoaxes. Guess that'd be Bill

Clinton. ...I'm going to recommend that they be confronted with a premier Objectivist philosopher — Malcolm X — who was recently trained by Socrates in the methods of educating corrupt minds.

Ann: My God!  Malcolm X a premier Objectivist philosopher! I'm going to have a stroke. ...And, who's Bill Clinton?

Helen: Bill Clinton is the 42nd President of the United States. He's a kamikaze agent working to vanish Earth's anticivilization.

— to be continued —

# Dialogue #2

Malcolm X and Socrates
bankrupt the
Great Cosmic Poker Game

Tending the gates to the Civilization of the Universe, light-bearer Jay Gould Zon is a commercial protector of conscious life. He discovers an interloping entourage of professional neocheaters: parasitical elites from Earth's past history.

Those interlopers have disguised philosophy, politics, education, and religion in the forms of Jean Jacques Rousseau, Abraham Lincoln, John Dewey, and Martin Luther King, Jr. Zon sends Malcolm X and Socrates to intercept the interlopers who are aboard a stealth flagship named *Sluos Daed rof Sedah* — a ship upon which the dishonesties of the living and dead meet. Those aboard seem to be united by souls so corrupt, so dead that they cannot recognize much less empathize with honesty and virtue. But are they all corrupt and dead? Are there counteragents aboard planning to profit from that boatload of ghostly neocheaters? ...The giant ship is captained by a peg-legged man named Ahab seeking revenge against the great white neocheater whom he believes is hiding in the Civilization of the Universe (C of U).

The ship will sail under the camouflage of tollbooth compassion built upon sophistic rhetoric. Malcolm X and Socrates locate the ship. They quickly talk their way past the eunuch guarding its gangway. Once aboard, they find the ship filled with lawyers, preachers, politicians, professors, and sophists lounging around, all talking at once. Malcolm X and Socrates joined by Plato seek out the crew's most persuasive leader, the champion sophist —

Protagoras. ...Socrates challenges the sophist maxim, "Man is the measure of all things". Socrates then convinces Protagoras to organize a huge poker game so the entire crew can win easy money for spending in the Civilization of the Universe.

Divine-poet Dante and loin-clothed Gandhi bring the game to an unexpected end. Through Plato, Zon reaps business profits by winning the potential value producers in that poker game. Zon wins them not as Morrison's dead *Beloved* slaves, but as Wallace's living *Neo-Tech* entrepreneurs. Plato sends the rest — the irredeemable criminals — back to Earth, into their domain of forgotten graves, dark dishonesties, and hidden criminalities.

In Dialogue #3, Helen of Vegas discovers that commercial profits can be generated from anyone — even from irredeemable losers. She, therefore, buys the rights to their labors with a cache of "illegal" whale oil discovered in the bowels of Captain Ahab's ship. With those losers, she creates a super-growth civilization on Earth.

## Act 2 of 3

Zon: Look at this cyberspace data. Is it really a black man who's posing as the capitalist, Leona Helmsley?

Malcolm X: Yes, it's Martin Luther King all right. That rascal.

Zon: Do you know him?

Malcolm X: Yeah, sure do. Love the guy. He had guts. Did good in confronting Earth's bigots. But, alas, he was an ol' neocheater — a bluffer par excellence. Still, got to tilt my hat to him. He and Gandhi taught me the impotence of hatred and force. They taught me the power of nonforce when combined with emotional rhetoric. But, ol' Martin sought to end racism so he could bilk whites as well as blacks. Gave stirring Dream speeches — like William Jennings Bryan's Cross-of-Gold/Crown-of-Thorns speeches. Everyone cheers, throws their hats into the air, and gives praise without knowing what he said. ...Hitler mastered that technique.

Zon: King's a neocheater?

Malcolm X: Of course! Martin was out to bilk the working classes, blacks and whites alike, for his own power and glory. He worked to enslave 'em with criminal socialism and fraudulent religion. He never learned to be a competitive value producer. That's why he never made it to the C of U.

Zon: He's trying to get in now?

Malcolm X: Yep. That's why he's here disguised as Leona Helmsley. Clever of Martin. But, he miscalculated. Didn't realize she's still living on Earth. That's why her husband, Harry Helmsley, and born-again entrepreneur, Socrates, are with me as advisers. Harry will confront King. Then marketing savant, Socrates, can teach ol' Martin about the morality of business and profits — the morality of being a competitive value producer rather than a parasitical neocheater.

Helen: I think your view that Dr. King is a neocheater needs adjusting.

Mr. Helmsley: Right. The Reverend King was the renowned civil rights leader who won the Nobel Peace Prize in 1964. ...Still, you say he's disguised as my wife? He's now white-faced and in drag? That's hard to swallow. Besides, I always thought the Nobel Peace Prize was a fraud. A socialist peace prize is not what capitalist Alfred Nobel intended when he funded his prizes in 1896.

Malcolm X: Sure, the Nobel Peace Prize is a fraud. And, look how King, that black-hat bluffer, is trying to infiltrate this business realm. He even cheated to get his Mickey-Mouse doctorate degree. Anyway, I can outflank his ploys with white-hat tactics that'll vanish his socialist criminalities and religious frauds. Then we'll educate him into becoming a value-producing entrepreneur. King's too talented to stay dead as a neocheater. Besides, we need him to profit from certified bad-guys like Rousseau, Lincoln, and Keynes.

Mr. Helmsley: What do you know about Keynes?

Malcolm X: I know his bogus socialist/fascist economics did more to hold down blacks and drain the working classes than anything else in history.

Mr. Helmsley: Didn't Keynes care about crashing the future and harming billions of people?

Malcolm X: No. In fact, he relished in that thought. Keynes and his elitist Bloomsbury group never cared about the destruction and suffering his corrupt economics would ultimately inflict on the world populations. Consider his evil response when confronted with the fact that his pragmatisms would in the long run impoverish and enslave the working class: "So what", Keynes would laugh. "We're all dead in the long run". The same attitude was displayed by Martin.

Helen: Slow down, Malcolm. Let's bring some fairness into your accusations. Dr. King was nothing like that elitist Keynes. If you study King's later years, you'll see that he backed away from his socialist ideas. Increasingly he was focusing on individual rights. King was moving beyond his book *Stride Toward Freedom*. He was moving away from bogus "spirit freedom" promoted in the totalitarian, mystical sense of Rousseau. King was moving toward free-enterprise liberty promoted in the natural-law, objective sense of John Locke, John Stuart Mill, and Milton Friedman.

Mr. Helmsley: Then he was killed.

Helen: Yes, he was killed at only 39 while abandoning the manipulative biblical "Truth shall set you free" ploys of Rousseau, Hegel, and Marx.  King was reaching for the inviolable laws of nature, physics, and the Universe.  He was evolving like you, Malcolm, when you too were killed at only 39. ...Both King and you were moving toward Objectivism in your final days on Earth.

Ann: King moving toward Objectivism?  I doubt it.

Malcolm X: What about his fake bus-boycott and dream-speech ploys?

Helen: They weren't fake or ploys.  I lived in Montgomery, Alabama when he accomplished his spectacular victory in that bus boycott.  That's when King began changing from seeking unearned power through religious frauds and socialist criminalities to genuine power though nonforce moral suasion and the natural rights of individuals.  His new idea was to undermine anticivilization injustice through civil disobedience while eschewing force in every action. ...Dr. King actually deserved the Peace Prize.

St. Aug.: Eschewing?  What's that mean?

Malcolm X: It means shunning or avoiding.  Where'd you get educated?  In Uganda?

Ann: Cut the ad-hominem insults X.  My friend Augie is a lot smarter than you.

Helen: King realized force was the essence of Earth's anticivilization. One could undermine the crimes and injustices of the anticivilization by rejecting its political-agenda laws backed by force. King's new tool was to direct neither anger nor hatred toward anyone, but to direct anger and hatred toward the anticivilization and its bogus political-agenda laws. ...In the anticivilization, everyone, including its villains, are its victims.

Malcolm X: What about his Dream speech?

Helen: His Dream speech is not only void of anger and hatred, but is filled with a dozen references to freedom and liberty. Those references point not toward socialism, which requires force, but point toward individual freedom, which requires liberty upheld by justice and natural law. ...King was rejecting injustice and political-agenda laws that corrupt everyone on Earth.

Mr. Helmsley: What was his view of justice and law at the end of his life?

Helen: As I said, King was moving from a socialistic political-agenda to the natural-law view — to the Civilization-of-the-Universe view of law by extending St. Augustine's proclamation that "an unjust law is no law at all".

Ann: Bravo, Augie! I didn't know you thought that way. ...I'm getting warmer toward you.

St. Aug.: We'll keep getting warmer to each other till our hearts become aflame. And, I'll never leave you 'cause of your age. ...We're soul mates forever.

Ann: Yeah, sure. Like some Objectivist heretic said that I'm a soul mate of that commie Sartre. ...Besides, I no longer blame Randon for leaving me because of my age.

Malcolm X: You know, I see that soul connection between you and Sartre.

Ann: Shut up! A soul connection with Augie is bad enough. ...Anyway, let Helen continue. I'm learning something.

Helen: Dr. King extended Aquinas's view that "an unjust law is that which is not rooted in eternal natural law". King stated, "any law that upholds the human personality is just and should be practiced". He also stated that "any law that degrades the human personality is unjust and should be rejected".

Malcolm X: I agree. Good thinking by my man, Martin.

Ann: Sloppy thinking, if you ask me. Such thinking leads to totalitarianism.

Helen: Regardless, Dr. King grew past Gandhi's naive ideas of *swaraj* freedom. King was moving away from that trap of false, socialistic freedom. He was moving toward sophisticated ideas of *capitalist* freedom. ...King was scrapping Eastern mysticism for objective reality.

Ann: King scrapping mysticism. Great!

Helen: Still, King never reached Malcolm's level of identifying that business entrepreneurs were the keys to freeing blacks and everyone else.

Malcolm X: You're right about me. And, maybe I've been off in my views about Martin. Maybe I was jealous of his blow-away Dream speech. I'll have to study that speech and his later years more carefully. ...Thanks for the facts and context about my friend Martin.

Ann: We learn and change by seeking new facts in ever wider contexts. ...My cult followers need to learn that idea, just as I'm now learning.

St. Aug.: You know, Ann, we'll be setting up a competitive business to teach them.  Should be a hot market, especially with you endorsing our infomercials.

Ann: Still can't see sleeping with a Moor.

Malcolm X: Knock off the racism.  Besides, Augustine is no Othello.  He's dark, but a honky just like you. ...Anyway, for now, what do we do about Martin whose heading this way dressed in drag as Leona Helmsley?  Call me Big Red, but look at this computer simulation.  King's not only white-face, but he's dressed in spike heels and a mini skirt.  Barf, he looks more like J. Edgar Hoover in drag than Leona.

Zon: My search-engine report says both you and King were assassinated in the anticivilization.

Malcolm X: That's right. Martin was killed by government spooks. They wanted to increase their bureaucratic powers by escalating racial violence.  They infiltrated the KKK and planted stories about King having sex with white wives.  Those rednecks were inflamed into killing King.  Government agents then duped some sucker into taking the rap alone. ...Sounds paranoid, but that's the fact.

Helen: Well, radio-talk-show fact, maybe.  More precisely, government-dependent parasites were threatened by King's radical change toward individual liberty in the final months of his life. His change was like Malcolm's change in his final months that threatened the Black-Muslim parasites.

Ann: What was King's threat?

Helen: He could have become the mirror image of Elvis Presley. Elvis took the country by storm by being a white person with the moves of a black person. They saw Dr. King taking the country by storm as a charismatic black person with the ideas of white libertarians like Locke, Mill, and Brand.

Ann: Don't link my name with libertarians!

Helen: Ann, try to overcome that irrational hostility toward your natural allies.

Ann: You're right. It's a dishonest habit. Look what I taught my followers. The closer the competition, the greater the dishonest hostilities they exuded. ...What a bunch of losers they made themselves with my help.

Helen: Getting back on point: King could have become a wildly popular president. He could have swept away the coercive elements of government that violated natural law and individual rights. ...Of course, the parasitical-elite ruling class had to eliminate King.

Mr. Helmsley: Did Louis Farrakhan order your assassination, Malcolm?

Malcolm X: Don't know. My daughter thought so. But, it was definitely a hit by the Islam Nationalists. They gunned me down after I discovered the power of individual value producers over racism, dogma, and hypocritical hoaxers like Elijah Mohammad.

Mr. Helmsley: You were promoting individualism?

Malcolm X: Yes, individualism and honesty, not collectivism and dishonesty. I found individual freedom through integrated honesty in the last year of my life. I discovered the Truth that Plato promoted in his Ideal Forms was fake. That Truth with a capital T was a tool of manipulation used by con-artists from Pericles to the Bible authors, to Popes, to Lenin, to Elijah Mohammad. I dumped the entire Truth dogma and began pursuing objective reality as a never ending journey on the highway of honesty. I learned that life must be lived as an individual through integrated honesty. Such a journey brings eternal prosperity and happiness.

St. Aug.: What happened on your journey?

Malcolm X: . My fast-changing life turned 180 degrees. I was no *Invisible Man* like Ellison wrote about. I was an individual — an individual brother who rejected collectivist brotherhoods. I began exposing the Nation of Islam hoax and liberating those oppressed by Black-Islam's criminal elites. They had to snuff me. Secular Jesus was snuffed when he made the same discovery. He was crucified when he began liberating the automaton minds of the populace. He pointed them toward the free will of conscious minds. ...Today, honest-carpenter Jesus would be building skyscrapers. He'd also be liberating the working classes by busting both fraud-backed religious hoaxes and force-backed government hoaxes.

Mr. Helmsley: Don't forget, the democratic mob made Socrates drink hemlock because of his lack of piety and political correctness.

St. Aug.: Remember, the democratic mob voted for Jesus' death because of his lack of piety and Jewish correctness.

Socrates: Look what the Catholic mob did to Bruno for his lack of piety and Catholic correctness.

Malcolm X: The democratic mob elected Hitler for his "moral" strictness — for his blame-the-Jews, get-something-for-nothing

276

harangues.

Helen: And, President Clinton for his "moral" blame-others, get-something-for-nothing sweet talks. ...Yet, don't blame Clinton. He's a decoy working in a lovely *Leaves of Grass* disguise. He's a valuable, illusion-breaking agent. ...Justice will come as citizens abandon their respect for political leaders.

Zon: This report says Plato and Lincoln will be cruising with King.

Malcolm X: I can outfox those guys. Lincoln, the liberator of slaves? Ha! That power-seeking lawyer wanted to keep the blacks and the laboring class from being liberated by America's rising free enterprise. Lincoln was out to enslave everyone through gun-backed force with his totalitarian time bombs. And, he's succeeding. On planet Earth today, Lincoln time bombs are exploding in everyone's face. ...Just look at the gun-backed IRS instituted by Lincoln. Look at his slave state of government dependents — mostly blacks.

Socrates: I don't know about Lincoln or King, but don't be so cocky about outfoxing Plato. He had no match on Earth. ...Anyway, don't worry about Plato. He's with us.

Zon: What do you mean, he's with us?

Socrates: He's from the C of U.

Zon: I'd forgotten about Plato. That's why I never looked for him in the Civilization of the Universe. Now, my memory is back, thanks to Helen of Vegas. Must admit that I never read Plato. My knowledge and opinions of him were secondhand — gleaned mostly from Ann Brand's works. I didn't think on my own. Because of her ad-hominem criticisms, I automatically dismissed Plato and then forgot him. I erroneously assumed he vanished as an irretrievable neocheater. I assumed he was never able to create honest values through business. So, I forgot about him. ...Guess Miss Brand, like me, had no wide-scope knowledge of Plato's work and accomplishments.

Ann, You're right. My knowledge was cherry-picked to fit my biased anticivilization agenda...and to drive my cult followers into worshiping me and my ideas exclusively. Damn, I not only closed their minds, but I closed my own mind. ...Augie showed me that I was miles off about Plato.

Socrates: I'll tell you a secret. I'm in a business partnership with Plato. We sell learning tools in competition with Zon. Next year we're going to rollout an IPO stock offer that'll raise capital to expand our markets into this Purgatory realm. Such a clueless realm should be a red-hot educational market.

Mr. Helmsley: I agree. It'll be a great market. ...Phone my CFO, Jim Fisk, on Monday morning. I'll subscribe to 20% of your offer.

Zon: What's King still doing in the anticivilization?

Malcolm X: Probably he's cultivating its value-destroying losers. That's his specialty. Maybe he's crafting white-hat business moves to cash in on Earth's neocheaters.

Zon: If Plato's in the C of U, what's he doing cruising with Dr. King?

Socrates: Plato's in a higher C-of-U realm of knowledge. He's beating us to a new market by turning back the neocheaters' assault on young minds. Plato's developing a business plan to expand his market reach. ...I'm emailing him now so we can coordinate business plans.

Malcolm X: In my realm on Earth, Plato was considered as nothing more than a dead, white male not worth reading. Maybe now I can learn something about business from him.

Socrates: You will. And he'll learn about Objectivism from you.

Ann: Plato learning Objectivism from Malcolm X...oh, no.

Socrates: Wait...Plato's responding to my email. Listen to this....

Malcolm X: I'm listening. Out with it, Socy!

Socrates: He found the great ship from Hades. It's packed with lawyers, politicians, bureaucrats, religious leaders, dictators, and university professors. Plato was stopped at the gangway by a eunuch guarding the entrance with a long curved sword. The eunuch accused Plato of being a gay politician from Rome. When Plato told him he was head of the Academy in Athens, Greece, the eunuch insisted he answer Aeschylus's riddle. You know, from the Sphinx in *Oedipus Rex*, "What walks on four legs in the morning, two at noon, and three in the evening?" Plato gave him the correct answer — "man". But, the guard rejected that answer and is threatening Plato with his sword. ...We've got to help him now.

Zon: What answer is that guard looking for?

Malcolm X: He's looking for a dirty-joke answer about eunuch power that uses missing genitals as metaphors.

Socrates: How do you know that?

Malcolm X: Street smarts, my sheltered man. ...Zon, send me, Harry, and Socrates to help Plato. We'll get him past that guard.

Zon: I'll put you into the pixelating program right now.

* * *

Socrates: Plato, my bisexual son!

Plato: Socrates, my dear mentor! I knew you were the one to get me out of this problem. ...Who's that handsome gentleman with you...and that black-African slave?

Malcolm X: Black-African slave! Damn, where's this guy been? And, where does he think I got my red hair? Maybe they were right telling me Plato's nothing more than a dead white Greek from whom you can learn nothing. No wonder he wrote *The Republic* — his manual on "How to be a Slave-Master Totalitarian". His society of parasitical-elites rulers wielding lawyer-like dishonesties needed slaves to survive. ...I ought to punch Plato's beautiful Greek face to a pulp.

Socrates: Cool it, X. Remember your lessons from King. Put Plato's question in historical context before shooting you're mouth off in a trouble-making reaction. During his time, the majority in Athens were slaves. ...Exercise a little DTC.

Malcolm X: DTC?

Socrates: Discipline, Thought, and then Control.

Malcolm X: You're right. I was out of control. I reacted like an anticiv loser. Still, such an ignorant statement from this noble-lying, philosopher king pissed me off.

Plato: Am I misunderstanding something? Socrates, help me on this. I'm not only in trouble with this guard and his sword, but, now, I've upset your servant.

Malcolm X: Whoopee, I've been promoted to a servant. Double damn. And, this guy is in an advance C-of-U realm? Seems like he's still mired in the anticivilization. Man, I can run competitive circles around this guy's business no matter what realm he's in. ...And, mark my words, I'm going to do just that. He's easy. I'll definitely take some put options against this guy. If he weren't involved with Socrates, I'd sell short his entire IPO.

Plato: First, let's handle the problem with this genital-challenged bureaucrat. I tried to help him by promising psychological counseling so he could adjust to his ejaculation-deprived condition. He ungratefully responded by threatening to make me like him with his phallic sword.

Malcolm X: Can't believe you're from the C of U. You sound like an anticiv liberal wielding hypocritical political correctness combined with malevolent toll-booth compassion.

Plato: Old habits are hard to break. But, what should I do about this eunuch guard?

Malcolm X: I'll handle it. ...What's your name, my good man...errr, my good eunuch?

Eunuch: Jennifer.

Malcolm X: Nice name. Now, put away your sword. Tell me who castrated you. It's time justice was done. It's time to make you whole again. It's time your name was changed to Sluggo. ...Would you like me to help you?

Eunuch: Oh, yes! No one ever before offered me justice or help. No one cared what happened to me. No one ever cared about the great crime against me as a defenseless little boy. ...Sluggo. What a beautiful name!

281

Socrates: Sluggo?  Gandhi wouldn't approve.

Eunuch: So what!  That loin-clothed skeleton is the biggest wimp on this ship. ...Oh, please let me keep the name Sluggo.  It's so macho.

Malcolm X: Here, here, my dear Sluggo.  Let me help you off the ground.  Let me wipe away your flood of tears.

Eunuch:  Thank you, thank you.  You're so lovely.  It's the tears held back for two-hundred years.  I was nine when the church cut me to sing soprano in the Vatican choir.  Didn't make the choir so they cast me onto the streets.  I survived by selling my neutered body to perverted men and jaded women.  I've never felt or experienced sexual joy...only horrible misery.  Can't even masturbate.

Malcolm X: Who's responsible for this great crime of mutilation?  Who's responsible for cutting you?  Was he ever punished?

Eunuch: Pope Pius was responsible.  Popes are responsible for millions of capital crimes.  They're never punished.  There's no justice.  Even the Popes who kept harems of little boys and girls go unpunished.

Malcolm X: He'll pay for his crime against you.  He'll be punished, I promise. ...Is he on this ship?

Eunuch: Of course he's on this ship.  Every Pope who ever lived and died is on this ship of dead souls along with every other criminal who harmed others on Earth without paying for their crimes.

Malcolm X: Okay.  Here's the plan for justice and profits.  With Zon's dynamic, we can even cash in on Hitler and Mao while bringing everyone to justice. Retribution and restoration shall prevail for their victims, including you, Sluggo. ...My fee will be reasonable.

Eunuch: Sluggo. What a beautiful name. Any fee I'll gratefully pay for justice. I almost feel an erection coming on. ...Will you change the Pope's name to Jennifer?

Malcolm X: For a slight additional charge.

Eunuch: Your on! Let's go aboard.

— to be continued —

# Dialogue #3

Vanishing Earth's Anticivilization
for eternal
Business Profits and Romantic Love

Dialogue #3 shows that those at the entrance to the Civilization of the Universe can vanish an anticivilization. By marketing through integrated honesty, people can profit by vanishing Earth's lethal dynamics of irrationality, mysticism, and political-agenda laws.

### Act 3 of 3

Helen: Good job by Malcolm X, Socrates, and Plato. They hired the potential value producers — put them under contracts from one to a million years. Malcolm X returned the irredeemables to Earth's anticivilization — the only place in which death and graves exist.

Zon: How can we profit from those irredeemables. How can we profit from the time, energy, and thinking spent intercepting and repelling them?

Helen: That's where my business plan comes into play. My plan cashes in on those irredeemable losers.

Socrates: Can you reconcile business profits with irredeemable losers and an eternal future?

Zon: Of course. Competitive profits woven from honesty *is* the mechanism of an eternal future.

Socrates: If I'd known that 2400 years ago, I could've vanished Pericles' lawyer-like dishonesties and terminated his war that ended Athens' advance toward the Civilization of the Universe.

Ann: Amen.  Recognizing the heroic genius of business profits was the missing link to my knowledge.  Realizing that single fact could have prevented the most disastrous errors in my life.  Despite my admiration of business reflected in my novels, I never appreciated the links between business genius, happiness, and the success of Objectivism on Earth.  Without that appreciation, I harmfully slammed movie producers and book publishers who delivered my work into the middle-class marketplace.  Worst of all, I never appreciated the crucial role to my success heroically played by my business manager, Dr. Bate Randon.  He commercially launched Objectivism worldwide.  Yet, I trashed him out of irrational jealousy and ruined our booming business. ...My emotionally destructive reactions wrought my worst injustices and errors.  Aristotle was right: Success on Earth lies in middle-class businesses.

St. Aug.: Looks like Ann and I are on a steep learning curve about competitive value production, marketing, and profits.  With that knowledge, our business partnership to mass market Objectivism at discount prices to the proletariat will outcompete Neo-Tech Publishing. ...We'll make a bundle, elope, and live an eternally exciting, romantic life by endlessly expanding our C-of-U businesses.

Ann: Not so fast, Augie.  Like I told you before, I cherish my husband.  You're not going to break the love investment I've built for decades with my handsome man.

St. Aug.: Who wants to break such a wonderful relationship?  Not me.  For that would portend disaster for our marriage.

Ann: Our marriage?  No way, ever.

St. Aug.: Wrong.  Like I told you before, I know of ways and arrangements, especially for your husband.

Ann: Ways and arrangements for my husband?  Like what?

St. Aug.: Like arranging for a happier, more compatible romantic partner that'll bring him eternal happiness.

Ann: My husband paired with someone better than I?  Like whom?

St. Aug.: Not better than you, Ann.  But, someone better for him. Like Cleopatra or Mary Magdalene.  They're much different than you might realize from your distorted twentieth-century history. Both are incredibly sweet and effective entrepreneurs.  Either would be a wonderful romantic partner for your husband.

Ann: Mary Magdalene?  You've got a lot to learn about romantic love, Augie.

St. Aug.: Consider your husband's happiness.  Then we'll see who has the most to learn about eternal love and happiness.

Ann: You'll be shocked over what you need to learn about romantic love, especially from Dr. Randon.

St. Aug.: Maybe it's you who'll be shocked.  But, first, we both need to learn about business before we can think about me as your eternal penetrator

Ann: What do you mean, you as my eternal penetrator?

St. Aug.: You know the answer from Dr. Randon's teachings.  It's about you being the penetrated and me being the penetrator — exclusively, forever — without ever needing Viagra.

Ann: I'll never think about that, unless my husband approves.  So, quit talking about it.  ...And what's Viagra?

St. Aug.: Don't know for sure.  Helen prescribed it for Sluggo.

Ann: I'm interested in having Zon teach us about the dynamics of universal business profits.  ...Then we'll see what happens between us.

Socrates: Universal business profits are linked to romantic love?

Zon:  Yes.  ...But, I am not the best person to teach that business dynamic.

Ann: If not you, one of the greatest businessmen of the nineteenth century, then who?

Zon: Helen of Vegas and her friend Harold Geneen are more qualified to teach those dynamics.  They're the closest to what's happening on Earth today.  ...Helen, what's your plan for profiting from the time and energy spent on returning that ship of dead souls to Earth.

St. Aug.: Yes, I want to understand.

Helen: First, to understand the dynamic for eternal profit, one must understand the lack of that dynamic on Earth for the past 2300 years.  As Zon said, I'm summoning my friend Harold Geneen. He simultaneously orchestrated two-hundred profitable companies for the conglomerate ITT on Earth.  He's bringing his C-of-U partners — airplane-titan Howard Hughes and french-fry-titan Ray Kroc.

Mr. Helmsley: Wow! Geneen, Hughes, and Kroc — talk about value-producing, civilization-benefiting powerhouses!

Ann: Handsome Howard and Ray's french fries...yum.

St. Aug.: Cool it Ann.

Ann: Don't get jealous Augie, but my pants just got wet thinking about meeting those heroes.

St. Aug.: I'm not jealous. For, I'm catching on fast as to what's the ultimate aphrodisiac. That's why I'm going to win you forever. When I capture that aphrodisiac, I'll outcompete 'em all. Then you'll soak your pants over me forever.

Ann: A while ago you mentioned the word Neo-Tech. Augie, is that your secret aphrodisiac?

St. Aug.: Perhaps.

Ann: Why are you smiling so slyly? I heard the word Neo-Tech in 1981 when my cult followers trashed a book about it that my secretary had acquired. They called it wacko, banned it for all Objectivists, and refused further discussion. ...What's it about?

St. Aug.: Ever hear of psychuous sex?

Ann: Vaguely, in 1976. ...Tell me about it.

St. Aug.: You'll find out soon enough. I've been learning from Helen. She knows firsthand about psychuous sex and Neo-Tech.

Ann: Oh, so you've been secretly seeing Helen?

St. Aug.: Now, Ann, don't get jealous. Helen has all she can handle with overtures from Geneen, Kroc, and Hughes.

Helen: Yes, Ann, you'll learn about Neo-Tech when I reveal the business dynamics for profiting from Earth's anticivilization. The opportunities can make you and Augustine prosperous and happy beyond your Earthly dreams.

Ann: How'd you learn about Neo-Tech?

Helen: In 1956, I was working toward my Master of Fine Arts degree at the University of Iowa. Sitting in the Student Union, opening to the first page of Melville's *Moby Dick*, a hand fell lightly on my shoulder. I looked up "Call me Wallace", he said. ...My life journey toward psychuous sex, Neo-Tech, and the Civilization of the Universe began.

Ann: Did he have blue eyes and blond hair?

Helen: Yes, but that made no difference.

Ann: Then what happened?

Helen: I asked him if he had a story to tell. "The grandest story in existence," he answered. ...Thus began my journey toward integrated honesty.

— to be continued —

290

*The New Gods*

DIALOGUES #4-100 (1999-2008)
DIALOGUES COMING IN 1999

*Completion of Dialogues #1-3.

*Two unexpected romances in Zon's "Purgatory". An unforgettable wedding party thrown by the Robber Barons. The birth and education of a baby Zon.

*The withdrawal of Neo-Tech from Earth's anticivilization.

*Discovering intellectual gold — discovering the universal mother lode — discovering a radically advanced Neo-Tech that vanishes philosophy, including Objectivism.

*Discovering universal justice — discovering universal laws — discovering an unexpected, ad-hominem protocol for judging morality.

*Shakespeare, Moliére, and Verdi form the AwakeWorks Production Company to dramatize the C of U in a galaxy-wide, mega-profit, holographic opera.

*Ann Brand and Saint Augustine buy advertising spots during that holographic opera to market their aerobic-fitness drink "Atlas Shape Up".

*Sam Walton and Ray Kroc profitably convert Al Capone, John L. Lewis, Jimmy Hoffa, and a host of professional parasites into a phalanx of value-producing entrepreneurs.

*Traveling back to Earth, Jay Gould and Malcolm X help the harassed-publisher Larry Flynt and the disgraced-agent Bill Clinton bring laissez-faire capitalism to planet Earth, starting in Nigeria, Africa. Together dirty-tongue Flynt and golden-tongue Clinton create an international chain of exotic, new-concept businesses that black-market combinations of erotic art productions, commercial romantic love, and low-cost sexual immortality. ...Through untaxed, unregulated businesses they vanish the boundaries of nations to end wars and flourish economies. ...They jointly win the newly instituted Nobel Prize for entrepreneurial-business achievements.

*The anticivilization's final war: Who wins? Who stays? Who vanishes?

\* \* \* \* \* \* \* \* \* \*

# In Memoriam

Humanity's greatest evil is anticivilization-caused death that is inflicted upon everyone living on Earth. Consider the unnatural, anticivilization death of a real-life hero — Helen Ward: On March 23, 1998, Neo-Tech Publishing Company suddenly, unexpectedly lost its quietest yet perhaps most important person. Neo-Tech Publishing not only lost her, but mankind lost the key role she was playing in switching conscious minds from mortal/irrational perspectives to immortal/rational perspectives — from dishonest anticivilization perspectives to honest C-of-U perspectives. ...Helen Ward is irreplaceable in this world. She is gone forever from its anticivilization. Yet, ironically, her life is now celebrated. For, still to come is her greatest gift — a magnificent gift to mankind — as reflected in the following eulogy delivered at her funeral on March 29, 1998:

### Discovering Helen of Vegas

*Helen was the deep, quiet heartbeat of Neo-Tech Publishing Company, secretly playing a heroic role of protecting us all. No controversies surrounded Helen. Her goodness blessed everyone, including our employees, even our ex-employees. And, now, we have lost this irreplaceable, precious person. But, have we really lost her? Or is today just the beginning of ever greater love and values that we shall gain from her immortal spirit.*

*Five days after she physically left us, I suddenly realized that perhaps Helen, years ago, unknown to everyone, had stepped beyond Earth's anticivilization, leaving behind its dishonesties, deceptions, and injustices, beckoning for us to do the same. Helen was a sweet, kind woman of pristine benevolence and untainted justice. I've never heard a dishonest word come from her lips. I've never heard her say a hurtful or unjust word toward anyone. She had no enemies. Had she, all along, been living in an honest civilization that each of us have yet to discover? If so, she will rise mightily in our lives — in our future works and publications in print and on the Internet. Her son, Eric Savage, will now complete her life work, which was nearing its conclusion after two decades of labor. Her great work will be published both as a book and on the World Wide Web under her pen name, Tracey Alexander. That work will torpedo and eventually sink dishonest mysticisms and religions around the globe. Already, valuable pieces of her writings are published on the Web, having their beneficent effect, doing their valuable work for mankind.*

*In the months and years ahead, through cyberspace featuring her posthumous masterwork, Helen will rise to show us how to abandon hidden deceptions, injustices, and dishonesties that harm everyone. So, let us celebrate Helen's life that will bring increasing prosperity, strength, and love into our futures.*

# APPENDIX I
## Ending the IRS

# ≈ Internet ≈

email: sue@irs.class-action.com
see web site www.neo-tech.com/irs-class-action/ for current IRS Abuse Reports

# IRS Abuse Reports

prepared for the committees
in the

## *United States Senate*

and the

## *House of Representatives*

investigating the
Internal Revenue Service

This Report is also Furnished
to all
Federal Judges in America

Prepared and Maintained
by the
Kenneth A. Clark Foundation

# Brace Yourself Before Reading
## the
# IRS ABUSE REPORTS

Are you
- a hard-working, middle-class American?
- a law-abiding, taxpaying citizen?

Do you believe that no harm can come to you and your loved ones from the Internal Revenue Service (the IRS)? Any such belief will change after reading the following IRS Abuse Reports. Those reports are from law-abiding, hard-working taxpayers like you -- honest taxpayers who suddenly found themselves being methodically, cruelly, criminally destroyed by an out-of-control bureaucracy. Indeed, the IRS is a juggernaut, not for tax collection, but for power expansion through fear and destruction.

Reports documenting the IRS's often brutal and criminal abuses inflicted on innocent Americans[1] are received daily as part of evidence gathering for Congressional hearings and potential class-action lawsuits. Through the dynamics of email combined with Internet Newsgroups and World Wide Web sites, unjustly ruined citizens finally have a way to come together for redress.[2] They will be coming together first by the thousands then by the millions seeking redress for the life-destroying injustices, criminalities, and cruelties inflicted upon them by the IRS.

---

[1]To protect identities of the victims, initials instead of actual names and email addresses are used on all IRS Abuse Reports. But, the Kenneth A. Clark Foundation can contact any of those victims to provide court and congressional testimonies — to act as witnesses against the brutalities and destructions of the IRS. ...These and other IRS Abuse Reports are systematically posted on various Internet Newsgroups and some are permanently displayed on the World Wide Web site www.neo-tech.com/irs-class-action/

[2]All Abuse Reports have come via Internet email. The vast majority of abuse victims and their families who have been devastated by the IRS have no means to access the Internet. Thus, these reports represent only the tiniest fraction of those citizens whose lives have been criminally destroyed by the IRS.

# Sample of Abuse Reports

**Date:** Sat Aug  20 20:07:06 1997
**To:** sue@irs.class-action.com
**From:**  JM

## New Hampshire IRS Horror Story

### By Joseph Daniel McCool
### Union Leader Correspondent

DERRY -- The IRS has formally denied a Derry widow's allegations that its tax debt collection activities pushed her lawyer husband to commit suicide one year ago today.

And in other court documents filed in U.S. District Court in Concord yesterday by the IRS, Donna Greeley, the collection agent who has been sued for violating Shirley Barron's civil rights and those of her late husband, Salem-based attorney Bruce E. Barron, has answered the family's lawsuit by asking the court to dismiss the case and claiming "qualified immunity" from prosecution.

Mrs. Barron recently sued the IRS in a civil action for $1 million in damages for what she claims was the pattern of illegal, intimidating and stress-causing harassment her late husband and family suffered at the hands of Greeley and her IRS supervisors, who were working to recoup hundreds of thousands of dollars in delinquent federal taxes owed by the family.

Lawyers for Mrs. Barron are seeking to prove the IRS pushed Mr. Barron to suicide by employing unlawful collection activities and by delaying an alleged settlement that he could have otherwise avoided simply by declaring personal bankruptcy.

The Taxpayers' Bill of Rights, which was amended in Congress last year, grants taxpayers the right to seek up to $1 million in damages if they can prove that the IRS "recklessly or intentionally" resorted to unauthorized tax-collection measures.

In previous documents filed in Concord court, the IRS has denied the allegation that Greeley sought to "intentionally embarrass, harass, or humiliate" Bruce or Shirley Barron.

David Hatherley, of the IRS' Boston appeals division, wrote in an internal memo obtained by Mrs. Barron's lawyers that "I do not believe that the IRS was responsible for Mr. Barron's death."

In the documents submitted to the court yesterday, the IRS has denied that Greeley ever violated the law in her attempts to recover more than $200,000 in delinquent federal taxes owed by the family.

The IRS answer to Mrs. Barron's lawsuit also denies that an IRS officer in Manchester indicated to Mr. Barron and his representatives that the agency would accept a settlement offer discussed during a meeting in September 1995.

In answering claims by the family's lawyers, the federal agency also denies that Greeley was told that her collection activities were pushing Mr. Barron toward suicidal tendencies.

It also denies that Greeley was aware of the claim that the ongoing tax collection case was causing Mrs. Barron "extreme psychological harm and loss of sleep."

To many of the family's charges, the IRS has replied that it "lacks sufficient knowledge or information to form a belief as to the truth of the allegation."

Mrs. Barron said she and her husband claimed substantial losses from the closure of a business, but that when the losses were recaptured and levied by the IRS, they were left owing about $80,000 in back taxes. But the family's tax debt, covering unpaid taxes from tax years 1986 through 1992 and including penalties and interest, grew to $233,268.

In 1993, the Barrons' tax collection case was assigned to Greeley, who mounted a debt collection campaign during 1994 and 1995 that included her placing liens on the family's home in Derry and its summer vacation home in Chatham, Mass., in an attempt to recover the taxes.

The lawsuit claims that Greeley demanded that Mr. Barron's legal clients pay the IRS directly for their legal services instead of him, a measure that caused Mr. Barron great embarrassment, humiliation and stress over the potential downfall of his legal practice.

On August 5, 1996, Mr. Barron opened a certified letter containing the bad news that his home was being foreclosed on. He penned a suicide note at his law office in Salem blaming the IRS for his demise, telephoned his wife that he'd be late coming home that night and drove two-and-a-half hours to the family vacation home on Cape Cod.

There, the 47-year-old attorney, who grew up in Salem, pulled his car into the garage, closed the garage door and let his car motor idle until he was overcome with deadly fumes. An autopsy confirmed that he had died from carbon monoxide poisoning.

Since Mr. Barron's suicide last summer, the IRS has foreclosed on the family's vacation home in Chatham, placed a lien on the home in Derry, seized Mrs. Barron's 1996 tax refunds and placed a claim against the $200,000 that she has received thus far from one of her late husband's two life insurance policies and also the outstanding $200,000 policy.

# **Reactions to IRS Abuse Reports**

Below is a typical reaction by those who have read the IRS Abuse Reports. ...A rebellion is brewing — a rebellion that can be quelled only by replacing the malignant, irrational IRS income-tax system with a beneficial, rational consumption-tax system.

**Date:** March 20, 1996
**To:** sue@irs.class-action.com
**From:** KS
I just finished reading all of the IRS abuse reports. I feel so very sorry for each of these people and their loved ones.
About three-quarters of the way through reading the reports, I had to take a break and lie down as I had become so nauseated from the vile destruction of these innocent victims.

---

# Evidence for Abolishing the IRS

is building on

## Internet/Usenet Newsgroups

Below is an example of Usenet Newsgroup postings that are appearing across the Internet.

Newsgroups: alt.irs.classaction,misc.taxes,misc.legal,us.taxes,us.legal, alt.society.civil-liberty
From: MC
Subject: Cyberspace Termination of the IRS
Date: Thu, 20 Jun 1996 20:33:02 GMT
In article <mk@netcom.com>wrote:
> Have you, a family member, a friend or loved one ever been
> defrauded, looted, hurt, injured, brutalized, or destroyed by the
> Internal Revenue Service (IRS)? Did no one help you, sympathize
> with you, or even listen to you, even though you were innocent --
> even though you and your family were criminally violated, badly
> injured, perhaps even destroyed or murdered?

When I read this I felt like you were writing just to me! My family members were brutalized by the IRS several years ago. My friend was destroyed just last week. Nobody sympathized with me, or even listened to me. My loved one was criminally violated, and nobody helped me. I didn't know where to turn but now I have this. Thank you.

---

**IRS Abuse Reports**
prepared for the
**United States Congress**
February, 1998

## Warning

Warning: These IRS Abuse Reports start mildly and build slowly. After awhile, these reports build into such a crescendo of sickening horror, criminal destructiveness, and unbearable evil that a sedative may be required to read them all:

## IRS Abuse Report #31

**Date:** Nov. 14, 1995
**To:** sue@irs.class-action.com
**From:** S
The IRS has illegally charged me $20,000 for a US Treasury Note which I purchased in 1989 for $10,000. They are saying that the Note was income which I did not claim. So, I am being penalized 100% for this Treasury note. They have notified my employer to garnishee my wages and they have placed liens on my property.

## IRS Abuse Report #32

**Date:** Nov. 18, 1995
**To:** sue@irs.class-action.com
**From:** SY
I received notice on 11-10-95 from my employer, that the IRS had garnished my wages. I certainly did not receive the 30-day notice as supposedly written into IRS policy.

## IRS Abuse Report #33

**Date:** Nov. 19, 1995
**To:** sue@irs.class-action.com
**From:** JC
In my experience with the IRS, if you don't

know what you are talking about, they will lie to confuse you. If you know what you are talking about, they take the fifth by refusing to answer.

## IRS Abuse Report #34

**Date:** Nov. 26, 1995
**To:** sue@irs.class-action.com
**From:** GT
The following happened to two friends of mine: BEWARE OF THE OVERPAYMENT SCHEME!! Each, having been overpaid by the IRS after filing a yearly statement, sent the excess back to the IRS. The IRS proceeded to bill them for interest, penalties and interest on penalties!!!! FOR THEIR OWN MISTAKES!!!!!

## IRS Abuse Report #35

**Date:** Nov. 27, 1995
**To:** sue@irs.class-action.com
**From:** SA
In 1992 I received a letter from the IRS that they had not received a tax return for me in the years 1980, 1981, and 1982. I said I had sent the returns when due (10-12 years ago), but I had no copies after so long. They maintained that there were no returns on file for those years. Subsequently, they levied against all my assets for over $80,000 and placed liens on my credit records which are still there. The liens keep me from getting work, getting anything on credit, etc.

## IRS Abuse Report #36

**Date:** Nov. 28, 1995
**To:** sue@irs.class-action.com
**From:** RB
Have taken my money, my businesses, (cost me 4 years of court time, my time, and my family's time). Am appealing in the Federal court.

### IRS Abuse Report #37

**Date:** Nov. 29, 1995
**To:** sue@irs.class-action.com
**From:** BH

During the 91'-92' tax years, apparently our CPA had entered false statements on our return so that we could get more money back. There were a lot of people in our area that she did this to. She took deductions that weren't legally acceptable, and we had no knowledge of what our legal deductions were -- after all, that was why we were paying a CPA. Then came the IRS and the auditors. About 50 people I know were audited. After the audit was over and they figured out how much we owed the IRS, they put us on a payment plan to pay them back. I thought that would be the end of the terrible ordeal, but no. Six months after the audit the IRS criminal investigators called and wanted to setup an appointment to discuss our CPA. So we told them all we knew, and again we thought surely this would be the end of this ordeal with the CPA and the IRS. After a year of making monthly payments to the IRS, which my wife made on time every month, they sent a letter saying that we had defaulted on our balance owed to them, and they were giving us 2 weeks to pay them or they were going to seize our assets and place a lien on us. So I went to the bank and got the money and paid them off. Again thinking, damn this has got to be the end of this situation with the IRS. Tonight an agent from the Charlotte, NC IRS criminal division called wanting to setup another appointment to discuss our tax returns again. I'm sick and tired of this and want it to stop. What options do I have? Help me.

### IRS Abuse Report #38

**Date:** Fri, 01 Dec 95 12:21:46 -800
**To:** sue@irs.class-action.com
**From:** S

Approx. 24 months ago I contracted a rare pneumonia, I was on disability for 8 months.

At the same time the company I had worked for was experiencing restructuring. They required that I move to San Francisco. We agreed on a cash settlement. This gave me the monies needed to learn and establish a new career. My monies were budgeted to give me adequate time for transition. I set about the career transition without asking any assistance.

Recently the IRS took $3200 out of my account. This was the last of my cash reserve. I now have no means of paying rent, electricity, or phone. The IRS could literally be the reason I become homeless.

### IRS Abuse Report #39

**Date:** Tue Dec 5 20:10:41 1995
**To:** sue@irs.class-action.com
**From:** MP

After filing bankruptcy in 92, because of a bad divorce, I went to the IRS for an offer of compromise, then the fun started. They denied my application. I still can't get them to stop harassing me with liens and levies.

### IRS Abuse Report #40

**Date:** Thu, 07 Dec 95 21:48:01 -800
**To:** sue@irs.class-action.com
**From:** IRS R.I.P.

Back in 1988 the IRS took all but $260 a month from my paycheck, via a levy. This was for the year 1982. I had been filing exempt on the w-4. Which is my lawful right. In 1992 I was convicted on two counts of tax evasion for 1986 and 1987. And for 1985 they are getting ready to send another levy to my employer for about $15,000. And before I forget, I am now in tax court for 83, 84, 86, and 87. Did I leave anything out? Oh, I am on probation until 1997. I did not see any prison time, am I lucky or what? I have been just this side of hell.

## IRS Abuse Report #41

**Date:** Sat Dec  9 10:48:32 1995
**To:** sue@irs.class-action.com
**From:** PG
The company where I am the Business Director was seized after the I.R.S. had entered into a payment agreement and we had given them $55,000.   The majority of the money owed now is penalty and interest.   However, to get the business back, we had to file a Chapter 11.

## IRS Abuse Report #42

**Date:** Mon Dec 11 12:51:45 1995
**To:** sue@irs.class-action.com
**From:** TR
My home belongs to the IRS and every attempt to negotiate is met with a brick wall.   In 1982 I was brought an investment, by an investment counselor, that would allow me to enter into the music/record business.  This investment promised some tax advantages so I met with the IRS to insure legality.  I was informed by the IRS that the investment was sound.  Upon making the investment and taking the tax credits in 1983, I was audited in 1986.  The tax credits were denied.  The IRS applied interest and  penalties which made the amount owed impossible to pay.  Liens were placed on my home.  Because of the liens my credit was ruined.  Because of this I was unable to get loans to pay off the liens.  This year I found a funding company that would work with the IRS to negotiate the amounts owed and give me a second mortgage.  The IRS refused to negotiate and instead is in the process of increasing the lien amounts for additional interests and penalties.  So far, an $18000 tax savings, originally approved by the IRS, has resulted in $62000 debt to the IRS.  During my last conversation with an IRS agent, I was told that the only way they would negotiate was if I sold my home and gave them all of the equity plus $1500.  When I asked the agent where he expected me to find housing, I was informed "that's not my problem".

## IRS Abuse Report #43

**Date:** Fri, 15 Dec 95 08:17:01 -0800
**To:** sue@irs.class-action.com
**From:**  MY Story:
I was audited by the IRS for Income Tax Filing Years 1980, 81, 83, and 84 and through this audit I lost a vehicle by IRS seizure while I was on an out of state work assignment in 1985.  In 1988 I had some military trauma flash backs which ended up with my being incarcerated from June 1988 until November 1994.  During this period of incarceration I was able to pay in-full the tax owed for the years of 1983 and 1984.  I had an attorney represent me before the IRS in an effort to settle the tax debts.  Through delays caused by the IRS not answering his inquiries, it took over 18 months, as well as red-tape run-arounds, to finalize payment for years 1983 and 84.  We asked for a waiver of interest for the period of my incarceration [only].  The waver was denied.  My tax debt for the unpaid years, was originally somewhere in the areas of $1100 for one and $2500 for the other.  With the IRS disallowing the waiver of interest during my term of incarceration, the total tax debt for those 2 years is just over $10,000.  The IRS has agreed to installment payments of $247/month for 3 years.  I do not object to paying the original amount plus interest and penalties for the years prior to my being incarcerated.  My payment of some $4,000 for the years of 1983 and 1984 while incarcerate is evidence that I am trying to settle my tax obligation.  I just have a real problem with the IRS incurring interest upon my remaining debt during a time of incarceration.

I am also disabled and receiving Social Security Disability Income monthly payments, a 10% VA monthly Compensation, and monthly payments from a trust my deceased parents setup for me.  This is my total source of income other than my wife's Social Security Retirement income.  I am just getting my family back into a stable living environment and this $247 monthly installment payments for 36 months will be a considerable burden. If the interest were adjusted to waive the period of incarceration I would likely be able to settle in full, 6 to 8 months, though with some short-term hardship. I could then continue my productive, tax paying life without the anxiety of continually looking over my shoulder for the feared impending ambush coming.

### IRS Abuse Report #44

**Date:** Sun Dec 17 11:05:15 1995
**To:** sue@irs.class-action.com
**From:** JK
Audited tax return from 1983 in the year 1989, then demanded that copies of checks, rather than actual bank statements which matched Merrill Lynch Cash Management Account statements, be provided. Merrill Lynch did not have the cancelled checks even though their literature states that they keep them on hand and will provide them, or copies of them, upon request.

IRS then rejected clearly legitimate deductions and demanded immediate payment of $250,000 in "unpaid taxes, interest, and penalties" which now adds up to more than $450,000.

### IRS Abuse Report #45

**Date:** Thu, 21 Dec 1995 00:42:54 -0500
**To:** sue@irs.class-action.com
**From:** BE
My life has been made miserable and my credit ruined by IRS liens relating to a business that I operated from 1978 to 1984. I always had an accountant do my withholding taxes and to the best of my knowledge, except for the last quarter of operations, when the company had no funds, I eventually made all payments. I have never had any conversation or correspondence with the IRS regarding these liens, but now they have seemed to multiply out of nothing into more than $80,000, and a couple of them

have expired, meaning that probably more than $100,000 has been assessed against me by the IRS for nothing that I can figure out.

It is my belief that the IRS misapplied payments that I made while the business was operating and did not credit them to my company, as I did change the name of the business twice. After that, penalties and interest applied by the IRS to mistaken claims have simply escalated, and continue to do so. There is nothing I can do to fight this, as all of the records from that business were given up when the business' lease was terminated in 1985. In any event, I have not been able to buy a home or a car, or anything on new credit as the IRS liens are viewed as the worst kind of credit liability. To make matters worse, due to my age, I have been unable to find suitable employment although I am doing important volunteer work which means that I am capable if I could get hired.

### IRS Abuse Report #46

**Date:** Fri Dec 22 22:14:23 1995
**To:** sue@irs.class-action.com
**From:** AS
The IRS has garnisheed wages three times. The IRS attempted once for $50,000. I am so sick of these people not answering my letters and stealing my property (wages).

### IRS Abuse Report #47

**Date:** Wed Dec 27 13:23:52 1995
**To:** sue@irs.class-action.com
**From:** LS
They have made so many mistakes on my account and charged me with monies I do not owe. Every time, they send me two and three letters about the same thing. They have made my life a living hell.

## IRS Abuse Report #48

**Date:** Wed Jan 10 13:12:38 EST 1996
**To:** sue@irs.class-action.com
**From:** JS
IRS has Fed.Tax Liens filled against my property. I can't even go on living, with this over my head. 56 years old..no way to ever pay off..Taxes paid..penalties and interest keep building. No way out..P.S. Probably dropping E-Mail address soon..Suicide the only answer to forgetting this problem. Help...

Can't purchase house, mine falling down..Can't even make any major purchase..Life not really worth going on 56 yrs. old and no end to this mess....Also, they took a friend of mine, house and everything he owned..ruined him forever. Help me...

## IRS Abuse Report #49

**Date:** Sat, 13 Jan 1996 21:49:29 -0500
**To:** sue@irs.class-action.com
The IRS is currently attempting to audit me on fictitious income they claim was suppose to have been reported on my 1985 Tax return. I am using the IRS Ombudsman to assist me in responding to the IRS. With interest and penalties, they turned a few hundred dollars dispute it into a $30,000 dispute. They have also Garnished my wages. Understand, my first claim against them was not prior notice (even about the garnishment) and the IRS states they sent notice to the address on the form. Well I haven't lived there since 1986 and the IRS has (from a print out of their own system) my current address as well as my current and previous employers. I wish I could afford a really good attorney. I'd like to put the IRS in their place.

## IRS Abuse Report #50

**Date:** Thu, 18 Jan 1996 02:01:12 -0800
**To:** sue@irs.class-action.com
Five years ago, my brother was married to a woman who filed a tax report owing $1,100 . She did not pay it. A year later my brother divorced this women. Now, the IRS wants my brother to pay taxes, interest, and penalties for his ex-wife.

My brother had bought a "dollar" home and lived in it for a few years and really fixed the place up and when he moved he sold it for 17,000 dollars! That's a real good improvement and the place really did look nice, but all the other homes in the area are worth about $10,000 dollars. He lived in a ghetto. Well, the IRS now says that the house was sold for $54,000 and not $17,000 and they want there cut of the action.

My brother now lives with a woman he is not married to. He has 4 boys that are living with him, ages 2 to 14. The IRS says he can't claim them as a deduction. He also has 2 children of his own which live with their mother, ages 8 and 15. He doesn't claim them but does have to provide support for them.

The woman that he lives with made 3,000 dollars last year as a janitor. He brought in a whopping $20,000 last year. My brother works very hard to support the family the best that he can. Last week he went to pick up his paycheck and to his surprise, its only for a hundred bucks for two weeks work. The IRS put a levy against his wages for 1,800 hundred dollars. He lives paycheck to paycheck as do a lot of Americans.

My brother NEEDS help and advise. I told him to pick up a second job until the IRS finds him and then move on to another job. He is 40 years old and has no savings, no retirement, and no future. What do you think is going to happen if no release comes?

## IRS Abuse Report #51

**Date:** Fri Jan 19 18:19:46 EST 1996
**To:** sue@irs.class-action.com
**From:** DS

During 1992 and 1993, my wife and I did not have enough tax withheld from our paychecks. As a result, we ended up owing the IRS almost $10,000, a large portion of which was penalties and interest. We set up an installment agreement, and have been paying on it for over three years. On TWO occasions during this time, we were late (by less than 5 days) in making our payment. This prompted someone in the IRS to decide that we are a "nonpayment risk." So, they seized our bank account and filed a public tax lien against us. They did not notify us of this action, and we found out when we received a call from an organization that helps out people with tax problems. We were able to get our bank account released, but only after dozens of phone calls to every IRS office whose number I could get, and a visit to two IRS offices. I was not able to get the lien released. In fact, they couldn't even tell me who in the IRS had taken the action. The bottom line? Because of the lien, we are not able to get a loan for a car, and were even turned down for renting a house. All because the IRS "seized" our credit for two late payments totalling $430. I know this may sound trivial compared to some horror stories, but every act of unconstitutional aggression by our government hurts us all.

## IRS Abuse Report #52

**Date:** Fri Jan 19 21:28:33 EST 1996
**To:** sue@irs.class-action.com
**From:** JK

I made a typo when filling out my forms making my sons social security number invalid. Because of this, they refused to let me claim him as a dependent. They ordered me to produce all kinds of paper work to prove that he was my son and that he lived with me. While I was getting the paperwork, I wrote them numerous letters explaining the typing error and asked if they would simply check their records they would see that I had been claiming him for the last 16 years and that his status hadn't changed. They would not accept him as my dependent. Each time I would send them the papers they requested, they would take several months to reply, always informing me of more papers they wanted, which in turn, I would send. When they decided that I had sent enough paper work, they sent me a notice saying to much time had elapsed and that the case was closed. Now, not only do I owe them the original amount, they assessed a penalty of 25% for late payment.

## IRS Abuse Report #53

**Date:** Tue, 23 Jan 96 00:23:43 -0800
**To:** sue@irs.class-action.com
**From:** JB

In the late 70's and early 80's I was behind on filing my returns. In 1984, I filed 8 years all at once and paid the fines. Now in 1994, the IRS has said that they did not receive my 78 return until 1989, and my 1981 return until 1986, and when a refund was due me, they kept the refund. Now can you believe what the IRS has done regarding penalties and interest since 1978 and 1981. The amounts they are claiming, you would not believe. I have dealt with seven offices, and at least 21 IRS employees. The left hand doesn't know the right hand. The Problem Resolution Program (PRP) only sends letters saying pay.....You mail these people proof of your filings, and they lose those documents and the process starts over again. The IRS should be eliminated, and I am sure persons in the private sector could do a much better job.

## IRS Abuse Report #54

**Date:** Tue Jan 23 02:13:01 EST 1996
**To:** sue@irs.class-action.com
**From:** GC

It is time to stop the unconstitutional powers of

the IRS. They need to be put out of business, along with anyone who supports them. They took my father-in-law and put a levy on him for my tax problems. No due process, they come and spit on your due process. It is time to shut them down and do America a great deed.

## IRS Abuse Report #55

**Date:** Sat Jan 27 01:37:45 EST 1996
**To:** sue@irs.class-action.com
**From:** TA

The money extorted from my paycheck and personal finances every day by the IRS has cost me freedom of movement, basic human comfort, a Chapter 11 Bankruptcy, and continual involuntary servitude. The presence of the IRS has created underlying fear in my personal life and the lives of my family. This fear has prevented productivity and the ability to live up to my highest potential as a human being and to exercise personal freedoms awarded me at birth. The money extorted every day prevents me from investing in the future, specifically my health and financial well-being when I become a senior citizen, and prevents my family the basic human right of safety and well-being in their future years. The IRS is a threat to my safety, both physically and mentally, and should be charged with endangering the health and well-being of every American citizen.

## IRS Abuse Report #56

**Date:** Thu Feb 1 18:39:39 EST 1996
**To:** sue@irs.class-action.com
**From:** RC

The IRS is taking $1800 of my $2000 pension which leaves me fairly penniless and unable to support myself in retirement.

## IRS Abuse Report #57

**Date:** Fri, 9 Feb 1996 02:39:02 -0500
**To:** sue@irs.class-action.com
**From:** BL

I am now engaged in a payment plan, which may not retire my IRS obligation before my death. The taxes in question, which I agree fully I owe (however, I strongly dispute the moral and legal basis for the penalties accruing thereto) were incurred in just two years, during which I was separated from my wife and trying to negotiate a divorce agreement. This period of time also saw the swift downturn of work availability in my profession, and in the general economy of the State of California. I was faced with providing necessary living accommodations for myself, my children, my to-be ex-wife, while trying to maintain a level of earning in a diminishing economy. It became clear to me that there simply wasn't enough money to satisfy all demands. I was eventually forced into bankruptcy.

Realizing my dilemma, I sought advice on how to deal with tax problems. One fact was perfectly clear: Filing tax returns when the means to pay was not at hand was tantamount to subjecting oneself to the most horrific torture. So, I did what was the proper thing to do: I delayed filing until I felt I could "face the music". Of course, the penalties and interest attached to the taxes have made the debt most burdensome.

Well, I was unable to pay the tax, and now I am on the aforementioned payment plan which will probably follow me to my grave -- if I can earn enough to stay a half-step ahead.

When I declared bankruptcy, my income taxes should have been discharged along with my other debts. I would now be a clean, productive citizen. Instead, I have a monstrous tax lien filed with the County Recorder, and the cloud of pernicious, untamed collection actions of the IRS hanging over me. The IRS doesn't have to live by any laws but their own. (And they hire the most obnoxious people -- but what normal person would want such a job?)

What possible good does this system serve? How does this differ from the time of indentured servants, "servants" who often paid with their lives when the tax collector paid his visit? Where is the constitutional authority for the establishment of an agency of the government which can disregard all the restraints of our constitution to achieve the ends of its mission? Where is the popular media exercising it's constitutionally protected grace to discuss this obfuscation of our rights? When will we all wake up to the fact that the IRS is, simply the armed servant of the power-grubbing, do-gooders -- social engineers, bureaucrats, and generally those who think their ideas and social mission is more important than individual rights and responsibility?

**IRS Abuse Report #58**

**Date:** Thu Feb  8 15:47:52 EST 1996
**To:** sue@irs.class-action.com
**From:** SR
In approximately 1983, I was asked by an employer to fill out a w-4 form. A few weeks later the IRS said the information I provided was false. They fined me $1,000 for providing false information. The IRS acted as judge and jury and convicted me without allowing me to redress my grievances. I refused to pay so they took all the money I had in my bank account and then they put a lien on my land and levied my wages.

**IRS Abuse Report #59**

**Date:** Thu Feb  8 19:58:37 EST 1996
**To:** sue@irs.class-action.com
**From:** JW
The income tax as presently levied makes us all slaves to politicians, IRS agents, state taxing agents, and their police state thugs. In reading

Kahriger v. U.S. the supreme court states that a tax return, like the 1040, is a confession. If we are compelled to sign confessions in this "land of the free and home of the brave" then we are slaves! Even the Geneva Convention outlaws the use of torture, physical or mental, or any form of coercion to force a prisoner of war to sign a confession. We are worse off than prisoners of war; WE THE SLAVE PEOPLE in order to form a "more perfect union"? The IRS wipes their butt with the U.S. Constitution every day...they think its a piece of toilet paper...and the bulk of Americans seem satisfied being the tame little Slaves for these supercilious rats.

The IRS seized my car in 1988. I paid to get it back and I asked the agent, if this was the end of it for the 1984 year. He responded with "yes." A year later the agency was back rejecting the settlement because the agent had used the wrong form!

The agency then treated stock sales as total profit, disregarding the obvious purchase price, and in 1987 they proceed to turn what was less then $12k (before inflation) gross profit on sales of $40k investment over 10 years into in excess of $150k taxes with penalties and interest! I lost to the tax court judge. I spent over $2k on an attorney to file  bankruptcy. The IRS accepted all but 1985, which they now claim as over $35k.

**IRS Abuse Report #60**

**Date:** Tue, 13 Feb 96 09:14:20 -2400
**To:** sue@irs.class-action.com
**From:** JM
The IRS has cleaned out our two IRA accounts and molested us in numerous other ways.

## IRS Abuse Report #61

**Date:** Mon, 19 Feb 1996 18:50:28 -0600 (CST)
**To:** sue@irs.class-action.com
**From:** NM

In 1989, my ex-husband left me. I have a son (not his). Within 6 months of his leaving, I was laid off from my job. (I also do not get child support -- his father refuses to pay.) My husband talked me into filing joint since we were still married in '89. I signed the form he worked up; it looked fine to me. Well, after he mailed it in, I found out that he had not paid ANY taxes for the year. Needless to say, we had to pay. Well, I ended up paying about three thousand dollars for him. He didn't file his taxes for at least three years, because it took me that long to pay it off. I asked the IRS why I had to pay his debt and I was told that 1) we were still married -- separation didn't count; and 2) "we take easy money, whoever we can get to pay first -- we don't care who pays." I ended up filing bankruptcy -- against my better judgement. I asked the IRS the second year why they weren't taking any money from him, too. I didn't get an answer. I asked if my ex was even filing his taxes: no answer. The second year I was paying his debt, the IRS sent me a letter saying I owed a little over $7,000. Since I had only made $9,000 that whole year, I laughed, then I got mad because they were serious. I was going through the bankruptcy, so my attorney also called the IRS to find out what was going on. She and I both fought them for a year just to get answers. We both got a different person every time we called. I got a letter about every month, and we called the IRS every week to find out what was going on.

## IRS Abuse Report #62

**Date:** Sat Feb 17 20:11:03 EST 1996
**To:** sue@irs.class-action.com
**From:** BR

I ran a successful contracting business for over ten years and had many employees. Due to an error in math I underpaid withholding taxes. I told the IRS this at the end of the year when I discovered the error. They fined me $40,000 and forced me into bankruptcy. Even after going bankrupt I still owe $16,000 personally and have had my accounts cleaned out and my wages garnished.

## IRS Abuse Report #63

**Date:** Mon, 19 Feb 1996 00:39:37 -0500
**To:** sue@irs.class-action.com
**From:** RM

The federal income tax and the IRS is destroying the very principles this country was founded on.

## IRS Abuse Report #64

**Date:** Fri, 20 Feb 1996 12:11:19 -0800
**To:** sue@irs.class-action.com
**From:** RV

Recently the IRS has adopted a new set of rules taxing tuition waivers for employees. Many university employees work for reduced salaries, like myself, because they are going to school to better themselves and the university gives them free tuition to compensate the difference.

IRS is collecting millions if not billions of dollars with this new law that is probably making many unfortunate people have to discontinue their graduate studies because they cannot afford to give the IRS several hundred dollars a month in tuition waiver tax. Please help!

## IRS Abuse Report #65

**Date:** Wed, 21 Feb 1996 11:45:28 -0500
**To:** sue@irs.class-action.com
**From:** DM

I have been battling the IRS for about 10 yrs now. They have a lien on the house, and until recently had a lien on my wife's salary. Last year we managed to make a (over 10% reduction) "contribution" to our tax liability. Seven months after this activity we receive notices of "WE HAVE CHANGED YOUR ACCOUNTS" where they added over $8,000 in "late payment penalties" and over $40,000 in interest! This interest figure represented, in a 7 month period, a 31% rate!

I have other information available if I can be of assistance in your fight.

## IRS Abuse Report #66

**Date:** Wed, 21 Feb 1996 20:26:52 -0500
**To:** sue@irs.class-action.com
**From:** BK

Recently I received a notice of levy from big brother of over $1500. The interesting part is that they are holding $1000 that they won't apply to this levy, and they refuse to let me make payments. They say that they won't release the cash because of the chapter 13 filed to prevent them from getting money from my trustee . It seems to me that if they are holding money that they owe me, it should be applied to the new levy, then I could afford to pay them off. This is the first notice that I have received on these new owes they say they have sent four. Any help or advice you can offer would help, what's next, be forced into homelessness?

## IRS Abuse Report #67

**Date:** Thu Feb 22 18:52:17 EST 1996
**To:** sue@irs.class-action.com
**From:** LE

When the IRS, allegedly, could not reach me at my N.Y. address that I had lived at for almost 8 years, they put a levy on my salary taking 90%. This left about $134 a week to live on. I lived on Long Island and used the Long Island Railroad -- that alone cost $140 monthly. Rent was $1330 and I won't even add in all the other expenses, phone, utilities, credit payments,

loans, food, etc... Since I couldn't afford to work I had to resign. I had about $18,000 saved so I moved to North Carolina where the cost of living is less than N.Y. and immediately hired a tax specialist to see what they could do. After almost a year of negotiations, the IRS 'AGREED' to allow me to make monthly payments of $740 to pay off my alleged underpayment of taxes since 1990 of $40,635.25. If I had $740 extra a month I'd have a nice sized savings account but as it happened I couldn't find a job for 10 months, exhausted all my savings and don't have a bank account at all.

I am to start making this payment in 2 weeks. If I make this payment I will not be able to pay all my other monthly bills. I am now shopping for a good, cheap bankruptcy lawyer. I am going to miss payments so I might as well go bankrupt before the harassing creditor calls start. How is it they could find where I worked to levy my salary but couldn't call me there or get my address from my employer?

The IRS is definitely more dangerous than most of the criminals in jail today. They don't kill you or maim you, they just rob all of us daily in the name of government, rape us, ruin us financially and make our lives a living hell.

## IRS Abuse Report #68

**Date:** Sat Feb 24 08:46:03 EST 1996
**To:** sue@irs.class-action.com
**From:** JB

A couple in Dayton Ohio saved for years to buy a dream home. The IRS had several properties advertised for sale at auction (seized properties). The IRS assured everyone that all the houses had clear titles.

The couple bid on a house and were high bidders. The IRS required $24,000 down payment. The couple put the $24,000 down and went to the bank for a mortgage for the balance. This wasn't a problem until they did the title search. The house had $150,000 in liens against it. The couple demanded that the IRS return their $24,000 but the IRS refused, saying the couple should have checked for liens (even though the IRS had assured them previously there were no liens).

If a real estate agency in the State of Ohio had done this, everyone involved would have been jailed. How can IRS agents get away with breaking fraud laws just because they happen to be employed by a Federal agency? This is the ultimate in sleaze.

## IRS Abuse Report #69

**Date:** Sun Feb 25 16:21:55 EST 1996
**To:** sue@irs.class-action.com
**From:** RI
The IRS claims to have a lien on my entire personal estate due to 'unpaid taxes for the tax year 1987. But I am unable to "make a return of income" because I have been very poor for the past 3.5 years

## IRS Abuse Report #70

**Date:** Tue Feb 27 17:02:56 EST 1996
**To:** sue@irs.class-action.com
**From:** TE
Where to start the list??? 1. Wage Garnishments. 2. Bank Acct Seizures. 3. Home Foreclosure & Forced sale for 20 % of true value . 4. etc...etc...etc...

I have been victimized, abused, lied to, cheated, and now I am being thrown from my home. This is all in the name of "for the good of the Government".

HELP !!!!!

## IRS Abuse Report #71

**Date:** Wed, 28 Feb 96 10:37:53 -0800
**To:** sue@irs.class-action.com
**From:** RU
We are in the mist of some serious charges, and nobody seems to care that we are innocent.

## IRS Abuse Report #72

**Date:** Wed, 06 Mar 1996 22:08:36 -0600
**From:** RH
**To:** sue@irs.class-action.com
Our trouble started in Jan.1985. We can't own anything, get credit etc... This last year they have been really bad. Garnishing wages illegally, Levies, false payment agreements. The told us to move out of our house in to a small apartment with our 2 sons. One of our sons is Attention Deficit with Hyperactivity and is under care. That is just part of the things they have done. I could write a book. The lies and deceit are unbelievable. Our legal bills are growing and our Attorney has recommended we file suit for damages and legal fees for all the hell we have gone through.

## IRS Abuse Report #73

**Date:** Sat, 09 Mar 1996 23:32:11 -0800
**To:** sue@irs.class-action.com
**From:** IR
The IRS's repeated attempts to audit me in person even though I was incapacitated at the time from an automobile accident is typical of the IRS.

The time and money I am spending due to their corrupt and inhumane bureaucracy could be spent in producing productive goods and services. They are crippling our country.

## IRS Abuse Report #74

**Date:** Tue Mar 12 09:34:05 EST 1996
**From:** MK
I voluntarily served in the armed forces, and after my final year of service, I was not given a W-2 form by the navy. I could only file on the other income which I earned that year. For 3 years now the IRS has harassed me, threatened me with liens and garnishings.

## IRS Abuse Report #75

**Date:** Thu, 14 Mar 1996 18:38:36 -0600
**To:** sue@irs.class-action.com
**From:** DP
I have been diagnosed as Atypical Bipolar-II Rapid Cycling. In simple terms this means that I suffer from an "atypical" form of manic-depression.

Over the past 10 years, I have been hospitalized approximately 12 times in both private and state hospitals. At least three of my hospitalizations occurred during tax time (Jan 1 through April 15). When you are hospitalized, voluntarily or by judges order (I have experienced both), there is no way you can comply with the tax laws or IRS policies.

The tax laws require (mentally) disabled people to do things they cannot do. (We are not on a mental/fiscal schedule, when we're ill, we're ill.) That sort of makes the ADA and the tax laws contradictory. When a person like myself goes into remission and does file his/her return after April 15, without an approved extension, we are subject to financial penalties and interest through no fault of our own.

There IRS offers no accommodation to and for the mentally ill. The IRS has ignored the reality of our needs to help us comply with the law. They however hold us 100% accountable for their unjust penalties and interest.

Communication from the IRS is a pretty scary

thing for all of us, but it can be a precipitating factor to someone like myself. I recently received a letter from the IRS advising me that they will soon place levies on my car and possibly my wages. Well I am living with that for now, but if I were in a degenerated state, it might be just enough to cause a psychotic episode resulting in anything from running to nowhere and putting myself in harms way, to hospitalization, to suicide. All over tax laws and their unfair means.

## IRS Abuse Report #76

**Date:** Thu Mar 14 00:22:49 EST 1996
**To:** sue@irs.class-action.com
**From:** KA
They put a lien against me for back taxes they said I owed, I did not. When I tried to prove this they told me I had to pay them in full before I could get my money back even though they agreed with me. They have damaged my credit record with this injustice. If this was the private sector of business the people involved would all be fired for malice, slander, mental anguish etc. and a lawsuit would be won hands down!

## IRS Abuse Report #77

**Date:** Mon Apr 1 16:30:23 EST 1996
**To:** sue@irs.class-action.com
**From:** MK
I have been nearly sequestered in my home since November 1994 due to actions of the IRS.

They stole the contents of my personal bank account in 1994 and demanded immediate payment of alleged underpayments; fines and penalties in the amount of approximately $180,000.

I have since gone through my records -- I have all records from all years. It turns out they owe me over $30,000, none of which I will ever see, and that doesn't include any interest calculations.

In the process of proving this, I have been unable to continue my business causing economic loss to not only myself, but my customers and my employees.

### IRS Abuse Report #78

**Date:** Tue Apr  9 03:27:03 EDT 1996
**To:** sue@irs.class-action.com
**From:**   RC
I had an attorney, specializing in tax matters, tell me that, "in this country, one can pay whatever the IRS claims or go to jail or get shot." This from an attorney working "within the system"!

### IRS Abuse Report #79

**Date:** Tue Apr  9 19:35:42 EDT 1996
**To:** sue@irs.class-action.com
**From:**   CM
We have been under the thumb of the IRS for over 10 years now. Currently, we are at the end of our 45 day stay against collection action while we are scrambling to put together our offers in compromise.

I was told by one IRS phone agent that I should get a real job and finally become a responsible taxpayer. When I call seeking help to solve our long term problem, all I get are standard form letters. When I call the IRS office I get abusive, patronizing, condescending slurs to my character and my responsibilities as an American.

When I asked for names, I was most often refused the information with comments like "it was of no value to me to have their names and therefore it's unnecessary".

After going bankrupt over five years ago from my first encounter with these people, I have never dug out. Now they have added 100% in interest and penalties and the interest is still

compounding -- yet no one will help us. This agency is absolutely out of control and needs to be abolished.

### IRS Abuse Report #80

**Date:** Thu, 11 Apr 1996 20:32:27 EDT
**To:** sue@irs.class-action.com
**From:**   DP
In 1988, I received a computer-generated IRS form letter about an over-refund from a couple of years before. The signature was a totally illegible inkblot. I called the 800 number on the letter -- every day for 6 months. No answer. I called the local IRS number. No answer.

I wrote to the IRS at the address on the letter. My response was another letter, identical to the first one, with the same inkblot signature.

Without any further warning, they began levying my salary -- 100% of it. I took home $0.00 paychecks for three and a half months. My home and car were both repossessed because I fell so far behind in my payments. The only reason I survived was through the kindness of a co-worker.

### IRS Abuse Report #81

**Date:** Thu Apr 11 01:37:19 EDT 1996
**To:** sue@irs.class-action.com
**From:**   JB
The IRS has decided to withhold refunds due me as they say I owe taxes back to 1981.  After three years of dealing with these people, the IRS is trying to attach liens against everything I own.  The problem resolution office will not even meet with me.  I filed suit in the Tax court against the IRS.  Since I constantly receive collection notices (totally incorrect) I though a law suit would finally settle the matter.  WRONG.  The tax court accepted a motion that the IRS filed to throw my case out as I did not have a proper NOTICE OF DEFICIENCY form.  They can still send collection notices, and I have asked for a proper

NOTICE OF DEFICIENCY form, but they will not give this form, just collections notices and attempted liens.

## IRS Abuse Report #82

**Date:** Thu Apr 121 20:06:23 EDT 1996
**To:** sue@irs.class-action.com
**From:** HN
The killed my father and put my family in the streets.......must I say more?

I have been left with nothing and have nothing.......thank you America!!!

IF THERE IS ANYTHING THAT I CAN DO TO BRING DOWN THESE BASTARDS PLEASE LET ME KNOW....I HATE THEM WITH ALL MY HEART AND SOUL!!!!!

## IRS Abuse Report #83

**Date:** Sun Apr 14 07:15:33 EDT 1996
**To:** sue@irs.class-action.com
**From:** RG
These thugs have to be stopped. The IRS through, fraudulent "Notices of Levies", have attacked my spouse and my wages, along with our bank accounts. And, because of these fraudulent leans, they have prevented me form getting credit for my daughters college education.

We are powerless to stop this tyranny and extortion.

## IRS Abuse Report #84

**Date:** Mon, 15 Apr 96 12:14:10 -0700
**To:** sue@irs.class-action.com
**From:** JG
After I was laid off from my occupation of 22 years in the aircraft maintenance field. I found out that the Federal Govt classified aircraft maintenance as an obsolete career due to the number of mechanics and the faltering airline business.

I proceeded to try and find a new career. Now, the IRS tells me that all expenses I spent trying to find a new line of work, while trying to support myself, my wife, and 4 kids on unemployment, is not deductible because it's not in the same field I was working in -- which they themselves classified as obsolete!

On top of that, in order to feed and house my large family on $125 per week, and trying to find a new job, I had to cash in my K401 to save my house... Now I'm taking a $1476 penalty off the top off my return. Plus paying the taxes on unemployment..

No wonder I can't catch up or get ahead, I wasn't even allowed food stamps because I had a 1 year old Mazda MPV that I owed the bank $23,000 on -- that disqualified me...Where is the justice!

## IRS Abuse Report #85

**Date:** Mon Apr 15 19:11:37 EDT 1996
**To:** sue@irs.class-action.com
**From:** GY
We have received liens on money they say we owe them! They have taken money out of credit union saving! And, they are trying to take money from my pay check!

## IRS Abuse Report #86

**Date:** Thu, 18 Apr 1996 18:02:54 -0400
**To:** sue@irs.class-action.com
**From:** VMD7493@aol.com
My parents committed suicide the first of this year to avoid further problems from the IRS.

## IRS Abuse Report #87

**Date:** Tue Apr 16 21:37:37 1996
**To:** sue@irs.class-action.com
**From:** MD

The IRS went after my brother and assessed him $19,000. He owed about $3000, so the balance was penalties and interest. Further, the IRS agents have refused to let him deduct his children, even though he has a court order that states he is the sole guardian. They also will not let his ex-wife deduct the children. This case proves they are not above breaking their own laws or above using harassment against others. By the way, my brother has been unemployed for the last two years and the $19,000 they took from him is from his retirement that he spent 20 years working for.

## IRS Abuse Report #88

**Date:** Thu Apr 18 11:36:37 1996
**To:** sue@irs.class-action.com
**From:** VN

I received a refund of $57.00 for 1988. Now, for the past four years, the IRS has insisted that I did not file. They have been adding interest and penalties continuously. I have been continuously sending them copies of the forms I originally sent to them. They refuse to admit they are wrong.

They have threatened me with all kinds of things from garnishments to taking my possessions. Where do they get the right to take more than they should. I have been paying taxes for many years and my ancestors paid before.

## IRS Abuse Report #89

**Date:** Thu Apr 18 22:27:50 1996
**To:** sue@irs.class-action.com
**From:** Anon

The IRS Has:
 *violated my power of attorney

*filed liens without notice
*threatened my pregnant wife
*routinely "lost files"
*refused to examine evidence
*told one of my attorneys to go away
*threatened me if I didn't fire that particular attorney.
All at a cost of time and money (a hell of a lot more than the bogus assessment).

## IRS Abuse Report #90

**Date:** Sun Apr 21 16:40:49 1996
**To:** sue@irs.class-action.com
**From:** JH

The IRS does not respond to any of my inquiries, letters, or statements. I have only received unscheduled visits at my home and office by agents threatening to charge me with crimes, stating that they do not have to respond to any of my questions. They sent summons to my banks, and credit card institutions.

## IRS Abuse Report #91

**Date:** Mon Apr 22 10:11:08 1996
**To:** sue@irs.class-action.com
**From:** TV

The IRS lost or misplaced my tax return for 1992 and then two years later notified me that I owed back taxes and penalties -- the penalties are approximately $6,000. When I pointed out that I had filed my return, their response was PROVE IT. How can I prove that I mailed a return? All I can do is show a copy of what they claim I did not send to them to begin with!!

## IRS Abuse Report #92

**Date:** Fri Apr 12 13:22:58 EDT 1996
**To:** sue@irs.class-action.com
**From:** anonymous

They claim I owe $75,000 and if I don't come into their offices to take care of it that they will begin to garnish my wages! I told them that I have never even earned that much money throughout my whole life as I have been a college student until this year. The majority of their claim came from a stock purchase of my fathers that had erroneously ended up with my social security # on it during a time while I was in Japan for two years doing volunteer missionary work with no pay! Letters were already on file with the IRS documenting the error and placing the tax liability with my father. All they were apparently doing was trying to discover something to come after my father with and scared the hell out of me in the process.

If that is not harassment then I don't know what is! They came after me for something they already knew wasn't my liability. I've had probing calls before, but that threat was just going too far!

I would love to give the IRS a taste of their own medicine but don't feel I can afford to because they have so much influence over my family's life. As we run a family owned business, they cannot only hit our personal lives, but come directly after our companies as well, so we quietly grin and bear it while shaking in our boots everyday.

No one is safe from the IRS!

(scared to give my name!)
P.S. I'd like information on the lawsuit, but I really don't want the IRS coming after me or my father, so I don't want U.S. mail sent to me on the subject. I'm not even sure e-mail would be safe. I'm really paranoid. The IRS makes life a living hell! I think I'd just as soon deal with the KGB.

## IRS Abuse Report #93

**Date:** Fri Apr 26 18:44:22 1996
**To:** sue@irs.class-action.com
**From:** GW
Here is a list of IRS abuses inflicted on me and my family:
*My 1993 taxes are currently "under audit" by an IRS Revenue Agent. He has been auditing our tax return since November, 1995. It is now near the end of April and we still have not gotten the audit finished.

*At first he said the audit would take about two half days. Then he wanted two full days. I run a business from my home, just me, I did not want this guy holding up my business for two full days.

*Neither we nor our attorney heard anything from him until a month later, when on February 29, 1996, I got a phone call from our attorney saying that the IRS agent had 13 questions he wanted us to answer. The questions were all answered in our amended return – which apparently he did not even look at.

*The IRS Agent then said there would be an additional $9000 plus my self employment taxes all payable in 10 days. I had to stop work for an entire week, trying to track down information to document his requests.

*When the 10 days were up, my husband went to the meeting between the IRS agent and our lawyer. The IRS agent was pretty hostile. He basically disallowed everything. He refused to look at any documentation my husband tried to present.

*From what my husband could figure out, it sounded like our tax bill was going to be even bigger than the $9000. So, the more we tried to comply, the worse it got for us. Now, we don't know what is going to happen. The IRS Agent even said that I had committed some kind of crime because I paid my kids to work for me in my business (which he doesn't believe--he said we just put the money back in our own pockets). My kids filed tax returns and paid taxes on their earnings, as well as tax on the interest in their bank accounts

*We live in a small town, our tax lawyer has to do business with the IRS all the time. Plus, he has been audited three times himself. He doesn't want to rock the boat.

*It's now April 26, I have no clue what's going on with our audit. I've paid my taxes for 1995 but filed for an extension because I don't know what's going to happen.

## IRS Abuse Report #94

**Date:** Tue Apr 30 11:16:24 1996
**To:** sue@irs.class-action.com
**From:** MR
I was a member of a partnership that was audited back in 1984.

The case took six years to settle. I signed an agreement accepting the settlement. Nothing happened for over a year. Then out of the blue the IRS came at me with both guns blazing. Assessing all kinds of penalties and claiming that the time to reply to their claims had elapsed.

This same event happened to everyone in the partnership, however, all members had signed and filed the paper work prior to final agreement. Each member had to individually prove to the IRS that the IRS had made the mistake.

It's very involved and involves several instances where the IRS misplaced, lost or outright deceived us. This also precipitated a nervous breakdown for me. The financial distress was enormous and to this day I haven't recovered from the problems the IRS caused due to their negligence.

## IRS Abuse Report #95

**Date:** Tue Apr 30 23:26:54 1996
**To:** sue@irs.class-action.com
**From:** PM
The IRS confiscated my wages. I was working on an $80,000 year job and had to quit, dispose of all I owned, and have not been able to work since, except odd jobs. I did not owe IRS the money they said. It was due to a tax shelter that went bankrupt and not only did IRS come after me, but about 200 other people. I filed bankruptcy against the IRS and was discharged of my debt. However, I still owe for the past 4 years and feel it is unconstitutional the way they harass me. I have not been able to get a real job or own anything because of the IRS.

## IRS Abuse Report #96

**Date:** Thu May 2 1:23:54 1996
**To:** sue@irs.class-action.com
**From:** CCl
"The IRS has harassed me for 16 years".

In 1980 a previous employer erroneously reported my income by reporting that I earned $10,000 in 1980. I explained to the IRS that I did not earn the $10,000 because I only worked two weeks in 1980 at the rate of $750 bi-weekly. I further explained that I was the accounting supervisor for that company that reported the error and it can be very easily corrected. To no avail, the IRS ignored my request to ascertain the facts and eagerly tried to destroy me. The IRS subsequently seized my house, my car, my retirement account, and everything I needed to sustain life. The IRS has hounded me for 16 years. This year in 1996, the IRS seized my bank account, and tax payments I made. The IRS told me the seizures were for payments on the 1980 taxes that they say that I still owe. The IRS seized everything I owned making it almost impossible to cope and they are still harassing and intimidating me.

I'm not rich nor do I own anything worth

having. The IRS has really hurt me in a very serious way. I mean in the way that you hurt inside where the pain is so deep that all the tears stop flowing and all that remain is the moan! I remember on one occasion the IRS came on my job and thus caused me to lose my job. I have not been allowed to get credit, or live a comfortable life for 16 years. I am a Vietnam veteran and I have not been able to use my G.I. bill to buy a house because of what the IRS has done to me, my name, and my credit. The IRS has caused me and my wife to suffer great depressions in our marriage and the IRS has caused disharmony among me and my friends.

## IRS Abuse Report #97

**Date:** Thu May  2 16:06:48 1996
**To:** sue@irs.class-action.com
**From:** Anonymous
I just received a tax examination change report for 1993 and 1994 which bills me for $25,000 due to disallowing alimony I paid.  I didn't even get a chance to show my canceled checks, court order, etc. I was presumed guilty without the right to show proof.

## IRS Abuse Report #98

**Date:** Sat May 18  0:54:48 1996
**To:** sue@irs.class-action.com
**From:** T.M
We are being audited for 1993 and 1994 in spite of losses totaling $ 70,000.  We have already been billed for almost $ 6,000 plus penalties and interest.  They are also accusing us of hiding income due to $ 25,000 in loans from relatives.  All this has caused much stress and sleepless nights so far.

## IRS Abuse Report #99

**Date:** Sat May 18  9:31:27 1996
**To:** sue@irs.class-action.com
**From:** PB
I am being persecuted and harassed by the IRS -- have been for years because I am trying to stop their abuses which are the same tactics and methods used by gangsters, the Mafia, the Gestapo, Al Capone -- collect through fear.  I have written to Congressmen, the IRS Commissioner, the president, everyone I think could help and called for a Congressional Investigation into the abuses of the IRS and its collection methods.  Without exception, they passed the buck and in effect laughed at me.

I am a tax accountant for many years -- have seen abuses first hand in my family and clients. Now for the tenth or 11th time I am being audited -- have had a deficiency judgment issued against me and am in the process of filing a brief in the tax court.  This will do no good.  How can we get justice in the tax court when the judge him or herself is in the pay of the same entity we are fighting.  It is to their interest to find for the government for their paycheck is at issue.  We do not have the right to a jury trial guaranteed us by the Constitution. The IRS violates every constitutional right -- they are the Gestapo run rampant.  I expect to lose everything for there is no justice here and I will go to jail before I will pay a tax I do not owe.  In the audit and appeals court I provided every proof of my deductions they called for, answered every question -- yet they disallowed everything.

I am not against paying taxes and in the last two years I was audited, I paid over $10,000 in taxes willingly but the IRS is trying to collect $10,000 more and I am just a small wage earner -- very middle class.  Please enter me in this class action law suit.

## IRS Abuse Report #100

**Date:** Thu May 23 14:38:12 1996
**To:** sue@irs.class-action.com
**From:** BW
My mom works for the IRS. She has told me numerous stories of how the IRS has taken things from people and even put them in jail. One particular story really made me hate the IRS:

An elderly woman lost her husband in 92. She had never written a check or paid a bill in her life. Her home was completely paid for. Her family was helping her pay her bills. In 1994 the IRS seized her home and all of her worldly belongings for back taxes. She died two months later. Her family fought with the IRS for a whole year to find out why no one was notified of this seizure before it occurred and why the family had no idea what was going on. After 5 months of investigation the IRS has sent the family a letter stating their apologies for a miscalculation which in turn made it look like the elderly woman owed $1750 in back taxes when it should have read a $17.50 due to her. Because of their misrepresentation and false information the elderly woman died of a heart attack at her home the day it was sold. The IRS has gone too far...these people think they are the answer to GOD himself. They need to be stopped.

## IRS Abuse Report #101

**Date:** Fri June 7 1:42:57 1996
**To:** sue@irs.class-action.com
From CW
I owned a cleaning business as sole proprietor. Incorporated after first year. Neglected to vacate first employer ID number, so IRS decided that I have two identical businesses simultaneously and estimated my so-called unreported income for two years. After six years I ran out of money to fight them and had to pay $16000 for a business I never owned?

## IRS Abuse Report #102

**Date:** Sat June 8 12:26:54 1996
**To:** sue@irs.class-action.com
**From:** RB
My uncle made a mistake over a period of ten years concerning deductions that should have been extracted from his farm workers wages. After repeated threats to take everything he had, and put him in prison, he committed suicide leaving a wife and children to fend for themselves.

He was goaded into it by the IRS, the GESTAPO and STORM TROOPERS of the UNITED STATES OF AMERICA. I have since found out that the threat of prison was used falsely.

I personally believe my uncle killed himself because of the shame he thought he'd endure by going to prison. He was wrong. To go to prison because of the IRS is a RED BADGE of COURAGE! Down with the IRS. If you work for the IRS, never let your shadow darken my path!

## IRS Abuse Report #103

**Date:** Sat June 10 23:19:06 1996
**To:** sue@irs.class-action.com
**From:** LT
Consider the "people" who are working for the "IRS". What makes them so heartless, so eager to destroy and cause pain and loss to so many. I don't consider these beings human in any sense of the word except that they appear in human form.

## IRS Abuse Report #104

**Date:** Sat Jul 13 17:14:31 1996
**To:** sue@irs.class-action.com
**From:** Anon
What happened with myself and the IRS is unforgivable. For the first time in my life I

truly know the feeling of hatred for another.

If you ever want to be free, then realize that the IRS must be destroyed. Shame them, turn your backs to them, make them and their families hate to go out in public, make sure they feel unwanted, let them know they are not welcomed anywhere. Stand up and fight with anyone who will stand with you against these monsters.

Anyone that has ever had any contact with the IRS must wonder what type of people they are. Just patriots following orders? So were the guards in the concentration camps. How do they look at themselves in the mirror? They provide nothing to society but misery and despair. They can look at themselves because they enjoy the limitless ability to abuse power.

If there is evil in the US, it is the employees and judges of the IRS. Do their neighbors and family know were they work? If they don't, they should. We should all know their ID's. If we are successful and true freedom is restored to every citizen of the US, do we simply forgive these parasites? Do the former IRS elite simply to go out among us as if they had done nothing but follow orders? Why don't you post lists of these employees with pictures, names, and addresses so we all know who they are? I don't want my children playing with the children of parents who think nothing of stealing food from the mouths, along with the shirts off the backs, of other people.

If your neighbors son or daughter works for the IRS, shouldn't you know? You would want to know if a pedophile came to visit the neighborhood, wouldn't you? Send them statements that they are not welcome in the USA any longer. Post their pictures and their identity in their neighborhoods. Ostracize them and their families. Start making *them* miserable for a change. Force them out! Don't feel pity for them. No one forced them to work for the IRS. They did it willingly, all on their own. They are not good people. If they were, they would recognize the evil in what they do for a

living. If they had an ounce of decency in them, they would never have taken a job with the IRS. Don't hold your breath waiting for a politician to give up their greatest political tool just to end our suffering. Like the IRS agent, if the members of the congress and senate had an ounce of decency in them, their first priority would be to free us, repeal the 16th amendment, and brand the bastards working at the IRS as criminals, jail them and take away everything that they bought with the money they stole from us.

Until we stand together against them, they will continue to intimidate and harass us and we will never realize freedom. All future generations of children in the US will be born into slavery. Never to realize any form of hope, prosperity, or the right to privacy.

### IRS Abuse Report #106

**Date:** Wed, 31 Jul 1996 19:54:35 -0400
**To:** sue@irs.class-action.com
**From:** EB

They have got me running in circles. They have even attached my customers accounts and now my customers don't want to have any contact with me. My livelihood is going down the drain. If I owed them, why don't they at least offer some type of explanation, instead of just saying you have been assessed -- now pay-up or we'll take everything you own.

### IRS Abuse Report #107

**Date:** Fri, 09 Aug 1996 15:34:33 +0000
**To:** sue@irs.class-action.com
**From:** HE

The IRS audited me. My wife who was not employed at the time, is now our only means of support. Without notice, they levied her bank account and took our rent money. The IRS collection agent admits that they only want me and that my wife is not involved. But they refuse to release her money. Between the IRS and the FTB they say I owe over one million dollars. I have been unemployed for almost 3 years now. I don't even own a car anymore. The agent wants me to meet with her by the 15th of August. Is there anything I can do? I no longer have any money to have representation and I am scared...

### IRS Abuse Report #108

**Date:** Thu, 5 Sep 1996 13:32:49 -0400
**To:** sue@irs.class-action.com
**From:** TT
My fight with the IRS has been going on for over 10 years. Presently, I am in the appeals process for the rejection of an "Offer-in-Compromise" of $30,000. The IRS rejected the offer based on the reasoning that I could pay the amount in full, if I sold my home and all of my assets. This of course is true, but to lose everything I have, just to pay for massive interest and penalties on an original tax debt of approximately $18,000, is untenable at best. The debt has now grown to about $63,000. I will fight them until they physically come and separate me and my family from what we have spent 23 years building. Which I expect to happen one day.

### IRS Abuse Report #109

**Date:** Sat, 14 Sep 1996 07:17:30 -0700
**To:** sue@irs.class-action.com
**From:** fed up
I have been fighting the IRS for one thing or another for the last ten years. They have audited me over eight times and each time I have shown and or proven my deductions. But they still harass me. They now say I owe some $7000 for tax year 91. I have a lien on my house and they currently want $3000 for tax year 93. I am at my wits end with this group of losers. I have tried talking to them but they are out to destroy my life, family and my pursuit of happiness. I thought indentured servitude was against the law in this country? I

am about ready to say the hell with it, at this point I have nothing left to give and I am tired of working for this government. It's time to exercise our constitutional rights and take this government apart.

### IRS Abuse Report #110

**Date:** Wed, 18 Sep 1996 12:42:37 -0400
**To:** sue@irs.class-action.com
**From:** JB
The IRS has a lien on my house, I wish to sell my home, but can't because of this lien. In 1987, I got out of the family business. In 1990-91, the owner did not pay taxes, the business used my tax ID number, so the IRS filed the lien against me. There was no warning and no chance to explain. I have since showed them my tax returns and all other paper work showing that I was not involved in the business. All with no result. They have to collect from someone, so they are picking me. If you can help in any way please contact me!

### IRS Abuse Report #111

**Date:** Wed Sep 4 0:45:42 1996
**To:** sue@irs.class-action.com
**From:** anonymous
Impossible to tell this BRIEFLY, but have been fighting the IRS for more than ten years. It started with less than $4,000 they claimed we owed. There own figures show that we had a TAX CREDIT at the time! We said we didn't owe anything, and fought them. It is now up over $280,000.00 with NOTHING to prove we owe any taxes!

I served in Vietnam and got two purple hearts. I shed MY BLOOD for this country. The IRS took EVERY CENT of my retirement pay for THREE YEARS! We had to sell everything we owned just to live. This includes my wedding ring and our family pets. Our kids let us move into their cabin and then the IRS went after THAT. They sold our kids cabin and land at auction! We tried to apply for food stamps, but were told the money the IRS was stealing every month had to be counted as "income". We couldn't get food stamps because we had "too much income" -- and the IRS takes ALL of it! An agent came out to seize our old car, he saw two cars belonging to our kids, so he hauled them off too. We went and got them back and were slammed with criminal charges of "FORCIBLE RESCUE"!

After 4 months of expense...paid for by the government, the day of the trial they asked for the case to be dismissed! This dismissed case cost the taxpayers more than $75,000.00!

When we said we were going to write our congressman, the agent sneered and said "go ahead". They do not fear ANYONE. They will not SIGN anything! One little self-important twirp can RUIN your life without any evidence at all.

## IRS Abuse Report #112

**Date:** Tue Sep 10 21:52:03 1996
**To:** sue@irs.class-action.com
**From:** BM
After making over nine years of on-time payments to the IRS on an installment program, the IRS levied my wages without any warning. Their reasoning for this? They lost my installment agreement! The original debt was $25000. I have paid more than that amount and now the debt is $33000. I will never live to get this debt removed. Due to the liens, I have had no credit, cannot buy a home, cannot get loans for my children to go to college, I can't even live a normal life. I am not as well off as an indentured servant -- at least they could work their way free.

## IRS Abuse Report #113

**Date:** Tue Sep 10 23:10:50 1996
**To:** sue@irs.class-action.com
**From:** LB
The IRS raided a private and legal business at gun point. It took five years to decide whether to try the case in court (since no one would plead guilty). They confiscated thousands of dollars, 6 vehicles, 4 big-screen TV's, stock, equipment, and I can't remember what else. All books, records, receipts, etc. were seized, and five years later we were put on the witness stand to answer questions about things we hadn't seen for five years!

## IRS Abuse Report #114

**Date:** Thu Sep 12 12:17:43 1996
**To:** sue@irs.class-action.com
**From:** anonymous
My father-in-law is 72 years old. He has rental property, and the IRS grabbed a figure out of thin air as to what his income should be from that property versus what he actually received (and had documentation for). That doesn't matter to them. They had no documentation, no proof of any kind that he underpaid, yet, the burden of proving his own innocence falls on him!!! In other words, to the IRS, you're GUILTY until you can prove yourself innocent. That's outrageous, and contradicts everything the judicial system supposedly stands for!

## IRS Abuse Report #115

**Date:** Sun Sep 22 16:40:27 1996
**To:** sue@irs.class-action.com
**From:** JG
The IRS said I owe them $70,000 from ten years ago. Even with legal help, they will not leave me alone. I've lost jobs because of them, they've taken refunds I have been entitled to, and they've put my health at risk. I don't owe them anything!! I need help.

## IRS Abuse Report #116

**Date:** Sat Oct 5 2:15:55 1996
**To:** sue@irs.class-action.com
**From:** DL

A Mr. W.H. has a goal in life to reduce me to nothing. He actually threatened me by vowing to "...lien me to the fullest extent of the law".

Mr. W.H. levied my business checking account for $ 70,000.00. Yet, a letter from the IRS, sent to me the prior week asked for $ 69.37 -- for the same time period as Mr. W.H.'s levy. I have the canceled check proving payment of this levy amount. Because of this, and my phone call to his supervisor, Mr. W.H. was embarrassed and forced to apologize to me (although he did not apologize to my bank). His supervisor claimed that the Levy Notice was sent by a different department and Mr. W.H. had no knowledge of it. I replied, how could he know nothing about it, HIS SIGNATURE IS ON THE BOTTOM LEFT SIDE OF IT?

Since then, Mr. W.H. handed me warrants for my personal taxes for 1990, 1991, 1992, 1993, 1994, 1995 and allowed me 10 days to get material to him. He started asking about ownership of everything he saw. I sent his requested material on time via FEDERAL EXPRESS. When he contacted me again, he claimed to not receive the information. However, Federal Express was kind enough to provide proof of his signature. More egg on his face.

Next, I got 14 notices in 3 days informing me that the IRS has taken the liberty of changing my returns and now I owed them. A few years ago this happened and they informed me that I owed them $ 45,000.00 for 1991 alone, although my original return showed a refund of $ 13,500.00.

It seems the IRS decided I was "Married filing single" instead of "Married filing Jointly". They assigned all of the income to me and credited NONE OF THE TAX PAYMENTS to me. Therefore, according to them, I made all the money and paid NO taxes. It took 3 years to clear this up. They finally credited me for all the penalties and interest and credited me for the original $13,500. What a joke. I haven't seen any money yet. Now they say they are keeping the money because I owe taxes for 1992.

Well, low and behold, last week I had the pleasure of receiving 18 copies of Notices of Levy's to every financial institution in the State. Wow, I thought I must be important. I don't even know half of these banks. Unfortunately, the amount that I am told I now owe is $ 70,000.00. I have the canceled checks to prove payment of taxes, but I think I will have to go over Mr. WH's head
because he might get egg in his face again, and the next time he might come after me with a gun.

## IRS Abuse Report #117

**Date:** Sat Oct 5 23:50:48 1996
**To:** sue@irs.class-action.com
**From:** JR

The 1982 taxable year was held open by my signing of a waiver at the insistence of the IRS. Meanwhile, they turned my account over to their collection division and placed a $60,000 lien against my home. After a year, they acknowledged that they found my tax payment check. However, all effort to get the lien released or acknowledgment of payment has been met with no success. They continue to hound me for the alleged taxes. They contacted my employer and entered a lien against my wages. They contacted my life insurance carriers and placed a lien against the cash value of my policies. They finally contacted Merrill Lynch, where I had an Individual Retirement Account, and removed $37,000! There was no hearing, no due process -- they just took my retirement money.

In the meantime, my 10.5% mortgage could not be refinanced because of the lien. I have paid thousands of unnecessary dollars in home payments. Despite efforts by my accountant, I can not get the matter resolved. I lost my job, my home, and my wife filed for divorce on 5-5-96.

### IRS Abuse Report #118

**Date:** Sun Oct 6 13:00:52 1996
**To:** sue@irs.class-action.com
**From:** MA
Without any notice, my checking account was seized, leaving me penniless. I'm now two mortgage payments behind, and I am in constant worry about how soon my electricity will get cut off. I like so many others, can only feel that my productivity as a tax paying citizen has certainly been diminished. Suicide is not the answer. It's reading these other letters and knowing I'm not the only one being dealt a great injustice that makes me strong. Please keep the faith and God Bless.

### IRS Abuse Report #119

**Date:** Wed Oct 9 14:58:45 1996
**To:** sue@irs.class-action.com
**From:** anonymous
Thank you so much for giving people a place to vent, a place to share, a place to learn! We empathize with all of you who have described your own personal horror stories.

My husband and I have been battling the IRS for several years now. He had a severe downturn in his business, which kept us from paying self-employment taxes one year. We've never been able to catch up. And now the penalties and interest have grown so large, we'll go to our graves owing the government! Our home, our health, and our sanity are crumbling around us. Trying to raise a child in this nightmare is horrific! Our bank accounts were wiped out, we were forced to file a Chapter 7

bankruptcy, and still the IRS keeps trying to get blood out of this turnip! We would love to pay the taxes we owe, but the penalties and interest prohibit that, and they are grossly unfair. The IRS is destroying businesses, families, lives. It's time for it to end.

### IRS Abuse Report #120

**Date:** Tue, 25 Jun 1996 00:30:45 -0800
**To:** sue@irs.class-action.com
**From:** KT
My husband and I have been on a payment plan since 1991. Our original debt to the IRS was just over $15,000. To date we have paid over $16,000, and because of interest and penalties, the IRS says we still owe another $16,000. We are almost 50, we cannot own a home, have no disposable income, and most heartbreaking, we can really do nothing to help our children and grandchild. My husband works an extra job to make the IRS payment, and I'm afraid he can't do it much longer. I don't want to end up a widow -- but no one at the IRS seems to care.

### IRS Abuse Report #122

**Date:** Mon, 06 May 1996 13:17:00
**To:** sue@irs.class-action.com
**From:** CC
I would like to reiterate that the IRS railroaded me, extorted thousands of dollars from me, hoodwinked me and seized my house, my car, my retirement account and everything that I need to sustain life.

I have documented evidence that the IRS has harassed me for 16 years, that the IRS fabricated documents and called it a deficiency.

Most people don't know the hurt and pain one endures at the hands of the IRS.

They don't know that the IRS is guilty of murder, extortion, bribery, organized crime, and destroying American families.

So, I say to you my friend--hold on, don't let go, the only hope we have is to reveal them to the world.

## IRS Abuse Report #123

**Date:** Mon, 28 Oct 1996 23:14:38 -0500
**To:** sue@irs.class-action.com
**From:** Anon
I am a firm believer that the IRS is the ultimate evil. How can I help in your quest to abolish this demon?

People that say they're tired of hearing about IRS abuses should know that such a statement would be like the judges at the Nuremberg Trials after WW II saying they're tired of hearing from concentration camp victims about the mistreatment they suffered at the hands of Gestapo thugs.

## IRS Abuse Report #124

**Date:** Sun Nov 10 8:24:40 1996
**To:** sue@irs.class-action.com
**From:** CS
My story starts like so many others, a Final Notice of IRS Action that I received 2 days before payday. When I called the local IRS for information, they gave me an appointment the following week. You can imagine the shock I received when I was notified by payroll that my check had been seized by the IRS. Further, my checking account had been levied.

My appointment with the IRS turned out to be the best meeting, to date, of any that I have had with them. The Agent was understanding and considerate. She worked with me and made arrangements to make payments on my debt of $19,000 for three years of back taxes.

Unfortunately, the story does not end there. Four years later, after paying $500/mo, I get another attachment. It seems that IRS Collection Agent PJ had taken over my file. One day, out of the blue, my banker calls to inform me that my checking account and savings account had just been levied. I called my employer's payroll dept. and was advised that my paycheck had also been levied.

Later that afternoon, PJ made contact by serving me with a Final Notice of Collection - after the levies had been made. She advised me that I now owed $56,000 and requested that I give her a check in that amount. I asked her how I was going to do that as she had just levied my accounts. Besides, she knew I didn't have that amount of money.

At this point, PJ seemed a little upset that I knew that she had made the levies...surprised might be a better term. Anyway, PJ informed me that if she didn't have a payment-in-full by close-of-business, this day, she would have a moving company in front of my house in the morning to impound my personal property for sale at auction to satisfy the debt.

Now let me explain what this debt consisted of: I had a business in 1979 through 1981 and had a CPA Tax Accountant looking after my books and insuring that my taxes were paid. Unfortunately, my accountant turned out to be a criminal that took off with three years of my taxes. The IRS is about three years behind in auditing so I didn't get a notice of anything wrong until the Spring of '82. I tried to contact my accountant but received a "disconnect" on his phone number.

Well, to make a long story short, I was contacted by the State Attorney General's office advising that some of my records had been found in a burn barrel on the ranch of my accountant and would I testify against him when they found him (which ended up to be in 1992).

I filed bankruptcy in 1991, the next day from when PJ announced her intentions. My attorney advised that my Chapter 13 filing would end this episode of my life. Little did he know that the problems were just starting.

In May, 1996, the bankruptcy was over and I was just starting to take easier breaths when I received a notice from the IRS that I still owed for my back taxes. The amount is now $186,000 on a $19,000 debt.

My attorney says that they have violated a Federal Court Order of adjudication. Somehow, I don't think the IRS is concerned with a little thing like a Court Order.

This has all led **To:**
10 years of aggravation, great stress,
12 years of marriage down the tubes
Sold a house at considerable loss
Had to move out of the area because of
   neighbors
My reputation has been greatly damaged
My credit is nill, had to file bankruptcy

### IRS Abuse Report #125

**Date:**  Wed Nov 13 19:21:57 1996
**To:** sue@irs.class-action.com
**From:** DD
The IRS has turned my life into a living hell since 1988, and I am so tired I don't know how I'm going to continue to stand up for my rights. I made errors on my tax returns in 86 and 87, which were discovered in an audit. I've been through a criminal investigation which destroyed my business, frightened me and my family and friends ("surprise" visits from G-men), and almost drove me to suicide. My husband was fighting cancer while this was going on, and when the IRS decided to try to prosecute me, I was broke and had a public defender, who advised me to accept a plea bargain (presented to me with less than 24 hours to decide) and plead guilty to a misdemeanor and pay a $25 fine, plus taxes and penalties, totaling $23,000. That was in 93 and I know now what a horrible mistake it was not to stand up for my innocence in court.

I paid it all off, and thought it was over. Now, 3 years later, they are back with a civil fraud charge, looking for $100,000 plus in additional penalties, penalties on top of penalties, and tons of interest dating back to 86. I've had  2 lawyers who ripped me off for big fees and did nothing. I have to find a good lawyer very soon, but am terrified of making another mistake, running out of money, and becoming totally paranoid about the IRS and their completely unchecked power and sick sadistic tactics.  Today, I understand I made errors on my return because I have a severe math anxiety, and have taken steps to get help with my tax records and filings.  But I've been told this defense will be laughed at in tax court, and that I don't stand a chance. Sometimes I just want to die.

### IRS Abuse Report #126

**Date:**  Sat Nov 16 16:02:26 1996
**To:** sue@irs.class-action.com
**From:** KM
Husband passed away, was only married for 8 months, he owed a large sum, and I have to give up my house, car, etc. I should not have to give  up anything because it was not my debt!! The  house is in his name and they are putting me out  on the streets because they said that I am  responsible for him not taking his responsibility.

### IRS Abuse Report #127

**Date:**  Tue Nov 19 14:26:42 1996
**To:** sue@irs.class-action.com
**From:** LP
The IRS has almost held me captive since 1984. Today is 1996. I have lost everything, have been unable to ever pursue real employment because every time I do, the IRS wants more information. Their vindictive audit of my life has caused such unspeakable financial damage I will never recover from it. They must be stopped. I was chosen' to be the First American to enter  into the 'new' process of Mediation with the IRS. It is a horror story of

incompetence run amuck. If I can help in some way, to further your project, I will try.

## IRS Abuse Report #128

**Date:** Fri Dec 6 9:47:30 1996
**To:** sue@irs.class-action.com
**From:** MD
Lets go get them!

A Client of mine failed to file and pay his taxes on April 15,1995. May of 1996 his taxes were finished by the accountant. He owed $32,000 for the year 1994. We obtained a payoff from the IRS for these taxes that were owed. The payoff amount was $54,584.00

Now, to calculate this to determine the interest paid on the this amount owed the factors are:

Taxes due April 15, 1995 and paid off May 1996 would be considered by a bank a 13 month loan. Borrowing $32,000 for a period of 13 months and paying back $54,000 the remaining unknown factor is what interest rate did he pay. The interest rate he paid was 77% interest rate.

## IRS Abuse Report #129

**Date:** Sat Dec 7 12:49:12 1996
**To:** sue@irs.class-action.com
**From:** LS
I have litigated extensively against the IRS, providing documented evidence of fraud, document falsification and perjury on the part of the IRS and D.O.J. The judges don't want to hear it because they have a vested interest in supporting the IRS. My story will curl your hair and I would be pleased to continue fighting and assisting with my experience - but I think we should understand what we are up against and keep our hopes in perspective. Life goes on and so does the IRS with their bodyguards - the judges.

I became a target to the IRS when I went on TV to expose IRS corruption. I had a $17,000.00 debt to the IRS for a capital gain tax which I self reported when I "bought down" instead of choosing bankruptcy. Incidentally, new 1996 legislation has remedied this ridiculous tax. I challenged the tax as illegal, (with supporting documentation), unfair, etc. but lost. The IRS began garnishing my ex husband for the tax. I became very politically vocal in criticizing the IRS, exposing corruption, learning the tax laws and assisting others to fight for the meager rights they have under the code.

To punish me, the IRS scheduled a sale of my home, at the same time they garnished my ex. I told them that they couldn't sell the principal residence - especially since the debt was being satisfied through wage garnishment. I also pointed out that they violated the noticing requirements by not giving me the 40 days to secure financing prior to sale. They ignored me and held the sale - selling my $250,000.00 house with $140.000.00 equity for the debt. I did not despair because I figured the sale would be deemed illegal when I did the inevitable action to quiet title, whereby I would prove that the noticing requirements were violated, the garnishment was in place, the house was exempt, etc. At the quiet title hearing, the special judge assigned to the proceedings scheduled two hearings. The first was an eviction hearing, the second - two months later was a trial to present evidence to challenge the title illegally conveyed to the investor. At the first hearing, I pointed out that eviction COULDN'T take place until AFTER the trial. The judge simply denied my objection and signed an eviction order - violating the automatic stay and denying me my motion to post bond pending appeal. They got armed deputies to evict me.

At the trial - two months later - I had an IRS expert to testify why the sale of the house was illegal. The judge dismissed my witness saying that since I was already evicted - the trial was moot. And yes, this is all in a certified transcript. They converted my equity to the investor leaving me destitute and homeless. I brought charges against the judge - the A.G. wasn't interested - I did a Quo Warranto and took it all the way to the W.D.C. Supreme Court. They denied it - saying my remedy is appeal. I brought an unlawful collection action in federal court - they said "dismissed" - the state court has discretion to decide federal violations and the state court did not find any (notwithstanding there was no trial!) The funniest part of the whole story is that people are being evicted from their homes with IRS Director's Deeds - which are obtained through IRS sales not judicial sales - even though the law says a JUDICIAL procedure is imperative for due process. The judges ignore this fact. I am before the State Court of Appeals showing that an IRS sale CANNOT convey property rights - if the law is to be followed - and that everyone who has been evicted after an IRS sale has been illegally evicted if a foreclosure action wasn't done first. IRS never does proper state foreclosure actions. Anyway - I know of four other horror stories....but I think I've taken up enough space for now.

## IRS Abuse Report #130

**Date:** Sun Dec 8 0:34:41 1996
**To:** sue@irs.class-action.com
**From:** DC

If I can support the class action suite or contribute in any way, please let me know. I could write for pages and pages. My life, my livelihood, my marriage, my children's education, my lost half million dollar home, my levied bank accounts start to tell the story. You can add Chapter 13 and 7 bankruptcies, and a destroyed two million dollar business that employed up to 20 professionals that I built from nothing.

This business was destroyed because the IRS levied my bank accounts for over $40,000.00 without notice for taxes that I had paid in full less than three months before. An error by an agent that I would not consider hiring for the most basic tasks in my company. I honestly think she was jealous of my success. And after this... all their liability is to reimburse the bounced check fees IF I FILLED OUT THE PROPER FORMS! This caused PhDs and technical staff to leave for other jobs, with my clients in hand. If any other entity had done this I could have sued and easily been awarded multiple millions in damages. But you can't sue the IRS for enough to pay for the case! And guess who runs the tax court????! There is no accountability. No consistent line of communication. No way out once you are in their claws. I know the horror and the impossibility of dealing with the IRS. Now they are after my wages.... So I have been fired from a decent job. Now I am the criminal! I was a strong, law abiding, tax paying citizen creating jobs and economic growth. Now I am a cynical, beaten down, rapidly aging 42 year old, with estranged wife and children. These are the things that I thought nothing could take away. Not even the IRS. I was wrong......There is no winning, no breaking even and no settling the matter. IRS agents advance their careers by destroying citizens. It does not matter if the citizen is Right or Wrong. It is just how many brownie points the agent gets to advance up the ladder. No not even getting a congressman involved really helps. You just become a favorite target. There is no way to catch up with the exorbitant, useross interest and penalties..... so why try?

Then after all of this the accountants and attorneys and congressmen are all afraid to attack the IRS for fear that they will be next. It must stop. If I have to walk to Washington to testify, Count me in.

## IRS Abuse Report #131

**Date:** Mon Dec 9 1:21:30 1996
**To:** sue@irs.class-action.com
**From:** MJS

I am stating here and now to use any of this information I am giving you in any way you see fit to fight against the enemy! Use at will with no hesitation.

In 1982, when I was a sophomore in high school, my parents took out a second mortgage on their house to assist them in starting a audio/video business for me to eventually take over. In more recent years we got audited for not making enough money. Because the auditor was not familiar with the audio industry, she wanted to see everything, as if we needed to take her through business school 101 for the audio industry. In approx. October 1993 my dad and I had to show up for this audit. After insisting that they needed more documents that we had not brought to the meeting, they said they would send us a list of required documents within two weeks, without which they could not possibly finish the audit. Five months later, without ever sending us the list of required documents, they sent a revised assessment, showing how we no longer owed them the $86K of disallowed expenses, but just $35k, what a deal -- I'll go get my check book and take them up on that offer before they change their minds.

They proceeded to charge us interest on the five months, while we were waiting for them to get us this list of required docs. Obviously, they make stuff up to suit their wishes or "creativity". This idiot auditor had, in the more recent assessment, given the entire company to me, without any contract or anything, because I signed more checks then my parents. My parents and I had always been operating under the bizarre general thought that because they funded the venture in the beginning, they would remain the owners until I might, in the future, buy it from them. By the auditor "giving" the audio company to me, she gave my parents a

$86K tax liability and me an $181K liability for the total income of the business for 1990. So, we hired a well recommended attorney, a former IRS agent, as we thought we would have an advantage getting someone who had been on the inside. After 13 months, he has managed to take $3k from us, totally ignore my dads portion of the case, and take me into the lions den, the "tax court", delivering me up to the vipers for strangulation. Though we just fired him, he intended to get paid another $3k to get me into "court" and another $3k to get me out and briefed. Of course, no promises that we would win or that he could minimize my penalty.

The IRS is a loose cannon on a deck of the titanic, heading for deep water. We must all fight to kill them asap. We are all allowed to legally audio record all of our meetings and phone calls with them, they will say crap like "there will be no recording here today" or "there will be none of that", you can quote them regs, not statues. Regs are enforcing empowering rules that allow enforcement. They usually quote statues or "code" as scare tactics, for the average person, who knows nothing of codes and regs its pretty intimidating, but you can fight, you must. You must hold them accountable for their actions. We are taking this to the end, or the top-which ever comes first-with help from all of you, together we can kill the whole mess!!! Stay alive and well, don't get off track and focus on the regulations-hold them accountable.

## IRS Abuse Report #132

**Date:** Mon Dec 9 23:48:37 1996
**To:** sue@irs.class-action.com
**From:** SS

My SO (significant other) had been a nonfiler, even though we are not and never have been married the IRS has attached my checking account twice... I do have a letter from them stating I'm an innocent victim...but how do you explain how my SO and my 8 year old daughter can live on a take home of $150.00 per month...From May until September that is what they had to live on. I feel I am a responsible parent so unfortunately, my credit has been shot to crap since I had to make sure we had a roof over our heads...

My SO has filed bankruptcy to get them off his back.

This is just the tip of the iceberg for what the IRS has put my family through... They have come very close to ruining a family.

How can the IRS agents live with themselves for what they do to people...

I've read all the abuse reports and it just amazes me how they can get away with it...

If more people stood up to them and weren't so paranoid against them, we could put a stop to their inhumane ways....

### IRS Abuse Report #133

**Date:** Thu Dec 19 17:20:08 1996
**To:** sue@irs.class-action.com
**From:** CV
If at all possible I would like to see every IRS agent, Director or any or all of the higher officials  PROSECUTED TO THE FULL EXTENT OF THE LAW !! Using only Objective law and fully integrated honesty. Subjective laws shall be considered as an atrocious evil crime against all citizenry.

### IRS Abuse Report #134

**Date:** Fri Dec 20 12:09:41 1996
**To:** sue@irs.class-action.com
**From:** JD
A 1979 TAX SHELTER THAT THE IRS DIS ALLOWED. WE LOST IN COURT AND THEY HAVE IMPOSED TAX WITH INTEREST AND PENALTY IN THE AMOUNT OF $561,000 THE AMOUNT OF THE

SHELTER WAS $94,000.

EITHER I SELL EVERYTHING AND PAY OR THEY WILL TAKE EVERYTHING I HAVE SPENT ALL MY LIFE WORKING FOR . I AM ON SOCIAL SECURITY NOW AND THIS WOULD WIPE ME OUT. I AM A PROUD FATHER OF 5 AND I THINK THIS IS VERY UNFAIR AND I DON'T KNOW IF THERE IS ANY GROUP THAT HAS BEEN STUNG BY THE IRS IN THE SAME WAY AND IF THERE IS SOMETHING THAT I DON'T KNOW ABOUT THAT COULD HELP ME . OR IF THERE IS A GROUP THAT I COULD JOIN IN A FIGHT WITH ?

### IRS Abuse Report #135

**Date:** Sun Dec 22 20:43:21 1996
**To:** sue@irs.class-action.com
**From:** TL
I am a retired Air Force Master Sergeant currently  working and paying taxes as a teacher and service engineer and the IRS has got to be stopped NOW!!!!

In the middle 1980's I decided to start my own business.  I knew a lot about this business but not a lot about being in business.  I had no idea that I had a silent business partner-THE IRS.

To make a long story short, I've ended up owing them 32K with not much ability to pay. The IRS has harassed me by liens, garnishments, levies, checking and savings accounts swept clean.  I will never be able to repay these taxes because of the interest and penalties.

### IRS Abuse Report #136

**Date:** Tue Dec 24  2:17:06 1996
**To:** sue@irs.class-action.com
**From:** GV
There was a law passed which was supposed to have stopped random auditing.  Because of this

law, some 300 to 400 IRS employees from the Omaha, NE. and Council Bluffs area have either been terminated (Amen) or a few had been given the option to move to Milwaukee, WI. Back in 1993, I was audited on my "in home business - schedule c, for the years 1990, 1991, and 1992. After much hassling and proving over again that my schedule C was correct for 1990, 1991, and 1992, I thought that I was finally rid of their harassment.

Oh sure, guess what? I received correspondence in Feb of 1996 that I was being audited for 1994 on my schedule c for my in home business. I was to report to the Council Bluffs, IA. office in Feb., however, I explained to the agent that I was extremely busy during tax time until Apr 15th, and could we move the date to some time after that. He gave me until Mar 28th over a phone conversation. To top it off, he asked me to bring along my 1993 tax return also. Now, if I remember the tax code and laws passed by congress about "NO MORE RANDOM AUDITS AND NO MORE AUDITS ON THE SAME ITEM FOR MORE THAN 3 YEARS IN A ROW!" Well, I asked the agent if he could send me his request in the mail. Sure enough, on the original request dated Feb, the agent added his request for me to bring my 1993 tax return, so that he could audit both 1993 and 1994.

NOW, this should be evidence enough that they are auditing me for more than 3 years in a row on the same item, WHICH IS A "VIOLATION OF THE BILL PASSED BY CONGRESS IN THE NO HARASSMENT LAW." I went to my audit and the auditor said that he wouldn't allow this and that as a deduction. He had the very same PARSONS TECH TAX CD ROM KIT that I used, however, he didn't know how to use it. So, he did it by hand and said that he would get back to me with what he thought was what I would owe in back taxes and interest. When I received his statement a few months later, he had several transposition errors and he had also used some wrong numbers that he was supposed to have received from my

local court house. He was wrong on some of those figures, and I responded to him by mail. He never replied, and I responded again. I still hadn't received any correspondence from him. Now he is no longer working for the IRS because of cutbacks (I guess).

Just now, the later part of November, I receive another correspondence from an IRS agent in Milwaukee, WI. saying that I have 90 days to pay up even more money or else the IRS will take action to collect by whatever means. I so damn mad now, because I have to go through this crap all over again with someone, hundreds of miles away, who doesn't know squat about this whole situation. And the IRS is actually the one breaking the law, by auditing me more than the allowed 3 years on the same item, by requesting what now turns out to be a 5 year in a row audit on the same item. Just where the H___ is justice? I am at my wits end and they are approaching a $5000 figure amount that they say I still owe them. What, what...does someone at the IRS need new golf clubs? Do they know the new law that says that a taxpayer cannot be audited for more than 3 years in a row on the same item? Who hires these kind of people? Larry, Curly, and Moe?

### IRS Abuse Report #137

**Date:** Fri Dec 27 11:40:32 1996
**To:** sue@irs.class-action.com
**From:** GP

My husband and I recently settled a 7-year battle with the IRS with an Offer-In-Compromise. We had to refinance our home and are now having problems making our monthly payments to our creditors. The IRS lost my husband's files for over 2 years after we moved from Texas to Tennessee. I have written my US legislators and even the White House trying to seek governmental intervention. We retained a tax attorney that worked on our case pro bono because he felt we had been repeatedly screwed by the IRS. My husband's wages were levied in February 1995 without written notice from the IRS. Our bank account was seized in November 1995 without written notice. Our attorney (who had Power of Attorney) never received notification either. I feel the IRS should have written our liability off due to their blatant ignorance and mishandling of our files for 7 LONG years. The Offer in Compromise was drawn out over 2 years -- IRS regulations changed and new forms had to be completed again and again. I think we submitted this information to the IRS 3 or 4 times before it was finally settled. The IRS took 7 years of our lives, created hardship financially, created emotional devastation, and we still had to pay through the nose to resolve the problems the IRS kept having with our files. I can't begin to describe the agony my husband and I have gone through. He has been hospitalized several times because of stress. I have hundreds of pages of documentation that an attorney thought was good enough to take our case, but the IRS will do what the IRS wants, when they want, and how they want. They make rules as they go. PLEASE HELP abolish this farce of a governmental agency called the IRS.

## IRS Abuse Report #138

**Date:** Sat Dec 28  1:25:01 1996
**To:** sue@irs.class-action.com
**From:** JP
I was hired and worked as an IRS Agent in the Jacksonville (FL) District. My work was fine until I helped a taxpayer get a previously closed case reopened due to the sloppiness of a Collections Officer. I also discovered a refund amount due her that was nearly barred by the statute of limitations (her tax accountant had failed to file her claim for refund). The combined amount she was refunded should have been around $30,000. After I closed this case, I was belittled, chastised, and hassled by the group manager and the branch chief. I resigned.

The lip-service about taxpayer rights is a source of great mirth in the bowels of an IRS post-of-duty.

## IRS Abuse Report #139

**Date:** Sat, 28 Dec 1996 23:05:46
**To:** sue@irs.class-action.com
**From:** RS
The following is in reference to my parents:
People With Homelessness

Paul S. is a 77 year old man. He has had a heart attack and has had heart surgery (angioplasty twice). He has had a stroke. He has a pre-diabetic condition and circulatory problems in his legs and feet. He has trouble walking and talking. He is married to Florence, his wife of 55 years. Florence is 78 years old. She has osteoarthritis, high blood pressure, and a hearing impairment. She has a broken rib. The IRS says Paul and Florence owe $62,203 in taxes for 1973-1980, $32,949 in penalties for 1973-1980, and $$286,362 in interest for 1973-1980. The IRS says they owe $264,000 in taxes, penalties, and interest for 1981-1988. For a total of $596,514. Plus compound interest for 1995 and 1996. The IRS is currently seizing Paul's entire ERISA pension by a continuous levy for the past year and a half. The amount so seized does not even pay the accumulating compound interest, or reduce Paul's tax liability. The IRS has filed suit in federal court to seize Paul and Florence's home of 33 years. The Taxpayer's Bill of Rights section of the IRS code (passed by Congress in 1988) provides that a taxpayer's home is exempt from seizure, except as authorized by the District Director or the Assistant District Director. The Chicago District Director of the IRS has authorized the seizure of Paul and Florence's home. Their home has been appraised at $95,000. Net proceeds from seizure and sale of their home would not be sufficient to pay the interest, nor extinguish the penalties, nor extinguish the tax. After seizure and sale of their home, Paul and Florence would be homeless and destitute.

## IRS Abuse Report #140

**Date:** Wed Jan  1 12:22:44 1997
**To:** sue@irs.class-action.com
**From:** LF

By missing 2 quarterly payments of under $3,000, The IRS filed liens on the property where I had my business. With the excessive penalty's and interest the less than $6,000 tax bill turned into over $20,000. One day an IRS agent came to my business and told me that if I didn't give him a check for $5,000 tomorrow he would come and padlock the door so I wouldn't be allowed in the building. So in order not to be shut down I had to take the money from deposits of jobs that had orders for. This eventually left me with no money to do these jobs, therefore I had to shut down my business and have a sheriff sale to repay the people whose money I had used to pay the IRS. I am now out of business, with no equipment and still owe the IRS around $20,000 after years of payments.

## IRS Abuse Report #141

**Date:** Wed Jan  1 19:27:39 1997
**To:** sue@irs.class-action.com
**From:** KF

As a successful entrepreneur in a technical field, I used to earn over $100,000 in compensation for labor while providing highly technical services which I estimated generated from 10 to 20 new jobs a year. My clients went from little shops of under 10 to international concerns with hundreds of workers; a growth to which I was proud to be a major contributor. The IRS is now on the attack and have fraudulently liened my home while arrogantly ignoring my correspondence over the last five years. The people in my Congressman's office speak with pride how the IRS is 'above the law'. At present, I figure it is of no value to be a wealth/ job producer if my fruits are to be stolen in direct violation of the Constitution and decisions of the Supreme Court. Some of my associates have quietly reduced or terminated their businesses, moved their fruits and sometimes families to places providing greater liberty, or have reduced their expenses to live moderately on early retirement. Over 3/4 this countries productive effort is now consumed by the IRS scam. That is a lot of lost 'quality of life' for all. Look at my case, over $100,000 and 10-20 jobs per year are now lost. And I use to buy a lot of products and services!

## IRS Abuse Report #142

**Date:** Thu Jan  2 22:24:03 1997
**To:** sue@irs.class-action.com
**From:** AT

THIS SITE NEEDS GREATER EXPOSURE TO THE PUBLIC EYE, THEN WOULD GET MORE SUPPORT. In 1984 the computer where my (ex)wife was employed 'hiccuped', reporting a second 1099 and a second stock dividend payout, each with the decimal place moved to the RIGHT 2 decimal places, appearing as a total of around $16,000 additional income. I was totally unaware of this situation until two years later when the IRS sent a letter stating the basic financial 'oversight' on my part and of course adding P & I onto those increased tax figures. As my wife was now estranged and non-locatable, of course I became the chicken to pluck. To make a long story short, I have been going through financial hell since then (I lost my due to levies, lost my house and am currently so stressed if I have a heart attack in the near future it will be because of the IRS. I have tried to deal with these things called IRS agents. It is impossible. It is time for the American people to stand up and fight while we're still allowed to bear arms against this Gestapo dept. Thinking I would get resolve through a so-called tax lawyer, I contracted with him only to learn he is a 'former'? IRS agent who simply assisted me in filling out forms and then sent them off to his IRS buddies. I think a flat sales tax with out the IRS would work better than what we got. When will this wanton oppression be stopped? Where is help?

## IRS Abuse Report #143

**Date:** Tue Jan  7  9:27:07 1997
**To:** sue@irs.class-action.com
**From:** PA

We are presently in a negotiation process with the IRS and we feel that we have no control over the IRS official that we deal with.  He is unprofessional, disrespectful and nasty.  I can not see how we will be treated fair in anyway and we expect the worst. Thanks, a struggling small business.

## IRS Abuse Report #144

**Date:** Sun Jan 12 15:34:13 1997
**To:** sue@irs.class-action.com
**From:** RA

Reading the abuse reports made me realize I'm not alone.  I know now that my life is truly ruined I have no future.  January 9, 1997 after several months and a notice of intent to levy, 2 IRS agents came to my house and gave me a deadline of 3:00 p.m. Jan. 10th to pay back payroll taxes.  They left signed paperwork that plainly stated we had until 3:00 p.m. Friday. We had assured the agents that the funds were in place and offered to let them speak to the attorney to confirm, they declined. At 10:45 a.m. Friday Jan. 10th 6 agents showed up at my business and told my employee and customers that the business was being seized.  I spoke to the IRS supervisor who was on our property and asked him why IRS was taking this action, when I had made arrangements the day before to be at IRS offices at 3:00. The supervisor, DQ, told me that when his agents got back to the office he decided that the agreement wasn't to his satisfaction and he made the decision to seize the property Friday morning.  I asked why no one told me about the change, DQ said WE DON'T HAVE TO CALL YOU.  I said I could get the funds and be there in about an hour, since IRS was demanding certified funds I asked for releases, which DQ said they had. What a lie.

These people threatened my employee if she didn't answer their questions, I mean really scared her, they asked about her where she banked told her that I had refused to talk to them, a lie I had never spoken to this man. When I arrived with the funds, I asked for the releases again, this time they said they did not have them I said then let's go to your offices with this check and finish our business.   The agent told me that I either hand over the check right then and quit asking about releases or they would seize the property regardless of the check.   I point blank asked one agent, CB, if she would type the releases when she got back to the office and she told me that yes, she was going back to the office that afternoon and she would do the releases and she asked me for the bank's fax number.   She lied, my accounts are frozen and come Monday morning I'm probably out of business.  I've been called 'fair game', stupid, a liar.  My property was damaged, my credit ruined, everything we've worked for is gone.  I paid the tax. After reading other horror stories, I know in my heart that no one will help us.  I e-mailed every senator and house member, not just the people from my state, and I begged for help and hope for at the least one response, but as of now no one has.  How can this government allow the IRS to completely destroy a family.  It does not make sense to me to take a persons livelihood thereby guaranteeing that the taxes the IRS claims you owe will never be paid.

These people want to sell my inventory, which is less than  $2,000.00 retail, for whatever they can get and then come to me personally for the balance.   We were never sent a notice by certified mail, which I believe IRS is supposed to do.  Our bank accounts are frozen, since I paid the tax this means the IRS has levied for more money that is owed, that is illegal as well I believe.  The screaming, name calling and intimidation are unbearable.  All this heartache from our government not a foreign power but our own UNITED STATES GOVERNMENT. Our dreams are shattered, our lives destroyed. My heart goes out to all the people who shared their stories on this service, I cried for you, I cried for myself.

## IRS Abuse Report #145

**Date:** Thu, 16 Jan 1997
**To:** sue@irs.class-action.com
**From:** CA

I don't know if you saw a senate/congressional hearing about the IRS that was broadcast on C-Span a few months ago. In it congressmen told horror stories of how people in their districts ended up committing suicide after the IRS ruined their finances for no reason. They also mentioned about how the IRS code, which as Jack Kemp noted is 83 years old or something like that, is so many millions of words and pages long that it would take 2 1/2 years of full-time reading just to go through it once! As a result, every agent has their own idea as to what the code actually means and how it is interpreted.

The IRS employs 5X as many people as the FBI, 3X as many as the CIA - more people than the military! It is definitely an out of control KGB like operation, unjustly shutting people down and seizing their property. I'm glad you are fighting them -- they are truly evil and can not even balance their own books year to year! Good luck with the lawsuit!

## IRS Abuse Report #146

**Date:** Fri Jan 17 11:57:13 1997
**To:** sue@irs.class-action.com
**From:** JS

After operating a profitable business for four years, the IRS decided that I could not take a full deduction for a piece of equipment I had purchased, but instead must amortize the expense over a 3 year period. The fifth year, due to the amortization, the business showed a loss.

Apparently, an agent at the Van Nuys IRS office decided that, while I had been a business for the first four years, for the fifth year I was not a business, but a hobby! I had made a gross income that year of about $35,000, and had deductions totaling $25,000, which included my home mortgage and medical expenses.

The agent decided to disallow all of the expenses. But instead of just disallowing them, he took the $25,000 from the schedule C, and added it to my gross income of $35,000, so that now in a year that I made $35,000 I owed taxes on $60,000. Then, in order to make sure that I could not appeal (Bear in mind that the IRS did all of this without contacting me), since you only have 30 days since the first notice is mailed, they mailed my first, second and third (and final) notice to a place I had not worked in over 10 years. Then, after waiting a year for the penalties and interest to accrue to nearly $20,000, they seized my home and everything I owned except for the truck I was driving and the clothes on my back. I contacted several attorneys before I could find one that would work on credit, since my checking and savings accounts had been cleaned out simultaneously with the seizure of my home. IT took the agent nearly 6 months to get the IRS to even tell me why I owed the taxes. When he finally got a copy of the tax return that the agent had modified, he could not believe what they had done. He said we had a good case, and that I should have my house back in short order. Then the IRS explained to him that if he didn't drop the case, every one of his other clients would be subjected to 'strenuous' audits. I now had no attorney, and was out the $5,000 I had borrowed from my father to keep him on the case for the 6 months. I ended up living in my truck in a parking lot for a year, while the IRS held my house and everything I owned.

They even denied me access to my safe deposit box, which held my passport, birth certificate and adoption papers, and my social security card. Because I could not even prove I was a citizen of this country, I could find only the most menial of jobs. After fighting with the

IRS for over a year about the way they had wrongfully altered my tax return, they agreed that, yes, I really didn't owe them the money, but since it was in the computer the only way to straighten it out was for me to pay them the money that I was wrongfully charged, then re-file my tax return the way it was before it was changed by their agent. They would then re-audit me and return the moneys due me. My dad helped me finally get the $20,000 together to buy back my house from them, by co-signing on a loan at a very high interest, with the house as collateral. When I finally was given permission by the IRS to re-enter my own home, I drove to Simi Valley to see it for the first time since I had been denied access, almost exactly a year earlier. As I walked up to the front of the house, past the overgrown front yard, I noticed that the front door was missing. Not open, missing. I took one look inside the house, just about threw up, and went next door to phone the police. They spent over 4 hours writing their report on the damage to the house, and taking photographs. There was approximately 3 inches of water on the floor in most of the rooms, and every thing I owned that had not been stolen was now in that water. All of my clothes, and my book collection of 40 years, which included a family bible that pre-dated our country's Independence Day. A few days later, I got a call from the IRS, stating that I had to drive into downtown Los Angeles to sign some papers to get title to my house returned to me.

When I got there, they had a legal-size green form, stating that they were returning my house to me in the same condition as when they took it. I tried very hard to control my anger while I explained to the lady that not only wasn't it in the same condition, but there was thousands of dollars worth of damage. She said they would have to send an investigator out. I told her I'd make it easy for them, and not replace the front door until after I heard from them. A week later I got the form in the mail. Where they had wanted me to sign it, there was now an official stamp: 'TAXPAYER NOT AVAILABLE FOR SIGNATURE. CASE CLOSED'. I contacted the IRS to find out when they would audit me, so I could recover some of my losses. I was informed that THEY decide who get audited, and when. Needless to say, I didn't make the list. It cost me over $65,000 to repair the damage, which included replacement of several walls, wall heaters, and most everything that came within 6' of the floor. Everything that was in the house when I finally got it back had to be thrown away. Things that I and my ancestors had spent lifetimes preserving, all went into 3 roll-off dumpsters. Even with this expenditure (for which I have every receipt), I still had to sell my home as a distressed house, since I couldn't make the payments long enough to finish the necessary repairs.

It sold for about $20,000 less than the value of the homes on either side. Now, as if to add insult to injury, the IRS has decided that I can't deduct the expense of repairing their damages, I can't deduct the 50% of the selling price that I had to give my ex-wife, and I can't deduct the damage done to my personal property. The net result is that, on a house I bought for $22,000, held for 10 years and sold for $117,000, I have now been forced to pay the IRS for 'Capital Gains'. Owning my own home in this country has cost me over $200,000, and forced me to live on the street for a year  Now I am living on a small boat, which is all that I can afford, since I am now making payments on $48,000 worth of credit card bill run up repairing the house and paying the IRS their blood money. The bank that held my safe deposit box decided to move while all this was going on, and gave me 60 days to remove my stuff from the box - yet wouldn't let me remove it until the IRS said OK. They never did allow it, now the bank doesn't know where the stuff that was in it went. All of my papers, etc. are now gone, and are impossible to replace. Thank you, IRS.

I hope someday to be able to repay you for what you have done to me. I heard that about a year after this was done to me, the head of the Van Nuys IRS was sent to jail. Apparently, he and several of his agents had been screwing up peoples lives, and then accepting bribes to straighten out the mess they had made. I guess I just didn't realize that a bribe could have saved me thousands of dollars, and years of grief.

## IRS Abuse Report #147

**Date:** Fri Jan 17 15:11:14 1997
**To:** sue@irs.class-action.com
**From:** RG
It started with a request for verification of expenditures regarding Lease/Repairs and maintenance expenditures on my Schedule C for some space I had leased for my business. Once I satisfied this request I was told that I could not use part of my residence as a business. I guess they figured out that accusation wasn't going to work since my residence was in a different location. They then went on to accuse me of not having a profit motive. Personally, I don't know too many people who start a business without a profit motive. Now, they've got a whole laundry list of records and other personal information that they want from me. It seems to me that the more information you give these people, the more they hassle you. They have been harassing me for the past four years and I don't see any end in sight. I guess what it comes down to is that the IRS is accusing me of perjury since I signed their tax forms under penalty of perjury. I have been an honest tax paying Citizen for over 20 years and I think this sort of behavior on the part of the IRS is abhorrent. It's like some kind of torture technique they use by leveling these accusations and persisting for years (reminds me of the Chinese water torture).

I think somebody has got to stand up to them. I'm willing to do whatever I can to help out in this class action lawsuit. Sign me up and let's do whatever we can to get rid of this rogue agency.

## IRS Abuse Report #148

**Date:** Mon Feb 3 16:14:41 1997
**To:** sue@irs.class-action.com
**From:** BS
The Internal Revenue Service is using strong-arm tactics to collect $3,000 from me that I don't owe. It falsely accuses me of receiving an undeserved $1,740 refund for tax year 1993 without evidence. It has nearly doubled the assessment with penalties and interest, even though I have followed its appeal procedures to the letter. It now threatens seizures of my property, bank accounts and paychecks, although the case awaits a Federal Tax Court hearing. All IRS's actions are violations of Federal laws, IRS policies and taxpayer rights.

## IRS Abuse Report #149

**Date:** Thu Feb 13 13:49:19 1997
**To:** sue@irs.class-action.com
**From:** DL
Upon being honorably discharged from the Army I started a small construction company, that I operated until 1984. My inability to collect earned receivables caused me to close the doors. When the company was closed neither the company nor I owed any IRS related taxes. However, the IRS alleged that there were employee wage tax deposits outstanding and they informed me that they would be imposing a 100% penalty upon me for same. I formally informed the IRS in 1984 that until such time as they afforded me due process of law, that I would not be filing subsequent returns and voluntarily giving them financial information.

In 1986 the IRS stole monies from the settlement of law suits pertaining to the construction company that equaled the total alleged indebtedness that they claimed I owed. Later in 1986 the IRS claimed that they had no record of receiving the payment and informed me that I was under investigation for criminal activities. In 1988, for years after the alleged indebtedness, I filed a personal bankruptcy and claimed the amount purported by the IRS. The bankruptcy court formally DISCHARGED the debt. Starting in 1990, six years after the alleged indebtedness incurred and two years after the alleged debt was discharged, the IRS informed me that they did not recognize the discharge, and at that time finally filed a lien against me. Also at that time, the IRS contacted all major credit reporting agencies and sent them a copy of the lien. All during the last thirteen years, the IRS has made my life a living hell and purposely tried to cause me total financial ruin. Also, for the last eleven years I have been branded a criminal by the IRS.

### IRS Abuse Report #150

**Date:** Sat, 15 Feb 1997
**To:** sue@irs.class-action.com
**From:** JW
Recently, I was told the following by an IRS employee, and I quote: 'We at the I.R.S. are doing the job we were commissioned by Congress to do. We are people, like you and your neighbors, and we don't deserve abuse and attacks from the citizens we serve.' Thanks to your web site, I looked him square in the eye and said: ...You moron, blaming your employer for making you steal people's money and harass them is the biggest cop-out I have ever seen. YOU are responsible for your own actions. If it weren't for robotic nitwits like you to carry out unjust laws, we would live in a free society. It is not just Congress to blame. Any honest person would find employment elsewhere where he could PRODUCE profit instead of coercing profit away from those that do. There is no escaping the fact that YOU are to blame for assisting in the carrying-out of any injustice your employer/government asks of you. Fully-integrated honesty makes it dreadfully clear. I think it's time you use it and become a valuable, productive, and conscious MAN. Earn an honest living instead of destroying what others have worked so hard for.

Blaming what you do on your employer absolves you of no guilt at all. The admonitory finger of Reason still points right at you, mister. You absolutely deserve to be "treated shabbily for doing [your] job," for by doing it you show yourself to be nothing but a shabby excuse for a man. Thanks to Neo-Tech your days are numbered.

### IRS Abuse Report #151

**Date:** Wed Feb 19 14:48:20 1997
**To:** sue@irs.class-action.com
**From:** GP
My husband and I recently (October 1996) settled with the IRS by an Offer-In-Compromise. This ended a 7-year battle where the IRS lost files for over 2 years, lied, never had any accountability, ruined our credit, seized our bank account WITHOUT prior notification, levied my husband's income WITHOUT prior notification, and so on.

To be able to pay for the amount as defined by the IRS as to what they would accept for an Offer In Compromise (which really didn't compromise anything on the IRS's part), we had to refinance our home.
 We closed on 10/8/96 and a check for $23,116 was sent via Federal Express for delivery on 10/9/96. Today (2/19/97) I find that there are still liens filed against my home. I contacted the IRS and was advised that the Collections division that handles Offers still show in their computer system that our debt is OWED!!! THIS IS AN OUTRAGE!!!! We paid our debt and the IRS is still inflicting their pain on me and my husband. Our credit is still being flagged for debts that we don't even owe. I either want the $23,116 that we paid out PLUS interest OR I want to see the IRS done away with.

Congressional IRS Abuse Reports

## IRS Abuse Report #152

**Date:** Thu, 27 Feb 1997
**To:** sue@irs.class-action.com
**From:** ANON
I too am on the payment plan with the IRS. I am also permanently disabled with a congenital cardiac condition that I recently had surgery for. I waited too long for the surgery so there was permanent damage to my heart muscle. I am 49. I do not receive public assistance, I was fortunate enough to have private disability insurance coverage. I have worked since I was 14 and never received any public assistance. A large part of my insurance payments each month goes to the IRS on a payment plan to pay back taxes they say I owe. I cannot afford a tax attorney so I keep paying but with penalties and interest the principle doesn't go down. I have been threatened with bank account seizure, which doesn't amount to much but my credit is still good and I want to protect it. I don't have property for them to seize except a car that my wife needs for work. So I will keep paying, probably for the rest of my life. I thought the amendment against slavery passed. I suppose the IRS overseers haven't read the constitution.

## IRS Abuse Report #153

**Date:** Fri, 28 Feb 1997
**To:** sue@irs.class-action.com
**From:** RF
Dear Sir: On February 12 1997, I had the unfortunate opportunity of the IRS to enter my place of business and proceed with the closure of same. I was sent a certified letter on Jan 09,1997 stating that I had thirty days to respond and I did on Jan 20, 1997 with a registered letter. The next communication that I had with the IRS was on February 12. When they entered my business and proceeded to close such business. They had the locks changed, put out bids on merchandise that had cost at wholesale $1919 for $638. Made the community think that I had done something

Illegal and almost destroyed my creditability as a business. What really angers me is their ability to enter a business and do whatever they like whenever they like. My business is a florist and bridal, needless to say that the week they entered my business was the week of Valentines, a florist's busiest week of the year. By entering my shop, the IRS, cost me approximately $8000 of business. Is there nothing we as business people and taxpayers can do other than go along with the GESTAPO of THE UNITED STATES??? Is there not a new law that was passed in '96 that prevents the IRS from Malicious Collection?

## IRS Abuse Report #154

**Date:** Tue Mar  4 18:39:38 1997
**To:** sue@irs.class-action.com
**From:** ANON
My 73 year old mother (who lives alone on a low fixed income). She was audited by the IRS last year for her 1993 tax return, which had been prepared by a tax accountant. She had never been audited before and has never done anything out of the ordinary or dishonest on her tax returns. According to the tax accountant in 1993, she owed the IRS about $800, which she scraped together and paid on time with her return. The IRS wrote back and said her return was in error. THEY actually owed HER $1300, they sent her check back and included a check to her for the $1300! She happily put the check in her bank account and counted it a blessing. Now, after last years audit, the IRS told her they had made a mistake on her 1993 tax return, and that she actually owed them $3000 plus the $1300 they had paid her WITH INTEREST!!!, and they wanted the full amount IMMEDIATELY, or large penalties would begin to accrue.

She had no say in the matter whatsoever. After consulting with a known good tax accountant, she had to take the money out of her retirement savings to pay off the IRS, and the whole incident cost her a great deal of stress and grief, not to mention the money. Do the heartless thugs at the IRS have nothing better to do than harass an elderly woman out of her retirement savings, because they and/or an accountant screwed up? These thieves should be put behind bars where they belong, not running the most corrupt and feared government institution in our country. Abolish the IRS!

## IRS Abuse Report #155

**Date:** Fri Mar  7 15:33:57 1997
**To:** sue@irs.class-action.com
**From:** ANON

My wife and daughter were maced and arrested in front of my 2 1/2 year old grand daughter by local police in Billerica Ma. on feb12,1993 when the police decided to they would help the IRS "American Gestapo", seizure my wife's car and my Truck Tractor . My wife was home alone when the IRS came demanding she pay them $56,000 or they would take her car and my truck after an hour of bullying my wife and daughter the police came.

## IRS Abuse Report #156

**Date:** Tue Mar 11 10:05:03 1997
**To:** sue@irs.class-action.com
**From:** PH

I did not know there were so many people like myself that the IRS has destroyed.

In 1993 my husband suffered a massive heart attack and was unable to work after 27 years in the work force. I had to claim extra depends so I could get as much of my check as possible to cover medical services, prescriptions and keep a roof over our families head and food on the table. The kids had to be taken care of along with my husband and I didn't know what else to do.

Well we ended up owing the IRS over $2000 and of course we couldn't come up with it, so we made payments and that got us no where.

It took from 1994 to the end of 1996 to finally get my husband's disability. All this time, we owed the IRS more and more. We finally paid off the IRS in 1996 when we got our disability back pay. Then we filed our income tax for that year, they got us even worse then before. The IRS claims we owe them over $6000 plus they penalized us for not taking enough money out for taxes! How were we to know that? It took me three years to pay off $2000 and the only way I could do that is because of the disability back pay. I will never be able to pay off $6000 plus penalties and late charges. They have taken all of my savings for my retirement and most of my paycheck. I don't understand how such a great country as ours could be so unfair and do such awful things to people.

## IRS Abuse Report #157

**Date:** Tue Mar 18 12:01:59 1997
**To:** sue@irs.class-action.com
**From:** CJ

Before my husband and I got married, he was in business with a partner that turned out to be a con man. Unbeknownst to us, the con filed a 1099 falsely stating that my husband had earned a certain amount of money for that year. The con skipped town. Two years later the IRS says my husband owes back taxes, penalties and interest. He disputes this and the IRS says the burden of proof is on him to show he didn't make the filed income amount. After much gnashing of teeth in an effort to prove this fact, he was told it didn't matter, he owed the money. Since we got married and filed jointly, now I also am responsible for this 'debt.' Penalties and interest have escalated the total owed to over $11,000. We have been trying to work this out with the IRS for over 9 years!!! The paper work is astounding. We send it in, they send it back saying oops we also need this information. We send it in, they send another form. We follow up with visits and phone calls to jerk after jerk...no one knows anything. It's a continuous circle of never-ending hell.

We got a tax attorney to handle this finally.  So what happens?  We send in $5000 for compromise, which includes some interest and penalties.  The IRS cashes our check, plus puts a levy on my wages!  The check was sent in with all the information they required.  Our attorney says it's against the law for them to have done this, but it doesn't sound like the IRS has to follow any laws!  He said they should have accepted the compromise and then cashed the check or rejected the compromise and returned the check.  So now they have our $5000 dollars and my pay is being garnished.

Needless to say our credit has been ruined by this whole ordeal.  There is a lien on our house.  I can't get a car without a co-signer.  The only credit card I have is secured.  I'm in sales and have to have these things in order to do my job!  My husband is about to have a nervous break down!

The IRS employs people that have a total disregard for the humane and just treatment of others.  I pity anyone who has to deal with the IRS.   The IRS has gotten completely out of control.

If we don't do something, the IRS will get worse!!!!!

## IRS Abuse Report #158

**Date:** Thu Mar 20  0:48:07 1997
**To:** sue@irs.class-action.com
**From:** AW
I am absolutely terrified, have just had wages levied for $46,000.  I am 50 years old and a single mother with two 17 year old children still at home.   I have no assets and have considered filing bankruptcy.  But after reading about IRS abuses where they don't honor bankruptcy....this morning I considered suicide.  Have never taken an active stand politically, but would now against them.

## IRS Abuse Report #159

**Date:** Sat Mar 22 21:45:17 1997
**To:** sue@irs.class-action.com
**From:** KE
The IRS says I owe them $75,000 in taxes, fines, and penalties.  I an just a porter.  I can not get credit, a loan, or have a savings account.  The company I worked for 22 years went out of business and I lost my pension.  I am 51 years old, have nothing for retirement, and the IRS wants everything I make.  I am a Viet Nam vet.  Is this the way America takes care of its own?  I have friends that come from Russia and they can't believe it.

## IRS Abuse Report #160

**Date:** Mon Mar 24 10:03:54 1997
**To:** sue@irs.class-action.com
**From:** HB
I have been trying for ten years to get caught up with the IRS.  The last payment of some 33K from a house I sold 3 days prior to them seizing it.  Now I am unable to pay the capitol gains and subsequent assessments from that sale of which all went to the IRS. My operating capitol has never recovered.  I have a continuing -- all ensuing trepidation in all that I do.  I am afraid to make money, hire employees or pursue any enterprise as this will only exacerbate the bleeding process.  They will be over me for the rest of my life as long as I have a social security # and attempt to own property.

## IRS Abuse Report #161

**Date:** Tue Apr  1  4:00:28 1997
**To:** sue@irs.class-action.com
**From:** DD
In 1986 I was a partner in a corporation.  The partner that paid the bills and did the accounting neglected to pay tax on my income for three years (later I found he had used that money for repaying his personal loan) though I

was under the impression my taxes had been paid as his actually were. In 1990, I began receiving the IRS form letters stating that I owed back tax and penalties. The amount had escalated from $60,000 dollars to over $225,000 w/penalties and interest. The next step was the forced sale of my home. It would be seized and auctioned if I did not sell it voluntarily. The house was sold and the equity was given to the IRS at close of escrow. $160,000 dollars all told. Remember the original amount owed was $60,000. So the IRS is now up $100,000 dollars. At this point, you'd think it would be resolved but no.... I still owed $65,000 dollars (interest still accruing w/ penalties).

The next step suggested was to file an 'Offer In Compromise'. That's an offer based on your net worth. So, I was worth about $8,000 now. I offered $10,000. (I arranged a personal loan from a family member). The IRS rejected my offer. I felt as though my entire life was ending. I was suicidal, depressed and exasperated at the process and bewildered at the ruthlessness of the IRS. I began seeing a psychiatrist at the recommendation of a friend. I was diagnosed as being depressed and having Delayed Stress Syndrome. The Doctor put me on disability and suggested I try to enjoy myself in the midst of the turmoil.

Then in about 2 months, I received yet another bill from the IRS. A bill for $27,000 for the capitol gains tax on the sale of my home. They have levied two checking accounts. They do not respond to my letters as required by the uniform commercial codes. I cannot own property as it would be seized. I can have no savings account or any dealing with a bank. Sometimes I wonder if I'll ever have a home again. Thanks for your efforts to fight these tyrants.

## IRS Abuse Report #162

**Date:** Mon Apr 7 14:37:56 1997
**To:** sue@irs.class-action.com
**From:** ANON

THE IRS IS OUT OF CONTROL. THE IRS AUDITED MY WIFE AND I. THEY SAID WE WERE OWED MONEY. NINE MONTHS LATER, WE HEARD FROM THEM AGAIN, THEY LOST OUR PAPER WORK. THE PERSON WHO DID THE ORIGINAL AUDIT WENT ON VACATION, NOW THEY SAY WE OWE $8,000 AND WONT LET US SHOW THEM PROOF THEY ARE WRONG. THEY ARE WORSE THAN ANY BANK ROBBER.

## IRS Abuse Report #163

**Date:** Tue, Apr 8, 1997 1:32 PM
**To:** sue@irs.class-action.com
**From:** BG

In 1993 my husband and I were notified, due to an audit, that there was a problem with one of our previous tax returns. My husband, Bill, contacted the IRS many, many, many times (over a two year period in an attempt to remedy the situation. He was laid-off from his job in 1992, and after 3 months found another job at 1/4 of the salary he had been making. Needless to say, things were very hard on us. He tried very hard to make the IRS understand this and tried to work out this situation with them. The IRS was VERY difficult to work with. In March, 1995, my husband committed suicide (shot himself in the head), leaving our son, Justin (12 years old) and I in unbelievable GRIEF (not to mention the terrible financial situation). Since Bill's death I had to put my son in a 'special' school in Irvine and he has been seeing a psychologist every single week since then. He is still devastated. Bill left me a suicide note mentioning that he just couldn't handle dealing with the IRS, etc., etc. any longer, and hopes that some day I'll be able to forgive him.

If only they (IRS) had worked with him, none

of this would have happened. I rest my case.

Below is a response to the above Abuse Report

This is almost routine (at least the part about the IRS failing to respond or being hard to work with). One of my best friends committed suicide after the IRS ruined his thriving business (destroying 25 good jobs in the process) and essentially caused his wife's premature death from cancer. After he contacted them in good faith (BEFORE his liability was due) and asked them for more time or some kind of payment plan to handle his tax bill, to which they said 'no problem', they seized his bank account and padlocked his business doors. His cancer ridden wife was then told to 'go home' by the hospital because this man's entire fortune had been seized by IRS thugs and he could no longer pay her bill.

Then of course there is the famous Alex Council story from Winston-Salem, NC. This was another man who committed suicide so his life insurance could be used to pay off what later (in court) turned out to be a erroneous lien on his family's home. This one was covered on 20/20. It is the one where and IRS regional director arrogantly told the 20/20 interviewer: 'Just because a judge says we're wrong, doesn't mean we are.'

### IRS Abuse Report #164

**Date:** Sat Apr 12 22:57:31 1997
**To:** sue@irs.class-action.com
**From:** GF
They sent me a letter telling me that I needed to sign a paper allowing them to go back further than was required to audit me . If I didn't sign, they would fine up to $10,000 dollars. I signed it all right stating that it was signed under threat. Later they claimed that I couldn't claim my kids as dependents on my 91' files and I owe them from 91 with penalties $2000 and its growing daily . They are going to garnish my wages. THEY have taken all my

savings and DESTROYED my credit.

### IRS Abuse Report #165

**Date:** Mon Apr 14  8:50:20 1997
**To:** sue@irs.class-action.com
**From:** KH
Please withhold personal information from any public reporting...IRS harassment techniques seem to be unlimited and their power out of control. In spite of the fact I held no ownership or stock in a company I worked for I was held liable by the fact I had signatory ability on the payroll account. With penalties and interest I now owe over $250,000. Through IRS actions I have paid over $20,000 to date with no end in sight. My ordeal began in 1985 and because of time, penalties accessed for having made offers in compromise, my statute will not expire until the year 2002. The icing on the cake was to find (from reliable inside sources) that no compromise will ever be accepted because I had the nerve to consult my local senator when this whole thing began. In effect, I am being blackballed by the IRS. The source I mention was never given my history so his findings had to come from my file. How would Congress feel to know that if a constituent contacts them, the IRS applies unlawful harassment tactics? If I could prove this I'd be a good case to cite.

### IRS Abuse Report #166

**Date:** Mon Apr 14 16:39:45 1997
**To:** sue@irs.class-action.com
**From:** LC
I (a female) owned a business in 1989 & 90 with two others (males). I left the company in 1990; my then partners took full responsibility for all the debts and taxes. The IRS came after me in 1993 for $18,000 in taxes that they have not paid. They haven't stopped since; they have drained my checking account, they have put a lien on my house, taken all my tax refunds and made my life miserable. The infuriating part is that they haven't bothered my

ex-male partners at all. They go for the easy kill -- females.

## IRS Abuse Report #167

**Date:** Fri Apr 25  9:02:18 1997
**To:** sue@irs.class-action.com
**From:** LB
 A payment plan was set up. For the first 6 months of this plan there were levies issued against my accounts and clients before I could even send a check to them. The payment was 2 times what I had said was disposable income. Now they say I am not paying enough (even though they set the amount) and are preparing to seize all my property. What the hell ever happened to life and liberty, the penalties and interest are about equal to a loan sharks rates.

## IRS Abuse Report #168

**Date:** Fri Apr 25 19:50:38 1997
**To:** sue@irs.class-action.com
**From:** DD
IN 1990 The IRS audited John for 1988 and 1989 They concluded since our two children had been on welfare since 1986 John had no right to claim them or get an earned income credit. There is only ONE BIG PROBLEM neither of the children were even born yet and were never on welfare, my other children were.

We have sent them all the paperwork they have asked for yet they still continue to take JOHN's income tax plus penalties and interest. WE cannot afford to hire a tax attorney, which I am sure the IRS knows.

## IRS Abuse Report #169

**Date:** Tue Apr 29 21:03:48 1997
**To:** sue@irs.class-action.com
**From:** ANON
Something must be done to stop this. How can the IRS get away with all they do? I am now

scared to death. I owe about $200. I am afraid that if I send it now, they will audit me. I just didn't file on time, thinking I would get a refund, but then I found out that I owe. Now it's too late to send the money in. I don't know what to do.

## IRS Abuse Report #170

**Date:** Wed Apr 30 23:44:58 1997
**To:** sue@irs.class-action.com
**From:** TP
I am an Attorney. I have three clients that were given Notices of Levy and either had their account seized or were verbally abused by collection agents. No hearings were held or Notices given prior to the Levy notices. I had no idea that this was as widespread as the site indicates.

## IRS Abuse Report #171

**Date:** Sun May  4  1:54:31 1997
**To:** sue@irs.class-action.com
**From:** TT
Our lives have been ruined by the IRS. We have been accused of not filing income taxes and being govt. protesters. The IRS wants nearly $200,000 and will not tell us why. We did not make even close to what they say we owe. They levied our salaries, put liens on our property and have demanded we pay them over $800/mo. for the rest of our lives, We do not make enough money to do this. I have two choices: suicide or fleeing the country. We have three children so leaving is definitely difficult. There is no point to working anymore. Why is this happening? We have committed no crime, yet the IRS has definitely threatened jail. No one believes us and there is no help. If we had committed murder we would at least have an attorney. Our Congressman has not even helped as he could. We are considered guilty. We have not had a day in court. The IRS has all our money if we do not pay them all and more of our money. I

am angry and want to do something.

## IRS Abuse Report #172

**Date:** Fri May 9 11:53:01 1997
**To:** sue@irs.class-action.com
**From:** MC
I have been married for 13 years and have three beautiful daughters. I work for a state agency so my income is barely enough for us to make ends meet. We have just entered into an installment agreement and I know will never be able to pay off. We also tried to get an agreement for the current taxes and they refused it. My credit is maxed out, therefore, no institution will loan us the money. My income last year alone was under 20K. How can one branch of the government have so much power? We fear for the worst but we will not give in. I will fight, literally, to the end before they destroy everything I have worked for. My only recourse now is to research and gather solid facts and information so when I do go and battle them my effort will be valiant. This is like the final straw that has destroyed my belief in the U.S. government and system. There is no fairness, not for the working-class, the low-income - we are the ones to bear the load for those that can and do manipulate the system to their benefit. God bless and help us all because we know the government we have entrusted so much in will not.

## IRS Abuse Report #173

**Date:** Sat, 10 May 1997
**To:** sue@irs.class-action.com
**From:** WW
I hammered out an agreement to pay the IRS $400 a month for one year, while I 'reduce my standard of living.' My wife again lost her job in January of this year. I called the IRS agent and told her I needed a new more reasonable payment agreement. She scheduled an appointment for me to come in, but later cancelled it. I heard nothing further from her

until I received a notice in the mail that they were proceeding to levy my income. Now my job and an upcoming promotion are in jeopardy. I have no economic future. I can't own a home, put my children through college or save for our retirement years. I have no credit. The only way I could ever come up with the money would be through a loan, which, obviously, I don't qualify for.

My point is that, although I shouldn't have fallen so far behind in my taxes, I have always tried to work with the IRS. They now say I owe them over $200,000. I am struggling to keep food in the house for my wife and two daughters. Throwing money at lawyers doesn't help. The IRS doesn't help. Some days all I can think of is blowing my brains out in front of the IRS office. Maybe that would prompt some much needed tax collection reform. I've had enough.

## IRS Abuse Report #174

**Date:** Sun May 11 7:48:43 1997
**To:** sue@irs.class-action.com
**From:** GW
My employer received a Levy from the IRS. I called the phone number on the notice and told the agent that their own regulations were violated by not granting a hearing. He told me that nothing I said would dissuade him. I asked to talk to his supervisor. He said he would not allow me! I called others at that office and got similar treatment.

## IRS Abuse Report #175

**Date:** Wed May 28 16:34:10 1997
**To:** sue@irs.class-action.com
**From:** SC
My husband, when married, forged my name on taxes. We divorced, he is told by courts to pay this debt of $917.00. I was eligible for earned income credit the following year as a single parent with 2 children. They seized my return

for his debt with the forged signature. And even though he set up a payment schedule with them, he never paid one dime to them at all, never made a payment. And they threatened to take my things and garnish my wages...and with a forged signature.

### IRS Abuse Report #176

**Date:** Fri May 30 11:50:35 1997
**To:** sue@irs.class-action.com
**From:** MF
I have been under a personal attack since Sept. 1996, wherein, the IRS has taken my salary and personal vehicle. Within 4 weeks after stealing my car it was sold with a minimum bid of $520 even though its value at the time was over $12,000 and would have cost over $32,000 to me. When the IRS agent was confronted to show his delegation of authority order he could not present, only directing me to another office of the agency. I was reduced to driving a rental car for several months until my parents lent me one of their vehicles. When the lien against my salary went into effect I placed several hardship dependents on the form. The IRS agent changed my deductions which reduced my take home pay to virtually zero and was forced to borrow money from friends. I have corresponded with several congressman and senators, most have not even acknowledge receipt of my letters. Those that do weasel out of their responsibilities by referring my questions and concerns directly to the IRS for response. What a security system, send the chickens to the foxes den for support.

### IRS Abuse Report #177

**Date:** Mon Jun  9 22:33:44 1997
**To:** sue@irs.class-action.com
**From:** BK
I own and operate a small accounting firm. As I write this, I have been on hold with the Ogden, UT service center for 1.25 hours. In the past two years, the degree of incompetence at IRS

has been astounding. I am dealing with a notice tonight for a client, that is a demand for his 3rd Qtr '96 941 return (Federal Payroll Tax Report). I have in my nicotine-stained fingers, the signed file copy of the form we submitted back in October 1996. The client called me tonight, panic stricken, because of the abusive letter he got from IRS that threatens to imprison him if he does not file the required forms. The tone of this letter is amazingly nasty and highly abusive.

### IRS Abuse Report #178

**Date:** Sun Jun  8 10:16:49 1997
**To:** sue@irs.class-action.com
**From:** SW
The Internal Revenue Service, Criminal Investigation Division (IRS - CID), Houston District, is truly a place where the lunatics are running the asylum. The managers rule by psychological warfare and intimidation. So pervasive is this method, that a special agent in the Houston District killed himself because of it, and the other employees did not dare to speak out about it.

I have seen first hand the way that IRS - CID management is willing to lie to achieve their goals. Management has turned Civil Service, into Self Service. I have seen how GS 13 special agents are promoted to GS 14, and sent to Washington in their last years of semi-retirement, so that their pension is based on a grossly inflated high three. These individuals contribute absolutely nothing, while padding their retirement package.

I have seen how IRS - CID employees learn quickly that integrity is not a luxury you can possess, if you want to survive in the Houston, District. The only quality a employee needs to survive, is blind loyalty to the IRS - CID agenda. Houston District IRS - CID special agents MUST be willing to lie, and participate in internal lynchings of others who refuse to go along with this corrupt program.

IRS - CID Management in the Houston District are blind to the fact that they are as criminal as the people they lamely attempt to jail for lying on their tax returns. It seems individuals of such questionable character are the only ones willing to enforce a unfair, out of date, and unnecessarily complex tax system. IRS employees are nearly completely devoid of integrity, because they must enforce a tax system which lacks integrity.

## IRS Abuse Report #179

**Date:** Sat Jul 5 10:01:11 1997
**To:** sue@irs.class-action.com
**From:** JB
The IRS has got to be stopped!!!!!

Recently I received a phone call from the IRS demanding that I pay taxes of approximately $4700. I had no idea what they were referring to and asked for returns that showed that I owed the money. After a week I had not received any paper work so I called the agent and asked when I would receive the documents that he told me he would send. He told me that he would fax them but I had to start paying now or he would attach my wages. I told him that until I had some proof that I owed taxes I wouldn't pay anything. That afternoon I received a fax of a form demanding payment and pages of questions about my personal finances and property. I again called the agent and told him that I needed copies of the returns that showed that I owed the money not just a form demanding it. He told me that would take time and demanded that I pay the taxes immediately or my wages would be attached the next week. I again told him that I would not pay without proof that I owed the money.

Guess what folks. Without any proof my wages were attached. The IRS was going to allow me to keep a whopping $253 a week to live on. That's not much when you have two kids. Needless to say I had to come up with the money. I had to borrow money to pay taxes that

I didn't owe.

By the way, I never did receive tax returns.

## IRS Abuse Report #180

**Date:** Tue Jul 8 1:22:12 1997
**To:** sue@irs.class-action.com
**From:** RB
I love this country, but the IRS is bent on destroying taxpayers with no regard for human rights.

The IRS own errors and delays were responsible for creating a terrible tax audit and inaccurate tax assessment.......(O.J.'s murder trial was on for one and a half years)....My audit was on for 9 (nine) years. While focusing my attention on reducing the erroneous tax assessment --I was buried with interest.

The IRS often terrorize tax advisers by threatening to audit all their clients, bar them from practicing and a host of other frightening possibilities. As a result, some tax advisers will actually incriminate you before they risk an IRS vendetta.

The IRS put a LIEN/LEVY on my home which was illegal, because my case was still in appeals. How could they do this?

## IRS Abuse Report #181

**Date:** Fri Jul 11 16:37:06 1997
**To:** sue@irs.class-action.com
**From:** JF
The IRS determined that I owed $10k for tax year 1992. I asked for detail on this amount, and was refused. When I pressed, in writing, the only response I got basically told me to put up AND shut up. I apparently don't have the right to know where the IRS' figures come from, and I don't have the right to challenge them. When it came down to a lien and levy, I was called into the Jax, FL office, where I

spoke to an officer Curry and her supervisor. I tape recorded the meeting (yes, I provided written notification before I did so, even though title 26 only requires 'advance notification', not '10 days written notification' as IRS collections flyers indicate) and had a CPA present.

I, as others have done, asked to see the agents' delegations of authority. The agents responded that they didn't have to show ANYTHING to me, declared the interview over, and stated that enforcement would begin (I have a transcript of the meeting should anyone be interested). Again, in violation of the law, a levy against my salary was issued the same day. I was allowed $566 a month to survive. Nothing else has been seized, but it might as well have been. The money is still being siphoned, to the point that I 'visited' a mental hospital for a month. I am working with a CPA to get several past years straightened out, but that's the only way I can find to communicate with these monsters. I would like a straight answer from the IRS for once. I read on this site that there is a decent, fair, IRS district director somewhere in this country. Sorry, but I don't believe it. Such an individual would be eaten by the rest of the sharks that run the organization.

### IRS Abuse Report #182

**Date:** Tue Jul 22 22:11:29 1997
**To:** sue@irs.class-action.com
**From:** TT
Your intentions are commendable. I myself have numerous stories about IRS abuse, including IRS's flagrant and unlawful refusal to comply with the Freedom of Information Act. I have evidence of falsification of evidence by IRS and DOJ officials, of back-dating of notices of deficiency by IRS employees, of computer fraud committed by IRS against myself and many others.

### IRS Abuse Report #183

**Date:** Wed, 23 Jul 1997 21:40:54 -0400
**To:** sue@irs.class-action.com
**From:** SS
I am a high school teacher of government and economics; a former USAF pilot with a combat tour (1 year) in Vietnam.

For over 15 years the IRS has been holding a lien on me for a tax debt that began as a mistake and eventually was over $100K. My lawyer, Hayes Young, Shestack & Young, 212 766 1200, did a bankruptcy which was supposed to discharge the IRS debts, but they refuse to vacate the lien they hold on me. This, combined with the State of New York's Department of Taxation and Finance taking their lead from the IRS, has me with no credit rating. I am unable to replace my defunct 1983 Olds, so I have no car. I am unable to try to get mortgage for a house or a coop or condominium.

They have, in the past, levied my pay, garnisheed it and seized my pay and my checking accounts, costing me large fees to have these reinstated.

### IRS Abuse Report #184

**Date:** Sat Aug  2 11:57:34 1997
**To:** sue@irs.class-action.com
**From:** KA
This is the best news we've heard of in a long time!!

In 1991 my husband and his ex-wife filed taxes using 1040-short form. Because she did not include several expenses, they were left with a large debt. ( In 1989 they owed 872.00 that she was paying on installments of $50.00 monthly.) When the '89 debt was paid her payments began applying to '91. She paid for about six months and then stopped. When my husband and I filed separately in 1993, half of my return was seized for the 1991 debt that my husband

and his ex-wife owed! This occurred again in 1994 and in 1995.

In 1996 the IRS told me that I owed back taxes for 1990 and that I had never filed a return for that year. My taxes were done by a CPA due to the business expenses I had that year. That same tax return was handed to a banker for and expense loan in 1991. How could I give him my taxes if I hadn't filed them?

The IRS sent a refund check for 50% of my 'married filing separate' 1995 refund and applied the remaining amount to my husband and his ex-wife's 1991 debt. Then in October of 1996 we received a letter stating that my refund was being held because I owed for 1990. Then they sent a letter to my husband saying the entire amount of my personal refund was being applied to his 1991 tax debt. I called to find out about this and they would tell me nothing, due to the fact my name was not on his tax return. We then received a letter saying 1991 still had $799.00 owing. Numerous phone calls have ended in confusing information, too many people in on the conversation, unanswered questions, CONFLICTING information, and rude comments. I asked one employee why I should be responsible for my husband and his ex-wife's debts. She stated, "You should have done a credit check before you married him." I asked to speak to her supervisor and was told "My supervisor doesn't want to talk to you. " she then hung up on me. There is no way to call back without an entire day on the phone, they cannot put two pieces of paper together. My ex-husband even managed to file two returns for the same year, leaving me out to dry. This whole mess has caused many problems in our lives. The IRS is an illegal agency and needs to be rid of. What would happen if everyone didn't work for one day? What would the American public gain? Everything, including freedom from these people!

## IRS Abuse Report #185

**Date:** Wed Aug  6 11:12:03 1997
**To:** sue@irs.class-action.com
**From:** LS

Too many families in Hawaii are being harassed and driven into the streets by the IRS - I have seen people driven to the brink of insanity and destitution because of the strong arm tactics.

I personally was hit with a $1 million + lien, levy, threats, the whole routine. Presently, I am working with several families whose paychecks have been snatched, they have children to feed, and the usual obligations and are unable to meet them because the IRS TAKES ALL THEIR MONEY. I have been the witness to too many people being devastated by the financial ruin the IRS heaps on them.

## IRS Abuse Report #186

**Date:** Sat Aug  9 22:57:16 1997
**To:** sue@irs.class-action.com
**From:** CB

About five years ago, my marriage broke up, friendly, for what it's worth. Being the primary wage earner, I took it upon myself to maintain the majority of our bills, as she was unable to do so. Coupled with that, I was paying a federal and state tax, that was killing me, forcing me to borrow money, just to pay these raping illegal direct tax on my labor. Well, it was only a matter of time, that my savings were depleted, my retirement, I lost our home, I lost two (2) pieces of dirt that I was hoping to have for retirement purposes, I was homeless, and lived in my office for 4 months without kitchen or shower, Pretty humiliating, but that was the result.

Hey, I am flat broke. I can't afford insurance, and am about to lose my job. I am so depressed, stressed out, because I can not learn the legal system fast enough to counter these thieves. The courts have gone astray, and I have nothing to go on, but case after case being

LOST. I fear I will end up in PRISON and for what?

Our congressmen/women do not care. I have sent info. to two without a peep of a response from them.

I want to know, while I still have a few resources, and haven't gone completely crazy, what can I do. There must be blame somewhere, someone has to be responsible that I can at least seek justice.

## IRS Abuse Report #187

**Date:** Tue, 26 Aug 1997 14:12:49 -0700
**To:** sue@irs.class-action.com
**From:** JK
My Mother, now 80 yrs old in a nursing home, was a diligent taxpaying citizen all her life. The tax return she filed for 1993 was audited in 1997 and found to have numerous math problems, plus she used the wrong tax table. She owed an additional $1,200 but was fined an extra $5,014. in penalties plus "statutory interest" for a grand total of $8,700! The IRS sent notices to an old address, even though her recent tax returns had the correct address. They would not talk to me about her case until they received papers of showing I had power of attorney. I sent them twice through the mail. They insisted the paperwork was not received. Finally, they gave me a FAX number to send it. Then I had a receipt. All this time, the interest was mounting. They don't care that my Mother was obviously incapacitated and incompetent to complete such complex returns. She has been fined all this money for being ill and unable to understand. She needs this money for her care.

I am sending the check because I was told by Miss Adams of the IRS that resistance was not only useless but also costly. She said even though she had the power to rescind the penalty, she was not going to do it. Meanwhile, interest is mounting.

## IRS Abuse Report #188

**Date:** Thu Aug 28 10:25:13 1997
**To:** sue@irs.class-action.com
**From:** DG
On Friday, August 8, 1997, at approximately 8:30 a.m., as I and Russel and Richard, my neighbors two sons who were in my care, were returning to my car at the vets office at 300 S. Dixie Highway, I saw two or three police cars, and a big flat bed tow truck blocking my way out of the parking lot. One police officer (James Schott) came over to my car and asked, "How are you today?" I answered, "I'm happy and joyful". He seemed nervous, looking around at other people who were coming closer to my car. I didn't know what was going on and I thought they're going to have to move those vehicles so that I can go home.

The officer Schott then asked me nicely to get out of the car I said "why" Before he had a chance to answer, another man (Daniel Dockum) very rudely commanded me to get out of the car. I said to him, "who are you?" he answered in a very intimidating manner, "you"ll find out, just get out of the car and tell the boys to get out too." I grabbed my purse and opened the door. I told the boys to go ahead and get out also.

Officer Schott asked "are you Denise" I said yes, then he said, "these are federal agents, do you know her?" pointing out a girl who was walking towards me, I said "yes" after recognizing her to be Revenue Officer C. Barron. Ms. Barron walked up to me and handed me a copy of Publication one. She said, "Are you prepared to pay six thousand three hundred ninety nine dollars and eleven cents". I answered "For what, I don't even have a checkbook with me". She said, "I am taking your car".
Three more people in suits came walking towards me. Some from a dark blue car and others from a gray van. I did not know these people. No one introduced themselves or showed me any identification even after I asked.

"Do you have a court order signed by a judge?" I asked. Daniel Dockum got right in my face, I could feel and smell his breath, and said, "she doesn't need a court order, here is her authority", and somebody handed me IRS Form 668-B, Levy. Turning to officer Schott, who looked confused, I said, "she can't take my car, without an order from the court signed by a judge, don't I have any rights?" Daniel Dockum shouted "NO". I said to officer Schott, "We have not been in front of a judge yet, she has no court order, are you going to let her steal my car? Officer Schott faced me. I think I saw a little compassion in his eyes, and he said, "Look I"m just a Pompano Beach police officer, these people are federal agents, you will cooperate with them and not give anybody any trouble or I will have to put you under arrest". With the boys in my care for the day I knew at that moment that it was useless to assert myself or insist on my rights. I felt like I was starting to cry. I was very angry, like I was being violated by this gang of thugs and there was no one to help me.

## IRS Abuse Report #189

**Date:** Tue Sep 2 15:04:10 1997
**To:** sue@irs.class-action.com
**From:** GB
Because they ignore the laws of America, they have made it impossible to buy a home or raise my children. They have put a lien on me and harassed me to no end. They threaten to take everything I own. Where is the protection of American lives that we the citizens of America work for?

## IRS Abuse Report #190

**Date:** Mon, 15 Sep 1997 02:23:01 -0400 (EDT)
**To:** sue@irs.class-action.com
**From:** AL
My father had a heart attack last year and passed away due to IRS attacks. He was also an attorney. He was a 54 year-old healthy, athletic husband and father to four daughters. The IRS still calls and harasses my mother.
I would love to be able to do something about this so others don't lose their loved ones due to IRS stress.
Thank you

## IRS Abuse Report #191

**Date:** Mon Sep 22 22:03:56 1997
**To:** sue@irs.class-action.com
**From:** GP
I challenged the IRS several years ago over an alleged corporate tax debt of less than $30K. My argument? The corporation couldn't possibly owe money for employee wage taxes since the tax years for which the debt was assessed was when the cooperation was defunct. It had no employees to tax; therefore, it could not possibly owe any wage taxes.

The IRS refused to listen to reason and common sense. They had one mission: to collect the alleged tax regardless of whether it was legitimate or not. Why? Because I questioned the IRS's authority to act outside of the law.

My punishment was swift. The IRS seized and sold over $1/2 million of my personal property for $16K. The IRS performed no inventory since it would show the value of the seized property to be far in excess of the alleged tax debt. The IRS took over $60K in cash from my personal safe, family heirloom jewelry, savings bonds being held for my children's coin collection and personal papers. To show their arrogance, the IRS never even admitted taking the cash or other items. It just disappeared.

My wrongful levy suit was an exercise in futility. District and appellate courts denied my wrongful levy suit. The courts said I had to prove the property seized and sold was my personal property and not that of the corporation, yet the IRS allowed my records that would prove such to be lost or destroyed. Because the IRS refused to take an inventory of the property, I attempted to photograph the seized items and was threatened with arrest despite the fact no such law exists preventing me from taking pictures. The IRS was intent on burying me for questioning their authority, pure and simple.

I couldn't even sue the IRS. The US government replaces the IRS as a defendant in such matters. What this means is that the US Justice Department argues in favor of the IRS and against the taxpayer, right or wrong. It's a mismatch of biblical proportions. A pro se litigant versus the tax attorneys of the US Justice Department. You're financially devastated following a tax sale so you couldn't afford counsel IF you could find one to even take the case! You're left alone to battle the government Goliath in matters so incredibly complex even the IRS admits it does not understand the laws it is charged with administering.

In federal court, you are asking a judge to go against his employer and the US Justice Department attorneys, something only a rare few have the courage to do. Those jurists that demand IRS accountability can expect to encounter the IRS's wrath for enforcing constitutional rights of the taxpayers.

The time to end IRS arrogance is now. The IRS is not above the law, but it will continue to act this way until Congress steps in and acts to protect citizen rights. The IRS does not recognize the US Constitution, so beware if you think the law will protect you against the IRS. I tried it. I lost everything and I live in fear they lurk in the shadows waiting to attack again. And they will. As long as I demand accountability.

Keep your doors locked if the IRS comes calling. They can take what they want without a search warrant. The jurist in my case said the IRS does not have to comply with the provisions of a criminal search warrant since the case is a civil matter. I petitioned him and

the appellate court with the actual federal procedural rules and case law showing IRS entry warrants MUST conform to these rules, and my pleas fell upon deaf ears. Translation? The Constitution will not protect you from the IRS. If you prove the law is on your side, both the IRS and their courts will simply look the other way. They both have tunnel vision, to collect taxes and the laws be damned!

As a sidelight, please note that even the IRS has a sense of humor. Of all the property it seized and sold, the only thing it left was some books explaining how the IRS illegally collects taxes. I guess they didn't want to publicize the fact they are at-large criminals wreaking havoc on decent, law abiding citizens. Could you blame them?

## IRS Abuse Report #192

**Date:** Tue Sep 23 1:48:34 1997
**To:** sue@irs.class-action.com
**From:** SF
We lost our entire focus of life for ourselves and our children. We have no incentive for working towards a better life and securing our future since we are living proof that IRS can walk in and find millions of reasons to keep us in debt to the government forever. We are a family of five, 44 and 38 year old husband and wife, self employed working in excess of 60 hours per week to just keep up with our current bills and have no time to supervise our children due to work load. Psychological effect of our faulty prosecution from the IRS has caused us to make insurmountable amount of mistakes, errors and misjudgments that has been hurting everything and everybody around us including ourselves. We just feel we are only a small part of a very, very sick system.

The easiest way out would be to commit suicide and the debt would not be inherited. We have absolutely no retirement plan, no savings account, no life insurance and no hope. Our American dream was destroyed by dark forces of the IRS, the destroyer and executioner of the weak, and defenseless small business owner.

## IRS Abuse Report #193

**Date:** Wed Sep 24 13:20:57 1997
**To:** sue@irs.class-action.com
**From:** BR
I am glad to see that someone is finally doing something about the IRS and their abuse of power.
In 1976, my mother owed $300 in taxes. They were not paid due to the fact that she was diagnosed with cancer and given 12 weeks to live. In May, as she lay dying, two IRS agents showed up at my house where we had moved my mother to take care of her. They told me they were friends and had come to visit.

I took them to her room where they introduced themselves as IRS agents and served her with papers to confiscate everything she owned. She was to weak to sign the paper but did make an X and I signed for her. On that day, they took everything she owned....even the soda bottles at her place of business! She died within the week. Glad to see someone is doing something about their abuse of power.

## IRS Abuse Report #194

**Date:** Wed Sep 24 19:15:50 1997
**To:** sue@irs.class-action.com
**From:** SV
When I filed my tax return few years back there was a simple error (i.e., #1 was not entered in the personal exemption column, but the number of exemption claimed etc., and the final amount to be returned by the IRS were correct. But the IRS got confused by this and sent my return for audit.
After the audit and many letters/faxes to the IRS, I still had to take my case to Tax Court. I can 100% say that the people working in IRS don't really don't know what they are doing. I can provide detailed information of my

experience that relates to how people are chosen for audit and what a poor job IRS does in handling even simple returns.

## IRS Abuse Report #195

**Date:** Wed Sep 24 21:04:26 1997
**To:** sue@irs.class-action.com
**From:** DS
All I'm doing now is going in circles paying the compounding interest and penalties! The IRS seized my checking account 3 years ago and forced my son and I to move out because the rent check bounced!

There has to be some way or someone that could help put a stop to this merry-go-round we're all on. Can't they give amnesty to the interest and penalties and have us pay what we owe in TAXES? Or at least change the structure of the installment agreements to stop the compounding penalties and interest once the agreement is in effect. I owe $12,000 to them...but more than 50% is their compounding penalties! I will never in my life be able to pay them off, never be able to purchase a home. I'm sick and tired of it!

## IRS Abuse Report #196

**Date:** Wed Sep 24 21:56:04 1997
**To:** sue@irs.class-action.com
**From:** GB
I hope no one will ever have to go through what I did. The begging, crying, pleading for someone to help me, I never felt so hopeless, when you know you are right. If I had not fought, I would be closed today, I would have lost clients and employees

## IRS Abuse Report #197

**Date:** Thu Sep 25 0:05:15 1997
**To:** sue@irs.class-action.com
**From:** MS
IRS agents came to my house threatened my wife with garnishment of her wages,

embarrassment at her employment, taking her house and car, they filed tax liens against her on the possibility she was involved in management of my bankruptcies. I eventually proved her innocence after loosing her and my children, and they withdrew their liens against her. Their attitude: "TOO BAD SUCKER -- WE DON'T CARE IF WE WRECK YOUR LIFE."

## IRS Abuse Report #198

**Date:** Thu Sep 25 1:34:10 1997
**To:** sue@irs.class-action.com
**From:** KA
I have been audited every year since 1977. I have put hours of work and money into each audit. But soon, the audit for the next year arrives. I have just finished fighting 94 and am currently fighting 95 and 96 -- all because I am a hard working, small business person. The auditor who keeps recalling me, admits she wants to put me out of business. I am exhausted -- though I have not lost what many have -- this harassment has been going on much too long.

## IRS Abuse Report #199

**Date:** Thu Sep 25 6:52:24 1997
**To:** sue@irs.class-action.com
**From:** TW
1992 my So. Cal. home and home based business was heavily damaged by a drought ending rain and mud slide. The damage was inspected and I applied for, and received a $5000 SBA loan for personal effects, and a $5000 SBA loan for my business, a sole proprietorship making enough to survive on. During the next two years I started to rebuild by applying the SBA loan for its intended purpose. I was making the monthly repayment on the SBA loan. I reconstructed lost records from the mud slide and got up to date with the IRS. They immediately levied the $4000 remaining from the SBA loan. I lost two employees, could not pay any bills, and eventually had to file bankruptcy. This was in spite of the fact that I was making quarterly payments to the IRS. This was followed by an audit of my next two years returns, including threats of seizing everything. They even contacted my clients and demanded they send the IRS my accounts payable. I lost that client. I am a U.S. Army veteran and a former Peace Corps volunteer. I see no reason to try to increase my income with the IRS Gestapo using illegal shake downs, thugs, and criminals.

## IRS Abuse Report #200

**Date:** Thu Sep 25 9:50:31 1997
**To:** sue@irs.class-action.com
**From:** LM
The issue still under scrutiny is the security deposit issue. I have a tape of an IRS representative stating that my position is correct and I have sited the IRS publication in support of my position and they will still not let the matter rest. I have been told twice by 2 different IRS people associated with my file that it does not matter what we say OR what our own publication states, it is a court that decides the rules!! This to me is incredulous! I have relied on professional advice, IRS publications and the IRS itself for my position and this is not enough. I am continued to be harassed.

Just last week, in this continuing nightmare, I received a form letter from the IRS wanting documentation on some mortgage interest deductions that supposedly do not match up with their records. I have talked to several tax professionals who have told me that I have for some reason made somebody at the IRS mad and that this is not good. I have been told "Do not underestimate them they are a VERY powerful organization."

I also have had CPA's refused to represent me as they are afraid for themselves. I am a law biding tax paying middle income citizen that has not cheated on my taxes. We need to stop this abuse. This is chillingly similar to the days of J. Edgar Hoover.

## IRS Abuse Report #201

**Date:** Thu Sep 25 10:18:16 1997
**To:** sue@irs.class-action.com
**From:** PS

I too am a victim of the vicious IRS. In 1987, I worked for several temp. agencies, during tax filing, I mistakenly forgot to add one of the W2 forms (1 out of 6 of them). I was notified by IRS in 1990 that since I did not add this with my 87 filing I would be penalized. The taxes on the W2 was $225. After my numerous calls and letter writings, the IRS in 1993 decided to contact my new employer and put a lien on my salary. I have been paying the IRS $150.00 a month for the past 3 years. Plus, they have been taking any refunds that I should have gotten from IRS. I was told at the time that it would take only 3 years to repay the $6,000. But I have now come to find out that I have been penalized with interest and penalties. Well in the past 3 years I have paid almost $6,000 for a $225 tax mistake (and still paying). When does it stop.

## IRS Abuse Report #202

**Date:** Thu Sep 25 12:17:19 1997
**To:** sue@irs.class-action.com
**From:** TA

Thank God someone has the courage to create this site and send the results to lawmakers. I had a letter to the editor published in a large metro newspaper earlier this year complaining about this very subject. I should not be surprised that I'm now being audited.

## IRS Abuse Report #203

**Date:** Thu Sep 25 12:48:36 1997
**To:** sue@irs.class-action.com
**From:** KT

Thank God someone decided to start this campaign. I have called this organization the SS for years. Not that I resent paying taxes. They are feared and allowed to go wild enforcers, supported by our government under the guise of democracy.

I have seen first hand the outrageous abuses that have occurred as a result of this organization. Brutality beyond belief, suicides, homes taken from the elderly, just the most ungodly type of free reigning organization.

## IRS Abuse Report #204

**Date:** Thu Sep 25 15:15:43 1997
**To:** sue@irs.class-action.com
**From:** VN

I am retired and I should not have much fear of the IRS but before I die, I will only be happy if America can rid itself of this terrible abusive agency. How can anyone consider himself free if he must undergo this terrible Nazi-like abuse? It is not necessary to go into the abuses on me by the IRS unless it will help the cause to eradicate this demon. I will definitely unleash my story if others are interested and will facilitate the fall of the IRS. I am not a Democrat nor really a Republican. I was actively interested in Forbes because of his Flat Tax in 1996; otherwise, he did not interest me much as a candidate.

I will do anything to help America purge itself of this nefarious outrage.

## IRS Abuse Report #205

**Date:** Thu Sep 25 13:39:06 1997
**To:** sue@irs.class-action.com
**From:** Anon

I am on a payment plan that will never be paid off. There was not enough taxes taken out during the year (it seems each year I change my withholdings to have more taken out and it is never enough)! I don't mind paying what I owe, but the penalty and interest are astronomical (what is the rate anyway?) If loan sharking is illegal, then why isn't what the IRS does illegal?

## IRS Abuse Report #206

**Date:** Thu Sep 25 17:17:12 1997
**To:** sue@irs.class-action.com
**From:** EP
The IRS put a hold on our checking account twice this year because we defaulted on our installment agreement. For a family of four living from paycheck to paycheck, we were simply left without any money to use. Checks we have written bounced. Even when our account was negative and we had to borrow money to pay debts, the borrowed money was taken by IRS! The people running the IRS are ruthless and heartless. Congress must do something to curtail and control this ugly giant. This is a good time to ask for a flat tax with no loopholes.

## IRS Abuse Report #207

**Date:** Thu Sep 25 19:17:28 1997
**To:** sue@irs.class-action.com
**From:** DK
I got an unsigned notice of levy. I answered it and asked for a hearing. What I got instead was a levy on my paycheck and my bank account for about thirteen thousand dollars. No assessment, no court hearing, no writ to enforce the levy, nothing.

## IRS Abuse Report #208

**Date:** Thu Sep 25 23:34:33 1997
**To:** sue@irs.class-action.com
**From:** LE
I Purchase my business in 1985, at that time the business was using Independent Contractors. I kept going with the same setup.

In 1987 the IRS came in and said that they were going to do an audit to determine if the workers were employees or Independent contractors. At the end we received a letter from the agent stating that the company was in FULL COMPLIANCE.

In 1988 the Department of Labor came in to determine if the workers were employees or Independent contractors, when they looked at everything and talked to everyone they said they were satisfied.

In 1989 the ILLINOIS Department of Employment Security came in and said that they were going to do an audit to determine if the workers were employees or Independent contractors, at the end we received a letter stating that we were correct.

In 1995 the IRS came and said that they needed to do an audit, after this audit they said that the workers should have been employees and that we, the company, owes back taxes for payroll of $3,000,000.00 -- yes THREE MILLION DOLLARS

A. The IRS said they lost there records of the audit of 1987 B. The IRS said the other audits we had didn't have any bearing. C. The IRS started collection and locked up my business D. The IRS then said that I personally owed the $3,000,000.00

Since this started in 1995 The IRS has made my life a nightmare, and cost us hundreds of thousands of dollars.

## IRS Abuse Report #209

**Date:** Thu Sep 25 23:44:56 1997
**To:** sue@irs.class-action.com
**From:** DT
In 1981 the bottom fell out of the oil field. I had worked in this industry for a number of years. Being a driller, I was responsible for providing transportation for myself and my crew. When starting with a new company it was common practice to take these travel expenses out of pocket until receiving the first payroll check and then a separate travel check to reimburse me for money spent. This check was tax exempt and did not require a 1099 to accompany my yearly return.

This practice worked fine until in 81 when a large number of drilling companies went bankrupt and filled this expense as taxable income in order to diffuse their liabilities. The IRS then began attacking the receivers of these checks, myself included. Going back to the very first year I received money of this type, adding penalties and interest and sending us a statement against money we didn't even know we owed . This continued for years, each year brought new penalties and interest on the next year and so on.

After quitting the oil field in hopes of putting a stop to this and getting a lesser job, paying what they said we owed, my hopes were shattered, they continued to hound us, year after year going back and refiguring and refiguring these returns and always finding yet another way that we owed more money. No one could help us, not only were they taking aprox. 1/3 of my pay in withholding on my payroll... We were destined to pay another 10-15% of my take home pay year after year without any sign of relief.

I have been unable to get out from under their scrutiny for 16 years now. I am now making close to half of what I was in 1981, and I'm still subject to the wrath of the IRS.....

My family suffers as I cannot provide for them properly we have had many troubles due to our financial standing, cannot acquire credit, because we can never get ahead, and it has caused many personal problems as well within our household. And this continues even today, as we received yet another statement from the IRS says that we now owe 3,300+ dollars for 1988. Here it is 9 years later (can they do that????????).

Why can't something be done?? When the system can go back again and again over the same years and refigure and recalculate and deem that they want more and more money from the meek of this country!! My family can starve and live on the street and they don't

care, we have fought off levy after levy and attachments to my wages .... we have suffered over and over ... year after year ... we live each day from pay check to pay check ... with no end in sight .... The mental anguish, stress, and financial deprivation, the suffering they have caused. IN GOD WE TRUST, and someday GOD will deliver us from this hell we call the IRS !!!!

## IRS Abuse Report #210

**Date:** Wed, 24 Sep 1997 11:55:21 -0500
**To:** sue@irs.class-action.com
**From:** GR
In 1976, when my mother was dying of cancer, two IRS agents came to my home and confiscated all that this woman owned. She was so sick she could not even sign the papers they gave her.

## IRS Abuse Report #211

**Date:** Fri, 26 Sep 1997 21:19:41 -0400 (EDT)
**To:** sue@irs.class-action.com
**From:** KA
I have been annually audited by the IRS since 1977. Each year after many hours of work and much expense, I am audited again. I just finished 94 and we are currently working on 95 and 96. The IRS auditor here has stated that she wants to put me out of business -- is the IRS's job to destroy small businesses?

## IRS Abuse Report #212

**Date:** Fri Sep 26 0:11:44 1997
**To:** sue@irs.class-action.com
**From:** TK
In 1990 I was treated so poorly by the IRS that I and my wife were in tears. It was a case of mistaken identity, something that should have been easily cleared up. They called me a liar on the telephone and refused to do the checking that would have cleared us.

On September 17, 1990 I received a notice of levy from my bank indicating that the IRS had taken our total checking account--$2397.46. We received notice, then, in an official notice of levy from the IRS, dated 9-16-90 that we owed them a total of $15,585.54.

We had no idea what this was all about. I was caught in an IRS snafu that accused me, as it turned out, of being another T. K. who lived in Florida. They had not an ounce of proof to back them up, nor, apparently, did they need any.

When I called the IRS, I told them that they had made a bad mistake. I was told by an extremely arrogant agent, "You don't fool us, Mr. K. We know you--we even talk to your neighbors." I told the agent, "I am sure you did not talk to our neighbors--I certainly wish you would.

## IRS Abuse Report #213

**Date:** Fri Sep 26 12:11:23 1997
**To:** sue@irs.class-action.com
**From:** JC
The IRS has kept me from making a living for the past 17 years! I am a firm believer that IRS CANNOT be fixed; it must be abolished! In addition, MANY people need to be brought to justice for the wrong doing done citizens for all these years. This includes every Congressperson, Senator, all government officials, and everyone who has taken part in ruining peoples lives participating in this illegal and unconstitutional activity.

## IRS Abuse Report #214

**Date:** Fri Sep 26 12:27:32 1997
**To:** sue@irs.class-action.com
**From:** DW
I have been being harassed by the IRS for almost 2 years. They are auditing me for 92,93, and 95. They disallowed my children and my head of household status. It took over a year

before they would acknowledge them. After that was settled, they decided that they would try and find something else to get me for. It's like a never ending battle. I am still trying to correct their errors. I have managed to hold off the various lien threats but this whole situation could have been totally avoided. They had no proof that my children weren't my children, yet they could manage to negate their existence for no reason. They can basically do whatever they want and get away with it. I'm glad that the IRS is finally being shown as the bully's that they are!!!!!

## IRS Abuse Report #215

**Date:** Fri Sep 26 13:34:42 1997
**To:** sue@irs.class-action.com
**From:** MA
My husband and I were harassed and humiliated for a long period of time.

In December of 1991 I took early retirement. In 1993 when filing our tax return, we found out that we owed $17,000 dollars in taxes due to this early retirement. The IRS attached our checking and savings accounts without notifying us (the bank notified). We called to see how we could resolve this situation since we did not have the money to pay it in full. We were told to fill out numerous forms on our finances and send it in. We did so, and then called them. We were told that we could make monthly payments to pay this bill off. We were told an amount to pay and we agreed to do this. We asked for the person's name that we dealt with in case there were any problems but was told this could not be done. We then asked for a statement to be mailed to us showing this agreement so we would have something to refer to. Again we were told this could not be done. They said everything would be in the computer if there were any problems.

We made the payments and a few months passed and our checking accounts were attached again. We called the IRS to find out why and the person that answered said they were reviewing the files and decided to try to collect the money due. We explained the agreement we made with the IRS and we had to go through the whole scenario again. One clerk actually laughed at us after reviewing our income and the situation. We went through this several times and our nerves were shot because we never knew when they would attach our accounts again and cause us additional problems. We finally went to the bank and refinanced our house in order to pay off the debt which at that point was up to $23,000.

We were treated like criminals and felt totally defenseless in this whole situation. After all, who was going to protect us from our own government? My husband and I have always been behind our government 100% but after this situation occurred we realize how vulnerable we are and how little protection we have in defending ourselves from government agencies such as this.

## IRS Abuse Report #216

**Date:** Fri Sep 26 14:36:25 1997
**To:** sue@irs.class-action.com
**From:** MN
I have become one step above homeless because of the IRS, I am forced to live off my friends and relatives because the IRS has taken just about everything I have. I can't drive anymore get a decent job. Or work on the books for anyone. Thank you IRS you have turn yet another potentially useful citizen into a drop out of society. Just think if you had notified me before you stacked on impossible to pay fines & penalties I might have been able to pay you! Now you have made it impossible for me to pay back, or find a decent job who would hire me in this predicament!

AMNESTY NOW !!!!!!!!!!!!!! CITIZENS TAKE BACK AMERICA!!!!!!!

## IRS Abuse Report #217

**Date:** Fri Sep 26 14:41:01 1997
**To:** sue@irs.class-action.com
**From:** GA
I believe the reports that I have read, but am afraid to tell my story because they have also abused me. I will never be out of debt because of it; even though initially I never owed them any taxes. I was not able to get any help to resolve the matter so I began to pay them every month because of the threats. They prey on women with kids who are defenseless, and no one can help you. They can have you paying a debt until the day you die and after because of their penalties, interests, and any other thing they want to add to torment you.

## IRS Abuse Report #218

**Date:** Fri Sep 26 15:37:55 1997
**To:** sue@irs.class-action.com
**From:** KH
Already thousands, if not tens of thousands of Americans live out their lives in fear of "big brother..." To learn the IRS is even able to intimidate members of juries sitting in judgment of IRS cases is chilling to every thought of justice! I also took note of the fact that one agent testified about a poor soul who became the focus of IRS attention for exercising his constitutional right to free speech! (writing a letter to the editor!) When will this stop?? Will it end only when the IRS begins putting us all into special "Tax Camps?" Once that happens, how long will it be before IRS agents are given the right to "liquidate" non-filers, or those who owe too much? Sounds ridiculous, I know... but the atrocities of Nazi Germany would have sounded pretty unlikely in 1933....

Only when the IRS is eliminated will America be free again. I don't oppose taxes, I oppose the oppressive and unconstitutional ways used by the IRS to punish those who dare to use their minds to think. In the 17th century one could be punished for "thinking about the death of the King.." Today, we learn, one can be punished for daring to think about the dismantling of the IRS

The IRS has damaged me and every other American citizen by forcing us to live in constant fear that one day there will be a knock at the door, or a letter in the mail demanding payment. Millions of American citizens live in constant fear of the IRS... The agency is guilty of, if nothing else, inflicting severe mental stress on honest, law-abiding citizens by conducting its campaign of terror and intimidation.

## IRS Abuse Report #219

**Date:** Fri Sep 26 16:24:09 1997
**To:** sue@irs.class-action.com
**From:** TB
I owed them $4000, came up in audit .. was willing to pay as a result of the fear of going to jail .. had no real idea of what could happen .. was not aware that a lawyer could help

As a result I agreed to pay in full .. thought that I could pay off $4K in 2 years .. wrong!! penalties and interest came to almost 200% of original .. still agreed to pay

Twice during the course of paying this off (5 years) I received letters threatening to seize my bank account due to non-payment .. I had been paying all along .. I had to contact the regional director in Denver to investigate (this after calling D.C. to find out what to do) .. turned out my payments went to someone else's account!!

I think the penalties and interest were way too high .. I did wrong but my total payout for $4K was close to $16K with all the interest!!

I felt threatened and abused but what could one do as the IRS carries a lot of weight and the little guy like me always pays up ..

## IRS Abuse Report #220

**Date:** Fri Sep 26 17:27:57 1997
**To:** sue@irs.class-action.com
**From:** FC
My business and my family were badly damaged in 1985 by IRS agents. They foreclosed my business and it ended up costing me over $12,000 in interest, penalties, and loan fees to pay over next 5 years. We wish to recover some of the money due but couldn't afford the attorney fees.

In 1984 my business was doing well. Because I installed and repaired appliances and my wife was attending college we hired an accountant to see to the IRS quarterly payments, etc. I was signing checks to have the taxes sent and the accountant was not forwarding the money to the IRS. We got a notice in May of 1985 that we were in arrears with out quarterlies. This was the first we had heard of this and I immediately contacted the accountant who said we should "write to the IRS" and ask them about the letter, "it was surely a mistake." Before I had any word back two IRS agents appeared at my door and stated that they would be back at 0800 the next day and if we didn't "have $8,200 (approx.) he would "lock the doors and ruin the whole thing!" He came back next day with a locksmith to change the locks, drove by our home every few days and called our home to remind me that I was not allowed to function in my business.

Other than this harassment of me and my family we did not hear from the IRS for something over two months. It was at this time the agent informed me they would be taking bids on my business the next day. He received no bids and offered to "sell" the business back to us--I can't recall the sum--and finally ended up giving us the keys and set up a payment plan. We paid on this plan for a year and when I received no paperwork to confirm my payments I requested a summary. It was at that time we discovered that the payments were falling way short, the penalties and interest on what we owed were still accruing. We contacted the IRS office and were told Mr. G. was no longer there. The woman who met with my wife and me was very nice and was admittedly shocked by the plan setup. She advised we secure a loan to pay the money off. Of course no one would give us a loan to pay off the IRS!

## IRS Abuse Report #221

**Date:** Sat Sep 27 12:56:34 1997
**To:** sue@irs.class-action.com
**From:** ED
Through misunderstanding the tax laws, I failed to pay a portion of tax owed.. The assessment came to about $16,000. In accordance to a phone conversation with the IRS, it was agreed that I would pay $350 a month. I requested, but did not received, anything in writing from the IRS, such as a breakdown on the penalties and the payment agreement. After paying the $350 a month for eleven months, I received a notice from the IRS that I now owed close to $30,000. I ended up declaring bankruptcy and paying $600 a month for five years and a balloon payment of $6,000 at the end.

## IRS Abuse Report #222

**Date:** Sat Sep 27 12:56:34 1997
**To:** sue@irs.class-action.com
**From:** JD
I commend you on your initiatives against these parasites of our society called the IRS. They have certainly destroyed everything I have worked for over forty years in just a couple of years. They have made my and my family 's life pure misery. They have contributed extensively to the destruction of my business and extensive family problems. The IRS be immediately dismantled and a national consumption tax is instituted instead. This can save this country and create another Switzerland. The IRS is worse than a bad nightmare that has plagued this nation for over forty years and is about to destroy it unless the IRS is eliminated and all its parasites are put to

do something productive; like work!

## IRS Abuse Report #223

**Date:** Sun Sep 28 2:27:54 1997
**To:** sue@irs.class-action.com
**From:** BW
Due to an error 20 years ago, I have incurred a tax levy that leaves me $130.00 a week to live on.

## IRS Abuse Report #224

**Date:** Sun Sep 28 8:16:00 1997
**To:** sue@irs.class-action.com
**From:** Anon
I am presently going through hell with the IRS. I am continuously being lied to and when I complained to the supervisor the agents actions increased from bad to worse. I was born in Germany after the nazi years only to live them now.

I owed some back taxes. I tried to do an offer of compromise, but was told to withdraw it and borrow the money instead or they would make me pay $3500 a month. Our monthly income with 5 children is $ 4500. I was called continuously and threatened, I owe the back taxes, my husband paid all his. The IRS agent went to his work place and threatened him, while I was meeting with another agent from the same office!

One agent said they would turn over the financial information to the other agent to work out a monthly payment. I was waiting for this payment amount to be told to me. They then seized our total paychecks two days before the end of the month. Which left us no money for rent, food or child care. I have developed an ulcer, my blood pressure went from 120 over 70 to 199 over 97, I have lost over 35 lbs. and had to see a doctor for depression. I was a healthy well adjusted individual before the IRS became involved.

I want to pay the money I owe but they don't want to work on any payment plans. A tax year bill of $325 has became $2500. The IRS calls my office and announces it is the IRS calling, just to embarrass me. The IRS agent knew this would harm my husbands career as a financial manager, so she went after my husband and told me she would call his boss if I did not come up with the money. I did not have the money, if I did, I would not have to live through this hell.

## IRS Abuse Report #225

**Date:** Sun Sep 28 8:16:00 1997
**To:** sue@irs.class-action.com
**From:** LM
I started with a $400 IRS debt. I ended up paying almost $14,000 when it was finished. Is there anyone I can contact in order to find out what happened? Where do I go for help?

## IRS Abuse Report #226

**Date:** Mon Sep 29 2:39:15 1997
**To:** sue@irs.class-action.com
**From:** Anon
By being honest and returning the refund of slightly over $400, I was charged more than $2000. I guess that shows you how much the IRS values honesty. I'm sure they had quite a few "yucks" around the office over this one.

## IRS Abuse Report #227

**Date:** Mon Sep 29 15:45:19 1997
**To:** sue@irs.class-action.com
**From:** LJ
1. Blocking my credit rating because of a lien attached on my house they are claiming my husband owes. (Separated for seven years) 2. Caused me to have serious financial problems. 3. Very stressful, I have developed high blood pressure. 4. I cannot get a loan because of the $50,000 lien on my house owed by my husband. 5. IRS refuses to talk to me about it.

6. Harassed and audited by the IRS for the last seventeen years. 7. IRS still has old liens attached to my deed that have been paid.

## IRS Abuse Report #228

**Date:** Mon Sep 29 23:39:42 1997
**To:** sue@irs.class-action.com
**From:** MM
My husband was self employed and did not pay the right amount of taxes. We were divorced some time later. My divorce decree designates my husband as the one that is suppose to pay the IRS. Because he has held a job only sporadically the IRS leaves him alone. I have all four kids and have held a job since the divorce. The IRS refuses to go after my x and keeps my income tax. I have four kids and am barely able to keep our heads afloat. I have shown my debt to income ratio and the IRS refuses to listen. They said there is no reason to settle this because they can continue to take my tax refund. How is this possible?? I am at my wits end. Can someone please get this bully off my back!?

## IRS Abuse Report #229

**Date:** 97-09-30 16:05:02 EDT
**To:** sue@irs.class-action.com
**From:** BL
Dear Sue:
Thank you for the reply to my email inquiry about the class-action lawsuit. I do consider myself a potential plaintiff in this case. Here's why:

In 1985, when I was an 19-year-old waitress, my employer failed to withhold enough from my wages. During some type of audit later, I (along with a few other employees) ended up having to repay the IRS a fairly small amount of money - around $117.00, I think. I did so promptly when I received a bill. But several years later I was contacted by the Michigan automated collection system, with the IRS trying to collect this money from me again. I called them when I received the collection letter, explaining politely that they were mistaken and that I had settled this debt years ago.

I was informed that I had better produce some proof or pay up. I began receiving letter after collection letter along with harassing phone calls from collection agents who yelled at me and intimidated me - not to mention did not listen to what I was saying - I HAD ALREADY PAID. I ended up in tears, screaming at one of them to "never contact me again." I threatened to call a lawyer if the abuse did not stop. I also produced and mailed copies of the (by then several years old, by the way) cancelled checks that proved my innocence. Incidentally, I was informed several times that the records detailing this debt had long since been destroyed because of the age of the claim. All they had left was my name and a number that they felt I owed.

They stopped calling me, failed to acknowledge my efforts and WITHHELD this money erroneously from my next refund. I gave up contacting the automated collection system since no one there seemed to have a brain in their head. My tax preparer took over for me. He contacted state rep. Don Gilmer at that time and insisted that the abuse stop and my money be refunded. Lo and behold, it was refunded shortly afterward. I thought the problems were over.

Later that same year I began receiving collection letters AGAIN for this same amount. It was withheld in error a SECOND time from my refund. That was two years ago. Since then my tax preparer has had no luck getting my money back for me; he has been in contact with Don Gilmer again and again without results.

I contacted two attorneys who both advised me that it would cost more than it's worth to collect the money for me - they bill at $100.00 per hour and the debt isn't much more than that (although they did add "late" penalties!)

I sincerely hope you can help end this nightmare for me; I may not be one of those wealthy people who have lost hundreds of thousands to these creeps, but it is MY MONEY that they have stolen. I have a family of four living on a heavy equipment operator's salary. I lost my job last year and have more than my share of financial problems as a result. Even this small amount would be a tremendous relief to me.

### IRS Abuse Report #230

**Date:** Tue Sep 30 11:00:44 1997 **To:** sue@irs.class-action.com
**From:** RM

I am a retired CPA, so nothing that I hear about the IRS and Congress's lack of control of this agency surprises me. However, why the American people in their complacency continue to put up with the complexities of and abuses from such a power-hungry, Congress-sponsored agency never ceases to amaze me.

Since retirement, any professional focus on my part in this area has been in supplying tax and financial planning services (gratus) to family members and surviving spouses of close friends. Having "removed my biased hat", I have really begun to realize just how far-reaching IRS abuses are and, even more importantly, that these abuses are primarily Congress-created and Congress-supported.

The IRS is only partly to blame. Congress, with the IRS following suit, has created the most complicated reporting and compliance system known in the history of the world, affecting some 265 million+ people in the US and millions more abroad. If members of Congress are indeed representatives of the people, then I can only paraphrase a well-known Biblical quote: "Forgive them Lord, for they know not what they do". Regrettably, they don't.

When Congress suggests changes, additions and deletions to the tax system, members, not having the experience and foresight, never realize just how complicated implementation of and compliance with their actions become. The IRS follows through with implementation and clearly believes that it has a mandate from Congress to force compliance.

Consequently, the changes are made, the IRS complies and the American people suffer. Shame on us for our complacency.

The IRS feeds on the lower-to-middle income taxpayer. These are the ones who in the main do not understand the tax system and for the most part cannot afford professional help. Seizure of assets, without due process, is common. A family's home can be seized with no prior notice and no hearing, and only requires the signature of an IRS District Director. No where else in our judicial system would that type of injustice be allowed.

When a system becomes so complicated for the masses that compliance can only be purchased from professionals, and only by those who can afford it, it is time for a change. The system, at a minimum, must be greatly simplified, due process and oversight must be required and atrocities eliminated.

More appropriately, it should be replaced, possibly with a much-simplified, consumer-based tax on spending. Do away with the IRS as we know it. Eliminate tax reporting. Divert our tax dollars to areas that are meaningful and stop paying for an agency that feels it has a mandate from Congress to simply do as it pleases.

Shame on us.

## IRS Abuse Report #231

**Date:** Tue Sep 30 11:13:24 1997
**To:** sue@irs.class-action.com
**From:** RB
The IRS has no human soul. It is an agency

made up of bureaucrats who neither know the person they are devastating, nor are they responsible to anyone for damage they have done. The net result is the alienation of citizens from their government.

## IRS Abuse Report #232

**Date:** Tue Sep 30 15:59:34 1997
**To:** sue@irs.class-action.com
**From:** Anon
It seems that the IRS is above the law of our land, they should therefore be treated as the TERRORISTS that they are.

## IRS Abuse Report #233

**Date:** Tue Sep 30 15:59:34 1997
**To:** sue@irs.class-action.com
**From:** SA
After getting my bill from the IRS and knowing I have no way of paying except selling my home, I found your page. I feel suicide is the only answer. All I have left is my home and at 50 years old and on disability, I will be in the street. There is no future in this life for me. Reading others problems only makes me feel worse. Where can a person go for help?

## IRS Abuse Report #234

**Date:** Wed Oct 1 14:39:13 1997
**To:** sue@irs.class-action.com
**From:** SP
Taxes not paid because the person responsible for paying the taxes was not paying them but telling us that the taxes were paid. The same person with held any information the IRS sent about paying said taxes. An offer in compromise was made (just trying to end the abuse and verbal attacks) the offer was to be a five year contract which has now extended to 6 years because of wording in the contract.

Through all this my wife who was the second

income in my family became very ill with a cardiac disorder (which, not proven, could have been accelerated by the stress from years of abuse by the IRS.) she was told she could not work any more or it would kill her . I have to replace her income now, and the IRS will get 50% of that because it is over what I was making myself in 1991.

Since 1987 when this all started, we have been through audits, inventories of personal property, levies, liens, 9 IRS agents, 2 attorneys, an appeals process that was a joke, and a hearing with an agent that told me he knew I was not responsible. But he said the person that was responsible is to old to go after and he will die soon. He said I have a lot of years left to work, and he would haunt me until I was 65." I have paid more than the amount the IRS felt I was responsible for. But the abuse and seizure of my income and my life has not stopped. I am a firefighter with three jobs to replace my wife's income and to pay the IRS. I cannot afford to pay this amount, but if I don't, the IRS will take everything I have worked so very hard to build including income I need for my children's future education and my wife's health.

## IRS Abuse Report #235

**Date:** Wed Oct 1 19:43:17 1997
**To:** sue@irs.class-action.com
**From:** AK
The IRS is abusive and I feel I was emotionally raped and physically robbed of all my money.

My father died in late 1988 when I was only 18 years old. He left me an inheritance of life ins. proceeds, stock portfolios and real estate. I did not receive these until 1989. I did file my tax forms and paid the tax that was due. 3 Years later I received a letter from the IRS saying that I owed them a few thousand dollars more. I was unable to pay this according to the terms they demanded. Penalties and interest was assessed and the amount grew rapidly. I consulted a tax attorney and he agreed that my

taxes were done properly, but he was unwilling to represent me for fear that the IRS would retaliate against him. My wages were garnished and my bank accounts were seized and I was left to support my two babies on $25.04 a week. The IRS pushed me into Chapt. 7 and onto welfare. My life, reputation, credit worthiness, and children were ruined. We still suffer great humiliation every time we try to buy something.

## IRS Abuse Report #236

**Date:** Wed Oct 1 22:40:42 1997
**To:** sue@irs.class-action.com
**From:** MS
Our name was given to the IRS by our bookkeeper along with every client she had (why, you ask - makes you wonder huh). Along with these clients, we were subjected to an audit that started out as a 2 year and ended up being a past 10 years audit covering the years 1984 through 1993. Each and every year was audited and if we were unable to produce receipts for any item, it was disallowed. The audit took approx. 2 years to complete. However, each year completed, we received a huge tax bill for. The end result was a meeting in the IRS office with our tax attorney (by then, we had hired someone to help relieve the burden of the IRS being in our place of business) and our CPA (who cost us $35,000 per year). We were told by the IRS agent 'well, we have decided not to file criminal charges against you'. My immediate response was well that's good because we haven't done anything criminal, at which point I was taken aside by the attorney and told not to say another word, be grateful. An agreement was reached between our attorney, accountant and the IRS that we owed over $176,000 based upon the IRS audits. We were told to refinance our home and give IRS the proceeds, a lien was placed on our home and all property and we were to pay $50,000 per year with 'after tax' money only.

After paying this amount for three years, we

still owed $152,000. Our business was suffering because we were draining out the operating money, paying personal tax on it and giving it to the IRS. Our attorney knew what was happening and talked to the IRS, even sending them a letter stating we were headed for bankruptcy unless the payments were reduced. The answer was absolutely no. We sold property, the IRS took the proceeds, we sold our condo, the IRS took the proceeds, there was no place left to go after we cashed out our retirement, borrowed on our life insurance and sold personal belongings.

In the end, we had to default on the agreement and file bankruptcy on our business. Now we were left with no source of income (along with our 15 employees) after 15 years of building our business. Therefore, we now had to file personal bankruptcy. However, since we had refinanced our home, now the payments were twice as much as they were when we bought it and without an income source, we were forced to sell more of our personal items just to eat and make house payments. The bankruptcy court assessed our situation and made the following plan: we are to pay the bankruptcy court $700 per month for five years. The money will be distributed as follows -- $45,000 to the IRS and the balance to the trustees for costs. No other creditor will get one dime. We have no health insurance, no business, no savings, no property and no relief after all. God bless America and our rights to the pursuit of happiness. If this is where hard work and 10 hour days building one's future get you, guess welfare is a better option.

### IRS Abuse Report #237

**Date:** Thu Oct 2 14:10:25 1997
**To:** sue@irs.class-action.com
**From:** JF
1st worked for man having open heart surgery, paid all taxes on his business, while he was in the hospital. After about 3 months of being in the hospital, he closed the business. So the IRS

came to me and said I owed $2,500 because it covered the months I was there. I didn't own the business, I was only there to help out a sick friend. I asked why didn't they go after the owner of store. They said he had moved and had no forwarding address for him. But they could find me. I told them I could find the owner but the IRS said (we don't need him we got you) quote!!!!! They are like Loan Sharks they never leave you alone, I would never open a business in this country, the IRS will close you down.

### IRS Abuse Report #238

**Date:** Thu Oct 2 15:15:35 1997
**To:** sue@irs.class-action.com
**From:** A Taxpayer
After having served four years active duty in the US Navy I was attending college using the GI Bill benefits. During my sophomore year I lived at home with my parents, and worked to pay for additional expenses associated with commuting to the University. I worked part time and earned just enough to meet those expenses. When I filed my tax return a refund of around $50.00 due me...for some reason I was audited and required to report to the IRS local office where a 'Gestapo like' snotty IRS agent took great delight in informing me that I owed $74.00 and was not getting a refund. (I did not agree with this, but based on his tone and demeanor arguing the fact would have been futile)... I only had a few dollars with me and I didn't have a checking account at that time, which I explained to the agent. Naturally I asked if I could pay it the next day which seemed a reasonable request to me...but not to this little 'Nazi' who DEMANDED I pay immediately, before I left his hole in the wall office, or he would get on the phone and cancel my GI school benefits.

It was frightening and extremely upsetting...It is still clearly impressed in my mind how close I came to punching him in the face...which if I had done I would probably be writing this from

Leavenworth.. I called my Dad and he came down and paid the $74.00...he also had a few words for the agent, who asked my father if he would like his return audited...a not too subtle threat, and in fact for the next three years my dad was audited without fail.. As a side note: He seemed obsessed with the fact that my car was 'newer' than his, and he commented several times that a student shouldn't be driving such a 'new' car. It is hard to understand how such an evil jackass could represent the US Gov't, but in light of the recent hearings I expect this little snot nosed 'nazi' agent is probably a department head somewhere in the IRS's bureaucracy...

## IRS Abuse Report #239

**Date:** Thu Oct 2 22:22:46 1997
**To:** sue@irs.class-action.com
**From:** JC

Because we were new to the business world, we didn't understand many of the IRS forms that applied to business. We put everything on a 1040 IN. The IRS should have corrected us the 1st year, but in fact we believe they purposely did not do this so they could build interest and penalties.

The stressful moments between my wife and I during this time has been hard. How was I impacted? There's no way to even count the hurt and the pain that the greed of the IRS has caused me.

## IRS Abuse Report #240

**Date:** Sat Oct 4 22:20:37 1997
**To:** sue@irs.class-action.com
**From:** Anon

My brother is having a horror story with IRS. He is in the low income bracket ... poverty level. He, with good honesty, completed his 96 taxes claiming EIC because he has a dependent child and not married. He went to the local IRS office to be sure that he qualified. The IRS now says he does not qualify, but will not tell him why.

There is no way he can pay back $2000 and the IRS wants him to pay up. There is no way he can ever pay it. Besides, he doesn't know why he does not qualify. He has no resources to pursue the case. Currently he receives no state or federal aid. He feels that he will have to go on welfare. He feels he is an innocent taxpayer who is a victim of the IRS making up rules as they go along and picking on the low income people who have no resources to fight back and don't know what to do. He barely scraps enough to minimally feed his son and himself. He believed that the EIC was designed for honest people like him who are good citizens and try to do right. He no longer has any trust in the US government.

## IRS Abuse Report #241

**Date:** Sun, 5 Oct 1997 13:06:45 -0400 (EDT)
**To:** sue@irs.class-action.com
**From:** DP

IRS has refused to allow me to make a settlement with them in the past on "mistakes" that my ex-husband made on our joint tax returns back in the 1980's. Now penalties and interest have increased the amount owed to $63,000 plus. And I have been informed that now that the amount is above the $50,000 mark, that it will be twice as difficult to resolve my case.

I can't get credit, my house is in jeopardy, my life will never be what our founding fathers envisioned, I am facing old age with the real possibility that I will be out on the street. I have no money. It occurs to me that IRS's investigative agents are waiting to see if I ever have anything....then they will swoop in and take it. It surely removes any hopes for better days. What can I do?

## IRS Abuse Report #242

**Date:** Mon, 29 Sep 1997 15:12:42 -0700
**To:** sue@irs.class-action.com
**From:** JL

I have been a victim of IRS abuse since the 80's. My husband and I separated in 1990. The IRS just garnished my check because they claim they could not get payments from my husband because he ownes a business. I applied for a loan to consolidate my first and second mortgage. I discovered the IRS had audited my husband and attached $25,000 onto my mortgage. This made my loan higher, but it was still approved until Mrs. A. H., from the IRS went to court and obtained a subpoena to force the loan company to see if there was enough equity to add another $25,000 to the loan. This caused my loan to be denied because I no longer qualified with this extra sum of money added to it. When I confronted her to have her remove said amount, she was very rude and told me she was not going to let me have the equity in the house. I am held responsible for my husband's taxes, yet no one at the IRS will discuss anything with me because I am not listed on his tax return. At the present time my house and I are being held hostage by the IRS. They have constantly been trying to hold me responsible for my husband's taxes. The stress of all of this has caused me to have high blood pressure, asthma, and I have had two blood vessels break. No one will lend me any money until this lien is paid. I worry daily thinking that they are going to take my house.

## IRS Abuse Report #243

**Date:** Tue, 30 Sep 1997 17:54:09 -0400
**To:** sue@irs.class-action.com
**From:** JS

At times it seems easier to escape the wrath of God than it is to escape the wrath of the Internal Revenue Service. In fact I fear them much more than burning forever in damnation.

My husband and I have tried repeatedly to resolve things with our tax debt, but the harder we try the worse things get. To date all we have lost through levies was the balance in our bank accounts which amounted to 60 dollars.

We have been told by IRS workers to apply for food stamps and disability. My husband is unable to get work due to his health. He has suffered several heart attacks in the past few months.

We have been constantly lied to by IRS representatives, one telling us one thing and another saying that what the other said was not true. I set up a payment plan while I was pregnant and the official said I could call back after the baby was born and have my payments lowered since there would be another dependent. When I called back to have my payments lowered, the representative I talked to said it was impossible to lower the payments.

At this point I can understand why so many have opted for suicide rather than deal with paying forever on a debt that can never be paid and that only grows with time. My daughter lives in a shed in the backyard because we are unable to get decent housing, we often go for long periods of time only eating potatoes and pancakes during the winter when there is no income and every year we get further in debt paying taxes on money that goes to the IRS which is non tax deductible. I would like to see anyone working as a representative for the IRS live for one year in my shoes. Only watch their own loved ones go without, and watch their own spouse dying before their eyes as they open the notice of levy against the last $60 to their name.

## IRS Abuse Report #244

**Date:** Mon Oct 6 1:03:39 1997
**To:** sue@irs.class-action.com
**From:** DW

I have been through a 15 year battle with the IRS in which there were great periods of despair for my family. They have insulted my wife and myself. They have called my employer and have taken my salary. They have broken agreements and caused me to file for bankruptcy . We have to end this now.

If you need more write me. It is a long sorted story.

## IRS Abuse Report #245

**Date:** Mon Oct 6 20:52:33 1997
**To:** sue@irs.class-action.com
**From:** KS
In 1992, my wife and I filed separate 1040 returns. On 4/1/95, we filed amended 1040X returns for the tax year 1992. Nearly 18 months later, IRS adjusted the returns and came up with over a $3000.00 balance owing. During that 18 month waiting period, I was forced to call IRS every 4 weeks so they could place a temporary stop on any collections. During that 18 month period, 3 levies were placed against my wife employer. Three times they were lifted due to the pending 1040X returns. Countless number of calls resulted in the most rude and incompetent people I have ever come across in my lifetime. I find my calls eventually getting disconnected. No one seems to know anything. It appears that most of the operators are using alias names.

## IRS Abuse Report #246

**Date:** Wed Oct 8 5:19:20 1997
**To:** sue@irs.class-action.com
**From:** SH
It seems too long to write about. Too painful. The result is that I just quit! I don't 'work' for wages, I don't plan, I exist in the here and now. IRS ruined my life and my future. I did nothing wrong. Nothing. Sleazy expensive lawyers advised me that it would cost too much to fight them. Even though I would eventually prevail, in the meantime I would have to finance the war -- which I wasn't able to do, given that the entity I was battling had the power to

disempower me in the process.

Friends: Far too many of them, good people, formerly 'main stream professionals, have quit also. I vowed that they would never suck another dime out of me, never tap another of my phones. I would never have another business for them to send their goons to take over, employees and clients to harass and intimidate and never own another piece of real property, bank account or safe deposit box or any tangible personal property for them to steal. There are many of us out here who just 'dropped out', forced out because of this enemy. The ultimate reality is that I'm not unhappy. I'm just leading a very different life than that which I was raised and educated to believe in and live within/for. IRS targets widow(er)s! Sometimes they make you one. It's a frightening organization, worthy of RICO action. Do we all have to have zero assets so we can collectively just say: 'Go ahead, repossess my body?' I think that a National Sales Tax should be enacted and all tax collection action should be caused to cease with amnesty given to all individuals who have not committed criminal acts which have been proven to be prosecutable. And let our people go.

## IRS Abuse Report #247

**Date:** Wed Oct 8 11:11:25 1997
**To:** sue@irs.class-action.com
**From:** Anon
I was on the verge of being homeless, ready to file bankruptcy, and had filed for food stamps, just so I could pay the IRS. I lost my home, relationship, school, and would have become homeless if I did not have relatives.

## IRS Abuse Report #248

**Date:** Wed Oct 8 23:37:59 1997
**To:** sue@irs.class-action.com
**From:** RE
I am a lawful citizen who has always paid my taxes but have been forced by the IRS to go

'underground' and become a fugitive. Due to illness in my family I was forced to sell a rental property in a very stressful situation which I later found out resulted in a large 'paper' profit. I ended up owing the IRS taxes on money I never got and did not have. The IRS has offered me a payment plan which doesn't even cover the interest so that the more I pay, the more money I owe the IRS. The IRS has forced me to be a fugitive and is 'punishing' me with monthly payments (that contribute nothing to what I owe the IRS) by threatening my only means of livelihood (my pension). This is a Lose-Lose situation for both myself and the IRS. It is unfortunate that people in my situation (and similar situations) cannot openly complain and therefore this abuse will never be heard in an IRS hearing or open forum on the tax system and will probably never be fixed. How much of the $120 Billion in 'uncollected' IRS taxes could be collected and how many people could be 'honest' taxpayers if the IRS's objectives were to maximize the collection of revenue rather than punishment.

## IRS Abuse Report #249

**Date:** Thu Oct 9 21:27:04 1997
**To:** sue@irs.class-action.com
**From:** YA
This is in reference to my client. He is among the many taxpayers I represent with problems with the IRS. This case is the most serious I have encountered in my 10 years of practice. I will be brief here but have aprox. 100 pages of testimony and documentation.

This client has endured 18 code blue audits, 2 attempted audits, one audit from Ogden Utah, since 1970. Twenty seven years later we are still doing battle with the IRS. The current disputed years are the result of records that were stolen and could only be partially reconstructed. The local IRS office is currently attempting to enforce collections, without regard to the age health and financial status of the taxpayers. They have separated the taxpayers,

who have been married and filed jointly for over 35 years. The IRS refuses to acknowledge receipt of their returns, although they are sent certified and in some years they have sent as many as three copies. The details are to many to list here, we will be happy to provide copies of this case.

## IRS Abuse Report #250

**Date:** Fri Oct 10 9:01:41 1997
**To:** sue@irs.class-action.com
**From:** SC
The IRS took $900 of my refund this year to pay my ex-husbands debt from last year after he forged my name on the taxes. The IRS sent me letters threatening to garnish my wages, etc. even though my ex has a job, too. Not one letter to him. He had set up a payment schedule with them and never paid so I guess they decided to get it from me and my wages. Why they never garnished his, is a good question? Of course, IRS won't address that question. I retained a tax atty. and after submitting my signature for verification as requested by the IRS and a lot of letters, etc., it has been at least 6 months and they still haven't refunded my money or have acknowledged any further correspondence sent them by my tax atty. I went into their web site and asked their procedure on such a matter and they even responded to me via e-mail that I would be due a refund of the money. So where is it? Now that they owe money, they just ignore the taxpayer. To top this off, my new husband's refund was used to pay his ex-wife's debt that she had incurred 2 years before he even knew or met her, that he was not even aware existed. They make me feel like in past history when the tax collector would just come take every goat and child in payment for back taxes that they just think you owe or that someone else owes or burn down your house. Just so they can get money, it doesn't matter who they hurt or get it from. It is like stealing.

## IRS Abuse Report #251

**Date:** Fri Oct 10 12:03:38 1997
**To:** sue@irs.class-action.com
**From:** JR
I can't believe that there is not one person who can fight the IRS. Why is this?

My mother died of cancer two years ago. About one year before her death, she went through a divorce after 42 years of marriage. She had no income and many bills to pay. Her first priority was to sell her house, which was LEGALLY in her name only. At the closing of her home, the IRS came and took 1/2 of the money she was supposed to live on. They took it because her husband owed business taxes. And they claimed since she was married to him they were her responsibility. (Even though she had a piece of paper proving non-attachment by the IRS) They stole her money anyway, because they knew she would never come back for it. Well, through all of the heartache with divorce, sickness and no money, she had no will to live and passed away. Its been more than two years, so by law we can't fight it even though we would win the case. And if we went to court, it would cost more money in attorney fees than what the money is really worth.

## IRS Abuse Report #252

**Date:** Fri Oct 10 13:34:52 1997
**To:** sue@irs.class-action.com
**From:** Anon
I am at the point with the IRS that I am ready to take my own life. I figure that maybe they will "feel sorry" for my husband and kids and finally resolve this case. But of course it would make no difference to the agent handling our case...he undoubtedly would serve my husband with a levy at my funeral! In 1993, my husband and I went bankrupt, losing our farm and livestock, and all we had worked for all our lives. We take full responsibility for this. At the time of our bankruptcy, we owed the IRS $26,000 in back taxes. We did not dispute this either. Due to incompetent lawyers (one

embezzled money from the estate), and the fact that we were broke, the case took 2 years to come to resolution. But it finally did, and the IRS received all of what was left...$31,000. During this 2-year period, we would occasionally receive notices of taxes due from the IRS, and we would always, ALWAYS, call and try to explain the situation. One time, they would say, "Oh, okay, well we see where it's in litigation, and we will put a 'hold' on this...don't worry." The next time, it would be, "You are liable for this amount, and if you don't pay the $26,000 RIGHT NOW (plus ballooning interest and penalties), we will immediately levy. After the payment from the bankruptcy court, we heard nothing for several months, and thought everything was resolved.

I'm beginning to think that once you have a problem with the IRS, it is never resolved. We moved to another state to be closer to my husband's work, and to start over. We had been here just a few months, when we received a notice from our new state's IRS office, that we owed over $60,000 in taxes!! And the agent disputed the fact that the IRS had ever received anything from the bankruptcy estate. He will not return our calls, and has levied our paltry bank account 4 times in the past year. As I write this, he has levied my husband's employer. When that happens, you have no income. I fully believe that this agent would love to make us homeless. He marched through my house, and smirked at my tears. He also made the comment that we were "scum" like 95% of people who don't pay their taxes, and that we were "not going to get away this time." We have filed faithfully since the bankruptcy, and have nothing for this man to take. We finally employed a tax advocate, but he refuses to acknowledge the paperwork she has sent him...even sending it back to her and slapping a levy on us because she misspelled one of my children's name! This man is not a professional. He is retaliatory, and almost rabid in his pursuit. He is about to break me emotionally, and of course that is his aim. If I had the money today, I would hand it to him, just to end this agony, and clear our names. And that is just what he wants me to do...whether I owe it or not. We are so very very tired.

## IRS Abuse Report #253

**Date:** Fri Oct 10 20:05:22 1997
**To:** sue@irs.class-action.com
**From:** DM
Thank you for appropriately citing the criminal acts of a monstrous cancerous appendage clinging like a parasite to the spine of the greatest nation under the stars.

With 12 children in our Family my father worked very arduously to provide opportunities among the necessities to each of us. So after his untimely death with the youngest at 12 months the strains of my educated and devoted mother were overwhelming. After years of uncertainty concerning finances she ventured to invest some of the life insurance benefits into projects of her developing children. After the investment and tax period the IRS came in saying she owed a monstrous sum. If she did not comply within 90 days of the notice, confiscation of her house would compensate for unpaid dues. ( and what leave her and her children fearful, and homeless). Get a consumption tax!

## IRS Abuse Report #254

**Date:** Fri Oct 10 20:05:22 1997
**To:** sue@irs.class-action.com
**From:** Anon
Most IRS Agents are non caring people. An agent once told me that they have nothing but time and that they can wait you out until the penalties are so high that there is very little that you can do.

## IRS Abuse Report #255

**Date:** Sun Oct 12 1:44:09 1997
**To:** sue@irs.class-action.com
**From:** JD
My brother in law has been fighting the IRS for five years. He worked as an independent contractor for a builder, and paid the taxes he thought he owed. Two years later, the IRS came calling, wanting four thousand dollars. The tax amount was less than a thousand, but the IRS can charge interest and penalty amounts that would embarrass a loan shark. I researched the matter for him, and found the exact page in the tax code that said he didn't owe this. During the next three years, we amassed a stack of documents two inches thick, including one copy of the exact same tax code page, sent to him by the IRS, with a different passage circled that had no relation to the problem. Unfortunately he was unable to afford a tax attorney, which seems to be the type of person they go after -- ones with a job so there is some money to be had, but not enough money to fight them. We even got one letter from an IRS employee -- a handwritten note actually, explaining that she'd reviewed the matter, and he didn't owe anything. Two weeks later, he got a collection notice, so he sent the problem resolution office (what a joke) a copy of the note, and they said, sorry, that was only her personal opinion, not an official position.

## IRS Abuse Report #256

**Date:** Sun Oct 12 6:05:36 1997
**To:** sue@irs.class-action.com
**From:** BH
I am a mother of 4 children, I get no support for any of them and up till 1994 I could barely put food on my table. My sister died in 1994 and left me money which was from her job it was a saving plan from her work. I have never had to deal with money or the IRS except in my early teens my father would file an income tax return because I had part time jobs. I not only was in a state of shock at losing my sister

but also at getting the money. I filled my taxes that year with a local tax man and he told me that I didn't have to claim the money it was an inheritance gift how did I know. 2 years later I get a notice in the mail from the IRS and they ask me why I didn't claim the money. I immediately notified my sister's old CPA he said he would take care of it. Yet, so far I have had to send the IRS $60,000 to avoid any further penalties and the CPA has got me for $3,000. The IRS still hasn't decided what I owe and if any penalties will be charged I am scared. How can they do this to people? I have 4 children and myself to support besides the fact I should not be penalized. I didn't purposely avoid them, it was an honest error, I couldn't think straight, my sister had just died.

**IRS Abuse Report #257**

**Date:** Sun Oct 12 21:44:50 1997
**To:** sue@irs.class-action.com
**From:** Withheld
This is a nightmare just beginning, I am afraid. Friends of mine lost a business about four years ago and apparently were unable to pay about three thousand in taxes. In Jan of '96, she was in a car accident which left her a quadriplegic. They have three kids and he quit his job to stay home and take care of her and the children. (The youngest just turned four ...) She apparently received a visit from the IRS last week and was told that she would be receiving a statement indicating a lien against their property. She received it! For $71,000 -- give or take a few dollars. They are in no way rich people -- in fact one might put them close to poverty level. What more can be taken from them?

**IRS Abuse Report #258**

**Date:** Mon Oct 13 8:40:19 1997
**To:** sue@irs.class-action.com
**From:** SA
I have had an ongoing battle with the IRS since

last summer. In 1994 the IRS started the additional earned income proof sheet. I don't even remember anymore what this is called. It is an additional sheet that you must file with your taxes with your child's social security #. I filed my taxes that year with H&R Block. IRS took away my head of household and dependent exemption until I could prove that I was responsible for most of her living expenses. I am the only one listed on her birth certificate and am the only one who has always paid all of her living expenses. Not only that, she is 9 years old and I have claimed her every year. I have spent numerous hours sending them all the papers they say they need and I still have not had this resolved. I have sent them her birth certificate, school records, doctor records, bank account records, child care records, personal affidavits from friends and family members, canceled checks, old tax statements, etc.... They still never seem to have enough. I am so sick of this. I have spent lots of money sending them duplicate copies because it is never the same person working on it. Not to mention the long distance bills.

The IRS has taken money from every year's tax refund to pay this enormous amount of taxes that they say I owe them. They have deducted from 1993 1994 1995 and even deducted from my new husband's refund for last year! This is abuse. I have sent them all that they could possibly need and even made a personal visit to the IRS office to make sure that they have everything. So far they say that I owe them $3,000. They actually owe me $84 from that year $400 from 1995 and $500 from 1996 and this stupidity continues. They are stealing money from single mothers and the small children that are supposed to benefit from this money. I only made $17,000 that year as a single mother and this is the insanity that they put people through. They are stealing from the poor and the children.

## IRS Abuse Report #259

**Date:** Mon Oct 13 13:12:46 1997
**To:** sue@irs.class-action.com
**From:** SP

The IRS is attempting to collect on tax years 1991-1996. They sent me a bill recently and I responded with a where, when and how much? They didn't respond other than to send an intent to levy notice. When I went to the local office to clear up the confusion, I was told, no problem, we will wait until you get the information you need to file an amended return and to file a missing return. Two days later another letter of intent to levy and garnishee. I hired a lawyer, he says he has never seen anything like it in 30 years of dealing with the IRS, they sent me a letter of intent to levy based on my 1996 return!! We have been making payments of over three hundred a month since we first received the bill, in good faith, in hopes of stopping a levy or garnishment. After each contact with the local IRS office, we get a notice of levy or garnishment. Our lawyer talked to the local agent handling our case and she assured us that they would wait before doing anything drastic and then I received another letter of intent to garnish my wages. Our lawyer was stunned and is meeting them again tomorrow. They say one thing to us and then go right ahead and attempt to tie-up my income. We are on the verge of filing Chapter 13 or applying for a medical retirement, but those are last resorts. We are determined not to loose our home! But right now we are one step away from serious damage.

## IRS Abuse Report #260

**Date:** Mon Oct 13 23:09:13 1997
**To:** sue@irs.class-action.com
**From:** HT

I been working for more than 20 years, but I never get to earn more than $18,000 a year until just recently. I work I filed my tax every year, but yet I was audited by IRS twice and

was forced to pay the IRS about $3000. My English is not so good, so when I receive the letter from the IRS, I was not so clear why I got the penalty. In order to stay out of trouble from the IRS, I decided not to question or challenge them and went ahead pay them, even though I was not so happy about it and have no money to pay. Now, every time when the tax season come, I feel like the nightmare is about to haunt me again. I just don't know if I am going to receive any more of that letter "demand for payment" from the IRS. I wonder if I better off working under table!! That way I will never have to deal with the IRS again in my life.

## IRS Abuse Report #261

**Date:** Tue Oct 14 17:15:39 1997
**To:** sue@irs.class-action.com
**From:** TV

You can't deal with these people. You never get a real person to talk to, you only talk to a touch-tone computer. There is no recourse and no one to go to about problems like this. I cannot believe how corrupt our governmental system has become in the last few decades.

## IRS Abuse Report #262

**Date:** Wed Oct 15 13:59:51 1997
**To:** sue@irs.class-action.com
**From:** JC

Everyone I know has either been through an unpleasant experience with the IRS (not just owing taxes) or knows someone who has been screwed by the IRS. This BS about the congress just finding out (and apparently buying into their contention) that there have been "a few abuses" in how the IRS deals with taxpayers is insulting and is evidence of congressional incompetence (or just plain stupidity).

I've been through several audits. The worst was the first. It was an office audit. The agent refused to tell me the notes he was making in my file ('these are my notes and none of your business'). After several hours reviewing my records (I generally keep good records and receipts) and not finding anything substantial, I was told that the agent would 'settle' for $800-- not based on any particular items, just a 'general' settlement. When I asked to have my accountant review the information, the agent became agitated and abusive, slammed my folder shut, and retracted the offer 'unless I agreed to it immediately.' I ended up walking out of the audit as he would not continue our 'conversation'. They sent me a bill for about $1200 and I figured it was not worth my time, effort, anger or frustration to fight it.

## IRS Abuse Report #263

**Date:** Thu Oct 16 8:21:41 1997
**To:** sue@irs.class-action.com
**From:** SS
I am supplying my name and address. That way I can, in some small way, register myself as a member of the resistance to this very real danger to America and Americans.

My parents are in their mid-sixties. They have worked 10-14 hours a day since they were in their teens. Their philosophy has always been to give to others, and to do an honest days work for an honest days pay. Their integrity has been unquestioned by everyone except the IRS in all these years. About 6 years ago, during some sort of feeding frenzy, the IRS got the name of my father's construction business, and evidently targeted it for a collections blitz. During the past 6 years my family has had their checking account levied, their property liened, and had 'scare' packets left at their front door by IRS agents. This has not been a single incident. When one round of requests has been fulfilled, the IRS finds something else to look for. You should also understand that in none of these incidents has the IRS ever found that my parents ever missed a tax payment. They have had to go back 5-10 years and find paperwork that would support their payments, and have

done so. At one point in time, they actually paid the IRS $6000. Because the agent said '...well, it appears that you paid these returns correctly, but understand, we are paid to bring in money. If you don't pay us something now, I'll just come back with another list of requests...' My parents logic in paying was that 'maybe now they'll leave us alone...'

Now it's 1997, and a new batch of requests was delivered to my parents home. Seven pieces of paper going back seven years. All items listed have exact amounts, indicating that the IRS has the returns. But my folks were told, unless you produce these documents you are liable for the taxes listed. The IRS then put a lien on my parent's home, in August 1997. The family accountant dug out all the documents and faxed them to the IRS office three separate times. The agent refused to acknowledge that they had been received. Finally, in September, my mother suffered a complete mental breakdown, and had to be hospitalized for a day and then placed on a 24 hour "family supervised" suicide watch, which is still in effect. I took over as spokesman for my parents and began dealing with the IRS agent. I have now been told that the paperwork is in his hands, but that the agent is "too busy to get to it for a while, and that at any rate, even after he 'gets to it', it will take 30-60 days to lift the lien" IF he is happy with the way we submitted the documents.

I am afraid to proceed in the normal "let me talk to your supervisor" method, because of what I have been led to believe about IRS power. In other words, I believe these people can, without provocation, initiate a collection campaign against anyone they wish. It's their word against mine, and until I have proved I'm right they can make my life as miserable as they want to, to the point of total attachment of property and income. Well, I think it's time to fight back. The IRS collection operation is out of control, and the agency has a perverted reward system, i.e. "you are rewarded for collecting money in any way you can", as opposed to "you are rewarded for collecting money from those who owe it, using the due process of the (as yet unwritten) law." Thanks for providing a forum for me to vent.

## IRS Abuse Report #264

**Date:** Sat Oct 18 10:26:34 1997
**To:** sue@irs.class-action.com
**From:** Anon
The IRS has made our life a nightmare. But the most recent incident is simply typical of this screwed-up group of legal loan sharks. The interest on our payment plan is so steep we decided to double our payment when possible & try to pay this off sooner. We doubled our payment and sent in a check for the doubled amount. Within a month our accounts were levied for non-payment of our payment plan. When I took off work and spent 6 hours talking to people from this group I was finally told their computer can only read the amount scheduled therefore, by sending double the amount it appeared we had not made a payment. The checks that bounced and bank charges were my responsibility and I was also responsible for the reinstatement charge due to the IRS. Don't try to be sensible. They can't compute.

## IRS Abuse Report #265

**Date:** Sat Oct 18 11:02:32 1997
**To:** sue@irs.class-action.com
**From:** DH
The IRS fabricated a $15,000. tax on me and confiscated my home, car, van, business, all bank accounts for not paying the phony tax. Then when I had the phony tax discharged in a chapter 7 bankruptcy their agents appeared in court and petitioned the judge not to grant the tax discharge. But the judge granted the discharge. To get even, the IRS made up a new law just for me that no tax attorney has ever heard of. The IRS taxed me with a punitive tax on the discharge of $15.000, claiming the discharge was a capital gain.

The IRS has literally destroyed my life in a sixteen year long battle forcing me to file five bankruptcies to stop their horrible, unrelenting harassment of liens, garnishments, bank account seizures, stealing my car from my driveway, threatening letters & phone calls, audits, and destruction of my credit rating preventing me from ever buying property, or cars, or renting apartments -- all to prove they can hate bigger and better than anyone.

## IRS Abuse Report #266

**Date:** Sun Oct 19 23:28:47 1997
**To:** sue@irs.class-action.com
**From:** RN
In 1983, I became a limited partner in an oil and gas venture. I became involved in the venture with the belief that it was above-board and the intent was to drill for oil and gas. This was during President Carter's administration whereby there was widespread talk about oil shortages and the need for creating underground storage facilities for emergency situations. Consequently, under these circumstances, I certainly did not have any reservations about investing in a venture that had purposes of discovering a much sought after commodity. I gave the prospective to my accountant to insure that the venture was a legitimate investment and was informed by him that everything appeared to be in order. However, he did emphasize the risk in oil and gas drilling and the possibility that it could result in 'dry holes'. Being this was the only concern I might face, I decided to invest a total of $16,000 in the venture. In December of 1989, I was informed that the tax deduction for the year 1984 was being disallowed, and I can say that this was the beginning of what has been an 8 year nightmare. I ended up paying approximately $28,000 on a $6,000 tax debt. This resulted in my having to pay $800 per month for 3 years. Consequently, this burden forced me to file for bankruptcy. The point to remember here is that I was informed 5 years after the filing of the 1984 return and there was no mention of any

problems with the 1983 return.

In March of 1996, thirteen (13) years after the original investment, I received a letter from the IRS informing me that I owed $65,000 based on a disallowance of a tax deduction on my 1983 tax return. This represented $16,000 of original tax with the remainder being penalties and interest.

On January 1, 1997, a Notice of Levy on Wages was sent to my employment whereby they were advised to hold all income other than $800 a month. Through endless hours of trying to receive some type of understanding, an agreement was reached to set up a payment plan of $500 a month which, based on my calculations, will take twelve years to satisfy.

Since I am 55 years of age with very little retirement, I feel this tax burden will force me to live off of the government which I do not want to do. In addition, a Federal Tax Lien was issued in February 1997 and because of this lien it has made it impossible for me to purchase a home after my job relocation in April 1997, not to mention what it has done to my credit rating. I am more than willing to pay my taxes but feel there is an injustice to burden me with 13 years of penalties and interests of which I had no knowledge. When assessing interest and penalties some consideration should be given as to the nature of the tax debt, how it was incurred and under what circumstances. The objective of the IRS should not be to cause as much misery as possible on a citizen of this country who has obeyed the laws and contributed the maximum to the tax coffers over a period of 35 years. To summarize the situation:

Due to an investment that I made which I thought was legitimate, I am being forced to pay 500% more than was originally due on my taxes, forced to declare bankruptcy, ruin my excellent credit rating and endure personal embarrassment with my employer due to the filing of a tax lien on my wages. I really don't

believe that a taxpayer who has religiously paid his taxes for 35 years should be treated in this manner. I trust that the investigation into the conduct of the IRS and their unlimited power will bring about changes to the system and how taxpayers are treated. I also would appreciate any assistance that your office may offer to reduce the financial burden and hardship that the IRS action has created in my life.

### IRS Abuse Report #267

**Date:** Tue, 14 Oct 97 14:37:54 PDT
**To:** sue@irs.class-action.com
**From:** TS

My family was put through "hell" by the system to the point of almost a nervous-breakdown. The IRS "dogged" us for years, demanding that we pay money, (money that we didn't owe to begin with) or they would seize our house and other assets. When you are struggling to feed your family, these threats can be devastating to your mental health. By the end of the whole fiasco, I was left with doctor bills and medical bills that were brought on by the system.

### IRS Abuse Report #268

**Date:** Mon, 6 Oct 1997 23:57:12 -0400
**To:** sue@irs.class-action.com
**From:** PC

My husband & two daughters are victims of the IRS. The IRS stated what we owed, we offered to pay them, they refused. Our daughters house was sold by the IRS because they were told that they would be held responsible for our debt. The house was bought for $55,000 The IRS sold it for $29,000. Before the IRS sold the house, our daughters had a buyer for the house for $55,000. The IRS would not let them sell the house. Our one daughter was called at work by an IRS agent in Washington, (who's name I have), threatened her, told her that he was suppose to be taking his children out Halloweening, but instead he had to call her, when he called, he identified himself as an IRS agent to her manager.

Within two weeks, our daughter was fired from her job. My husband's disability check was taken from our account, his check was electronically deposited on the 3rd of the month, I send out our bills on either the 3rd or the 4th of the month, on the 4th of the month, we got a notice from our bank stating that the IRS had levied our account, which left us with nothing to live on for the rest of the month, plus try to make up what we had sent out to pay our bills. The IRS agent stated that "It was fair game", once it was in the bank, it was fair game. We borrowed money from our daughter to hire an atty. to file bankruptcy to try to settle the debt with the IRS, the IRS agent told our attorney & myself in a 3 way conversation that this would be the best thing to do to settle the debt. When the bankruptcy was finalized, the IRS would not accept the bankruptcy, this ruined our credit & still did not settle this case. An atty. that we had had in 1986 was threatened by the IRS agent in Washington DC. That agent told him & my husband that he was going to make an example of him. Since then, my husband has had a heart attack, our nerves are shot, we didn't know which way to turn. This is only a little of what they have put us through. I'm hoping that something will be done with the IRS.

## IRS Abuse Report #269

**Date:** Thu, 9 Oct 1997 19:05:15 EDT
**To:** sue@irs.class-action.com
**From:** ANON
May, 1985 I was in an accident in Myrtle Beach, S. Carolina. As a direct result of the accident I was out of work for one year. Lost my employees/business, lost two condominiums, lost 4+ acres of property contiguous to my residence, used up all my savings to live on until I was devastatingly broke. I applied for unemployment but was refused because I was self-employed; I applied for welfare but was turned down because I owned a home, etc.

In December the IRS froze my Bank accounts and attached my wife's wages. In order to protect myself, my family and my property I filed a chapter 13 plan. The IRS rejected the plan because the initial tax debt with penalties and interest added had increased the amount by $8K. The plan was revised in January to accommodate the IRS demand for $33K. The plan was again rejected by the IRS because the amount was now $50K. My accountant prepared an offer in compromise for $20K which was rejected by the IRS.

In September 1994, The IRS sent notice of levy on salaries and wages to my employer for $99,890. In December 1996 the IRS again sent notice of levy on salaries and wages to my employer in excess of $100,000.

In January 1997, I was fired from my job. I collected N.Y. State unemployment ($300 per week) until it ran out in July. In July, the IRS again froze all of our accounts and garnished my wife's salary and wages for $98,734. (We received $21.70 a week since August 22nd, until this coming October 17th.)
On September 12th, we received notice that a Sheriff's sale of my home is scheduled for this coming Tuesday, October 14th.

## IRS Abuse Report #270

**Date:** Fri, 10 Oct 1997 17:33:33 -0700
**To:** sue@irs.class-action.com
**From:** TK
I have been warring with the IRS since an audit in 1981, and was so out gunned that in 1993 I committed financial suicide by trying to rob a bank with the thought of paying the IRS debt that they just wouldn't let go. Even after losing my business, my career, and my pride the IRS is still in pursuit of moneys from me. I would love to get involved in a lawsuit against the IRS and wonder how I could get involved and help put an end to this runaway death train called, the IRS. Any and all information is greatly appreciated.

## IRS Abuse Report #271

**Date:** Tue Oct 21 14:25:30 1997
**To:** sue@irs.class-action.com
**From:** DS
IRS has levied my bank account again! I can't even count anymore how many times this has happened to me. I am having problems because of a past business that I owned with my ex-husband. Back in March 1993 I was divorced. Gave the house to my husband and walked away with nothing from 28 years of marriage. I gave him the house to settle the IRS debts. IRS this past September seized the house. My ex-husband was living there at that time. They sold it and received the money from the proceeds. He then proceeded to do an offer and compromise with them. I also proceeded to do one. His offer and compromise was presented mine was not. My divorce decree states that my husband is totally responsible for all these debts!!!

I know for a fact that divorce decrees do hold up. But unfortunately I don't have money to pay big attorney's to fight this case. So instead they go after a Divorced woman who is just trying to make a living. Now they want my car. It is a 1992 Chevy with 80,000 miles on it. I sell Real Estate for a living, how am I suppose to work? I offered them my life savings of $1500 even though I shouldn't be doing this. How does this government really work? Do they want people killing themselves. Do they really sleep at night?

## IRS Abuse Report #272

**Date:** Tue Oct 21 19:58:26 1997
**To:** sue@irs.class-action.com
**From:** DH
I was involuntarily separated from the US Army in 1988, for non-selection to the grade of Major (Thanks to Senator John Glenn's committee downsizing the active officer corps). As I was a USAR officer, OCS graduate, I had a Statutory Entitlement under Title X, USC to reenlist, which I did, in my previous enlisted grade.

Being Released From Active Duty (REFRAD), I became a Dual Component soldier (officer in the reserves, sergeant on active duty) and I received a Separation Pay of $30,000 (minus $6,000 in withholding), net $24,000. I continued to serve until June, 1993, retiring at my officer grade, USAR Major. I had served the last four years and ten months at the grade of Sergeant E-5 and Staff Sergeant E-6, a 55 percent pay reduction. I retired with twenty years active duty (eleven as a commissioned officer) and three years active reserve, for a total of twenty-three years of my life. Under Title X, the Defense Finance and Accounting Service "recouped" the $30,000 from my retired pay starting with the first check and continuing until they had collected the entire amount (June 1995). The $30,000 was reported in my income for the 1988 tax year and I paid Income taxes on that amount (approximately $8,400 at the 28 percent tax rate). For the 1993 Tax year, I called the IRS "Hotline" for advice on how to recoup the taxes paid on the amount that I was repaying to DFAS. I was told first to file a 4558 to extend the tax deadline while they researched the problem. I did so, and they called back and told me to use IRS Pub 525 and IRC 1341 "Repayments" to determine the deduction for the amounts repaid each year. I got the Publications, figured my tax deduction and submitted my returns in 1994, 1995, and 1996 (for the previous tax years).

In August 1996, I received the first letter from the Austin, Texas IRS "Service Center", they asked for additional information about my IRC 1341 entry and sent a "Business Depletion" form to fill out. I sent another complete copy of my tax return and the letter I had enclosed each of the previous years. Five weeks later, I received my notification that my deduction was denied, and that, due to my letters, my 1993 and 1994 returns were being audited with the intent to deny the deduction. Letters to the Austin, Texas IRS go unanswered, they don't have a phone listing, and the "Help Line" is not able to give out their phone number. An ATT Operator (after four tries) finally gave me a number that is an answering machine that tells you "You've reached the Austin IRS Service Center. No one will answer this phone.", then hangs up. Meanwhile, we received the usual, "Pay Immediately, or "LIEN, SEIZURE, GARNISHMENT, ATTACHMENT!!" letters. They say I owed $11,300 with penalties and interest. I went to Oklahoma U.S. Congressman J.C. Watts Lawton office, his staff took the complaint and sent it to the Congressional Liasion, the reply letter came from the Oklahoma City IRS office. Basically it said that I hadn't "repaid" anything, and so, I wasn't due a deduction. I continued to try to get an answer based on public law about the "Claim of Right" cited in IRC 1341. Congressman Watt's staff said, "All we can do is refer it to the Liaison Office" and "You know, the IRS is a law unto themselves."

They did, I think, manage to get my wife and I an appointment with a Mr. Baty of the Oklahoma City IRS office to hear our grievance and "try to explain the IRS's position". Mr. Baty would not listen to the simple facts that I was being taxed on money that had been repaid to the Federal government. At the end of two hours, he handed us his prepared reply that he had not shown us, but had when we came in. I went to the Lawton IRS Collection Agency in February, 1997 and entered into an agreement to pay $2500 initially and $700 a month until my tax, penalties, and interest are paid (now approximately $12,800). I make my payment each month by the 5th, because they have filed a Lien against my house. At the end of the day, the DFAS has back their $30,000 and the IRS will have their $12,800 for the four-year, $24,000 loan Uncle Sam made to me. They've made my wife cry, they've eroded my faith in the Constitution that I swore to guard, and they've shown themselves to be the "Law unto themselves" that Congressman Watts staff told me they are. I thought that this country was established on the basis of the rights of the individual over the rights of an oppressive government. I guess I'm wrong; "The rules are what I say they are!", as the Red Queen said.

## IRS Abuse Report #273

**Date:** Tue Oct 21 20:22:58 1997
**To:** sue@irs.class-action.com
**From:** OL
In my business, I had government contracts with accounts receivable of $100,000 per month on one side (not paying me for sixty days) and the IRS on the other side (charging penalties every two weeks for late payment of taxes). Contract default was not an option, as it carried a million dollar penalty. After $60,000 in late tax payment penalties and interest, we were forced into bankruptcy and lost the entire business. All taxes were paid. However, the IRS has liens against my wife and me and we are sending them $230 per month out of our social security for the next ten years or until age 75. Penalties and interest continue, and every month we go deeper in debt.

## IRS Abuse Report #274

**Date:** Tue Oct 21 20:53:32 1997
**To:** sue@irs.class-action.com
**From:** GM
I've had an ongoing problem with the IRS over the last two years. When I filed my 95 tax forms I forgot (or so they tell me) to put the amount of tax that I paid when I was figuring out my tax return. In the end I figured I owed them 26 dollars, so I wrote the check and sent it...everything should have been fine. While doing my 96 tax return, my payment center advised me they had received a letter from the IRS to withhold over 2K from my paycheck! But they gave me a chance to call the IRS to take care of it before they held my paychecks. After calling the IRS and getting the run around and sending several letters describing my predicament, I did receive some satisfaction.

They finally believed me, and sent me a letter stating that everything was okay...Last week I started to get letters again from the IRS about the same account....The really ironic thing is I work for the federal government. I'm in the Navy. For the IRS not to think that I paid my federal income tax is nuts!! The first thing that comes out of my check is federal taxes....I've called and waited forever on hold, to finally have someone get on the phone, who I have to tell the entire story to again, and again....They seem not to care...and they never believe that gee maybe it's there mistake!!! I'm guilty until I prove myself...but I did, and now I'm going through the same thing all over again....sometimes I wonder why I'm in the Navy protecting our rights and freedoms while getting shafted by those I'm trying to protect.

## IRS Abuse Report #275

**Date:** Wed Oct 22 9:18:44 1997
**To:** sue@irs.class-action.com
**From:** RF

After being laid off in July and collecting unemployment, I contacted the IRS in response to a 'Notice of intent to Levy'. I am paying back taxes and interest for several years, beginning in 1987 when for most of the year I was unemployed and lived off of a retirement fund from my previous job. Around the first week of October, a representative said they would hold any action until the end of the month when I was to contact them to report whether I was back to work. On October 21, they cleaned out my account thereby causing my rent check and several others to be returned for insufficient funds.

## IRS Abuse Report #276

**Date:** Wed Oct 22 18:18:00 1997
**To:** sue@irs.class-action.com
**From:** RP

My mother who is 62 years old has been abused and harassed by the IRS. It started when she filed the wrong tax forms in 1992. At that time she was separating from my dad and was emotionally stressed. It might have been overlooked by her. The IRS hounded her for years about the taxes she owed. She has long been retired and is on disability. She is not in

the best financial situation. She was not able to pay the entire amount, so they garnished her disability pension. Now she works in order to live because they garnish her pension. Yesterday (October 22, 1997) she received a letter from her employers stating that the IRS will garnish her paycheck of 25%!!! This action is supposedly from the 1995-96 taxes that she paid off in June (from her minimum wage job in the kitchen of a restaurant). She is not in her best years of age to work. Her problem with the IRS has existed now for five years. We are trying to get a summary from the IRS to understand the amount they claim she owes. Because the IRS keeps finding another reason to send letters saying they have found more taxes that she still has not paid for. So where are they finding this unpaid and owed taxes??? She has suffered unduly by this situation.

It seems like this period of her life should be her golden years. Yet, when she sees an IRS envelope in the mail she shakes from fear. When she received the letter from her employer saying that the IRS was going to garnish 25% of her paycheck, she broke out in tears and had to take her high blood pressure medicine to maintain her heart. I've seen this happen many times. Please HELP.

## IRS Abuse Report #277

**Date:** Sat Oct 25 18:26:32 1997
**To:** sue@irs.class-action.com
**From:** DW

Good Afternoon, If I did not have experience fighting for clients who have problems with the IRS, I would think these accounts were about people in Hitler's Germany or some communistic country. But, my experience with clients helps me to believe every word I read in your abuse reports. When you see that 52% of our income is now being paid to taxes, where do normal people go, those trying to make a living, mostly with both parents working??. Where are businesses going to be, when every penny made is going to pay some kind of tax

?? As management consultants, we are asked time and time again, "What is wrong with businesses today??? Why can't small businesses make it" ??? Our findings points directly to excessive taxes on businesses and abusive tax collectors. Thanks for allowing me a few lines. I have so much to say, but for now, I'll be still.

## IRS Abuse Report #278

**Date:** Wed Oct 29 16:34:58 1997
**To:** sue@irs.class-action.com
**From:** KT
I am accused by the Internal Revenue of not filing taxes for two years 8 years ago. They were totally wrong. So far they have cost me my marriage, ulcers, sleeplessness, and a massive case of depression. For 18 years I worked to raise two children on my own and pay my bills and taxes, they now claim I owe them $85,000 in back taxes, and penalties. They refused to supply records of what they based their figures on and also refused to cross reference 1099 information that was filed by me at the time in question....I now own nothing but the clothes on my back and am struggling to make a living and get back on my feet from my marital separation. After filing what they asked me to provide. I was not given a chance to prove my innocence. Then they gave me two days to provide more information -- information I had already given them. I am sincerely ready to commit suicide. What is the sense of having a job and trying to work and be honest all your life if this is what you get?

## IRS Abuse Report #279

**Date:** Thu Oct 30 9:47:08 1997
**To:** sue@irs.class-action.com
**From:** BL
I had been divorced a few years. Around 1988, I did not receive my refund. I called the IRS, and a woman informed me that I had been notified they were keeping my refund because my husband lied on our 1986 joint tax return. (I

never received such notice.) This was quite a blow. I had divorced him because he not only had begun beating me, but molested my daughter. I gave the IRS his work number, work address, and any other information I had on him. I told them to go after the guilty party and leave me alone. She told me they could not do this. They kept my refund the following year also. I sent them copies of my divorce decree and court papers proving he was barred from seeing my children. I had been through so much, and just as I was trying to make a new life. It seemed that he was reaching out to antagonize me again through the IRS. Somehow they accidentally sent me his address. I was terrified that somehow, they would accidentally send him mine. The IRS wrote me that they put a lien on his property. Then they wanted to know what I had of any value. Since I was afraid of him and his abilities to find me were so good, I had very little (which allowed me to put everything in my car and run at a moments notice). All I had of any value were an antique bed my mom paid $10 for at a yard sale, and an LTD which I had paid $400 or so for. I was told they would leave me alone for the time being, but if I ever bought anything of any value, they would put a lien on it. The last agent told me this collection process would go on for 11 years. I still to this day can hardly stay put for any length of time, and am terrified he may find me. I still own very little of any value so I will not have to pay for his lies. I can't tell you how hard it has been to try and have a life without wondering if the IRS is going to come after me again, or accidentally send him my personal information.

## IRS Abuse Report #280

**Date:** Thu Oct 30 13:26:15 1997
**To:** sue@irs.class-action.com
**From:** BD
Up until about 10 years ago I was a dumb and happy taxpayer. Play by the rules, pay whatever they say and all will be well. That was until my paycheck was seized, along with all other liquid

assets, meager as they were. Seizing my assets was the IRS's first attempt to contact me. After calling them, it turns out that this person, new at the job, and with the stroke of a pen, forced me to the brink of bankruptcy. Her first words I will never forget..."I guess we have your attention!" ...I almost lost my job.

## IRS Abuse Report #281

**Date:** Thu Oct 30 19:28:05 1997
**To:** sue@irs.class-action.com
**From:** SM

I am a self employed attorney. My accountant did not pick up that I was earning more than anticipated. At the last minute we [wife and I] learned to our astonishment that we owed a payment of $19,000 more in taxes. We obtained a home equity loan, fired our accountant, and sent in our return with a bank draft in the correct amount enclosed. Prior experience caused us to obtain proof of mailing, take pictures of the draft, and send by certified mail. A month passed. Then we received a letter from IRS claiming the draft was not enclosed. The bank draft had not been cashed. We sent the proof and got back a letter threatening awful things. We began calling IRS. One cannot reach the agent you talked to last time. You get IRS's random choice. Talked with another agent based in Phoenix. This lady found the return and proof of mailing. She was not impressed. She said that the Post Office must have lost the draft. Inasmuch as IRS was not at fault we would have to pay the $19,000 again together with penalties and interest. Penalty for what... borrowing money so that I could timely file my tax return, and sending everything in plenty of time? More calls. We reach a brighter employee. She pulls up file on computer. Says that our file shows that the draft did arrive. Though some error at IRS the draft was never cashed (nor returned). The lady promised to get us out a letter that day. A month has passed. The draft is at the IRS service office. I expect another letter outlining penalties and interest. I know this is just the beginning of a nightmare.

## IRS Abuse Report #282

**Date:** Sat Nov 1 6:42:23 1997
**To:** sue@irs.class-action.com
**From:** RD

The stories I've read here are all so familiar in regards to IRS abuses of people & small businesses. You wonder, what does it mean to be an American these days?, what do they want from us?, I served my country, spent 20 years in law enforcement, have been a good citizen. I started a small security business in 1991, from the beginning I had troubles with IRS, for 6 years now they claimed I owed money even after I paid my accountant to prove I didn't. It did come to a point where I fell behind due to increasing medical bills for my mother but I made every attempt to catch up, sending them thousands. I finally set up a meeting with an IRS rep. in hopes of an "arrangement"..this was the text of the conversation..I was told "You don't belong in business", The IRS doesn't want you in business", "you need more accounts", "do you have a check on you?", "do you have overdraft checking?", it looks as if you have an $11,000 or $12,000 credit but that takes 3-6 months because only "special" people are allowed to credit you account. The end on 10/25 they took every dime. The next day, on 10/26, my mom died. I now have no business, no job, no income except some savings. Its too late for me, but I strongly suggest to all "Keep fighting", don't commit suicide over these idiots, you only hurt others, don't take "radical" actions or plan overthrows of our government. Instead, "wake" up, we are the people, we are the people, we have the power to force the government to stop the "Gestpo" tactics of the IRS, take a serious look at Nazi Germany and what goes on in the IRS today..The Nazis felt Jews had no right to be in business, so they "took" everything they owned, it's no different here today in America just a different decade and a different flag.

## IRS Abuse Report #283

**Date:** Sun Nov 2 3:51:39 1997
**To:** sue@irs.class-action.com
**From:** SB

Hard to believe we live in America, the land of the free, and have an agency with the power to destroy lives.

It began in 1983 when my husband's business was audited because the IRS was conducting audits on "like businesses" in our area. He responded by turning over all records and complying with all requests from the auditor.

After two years, now 1985, and two auditors later, the result was $500,000 owed by him as a individual - all moneys received were considered his income. It was never suggested that he issue 1099's and a penalty be filed against him. His business folded before the completion of the audit and he tried to explain to the auditor that he did not make the income the audit resulted in - the auditor fully agreed but did nothing. My husband begged them to take our home as settlement. That $500,000 eventually became $2.9 million. In 1986, at age 40, my husband suffered a severe aorta aneurysm which resulted in emergency surgery for repair of the aorta and heart valve replacement and another aneurysm was found which could be repaired because of the risk of his death. I was told his condition was a result of severe stress and hypertension and that he may not be able to live a normal life again. I went to work because he could not work - we had no income, no savings, no retirement, - nothing. We received letters monthly demanding payment of the $2.9 million. 1990 a revenue officer was assigned and as a result of our meetings I voluntarily agreed to have $160 weekly garnished from my earnings - I was told the amount I owed was too large to garnish and I would have to volunteer if I wanted to keep the IRS away. The debt would be paid in approximately 257 years. Our "offer in compromise" was rejected because they could take everything we offered - we only had our

home. We were again told that they knew we did not make the money suggested by the audit. My husband was able to return to work, however he suffered several TIA strokes which resulted in hospitalizations. I begged the IRS to only deal with me because I was afraid the continuing stress of the situation would result in his death. In Aug'93 I was assigned a new revenue officer -HM and she demanded a new financial statement and no compassion for my situation. She would call and demand a response and threaten further severe action. Because of the fear I had for HM, I desperately searched for help and was finally represented by council, pro bono. We filed bankruptcy on the amount owed - maybe we could now have some peace of mind. Wrong - in May '96 I started receiving demand letters again and a new levy on my earnings. In June '96 my husband suffered a severe heart attack which resulted in his death (at age 49) in Aug. '96. In Nov '96 I started receiving demand letters again and another garnishment. In April '97 my checking and savings was levied and another garnishment on wages. I called and cried, screamed and hollered until they released the levy and assigned a new officer. Guess what, this new officer knew nothing about my history and I had to supply her with my records and information about my case. The last time I spoke with her was 10/31/97 and I became so distraught I could barely speak. She seems to be trying to sort things out but she still says they may seize my home. I am now on medication for irregular heart rhythm and the stress is unbearable. I grieve not only for the loss of my husband but for the feelings of worry he had before he died knowing the mess he would leave me in. He was very alert and aware until two days before his death - even told his doctors' about his concerns with the IRS.

## IRS Abuse Report #284

**Date:** Sun Nov 2 9:38:44 1997
**To:** sue@irs.class-action.com
**From:** BB
Thank you for creating this web site. Together we can expose the IRS for what it truly is. A monster out of control!

This will be the second year in a row that I have been audited and the IRS for some unknown reason refuses to acknowledge the existence of my son (age 12). I file my taxes in timely fashion and in both audits (tax years '95 & '96) they deny my eligibility for the "earned income" tax credits available to me as a poverty-level single parent. The IRS has for the second year in a row sent me a letter stating that they have RE-DONE my taxes for me and disallowed my claim for earned income credits and are now charging me , with interest penalty, for unpaid taxes. Citing their reasons that my son does not exist!! and I am not qualified to receive the credits due me. For the tax year of '95 I filed a total income of $6,005. And now they are saying I owe $3,343 in unpaid taxes! more than half of my poverty-level income. I include in my tax forms the form they request for eligibility for the earned income credits wherein I give the appropriate information about my son. Beyond any doubt I do qualify for the credit and they never give reason as to why I do not qualify. It is as though they, the IRS, have lost some paper work and now I have been compelled by them to prove that they are wrong in the form of notarized documents and excessive and expensive mailings to prove my tax status. A status of which I have sent them each and every tax year.

The IRS blindly go about their business of sucking poor hard working taxpayers who don't have the money to defend ourselves. It should be illegal for anyone, IRS or otherwise, to RE-DO someone's taxes without that person's knowledge or input. The whole idea that the IRS can do this is ludicrous and totally outrageous! The stress of all this brought about by a clerical error on their part is overwhelming at the very least, the matter in which they attempt to resolve these problems is unconscionable.

## IRS Abuse Report #285

**Date:** Sun, 2 Nov 1997 19:20:10 -0400 (EDT)
**To:** sue@irs.class-action.com
**From:** JD
In 1987 I closed down a business. Subsequently, the IRS billed me for 1988 & 1989 taxes. I have requested that they support their claim and was told that they did not have to prove I owed the $, I had to prove I did not owe the $. When I asked where they got their figures from I was told it was off returns I filed. Naturally, I asked them to produce the documents. Guess what? The documents are in archives and can not be located! But none-the-less I owe the $ and must pay.

This nightmare has been going on for 8 years. I can not own anything, every 6 months or so a new agent is assigned to my case and with each new agent I go through the same process. They do not have to support their claim, I must prove they are wrong.

I now pay $550 per month against a bill of over $250,000, the IRS has never produced one document other than a computer printout to support their claim. I can not own any property, my bank accounts are subject to levy, I can not borrow $.10, my entire life is under their control. And they still have not supported their position.

I have hired lawyers to attempt to resolve this matter, the net result is that I have paid lawyers to get the same result. I can not afford to fight them alone.

## IRS Abuse Report #286

**Date:** Sun, 2 Nov 1997 06:32:28 EST
**To:** sue@irs.class-action.com
**From:** QP
The IRS has levied our wages (mine and my spouse), our life insurance policies, our bank accounts. This was done by them without following the laws of the United States.

## IRS Abuse Report #287

**Date:** Sun Nov 2 23:03:14 1997
**To:** sue@irs.class-action.com
**From:** TK
This may or may not qualify as an abuse report but the IRS has certainly cost me years of my life, much of my peace, and a substantial chunk of money over the years.

I've had liens and garnishments and collections pending since 1990. Not one day of peace. This, despite my most scrupulous efforts to satisfy every request by the IRS, and to file detailed and accurate returns every year. The anger and frustration resulting is enough to drive one to distraction.

## IRS Abuse Report #288

**Date:** Sun, 2 Nov 1997 06:32:28 EST
**To:** sue@irs.class-action.com
**From:** QP

The IRS has levied our wages (mine and my spouse), our life insurance policies, our bank accounts. This was done by them without following the laws of the United States.

## IRS Abuse Report #289

**Date:** Fri Nov 7 15:05:56 1997
**To:** sue@irs.class-action.com
**From:** Anon
For some reason, the IRS sent my mother in

law a check in excess of $80,000 that she didn't have coming to her. A complete and undeniable error on their part. When she gave it back to them, they said "where's our interest?" And they still won't back down! They keep insisting they are required to collect this interest.

## IRS Abuse Report #290

**Date:** Sat Nov 8 19:16:14 1997
**To:** sue@irs.class-action.com
**From:** Anon
I work for an owner of a company that had an 'encounter' with the IRS. To make a long story short, the business owner and the IRS had an agreement that the business owner would pay a certain amount of money until the tax bill was paid in full. It was only a short period of time until the IRS walked into his place of business and demanded the full payment. The IRS was reminded about the agreement that both parties had, but that did not seem to matter. They demanded the remainder of the money or they threatened to close down his business. The owner paid the money but it took all his operating funds.

## IRS Abuse Report #291

**Date:** Sat Nov 8 22:40:32 1997
**To:** sue@irs.class-action.com
**From:** PB
I went through a nasty divorce. My ex-husband never paid taxes but mine were taken out of my paycheck. In the divorce the judge ordered him to be responsible for his taxes amounting to thousands of dollars. He simply left the state. The IRS didn't know where to find him, but they knew where I was. So they started with my car and my checking account. I had checks bouncing everywhere because they simply took what little I had. Then when I filed my tax returns they kept what they were supposed to return. They did that until they had all the money he owed them. I was raising three children myself. I explained to them what had

happened. They said oh that is really too bad, I feel bad for you but we can do this because your name is on the taxes since you had filed a joint return while you were married. My ex-husband never had to pay one dime of his taxes, I had to pay them all.

### IRS Abuse Report #292

**Date:** Mon Nov 10 23:45:26 1997
**To:** sue@irs.class-action.com
**From:** PC
I ran into trouble with the IRS because for the first time in my life I actually got some extra income other than my annual salary. The company that I was working for at the time rewarded my performance with some stock options which I took advantage of and used the money to put a down payment on the purchase my first home. Well for the first time in my life when it came to tax season I owed money approximately $4000 which put me in a panic because I did not have the funds to pay this. I was advised to enter into a payment plan which I saw as only fair since I owed the money. I thought I was safe as long as I made my monthly payments which I did!! Well it was a week before Christmas the actual date was 12/17/96 and I had about $1700 in my checking account, I had just sent my mortgage payment, we just had our first child 4 months old at the time and were looking forward to Christmas. On a trip to make a small withdrawal from my account I was denied and I then made the discovery my account was empty, and my mortgage payment bounced!! I called my bank and they informed me that my account had been levied by the IRS! I had no notice and NO reason to suspect it since I made my monthly payments!! I called the IRS and spoke to a woman whom I asked why was this done -- " I made my payment?!!" She confirmed that I made my payment and that it I should not have been levied but it was "just" the computer!! She said the funds could not be returned but it would be credited towards my outstanding TAX DEBT, I pleaded with her, trying to get the IRS

to put it back -but it was useless!! Well that little random act of kindness from the IRS caused me a black mark with my Mortgage holder who was to remove the PMI off my mortgage which would have saved me almost $200 a month, but because of that bounced payment they would not remove it. But the worst part of it was how depressed I became, and we just let Christmas pass with no celebration. I am still paying every month but I can not catch up -- they continue to hit me with penalties and I have pretty much given up hope on ever getting out of the hole!! I am in fear that they will do that again and I feel that there is nothing I can do about it!!

### IRS Abuse Report #293

**Date:** Mon, 10 Nov 1997 17:35:32 -0500 (EST)
**To:** sue@irs.class-action.com
**From:** TB
I filed as head of household for the 1996 tax year, rightfully so, and now I have been audited. They have sent me a determination that I currently owe $4190! (All of my 1996 return plus penalties) They never gave me an explanation to this decision, even after I sent them school records, court records, lease agreement, receipts, doctor bills, dental bills, the works.

The IRS is very powerful against a single mother of two with an income of less than $20,000 a year (that includes child support)! I do not have the resource to fight them and have read these horrifying stories similar to mine. Thank you for your time.

### IRS Abuse Report #294

**Date:** Tue Nov 11 21:14:54 1997
**To:** sue@irs.class-action.com
**From:** SS
This is a case of IRS harassment and extortion. I am a 79 year old man, and the IRS is suing in federal court to throw me and my wife out

of our home. The suit has no merit. This is a matter of life or death for me and my wife who is also 79. We have no place to go when our home is seized. The IRS wants to throw us into the streets. We have no money to hire a lawyer, because the IRS is levying and seizing our pension, after the legal time for levying has expired. The IRS claims that we owe taxes-- based on defective and improper dummy returns which they prepared.

## IRS Abuse Report #295

**Date:** Tue Nov 11 23:10:33 1997
**To:** sue@irs.class-action.com
**From:** PM
In 1986, after my father begged me, I went into business with him as his secretary. My father was totally responsible for deciding what bills got paid and what ones didn't. Although I physically wrote the checks, all checks were written under his direction. In May, 1987, I found employment elsewhere and resigned. I have been with the same employer since 1987. In 1988, I received my first visit from the IRS. Apparently, my father did not pay withholding taxes for one quarter of 1987 for his company. I was told that as a single parent with a disabled daughter, practically on welfare, the debt would be declared uncollectable and that for 7 years, the IRS would seize my tax refunds and hold a lien against me. In 1989, they came after me a second time with threatening notices -- at the time I was living on subsidized housing, working 3 jobs to pay my bills and still receiving no support for my daughter from my ex-husband. Since that time, the IRS has come after me and harassed me 3 or 4 times. In 1993, the sent a notice of levy of wages to my employer. The IRS has been attaching my wages taking approx. ($50) per week. They are now demanding payment for nonpayment of withholding taxes for a quarter in 1988 when I wasn't even with my father's company and I can prove it and have told them so -- only to be ignored! For the past 9 years, the IRS has seized close to $10,000 in tax refunds, wage

levies, etc. from me. They say I owe a total debt of over $50,000 now. Last month, still having a levy on my wages, I was contacted by a local rep of the IRS saying it had been turned over to her for collection because the debt was too large and $50 per week wasn't enough money! I am so tired of being harassed and abused at every corner. I cannot own anything, cannot have a bank account! How can we stop this abuse? Signed -- a very frustrated, innocent taxpayer.

## IRS Abuse Report #296

**Date:** Wed Nov 12 18:08:07 1997
**To:** sue@irs.class-action.com
**From:** TH
My IRS problems began years ago when someone else was given my tax identification number by mistake. With the first piece of IRS mail sent to me with the wrong name but the right social security number and address, I let them know. I also checked with the Social Security Administration to see if they had the error too. No. When I did not get my tax refund for 1988, I called. 'We'll get back to you.' I called back. This time I was asked: Are you sure this is your Tax ID number? Yes. Then I explained again and again the error. 'We'll get back to you.' When I didn't get my refunds for 1989 and 90, I went through the whole song and dance again and again. By now I was owed $1,100 in refunds. I move to the Pacific Northwest in 1991. That December, my employer served me with an IRS wage garnishment Notice of Levy for failure to pay taxes in 1988. What! The notice was from the IRS in Fresno, California. The next day I called IRS Fresno and told the agent I that had filed the 88 return, and had contacted the IRS numerous times about my meager refund. I also asked about my other refund. 'I'll inform out Seattle office.' I faxed the 1988 return to him and within a day, the levy was released. In March 1992, I got another Notice of Levy for failure to pay 1988 taxes. This time the notice was from IRS Seattle. I told the agent I had

faxed a copy of the return to Fresno, and could fax one to Seattle. I did. A week later the notice was canceled. I inquired about my 89, 90, and 91 refunds. 'We'll check into it.' In 1994, when the construction cost on my new house was over budget, I went to the bank to borrow $20,000 more. At that time, I learned my property had been liened by the IRS for $8,000 for 1988 taxes! I contacted IRS Seattle, which told me to contact IRS-Vancouver, WA. The agent there told me that there were now new liens against the property, totaling $29,000 for failure to pay taxes for the years 1989, 1990 and 1991. I showed him my tax returns and said I've been trying to get my refunds. The agent said he would not look at any of my returns unless I paid the $8,000 for 1988. I had no choice but to pay the IRS to get the liens released for the bank loan. I gave him copies of my other tax returns and asked to please get my refund. Common sense went out the window. Consequently, they disregarded my returns-- except for 1990 where I received refund credit-- and made up their own showing that I owed not $29,000 but $14,000 to be paid immediately.

### IRS Abuse Report #297

**Date:** Thu Nov 13 17:30:21 1997
**To:** sue@irs.class-action.com
**From:** WM
I just got off the phone with the IRS (13 Nov 97/1615 ET) where I was told I have a new monthly payment to them for just under $500. This is to increase another $300 upon final payment of a garnishment caused by one of their levies emptying my bank account last year. This action, caused checks to bounce and my daughters and I receiving eviction notice. They've done this to me four years in a row now, emptying my bank account without notice. When I call, I was told once, 'We did that to get your attention.' I have been slandered, have suffered defamation of character, and had to file bankruptcy. Ten years ago I noticed a problem with the IRS and called the so called 'Problem Resolution Office'. I was told, 'You have no

problem with the IRS.' A couple of years later, I received a letter from them, 'You have a problem with the IRS!' I started a writing and calling campaign to get this straightened out. It took 10 years, plus writing to the White House, the Commissioner of the IRS, and the Speaker of the House before I received a call from the IRS purporting to help. By this time, my bank account had been emptied thrice, 'to get my attention', had been evicted once, had three vehicles repossessed and had my pay levied.

I recently had to resign from my career job as another judgment was levied against me causing a lot of concern with the folks holding my employment. These types of continuing actions and threats cause great pain and heartache to myself and dare I say millions of law abiding citizens of the United States of America. As a friend (they can't take these away, yet), stated a couple of weeks ago, except for the lack of black coats and saucer hats, you'd think we were in 1930's Germany. Because of these actions, I have suffered physical health problems associated with heart and stress levels. I've not reached any self destructive conclusions. However, one of my daughters ended up in the hospital because she thought one less mouth to feed would lighten the burden. I've been able to convince her through Love and hope that the heaviness placed on my heart by losing her would not lighten my burden one iota. Thank you IRS for driving my little girls to ask if we can afford school lunch today, thank you for making me walk for weeks until I could find someone who would finance a car (at 24%) after losing our only transportation by repossession not once, not twice but three times (so far). Empty my account again and I'll lose the next one too. According to IRS math, I owe in back taxes and penalties a little over $50,000. Not bad for someone who didn't make near that much to begin with.

In the last two years, I have been called a criminal, a burden to society, a deadbeat and just last week I was told by one individual he didn't care about my children or myself and he wasn't only going to take my bank account but my next paycheck as well.

## IRS Abuse Report #298

**Date:** Mon Nov 17 8:29:11 1997
**To:** sue@irs.class-action.com
**From:** DD
Began in 1986, was sick for several years. Became unable to file for 2 years, 1986,88. In 1992 realized in my records I had not filed, and filed those two years. Found that for 1986 IRS owed me $2600, for 1988, I owed IRS $1400. They refused to offset debt due to Statue of Limitations. So they owe me nothing! However, I still owe them $1400, plus interest! Things have gotten worse...I get different stories from different IRS agents, no consistency, no help. Threatening phone calls to my employer, stating our bookkeeper would be personally responsible if I didn't pay immediately! Agents telling me not to appeal because/c I'll lose. Once I tried to make arrangements for payment on what I could afford, an agent told me "We don't accept arrangements, it must be paid in full or we'll take you to court" HELP! I can't afford to pay $3000+ plus they have my refund I worked hard for!

## IRS Abuse Report #299

**Date:** Mon Nov 17 11:45:19 1997
**To:** sue@irs.class-action.com
**From:** FS
Wrongful levy/seizure of unrelated company income funds to satisfy an unrelated individual's TAXES OWED!!!!!!!. IRS field agent created fictitious company/partnership, i.e. assigned new EI number. Caused financial devastation.

## IRS Abuse Report #300

**Date:** Mon Nov 17 11:46:08 1997
**To:** sue@irs.class-action.com
**From:** MD
I am a single mother. I claimed my three children on my 1996 tax return and was to get a refund. I received a check from the IRS for only part of my refund, along with a letter stating that I needed to send all kinds of papers and proof that my children were with me during the period stated on my return. I got copies of all the paper work, school papers on my children, immunization records, anything and everything they wanted. I even had letters written to them by friends and family members testifying to the fact that I did have my three children at least 6 months of the year.

Because I did move some during the year, even to a different state to get a better paying job, the IRS told me I did not furnish my children with a stable home. What has that got to do with paying taxes? I did pay taxes and did file a return and did have my children with me. They were not abused and they are loved dearly. The IRS has no right getting involved in that part of a persons life. I was, and am, doing the best I can. I was one of the mothers trying her best to stay off of welfare, and I still got penalized. I finally gave up trying to fight IRS, because I knew I couldn't win. They withheld my earned income credit for that year, plus, I am now having to pay back the refund I received, and all the penalties and interests; so I ended up with nothing and in debt to the IRS! What is the point in even working and trying to make an honest living and raising your kids when you get stabbed in the back by your own government?

I am using my brother's computer, in case you're wondering. I can't afford one of my own. I am now living with him and his wife. I have started a new job, in a new location, I wonder if I will get penalized again this year? My family has supported me through this and my brother has taken me and my two children into his home to help me, but I sure can't get help from a government that is suppose to be "of the people, for the people and by the people". What a joke! Yes, abolish the IRS.

## IRS Abuse Report #301

**Date:** Mon Nov 17 13:30:17 1997
**To:** sue@irs.class-action.com
**From:** LH
The IRS keeps levying my check account. Every time there is a levy, I call and they request inf. I send the inf., the levy is lifted, then they levy again and say the inf. sent was not the issue, it is some other type of verification. I send the new material out, the levy is lifted. Many weeks later, they levy again leaving me $159.00 in my check. I had just moved on the Friday they levied my account, I was supposed to give my new landlord the first months rent but was unable to due to the levy. Someone else moved in. Now I have to find a new place to live. I don't get paid for another 2 weeks. The IRS representatives I spoke with were the rudest people I have ever talked to.

## IRS Abuse Report #302

**Date:** Wed Nov 19 2:21:33 1997
**To:** sue@irs.class-action.com
**From:** MS
I am currently being audited for 1994 and it is a mess! I have all my receipts and an accountant. The audit has been going on for one year. They write me and ask for info., I send them the information, but they still are not satisfied. They have made me completely restructure my business. You would not believe what a Hell of a mess that made for my payroll reports and everything else . The I R S does not know what the Right hand is doing with the Left hand! Anyway to make a long story short, it looks as if I will have to pay the IRS 10,000 for 1994 and I am so confused as to how they were able arrive at that figure. I believe in paying taxes, but I do not believe in being

manipulated into paying them. I am a small struggling business and cannot afford a high priced attorney to fight for my rights and to prove to the IRS that my records where accurate. The IRS is so complicated and has so many laws and regulations they can manipulate anything and get away with it!

## IRS Abuse Report #303

**Date:** Fri, 21 Nov 1997 18:37:07 -0600
**To:** sue@irs.class-action.com
**From:** MB
My family and I, have suffered, for well over a decade now, at the hands of the IRS. My husband and I at that time (the early 80's) were young and full of ambition. We were successful at our businesses, marriage, and raising 2 children, until one day the IRS decided to be judge and jury and put us on death row without a fair trial. I am currently still living on IRS's death row. These are some of the things I have had to endure: Watch in horror as the IRS humiliated me and my husband in front of my children, employees, friends, and associates. Watch my bank accounts be levied. Saw my home ripped from under us. Income property seized. How in god's name if you did owe the IRS any money could you pay? There is no way you can keep your businesses or life going. Doesn't the IRS know if they shut down a persons business they won't get any money? Don't they understand that they are ruining America? I no longer am married and have not been for many years. I can never own anything or work anywhere for long periods of time or the IRS will come and take it all. It is impossible to have a career under these circumstances. There are many more events that took place than this, and those of you that have suffered at the hands of the IRS know what I am talking about.

## IRS Abuse Report #304

**Date:** Mon Nov 24 18:35:56 1997
**To:** sue@irs.class-action.com
**From:** KE
The IRS has levied my Social Security for eight years; month by month...from an original notice of deficiency of $8,000 they tricked me into an "assessment" from Tax Court of some $135,000 which became $235,000 with their usury and penalties..levied $55,000 and the balance remains about $240,000. Oh yes, I'm 75...World War II Vet. Nothing matters...nobody cares. Land of the FREE and Home of the Brave? Sure.

## IRS Abuse Report #305

**Date:** Mon Nov 24 18:35:56 1997
**To:** sue@irs.class-action.com
**From:** AK
Why IRS cannot be saved: It's bad enough that IRS would support a company issuing me a fraudulent 1099 and then do their stonewall act to perfection when challenged to justify this travesty of conduct. But I shouldn't be shocked. It's the standard operating procedure for Internal Revenue, whether Orlando, Jacksonville, Atlanta, Andover, or Covington. Lie, cheat, mess up, and stonewall -- it's all IRS knows. This latest absurdity is just to be expected. It's the reason that IRS cannot be reformed -- extinction is the only solution. Too many bad eggs to ever fix the people, even if the system could be salvaged. Long before my son wanted to major in accounting, he filed his first 1040EZ (with Dad's help) while in high school. Two W2's for part-time jobs were all there was to it. The IRS keyed in the wrong withholding amount from his typed 1040, and from that mistake kept his refund. Should have been easy to get corrected. After I made five tries, and after being told that either there was no mistake (obviously there was) or the check was in the mail (it was not), I contacted the regional IRS director in Atlanta. My son got his check 3 months latter. One of the "problem resolution" people who called me had NO information on the case, but was told to call me and convince me that there was no error. IT IS AN EXTREMELY CORRUPT SYSTEM that tells people to go out and con others; I felt more sorry than angry at the woman with the con-job assignment. All the same, people who work in the real world go to jail for crooked things like that. My favorite aunt on Cape Cod paid her annual tax bill with a check. It didn't get registered in the IRS computer one year, so they yanked one of her savings accounts for the amount. No notification. She only discovered the bank debit via her savings statement. With bank statement and the canceled check in hand, she tried writing and calling the IRS about the double payment enforced upon her. They stonewalled her letters and passed the buck on the telephone. So, this elderly lady (70 years plus) drove almost 100 miles to Andover to get things straight, but IRS refused to talk with her because she failed to make an appointment first. I begged her to let me contact Tip O'Neil's office. (His summer home was two doors down from my aunt.) But as a good New Englander, she wouldn't "impose." This dear old woman -- who never cheated anyone, much less the government, simply ate what the IRS did to her. I should have called Tip's people anyhow! My best friend in Florida had a small business he was starting. Trying to keep it in the black, he took no salary for his work there. (He had other income, and everything was reported honestly.) The IRS decided that he "should" have a salary, and determined the FICA tax and penalty he had to pay based on their imaginary salary. He had to pay it all, including the expensive accountant who filled his original and "corrected" tax statements. The first time an IRS agent told me: "There is nothing in the rules that says we have to be fair" was when the IRS waited 2´ years to arbitrarily determine that 40% of the payout on a defaulted Wickes bond was interest and not capital gains. It was unreasonable to start with, and I had no way of knowing or suspecting they would come up with such an absurd determination; but I had to pay both taxes and "interest" (at a usurious rate) for this arbitrary and delayed decision. It

didn't seem worth fighting, at the time. I got the same response ("we don't have to be fair") from the IRS after they were asked about my opening an IRA account and was told -- by an IRS agent (a Jacksonville, FL pension plan specialist, no less) that I had until April 15 to open it. When I went to open the account in March, I was told I could add to the account until April 15, but I had to open the account in the year the money was earned! I said it was not fair to penalize me ($600 in extra taxes) because the IRS gave out bad information (in the year the money was earned). The IRS people could care less, even if I had it in writing. IRS doesn't have to abide by what they say or write. Even so, they prefer to tell it by telephone so they can claim that I "misunderstood" them. The poor guy I played cards with in Florida; a carpenter who worked out at Disney. Thought it was good luck when he and his wife won a new home in Orlando as part of a radio station contest. Then the builder demanded extra payments before he would give up title, and IRS demanded about 1/3 the value of the house as taxes -- NOW! Without title, he could not occupy or obtain a loan to payoff IRS -- but IRS considered the title just "his problem." He really was afraid of being destroyed by IRS, but finally a local TV station put the spotlight on both the IRS and the builder. That got IRS to hold off long enough for the builder to fork up the title he contractually owed. My friend was then able get a bank loan to pay the IRS' tax and interest, and he and his family could again sleep at night. Maybe this sounds like small stuff. But the composite adds up to a consistently inept and corrupt organization, called Internal Revenue. They abuse what they do, and should not be called a "service." I cannot imagine any decent person wanting to be part of such an organization. That must be why the good people get out and the Internal Revenue sinks deeper and deeper into the muck every year. Rossotti needs more than luck -- help eliminate the IRS, it's un-American.

## IRS Abuse Report #306

**Date:** Mon Nov 24 13:13:19 1997
**To:** sue@irs.class-action.com
**From:** MN

The principle that we owed was bad enough, but it was all the interest and penalties that they kept piling on top of us that drove us into bankruptcy! We honestly tried to make payments and keep up, but they just wouldn't let go! When I called to make payment arrangements of $2,000 a month, thinking I could have it paid off in a year or so, she informed me that interest and penalties would amount to $500 PER DAY!! You may as well be dealing with criminals!

## IRS Abuse Report #307

**Date:** Mon 24 Nov 1997 19:17:44 EST
**To:** sue@irs.class-action.com
**From:** PS
Report on IRS "PROBLEM SOLVING DAY", Nov. 15, 1997

"national day of redress" [Chicago Tribune, Nov. 12, 1997]. Many IRS employees attended, all wearing 3-inch buttons proclaiming in colored art-work: "At the IRS We Work For You Problem Solving Days"

A large colored poster with the same message adorned the waiting room.

### SUMMARY
For me, the event was a complete waste of time. Absolutely nothing was accomplished that could be called "problem solving".
The hearing officer was officious, insolent, irritable, pushy, and did not give me a chance to present my case.

She grasped at the fact that the IRS is suing me (for some of the years) to foreclose on my home, taking the position that "we can't handle it" because the Justice Dept. "is controlling the case".

## INTERVIEW NOTES

- The interview was with Miss G. Reed, IRS Collections (?).
- She had a computer printout of my file, and a handwritten memo.
- She said that there was mention of a suit (on the memo) but nothing on the computer printout about a suit. She immediately began to question me about the suit. She asked several times if I had brought any documents about the suit. I answered that I did not.
- She continued to question me about the suit, repeatedly asking for documents pertaining to the suit. •Finally she phoned the US Attorney's office. She said that they confirmed that there was an IRS civil suit against me (to foreclose on my home for taxes in certain years).
- She said that since "the case" was in the hands of the Justice Dept., "we can't handle it", because the Justice Dept. "is controlling the case" and "have jurisdiction".
- I showed her the substitute return for 1973 prepared by the IRS. She admitted that it contained no financial numbers and no signature.
- I asked if she would pass on the information about this procedural irregularity to the Justice Dept. She said no. I tried to show her some documents pertaining to other years beyond 1980. She refused to look at then, declaring the meeting over.

(End of interview.)

## COMMENT

This interview illustrates the IRS attitude that the IRS is under no obligation to correct its mistakes.

By refusing to point out to the Justice Dept. the procedural irregularities which might have the effect of rendering the government's case untenable, the IRS compounds the injustice caused by the original filing of the suit based on false "facts" (which the IRS certified to the Justice Dept. as "true"). By refusing to correct the information, the IRS lets stand a lie: "information" that the IRS knows to be false.

By its action, the IRS in effect claims the right to violate the law with impunity, disregarding and trampling on the right of a citizen to fundamental due process, to the facts and to a hearing. By its action, the IRS protects its rear at the expense of the citizen's rights.

If the IRS violates the law in the course of imposing a tax, as in the present case, justice requires that the IRS should be held accountable and should make amends. Instead, it offers the lame excuse that one IRS error (filing suit based on faulty information) makes it "impossible" for the IRS to correct that very error. Catch-22 or cover-up?

Thus it appears to be IRS policy to file suit against the victim of IRS irregularity and lawlessness, in order to cover up that very irregularity and lawlessness.

It appears that there is no mechanism within the IRS for correcting mistakes or information once that false "information" becomes part of an IRS-instigated suit. This puts an intolerable burden on the target of such a suit.

Justice demands that the IRS be required to provide to the Justice Dept. any exculpatory evidence relating to any suit that originated with the IRS.

### IRS Abuse Report #308

**Date:** Fri, 28 Nov 1997 01:38:07 -0700
**To:** sue@irs.class-action.com
**From:** HB

I recently filed a FOIA request to get a copy of a imf transcript. I was surprised to learn that I apparently own a gun and pistol manufacturing plant in the Virgin Islands and that I failed to pay some excise taxes and employee pension plan taxes etc. Having been employed at my boring old job forever, I found this bit of information in my file to be very interesting. But when I told the IRS that there must be some kind of error, they ignored me. My many letters have all gone unanswered. To make matters worse, they have begun increased withholding from my paycheck (wages) and they have ordered my employer to Withhold, or else face criminal charges. At this point I barely have enough money left to eat and buy gas. All my bills have fallen delinquent and my credit is now mostly ruined. Thank you IRS for destroying another citizen's life, liberty and pursuit of happiness

## IRS Abuse Report #309

**Date:** Fri Nov 28 10:05:45 1997
**To:** sue@irs.class-action.com
**From:** HM
My story takes up too much space for this site. I am an ex-spouse who has been harassed and tortured my the IRS to the point I live with fear from day to day, until my ex-husband pays them off. And I know that he'll die before that happens.

## IRS Abuse Report #310

**Date:** Fri Nov 28 11:11:23 1997
**To:** sue@irs.class-action.com
**From:** SS
My IRS abuse story is one that I thought could be avoided. --WRONG-- Back in the early 1980's I had an addiction to cocaine, granted that was my fault. As a result of all this abuse TO MYSELF I did not file taxes for a number of years. Finally after receiving numerous IRS notices and the rest of my life falling apart. I had often heard that there were ways to "straighten up" my act. I was either going to die addicted to cocaine, or pick myself up and try to live. I chose the latter. Now I don't know if I made the right choice. In 1989 I contacted the IRS, and told them I was willing to accept whatever as long as I could get back on my feet. I asked them if there was a way for me to get things worked out, they assured there was. I went to the IRS office with all paperwork needed to have my case handled. We worked out a payment plan and an agreement and I was

feeling better about myself for taking this first step. The total bill to me for all back taxes with penalties and interest was over $70,000. Even though I owed all this, I still had paid all my taxes for each year I was delinquent, through regular Payroll deductions. My problem was that I did not file my taxes. Through the years since 1990 I have had to file bankruptcy twice and hire a few attorneys to stave off any collection action to allow me to pay bills and LIVE as was my ultimate goal after my addiction. Well the IRS finally got to me and demands payment of about $45,000. Of course I have no way to pay that amount, so the IRS levied my checking account. So be it, my fault. That was not the worse. In 1994 my mother passed away, leaving my father to care for himself and pay the bills. Dad had never written any checks, and needed my sister and brothers and myself to help him sort things out, which we obviously were ready, willing and able to do. Never knowing I was about to make a big mistake. My sister and I went to my fathers bank, and were put on his checking account to help him pay his bills, until he could manage on his own. Forgetting I was on his account along with my social security number, The IRS searched my SS# and found me on that account and as a result has now levied my fathers account. He is 81 years old. That account he has is only from a small retirement check and a social security check that he receives each month. He has no other income whatsoever. So now I am back where I started. Will I live or die? After all this embarrassment to my family, for my problems, affecting their lives without their knowledge of my IRS problems, why am I trying to fight this? Too many times lately I have considered the ultimate sacrifice, suicide. I want to live but the IRS won't allow me that option. If the IRS would just deal with me, I can accept that, they can have everything I own and I'll go homeless. My father who has always worked hard and been a law abiding American citizen is now being harassed by the IRS, through no fault of his. I can't deal with the IRS hurting the only things in life that I love. They have done nothing. God help us all.

## IRS Abuse Report #311

**Date:** Sat Nov 29 20:21:58 1997
**To:** sue@irs.class-action.com
**From:** GG

The year was 1995 when the IRS locked my bank account and withdrew all of my funds leaving me with nothing. Previous to this event, I owed 5000 in back taxes, but had an agreement to pay in installments. After a year had gone bye the debt was half paid off per our agreement and at that time the IRS levied a fine which canceled out everything we had paid for the year. In a panic I borrowed 5000 dollars from my in-laws so I could pay what I owed, that's when they IRS cleaned out my account. What kind of Democracy lets this happen to its people. This agency is out of control.

## IRS Abuse Report #312

**Date:** Sat Nov 29 20:21:58 1997
**To:** sue@irs.class-action.com
**From:** EH

To The Joint Committee on Taxation: In re: the hearings on tax abuse, please forward my husband and my testimony as a part of the record of these hearings before the Joint Committee on Taxation. Our problem started in approximately 1984, when we received notices from the IRS stating that they could not 'accept' our 1040 forms because they did not 'contain information' 'required to be given'. We immediately sent them a response requesting that they send us the specific 'information required to be given'. Upon no response from the IRS and upon several status and duplicate requests back to the IRS, we finally received a postcard wherein it stated that there would be a response within '90 days'. We are still waiting. In the meantime, IRS employees have stolen and taken everything we own and put us in jail, broke and entered into our home while we were away and other heinous acts that can be testified to. The thefts started on 10 October 1986 when IRS "agents" and county sheriff deputies and city policeman came out into the

county into our yard and took our sweeper truck and a pickup, all being done without a warrant, without our consent, and without a court judgment.

From that point on, these same brutal people have taken the following:

* Feb. 3, 1987: 1977 Pontiac
* Aug. 10, 1987: Attempted to take 1979 Pontiac -- No administrative hearings or court orders
* May 18, 1988: Our home -- No administrative hearings or court orders
* Nov. 25, 1988: 1979 Pontiac -- No administrative hearings or court orders
* Sept. 10, 1990: Two (2) Cruise Tickets -- No administrative hearings or court orders
* Nov. 20, 1990: 1977 Pontiac, Computer, Computer tables, TV, VCR, 2 copy machines, 40.00 cash, misc. items This was done by breaking and entering into our apartment without our being there.

This entire matter has been a nightmare from 10 October 1986 to the present date and has devastated our family life, depriving us time for our children and now our grandchildren for 11 years now. In fact, it has set the mind set of at least 4 of our grandchildren because of the acts of reckless disregard as to our little ones watching their grandma being taken away in handcuffs and leg irons. It is a tyranny that must be stopped. I love my country and I want to keep the basic principles that made it great.

This is an outrage. We could see it if there was an honest mistake, but upon review of the rules and law, the acts by these people (our employees to be serving us) have blatantly ignored the law and their own procedures for over 10 years now. We are like little ants to them. And by the way, who are "them" and "they" and "their"? And by what authority have they done the horrendous acts against my husband and I, and now trying to bring my 78 year old mom and daughters and brother into their scheme of things, all in order to gain "power", I guess. We were merely private people out here in California with a little sweeper truck and a pickup sweeping parking lots and living on a 2 acre place. That was our dream at the time, and we were just raising our family and living the way of life as we were brought up in Iowa. Where did it all go? Just for our standing on what is right, we have been devastated by all the fraudulent acts perpetrated upon us by over zealous employees of government.

## IRS Abuse Report #313

**Date:** Mon Dec 1 22:48:23 1997
**To:** sue@irs.class-action.com
**From:** WM
My problems with the IRS started in 1992. After serious personal problems, I was unable to stay completely focused on managing my practice. The result of these actions forced me into foreclosure on my office building. The foreclosure then created a massive PERSONAL income tax problem. This summer, the agent closed my business for one week. He told me what I needed to do to reopen, but changed it every time I met those conditions. He allowed me to reopen, but every time I get back on track, he seizes my accounts and payments and I fall behind again. My credit is ruined, and I don't have funds to make my practice grow. So I'm stuck in this nightmare. He can't close me, just make my life a nightmare.

In addition, the agent has come into my office, waved his badge in front of a reception room full of patients, identified himself as an IRS agent and demanded to see me immediately. I was told on another occasion that if I didn't give him all the funds in my IRA that he would close my business. I had been advised that he couldn't do that, and when I challenged him on that point, I was told that I was correct. However, he told me that if I didn't give him the funds, he would close me anyway, it would take months to reopen, and I would have no business by then.

## IRS Abuse Report #314

**Date:** Tue Dec 2 11:05:08 1997
**To:** sue@irs.class-action.com
**From:** SH
I am really scared of this group! They are way out of control. I received a Notice of Deficiency last week because of their error. They doubled my salary for last year and completed their own 1040 for me. I've tried to tell them that they have messed up the amounts that I made last year, but they refuse to listen to me. I even have the correct amount on my W2, but they refuse to admit that they have made an error. So now I am off to Tax Court, which I will probably lose because of the corrupt Tax Court Judges in this country! The media is also to blame for the fear that US Citizens have regarding the IRS. They perpetuate the fear! The IRS is above the law! They neither adhere or even follow their own laws. They are the most corrupt, evil group of the century! The IRS is a killer of the American dream and they must be stopped before more peoples lives are ruined by this evil group!

## IRS Abuse Report #315

**Date:** Wed Dec 3 0:25:27 1997
**To:** sue@irs.class-action.com
**From:** RP
Sue them. Sue them and make them pay. Sue them and make them stop.
I was embezzled by a dishonest employee who absconded with 60K plus and left 60K in unrecoverable billing. The employee taxes were not paid. I and my partners paid them, drawing money from our own retirement accounts, credit cards and other resources, as well as limiting what we took from the business. But due to poor judgment on my part, I did not pay my personal taxes in order to pay for the business expenses. The IRS sent collection letters. I obtained an attorney to negotiate with the IRS. All efforts failed. Because they claimed I owed 50K, they garnished my wages. The IRS believed that I was withholding income, evading

taxes, and refused to negotiate with my attorneys.

Demoralized, I walked from my business, almost committed suicide, put my family through hell, and took a job much below my ability to earn. I lost my business, almost my life, my respect for the government agencies, and became embittered at the complexity and inaccuracy of the IRS agenda. There was no reason to go after me with the vengeance they used. As a measure of good faith, I had been making voluntary payments of $500 per month, showed good faith in getting my house in order by using my attorneys and accountants, and attempted to negotiate with the IRS. All was stalemated by one individual in the Olympia, Washington office who believed that I was worth more than I was. Now, I am poor, lost my house, lost my credit, lost all that I had worked for, have no savings, and have nothing to give to my children for their college. I have struggled not to feel bitter, but I am.

## IRS Abuse Report #316

**Date:** Sun, 7 Dec 1997 12:37:51 -0500
**To:** sue@irs.class-action.com
**From:** JD
The Congressional hearings were a 'commercial' for IRS which reinforced these points:

1. If you fall into IRS scrutiny, the US Constitution is suspended, and: a. your economic life can be terminated with no redress b. IRS will seize assets and wages with the stroke of a key. All you get is a voice on an 800#. c. any claim of hardship due to illness, unemployment, etc., will be ignored. -- witness the many reports shown on this newsgroup. d. IRS personnel will treat you with sarcasm, attitude, and arrogance. It's their job. e. IRS will set all the rules, you be assimilated. See because. above.

2. This treatment is reserved for the middle class and lower middle class.

3. Congress does not care to reverse this treatment.

Evidence: how many citizens have written their Congressman for help in a personal tax situation and GOTTEN HELP? How many have not received even a reply?

## IRS Abuse Report #317

**Date:** Mon Dec 8 22:00:52 1997
**To:** sue@irs.class-action.com
**From:** HR
After current IRS Hearings on IRS Abuse, I have regained my anger after about 4 years after being forced to settle with the IRS on a 100% Penalty action.

I lived in fear under threats of losing my home, job, and wages until I agreed to give up. I have slept better, but it cost me $65,000 for something that I should not have had to pay. I had to move, sell my home and borrow from hard-working relatives in order to rid my life of the tyranny of the IRS.

## IRS Abuse Report #318

**Date:** Mon, 08 Dec 1997 14:01:48 EST
**To:** sue@irs.class-action.com
**From:** PS
Congress spends untold millions on "pork" projects that benefit favored clients, while the IRS liens or seizes the homes of 70,000 citizens, rendering them destitute and homeless. And Clinton professes concern for the plight of the homeless, while refusing to support any meaningful tax reform.

We need an end to this hypocritical thievery in the name of government. A law prohibiting the IRS from liening and seizing homes would halt the making of 70,000 government-created homeless families, the victims of government's disgusting criminalities.

## IRS Abuse Report #319

**Date:** Mon Dec 8 11:06:46 1997
**To:** sue@irs.class-action.com
**From:** JA

In 1994, my company had been given a refund of $53,000, approved by California, Texas and Pennsylvania IRS. In May, 1994 the Revenue Agent we were dealing with retired and my account was transferred to Lancaster, PA IRS Office. The new revenue agent immediately stopped the credit and charged this back to our account. While doing this she took an extra $23,000 of funds that were paid our account. A few months latter she came into our offices and ordered my accounting clerk that she must file our 941 forms in three states, and send the employees taxes to those three states. The revenue agent then levied my company for the taxes in these other states. My wife and I were assessed over $245,000 each for recovery penalties. I finally hired an ex-agent of the IRS. It has taken him over a year to track down the money that was paid into these different states where the IRS had placed these funds into suspense accounts. In 1996, this same revenue agent, which I was required to send my 941 reports was filing her own 941 reports showing twice the amount owed. The IRS has just levied all our bank accounts, stopping our business. The American people must take legal action to bring this agency back in line.

## IRS Abuse Report #320

**Date:** Tue, 9 Dec 1997 09:40:10 -0500 (EST)
**To:** sue@irs.class-action.com
**From:** MW

In 1990 I worked for an employer as an employee. He filed a 1099 claiming I was an independent contractor and not an employee. I contacted IRS investigations in Van Nuys CA who prosecuted the employer and collected over $300,000 in fines and penalties which I was told would be used to offset any penalties assigned to me. Later I would be told that IRS criminal investigations never communicates with IRS audit departments and that any money recovered from a criminal investigation go to the US Treasury and not to the victims of the crime. The IRS would not give us a clear guideline on whether to file returns as an employee or independent contractor for Calendar Year 1990. We got different answers from everyone at IRS that we spoke to. We finally filed as an employee based on the larger number of responses we received from the IRS to that effect. The IRS rejected our return and filed one of their own. An auditor, Clifford Chase, claimed to not be able to get in touch with me and filed a warrant for my arrest on tax evasion charges. We finally got in touch with him and arranged an audit where he threw out every deduction I had (though we provided legal chapter and verse backing up our deductions) and demanded an additional $16,000 in taxes plus penalties and interest, in addition to the $36,000 I had paid through my employer (on a gross salary of $102,000). We challenged the audit and the IRS became very nasty. At first, the auditors refused to attend our scheduled appointments for appeal. On one occasion myself and accountant (at $120/hour plus travel) were left sitting in the waiting room for four hours before we were told that the IRS auditor 'was not coming in today because he was mowing his lawn'.

After this, I could no longer afford an accountant or attorney so I decided to just pay the additional taxes. I borrowed money from family and sold off personal belongings to get the required amount. When I went in to pay the taxes, the IRS refused to accept the money on two occasions (payments by cashier check) saying that at this point I could NOT pay the taxes and had to 'follow their procedures' before I would be allowed to pay and then I could only 'pay when they say it is OK to do so'. Their 'procedures' led to a Tax Court judgment which I was forced to sign after an appeal. We were told that we could either sign the judgment or the IRS would show up in seven days with a US Marshall and confiscate our home and all our personal belongings. It was made VERY CLEAR that we DID NOT have any choice in the matter. We were also told on several occasions that the IRS would NOT negotiate any payment or settlement until we signed this judgment, so we signed. This whole procedure took 5 years. In this time, our penalties and taxes increased to over $45,000. During this time, the IRS confiscated all our tax refunds and we had made additional payments of around $13,000 by mailing in checks to the IRS, all of which were always applied to interest and never to the tax principle amount. The final tax judgment was for $27,000 + at which time the IRS put a lien on our house and garnished my wages. During this time, I was threatened by the IRS on numerous occasions. On one occasion in Laguna Beach after I had filed a protest, as I was getting into my car, a lady came by and shouted at me that if we continued to protest their actions, everyone in my family tree would be audited for the next five years. In addition one gentleman at the IRS in Santa Ana casually asked if I had life insurance and for how much. When I said that I did have a $200,000 policy and asked him why he wanted to know, he suggested that the IRS should consider killing me to collect my insurance money rather than deal with my protests. When I called his supervisor, the man denied ever saying such a thing and was backed up 100% by his supervisor who called me a liar.

They take $1700 per month out of our $3600/month GROSS income leaving almost nothing for my family to live on. As a side note, I once spoke to a gentleman who claimed to be a retired IRS auditor. He said that what the IRS does is at the time they get a case, they check out your financial history and then decide how much total money they think they can get from you. From that point on, they squeeze you and torment you until they get every last dime of that amount. He told me this 'after the fact' and the procedures and methods he described were

exactly what had happened to me over the past five years, almost to the letter.

At this point, my wife and I have taken out a second and third mortgage on our home. Unfortunately, the company we both work for is going out of business and we are going to have to file bankruptcy (which will still not release the IRS judgment because even though the case is seven years old, the judgment is only one year old and cannot be released from a bankruptcy.

The final tally is that out of a $102,000 salary, I have paid or will pay nearly $98,000 in taxes, penalties and interest plus I paid another $15,000 in accounting and legal fees trying to fight this situation. The final stab was that it wasn't enough that the IRS had to add another $16,000 in taxes to my 1990 calendar year, they then decided to audit my 1991 taxes and added another $7000 there as well, throwing out every claimed deduction here as well. In addition, in 1993 and 1994, I brought cashier checks to the IRS in Santa Ana offering to pay the taxes in full, but the payments were REFUSED by the IRS which led to nearly $35,000 of ADDITIONAL penalties and interest being charged to my account which would not have been if they had accepted my payments. Add to this the nearly $13,000 they took from me in confiscating tax refunds and other payments I had made and you begin to see just how out of control this situation has become. The IRS has destroyed our lives, ruined my career and are in the process of bankrupting my family. All for something I didn't have anything to do with or any control over.

### IRS Abuse Report #321

**Date:** Mon Dec 15 1997 17:11:06
**To:** sue@irs.class-action.com
**From:** WD
I'm sorry I don't know how to put into words the unnecessary destruction of a family, their careers, their good name, their whole lives.

Maybe you can help me categorize humiliation, terror, bankruptcy, divorce, and unfair injustice.

## IRS Abuse Report #322

**Date:** Tue Dec 16 14:45:31 1997
**To:** sue@irs.class-action.com
**From:** RJ

In Oct. 1993 I was laid off. My position required me to travel all over the globe training military customers in the operation and maintenance of the F-16. Due to changes in the IRS code all moving expenses that were incurred were passed on to me as income even though I was required to move because of my job. When I was laid off, I virtually had no place to live and had difficulty finding another job. I had to cash in my 401k plan in order for me and my wife to survive. At the beginning of 1994 the IRS demanded an extreme amount of income tax that amounted to more money than I had made for the entire previous year. This was because the company inflated the moving expenses they reported along with the cashing in of my 401k had placed me in an unbelievable income tax bracket. And not having the means to pay, the IRS has placed a lien on my otherwise excellent credit. Starting in 1994 I decided to go back to school to get my Engineering Degree so I could get appropriate employment. Since then I have barely survived for four years due to the IRS lien. I cannot buy anything or get a decent job because the IRS has given me a bad credit rating even though I have always paid my bills. The IRS has never given me the opportunity to talk with them and explain what is going on and the hardship I am going through. I am now 48 years old and have almost no hope of a future due to these unusual circumstances beyond my control.

## IRS Abuse Report #323

**Date:** Sun, 21 Dec 1997 14:15:47
**To:** sue@irs.class-action.com
**From:** JO

An illegal immigrant is allowed an interview/evaluation with an immigration officer, followed by a judicial hearing. And an appeal. Only then can he/she be deported. [ref: Dec 21 NY Times]

Too bad US Citizens aren't treated similarly when IRS is involved:

A US Citizen can have salary and other assets summarily seized by IRS/Treasury without a court order, a hearing, or an appeal. And, AFTER the seizure occurs, no matter what hardship may be involved, there is no _reasonable_ way to get due process.

If you have had IRS trouble, and have written your Senator or Congressman, have you noticed that the response, if any, has been that these representatives have said that they 'have asked IRS to review' your situation? They are apparently powerless to stop IRS action. There are no provisions for hearings?! Just whatever the IRS wants to do.

Why do we allow this? This, lack of due process?

It certainly is time to organize, to lobby, to get our local representatives to change IRS from what it is, to an accountable agency, subject to due process rules of justice that is supposed to be our guarantee. IRS is operating outside the bounds of the US Constitution, and this must be legislated to a halt, now.

Write, fax, phone your representatives, asking them for change, and if you want to be specific, then demand that IRS seizures be subject to PRIOR hearing/court order, with the taxpayer involved PRIOR to seizure authorization by a court of law. US Citizens demand to be protected under the US Constitution.

Let's not drop this issue, it is too big, and too damaging to millions of people, US Citizens.

## IRS Abuse Report #324

**Date:** Sun Dec 21 10:03:44 1997
**To:** sue@irs.class-action.com
**From:** SE

The IRS informed my that THEY have taken it upon themselves to change my filing status on my 1996 income tax return, from head of household to single. They have also stated that I can not claim my 2 youngest children under Earned Income Credit. They have now said that I owe them over $5,000. I am a not-yet-divorced mother of 3 children. My husband left me in 1995 and I raise my children on my own. I worked the whole year and raised my children on less than $15,000. When I went to file my tax return, an H and R block employee informed me that I could claim head of household and Earned Income Credit, (my 2 youngest were 5 and 6 at the time). Why did the IRS take it upon themselves to change my filing status? Why are they harassing a person trying to survive living under the poverty level?

## IRS Abuse Report #325

**Date:** Mon Dec 22 14:55:03 1997
**To:** sue@irs.class-action.com
**From:** SZ

My circumstances are complicated and when I attempt to explain the many 'arms and legs', it causes confusion. This is a much simplified summary. I am a nurse. I have been self-sufficient and self-supporting since age 15. I have always been a model citizen, had excellent credit, never accepted help from anyone, supported an ex-husband voluntarily and have a spotless past. I have moved far in my career and been successful and highly respected by the medical community. In 1991, I thought of a way that would save lives, significantly reduce unnecessary hospital admissions and emergency room visits and save Medicare and private

insurance companies large amounts of money. I started a tiny company in my kitchen, using my own moneys. It was a huge and rapid success. After nine months, I brought in a financial expert as my partner because I have no knowledge of finance. Two years later, the company was public and trading on Wall Street and I was the recipient of prestigious awards for my contributions to the improvement of health care. I then discovered my partner had embezzled $2 million through bogus expense reports. I confronted him, notified the government, and he fled to New Zealand. I hired attorneys and it didn't take long for me to learn that he and several insiders used my naiveté and trust in order to use and defraud my company. The only funds that they did not steal was my personal $225,000 pension plan. I spent all of that myself during the past three years on relentless investigations, gathering 1500 lb of evidence, paying lawyers to persist in efforts to get the government to follow up on the 1994 criminal referrals that I made, being voluntarily polygraphed, paying lawyers to pursue countless leads I provided to various government agencies. Each pursuit was totally fruitless. I developed a disabling illness and am now bed-ridden. I have no income and have had none whatsoever throughout this entire ordeal, I was solely dependent upon receiving my 1994 tax refund on which I anticipated living frugally for the remainder of my life. The IRS has stolen my $66,000 refund and attached an additional $212,000 fee in addition to undisclosed penalties. Despite having met with me in 1995 and agreeing to accept $5000 and asking for nothing additional, they have decided to hold me accountable beyond their 1995 agreement, and for the tax fraud committed by my previous partner. They denied my appeal this week, for which I provided them with a substantive package of evidence of his guilt and not mine, including several dozen sworn affidavits of witnesses, not one of which they contacted. I discovered his crime, I reported his crime. No efforts have been made to even interview him. I have evidence that would be sufficient for the indictment of no less than six people, all of whom have been ignored by the government. I have done nothing wrong and have repeatedly offered myself to the government for their scrutiny, which they have declined. I have never managed to get any audience from the government to review the evidence. I believe that I have left no stone unturned in my efforts to initiate proper criminal investigations but have met with unexplainable apathy. Now, I am preparing the detailed arrangements for my suicide, in 4 - 6 months, at which time I will be totally penniless. I am organizing loose ends so that my two dogs will have a loving home and someone who will take good care of them. I am a 48 year-old, attractive, loving, giving, talented and vivacious woman who has lived my life very much dedicated to service. I have always offered my outreached hand to anyone who could benefit from my help.... So much for my healing the sick!!!! The truth does NOT prevail and what goes around does NOT come around and the police do NOT protect and serve. This is my penalty for having worked full days and evenings throughout my life, without vacations, always contributing toward the improvement of health care. I will die disappointed, still shocked, and in rage and disgust.

### IRS Abuse Report #326

**Date:** Tue Dec 23 13:24:36 1997
**To:** sue@irs.class-action.com
**From:** AY
I AM A FATHER OF 8 DEPENDENTS. I HAVE BEEN FORCED BY THE IRS TO FILE BANKRUPTCY TWICE. ACCORDING TO THE IRS, I OWE ABOUT NINE THOUSAND DOLLARS. ALL MY CHILDREN LIVE IN MY HOUSE, BUT THE IRS CLAIMS THAT THEY ARE NOT MINE. THE LAST TIME MY WIFE AND I RECEIVED A REFUND WAS 1989.

AT FATHERS PASSING IN 1993, THE IRS KNEW OF HIS PASSING AND MY RESPONSIBILITY TOO BURY HIM, BUT

THEY STILL LEVIED MY CHECKING ACCOUNT

### IRS Abuse Report #327

**Date:** Tue Dec 23 23:58:58 1997
**To:** sue@irs.class-action.com
**From:** WC
In 1985, After 21 years of marriage I was divorced, on my own, with three sons. No child support and an ex spouse that ran off with another woman to another state. He had not filed taxes for 5 years before the demise of our marriage, had told me not to take taxes out of my check, he would take them out of his and it would even out at the end of the year. After the back taxes, penalties and interest, and hiring an accountant to re-file for me, I owed over $8,000. I was told nothing would be done about my exhusband. They had me, I was working and they knew where I was. They garnished my salary, and put a lien on anything I had of value. The debt was finally paid. The part of this I have the most problem with, is the IRS told me if I had not filed after my ex sent his threatening letter, I could have filed under an exception for ex-wives and wouldn't have owed a dime. I didn't have a clue that such an exception existed -- now they tell me about it after it is too late! This is grossly unfair and wrong.

### IRS Abuse Report #328

**Date:** Sat Dec 27 13:51:48 1997
**To:** sue@irs.class-action.com
**From:** LS
I've been making monthly payments against back taxes for over four years. Now, IRS people are finding me in the computer with a balance owing and writing demanding payment in 10 days. They fail to see any record of my ongoing payments. The most recent incident resulted in the agent setting up a new installment payment agreement as though none existed and sending a demand for a "user" fee, stating I would owe

my entire balance immediately if I fail to pay the user fee. This most recent incident occurred at the very IRS center that has been processing my payments and sending me statements every month for over four years! Bottom line seems to be that IRS's computer software is flawed so badly that employees all over the country are spending time and money on witch hunts against people who are making regular monthly payments. Multiply the time and effort spent harassing me by several hundred or several thousand similar situations, and we're talking massive squandering of IRS's operating budget-- all because they fail to see anything in the computer except "balance owing." I wonder what other budget-squandering goose chases are going on due to procedural or programming deficiencies!?

## IRS Abuse Report #329

**Date:** Fri Dec 26 14:02:15 1997
**To:** sue@irs.class-action.com
**From:** RM
At the time this started, I was a single parent, raising a daughter free of welfare and trying to give her a better life In 1992, I was audited for 1989. I was disallowed the write-off of expenses in completing a Master's Degree. I sent in tax returns--enough to pay off the debt. The IRS said it was applied to outstanding student loans, then recharged me.

Due to a car accident, I was off work for 1 1/2 years, I was finally able to get disability pay -- it was sent to me in 1 payment. The IRS levied tax on it, stating I failed to claim it as income. I was disallowed a hearing about taxes. I was warned I should contact them and etc. In July I did...the rude, ruthless woman at the other end would not help me. She hung up on me TWICE. In August, my husband's, my, and my Daughters checking and savings accounts were frozen. I was not notified, my husband left me. Due to the stress I had a severe asthma attack. I made arrangements to pay. I only stopped paying when the amounts demanded were more

than I made, and they had threatened and scared my 9 year old over the phone. I have always intended to pay the debt, but now with collection fees and other costs, I will not be debt free from student loans until I am 68 years old!!!! Please help remove this abuse of power!

## IRS Abuse Report #330

**Date:** Mon, 29 Dec 1997 10:29:41
**To:** sue@irs.class-action.com
**From:** RS
For two months I have been seriously contemplating a lawsuit on my own, but need advice as to how to achieve positive results which could be beneficial to your class action suit and all Americans as well. Since 1995 I've been working through Newt Gingrich's office here in Georgia and have numerous complaint letters about the IRS on file with Newt. At his Town Hall meetings, Newt has warned that overhauling the IRS is a long process because repealing the tax amendment will take 7 years minimum.

My fundamental complaint is not about money, as my pending issue is over two matters totaling $97, which are not due. My complaint is about the IRS's gross mistreatment of U.S. citizens without due process of law, bully tactics, etc. Having responded in writing to each IRS letter demanding payments, the IRS threatened me with two separate tax levies anyway, and demanded my payment within 5 days. In numerous letters, I've urged Newt to do whatever it takes to get results NOW to stop the IRS from unlawful tactics against U.S. citizens. There's no reason to wait for the IRS to obey the law, while the lives and fortunes of some continue to be ruined.

Having achieved no results since August, I feel it is my patriotic duty to report on such continued abuses to the Judicial branch to obtain a Court order mandating the IRS and their computer cease all such unlawful practices threatening "life, liberty, and the pursuit of happiness" without due process.

I also have a great paper trail on my latest IRS problem, which clearly demonstrates how fouled up the IRS's "system" is. I have numerous complaint letters to which the IRS never responded. At the urging of Newt's office, I participated in a problem resolution session in Mid-November, which yielded no result. No reply, no phone call, etc. The IRS's records regarding employee payment dates are all fouled up. IRS has sent numerous letters threatening tax levies, etc. over one matter totaling $22! What really irks me is that I've tried to work within their system and the IRS has rewarded me with letters threatening tax levies over two silly matters totaling $97.

I didn't want the IRS to ruin my excellent credit record over such a small amount of money, so I personally delivered my $97 check to the IRS District Director's office with a protest letter. He never responded in writing. I've never sued anyone, but in this case I want to file a lawsuit to get my money back and embarrass the IRS in the process. Actually, my primary objective is to expose unlawful IRS tactics which I have repeatedly demanded the IRS to stop!

I fail to understand your philosophy of a class action suit, as it appears from your Web page that Federal judges are unsympathetic to such actions. My approach until now has been to do everything I can within the law to embarrass the IRS and its employees with facts about their repeated incompetence, failure to respond when promised, etc. and to demonstrate unlawful action to Newt's staff. I will make no broad claims, but can cite specific cases which reiterate the IRS's unlawful abuse toward me.

I also wrote two letters to the IRS District Director Nelson Brooke, protesting the IRS's threatening letters and charging his agency with violating my civil rights. I also took notes during their highly publicized "Problem Resolution Day" and sent a full report to Newt

indicating that many folks never even got through IRS Security to discuss their problem. I also called the local V news media with this report as well. Mr. Brooke tried to call me at work over Thanksgiving. I tried to call him back on December 1 and was lied to by his assistant that he would return on December 2, when I called again. Finally, I was promised he would call me on December 5. He never called; I have voice mail, so there is no possibility that I missed his call. So never had the opportunity to discuss my complaints with him.

I would love to have the opportunity to present my impressive array of facts, reply letters, and written documents which prove I am in the right. It will cost $150 to file suit, plus attorney's fees. I believe that if only 1% of the 100 million taxpayers (I don't know how many) have legitimate cases of IRS abuse and were to file suit, the courts would be so clogged that the government would be forced to take alternative action to resolve IRS complaints. IRS management is so stupid that their "problem resolution" program has yielded more fuel for me to embarrass them even further.

Can you identify a tax attorney sympathetic to our gripes against the IRS and would be willing to provide modest assistance such as strategic planning at reasonable cost? Even if I lose, it wouldn't break my heart or my pocketbook if I were to give up the $97 I've already paid, the $150 filing fee, and modest attorney's fees. I would like to file suit before year end 1997. I feel I can make substantial progress on the civil rights issue, as the IRS clearly made unreasonable demands. Each time I replied to the IRS very quickly with another letter, but the IRS never kept any of their own self-mandated reply dates. If I were to make progress as a test case on the civil rights issue, I'm certain it would greatly boost your class action suit as well. This is important!

Although I believe I have a strong case, what is you opinion of my overall strategy to file suit myself? Have others tried this strategy? What are the traps to avoid? I will truly appreciate any comments you may have. Thank you.

Also, I heard the tail end of a discussion on Tony Brown's Journal about something called a "214?" whereby citizens can sue IRS employees for failing to do their jobs. It would be pretty neat if I were to sue the IRS District Director or Problem Resolution agent for failing to do their jobs (reply). Where can I get inf. on this, and what showing (damages, incompetence, etc.) would I have to make? Can you provide any strategic advice?

I'm going to hand-carry another letter to the IRS District Director in a Christmas card envelope, to remind him that the IRS still owes me a reply regarding the Problem Resolution meeting I attended five weeks ago, that I continue to demand my money back, that the IRS continues to request forms I gave in person the problem resolution agent, etc. With a copy of Newt, of course.

Please respond. Thank you.

## IRS Abuse Report #331

**Date:** Mon, 29 Dec 1997 21:07:23
**To:** sue@irs.class-action.com
**From:** RR
My wife and I have been continually pursued by the IRS. It is truly amazing. We lost everything, including our health, we have spent countless dollars on so called specialists. They came into our business told us they are going to close us down, seized our bank accounts specifically used for tax reserves, leined us again and again. We gave up destroyed. Then they took all of the business assets and sold them....they still will not answer where and how much...should have taken care of tax liabilities.

## IRS Abuse Report #332

**Date:** Mon, 29 Dec 1997 12:31:54
**To:** sue@irs.class-action.com
**From:** CC
I just saw this e-mail address and the multiple letters of abuse. I worked for the IRS for three years (only two of which I was actually working and getting paid). I can not even put into words what the IRS has done to me as an employee for exposing their violations and intentional disregard for the laws that protect employees. They are experts at the cover-up game -- yet they are not so smart -- they are just cruel, cold hearted people.

There were employment issues, not even issues of mine, in which I vocalized. The story of how my life ended from their games and lies and deceit can not be explained in a page or too. I have lost my home, car, possessions, savings, health insurance, marriage, and I can not get a job.

Oh yeah, it is obvious that all of the complaints and stories I heard while I worked for the IRS must have been true. I had no idea that those stories could even possibly be true, at the time. No doubt, the management of the IRS has misused their authority, ruined lives, ruined the lives of employees who refused to join their violations against mankind, and have totally misused the moneys of the taxpayers (that includes me) for their own benefit and gain, and they have not remained impartial in their selection of which taxpayers to hit the hardest and put forth their eight (usually less) hours a day -- they also have little clicks on the outside in which folks that should have their taxpaying but put in a sling for life are let go because -- isn't it funny that those folks let go use to be acquainted with the managers or other revenue agents or collections officers?

Two employees I knew were suffering reprisal for testifying on behalf of themselves or other employees. They would not say anything for fear of becoming a ruined mess like me and near the streets to live.

Then, my spouse has almost sold out for fear that he would be blackwalled from the job market. I am all alone. Everyone is so afraid of the IRS, which by the way, most management employees can not even handle their own finances even though they are supposedly accountants!

These IRS Management and Some Revenue Agents play this game with fervor. It is the only thing they do well--deceive, lie, trick, and damage lives.

## IRS Abuse Report #333

**Date:** Tue Dec 30 8:42:07 1997
**To:** sue@irs.class-action.com
**From:** FC
The IRS was attempting to levy all our assets from 1988 to 1994 when I was forced to file bankruptcy because they had garnished my wife's account which almost caused the end of our marriage. They continue to audit me every year since then.

## IRS Abuse Report #334

**Date:** Wed Dec 31 9:49:33 1997
**To:** sue@irs.class-action.com
**From:** TK
I now have a $10,000 bill with IRS, I am in disagreement because it's not the truth. In 1994 is when this started when I heard about IRS billing me and giving me penalties that I will never be able to over come. At first having this bill thrown on me when I tried to stay in compliance with the laws of our land and always being truthful with the IRS. It affects my thinking and is destroying my belief and my life. It's like they are making me out to be a crook. The problem is a technicality in the writing up of a contract for a house I bought, and not that anything was done with dishonor. They are destroying people to get a promotion at the cost of anyone.  This is the horrible

nightmare I am stuck.  I am covered with Psoriasis, this disease has really taken over, it's from stress, nervousness, fear of what to do, and almost covering my body, where pretty soon I won't be able to work, then I'll be on welfare all because IRS won't budge from their decision.

## IRS Abuse Report #335

**Date:** Thu Jan 1 14:15:26 1998
**To:** sue@irs.class-action.com
**From:** WJ
The IRS unlawfully seized and disposed of my Texas family Homestead, unlawfully seized wages, unlawfully seized Social Security entitlements, unlawfully seized bank accounts and made an attempt to seize loan value of insurance policies. I have a file of communications with the IRS which have been ignored or otherwise neglected. I suspect I am a victim of the quota "scam". I have been unlawfully raped, pillaged and otherwise mistreated by a band of thugs allowed to operate unimpeded in my country. IT IS CRIMINAL WHEN AMERICANS ARE ALLOWED TO ABUSE AMERICANS.

## IRS Abuse Report #336

**Date:** Thu Jan 1 22:35:24 1998
**To:** sue@irs.class-action.com
**From:** GM
In Sept., 1993, while in the midst of a divorce proceeding, I decided to modify my withholding exemptions to make for a smaller refund (consequently smaller "gift" to the soon to be ex-) and submitted such, along with proper documentation, to my employer, a major airline where I work as a pilot. Much to my surprise, I came home to a very reduced paycheck, on January 1st. A call to the payroll desk said they had received word from the IRS that I was to be withheld at the maximum single rate, UNTIL THEY DEEMED OTHERWISE!! A call to the IRS office in Detroit yielded little help except

for one rather inept female gov't worker. She told me they had mailed me a letter in October and I should have known better. (Interestingly enough, the original letter showed up a week later, postmarked Jan 5th, 1994.) I was somewhat curtly informed that I could fill out some forms, which they agreed to fax me, and I was assured that if I faxed them back, all would be right within days. I got the forms that afternoon and faxed them back. Needless to say, nothing much happened, and for another 2 months I was treated to wages resembling those of a fast food worker, and no way to pay the bills. After repeated phone calls to the woman's supervisor, I was told by him that he hadn't thought it was very important, and that he had given it back to her to "..work on."

As I was on the phone that day, they finally cleaned up my "surprise" withholding adjustment, I was referred to the original lady, and her parting words to me were..."just remember, we can get you anytime, and anyplace we want to." At the time, I was just happy to be rid of them, and I do not fear these people. Loathe them, and feel that they are totally incompetent, but no fear! As luck (?!?) would have it, guess who got an audit notice for 1993, in October of 1996? This was so far out of the ordinary audit sequence, that my accountant (an ex-IRS Criminal enforcement agent himself) went to the director to find out what was going on? Nothing yet, but a coincidence...hardly. The worst part was that I was subjected to an audit (they wanted a field audit of my home, and I refused) far beyond need. Then they realized they were out of time to apply the statutes, and asked me for an VOLUNTARY extension to prosecute me! We gave it to them (much against my feeling) and it was the Keystone Kops in action. The audit is another story all unto itself, and I will provide such fodder if you feel it would be useful. Suffice it to say that it cost me another $10,000 to argue the case, for the Gov't to collect $3200.

**IRS Abuse Report #337**

**Date:** Fri Jan 2 1998
**To:** sue@irs.class-action.com
**From:** AT

1990 & 1991 my CPA filed my return listing that they owed me money. IRS said the returns were subject to audit (I was now in collection without the right of audit) but that I could not get any money back because it was a closed year. I said fine, wait for the audit. IRS came back and ordered and threatened me with future audits and prison if I did not sign a waiver stating that I owed the assessed amounts. I said no and they told me that they liked to take care of people like me who did not want to play ball. I was ordered to give them employer inf. but I refused fearing harassment. I wrote to my Congressman Shaw whose aid was considerably less than totally unacceptable. The first thing Shaw did was to sent my letter of complaint to problems & resolution with my phone number. P&R gave it to IRS collections who immediately started harassing my employer. The IRS levied 95% of my wages INCLUDING CHILD SUPPORT. IRS told me they were levying wages not child support and some jail time would do me good. Oh, P&R called me and started yelling at me and my roommate saying that I owed the money and it did not matter what audit said I had to pay. They have threatened me, my accountant, my roommate, harassed my employer, and a collection agent stalked me at worked, followed me around. Mad as hell, I cut my own wages so the IRS would get nothing and despite me being placed in an uncollectable state, the IRS seized my bank account. My Co. finally got tired of the problem and having IRS parked in front of the office and fired me. I have been out of work for 4 months. I have written to Senator Roth -- no response. I followed up 3 times in the last 3 months and still no response.

## IRS Abuse Report #338

**Date:** Fri Jan 2 1998
**To:** sue@irs.class-action.com
**From:** JS

I too am having problems with the IRS. Seems they think I owed them around $1,200 from the years 84, 85 & 86. As of their last letter 12/19/96 they indicate that I now owe them over $19,000.!!!! I do not know how they can turn a simple $1,200 dollar debt into an amount that will put a major financial burden on myself and my family. They have already put a lien on any property I own and are threatening to garnish my wages. I have my own family and obligations to take care of as well as my parents. Garnishing my wages would cause severe consequences to both. I am in a position now to pay off the original amount they "say" I owe, but I do not feel that I should have to pay over $18,000 in penalties and interest!

## IRS Abuse Report #339

**Date:** Fri Jan 2 1998
**To:** sue@irs.class-action.com
**From:** AM

The IRS is currently harassing me for an amount they say I'm responsible for. It deals with the Trust Fund Penalty (payroll taxes), they are billing for amounts which are due on Bankrupt co. of which I was just an employee. For one of the periods in question, I wasn't even an employee for the co. The other period in question, I wasn't a signatore at the time the period ended. When I appealed to the IRS agent in Florida and told him my side of the story, his comment was "I don't care if you're innocent or guilty, I'm here to make someone pay". This harassment has been going on since 1993, the bill is for 1990 & 1991. Since that time, the then sole owner of the co. has opened many different business, and the IRS has not gone after him for the money. I am extremely frustrated with this and its ruining my life. I can barely make ends meet with my day to day expenses.

## IRS Abuse Report #340

**Date:** Sat Jan 3 1998
**To:** sue@irs.class-action.com
**From:** LP

The IRS has created Hell and Havoc for us for over 2 years now, using trumped up, concocted, evidence as to how we understated our expenses for the years 1993, 1994, 1995, and 1996

In August 1995, we were first audited by the IRS. We were told that we had to have the audit in our home. This, our accountant told us was the first year that they had decided to go into peoples homes to see if they were living lifestyles above what was indicated on their tax returns. The first thing the Lady did was ask questions about how much money my wife withheld from bank deposits in the form of cash. Where did she hide it...wrapped up in the freezer? Buried in the back yard? She asked, "if you need any cash money where would you find it in your home? I told her that if I did, I'd have to ask her for it. She asked to use the rest room and cased our home as she went. She demanded that I show her the inside of my garage suggesting that we were hiding inventory or other items for sale. When she looked through our records, which had been stowed away in my garage for over two years (1993), she told me that she didn't like the way that we recorded the information and wanted to take some of it to her office so she could complete the audit. Like an idiot, I allowed her to. She sent several summons' to us via the mail asking for bank records and check copies for the year 1993. Then she increased the audit to include 1994, resulting in more summons for records. Later, she wanted copies of all checks that we wrote from personal accounts. With this information, she was attempting to track movement of all our money. With this, she concluded that we made more money than we really did. She explained to me initially that the IRS has a formula which applies to everybody when used could accurately determine their taxes even if the person didn't have good records. She certainly must have used it. When

I was laid off in 1991 from my regular employment, I was unemployed during that year, all of 1992, and most of 1993, and some of 1994. During 1993, and 1994, I was attempting to expand my wife's maintenance (business and homes) to schools, maintaining (cleaning and changing lights, etc.) their basketball and football score boards. This required the purchase of lots of specialized equip. and tools that are not normal to a cleaning service. This also required a lot of trial and error (and loss of money) trying to learn how to fix these items. Also, it required a lot of mileage on my aging pickup. She disallowed mileage thinking it was unreasonable and excessive, she disallowed travel and lodging for my wife's Mary Kay business, because on a couple of occasions, she allowed me to travel with her saying that most of the time she probably was with me rather that doing Mary Kay. She basically made up her own mind, what she wanted to use and denying the claims made by us for the write-offs. Our second visit was to be in the home again. She delayed that meeting 3 successive time until the following February, and changed that audit to the IRS office downtown in San Jose, CA. We arrive at the building, there were no nameplates, just a cipher lock on the door. I had to go ask people where I was to go. Somebody finally let us in. We were ushered to a auditor room. During that time, she told us that she needed to make copies of all of our bank records and that she would be gone for some time. We were suspicious that there was a listening device, or a video camera in the room...and sure enough, my wife found a recording device taped to the underside of the table, just above my lap. When she entered the room, I demanded it be removed, and the security manager came and removed it. She later showed up at our house, did not ring the doorbell, walked past it into our entry and up to our kitchen where we were standing. She tells me that she was delivering another summons and that she knew that I was now working a 2nd job. My wife kicked her out. That is when we decided to hire and attorney and keep her from coming to our home

and hassling us. To date, we have spent over three thousand dollars and the little black cloud of owing what she said we owed (over $35,000 for 1993 and 1994) is still over our head. During this time, they have refunded money from 1993 (a year they say I underpaid over $9,000, and applied it to 1995 (explain that). They asked for an additional $1600 penalty for 1995 because our Wells Fargo Bookkeeping service apparently had not sent in our W3s and W2s. We paid it, only to have them ask to get it back. I made numerous calls for explanation, and was basically told pay it, don't question it. We do not have to explain before you pay. Pay and then maybe we will explain. Next, I found a garnishment of about $500 from my paycheck. I called and promised to pay the money back that was remaining. I was given a letter from my attorney that while I was trying to work out a payment plan with them on these issues, the IRS would stop all collection activity on me, So I did not pay the remaining...only to have them levy this account out of my wife's personal bank account, causing a whole bunch of checks to not clear. IT aint over yet. Our marriage, because of all this stress is on the rocks.

It seems that these guys know they can damn well do anything they want on the small business person, because they know that they can use taxpayers money to push and push and push and the taxpayer can't afford to hire a high priced lawyer like large corporations. This is bad, really bad. I do not trust them, and in the future, no matter what changes they make, I will not talk to them without a lawyer. I hate living in this country, where congress allows this Mafioso band of guerrillas to rape its citizenry.

### IRS Abuse Report #341

**Date:** Sun Jan 4 1998
**To:** sue@irs.class-action.com
**From:** RS
To this day the IRS is seeking to collect business and personal tax for a business that my

dad had before and after their separation (which my mother had no part of). Also, they are trying to collect personal income tax from her which my father owed during the time they were separated.. Granted they are only looking at about 4,000 dollars but to me and her that is a lot of money! She has since remarried and has to work 2 jobs because the IRS says they can't find my father to collect the debt.....since she doesn't want to go to jail cause she can't pay the debt she is working about 80hrs a week to save money so she can pay the debt (and I am worried that this may have severe effects on her being that she is 45 and having to start her life all over again and now has to worry about paying this before she can start saving for retirement).

## IRS Abuse Report #342

**Date:** Mon Jan 5 4:14:31 1998
**To:** sue@irs.class-action.com
**From:** TW

In 1992 my home and home based business was heavily damaged by a drought ending rain and mud slide. The damage was inspected and I applied for, and received a $5000 SBA loan for personal effects, and a $5000 SBA loan for my business, a sole proprietorship making enough to survive on. During the next two years I started to rebuild by applying the SBA loan for its intended purpose. I was making the monthly repayment on the SBA loan. I reconstructed lost records from the mud slide and got up to date with the IRS and was making payments. I had a power of attorney in effect through a CPA but the IRS immediately levied the remaining $4000 from the SBA loan. This was followed with two CONCURRENT audits, including threats of seizing everything. They even contacted my clients and demanded they send the IRS my accounts payable. The bottom line is that I made an effort to get right with the IRS. The result was a levy of money that they loaned to me, (which I was repaying), and two CONCURRENT audits which netted the IRS an additional $800 ($400 per year). Would a sane

person volunteer to go through that again? The IRS is a festering sore. I am a U.S. Army veteran and a former Peace Corps volunteer. There is something very wrong.

## IRS Abuse Report #343

**Date:** Mon Jan 5 4:14:31 1998
**To:** sue@irs.class-action.com
**From:** LM

The IRS has ruined my credit. They've placed liens against me and are threatening to seize my assets.

Although I was a signatore for a very short period of time during 1991, all checks had to be approved by the owner. All of the facts were presented to the IRS Appeals Officer (Jorge Moral) back in 1993, just before they assessed the taxes against me. The appeals officer refused to hear my side of the story, his comment was "I don't care if you're innocent or Guilty, I'm here to make someone pay", his main concern was that he had to close the case before the end of the year. Even before I went into his office, he had already found me guilty. He told me to agree to pay approx. 75% of the taxes or he'll make me pay for everything (approx. $29,000.). I signed nothing, and the result was a bill for approx. $29,000.

Just recently, I tried reopening the case, but the IRS refused to do so. They claim that I already went through the appeals process and that the only thing for me to do is file suit against them. Also, I received another demand for payment. The new bill comes to approx. $44,000 including interest.

It his hard for me to function on a day to day basis while this is hanging over my head.

## IRS Abuse Report #344

**Date:** Jan 6 1998
**To:** sue@irs.class-action.com
**From:** WM

After being told by the IRS agent I was a nuisance and they raised my payments from $200 a month to $498 (as a disciplinary move), I was told they would NOT place another levy on my bank accounts because I was making payments as "directed". Last week I received a certified letter from the IRS, a "Notice of Levy". Oh well, further proof the IRS follows the guidelines of Karl Marx rather than our forgotten Constitution. Right after receipt of the "Notice of Levy", I went to bed. The next morning I was transported via ambulance to our neighborhood hospital for heart attack symptoms. After three nitro pills and two nitro patches and lots of blood letting, it was determined I was under an "UnGodly amount of stress," and it will kill me without relief. My doctor put me on beta-blockers and a new ulcer medicine to help relieve the pain. Thanks IRS for again scaring the blazes out of my family!

## IRS Abuse Report #345

**Date:** Wed Jan 7 14:25:17 1998
**To:** sue@irs.class-action.com
**From:** RC

I have been trying to settle with the IRS for several years. Because the issue is a joint return with a divorce in between, because my now ex-wife will not sign anything, the IRS has never acknowledged my attempts to settle, and is now seizing my accounts, selling my stocks, and doing everything else to get it's money. I have never disputed I owe them money, just how much. I am now borrowing from my retirement to settle with them before they seize my house.

## IRS Abuse Report #346

**Date:** Thu Jan 8 10:38:13 1998
**To:** sue@irs.class-action.com
**From:** MO

My business took a hard hit due to the recession, and I was unable to pay the IRS taxes for 1989, 1990, 1993. In 1993 I submitted an Offer in Compromise after extensive documentation was submitted, it was denied claiming to be missing documentation! I resubmitted the documentation and was a few days delayed, but I had spoken to a revenue agent who informed me that the deadline was extended. The offer was denied due to late filing! I took the liberty to send all documents w/return receipts and recorded the conversation w/the revenue agent extending the deadline due to the volume of documentation requested. The offer was still denied and I was informed that I had to resubmit and all of the documentation was lost so I needed to prepare it again! My . employer recently received a garnishment levy from the IRS, but since I am currently a full time student my earnings are meager, yet they take it all!! I originally owed $5916 in taxes and have paid the IRS $7290 at my families expense. I still owe, according to the IRS over $10,000. I am at a point were I'm not even working since I will never be able to get ahead on the mounting penalties and interest. In summary the IRS is crippling my financial future at this time with no end in sight!

## IRS Abuse Report #347

**Date:** Sun Jan 11 8:56:50 1998
**To:** sue@irs.class-action.com
**From:** MN

Our lives are pure hell. 2 years ago we got a letter from IRS saying we were getting audited. We have a friend that does taxes on the side to earn extra money. She assured us that she was highly qualified and would do our taxes but that she couldn't sign them because she wasn't licensed, but that it was still legal for her to do them for us. We trusted her and she did them for 8 years. We paid her a fee for this and they were done every year. We had no idea she was doing them wrong.

When asked to come into the office for audit I was told I could bring a friend, my auditor, CPA etc. Not knowing the laws I went by myself knowing we did nothing wrong. I was showed one line that they felt was in error. The auditor said if I could clear this up the audit was over. I was in great relief and explained to him that my husband just had a heart attack and was recovering and that this really had us upset and scared. He assured me that it could be over if we could clear up that one matter. I called my friend and she said she would come in with me to explain any problem as nothing was wrong. She did, and the auditor admitted that she was right. The audit should have been over from what he had told me. However, he dug into some other issues, she explained them and so on. He asked to see my files which I was requested to bring in with me. I gave them to him and he questioned our deposits in the bank.

I tried to explain that I bought jewelry supplies for my friend and did some craft shows once in awhile. He said that it was never put on the tax papers. So I again got my friend we went in and tried to explain everything to him, he said that he understood where the money came from and that we were about at the end of the audit, he had to turn it into his superior and she would say whether we would be audited for the prior year. Before leaving I told him this was making me a nervous wreck and my husband and asked if this would go on much longer? He said no, it was just about wound up. I said I know you have an idea if this will be closed or if they will audit us for the prior year and he said in his opinion it looked fine to him and not to worry that it was almost over. I was so relieved.

The fear of going in there was so hard. I was brought to tears numerous times and voices were raised, and this was mostly over my book keeping. He made me go home and redo my

files 2-3 times. I was really upset. I had always heard you just take your receipts and w-2s in and they audit you. He made me completely re-do my files the way he wanted them. Not being a book keeper, I didn't understand, this made him mad at me when I came in the next time. IT got worse and worse at each appointment he said take them home and re-do them again. I was a nervous wreck. Well he finally accepted them and he assured me that everything was going to be ok. That I would get a letter in the mail telling me if the audit was over or if they were going to audit us for another back year he said within one week. I waited and waited and no word. We were a nervous wreck watching the phone and mail and nothing came. I called his office and they would say 'yes he is in just a minute' then they would get back on the phone after telling him it was me and say that He is not in right now'. This happened a few times so I just went into the office and asked to see him. He had kept my files and I needed them and we wanted to know what was going on. He came to the outer door and told me that everything was fine I had nothing to worry about. If I didn't hear nothing that was good news that his audit was over. We waited and nothing came so we assumed it was over.

Just prior to the audit, my husband had a heart attack, was told he was diabetic, and we were forced into bankruptcy. Everything hit at once. Then things started going a little better and my husband broke his ankle, just before Christmas and my daughter passed away from cancer 2 days after Christmas. I can't tell you the pain and mental state we were in. We have never had more pain in our lives to handle. Then I got a call from the audit man and he said that I needed to come into the office. I called the day of the appointment and asked them to make a new one because I didn't feel well. She said the auditor wasn't in but she would make me a new one. A little bit after that we were sitting in our home that day and 2 men came to the door. IT was the auditor and an "FBI" man and they said if I couldn't come to them that they came out to see us. We invited them in and they told us that it was serious and that we could be in great trouble and that they had a case against us. We were so shocked and terrified. They explained that because of the extra income not reported on the taxes in a schedule C for 4 years that it was fraud. We tried to explain that a schedule C was always filed. They said no and that was fraud and we were really in trouble. That we could get our files and if we could prove where we made the money and if we could prove we filed a schedule C on it that it would help . They gave us a chance to bring in our files for the 4 years and I called our friend that did the taxes and she assured me that the schedule C was filed every single year. We thought it was all a mistake. If we owed money we just wanted to pay it on a payment plan and try to get back a life. We got a CPA that we were told was really good in matters this serious.

We went with our CPA into their office and the federal men were there we were told, and ready to handcuff us and take us away. I started crying and tried to think who I could call to go get my dogs and some things out of our house. Prior to going into the office meeting our CPA told us that this was not just an audit but that we were going to be indicted for fraud. We were petrified. He said that we could get an attorney but the IRS said they had a closed case on us and that if our records were not perfect we would lose. We were taken to a little room where the auditor sat across from us and our CPA at the end of the table and informed us that the government wanted to indict us for fraud and that we were looking at 20 years as it stood. We were told what was going to happen, they were going to file fraud charges against us and that we would have to get an attorney and that even if we got one there was no hope that we would win as they had an air tight case against us and fighting it in court would run into the 100's of thousands of dollars and did we have the means to fight it and try to win a case that we were going to lose anyway? We sat there and had no idea of what to do or say. We said we couldn't afford the attorney and

would do anything they wanted to keep us from going to prison! Anything. They left the room and came back and asked our CPA what he proposed. The CPA said he would like to offer a compromise. They left the room and we sat on pins and needles while our life hung in the balance and our CPA had to tell me to be quiet because we were being recorded in that room. My husband and I had no idea of that. We were so shook up. They re-entered the room said they had talked it over and they would listen to a compromise.

At this point they left the room and our CPA told us he was going to offer them a cash total that we would owe and that we would pay it. He said no matter what the amount was if we would trust him and go along with it. We had no alternative, we both said anything you can do. They came in the room and the auditor asked for the offer and the CPA started writing things down. The auditor took it out of the room to his superiors for an ok and then came in the room again. He said that they could start the offer. He then showed the CPA a bunch of paper with numbers and said this is what we want. The CPA asked for conference, the auditor left the room and the CPA showed it to us and it was ridiculous but he said we had no room to argue it was that or prison and that they would dicker to get a lower sum. The auditor came back into the room and they would do some figuring push an amount back and forth to each other and disagree. We had no idea what the amounts were still. At the time that didn't matter to us.

You have to understand that my husband and I felt like we were Americans and the Gestapo was interrogating us. It was much more intense and terrifying then what I can put on paper, I couldn't quit shaking and I urinated in my pants. I would look at my husband and he was as pale as a ghost. I was so afraid he was going to have a heart attack. He was so nervous he was speechless. We both were like robots and did whatever they suggested, the fear was that bad every time he left the room. When he would close that door we were waiting for a death sentence when he walked back in. He would be gone for quite a few minutes. Which to us seemed like forever and the fear we felt when he re-entered was unbelievable. Any time he left the room he could have come back in and said 'No they won't accept this' and we were going to prison. My heart stopped several times and I know my husband's did, I was so worried for him. It didn't even matter that they had scared me to death or into urinating on myself. It just didn't matter I was terrified beyond caring about anything but my husbands health. When the auditor re-entered again which seemed like the 100th time but was probably the 6th or 7th, I don't know, they started bartering back and forth with our lives in numbers. With sums we knew we couldn't pay. But from the insinuations we got from them we had nothing to fight with and had to sit there and let them take our lives over.

They would total figures, show them to each other and then finally they both agreed on an amount. It didn't come to us then but they each had an amount written on a piece of paper at the beginning, I guess the auditor said isn't that funny we both had the exact same amount written down. The auditor took it out of the room, again we waited with the fear of god in us and he finally re-entered and said that it was acceptable. They showed it to us and then he left the room again. Awhile later he came in with contracts and papers to sign and our CPA told us to sign everything he had our power of attorney and he signed them and that in the deal we would not be audited for the prior 6 or 7 years if we agreed to pay this amount and that our CPA would amend 2 years of our taxes and submit them for approval and then we would get a payment plan. Our CPA said yes and the signing was completed and the meeting was over.

The ordeal that my husband and I was submitted to was no less then what we see in the movies in a Nazi story. We didn't know what we were doing and didn't care at that point, due to what they told us. We just gave them anything they wanted. We left that day so scared we didn't know what to do. We have an average home that we are buying, we kept our bills up after the bankruptcy, my husband drove truck and was gone 22 days out of the month. Not knowing in between all of this if he had a home, wife or dogs to even come home to. His time on the road was stressful to his health and the conditions he worked under made him a nervous wreck. We were told by the CPA that the papers would come in the mail for a payment plan. They never came and I got letters from the IRS saying they were going to attach the pay check, lien the house and vehicles and anything we owned. I called the CPA and he said that he submitted it to the IRS and to disregard the letters it was automation that was behind. We couldn't let it go it was our life and they were serious so I went in and talked to the CPA and he resubmitted it to make sure they had it and I was told not to worry, again I got a letter saying that because we have neglected to make a payment plan and answer their letter that they were attaching the paycheck seizing the vehicles and home etc. I was terrified again and went to the CPA, he was out of town. I called the number on the IRS letter and explained that he had our power of attorney and that I couldn't do anything and she said they had no correspondence from our CPA on record let alone a power of attorney and that she would give me 2 days to get it to her and the forms for the payment plan. I again went to the CPA and he gave him the financial status and he resubmitted it again and we got another final notice saying we have failed to make any attempt to pay this bill and that they have written us numerous letters and given us numerous chances to clear the matter up with installments and we have ignored them and that this time it was the last attempt to let us have a payment plan and action was being taken place. I called the CPA, he called them and he called me in the morning and told us that it was straightened out that a payment plan would be in the mail.

This was all over several weeks and the harassment from the IRS not applying the papers that our CPA sent in put us through hell again. It had started almost 2 years ago and seemed like it was not going to stop. Then a payment plan came in the mail and we were told we had to also pay estimated taxes at the same time in a different check by our CPA. The amount to us was unbelievable. We have been in a nightmare for almost 2 years and are still not out of it. The penalties and interest they added on made the amount bigger and bigger and this keeps going and there is no way we will ever get it paid at this rate. The depression they have put us in has driven each of us at separate times to the point where we actually thought about committing suicide. We had no life, our health was bad, different situations drove us to the limit because the IRS couldn't treat us like human beings and Americans. In that whole time we endured the stress they put upon us, my husband broke his ankle, I lost my daughter to cancer, this is very hard for me to write these things, my husband lost both of his parents a month apart from each other.

Our CPA finally got them to straighten out their files and get us the payment plan but we were at the end of our rope. I even had a conversation with my CPA that was trying to help us that was so emotional that he threatened to quit us and drop the whole compromise. I can't tell you or put in words what this has done to my husband and myself. We now wait each day to see if we can make the payments. If not we know that they will take our home, truck, and everything.

This is not what America is supposed to be. If we knowingly set out to cheat the government out of money then this would be so different but we had no idea that our friend didn't file a schedule C all those years and that we were guilty of anything. If we owed them money we wanted to pay it and get on with our life. We always wanted to pay what we owed that wasn't the problem. It never entered our minds not to pay it. We just wanted to pay what was

reasonable considering the circumstances and see if we could go on with a life. We don't feel the amount is fair to us. But they didn't' care, they were taking us to prison and we had no alternative. We are paying an amount now that is unfair and the interest and penalties are astronomical. I see no end to it if my husband becomes ill or he loses his job. There is no life when you owe IRS, they are in every day that you live, making it harder and harder to see an end for or a time for peace again. IRS has an un-American system that only tears down the average working American that is the backbone of the country. These laws weren't made for us they were made for higher ups that don't care about the working man or family. The methods they use are Communistic, that's the only word I can think of to express what we are going through. My husband still goes to work as long as he can and we hope that something or someone can make a difference in our life and people like us. Something must me done to take the outrageous power that they have bestowed upon themselves away. It's Un-American and I am ashamed to say they are part of our United States because they are not. They belong in a country where these tactics and methods belong. Not here in American.

I have dates and times for almost everything but am still missing papers that the auditor has and the CPA. I can get them if they are needed for precise situations if needed. I asked the IRS for them back and my CPA but I have got nothing from them. I have most of the papers proving my situation and have made notes through the whole time period in case something happened or if we were offered help I would have something to go by. Please let me know if there is any hope for us, and people like us in the same situation? Thank you so much for letting me tell you our nightmare. It's still not over.

## IRS Abuse Report #348

**Date:** Sun Jan 11 22:28:11 1998
**To:** sue@irs.class-action.com
**From:** RL

I got a notice of audit in mid 88', agent came to my small Business and ask questions, one was "how long have you been doing your books this way"? I replied, 'Since I bought the business in 80'. She wanted to see business and paper work back to 80', I let her, stupid me. In 89' she and her supervisor handed me a bill for $80M. I fought it for 6.5 years, proving 8 different times that they were wrong in their assumptions and accusations. I appealed twice, finally took them to federal court, then they wanted to settle for a credit to me for $32. They lied, took my books for 2 years, made dozens of errors, billed me w/o written audit, threatened, liened, criminalized me, separated us on paper, basterdized our 5 children, informed everyone in our small town, ruined my business and reputation. In mid 95' it started all over again and now I'm going back to tax court. It's never over is it? If it wasn't for a wonderful family and a great Lord, I would have given up years ago.

## IRS Abuse Report #349

**Date:** Wed Jan 14 1:26:23 1998
**To:** sue@irs.class-action.com
**From:** RH

Have been unemployed since 1985 and have not filed since then. This is because a zealous agent refused to let me see a supervisor after requesting four times. The IRS then claimed I owed $203,000 and I had better pay immediately or a lien would be placed against our home. I am 50 and have never made more than 10,000 in any year.

## IRS Abuse Report #350

**Date:** Mon Jan 19 13:29:12 1998
**To:** sue@irs.class-action.com
**From:** FN

The IRS has harassed and abused its power. The IRS single-handedly disagrees, unilaterally, without any reason, every piece of proof that I submitted for deductions. Legitimate deductions for dependent expenses, business purpose and business deductions. This IRS thing is pretty scary. The IRS plays the role of collector, judge, and enforcer. The IRS, in other words, represents classic Communism—which I fled Vietnam to avoid. The first thing a taxpayer hears from an auditor is: 'you are a liar, whatever documentation you provide to me, I will need further proof'. Such proofs are very time-consuming, humiliating and sucks all livelihood out of a person. We must dramatically reduce the IRS role ASAP. The IRS must be nothing more than anyone else, i.e., it must go through the court system to prove anyone is guilty before collecting a penny. We must turn around the system, we must turn the system upside down:

## IRS Abuse Report #351

**Date:** Mon, 19 Jan 1998 14:48:44
**To:** sue@irs.class-action.com
**From:** JO

The submissions to this list seem credible to me, NOW. At the time I had a banking levy placed against me by IRS, I began reading the IRS abuse reports on this group, and I wondered if these were actually true.

Then, the IRS levied my SALARY without notice in writing, and my attempts to get this levy cleared are entering their third month, so far without success.

I've written US Senators in my state and have received polite replies that they will look into the situation. My CPA has been unable to connect with the IRS agent who is handling the levy and other details. CPA calls, the agent is 'out.' etc. Attorney's don't work for free, etc.

What I mean is, I am experiencing what I observed in the abuse reports. I am experiencing the same invisibility and lack of cooperation from IRS, and the same powerlessness of US representatives. My case is no different from the hundreds of others reported -- lost job, used savings to subsist, etc., and now IRS has levied the job it took me a long long time to find, and has made it impossible for me to survive. So, my story lines up with that of others who have written: powerless Congressmen, aloof IRS agents, all of it.

I no longer have ANY doubt that the abuse postings are for the most part, real and authentic, and I also conclude that our US representatives are fully aware and fully supportive of what the IRS is doing. This should scare ANYONE: IRS apparently has permission to do exactly what they are doing. This is an X-files script. How do we stop this economic slaughter? I read here that many consider suicide as an option, and frankly I am beginning to also. The state of Michigan, for example, seeks to jail Dr. Kevorkian for his helping to euthanize patients, but at the same time, IRS can push people to taking their lives and that is OK?!

The ethics behind IRS actions are simply outrageous. I do not say that taxes are unconstitutional, but I do say that the IRS should not operate outside the Constitution, and our elected officials have apparently allowed it to do just that.

### IRS Abuse Report #352

**Date:** Thu Jan 22 11:12:01 1998
**To:** sue@irs.class-action.com
**From:** SB
After having observed the development of this web site over the last six or so months, I have refrained from entering my truly horrific IRS abuse story. But JO's entry on 1/19 of his/her abuse inflicted by the IRS (See IRS Abuse Report #351) where JO mentions that he/she questioned the validity of the previous 350 reports, has prompted me to add my thoughts. Yes, these things happen all too often and No, suicide is not the answer. The IRS will not let a taxpayer's suicide abuse stand in their way of collecting $. My husband of 23 years committed suicide due to several years of IRS' very abusive tactics. They did to us all of the usual things mentioned in the previous 351 reports ... and more. The first line of my husband's suicide note cited the IRS .. ' they sit, do nothing and watch you die.' He left behind me a widow at age 48, a sixteen year old daughter, his mother, father, sister, brother, many relatives and friends. To keep this brief, I will not delineate the years & years of IRS abuse. What I would like to tell everyone out there in the same boat, is that suicide not does stop IRS collection agents. Since my husband's suicide, I have been harassed by two agents -- one of whom lined my husband's life insurance policy and the other agent levied the unspent proceeds from another life insurance policy. In essence, not only did the IRS kill my husband, they have taken his life insurance money which was intended to support me and my daughter. Suicide is not the solution. The surviving spouse then has to deal with the IRS alone, and in a very vulnerable emotional state. The loss of my husband is almost more than I can bear, and now I have to deal with the IRS as well. My senator Judd Gregg has been most helpful, but even he couldn't get the IRS to back down. I may be a meek & quiet individual (who's also an emotional wreck), but when the IRS took my husband away I decided to let the IRS have it back with both barrels. I will fight ... and I plan to win. Yes, 'JO' these IRS abuses are real, even in this 'free' country and the sad thing is that they are allowed to continue even to this very day. We'll be reading about them in subsequent IRS Abuse Reports, I'm sure. I have had quite enough, haven't you??

## IRS Abuse Report #353

**Date:** Sat Jan 24 17:47:25 1998
**To:** sue@irs.class-action.com
**From:** RC

I have been in battle for over twelve years over tax returns from 1983 and 1984. I have been lied to, given false information on how to absolve problems leaving me with even greater penalties and interest. I have been forced to sign away my Statute of Limitations. I have had my credit ruined and my marriage almost ruined. They have burdened my new wife with monetary obligations that have absolutely nothing do with her. Her credit has also been ruined. At every step of the way there is harassment and threats. The almighty "Intent To Levy Wages" letters keep coming especially if you make any attempt to disagree or complain. I have lost two good jobs due to these letters to my employers. Although illegal to fire you because of them it happens and can be easily covered up. Taxpayer assistance and problem resolution is a farce and a lie. It gets you nowhere but in deeper crap the next time you have to talk one of the heavy weight crooks on the end of a phone line which takes hours to get to. How can we ever hope to get out of the trap we are in? The penalties and interest keeps you from ever paying it off. You can't get a loan because there is crap on your credit report and liens on your property. It is worse than owing Guido the loan-shark. WELCOME TO HELL ON EARTH!

## IRS Abuse Report #354

**Date:** Sat Jan 24 22:40:15 1998
**To:** sue@irs.class-action.com
**From:** LP

After reading through the many examples of IRS abuses, I now have some solace and peace of mind that I am not the only one disgusted with this organization that has been given license to steal, badger, and kill the American spirit.

Between 1986-1989, I was an office manager for a Chrysler dealership, in a depressed marketplace in urban new jersey. For a period of time, I was a signatory on the checking account. The owners began to have financial difficulty, federal liens were placed on the business. The IRS never informed me personally that I was a responsible party for the unpaid tax. the owners were fortunate to sell the business for enough money to cover the unpaid tax bill. Since I was not a corporate officer, I was not present at neither the first, or second, closing of sale. However, by the time these closings occurred, a 100% civil penalty had been imposed upon me, and of course, I hired an attorney to represent me. My attorney informed the IRS of the sale of the business, and that if they pursued the corporate attorney, they could collect the money at the closing. After all, they had liens on the business. for some reason, probably a monetary one, the IRS agents ignored my attorney. Ten years later, I am still pursued by the IRS. They have garnished my wages and made my life and my family's life miserable. This debt is not mine, but no one cares

## IRS Abuse Report #355

**Date:** Mon Jan 26 19:33:10 1998
**To:** sue@irs.class-action.com
**From:** SE

As a self employed citizen, I Have been harassed and abused by the IRS for many years. I strongly believe they are out-of-control with power. They are the America's Gestapo! The IRS should be abolished entirely.

I am currently in the middle of a major battle with the IRS over an audit for my 94 and 95 taxes. I gathered all my documentation to prove I did not owe taxes for those years, and my CPA (who I have had for 9 years, and has done an excellent job at my other audits), was suppose to go to the audit for me. Evidently, he did not show up for my audit, (we still don't know why), and 50 of his other client's audits, too! A short time later, much to my surprise, I received an "URGENT" letter from the IRS stating that I owed in excess of $20,000 for 94 and 95, and if not paid, liens and garnishment was the next step. I was contacted by a Tax Attorney shortly thereafter. He told me I had very little chance to be able to go back and be audited now, because it has already gone to collections. Although he agreed I have a "cut and dried" malpractice against my CPA, the IRS doesn't care about the circumstances, and I am now liable for the $20,000, which will literally put us into bankruptcy! So far I have spent over $2,000 in attorney's fees, and this is only the beginning of our fight. I am sick, not knowing what the future will bring.

## IRS Abuse Report #356

**Date:** Tue Jan 27 17:44:03 1998
**To:** sue@irs.class-action.com
**From:** ANON

For anyone who believes that the IRS only abuses the average taxpayer, I suggest that they go to work for this organization. What the IRS does to the average citizen is gentle compared to the stresses it imposes on its own employees. By the time an individual rises to permanent employee status, he or she has become so cynical that screwing taxpayers is just the way it is. Phony performance evaluations to get incompetent personnel out of a department is the norm, yet the competent employee is continually ignored in the awarding of promotions and performance awards. Training is done by the most boring speakers imaginable. And even then is inadequate to perform the job. Horror stories? No, part of the Reagan tax reduction program. Here's how it works. Take the most widespread tax benefit program and perform a 100% review of all the returns that claim it. Don't tell anyone that you are doing it. Delay issuing the full refund so that you have to pay interest, especially on those cases that the taxpayer got a refund loan. While you go after these poor people, let the top 20% incomes have a free ride on a program in which

there may be up to 40% fraud. Sit back and laugh as the citizens BEG for a tax reform that will result in an increase in the tax burden for 62% of the population and the top 15% will have a tax reduction of up to 49% and more. When the people realize what is happening, you get to blame the 'lazy, incompetent and untrainable' employees. Way to go!

## IRS Abuse Report #357

**Date:** Sat Jan 31 15:31:51 1998
**To:** sue@irs.class-action.com
**From:** JK

We have been in the process of solving a tax problem for my brother since September 1997. With telephone advice from 4 different IRS representatives (we have their names and dates of conversation) we thought we had an agreement that we would put an agreed upon sum of money in the mail by February 2, 1998, to the IRS and when they received that sum, they would send us an agreement for us to make payments beginning in March 1998, to retire the balance they claim is due. In the meantime we had written a letter to the Penalty & Interest Abatement Service in Ogden, UT, certified, return receipt requested, for which we have a return receipt stamped 12/24/97. There has been no reply. So, we were prepared to deposit the agreed upon sum of money on Monday, February 2, 1998, just like we promised. Today, January 31, 1998, my brother's employees went to cash their paychecks and the bank couldn't honor them because the IRS had confiscated all the funds on Friday, January 30. This has virtually put him out of business and destroyed his credibility with the bank. Congratulations to the IRS, they have now destroyed one more family and business.

**IRS Abuse Report #358**

**Date:** Wed Feb 4 20:39:16 1998
**To:** sue@irs.class-action.com
**From:** SS

The taxpayers of this country need relief from the biggest power hungry criminal organization created, the IRS.

Just one week ago, my husband and I attended our very first audit request by the IRS. I was very uncomfortable about going when we first received a letter from them because of all the horrible stories we heard from various people. So I purchased several books and read several reports about what to expect and what to beware of. I read how the IRS tries to threaten people and purposely look for ways to disallow items on a return. Well, after attending our meeting with an IRS agent, I want to say that the stories are true. Being a former government employee, I had an idea of how the IRS wanted to receive the requested information in the letter they sent us, so I prepared and organized every document and dotted every i. However, I suspected that there was going to be one problem, some of our receipts were lost by our moving company during our recent move to a new city. To make a long story short, After the IRS representative reviewed my organized documents, she seemed removed that she did not see a weak spot in our return to disallow, and then the big question came. Where are all of your receipts, I provided a letter from the moving company verifying that they lost some of our household items etc. etc. and of course, at that time, the IRS agent indicated that she was going to disallow everything without a receipt. One week later, we received a letter from the same IRS agent that she now wants to audit our following year tax return. Can you see where this is going??

**IRS Abuse Report #359**

**Date:** Sat Feb 7 12:18:49 1998
**To:** sue@irs.class-action.com
**From:** SY

I need to give you a bit of background information about myself. I am a 31 year old, single female. I am from a small town in East Tennessee. My father worked in a factory and made about $22,000/year until he died in 1992. I have two sisters. Each of us worked hard and paid for our education's while pursuing "the American Dream". I worked two jobs in the summers and one full-time job each school year while I was in college. Wanting more, I went to graduate school. I never received one grant, one free lunch or one handout of any kind. I did however receive student loans, for which I am paying dearly. I admit, that I was neglectful in paying my taxes for 1994 and 1995.. and in 1996, I filed late for 1994.. paid it in full $7,569..which included about $4,000 in penalties and interest. I paid 1995 in full, I had an outstanding balance for that year of $4357, which included about $1200 in penalties and interest..I sent $4,700 for my 1996 taxes and began to pay installment payments of $500. per month.. ( this does not include the withholdings from my paychecks or the multiple "partial payments that I sent them). Trying to do the right thing, I sent them a total of $15,000, I have had $13,000 withheld from my paycheck this year..I made payments of over $3,000. My accountant advised me to send the payments, and I would be sent an agreement to sign.. the agreement never came. In short, I have paid the IRS over $31,000 over the last 10 months.

So, here I sit...the American dream...emotionally battered, no money, no savings.. no nothing..the electricity is still on.. I did get them to release $157 to pay my electric bill since it is 20 degrees outside. I realize that I must be the lowest form of life.. well that is how they made me feel.. I do not know what kind of fallout from the bounced checks that I am going to have to endure.. the hag from the IRS would not even acknowledge that I had paid over

$30,000 in less than a year. I, this point, have cried for about 14 hours.. and I do not know what I am going to do.. the phone is still on, for now.. when I tried to get the money released to pay the phone bill.. the woman wanted to discuss with me how I could possibly have a $300 phone bill. Work hard, make sacrifices.. and you will be rewarded..that is what I was taught.. I worked hard, made many, many sacrifices.. and look where it has gotten me.. Thank you IRS.. I am the American dream.. I suppose I would not have to worry about my electric bill or my health care, or my housing.,. if I laid at home.. and had kids.. hell, I can't afford a kid.. nor, do I have the time.. so, I guess the two jobs I have now are not enough.. I will be seeking employment at a third job.. so that I can "stay afloat". I am tired.. worn out actually.. and can not take it anymore, I have no groceries and do not know how I am going to get to work.. because I do not have any gas money.. to receive this treatment.. I have scrimped, eaten Ramen noodles for the past year.. and paid over $31,000.. which has put me in financial ruin.

## IRS Abuse Report #360

**Date:** Mon Feb 9 3:38:48 1998
**To:** sue@irs.class-action.com
**From:** CC

The IRS has harassed me since 1990, first by removing the dependent deduction for my niece (even though I cared for her and kept her), and second—by accusing me of failing to report income that I never even received. As late as today, I am still battling through numerous Problem Resolution Offices against a recent levy of one of my accounts, tax refunds, and now intensive collection actions. I am so frustrated and angry with their arrogant, rude and illegal tactics. No one to date has taken the time or energy to investigate the validity of the IRS's initial claims against me, and an amount originally totaling $3,000 has climbed towards $10,000. I am bright, articulate, extremely well-educated and traveled, and have spent my entire life being diligent, conscientious and law-abiding...and now I am being treated like an evil, low-life crook. The IRS really needs to be stopped (beyond simple rhetoric), or something drastic will begin to happen as the American taxpayer revolts.

## IRS Abuse Report #361

**Date:** Wed Feb 11 19:35:40 1998
**To:** sue@irs.class-action.com
**From:** JG

I am a divorced 34 year old mother of one. I was married for six years before I discovered the extent to which my husband had deceived me. I received notification from the IRS of over $400,000. dollars worth of taxes from the company that I owned. There was one large problem with this debt. I never owned a company in my life. I have been a flight attendant for thirteen years and do not even understand the 941 taxes that the say I owe. I know what your thinking. How could this happen? The answer easy. My husband put two different companies in my name and forged my signature on the state of Illinois registration, a bank loan document, credit card applications, income tax returns, checks, offer in compromise to the IRS, ect... I requested copies of my taxes so I could see how in the world a woman who makes less than 24,000 a year could be 400,000 in debt. I was unable to get copies of those tax returns because my signature did not match. At this point the IRS began garnishing my wages leaving me at poverty level. I could go on telling my sob story but I will bring you to the results. The IRS agent is aware of the debt not belonging to me but surprise, surprise he does not care. He has asked for an offer in compromise of at least 75% of what I am worth. At this point that does not seem that bad considering I have paid over 30,000 of legal fees and am not worth much.

## IRS Abuse Report #362

**Date:** Fri Feb 13  3:18:44 1998
**To:** sue@irs.class-action.com
**From:** VM

The IRS is forcing me to sell business or Pay all now. They led me to believe that if I made payments they would give me time. Now they say I have paid enough that if they "liquidate me", they will get their money faster.

Been running a successful business since 1975. In 1993-4 became deathly ill and was absent for 18 months. Employees desperately tried to keep business going and did, but failed on some tax payments. They never even told me as I was so ill. When I returned to work, I rebuilt the business, kept taxes current, paid off the state, all vendors and 20% of what I owed the IRS. Now, I am all caught up and can concentrate on paying them off within 2 yrs. But, they say "Liquidation" is faster, now that I have lowered the amount owed, they can get the rest by liquidating.

They let me stay open for these 2 yrs so I could pay down to the value of my assets. Am 54 and primary support of family, husband 62 and limited physically. Have 10 long time employees who will also suffer.

## IRS Abuse Report #363

**Date:** Fri Feb 13 12:58:46 1998
**To:** sue@irs.class-action.com
**From:** KW

When I was teaching at AUB in Beirut, Lebanon and making about $16,000 per year, I paid Lebanese taxes but was told I didn't have to pay US taxes because I was working in another country and making far less than $80,000. There was a civil war in Lebanon at the time and I didn't file an income tax return until returning to the US in 1986. Several years later, I received a notice to pay $9,000 penalty and interest because I hadn't filed while I was in Lebanon. I tried to explain the problems

involved at that time but my arguments fell on deaf ears. I paid $100 every month for years! Ever since that time, I feel that my tax return has been examined with a microscope. I have received so many penalties since then. I earn only about $18.000 per year and am having a very difficult time just making ends meet. I'm now 63 years old and my income will only go down! What can I do? I would like to sue the IRS.

## IRS Abuse Report #364

**Date:** Sat Feb 14 18:46:33 1998
**To:** sue@irs.class-action.com
**From:** CS

I am only 20 years old, but I grew up in a house darkened by the aggression of the IRS. I was never totally aware of what was going on until recently when my parents told me of the unnecessary cruelty that they have been subjected to since 1983, when I was six. My parents have their own business, and have since 1980 when my father began an oil and gas company out of nothing. The American dream, right? Wrong. My mother tells me, with tears in her eyes, about how the IRS has destroyed everything in our lives by placing countless liens upon everything we owned. And for what reason? Well, my father filed incorrectly in 1980 because he couldn't afford the benefits of a CPA. Well, the IRS didn't tell him until 1985, after five years of filing incorrectly. The money owed wasn't anything outstanding, just around $15,000. But, that wasn't what was owed. By use of the IRS's fabulous penalty scale, the price was jacked all the way up to $425,000. And I want to know why? Why have they been allowed to destroy my hard working father to the point that his health is beginning to fail? Because of their tyranny, my children will not know their grandfather. I would like for anyone at the stinking IRS to show me where in the Constitution they are given these omnipotent powers. 222 years ago, Americans fought a war because of tyrannical taxes. This will be looked back upon as a period of oppression, and the

IRS will be compared to the Nazi party. No other family should ever suffer like we did.

### IRS Abuse Report #365

**Date:** Sun Feb 15  0:57:48 1998
**To:** sue@irs.class-action.com
**From:** JF

I am a Bankruptcy lawyer. In 1994 I filed a Chapter 11 reorganization for a client and saved it from financial ruin. I had no prior relationship with this client and did not have any contact or communication with them after I completed my services. Over 3 years later, in November of 1997, I received notice from the IRS that they intended to hold me personally responsible for taxes that my client had failed to remit. I had no involvement with this client other than to serve as its legal counsel. The IRS continues to pursue me despite my having filed a protest and to date, has refused to provide me with the basis or rationale for their position other than to provide me with vague and cryptic allegations that I am "responsible" for the taxes.

### IRS Abuse Report #366

**Date:** Sun Feb 15 16:15:42 1998
**To:** sue@irs.class-action.com
**From:** AH

You must get this Agency under control... But what about all the people behind Prison Bars that the IRS has abused, threatened, intimidated while the Criminal Courts don't deal with the abuse? It has been programmed into the People's minds that the Government is ALWAYS right, you're guilty for just being in the court. How can the courts be fair and unbiased when they are protecting the Government? In my case, it was proven that the IRS and government were wrong, they even destroyed documents. But, still the Jury Convicts of Conspiracy to impeded the IRS because there is no recourse for the People to Address the IRS's Abuse. Why are they immune to punishment? I think the Conspiracy laws

need to be changed, the seizure and lien laws, and government immunity from prosecution.

Thank You for exposing the Truth!!!! I just wish there was something I could do about my own situation...I am scheduled to surrender to the Bureau of Prisons February 23rd...."sigh" .

### IRS Abuse Report #367

**Date:** Wed, 18 Feb 1998
**To:** sue@irs.class-action.com
**From:** SF

To whom it may concern: Please add my name along with my wife's name to the class action case as a plaintiff.  We feel that we were victims of harsh, unfair treatment from the IRS. Please feel free to contact us.

We were audited for the years of 1991 and 1992, we were told that we owed $29,000, of which more than 75% was penalty and interest and the other 25% was tax assessed on hypothetical assumption of income to our real income by the IRS employee.  We had no idea of where we could have ever owed so much considering that our net worth and revenue was in the negative.  We did not take legal action, but did later talk to a lawyer and found out that to fight it in court would exceed $29,000.  My wife was threatened to be sent to jail, we were told we were liars and that what we did was a criminal act, that our home and car would be taken to pay the tax since we had no savings of any kind and these items were the only valuable assets that we had.  We have no savings, no retirement, we have a small self employment income, supporting three children.  I, myself, have been sent to the hospital because of the fear that I was having a heart attack.  I was admitted and spent a week in the hospital. My wife has had several anxiety attacks and caused herself to become very ill to the point that she could not even speak.  We work very hard, just to make ends meet, sometimes to the point of working everyday up to 14 hours with no break. Please do not hesitate to add our names to any list that may help fight the unfair actions of the IRS.

## IRS Abuse Report #368

**Date:** Wed Feb 18 1998
**To:** sue@irs.class-action.com
**From:** KA

I am paying my ex-husband's taxes. The IRS doesn't harass him but goes after me because my money is easy target. The most stupid thing I have ever done is to file my taxes with this man. For this reason I have been paying for the last four years. I recently came down with a serious disease but still must pay the IRS their precious money every month. I am very bitter about the way I have been treated by these unsympathetic, uncaring people. I hope and pray the laws will change for all the people who are unfairly accused of owing taxes that they do not owe. I hope the IRS will be put out of business.

## IRS Abuse Report #369

**Date:** Thu Feb 19 1998
**To:** sue@irs.class-action.com
**From:** LS

Our small business has a lot of ups and downs, but we have been dedicated to serving our poverty level clients and being fair to our employees. We used to have 10 employees, but now we have one due to the IRS seizures we have been subjected to. We were damaged by the elimination of the 3 year income averaging. We borrowed heavily to stay. The IRS collection department slashed and seized. We were the subjects of a newspaper article and told the information was obtained from a tax agent. We have had a levy placed on our gross income of 25% for the past two years. Our income has declined dramatically. We have also been audited for 1993, 1994, 1995, and 1996 during the past year. But my husband and I are left working the jobs of 10 people. The liens on our property have led to foreclosure on one property, the short-sale of another, and our

home is scheduled for this month.

## IRS Abuse Report #370

**Date:** Thu Feb 19 1998
**To:** sue@irs.class-action.com
**From:** ANON

I'm a 17 yr. old kid who was looking forward to going to college. I started working for a hotel when I was 15. I set it up so that I would not have Federal taxes taken out. I was told because of my age and working part time that I would not owe any taxes. Wrong. I got a letter from the blood suckers in the IRS that I was to be billed $600 because I made over $3,500 that tax year, which is supposed to be some kind of limit for minors. I asked my employer to please correct whatever mistake is on my forms and I will go ahead and pay that 600 dollars (I'm still paying). Now the IRS wants to charge me $1000!!! And people wonder why everyone wants an uprising against the government. STOP OVER TAXING!!!

## IRS Abuse Report #371

**Date:** Sun Feb 22 1998
**To:** sue@irs.class-action.com
**From:** DH

In April of 1996 I received a Notice of Deficiency on a 1992 income tax. I answered it. They answered me. I in turn answered them. All done via a working, valid address. In August of 1997 two IRS agents and a Sheriff trespassed on private property and illegally seized my car, tools of my trade and all personal items contained in the car. They claim to have sent the required notices to a very old (about 12 years old) address. But, In June of 1996, in my last contact with them before the seizure, I had mailed them (via certified mail) an Affidavit of Citizenship and Domicile and a written request for a verified determination letter. This letter contained my complete working address. They ignored this address and claim to have sent notices and attempted manual delivery to an address they knew was not valid, completely ignoring the valid one. Their lies get deeper and I have documented proof of their lies. Yet, I currently have no car, I am only allowed 75 dollars a week of my pay to live on, and I have a Federal Tax lien against me. Yet, to this day, they will not give me a valid assessment for ANY YEAR. There is more to this story. But, that is the basics of it.

### IRS Abuse Report #372

**Date:** Tue Feb 24  1998
**To:** sue@irs.class-action.com
**From:** AE
The IRS, without any notice took my husband's death benefit and refused the 911 hardship clause despite the fact this monthly payment is only money have to eat and live on.  I have liens on all property, tied up cars so can't drive to work, can't get insurance due to liens.  The IRS says a retail business with three locations is not a business so wont accept filings. Have not worked in 6 years -- the farm I live on has appreciated, the IRS has their sites on this...even though I do not have an income. Agent doesn't think farm or retail stores were a business so will not allow my  filings -- only the governments filings. Since they have all my assets tied up, I can't find any legal representation to help. House is now in foreclosure with a hefty gain to their benefit. Is there any help out there?

### IRS Abuse Report #373

**Date:** Thu Feb 26 1998
**To:** sue@irs.class-action.com
**From:** ANON
The IRS has forced my wife to pay $300.00 a month on a $275,000 IRS debt incurred by her EX husband. She works, pays taxes and does not cheat. He lives in Hawaii, owns art galleries and even has a web page asking for 1 BILLION dollars to feed the hungry of the world. This is the man who never fed his own kids when he

walked away from his family. With interest & penalties her debt is $1855.00 per month less the $300.00 she pays, she runs negative $1555.00 per month. We have given the IRS her ex's addresses, web site etc. they refuse to go after him. They say he's to tuff to get, she is working and filing taxes so they will take from her. THE IRS ARE THIEVES

### IRS Abuse Report #374

**Date:** Fri Feb 27 1998
**To:** sue@irs.class-action.com
**From:** LR
In 1994 I filed my taxes, in return the IRS sent me a letter stating I could not claim my children.  I was due a refund of $3300.  I didn't receive anything.  They did the same thing in 1995, 1996, and 1997.  Each time I called to find out what the hold was for, no one could tell me.  Someone please help.  I only make $17,500 a year.

### IRS Abuse Report #375

**Date:** Sat Feb 28 1998
**To:** sue@irs.class-action.com
**From:** TR
I work at the IRS, in collections, and I have reviewed some of the abuse stories. While I must try to collect unpaid taxes, if possible, I try to treat taxpayers as human beings and I also do not assume that they are liars and cheats until it becomes a solid fact. I am not appreciated by management and I don't fit the agency "norm". The agency has become bigger than its mission, and I believe the Congress wants it that way. It is a power system that the Executive and the Legislative Branches can use for their own purposes. The Examination Division is virtually an entity without reporting responsibility to anyone. We, in collections, are given the task of collecting from individuals (and businesses) that never knew they were being audited. Examination correspondence records are not available to any other division

in the agency. It is common practice to correspond with the taxpayer by using an old address when there is a new address on the system. (They use the address on the return in question.) Throughout the agency, Tax Examiners are on a quota or measured production system that invites errors by not allowing time to accurately complete a case. In fact, any employee that takes time to try to clear up any questionable items will be given poor performance evaluations. Only blind loyalty to the management clones will be rewarded. I cannot relate any stories that I have personal knowledge about, but I can verify that the stories on this site are no surprise.

## IRS Abuse Report #376

**Date:** Sat Feb 28 1998
**To:** sue@irs.class-action.com
**From:** KS

I have found the representatives of the IRS to be deceitful, arrogant and condescending. I found it ironic that I was watching the head of the Treasury on CSPAN testifying to Congress about how the IRS was improving while I was being hung up on by IRS representatives who had just lied to my accountants. I have been promised three times that I would receive my refund ($1,250) for the 1996 tax year. I still don't have the refund. Each time I wait the number of weeks they specify. When I call, I'm told there is no matter to resolve and I'm not due anything. I have to start all over again. Usually these calls are long distance and I have to pay the charges. In this case, it appears that the only party that has made any mistakes is the IRS.

## IRS Abuse Report #377

**Date:** Sun Mar 1 1998
**To:** sue@irs.class-action.com
**From:** RF

The following conversation took place between myself and Debra J. at the IRS. After this conversation I wrote to Public Affairs Officer, Mr. E.: I am need of your help and understanding. I cannot live with the garnishment placed on my income. I will not be able to pay my bills. I can only ask that you allow my accountant to straighten this mess out and if there is any money I owe, allow me to make payments that I can afford. Please read the below conversation I had with your agent yesterday. I am surprised at her lack of understanding and compassion for another human being. I have asked reasonable questions and received only the answer that "no one within our organization needs to respond to them".

Here is that conversation: Ms. Debra J. Revenue Officer, Date: Tuesday, February 24, 1998 Time: 12:36 pm. Ms. Debra J.: Hello, may I help you? R. F.: Hello, my name is Robert F., my SS No. Is xxx and I believed we have a matter that needs immediate attention. I have received a notice from my employer that you are garnishing my wages. Ms. Debra J: That's right. R. F.: Ms. J, I have yet to understand the liability you say I have. I have tried in good faith to understand and I am unable to get any answers from anybody about the liability. Ms. Debra J.: Well sir, we sent you a letter with the amount you owe and I don't have to answer your questions with regards to your not understanding the letter, so I sent your employer a notice of levy. R. F.: But Ms J., I don't understand why I owe the IRS any money. I just received a packet on Jan 22, 1997 with a copy of the tax return that was filed in 1990. The papers show that the audit was sent to the wrong address in 1992 so I never had a chance to respond because I never knew I was being audited until a few months ago. So I gave them to my accountant and he also is confused about the disallowed amount of exemptions in your findings. Ms. Debra J.: Well that is not my problem. I said in my response to your ridiculous questions that no IRS agent is required to answers your questions. R. F.: Well, about the garnishment, I have not received any of what "6331 Levy and restraint" says I or my employer should receive. Ms. Debra J.: Sir, I do not need to do anything other than what I did. I do not have to prove anything to anyone, that is your job. R. F.: But I am looking at 6331 right now and it says (I was cut off by Ms. J.). Ms. Debra J.: I don't have to follow those laws Sir. If you don't like it then I will just see you in court. R. F.: This is not right! This is how wars get started! Ms. Debra J.: Good "Click"

## IRS Abuse Report #378

**Date:** Sun Mar 1 1998
**To:** sue@irs.class-action.com
**From:** PT

 I was contacted by IRS through my payroll clerk at work last year in January. They threatened to garnish two thirds of my monthly pay. The IRS representative could not give me any type of balance information or origin. I ended up paying an undetermined amount over a six month period (paying $300 per month). That amount was not including any refunds not received for three years. I am being audited again this year and my refund is being held. My anxiety level is at its limit. My fear of "Big Brother" is overwhelming. These people have the power to ruin people. I'm just a small fish in this ocean of politics. My current husband is disabled and I am in a position to have to fight still another bureaucracy. His medications alone are about $800 a month.

## IRS Abuse Report #379

**Date:** Wed Mar 4 10:09:11 1998
**To:** sue@irs.class-action.com
**From:** LN

After 10 years of marriage, I went through a messy divorce. In the divorce decree, my ex-husband was responsible for paying any due taxes, after all, he was self-employed. After going through a rough 3 year period, and filing my first single tax return, I learned that my ex-husband had not filed the taxes for several years and the IRS was going to take every

refund I would be due, for the rest of my life. It has been 12 years since my divorce. My ex-husband ran his business for 6 years without ever filing taxes again. I have spoken with the IRS many times, with absolutely no results.

## IRS Abuse Report #380

**Date:** Fri Mar 6 9:53:42 1998
**To:** sue@irs.class-action.com
**From:** RK

I am being harassed by a zealot in the IRS collection department. He is totally a zealot. I have borrowed money to make my house payment because the IRS takes anything it can find.

Even though I have supplied documents to show that I have no money, the local agent continues to levy my checking account and anything else he feels might have money in it. He rejected my offer and compromise so what can I do? I have nothing, but the IRS does not believe me. Is there no policy that the IRS agent must follow? The IRS has taken my IRA and my savings. I mean every penny. I have 0.00 dollars in the bank or anywhere else. The latest levy was against my associates checking account. The IRS demanded 1/2 of the balance even though I do not own the account. I cannot sign on the account, yet the IRS wants to say that it is mine. Now I must prove that the $750 that was taken was not mine. How can this be the American Way? The IRS can just walk into the bank with numbers on a sheet of paper and take anything they want.

## IRS Abuse Report #381

**Date:** Sat Mar 7 8:34:42 1998
**To:** sue@irs.class-action.com
**From:** KA

I made the mistake of filing a joint return with my now ex-husband, back in 1989. I have not been with the man in 7 years. I paid my taxes in 89 and he did not finish all of his. Hence because of this, they took my return from me this year. I don't receive child support, or anything from this man. Now I have to spend the next, however many years, paying off his debt with the IRS. It is not fair...my children and I have suffered enough because of this man and now the IRS is making us suffer more. Why should I have to pay his debt with IRS when I have none of my own? This has to stop, if is not fair.

## IRS Abuse Report #382

**Date:** Mon Mar 9 16:51:59 1998
**To:** sue@irs.class-action.com
**From:** RJ

I was audited for my 1994 taxes. I went to the audit and presented a copy of what I had submitted to the IRS with my taxes for 1994. The auditor asked me to gather up all my business receipts. I did this and called the auditor back requesting another meeting to present my documentation. He told me I would be receiving a letter from the IRS in a few days/weeks and to just sit tight, wait for the letter then call him for a new appointment. Suspecting he was giving me a line just so the 90 day appeal date would expire and I would have not recourse, I wrote a letter to his field auditor saying the original agent would not give me a new appointment and that the appeal date was drawing close. I received a letter back saying they were checking into it. I never heard from them again regarding a meeting. I then started getting letters saying I owed the IRS $4000 in taxes plus $4000 in penalties and interest. Every time I receive one of these letters, I call the 1-800 number at the top of the form and explain my plight. I am repeatedly told I should have just had another appointment originally, but they will check into it. My last correspondence was in September, then last week when I opened my pay check, the IRS had placed a levy on my pay.

How can they do that? Everything was still being reviewed! How can they levy without any notice? I have an appeal date of 3/21/98, but it

really doesn't help, all my finances are screwed up. I am now unable to pay all my bills, I am being charged late fees, my credit is quickly being ruined. The IRS sucks, they should not be able to do this.

## IRS Abuse Report #383

**Date:** Wed Mar 11 15:39:11 1998
**To:** sue@irs.class-action.com
**From:** DT

About three years ago I filed my taxes as usual through the same CPA I have had for 15 years. I was due a little over $2000 dollars which at the time we needed badly. I corresponded with the IRS agents by phone (holding any where from 45 minutes to 1 1/2 hours just for a 3 to 8 min. conversation). They first wanted me to prove my three kids existed before they would send my refund. I sent birth certificates and school records. I then waited for 6 weeks and was required to prove my kids lived with me during the years I was claiming. I sent them letters from my co-workers, employer and landlord. I was then asked to prove this all took place in the United States. Again letters from school and landlord. Now it has been almost a year since I filed. The last thing I got from them was a check for $50 dollars and a note saying if I wanted to dispute their decision, I needed to prove my children existed. They don't care who they stomp on. I am afraid of their power and just gave up fighting them.

## IRS Abuse Report #384

**Date:** Wed Mar 11 16:28:29 1998
**To:** sue@irs.class-action.com
**From:** TS

I am on permanent disability after back surgery and heart problems. I receive a pension from the Ironworkers and monthly SSI. The IRS said I owed them $60,000+ including taxes and interest. They began by taking 1/3 of my pension check and then without prior notice they began taking approx. 5/8 of my SSI. This does not leave me with enough money to survive on. Is it legal that they take so much of a portion of my SSI? I didn't think it was even legal for them to take part of my SSI. How do I fight this?

## IRS Abuse Report #385

**Date:** Wed Mar 11 19:59:23 1998
**To:** sue@irs.class-action.com
**From:** ANON

The Internal Revenue Service, Criminal Investigation Division, Houston District is truly corrupt. Not only do these evil civil servants disgrace the IRS, but the United States Government. A Houston District IRS Special Agent by the name of Nancy A., really takes the cake. A. was the case agent on a IRS criminal investigation worked jointly with the FBI. During the trial in Houston, nine of the witnesses for the defense, received audit letters from the IRS. This was meant to intimidate these witnesses into giving false or incomplete testimony during the trial. Well it backfired and the Federal Judge chastised A. in open court. A. lost the case and the defendants went free. Well this was too much for A. to bear, so she had a friend, another agent in the District open a investigation on the defense attorney in the case. The IRS is fully aware of A.'s transgressions.

## IRS Abuse Report #386

**Date:** Wed Mar 11 02:01:09 1998
**To:** sue@irs.class-action.com
**From:** RG

On March 4, 1998, I received via mail a notice that I owed the IRS $ 8,412.76 from the years 1986, 1987, 1989..... On March 6, 1998 my employer received a levy for my wages. What happen to due process?

## IRS Abuse Report #387

**Date:** Wed Mar 11 02:01:09 1998
**To:** sue@irs.class-action.com
**From:** SP

I wholeheartedly support your efforts, and I believe that there must be something seriously wrong going in the IRS. I will continue to pay my taxes, like a good little citizen/subject of the U.S.A., but I will help in any way that I can to GET RID OF THE IRS!!! I believe that corrupt politicians have given them this power, just to make themselves feel good, and it must be stopped.

## IRS Abuse Report #388

**Date:** Tue Mar 17 20:14:52 1998
**To:** sue@irs.class-action.com
**From:** PB

I have been hounded, harassed and victimized by the IRS and its paid Gestapo for many years because I write letters. I am a tax consultant and the IRS has audited not only me many times but most of my clients. I am in tax court now. The judge entered a completely biased and prejudiced opinion and I of course am appealing. I do not have much hope of winning as the IRS cannot let a taxpayer win. I will lose my home for I cannot and will not pay a tax I do not owe and by now, since 1992 and 1993 it amounts to over $10,000 and is growing fast because of the interest that keeps accruing.

## IRS Abuse Report #389

**Date:** Tue Mar 17 22:01:39 1998
**To:** sue@irs.class-action.com
**From:** JJ

This is a real disaster story of criminal behavior by the IRS. Six years ago someone stole my purse and engaged in "identity theft." He worked using my social security number and name. Apparently, he was a freelance artist and earned over $80,000 working for different advertising agencies. He never paid any taxes.

A couple of years after the theft, I received a notice telling me that I owed taxes. I telephoned IRS and told them about the theft of my purse. They flat out told me I was a liar even though I could prove the theft had been reported to the police and to the various credit bureaus. An agent came to my house, threatened me with prison, seized my checking and savings accounts, placed a lien on my home and screamed obscenities at me whenever I protested. It took four years, more than $200,000 in attorney's fees and untold stress before the IRS admitted it was wrong. I lost all my savings, I lost my home and I lost my health. These people are no different than the Gestapo in Nazi Germany or the KGB in communist Russia. They are monsters and they should all go to prison. This is no longer a free country. We are ruled and abused by vile, filthy government assassins.

### IRS Abuse Report #390

**Date:** Wed Mar 18 1:14:14 1998
**To:** sue@irs.class-action.com
**From:** CL
THE WORST PART IS THE ALIENATION THE IRS CAUSES THE AVERAGE WORKING MAN. IT IS NOTHING SHORT OF TERROR TO HAVE TO DEAL WITH THE I.R.S. THIS DIGS INTO THE HEARTS OF MEN WHO CARE FOR THIS COUNTRY. I TRY TO MAINTAIN SOME ORDER IN MY LIFE BUT THE GOVERNMENT KICKS ME IN THE PANTS EVERY CHANCE IT GETS. THE IRS LETTER I GOT HAS ME SO STRESSED OUT. PEOPLE SHOULD NOT LIVE IN FEAR. I SUFFER FROM ANXIETY ATTACKS. I'VE GOT THE POINT I DON'T WANT OPEN MY MAIL, IT IS TOO MUCH.

### IRS Abuse Report #391

**Date:** Wed Mar 18 8:28:01 1998
**To:** sue@irs.class-action.com
**From:** SD
IRS does not respond in writing. IRS did not explain status of my documents. They pushed me in tax court without a review of my documents.

### IRS Abuse Report #392

**Date:** Wed Mar 18 9:38:40 1998
**To:** sue@irs.class-action.com
**From:** ANON
As an employee of the IRS for 17 years in the field, I will not argue that these alleged abuses may have merit.

### IRS Abuse Report #393

**Date:** Wed Mar 18 21:55:45 1998
**To:** sue@irs.class-action.com
**From:** TT
The IRS is the most evil group of goons this country has ever seen. In 1992, my father who was 81, received a notice of deficiency from the IRS. My father was incontinent, suffered from Alzheimer's and was in a nursing home. He had not worked in many years. His only income was from a small pension and social security. I also helped him with expenses. I immediately hired a lawyer from a senior citizen's group and he telephoned the IRS. They said they had to talk to the next of kin. That was me. I called a woman who refused to identify herself on the phone and told me that she thought my father was faking Alzheimer's. They seized his tiny bank account and he was forced to leave the nursing home. He died two weeks after the outrageous murderous activity of the IRS. Obviously, IRS discovered that they had made an error. When I called and told the monsters what had happened I was told that "old people die all the time" and I was hung up on. This group of thugs must be stopped.

## IRS Abuse Report #394

**Date:** Thu Mar 19 3:17:49 1998
**To:** sue@irs.class-action.com
**From:** AV

I received letters from the IRS stating that I owed over $6000 in taxes for unreported income of $3000 in 1994. How could my tax be so high on that amount of money? When I called the number, the IRS representative yelled and screamed at me and told me I better just pay it because if not the IRS is going to take everything I own. They're sending letters to my job now. I admit I made a mistake in not reporting the income, this is something my tax advisor told me not to worry about. I am willing to pay taxes on the $3000 unreported income but think that $6000 is a wrong amount, it's too high. I have a wife and two small children and I work full time. I do not know how I am going to pay $6000 in taxes. It's seems unreasonable but they do not want to explain to me how the $6000 was calculated. The representative screamed at me and threatened me on the telephone and now I am not sure what to do. I am afraid they will garnish my wages and take my belongings. I'm afraid. It's very hard to get answers and I'm afraid to go into the office to try to work things out after listening to the threats on the telephone. I think maybe I could get arrested if I go into the office to explain my problem.

## IRS Abuse Report #395

**Date:** Fri Mar 20 9:26:24 1998
**To:** sue@irs.class-action.com
**From:** SW

Having worked for the IRS, I can sympathize with the taxpayers fears of this out of control gov't agency. The terror this agency instills is not limited to the taxpayer. Employees of the IRS, are confronted by the same terrorist tactics. The IRS has a division know as Internal Security (Inspection). One of Inspections functions is to investigate allegations of corruption within the IRS. Instead, Inspection has become a Gestapo tool of IRS management, which is used against its own employees. Whenever a IRS employee makes an allegation about the IRS to Inspection, the employee making the allegation becomes the target of the investigation. The IRS does this to cover up any wrong doing of the agency and to intimidate its employees into not reporting IRS corruption.

## IRS Abuse Report #396

**Date:** Fri Mar 20 16:02:23 1998
**To:** sue@irs.class-action.com
**From:** MC

My husband has worked for the IRS for 14 years. In 1995, he tried to report Waste, Fraud, and Abuse by his project's management. They found out, and began a long campaign to harass him and undermine his reputation with false allegations and discrimination. The stress was too much—in June 1997 he had a nervous breakdown.

## IRS Abuse Report #397

**Date:** Sat Mar 21 12:03:39 1998
**To:** sue@irs.class-action.com
**From:** ANON

IRS started auditing us four years ago. The agent suddenly stopped, disappeared, and then some sixteen months later, armed agents appeared at our office. We are a family run business which includes farming and construction. We have been through audits before with little change on the returns. Now some four years later, we are in tax litigation through the appeals office. They claim they do not have some of my returns. I was never notified by them that they had not received them, as well as I paid tax on one of the years in question. Of course they have tried to refund that money, then turned and wanted it back with penalty and interest, even though they say I never filed. I never cashed the check as I knew it was not mine. I am sick of their games. I gave the agent a copy of the returns when he asked for them. How can I prove that they have these returns? The auditor has totally lied in his paperwork. Numerous comments of his can be documented by the source as lies. We realize that the agent just wanted to make himself look good. We have spent thousands of dollars, simply trying to get an audit over with. We furnished him with anything he needed. We had nothing to hide. We did not mind the audit. Our only request was that he did it in a timely manner, as my father was critically ill. He had had a rare immune disorder since Feb. 1993. This audit all began in March 1994. I have since lost my father (Sept. 97) and my mother is very fragile. I am hopeful that the IRS will be able to finish this and let us alone. I am sick of the waste of taxpayers money. This has been a nightmare and the most absurd experience of my life. I can not understand their tactics. We have been threatened, lied about, lied to, and intimidated. I am tired of it. I am afraid.

## IRS Abuse Report #398

**Date:** Sun Mar 22 18:38:00 1998
**To:** sue@irs.class-action.com
**From:** SW
IRS Criminal Investigation Division managers can do no wrong! Group manager Darrel S. was investigated by IRS inspection division (internal security) for falsifying earned income tax credit statistics within IRSCID. Result; Darrel S. is now a chief at the Austin Service Center. Group Manager Terry C was indicted for fraud and conspiracy for his involvement in switching price tags and returning cheap clothing to Neiman Marcus. He was caught on video tape and reported by his X wife for failing to pay child support. Terry C., is now teaching at the Federal Law Enforcement Training Center, in Glynco Georgia. Bill K was involved in a conspiracy to create a hostile working environment for special Agent Hirose. Hirose was disliked by the Houston IRSCID staff because he was different: he was a Japanese American. Hirose committed suicide as a result of the IRS CID sponsored abuse. Bill K. is now

the reigning manager over the most sensitive area in IRS CID, the drug money laundering group!

## IRS Abuse Report #399

**Date:** Tue, 24 Mar 1998 23:18:04
**To:** sue@irs.class-action.com
**From:** HG
The IRS has taken my bank account and are planing to take away SSI from my sister & nephew. Why are American tax payers paying to have the government steal from us? We must ban together and abolish this system.

## IRS Abuse Report #400

**Date:** Tue Mar 24 19:03:59 1998
**To:** sue@irs.class-action.com
**From:** KM
Ten years ago my husband and I got burned by a fraudulent investment company and we notified the IRS that we suspected this company walked with our tax moneys that were supposed to be invested. They never contacted us until approximately 6 months before the statue of limitations. An auditor showed up at our front door and demanded that we sign papers agreeing that we owed approx. $51,000 and if we didn't they would start action to take everything. He wanted payment in full that day! Needless to say we signed the papers. To make a long story short, we agreed to a payment plan and for the last 10 years we have paid faithfully. Never late. Of course there was a lien placed on the house and we just discovered that a second lien was placed after six years for the same amount, so now it shows as double. Well our latest payment statement from the IRS shows that we have a balance of $16,000 to go. But guess what! We wanted to refinance the house — the IRS informed us that what we've been paying for the last ten years was only principle and penalty. The interest still stands at $33,000 and is compounded daily. Hell, I'd be better off blowing the damn house up, walking

away and just drop out of society. We can't take advantage of lower interest rates, we can't get money to help put our kids through college, we are trapped.

## IRS Abuse Report #401

**Date:** Wed Mar 25 19:36:19 1998
**To:** sue@irs.class-action.com
**From:** VN

In 1989 I filed my return for 1988. I received a $57.00 refund. In 1990 I filed my return for 1989. That year I owed some taxes (no dispute there). Two years after the IRS sent me a bill for both years amounting to over $25,000. They have tried to take everything I have. Every time they threatened to Levy me, I sent copies of my tax forms and W-2's. They kept insisting I never filed and even asked me for a copy of the canceled check for the $57.00. It's their check and I have no access to it. I paid them so much money, but they kept adding penalties and interest so I never did get to any of the original taxes paid. Well, in 1996, I had to take drastic measures and filed bankruptcy (just the IRS, I didn't even have credit cards or loans). The court discharged all taxes, penalties and interest — the whole thing. Now, almost two years later, the IRS sent me a "FINAL NOTICE" saying that they will take my salary, car, and home because I still owe them. I don't know how to fight them anymore! They are experts at breaking people.

## IRS Abuse Report #402

**Date:** Wed Mar 25 19:36:19 1998
**To:** sue@irs.class-action.com
**From:** TK

I was partners in a restaurant business with my girlfriend and made the mistake of including her on the deed when I bought my family summer cabin from my three sisters. Years later my girlfriend went bankrupt and the bankruptcy trustee sold me her share of the house. What he didn't tell me was that her portion of the deed was encumbered with liens for allegedly unpaid 940 and 941 taxes (after I had left the business). Through my attorney I began negotiations with the IRS. An agent came to visit, he wrote up an agreement, $500 would clear the title. I sent in the check, and then got it back. The IRS is now trying to take my house away, and the only documents they'll provide me or my lawyer are 7 sheets of totally incomprehensible numbers that the Justice Dept. attorney claims that he can't understand either, but he can't settle the case because his superior wouldn't approve. My wife, a high school history teacher, is in tears every night, our money is gone, and the IRS is threatening to take our house for money we don't owe them. My lawyer says our legal arguments are airtight, but we're facing an opponent with infinite resources, no morals, and no incentive to settle.

## IRS Abuse Report #403

**Date:** Thu Mar 26 1:38:04 1998
**To:** sue@irs.class-action.com
**From:** LM

THE IRS IS CURRENTLY TAKING APPROXIMATELY 80% OF MY WEEKLY LIFE SUSTAINING RESOURCES WHICH HAS CAUSED MY MEANS TO SURVIVE TO BE IN JEOPARDY. THIS SICK ACTION IS CRUEL AND UNUSUAL

## IRS Abuse Report #404

**Date:** Fri Mar 27 14:06:14 1998
**To:** sue@irs.class-action.com
**From:** CB

The IRS is holding my refunds without interest and refuses to relinquish them. (this is several years worth. Soon I will lose my home and everything I have ever worked for. My income is less than 10,000 dollars a year and there is no excuse for this.

## IRS Abuse Report #405

**Date:** Fri Mar 27 23:44:45 1998
**To:** sue@irs.class-action.com
**From:** CA

In 1989 my husband entered a partnership in which the only thing he made was his weekly paycheck. After a year, we were forced by the major stockholder to sign our part of the stock over to them. In an effort to gain the stock we financed everything we had to raise 7,000. We never made anything off this company except my husbands weekly paycheck. In 1992 ,the IRS said we owed 180,000 due to signing our part of the debt and stock over to the major stock holder. We hired a lawyer and had the debt reduced to 30,000. Our lawyer said if we could get proof that forgiveness of debt was given by the creditor our tax would be dismissed. We provided this proof and the IRS contacted the stockholder and had them rescind the letter. They are now garnishing my husbands wages $4,000 a month. We do not make $4,000 unless he works 7 days a week-12 hours a day. We have tried to have the levy lifted by filing all proper paperwork and an appeal, but have only been lied to and ignored. Our lawyer has informed supervisors and problem resolution of the our treatment by the IRS agency. According to p.r., the levy is lifted but they continue to garnish my husbands wages. Today they offered us a payment plan of 1,500 a month. I wish I could pay this kind of note. I live in a 14 year old trailer house not a mansion. The IRS is destroying my life and the lives of the people around me. My children are affected by our stress. We do not live in a free country, we live in a prison controlled by the IRS.

## IRS Abuse Report #406

**Date:** Sat Mar 28 15:15:13 1998
**To:** sue@irs.class-action.com
**From:** JG

The IRS is damaging me. How can they impose a levy on 1991 when I did not even get one paper from them. I have just read an article about people from NY who took the IRS to court concerning "last known address" (Sicari,U>S> Ct.App.(2nd Cir.;2/7/98)] I moved three times in the last 8 years, I had all forwarding address in local post offices, (I stayed in the same county) every other bill collector found me, no problem. I might add I was at the same address for 17 years in 1993 moved 12 miles away, never heard from them. How can they levy me without some kind of notice? The agent said she will start collections after the 15th of April. They are going to put a lien on my home and my salary. I would like to pay them back, if they lien me I will never get a loan, my credit is bad. I know I am dead. Can't sleep or eat, I am a nervous wreck.

## IRS Abuse Report #407

**Date:** Tue Mar 31 17:58:53 1998
**To:** sue@irs.class-action.com
**From:** MM

We have more IRS agents than we have armed forces personnel! In 1989, my 1986 return underwent the dreaded Taxpayer Compliance Audit. The IRS disallowed about $400 worth of deductions, so I paid it. Last week (now, a decade later), N. J. of the Sacramento Office overturned that audit and assessed me for more tax payments—to the tune of about $9,000! This CAN'T be legal. Also, Norm sent me a letter along with a newspaper clipping saying he put a lien on the home of an 89-year-old woman! He's proud of it!

## IRS Abuse Report #408

**Date:** Wed Apr 1 3:44:36 1998
**To:** sue@irs.class-action.com
**From:** ANON

An informant (I thought he was a friend) introduced us to a person who, unknown to us, was an undercover agent for the IRS. This person (agent) claimed he would make our taxes disappear and provide documented proof, all for

10% of the dollar amount owed in taxes. Because of timing and slow business, four people fell for this trap. They are now going to jail and are subject to large fines. Until this happened, these people had never done anything wrong or illegal regarding taxes. Is the IRS so desperate that they have to entrap people, encouraging or bribing them to cheat? We had no intentions of not paying our taxes until they came to us with the idea. Please let the people know that the IRS is setting up sting operations. Since this happened, over four years ago, we have all paid our taxes along with penalties and interest. Yet, we are still going to jail. I will not use my name here because they are vindictive and will make it worse for me. The country must know that this sort of thing is happening here in America.

## IRS Abuse Report #409

**Date:** Wed Apr 1 22:08:17 1998
**To:** sue@irs.class-action.com
**From:** TP

My x ran his own business in 1987 and 1988 and didn't pay taxes. I filed a joint return knowing I had sufficient taxes taken out. I paid the IRS monthly installments from 1987 through 1991 when the court ordered him in the divorce decree that he was 100% responsible for these taxes (what a joke this court document has turned out to be). The day I got back from my honeymoon (with my husband of 5 years) the IRS called and said I again had the ability to pay because of my new husband's profession. They have never garnished my x's wages in all these years. I have paid $4,400 on an original debt of $3,000. Now after a failed offer in compromise and appeals, my new husband is going to have to pay (because I'm a homemaker with no income) an additional $6,200 to the IRS for my ex-husband's taxes. Where is the justice in this???

## IRS Abuse Report #410

**Date:** Thu Apr 2 22:10:57 1998
**To:** sue@irs.class-action.com
**From:** CS

The IRS did not hesitate to take our two children's savings, every dime out of our checking, and attack our wages. The result of many months of this we have had a car repossessed, we can't keep our utilities turned on, we are on the verge of losing our house. I am so stressed out about where we will come up with the money to keep from having everything taken that we have worked so hard for. The IRS knows that the money they took is due to us instead. They are taking their own sweet time returning it. This has been dragging on for 9 months and our file still has not left the auditors desk. The audit showed that we didn't owe the money, yet I received a letter stating that they were going to start garnishing my paychecks.

## IRS Abuse Report #411

**Date:** Sun Apr 5 18:05:41 1998
**To:** sue@irs.class-action.com
**From:** CS

In 1981, I worked overseas in Indonesia. Taxes were paid on my behalf to the Indonesian government and reported as income to me to the IRS, but I was not told about them. After repeated instances of abusive letters, I was conned into signing forms at an IRS office which were apparently a waiver of going to Tax Court, I finally found out that I could have filed an amendment showing the amount due in taxes; when I did, the IRS refused it saying it had been too long since my original filing. I now have a tax lien that I have no hope of ever paying off hanging over me and ruining my credit. If my amendment had been accepted, the IRS would have wound up owing me money.

### IRS Abuse Report #412

**Date:** Mon, 06 Apr 98 23:14:39 EST
**To:** sue@irs.class-action.com
**From:** MF

I have read some of your material on the IRS and am quite interested. I am personally going through a nightmare situation with them. They mistakenly placed a $100,000 plus tax lien on my property without my knowledge. I started getting turned down on credit card and loan requests and I didn't know why. Finally I requested a copy of my credit file and found out. I had paid my taxes up and yet someone with the IRS put the tax lien on me anyway. My credit report used to be very clean and now I cant get a loan for anything. I am self employed and depend very heavily on a good credit record of which I have worked very hard to maintain and now my whole life financial efforts have been destroyed by someone that I don't even know. It is a much longer story than what I have wrote here. Probably a horror movie could be written about what I have gone through. I contacted my US Senator and quite frankly didn't get anywhere.

### IRS Abuse Report #413

**Date:** Mon, 06 Apr 98 19:26:17
**To:** sue@irs.class-action.com
**From:** HG

I was informed in 1994 and 1995 that I could claim as dependents my mother, sister, and nephew because all three are handicapped. In 1996, I was audited. At the time of the audit, I was informed that I could not claim my mother, sister, & nephew all three are handicapped. I produced evidences in both arguments but was denied dependents. I went to the office that assisted me in the filing of the returns. I was treated like a criminal. I was told to get various documents and that if I did not have them not to come back (Employees Name: Brenda. ) I finally had the case presented to a reviewer. The individual that reviewed the case went on leave and did not place the account on hold. I

then received a call from the bank saying my account had been seized by the internal revenue service. Also a letter from the IRS was faxed to my employer. I owe $1811 and that it is to be deducted from my pay. I had to Pawn my Vehicle to come up with the funds to pay my utilities. Now I'm further in debt. How can the government take from people like this?

### IRS Abuse Report #414

**Date:** Mon, 06 Apr 98 18:54:49
**To:** sue@irs.class-action.com
**From:** RF

Please see my web site www.ixpres.com/lancewill. It is my first filing in federal civil suit 980318H (San Diego, California). I posted the court filing because I want more evidence before serving the Secretary of the Treasury with the complaint. I was forced out of my job as an IRS auditor. I believe I suffered retaliation for my complaints about illegal penalties imposed wholesale, on mostly farm workers. The lawsuit says the Secretary of the Treasury was negligent in training and supervising IRS managers. The lawsuit indicates: IRS managers were negligently permitted to "hijack" the IRS and keep control through unlawful acts; Some of the unlawful acts were in violation of the federal racketeering statute (extortion and assault).

### IRS Abuse Report #415

**Date:** Mon, 06 Apr 98 03:37:35 GMT
**To:** sue@irs.class-action.com
**From:** JF

The following report is technically not an IRS Abuse Report. But, its 13 suggestions to FIX the Internal Revenue is included among these reports.

1 EFFECTIVE OVERSIGHT: Present IRS Oversight committees do not work. The public needs people who have never received special handling from IRS. Real taxpayers should make

the judgments on the appropriateness of IRS decisions; people who have filled out their own forms and attempted to communicate with IRS as just ordinary tax payers. Current congressional oversight committees are mostly made up of "IRS protectors" who are either protecting themselves from IRS audits, or more interested in revenue than basic justice for the general public. There can be no effective oversight of IRS as long as IRS can use 6103 to effectively block real examinations of IRS conduct. Anyone affected by an IRS agreement or policy should have a right to see what that agreement or policy is; currently, that is not true.

2 FAIRNESS: The de facto motto of the IRS is currently "There's nothing in the rules that says we have to be fair." Although "fairness" is the last word in Internal Revenue's own mission statement, they ignore it at every opportunity. Tax law should be changed to make fairness a requirement, and punish those agents that cannot conform.

3 ATTITUDE: The majority of IRS people have one - a bad attitude. The "how dare you question what we do" attitude from inept and unreasonable IRS people is exasperating to deal with. Until Congress can get it across to these bureaucratic people that the public is their customer, and they are NOT above the LAW and over Congress - until then, we must endure their unacceptable insolence.

4 DRUG FREE: With IRS people selling dope from the local (Covington) IRS building, and drug impaired IRS policy makers working inside the DC beltway, it is obvious that the IRS has a major problem with drugs! Total entry-hiring screening, along with random drug testing should be required. The testing should start with the Commissioner and go right down the line. People operating with less than their full faculties are a menace; the public has a right to deal with only sober government workers who have not damaged their thinking process with dope and alcohol. Industry tests for sober workers, so should government.

5 ACCOUNTABILITY: The most feared word at the IRS. That's why they won't post mark their letters, sign the return receipt on certified letters, put anything of substance in writing, or face the press when they have been caught. The masterful ways of covering itself from investigation and wrongdoing must be stopped. IRS works very hard at not leaving any paper trail; this should be made a criminal offense when it is done to cover-up IRS abuses.

6 RESPONSIBILITY: IRS must be held responsible when they unjustifiably foul up peoples lives. The IRS individuals who fail to do their job properly should be held responsible for improper activities. IRS individuals (not taxpayers via government money to defend IRS criminal acts) should have to pay to defend their unlawful acts. Both those who give the orders, and those who do the dirty work should be responsible - and jailed, as appropriate.

7 PROFESSIONAL: Congress should not tolerate the amateurish and unprofessional conduct which permeates the majority of IRS personnel. IRS should be employing people who can read and write English, and who have professional business and finance backgrounds. Get rid of the political science and law majors who don't know the first thing about business and decency. The IRS should not be run by the political hacks.

8 ETHICS: The IRS should stop their lying. If they won't answer, they should so state. This "we can't" and "unfortunately" stuff MUST be stopped. Ethics means an end to taxes on moneys never received. Ethics means no longer dating time-critical letters a week before they actually go to the post office. Ethics means being honest! Ethics does not mean waiting almost three years to notify someone of a mistake, hoping that the taxpayer has lost their backup! Ethics does not mean making late determinations and charging a usurious rates based on the amount due from some date years

before the taxpayer is notified. Ethics does not mean telling people you will do something, and not doing it. Intentionally embarrassing, harassing, and humiliating people are acts of a bully, not ethical professional people. As an enforcement agency, IRS demonstrates no visible ethics; it's frightening.

**9 HIRING:** The IRS must start hiring qualified people. For years, they have been hiring people for every reason, except their ability to do the job. These non-qualified people are difficult to train and unable to deal reasonably with the tasks before them. Union seniority assures inept managers and drives out the good people. IRS needs people with accounting and business skills, as well as big dose of common sense. They don't need more people with law degrees! Diversity is great - but not if it means hiring unqualified people who ultimately will abuse the public.

**10 WORK ETHIC:** Most of us in civilian work put in at least 40 hours of actual work time (as opposed to cooler-time or telephone time). Real jobs don't pay for "travel time" (driving into work) or include lunch time as work time. Is it too much to expect government workers to put in something that approaches 40 hours for their regular weekly pay? Much of abuse coming from IRS is just a matter of laziness and poor work ethic; it's easier to not listen, not look, and not care.

**11 TRAINING:** Instead of training employees how NOT to answer questions directly, or how to NOT answer at all - IRS employees should be trained by people who really know the tax system. H&R Block, or someone outside their sick system should assist the IRS in teaching how to competently answer questions, operate computers, and answer the telephone. This should put an end to the IRS's non-sequitur check-off box forms.

**12 INTEREST:** Interest should be interest, not penalty. The old policy of the IRS paying what they charge helped to keep them honest;

now IRS intentionally waits almost three years to rip you with their so-called "interest". Interest should be pegged to the 4-year car rate interest (or some real-world interest rate), and be charged at 1/2 that rate (or zero), up until the IRS actually decides to notify the taxpayer.

**13 BILLING:** When someone owes money, or at least the IRS thinks they do, the IRS should be required to provide a proper bill. That means a statement of the error, the date and amounts of interest. A simple, and complete accounting of how the final number was arrived at. The taxpayer should not have to put up with anything short of this. The IRS doesn't know how to send a proper invoice; or if they do, they certainly have never done it. Internal Revenue's unexplained bills are just part of their "normal" devious and corrupt operation. It must be changed.

### IRS Abuse Report #416

**Date:** Mon Apr 6 21:56:02 1998
**To:** sue@irs.class-action.com
**From:** DM

In 1989 My wife died of cancer and in the same year I retired as a police officer (22 YEARS). I filed my taxes. The IRS said I owed them money from insurance. Now that I have retired, I pay $2000 a year in taxes, I had to get a job to make ends meet. All I want to Know is what is going on with our government. The IRS has more power than your local Police department in a murder case. There is something wrong in the USA The murder suspect has more rights than the average city and or country people of the states. But I.RS can come in and sell everything you have (AND LAUGH ABOUT IT). They are above the LAW.

## IRS Abuse Report #417

**Date:** Tue Apr 7 12:05:53 1998
**To:** sue@irs.class-action.com
**From:** MR

In 1991 I received notice from the IRS that I owed self-employment taxes from working in 1988, 89 and 90. It took me 3 years to prove to them that I was in fact an employee and not an employer! Because they could not locate my former employer to get them to pay my FICA, they tagged me with it. They said I originally owed $1500 but after penalties and interest accruing over 5 years, I owed near $9,000. My file was lost several times and I was threatened with tax court and garnishment of wages. I was a single mother earning only $16,000/yr.. They wanted to assess my personal belongings and take my only car. I told them my furniture was purchased at garage sales and held no value. I had no money in the bank at the time so that is why they wanted the contents of my apartment. Including my children's belongings! They placed a tax lien against me instead. It ruined my credit and I filed for bankruptcy soon after. I was humiliated and intimidated for several years.

## IRS Abuse Report #418

**Date:** Tue Apr 7 19:30:51 1998
**To:** sue@irs.class-action.com
**From:** ANON

I want to start by saying that what I have read on these pages has horrified me. I am beginning to have problems with the IRS, and it looks as though it will probably get worse. It seems to me that if any "ordinary" citizen tried to do what they are doing, that person would immediately be arrested. Why is our government allowed to get away with actions like these? Is the government not for the people, By the people? Why has this been allowed to escalate to these proportions? How can we call ourselves free when we have to live with the knowledge that every year we may be subject to inhumane treatment by our own government? Living in

fear makes me wonder how free I actually am. I am, or was proud to be an American. I stood up for the government as a whole. But why have I wasted so much time, energy, and hard work, just to satisfy a fiendish government office? I now sit sickened by what I have seen. Hoping, and praying that it will not continue on its live destructive path.

## IRS Abuse Report #419

**Date:** Sat Apr 11 21:58:07 1998
**To:** sue@irs.class-action.com
**From:** ML

In my mailbox today (March 10, 1998), I received notices that the IRS recently audited me for 1982, 83, 84, and 85. The notices included bills totaling $26,000. The IRS has also (this year) RE-audited me for 1986 (the original audit was in 1989) and sent a bill for nearly $10,000. The IRS kept my refunds for 92, 93, 94, and 95 ($15,000)—and each year has rebuffed my inquiries with the attitude "resistance is futile.' I have an audit for 1996 scheduled for next month. Does something seem a little out of whack, here? Isn't there a statute of limitations on tax audits? I can't possibly take the IRS to court over each of these tax years. I doubt even Bill Gates has enough money to do that, nor Methuselah the time. I work 60 to 70 hours a week on a salary of about $50,000 a year. Just responding to all this intense harassment is ruining my life. This nonsense is originating from the Sacramento office of the IRS. The fellow causing all this is N.J. Is there any way to put a leash on him? I have been trying to get in touch with someone who is a Problem Resolution Officer. It's about like trying to find a needle in a haystack. The PROs are probably tied up trying to assist N.J.'s 1100 other victims! By the way, one of those people is a 90-year-old widow. She exhausted her life's savings beating Mr. J. in court, only to have him place a lien on her house when she was 93 years old. I am deathly afraid of anyone who can and would financially ruin someone no longer able to earn a living. Pretty cold and heartless, wouldn't you say? The real rub is, he was wrong on the tax issues -- just as in my case. This kind of abuse is too much for a private citizen to handle. I sincerely believe I cannot take much more.

## IRS Abuse Report #420

**Date:** Sun Apr 12 0:13:41 1998
**To:** sue@irs.class-action.com
**From:** RF

I am tax practitioner: An attorney friend told me this story a few days ago while we were visiting: He was retained briefly to help a bar owner out of a tax audit assessment. His client had owned a bar for some 20 years in Palm Springs. She [in her 70's] was now going out of business [for health reasons], but was informed that she owed something like $700 in taxes, but that she only had $200 to pay immediately. The attorney called the local IRS office, and requested a payment plan from the IRS officer taking the call. Before the attorney could finish his call with the IRS officer, was asked to hold for several minutes, while the IRS officer checked out the attorney. It turns out that the attorney had a pending dispute with the IRS for some $20,000 in tax assessments against him personally. When the IRS officer came back on the line, she told the attorney that he owed the IRS $20,000 and that she was coming over to his office to collect a check. The attorney said he didn't have that type of money on hand, but that he was working with the IRS on a resolution of the dispute [the attorney had already retained a tax attorney to represent him, and a Power of Atty. was on file to that effect], and that he was not interested in discussing his problems while calling for a client. The attorney said there was a correct time and place for any such discussion [and that was with his representative], and now was not the time to discuss his matter. The IRS officer refused any further discussion on the phone, and within 48 hours, the IRS officer was at the attorneys office door with a policeman and a tow truck. The IRS officer demanded the full payment, which the attorney said he couldn't pay just then, so the IRS officer then ordered the tow truck to hook up the attorney's auto, and tow it off. The police stood by to ensure law and order.

The attorney was represented via a power of attorney on file specifically for this dispute [and he was actively engaged in resolution of his dispute with the IRS via his tax representative], but the local IRS officer completely ignored that power of attorney and commenced collection activities without contacting the taxpayers representative. Secondly, the IRS officer refused to discuss the taxpayers' client underlying case during the inquiry, which would have helped the original client to get out of her initial problem, that being the bar owners tax problem. The IRS officer was retaliating against the attorney for representing his client.

## IRS Abuse Report #421

**Date:** Sun Apr 12 6:16:24 1998
**To:** sue@irs.class-action.com
**From:** DJ

Refund disallowed, "$4,634". IRS showing date received not date mailed. One days past 3 year limit, mailed Apr. 14th (certified) IRS received 16th Apr. States this on letter received from IRS. !!!IRS NOT GOING BY THEIR OWN LAWS!!!

## IRS Abuse Report #422

**Date:** Tue Apr 14 22:49:44 1998
**To:** sue@irs.class-action.com
**From:** MN

When I was living in Virginia, my best friend lost her home. She had 3 sons and 2 daughters and they moved in with my daughter and me. I claimed her sons on my income tax return because they stayed most of the year. I was the sole provider, but only claimed two of her children. Upon moving to Ohio I learned that I was being audited by the IRS. I was not well and was scheduled for surgery and I told the IRS of the situation. The audit went forth without me ... I lost, of course, and have been losing returns ever since. My daughter could be in college, but I get no returns. I could pay some debt off, but I get no returns. Keep in mind that I have paid the original "tax owed" several times over. It is the penalty and interest that will keep me from being able to receive my tax refunds. This year I needed surgery and was unable to work. I have medical costs and can not pay my rent, and my refund would really help me right now. I was in ICU for three weeks.

I have not been able to put my daughter in college. I have not been able to pay rent this month. I have not been able to get anyone to listen to me. I am paying the same debt over and over ... a debt I do not owe.

## IRS Abuse Report #423

**Date:** Fri, Apr 14 1998 21:33:21 PDT
**To:** sue@irs.class-action.com
**From:** JW

I and my husband have been paying back taxes for the past 5 years. My husband and I were self-employed providing shoe repair to our community. We have three children and didn't make enough money to support our family. We filed late and were charged penalties. We owe for 1989, 1990, 1991, 1992. We are currently paying penalties on the 1989 taxes. IRS sent us a letter saying that we could ask to have the penalties removed and so we did. IRS sent us a letter back stating that we had to pay these penalties. We inquired about the 1992 taxes and the penalties are over $5000. On that year. I was not employed for 6 months yet, the next year (1993) we owe over $10,000. To IRS. We filed our taxes for 1993 but, IRS said that we didn't, they added more penalties for that year than the taxes due. IRS placed liens on the home. We are going to lose our home in February of 1999 due to a balloon payment

being due and the property will go back to the owner.

## IRS Abuse Report #424

**Date:** Fri, Apr 14 1998 23:49:50 EDT
**To:** sue@irs.class-action.com
**From:** S

This all started when I sold my business in 1986, a gas station. I sold it I did not pay the capital gain at the time. I went to the IRS office to pay the capital gain which was $18,000. At the time and they said get a lawyer. Repeatedly I said I would like to pay for this at the time. I had a cashiers check, no one accepted the check. After getting three lawyers as of today, they all ripped me off completely. The IRS has taken my retirement, the balance is zero. I have no retirement now. I am making payments every month, there is a lien on my house. I am 64 years old, my wife is very sick with lupus from all this stress. The IRS has being giving me the run around for almost 12 years of my life, I have suffered. I am exhausted in getting this situation resolved.

## IRS Abuse Report #425

**Date:** Wed Apr 15 1:34:22 1998
**To:** sue@irs.class-action.com
**From:** JW

The IRS is totally out of control, with agents capitalizing on targeting poor people who are unable to fight back. We should ask for severe criminal penalties to be brought against all those involved in abuse of office.

Since 1984, a tax liability of less than $500 has BALLOONED into a geometrically impossible debt that we will never be able to satisfy. The IRS has taken about $10,000 dollars from us since then and the debt hasn't shrunk. They refused to allow us to make payments, telling us we couldn't afford the monthly payment, but that "we should make payments to minimize failure to pay and interest charges". Is this double talk nonsense or what? They have acknowledged that we don't owe the calculated amount but say we MUST PAY IN FULL before we can have the matter adjudicated (someday). This action by the IRS has caused us significant hardships for 13 years with the promise of a LIFETIME more to follow. This is an injustice of overwhelming proportions, especially in light of new evidence that IRS agents are getting easy commissions by targeting impoverished people such as ourselves. We have got to do something to those elected who don't fix the IRS now, this situation is intolerable.

## IRS Abuse Report #426

**Date:** Wed Apr 15 13:32:15 1998
**To:** sue@irs.class-action.com
**From:** MC

The IRS has no one they are accountable to. My congressman tried to intervene for me, and they sent him a very condescending letter about how they are handling my case and I shouldn't be concerned it will be taken care of. It's been 13 years.

## IRS Abuse Report #427

**Date:** Wed Apr 15 14:39:29 1998
**To:** sue@irs.class-action.com
**From:** ANON

Since 1986 when I returned from serving my country for 8 years in the U.S. Marines, I was forced to: 1) Go hom,eless for 6-months. 2) Lose my bank/checking accounts. 3) Forfeit every refund to pay off a debt that NOT ONE IRS person can even inform me as to what/ when I failed to file. 4) I've proven through my DD-214 and pay check stubs from my service days that I never did fail to file. 5) To this day I get letters that are more of a threat than an offer at a resolution. 6) In spite of proving my case it has only landed me in hotter waters than before.

## IRS Abuse Report #428

**Date:** Wed Apr 15 17:15:45 1998
**To:** sue@irs.class-action.com
**From:** RB

There is no question that the IRS needs a bloody nose! I love this country — risked my life in the military, when called. Only to come home and fined that the IRS is bent on destroying a taxpayer with disregard of human rights! The IRS errors and delays were responsible for creating a terrible tax audit and erroneous tax assessment. My audit and appeals was on for 9 years in which the assessment was greatly reduced — but in doing so — I was buried with interest, which was greater than the tax bill! My tax advisor was a wimp! You see, the IRS doesn't hide the fact that they are not too fond of professional tax advisors. Why? Because they save people money. So the IRS often terrorize tax advisors by threatening to audit all their clients, bar them from practicing and a host of other frightening possibilities. As a result, some tax advisors will actually incriminate you before they risk an IRS vendetta. I finally took out a bank loan and paid the erroneous tax bill in order to stop the clock from running and filed a 'petition' to go to tax court. Guess what? The IRS made a motion to block me from going to tax court to argue my case. The tax court (thank god) overruled their motion and allowed me to go to tax court. The date for trial has not been set yet.

## IRS Abuse Report #429

**Date:** Sat Apr 25 7:56:31 1998
**To:** sue@irs.class-action.com
**From:** LN

When we divorced, my husband was self-employed and agreed per divorce decree to pay all due taxes. Not only did I not sign the tax papers (someone else signed without my knowledge), but my ex-husband did not file for several years. After being audited, they said he owed them over $6000. The IRS insists that I must pay for my ex-husband's stupidity. Every year the IRS takes my refund and the interest and penalties just keep adding up because my refund is less than the accrued. The IRS has threatened to garnish my wages. My ex-husband has not filed taxes since 1988. Why do they not go after him? I know that he works for someone else now.

### IRS Abuse Report #430

**Date:** Wed Apr 29 22:47:47 1998
**To:** sue@irs.class-action.com
**From:** BC

IRS PLACED UNJUSTIFIED LIENS AGAINST MY FAMILY FOR 1983 returns in 1992. Even though the liens were released shortly after being placed against us. The IRS will never admit they wrongly accused our family of not paying our taxes. They will never provide a letter stating such so we can have the local court docket expunged from our credit reports. Even the Credit Bureau's and Banking institutions pile on US Citizens when IRS Officials abuse their powers. No credit, no life in this country, I can't rent a car, and a hundred other civil rights violations are removed due process due to the unjustified IRS lien on my financial record. The courts and congress both ignore the abuses by hiding behind the rule of law they created to empower abusive and arrogant IRS employees. For our Vice President and President to defend these people and their organization is a criminal act in it self.

### IRS Abuse Report #431

**Date:** Wed Apr 29 22:47:47 1998
**To:** sue@irs.class-action.com
**From:** BB

I've only read a few of the abuse reports, I intend to read them all, but for now I've heard enough to reinforce my hatred for the IRS. I formed my negative opinion of the IRS a long time ago. I am glad that people are starting to speak out against the IRS. I've always felt that

the IRS was much to powerful. They could do whatever the wanted to whoever they wanted. I've also wondered if the IRS agents had to have their conscience removed when they started their jobs. I think the IRS should be completely abolished, because it does more harm than good. Plus, the agents are non-human life forms. Doing away with them would end much pain and suffering of the American people. I apologize for the way this sounds, but I'm so angry I can't think rationally. But it felt good to say whatever came to mind. Thanks.

### IRS Abuse Report #432

**Date:** Thu Apr 30 12:51:41 1998
**To:** sue@irs.class-action.com
**From:** LS

An Internal Revenue Agent without looking at any of my records sent me a Notice of Income Tax Examination Changes indicating a balance due the I.R.S. of $259,372.50. I worked as an Internal Revenue Agent from 1965-1970, so I know this is totally inappropriate to issue a notice before an examination is started. It is a scare tactic, totally abusive and it nearly gave me a heart attack when I received the notice.

### IRS Abuse Report #433

**Date:** Fri May 1 20:42:21 1998
**To:** sue@irs.class-action.com
**From:** KA

I worked for a company for four year that had two restaurants. When the IRS closed one of the restaurants I was sent a notice by the IRS. I went to the company attorney and gave him the notice. He said not to worry I was just an employee and not a officer of the corporation. A few months later I received a judgement from the IRS for $80,000 I went to a tax attorney and he said it would cost me 15 to 20 thousand dollars to take care of it and I should wait for 6 years and it will go away. I went back to the company lawyer, he said he knew nothing about it. I went to the State bar association, couldn't help me. I the company gave me two thousand dollars to help with the attorney fees. My wages got garnished. I was summoned to the IRS in Riverside CA, This lady should of had a Nazi uniform, because she acted like one. She yelled and threatened me. I said just let me have a hearing I know I can clear it all up. She said it was too late we have a judgement and you are ours. I cried, she just laughed, I was forty eight years old and she humiliated me. I got a letter the next week, they were taking possession of our house and cars the following week. We were trying desperately to sell the house and find a place to stay. The day we were suppose to be evicted, they didn't show, however they said they could come any day. My wife went crazy and we had to leave the house that week, we sold the house and the IRS got 7,000 we lost 30,000 dollars. They kept hounding us I would have to take work where I got paid cash, We were like fugitives, My marriage went to pieces, and I must tell you for the first time in my life I was contemplating violence.

Six years went by, I paid my taxes, started a job and started to get my life together. Another call from the IRS, six years has been changed to 10, here I go again, another fours years of hell, my wife left me, and more hell. Finally I got a good job, life started looking good I had three months to go before the ten years were up. My wages were garnished, 40% of my pay gone. If it hadn't been for the company I was working for giving me a loan to get through those three months, I honestly feel I would of gone over the edge. Ten years were up I called the IRS. They said it was over. I will swear to you that if I owed that money I would of made arrangement to pay it. The only thing that saved me was that I never signed anything. I have been raped, sodomized, and humiliated. I will never forget what the IRS did to me and my family. If you need data I am more than willing to give it to anybody that can get this to the IRS. I would still like my hearing.

## IRS Abuse Report #434

**Date:** Sun May 3 20:22:25 1998
**To:** sue@irs.class-action.com
**From:** ANON

The IRS is absolutely out of control. The abuse of power is simply unbelievable. My own problem with the IRS seems insignificant in comparison to other stories I have read so far. They seem to take sadistic pleasure in ruining people's lives. I have little faith that the recent hearings will lead to anything since this agency seems to be such a wonderful tool for the government to suck its citizens dry.

My problems with the IRS started a couple of years ago. I could write books about their ignorance, rudeness, incompetence and their ability to act above the law, but choose to only show you the most recent incident. In the beginning of February this year I noticed, after trying to withdraw money from an ATM machine, that my bank account had been completely emptied out. I contacted the bank and found out "somebody" had levied my account and literally took every penny in it. They gave me an 800 number, the only information they had regarding this levy. I proceeded to call this number and found out that it was the IRS's Collection Agency. Though the circumstances of this levy was highly dubious, I caved in and did not dispute the levy. The bank, after a waiting period, sent a check to the Ogden UT office at the end of February. A few weeks later I received a statement from this office, letting me know that they applied my refund check to my account. I called for a couple of weeks straight trying to get some information on what happened to the money taken by the levy. Both offices initially blamed the other office for the problem. I was then told that it simply was my problem to find out what happened to the money. The bank confirmed that it was sent out. The IRS was not willing or capable of tracking the check. Without their help, it is impossible for me to straighten this out. As it stands now, the IRS stole that money from me and only God knows what account they applied this money to. I am filled with anticipation on when they will place another levy on my account to suck me dry again. And who knows, maybe they'll loose that money too. And so on, and so on....... I cannot afford a lawyer and for now all I seem to be able to do about this is to keep building up anger.

## IRS Abuse Report #435

**Date:** Sun May 3 20:22:25 1998
**To:** sue@irs.class-action.com
**From:** JT

My wife and I had a severe run in with the IRS in 1988 over the order in which our social security numbers appeared on our 1040 form. Apparently, it makes a significant difference if, after many years of filing with the husband's name and SSN first, that if the wife's name and SSN are placed first on the 1040 return form, they have no way of verifying that you have filed. We were advised that we hadn't filed and we said we did, and they said we didn't. This went on for a year. We sent them a copy of our return after they said it was lost. Finally, they said "our problem" (actually, my wife and I's problem) was, in fact, that my wife's SSN was first on the return line and "how dare we file a return in that manner and that we should have known better."

## IRS Abuse Report #436

**Date:** Tue May 5 22:58:59 1998
**To:** sue@irs.class-action.com
**From:** MP

I worked for inspections within the IRS. As I was trying to get a company audited. The IRS went after me, at the time I never thought that requesting an audit of a company could cost me my job, but it did. They found someone to lie and make allegations against me that were not true. The Dept. of Treasury IG did an investigation five years after my allegations were made, the investigator was ordered by his bosses not to find in my favor. The witness that

could totally clear me was never contacted. I have a sworn statement from the woman that the investigator told this too. Inspections never investigate, they cover up. If you need more, or would like to check this out please contact me.. My bosses received a bonus for hiring me, keeping me on, and then one for firing me. I did an audit in Feb. 1989 that hit the Wall Street Journal. No one else wanted to do it because the taxpayer benefited and there would be no bonus for the work, so I did it.

## IRS Abuse Report #437

**Date:** Thu May 7 11:14:39 1998
**To:** sue@irs.class-action.com
**From:** BH

Personally: I worked for a company as a secretary/bookkeeper. During my employment I was added to the bank account as a signator authority so I would obtain balances for my employer otherwise the bank would not disclose information to me. After being laid off almost a year later, I start getting notices from the IRS that I am liable for the payroll taxes the company never paid. I told them I never signed any checks or performed any transactions but they said too bad we think that you had the ability to pay the payroll taxes being a signatory on the account. Now they have filed a $25,000 tax lien on me and subsequently any future refunds or potentially any assets I may obtain or whatever are in jeopardy of being seized or garnished.

## IRS Abuse Report #438

**Date:** Sat May 9 1998
**To:** sue@irs.class-action.com
**From:** DB

This past January, I filed our federal tax return as usual. After I completed our tax return and triple-checked everything, we were due a refund of $670. We filed our return. Three weeks later we got a letter from the IRS -- the FIRST such notification that we had EVER received -- indicating that our $670 refund was being applied to back taxes. In the same mail run there was another envelope from the IRS informing us that we owed $4,590 in back taxes, interest and penalty for 1988 and $1,750 in back taxes, interest and penalty for 1992. This was certainly news to us and the first we'd EVER heard of such. There was a notice claiming the IRS had attempted to collect the amount we allegedly owe (Really? When? We NEVER received ANYTHING before this at ANY time) and informing us that if we did not respond the IRS "may seize your paycheck, bank account, auto, or other property....may also file a Federal Tax Lien.' Terrified and shaking, I immediately called an 800 number for the IRS. I explained that we had a modest income for the last thirteen years after my husband was "down-sized' out of his former job in 1985, own no property except our 1989 vehicle, have no interest bearing accounts, stocks, bonds or other assets except our household furniture. I was a nervous wreck. She told me that the IRS had no record of our 1988 or 1992 tax returns on file and had therefore calculated them for us, hence the amount of back taxes, interest and penalty owed. I was shocked. How does the IRS lose your tax returns and then tell you they were never filed?

I made copies of our 1988 and 1992 tax returns and mailed them off in two separate envelopes. I waited six weeks and phoned the 800 number at the IRS again and went through explaining everything all over again. This lady, not the same one, indicated that the copies of our 1040s I'd mailed in had not yet been processed into the computer. She asked for my social security number as well my husband's, she then informs me that IRS records indicate there are also delinquent taxes (of an outrageous amount) under my social security number for 1985 and 1986 to the tune of $17,000+ with interest and penalty. If you think I was a nervous wreck when I opened the first IRS envelope, you should've seen me at that point. In 1985 I made $15,000 with my employer withholding all the taxes from my paycheck (I

claimed single and no dependents on the withholding to ensure we'd never come up at the end of the year owing taxes), there is no way we could possibly have any unpaid taxes for those years. Every Monday I call to see if they received the copies I mailed. They were to send proof that I owed taxes for 85 and 86. So, here we hang in limbo.

Here we are on the verge of the 21st century living in what is supposed to be a democracy where all citizens are guaranteed due process and presumption of innocence and we find ourselves stashing our savings, grocery and rent money in a box under the bed because we're too afraid to leave it in our bank accounts for fear the government will levy it for taxes we can't possibly owe. (But of course, whether we owe taxes or not, if the IRS ultimately determines we owe them, then we owe 'em, right?...plus outrageous interest and penalties at a rate the Mafia's own loan sharks can only envy from afar, of course.) Unless and until Congress deals with the IRS and strips it of its arbitrary power to ruin the lives of honest American citizens, we will never be free of this fear.

We have made and paid our own way, paid our share of taxes through payroll deductions and we are good citizens. But now, every day of our lives we live with the fear in the back of our minds that we could lose what little we do have because of a single government agency that has all the power of Hitler's storm troopers coupled with zero real accountability. What and when will Congress tangibly do something to bring this horrible malignancy called the IRS under control and to a level of accountability beyond itself so that the rights of American citizens cannot continue to be demolished without due process? This is America, once truly a great democracy whose citizens enjoyed certain inalienable rights, one of which being the presumption of innocence unless and UNTIL proven guilty. Today, I fear what the IRS can do to me and my husband immeasurably more than I fear what this cancer in my physical body can ultimately do to me. We still love our country and we will continue to obey the laws of our land as we always have, but now we know what it is like to live in never-ending fear of our own government every single day of our lives.

## IRS Abuse Report #439

**Date:** Sat May 9 1998
**To:** sue@irs.class-action.com
**From:** MQ

I was alerted that I had been subject to review of my 92 Head of Household status as I was divorced during that time. Then without warning the IRS seized all my bank accounts and levied everything for a $5500 assessment.

## IRS Abuse Report #440

**Date:** Sat May 9 12:06:07 1998
**To:** sue@irs.class-action.com
**From:** VE

I was married to a general surgeon for 18 years. We divorced in Sept. 1993; as part of the divorce settlement agreement he was responsible for federal taxes owed for one year (1991) we filed jointly. By March 1994, 6 months to the day, he filed bankruptcy. He has not paid a dime on the 1991 taxes to date, he did not pay me one dime of alimony or the distribution that was part of the signed agreement. The IRS does not pursue him. They find it easier to come after me. I have called problems & resolution offices and have been told to simply pay the bill; that is the only way to eliminate the problem. You talk about maddening; I feel that I am truly at wits end.

## IRS Abuse Report #441

**Date:** Mon May 11 0:30:42 1998
**To:** sue@irs.class-action.com
**From:** LW

I was forced out my job as IRS auditor because I complained about illegal penalties. My favorite quote, from my manager, about taxpayers: "A little fear is good for them."

Damage to me: four years of fly specking and hiding my cases. Illegal surveillance, stalking, extortion, common-law assault. Damage to audit customers, observed by me: illegal penalties; extra interest due to delaying my cases; Please see my racketeering lawsuit against IRS bosses, at www.ixpres.com/lancewill. It has 20,000 words about the Behavior of IRS Bosses, observed during my eleven years on the job. /s/ Lance Williamson, Attorney at Law (I should hand my case over to a different attorney, instead of doing it myself). You may quote any part of my web page statement.

## IRS Abuse Report #442

**Date:** Tue May 12 20:04:38 1998
**To:** sue@irs.class-action.com
**From:** AS

We must remove the power of the IRS to destroy people's lives. Such power is not given to a common merchant who must take action through the legal system to collect monies owed. The IRS should follow the same rules as apply to the merchant. The outrageous penalties they charge are not only unreasonable, they would be criminal if a commercial entity assessed them.

I resigned as partner in a small business due to irreconcilable differences with my 2 partners. At the time of my resignation the company was profitable and was current in all its tax liabilities. Over the course of 9 months following my departure, the company came under severe financial pressure. Unknown to me, they ceased paying their obligations, including taxes. Within 12 months the company and the 2 partners were bankrupt. Even though I was not involved and had no control of the company (nor was aware or interested) in their operations, the IRS held me responsible for their failure to pay taxes and penalties. They attached my home and made my life miserable with threats, notices and meetings at the IRS office. After two years of legal battle, and attorney's fees of several thousand dollars, the IRS finally admitted I was not liable. I received no apology from the IRS, much less reimbursement for damages. I suffered legal expenses, stress, anxiety and a black mark (IRS lien) on my credit report.

## IRS Abuse Report #444

**Date:** Mon May 18 2:19:55 1998
**To:** sue@irs.class-action.com
**From:** BC

1) divorced 1994 from an attorney 2) separated Oct 92 3) sold residence 1996-bought smaller, cheaper home 4) full custody 4 children 5) put all the cash from sale of previous home into this one after paying off my debts 6) less than a month after we moved in...IRS slapped an $83,000 lien on me for his unpaid taxes for 92, 93. (He also hadn't paid taxes in 94,95,96) 7) My divorce decree said I wasn't responsible IRS taxes. 8) My ex-husband is self-employed and always kept his own books 9) I knew when I bought this house I would have to access the equity at some point to be able to pull off staying here until my youngest was ready to leave for college 10) at this point, my house is falling apart, I'm on the verge of bankruptcy, have no money to hire a tax attorney 11) My divorce attorney said to file suit and hold my ex in contempt...I tried for 2 years to divorce him and never saw the inside of a courtroom or receive any temporary support. 12) If I file suit it will be years before I see the inside of a courtroom and I will have lost everything by then 13) In the mean time he is paying IRS $500 per month less than the interest due mths 14) He also has completely redone his home inside and out, landscaped his yard, owns numerous vehicles, a boat, see-doos, etc. 15) to my knowledge IRS has never even checked on the worth of his home or his assets 16) I have not worked since he got out of law school and

only have my alimony and child support to live on. I will never have that kind of money. 17) Have tried to talk to IRS...have been transferred to every department that exists I think, and yet have gotten nowhere. Did finally talk to someone in Memphis who basically laughed in my face 18) don't know where to turn...my credit is already ruined but I can't loose this house, it is our home. The kids have been through enough.

## IRS Abuse Report #445

**Date:** Wed May 20 15:17:22 1998
**To:** sue@irs.class-action.com
**From:** EM

I have been out of work for 2 1/2 months I have paid the IRS $9000 over the past 8 years on a $4500 tax debt. I am living with a friend as I had to give up my residence due to lack of work. When I called the IRS on 5/20/98 I got the usual 12 person shuffle.

When asked by me why, due to my circumstances, couldn't we call this account satisfied, being that I had already paid $9000 on a $4500 debt. The agent said we want to collect as much as we can. How can we allow this abuse to go on? Lets dismantle this power hungry machine.

## IRS Abuse Report #446

**Date:** Wed May 20 15:17:22 1998
**To:** sue@irs.class-action.com
**From:** VW

To whoever can help, I am being forced to pay 84 percent of my take home pay to the IRS because I owe them $3,700 dollars. They have kept me from paying my rent this month, as well as my car insurance, and I am backed up on numerous bills because of this!! I can't get them to resolve this until they get information which they lost!! I am at totally the end of my hopes. This can not be right!!!!

## IRS Abuse Report #447

**Date:** Wed May 20 13:44:55 1998
**To:** sue@irs.class-action.com
**From:** PR

In January 1986, I was deployed to the North Atlantic while serving in the US Navy. Before I left, my ex-wife and I discussed the fact that I would do our 1985 income tax when I returned in March.

I returned to find out that my spouse had "done" the taxes herself, having never done them before, and we were going to get a $300 refund. She admitted forging my name and sending in the document but had not made copies for our records. I called the IRS office and was told there was no problem and I did not have to refill. We received a refund (I never saw the check) for $300 and bought a washing machine.

Two years later, after leaving the Navy and getting divorced, I received a notice from the IRS that I owed them over $3000 due to an incorrectly filed return for 1985. I promptly went to the offices of the IRS in Arlington, VA to clarify that I had only received $300. I was "enlightened" and told if I did not pay, I would lose everything. I was also told that my ex was not liable for this debt because my name was listed as head of household.

I requested several times copies of both the return and the canceled check. I received neither. I was told to contact a tax crimes investigators office, which I did in writing and numerous times by phone. I never actually got to talk to a person or received a response. I paid the bill in installments over almost 3 years. My taxes prior and since have been extremely accurate, even when, like this year, I owed a substantial amount. I just happened to be the easiest one to harass and the most likely to pay.

## IRS Abuse Report #448

**Date:** Wed May 20 15:17:22 1998
**To:** sue@irs.class-action.com
**From:** BS

Rec'd a tax levy unknown to me. Years in question are 1986, 1990 and 1991. They seized my bank accounts and did not make an accounting for what they claim I owe. In 1990 and 1991 it appears that I owed no taxes and then in 1994 there is an entry that shows I owed something like $1300...the person looking into this said either I filed these years late (which is not the case) or they audited me...if that is the case, aren't you suppose to KNOW about the audit?

They also claim I did not file in 1994 and when an accountant came to me showing income earned, they have income listed twice in several instances to make it look like I made more then I did...how can we ever trust these people?

## IRS Abuse Report #449

**Date:** Mon May 18 2:19:55 1998
**To:** sue@irs.class-action.com
**From:** BC

1) divorced 1994 from an attorney 2) separated Oct 92 3) sold residence 1996-bought smaller, cheaper home 4) full custody 4 children 5) put all the cash from sale of previous home into this one after paying off my debts 6) less than a month after we moved in...IRS slapped an $83,000 lien on me for his unpaid taxes for 92, 93. (He also hadn't paid taxes in 94,95,96) 7) My divorce decree said I wasn't responsible for IRS taxes." 8) My ex-husband is self-employed and always kept his own books 9) I knew when I bought this house I would have to access the equity at some point to be able to pull off staying here until my youngest was ready to leave for college 10) at this point, my house is falling apart, I'm on the verge of bankruptcy, have no money to hire a tax attorney 11) My divorce attorney said to file suit and hold my

ex in contempt...I tried for 2 years to divorce him and never saw the inside of a courtroom or receive any temporary support 12) If I file suit it will be years before I see the inside of a courtroom and I will have lost everything by then 13) In the mean time he is paying IRS $500. per month less than the interest due 14) He also has completely redone his home inside and out, landscaped his yard, owns numerous vehicles, a boat, see-doos, etc. 15) to my knowledge IRS has never even checked on the worth of his home or his assets 16) I have not worked since he got out of law school and only have my alimony and child support to live on. I will never have that kind of money. 17) Have tried to talk to IRS...have been transferred to every department that exists I think, and yet have gotten nowhere. Did finally talk to someone in Memphis who basically laughed in my face 18) don't know where to turn...my credit is already ruined but I can't loose this house, it is our home. The kids have been through enough.

## IRS Abuse Report #450

**Date:** Wed May 20 15:17:22 1998
**To:** sue@irs.class-action.com
**From:** EM
I have been out of work for 2 1/2 months I have paid the IRS $9000 over the past 8 years on a $4500 tax debt. I am living with a friend as I had to give up my residence due to lack of work. When I called the IRS on 5/20/98 I got the usual 12 person shuffle.

When asked by me why, due to my circumstances, couldn't we call this account satisfied, being that I had already paid $9000 on a $4500 debt. The agent said we want to collect as much as we can. How can we allow this abuse to go on? Lets dismantle this power hungry machine.

## IRS Abuse Report #451

**Date:** Wed May 20 15:17:22 1998
**To:** sue@irs.class-action.com
**From:** VW
To whoever can help, I am being forced to pay 84 percent of my take home pay to the IRS because I owe them $3,700 dollars. They have kept me from paying my rent this month, as well as my car insurance, and I am backed up on numerous bills because of this!! I can't get them to resolve this until they get information which they lost!! I am at totally the end of my hopes. This can not be right!!!!

## IRS Abuse Report #452

**Date:** Wed May 20 13:44:55 1998
**To:** sue@irs.class-action.com
**From:** PR
In January 1986, I was deployed to the North Atlantic while serving in the US Navy. Before I left, my ex-wife and I discussed the fact that I would do our 1985 income tax when I returned in March.

I returned to find out that my spouse had "done" the taxes herself, having never done them before, and we were going to get a $300 refund. She admitted forging my name and sending in the document but had not made copies for our records. I called the IRS office and was told there was no problem and I did not have to re-file. We received a refund (I never saw the check) for $300 and bought a washing machine.

2 years later, after leaving the Navy and getting divorced, I received a notice from the IRS that I owed them over $3000 due to an incorrectly filed return for 1985. I promptly went to the offices of the IRS in Arlington, VA to clarify that I had only received $300. I was "enlightened" and told if I did not pay, I would lose everything. I was also told that my ex was not liable for this debt because my name was listed as head of household.

I requested several times copies of both the return and the canceled check. I received neither. I was told to contact a tax crimes investigators office, which I did in writing and numerous times by phone. I never actually got to talk to a person or received a response.

I paid the bill in installments over almost 3 years.

My taxes prior and since have been extremely accurate, even when, like this year, I owed a substantial amount. I just happened to be the easiest one to harass and the most likely to pay.

## IRS Abuse Report #453

**Date:** Wed May 20 15:17:22 1998
**To:** sue@irs.class-action.com
**From:** BS
Received a tax levy unknown to me. Years in question are 1986, 1990 and 1991. They seized my bank accounts and did not make an accounting for what they claim I owe. In 1990 and 1991 it appears that I owed no taxes and then in 1994 there is an entry that shows I owed something like $1300...the person looking into this said either I filed these years late (which is not the case) or they audited me...if that is the case, aren't you suppose to KNOW about the audit?

They also claim I did not file in 1994 and when an accountant came to me showing income earned, they have income listed twice in several instances to make it look like I made more then I did...how can we ever trust these people?

## IRS Abuse Report #443

**Date:** Wed May 13 9:47:30 1998
**To:** sue@irs.class-action.com
**From:** JK

Note: This is the only Abuse Report that compliments the IRS. Here, the IRS stiffed this snitch out of his blood money. Congratulations to the IRS.

The IRS has a Form 211, which basically is a 'snitch' form that 'promises' to pay a person who has accurate and qualifying information about a tax-cheater, to be rewarded for their information. I submited such a form. The person was audited and given a substantial penalty. Contacting the agency they claim: 1) They lost the paper work and could/would pay. 2) I required proof that such a form was submitted....so goes the 'promises' made by US government.... ...an agent who wishes not to be identified said, 'One would only receive the reward, if litigation was actively pursued.'

## IRS Abuse Report #444

**Date:** Mon May 18 2:19:55 1998
**To:** sue@irs.class-action.com
**From:** BC
1) divorced 1994 from an attorney, 2) separated Oct 92, 3) sold residence 1996-bought smaller, cheaper home, 4) full custody 4 children, 5) put all the cash from sale of previous home into this one after paying off my debts, 6) less than a month after we moved in...IRS slapped an $83,000 lien on me for his unpaid taxes for 92, 93. (He also hadn't paid taxes in 94,95,96), 7) My divorce decree said I wasn't responsible for IRS taxes, 8) My ex-husband is self-employed and always kept his own books, 9) I knew when I bought this house I would have to access the equity at some point to be able to pull off staying here until my youngest was ready to leave for college, 10) at this point, my house is falling apart, I'm on the verge of bankruptcy, have no money to hire a tax attorney, 11) My divorce attorney said to file suit and hold my ex in contempt...I tried for 2 years to divorce him and never saw the inside of a courtroom or receive any temporary support, 12) If I file suit it will be years before I see the inside of a courtroom and I will have lost everything by then, 13) In the mean time he is paying IRS $500. per month less than the interest due, 14) He also has completely redone his home inside and out, landscaped his yard, owns numerous vehicles, a boat, see-doos, etc.,

15) to my knowledge IRS has never even checked on the worth of his home or his assets, 16) I have not worked since he got out of law school and only have my alimony and child support to live on. I will never have that kind of money, 17) Have tried to talk to IRS...have been transferred to every department that exists I think, and yet have gotten nowhere. Did finally talk to someone in Memphis who basically laughed in my face, 18) ...don't know where to turn...my credit is already ruined but I can't loose this house, it is our home. The kids have been through enough.

## IRS Abuse Report #445

**Date:** Wed May 20 15:17:22 1998
**To:** sue@irs.class-action.com
**From:** EM
I have been out of work for 2 1/2 months. I have paid the IRS $9000 over the past 8 years on a $4500 tax debt. I am living with a friend as I had to give up my residence due to lack of work. When I called the IRS on 5/20/98 I got the usual 12 person shuffle.

When asked by me why, due to my circumstances, couldn't we call this account satisfied, being that I had already paid $9000 on a $4500 debt. The agent said he wanted to collect as much as he can. How can we allow this abuse to go on? Let's dismantle this power hungry machine.

## IRS Abuse Report #446

**Date:** Wed May 20 15:17:22 1998
**To:** sue@irs.class-action.com
**From:** VW
To whoever can help, I am being forced to pay 84 percent of my take home pay to the IRS because I owe them $3700 . They have kept me from paying my rent this month, as well as my car insurance, and I am backed up on numerous bills because of this!! I can't get them to resolve this until they get information which

they lost!! I am at totally the end of my hopes. This can not be right!!!!

## IRS Abuse Report #447

**Date:** Wed May 20 13:44:55 1998
**To:** sue@irs.class-action.com
**From:** PR
In January 1986, I was deployed to the North Atlantic while serving in the US Navy. Before I left, my ex-wife and I discussed the fact that I would do our 1985 income tax when I returned in March.

I returned to find out that my spouse had "done" the taxes herself, having never done them before, and we were going to get a $300 refund. She admitted forging my name and sending in the document but had not made copies for our records. I called the IRS office and was told there was no problem and I did not have to re-file. We received a refund (I never saw the check) for $300 and bought a washing machine.

2 years later, after leaving the Navy and getting divorced, I received a notice from the IRS that I owed them over $3000 due to an incorrectly filed return for 1985. I promptly went to the offices of the IRS in Arlington, VA to clarify that I had only received $300. I was "enlightened" and told if I did not pay, I would lose everything. I was also told that my ex was not liable for this debt because my name was listed as head of household.

I requested several times copies of both the return and the canceled check. I received neither. I was told to contact a tax crimes investigators office, which I did in writing and numerous times by phone. I never actually got to talk to a person or received a response.

I paid the bill in installments over almost 3 years.

My taxes prior and since have been extremely

accurate, even when, like this year, I owed a substantial amount. I just happened to be the easiest one to harass and the most likely to pay.

### IRS Abuse Report #448

**Date:** Wed May 20 15:17:22 1998
**To:** sue@irs.class-action.com
**From:** BS

Rec'd a tax levy unknown to me. Years in question are 1986, 1990 and 1991. They seized my bank accounts and did not make an accounting for what they claim I owe. In 1990 and 1991 it appears that I owed no taxes and then in 1994 there is an entry that shows I owed something like $1300...the person looking into this said either I filed these years late (which is not the case) or they audited me...if that is the case, aren't you suppose to KNOW about the audit?

They also claim I did not file in 1994 and when an accountant came to me showing income earned, they have income listed twice in several instances to make it look like I made more then I did...how can we ever trust these people?

### IRS Abuse Report #449

**Date:** Fri May 29 14:32:16 1998
**To:** sue@irs.class-action.com
**From:** MM

We received a letter from the IRS stating that we wouldn't be receiving the refund because they said I hadn't filled my return for the year 1989 and I'd "likely owe money for that year. I contacted them, they finally found the 89 return, it was accidentally attached to the 90 return. I received a check a week later. Then about three months later, the Controller at my job approaches me with a Levy of Wages from the IRS. I called them and they said it was for taxes not paid on my 89 return. They claim I never paid the $2,100 owed. I don't have any records back that far to prove otherwise. The

criminals now claim that with penalties and interest it's gone from $2,100 to nearly $7,000 and if I didn't agree to pay it, they'd levy my wages. So, I'm stuck sending them $100 a month I can't afford to be sending them. This is outrageous!

### IRS Abuse Report #450

**Date:** Sat Jun 6 18:23:08 1998
**To:** sue@irs.class-action.com
**From:** AP

I think the IRS is very wrong to do what they do to the average working person. I owe the government, but I started out owing them 8500 dollars. I have been paying them 200 a month since 1992 and I'm still paying. My calculations show I have paid 15 thousand dollars and they say that I still owe them 8700. Something is very wrong with this. How many other people are they doing this to and why?

### IRS Abuse Report #451

**Date:** Fri Jun 12 12:21:14 1998
**To:** sue@irs.class-action.com
**From:** WG

Prior to doing business with a foreign entity, I retained a high profile IRS tax specialist to advise. After conducting the business, someone with the criminal investigation division tried to get me indicted on criminal charges. It is obvious he did not understand the code. This did not deter him from huge wide spread confiscation of documents and my cost of $92,000 to date in defense cost. I ultimately had to hire an expert to explain to the US Attorney the facts of law. I still don't know if it's over, but I am. After 30 years in business (always paying taxes of every sort) I am now having to sell due to the huge attorney fees. I am broke. The IRS cannot yet explain why they had the off the wall notion they did about the meaning of the code they may still be attempting to prosecute/persecute me for.

## IRS Abuse Report #452

**Date:** Tue Jun 16 3:09:57 1998
**To:** sue@irs.class-action.com
**From:** RA

In 1982/83 I went through a divorce and was laid up in the hospital for six months after a major auto accident. I failed to file my taxes for those two years and did not go back to straighten out my IRS obligations until 1989. By then I had re-established my career and felt secure enough in my life to face up to my past indiscretions and mistakes. I retained a CPA to help me compile my returns and sent them off to the IRS. The next thing I knew my paycheck was attached and my checking account was cleaned out. When I went to my CPA to find out what had happened, he informed me that he didn't know, and was as surprised by the action as I was. Upon further investigation he found that the IRS had filed my returns for me for those two years (Congress gave them that authority), and with interest and penalties the IRS claimed that I owed them more than $97,000. It would serve little purpose to itemize the absolute hell the IRS has put me through since then. I have gone from openly fighting them to absolute submission. I have no future, but to pay the IRS whatever they demand. My credit is destroyed. I am nearing the end of my working career and the IRS has taken every little bit I have put away for retirement. They don't send me any accounting except when they come out and attach my property (which they claim is theirs). The IRS has informed me that with interest and penalties and my present payment plan I'll never pay off my debt to them. Will they go after my children when I'm gone? Our Congress, the people we elect to run our country have created this monster. They have allowed these injustices to be perpetrated upon the citizens of this country. The IRS acts outside of our justice system with immunity, and there is no recourse to redress grievances. Is the Congress of the United States also powerless before the apparently omnipotent IRS or do they just not give a damn?

## IRS Abuse Report #453

**Date:** Tue Jun 16 20:13:09 1998
**To:** sue@irs.class-action.com
**From:** CF

June '96 I filed for a divorce, it was finalized Feb'98. Mar'97 filed my single IRS return and had the tax preparer verify what was reported by my husband on our 1995 joint return. I was advised he did not report income on a Lawn Service started that year. Per my attorney, I immediately reported this to the IRS, advising them of the situation and how I could be reached.

The IRS now says I am responsible for $50,000 in under reported taxes, fines, and penalties for his business.

I was advised by the auditor that if "fraud' were considered the penalty could be accessed at a higher fee. The IRS will not cooperate with me, even thought I have cordially supplied them with all information available to me.

Previously, the IRS told me under "innocence of spouse' I was not liable for my husbands taxes. I DO NOT understand how they can now refuse to consider that "innocence of spouse' status. I didn't even know the business existed.

As of today, I am still considered liable for his taxes, interest, and penalties!!!

## IRS Abuse Report #454

**Date:** Tue Jun 16 20:13:09 1998
**To:** sue@irs.class-action.com
**From:** JP

The stories at this site really hit home. My parents have had a horrifying experience with the IRS and I have watched them go through so much because of it. I guess I grew up believing that I would never have to worry about The IRS coming after me because I would always follow the rules and do the right thing. That's how I felt until my parents made a honest mistake that ended up taking their retirement, put a lien on their home and made them go through more grief than any human should endure in a lifetime. The sad thing is that my father should be retired now and must continue to work to pay an IRS dept. that has INCREASED since he began paying $4000 a month 5 years ago! I don't even know how to describe how I feel toward this agency. It makes me physically ill to think about what the IRS has done and will continue to do.

## IRS Abuse Report #455

**Date:** Fri Jun 19 10:46:03 1998
**To:** sue@irs.class-action.com
**From:** JL

I am currently going through heck with the IRS. In 1994 I did not receive a 1099 from my employer. This 1099 only covered 1 1/2 months of the year (the time frame I was self employed) The rest of the year I worked for the company. So I did receive a W2. I filed my taxes and did not think about the 1 1/2 back in Jan and Feb that I should have received a 1099 for. So 4 years later, I get a letter stating that I owe 1600 plus dollars. Before this letter however, a gentleman working for the IRS called my place of business and threatened the Payroll dept. and hung up on them several times simply because he was told by them that all of this had to be done in writing. I then called him after receiving the letter. After numerous messages left, I finally got a hold of him. He told me to fill out a 1040X and then it would be reviewed. Now, I am being told that I did not fill out all the needed forms so I still owe them a sum of money that they will not disclose to me. It took them 4 months to get back to me, so now I am sure to owe even more in penalties. How does somebody protect themselves against the government?

## IRS Abuse Report #456

**Date:** Fri Jun 19 10:46:03 1998
**To:** sue@irs.class-action.com
**From:** CP

In the majority of cases there is an apparent commonality (in addition to the blatant and rampant abuse): this agency and the actions of its employees are not held accountable to the same laws by which the rest of us are bound - nor is there any recourse available when laws and civil rights are broken and abused. My family has also been, and still is, a victim of this agency; therefore, I speak from personal experience. I also speak as a former auditor with a state revenue department, and in this capacity had the "opportunity" to work closely with IRS located in our building. The personalities and attitudes pervasive throughout your reports are indicative of the attitudes which I encountered in my dealings with them on a professional level. This web site is most informative and disturbing, yet is a most effective means of letting others know that they are not the only victims. Perhaps it will give them some hope of obtaining satisfaction - or even hope that their "day in court" will come. Your web site could be an effective means of increasing the pressure on Congress, not only to bring to their attention just how deplorable and criminal this agency is, but to convey just how out-of-control the IRS is. I cannot envision reform as an alternative, particularly since this has been a popular "political" theme for many years. For the majority of Americans, probably any plan short of "scrapping" the IRS will not be acceptable. I wish that I had a suggestion for expansion of your site to make sure that your reports, messages/comments, etc. reach our lawmakers. Somehow it must be impressed upon them the destruction and devastation that has occurred at the hands of this agency. Although there have been investigations and testimony, I doubt that the full extent of the unlawful actions of this agency have had the impact to elicit serious thought and actions. Realistically, this agency cannot be reformed. This agency exemplifies the victimization of average

American citizen. If this Congress wanted to take on a cause that would be historical and to their credit, they would accept the challenges of disarming the IRS. If the testimonies have left any question in their minds as to the right action to take, then they have no conscience.

### IRS Abuse Report #457

**Date:** Wed Jun 24 9:35:22 1998
**To:** sue@irs.class-action.com
**From:** WM

I received a notice from the IRS stating that I did not pay sufficient estimated tax. A penalty was assessed. A colleague suggested I file Form 2210, "Underpayment of Estimated Tax. . . ." I got the form and noted that the penalty could be waived by the IRS due to something in the Taxpayer Relief Act of 1997. But, the instructions did not elaborate. I had no idea if or how the act affected my situation. I called and spoke to a man who identified himself as "Mr. H." Mr. H informed me that the TRA of 1997 was a 900-page statute and he "didn't have time" to explain the act to me." I said that I was only concerned with one aspect of the act. He, quite gruffly and very obnoxiously, informed me that the responsibility to interpret the act was mine. I asked why, then, was he answering the phone? He said he was "only doing my job." I asked him what his job was and suggested that his job was to help hapless taxpayers. He hung up.

### IRS Abuse Report #458

**Date:** Wed Jun 24 21:53:39 1998
**To:** sue@irs.class-action.com
**From:** VH

I recently made an offer of compromise to the IRS. They have rejected the offer I made and have made me a counter offer. The agent has told me they will take my 401K retirement fund investments and the cash value of my life insurance policy I have started to help with my five year old daughter's education. I have been penalized and levied by the IRS for the past twenty years. I have very little money and no personal property because the levies have prevented me from being able to buy. The agent has told me should I not accept this offer that they make me which doubled from my original offer, they will garnish my wages, still take my 401K retirement investments and my life insurance cash value. They also want to take any inheritance my family might leave me. I have filed prompt returns since 1994. I have gotten refunds, which they have taken since that year. The penalties and interest for some of those years are in excess of the amount of money I made for the entire year they penalized me for. When does justice and freedom for all take effect?

### IRS Abuse Report #459

**Date:** Fri Jun 26 10:41:16 1998
**To:** sue@irs.class-action.com
**From:** SW

The Office of Inspector General, Treasury investigated IRS abuses in the Houston District. The OIG Treasury determined that all IRS employees are afraid of retaliation by management if they speak out about IRS abuses. Retaliation at the IRS is swift and severe. With all the evil that is promoted at the IRS, a agency of the United States Government, how can Americans have the nerve to point fingers at another gov't? IRS Houston District is the poster child of IRS abuse in our country. Yet, IRS management's repression of ethical employees works though the threat of a campaign of terror against the honest IRS employees.

### IRS Abuse Report #460

**Date:** Tue Jun 30 2:38:42 1998
**To:** sue@irs.class-action.com
**From:** ANON

I didn't put my two children's Social Security numbers on the return. Thus, they took away my dependents and my child care benefits. While getting ready to file an amended 1040x for 1996, they decided to clean out our savings accounts. Totaling just over $4000 dollars. This is money My wife and I have saved for medical expenses for the baby we are expecting in August. What kind of country is this? No one should have the right to get money out anybody's bank accounts! This should be against my constitutional rights. If this is how our Government treats its citizens I am ashamed to call myself an American. It's high time the people of the United States stand up and fight this injustice. The IRS must go!

### IRS Abuse Report #461

**Date:** Tue Jun 30 2:48:50 1998
**To:** sue@irs.class-action.com
**From:** ANON

I had gone to Europe to visit an Aunt I hadn't seen in a decade. During my visit she became ill and I had to stay to help take care of her. I had some self-employment income the end of 1996 and wasn't able to file until Nov. 1997 as the paperwork had been put into my storage room. When I returned in late Oct. 97, I noticed had received a letter from them requesting my 1996 return and promptly filed my return, paid the taxes in full, paid interest, and to show good faith paid a 100 dollar late filing fee. A few weeks later I received a letter saying that I owed them $20,000 (the self employment income was $30,000 and out of that I paid around $12,000). They said they would reposes my car, garnish my wages, and possibly prosecute me (It was a form letter !) if I didn't pay. After the initial shock wore off I sat down and figured out what they had done. Included in the new tax bill was a 50% penalty (~6000)

AND another ~13,000 in taxes - they mistakenly had added my self employment income in TWICE. I went to a tax person and we filed another return with everything in it and waited. They wrote back saying that they had corrected my account but that I still owe them

$20,000 with added interest and penalties !!! I got up enough courage to go down to the IRS local office to put an end to this. I was greeted by a gentleman who apologized and actually filled out a correction form for me. He said that I would have to pay the penalty - which is automatically assessed. I explained my case and received a 'sorry but our hands are tied' reply. I told myself -

FINE I PAID IT JUST TO GET THIS OVER WITH. ...Last night I received a letter saying that they are now beginning backup withholding because I haven't paid the $20,000 yet.......
WHAT NEXT ????

### IRS Abuse Report #462

**Date:** Tue Jun 30 11:29:08 1998
**To:** sue@irs.class-action.com
**From:** TM
THE IRS SENT COLLECTION LETTERS, REFUSED TO LISTEN TO ME, DEMANDED MORE MONEY, GARNISH MY BANK ACCOUNT, AND THE RENT CHECK BOUNCED. THE IRS IS A CRUEL GESTAPO ORGANIZATION THAT WORKS OUTSIDE THE LAW. IT IS BIG BROTHER AT IT'S BEST, THE POLITICIANS HAVE TO GET OFF THEIR ASS AND DO SOMETHING ABOUT IT.

### IRS Abuse Report #463

**Date:** Thu Jul 9 15:45:00 1998
**To:** sue@irs.class-action.com
**From:** MK

While working as an office manager, an audit was done, the IRS claimed we owed more money than the accountant had figured. Next thing we knew, an IRS agent came into the office, asked to see the Dr., I told him the Dr. was with a new patient and could he wait. It would be about one hour. He waited about fifteen minutes, he then came and told me that I would wish I had told the Dr. to come see him.

He said we would now do it his way on his terms and time. He told me, do you see that truck and car outside the building that belong to the Dr. "Well all that will be gone when we close your doors.' We will audit you, the rest of the staff, and even your parents. Then over a period of months, he continued to send letters of demands for moneys, collected some by attaching the bank account. Finally one day my nerves just went and the Dr. put me on work comp for nearly two yrs. I took medication for nerves and lost my job. By the time work-comp checks started coming in we were too far behind to catch up and had to declare bankruptcy. I had to undergo one yr of mental health counseling to get a grip on things. No one should have the ability to do this to another human , I don't care who he is. It was not money owed rightfully and he was not within bounds to threaten us in this way.

## IRS Abuse Report #464

**Date:** Thu Jul 9 22:33:51 1998
**To:** sue@irs.class-action.com
**From:** JC
I was crying earlier after coming home from work and receiving a hefty envelope containing IRS documents. I feel a little less frightened and alone since I read several of these articles. I pray the IRS is abolished. I am all for a flat tax.

I was divorced 5 years ago. Not only did I suffer from an abusive ex-husband for 17 years and endure his reign of terror for eight months following our separation in which he threatened to kill me and our two children. I have two bullet holes in my ceilings to prove it and an old newspaper clipping describing the "hostage' situation in which we found ourselves. I ended up on welfare because no one would hire me for fear he would come to my employment and "cause' trouble. On top of this I was also left with IRS debts. Two years out of the 17 where I filed jointly with him the IRS states a balance is owing for 1988 + 1990. Since then the

balances of $1200 and $3800 have escalated to over $43,000. I have a lien against my house which is my only property. The house is old but paid off so the IRS wants it. The market value is approx. $25,000. This is nowhere near enough to cover the total tax. For the past five years they have been more than repaid for the original tax amount (of which I am only liable for half) but my ex-husband is physically disabled due to heart disease and has had two open heart surgeries. They know he owns no other property. An agent came recently to check out my status. I explained that I filed an offer in compromise four years ago with another agent but it was turned down. He said it was because they knew that I had this house and they could therefore collect more than what I offered. I am remarried, finished my Bachelor's degree last year and thought life would start to improve. I was looking to the future with hope. NOT ANYMORE. My new husband is standing by me but I ask myself "HOW LONG?' before he can't take it anymore. They want me to sell my house or they will seize it. My ex-husband and I went bankrupt in 1990 so I don't have any credit and only work part-time. I don't have any means to pay except sell the only thing I own. We can't afford to move out, pay rent and fight this thing. My new husband has helped me out financially to keep my home, but he has his own bills to pay. I can't get a loan even if I wanted to because of the IRS Liens. My expenses exceed my income and that's by their own agent's analysis. Despite what they have received from me they say past moneys do not count towards the amount owed. That paid interest only. I don't know what to do except abandon my home. Even if I do an offer in compromise again it will only cover my share. My ex-husband's name is on the house and the liens are in place so if I pay my "share' his half will be unpaid and qualify them to seize my home. I know its only a matter of time. The agent told me a good lie "he said that the IRS realizes how bad they look right now and will probably not turn down any reasonable amount.' Then stated that a reasonable amount could not be less than 60% of the value of my home which is what they would sell it for it they seized it. I explained I have no credit so how can I get that kind of money. He just looked at my new husband. I told him forget it. My new husband was not going to pay for debt's owed by the old "no matter what'. He left saying that he would do his report and that he would recommend the IRS just let this ride out until the Statute of Limitations rides out. That was two weeks ago. I just received this packet which contains an "Offer in Compromise' form, a form waiving the normal Statute of Limitations that they want me to sign so they can extent collection time until the year 2006, a 433A form so they can determine if I have any other assets they want to seize. So much for "riding it out.' That was just another lie. Because their knowledge of my new husband raised their interest in me considerably and I know they won't accept anything less than my 90 year old home.

## IRS Abuse Report #465

**Date:** Thu Jul 9 15:45:00 1998
**To:** sue@irs.class-action.com
**From:** GP

It seems too long to write about. Too painful. The result is that I just quit! I don't 'work' for wages, I don't plan, I exist in the here and now. The IRS ruined my life and my future. I did nothing wrong. Nothing. Sleazy expensive lawyers advised me that it would cost too much to fight them. Even though I would eventually prevail, in the meantime I would have to finance the war — which I wasn't able to do, given that the entity I was battling had the power to disempower me in the process. Friends: Far too many of them, good people, formerly 'main stream professionals, have quit also. I vowed that they would never suck another dime out of me, never tap another of my phones. I would never have another business for them to send their goons to take over, employees and clients to harass and intimidate and never own another piece of real property, bank account or safe deposit box or

any tangible personal property for them to steal. There are many of us out here who just 'dropped out', forced out because of this enemy. The ultimate reality is that I'm not unhappy. I'm just leading a very different life than that which I was raised and educated to believe in and live within/for. IRS targets widow(er)s! Sometimes they make you one.

It's a frightening organization, worthy of RICO action. Do we all have to have zero assets so we can collectively just say: 'Go ahead, repossess my body?' I think that a National Sales Tax should be enacted and all tax collection action should be caused to cease with amnesty given to all individuals who have not committed criminal acts which have been proven to be prosecutable. And let our people go.

## IRS Abuse Report #466

**Date:** Sun Jul 12 14:50:18 1998
**To:** sue@irs.class-action.com
**From:** MI

After several years in an abusive marriage I contemplated suicide and went into therapy which helped me to leave. At that time I found out that my ex had not paid taxes on income that he earned as a self-employed contractor. Levies where placed on my income. At one point my take-home pay, after being levied, was $44 week. I was unable to pay my rent, utilities, and car payment. I sold anything I had of value to survive, which did not amount to much since I left everything when I left my husband. I borrowed money from family for an attorney which did not help at all.

I am constantly worried about where I will live, what I will eat, my car only has 2nd gear and bald tires. I pray every day that it will just hold out until I can figure out what to do. I found out that the IRS is not attempting to collect from my ex because my income is easier to get to. I don't understand how that justifies what the IRS has done to me. I am a registered nurse and have always filed with excess withholding at the hospital so that I would not owe taxes at years end. I do not see an end because penalties and interest keep piling up. Don't know where to turn, totally lost.

## IRS Abuse Report #467

**Date:** Sun Jul 12 17:40:07 1998
**To:** sue@irs.class-action.com
**From:** AK

I used to own a business. I sold it. The lady who bought it did not pay the taxes she was supposed to. She used my tax id number. Several years after I sold the business, I got a notice of intent to foreclose and threats of seizure of property. I contacted the IRS and sent them a copy of the contract between me and the party that bought the business. It showed that the taxes were due after the business was sold. But they said I have to pay, and the 120% penalty and the interest. The whole time I had the business, I paid my taxes on time and in full. This other person was already in debt to them for tens of thousands of dollars and they were having trouble getting it from her. I now send them a check every month and keep my mouth shut for fear of repercussions. I work on a farm and don't make a whole lot. It seems strange to me how anyone that works at the IRS can live with themselves.

## IRS Abuse Report #468

**Date:** Sun Jul 12 17:44:34 1998
**To:** sue@irs.class-action.com
**From:** JF
This EVIL EMPIRE had threaten me with garnishment and declined my offer of payments methods, they put a LIEN on my house, interest continues to accrue.

They damaged my reputation beyond recognition since 1993. No wonder many of us are rebellious toward these EVIL EMPIRE. They are nothing more than a pack of Hungary

WOLVES, eager to chew up anything that comes against THEM.

## IRS Abuse Report #469

**Date:** Mon Jul 13 17:16:48 1998
**To:** sue@irs.class-action.com
**From:** ANON
We can't pay our bills. My wife and I work 40 to 80 hours each week to feed, house and feed our children. The IRS has too much control of the American People, we are no longer a free country. The IRS is rude, insensitive, and not caring. Our country is in trouble and the IRS is a large reason.

## IRS Abuse Report #470

**Date:** Mon Jul 13 17:47:26 1998
**To:** sue@irs.class-action.com
**From:** KM

My home was sold in 1994 for an alleged assessment not owed by myself and husband. I continued to fight them and they sold the homes of all of my brothers and sisters and my parents in June of 1995, who had been retired and on social security for over 6 years at the time. They alleged that my parents owed $958,000 during the years they had no income and claimed my siblings owed as much as 1.25 million dollars each. The agent involved violated the IRS disclosure laws by submitting statements to the local press to defame my parents and family. My parents won their home fight in court. We were lucky enough to have a judge who went by the law! However, it's been so costly, they now have nothing for retirement. The agent perjured himself on the witness stand, as verified by the files we obtained. He has bragged of selling over a hundred homes in Idaho.

We did testify at the hearings in January of this year — but nothing came of it and we were informed by Congress that the IRS is not even bound to the Administrative Procedures Act and apparently not the law. If Congress will not address renegade agents who have violated their own laws and the Constitution- who will?!

My father is dying of lung and heart disease, and this battle without foundation in law, according to our family Dr., has cheated him out of even more time with his family.

The laws have been clearly broken and tromped on, the hearings and these inclusive horror stories have proven that over and over. No wonder these agents feel themselves to be above the law. If our lawmakers and courts refuse to demand enforcement of those laws- then they are! We should be demanding performance from our leaders and judges. They're the ones at fault here for allowing this agency to continue to run wild- even with the facts made clear. I have not heard of one indictment against an agent to date.

### IRS Abuse Report #471

**Date:** Sun Jul 12 11:32:39 1998
**To:** sue@irs.class-action.com
**From:** SW

They have violated my wife's civil rights by refusing her the extra exemption for being blind she has been getting all her life. Proper forms were filed with them. Also, they have broken federal law by not allowing her the extra exemption allowed under federal law. I have sent them 2 certified letters demanding my wife's legal rights and her refund as a result of their "decision". They have not replied to my letters. My wife is blind and they took away her rights and have broken federal laws. They "STOLE" from her what is not theirs!!!!!

### IRS Abuse Report #472

**Date:** Mon Jul 20 17:39:07 1998
**To:** sue@irs.class-action.com
**From:** SB

Happy to know we are not alone in our struggles against the IRS. My heart goes out to all that have suffered, we have been homeless on 2 occasions from their actions.

We did owe the IRS taxes. They forced us to sell our house for money owed. They were not willing to settle. They had a lien against us for $56 and at the closing received over $66,000. We disputed the $56000 showing dates money paid, they said their dates were typos! and I really did owe the money sometime. 8 months after they rec'd the $66K, they filed another lien against us that stands today for $34,000 for the same taxes. Only now the amount is over $66,000 again. They had 2 years from the close of the business to get the figures together to collect from our home sale. The newer lien shows the same amounts that were collected from the Title Company. They call it "our sad old woes" now and have no paperwork to back up what they are trying to collect.

### IRS Abuse Report #473

**Date:** Wed Jul 22 1998
**To:** sue@irs.class-action.com
**From:** DB

Incredible factual stories.... Somebody should make a movie about this abuse...

### IRS Abuse Report #474

**Date:** Sat Jul 25 14:39:30 1998
**To:** sue@irs.class-action.com
**From:** RW

In 1993 I "won" legal and physical custody of my 2 year old son, after a rocky marriage. Shortly after that, I was filing returns (like a good slave) and claiming head of household with my son as a dependent. I didn't put his social security number on the returns as I didn't have it or know it. It didn't seem like a big deal at the time. Well here it is 5 years later and I'm still fighting the IRS over my son's existence. They don't believe that he exists, they claim that he could be my dog or something, I am trying to get the deduction. I have given them his social security number about four times now. I have sent them court papers, school records, and birth certificate. To no avail, they have removed my head of household status and penalized me with interest and penalties.

## IRS Abuse Report #475

**Date:** Sun Jul 26 17:04:44 1998
**To:** sue@irs.class-action.com
**From:** KL

My parents always filed joint returns, my father decided to file a second return filing single (for a rapid refund). The IRS said he owed over $10,000 in back taxes. My father and mother maintained separate households and my mother did not know my father had done this. The IRS put a lien on my mother's salary for my father's IRS debt. My father died in 1994, mother is paying $150 per month. She's 71 years old and wants to retire but is afraid of the IRS coming to take her house and pension.

## IRS Abuse Report #476

**Date:** Thu Jul 30 1:24:04 1998
**To:** sue@irs.class-action.com
**From:** BS

From 1980 to 1994, my husband and I were victims of the IRS. We didn't file our taxes on time for 78,79,80 and turned them in on time in 1981, and 1982, and the IRS came back and said we owed hundreds of thousands of dollars, a total of $293,000. My husband lost his job due to IRS liens. The IRS has followed us all these years. We were harassed by calls to our home, work, tenants, my family and even tenants of my sister. They took rent money

directly from tenants living in my brothers house, which they thought was mine. The money was taken illegally and with no cause. They liened all of our paychecks, and we were unable to pay bills, rents, etc. We lived on borrowed money for those years. My husband was only able to get odd jobs, but he was in a very depressed state and could not really work. I had to get a lawyer to help us (of which we still owe $9,000), and he was able to get a settlement for $48,000, of which we I borrowed from my sister to pay them off. This was still incorrect, but I had to get them out of my life. We kept asking where the amount came from and they would not answer. They kept moving us from one agent to another, starting over, audits, etc. They then said they just put in an amount and then added a percentage over the years to assign to our debt. I can tell you much more of the horrors, but this is a brief description. The reason I am writing is that I still have them in my life. Even though all of the liens have been paid off, they are still on my credit report and I cannot buy a home.

## IRS Abuse Report #477

**Date:** Sun Aug 16 18:30:39 1998
**To:** sue@irs.class-action.com
**From:** LL

The IRS auditor and I played tug-a-war, he said, "the federal government does not lose records, nor do they owe you money. You owe them, and you should feel bad you are not paying taxes like everybody else.' I knew I was in trouble, and it got worse. He said I owed $180,000 and didn't want to discuss things with me. He told me I shouldn't be in business, and needed a new accountant. He even discussed my problems with my landlord, who had been wanting my business since he bought the building. Thus enabling the landlord to take my business from me. He wouldn't take payments, talk about or work out this thing, called me a total and complete liar. Needless to say, they had everything taken from me. I lost ten years of sacrifice, my honor, and nearly my life. Not to mention my wife's and my heart attacks, I had major neck surgery on my 4th and 5th vertebrate. Money has been taken from my wife's accounts under her maiden name, under our name, and from her paycheck at Princeton University where she has been employed over thirteen years where taxes are already deducted, my records have been mixed with others lost or whatever.

### IRS Abuse Report #478

**Date:** Mon Aug 17 3:31:06 1998
**To:** sue@irs.class-action.com
**From:** RS

The IRS is trying to collect for a debt that has been paid in full by my ex-husband. I was assured by SS of the IRS that the taxes owed with my ex-husband for 1984, 85, 86, 87, and 89, 90...were paid in full. While my ex was in bankruptcy...SS came after me and my current husband. They wouldn't listen to me that the debt was being paid in full. Due to lack of communication with the computer system's...there are several liens on our property that the IRS is suppose to release and haven't done. It is creating great stress and putting our marriage to the test. I want some closure to this matter, we have two small children to raise, and we don't have a lot of income as it is. It's pretty hard to keep going when the bloodsuckers are draining our sanity and livelihood for no good reason except for the harassment of it all.

### IRS Abuse Report #479

**Date:** Mon Aug 17 6:31:28 1998
**To:** sue@irs.class-action.com
**From:** GC

My partner's bank account was levied, leaving us with five dollars with which to feed and clothe us and our child. Loud amateurish phone taps were used to determine our whereabouts prior to serving a summons. The summons was issued as far as we can tell without proper authority as required under federal law. Financial threats were made against us by IRS officer at that summons. We were refused permission to record the details of the summons. Our house was seized using the mortgage company to provide a smokescreen for the IRS. The mortgage company claimed payments were missing which was nonsense. It appeared that the IRS was short-circuiting the payments into its own accounts. The house was auctioned from under us and my family (including a 3-year old boy) were evicted. Fifteen months later in another summons against my (financially uninvolved) partner, the I.R.S. admitted it had caused the foreclosure, seizure, and eviction.

### IRS Abuse Report #480

**Date:** Wed Sep 2 10:04:01 1998
**To:** sue@irs.class-action.com
**From:** GL

The IRS along with the courts, have taken over $1 million, I have sold one home, truck, a home belonging to my daughter, am in the process of selling another all at bargain prices. All over a tax liability of $500,000, which the IRS allege is over $2 million. They put me in jail for 355 days, took all of our funds so we could not retain an attorney, thereby causing us to defend ourselves, with no knowledge of the law or IRS. In my first appearance in court, I was told by the federal judge that I had no rights in this court, also that I had no rights to an attorney. This is documented in court transcripts. I was kept in jail for 355 days.

### IRS Abuse Report #481

**Date:** Sat Sep 5 20:39:12 1998
**To:** sue@irs.class-action.com
**From:** AJ

They have a lien on my wages, I did not know I even owed them money. Tried to talk to them about payment plan, the lady was very ugly and told me I should have known I owed them.

### IRS Abuse Report #482

**Date:** Wed Sep 9 1:13:39 1998
**To:** sue@irs.class-action.com
**From:** ANON

After reading these IRS abuse reports it actually nauseates me. The news media needs to be flooded with these stories, these reports must constantly be made public so that the American public can react. Something has to be done, our system is in dire trouble. The IRS can put a honest, decent taxpayer in prison for a tax bill. The more I talk to other people the worse the stories get and everyone is afraid to do anything for fear of reprisal. If such stories were kept in the news limelight, maybe things would change...something needs to be done, not only for us but for our future and our children.

### IRS Abuse Report #483

**Date:** Fri Sep 11 23:26:38 1998
**To:** sue@irs.class-action.com
**From:** J

I cannot believe such evil. I cannot and will not understand how IRS can sit by and watch fellow Americans — neighbors be tortured. Where's the faith and the freedom? It saddened me so to read these reports and yet it also pushed me to madness and compassion all rolled into one. The devastation that my fellow Americans go through in such hatred and selfish ways. I do believe people need to read these reports. They need to learn and to stand up for your neighbor and your family. Stand up for what's right. There's people in this world, including myself that didn't really know about such things until I came across this page. It needs to expand. It needs to known. It's a shame that we have to place these hard working souls up on a stand for all to see just because we're not informed and yet it's so brave of those that tell their story because if they hadn't, we'd be fools and our children would be fools. I don't think I could lay still in my grave knowing that our children are toys and slaves. It's time we all take compassion and strength

and pass it on to those beside us. Thank you.

### IRS Abuse Report #484

**Date:** Sat Sep 12 8:39:33 1998
**To:** sue@irs.class-action.com
**From:** LR

I had a business loss, the IRS has disallowed my loss and has repeatedly levied my paycheck for several years and has refused a face-to-face meeting to clear the matter up with me. Their response was to mail an inapplicable code and to state they were denying my request for a case-worker based on this inapplicable code. In addition, their employees are emotionally abusive. If you need specifics (years, dates, amounts of penalties, etc. Let me know and I will provide.)

### IRS Abuse Report #485

**Date:** Fri Sep 18 14:10:24 1998
**To:** sue@irs.class-action.com
**From:** ANON

My father's wife, whom he married in 88', owed the IRS back taxes, but just like the IRS they don't bother to inform you that you owe until years later. Now the amount of her taxes has grown to about $20,000. They garnished her wages and my father's. I am named after my father, I am the 2nd. So now the IRS is after me. They have sent notices to me saying that I owe them $7515. I have never owed the IRS. Try getting a hold of a live person at the IRS, much less one that will listen. They have now put a lien on my property, and I'm sure the hassle is just starting.

### IRS Abuse Report #486

**Date:** Sat Sep 19 13:01:36 1998
**To:** sue@irs.class-action.com
**From:** BC

I was under an IRS audit for 3 years. They constantly had me bringing items to their offices and needless to say it was very frightening and disturbing. After spending tens of thousands of dollars I finally received a letter in the mail that they accepted my taxes as filed. However, at this point I had lost my business and nearing a nervous break down! Can I write off the money I spent defending myself -NO- Do they care that they drove me to the brink of considering taking my own life, fat chance!

### IRS Abuse Report #487

**Date:** Mon Sep 28 1:14:38 1998
**To:** sue@irs.class-action.com
**From:** DT
The IRS is threatening to garnish my $6.25 per hour wage. Interest climbs faster than what I earn, at their rate of interest, the debt/tax can never be paid.

### IRS Abuse Report #488

**Date:** Mon Sep 28 9:22:00 1998
**To:** sue@irs.class-action.com
**From:** JC
When I got out of the military, I got a letter saying that because of the additional manpower called back in for Desert Storm there would be a delay in getting the w-4 forms to us. The letter also said this letter is reason enough for an extension. Well I never got my w-4. When I called the next year, they said it was my fault and that I had to pay any past due taxes with interest and penalties. I would like to set this straight, but all they do is scare me by telling me they will take everything I own. What started as a small problem, has now snowballed into a huge one.

### IRS Abuse Report #489

**Date:** Wed Sep 30 19:59:34 1998
**To:** sue@irs.class-action.com
**From:** WM
My husband and I have had problems with the IRS since 1988 when we started our own Dry-

wall Company, during that time things got bad due to the recession. At the time we filed bankruptcy. We owed around $26,000 in taxes. Since that time, the figure has gone up to over $256,000. During this time, we were intimidated into signing forms that we should not have signed — this extended the amount of time the IRS had to collect this debt. The agent said that if we didn't sign them, he would immediately come after anything that we owned. We did make an offer in compromise which was turned down. We then entered into a payment arrangement, of course, the debt will never be paid off. In 1996 we tried going into business again, the same agent got a hold of our account and started levy proceedings against all of our builders. When we tried to set up arrangements to pay the outstanding taxes, he said "no way, I haven't forgotten about you hiring a lawyer the last time' He just won't work with us at all. He has made our life a living hell. We never know what he will do next. My Husband's and my health are suffering because of this Revenue Officer.

---

Editor's Note: Due to its longer length, the next testimony was placed at the end of this report. This final testimony helps identify the attitude of the IRS concerning its horrendous behaviors toward innocent people.

---

### IRS Abuse Report #105

**Date:** Mon 11 Sep 1995 08:08:36 -0500
**To:** sue@irs.class-action.com
**From:** RD
The following was written a few days after the incident happened.

Around 10 A.M. January 19, 1995, my bookkeeper came to my office and said a QW from the IRS was there and wished to speak to me.

I told her I did not want to talk to Q because I had no idea what this was about. As far as I knew, we had no outstanding issues with the IRS, and all old issues had been settled. Since she was obviously frightened by Q's attitude, I knew I'd have to handle it myself.

I went to the door, this lady shook my hand and said "I'm QW with the IRS". I said she could come in and motioned her to a chair in my office. I took my chair, and she asked as I sat down, "Who am I speaking to?". I replied, "My name is RD". She said "Then you are who I need to talk to." I thought it strange the way she asked and responded. If she didn't know who I was, I thought, "Perhaps this is a scam artist, or, who knows what??? I'd better be careful, 'til I can tell what's going on here. She didn't offer me any identification, and since I don't know of anything wrong with my relationship with the IRS, this might be 'some type of out-of-the-blue' scam. I figured I had better find out if this gal is real, or yet another nightmare."

She then asked "Who owns this building?" I thought "What the heck business is it of yours?" but replied, "What is your authority and what is your purpose." She did not reply, but instead asked if JK was my attorney. Now, this really put me on edge. If she really was IRS, she should know who my attorney was. And if she knew that, she knew it was a breech of the IRS code to talk to me directly. If she wasn't IRS, then she'd ask that question to set us up for something -- but what? Maybe She'd been routing in our trash and found an old bill and come up with a scheme to bilk us. But if she is IRS, she should have already talked to Jim before showing up, and he hasn't called. So, who knows what's going on here! This lady is apparently up to no good. So, I cautiously replied, "I haven't talked to Jim in a few months. But I notice you haven't answered my question, what is your authority and what is your..." She cut me off! I was getting very stressed and thinking I need to call the police and get this lady out of here. "She said, what I

notice is you didn't answer my question -- WHO OWNS THIS BUILDING!" I think I asked why she needed to know, and incredibly, she said, 'Cause I checked and it isn't listed with the county records office!" I wondered what that had to do with anything, and how it could be that the records didn't list the owner, when all filing and insurance paperwork was paid for back when NM purchased the property. Again, her conduct and responses did not match what I thought to be the truth.

Then, I thought about the two "POSTED: No Trespassing Signs" on the corners of the building. And also the "KEEP OUT PRIVATE PROPERTY" sign in the yard. A few minutes before she arrived, someone had been walking on the property taking pictures and I had debated going out after them and throwing them off. But having been shot at before, I returned my thoughts to her and said, "Listen, you're on private property without an appointment or an invitation..." I was preparing to order her off the property, but she didn't wait for it to be stated. "That's fine," she said, "that's all I need to know." And she got up and walked out.

I was pretty miffed. If she was IRS, what had she wanted and why wouldn't she tell me? If she wasn't, which sure seemed to fit her actions better, then I was the target of some kind of scam. I told my bookkeeper to bring me that old IRS file. I needed to talk to MZ. I had worked with Mark before and trusted him, and I think he trusted me as well.

I called and asked the gal who answered the phone if QW worked there. I was told she did. I asked this gal for Q's supervisor. I was told it was Dave someone. I was surprised it wasn't Mark. I asked to talk with Dave. The operator said Dave was busy. I said, fine, who is his supervisor. She said MZ. I said "Oh good, I know Mark, let me speak with him!" I was put on hold again. Then a fellow came on the line. He identified himself and I said, "Is QW one of yours?" He took a hostile stance and said "What do you mean, is she one of mine!" I said, "Is she one of your employees? Are you her supervisor? Is she an IRS agent? He said, "Well, who am I talking to?" or perhaps "Who the hell am I talking to?" the intonation was consistent with either answer. I said, "My name is RD. A lady just popped up out here, saying her name was Q that she was IRS." He informed me, "Yes, she is a IRS collection agent, and she must be working on a collection case." I said, "Well, she just popped up out here and refused to answer any questions about who she was and what authority she had." He snapped back, "She's a field agent and us field agents can pop up wherever we want to." I asked, "Why wouldn't she tell me what's going on? and why isn't she talking to the people I pay to handle these matters..." He asked, "Well, does she have a paper with her where you assigned your power of attorney?" I replied, "Well how should I know, I've never seen this lady before in my life and...". He replied, "Well, she's got to have a power of attorney to be able to talk to your attorney." I said, "As far as I know the IRS has a power of attorney on file for JK...", He again belligerently asked, "Well, does she have that piece of paper?" I answered, "How I am supposed to know? I asked her about her authority and she left!"

He seemed to drop his hostile attitude, a bit. He said, "She's working on a case." I was confused. I thought we were all caught up with the IRS and, frankly, proud of it, and how we had handled our obligations at the time. I said, "I don't understand, I worked with MZ in the past..." He spouted, "What do you mean you worked with MZ!" He was fierce. This news really took him by surprise. It frightened me. I had no idea where he was coming from, or why he'd be mad at me for having worked with Mark. I said, I worked with Mark in the past, we had some trouble and we worked it out.. He was clearly confused by what I was telling him. I again complained about Q's refusing to identify herself and her authority and purpose. He asked, "She showed you her credentials?" I said "No, I asked her what her authority was, and what her purpose was, and she refused to

answer. She didn't show me anything. I told him someone remembered a QW from the past coming out, but I had never met her. After that, he calmed down again. I think he then asked to talk to Q. I told him she had left the property. At this point, I noticed a surprise in David's voice. He must have thought she was still in front of me. He said "If she comes back tell her to talk to me." I wondered why she would be coming back. I told him, "Look, whatever the case, my position is, if she is here without an invitation and without an appointment, she is trespassing. She's supposed to talk to my attorney, and it's still my opinion she should do so." He acknowledged, reminded me if she were to come back he wanted to talk to her first. I took this for an acknowledgment of my complaint, and an indication he would see after it. I thanked him and hung up.

I thought there was more to this story. I didn't feel safe any more. I called my attorney and explained the strange thing that had just happened. He said he hadn't heard anything, but he'd find out and if something was really happening, he'd fill a 911 with the IRS, because as far as he knew, there had been no communications with the IRS since filing the affidavit. Clearly proper IRS procedures were not being followed, and someone was out of line, and way out of control.

At that point, one of the employees appeared at my office and said "she's back". She stormed in and said they were taking the building and changing the locks. She started down the hall, I said you need to call David. She wheeled at me and shouted, accusatory, "I know you talked to David." I thought this was probably a lie, she was probably surprised I knew her coworker's name and was bluffing. I asked, "Have you talked to David since you were last here?" She wheeled and again headed down the hall without answering. I said, "David told me to tell you to call him." She ignored me and started to peel the back off of some kind of sticker. Clearly this person was not interested in Law, Justice, Due Process, or IRS procedures and Code. Nor was she interested in hearing what her supervisor had to say to her. I began to suspect Dave wasn't her supervisor at all. What was going on here?

She threw out a Notice of Levy on my desk. Then she walked away and turned around again and threw out a Notice of Seizures. I looked at it. It was getting pretty clear at this point. The notices were to CA-PC. I asked "What do you think you're doing here?" She shouted, "We're shutting down the business!" I asked, "Which business?" That pretty much threw her into a rage. She sputtered and shouted, "This business here!!!" and pointed at the floor in my office. So, I asked, "And what business do you think this is?" She refused to answer and stormed out of my office.

My attorney and I continued to talk. I began digging for the sales contract proving NM owned the building she was seizing in the name of PC's back taxes. She went to every NM employee and told them they had to leave. She ordered one to get off the phone, who was having a conversation with a NM customer. I am told no one believed her. She was so rude and irrational, no one could imagine what her problems was.

I was talking to my attorney one time when she came stomping through, and I was telling him I had asked for her identification several times and she had refused. At this, she finally produced a wallet with two pieces of paper in it. I began to read the paper, and had read the first half, with various IRS information on it while still holding the phone so my attorney could hear, and as soon as I reached the personal information, she snatched it away and stomped off. I said "wait a minute, I didn't finish. Hey, Q, can we get a copy of that?" She didn't answer. It's becoming apparent to me this woman does not want any personal identification numbers to become part of the record.

I decided I'd better talk to Mark at the IRS, since he was the only one with enough integrity to be trusted. It seemed nearly every other agent I had talked to, had lied. I dialed Mark. I had to wait quite awhile. When Mark answered the phone, I asked if he remembered me and that we had worked together in the past. He said he thought he remembered the name. I began to explain the situation as best I understood it. At that moment, the police we called arrived in my office. I told Mark, "Oh good the police are here, hang on." I then addressed the officer, still speaking into the phone so Mark could hear, and said, "Thank you for coming out, today. We've got quit a problem here. These agents have come out to serve a Levy and Seizures, but as you can see here on their documents they have the wrong company listed. This property is owned by another company, here.." and I offered him the sales contract showing NM owned the building. The officer began examining the two documents. I turned my attention again to Mark. I said, "Did you copy all that Mark?" He said he wanted to speak to Q. I told the bookkeeper to go tell Q she was wanted on the phone. She said, I don't think she'll come. I said please go tell her MZ is on the phone and wants to speak to her. She said she'd try.

Both agents were in my office. Q began listening to Mark. She made several objections. She said, "I sent it to them here, and I sent it to them there" I assume she meant PC, "and these guys sent back an affidavit and the other guys didn't send back anything." I thought, "Great, cooperate with the IRS, follow the rules, and what do they do? Jump on you for the effort. If the other guy DIDN'T respond, why did you assume the guys who did respond, followed IRS procedure and filed affidavit, which went unanswered by the IRS for months, were the ones who needed to have things seized?

She said to Mark, "I was out several times and I spoke to Mr. RD several time..." My blood boiled. She was a liar. To the best of my knowledge, I had never seen this woman before. She may have called several times when I was out, but she sure didn't talk to me. I had a power of attorney, and they were supposed to talk to him. I was so mad at the way I had been treated by the IRS that I wanted no personal contact. Nothing in the world burned me more than dishonest IRS agents, and here in my office on posted private property was a jerk using my phone to lie to her supervisor while disrupting the business of a company in complete compliance with the IRS. She was busily trying to deprive more than a dozen people of their salaries, and thereby about to deprive the U.S. of $100,000 a year in revenue. Let alone the other companies who would go out of business and have cause to sue. We were already warned that day, if we allowed interruption of parts shipments to RJS, they would go out of business and be forced to sue. She had usurped so many powers of the Constitution, let alone violated so many rules and procedures of IRS code, that she was, well, either criminally negligent, or worse, acting with full criminal intent.

She and Mark went on talking, "but I'm looking right at a business card with CA on it in his office." I said, yes, but that's CA-I. That's an entirely different company from CA-PC." By her reasoning, Joe Getz could be held accountable for Joe Gonzales taxes, even if their Federal Tax Identifiers were different. Why? Because they had the first name? Oh Brother! I got up and took one of the cards and offered it to the other agent. I said, may I present this for your examination. Now, this other agent was sitting wide eyed and in general looking amazed at what was going on. She looked at the card. Q on the phone said something to Jim about "International". Sensing there might be some reason coming to the other agent, I returned to my desk and took out the sales contract and took it to her and told her this property was owned by NM. She almost grabbed this out of my hands. I held on to it as it was the only copy I had. She asked, "When was this?" I helped her look for a date and found the 4th of November 1986.

I went back behind my desk and was able to find an inventory list from PC works which was labeled as such and returned to show her. I said, "These were the assets of PC," and I pointed out, "there's not a single piece of anything on that list in this building."

She said, "JK is your attorney?" I said yes. She shook her head and said, "I've worked with Jim before, he's a good guy." I began to pipe in how I thought so too and Jim was an ex-agent himself and I almost missed her next comment, half under her breath and in total disbelief. "How did this ever get this far?"

Q jumped in, still on the phone with Mark and said, "Can I have a copy of that?" I said, "Sure, I'll be more than happy to give you a copy -- just as soon as you agree to stop this illegal action.." Oh! she glared at me. She turned around and didn't ask again, nor did she acknowledge my offer. She finished with Mark after a quite a few more minutes. She closed saying, I'll see you back at the office." I said, Wait! I still want to talk to Mark. She hesitated and sneered at me.

A little later, or perhaps still during the phone call, this agent who had seemed reasonable asked about NM. She asked if I was the president of NM. I said yes, and she said, "Q he's the president of NM too, Q! Q!" But Q was getting an earful from Mark at that time, or just ending her call, and waved her off. I thought great, you still are outside due process and you're grabbing at straws, and you're going to do the seizure anyway. You've got no concept of the meaning of "legal entity" and due process of law. Another attempt at illegal seizure. These agents are either ignorant of the law and the IRS code, or deliberately ignoring it. They don't know who they can proceed against and they don't care. They don't even know the difference between private property and personal property.

When I got the phone back, Mark had already hung up. So, I dialed him up again. He asked about my relationship with PC. I went on and told Mark that I was willing to pay every cent I owned, and he should know that from working with us before, but in this case, that wasn't it. I told him I'd been involved with Pat of PC for only a few months. Pat had told me where break-even was, and I helped get the sales there. I then found out break-even was MUCH lower. I told Pat we could either shut down the business and sell off the assets or he could buy it back and take over all obligations. Mark asked about my relationship and I said I basically gave business advice and had pumped in some money. I told him I never had signature authority on the PC account, that Pat was the manager before, during and after my involvement with it. I think this was all in accordance with the affidavit we filed. He asked me if I knew where the bank account was, then there was another commotion. Someone shouted at me, they're changing the locks. Q walked back in. I asked if we were done? Was it over? Could the police office go? She gave half a nod and a sneer, but no solid answer and walked out.

Mark asked if I minded answering a few questions from time to time. I told him I didn't mind talking to him personally but... He said, okay, what if he called and asked a few questions from time to time, would I mind. I said, no I wouldn't mind, but, this in no way was meant to waive my power or attorney I had with JK. He acknowledged he understood, and then we went on to discuss what a good guy we both thought Jim was. That was the end of our conversation.

Q was standing outside. I opened the door to ask her if she wanted copies as I had promised, and she sneered, I'll be back in a minute. So I went back to waiting. All the employees were standing around trying to figure out what happened. She came back in with two sets of keys and said here's your keys to the locks. Sign this. I asked what it was. She said it was just a release form, saying we got our building back in the same condition it was in. I insisted on reading the type above my signature. There

were two sides to the page. I didn't know it at the time I signed. When I tried to pick up the papers, she scolded me. Ooh, there's two copies there be careful. Don't get them out of line. Above my signature was the line she said certified the building had been returned in the same condition it was taken. There was also a release clause that I held the government blameless for damage to the building. I turned to the locksmith and said, are those my original locks and keys. He said he had to re-key the locks and he couldn't put them back in the same order without seeing our original keys. I said, we had lots of keys out and if we didn't have keys we didn't have our building back. She said, Well you're going to have to pay for that. All I paid him to do was to change the locks and then give you the keys. If you want them changed, you're going to have to pay for it. I scowled at the paper. The locksmith chimed in, how many sets of keys? I said about ten. He said he'd make them. I asked how much. He said he'd throw them in no charge. I accepted his offer and signed under that condition. As far as I know, they did not damage the building. It wasn't the building I was worried about anyway. We'd been knocked off our schedule, suffered lost production and sales, I was suffering chest pains and could feel my blood pressure was at a dangerous level, and I thought if I didn't have that release, I'd be sleeping there overnight with as many employees as would stay with me. And there was no release clause against her as an individual. After all, as I understood the situation, the government had rules she had broken and the majority of illegal action had been on her part, the assisting agent, and the supervisor, Dave. So we were free to sue for anything as long as we weren't claiming damage to the building.

When I had the keys, I made copies of the Sales Contract between NM, Inc., and PC along with the inventory list of PC equipment. She told me she was going to send a letter of some kind and to be sure I filled out every question on it. Then she said I was the only registered officer of the company so they were still going to hold me responsible for the back taxes. She then left.

Well, I was so upset I was only able to sleep about an hour that night. Most of the night I spent working on this recording of the events as they were fresh in my mind. My wife told me she could hear the stress in my voice and she can see it in my color.

The experience of trying to deal with an irrational QW and IRS has been detrimental to my health. I checked my blood pressure Friday morning and it was up ~150% above previous highs. The readings I took were 214 over 114 with pulse of 110. I called my Doctor's staff, with the numbers. They told me to come in immediately. I went to the hospital Friday before noon. My doctor told me anything over 200 was an emergency. He told me no matter what was going on, "At some point you've just got to calm down and tell yourself, 'I'm not going to let these people kill me.'" He told me he was certain I'd had suffered some injury to my heart during that session. He felt the IRS should be made to pay for such a serious intrusion into one's life.

I am now on blood pressure medicine. Prior to this, I had maintained a reasonable pressure by natural means -- reduced salt, low sugar, low fat diet, exercise and weight loss. This is no longer possible. Monday, five days later, under medication, my pressure is still 177 over 93, higher than any other point I have a record of prior to Q's illegal action.

# APPENDIX II
## Messages from Cyberspace

# APPENDIX II

# Messages from Cyberspace

See www.neo-tech.com/feedback/ for current messages

The first three pages of messages are from female readers in 1998.
The balance are not sorted by gender.

---

### Special Instruction

Do not skip these messages. Pay close attention. Read each message plucked from cyberspace. By studying messages that come from every possible perspective, you will gain confidence, knowledge, and power available from no other source. These broad-spectrum messages from ordinary people encountering Neo-Tech for the first time in cyberspace are crucial for understanding:

1. How, through cyberspace, Neo-Tech will vanish Earth's anticivilization.

2. How, even without cyberspace, one gains unexpected powers and competitive advantages in every area of life through Neo-Tech.

3. How, by infusing the whole of these messages, one gains much more than the sum of their parts — one gains every imaginable advantage for the present and on into the future.

Sarah V., prodigy.net, 6/1/98
Nothing can stop my quest for eternal life here on Earth. I always thought we should never die or get sick — to live eternally with love over flowing. I love your Outcompete book.

Melissa P., softhouse.com, 5/12/98
This is a great site it was really helpful with a relationship problem I had.

Maria G., ny.us, 5/5/98
Your work is the finest thing that I have ever read.

Liana M., erols.com, 5/2/98
This is information that requires the widest possible dissemination.

Georgia G., mainnet.net, 5/1/98
It is very important that Neo-Tech stay on the web in order to continue to educate the honest value producing members of society with regard to how to advance in every aspect of human life and how to un-stagnate oneself. We must spread the knowledge of opportunities that await us shall we break through the barriers that inhibit and control us. I admire the courage of your organization and I support all your efforts. Someone has to help the value producers progress. The powers that be can't afford for the value producers to become knowledgeable. Keep up the excellent work.

Gayle G., millikin.edu, 4/28/98
This site must never, ever, be taken off the web. Unlike so many deleterious influences in the world -- media, television, family, peers, associates, tricksters, clergy, politicians, advertisements, and literature, every integrated word is truth. Nothing else in the world is like that, and I can not explain to you the affect this has on my entire being except that upon reading it, something in me cries in joy and relief. The majority of our society is urgently in need of being de-programmed. Unfortunately, most are sadly resistant to changing a self-destructive way of thinking that is deeply embedded in their minds and souls from childhood. So the more Neo-Tech people there are, the easier it will be for the rest to change. Neo-Tech has given me the wings with which to fly out of the muck.

Tammie F., aol.com, 4/23/98
The information contained herein is what most of us know but do not think about nor use. It is an inherit ability that we have lost. If anyone is afraid of the contents of the materials herein, then it is because they are closed-minded and do not want others to think for themselves or have the ability to think about something beyond what we are taught through school or television, or what politicians or people of power want us to believe.

Diana R., aol.com, 4/10/98
WOW!!! So exciting!

Christina B., mcmail.com, 4/9/98,
United Kingdom
From what I have read so far, I believe that this approach to life is extremely valuable both to me to the general welfare of humanity.

Beth R., hotmail.com, 4/2/98
I was first introduced to Neo-Tech in 1993 by a very bright, yet still, very mystical young man. Together, we read and re-read the literature, ordered new literature, and slowly we grew into a fully integrated, honest Neo-Tech couple, with our only commitment being towards mutual growth and total honesty. Our continuous value reflection has benefited our lives greatly. Our genuine love for one another is reflected so clearly that it touches every life we touch.

Associates and peers are often amazed at our honesty and compassion for one another, not to mention they are envious. By integrating the facts presented by Neo-Tech and consistently sticking to THE point, rather than being distracted by A point, we have become the gods of our own universes. The flow of the good is beginning to come to us. We could not have done these magnificent feats without the help and wisdom of Frank Wallace, Mark Hamilton, and Eric Savage. Your endurance to the continuous struggles in the anti-civilization serve as a beacon for all honest value-producers in the world. My eternal gratitude goes out to all of you and your staff at Neo-Tech Publishing for all your hard years of effort. Thank you for making my life a pleasure to live and for giving me a future I can look forward to.

Cathy W., wlc.com, 3/24/98, Canada
Thank you for having the courage to create and maintain this site.

Laura J., psi.net, 3/12/98
What an eye opener your materials are. I would like to know that everyone has access to them.

Sheila M., aol.com, 3/11/98
Neo-Tech is the breath of life to which nothing else can compare. As Buzz Lightyear might say, 'Expand this web-site to Infinity and Beyond!!'

Pamela M., webtv.net, 3/10/98
Since discovering Neo-Tech I feel hope again!

Flora K., prodigy.net, 3/5/98
A lot portrayed in Neo-Tech are things that I knew about, but did not know how to put in words. I did not know how to stop professional mystics and neocheaters from usurping my

values. I could see, feel, and experience the why's, when's, and where's (effects) but I have always looked for the 'how's' and Neo-Tech is the first to show me the how's (cause). Neo-Tech is the way. Keep on keeping on (Bravo).

Maria D., aol.com, 3/5/98
I really love my Neo-Tech Manuscript. I would not sell it even for $6,995. When I am angry and disappointed I run to my best friend and read for about three or four hours without stopping, not even to drink water. I read, reread, and reread Neo-Tech Manuscript because I feel so relaxed and at home when I am in company of my best friend. I find very much truth in it. It is like I moved from one world to another world. Thank you again, and keep up the good work.

Marilyn P., netcom.com, 2/22/98
I would be very interested in the latest research/ planning of Neo-Tech schools, and all work being done concerning the education of our children. I am finally learning what I longed all my life to learn for myself, and also when rearing my children. These readings are the most valuable I have ever encountered. Thank you for making them available.

Jenny W., aol.com, 2/22/98
I definitely want this site to remain on the web. It offers invaluable information that may not be available through the marketed Neo-Tech written literatures (for example, Rosa Maria's articles). Please do expand this site. This site has gone a long way since I visited it last year—more info, more articles, more art, and thus more power.

Ann H., aol.com, 2/21/98

You have opened a whole new world of understanding for me, I hope that I can continue to grow in the neo light that you have lit...I have always tried my best to be honest, and compassionate...but grew extremely dismayed at the lack of concern others had with the way the world has turned...corrupt leadership with no morals...I hope many more people read your web site and realize that we are the only ones who can change things...

Janet K., ntt.it, 2/21/98, Italy

I am extremely fascinated. I look forward to learning more to improve my life and those who are close to me.

Miranda T., advsol.com, 2/21/98

I am anxious to learn more about Dr. Frank Wallace's discovery. It is indeed powerful and ingenious.

Susan E., ark.com, 2/18/98, Canada

I admire Neo-Tech quite a lot. YOU MUST CONTINUE THIS WEB SITE. It has taken me 6 months to find a view that is rational, thoughtful, and fair.

Sheila M., att.net, 2/18/98

God's pajamas!! Neo-Tech is more fun than a barrel a Jell-O!

Barbara C., stc.net, 2/10/98

I'm telling everyone I can about Neo-Tech, even those really hung up on the god thing. We have been successful in this country in spite of the government not because of it.

Sherri I., co.za, 2/4/98

I think it is fascinating information and extremely beneficial. It allows you to think for yourself and think in a very positive manner.

Dawn K., net.za, 2/4/98, South Africa

From the little information I received from a friend, I know that I need this information in order to change my life and make it meaningful. The benefits she has derived from Neo-Tech are unbelievable. I have always been the type of person who wants more out of my life, and I have tried almost every self help, motivation, positive thinking books on the market and none seem to work. I need Neo-Tech so that I can start living!!

Lynda L., swbell.net, 1/29/98

I need more information. I am soaking this up like a sponge.

Elizabeth P., aol.com, 1/14/98

I FELT REFRESHED AND SET FREE AFTER READING CERTAIN PORTIONS OF YOUR WEB SITE.

A.B., mnsinc.com, 12/31/97
"I feel grateful for having found this information and to apply it in my life. I only wish I could have came across it sooner. I hope that you will continue to keep your web site up, more people need to seriously sit down and read your material and to expand their thinking."

R.S., gnt.com, 12/31/97
"WE SHALL DANCE AMONGST THE STARS LIKE ANGELS, NOT IN DEATH, BUT IN LIFE. EVERLASTING LIFE!!!"

R.W., flash.net, 12/31/97
"You have to read Neo-Tech in order to see it in the news. I see Neo-Tech in the news around the world today more than ever before. I am proud to be a Neo-Tech owner."

D.S., aol.com, 12/31/97
"Time spent at this site is definitely value-added-time. Thank You."

L.L., caribsurf.com, 12/30/97, West Indies
"I Find the Neo-Tech literature to be very eye opening, with Neo-Tech one feels totally in control of everything."

S.B., cedarnet.org, 12/29/97
"I am still working at tearing out the roots of my mysticism. This site helps."

G.M., netcom.ca, 12/28/97, Canada
"Neo-Tech is the way of the future. No other way is possible or acceptable. We must get the word out that Neo-Tech is the answer we've all been looking for."

G.M., netcom.ca, 12/26/97, Canada
"I think Neo-Tech is a visionary's masterpiece. Everyone who reads, understands and believes in the writings contained in this book is sure to realize that there is more to life than what we are settling for today. We can't be held down, we can't be pushed back and we can't be controlled by the short-sighted, narrow-minded leaders that are in control of the world today. If people would just open their eyes to Neo-Tech."

R.W., flash.net, 12/25/97
"I am happier now than any time in my adult life. I find more people being honest today than ever before. The God concept and politicians have to go and be forgotten. WE OWE YOU MORE THAN THAN ALL THE GOVERMENTS IN THE WORLD ARE WORTH. HOW CAN I HELP?"

H.H., co.nz, 12/24/97, New Zealand
"All the best for 1998 to all NT value producers. 1998 is the year we receive the QS from Dr. Wallace and other great works from his revolutionary colloquies. It seems the parasitical elite are hell bent on destroying economies around the world as fast as they can before their hoax is finally put to an end by the honest hard working value producers of the world. I remember telling individuals as early as May/June 1997 that Dr Wallace had predicted what is now happening. At the time individuals without the NT knowledge I had, could not see it and it is only now becoming obvious that Neo-Tech Publishing will be the greatest company of the 21st century. Bigger and faster growing than Microsoft and Bill Gates. In 2598 when I am living in my own galaxy and commuting to Planet Earth for business purposes, I will think back to this time in the nuclear decision threshold and think of one individual, and he is Dr. Frank Wallace. Someday I hope to have the privilege of meeting with this great value producer, it will be an incredibly humbling moment."

Heather S., uu.net, 12/23/97
"Neo-Tech sounds as though it may become the mainstay for my life. thank you."

J.M., megsinet.net, 12/23/97
"Your approach genuinely impresses me. You guys do a fantastic job. Thank you for taking the time to teach people how to help themselves. It is this type of conscious effort that is necessary for humanity to change our nihilistic course."

S.M., megsinet.net, 12/23/97, South Africa
"I like the site. Keep up the work, and let us take this info. to the world!"

J.D., aol.com, 12/22/97
"I think a site like Neo-Tech gives people the opportunity to expand their vision. To see what can

be and what is. I feel this information will enlighten my future. A future to improve the world for mankind. A future to give anyone who can dream, a source to improve their lives and the lives and futures of their loved ones."

C.K., mich.net, 12/22/97
"I like the way Neo-Tech shows me what is really happening in the world and in everyday living. After reading Neo-Tech, I can usually tell if a person I am talking to is being honest or not. I feel I am much more in touch with reality than I was before I read Neo-Tech."

W.B., compuserve.com, 12/21/97, Canada
"NEO TECH IS A VERY POWERFUL THOUGHT PROCESS. USING IT BROUGHT ME TWO RAISES AT WORK WITHIN THE LAST YEAR, AND, I NEVER EVEN ASKED FOR THEM!"

H.S., ac.uk, 12/20/97, United Kingdom
"Your web site and its information is simply awesome. It was mind-blowing. A zillion thanks for the brilliant effort you have put in over the years."

J.M., co.za, 12/18/97, South Africa
"Neo-Tech provokes the mind and generates new thoughts."

M.L., com.au, 12/18/97, Australia
"With Neo-Tech I have changed so much for the better. My thinking is clearer, my opinion stronger, and I try to help Neo-Tech bring in a new and better world. We are all in it for the betterment of our lives and this world. I am very grateful for the enormous gift that Frank Wallace has given me."

S.H., webtv.net, 12/18/97
"I have gained so much from Neo-Tech I cannot thank you enough."

A.M., asu.edu, 12/17/97
"My father taught me how to be an honest person. That is why I feel that Neo-Tech should stay on the web — it promotes honsty! I like Neo-Tech because it makes me happy!"

M.H., asu.edu, 12/17/97
"I consider this site to be one of the most valuable

in existence. The information provides answers to many questions which arise as we try to cope with the difficulties encountered while struggling with life. Whether the problems are occupation, financial, emotional, or love relationships, I find the answers in your articles. You indeed provide a service to humanity."

M.W., cass.net, 12/17/97
"Neo-Tech has been my anchor these last 2 years. It pulled me out of a long downward spiral of religious guilt and depression that nearly killed me. I think NT publishing is accomplishing the greatest feat for mankind for all the future generations of the entire human race. Frank Wallace and his family will be recognized for thousands of generations as heroes and mighty warriors that saved the Planet Earth from its self-destruction."

S.L., aiusa.com, 12/17/97
"It's absolutely imperative for mankind's evolution that this site stays on the web and the Neo-Tech literature be circulated worldwide. All I can say is this literature has opened my mind and I can't wait to leave all these government authorities and false guilt inspiring religions behind and start my empire of wealth, power, and romantic love. As Frank R. Wallace wrote 'Truly great days are coming.'"

J.M., aol.com, 12/16/97
"Dear Mr. Wallace, I am 27 years old, and I have read literally 1000's and 1000's of pages of self-help material. I've taken years of college classes in both business and psychology. I've attended numerous seminars. Yet, while all of them where interesting, not one class, not one speech ever gave me the answers I was looking for. What I did know was that at 27 years of age, I was extremely depressed because I was not financially where I wanted to be in life, I was in an emotionally draining relationship and I was just completely unhappy. Unfortunately, I pretended to be happy, but inside I was dying everyday. The guy that I was in this roller coaster relationship with was reading Neo-Tech and he told me I should read it. So, I started to, because that was what my life was made of. Constantly doing things that other people wanted me to do. I could never say NO to anyone. Anyway, I started reading it, but I had to stop. I was completely petrified of just reading the definitions and the first 25 pages of the Neo-Tech Advantages. After that, I wasn't able

to focus on what I was reading, and it took me about an hour to read 4 pages. I told myself that the way it was written, made it too confusing. It wasn't written like all the other books that I was used to reading. If there was an excuse I could give myself, I took it. I continued to read, even though I didn't allow myself to get anything out of it, because what I was reading would completely turn my life upside down, if I let myself believe it. That was something that I wasn't sure if mentally, I was strong enough to admit that to myself let alone anybody else. So, I continued to read for this guy because it was what HE wanted and I thought it would make HIM like me more. Then, one night I was sitting on the couch completely feeling sorry for myself and being told so, I just emotionally hit rock bottom. Physically feeling ill, because I just could not stand my life, I didn't know what else to do. I was so lost, alone, and completely miserable, so I picked up Neo-Tech and started reading it for ME. Starting from the beginning and reading clear through to page 50, I realized things about myself that at certain points it felt like someone was squeezing my heart so hard that I couldn't breathe. I forged ahead though, as hard as it was, I had finally found the book to give me the answers that I had been looking for my whole life. After spending my whole life being a dishonest, pathetic little whimp, a total mystic through and through, I finally realized that being that way was the cause of all my unhappiness. I use to blame my past, my family, my friends, my relationship for all the unhappiness in my life. They were the reason, I wasn't as successful as I wanted to be. Neo-Tech though, has made me stand up and be responsible for myself, my actions and my feelings. Neo-Tech has made me realize how much of my life I have sacrificed for other people. I made those sacrifices to justify all of the dishonesty in my life. By sacrificing myself, it gave me a false sense of being a good person. A BIG FAT LIE !!! It hurt so much to have to admit to myself, that I was nothing but a mystical liar. So, complete honesty has been a struggle for me on a daily basis. But I never new how good it felt to be honest. I have come a long ways since that night. I know I still have a ways to go. Now, Neo-Tech excites me beyond my wildest dreams. I always knew that I would be successful, but because I was spending all of my productive time in the past feeling sorry for myself, I was missing all of my opportunities. Fortunately, thanks to Neo-Tech, that is no longer happening. I have taken my mystic filled, non-

productive life and turned it around. Again, I'm not even remotely close to where I will be, but now, because of Neo-Tech, I have not doubts that I will get there."

M.S., aol.com, 12/15/97
"I have read The Neo-Tech discovery and there is more honesty contained in that book than any religion would ever want people to know. It is hard to believe there are people out there who actually want to feed off the productive activities of others and want to control them by force to benefit their parasitical ways. I will commit myself to honestly producing more than I consume and rendering neocheaters powerless. We have the power! Not religion or government parasites!"

D.W., aol.com, 12/15/97
"Neo-Tech informs those who wish to have a better quality of life."

C.K., mich.net, 12/15/97
"I believe Neo-Tech truly shows a positive way of viewing life on earth. The information gives a person a clear understanding of how the world really works."

M.H., starent.com, 12/15/97
"I think this website provides a valuable service. Keep up the excellent work."

S.F., diginetusa.net, 12/14/97
"Neo-Tech helped me to begin to really live."

R.D., syr.edu, 12/13/97
"This web-site has blown my mind! It is the best one I have ever read."

J.J., aol.com, 12/13/97
"Magnificent work! The strength of Neo-Tech is impressive! I know that Neo-Tech will grow and penetrate this anti-civilization and bring eternal wealth and happiness to all mankind!"

T.G., ctonline.it, 12/13/97
"There is some very valuable Information on this web site."

W.P., compuserve.com, 12/13/97
"I just wished I had found this incredible information earlier. I will be spreading this ideas whenever I can."

C.P., aol.com, 12/11/97
"To be brief, Neo-Tech pulls no punches. It appeals to the open mind. Weather one agrees with it or not, it stimulates one to consider."

W.D., laplaza.org, 12/9/97
"The main crux of Neo-Tech is integrating into you life absolute honesty and integrity. In so doing one aligns his/her very inner core or being with the consciousness that powers everything that exists!"

K.G., aol.com, 12/8/97
"So far it has been a great experience reading the contents of such a great and interesting work of literature. I have learned a different perspective about life. I will continue reading to improve my life."

R.A., psi.net, 12/7/97
"The profound effects of Neo-Tech are indeed visible in the general society and will be long into the future. As a 'cyber-citizen' I feel this is one of the best sites on the web and integral to the advance of our universal civilization. So many people need to wake up to what has been done to them and it is exciting to me that these ideas are now so succinctly put forth through these pages. Onward...!"

P.B., mindspring.com, 12/5/97
"People are waking up to Neo-Tech!"

A.A., swbell.net, 12/5/97
"The subject matter is absolutely profound."

D.L., ibm.net, 12/5/97
"I just finished reading the Neo-Tech discovery manuscript. The book left me with the feeling that I was already heading in the right direction. I can't wait to expel mysticism entirely from my life and take over my own destiny."

R.N., webtv.net, 12/5/97
"I love the Neo-Tech concepts! Can we open an Neo-Tech education center?"

M.R., aol.com, 12/3/97
"Any attempt to remove Neo-Tech from the web would be purely a criminal act. Honesty speaks for itself. I was just reading about the Honesty Oath being Law of the Land. Excellent success! It is good to see NT working in the courts. The IRS is indeed crumbling—keep up the great work."

B.C., aol.com, 12/3/97
"I am compelled to write to Neo-Tech to let you know what has happened in my life. I see the hoax and events of our Anticivilization in the newspapers and on television. I hear the negative and stupid words and actions people use to mess up their life. Without Neo-Tech this is possible. I'm going to read Zonpower and take a serious approach to learn this information and change my life once and for all!"

M.L., mindspring.com, 12/1/97
"Neo-Tech works wonders. NT has shown me how to apply my mind to destroy any mystic in my way and how to make lots of money."

W.S., aol.com, 12/1/97
"Neo-Tech changed my life. I went from fat to thin, sad to happy, from a value destroyer to a value producer. I once asked Neo-Tech how do we know who are the parasitical elite, I thought about it and realized how: Once someone tastes the sweet water of life, they either enjoy it or vomit. Then they will come face to face with the final decision: get busy living or get busy dying."

C.D., execpc.com, 11/30/97
"The POWERS that be have limited the minds of the people across the globe with its doctrine. Neo-Tech will unlock the mind and give individuals a new way of thinking— let Neo-Tech circulate worldwide."

N.W., thefree.net, 11/30/97, England
"Certainly opened my eyes to areas of life I never knew existed. Keep up the excellent work and get rid of government interference."

A.S., aol.com, 11/30/97
"This site gives me a new outlook on everything I thought I knew. Keep up the good work."

S.B., servtech.com, 11/30/97

"I think that governments would have to ban Neo-Tech (NT). NT poses too great a threat to their bogus power structure for them not to ban it. It's a good thing that they ban NT. For they will have publicly, and widely, demonstrated their disregard for peace, prosperity, love and happiness. NT will gain an instant and many fold increase in readership. Of course, governments know the above is true, thus, is the reason they've done their best to avoid Neo-Tech as much as possible. Governments do not want people to have NT. For governments, it's Catch 22."

L.S., iav.com, 11/30/97

"You present a different perspective and stimulate intelligent thought, e.g., the article on Princess Diana & Mother Teresa. The Media had us weeping over the 'tragic' loss of Di. Any other woman in a similar situation would have been considered a drunken slut out gallivanting around who reaped her just dessert."

K.L., att.net, 11/30/97

"This seems to be a very cool site that allows the individual to study the world in a different kind of light... and helps to better themselves with a true understanding of the experiences of life."

S.V., asdc.kz, 11/29/97, Kazakhstan

"I looked for information like at this on the web a long time. So I was exciting to read it and hope to stay here to understand your ideas... Thanks!!!"

P.C., pdq.net, 11/29/97

"Great site...have benefited enormously from Neo-Tech...only fools would want to ban Neo-Tech..."

T.Q., aol.com, 11/29/97

"NT opens people's eyes to standing up for the universal rights of humanity."

G.B., hud.gov, 11/28/97

"We desperately need your message. I hope every person on earth gets the chance to hear it."

R.A., edu.au, 11/26/97

"I enjoyed reading the content of the present site and found it a breath of fresh air in the face of present dishonesties."

R.O., dialsprint.net, 11/26/97

"Neo-Tech has changed my life. I have developed a bull detector and it is mind boggling the amount of garbage is spewed out from various sources on a daily basis. Anybody who wishes to live life to its fullest needs to read Neo-Tech and be active minded instead of open minded."

T.T., aol.com, 11/25/97

"The more I read and understand these concepts, the more I understand myself and the coming Civilization of the Universe. Self-pity and depression are dreadful and un-necessary for me or anyone. I long to be 'sublimated' and 'flipped' but know there is no magic, messiah, or miracle... Only effort and honesty and _action_. I started with 3 blocks of jogging and a shower today."

M.T., pipex.com, 11/25/97, England

"Hey, this is a wild, fantastic, deeply meaningful site."

Anon, co.kr, 11/25/97, Korea

"Excellent sites for clear-cut objective views."

D.W., uu.net, 11/23/97

"I have just tried to finish reading the Abuse Reports, again.. Your cautionary words at the beginning are very appropriate. I have not been able to read all of them yet. Are you certain we live in the United States???? I am a management consultant, whose one area of business is working for clients that are being 'attacked' by the IRS. When it comes to the IRS, ALL legal, ethical and humane laws and rules are done away with. The IRS does not listen to the courts, our legal systems or the Constitution. And, worse yet, the government of this country allows them to do this to the United States citizens. Again, I ask, Are you certain we live in the United States??"

J.E., worldaccessnet.com, 11/23/97

"Neo-Tech is valid and the world needs to know honest facts. Pricelessly honest information. I will be starting a business very soon with a patented product I have developed. I will use what I've learned from Neo-Tech.... The only dynamics that are fail proof. thank you Neo-Tech."

A.G., net.my, 11/23/97, India
"I'm a computer programmer living in India and I discovered Neo-Tech recently. Of late (the last 3-4 years) I was disillusioned, depressed, and moving towards self-destructive habits such as drugs and alcoholism. I was so intellectually stymied by the overwhelming 'power' of neocheaters in India, and so frustrated by the completely anti-civilization social environment I almost lost all my power and will to continue to produce values. Neo-Tech has rejuvenated me."

T.S., compuserve.com, 11/22/97
"Neo-Tech breaks through dead-end mysticism and reveals an unlimited success formula."

J.M., pipex.com, 11/22/97, United Kingdom
"I can say honestly that my life is changing. Your frankness and honesty in the information you provide is appreciated."

C.C., net.my, 11/22/97, Malaysia
"NT books is the best thing that ever happened to me. At the tender age of 19, I am all go for Neo-Tech — for the rest of my life!! I will go all out to fight with Neo-Tech against the anticivilization of today and tomorrow. Long Live Neo-Tech!! Down with mysticism and lawyer-like dishonesty!! Truly great days are coming!!"

J.R., netcom.com, 11/21/97
"Your work is absolutely amazing. Without your work, I would have no clue as to what really is happening on this little planet of ours. Thanks again for the most VALUABLE information I have yet to come in contact with."

J.S., ac.uk, 11/19/97, United Kingdom
"A wonderful insight into the way of human relationships and communication."

G.M., aol.com, 11/19/97
"I like how Neo-Tech encourages honesty among people. Anyone who attacks Neo-Tech is already doomed."

D.F., ij.net, 11/17/97
"A shining light in a very dark age."

P.M., gov.au, 11/17/97, Australia
"N-T is very explosive material. It looks like a pebble but has the strength of a mountain. Many friends I know say that this literature is very dangerous, whilst the opposite is the fact. Insanity seems to be growing at an alarming rate through mystical belief by which people's minds have been imprisoned. Only N-T can strip and shred this stupidity. The good aspect about N-T is the healing mechanisms that it has to purge mystical rubbish, it actually heals the brain."

M.B., usc.edu, 11/16/97, Brazil
"As a whole, view is very impressive."

M.F., usc.edu, 11/16/97, UNITED KINGDOM
"It is imperative that this web site remain open, to remove it would be akin to removing a chromosome from the nuclei of all living cells in the body. THIS NEO-TECH/ZONPOWER WEB SITE ENSURES A PROSPEROUS FUTURE FOR ALL WHO ARE NOT INVESTED IN THIS ANICIVILIZATION."

D.W., prysm.net, 11/16/97
"Neo-Tech will fulfill everything the bill of rights promised but couldn't deliver. VIVA LA NEO-TECH!!!!!!!!!!!!"

S.H., prysm.net, 11/16/97, Australia
"Neo-Tech information is invaluable. Everything said has complete logic, and it really opens your mind. It really does change your life. Of course, governments want to ban it! They'll lose all their power!"

R.W., flash.net, 11/15/97
"Neo-Tech is all we need. I cannot read enough. No one can compete with Honesty. I know we owe Neo-Tech & all people connected to Neo-Tech more than we can give for a FREE World arriving sooner than expected. I want to be a Neo-Tech man. Crime is slowing down. Thanks to Neo-Tech, Honesty is working. Try it you'll like it."

R.J., aol.com, 11/15/97
"I have read only pieces of Neo-Tech and it has greatly changed my way of thinking thus far. I am really starting to think on my own and be aware of things that are going on in the world."

L.N., aol.com, 11/15/97

"Unusual but brilliant insights in many areas including your concept of neocheating, how to handle a job (treating it as a mini company), how CEOs should stick to running their businesses, IRS abuses, biological immortality (overdue for serious discussion), discussion of the bicameral mind (Julian Jaynes)— never heard this one before!, the splintering of businesses into small but viable economic entities run by individuals empowered by high tech, ideas on the creation of the universe (created by a person—not so far out if you extrapolate the exponential growth of technology over millions of years !).... keep it going."

C.C., ctc.edu, 11/14/97

"I am absolutely blown away by this knowledge! It 'jiu-jitsu's the forces of evil by exposing its means and tactics! What has operated in the night has been exposed to the light!"

K.W., aol.com, 11/13/97

"Yes! By all means, Neo-Tech should definitely be made available to all those that wish to acquire the knowledge this incredible program has to offer. The fools that wish to throw away this once-in-a-lifetime opportunity may do so but they are only hurting themselves by continuing their daily pattern of mediocrity."

J.H., aol.com, 11/13/97

"Nothing I have read has been able to maintain my full attention such as this site."

F.T., prodigy.net, 11/13/97

"I cannot begin to explain the help Neo-Tech has brought to my life. I was forever trapped in the inevitable demise of my existence with my mystical beliefs. YES! The world, as we now know it, is doomed without the knowledge contained on these web pages. This is the greatest vehicle to the resurrection of mankind. I, for one, owe my life to the valuable information I gained for myself and my family."

J.G., utilicorp.com, 11/12/97

"You are absolutely awakening the human mind to an alternative awareness that all is not what it seems, but only what one has been brainwashed to believe by big brother."

W.S., aol.com, 11/12/97

"Damn straight Neo-Tech should stay on the web, lest we wish to die, I for one do not."

A.S., co.uk, 11/12/97, United Kingdom

"AMAZING! What a concept! What content! Blown away!"

K.J., shentel.net, 11/11/97

"I am a reader of Neo-Tech and I have women hit on me all the time."

R.C., aol.com, 11/11/97

"Neo-Tech is the most valuable thing available today. There are still to many people out there that don't know the greatness of Neo-Tech."

G.S., co.uk, 11/11/97, ENGLAND

"I SINCERELY WANT TO SEE MYSTICISM FALL BY 2001."

B.K., centuryinter.net, 11/11/97

"This is a great site. I think I will implement the principles in my life and show them to my relatives so they can use them too."

S.H., aol.com, 11/6/97, Germany

"The Neo-Tech book was the best book on business management I have ever read."

J.S., tusco.net, 11/6/97

"I am so glad that the IRS tax reform bill will shift the burden of proof in civil cases. The Tax Code was a Law in itself, and was designed to oust every taxpayer who challenged their Code. In almost every case, the taxpayer loses. Do you believe Neo-Tech was the forerunner in this shift? I do."

K.M., msn.com, 11/10/97

"I'm very grateful this site exists so I can express concerns regarding our laws and how the IRS abuses it's power!! It's a growing problem that must be resolved!!! Please keep this page available for those that need this kind of support!!!"

G.B., flash.net, 11/9/97

"Yes!! Neo-Tech in cyberspace!!! Neo-Tech should ABSOLUTELY remain on the Internet! Down with the neocheaters!!! Banish every pathetic, wicked little mystic OFF THE FACE OF THE EARTH!!! Infinite gratitude to Frank R. Wallace for providing a clear, RATIONAL, and HONEST 'path' out of the cold, dark catacombs of evil and oppressive religions, force-backed governments, and other abominable, irrational, and dishonest monstrosities. LONG-LIVE CAPITALISM AND BUSINESS!!!!!!"

P.C., hhs.net, 11/9/97
"This site should stay on the web. It is giving many many people including myself the hope that something can be done about the abuse the IRS has done to people. There are people out there that do not believe just how abusive the IRS has and can be. I only hope and pray that they will not have to go through what I and others have gone through."

Q.S., uu.net, 11/9/97
"Many thanks for having the guts to make the IRS an issue — something that 3 generations of senators and representatives have had neither the will nor the fortitude to do. We fought a war to rid ourselves of a king who had less arbitrary power in his entire realm than this misbegotten agency has. Perhaps it's time for another. There is no reforming what is criminal and malevolent to its core."

A.G., compuserve.com, 10/31/97
"Let the truth about LIFE be told!! We are conditioned to think we are not worthy of a better life. We are programmed to believe there is no other way."

R.B., hp.com, 10/30/97
"Fully integrated, fact-based, honest literature is a welcome relief from the status quo, politically-correct, biased literature in the straight press."

J.K., com.sg, 10/30/97, Singapore
"Neo-Tech is the blueprint that all of us need."

D.E., ibm.net, 10/30/97
"What I have seen so far on the web-site is absolutely astonishing!"

C.Z., gte.net, 10/29/97
"When I began to read Neo-Tech it scared me. Neo-Tech is the best gift I have ever received. Now I realize what mysticism has being doing to the human mind."

C.F., adams.edu, 10/29/97
"This might be what I need in my life. Neo-Tech seems like a dream I have longed for."

Z.Z., net.my, 10/28/97, Malaysia
"The time has come for everyone to experience true living. Down with all the neo-cheaters now. What a revelation of truth! I am fascinated."

R.C., csuchico.edu, 10/28/97
"The power of cyber-space is the rapid and mountainous delivery of information. Neo-Tech is a body of knowledge unlike any other."

G.M., ornl.gov, 10/28/97
"I like the benevolent ideas aimed at a greater good for mankind in business, political, religious, and social operations."

C.B., nf.ca, 10/27/97, Canada
"I think that this is the best thing that has ever happened to the web. Keep up the mysticism cleansing!!!"

T.R., unitedgrain.ca, 10/27/97, Canada
"I have just finished re-reading Neo-Tech and I am absolutely astonished how my thinking has been changed. I can now easily spot a neo-cheater and their ways in my daily life with little effort. I want to thank all those who have enabled the truth to reach me. I look forward to growing Prosperity - Money - Power and Romantic-Love which is in the reach of any individual armed with Neo-Tech. We shall succeed in driving the neo-cheaters to their much deserved demise."

J.F., aol.com, 10/26/97
"I found the information riveting and exciting. Do what you have to in order to stay on the web!"

A.O., pace.edu, 10/26/97
"This is a great site. It gives a lot of valuable information, it opens the secrets of Universe. It's exiting and breathtaking..."

C.M., net.au, 10/26/97
"Excellent, thought provoking material."

R.P., netcom.com, 10/26/97
"This is very thought provoking. It is very well thought out."

Y.O., net.id, 10/24/97, Indonesia
"You have a good idea of making a good life."

S.C., baf.com, 10/24/97
"This is the only literature I have read in the past 20 years that has really made sense. I have exhausted many efforts in 'Money Making - Get Rich Schemes' for the past 10 years and only wish I had used that effort towards Neo-Tech. I now know where to put my efforts."

D.K., bc.ca, 10/24/97, Canada
"Neo-Tech is so different from other points of view, it stimulates thinking. One may not agree with what is being presented or may be shocked or outraged, but that kind of challenge is necessary."

D.U., aol.com, 10/23/97
"Neo-Tech has changed my life for the better. In just three days, I had total control of my life, love life and financial problems. I am now out of financial debt. I have no fears or worries of any kind. Neo-Tech most definitely benefits those who are looking for a better life"

D.K., aol.com, 10/23/97
"Any organization that brings forth the truth is phenomenal and unusual."

K.L., saber.net, 10/23/97
"I believe Neo-Tech is an excellent learning tool."

R.T., direcpc.com, 10/22/97
"Wow! What a vast amount of information!!!! This is Awesome."

D.B., webtv.net, 10/22/97
"This is mind boggling stuff!!! I WANT TO BE A NEO-TECH MAN!"

D.M., webtv.net, 10/22/97
"Make's more sense to me than anything ever read. I have a much clearer view of the universe."

F.P., psi.net, 10/22/97
"I sure like what you say. It has changed my life. Now I am happy. Before I was despondent."

S.D., msu.edu, 10/22/97
"By all means, this web site should stay on the web as an aid to mankind. It opens up man's mind and awakens him the higher meaning of life. I support

your research and the work Neo-Tech is doing."

R.Q., bellatlantic.net, 10/22/97
"My view of Dr. Wallace is that he's a thousand years ahead of his time."

T.M., swbell.net, 10/21/97
"All I can say so far is WOW. Thanks Dr. Wallace and all Zons who make this life liberating material available to all those who want to wake-up and take back control of their lives from the neo-cheaters and mindless-cattle-society types."

Anon, swbell.net, 10/21/97
"Your work is both good and original."

M.F., tek.com, 10/21/97
"Great site, The world needs more information like this, not less!"

D.W., aol.com, 10/21/97
"Very Impressive!! Stumbled upon your site by accident. but what a gracious accident. Myself and my friend, read so much so fast, it was a bit exhilarating. We are still absorbing the input. The search for truth takes one to mysterious places, even in the ether. One cannot deny REALITY. Reality is TRUTH, and that TRUTH cannot be false. NEO-TECH impresses me as fundamental truth, common sense, and logic. And my eyes were open wide the whole time I was here. Bravo! Thanks.."

R.J., webtv.net, 10/19/97
"All this scares me, but I truly like what I have been reading and I need more!!! How can any of this be harmful to man when it is for the good of man?"

B.M., webtv.net, 10/19/97,
"Here is to truth and honesty. May it prevail!"

J.S, swbell.net, 10/19/97
"What your site does is to awaken a sleepy mind to start thinking."

B.M., ne.us, 10/15/97
"Neo-Tech is the greatest discovery since man discovered fire. In fact, without Neo-Tech, man will most likely *digress* to his former Neanderthal self. That is, if he doesn't annihilate himself first. We have come a long way since the days of our cave dwelling ancestors. To progress further, to unleash

the life-saving, life-building, life increasing discoveries of the future, we must wipe out every trace of mysticism from the mind of man. Neo-Tech is man's one and only hope. Only Neo-Tech can save man from eventual extinction. Only Neo-Tech can provide each and every individual with a life he will want to live forever—a life of limitless happiness, prosperity, and romantic love. Viva Neo-Tech!"

Tony C., hula.net, 10/15/97
"I want what Neo-Tech offers."

P.D., unlimited.net, 10/15/97
"I found this web site to be very enlightening and worthwhile, I would like to learn more about the awesome effects of these powers and how they can be applied to my every day life."

E.E., unlimited.net, 10/14/97
"People can gain many things from Neo-Tech including power, money, happiness, and the ability to do what you want."

I.N., flash.net, 10/13/97, Germany
"Neo-Tech is the revelation of the century. This site is spectacular and exciting."

R.H., highfiber.com, 10/13/97
"Just enjoying reading truth"

F.M., lvdi.net, 10/12/97
"I have recommended Neo-Tech to many people and the web site makes it easy to refer other people to this valuable resource."

E.S., aol.com, 10/12/97
"Definitely helped me to break the chains of guilt and oppression of 'friends', family and parasites....I FINALLY GET TO BE ERIC!!!!!!! I look forward to love, romance and excitement Thank you"

S.C., net.my, 10/11/97, Malaysia
"Excellent material. Gives hope to life with new ways. Just love it."

K.A., ptialaska.net, 10/11/97
"Truth and honesty for all and to all."

E.P., skyinet.net, 10/11/97, Philippines
"This is the most useful invention ever created since the beginning of time!!! Thank you very much in advance for the most-recent Money/Power/Romantic-Love information."

R.P., skyinet.net, 10/11/97, India
"I just got a net connection today. I found your site through Ayn Rand. Boy has it freshened me and exited me. Please inform me more of Neo-Tech, what I can do to spread what you are doing?"

E.S., uconn.edu, 10/9/97
"I was a sophomore in high-school when I first ordered 'The Neo-Tech Discovery'. I was too caught up in mysticism to integrate with it except as a philosophical/preach-this-as-the-right-way set of good-sounding information. Everyone thought I was a kook! Then I began to apply it and I got scared. I was trapped still in my mysticism and I burned all the books 'cleansing' myself. Then at the end of my senior year, I got rejected from the 'major' Ivy League schools everyone had always thought I'd get into. Depression hit as the mysticism-shattering, mind-de-lousing effects of Neo-Tech began to surface. Yet I still had too much invested in my mysticism and the anticivilization...I was prepared to enter the University of Connecticut and experience the 'finer' points of life that my childhood never offered: girls, sex, alcohol, and drugs. Those things blurred away the reality that Neo-Tech was asserting within me...I reached an all-time low in self esteem. I ended up hooked on pot by the end of my freshman year...people didn't respect me, my mind was blurred and the promises of college weren't being delivered.. During the summer, I got involved with AOL and the Internet. I also received a new Zonpower brochure in the mail I went to this web site, re-ordered the manuscript and now here I am: Drug free, alcohol-free, sugar free, caffeine free, self-hate free, and hard-working towards mysticism free. I am in the process of separating from this lazy professor-alcoholic/life wasting institution of the anticivilization to launch myself into the all-effort, zero mysticism life of reality... Life is Wonderful 'Death To Mysticism'"

C.B., mint.net, 10/9/97
"Neo-Tech is the greatest mind-expanding tool for fighting evil on the planet earth."

D.B., com.au, 10/9/97, Australia
"Well done guys! I have been a Neo-Tech fan for years now and hunger for every thing you write. Keep up the great work."

R.W., rowan.edu, 10/8/97

"I can feel the cracking whip of Neo-Tech destroying the evil that has ruled this planet for 2300 years!! Thank You Neo-Tech Publishing."

M.R., swbell.net, 10/8/97

"The information has made quite an impact on me. I have always thought there was a lot of corruption, but now I can see the big picture. My wife and I are still having trouble breaking away from this anti-civilization. Everywhere we go it seems no one is aware, or they just don't care. I appreciate the commitment and effort you all put forth in collapsing mysticism. Thank you in advance for saving the world."

J.W., uu.net, 10/8/97

"The future is here, we have the technology to live in a society of bliss, but it all is oppressed by the federal government and it's regulations. I agree strongly in the Neo-Tech philosophy and wish very much to progress with it."

M.A., com.au, 10/8/97, Australia

"I would definitely like the Neo-Tech site to remain on the Internet as it is invaluable. Neo-Tech has done wonders for both myself and my partner and I will continue reading whatever information you make available to the world over the Internet."

R.K., ca.us, 10/7/97

"Thanks for posting your IRS Abuse Reports. I've added your link to my homepage intending for our public school students to use the free flow of information as they mature into active participants responding to real current issues in our country. You've hit a hefty home run with your Web site!"

J.B., att.net, 10/7/97

"Excellent service to document the IRS abuses."

A.M., ksla.nl, 10/7/97, Netherlands

"I find the Neo-Tech material intriguing, and certainly different from mainstream thought. For this reason alone it is valuable. Is mainstream thinking so weak that it cannot withstand alternatives?"

T.H., netcom.com, 10/6/97

"I first came into contact with Neo-Tech about 5 years ago, All of a sudden the lights came on as a new perspective and paradigm unfolded. After reading the material, I was charged and excited. At the time I tried to share my excitement with my family and friends... they all thought I was mad and would burn in hell. After all who was this school dropout, starving kid to tell anyone that he knew better? Oh well so be it... At that time I was broke and starving, working in a job I hated. So I packed my bags, moved to America, partnered up with a few very talented and like minded people, started our own computer software business, and built it into a multimillion dollar concern."

T.D., bellsouth.net, 10/5/97

"As we grow up, we come to our realizations about Santa, the tooth fairy, ect. It floors me that so many people still base their entire lives on a 3000 year old fairy tale!!! The N\T Discovery should be shouted from the highest global rooftops! After one year of studying and applying N/T, I realize that the 'Jesus freaks' have no idea what it means to be born again. The only 'Supreme Beings' I know of are Dr. Wallace and Associates. I can never thank you enough."

M.T., prodigy.com, 10/5/97

"I think Neo-Tech is great! I am confident that these ideas will prevail in the future. I find that battling mysticism and self defeating behavior in myself more challenging and the ultimate battle is against myself more than neocheaters. One thing is for sure: Now I can spot a neocheater and refuse to give any value to these shitbags"

M.S., psi.net, 10/4/97

"I was 23 when I first started reading NT material, and I remember the day it arrived in the mail. I read the first few pages of Zonpower, and put it back in the envelope to return it because I felt it was evil. The next day I decided to take another look, and that began a life-changing journey into rational, mystical-free thinking. I'm grateful for the information, and what it has added to my life. Thanks for contributing to the betterment of the most important thing in society: the Individual."

D.E., co.nz, 10/4/97, New Zealand

"Neo-Tech makes more sense to me as each day goes by. I see the better world Mark Hamilton writes about in 'After2001: The New Code' and I want to be part of that world. The world needs Neo-Tech now."

C.B., aol.com, 10/3/97
"I FEEL THAT THE FUTURE OF SOCIETY DEPENDS ON THE SUCESS OF NEO-TECH."

R.J., flash.net, 10/3/97
"Neo-Tech takes the place of the Lone Ranger, everything comes out good and honest. You can bet on Neo-Tech, a real winner delivering health-wealth happiness, honesty and new light to the individual. Good bye IRS, FDA, deceit, deception and all other value destroyers. I can not find the words to thank Dr. Wallace and Mr. Savage and all others connected to Neo-Tech enough. Reading other positive comments I say ditto, ditto, ditto to all of them. Nothing short of scraping the IRS will be accepted and a consumption tax put in place with no other tax of any kind needed."

D.T., hotmail.com., 10/2/97, Australia
"I am deeply indebted to Dr. Wallace for all his work. I received Neo-Tech at 17 and I am now poised to conquer the world (in an honest business-like way). The medium of the WWW seems made for this information. Accessible to anyone, anywhere, at any time."

P.W., honeywell.com, 10/2/97
"Sometimes when I need some reinforcement, I can easily go to your web-site and read what I need to help me with the situation that is occurring or lift my mood."

J.W., ctc.edu, 10/2/97
"Neo-Tech is simply incredible."

B.R., aol.com, 10/1/97
"This is information that everyone needs to understand. Keep up the good work."

S.P., snip.net, 10/1/97
"Honesty Rules! Please expand the presence of Neo-Tech on the WWW. It is extremely important that all people know where to go to learn how to think for themselves — neothink."

C.C., pacbell.net, 10/1/97
"I find this information extremely valuable. The 114 advantages were inspiring and educational."

N.C., co.uk, 10/1/97, United Kingdom
"Yes! Yes! Yes! Yes! Yes! Yes! Yes! Yes! Yes! Yes! Yes! Yes! Yes! Yes! Yes! Yes! Yes! Yes! Yes! Yes! Yes! Yes! Yes! Yes! Yes! Yes! Yes! Yes! Yes! Yes! ........ A hundred Million times YES!"

G.S., ac.uk, 10/1/97, United Kingdom
"What an AWESOME web site, so much useful information it's almost mind-blowing."

J.S., tusco.net, 10/1/97
"Neo-Tech must remain on the web. For without Neo-Tech, disarming professional neo-cheaters, value-destroyers could not be possible by the year 2000 A.D. Neo-Tech is the future. I am pleased with the recent IRS exposure. While still in the very early stage of media attention, the IRS and their force-backed agendas will soon be expunged with Neo-Tech's forthcoming triumph over them."

S.A., map.com, 9/30/97
"I purchased one of the Zonpower manuscripts. Every aspect of my life has been enhanced. Zonpower in cyberspace has no equal. Removing it would do a severe disservice to humanity."

R.H., map.com, 9/30/97
"I've just finished reading Neo-Tech for the second time. The sense that it makes is astonishing. I can literally feel some of my internal mysticisms falling away. I now realize my own laziness and dishonesty that have plagued me in the past and hope to work hard and rid myself of these mysticisms. Thank you!!"

M.C., ptd.net, 9/29/97
"After years of alcohol abuse and 5 years of AA, I am looking for a new life that is objective. I never wanted to give credit to a god or anyone else for my 5 plus years of sobriety. I know I need to live a life of honesty, integrity, and guilt free life. Thank you for this important web site."

R.M., aol.com, 9/29/97
"NEO-TECH is REALITY. I only hope that one day people can see the world as it truly is and take FULL responsibility for their actions."

G.C., aol.com, 9/29/97
"Very enlightening. It is amazing how much the general public lacks the ability to see the layers of deception and deceit around them. Dr. Wallace's and Mr. Savage's works are a tribute to value producers

everywhere striving to accomplishment, success, and achievement. thank you."

D.A., aol.com, 9/29/97, Canada
"Neo-Tech is the most valuable site on the web today. Delivering health, wealth and happiness to the individual."

N.U., net.sg, 9/29/97, Singapore
"I never came across anything (information) like this before. I would like to see this site expanded.

R.E., aol.com, 9/28/97
"Neo-Tech/Zonpower is the greatest discovery since the computer itself. The two were made for each other."

Y.S., jumpnet.com, 9/26/97, Indonesia
"Neo-Tech is the only publication that dares to speak the naked truth of the present corrupt world that readily and happily exploits the ignorance of their fellow human beings."

S.G., richnet.net, 9/25/97
"Neo-Tech changed my life. The concepts I took away from reading the material are still manifesting huge changes in the way I interact with reality. I am beginning to operate my mind in an non-reacting mode whereby I feel I have the ability to effect the future. Without Neo-Tech exposing the cheaters I could never have defeated religion and the rest of the parasites to gain the freedom to think on my own."

L.P., bellsouth.net, 9/25/97
"This is most unusual, yet I have gained much more than enjoyment from your site."

S.D., sun.com, 9/25/97, Canada
"This inf. is amazing — I just 'ate' up the text. This site is vital to keep those of us alive who die a little every day at our mundane jobs...."

C.B., umn.edu, 9/25/97
"When I read idiotic messages like 'Neo-Tech will destroy our nation' I feel like I'm being held back, like someone else is trying to control me, keep me in line. I hope that Neo-Tech moves forward with their philosophy and makes further attempts to broaden the conceptual abilities of all mankind."

T.M., bell.ca, 9/24/97, Canada
"It is this type of readily available information that will help expedite the collapse of the neocheating infrastructure that exists today and at the same time open the eyes of those innocents that have been the real victims."

L.K., wl.com, 9/24/97
"I love any and all work that has been done on Neo-Tech/Zonpower. I've tried the techniques and they work wonders. Keep up the great work you're doing for humanity."

T.B., aol.com, 9/23/97
"Neo-Tech has been greatly beneficial to my life. The insight that I have gained through Neo-Tech has made me feel more alive than ever. I have undergone quite a transformation!"

C.D., aol.com, 9/23/97
"Without Neo-Tech we would have been completely devoured by professional neo-cheating lawyers, religious fanatics, etc. long ago. With Neo-Tech we are living again and know that life is getting better, fuller, richer daily. Neo-Tech literally saved our lives from total destruction & enabled us to see the chaos we were so deeply involved in & showed us a way out. Neo-Tech is our bible. THANK YOU NEO-TECH!"

K.E., netcom.com, 9/22/97
"A brilliant, zealously optimistic portrayal of humanity's potential. An infectious masterpiece."

C.C., accnorwalk.com, 9/22/97
"To all you critics of this site, before you judge you should judge yourself. You have to ask yourself, do I really understand this information being given to me (free I might add)? Am I really being brainwashed by the parasites of society? Am I so far gone that I don't even see the truth right in front of me? Like it or not changes are taking place, wether you understand why or not they are still going to take place. Don't you want to be part of it? Look at the world around you as you read each part of this site, and realize that its time to retool your brain for the future 'THE NEO-TECH FUTURE'"

R.R., aol.com, 9/21/97
"This information has been long in coming. Any person, that is aware, will leave all those behind that are awaiting guidance from the so called higher sources."

R.B., casema.nl, 9/19/97, Holland
"About 8 years ago I came into contact with your information. The volumes turned my life around. I am now a very happy self-employed human being and I travel the world doing what I like."

B.T., oz.net, 9/18/97
"All I would like to say is: 1. Your position against the IRS is right. 2. Your goal of eradicating the IRS is right. 3. Your web site can bring these 'rights' to the people. Thank you for publishing the evils of the IRS."

D.P., cattel.com, 9/17/97
"As an advocate of independent thinking, hard work, and continual efforts towards personal improvement, I, and many people I associate with, find sites such as Neo-Tech a refreshing and rewarding alternative to so much of the average, unthinking material available on the web. Good Job, great stuff."

N.L., ar.us, 9/17/97
"Dear Neo-Tech, I think it is very important for this site to stay on the web. It is a great source of information for all. Within days of first reading Neo-Tech, I was able to eliminate many unnecessary things from my life. And I effortlessly began making an estimated $1000 a week. I think all anyone has to do is read this and open their minds and the possibilities are endless. I owe a lot to Neo-Tech. I would like to thank Neo-Tech for making my life so much better and allowing me to do what I only before dreamed of. I am now live a life of total happiness and am able to get anything I want in life. Thanks again"

T.B., worldnetoh.com, 9/17/97
"I have long awaited this information to be available to the common person. After reading Neo-Tech, I realize that this IS the future of our world. There ultimately will be no stopping this, it has already begun. Thank you."

A.M., aol.com, 9/17/97
"There were times when I was reading that I felt like I had finally found what was missing in my life. Very enlightening."

D.W., bellsouth.net, 9/16/97,
"An amazing discovery. Neo-Tech is a better, healthier, more exciting way of living."

M.L., com.au, 9/16/97, Australia
"I see the changes that are occurring in this world. Neo-Tech has changed my life so much for the better. You are making a difference for the better for this world."

R.H., webtv.net, 9/15/97
"I am so excited about the future and what it holds for our civilization. I'm looking forward the next World Conference and the new book from Dr. Wallace. In closing, with Bill Gates buying Webtv and wanting to put a computer with Internet access into 95 million homes, and with Webtv expanding into the international market, this partnership will further the goals of Neo-Tech and bring the world to the Civilization of the Universe. To Dr. Wallace and all the people who have worked so hard to get this vital information out, THANK YOU!"

S.P., uu.net, 9/14/97
"The keys are here we just need to unlock the door."

J.H., uu.net, 9/14/97
"I can't get enough, I love reading all this stuff."

M.T., pipex.com, 9/13/97
"Neo-Tech is pure unadulterated honesty. The only people who have anything to fear from Neo-Tech are the dishonest."

S.J., att.net, 9/12/97
"Most informative and honest site I have ever visited on the Web."

D.C., mindspring.com, 9/11/97
"A genuinely sincere thank you to all involved with Neo-Tech and its goal of vanishing irrationality and mysticism worldwide."

S.K., froggernet.com, 9/11/97
"Neo-Tech is exhilarating, and powerful! Its hard to believe the absolute honesty written within the pages. Neo-Tech leaves me stunned with the new found thoughts of myself and world!"

R.W., clark.net, 9/10/97
"Neo Tech has given me the tools I've needed. ... The view through Neo-Tech eyes has removed the fog that has had me encased and shackled in this anticivilization. The view now is awesome, wide-scope and Iron Grip."

J.H., webspan.net, 9/10/97
"When I bought my discovery I was 17 years old, confused and zit ridden, and working in a public park hauling garbage. I have just turned 21, and am a professional actor. I have just finished an off-Broadway play in NYC, and will be shooting my first film in November. Hail life! And thank you for exposing me to Objectivism."

M.P., i-55.com, 9/9/97
"Welcome to the new world of peace and harmony!!!!!!"

M.P., i-55.com, 9/9/97
"Just finished Zonpower, will take deep breath and reread. See neocheaters everywhere now. Hide the women and children (and your wallet), there are a lot of bad folks out there. Keep up the good work. Great page, lets beat the 2001 goal..... Zon here we come."

B.W., webspan.net, 9/8/97
"For it matters not if Neo-Tech remains on the web. The seeds have been planted, germination taken root, and blossoming for all the universe to see."

L.W., uu.net, 9/6/97
"Just started reading the Zon/Neo-Tech site today and have not been able to stop. You've produced an expanded version of Rand's philosophy for the common man. Stay on the Web and spread the word. Keep the bastards in their non-productive place!"

B.M., iol.ie, 9/5/97, Ireland
"It is a refreshing way to look at a very clouded world"

M.M., net.au, 9/5/97, Australia
"Why shouldn't the best information in the world be available to everyone? Neo-Tech has/is and will continue to change the world. Neo-Tech has 100% of my vote because they are conducting a needed and moral service for all individuals. I constantly spread the Neo-Tech address over the Web. Down with Mystics/Neocheaters."

S.P., cyberstreet.com, 9/5/97
"Reading Neo-Tech gives me peace of mind, confidence, and self-esteem."

S.C., aol.com, 9/3/97
"The visibility of such information is needed. And more importantly WANTED. Light is best broadcast upon darkness from ABOVE...not below."

H.D., compuserve.com, 9/3/97
"Neo-Tech is a time bomb"

M.W., cass.net, 9/3/97
"Neo-Tech saved or rather is saving my life."

J.P., aol.com, 9/3/97
"I seem to feel more calm than usual during and after I read Neo-Tech information. Most people are blind and don't understand, they just walk through life doing as the government or 'society' tells them to do. With Neo-Tech, there is understanding rather than confusion."

D.S., demon.net, 9/2/97, England
"Neo-Tech is probably the greatest single human achievement since the invention of consciousness. The change it will bring can already be felt, and I think the neo-cheaters know this. They are running scared, and with good reason. Keep on battling guys. You're the only thing that will save mankind from itself."

Anon, aol.com, 9/1/97
"It's great to know the truth"

T.A., aol.com, 9/1/97
"In a world that seems to be on the verge of self-destruction, Neo-Tech offers hope. The reason Neo-Tech is so controversial is because most people cannot admit that their lives have been entrenched in a fallacy. I think that everyone should have the access to the cutting-edge information that Neo-Tech makes available. It is up to each individual to choose it or not."

H.B., uu.net, 8/31/97
"You have uplifted dark into LIGHT!!"

M.J., flash.net, 8/31/97
"The thoughts and rationality exhibited on these pages needs to be available to those who hold everyone or everything responsible but themselves. It allows for an personal review and reawakening."

M.T., netbiz.net, 8/31/97
"Finally!!! It is refreshing to find a group of people

who believe in Rationality, Individual Rights, and Capitalism!!!"

M.K., bellsouth.net, 8/30/97
"I have found what I have been looking for. I knew there was more to life than this anticivilization showed me: Neothink and Profound Honesty. Cyberspace is where I want to be."

P.B., bellsouth.net, 8/29/97
"This web-site is a significant find and has added greatly to the strength and diversity of my personal beliefs."

M.M., aol.com, 8/29/97
"This is prophetic information. Enlightening as well as captivating, resonating in truth."

B.E., pcisys.net, 8/29/97
"I checked out this so called MIRACLE (Neo-Tech) a friend tells me about! I have been reading this site now for about 1 month and have somehow been able to actually be a magnet to women. I will never stop reading this site. It's too valuable!!"

L.D., pinn.net, 8/28/97
"You are ushering in the new age. You have driven in a major nail in the coffin of this passing world."

A.G., aol.com, 8/28/97
"Absolutely, you should remain on the web! It may be the only hope left."

C.B., aol.com, 8/28/97
"There are those among your readers who can discern the sublime within your 'honesty'."

J.P., aol.com, 8/28/97
"I am pleased to find an organization dedicated to rationality and honesty."

L.K., erim.org, 8/28/97
"This is the true purpose of the Internet or world wide web, to finally provide a means by which tyranny can be broken. This is what the world has been waiting for."

M.C., dynasty.net, 8/28/97
"I think the web site is fantastic. I feel like I've entered another dimension."

N.S., mci.net, 8/27/97
"Neo-Tech has changed my life. I am a better person through it."

J.O., bendnet.com, 8/27/97
"After having read Zonpower manuscript 4 yrs ago my life went from drifter to capturing my own essence with the help of iron grip control. My fears have become exhilarated grasps of life. I manage many employees through D.T.C. and Neo-Tech."

S.P., total.net, 8/27/97
"In the year in which I have been surfing the web, I have never, and I mean never come across anything like this before. I must say that I am blown away by the presentation and huge content of this site."

A.M., att.net, 8/27/97
"Incredible. I can see in one reading that finally, someone understands the insanity and is ready to rise above it. I have searched and studied for years and all the time the answer was before me. We are all Zon!"

J.H., webtv.net, 8/26/97
"Vivid thinkers are the beacons of any advance. Congratulations!"

C.G., execpc.com, 8/26/97
"I think Neo-Tech has incredible, untapped potential! The sky is no longer the limit!"

Anon, execpc.com, 8/26/97
"Yes, please stay on the web for the sake of all that is right and human, keep fighting."

J.B., iadfw.net, 8/26/97
"It puts reason in an era without reason."

B.W., tinet.ie, 8/25/97, Ireland
"I think it's fantastic that someone has provided everything that someone needs to know."

B.T., teleport.com, 8/25/97
"EXISTENCE EXISTS... What a profound statement! When one lets that fact sink in, then out the window goes the God Concept and the Creation Concept which have been buzzing around in people's heads for centuries. Please don't ever leave the Internet. I would like to see more comments from readers and viewers of Neo-Tech with stories of their experiences."

H.B., aol.com, 8/25/97, United Kingdom
"The information which NT brings is essential for everyone and I am very grateful to everyone involved. NT has showed me the freedom, that we are entitled to it. I realize the advantages Neo-Tech offers. Nowadays I get so frustrated when I see so many people with their minds so full of mysticism, such a disease. But I learn to just stand back with the knowledge of the NT secret myself."

A. MacRae, aol.com, 8/24/97, Scotland
"After reading acres of flowery flim-flam on the NET, I'd just like to make the following comments and say that this Zon business is a real threat and will probably 'get the chop'. The reason is, it is robust, it is honest, it looks as though someone has been fishing in the right spot."

S.C., aol.com, 8/24/97
"Thank you, Dr. Wallace for changing my life."

J.W., net.id, 8/23/97, Indonesia
"Neo-Tech is incredible!"

T.M., wic.net, 8/22/97
"Neo-Tech has been the best thing to come into my life."

LSD, aol.com, 8/22/97
"This site needs to stay available, Definately!! No wonder there is so much poverty."

J.R., aol.com, 8/22/97
"The information that I have found on this Web-site thus far is tremendous! I have found, even though I have just begun integrating a few of its concepts, the information provides profound insight on how to move forward in all aspects of my life. This material should be published freely for all who have the insight to integrate it into their lives."

B.R., frognet.net, 8/21/97
"Neo-Tech is very valuable information that has added much to my happiness and well-being."

K.R., nothnbut.net, 8/21/97
"I think your page is very informative and is an asset to the world of knowledge. People need to understand things so that they will not be afraid of them. Keep up the good work."

M.V., aol.com, 8/21/97
"Neo-Tech is a wonderful thing, now that I've dropped the need for mysticism, I've quit drinking for good and have started to make a life for myself."

J.C., rutgers.edu, 8/21/97
"Neo-Tech is great paradigm shifting literature. Its vision of the real world is one of the most thought provoking I have read."

F.W., gov.au, 8/20/97, Australia
"Very interesting site. Valid points about society and the destructive way we are walking."

T.F., con2.com, 8/20/97
"This is the greatest site on the web. It will change and sustain every aspect of cyberspace and the world!"

S.F., mindspring.com, 8/20/97, Australia
"A fascinating site, bringing together in one place a wealth of facts and opinions that should be disseminated as widely as possible."

P.F., iadfw.net, 8/19/97
"This is an exciting new way of thinking that could unlock anyone's potential"

J.H., best.com, 8/18/97
"Fascinating. Herein lies the key information to vast resources of knowledge and power."

T.N., edu.au, 8/18/97, Australia
"How else will the world be changed? Everyone else has failed."

T.N., aol.com, 8/17/97, England
"I have to say that the information contained in your books has benefited me immensely, and the knowlege I have gleaned from them has purged me of, what were in retrospect, seriously harmful mystical tendencies."

D.F., swbell.net, 8/17/97
"I believe Neo-Tech is something new, refreshing, and truthful in the fullest extent. I can certainly understand why Neocheaters are doing everything in their power to ban this literature—it means the end to life as they now know it."

D.V., swbell.net, 8/16/97
"Wonderful information."

W.H., erols.com, 8/16/97
"Neo-Tech is a valuable life strategy for mankind. With the creation of cyberspace, it would be a crime to eliminate the greatest creation for man's future, NEOTECH."

D.D., erols.com, 8/16/97
"Please keep this site because it really keeps the common man in the light ,so to speak, of the propaganda of the so called 'media'. Please keep this page open at all cost!"

H.R., unicom.net, 8/16/97
"Having recently received the Neo-Tech manual and starting my study of its contents, I recoginize the powerful concepts that will change how mankind functions. Each day, as I go through the readings I get more and more excited. The information is presented in such an easy to follow format. Many thanks to Dr. Wallace."

J.M., iafrica.com, 8/16/97, Zimbabwe
"Very very exciting . You have got to stay on the Internet."

T.P., aol.com, 8/15/97
"Neo-Tech should stay on the web to further the lives of everyone and society as a whole. People need to be informed."

R.J., flash.net, 8/14/97
"Neo-Tech is everything you said it would be. I am very very very happy now. I am in love with Neo-Tech, cannot get enough. I am forever Grateful."

F.D., uu.net, 8/14/97
"Interesting stuff. You might also title your material 'Objectivism, a users guide'"

W.K., aol.com, 8/13/97, Africa
"Please, I and my people would like to see a Swahili publication in order for the masses of people who don't speak other foreign languages to become knowledgeable of this valuable information. After all, the more net value producers in this world means less net value destroyers there would be."

E.P., aol.com, 8/13/97, Australia
"Thank you for the Neo-Tech site. As I have recently started a new business, I am very interested in the business concepts shown on your site."

B.O., uu.net, 8/12/97
"The sections about the big money, job, and power thinking were fantastic."

H.D., aol.com, 8/12/97
"This is one of the best sites on the web. Don't you dare leave! This man is the hero of our time. If we could only spread this mind un-set through the air like un-pollution! I am ready to help! If I can do anything to remove the fly out of the ointment of humanity, let me know."

I.P., aol.com, 8/12/97, Indonesia
"Neo-Tech doesn't have anything to do with religion and that sounds good because it's universal and can be useful to anyone. But what I can be sure of is that Neo-Tech is a refreshing approach that's needed by anyone to live his or her life to the fullest and hopefully to help people to help others and make this world a better place for every being. We cannot afford to be uninformed about this very worthy knowledge."

C.J., alaska.net, 8/11/97
"I cannot believe that all of this information has escaped the general(ly anesthesized) Public for all these 2000 years. I know I am not the only person who has felt deep inside my heart of hearts that 'something' is wrong somewhere. And never before had this been more evident than in this country in this era of ever-increasing government intrusion into even an individual's ability to feed themselves. I would like to extend my personal thanks to the publishers, and also to Frank Wallace for bringing it all together for all to read. How did Dr. Wallace come to write such a phenomenal volume as the Neo-Tech manuscript? Please don't take this information off the web...it may be the only access some have to it."

M.B., compuserve.com, 8/10/97, United Kingdom
"I have been familiar with this knowledge of NT for over a year now. I agree that it is the most valuable information I could have ever come by. Please do carry on making NT available to lots of people. Only this can save us."

B.M., iol.ie, 8/10/97, Ireland
"I am interested in a great deal of your material. It

seems both radical and practical - a quality difficult to find."

G.G., qnet.com, 8/10/97
"YES! Neo-Tech will remain on the web. Neo-Tech can't be stopped, even if it were banned from the web. The Neo-Tech web site IS the most valuable web site in Cyberspace, and Dr. Frank Wallace is a genius."

ANON, net.mx, 8/9/97, Mexico
"Keep going! you are doing great! Can you do it faster?"

P.M., com.au, 8/8/97, Australia
"I think it is essential that N-T stays on the web. It is time to unplug the ugly waters of mysticism and free mankind from the sludge that we were in."

H.H., co.nz, 8/8/97, New Zealand
"The knowledge is unbelievably correct and has certainly created a clear rational mind for me. It will take time for people to clear their minds from irrationality to rational thought. But they will be the much richer for it. I am putting the word of Neo-Tech out for people to have a look at this information. All you guys are legends and I'm indebted for your tireless efforts in producing this valuable site and literature. Keep up the good work. Your Profound Honesty book received ten days ago is fantastic, and I am now into my second reading."

B.H., pcisys.net, 8/8/97
"Neo-Tech is definitely real! Neo-Tech makes you think and realize that we do live in a world full of liars, cheaters, hypocrites, thieves, and ignorance! Neo-Tech tells the logical and precise advantages to successfully taking control of your life without the headaches and heartbreaks of the neo-cheaters! We can all learn something better to improve one's future! Keep Neo-Tech alive and we will all live happier!"

E.S, cancom.net, 8/7/97, Canada
"Neo-Tech must stay on the web! Finally people will open their eyes to the corruption of politicians, lawyers and other dishonest humans."

K.C., valley-internet.net, 8/6/97
"Neo-Tech's philosophy succeeds brilliantly in applying Objectivist principles to daily life and work in the 'Get Rich By 2001' section. Its focus on

wide-scale integration and task structuring to concentrate on money-making purpose is brilliant."

L.H., sasol.com, 8/6/97, South Africa
"The only company in the world to save the individual from perishing under Neocheating governments!"

M.W., mich.net, 8/6/97
"This is a very neat web site and should be seen and judged by all."

C.R, school.za, 8/4/97, South Africa
"This site is an inspiration to all. Thank Zon that something as wonderful as Neo-Tech has been allowed to prosper."

D.H, aol.com, 8/3/97
"Suddenly everything is very clear."

R.K, uu.net, 8/3/97
"Why shouldn't your site stay on the Web? Any site that offers individuals an opportunity to take control of their lives should be promoted not oppressed!"

A.S., aol.com, 8/2/97
"Neo-Tech should definitely stay on the web. I am a completely different and extremely more productive person for it. This (new) knowledge I've gained is priceless."

J.W, newwave.net, 8/2/97
"You guys rock! Helped me a lot. Stay online!"

M.J, wwics.com, 8/2/97
"Thank you for expanding on Ayn Rand's ideas — especially the romantic-love idea. I am in a serious, monogamous relationship. We both want to love each other in a non-altruistic way. Some of your essays have been great tools."

K.C., valley-internet.net, 8/2/97
"The Neo-Tech site is thought-provoking, especially the sections on physics and the bicameral mind. As an Objectivist, the discussions of rational egoist ethics and laissez-faire capitalism were familiar ground, but I can see how they would shock the average collectivist or religionist."

S.K, ernet.in, 8/2/97, India
"I found Neo-Tech most progressive, scientific and

educative."

M.O, grolen.com, 8/1/97
"I cried when I read it. I will never feel guilty
again. I have regained the innocence that was taken
from me when, at age 5, I entered the local
'concentration campus for mind destruction.' Thank
you Neo-Tech for healing my mind. I am very
grateful."

A.M, jaring.my, 8/1/97, Malaysia
"Bravo!!! What a surprise."

B.R, aol.com, 7/30/97
"The truth is finally revealed. Neo-Tech and
Zonpower will wipe from existence all who wish to
destroy honesty."

D.B, aol.com, 7/30/97
"If honesty and effort are wrong, we live in a
strange world. Expand!!"

E.S, aol.com, 7/30/97
"I've been up for hours at night absorbing the
information on your web site....It's amazing!!!!! I
cried and laughed in excitement of what I've read."

K.L, bright.net, 7/29/97
"This is the most incredible document I've ever
read."

B.R., aol.com, 7/26/97
"I think Neo-Tech is the future of mankind."

M.V., mms.com, 7/25/97
"I believe Neo-Tech to be the world's most
important discovery and am grateful that there are
hard producing individuals willing to spread the
word and get rid of the disease called mysticism."

M.B., com.br, 7/25/97, Brazil
"It is a new awareness."

P.M., net.au, 7/25/97, Australia
"Neo-Tech offers many windows of opprtunities in
creativity and originality, it has worked for me and
it should work for anyone else. I am sick of
negativity in people and dead-psyche minds. It is
time these people were healed by Neo-Tech. Finally
let's continue to unplug the sludge of mysticism that
has soaked peoples minds for many years."

D.B., netcom.com, 7/23/97
"Neo-Tech confers unimaginable power to the
individual. Everyday I become more powerful using
this information. Mystics are now so easy to identify
and outcompete it's hardly believable."

R.R., netexp.net, 7/23/97
"Raised with some strict values and loads of guilt. I
have started on my journey out of the darkness ."

R.C., flash.net, 7/22/97, U.S.A.
"Neo-Tech should be on the sides of milk cartons
across the globe as the lost child of mankind's
survival-wise ancestors! It should be added to the
keys of all atlas and map makers by their own
conscience, to guide those who support their efforts
by purchasing their product(s)."

T.W., infi.net, 7/22/97
"I have been a fan of quantum physics for a long
time. The limited time i have been exposed to Neo-
Tech it has given me a new paradigm to non-linear
dynamics and mass to energy relationship. Only
linear thinking would fear this expansion of
thought."

L.B., net.au, 7/22/97, Australia
"Although I have read only a small fraction of the
information contained in this site, I feel a niggling
sense of relief from the debilitating fear and
confusion which has prevented me from achieving
anywhere near my true potential. As a mother of a
very young child I have been driving myself to
insanity wondering how I am going to help my child
achieve his potential, have love, health, happiness
and prosperity. Thank you for providing me with
another option, especially one which makes
absolutely, rational, logical sense."

D.L., yesic.com, 7/20/97, Canada
"Great Stuff! As a former alcoholic and drug addict,
I have used and continue to use many of the
concepts you so eloquently advocate, in order to
solidify the foundation of my recovery. I know that
by diligently applying the concepts herein, I will be
able to rapidly accelerate the process of achieving
my goals of financial freedom and total
empowerment."

M.A., aol.com, 7/20/97
"I've got to have this stuff...looks like the solutions
to my problems....and civilization's"

**J.W., byu.edu, 7/18/97**
"Your information is amazing. I'm a high school debater, this information is excellent."

**M.F., vir.com, 7/17/97, Canada**
"What you're publishing is very powerful. Disseminate your info discreetly via the Internet, but don't make yourselves become visible public targets for politicians. Cyberspace is blowing away all forms of government interference with the world, and I feel that it is only logical that you use it as a tool and an ally to promote your interests, and those of mankind as a whole."

**T.K., erie.net, 7/17/97**
"Should I be reading this in the closet? Its what I have believed all along, but were afraid to say. I had to read it over and over again. Neo-Tech will consume you because it is the truth that we already know."

**P.F., com.au, 7/17/97, Australia**
"Neo-Tech enables one to see the disintegrating activity of those mystics around him. Through that, one is able to protect himself consciously from the value destroyers which exist only to hinder the lives of the value producer."

**D.C., netcom.com, 7/15/97**
"You guys are the best. Terrific work. The Web Site is Phenomenal. Talk about being on the cutting edge! The Neo-Tech matrix is unstoppable."

**M.W., compuserve.com, 7/15/97, England**
"Please forward more information on how to raise children and young adults in this soon to be changed world. I want to thank Dr. Wallace because without his knowledge, I would be suffering trapped in a world without a way out. Thank You Thank You Thank You"

**R.K., netcom.com, 7/14/97**
"This site helps people understand the inner workings of one self and helps them move onto correcting the problem."

**A.P., aol.com, 7/14/97, Western Samoa**
"It will help to solve some of my problems."

**M.T., uu.net, 7/14/97**
"Expanding this web site would greatly help society. Thanks for exposing me to Neo-Tech, its knowledge is better than schools."

**B.N., pipex.com, 7/13/97, England**
"Neo-Tech is an eye opener for me. It seems that I have been waiting for it all my life. It is so fundamental. It's basis is so logical and reasonable."

**C.C., gd.cn, 7/13/97, China**
"It's simply one of the greatest web sites."

**E.E., aol.com, 7/11/97**
"I completely agree with you on the dishonesty and mystical thinking crap. I also like your readings on biological immortality because I think its completely possible. The only thing holding us back is the religions (mysticism) saying 'Its not right. We must die to go to heavens pearly gates'. Screw heavens pearly gates. I want to be immortal and completely free of mysticism to gain ultimate power and happiness the right way not the neocheat way. Thank you NEO-TECH. You better stay on the web. Your info really helps."

**S.K., webtv.net, 7/10/97**
"I am almost 21, thanks to Neo-Tech and the support of my father for Neo-Tech, everything about life is becoming crystal clear. Keep up the good work..."

**J.B., jpmorgan.com, 7/10/97, England**
"I have found this most useful reading."

**J.Y., hotmail.com, 7/9/97, Malaysia**
"I find that this homepage is very interesting, very powerful and convincing."

**D.D., compuserve.com, 7/8/97**
"Neo-Tech is the only chance we have......."

**D.H., hotmail.com, 7/8/97**
"By all means keep it on the web. For when the truth or the light is shining, people don't want to see it, they love to put it out. So by all means stay on the net."

**R.E., pty.com, 7/8/97, Rep. of Panama**
"After reading Neo-Tech, I am not afraid anymore. I am free of mysticism. I rely on myself and do not seek nor follow external authorities of any sort."

**M.K., dialsprint.net, 7/7/97**
"The Neo-Tech web site provides a fast and easy

way for me to share the information with others. I have turned on many people to the web site who have found the information to be extremely helpful in their lives. As time goes on, they will have the opportunity to learn more and more via the web site. They, in turn, have shared the information with others, as they suddenly wake-up to the fact that they are surrounded by mysticism and people who's lives are to a greater or lesser degree based on dishonesty, denial, and lack of self-responsibility."

P.B., thepla.net, 7/6/97, Australia
"I find it both enjoyable and interesting. I think that this site should be left open and tell all the neocheaters to make one more decision to get out in the real world, where the real power is!!"

G.C., dialsprint.net, 7/6/97
"Most fascinating site I have ever read."

R.P., nni.com, 7/4/97
"Zonpower controls all existence! Those humanoids who don't realize this will go on to live unhappy, pitiful, unfullfilling lives. Wake up society! Your in deep spell of mysticism which is currently making life hellish on Earth. Producing genuine values and love for people is what life is all about. We are not here to serve some mystical higher power. Neo-Tech is doing a great service and not only should stay on the web but expand their sites. Zonpower will win out and we can all live in a happy world!"

J.P., co.uk, 7/3/97, England
"I found your site very influencing, aiding me in all my decisions and allowing me to detect the menace of the neocheaters."

N.C., co.uk, 7/2/97, England, UK
"Insightful and wonderful, a truly unique web site unlike any other. Everyone should visit this site."

K.J. mmm.com, 7/2/97
"Reading the negative comments is an amazing reinforcement of NT ideas. The irrational arguments are blazing examples of the mystical fog that people live in. Thanks again for your benevolent information."

D.P., infinitytx.net, 7/1/97
"I now believe I have made what could be considered the discovery of a life time — Neo-Tech."

M.G., prodigy.com, 7/1/97
"Neo-Tech certainly is the way to go into the 21st. century. Innovative and reliable."

A.M., stratos.net, 7/1/97
"The truth *and* honesty on your site are refreshing."

M.B., virgin.net, 7/1/97, United Kingdom
"It has changed my life. Keep up the excellent work!"

G.W., uu.net, 6/30/97
"I first heard of Neo-Tech through Alan Grant's 'Anarky' comic (the reading list in back is a great idea). My first impression of the site was of the incredible amount of information it contained. My first day on I read through 'Zonpower from Cyberspace' and was very impressed. A first-class site all around."

H.R., uni-frankfurt.de, 6/29/97, Germany
"It is quite astonishing, a new world."

A.B., aha.ru, 6/29/97, Russia
"This is great, keep going"

A.C., att.net, 6/29/97
"Stay on the web? You bet! Go for it! Take over cyberspace."

D.D., psi.net, 6/28/97
"I am an avid reader, and I must say that the Neo-Tech/Zon information is the most integrated, realistic, powerful collection of literature and philosophy that I have ever encountered, or been exposed to. It totally shatters the misconceptions and outright, deliberate lies and B.S. that are, in many cases, purposely propagated by the 'powers that be.' It gives the average person a way to truly understand what is really taking place on planet Earth. The world seems to be in a deep freeze, and most people are fast asleep, having no idea of what is happening, and how the world is changing so rapidly. This web site is a great way to introduce people to the NT/Zon concepts. Most people will not ever hear about NT/Zon, but will still be affected by it. I think that eventually, a critical mass of people will start a cascade of rationality and production that will not be able to be ignored by the backwards anti-civilization inhabitants, and then, the anticivilization will be left behind forever. I would

like to thank everyone at the NT/Zon center for their work and dedication to the eradication of mysticism and neo-cheating. "

M.G., compuserve.com, 6/28/97,
United Kingdom
"Thought provoking Web-site, provides the mind with ideas that will change the essence of the current world ideology.!!"

P.P., jaring.my, 6/28/97, Malaysia
"I am using Neo-Tech every day in every way. Thank you for keeping this knowledge alive and please continue making it accessible to as many people as possible."

P.R., ituh.com, 6/28/97, United Kingdom
"Your ideas are extremely valuable and liberating. Please continue with your campaign to vanish the parasites and scum who leech off the honesty and effort of business-oriented people."

P.C., aol.com, 6/27/97, Germany
"It's really fascinating to me."

B.H., pobox.com, 6/27/97
"I am astounded as to how weird some of the writings seem but how much I realize that I actually agree with everything I'm reading. My mind is in a tizzy at this point and I'm anxious to hear/read much more."

M.H., huntleigh.net, 6/27/97
"Awe-inspiring"

N.T., usa.net, 6/27/97
"I have prospered by integrating and using this knowledge. I have seen the predictions of a neothink mind unfold and see the coming of the new age rapidly approaching."

M.C., dialsprint.net, 6/26/97
"Mysticism is truly useless. Let us all pursue its extinction immediately! Neo-Tech flows through my mind unblocked by mysticism! I am Zonpower. My children will be Zonpower. My business is Zonpower. My new international business hyperstructure will deliver Zonpower into the hands of 100 million individuals. The end of the irrational/mystical is here!"

J.W., hotmail.com, 6/26/97, U.S.A.
"As I read, I can feel myself gaining in power and strength. I am hungry for more."

J.S., megabaud.fi, 6/26/97, Finland
"All I can say is WOW! So motivational, I know that this will be one of my primary sites in the future, I will visit you often."

J.W., swbell.net, 6/25/97
"YOUR INFO IS POWER. KEEP IT UP! Love to read the stuff you have on your site. IT'S ADDING TO MY MIND AND MAKING ME RICHER!"

S.N., hotmail.com, 6/25/97, U.S.
"Free Your mind through Neo-Tech, and your soul shall follow. Unleash your unrealized powers with Neo-Tech. I love the values put forth through Neo-Tech."

C.G., compuserve.com, 6/25/97, Germany
"I love Neo-Tech material. Great stuff."

H.N., co.nz, 6/25/97, New Zealand
"Go Neo-Tech. Free Dr. Frank Wallace from the criminally insane parasitical elite so he can continue his incredible work. All value producing individuals and Neo-Tech readers must support Dr. Wallace in order to collapse mysticism and to enhance freedom and prosperity for all value producing individuals."

D.B., aol.com, 6/25/97, US
"Neo-Tech is valuable information that can help people transform their lives. Over the past two years I have scrutinized the information contained in the Neo-Tech Zonpower package. It has supreme value to those that apply it to their lives."

Z.M., jaring.my, 6/25/97, Malaysia
"It is just the best philosophical ideas I ever came across."

E.S., co.za, 6/24/97, South Africa
"I read through chapter 1-5 of Zonpower last night and was surprised and amazed by the information I found there. Finally something that makes me think."

T.L., aol.com, 6/24/97
"I would like to thank every one who helped bring out Neo-Tech. In a metaphorical sense, it has turned me right-side-up in an up-side-down world. Without

it I would be terribly confused about everything but with it, I have much WORTH IN MY SELF and a very controlled sense of direction and lots of self-esteem. Thanks! Oh yah, I'm only 23 years old."

J.S., gmeds.com, 6/24/97
"'Fascinating!!!' as Spock would say. I feel like I found a gold mine. I look forward to reading more to find out who put all this wisdom together. I love the vocabulary and perspective on this web page."

J.Q., co.uk, 6/24/97, United Kingdom
"The best and most valuable information I have ever read. Frank Wallace and Mark Hamilton and Eric Savage are worthy of a Nobel prize at least."

J.Q., co.uk, 6/24/97, United Kingdom
"It is an eye opener and the most valuable data I have ever seen."

J.C., uu.net, 6/24/97
"Thanks for what I estimate to be the world's most intelligent web site. There could be no more important and valuable site on the web. Thanks for assisting me in changing the world...NT forever."

V.C., edu.au, 6/24/97, Uganda
"Very well created. Keep up the good work!"

C.W., gf-net.com, 6/23/97, Monaco
"I am very enthusiastic about what you guys are trying to achieve. I would like to complement you on an excellent Web Site and your efforts to bring about the Prosperity Revolution."

S.P., jaring.my, 6/23/97, Malaysia
"Giving hope to life, and living life to our fullest potential. This is what I think describes Neo-Tech best. For there is no LIFE without hope, just mere existence."

K.P., aol.com, 6/23/97, US
"I have been reading and gradually integrating with Neo-Tech concepts since May 1993. Neo-Tech was THE pivotal point in my life. No longer could I look to some undefined, even unknowable heaven as my sole point of light to focus on in the vast darkness; now, I know fully that a.) my life is MY responsibility alone, b.) only I can decide to enter and prosper from or avoid and be out competed by the Neo-Tech World, and c.) the Neo-Tech World is worth holding out for.

My thanks to all Neo-Tech employees who unswervingly seek to bring Neo-Tech literature to the whole of the human race, but most especially to Dr. Frank Wallace and Mark Hamilton for originating the basic Neo-Tech ideas and making them accessible to all who seek such knowledge. I am currently working on what I consider to be a Neo-Tech album and look forward to the time when I will be able to work side by side with all of you in the battle to end mysticism and bring about the Civilization of the Universe on this planet."

R.J., co.es., 6/23/97, Spain
"The search engine is a marvelous way of looking up the vast amount of material published."

C.A., compuserve.com, 6/23/97, United Kingdom
"This is one of the most powerful sites that I have come across on the web, excellent"

S.Z., co.uk, 6/23/97, United Kingdom
"I was first introduced to Neo-Tech in 1989 -- since which I have held the philosophy with the deepest respect. Not one to take anything for face value, placing the concepts into action has produced a degree in mechanical engineering, straight into business in 1992, successfully sold out in 1996, and now committed to a direct-mail computer software business turning over UK£700,000 per year. I possess a powerful skill to test new boundaries and the business hence grows at accelerating speed while focus on the means allow the ends to take care of themselves. I feel so intensely for people who go through life not realizing their potential, indeed the accurate perception of the new civilization which will come, as sure as the sun will rise tomorrow. Everything in my life revolves around a central core of strength that is Neo-Tech. Thank you sincerely."

J.T., net.ve, 6/23/97, Venezuela
"Neo-Tech is invaluable."

G.S., att.net, 6/23/97
"You have some important insights that the mystic-minded people need to get well. "

P.C., auburn.edu, 6/23/97
"Don't you dare pull this site off the web. It's great. Keep up the good work and don't allow the statists and envy peddlers to intimidate you."

G.P., hotmail.com, 6/22/97
"It is my hope that the whole world eventually gets a chance to read the wisdom contained within these documents. Transformation of the entire consciousness structure would result and the world would irrevocably be uplifted from its dark and dismal plight."

D.T., np.com, 6/22/97, Nepal
"Neo-Tech is the right thing for people to live totally free. Neo-Tech will pervade over all in the next century."

J.B., du.edu, 6/21/97
"I believe it does an excellent job of exposing the deeply rooted problems of our civilization. I was extremely pleased to find you on the Web."

O.H., earthling.net, 6/21/97, Netherlands
"Very informative site."

M.P.L., wwwonline-ny.com, 6/21/97
"I read about this site in Alan Grant's recent comic book 'Anarky'"

P.L., or.jp, 6/20/97, Japan
"Your site is beautifully interesting and contains power-packed knowledge."

S.L., com.au, 6/20/97, Australia
"Very professionally done web site with indexes which makes it user-friendly."

D.S., bellsouth.net, 6/18/97
"I think this is very powerful material that should be learned in school"

L.H., aol.com, 6/18/97, Germany
"I've read Neo-Tech, there is no other way of thinking and living for me."

M.M., cam.org, 6/18/97
"You provide infinite values for ALL in the world who want to listen and apply the keys to freedom and happiness. Thank you for reviving and catalyzing my productivity, self-protection and passion."

L.H., aol.com, 6/18/97, Germany
"I've read Neo-Tech. There is no other way of thinking and living for me."

T.F., sympatico.ca, 6/17/97, Canada
"Your web site is a killer. My life is getting better."

M.L., mindpspring.com, 6/17/97
"This site is a wondrous abode of the finest facts that are necessary for living on Earth. Without this site, I would have spent much of my life attempting to discover reality."

M.S., samoatelco.com, 6/16/97
"Very interesting and thought-provoking."

Z.D., ac.uk, 6/16/97, England
"I think your site is a great asset to the Internet."

D.C., direcpc.net, 6/16/96, Canada
"The site is good. Very important to human kind."

M.L., mindspring.com, 6/16/97
"Neo-Tech seems to be the realization and result of ultimate truth i.e. justice. Leaving Neo-Tech on the web will allow more people to find the truth instead of spending their entire life in search of it."

R.E., aol.com, 6/16/97
"You offer the self to anyone who will listen and use their mind."

J.B., charleston.net, 6/15/97
"Neo-Tech is the first step in the direction to create a totally free world society."

D.T., com.np, 6/15/97, Nepal
"Neo-Tech is preparing me for the 21st century, with factual information that is really helping me."

R.S., netrevu.com, 6/15/97
"Outstanding! Finally, a no-holds-barred guide to practical living."

T.R., ccse.net, 6/14/97
"An interesting web site -- lots of information"

C.I., blackpool.net, 6/14/97, United Kingdom
"The Neo-Tech site IS by far the most valuable site on the web."

S.H., aol.com, 6/14/97
"NT has really helped me understand who I am. Now I am better able to control my life, to live happily and successfully! Thanks NT, I was lost, but now I'm found."

D.E., aol.com, 6/13/97
"I am in constant pursuit of self-development and financial improvement. Neo-Tech is very informative and enlightening, refreshing and direct."

Shannon S., metnet.edu, 6/13/97
"This site is a great help to people."

N.G., co.uk, 6/13/97, United Kingdom
"The only way for the survival of human kind."

J.V., millkern.com, 6/13/97
"Thank you for Neo-Tech, my life has changed drastically."

Lynn A., netcom.ca, 6/12/97, Canada
"This is powerful stuff, the stuff dreams are made of. Imagine the opportunities for those who embrace change and not fear it. This really is the new frontier for those with the vision to see it."

Z.S., ac.uk, 6/12/97, England
"I have been searching the Web for months, looking for a site that gives useful, important information. I think your site is great."

D.P., att.net, 6/12/97
"Neo-Tech has helped me think much clearer and I am doing much better in my business."

U.L., co.cr, 6/12/97, Costa Rica
"Power to the Value Producers!!"

J.G., aol.com, 6/12/97
"I know that I want to live for 100 or 200 years and only the philosophies of Neo-Tech will power societies and encourage economic values to a point where we will be able to survive that long. Mysticism brings down advancement by stopping people from doing things that seem 'godlike' (i.e. cloning)."

J.Y., bigfoot.com, 6/11/97, Philippines
"Neo-Tech helps people in their daily struggle for survival. More power and long live Neo-Tech! "

C.B., aol.com, 6/11/97
"I am enthralled, enamored by this wondrous/awesome system of knowledge."

J.E., netcom.com, 6/10/97
"The views expressed in Neo-Tech are both

interesting and bold. Neo-Tech could definitely be the radical step needed to project our society to the next level."

K.T., parksandhistory.org, 6/10/97
"Your web site is clearly the best value I've encountered. Your thinking is bold and revolutionary."

J.L., com.sg, 6/10/97, Singapore
"Well done! The articles in your web site are extremely practical, catering to the needs of many."

R.O., aol.com, 6/9/97
"Neo-Tech will be my 'guide' back to the singleness of purpose I once had. Only now, I know I am not alone, a 'voice in the wilderness'."

J.R., compuserve.com, 6/9/97, Mexico
"I find Neo-Tech amazing and interesting."

J.D., net.au, 6/9/97, Australia
"Knowledge of the caliber that you disseminate should be spread by all possible means. Although not everyone is ready for its vast implications, everyone needs it desperately. Stay on the net at all costs."

C.D., aol.com, 6/9/97
"The Web Site is very impressive. I like how easy it is to obtain the information. I have visited this site four times now and each time I find some very, very interesting points."

G.A., sprynet.com, 6/8/97
"I was looking for a great page like this one for long time."

G.U., juno.com, 6/8/97
"All of the information on this site has had, and will continue to have, a profound impact on my life, and the lives of those people in society that I come in contact with."

S.S., net.id, 6/8/97, Indonesia
"It is a nice and helpful web site."

Aainaa R., thepentagon.com, 6/8/97, Malaysia
"I must commend on a simple yet very effective mode of communication. Bravo!"

L.H., netscape.com, 6/7/97
"Very readable and understandable, I have learned a

lot from it."

**G.S., ac.uk, 6/7/97, United Kingdom**
"This web site is an invaluable source of information to any person wishing to lead a happy, successful life."

**A.D., net.au, 6/7/97, Australia**
"Neo-Tech really made me think. I have taken some remarkable steps and made a lot of mistakes, but I learned a lot. Now, I travel the world, expand my awareness, and make a good living."

**S.M., hotmail.com, 6/7/97, South Africa**
"Very interesting information, keep it up."

**M.G., co.za, 6/7/97, South Africa**
"I like the thorough indexing."

**S.O., sprynet.com, 6/6/97**
"The information is refreshing and very useful. This site is now my favorite and will be visited frequently."

**Carlie.G., nsula.edu, 6/6/97**
"By finding this site, I have found a new insight to a lot of different subjects."

**J.M., hotmail.com, 6/6/97**
"I am extremely glad I came across this information. I will apply it to my life."

**K.J., mmm.com, 6/6/97**
"Thanks again for your awesome information and exalted quest."

**S.J., net.tr, 6/6/97, Turkey**
"I just began reading your site a few days ago. Even in this short period it has added happiness to my life."

**L.L., aol.com, 6/6/97**
"The short time I spent at this site has really given me a new insight."

**R.S., uu.net, 6/5/97**
"What I have read is truly powerful. More people need to be exposed to these ideas."

**Lindy H., istar.ca, 6/5/97, Canada**
"Excellent site, if only every person with access to a computer could be able to explore it. So much truth

is portrayed here. I will endeavor to steer as many people as possible to this site."

**I.V., oz.au, 6/5/97, Australia**
"The ideas and topics you raised are quite fascinating."

**D.A., aol.com, 6/5/97**
"This is the Greatest Site on the Web because it provides the vision of Hope and light. The ONLY elegant solution to all human problems!"

**J.A., wright.edu, 6/4/97**
"I found this web site very interesting and informative. I have already told my friends to read this web site."

**K.A., nucleus.com, 6/4/97**
"If the gov't is trying to censor this literature, then it must be good."

**Z.Z., hotmail.com, 6/4/97, People's Republic of China**
"It's exciting to read."

**Marilyn O., net.au, 6/4/97, Australia**
"Neo-Tech is a fantastic concept and I fully support it. I can't stop reading it. "

**J.M., onramp.net, 6/4/97**
"Your site can help thousands. It is well prepared and easy to receive. Thank You."

**J.K., nauticom.net, 6/3/97**
"If these ideas are put into practice, success is guaranteed. I urge everyone to read this with an open mind."

**P.W., juno.com, 6/3/97**
"I believe that you are doing important work on this web site and I applaud your efforts. Finally someone has something rational to say and a real solution to so many problems in this country and world-wide."

**R.D., solarlabs.com, 6/3/97**
"I know your site will help me accomplish my business and life goals."

**T.A., hotmail.com, 6/3/97**
"I must thank you for the knowledge I have received on this web site and I shall spread the

word to others about this wonderful web site. "

Milly C., geocities.com, 6/2/97
"Very interesting. I hope you get it out to a lot of people. The more I read the more I think, and the more I think, the more I realize how wrong I might be about a lot of things."

ANON, nv.us, 6/2/97
"Neo-Tech is the most concise depiction of reality ever."

W.L., nv.us, 6/2/97
"This college student loves Neo-Tech. My college classmates want Neo-Tech."

ANON, nv.us, 6/2/97
"A fascinating site. It expands your mind and helps form new ways of thinking."

M.H., stratos.net, 6/2/97
"This web site contains powerful ideas."

B.L., on.ca, 6/2/97, Canada
"Without Neo-Tech, who will demystify people? Seems to me that the Net is THE WAY to spread Neo-Tech info."

P.H., com.au, 6/2/97, Australia
"What a brilliant idea the Internet is! It has become the perfect distributor for worldwide Neo-Tech knowledge. Producers of values may unite from anywhere to everywhere on our earth. LOVE IT!!!"

D.C., msn.com, 6/1/97
"Neo-Tech is needed for the maintenance of a free world for everyone."

C.B., netcom.com, 6/1/97
"I can only believe that sites such as yours will pave the way for the development of a new world that is not so filled with ignorance and hidden agendas."

S.K., hardin.com, 6/1/97
"I'm going to use Neo-Tech. Imagine, using honesty to solve all your problems."

ANON, nv.us, 5/31/97
"Neo-Tech is the only true serum that eliminates cerebral stagnation. Its power releases the individual to think happily and to create value for all."

P.R., hotmail.com, 5/31/97
"I love Zon."

I.C., net.pk, 5/31/97, Pakistan
"I'm very very impressed by ZON POWER and NEO-TECH."

J.H., webtv.net, 5/31/97
"Your site is very exciting and well put together."

R.M., cyber-wizard.com, 5/30/97
"I am relieved to have discovered it. Clearly, someone is thinking out there."

R.B., idt.net, 5/30/97
"Neo-Tech is the highest truth anywhere on this planet or any other planet in Space. Thank you, Thank you and Thank You."

J.S., nv.us, 5/29/97
"This information is immeasurable."

B.M., aol.com, 5/29/97
"I WAS VERY IMPRESSED WITH YOUR SITE, IT IS INFORMATIVE AND EASY TO USE. I JUST FINISHED READING ABOUT THE NEO-TECH DIET. I FOUND IT TO BE VERY WELL THOUGHT OUT. I SHALL GIVE IT A TRY. GOOD WORK."

Annette.D., octonline.com, 5/29/97
"Since I found you, my mind has opened up so much I can't consume enough knowledge. I feel like I've stepped into a new world. I've acquired more life knowing amazing human beings like you. I've always wondered where all the remarkable people were."

A.G., com.au, 5/29/97, Australia
"What a fantastic site. I have set it up as my web start page and cannot stop reading."

K.M., nv.us, 5/28/97
"This is the first time I've ever seen anything like this. It is fantastic. This info is the truth."

S.C., awwwsome.com, 5/28/97
"Mind-opening reading experience. Anyone who believes in freedom and individual responsibility will enjoy such insight and wisdom shared freely via the web."

D.D., icdc.com, 5/27/97
"This is a truly informative site. It contains true content. I believe it will enlighten many people. It should remain so it may serve its purpose."

L.M., juno.cpm, 5/27/97
"The information found on your web site is vital to anyone looking to start his/her own business."

S.E., ac.uk, 5/27/97, England
"Learning about Neo-Tech is becoming a really eye opening experience and is helping me to think in new ways. Your material has helped me to dispel all the ingrained negative knowledge I have been taught. I can now get on with my life as a happy, productive individual. Thank you very very much for opening my eyes, keep up the Excellent work."

N.E., co.uk, 5/27/97, United Kingdom
"This is a fantastic site!"

S.M., hotmail.com, 5/27/97, South Africa
"Excellent and interesting information that can change ones life completely."

J.G., aol.com, 5/26/97
"I think this site is really informative and a great source of knowledge."

Anna M., aol.com, 5/26/97
"This is so sensible to me. I tell all my friends to look at this site. This is the beginning of my exciting mind travel. Yes, I am truly excited about this plan."

S.B., aol.com, 5/26/97
"Awesome simply awesome."

H.L., sequel.net, 5/26/97, Philippines
"It is cool and usable."

B.M., nucleus.com, 5/26/97, Canada
"Overwhelmingly sensible."

D.D., hotmail.com, 5/25/97
"This is the most incredible thing I know about. Neo-Tech blew me away. I always new that somewhere in honesty was POWER...."

E.A., netcom.ca, 5/25/97, Canada
"This web site is needed to help all people receive a chance at changing their lives. Without Neo-Tech

we are all just empty beings. But with it, we can bring down all neocheaters and are masters of our own lives for a change. This web page has to stay because it will continue to grow and teach people the truth. It has to stay for the sake of all human beings who want something more out of life!"

E.A., netcom.ca, 5/25/97, Canada
"Your web page is incredible."

V.P., earthcorp.com, 5/25/97, United Kingdom
"Extremely interesting and thought provoking."

Joyce G., mozcom.com, 5/25/97, Philippines
"Thank you and more power to you!"

S.P., co.my, 5/24/97, Malaysia
"I think Neo-Tech could prove to be the Answer for living our true potentials and our dreams. I am awed by the limitless possibilities available with Neo-Tech. By all means, please remain on the web for the betterment of mankind!"

J.C., wic.net, 5/24/97
"Neo-Tech is the best. This is the moment of truth for our planet. Thank you."

K.G., virgin.net, 5/23/97, United Kingdom
"Good stuff! About time someone put the world to rights."

G.F., memmart.com, 5/23/97, United Kingdom
"If Leonard Peikoff's Objectivism: The Philosophy of Ayn Rand is 'Reality Unfolded', Neo-Tech is the ultimate 'set of guidelines' for living without/ dispensing with the need for guides."

A.M., com.au, 5/23/97, Australia
"Thank you for helping to free me from mystical thinking. I have only begun to experience the freedom of living. I realize now my potential is unbounding. Peace, love and eternal happiness to the free world!"

B.S., nv.us, 5/22/97
"Absolutely the most amazing thing that humans have thought of. I am ready for the Civilization of the Universe right now!!!!!"

S.W., co.uk, 5/22/97, England
"I have found the Neo-Tech advantages very helpful."

Joyce K., stlnet.com, 5/22/97
"Very exciting and totally sensible in an age that often seems the opposite. I definitely want to see more. Here is to a brave new world!"

D.S., gmu.edu, 5/21/97
"This is my favorite web site. Tons of interesting and insightful information."

P.S., net.au, 5/21/97, Australia
"Neo-Tech on the Net is the best thing yet."

P.N., aol.com, 5/21/97
"I've begun removing my own personal mysticism with the intent of becoming a competitive, honest, happy, value-producing Citizen of the Universe. I wish to thank everyone at Neo-Tech for their courage, perseverance, integrity and effort to break the chains of professional Neocheaters and Mysticism everywhere."

J.R., nv.us, 5/21/97
"I really like the articles on atheism, new-testament interpretations, and capitalism. Thank you and you have a very wonderful web site here."

E.G., mcione.com, 5/21/97
"I have greatly benefited from them Neo-Tech, especially in times of business and financial decisions. It is easy to access and readily obtain the desired guidance and help through the search engines or the various topic headings. Keep up the good work and make the world a better and more prosperous place for everyone."

T.C., aros.net, 5/20/97
"Neo-Tech has helped me build a vast puzzle in my mind. The final pieces are falling into place, just as predicted. I am Neo-Thinking. I am a Self-Leader. There needs no further explanation. Thank You to Frank R. Wallace, Mark Hamilton, and everyone else working behind the scenes to create the future we deserve!"

R.J., aol.com, 5/20/97
"Neo-Tech is what I've been looking for all my life. I'm hungry for more. Thank you."

J.M., acadiau.ca, 5/20/97, Canada
"This site has really made me think about who I am and why I am here. There is so much to learn about our way of life, and after reading most of the information here, I think that I will now look at everything I do in a whole new perspective."

E.B., aol.com, 5/20/97
"I have enjoyed the stimulation of the NEO-TECH influence in my life. Your web site gave me a shot in the brain when I needed it."

P.L., hotmail.com, 5/20/97
"This web site has a lot to offer. People need to see it. Keep up the good work!"

A.O., chilesat.net, 5/19/97, Chile
"This site is very interesting."

D.D., aol.com, 5/19/97
"NEO-TECH IS THE MOST STRAIGHT FORWARD AND TO THE HEART OF MATTERS MATERIAL I HAVE READ. IT PERTAINS TO GENUINE LIFE AND WELL BEING ISSUES."

E.F., aol.com, 5/19/97
"I feel that the Neo-Tech web site is a fundamental necessity in that it provides a library of wealth and knowledge that could not be accessed by mystic government libraries that don't care to express all points of view. In my humble opinion this web site will change the way people see their lives and ultimately save the world."

A.R., frontiernet.net, 5/18/97
"I never thought of our society as an anticivilization until tonight. To be honest, of all the Web sites I have visited, yours has been the most interesting an informative."

S.S., mci.net, 5/18/97
"Very informative and enlightening! A different way to look at the world today and to help alleviate boredom and stagnation which are epidemic."

P.J., aol.com, 5/18/97
"I think your ideas are revolutionary. Very insightful."

C.E., infi.net, 5/18/97
"It is wonderful to see Neo-Tech on the Web where it can be accessible to so many people. Keep it up."

B.G., or.jp, 5/18/97
"Very impressive! Glad to see someone thinking."

R.V., aol.com, 5/17/97
"I AM VERY GLAD NEO-TECH IS ON THE INTERNET. IT IS A WAY OF LETTING OTHERS KNOW OF THIS VERY POWERFUL KNOWLEDGE."

G.R., juno.com, 5/17/97
"As a long time Objectivist and Libertarian, I'm naturally in favor of anything and anyone that promotes rationality and true freedom."

K.V., votrex.is, 5/17/97, Iceland
"It is really interesting and there are a lot of topics where one can take exciting information."

L.T., wj.com, 5/16/97
"I find this web-site highly informative and of great insight into the human condition. I would recommend it to anyone interested in advancing their evolution."

J.E., aol.com, 5/16/97
"This is some of the most interesting concepts I have seen in years. I am ready to learn more."

J.H., nv.us, 5/16/97
"I BELIEVE THAT THE WORLD WOULD BE A BETTER, MORE CONTENT PLACE TO LIVE IF EVERYBODY WOULD ABIDE BY THIS HONESTY."

ANON, aol.com, 5/16/97
"Thanks Neo-Tech, for bringing light back into the world."

R.B., aol.com, 5/16/97
"Extremely intriguing. Thank you for being here for those of us who seem to be lost in the world."

E.M., oio.net, 5/15/97
"I found you site to be very informative, and in a very here-and-now way, quite easy to follow."

W.D., aol.com, 5/15/97
"I enjoy your site. Neo-Tech has made profound changes in my life. I continue to grow and expand as I read and re-read the material."

A.R., wired2.com, 5/15/97
"This information is a must for anyone who wants to control his/her destiny."

J.J., lullitec.com, 5/15/97, Peru
"Muchas gracias."

D.A., nv.us, 5/14/97
"Extremely informative and uplifting...an optimistic prognostication on world issues and economics!"

A.R., frontiernet.net, 5/13/97
"I cannot believe the contrast between what you are saying and what the liberal media would have us believe. I am really impressed by your Web site."

R.S., online.no, 5/13/97, Norway
"Really cool...interesting"

M.C., smyth.net, 5/13/97
"It is my feeling that there is no other truly honest, logical distillation of life applicable philosophy being espoused."

S.A., warnerbros.com, 5/13/97
"You're giving us a hope, a hope for better living in a better society."

K.R., lotus.com, 5/13/97
"This is a revolutionary and very, very important concept."

C.G., spacestar.com, 5/13/97
"Neo-Tech allows the 'average' person to succeed, where before they fail. It releases a lot of garbage from the mind."

M.F., com.au, 5/13/97, Australia
"I think this site is mind boggling! Keep it up Please!"

K.T., bellsouth.net, 5/13/97
"I have received more valuable knowledge from Neo-Tech than my previous twenty years of schooling. I now have the most incredible romantic-love relationship with the woman of my dreams. I have left a mystical profession and now am starting my own business. The web site is the most valuable web site on the Internet. Thank You Neo-Tech!"

J.S., aol.com, 5/12/97
"Your site has changed the way I think about life! Nothing is impossible with Neo-Tech!"

L.V., oz.au, 5/12/97, Australia
"This information is too powerful to remain on the

Web!!!!"

**P.M., hotmail.com, 5/12/97, Australia**
"Neo-Tech is a new state of thinking that strips and shreds mystical stupidity."

**C.W., com.sg, 5/11/97, Singapore**
"Zonpower confirms and puts into words what we all feel. We are all helpless puppets caught in this vicious circle with no way out. Zon is the answer!"

**K.M., caribsurf.com, 5/11/97, Barbados**
"This is nothing short of FANTASTIC. I feel as if I have found a TREASURE."

**P.M., usa.net, 5/11/97**
"Thanks for each and every word of wisdom that you've shared with us."

**R.M., flinet.com, 5/11/97**
"Your material is about the best reading on the Web. Very interesting."

**M.G., intel.com, 5/11/97, Philippines**
"The web page is very informative and triggers the mind!"

**E.C., co.ch, 5/10/97, Chile**
"You have awakened my curiosity and I would like to know more about Neo-Tech."

**M.R., aol.com, 5/10/97**
"Ban Neo-Tech? This idea could only come from an unevolved and ignorant mind. Not only is that NOT possible, but, who in their right mind would want to after reading this wonderful literature? Only the corrupt and the unevolved, and for very obvious reasons! Keep up the good work  --  mysticism is finished!!"

**G.G., msn.com, 5/10/97**
"Excellent site! I have finally started to integrate on a wide scale thanks to Neo-Tech. It's hard work and I love it! I am growing more powerful every day. I know that nothing can stop me now. You are right, the battle between good and evil has begun. It had to begin and there is no stopping it. Listen up everybody in cyberspace, you are a critical part of this battle. The time has come to ostracize the value destroyers from existence. Thank you Frank Wallace. You are one of the few heroes."

**R.E., pty.com, 5/9/97, Republic of Panama**
"Your material is great."

**A.W., aol.com, 5/9/97**
"Information is of huge value. None should be lost, destroyed, or otherwise censored."

**B.M., hotmail.com, 5/9/97**
"Very Important! Contains the information for independent thinkers who are looking for opportunity, to self-actualize and claim their power!"

**N.A., globalpac.com, 5/9/97**
"The insights and the clarity in which they are presented are magnificent. No one should be denied to evolve..."

**N.A., globalpac.com, 5/8/97**
"Amazingly accurate and informative."

**J.P., nv.us, 5/8/97**
"I can see the potential for the Neo-Tech mind to truly aid those who develop and use it. The entire theory of Neo-Tech is quite interesting, and perhaps I can use it to finally take control of my life."

**A.N., utdallas.edu, 5/8/97**
"This is a great web site. New information that helps others discover success in love, money, and power."

**Z.G., cwru.edu, 5/8/97**
"This is the best web sit I have EVER seen. It has practical applications that anyone can apply to improve their life!"

**R.A., lotus.com, 5/8/97**
"I think the Neo-Tech info on mini-days is great!"

**P.B., aol.com, 5/8/97**
"Thank you for printing TRUTH. I know that I have a long way to go but I am on my rightful path to being 'ZON'."

**N.A., monmouth.com, 5/7/97**
"The neocheating information is VERY useful and interesting."

**D.D., umass.edu, 5/7/97**
"I read your web site for hours. This is great info. It's time we did something for humanity!!!!!!"

S.B., nv.us, 5/7/97

"As to voting for Neo-Tech to stay online. Should we vote to eliminate the zero and go back to Roman numerals? Do we want to return to blood letting and leeches to treat our ill and infirm? Do we reinstate slavery in order to increase our work force? Sure let our anti-civilization suck us all into oblivion. That's what I need for my life. 'Cause I ain't been unhappy enough'. Mysticism Collapse!"

N.S., co.ma, 5/7/97, Malaysia

"This material is shocking but extremely powerful. Finally, the individual is free and powerful!"

D.V., voicenet.com, 5/6/97

"I just spent 2 hours in your site. I am captivated by how much sense this makes."

J.G., nv.us, 5/6/97

"Brilliant. Well written. You guys have helped me solve some of my personal problems and I thank you dearly for it. I offer any assistance that you may ever need."

T.Z., att.com, 5/6/97

"I'm absorbing everything I can from your web pages. Thank You."

A.K., co.jp, 5/6/97, Japan

"I am really very desperate to know about Neo-Tech."

M.R., hotmail.com, 5/6/97, Belgium

"Very good, important, interesting, and helpful."

D.W., hotmail.com, 5/6/97

"Neo-Tech is the New Way."

Z.Z., co.ma, 5/6/97, Malaysia

"Arise everyone and let's do what we have to do. And do it honestly. The Civilization of the Universe is already here! The web is here to stay. You have my total support."

G.P., nv.us, 5/5/97

"I see Neo-Tech as a way to live better."

A.B., webtv.net, 5/5/97

"I believe this to be TRUTH -- HONESTLY!!!!!!!"

K.R., lotus.com, 5/5/97

"If everyone was aware of the Neo-Tech information, this would be a healthier, more positive, and prosperous society for all of us."

K.M., hotmail.com, 5/5/97, Canada

"Neo-Tech is very well written, and has a lot of useful information."

J.S., nv.us, 5/5/97

"I was overwhelmed in shock and disbelief. Neo-Tech has answered my questions about life."

T.D., aol.com, 5/4/97

"No other information source has made such a profound and vertically rising difference in my life. I would heartily recommend this to anyone and everyone."

I.S., hotmail.com, 5/4/97

"It's brilliant, magnificent!"

L.L., com.au, 5/4/97, Australia

"Great work. Really a lot of people should read the information on your site."

J.S., nv.us, 5/4/97

"SINCE MY FIRST READING, YOUR SITE HAS INFLUENCED ME TO PUSH MYSELF FARTHER IN EVERY AREA OF LIFE."

A.M., webtv.com, 5/3/97

"I would just like to thank Neo-Tech for helping me get started on my Neo journey of life."

K.H., net.my, 5/2/97, Malaysia

"The best web site. Great Service to Mankind. Keep Up The Great Work."

R.O., psouth.net, 5/2/97

"Your information is a great value to many people, it is a great asset."

D.M., aol.com, 5/1/97

"If you can't find what your are looking for here, you can't find it anywhere."

J.C., airmail.net, 5/1/97

"Your site has to be the most informational packed site I have ever ran across over the web. The wealth of eye opening reading kept me for hours, I forgot about what I was researching and read from one

515

section to another. I appreciate your great works and continue with what you have started."

C.M., nv.us, 5/1/97
"The greatest site on the Web. My sense of self-control has increased 100 fold. Nothing or nobody mystical controls my destiny. I am in the beginning stages of starting a cleaning business. Before, that was a "ridiculous" dream, now it's soon to be reality."

B.L., on.ca, 5/1/97, Canada
"It's important that people who are looking to make positive changes in their lives, are able to access this information and become de-mystified."

R.T., mi.us, 4/30/97
"I find it very fascinating and refreshing. It has made me look at my own life in a different perspective. I believe the Neo-Tech system is relevant and will be a great power in the future."

S.W., co.au, 4/30/97, Australia
"I find the entire concept of ZON fascinating and want to know more, more, more."

C.T., idt.net, 4/30/97
"I think there is truth to be found here."

K.M., nv.us, 4/30/97
"What I have heard of this site is absolutely astounding. Let's put it to good use by all and all will flourish."

W.M., aol.com, 4/29/97
"The best site I've ever read, stop neocheaters forever."

B.T., teleport.com, 4/29/97
"Mark Hamilton's "2001: The New Code" blew me away!"

D.R., i-one.com, 4/29/97
"This is POWERFUL stuff. I can't ever remember reading anything that made so much sense. Thank you for putting this out. I will ensure that those who are close to me, and that I care about, read this."

M.P., ica.net, 4/28/97, Canada
"The Neo-Tech philosophy speaks of a universal truth that seems to benefit all. It brings optimism

into the hearts of those that listen. It makes obvious that which bewildered the naive for so long. Neo-Tech is an answer to the cry for help from those that are caught in the web of societal confusion. Thank you Neo-Tech for sharing your wisdom with all. Freedom awaits us all."

J.S., bgsm.edu, 4/28/97
"Congratulations on your discoveries -- I am excited about learning more about your concepts and look forward to becoming an efficient value-producer as opposed to a pawn in the destructive collective consciousness which permeates our individual psyches."

D.W., nv.us, 4/28/97
"I have the utmost gratitude for the efforts of Neo-Tech to rid our world of the plaguing anticivilization."

A.M., org.uk, 4/28/97, England
"Your web site is dynamite! No wonder its got the authorities spooked! I am intrigued by it's potential to revolutionize society."

J.G., aol.com, 4/27/97
"Neo-Tech is the future."

J.M., livingston.net, 4/27/97
"This web site is fascinating. I hope it stays up so more people can come in out of the darkness."

P.H., msn.com, 4/27/97, United Kingdom
"Thank you for waking me up and causing me to think. How can anyone handle their problems when they don't even know what they are?"

D.P., nv.us, 4/26/97
"Neo-Tech should be a common study for all mankind."

K.M., msn.com, 4/26/97
"I believe that Neo-Tech should stay on the web as it provides people with information on how to better their lives."

E.H., aol.com, 4/25/97
"THIS SITE HAS CHANGED MY LIFE....FOR THE BETTER! TAKING THIS SITE OFF THE WEB WOULD BE THE BIGGEST MISTAKE ANYONE COULD MAKE. I FEEL STRONGLY THAT THIS SITE IS THE BEST SITE ON THE

WEB, AND THE LITERATURE WITHIN IT IS VALUABLE BEYOND COMPREHENSION."

Z.Z., com.my, 4/25/97
"I have found the answer. Thank you. Let us together uphold profound honesty and vanish mysticism now and forever."

D.S., dec.com, 4/24/97
"This world needs Neo-Tech thinking if it is to prosper. Please keep promoting freedom oriented solutions to world problems and keep the web going."

M.M., hotmail.com, 4/24/97
"The information on the site has helped integrate my thinking. I had a flash, saw the new color mode, and now can manipulate the essence to brighten and control everything that moves."

A.P., mozcom.com, 4/24/97, Philippines
"I find many interesting details of earning money and becoming rich."

C.V., nv.us, 4/24/97
"VERY STIMULATING, WITH A DIFFERENT OUT LOOK ON LIFE. INFORMATIVE AND SINCERE ON DIFFERENT SITUATIONS THAT COME UP IN LIFE. A VERY GOOD MOTIVATION TOOL!"

S.B., wwa.com, 4/23/97
"I believe that Neo-Tech is a totally new idea that will revolutionize known thought in the world. It is a necessity to every man wanting to hold dearly a happy life free of worry and full of pleasure. Without stress, the world becomes much clearer and Neo-Tech has the ability to do that."

J.P., opman.com, 4/23/97
"I WOULD LIKE TO TAKE THIS OPPORTUNITY TO SAY THANK YOU VERY MUCH. FOR FORTY YEARS I HAVE STRUGGLED WITH MANY UNANSWERABLE QUESTIONS. THANKS TO YOUR SITE I HAVE A CLEAR PATH TO THE FUTURE."

J.M., hotmail.com, 4/23/97
"I think what you are doing is admirable, let's put the power back where it belongs."

H.A., netcom.com, 4/23/97
"Your site is very informative and helpful. I greatly appreciate the information."

L.E., nv.us, 4/23/97
"I thoroughly enjoy your web site. The combination of topics is unprecedented on the web. Thank you for the information."

A.P., co.ca, 4/23/97, Canada
"The most interesting Web sight I've read."

K.S., aol.com, 4/23/97
"I am amazed at how the success that I've had over the years is related to the concepts outlined in the site. Concepts like Objectivism, honesty, and integrity are powerful weapons against mystics and lazy people."

J.T., nv.us, 4/23/97
"The most mind-blowing information I've ever read."

R.B., hotmail.com, 4/22/97
"Very enlightening. Quite possibly the most innovative school of thought in history."

G.B., nv.us, 4/22/97
"Neo-Tech is pure human logic. It should be required reading for understanding humanity."

A.P., nv.us, 4/22/97
"I was amazed at how true the information is. Please keep up this wonderful self-help site. It's extremely interesting reading."

A.S., nv.us, 4/22/97
"I believe Neo-Tech is very educational and will do a lot of good for generations to come."

G.P., uh.edu, 4/22/97
"What you are doing is phenomenal and would be beneficial to many people. I hope that you open the eyes of many so that we may help create the Neo-Tech world."

J.R., com.au, 4/22/97, Australia
"This material literally changed my life in many ways by including making me feel good about myself and throwing off unearned guilt."

R.L., arizona.edu, 4/22/97
"This site is amazing and needs to remain available to anyone who feels the confines of social and religious correctness. I will point this site out to those I care most about. KEEP THIS SITE OPEN!!!!!"

D.S., sezampro.yu, 4/22/97, Yugoslavia
"Your site is absolutely essential."

A.K., geocities.com, 4/22/97
"A most amazing and intriguing site...The subject is one everyone talks about. The information is needed, there is definitely a need for more sites like this."

T.L., harvard.edu, 4/21/97
"I think you are doing a good thing by trying to help people realize their own power and identity as who we really are (you call it Zon)."

B.M., baylor.edu, 4/21/97
"I have found your site extremely enlightening. I have the feeling this material is really going to help me see."

J.B., juno.com, 4/21/97
"I feel like I have started a new learning process for the future."

A.B., co.uk, 4/21/97, United Kingdom
"Who could disagree with the need for this kind of information being made available to everyone? More power to you, keep up the good work."

S.N., msn.com, 4/21/97
"Great Web site... I especially find the topic search capabilities very useful."

C.H., hotmail.com, 4/21/97
"I am impressed with the information given here. The Web site's layout is superb."

J.U., pacifier.com, 4/21/97
"Your site should remain on the web so we can learn to live without external guidance...."

R.H., akera10.com, 4/20/97
"I am 67 & feel comfortable for the first time that I can throw off mysticism thanks to all you good, brave souls at Neo-Tech. Where was Neo-Tech years ago? How many lives could have been saved.

From my youth, I knew something was wrong, but could not find out till I read Neo-Tech."

S.C., nb.ca, 4/20/97, Canada
"Your site helped me understand a lot about what the hell is going on around me. THANK YOU NEO-TECH."

M.B., aol.com, 4/19/97
"What an abundance of truly helpful information!"

W.W., aol.com, 4/19/97
"This web site offers enormous value to anyone examining it. If this web site were removed, and enormous exponential value would be lost to everyone. The information contained here is so vitally important to the progressive survival and enhancement of conscious life, possibly the most positive life-changing, life-giving value on the net. 'Let there be Neo-Tech'"

R.T., hotmail.com, 4/19/97, Australia
"This site is very informative and provides much helpful information."

A.N., feist.com, 4/18/97
"It should be a prerequisite for anyone who wants there dreams to TRULY become reality."

A.K., co.za, 4/18/97, South Africa
"Sounds absolutely fantastic. I suppose I'll be sitting here the whole weekend going through this site."

D.T., sonic.net, 4/18/97
"Thanks for the web site, its an oasis, and I am once again encouraged to get on with goals rather than dragging my feet...buzzing out, following unknown paths."

B.T., teleport.com, 4/17/97
"For the past few years {I'm now 79} I have been attempting to fire up, and instill in my brain neurons this fantastic knowledge of the Neo-Tech concepts. Please never ever let this Web Page be removed until there is at least a hundred million or so on the Page visitor counter. Then by that time, it will be firmly implanted in everyone's mind. Good-bye neocheaters and all non-sense."

K.S., webtv.net, 4/17/97
"This is the first time I've seen anything that attempted to 'expand' upon Objectivism."

M.B., att.net, 4/17/97
"This is my first exposure, I find the content interesting. It seems to encompass the complete width and breath of life."

I.W., dux.ru, 4/17/97, Russia
"Your site is great! I enjoy it! Neo-Tech is the answer to all my questions. It's really an aid for my job and life. Thank you so much."

V.A., nv.us, 4/17/97
"Your site is trying to do something good for others."

I.M., co.uk, 4/17/97, United Kingdom
"Neo-Tech must be available to as many people as possible. It gives us a new way of seeing the world and our relationship to it. I find what you have to say exciting and I want to understand it more. The real issue is about encouraging more people to take control of their own lives."

W.B., mci.com, 4/17/97
"Please do not remove this site from the web under any circumstances. By removing this site you will deny millions access to Neo-Tech who want to free themselves forever from the chains of mysticism."

D.F., telepath.com, 4/17/97
"As long as individuals such as the brilliant writers who document reality are allowed to publish their information free of force, threat of force, and censorship, the prosperity revolution will proceed peacefully; almost without notice... THE FUTURE OF THE WORLD DEPENDS ON NEO-TECH (HONESTY) GROWING ON THE WEB... GO NT!"

V.G., thegrid.net, 4/16/97
"NT is the seed of the 21st Century and of all time for the Civilization of the Universe as it springs up here on earth. It is the essence of life for all of us."

G.F., dg.com, 4/16/97
"I think this WEB site is helpful and informative. I have already noticed clearer thinking. I haven't quite mastered the technique of integrated thinking but I think it is key and want to be able to use it daily. I've noticed how much mysticism is and has been involved in my life and I'm astounded...how did I ever get by?"

M.D., hotmail.com, 4/15/97
"Neo-Tech is invaluable, there is nothing like it on this planet. Neo-Tech and the Zonpower have changed my life, and should be allowed to change other's lives as well."

A.T., bigfoot.com, 4/15/97
"I think this is great stuff. I have never seen anything like it on the web or anywhere else."

T.O., awinc.com, 4/15/97, Canada
"I will be looking on your Internet site for guidance and support to a better me. I am about to embark on this great journey called life I think it would be a tragedy for a site such as yours to disappear."

D.M., idt.net, 4/15/97
"To the day I die (which will be never!) I will be asking myself why I fell for the mysticism."

W.H., or.jp, 4/15/97
"Keep on pushing toward victory NEO-TECH!!!! The world is about to be corrected by ZON!"

M.A., com.au, 4/15/97, Australia
"NEO-TECH SHOULD EXPAND FOR HUMAN GROWTH AND HAPPINESS AND PROSPERITY."

L.L., co.sw, 4/15/97, Switzerland
"POWERFUL EYE-OPENER WHICH IS THE TOOL TO A MUCH MORE PLEASANT WORLD AHEAD."

M.D., juno.com, 4/14/97
"The Neo-Tech home page gets a big thumbs up."

S.A., earthlink.net, 4/14/97
"The world needs Neo-Tech."

K.J., aol.com, 4/14/97
"Your site is very mind-stimulating."

T.B., qualcomm.com, 4/14/97
"Every body should read Neo-Tech. It is great."

A.B., org.au, 4/14/97, Australia
"What are these fools afraid of? Zonpower taught me to think in a way I never thought before."

ANON, co.nw, 4/14/97, Norway
"I most certainly want this site to expand on the web."

T.R., onlink.net, 4/13/97, Canada
"Neo-Tech is the most important thing in the history of our existence -- it must be available to everyone."

S.Y., nv.us, 4/13/97
"As a Neo-Tech owner for over 10 years now I can say that NT, Mark, Eric, and Frank have been the guiding light in a world full of Mysticism."

J.M., 1st.net, 4/13/97
"Keep up the good job, because if you don't we are doomed."

M.B., accessone.com, 4/13/97
"This is by far the greatest site ever and Dr. Wallace definitely deserves the Nobel."

D.B., netcom.com, 4/12/97
"Neo-Tech is on the cusp of a revolution. I now know something is tragically wrong in the universe."

L.L., netcom.com, 4/12/97
"Neo-Tech has helped me gain valuable advantages over the mindless mystics and dangerous parasites that exist in government, religion and business. I keep coming back for more. Philosophically centered in an off-centered world!"

G.M., nv.us, 4/12/97
"This site rocks. So much information, so little time. I love the Zon manuscript, it is intriguing. Also, the Global business section contains information I could use in starting up a global wealth empire. What a site! It has already helped me, and can help many others."

ANON, com.my, 4/12/97, Malaysia
"Neo-Tech is the answer to all the questions that I have been looking for. It is definitely going to change my life."

T.T., co.my, 4/12/97, Malaysia
" I found your site both informative and interesting."

P.S., co.uk, 4/11/97, United Kingdom
"Most definitely Neo-Tech can only be good for humanity."

K.G., community.net, 4/11/97
" I would like to put into practice the GOLDEN-

HELMET and help restore America back to the strong, moral and just nation it once was."

ANON, nv.us, 4/8/97
"I am proud to say that Neo-Tech works."

R.M., hotmail.com, 4/8/97
"Ever since I stumbled upon this site, I've noticed life bending itself to fit my will."

T.H., ctg.com, 4/8/97
"I was amazed at what I read -- I followed a link to read the IRS Abuse cases, and ended up spending most of the day browsing through your info. By all means stay online! And I'll be passing around your Web address..."

S.C., micron.net, 4/8/97
"The fact that the information you present here is so close to the truth, makes it extremely dangerous. You are offering people an explanation for their life and the world. You give people the truth. By giving people a better glimpse of the truth than they have ever had before, something so radically different from any of the mysticism or religions available, it is dangerous to their own mysticisms. Break the Bubble of Mysticism."

M.M., earthlink.net, 4/8/97
"Every American needs to be informed of this web site."

N.J., ac.za, 4/8/97, South Africa
"We have been taught to believe that a relationship is all about compromise, but that is only if you want to be happy for the moment and sad for the rest of the time. I think your DTC technique makes a lot of sense."

K.R., nv.us, 4/8/97
"The ideas expressed are eye opening and should be made available to the world in mass doses. The world we live in today is that of lies. We the people deserve the truth about all Neo-Tech has to offer. The books should be in every library in the world."

P.C., frontiercomm.net, 4/7/97
"We need Neo-Tech. It is too easy to become stale and vulnerable in our society of users and abusers. Thanks!"

J.P., workerbee.com, 4/6/97
"The information you are providing the world is of the utmost importance!"

G.W., execpc.com, 4/6/97
"This New World site must stay on the 'net' to help 'those who will inherit the earth' through the Civilization of The Universe, while ostracizing the pip-squeaks and parasitical elites from the earth."

J.H., intermind.net, 4/6/97
"I must say that I really enjoy this Randian capitalist spritzer with a twist of sarcasm and light sprinkle of earthy-crunchy clean living."

R.F., ibm.net, 4/6/97, Thailand
"This site is too cool for school."

B.S., johnstown.net, 4/5/97
"NEO-TECH HAS CHANGED MY LIFE. I AM THANKFUL FOR YOUR EFFORTS."

Y.D., jaring.my, 4/5/97, Malaysia
"I have found a lot of inspiration in NT."

M.A., aol.com, 4/5/97
"I want to learn more about taking responsibility and improving all areas of my life."

R.I., tnp.com, 4/5/97
"I think this is one of the best sites I have seen one the web."

ANON, nv.us, 4/5/97
"Neo-Tech will rule the world with it's legion of business leaders. NO FEAR."

T.R., trose, 4/4/97
"Wow!! What an eye opener!! Thanks a million."

L.W., nv.us, 4/4/97
"The growth of a person's potential is greatly increased when one's knowledge is expanded with Neo-Tech."

T.N., valpo.edu, 4/4/97
"I like the Plato-Aristotle comparisons. Very interesting. This is my first visit, I'll be back."

C.M., com.au, 4/3/97, Papua New Guinea
"I've never read anything like it! Its' almost unbelievable, the differences of the Neo-Tech era is

overwhelming..."

H.R., hotmail.com, 4/3/97, Canada
"I believe that ZONPOWER is the key to health, wealth, and happiness. Also, the fact that this web page has opened my mind as well as many others is great. This web page really does have all the answers. I looked into the matrix and almost fell over at the LIMITLESS amounts of information on everything."

J.M., seanet.com, 4/3/97
"Neo-Tech has now become another aspect of my up all night computer studies and as you report there is a profound liberation upon reading this text."

M.Y., chesco.com, 4/3/97
"With Neo-Tech I have the freedom that no one can take from me. I am safe for the first time in my life."

J.G., pipex.com, 4/3/97, United Kingdom
"I think what you have to say on this site is... well.....immense."

L.M., hotmail.com, 4/3/97, Brueni
"I found this web site an eye opener. I have surely learned a great deal."

C.B., nv.us, 4/3/97
"I am a devout Objectivist. This is all VERY impressive."

ANON, nv.us, 4/2/97
"I find Neo-Tech very useful in seeing through the ways of mystics and parasitical elites. It gives much added depth to life."

R.W., amworks.com, 4/2/97
"I am thoroughly thrilled with Neo-Tech. Neo-Tech continually improves my abilities to achieve happiness and prosperity in life. Go NT!"

D.M., fivearea.com, 4/1/97
"Neo-Tech provides a much needed approach to life. Instead of people thinking that someone or some government will care for them, Neo-Tech teaches about being self sufficient."

N.J., n8dog.com, 4/1/97
"This site has opened my mind to the truth about

life."

D.C., microcell.ca, 4/1/97, Canada
"It is rare to see anything this informative, here on the Web, or any place else."

D.E., co.uk, 4/1/97, England
"Neo-Tech is needed by all...."

S.B., sympatico.ca, 3/31/97, Canada
"I would like to thank all those involved with the continuing efforts and enlightening focus of the Neo-Tech instructions. I have studied various philosophies in my pursuit of life and happiness but none have opened my consciousness as yours. I hope Neo-Cheating and Mysticism crumble as this new tomorrow rises on a waking world!"

C.D., aol.com, 3/31/97
"This Web Site has tremendously changed my previously polluted view of existence."

D.C., drdons.com, 3/31/97
"It has already started to make an enormous impact on my life."

J.R., aol.com, 3/31/97
"This will change the world."

M.Y., net.pk, 3/31/97, Pakistan
"It is a tool for all humanity. I think it is especially helpful in business and love."

L.S., aol.com, 3/31/97
"Thank you very much. I have benefited tremendously from this information."

P.F., att.net, 3/30/97
"I find the information extremely compelling. I have found immediate use for the mini-day structure in my business."

M.M., cam.org, 3/30/97, Canada
"Neo-Tech information awakened me to my amateur, naive understanding of life and business. It dispels all mysteries about the process of creating, producing and distributing marketable values. Neo-Tech totally models how I, too, can produce and promote useful values, competently compete and voluntarily trade with others. Neo-Tech provides the process to achieve ever renewable health, prosperity, security, self-esteem and happiness. The keys:

Constantly applying integrated honesty and rational efforts to every department of my life. Thank you forever!"

J.R., msn.com, 3/30/97
"I feel the excitement of the 'answer is here!'"

ANON, nv.us, 3/29/97
"Jesus' secret message about discovering a Neo-Tech consciousness is super-duper...... Super! I love it!"

D.D., aol.com, 3/29/97
"Excellent, Just plain excellent."

C.M., worldnet.net, 3/29/97
"This could possibly be the ONE THING in life that I need to get ahead."

D.P., aol.com, 3/29/97
"The web is the PERFECT place to spread the word about Neo-Tech. The revolution is coming."

T.T., aol.com, 3/29/97
"I agree this is the best site on the world wide web."

L.F., nv.us, 3/29/97
"I am a 23 year old college student and new to your site. Neo-Tech totally changed the direction my life was headed. I am now ready and exited to begin a new life of discovery and adventure. I will be forever grateful for your information. Thank you."

P.S., aol.com, 3/28/97
"The one thing that interests me most about the philosophy of Neo-Tech is the fight to cure the disease of death!"

D.T., com.au, 3/27/97, Australia
"I have gained incredible advantages by using Neo-Tech."

P.C., frontiercomm.net, 3/26/97
"ZONPOWER/NEO-TECH was the precipitating factor in a major life improvement for myself and my best friend. Thanks!"

W.S., aol.com, 3/26/97
"Thanks Neo-Tech, your information helped me a lot. I think it's time for Neo-Tech to become a global awareness so that we can enter the

Civilization of the Universe. It is time to end pointless death and suffering."

D.P., djpelkey.com, 3/26/97
"With knowledge there is power. With an increased knowledge, we can more accurately aim our lives in such a way to become a more complete and effective person. Please continue publishing this most needed information."

S.S., erols.com, 3/26/97
"I like the idea of freeing myself from the external 'voices' of government and religion."

M.R., golden.net, 3/25/97, Canada
"In my search for truth, I have found that Neo-Tech has given me a feeling that there is hope."

R.A., arcticmail.com, 3/25/97
"This is a wonderful site. I feel that, if adopted, the principles espoused by Neo-Tech would certainly aid in the construction of a sane society."

M.Y., chesco.com, 3/25/97
"If Neo-Tech were not on the web it would be the dark ages descending upon the world."

K.M., iafrica, 3/25/97, South Africa
"Moral standards have declined to such an extent that good honest basic attitudes are regarded as 'weird'. Any attempt to set the record straight should be applauded."

L.R., bright.net, 3/25/97
"I did a search for integrity + honesty + value + commitment + persistence and found this site. It has to be a good thing!"

A.R., vvm.com, 3/24/97
"Your site is incredible. Thank you so much for providing this valuable information. You have taken the very best of Ayn Rand and Objectivism and moved forward into the future. Keep up the great work!"

B.H., pfi.com, 3/24/97
"This is truly the only hope our civilization has for eliminating mystics and neo-cheaters."

Z.S., aol.com, 3/24/97
"I just came back from Hungary, I was surprised to see in Hungary how strongly people desired this

kind of information."

D.S., entex.com, 3/24/97
"I find the information interesting and insightful. Isn't truth what you are telling?"

Y.S., nasionet.net, 3/24/97, Malaysia
"This site is great. It provides the valuable information I have been searching for all this time. Keep up the good work. :)"

L.C., prodigy.com, 3/24/97
"I think your web-site is great. I'm definitely going to put this site on my hot list. I'll be back!!!"

R.R., aol.com, 3/24/97
"All my life I have been a mystic. Reading Tarot cards since I was 13, born-again Christian at 19, sensitive new age guy at 21, ritual candle magic at 25, and so on. After reading this powerful material, my emotions range from anger to fear to sadness to determination. Is there a Neo-Tech support group? (Mystics-anonymous anyone?) I feel so stupid for letting the mystic neo-cheaters sap my life away. If anybody has similar trouble trying de-mystify themselves lets talk."

J.H., webtv.net, 3/24/97
"Neo-Tech has a great deal of value to offer people. Its emphasis on abolishing mysticism is its best aspect."

M.B., co.ph, 3/23/97, Philippines
"Thought-provoking information! Mind-opening information not found elsewhere!"

R.T., co.uk, 3/23/97, United Kingdom
"I love Neo-Tech ideas. Powerful, practical, hands-on, change-your-life stuff."

J.Y., msn.com, 3/23/97
"Whatever you do please don't take this site off the Internet. I think it's the best one that exists. What is, is."

S.M., msn.com, 3/23/97
"Neo-Tech stands for the correct way the human race should be living. Without Neo-Tech, our direction is toward unhappiness and death. Neo-Tech has taught me to except responsibility for all my action. Without Neo-Tech, we are just a group of losers. I'd rather be a winner. Even if Neo-Tech, is

removed from the web, which would be a great loss for the human race, I will always live through Neo-Tech. ...Biological Immortality, Romantic love, Happiness, and Lot's of earned money, for all the Neo-Tech people."

G.M., netcom.com, 3/22/97
"The greatest achievements of mankind were not discovered by some emaciated ascetic meditating on a mountain top; they were discovered by the hard work of dedicated, rational-thinking, human being striving to overcome the unknown. The Neo-Tech site goes to great lengths to address this very issue. You are to be commended for your diligence in the light of our society's spiraling descent into yet another Dark Age. Keep up the hard work!"

R.S., hotmail.com, 3/22/97, Australia
"Neo-Tech is the best source of information to improve our life. Thank you, Neo-Tech for providing this powerful information."

P.B., freenet.edu, 3/22/97
"I used to preach and teach the Bible in the Church of Christ, I find the values of Neo-Tech worth much more."

D.N., aol.com, 3/22/97
"It's honest to the core."

A.K., gate.net, 3/21/97
"Just reading a few pages here has set me to thinking and planning, but no longer dreaming!"

G.W., co.uk, 3/21/97, United Kingdom
"I look forward to the day when all human beings know Neothink (natural thinking for conscious beings). There is no compromise with Neo-Tech. Contradictions are easily identified and eradicated. The overwhelming beauty of recognizing the objective 'meaning of life' triggers an irreversible change in perceptions."

E.S., aol.com, 3/21/97
"I love your web site and visit it almost daily, the layout is great and the knowledge it provides is priceless."

D.D., iusb.edu, 3/20/97
"I believe this is the most valued information I have ever read!!"

S.S., aol.com, 3/20/97
"I just read Neo-Tech/Zonpower. Needless to say, it is not possible to achieve happiness under today's conditions. Neo-Tech will change that. I am amazed at the grip the mystics have over individuals. I guess that ignorance truly is bliss. But not for me. I am looking forward to the day we can get organized and stand as a united front against our common enemies of the mystics and the Gov't which oppresses us. If we can get organized, they don't stand a chance against us. Keep up the fantastic work, and let me know what I can do to help."

C.C., planetc.com, 3/20/97
"Keep up the fight against all the neocheaters and value destroyers."

P.A., com.uk, 3/20/97, United Kingdom
"I have read the information on your web site and I can honestly say my life HAS changed IRRETRIEVABLY for the better.....I have gone from severe debt to a comfortable situation and it gets better each day ....I found an intelligent, beautiful, young wife (of 30, I am near 50) who is crazy about me....and my dreams came true ...Everyone in the world knows there is a better way to live. I could go on all day about the benefits....suffice to say , whatever happens, don't go away, WE ALL NEED YOU."

F.A., istar.ca, 3/20/97, Canada
"I find your site infinitely inspiring. Your web site makes my day easier."

R.T., net.my, 3/20/97, Malaysia
"Neo-Tech sounds like it will have a significant impact on man's thinking and to the future of humanity. Man always fears the new and unexplored. This is adventurous territory. Keep it up and expand!"

S.N., dictatorsmurf.com, 3/19/97, Canada
"This site is the best. I am glad I found it and shall return often. I do agree that mystics are a great source of evil, and I think sites like this are needed to combat religious thinking. Neo-Tech needs to grow, it needs massive distribution, it needs to make a bible of it's own. If enough people hear of this, it might snuff out mystics permanently, so that we can usher in a new era. Science and futuristic idea's need to grow. I am a college student studying genetic engineering, and I have made it my life goal

to pursue biological immortality through human cloning and genetic manipulation. I would really like to thank the creator of Neo-Tech, and I hope it's values will soon be embraced by everyone."

T.M., net.ve, 3/19/97, Venezuela
"It was really interesting to read about Neo-Tech. I like it very much. Keep going!"

R.M., hotmail.com, 3/19/97
"This is a definite source of self-empowerment."

M.H., workmail.com, 3/19/97, United Kingdom
"This site contains the most valuable information on the Web."

R.K., lava.net, 3/19/97
"I think this web site is very powerful and exciting."

J.B., ycp.edu, 3/18/97
"Wonderfully enlightening."

L.D., aol.com, 3/18/97
"I HAVE BEEN IN SEARCH OF THIS DOCUMENT FOR THIRTEEN YEARS."

B.A., hp.com, 3/18/97
"I really like what is said here and think the 'neocheaters' most definitely do damage society. Thanks for all your great work."

M.A., pipeline.com, 3/18/97
"Wonderful insight and science. We need it."

ANON, nv.us, 3/18/97
"Neo-Tech Objectivism rules!"

C.C., univ-tlse1.fr, 3/18/97, France
"It's really fantastic!"

S.S., warehouse.net, 3/18/97
"The Neo-Tech/Zonpower Discovery is very powerful. I already see the world in a new light."

J.P., deltanet.com, 3/18/97
"This is the most honest information I have ever seen. It is time the politicians were be placed where they belong, under us, not above us. They have been elected to serve us, not us serve them. Keep up your work. I feel honored to have read and re-read your material."

J.C., aol.com, 3/17/97
"I am most interested in becoming a master of these arts I think the power of this literature will benefit me in my business ventures."

A.L., lmco.com, 3/17/97
"Important evolution in the works of Rand. Enlightening!"

S.D., cris.com, 3/16/97
"I will never regret adopting Zonpower in my daily life."

B.T., bgsu.edu, 3/16/97
"I want to learn the total benefits of Neo-Tech it is very important for me to succeed in life and I find Neo-Tech hard to resist."

M.A., smithville.net, 3/16/97
"I would like to see this web site expand. I would also like to see people realize that religion is fake and that we should only believe in ourselves. That's the real fact!"

W.J., bluebon.net, 3/15/97
"Can this be true? This may be too good to be true."

G.Z., aol.com, 3/15/97
"Fantastic site! Absolutely can't wait for interactive Zon. I predict that we will all begin to experience the final fall of the neo-cheaters when the 'hits' to this site increase geometrically. Permanently bookmarked as my favorite site."

S.N., wzrd.com, 3/15/97
"This is the most valuable information I can think of. It would be great if tomorrow, everyone would wake up with this knowledge."

L.B., netropolis.net, 3/15/97
"This is the most intellectually challenging site I found to date. Thanks for making it available."

R.M., co.us, 3/15/97
"Dominate the web. Scare every Objectivist out of his wits."

W.H., or.jp, 3/14/97
"Keep filling the net with your information. It has helped me discover the REAL ME that everyone told me not to listen to. Thank you for this site."

S.W., rcvideo.com, 3/14/97
"I think you are onto a universal truth."

D.C., nv.ux, 3/14/97
"This truth is needed!!!!!"

A.P., coqui.net, 3/13/97, Puerto Rico
"Very powerful information that properly applied can lead one to a positive transformation from traditional living and thinking."

B.P., nv.us, 3/13/97
"This site must remain on the web. If it were not for Neo-Tech, I would not be happy, rich, loved, or healthy."

W.V., bci.net, 3/13/97, Canada
"I am currently a high school student. This site assists me in gaining greater insight on the world today. (A 17 year old student)"

S.Y., net.my, 3/13/97, Malaysia
"The world of tomorrow is here. I will be backing this web site with all the efforts I can get. This is indeed the most valuable web site in WWW. The dawn of a new era is what I have been looking forward to an era of profound honesty and competitive business. Down with Mysticism and Rise with Neo-Tech. 'Great days are coming'"

J.R., juno.com, 3/13/97
"Everyone needs Neo-Tech -- Best Web site ever!!"

B.H., iname.com, 3/13/97
"There's nothing else like it! Have enjoyed tremendous gains since I first experienced Zonpower. It continues to build exponentially! Harm no others AND Produce values! Stop the Neo-Cheaters in their Tracks!"

B.W., bigfoot.com, 3/11/97
"This is terrific information; important and basic and insightful. Thank you for making it available. You are whetting a lot of appetites and undoubtedly changing a lot of lives with your concepts."

G.P., mea.com, 3/10/97
"It often takes eye opening, thought provoking material to nudge people in the right direction and this looks to be some of the best!"

B.K., campbells.ca, 3/10/97, Canada
"I like viewing your fascinating material through its hyper-linked web pages Keep up the great work!"

B.V., msn.com, 3/10/97, France
"I am very pleased to read one or two articles from time to time. It is a very interesting enriching encyclopedia."

J.C., nv.us, 3/10/97
"This site is changing my life."

S.S., net.au, 3/10/97, Australia
"Well well well, someone has finally got it right!!!! Neo-Tech is definitely the way of the future, this site should be available to everyone. I am going to make a link to it on my home page!!! Thank you."

C.O., rit.edu, 3/10/97
"I believe that your presence on the web is essential for both the elimination of the parasitical value-destroyers and for the removal of the current anticivilization."

V.L., hotmail.com, 3/10/97, Malaysia
"This site really helps me generate wealth."

R.K., co.ng, 3/10/97, Papua New Guinea
"I like seeing this offered worldwide so potential value producers can have access to this very important information. This is a doorstep service."

E.H., aol.com, 3/10/97
"I can clearly see the benefit of this line of thought and way of looking at life."

D.B., sympatico.ca, 3/9/97, Canada
"The Web is for the access to information, it's a natural 'home' for Neo-Tech."

J.C., aloha.net, 3/9/97
"I learn a lot every time I click into this site."

R.M., nv.us, 3/9/97
"NT is the only antidote to the worlds poisons. I want the universe to be completely free of criminal machinations."

J.S., online.no, 3/9/97, Norway
"It sounds interesting to explore a world of new possibilities."

J.C., ionet.net, 3/9/97
"Once I start reading it is hard to stop."

J.V., earthlink.com, 3/9/97
"This is the best reading I have done. I finally can see that logical thinking wins over our mystical brainwashing."

D.S., evansville.net, 3/8/97
"Has potential to free individuals from government, corporate, and any other form of slavery."

J.M., seanet.com, 3/8/97
"I have just visited this sight for the first time and I was greeted with a wave of relief that the knowledge is finally being let out."

F.R., form-net.com, 3/8/97, Kenya
"Super site -- beyond description/value!"

C.I., blackpool.net, 3/8/97, United Kingdom
"The Neo-Tech Web Site is by far the most valuable site on the Internet."

S.V., aol.com, 3/8/97
"Absolutely Best of the Web. I know this takes a lot of effort and I want to thank you for your hard work (not just the www but all the preceding development of Neo-Tech. I can't get enough. I previously had searched every corner of the esoteric universe for the 'most objective' type of (scientific) mysticism and it took Neo-Tech to show me the error of my oxymoron ways. It never occurred to me to dump the entire dishonest bicameral matrix. Doing so has improved my quality of life immensely and I have made several life-changing decisions and changes this year. Thanks again and Happiness forever! to all of you."

M.P., prodigy.net, 3/8/97
"Nice Work, and Thank You for helping me become a Neo-Tech man."

S.H., earthing.net, 3/8/97
"Thank you very much for the information that has helped me identify individuals in my life that have been neocheating me out of just about everything. Now I have some form of defense and can start to enjoy my life."

A.G., eot.com, 3/8/97
"There is no other web site that delivers more

values on the web. PERIOD! This web site is the reason I got an Internet account. That's how much I value it."

J.R., aol.com, 3/7/97
"You must continue your great job helping all of the revolutionaries."

J.L., nv.us, 3/7/97
"Keep up the good work for the most just of ALL causes.....honesty."

S.H., umn.edu, 3/6/97
"Neo-Tech information has been of tremendous value to me."

K.N., odc.net, 3/6/97
"Brilliant and Prophetic!!! 1984's 'Big Brother' is driven back by the slaves he subjugates. Ayn Rand's theory, 'Money is the root of all good,' emerges victorious."

J.P., ricochet.net, 3/6/97
"I have long believed that the government has lied, deceived, and cheated the hard working American people."

J.R., nv.us, 3/6/97
"I have found invaluable help and information contained within this site. I feel that it is instrumental to my financial and personal success."

N.N., phsmail.com, 3/5/97
"The most valuable information anywhere."

J.V., nv.us, 3/5/97
"This is the best way to reach the people of this earth who want a better way life!"

J.M., msn.com, 3/5/97
"The values delivered into my life via this web sight and related I&O publications are immeasurable. Prosperity and happiness seem to come to me almost effortlessly! Thanks to Neo-Tech I no longer have to search blindly and wonder 'why'. I simply cause things to happen, and due to the power of totally integrated honesty, I do so with a confidence never before known to me!"

N.N., swipnet.se, 3/5/97, Sweden
"Very nice site. I would like to read more about epistemology and ethics. Keep expanding

Objectivism and fight the orthodox dogmatists in that corrupt movement."

### C.P., nv.us, 3/4/97
"PEOPLE NEED TO BE EXPOSED AND EDUCATED ABOUT NEO-TECH."

### G.G., co.uk, 3/4/97, United Kingdom
"In mid chapter, I have to interrupt my reading to express the exhilaration I just experienced. I was bowled over by the following thought: At this moment, on both sides of every value exchange happening on Earth, society is benefiting. To add up all those values is one thing; but to realize that at some point in the future, I ALONE will have contributed more value to society than that TOTAL caused me to jump to my feet and proudly proclaim that I AM ZON. Then it dawned on me that as both parties in a trade benefit, to have provided all that value, I will also HAVE EARNED EVEN MORE!!! I flopped onto my bed overwhelmed by the prospect. You cannot possibly be aware of the extent of the value you are providing with this web site. Now that I have written this, I can get on with the chapter!"

### R.R., millionaireintraining.com, 3/4/97
"This is definitely the most powerful, useful, insightful, and informational web site that I've ever encountered. I hope that you continue to expand on the information presented here."

### C.F., nv.us, 3/4/97
"THE NEO-TECH WEB SITE IS MOST VALUABLE. IN FACT, THIS SITE IS WHERE I GO FIRST WHEN I COME INTO CYBERSPACE."

### J.S., globalthink.com, 3/4/97
"I have read your literature and understand it completely. It has definitely helped me incredibly!"

### J.S., wave.ca, 3/4/97
"Neo-Tech has greatly influenced my life."

### P.L., com.au, 3/4/97, Australia
"A definite must for the entire planet. No person should do without this information."

### B.R., co.nw, 3/4/97, Norway
"I'm very exited about this philosophy."

### R.L., ophi.com, 3/4/97
"I think what your doing is fantastic. It's so refreshing to see the principles of Objectivism being applied with your vigor and business savvy."

### S.A., smithville.com, 3/4/97
"From the time I was a very young child and first understood the concept of death, I thought why does it have to be this way? I have always appreciated greatly, the astounding odds of just being born, let alone the magical possibilities of living forever. I can't even begin to express my loving appreciation to all of you at Neo-Tech Publishing and your courage for getting the word out. I will forever be loyal to Neo-Tech and its causes. Thank you, thank you, thank you, for your knowledge has finally answered many of my life's questions!!"

### S.S., nv.us, 3/3/97
"Speaking as a common man who has been walked on his whole life, it does my heart good to see someone who actually cares for the little man who deserves more."

### K.C., earthlink.net, 3/3/97
"This upside down world needs Neo-Tech and it's fully integrated honesty."

### J.S., jsaml, 3/3/97
"I am glad Neo-Tech came about because I was so honed in the Word of God. With Neo-Tech thinking it helps me to live worthwhile. Thanks!"

### K.S., oz.net, 3/3/97
"Yes, I believe this site causes people to think for themselves and not allow others to think for them."

### A.P., co.uk, 3/3/97
"The value of Neo-Tech to me will very soon be countable in pounds. Until then -- I just feel it and act on it -- rationally."

### H.S., aol.com, 3/2/97
"As with anything so different to the mind-set, it takes time to clear the old and experiment with the new. I keep on trying to eliminate the 50 years of bogus teachings from my mind. Keep up the good work, and maybe someday we all will live in a world of honest peacekeeping, loving individuals that contribute to the best for mankind."

C.M., us-south.net, 3/2/97
"I think effort should be made to make a greater portion of the Internet community and the community at large aware of your works and the 'nature of the beast' that threatens every hard working, honest person and their families."

A.M., algonet.se, 3/2/97, Sweden
"I think this site is very professionally designed."

R.V., pacbell.net, 3/2/97
"HI, MY NAME IS RICHARD AND I'M 28 YEARS OLD I OWN FOUR PLASTIC MANUFACTURING COMPANIES. I LOVE EVERY WORD THAT I HAVE READ."

N.G., swipnet.se, 3/2/97, Sweden
"Neo-Tech is a must if we want to make progress and save our life from Neo-cheaters and the band of dishonest people. I'm with you."

D.G., idirect.com, 3/1/97, Canada
"Thanks for a mine of really incisive key ideas. You really see how the old order has become irrelevant and a complete drag on progress."

J.S., att.net, 3/1/97
"It's nice to know that there is still a viable struggle for an illuminated life."

S.P., compuserve.com, 3/1/97, United Kingdom
"After receiving Neo-Tech several years ago, I recently began to realize the importance of DTC. I cannot now overemphasize the changes that a person goes through after integrating DTC into their lives. Thank you Neo-Tech."

T.M., aol.com, 3/1/97
"A prodigious piece of work that is making a tremendous impact on *Thinking Individuals*. This *Objective Reality* is profoundly benefiting the remaining 95% of the individuals throughout the world that are currently sedated from Neo-Cheating rhetoric. Like the Sleeping Giant, they too will awaken. Fortunately due to Cyberspace & Neo-Tech this wake-up process has been accelerated by decades."

B.K., ab.ca, 2/28/97, Canada
"Skeptical at first but after I started reading some of the articles, I said to myself how can you argue with something that just makes sense."

D.W., nv.us, 2/28/97
"The world needs this web site. The Neo-Tech site now stands in a distinct class all its own. I would like to congratulate all contributors of Neo-Tech information and those who share its views on being the true benefactors to all humankind. My devotion and commitment to being a competent value producer is adamant and firmly rooted in my own self-preservation. For the sake of all that is or ever has depicted love, integrated honesty, and goodness, continue to make available your findings and publishing. Thank you."

R.E., com.au, 2/28/97, Australia
"Neo-Tech Discovery has changed my life. Neo-Tech has improved my memory power immensely, given me a diet which is logical as to why I was overweight (I'm now many kilos less), lowered my cholesterol and triglyceride levels and blood pressure and made me much fitter aerobically. These are the side effects. The main effects are that Neo-Tech has given me a whole new purpose in life that has led to a new business, a great increase in happiness and a future of certain success. Thanks to everyone at Neo-Tech, Frank Wallace and Mark Hamilton in particular, and please keep the best site in cyberspace going."

R.A., ncfcomm.com, 2/27/97
"It is good to have a resource such as yours being presented to the world. I am forwarding your site to several of my friends. There are pockets of people just waiting to bring forth a new set of physics that is not based on decay, but on continued renewal of matter. What is explained in Zon Power is a reality today. I am glad a voice is standing out. It is imperative you stay on the net!"

G.B., mb.ca, 2/27/97
"Your web site is fabulous and filled with life saving concepts. I have read the articles 'SILENCE the Ultimate Protector of Individual Rights' and 'Businessmen versus Neocheaters' by Carl Watner. Please keep up the good work. Honesty and Justice will prevail."

G.A., aol.com, 2/26/97
"I am really interested by your comments on living like a millionaire by the year 2001."

R.M., aol.com, 2/26/97
"I think Neo-Tech offers the right mentality of

honesty and integrity for one to prosper and be happy."

S.H., usa.net, 2/26/97
"Very eye opening. I have always realized there was a great injustice going on around me. However, I only realized it subconsciously. I have now been able to pin point some of the neocheaters and their methods. I will soon be on my way to unlimited prosperity and happiness. Neo-Tech will rule in the 21st Century and beyond."

F.F., tip.nl, 2/25/97, Netherlands
"I have already the NEO TECH in SPANISH. This is the BEST BOOK that I ever read."

A.M., co.il, 2/25/97, Israel
"Hi everyone! Your site is one of the coolest I've ever seen. It should remain on the web FOREVER!"

J.R., nv.co, 2/25/97
"Your new ideas are brilliant."

B.S., aol.com, 2/25/97
"I wish more people knew about this."

T.N., net.my, 2/25/97, Malaysia
"I read with much interest all your articles. I will be back to visit Neo-Tech again, as Neo-Tech is very unique and relevant to my daily life. Thank you."

B.H., gol.com, 2/25/97, Japan
"It is good to see it on the net, it helps to keep me focused."

O.R., com.au, 2/25/97, Australia
"It is necessary to develop a train of apolitical philosophy by which the political system(s) of the world can be rendered open to rational, positive process. As an owner/user of the Zon principles, I am currently investigating methods by which these principles can be brought to fruition in the (Australian) political climate."

M.H., metronet.de, 2/25/97, Germany
"It's great to know better times will come."

K.C., abs.net, 2/24/97
"Neo-Tech must not only remain ON the Web, but Neo-Tech must eventually BE the Web!"

R.B., net.au, 2/24/97, Australia
"Yes, this site is the best. I first came across NT in August '93 and have since not looked back. It has changed my life forever. Long live NT. We really need more of NT."

K.M., itt.com, 2/24/97
"Fascinating reading. Nothing more thought provoking has made it to the web yet."

J.N., topservice.com, 2/24/97, Costa Rica
"Neo-Tech has completely changed my life and thinking process."

S.B., aol.com, 2/24/97, Germany
"I think Neo-Tech is dangerous but great."

I.F., net.ae, 2/24/97, United Arab Emirates
"I have found it very interesting."

E.I., com.sg, 2/24/97, Singapore
"This site is very good. This is a well organized page, keep it up."

J.B., uidaho.edu, 2/24/97
"I think your ideas are great and more people should be informed of what Neo-Tech is about. I would like to put a link on my homepage."

A.B., bikerider.com, 2/24/97
"I am eager to study this so I can achieve integrated honesty."

F.H., pe.net, 2/24/97
"Neo-Tech/Zon helps people feel their true magnificent value in the universe. Through this, people can realize their power to fulfill their deepest desires in life -- wealth, personal power, control and romantic love."

S.B., servtech.com, 2/23/97
"It's been about 12 weeks since I last spent time at the NT web site. Rave reviews for the following: Justin Parkes 'Ten Mega Tips' Tracey Alexander's 'Developing a Neo-Tech Consciousness' Drew Ellis's 'Thus Spake Zon' 'Zon, Ruler of Universe' With special mention of John (Flint's) 'The Bible Decoded' I never read past the first three pages of the bible. After reading JF's decoding I integrated the joy of the other past and future readers of the article. I'm very happy for them. Please pass along my thanks and appreciation to the authors mentioned

above. And know that I appreciate everyone's efforts on this, the grandest of all journeys."

L.B., nv.us, 2/22/97
"This site lets the world know that sooner or later Neo-Tech people will rule the world!"

E.C., earthlink.net, 2/22/97
"I think that this is a very educational site for anyone that wants to learn how to avoid being cheated."

A.D., aol.com, 2/22/97
"This has the potential of being mind boggling."

R.C., infoave.net, 2/22/97
"This is the most thought-provoking information I have ever encountered."

F.C., aol.com, 2/22/97
"I find it to be very powerful and meaningful...It really puts into perspective the downfalls in all our lives."

T.K., hotmail.com, 2/22/97, Egypt
"A very cool site."

J.D., utk.edu, 2/22/97
"I have been carefully studying the information on this web site for the last few days, and I'm amazed at the implications this kind of knowledge holds for everyone. Neo-Tech confirms many long-held suspicions that I've been told were 'evil' and 'bad' by religious neocheaters. Your web site is wonderful."

D.A., netcom.ca, 2/21/97, Canada
"This is the most dynamic site on the web because It GIVES you the life changing information right on the Web. I have learned so much in a short period of time! The concepts are invaluable to all people that desire wealth, happiness and success in their lives!"

P.C., virgin.net, 2/21/97, Scotland
"I have not read much, but I am already intrigued. I shall read on!"

J.J., atlantic.net, 2/21/97
"It is the most thought provoking piece of literature I have seen in a long time."

G.V., kub.nl, 2/21/97, Netherlands
"I make printouts, just because I like to carry them with me while traveling."

E.C., earthlink.net, 2/21/97
"This is an eye-opening as well as a mind-opening and educational web site."

R.J., att.net, 2/21/97
"Your site speaks of many aspects of Life."

R.M., algonet.se, 2/21/97, Sweden
"This is superb source of information."

M.B., metrokc.gov, 2/20/97
"Just want to thank you folks for initiating the most divine mission available in this day and age. Also, now that a few of us 'out there' know the concepts, Neo-Tech will always be on the web -- in one form or another -- until irrationality is completely diffused. Here's to your endeavors!"

B.R., co.za, 2/20/97, South Africa
"This is a super site delivering a cornucopia of values to enrich me mentally, sexually, financially. I have just completed the all powerful, 'nuclear power-like' Mystic Busting Bible, I literally feel and sense how I am moving into a new dimension!! Today I made more money then most make in a week! As I walked back to my office I sensed a powerful force which I know with certainty will propel me into limitless wealth and power. I am like a hungry lion! I am hungry for more Neo-Tech!!! Please make the other 'To Appear' articles available soon! I'm looking forward to Maria's next article, hit me with your powerful integrations baby!!!"

J.L., aol.com, 2/20/97
"Someone has to keep telling the truth until the world wakes up to what is and has been going on for so long. Thank you for this site."

H.A., nv.us, 2/20/97
"I believe the Neo-Tech concepts work and I believe strongly that this is what has to be done to change this world and get the parasites out of power."

G.K., aol.com, 2/20/97
"Let Zon rule cyberspace!"

J.S., netropolis.net, 2/20/97
"I appreciate what you are doing for mankind."

F.C., aol.com, 2/19/97
"Excellent piece of information. The information and ideas expressed in this technology are completely riveting. I completely understand and firmly believe in these ways!"

J.L., monterey.edu, 2/19/97
"I am a student and have found that reading Neo-Tech/Zonpower books have been beneficial. I still have not completely destroyed all my inner mysticism, but cannot wait until I do. I also realized how alone I am in my age group. This does not matter to me, only that I do not understand why others have not been inspired as I have."

C.D., utk.edu, 2/19/97
"This is the most incredible thing I have ever seen. Such powerful information should be available to everyone."

C.C., univ-tlse1.fr, 2/19/97, France
"Good site, it must stay on the web."

L.A., msn.com, 2/19/97
"You are the most important people in the universe."

J.K., washjeff.edu, 2/18/97
"Neo-Tech has published the most useful books in history."

P.B., snet.net, 2/18/97
"Any organization or belief system that can upset as many bureaucrats as yours apparently has, must have a great deal of truth in it."

R.M., oneonta.edu, 2/18/97
"Thank-you for your very important site."

J.O., msn.com, 2/18/97
"Wow!! You've put into words the natural chain of events! "

T.M., aol.com, 2/18/97
"A wonderful piece of work. Keep up the great writing."

J.G., msn.com, 2/18/97
"I received great values and insights."

E.S., mvnet.de, 2/17/97, Germany
"It was great reading the information about Neo-Tech."

D.S., juno.com, 2/17/97
"Neo-Tech presents a great service and has a great deal of information useful to all. There should be no censorship on the web whatsoever. If anyone desires to remove this site from the web...send them my way. I'll convince them otherwise."

C.R., aol.com, 2/17/97
"I think that it is great that you are putting Ayn Rand and the Objectivist movement into perspective. It needs it. Keep up the great work. Thanks."

A.G., co.cr, 2/16/97
"Fantastic site! The information is a must for any high achiever."

A.T., aol.com, 2/16/97
"I stumbled across your 'Global Wealth Power' and simply couldn't stop reading it while online."

C.R., iafrica.com, 2/16/97, South Africa
"Brilliant Publications. Keep Up The Outstanding Work."

G.B., srce.hr, 2/15/97, Croatia
"This is definitely the most valuable site on the Web. Neo-Tech is clear and concise, Neo-Tech is more then a masterpiece. Neo-Tech is the future, and those who won't be able to deal with reality will fade away. Just keep up the good work."

A.D., octonline.com, 2/15/97, Canada
"Keep expanding for the survival of all honest, hard working, intelligent people with the desire to keep living, growing, producing and progressing in every way."

D.S., aol.com, 2/15/97
"I have become very personally involved with the philosophy of Objectivism. I think that Neo-Tech Objectivism will take me even farther. I think this is the philosophy for the 21st century and beyond."

R.D., islandnet.com, 2/15/97, Canada
"Incredible site, with a rational basis. Quite an antidote to the mystic disempowering drivel on the Net."

K.J., mmm.com, 2/14/97
"The ultimate in real information that answers many

of my lifelong questions. Anxiously awaiting the Civilization of the Universe and am working on eliminating my own mysticism (I had it big time!) thank you forever."

M.H., starent.com, 2/14/97
"This is the one of the most valuable web-sites on the Net. I hope that the master-crooks, Clinton & Gore, are successful in putting the Net in everybody's hand. It will be their undoing because honesty and objective rational thought will be unleashed to the demise of liberalism and socialism."

A.P., aol.com, 2/14/97, United Kingdom
"Wonderful site! It is amazing what can be learned here."

M.J., vertexinc.com, 2/14/97
"The Neo-Tech/Zonpower Discovery helped open my eyes as to who the REAL cheaters and criminals in the world are. I also am aware of many more 'control mechanisms' politicians have ingrained in our minds and can reject their government as big brother, father and mother."

A.L., com.au, 2/14/97, Australia
"THE most valuable web site on the Net. Neo-Tech literature is an enormously powerful weapon for the individual to rise out of the stagnation trap and trailblaze new values for mankind. This site is needed to reach that critical mass of value producers so we can ostracize the neocheaters off the face of the Earth and enter the Civilization of the Universe. Don't stop expanding. I would like to see an online NT community (Civilization of the Universe?) where value producers can interact."

V.T., edu.kw, 2/14/97, Kuwait
"I like your ideas and am very much interested."

N.K., aol.com, 2/14/97
"I thought Ayn Rand was the only one that ever understood this and her works were suppressed by the Altruistic Regime. It is very rewarding to see that someone has taken the next step. Keep up the effort. Keep up the example."

J.M., aol.com, 2/14/97
"This sight is a must. Should NT leave the web? That would be a dark day in cyberspace! These concepts have propelled me into a new world of

happiness and competence."

V.M., nv.us, 2/14/97
"Wallace's books are not just as a system of living but a system to prosper and grow by! ...Neo-Tech must stay on the web. We are losing to many freedoms, Neo-Tech must win."

P.K., pa.us, 2/13/97
"Greatest eye opener, mind expanding knowledge I ever received. Only wish I had it sooner."

G.G., spimageworks, 2/13/97
"I LOVE IT! KEEP GROWING! KEEP EXPANDING! KEEP INTEGRATING FOREVER!"

E.M., netcom.com, 2/13/97
"Reality is not easy for me but I am now grasping it by the horns."

T.W., aol.com, 2/13/97
"READ, IMPLEMENT, AND SPREAD we are almost there. Even though the fall of communism and the Berlin wall seemed to happen overnight, those events will seem glacier-like compared to the hyper-speed pace we are about to enter into with the final worldwide acceptance of the Neo-Tech philosophy. THANK YOU MR. FRANK WALLACE!"

G.G., pacbell.net, 2/12/97
"It is a true source of enlightenment and education. I would like to pursue studying this discovery for a more thorough understanding of the possibilities and power available with this knowledge. I have enjoyed researching and learning about suppressed information."

V.V., wwnet.com, 2/11/97
"I am a Neo-Tech owner and the thoughts behind this system are very useful. Anyone looking to make changes in their life, this is a great way to start."

K.W., null.net, 2/11/97
"Keep this site going and growing! I return to it often and have given out the url to countless people in high recommendation for what you are saying."

R.R., uc.edu, 2/11/97
"I completely love this site! I've been a Neo-Tech reader and user for about 5 years, and I find that I'm learning so much more on the site. Keep it

up!!"

R.L., compuserve.com, 2/11/97
"Your concepts about individuals make a lot of sense to me. Rational selfishness is the best tool to pursue happiness. The creation of surplus values seems to be the moral way to help one another."

S.B., aol.com, 2/11/97
"I must commend your courage and convictions for publishing what many might consider heretical and/ or anti-establishment opinions. And for that, whether we agree or disagree, we as Americans and free-thinking people everywhere must applaud your efforts. Keep up the good work, and thanks."

G.B., mb.ca, 2/10/97, Canada
"Great site...keep up the good fight."

D.D., telepath.com, 2/10/97
"I absolutely believe the honest values at your web site will be the key to ousting destructive, freeloading, parasites on a local, national, and global level. Keep up the 'Ultimate Battle' between honesty and effort vs. dishonesty and laziness."

R.W., erols.com, 2/10/97
"This site makes it easier for more and more people to learn about this incredibly valuable technology."

N.Q., utah.edu, 2/10/97
"Best site on the net. I have read a lot of it and hope to read it all. I spend more time on this site than any other site on the net."

T.M., hotmail.com, 2/10/97
"I LOVE THIS SITE."

S.H., aol.com, 2/10/97
"I have found your page to be thought-provoking and needed. As well, it provides a critical pause to status quo thinking."

A.C., com.mx, 2/10/97, Mexico
"I appreciate all the effort that you are doing to expose neocheating and mysticism, especially from the government. This site is very important to the advance and development of Neo-Tech all around the world. I live in Mexico, that is an unhappy country infected by the cheating and mysticism of the government and religious leaders. This web site is very important for the initial exposure of Neo-

Tech to Mexicans. This site can help improve the unhappy way of life for the people in this country. I think that sooner or later, Neo-Tech will win here in Mexico and all around the world."

T.D., www.aol, 2/10/97
"I do believe this work is extremely beneficial to all those who are fortunate enough to encounter it."

K.T., co.za, 2/10/97, South Africa
"I find the Zonpower web site invaluable as it keeps me informed of current values from Neo-Tech Publishing."

J.W., aol.com, 2/10/97
"Your web site is absolutely necessary, many people need to see this. To sum it up, CATALYST."

C.G., aol.com, 2/10/97
"I think you will change humanity. I have been telling all the people I know with access to the NET about your site."

T.N., dec.com, 2/10/97
"I immensely enjoy all of the information that you have on the Internet. I am very supportive of your efforts and demonstration of courage to expose the true realities in our world."

K.H., aol.com, 2/9/97
"This web site is, by far, the most profoundly valuable I've ever encountered. As a Libertarian and Objectivist, I find the content to be wonderfully thought provoking and intellectually stimulating. Thank you so much!"

V.J., thegrid.net, 2/9/97
"This is the most valuable web page going."

G.B., island.net, 2/9/97, Canada
"Looking forward to the Civilization of the Universe. Imagine a world without dishonest government."

M.M., cam.org, 2/9/97, Canada
"Your site promotes 'life, liberty and the pursuit of happiness.' The Neo-Tech literature literally saved me from suicide at age 48. Through Neo-Tech I am learning how to EARN self-esteem, protect myself from dishonesty, define my own mission, produce and market my own products and services, do my own accounting in non-traditional ways that

guarantee success. The happiness I long ago dreamed was possible is dawning again in me. I see how I can make a difference, starting by applying the right information (Neo-Tech) to transform myself and this world into the glorious Civilization that I know is possible for all."

K.P., msn.com, 2/9/97
"Great site... this is a great help...hope you are going to stay around and implement all that is proposed...keep strong."

M.O., webtv.com, 2/9/97
"I really enjoy your web-site. I have accessed it several times. I appreciate the fact that you present both positive and negative views on Neo-Tech. That proves honesty is at work here."

N.G., swipnet.se, 2/9/97, Sweden
"This site is the most valuable on the web. I want it to expand forever! This is the best and only way to let the humans around the world see how the world functions. This is the only site who tells you this in an honest way."

A.R., prtc.net, 2/8/97
"Neo-Tech has penetrated the knowledge boundaries of human existence. Subjects that benefit the human race. For the benefit of the whole world, this web site should remain intact for us humans to continue our knowledge growth and understanding of ourselves, and to stop once and for all the human suffering."

G.W., anewvision.com, 2/8/97
"I want this web site, I need this web site."

G.W., co.uk, 2/8/97, England
"I am a Neo-Tech owner since 1987 and have benefited incalculably since absorbing it and taking it on board in 1991. Thank you for Neo-Tech. I cannot over emphasize the benefits to my life from having come across it. Every moment I am living is now also enhanced by the Zone favorable diet thanks to your reference to Barry Sears' book."

G.G., msn.com, 2/7/97
"Excellent web site, one of the most valuable and powerful that I have found. It just may save mankind. I would like to see more intellectual ammunition like this. Thanks, keep up the great work."

L.M., hotmail.com, 2/7/97
"Neo-Tech is unstoppable. It is strange, but as a homosexual, I am experiencing desires for the opposite sex. I never thought this desire could be possible. Wow!!! I feel great, moving towards or expressing my biological nature makes me feel profoundly happy. AH! how good she looks, I can't wait to experience pleasures together. The more objectively productive I become, I experience these growing desires to the same degree."

L.R., dancris.com, 2/7/97
"'Dismissing Professional Value Destroyers' sounds like what I need. I have drawn much comfort since reading Mark Hamilton's latest book. I am still in the process of integrating and applying to my life all the new concepts your company has contributed to the people who long to be free of oppression."

R.R., aol.com, 2/7/97
"I love the web site, I just need to spend more time caught in it so I can fully consume it. I have much to learn, and I plan to use this site for my education."

J.P., nni.com, 2/7/97
"This site is a conch shell of rationality washed up on a beach of dishonesty. Good luck in keeping the beauty flow."

B.H., heald.edu, 2/7/97
"This IS the MOST VALUABLE site period. Neo-Tech is based on the Objectivist philosophy where you have to examine everything from all angles, all sides. You have to integrate all known facts with objective reasoning to benefit ALL. EVERYONE, including the people who want to ban this site, are being deprived of real happiness. After discovering Neo-Tech, I have made INCREDIBLE realizations about my life, our lives, and where everything's going."

D.D., usit.net, 2/7/97
"This is very important information that everyone needs. It will help to speed up the revolution."

M.I., fazer.com, 2/7/97, United Kingdom
"If this site was banned or ceased to exist the future would indeed be bleak."

E.S., aol.com, 2/7/97
"I am grateful this information is made available

period, but at no cost to the viewer, that's nothing short of amazing!"

D.P., specdata.com, 2/7/97
"Very informative -- mind blowing if I may say so."

K.E., aol.com, 2/7/97
"I find Zonpower tenets most intriguing food for thought. I just ran across it tonight. I think it's great for thinking people."

D.R., hotmail.com, 2/6/97, Canada
"Neo-Tech has changed my life and to this day is continuing to do so. The great power this gives an individual is exhilarating and contagious."

J.M., netcom.com, 2/6/97
"Neo-Tech has been the primary source of new knowledge for me as I'm sure it is has been for most that have ever read and understood a Neo-Tech book. My mysticism, is what lead me to Neo-Tech, and anyone who is mystical will eventually turn to Neo-Tech. Why? Because mysticism is a 'drug' and in time, you'll need more of it to make you 'FEEL' better about your life, money, health, love, and self-esteem problems. When one starts to have questions about their 'Higher Authorities', power to make their dreams or desires come true, one starts to look for a more potent mystical doctrine. I went from being a practicing catholic to Kahuna, to hypnosis and others, to finally arrive at Neo-Tech. This is real, it's not automatic, it works from your efforts to achieve what you desire and not, what some 'God' says is good for you, or 'God' has his reason for things being this way. Neo-Tech has been a very positive addition to my life, and will forever continue be a part of my life. Neo-Tech should always stay in Cyberspace, because as Neo-Tech expands, conscience life does also."

L.H., cup.edu, 2/6/97
"I believe this web site to be one of the most valuable and informative I have ever explored. It contains vast amounts of knowledge on virtually every aspect of my life and I continually refer back to it for more and more insight. The information presented has given my mind the 'pegs' to hang on to when I deal with those around me, who are submerged in mystical dogma. Being a college student, majoring in business no less, I am more susceptible to what my peers 'teach' me. It is vital that I continue to be exposed to this literature and

especially to this web site."

T.R., aol.com, 2/6/97
"I check this web site every day for updates, and make sure that I read one chapter each day. It has become an integral part of my daily life (fits right into one of my mini days. This sight should be part of the Internet until the Internet is obsolete."

M.T., dec.com, 2/6/97
"This site is very inspirational. I use it in my personal development."

ANON, nv.us, 2/6/97
"One thing I love about this web site is that it is not an evangelistic web site asking people to follow. Rather, it focuses on everyone's self-effort. Thanks for doing an excellent job. I sincerely hope that you will achieve the goal of eradicating mysticism. What a beautiful world that would be! Excellent work!"

G.G., pacbell.net, 2/6/97
"I love this site! Finally some real knowledge instead of that boring mainstream stuff! Great men are they who know that thoughts rule the World!"

T.B., aol.com, 2/5/97
"This sight is very informative in helping to share knowledge that is vital to the future of mankind. I hope that you continue to use this site to enlighten many unaware human beings of the parasitical elite. Keep up the good work."

A.J., com.au, 2/5/97
"This site is providing a valuable community service by allowing people to consider alternatives to the system that is being thrust down our throats by megalomaniac governments of this world. Stay on the net and don't bow to the pressures that must be being exerted upon you."

L.D., cvn.net, 2/5/97
"Neo-Tech is the only hope we have."

B.L., callutheran.edu, 2/5/97
"Almost everyday I come online to this web site and just browse for new information and to brush up on favorite works like Zonpower in Cyberspace. I really feel that this is a place I can commune in. I feel among friends here. It is a new and powerful experience for me to feel empowered over my life. I feel that there should be a lot of credit placed in the

hands of the many authors that contribute to this superior site."

M.B., daknet.com, 2/5/97
"I have found that the information in this site provides a totally new outlook to things, and has even helped me develop personally in my work and home environments. PLEASE don't take this site off the web."

J.D., sprynet.com, 2/5/97
"Keep on telling the truth!!! We are looking for it!!"

S.B., pol.net, 2/5/97
"This is an extremely valuable site. I fervently hope that it remains on the Web...the world desperately needs this information."

W.M., kmtnet.com, 2/5/97
"Please keep this site on the web. I have become quite accustomed to reading Neo-Tech during lunch at work. It re-energizes me and is very beneficial in this setting as I can immediately apply the concepts I have just read to actual situations at work."

P.G., mindspring.com, 2/5/97
"Take this off the web! BAH! the government just wants us to obey big brother and be slaves of one big brother! I can easily see their reasoning for trying to be rid of this. Obviously people are protesting this because they don't want good people to get a hold of it and turn the tables in their favor."

A.M., jetstream.net, 2/5/97, Canada
"This is the site of sites and should never be removed from the web."

C.B., hotmail.com, 2/5/97, England
"You have the most valuable site on the net. Only a sick mind would want it banned."

J.D., utk.edu, 2/5/97
"This is very exciting information!!! Everyone should have a chance to read this."

J.L., aol.com, 2/5/97
"If Clinton/Dole/Billy Grahmn types wish to remain in power, they must IMMEDIATELY squash this radical, 'we don't need you' message. What would they do without followers? What would followers do without leaders? Web sites like Neo-Tech must be nipped in the bud if the status quo is to survive. Stop this horror, NOW, before people use its power! If individuals are allowed to use Neo-Tech, then why would we need god or government? Neo-Tech will upset everything. Stop it NOW!"

R.K., erols.com, 2/5/97
"Your efforts are reaching individuals all over the world. The momentum is building. The writing on this site is needed to help turn this world right side up and it's starting to work. Keep going!"

B.C., pacbell.net, 2/5/97
"This is an excellent web site. As a student of Objectivism, this program of yours seems like the next logical step in the advancement of knowledge -- the implementation of Ayn Rand's ground-breaking work."

R.G., electriciti.com, 2/5/97
"The best site on the entire information highway. Let there be honesty."

E.R., aol.com, 2/5/97
"It would be tragic for every decent individual using the Internet to lose this site. The information is a treasure trove of powerful, turnkey information. Where else can a lowly person find information to fix most of his/her problems? This site continues to inspire. The information is too powerful to be stopped by any individual or group of individuals."

M.W., tiac.net, 2/5/97
"This web site should continue to expand until all mysticism has been uprooted and rejected. When the anti-civilization collapses and we all are Zon, then this site will no longer be needed. Until that time, this site must continue to grow."

R.A., aol.com, 2/4/97
"This site stirs people to thought and to contemplate their existence and likely futures? Hmmmmm. Sounds like a good use for Internet."

S.B, aol.com, 2/4/97
"This is definitely THE MOST VALUABLE WEB SITE IN CYBERSPACE."

D.V., naplesnet.com, 2/4/97
"I have been a reader of your materials since 1987...happiness is growing as my business grows! Thanks for your genius."

J.A., icanect.net, 2/4/97

"I've been a supporter of Neo-Tech for about 10 years now, It is one of the most important pieces of work ever created by man, for man. Neo-Tech has proven itself to me many times. It has given me great leverage in life. I went from a pizza delivery driver to a successful General Manager for a national Motel chain. Neo-Tech must remain on the web. And it must continue to expand without limit for the sake of humanity."

B.B., ohio-state.edu, 2/4/97

"Thanks to you, all of my questions have been cleared, and I have reclaimed clarity of thought and conviction of the soul, commodities that I once had but lost. Again, sincerely, thank you for clearing the mist in my mind, and allowing me to see what must be done so clearly."

G.M., netcom.com, 2/4/97

"This is a great site! I was introduced to Neo-Tech about eight years ago and it was truly a transformational experience. My life has not been the same since I was introduced to Neo-Tech. At first the information is very hard to take. In fact, the information is startling. But, once the initial shock wore off I realized I was reading the most important information I had ever come in contact with. The effects of Neo-Tech will never leave me. Thanks for this important work."

G.D., aol.com, 2/4/97

"I think you have a great web site. To remove it would be a great loss to mankind."

M.W., cass.net, 2/4/97

"This web site is a MUST! It would be a crime AGAINST humanity to REMOVE it. I NEED this web site. DO NOT REMOVE IT!"

R.K., nv.us, 2/4/97

"Of course this site should remain...at least until the dishonesty disease/epidemic is cured worldwide."

M.Z., hotmail.com, 2/4/97, Bolivia

"Cutting edge !! at last !!"

B.R., co.za, 2/4/97, South Africa

"This site is worth more than all the gold and platinum in the world!!! PRESERVE THIS SITE, IMPROVE AND KEEP ELEVATING IT WITH THE MAGICAL NEO-TECH FACTOR. YOUR HAPPY, PROSPERING NEO-TECHER FROM S.A."

M.L., lamp.ac.uk, 2/4/97

"It is without a doubt the most important web-site there is. Neo-Tech is 100% positive, constructive and pro-life. Neo-Tech creates REAL people, far removed from all the con-artists, manipulators, losers and general low-lifes who are merely parasites in human form [metaphorically AND literally]. Reading Neo-Tech is like putting on a pair of special sunglasses; one finally 'WAKES UP' to what is really going on; the neocheaters and all their dirty tricks are 'EXPOSED'."

M.L., spiritone.com, 2/4/97

"I am completely and totally at a loss for words. I have been reading and absorbing info like a sponge."

R.K., uia.net, 2/4/97

"This is beyond my wildest dreams. An absolute wealth of information. I truly wish I never had to sleep so I could spend many more hours on your Web Site."

L.J., micronet.fr, 2/4/97

"I can't spend more than a day without verifying what's new on this site. Thanks a lot for all the effort."

E.B., compuserve.com, 2/4/97

"Keep up the good work! Cyberspace is the only place that is possible to expand and move toward the Civilization of the Universe."

M.D., mafia.com, 2/3/97

"This whole Neo-Tech information like the money/ power/and love information has got me thinking about the future. Thanks for the insight of the Cyberspace Revolution."

K.K., doi.com, 2/3/97

"It drastically changed the way I think about things. Keep up the brave work."

T.H., csufresno.edu, 2/3/97

"I am amazed at all the free and honest information. I have always felt that lies have been masking the truth in the name of greed. It is obvious that there will no longer be a need for greed."

M.H., starent.com, 2/3/97

"I do my best to calm down and be patient for the end of big government and the return of rational thought especially when augmented with Neo-Tech Objectivism."

L.P., nv.us, 2/2/97

"To me, this web page is a beacon of light for all those who hope to see the birth of a society (or of a new world) in which the populous represents a body of individual men who live their lives by the use of their independent minds. Your literature outlines the principles which are the foundation of rational conduct in life."

Y.S., nasionet.net, 2/2/97, Malaysia

"This web site is great. Great for me to learn valuable knowledge."

D.H., swbell.net, 2/1/97

"I do believe in the principles you have mentioned. I have always thought through discipline and effort people may advance mentally, economically, and emotionally."

S.L., compuserve.com, 1/31/97, United Kingdom

"Stunning, excellent, and a breeze to surf. I have known about Neo-Tech since 1987. Since enlightenment, I have developed a direct marketing business currently turning over UK£691,200 per annum, with 52% net profits!!! If you require any testimonials of 'living proof' of the route to freedom, I remain on standby."

D.H., sircham, 1/31/97

"I was astounded. The information was so valuable that I just want to thank you for making it available. My New Year's resolution is to study ALL of these pages and to USE them!"

S.C., net.com, 1/31/97, Australia

"This is an amazing discovery by Mr. Wallace. Thank you for such powerful and mind blowing information."

P.O., pi.net, 1/31/97, Netherlands

"Absolutely very helpful in achieving several important goals in my life and work."

R.M., uiuc.edu, 1/30/97

"This web site is very informative and provokes new directions in thought."

J.G., co.k, 1/30/97, Kenya

"After taking one look from the colorful web pages one can't help envision the breathtaking scenery of what the future holds for those (very) lucky to possess this knowledge of knowledge. Objectivists and Libertarians, with all due respect, "Eat Your Hearts Out.""

J.B., aol.com, 1/30/97

"There is a wealth of information in this Web site! Timeless principles, when put into action, that really work. Plus, all of the information validates what many people truly believe in -- honesty, integrity, character and courage."

G.H., juno.com, 1/30/97

"I'm fascinated by what I've been reading! I had no idea about these concepts but I can see they are making sense. Thanks for a mind broadening experience!"

C.B., centuryinter.net, 1/30/97

"This makes so much sense, it makes you want to go out and start hammering the politicians."

E.S., aol.com, 1/30/97

"Everything I've read so far has caused me to look at life and wish I only knew about The Neo-Tech Discovery sooner."

R.L., webzone.net, 1/29/97

"I am glad that I was introduced because I am one who is providing jobs for others. I am getting punished by taxation instead of incentives to continue or grow. It really sucks that I always feel like if I screw up in my accounting ONCE, a person from the parasitic group is going to come down on me and take all I worked for and give it to a parasitic group who does not contribute. They don't even understand what a beneficial individual I am to our society. THANKS FOR YOUR QUEST."

J.L., webtv.net, 1/29/97

"I NOW LOOK FORWARD TO THE FUTURE."

N.S., house.gov, 1/29/97

"You have reminded me of how much I appreciated Ayn Rand when I first discovered her work years ago. Thank you."

A.F., att.com, 1/29/97

"Breathtaking in its profound significance."

N.F., nconnect.net, 1/29/97
"Never before have I come across a system like this. I have seen every kind of scam claiming to furnish you with the results that Neo-Tech actually gives you. And unlike scams, Neo-Tech is simple and has definite integrity. Neo-Power will definitely change my life."

R.F., aol.com, 1/29/97
"This (Neo-Tech) is without a doubt, a most fascinating work. There is so much to read I could stay on the net for hours and hours. I must think on all this exiting reality, and then begin the integration's you mention! Many thanks!"

W.S., infoave.net, 1/29/97
"I can use what I learned to help in all areas of life."

U.S., aol.com, 1/28/97
"I think this web site is absolutely fantastic. There is a wealth of information that is useful for self-development. Keep up the great work."

L.M., erols.com, 1/28/97
"I find the testimonials at this site to be an added source of enthusiasm and inspiration."

P.B., freenet.edu, 1/28/97
"I have never been so amazed by a web site as I am by this one."

S.C., co.m, 1/28/97, Malaysia
"This web-site is very important to spread powerful and no-nonsense knowledge. More and more people in this world are using the Internet and more people can be reached."

G.C., mind.net, 1/28/97
"WHERE IS THE NEO-TECH PRESIDENT?"

M.S., zianet.com, 1/27/97
"Neo-Tech is the optimistic opportunist's guide to the world."

L.B., concentric.net, 1/27/97
"Interesting prognostication. Hope it happens."

N.Q., utah.edu, 1/27/97
"This is by far the best page on the net!!!"

B.Z., compulink.gr, 1/27/97, Greece
"Good work."

T.G., miworld.net, 1/27/97
"A real asset to the WWW."

K.S., bigfoot.com, 1/27/97, Singapore
"The web site is well-arranged, offering a clear view of what is offered. The color mix is appealing and I look forward to new ideas that will be displayed."

P.O., stream.com, 1/27/97, Ireland
"I found this very interesting and will continue to learn."

D.W., travelin.com, 1/26/97
"What I have read so far is great. This just might be the info that I have been waiting for to take advantage of the opportunities that await me."

B.C., umontreal.ca, 1/26/97, Canada
"Your web site seems very exciting. I practice objectivism and understand many of your ideas and statements."

C.G., ternet.pl, 1/26/97, Poland
"This is a very interesting web site. I found a lot of fascinating information on different subjects. I hope you will maintain and keep this high Zonpower/Neo-Tech standard all the time. All the best to all of you working on it."

T.W., netcom.com, 1/26/97
"An absolute must read for those of us who have been made to feel inadequate and unworthy by religion. I am only through a small portion of the web site, but already I have a better realization of who I am, and more importantly, who controls my future -- ME."

R.J., mci2000.com, 1/26/97
"This is most likely the best site on the Web! This gives everyone hope for the future. Thank you for the guts to get the messages out you are espousing."

R.L., sprynet.com, 1/26/97
"One of the most intriguing web sites I have yet encountered. It provides valuable advice and the wisdom of the ages."

J.L., nv.us, 1/26/97
"I am sick of this world, I can see it in my face when I look in the mirror I can feel it in my emotions or lack of them everything in this world is so boring!!!! Is this the ANTICIVILIZATION that

you speak of? Like a nagging infected sore that reminds you when you bump it that the world is controlled by what you call the LEECH CLASS. If this is what you are talking about, I must know more."

M.D., gkb.con, 1/25/97, Switzerland
"This site is the greatest."

C.C., univ-tlse1.fr, 1/25/97, France
"This is the most interesting web site."

D.D., co.c, 1/24/97, Cyprus
"I have an unmistakable feeling that you know what you are talking about. You are good."

T.G., nv.us, 1/23/97
"Way to walk the talk!"

R.C., alaska.net, 1/23/97
"I have thought for quite some time that the whole problem with our country is 'big-government'."

M.F., com.sg, 1/23/97, Singapore
"Absolutely fabulous!"

D.S., aol.com, 1/22/97
"Excellently wonderful!! Objectivism is central to my life, and this site will be a big help. The mainstream Objectivists have caused me too many disillusions, and this site is beginning to feel rejuvenating."

T.T., vcu.edu, 1/22/97
"I would like to thank you for sharing this information with millions of people. I think it is really neat to give away something like this."

G.M., ac.at, 1/22/97, Austria
"This is exciting news for the world's working class."

H.A., net.id, 1/21/97, Indonesia
"What a great web site, it gives us intuition."

K.E., infi.net, 1/21/97
"It is the most interesting and intriguing site I have ever seen. As I read, my interest just keeps growing. It is fascinating. I want to know more!"

G.F., nv.us, 1/21/97
"The search for knowledge, understanding, and a

better way are obviously at the core of the web site."

T.B., hot-shot.com, 1/21/97, Thailand
"Very useful site. Thank you."

W.L., aol.com, 1/21/97
"I feel that I would be foolish not to look into this further. Everything mentioned I believe to be true, yet I have always felt powerless to do anything about it."

J.T., net.sg, 1/21/97, Singapore
"This web site is great."

C.H., edu.tw, 1/21/97, Taiwan
"Good Web!!!!!!!!"

F.K., edu.tw, 1/21/97, Taiwan
"Very interesting! Excited!! Magic!!! Powerful!!! One of Best Web-Sites I have even seen!"

C.F., imago.net, 1/21/97
"If I had to replace my 59 other books on success, personal development, management, and business planning, I would only keep the Neo-Tech manual. I have increased my productivity by 3 times in less than 30 days. This manual should be used in every high school in the world... I can't praise the teachings of this book enough. Thank you for making such a difference in my life. I have moved from existence to essence from lost to laser focused... THANK YOU!"

S.T., com.au, 1/21/97, Australia
"Through what I have read, Zonpower/Neo-Tech can fix many of the problems I have in life. Neo-Tech could make a great difference. I am excited that things will be brighter for me when I use Neo-Tech."

N.W., hotmail.com, 1/20/97
"I think it will open a lot of minds to opportunities in personal growth that most people aren't exposed to."

R.R., aol.com, 1/20/97
"I think this web site is immensely valuable to all who are interested in improving themselves and ultimately the human condition."

J.S., aol.com, 1/20/97
"Thoughtful and scholarly... I'm glad to see more people recognizing the dangers of blind faith and religion."

P.J., pwrnet.com, 1/20/97
"Very Impressive -- I can't get enough of this info. The site is arranged in an easy fashion to locate and to read. I very much like the search part and that you have so much info. available. Look forward to more."

M.M., hotmail.com, 1/20/97, West Malaysia
"I admire all the work you're doing. You've opened up a hidden self within me and now I'm fueled with desire to produce values and live life as it was meant to be."

S.B., wwa.com, 1/19/97
"This web site provides new insight on current beliefs about the cyberspace revolution. It tells of a power that most people only dream about. Neo-Tech makes dreams come true."

A.R., co.sg, 1/19/97, Singapore
"It's a gold mine. The truth of all truths for those who desire the wealth, prosperity, love and power."

G.S., aol.com, 1/19/97
"As a teacher, and a fan of "core knowledge" a la Hirsch, I consider finding your page (when I was searching under DREAMS) a piece of synchronicity and good fortune."

E.K., xensei.com, 1/18/97
"Applicable to many areas of life."

B.W., seidata.com, 1/18/97
"I think it is great that Dr. Wallace is making available this important information for free."

D.R., tel.hr, 1/18/97, Croatia
"Before the war in my country, I read the first book about Neo-Tech. Now, it's time to learn more."

D.S., helixbiopharma.ca, 1/18/97, Canada
"I find this to be a most interesting and well prepared web site. It keeps me reading and exploring with interest. There is a lot of truth and value in what is being written here."

V.S., techie.com, 1/18/97, India
"This site opens up an entirely new approach to thinking."

P.D., bellsouth.cl, 1/17/97, Chile
"Well organized, interesting, and entertaining."

A.R., mrsi.com, 1/17/97
"I find your Web Site intriguing. It caused me to question the source of my own potential-limiting modality. Neo-Tech, no doubt, has the answer(s)."

T.B., aol.com, 1/17/97
"I think this web site was very informative. I believe that Neo-Tech holds the key to the future."

P.C., compuserve.com, 1/17/97
"Interesting and profound ideas."

A.T., com.au, 1/17/97, Australia
"I found this web site through a search on 'world conspiracy', and it has certainly confirmed that the tools of wealth and progress have been withheld from the general population for the express purpose of narrowly defining the dispersion of wealth and knowledge to all but a select few."

B.P., co.za, 1/17/97, South Africa
"Thank you for a super web page and keep up the good work."

C.C., co.eng, 1/14/97, England
"Those damn parasitical neo-cheaters."

L.K., intercall.com, 1/14/97
"The topics are mind boggling. You can be sure I will be a frequent visitor. "

G.B., compulink.gr, 1/14/97, Greece
"Interesting...I will come back often, thank you."

J.R., aol.com, 1/14/97
"I have found this site to be a page of great knowledge and it has answered many questions I have had for my whole life. It is great and wonderful."

J.S., netropolis.net, 1/14/97
"The Neo-Tech/Zonpower web site offers the most complete formulas to happiness available anywhere in cyberspace. Not only has Neo-Tech changed my life, but its application is a never-ending growth

process for my self-esteem and personal happiness. Thanks a million, Neo-Tech!"

L.J., ata.com, 1/14/97
"THE INFORMATION PROVIDED HAS BEEN BEYOND MY IMAGINATION. I'M LOOKING FORWARD TO ITS IMPACT ON MY LIFE"

S.K., erols.com, 1/14/97
"I look forward to visiting your web pages to learn more about Zonpower and working harder to burst my mystical bubble to become Zon. Once again thank you for all the work you are doing. I look forward to joining the Civilization of the Universe."

C.M., com.au, 1/13/97, Australia
"It has changed my outlook on the way we think, invest and work."

D.B., spb.su, 1/13/97, Russia
"It's so strange... And is a great thing in the world of bytes and common problems. I like it."

J.C., bhis.com, 1/13/97
"This web site is one of the few on the entire Internet that has Actual Useful Information. By far, one of the best sites I have visited. I consider myself lucky to have found this place."

A.R., net.mx, 1/12/97, Mexico
"I think It is like a gate to the limitless abundance of the universe."

M.Y., ohiou.edu, 1/12/97
"This web site has it all. Innovative ideas to global marketing."

T.M., buffalo.edu, 1/12/97
"These writings express an interesting point of view on the nature of consciousness."

D.V., nv.us, 1/11/97
"Thought provoking. Truly revolutionary. Light years ahead!!!"

ANON, compuserve.com, 1/11/97, Germany
"I think what Neo-Tech basically does is to determine reality and truth. The way of accomplishing a successful life by using profound honesty is the best way ever (and the ONLY way to be productive and to receive Neo-Tech values). All I can do is re-state it: 'The most valuable site in cyberspace'. I am really looking forward to a Neo-Tech oriented world like you described it and I know that it is only a matter of time. All of us can do something to make the world a better place, and what might be more important: to improve our own life. And that is to be as productive as you."

C.W., aol.com, 1/11/97
"Absolutely Refreshing......there is a great sense of freedom and discipline in non-mystical thought. Thank you for helping me realize who I really am. I no longer feel out of place in an otherwise mystical society."

H.A., net.id, 1/11/97, Indonesia
"My most favorite web in the cyberspace and it's my number #1 web address in my bookmark. This web can give me more intuition."

M.S., gdsi, 1/11/97, Philippines
"Very informative and comprehensive as well!"

D.Y., bc.ca, 1/11/97, Canada
"I thought it was excellent. It taught me things about using the mind that I never thought possible. I am eager to learn more."

C.C., co.pr, 1/10/97, Puerto Rico
"THIS IS A WHOLE NEW WAY OF THINKING FOR ME AS I HAVE BEEN RAISED AS A CHRISTIAN CATHOLIC. I MUST ADMIT THAT WHAT I HAVE READ IS MORE LOGICAL THAN WHAT I WAS TAUGHT IN THE CATHOLIC RELIGION."

D.L., eunet.be, 1/9/97, Belgium
"I heard about this web site from my family. I must say it is very interesting and it gives a very refreshing view from another perspective. I use the power search a lot, to find out Zonpower's opinion. Thanks!"

B.A., aol.com, 1/9/97
"The stuff I've read already is incredible. The footnote concerning social security is already happening as we speak. This is great. This is great reading."

J.S., hlc.com, 1/8/97
"I am extremely impressed with your web site. This site proves to me that your organization believes in what it prints and sincerely plans to bring about

change."

C.L., msn.com, 1/8/97
"Thank you for updating the web site in response to my comments about homosexuality. As a gay man, I found the previous statement to be inaccurate, and it is a testimony both to you and to the entire Neo-Tech Publishing Company that you actually DO believe in fully integrated honesty. "

D.A., netcom.ca, 1/8/97, Canada
"This web site is full of information which can be used and applied. This site is more than just a place to visit on the web. IT IS A PLACE TO LEARN and PROSPER. EXCELLENT WORK "

D.K., co.uk, 1/7/97, United Kingdom
"I was overjoyed to see you in Cyberspace! All your publications are well written but this Web site surpasses you. You have continued to be courageous, honest and informative."

N.H., auc.edu, 1/7/97
"This web site brought about many different ideas to consider about the international market. I have never looked at expanding my life beyond the United States. After reading this web site, I will definitely try to expand my thoughts and business to other parts of the globe."

P.P., brain.com, 1/7/97
"Excellent! I've bookmarked this web site. It's 2am. After a bit of sleep I will have to spend a lot of time here in order to take in all the information. It's good to see someone taking on the tyrannical forces that is our present government. "

J.M., aol.com, 1/7/97
"Very interesting and enlightening. This does shed a new light on life itself and endless possibilities for a new future."

E.R., aol.com, 1/7/97
"FIREWORKS! FIREWORKS! FIREWORKS! This information will jump-start the Psychologically dead. MUST read for every honest person on this planet. The implications of Neo-Tech/Zonpower are earth-shattering. It will transform the most wretched loser into an unstoppable winner. THIS WEB SITE IS ALSO A TECHNICAL MARVEL!"

B.W., webtv.net, 1/6/97
"The first site that has kept me reading the text. Very thought provoking."

A.T., pemex.com, 1/6/97, Mexico
"I found it awesome!"

S.B., aol.com, 1/6/97
"I would like to say that Neo-Tech is the most powerful book I have ever read. Thank you Dr. Wallace for your hard work and your value production."

K.J., aol.com, 1/6/97
"I find this site a magnet!"

M.L., netrunner.net, 1/5/97
"Fantastic work! Amazing web site! I'm not done reading your material yet, but what I've read so far is very inspiring/exciting! Thank you for this web site!"

C.N., pcisys.net, 1/5/97
"Who wouldn't want such answers to many of Life's most central questions? Spreading such a word is both compassionate and generous."

P.V., aol.com, 1/4/97
"Very unique and informative. An alternative that is not at all alternative. "

F.M., cwconnect.ca, 1/4/97, Canada
"Very interesting. The information was very motivating! Would encourage anyone to start a business."

P.C., aol.com, 1/3/97
"Neo-Tech is the answer, I am glad that it is on the web. the site is a good one keep up the good work."

F.H., bigfoot.com, 1/3/97, West Malaysia
"I have found this web site to be too good. There's so much to discover and to know about reality. Zonpower has so much to offer, not many people know about it. I hope in the near future I will be able to know all that Zonpower has to offer. Keep up the good work!!!!!"

M.G., lkdllink.net, 1/3/97
"I enjoy visiting this place because of the cause: Individuality. I have been practicing Fully-Integrated Honesty for a while and found it to be great. At

first I used it in a mystical way and ended up losing some of myself, but over time, I am earning it back and I thank you, and hope that in the future all parasites will come to an end. Thank You"

M.W., nv.us, 1/3/97
"I have always agreed in full with the principles of Objectivism, but have been skeptical of its dictatorial leaders and their cult-like following. Neo-Tech is OBJECTIVISM APPLIED CONSISTENTLY to all areas. Thank you."

E.R., aol.com, 1/2/97
"Everyone with an ounce of sense should turn to it. A clear, powerful mind is the prerequisite to anyone's journey through life and this site provides the starting point. It is a technical masterpiece as well."

S.B., msn.com, 1/2/97
"My #1 Web site. You have opened doors which I knew not were there. Keep up the excellent work. Bravo."

L.W., dextergraphic.com, 1/2/97
"I am profoundly glad to have access to the most important information ever available to the human race."

M.C., clubi.ie, 1/2/97, Rep of Ireland
"I am an owner of Zonpower and I must say I find this Web site the perfect back up for the Neo-Tech advantages."

JS.M., gnn.com, 1/1/97
"I think Wallace is addressing some very important aspects of our culture which we all know, but often deny. Seems like what he is describing accounts from much of what we see in government, corporate business, media, etc. I enjoy his works very much and hope people become more aware of the issues he is addressing."

S.B., tivoli.com, 1/1/97
"Wow! I'm an Objectivist, but have recently been having some doubts about my Objectivism and Objectivism in general. There seems to be a missing link, something that indicated that Objectivism wasn't quite right, but I couldn't put my finger on it. The Neo-Tech stuff at least provides a metaphoric answer to that missing link. This is compelling stuff. A useful tool."